POSITION	PRIMARY RESPONSIBILITIES	REQUIREMENTS	AVERAGE STARTING SALARY	FOR MORE INFORMATION
JUDGE	Apply the law through hearings and trials, ensuring that they are conducted in fairness to all parties, issuing sentences and penalties to guilty parties. Judges hear the facts and evidence of each case from prosecution and defense counsels to decide whether a trial is necessary.	▪ Bachelor's degree ▪ Juris Doctorate degree ▪ practicing attorney experience	$79,000 to $141,000	www.abanet.com www.fjc.gov www.nisc.dni.us www.judges.org
ATTORNEY	Attorneys practice in either criminal or civil law as prosecution or defense counsel. Activities include researching and examining evidence and facts of each case and interpreting the law based on the purposes of the laws and prior judicial decisions.	▪ Bachelor's degree ▪ Juris Doctorate degree ▪ passed the state Bar exam	$40,000 to $80,000	www.usajobs.opm.gov www.abanet.com www.lsac.com
PARALEGAL	Research laws and prior cases, investigate facts and evidence, write legal documents and briefs, coordinate communications, keep records of all documents.	▪ Varies among firms and employers ▪ Generally a college degree or paralegal certification required. Certification requires an exam.	$32,900	www.nala.org
CORRECTIONS OFFICER	Monitor prisoners, enforce rules, maintain order, inspect correctional facilities and prisoners for illegal substances and weapons.	▪ 18 years of age ▪ U.S. citizen ▪ High school diploma or equivalent ▪ Federal Bureau of Prisons requires one of the following: Bachelor's degree, three years work experience, or combination of undergraduate experience plus work experience	Federal entry level: $20,000 to $22,000	www.corrections.com
PROBATION OFFICER	Counseling and rehabilitating criminal offenders without the use of incarceration. Probation officers also assist in sentencing by preparing presentence reports. Monitor and keep records of the offender's behavior for the Courts.	▪ Bachelor's degree and/or experience in probation of intermediate corrections ▪ U.S. citizen ▪ Valid driver's license ▪ Must pass drug, medical, and psychological screening	$20,000 to $30,000	www.appa-net.org
PAROLE OFFICER	Responsible for legal custody of offenders following release from incarceration and ensuring adherence to conditions of parole.	▪ Bachelor's degree or prior experience in parole or probation ▪ Written and oral exams typically required	$25,000 to $30,000	www.appa-net.org

CRIMINAL JUSTICE in action

LARRY K. GAINES
California State University–San Bernardino

MICHAEL KAUNE
Radford University

ROGER LEROY MILLER
Institute for University Studies,
Arlington, Texas

Wadsworth
Thomson Learning

Australia • Canada • Denmark • Japan • Mexico • New Zealand • Philippines • Puerto Rico
Singapore • South Africa • Spain • United Kingdom • United States

EXECUTIVE EDITOR, CRIMINAL JUSTICE: Sabra Horne
SENIOR DEVELOPMENT EDITOR: Dan Alpert
ASSISTANT EDITOR: Shannon Ryan
EDITORIAL ASSISTANT: Ann Tsai
MARKETING MANAGER: Christine Henry
MARKETING ASSISTANT: Ken Baird
PROJECT EDITOR: Jennie Redwitz
PRINT BUYER: Karen Hunt
PERMISSIONS EDITOR: Susan Walters
PRODUCTION: Bill Stryker
TEXT DESIGNER: Doug Abbott
ART EDITOR: Ann Borman
PHOTO RESEARCHER: Megan Ryan

COPY EDITOR: Patricia Lewis
ILLUSTRATORS: Stan Maddock and Bill Stryker
COMPOSITOR: Parkwood Composition Service
COVER DESIGNER: Doug Abbott
COVER IMAGES: Background fence image © PhotoDisc; courtroom © John Neubauer, PhotoEdit; drugs and money © Douglas C. Pizac, AP/Wide World Photos; guard tower © A. Ramey, PhotoEdit; courthouse © Chuck Pefley, Stock, Boston; police © 1997 Washington Post, photo by Bill O'Leary.
COVER PRINTER: Phoenix Color Corporation
PRINTER/BINDER: World Color/Versailles

Printed in the United States of America
1 2 3 4 5 6 7 03 02 01 00 99

For permission to use material from this text, contact us:
Web: www.thomsonrights.com
Fax: 1-800-730-2215
Phone: 1-800-730-2214

For more information, contact

Wadsworth/Thomson Learning
10 Davis Drive
Belmont, CA 94002-3098
USA
www.wadsworth.com

International Headquarters
Thomson Learning
290 Harbor Drive, 2nd Floor
Stamford, CT 06902-7477
USA

UK/Europe/Middle East
Thomson Learning
Berkshire House
168-173 High Holborn
London WC1V 7AA
United Kingdom

Asia
Thomson Learning
60 Albert Street #15-01
Albert Complex
Singapore 189969

Canada
Nelson/Thomson Learning
1120 Birchmount Road
Scarborough, Ontario M1K 5G4
Canada

Library of Congress Cataloging-in-Publication Data
Gaines, Larry K.
    Criminal justice in action / Larry K. Gaines, Michael Kaune, Roger LeRoy Miller
        p. cm.
    Includes bibliographical references and index.
    ISBN 0–534–56808–4
    1. Criminal justice, Administration of—United States
    I. Kaune, Michael. II. Title
HV7419.G35 1999
364'.0973—dc21   99–22187

 This book is printed on acid-free recycled paper.

Dedication

This book is dedicated to my good friend and colleague, Lawrence Walsh of the Lexington, Kentucky Police Department. When I was a rookie, he taught me about policing. When I became a researcher, he has taught me about the practical applications of knowledge. He is truly a professional in our field.
   —L.K.G.

I wish to dedicate this work to the people I love most: my intriguing wife, Kirsten Baxter, and my three children, Alexis, Aslynd, and (due in October) Cameron or Averon.
   —M.K

To Shawn G. Miller,
Who has become the world's greatest researcher (and many other things, too).
   —R.L.M.

Contents in Brief

Contents

2 Measuring and Explaining Crime 36

Criminal Justice in Action **The Growing Role of the Victim 64**

3 Criminal Law 74

Criminal Justice in Action Terrorism and American Criminal Law 104

Terrorism: Real and Imagined • The Anti-Terrorism Act • Tactics in England and France • "Little to Do with Terrorism" • Dangers in the Future

Key Terms • Chapter Summary • Questions for Critical Analysis • Selected Print and Electronic Resources • Using the internet for Criminal Justice Analysis • Notes

Cross-National CJ Comparison
"Honor Killings" in Jordan 87

CJ in Focus
WAS JUSTICE SERVED?
Drunk Driving and *Mens Rea* 89

CJ in Focus
MYTH VERSUS REALITY
Are Too Many Criminals Found Not Guilty by Reason of Insanity? 95

CJ in Focus
LANDMARK CASES
Regina v. Dudley and Stephens 99

Part Two The Police 111

4 Police: Agents of Law and Order 112

INTRODUCTION 114

A HISTORY OF THE AMERICAN POLICE 114

LAW ENFORCEMENT AGENCIES 123

Cross-National CJ Comparison
A Professional Police Force for Bosnia 121

Criminal Justice & Popular Culture
Star Gazing at the FBI 129

5 Policing: Organization and Strategies 150

6 Police and the Rule of Law 194

CJ in Focus
THE BALANCING ACT
Excluding Justice? 199

Cross-National CJ Comparison
French Identity Checks 202

CJ in Focus
WAS JUSTICE SERVED?
Rules of the Road 211

Criminal Justice & Technology
X-Ray Eyes and the Fourth Amendment 213

CJ in Focus
LANDMARK CASES:
Miranda v. Arizona 216

7 Challenges to Effective Policing 232

Careers in Criminal Justice
Peter John Mantello, Training Coordinator for the
Vermont Criminal Justice Training Council 239

Part Three Criminal Courts 267

8 Courts and the Quest for Justice 268

9 Pretrial Procedures: The Adversary System in Action 300

Criminal Justice in Action Legal Ethics on Trial: Defending the Guilty 328

Strong Feelings against Lawyers Have Long History • The "Truth" of the Courtroom • Privileged Confessions • On a Personal Level

Key Terms • Chapter Summary • Questions for Critical Analysis • Selected Print and Electronic Resources • Using the Internet for Criminal Justice Analysis • Notes

10 The Criminal Trial 336

Criminal Justice in Action Cameras in the Courtroom: Is Justice Served? 366

A Right or a Wrong? • The Simpson Shadow • The Effects of Public Opinion • Two Rights in Conflict?

Key Terms • Chapter Summary • Questions for Critical Analysis • Selected Print and Electronic Resources • Using the Internet for Criminal Justice Analysis • Notes

11 Punishment and Sentencing 374

CJ in Focus
MAKING WAVES
The Shaming Judge 385

CJ in Focus
WAS JUSTICE SERVED?
The "Good" Defendant 392

CJ in Focus
LANDMARK CASES:
Furman v. Georgia 399

Part Four Corrections 415

12 Probation and Community Corrections 416

CJ in Focus
THE BALANCING ACT
"Jason's Law" and Compromised Justice 419

CJ in Focus
WAS JUSTICE SERVED?
Probation and the Scarlet Letter 426

Careers in Criminal Justice
Scott T. Ballock, U.S. Probation Officer 429

Cross-National CJ Comparison
Swedish Day-Fines 435

Preface

Why are more students than ever enrolling in criminal justice programs throughout the country? No doubt, the sincere desire to serve the public and help others has motivated many students to major in criminal justice. Many are hoping to find lucrative and secure jobs in the criminal justice professions. Today, the career possibilities and challenges are greater than ever. Finally, some are simply drawn to the excitement of the field.

In this new text we have attempted to impart to the reader this excitement. Consequently, we have used high-interest examples throughout. We have developed numerous features, all guaranteed to keep student interest. These features have been explained in the first few pages of this preface. Even a cursory glance at this text lets you know that you are reading the introduction to criminal justice textbook that truly is for the twenty-first century.

As we enter the new millennium, more challenges than ever are facing our society, many of which involve our criminal justice system. Consider the following:

- School violence seems to be making the headlines on a regular basis. What can we do as a society to prevent not only highly publicized massacres, such as at Columbine High in 1999, but also the less well publicized shootings and other acts of aggression that plague many school districts?

- How will we adapt to increasing prison overcrowding? For the first time ever, those incarcerated throughout the United States exceeded 1.8 million, and the number is rising. Part and parcel of this problem is our overburdened court system. Is there something that the criminal justice system can do to alleviate this situation?

- The demands placed on law enforcement officers are greater than ever. The police have been redefining their role in society and, in many instances, actually reinventing the way they work.

- New technologies have influenced nearly every aspect of the criminal justice process. DNA techniques have allowed police to solve more crimes, sometimes years after they occurred. DNA investigation has even allowed some death row inmates to be freed based on negative DNA tests.

- The public's view of the criminal justice system has been increasingly molded by how the popular media portray it. Have the media been accurate? If not, is there anything we can do about it? How do we teach our students to become more critical consumers of the media?

These are the kinds of issues that face students going into the field of criminal justice.

THE GENESIS OF *CRIMINAL JUSTICE IN ACTION*

Of course you may be asking yourself why another introduction to criminal justice text had to be written. We believe we have the answer to this question: Our society is changing, as are the backgrounds and expectations of today's students. We decided to create a text that really speaks to today's students. We know from our own experiences and from those of our colleagues that many students are not really motivated to read traditional textbooks. We therefore realized that we had to come up with a book that would truly engage students while at the same time provide solid depth of content to meet course needs. That is also why we developed the fully integrated teaching/learning package for instructors and students alike (discussed below). In short, we believe that we succeeded in developing a text that students will want to read.

A COMPLETE LEARNING EXPERIENCE

While the text itself is filled with numerous eye-catching, instructive, and penetrating features, we have not stopped there. You will notice that the pedagogy extends from the first page of each chapter—with its outline and learning objectives—all the way through the end of each chapter, which includes a full array of pedagogical devices:

- **Criminal Justice in Action feature:** Every chapter ends with this important feature. It deals with major issues and controversies that require several pages to explain.

- **Cross-National CJ Comparison:** Because it is sometimes easier to teach by comparison, we felt it important to present the students with information about how our criminal justice system compares with those of other countries.

- **Criminal Justice & Technology:** The criminal justice field is changing so rapidly because of technology, we made sure that the student could not miss learning about the important technology issues used by practitioners in the field today.

- **Criminal Justice & Popular Culture:** Many aspects of the criminal justice system have invaded popular culture. We felt this feature was important to reveal these "invasions" while at the same time commenting on their accuracy.

- **Careers in Criminal Justice:** Most students reading this book are planning a career in criminal justice. We have provided them with an insight into what some of these careers will be like by offering first-person accounts of what it is like to work in the criminal justice professions.

- **CJ in Focus:** This generic feature title covers important topics such as excerpts from important Supreme Court cases and the age-old struggle between the need to protect society and the rights of individuals.

- **Concepts Summary:** This feature helps students to master essential concepts of criminal justice. Since it is often important to compare and contrast two similar concepts to help the student understand them, many of the concepts summaries are based on comparisons.

- **Marginal Technology Features:** Our teaching/learning package offers numerous opportunities for using technology in the classroom. In the margins you will find InfoTrac citations that lead students to very important research articles in this powerful private, password-protected, online database. In addition, there are relevant Web citations in the margins of every chapter. Finally, when appropriate, there is a CD-ROM logo displayed to show that a career feature is available in the text's companion careers CD-ROM.

THE SUPPLEMENTS

Our entire team—the three authors plus numerous individuals at Wadsworth—have put together a complete teaching package. In this package you will find:

For the Instructor

Annotated Instructor's Edition   Marginal annotations provide learning tips, lecture launchers, and references to test bank questions and PowerPoint slides for each chapter.

Criminal Justice Video Library   Qualified adopters can select from a variety of videos, including exclusive *CNN Today* videos for Introduction to Criminal Justice, Criminology, and Juvenile Delinquency, which are tied to chapters of selected texts; an exclusive Introduction to Criminal Justice video from the Films for the Humanities; eight dynamic *Court TV* videos profiling some of the most famous and current cases in the judicial system; the *A&E American Justice Series*; ABC News and MPI Home Video; and the National Institute of Justice Crime File Videos.

Criminal Justice Faculty Development: Teaching Professors to Teach   This supplement provides valuable tips on teaching criminal justice with suggested articles, worksheets, and sample syllabi.

Instructor's Resource Manual   One of the most comprehensive resource manuals to accompany *Criminal Justice in Action*, this manual includes detailed outlines, chapter summaries, key terms, student and research activities, and a test bank of over 1800 test questions.

PowerPoint Presentation Slides   Choose from over 500 engaging PowerPoint slides that correspond to each chapter of the text.

Transparency Acetates   Enhance your lectures with 50 4-color acetates that highlight some of the most important concepts in criminal justice.

Thomson Learning Testing Tools   This fully integrated suite of test creation and delivery includes Thomson Learning Test and Test Online it allows professors to deliver tests via print, floppy, hard drive, LAN, or Internet. Call-in testing is also available.

For the Student

***Careers in Criminal Justice CD-ROM* (automatically included with the book)**   This engaging self-exploration provides an interactive discovery of careers in criminal justice. The CD-ROM provides personalized results from a self-assessment of interests and strengths to help steer students to careers based on their profile. Students gather information on various careers from job descriptions, salaries, employment requirements, and actual video profiles of criminal justice professionals.

Crime Scenes CD-ROM   An interactive CD-ROM featuring six vignettes that allows students to play various roles as they explore all aspects of the criminal justice system such as policing/investigation, courts, and sentencing and corrections. Awarded the gold medal in higher education and silver medal for video interface by New Media Magazine's Invision Awards.

Study Guide   Includes chapter objectives, outlines, summaries, key terms and concepts, and a multitude of test questions in true/false, multiple-choice, matching, and essay format.

InfoTrac® College Edition   Students receive four months of real-time access to InfoTrac® College Edition's online database of continuously updated, full-length articles from more than 600 journals and periodicals. By doing a simple keyword search, users can quickly generate a powerful list of related articles from thousands of possibilities, then select relevant articles to explore and/or print out for reference or for further study.

The Internet Investigator II   This colorful tri-fold brochure lists the most popular Internet addresses for criminal justice-related Web sites, including URLs for corrections, victimization, crime prevention, high-tech crime, policing, courts, investigations, juvenile justice, research, and fun sites.

Internet Activities for Criminal Justice   This guide teaches students the best practices for utilizing the Internet for research and includes criminal justice-specific activities that are tied to each chapter of the book.

Internet Guide for Criminal Justice   Intended for the novice user, the first half of this 80-page booklet explains the background and vocabulary necessary for navigating the Web while the second half is customized for criminal justice related-Web sites as well as Internet project ideas.

Seeking Employment in Criminal Justice and Related Fields, Third Edition
This book is designed to help students develop a job search strategy through resumes, cover letters, and interview techniques; it also provides extensive information on various criminal justice professions.

Web Site to Accompany *Criminal Justice in Action*   Students and instructors will have access to the book-specific Web site that includes chapter links, discussions, Internet projects, homework, quizzes, scavenger hunts, and instructor resources. **http://cj.wadsworth.com**

The Criminal Justice Resource Center   This powerful criminal justice Web site contains links to over 3000 popular criminal justice sites, grants/funding, jobs, news, list servs, convention information, instructors resources, and fun links. **http://cj.wadsworth.com**

THE CHALLENGES LIE AHEAD

We believe that we have developed the most student-friendly and instructor-efficient learning/teaching package. We know that challenges await us, nonetheless. We are faced with a generation of visual learners. We believe that we have done all that is possible to interest them in our exciting and important field. We won't rest on our laurels, however. We will continue to observe how our text is used, learn about its strengths and weaknesses, and determine ways we can improve it.

TO OUR READERS AND CONSULTING EXPERTS

Numerous reviewers and consultants were kind enough to take time to help us throughout every phase of this project. We list them in alphabetical order on the following pages. We sincerely thank all of these reviewers and consultants. You performed above and beyond the call of duty. We think you will agree that your suggestions have made all the difference in this book.

Special thanks to the following individuals who made significant contributions to our development effort.

Mark Correia
University of Nevada—Reno

John H. Kramer
Pennsylvania State University

John Scheb II
University of Tennessee—Knoxville

REVIEWERS

We are especially grateful for the participation of the following reviewers, who read and reviewed portions of our manuscript throughout its development:

Angela Ambers-Henderson
Montgomery County Community College

Judge James Bachman
Bowling Green State University

Tom Barclay
University of South Alabama

Julia Beeman
University of North Carolina at Charlotte

Anita Blowers
University of North Carolina at Charlotte

John Bower
Bethel College

Steven Brandl
University of Wisconsin—Milwaukee

Charles Brawner III
Heartland Community College

Susan Brinkley
University of Tampa

Paula Broussard
University of Southwestern Louisiana

Michael Brown
Ball State College

Joseph Bunce
Montgomery College—Rockville

Paul Campbell
Wayne State College

Dae Chang
Wichita State University

Steven Chermak
Indiana University

Charlie Chukwudolue
Northern Kentucky University

Monte Clampett
Asheville-Buncome Community College

John Cochran
University of South Florida

Mark Correia
University of Nevada—Reno

John del Nero
Lane Community College

John Dempsey
Suffolk County Community College

Joyce Dozier
Wilmington College

M. G. Eichenberg
Wayne State College

Frederick Galt
Dutchess Community College

James Gilbert
University of Nebraska—Kearney

Dean Golding
West Chester University of Pennsylvania

Debbie Goodman
Miami-Dade Community College

Donald Grubb
Northern Virginia Community College

Sharon Halford
Community College of Aurora

Michael Hallett
Middle Tennessee State University

Mark Hansel
Moorhead State University

Michelle Heward
Weber State University

Dennis Hoffman
University of Nebraska—Omaha

Richard Holden
Central Missouri State University

Ronald Holmes
University of Louisville

Marilyn Horace-Moore
Eastern Michigan University

Matrice Hurrah
Shelby State Community College

Nicholas Irons
County College of Morris

Michael Israel
Kean University

J. D. Jamieson
Southwest Texas State University

James Jengeleski
Shippensburg University

Paul Johnson
Weber State University

Matthew Kanjirathinkal
Texas A & M University—Commerce

Bill Kelly
University of Texas—Austin

Kristen Kuehnle
Salem State University

Karl Kunkel
Southwest Missouri State

Barry Latzer
John Jay College of Criminal Justice

Deborah Laufersweiler-Dwyer
University of Arkansas—Little Rock

Paul Lawson
Montana State University

Nella Lee
Portland State University

Walter Lewis
St. Louis Community College—Meramec

Faith Lutze
Washington State University

Richard Martin
Elgin Community College

Bill Matthias
University of South Carolina—Columbia

Janet McClellan
Southwestern Oregon Community College

Pat Murphy
State University of New York—Geneseo

Rebecca Nathanson
Housatonic Community-Technical College

Michael Palmiotto
Wichita State University

Gary Prawel
Monroe Community College

Mark Robarge
Mansfield University

Matt Robinson
Appalachian State University

Debra Ross
Buffalo State College

William Ruefle
University of South Carolina

Gregory Russell
Washington State University

John Scheb II
University of Tennessee—Knoxville

Ed Selby
Southwestern College

Ronald Sopenoff
Brookdale Community College

Gregory Talley
Broome Community College

Kimberly Vogt
University of Wisconsin—La Crosse

Robert Wadman
Weber State University

Ron Walker
Trinity Valley Community College

John Wyant
Illinois Central College

CLASS TEST PARTICIPANTS

We also want to acknowledge the participation of the professors and their students who agreed to class test portions of the text. Our thanks go to:

Tom Arnold
College of Lake County

Paula M. Broussard
University of Southwestern Louisiana

Mike Higginson
Suffolk Community College

Andrew Karmen
John Jay College of Criminal Justice

Fred Kramer
John Jay College of Criminal Justice

Anthony P. LaRose
Western Oregon University

Anne Lawrence
Kean University

Jerry E. Loar
Walters State Community College

Phil Reichel
University of Northern Colorado

Albert Sproule
Allentown College

Gregory B. Talley
Broome Community College

Karen Terry
John Jay College of Criminal Justice

Angelo Tritini
Passaic County Community College

Gary Uhrin
Westmoreland County Community College

Robert Vodde
Fairleigh Dickinson University

SURVEY RESPONDENTS

Last, but not least, the following individuals participated in our introduction to criminal justice market survey. Their influence is reflected throughout this book:

Edward Abair, Madonna University
Samuel Ackah, Delaware State University
Charles Adams, Savannah State College
Leanne Alarid, University of Missouri
R. B. Allen, Anson Community College
James Amos, Alvernia College
Allen Anderson, Indiana University—Kokomo
William Arnold, University of Kansas
Kelly Asmussen, Peru State College
Thomas Austin, Shippensburg University
James Bachman, Bowling Green State University
Thomas Baker, University of Scranton
Gregg Barak, Eastern Michigan University
Tom Barclay, University of South Alabama
Allan Barnes, University of Alaska, Anchorage
Peter Barone, St. Thomas University
Thomas Barry, University of Texas at San Antonio
Elaine Bartgis, Fairmont State College
Lincoln Barton, Anna Maria College
Larry Bassi, State University of New York College at Brockport
Mary Ellen Batiuk, Wilmington College
Chris Beard, California State University—Sacramento
Frank Beck, College of the Sequoias
Joe Becraft, Portland Community College
Julia Beeman, University of North Carolina at Charlotte
Richard Bennett, American University
Charles Biggs, Oakland City University
Donna Bishop, University of Central Florida
John Bower, Bethel College
Gary Boyer, University of Great Falls
Chuck Brawner, Heartland Community College
Susan Brinkley, University of Tampa
Ronald Brooks, Clinton Community College
Paula Broussard, University of Southwestern Louisiana
Carolyn Brown, Fayetteville Technical Community College
Michael Brown, Ball State University
Joseph Bunce, Montgomery College
John Burchill, Kansas Wesleyan University
Tod Burke, Radford University
Michael Burnette, Southwestern Community College
Deborah Burris-Kitchen, University of LaVerne
Orman Buswell, Fairmont State College
Timothy Buzzell, Baker University
David Calihan, Longwood College
Paul Campbell, Wayne State College
Leon Cantin, Mount Marty College
Timothy Carboreau, University of Cincinnati
Joseph Carlson, University of Nebraska at Kearny
David Cary, Mary Baldwin College
William Castleberry, University of Tennessee at Martin
Darl Champion, Methodist College
Dae Chang, Wichita State University
Charles Chastain, University of Arkansas at Little Rock
Russ Cheothem, Cumberland University
Steven Chermak, Indiana University
Art Chete, Central Florida Community College
Steven Christiansen, Green River Community College
Charlie Chukwudolue, Northern Kentucky University
Monte Clampett, Asheville-Buncombe Technical Community College

Ray Clarkson, Kings River Community College
Kenneth Clontz, Western Illinois University
Jean Clouatre, New Hampshire Technical Institute
John Cochran, University of South Florida
Keith Coleman, Fayetteville State University
William Cook Jr., Westfield State College
Kim Cook, University of Southern Maine
Richard Cook, Evergreen Valley College
Tom Cook, Wayne State College
Walt Copley, Metropolitan State College of Denver
Gary Copus, University of Alaska at Fairbanks
David Corbett, Pensacola Christian College
Mark Correia, University of Nevada at Reno
Stephen Cox, Central Connecticut State University
Beverly Curl, Long Beach City College
Dean Dabney, Georgia State University
John Daly, Cazenovia College
Carol Davis, Indiana University Northwest
Rita Davis, New Mexico State University
Peggy De Stefano, Bakersfield College
Tim Dees, Floyd College
Darrel Degraw, Delta State University
John Del Nero, Lane Community College
Tom Dempsey, Christopher Newport University
Holly Dershem-Bruce, Dawson Community College
John Doherty, Marist College
Rita Dorsey, Shelby State Community College
Marion Doss, Jr., James Madison University
Yvonne Downes, Hilbert College
Daniel Doyle, University of Montana
Joyce Dozier, Wilmington College
J. C. Drake, Roanoke-Chowan Community College
David Duffee, State University of New York at Albany
Gary Dull, Mesa Community College
William Dunford, Erie Community College
Steve Dunker, Casper College
Tim Durham, Thomas College
Mary Ann Eastep, University Central Florida
Peter Eckert, Broward Community College
David Emmons, Richard Stockton College of New Jersey
Don Ernst, Joliet Junior College
Dave Evans, University of North Carolina
Tom Fields, Cape Fear Community College
Larry Field, Western New England College
Charles Fieramusca, Medaille College
Frank Fischer, Kankakee Community College
Terry Fisk, Grand Valley State University
Michael Foley, Western Connecticut State University
Walt Francis, Central Wyoming College
Carl Franklin, Cloud County Community College
Crystal Garcia, Indiana University
Barry Garigen, Genesee Community College
Godfrey Garner, Hinds Community College
Carole Garrison, University of Akron
Andrew Giacomazzi, University of Texas at San Antonio
John Gillespie, Pennsicola Christian College
J. Ginger, St. Mary's University
Mary Glazier, Millersville University
Dean Golding, West Chester University of Pennsylvania
Michael Goodman, Illinois State University
Dirk Grafton, Mt. Aloysius College
Charles Graham, Solano Community College
James Green, St. Thomas Aquinas College

Peter Grimes, Nassau Community College
Edmund Grosskopf, Indiana State University
Donald Grubb, Northern Virginia Community College
George Guay, Salem State College
Stephen Haas, California State University at Bakersfield
Jan Hagemann, San Jose State University
Sharon Halford, Community College of Aurora
Doris Hall, California State University at Bakersfield
Cynthia Hamilton, West Virginia State College
Hil Harper, Valdosta State University
Judith Harris, University of South Carolina—Spartanburg
Lou Harris, Faulkner University
Robert Harvie, St. Martin's College
Curtis Hayes, Western New Mexico University
Kay Henriksen, MacMurray College
Gary Hill, Cisco Junior College
Vincent Hoffman, Michigan State University
Joe Hogan, Central Texas College
Ronald Holmes, University of Louisville
John Homa, Murray State University
David Hough, University of Findlay
John Hudgens, Weatherford College
James Hudson, Bob Jones University
Wendelin Hume, University of North Dakota
G. Hunt, Wharton County Junior College
William Hyatt, Western Carolina University
Timothy Ireland, Niagara University
Michael Israel, Kean University
Mary Jackson, East Carolina University
Theron Jackson, Los Angeles Southwest College
Caron Jacobson, Wayne State University
J. D. Jamieson, Southwest Texas State University
Shirley Jarreo, Texas A & M University at Commerce
Denise Jenne, Montclair State University
H. Johnson, University of Iowa
Kathrine Johnson, Kentucky State University
Paul Johnson, Weber State University
W. Johnson, Sam Houston State University
Fred Jones, Simpson College
Ken Jones, Coastal Carolina Community College
Casey Jordan, Western Connecticut State University
Lamar Jordan, Southern Utah University
Judy Kaci, California State University—Long Beach
George Kain, Western Connecticut State University
Michael Kane, Coastal Bend College
Richard Kania, Guilford College
Mathew Kanjirathinkal, Texas A & M University at Commerce
Kimberly Kempf-Leonard, University of Missouri—St. Louis
Patrick Kinkade, Texas Christian University
Douglas Kirk, University of South Carolina—Aiken
Paul Kish, Elmira College
Dan Klotz, Los Angeles Valley College
F. Knowles, Jr., Central Methodist College
Junius Koonce, Edgecombe Community College
John Kozlowicz, University of Wisconsin—Whitewater
Fred Kramer, John Jay College of Criminal Justice
Pete Kraska, Eastern Kentucky University
Bob Kristic, College of the Redwood
A. Kuennen, Briar Cliff College
Karl Kunkel, Southwest Missouri State University

Lon Lacey, The Victoria College
Jerry Lane, Central Virginia Community College
Peter Lango, Gateway Technical College
Anthony LaRose, Western Oregon University
Michael Lauderdale, University of Texas at Austin
Deborah Laufersweiler-Dwyer, University of Arkansas at Little Rock
Alan Lavallee, Delaware Technical College
George Lawless, South Plains College
Richard Lawrence, St. Cloud State University
Nella Lee, Portland State University
Tazinski Lee, Mississippi Valley State University
Thomas Lenahan, Herkimer Community College
B. H. Levin, Blue Ridge Community College
Elizabeth Lewis, Waycross College
Walter Lewis, St. Louis Community College
Lee Libby, Shoreline Community College
Charles Linder, John Jay College of Criminal Justice
Bobby Little, University of North Alabama
Jay Livingston, Montclair State University
Robert Lockwood, Portland State University
Thomas Long, Vance-Granville Community College
Beth Lord, Louisiana State University
Albert Lugo, El Camino College
Dennis Lund, University of Nebraska at Kearney
Faith Lutze, Washington State University
Richard Mangan, Florida Atlantic University
Larry Marshall, Methodist College
Brad Martin, University of Findlay
William Mathias, University of South Carolina
Nancy Matthews, Northeastern Illinois University
Rick Matthews, Ohio University
Richard Mays, Cameron University
Michael Mc Morris, Ferris State University
Stephen McAndrew, Hessen College
Thomas McAninch, Scott Community College
William McCamey, Western Illinois University
James McCarten, Mt. Senario College
Kenneth McCreedy, Ferrum College
Susan McGuire, San Jacinto College North
Barry McKee, Bristol Community College
Maureen McCleod, Russell Sage College
M. McShane, Northern Arizona University
Jim Meko, Gannon University
D. Miller, Alvin Community College
Robin Miller, Sterling College
Al Miranne, Gonzaga University
John Mockry, Clinton Community College
Dale Mooso, San Antonio College
Karen Mullin, Southwest State University
William Muraskin, Queens College
Pat Murphy, State University of New York at Geneseo
Stephen Muzzatti, Clark College
Johnnie Myers, Morris Brown College
Alisa Nagler, Edgecombe Community College
Brian Nanavaty, Indiana University—Purdue University
Rebecca Nathanson, Housatonic Community College
Marc Neithercutt, California State University Hayward
Steve Nelson, University of Great Falls
Robert Neville, College of The Siskiyous
Deborah Newman, Middle Tennessee State University
Frederica Nix, Missouri Western State University
Robert Nordvall, Gettysburg College
Paul North, Spoon River College
Patrick O'Guinn, Howard Community College
John O'Kane, Adirondack Community College
John O' Sullivan, Mt. San Antonio College
Robert Oatis, Indiana Wesleyan University
Willard Oliver, Glenville State College
Ihekwoaba Onwudiwe, University of Maryland—Eastern Shore

Kenneth Orr, College of the Albemarie
Alejandrina Ortiz, Catholic University of Puerto Rico
Gregory Osowski, Henry Ford Community College
Ted Paddack, Midwestern State University
Don Palmer, Union County College
Michael Palmiotto, Wichita State University
Peter Parilla, University of St. Thomas
Dan Partrich, Mid America Nazarene University
Jill Payne, American International College
Michael Penrod, Ellsworth Community College
Francine Perretta, Mater Dei College
Morgan Peterson, Palomar College
Vincent Petrarca, Salve Regina University
Peter Phillips, University of Texas at Tyler
William Pitt, Del Mar College
Joy Pollock, Southwest Texas State University
Darrell Pope, Pensacola Christian College
Edward Porter, Halifax Community College
Harry Porter, Mississippi College
Wayne Posner, Los Angeles City College
Ronald Powell, Taylor University
Gary Prawel, Monroe Community College
Chester Quarles, University of Mississippi
Norman Raasch, Lakeland Community College
Alfred Reed Jr., Los Angeles Southwest College
Jack Reinwand, Ricks College
George Rengert, Temple University
Marylee Reynolds, Caldwell College
Jayne Rich, Atlantic Community College
Mark Robarge, Mansfield University
Matt Robinson, Appalachian State University
Herman Roe, The Victoria College
Darrell Ross, East Carolina University
Debra Ross, Buffalo State College
William Ruefle, University of South Carolina
Walter Ruger, Nassau Community College
Jeffrey Rush, Jacksonville State University
Gregory Russell, Washington State University
Carl Russell, Scottsdale Community College
Ronald Ryan, Bladen Community College
Julie Salazano, Pace University
Beth Sanders, Kent State University
Wayne Schaffter, Anderson University
Barry Schelzer, St. Ambrose University
Harry Schloetter, Napa Valley College
Patrick Schuster, El Centro College
Edward Selby, Southwestern College
Allen Settles, Mid-Plains Community College
Tim Sexton, University of Northern Iowa
Martin Seyler, San Antonio College
Stan Shernock, Norwich University
Daniel Simpson, Delaware Technical and Community College—Terry Campus
Barbara Sims, Pennsylvania State University
John Sloan, University of Alabama at Birmingham
Neal Slone, Bloomsburg University
Martha Smithey, University of Texas at El Paso
Beverly Smith, Illinois State University
Brian Smith, Northern Arizona University
Lynne Snowden, University of North Carolina—Wilmington
Diann Sollie, Meridian Community College
Ronald Sopenoff, Brookdale Community College
John Spiva, Walla Walla Community College
Phoebe Stambaugh, Northern Arizona University
Debra Stanley, Central Connecticut State University
Katherine Steinbeck, Lakeland Community College
Rick Steinmann, Lindenwood University
G. Stevens, Carteret Community College
Jeffrey Stewart, Howard University
Sandra Stone, State University of West Georgia
Thomas Stoney, Lees-McRae College
Danny Stover, Kaskaskia College
Gene Straughan, Lewis-Clark State College
David Struckhoff, Loyola University

Leslie Sue, Tacoma Community College
Thomas Sullenberger, Southeastern Louisiana University
Kathryn Sullivan, Hudson Valley Community College
Margaret Sylvia, St. Mary's University
Susette Talarico, University of Georgia
Michael Tatum, Ricks College
Carol Thompson, Texas Christian University
Shurunda Thrower, University of Arkansas at Pine Bluff
George Tielsch, College of the Desert
Amy Tobol, Empire State College
James Todd, Tiffin University
C. Toler, Coastal Georgia Community College
Bonnie Toothaker, Mt. Wachusett Community College
Lawrence Travis, University of Cincinnati
Cecilia Tubbs, Jefferson State Community College
Jarrod Tudor, Kent State University—Stark Campus
Steve Turner, East Central University
Gary Uhrin, Westmoreland County Community College
Prabha Unnithan, Colorado State University
Dean Van Bibber, Fairmont State College
Ellen Van Valkenburgh, Jamestown Community College
Eddyth Vaughan, Hillsborough Community College
B. Vericker, Honolulu Community College
Kimberly Vogt, University of Wisconsin—La Crosse
Ron Walker, Trinity Valley Community College
Anthony Walsh, Boise State University
Thomas Ward, New Mexico Highlands University
Glenn Ware, North Harris College
Gene Waters, Georgia Southern University
John Watkins Jr., University of Alabama
Ralph Weisheit, Illinois State University
Karen Weston, Gannon University
Christine Westphal, Mt. Ida College
Giselle White, South Carolina State University
Martin White, Garland County Community College
Paul White, Quincy College
Stephanie Whitus, Sam Houston State University
Terri Wies-Haithcuck, Lima Technical College
Robert Wiggins, Cedarville College
Frank Williams, California State University—San Bernadino
Kathryn Williams, Southern Nazarene University
Deborah Wilson, University of Louisville
Deborah Wilson, Ohio State University
Michael Witkowski, University of Detroit—Mercy
Grace Witte, Briar Cliff College
Kevin Woods, Becker College
Alissa Worden, State University of New York at Albany
Robert Worden, State University of New York at Albany
John Wyant, Illinois Central College
Lisa Wyatt-Diaz, Nassau Community College
Bert Wyatt, University of Arkansas at Pine Bluff
Coary Young Sr., Jefferson College
Dawn Young, Bossier Parish Community College
Rosalie Young, State University of New York at Oswego
Steve Zabetakis, Hagerstown Junior College
Edward Zamarin, Catonsville Community College
Otho Zimmer Jr., Essex Community College
Glenn Zuern, State University of New York at Albany

ACKNOWLEDGMENTS

As you can well imagine, this project was a massive undertaking. Not only did the three of us spend several years writing, revising, rewriting, and revising again, but we also had the help of numerous assistants. We wish to thank Shawn G. Miller for his research prowess, particularly his ability to find information on the Web and through Westlaw. We wish to thank William Eric Hollowell for his legal assistance at every turn. We are also appreciative of the incredibly detailed and astute development reviews that our developmental editor, Dan Alpert, provided for us during these several years. Our editor, Sabra Horne, provided encouragement from the very beginning and doggedly pushed us to improve the manuscript and the supplements. At the production end, we feel fortunate to have had the services of Bill Stryker, Doug Abbott, Ann Borman, Jennie Redwitz, and Megan Ryan. We think everyone will agree with us when we say that no other design/production team has ever put together a more compelling and user-friendly introduction to criminal justice textbook. Our marketing manager, Christine Henry, also made a significant contribution to this effort throughout its development. We also wish to thank our publisher, Susan Badger, for supporting many of our outrageous demands for this project.

This text is a living product. We know that we can improve it and we will do so with each new edition. But we need your help. Please do not hesitate to write us with any suggestions you have.

L.G.
M.K.
R.L.M.

part one
The Criminal Justice System

chapter

1

Criminal Justice Today

Chapter Objectives

After reading this chapter, you should be able to:

1. Describe the two most common models of how society determines which acts are criminal.

2. Define crime and the different types of crime.

3. Outline the three levels of law enforcement.

4. List the essential elements of the corrections system.

5. Explain the difference between the formal and informal criminal justice processes.

6. Describe the layers of the "wedding cake" model.

7. Contrast the crime control and due process models.

8. List the major issues in criminal justice today.

9. Describe how the media affect the public's view of crime.

INTRODUCTION

When Karla Faye Tucker looked back on the events of that Friday night in June 1983, she would comment on how "sick-minded" she had been. "I did *that?*" she would say in disbelief, still finding it hard to comprehend.

What Tucker did—as a significant number of Americans at the time were well aware—was murder a twenty-seven-year-old cable television installer named Jerry Lynn Dean with a pickax and help her boyfriend do the same to Dean's companion, Deborah Thornton.[1] Nearly fifteen years later, Tucker was executed by the state of Texas for her crime.

Tucker was the thirty-eighth death row inmate Texas had executed in a year, but none of the previous thirty-seven received even a fraction of the attention afforded her. In fact, not since 1977, when Gary Gilmore became the first person put to death after the Supreme Court ruled that the death penalty was not *per se* cruel and unusual punishment,[2] had an execution taken such a prominent place on the national stage. The morning of Tucker's execution, hundreds of reporters and protesters crowded outside the walls of the Huntsville prison unit that contained the death chamber. That same morning, Texas Governor George W. Bush's office heard from three thousand callers, 80 percent of whom asked him to commute Tucker's sentence. Tucker herself had done the media rounds in the preceding weeks, appearing on *60 Minutes, Larry King Live, Charles Grodin,* Court TV and, her favorite, *The 700 Club.*

At first glance, the reason for this attention is obvious. Tucker was the first woman executed in Texas since 1863, and the first in the United States in fourteen years. For many observers, however, the event had a significance that went deeper than its statistical rareness. For them, Tucker's execution was the culmination of a decade-long shift toward retribution and away from rehabilitation in the American criminal justice system.[3]

Opponents of the death penalty had hoped the shock of knowing that a woman had been executed would reverse, or at least give pause, to this national inclination. It became quickly apparent, however, that this would not be the case. Six days after Tucker's execution, on February 3, 1998, when Steven Ceon Renfro was put to death for the murders of three people, the Huntsville grounds were nearly empty. Debate over the next woman in line to be executed, Florida's Judias Buenoano, was similarly muted. Most of the media stories on Buenoano—dubbed the Black Widow for poisoning her husband in 1971 to collect life insurance—centered on the fact that she was *not* receiving much media attention. It seemed that Tucker was destined to be no more than the latest in a long line of true crime media sensations that included Charles Manson, Ted Bundy, Jeffrey Dahmer, the Menendez brothers, and O. J. Simpson.

WHAT IS CRIME?

For all the controversy surrounding Karla Faye Tucker's punishment, few disagreed that she had committed a heinous crime. In our society, and indeed in most societies, taking another person's life is considered the most serious of crimes and warrants the harshest penalty. The taking of a life is not, however, always considered murder. As we shall see in Chapter 3, homicide may be justified when the offender is protecting himself or herself. In some circumstances, discussed in Chapter 7, law enforcement officers may kill in the line of duty without invoking criminal penalties. The state may sanction killing in times of war or, as with Tucker, as punishment.

When, then, is homicide considered murder? The easy answer is: when the legal conditions are met that designate it as such. Therefore, a *crime* can be

British au pair Louise Woodward was found guilty of second-degree murder for her role in the death of eight-month-old Matthew Eappen, who had been in her care. Woodward apparently caused Eappen's death by treating him roughly in a fit of annoyance when the infant would not stop crying. Massachusetts Superior Court Judge Hiller Zobel, who presided over the case, disagreed with the jury and reduced the murder conviction to involuntary manslaughter, setting Woodward free in the process. How does this case show the flexibility in the punishment of homicide in the American legal system?

defined as a wrong against society proclaimed by law and, if committed under certain circumstances, punishable by society.[4] The problem with this definition, however, is that it obscures the complex nature of societies. A society is not static—it evolves and changes, and its concept of criminality evolves and changes as well. Different societies can have vastly different ideas of what constitutes "a wrong." In Singapore, for example, the sale of chewing gum is illegal, a law that many Americans may find incomprehensible.

To more fully understand the concept of crime, it will help to examine the two most common models of how society "decides" which acts are criminal: the consensus model and the conflict model.

The Consensus Model

The **consensus model** assumes that as people gather together to form a society, its members will naturally come to a basic agreement with regard to shared norms and values. Those individuals whose actions deviate from the established norms and values are considered to pose a threat to the well-being of society as a whole and must be sanctioned (punished). The society passes laws to control and prevent deviant behavior, thereby setting the boundaries for acceptable behavior within the group.[5] Use of the term *consensus* implies that a majority of the citizens agree on what activities should be outlawed and punished as crimes.

The consensus model, to a certain extent, assumes that a diverse group of people can have similar *morals*. That is, they share an ideal of what is "right" and "wrong." Consequently, as public attitudes toward morality change, so do laws. In colonial times, those found guilty of adultery were subjected to corporal punishment; a century ago, one could walk into a pharmacy and purchase heroin. Today, social attitudes have shifted to consider adultery a personal issue, beyond the purview of the state, and the use of heroin a criminal act. When a consensus does not exist as to whether a certain act falls within the parameters of acceptable behavior, a period of uncertainty ensues as society struggles to formalize its attitudes as law. (For an example of the consensus model at work, see *Cross-National CJ Comparison—Doctor-Assisted Death and the Dutch* on the following page.)

CONSENSUS MODEL
A criminal justice model in which the majority of citizens in a society share the same values and beliefs. Criminal acts are those acts that conflict with these values and beliefs and are deemed harmful to society.

At the Cannibus Buyers Cooperative in Oakland, California, "bartender" Pamela Powers picks out a marijuana muffin for quadriplegic Ken Estes. In 1996, voters in California approved Proposition 215, which allows those with a physician's approval to purchase marijuana for medical purposes. The U.S. Department of Justice declared Proposition 215 illegal, as it countered federal drug laws that prohibit the production and sale of marijuana. U.S. District Judge Charles Breyer agreed, ordering the closing of the Oakland Cannibus Cooperative. In response, the city kept the Cooperative open, with an official telling the federal government to "butt out." How does the debate over medical marijuana reflect the consensus model in action?

Doctor-Assisted Death and the Dutch

Physician-assisted suicide and euthanasia ("mercy killing") are technically illegal in the Netherlands. Since 1973, however, this European nation's courts have decided that doctors can help terminate a patient's life if certain conditions are met: the patient must explicitly request such an action; the request must be voluntary; and the patient's suffering must be unbearable and without any hope of improvement. Furthermore, the physician must notify local prosecutors of the decision to terminate a life. Nearly 6 percent of all deaths in the Netherlands each year are assisted by a physician.

In explaining why the Netherlands accepts actions that many other countries would consider insupportable, observers point to several characteristics of Dutch society. First, doctors hold exalted positions, and their actions are rarely questioned. Not only are doctors authorized to terminate "meaningless" lives, but they are also expected to do so. Second, the country lacks a strong religious influence, which might place the question of assisted suicide in a different moral perspective. As it is, hopelessly ill patients who fail to request euthanasia are seen as adhering to outdated ethical values. Third, and most important, is the Dutch emphasis on personal autonomy; the choice to die is considered the responsibility of the individual, not of the state.

In 1998, an elderly Oregon woman whose breast cancer left her unable to breathe easily became the first American to legally commit suicide with the aid of a doctor. Oregon's Death with Dignity Act—which is modeled in many respects after the Dutch system—was upheld by a Supreme Court decision that gives each state the authority to legalize assisted suicide.

WHAT'S THE EVIDENCE?

Describe how the Dutch laws on physician-assisted suicide and euthanasia reflect the consensus model. To obtain information on the Internet, visit the Dutch Voluntary Euthanasia Society Web site at **www.nvve.nl/ukframe.htm**.

The Conflict Model

Those who reject the consensus model do so on the ground that moral attitudes are not absolute. In large, democratic societies such as the United States, different segments of society will inevitably have different value systems and shared norms. According to the **conflict model,** these different segments—separated by social class, income, age, and race—are engaged in a constant struggle with each other for control of society. The victorious groups exercise their power by codifying their value systems into criminal laws.[6]

Consequently, criminal activity is determined by whichever group happens to be holding power at any given time. Because certain groups do not have access to political power, their interests are not served by the criminal justice system. To give one example, which will be elaborated on in Chapter 18, the penalty (five years in prison) for possession of 5 grams of crack cocaine is the same as for possession of 500 grams of powder cocaine. This 1:100 ratio has had widespread implications for inner-city African Americans, who are statistically more likely to get caught using crack cocaine than are white suburbanites, who appear to favor the illicit drug in its powdered form.

An Integrated Definition of Crime

Considering both the consensus and conflict models, we can construct a definition of crime that will be useful throughout the textbook. For our purposes, crime is an action or activity that is:

1. Punishable under criminal law, as determined by the majority of a society or, in some cases, a powerful minority.

2. Considered an *offense against society as a whole* and prosecuted by public officials, not by victims.

CONFLICT MODEL
A criminal justice model in which the content of criminal law is determined by the groups that hold economic, political, and social power in a community.

3. Punishable by statutorily determined sanctions that bring about the loss of personal freedom.

Types of Crime

The manner in which crimes are classified depends on their seriousness. Federal, state, and local legislation has provided for the classification and punishment of hundreds of thousands of different criminal acts, ranging from first degree murder to jaywalking. For general purposes, we can group criminal behavior into six groups: violent crime, property crime, public order crime, white-collar crime, organized crime, and high-tech crime.

Violent Crime. Crimes against persons, or **violent crimes,** have come to dominate our perspectives on crime. There are four major categories of violent crime:

- *Murder,* or the unlawful killing of a human being.

- *Sexual assault,* or *rape,* which refers to coerced actions of a sexual nature against an unwilling participant.

- *Assault and battery,* two separate acts that cover situations in which one person physically attacks another (battery) or, through threats, intentionally leads another to believe that he or she will be physically harmed (assault).

- *Robbery,* or the taking of money, personal property, or any other article of value from a person by means of force or fear.

As we shall see in Chapter 3, these violent crimes are further classified by *degree,* depending on the circumstances surrounding the criminal act. These circumstances include the intent of the person committing the crime, whether a weapon was used, and (in cases other than murder) the level of pain and suffering experienced by the victim.

Property Crime. The most common form of criminal activity is **property crime,** or those crimes in which the goal of the offender is some form of economic gain or the damaging of property. Pocket-picking, shoplifting, and the stealing of any property that is not accomplished by force are covered by laws against *larceny/theft. Burglary* refers to the unlawful entry of a structure with the intention of committing a felony such as theft. The willful and malicious burning of a home, automobile, commercial building, or any other construction, known as *arson,* is also a property crime.

Public Order Crime. The concept of **public order crimes** is linked to the consensus model discussed earlier. Historically, societies have always outlawed activities that are considered contrary to public values and morals. Homosexual acts, for example, have been designated criminal for most of this nation's history[7] and are still banned (though rarely prosecuted) in nearly half the states. Today, the most common public order crimes include public drunkenness, prostitution, gambling, and illicit drug use. These crimes are sometimes referred to as *victimless crimes* because they harm only the offender. As we shall see throughout this textbook, however, that term is rather misleading. Public order crimes often create an environment that gives rise to property and violent crimes.

White-Collar Crime. Crimes occur in the business world too. Business-related crimes are popularly referred to as **white-collar crimes.** The term

---

"Murder is unique in that it abolishes the party it injures, so that society has to take the place of the victim and on his behalf demand atonement or grant forgiveness; it is the one crime in which society has a direct impact."

—W.H. Auden, *Anglo-American poet* (1949)

VIOLENT CRIME
Crimes committed against persons, including murder, rape, assault and battery, and robbery.

PROPERTY CRIME
Crimes committed against property, including larceny/theft, burglary, and arson.

PUBLIC ORDER CRIME
Behavior that has been labeled criminal because it is contrary to shared social values, customs, and norms.

WHITE-COLLAR CRIME
Nonviolent crimes committed by corporations and individuals to gain a personal or business advantage.

In April 1999, John A. "Junior" Gotti, left, pled guilty to racketeering, bribery, extortion, and several other charges related to the illegal takeover of a topless club in Manhattan, New York. For committing these white-collar crimes, Gotti was sentenced to a seven-year prison term.

white-collar crime is broadly used to describe an illegal act or series of acts committed by an individual or business entity using some nonviolent means to obtain a personal or business advantage. Figure 1.1 lists various types of white-collar crime; note that certain property crimes fall into this category when committed in a corporate context.

The U.S. Department of Commerce estimates that white-collar crime costs corporate America $40 billion annually.[8] The consequences of these crimes are felt by thousands of citizens and businesses. After helping to uncover an $8 million telemarketing scam, a federal law enforcement officer commented, "When you look at the human tragedy of something like this, the impact on society is much greater than when somebody walks in and sticks up a store with a gun."[9] Some observers see the relatively light penalties given to wealthy white-collar criminals—in contrast to harsher penalties for poorer "blue-collar (or street) criminals" convicted of burglary, larceny, and the sale of illegal drugs—as supporting the conflict model of criminality.

Figure 1.1 White-Collar Crime

Embezzlement	A form of employee fraud in which an individual uses his or her position within a corporation to *embezzle,* or steal, the corporation's money, property, or other assets.
Pilferage	A less serious form of employee fraud in which the individual steals items from the workplace.
Credit-Card and Check Fraud	The unauthorized use of credit cards costs billions of dollars annually. This form of white-collar crime involves obtaining credit-card numbers through a variety of schemes (such as stealing them from the Internet) and using the numbers for personal gain. Check fraud includes writing checks that are not covered by bank funds, forging checks, and stealing traveler's checks.
Insurance Fraud	Insurance fraud involves making false claims in order to collect insurance payments under false pretenses. Faking an injury in order to receive payments from a workers' compensation program, for example, is a form of insurance fraud.
Securities Fraud	This area covers illegal activity in the stock market. It includes stockbrokers who steal money from their clients and *insider trading,* which is the illegal trading in a stock by someone (or on behalf of someone) who has inside knowledge in the company in question.
Bribery	Also known as *influence peddling,* bribery occurs in the business world when somebody within a company sells influence, power, or information to a person outside the company who can benefit. A county official, for example, could give a construction company a lucrative county contract to build a new jail. In return, the construction company would give a sum of money, also known as a *kickback,* to the official.
Consumer Fraud	This term covers a wide variety of activity designed to defraud consumers, from false advertising (claiming a juice is "100 percent pure" when it contains a high amount of chemicals) to offering "free" items, such as electronic devices or vacations, that include a number of hidden charges.
Tax Evasion	The practice by which taxpayers either underreport (or do not report) their taxable income or otherwise purposely attempt to evade a tax liability.

The Godfather Imitates Life; Life Imitates The Godfather

In both Mario Puzo's best-selling novel and Francis Ford Coppola's classic film, *The Godfather* was a tribute to a romanticized version of organized crime in America. Puzo's original story was a rewriting of the tales of the "Five Families," or the five main branches of the Italian Mafia in the United States (Bonnano, Gambino, Genovese, Luchese, and Profuci). The image that opens the film, of Don Vito Corleone (played by Marlon Brando) welcoming supplicants at his daughter's wedding, is a reflection of a practice fostered by the legendary Don Carlo Gambino, who used to hold similar audiences in cafés in Little Italy, New York. The character of Corleone was a combination of two Mafia dons, Vito Genovese and Joseph Profuci. Like the real-life Genovese, the fictional Corleone ordered his underlings not to deal in the new and risky market of illegal drugs.

The movie was so successful at delivering images of the American Mafia that the real Mafia began to copy what it saw on-screen. Only after *The Godfather*'s release was the prewar practice of kissing a don's hand as a sign of respect resurrected. The movie also proved to be a powerful recruiting tool for young men drawn to the ideals of honor and family it portrayed. Famed Gambino hit man Sammy "the Bull" Gravano decided to become involved in organized crime after seeing the film in Brooklyn in 1972. More than twenty years later, after being involved in nineteen killings, Gravano turned state's evidence against his boss, John Gotti. In explaining his motives, Gravano told prosecutors, "The only thing I can love about my life is the movie. There's no honor, there's no respect. Everything is a double cross."

Organized Crime. White-collar crime takes place within the confines of the legitimate business world. **Organized crime,** in contrast, operates *illegitimately* by satisfying the public's demand for illegal goods and services. Organized crime broadly implies a conspiratorial relationship between any number of persons engaged in illegal acts. More specifically, groups engaged in organized crime employ criminal tactics such as violence, corruption, and intimidation for economic gain. The hierarchical structure of organized crime operations often mirrors that of legitimate businesses, and, like any corporation, these groups attempt to capture a sufficient percentage of any given market to make a profit. For organized crime, the traditional preferred markets are gambling, prostitution, illegal narcotics, pornography, and loan sharking (lending money at higher than legal rates), along with more recent ventures into counterfeiting and credit-card scams.[10]

Thanks in large part to popular culture and the media, organized crime is often associated with the Italian Mafia. Indeed, to many, organized crime and the Mafia are synonymous, and the myth has become more powerful than reality. (See *Criminal Justice & Popular Culture—The Godfather Imitates Life; Life Imitates The Godfather*.) In fact, organized crime is an equal opportunity field of criminal activity, with nearly every ethnic group, including white Anglo-Saxon Protestants, represented. Organized crime has also developed global networks. Senator John Kerry (D-Mass.), who chaired the U.S. Senate Subcommittee on Terrorism, Narcotics, and International Operations, describes a "global criminal axis" dominated by the Mafia, the Russian mobs, the Japanese *yakuza*, the Chinese triads, and the Colombia drug cartels. According to Kerry, the "Big Five" have formed strategic alliances with each other and smaller operations in countries such as Nigeria, Poland, Jamaica, and Panama to streamline the international drug trade, among other things.[11]

ORGANIZED CRIME
A conspiratorial relationship between any number of persons engaged in the market for illegal goods or services, such as illicit drugs or firearms.

You can find a wealth of information on cybercrimes at the CyberSpace Law Center's Web site Go to:
www.cybersquirrel/com/clc/criminal/

High-Tech Crime. The newest typology of crime is directly related to the increased use of computers in everyday life. The Internet, with approximately 160 million users worldwide, is the site of numerous *cybercrimes,* such as selling pornographic materials, soliciting minors, and defrauding consumers with bogus financial investments. The dependence of businesses on computer operations has left corporations vulnerable to sabotage, fraud, embezzlement, and theft of proprietary data. According to one study, nearly 60 percent of American corporations surveyed reported that the security of their computer systems had been compromised in the past year.[12] The American Society for Industrial Security estimates that the nation's businesses may lose as much as $300 billion from the theft of intellectual property each year.[13] (See Figure 1.2 for several types of cybercrimes.)

Because little more is needed than a home computer and a telephone line, virtually anyone is capable of committing high-tech crime. The perpetrators range from a Russian "hacker"—slang for someone who illegally enters a private computer system—who engineered the theft of $10 billion from Citibank to two teenagers in South Brunswick, New Jersey, who lifted credit-card numbers from Internet users and used them to buy more than $15,000 worth of merchandise. Law enforcement agencies are forming specialized units in response to the increased incidence of high-tech crime. The Federal Bureau of Investigation's Criminal Squad 37, for example, is dedicated to apprehending criminals who attack computer systems.[14]

THE CRIMINAL JUSTICE SYSTEM

Defining which actions are to be labeled "crimes" is only the first step in safeguarding society from criminal behavior. Institutions must be created to apprehend alleged wrongdoers, determine whether these persons have indeed committed crimes, and punish those who are found guilty according to society's wishes. These institutions combine to form the *criminal justice system.* As we begin our examination of the American criminal justice system in this introductory chapter, it is important to have an idea of its purpose.

Figure 1.2 Types of Cybercrime

Cybercrime against Persons

- *Obscene Material and Pornography:* The selling, posting, and distribution of obscene material such as pornography, indecent exposure, and child pornography.
- *Cyber-stalking:* The act of using a computer and the Internet to continually attempt to contact and/or intimidate another person.
- *Cyber-harassment:* The harassment of a person through electronic mail, on chat sites, or by printing information about the person on Web sites.

Cybercrime against Property

- *Hacking:* The act of using programming abilities with malicious intent.
- *Cracking:* The act of using programming abilities in an attempt to gain unauthorized access to a computer or network.
- *Piracy:* Copying and distributing software or other items belonging to someone else over the Internet.
- *Viruses:* The creation and distribution of harmful computer programs.

Cybercrime against the Government

- *Cyber-terrorism:* The use of a computer and/or the Internet to further political goals of terrorism against a country and its citizens.

SOURCE: SUSAN BRENNER AND REBECCA COCHRAN, UNIVERSITY OF DAYTON SCHOOL OF LAW AT **www.cybercrimes.net**.

The Purpose of the Criminal Justice System

In 1967, the President's Commission on Law Enforcement and Administration of Justice stated that the criminal justice system is obliged to enforce accepted standards of conduct so as to "protect individuals and the community."[15] Given this general mandate, we can further separate the purpose of the modern criminal justice system into three general goals:

1. To control crime

2. To prevent crime

3. To provide and maintain justice

Though many observers differ on the precise methods of reaching them, the first two goals are fairly straightforward. By arresting, prosecuting, and punishing wrongdoers, the criminal justice system attempts to *control* crime. In the process, the system also hopes to *prevent* new crimes from taking place. The prevention goal is often used to justify harsh punishments for wrongdoers, which some see as deterring others from committing similar criminal acts. The third goal—of providing and maintaining justice—is more complicated, largely because *justice* is a difficult concept to define. Broadly stated, justice means that all citizens are equal before the law and that they are free from arbitrary arrest or seizure as defined by the law.[16] In other words, the idea of justice is linked with the idea of fairness. Above all, we want our laws and the means by which they are carried out to be fair.

Justice and fairness are subjective terms; different people may have different concepts of what is just and fair. If a woman who has been beaten by her husband retaliates by killing him, what is her just punishment? Reasonable persons could disagree, with some thinking that the homicide was justified and she should be treated leniently, and others insisting that she should not have taken the law into her own hands. Police officers, judges, prosecutors, prison administrators, and other employees of the criminal justice system must decide what is "fair." Sometimes, their course of action is obvious; often, as we shall see, it is not.

Society places the burden of controlling crime, preventing crime, and determining fairness on those citizens who work in the three main institutions of the criminal justice system: law enforcement, courts, and corrections. In the next section, we take an introductory look at these institutions and their role in the criminal justice system as a whole.

The Structure of the Criminal Justice System

To understand the structure of the criminal justice system, one must understand the concept of **federalism,** which means that government powers are shared by the national (federal) government and the states. The framers of the U.S. Constitution, fearful of tyranny and a too-powerful central government, chose the system of federalism as a compromise. The appeal of federalism was that it allowed for state powers and local traditions while establishing a strong national government capable of handling large-scale problems.

The Constitution gave the national government certain express powers, such as the power to coin money, raise an army, and regulate interstate commerce. All other powers were left to the states, including police power, which allows the states to enact whatever laws are necessary to protect the health, morals, safety, and welfare of their citizens. As the American criminal justice system has evolved, the ideals of federalism have ebbed somewhat; in par-

"The American people have been very clear; . . . [t]he most important job is to keep the streets and the neighborhoods of America safe. The first responsibility of Government is law and order. Without it, people can never really pursue the American dream. And without it, we're not really free."

—President Bill Clinton, 1994

FEDERALISM
A form of government in which a written constitution provides for a division of powers between a central government and several regional governments. In the United States, the division of powers between the federal government and the fifty states is established by the Constitution.

ticular, federal involvement has expanded significantly. Crime is still, however, for the most part a local concern, and the majority of all employees in the criminal justice system work for local government (see Figure 1.3).

Law Enforcement. The ideals of federalism can be clearly seen in the local, state, and federal levels of law enforcement. Though agencies from the different levels will cooperate if the need arises, they have their own organizational structures and tend to operate independently of one another. In addition to this brief introduction, each level of law enforcement will be covered in more detail in Chapters 4, 5, 6, and 7.

Local Law Enforcement. On the local level, the duties of law enforcement agencies are split between counties and municipalities. The chief law enforcement officer of most counties is the county sheriff. The sheriff is usually an elected post, with a two- or four-year term. In some areas, where city and county governments have merged, there is a county police force, headed by a chief of police. The bulk of local police officers—nearly 500,000—are employed by municipalities. The majority of these forces consist of fewer than ten officers, though a large city such as New York can have a police force of more than 35,000.

Local police are responsible for the "nuts and bolts" of law enforcement work. They investigate most crimes and attempt to deter crime through patrol activities. They apprehend criminals and participate in the trial proceedings, if necessary. Local police are also charged with "keeping the peace," a broad set of duties that includes crowd and traffic control and the resolution of minor conflicts between citizens. In many areas, local police have the added obligation of providing social services such as dealing with domestic violence and child abuse.

State Law Enforcement. Hawaii is the only state that does not have a state law enforcement agency. Generally, there are two types of state law enforcement agencies, those designated simply as "state police" and those designated as "highway patrols." State highway patrols concern themselves mainly with infractions on public highways and freeways. Other state law enforcers include fire marshals, who investigate suspicious fires and educate the public on fire prevention, and fish, game, and watercraft wardens, who police a state's natural resources and often oversee its firearms laws. Some states also have alcoholic beverage control officers plus agents who investigate welfare and food stamp fraud.

Figure 1.3 Local, State, and Federal Employees in Our Criminal Justice System

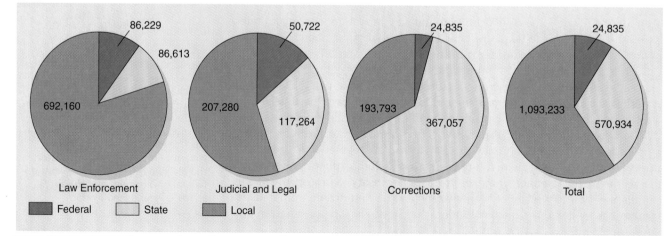

	86,229	50,722	24,835	24,835
Law Enforcement	86,613	117,264	367,057	570,934
	692,160	207,280	193,793	1,093,233

Law Enforcement   Judicial and Legal   Corrections   Total

■ Federal   □ State   ■ Local

SOURCE: BUREAU OF JUSTICE STATISTICS, JUSTICE EXPENDITURE AND EMPLOYMENT EXTRACTS, 1993 (WASHINGTON, D.C.: U.S. DEPARTMENT OF JUSTICE, 1994), TABLE 2.

Few states offer the law enforcement challenges that can be found in Alaska. Covering 586,412 square miles (one-fifth the size of the continental United States), the state is filled with mountains, glaciers, millions of lakes, and thousands of rivers, and has a coastline of more than 6,600 miles. The Alaska State Troopers, pictured here, must cope with blizzards, avalanches, subzero temperatures, and limited traditional transportation routes such as roads. Obviously, environment plays a large role in law enforcement on a state and local level.

Federal Law Enforcement. The creation of new national gun, drug, and violent crime laws over the past thirty years has led to an expansion in the size and scope of the federal government's participation in the criminal justice system. Federal agencies with police powers include the Federal Bureau of Investigation (FBI), the Drug Enforcement Administration (DEA), the U.S. Secret Service, and the Bureau of Alcohol, Tobacco and Firearms (ATF). In fact, almost every federal agency, including the postal and forest services, has some kind of police power. Many observers worry that this increase in federal law enforcement is counter to our constitutional dictate against the formation of a national police force.

The Courts. The United States has a *dual court system;* that is, we have two independent judicial systems, one on the federal level and one on the state level. Practically, this translates into fifty-one different court systems: one national court system and fifty different state court systems. The federal system consists of district courts, circuit courts of appeals, and the United States Supreme Court. The state systems include trial courts at the local and state levels, intermediate courts of appeals, and state supreme courts.

The *criminal court* and its work group—the judge, prosecutors, and defense attorneys—are charged with the weighty responsibility of determining the innocence or guilt of criminal suspects. We will cover these important participants, their role in the criminal trial, and the court system as a whole in Chapters 8, 9, 10, and 11.

Corrections. Once the court system convicts and sentences an offender, she or he is delegated to the corrections system. Depending on the seriousness of the crime and their individual needs, offenders are placed on probation, incarcerated, or transferred to community-based corrections facilities.

- *Probation*, the most common correctional treatment, allows the offender to return to the community and remain under the supervision of an agent of the court known as a probation officer. While on probation, the offender must follow certain rules of conduct. If probationers fail to follow these rules, they may be incarcerated.

- If the offender's sentence includes a period of incarceration, he or she will be remanded to a corrections facility for a certain amount of time.

Jails hold those convicted of minor crimes with relatively short sentences, as well as those awaiting trial or involved in certain court proceedings. *Prisons* house those convicted of more serious crimes with longer sentences. Generally speaking, counties and municipalities administer jails, while prisons are the domain of federal and state governments.

Community-based corrections have increased in popularity, as jails and prisons have been plagued with problems of overcrowding. Community-based correctional facilities include halfway houses, residential centers, and work-release centers; they operate on the assumption that all convicts do not need, and are not benefited by, incarceration in jail or prison.

The majority of those inmates released from incarceration are not finished with the correctional system. The most frequent type of release from a jail or prison is *parole,* in which an inmate, after serving part of his or her sentence in a correctional facility, is allowed to serve the rest of the term in the community. Like someone on probation, a parolee must conform to certain conditions of freedom, with the same consequences if these conditions are not followed. Issues of probation, incarceration, community-based corrections, and parole will be covered in Chapters 12, 13, 14, and 15.

The Criminal Justice Process

In its 1967 report, the President's Commission on Law Enforcement and Administration of Justice asserted that the criminal justice system

> is not a hodgepodge of random actions. It is rather a continuum—an orderly progression of events—some of which, like arrest and trial, are highly visible and some of which, though of great importance, occur out of public view.[17]

The commission's assertion that the criminal justice system is a "continuum" is one that many observers would challenge.[18] Some liken the criminal justice system to a sports team, which is the sum of an indeterminable number of decisions, relationships, conflicts, and adjustments.[19] Such a volatile mix is not what we generally associate with a "system." For most, the word *system* indicates a certain degree of order and discipline. That we refer to our law enforcement agencies, courts, and correctional facilities as part of a "system" may reflect our hopes rather than reality.

Just as there is an idealized image of the criminal justice system as a smooth continuum, there also exists an idealized version of the *criminal justice process,* or the procedures through which the criminal justice system meets the expectations of society. Professor Herbert Packer, for example, compared the idealized criminal justice process to an assembly line,

> down which moves an endless stream of cases, never stopping, carrying the cases to workers who stand at fixed stations and who perform on each case as it comes by the same small but essential operation that brings it one stop closer to being a finished product, or, to exchange the metaphor for the reality, a closed file.[20]

As Packer himself was wont to point out, the daily operations of criminal justice are not nearly so perfect. In this textbook, the criminal justice process will be examined as the end product of literally thousands of decisions made by the police, courtroom workers, and correctional administrators. It should become clear that, in fact, the criminal justice process functions as a continuous balancing act between its formal and informal nature, both of which are discussed below.

"What is legal is not necessary—not even usually—about what is right, just, or ethical. It is about order. Similarly, 'justice' is a process that makes things work, not necessarily a result that is good or moral or ethical."

—Charles R. Gregg, *President, Houston Bar Association* (1995)

The Formal Criminal Justice Process. In Packer's image of assembly-line justice, each step of the process "involves a series of routinized operations whose success is gauged primarily by their tendency to pass the case along to a successful conclusion."[21] These "routinized" steps are detailed in Figure 1.4.

The Informal Criminal Justice Process. Each step described in Figure 1.4 is the result of a series of decisions that must be made by those who work in the criminal justice system. This **discretion**—which can be defined as the authority to choose between and among alternative courses of action—leads to the development of the informal criminal justice process, discussed below.

Discretionary Basics. One New York City public defender called his job "a pressure cooker." That term could apply to the entire spectrum of the criminal justice process. Law enforcement agencies do not have the staff or money to investigate *every* crime; they must decide where to direct their restricted resources. Increasing caseloads and a limited amount of time with which to dispose of them constrict many of our nation's courts. Overcrowding in prisons and jails affects both law enforcement agencies and the courts—there is simply not enough room for all convicts.

The criminal justice system uses discretion to alleviate these pressures. Police decide whether to arrest a suspect; prosecutors decide whether to prosecute; magistrates decide whether there is sufficient probable cause for a case to go to a jury; judges decide on sentencing; and so on. (See Figure 1.5 on page 18 for a rundown of some of the more important discretionary decisions.) Collectively, these decisions are said to produce an *informal criminal justice system* because discretion is not enclosed by the rigid confines of the law. Even if prosecutors believe that a suspect is guilty, they may decide not to prosecute if the case is weak or if they know that the police erred in the investigative process. In most cases, prosecutors will not squander the scarce resource of court time on a case they might not win. Some argue that the

DISCRETION
The ability of individuals in the criminal justice system to make operational decisions based on personal judgment instead of formal rules or official information.

Although discretion is absolutely necessary in the criminal justice system, it can be abused. Damien "Pookie" Burris, at left with his young son, spent more than five months in a Los Angeles jail for a 1993 murder he did not commit. Witnesses to the killing said the assailant was nicknamed "Pookie," and, after several identified Burris from mug shots, he was arrested by the police. Burris claimed he was in church at the time of the murder, an alibi detectives chose not to validate. In fact, it took the discretionary intervention of a patrol officer to prove that Burris had in fact been in church and the police had arrested the wrong "Pookie." How can criminal justice procedure be seen as a system of "checks and balances" in which discretionary errors are eventually corrected?

Figure 1.4 The Steps of the Criminal Justice System

After an arrest, law enforcement agencies present information about the case and about the accused to the prosecutor, who will decide if formal charges will be filed with the court. A suspect charged with a crime must be taken before a judge without unnecessary delay. At the initial appearance, the judge informs the accused of the charges and decides whether there is probable cause to detain the accused person. If the offense is not serious, the determination of guilt and an assessment of a penalty may also occur at this stage.

Often, the defense counsel is assigned at the initial appearance. All suspects charged with serious crimes have a right to be represented by an attorney. If the suspect cannot afford a defense attorney, the court will provide one for him or her at the public's expense. A pre-trial release decision may also be made at the initial appearance. The court may decide that the suspect poses a threat to society, and place him or her in jail until the trial. The court may decide to release the suspect with the understanding that he or she will return for the trial, or release the suspect on bail (meaning he or she must provide the court with monetary payment [bail] which will be returned when the suspect appears for the trial).

In many jurisdictions the initial appearance may be followed by a preliminary hearing. The main function of this hearing is to discover if there is probable cause to believe that the accused committed a known crime within the jurisdiction of the court. If the judge does find probable cause or the accused waives his or her right to the preliminary hearing, the case may be sent to a grand jury. A grand jury hears evidence against the accused presented by the prosecutor and decides if there is sufficient evidence to cause the accused to be brought to trial. If the grand jury find sufficient evidence, it submits to the court an indictment, a written statement of the essential facts of the offense charged against the accused.

Misdemeanor cases and some felony cases proceed by the issuance of an information, a formal, written accusation submitted to the court by a prosecutor. In some jurisdictions, defendants—often those without prior criminal records—may be eligible for diversion programs. In these programs, the suspect does not go to trial, and instead must complete a treatment program, such as drug treatment. If he or she is successful, charges may be dropped and his or her criminal record may remain clear.

Step 1: Entry into the System

Once a law enforcement agency has established that a crime has been committed, a suspect must be identified and apprehended for the case to proceed through the system. Sometimes a suspect is apprehended at the scene of the crime; however, identification of a suspect sometimes requires an extensive investigation. Often, no one is identified or apprehended. In some instances, a suspect is arrested and later the police determine that no crime was committed and the suspect is released.

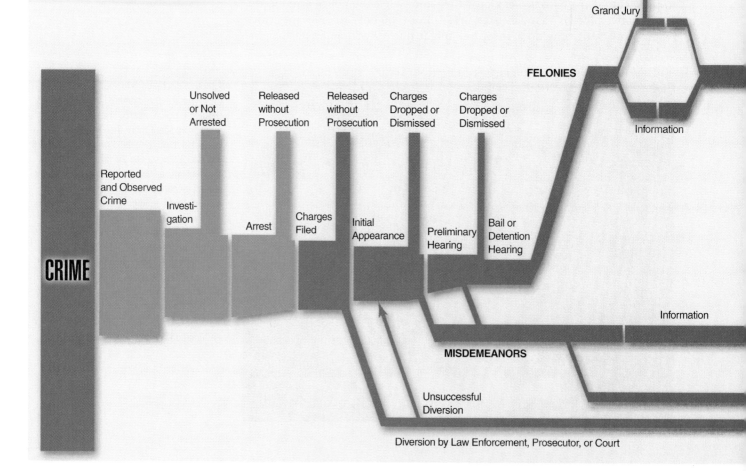

Step 3: Adjudication

Once an indictment or information has been filed with the trial court, the accused is scheduled for an arraignment. At the arraignment, the accused is informed of the charges, advised of his or her rights, and asked to enter a plea to the charges. Sometimes a plea of guilty is the result of negotiations between the prosecutor and the defendant. If the defendant pleads guilty and this plea is accepted by the judge, no trial is held and the defendant is sentenced. If the accused pleads not guilty, a date is set for the trial. A person accused of a serious crime is guaranteed a trial by jury. During the trial, the prosecution and defense present evidence while the judge decides on issues of law. The jury then decides whether the defendant will be acquitted (found not guilty), or convicted (found guilty of the initial charges or of other offenses). If the defendant is found guilty, he or she may request that the trial be reviewed by a higher court to assure that the rules of trial procedure were followed.

Step 4: Sentencing and Sanctions

After a conviction, sentence is imposed. In most cases, the judge decides the sentence, though sometimes the jury makes this decision. Some of the sentencing choices available to judges and juries include the death penalty, incarceration in prison or jail, probation (allowing the convicted person to remain in the community as long as he or she follows certain rules), and fines. In many jurisdictions, persons convicted of certain types of offenses must serve a prison term.

Step 5: Corrections

Offenders sentenced to incarceration usually serve time in a local jail or a prison. Offenders sentenced to less than one year usually go to jail; those sentenced to more than one year go to prison. A prisoner may become eligible for parole after serving part of his or her sentence. Parole is the release of a prisoner before the full sentence has been served. If released under parole, the convict will be supervised in the community for the balance of his or her sentence.

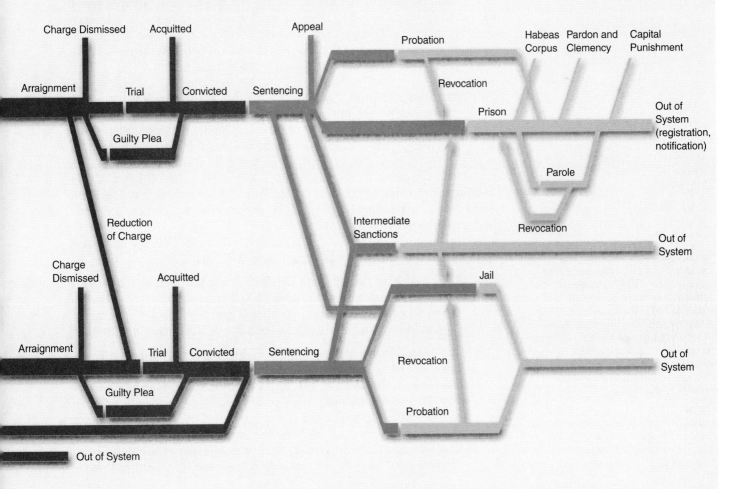

Figure 1.5 Discretion in the Criminal Justice System

Criminal justice officials must make decisions every day concerning their duties. The following officials must decide whether or not to make the following decisions, or how to make them.

Police	Enforce laws
	Investigate specific crimes
	Search people or buildings
	Arrest or detain people
Prosecutors	File charges against suspects brought to them by the police
	Drop cases
	Reduce charges
Judges	Set conditions for pre-trial release
	Accept pleas
	Dismiss charges
	Impose sentences
Correctional Officials	Assign convicts to prison or jail
	Punish prisoners who misbehave
	Award prisoners who behave well

SOURCE: U.S. DEPARTMENT OF JUSTICE, BUREAU OF JUSTICE STATISTICS, REPORT TO THE NATION ON CRIME AND JUSTICE, 2D ED. (WASHINGTON, D.C.: GOVERNMENT PRINTING OFFICE, 1988), 59.

informal process has made our criminal justice system more just. Given the immense pressure of limited resources, the argument goes, only rarely will an innocent person end up before a judge and jury.[22]

Of course, not all discretionary decisions are based on scarce resources. Sometimes, discretion is based on political considerations, such as when a police administrator orders a crackdown on public order crimes because of citizen complaints. Furthermore, employees of the criminal justice system may make decisions based on their personal values or morality (for an example see *CJ in Focus—Making Waves: A Prosecutor's Crusade*). For that reason, discretion is closely connected to questions of *ethics* in criminal justice and will be discussed in that context throughout this textbook.

The "Wedding Cake Model" of Criminal Justice. Some believe that the prevailing informal approach to criminal justice creates a situation in which all cases are not treated equally. They point to the highly publicized O. J. Simpson trial of 1994, during which the defendant was treated differently than most double-murder suspects. To describe this effect, criminal justice researchers Lawrence M. Friedman and Robert V. Percival came up with a **"wedding cake" model** of criminal justice.[23] This model posits that discretion comes to bear depending on the relative importance of a particular case to the decision makers.

As in any wedding cake, Friedman and Percival's model has the narrowest layer at the top and the widest at the bottom (see Figure 1.6).

1. The "top" layer consists of a handful of "celebrity" cases that attract the most attention and publicity. Recent examples of top-level cases include the trials of Simpson, Oklahoma City federal building bombers Timothy J. McVeigh and Terry Nichols, and nanny Louise Woodward.

2. The second layer consists of "high-profile" felonies. A **felony** is a serious crime such as murder, rape, or burglary that in most states is punishable either by death or by incarceration for a period longer than one year. This layer includes crimes committed by persons with criminal records, crimes in which the victim was seriously injured, and crimes in which a weapon was used, as well as crimes in which the offender and victim were strangers. These types of felonies are considered "high profile" because they usually draw a certain amount of public

"WEDDING CAKE" MODEL
A wedding cake–shaped model that explains why different cases receive different treatment in the criminal justice system. The cases at the "top" of the cake receive the most attention and have the greatest effect on public perception of criminal justice, while those cases at the "bottom" are disposed of quickly and virtually ignored by the media.

FELONY
A serious crime punishable by death or by imprisonment in a federal or state corrections facility for more than a year.

CJ in Focus
Making Waves
A Prosecutor's Crusade

To his critics, South Carolina attorney general Charles Condon is an example of discretion gone mad. To his supporters, he is a visionary fueled by the strength of his convictions. In either case, he is widely recognized as being at the forefront of a movement to charge pregnant women who use drugs with crimes ranging from child abuse to murder.

ONE IN TWENTY-ONE

Most states will convict a third party for causing harm or death to a fetus—inducing miscarriage by kicking a pregnant woman in the stomach, for example. But most states are not willing to levy criminal charges if the mother harms the fetus herself. As of 1998, twenty-one appellate court systems had heard cases charging pregnant women with a variety of crimes toward their unborn fetuses. Twenty of those states rejected the charges.

The only success story has been that of Attorney General Condon. In 1992, he prosecuted Cornelia Whitner for neglect after she gave birth to a baby with traces of cocaine in its blood. Five years later, by a vote of 3-2, the state supreme court upheld Whitner's eight-year sentence, ruling that a viable fetus is a person under the state's child abuse laws and that a mother using illegal drugs during pregnancy can be charged with neglect, manslaughter, and possibly murder. Two months after this ruling, another South Carolinian who said that she smoked crack an hour before giving birth to a stillborn baby pleaded guilty to involuntary manslaughter.

For Critical Analysis: How does this example highlight the possible pros and cons of discretionary power in the criminal justice system?

---

attention, which places pressure on the prosecutors to bring the case to trial instead of accepting a guilty plea for a lesser sentence.

3. The third layer consists of "ordinary" felonies, which include less violent crimes such as burglaries and thefts or even robberies in which no weapon was used. Because of the low profile of the accused—usually a first-time offender who has had a prior relationship with his or her victim—these "ordinary" felonies often do not receive the full formal process of a trial.

4. Finally, the fourth layer consists of **misdemeanors,** or crimes less serious than felonies. Misdemeanors include petty offenses such as shoplifting, disturbing the peace, and violations of local ordinances; they are usually punishable by fines, probation, or short jail times. More than three-quarters of all arrests made by police are for misdemeanors.

The irony of the wedding cake model is that the cases on the top level come closest to meeting our standards of ideal criminal justice. In these celebrity trials, we get to see committed (and expensive) attorneys argue minute technicalities of the law, sometimes for days on end. The further one moves down the layers of the cake, the more informal the process becomes. Though many of the cases in the second layer are brought to trial, only rarely does this occur for the less serious felonies in the third level of the wedding cake. By the fourth level, cases are dealt with almost completely informally, and the end goal appears to be speed rather than what can be called "justice."

Public fascination with celebrity cases obscures a truth of the informal criminal justice process: trial by jury is relatively rare (only about 3 percent of those arrested for felonies go to trial), and most cases are disposed of with an eye more toward convenience than ideals of justice or fairness. Consequently, the summary of the criminal justice system provided by the wedding cake model is much more realistic than the impression many Americans have obtained from the media.

I. The celebrated cases

II. Serious or "high profile" felonies

III. Less serious or "ordinary" felonies

IV. Misdemeanors

Figure 1.6 The Wedding Cake Model

MISDEMEANOR
Any crime that is not a felony; punishable by a fine or by confinement for up to a year.

VALUES OF THE CRIMINAL JUSTICE SYSTEM

If the general conclusion of the wedding cake model—that inequality is inherent in our criminal justice system—bothers you, then you probably question the values of the system. Just as individuals have values—a belief structure governing individual conduct—our criminal justice system can be said to have values, too. These values form the foundation for Herbert Packer's two models of the criminal justice system.

Crime Control and Due Process: To Punish or Protect?

In his landmark book, *The Limits of the Criminal Sanction*, Packer introduced two models for the American criminal justice system: the crime control model and the due process model.[24] The underlying value of the crime control model is that the most important function of the criminal justice process is to punish and repress criminal conduct. Though not in direct conflict with crime control, the underlying values of the due process model focus more on protecting the rights of the accused through legal constraints on police, courts, and corrections.

The Crime Control Model The **crime control model** begins with two assumptions: it is the role of the criminal justice system to protect and guarantee personal freedom, and if the system is to do so, law enforcement must be counted on to control criminal activity. "Controlling" criminal activity is at best difficult, and probably impossible. For the crime control model to operate successfully, Packer writes, it

> must produce a high rate of apprehension and conviction, and must do so in a context where the magnitudes being dealt with are very large and the resources for dealing with them are very limited.[25]

In other words, the system must be quick and efficient. In the ideal crime control model, any suspect who most likely did not commit a crime is quickly jettisoned from the system, while those who are transferred to the trial process are convicted as quickly as possible. It was in this context that Packer referred to the criminal justice process as an assembly line.

The crime control model also assumes that the police are in a better position than the courts to determine the guilt of arrested suspects. Therefore, not only should judges operate on a "presumption of guilt" (that is, any suspect brought before the court is more likely guilty than not), but as few restrictions as possible should be placed on police investigative and fact-gathering activities. The crime control model relies on the informality in the criminal justice system, as discussed earlier.

The Due Process Model. Packer likened the **due process model** to an obstacle course rather than an assembly line. Rather than expediting cases through the system, as is preferable in the crime control model, the due process model strives to make it more difficult to prove guilt. It rests on the belief that it is more desirable for society that ninety-nine guilty suspects go free than that a single innocent person be condemned.[26]

The due process model is based on the assumption that the absolute efficiency that is the goal of the crime control model can only be realized if the power of the state is absolute. Because fairness, and not efficiency, is the ultimate goal of the due process model, it rejects the idea of a criminal justice system with unlimited powers. As a practical matter, the model also argues that human error in any process is inevitable; therefore, the criminal justice

---

I N F O T R A C®
COLLEGE EDITION

Moore, Mark. Legitimizing criminal justice policies and practices.

CRIME CONTROL MODEL
A criminal justice model that places primary emphasis on the right of society to be protected from crime and violent criminals. Crime control values emphasize speed and efficiency in the criminal justice process; the benefits of lower crime rates outweigh any possible costs to individual rights.

DUE PROCESS MODEL
A criminal justice model that places primacy on the right of the individual to be protected from the power of the government. Due process values hold that the state must prove a person's guilt within the confines of a process designed to safeguard personal liberties as enumerated in the Bill of Rights.

system should recognize its own infallibility and take all measures necessary to ensure that this infallibility does not impinge on the rights of citizens.

Finally, whereas the crime control model relies heavily on the police, the due process model relies just as heavily on the courts and their role in upholding the legal procedures of establishing guilt. The due process model is willing to accept that a person who is factually guilty will go free if the criminal justice system does not follow legally prescribed procedures in proving her or his culpability.[27] Therefore, the due process model relies on formality in the criminal justice system. The *Concept Summary* compares and contrasts the two models.

CONCEPT SUMMARY
Crime Control Model versus Due Process Model

Crime Control Model

Goals of the Criminal Justice System:

- Deter crime.
- Protect citizens from crime.
- Incapacitate criminals.
- Provide quick and efficient justice.

Goals Can Best Be Met By:

- Promoting discretion and limiting bureaucratic red tape in criminal justice institutions.
- Making it easier for police to arrest criminals.
- Reducing legal restrictions on proving guilt in a criminal trial.

Favored Policies

- More police.
- More jails and prisons.
- Harsher penalties (including increased use of the death penalty) and longer sentences.

View of Criminality

- Wrongdoers are responsible for their own actions.
- Wrongdoers have violated the social contract and can therefore be deprived of many of the rights afforded to law-abiding citizens.

Case in Point

- *Ohio v. Robinette* (1996), which allows police greater freedom to search the automobile of a driver stopped for speeding.

Due Process Model

Goals of the Criminal Justice System

- Protect the individual against the immense power of the state.
- Rehabilitate those convicted of crimes.

Goals Can Best Be Met by:

- Limiting state power by assuring the constitutional rights of the accused.
- Providing even guilty offenders with full protection of the law, and allowing those offenders to go free if due process procedures are not followed.
- Assuring that all accused criminals receive the same treatment from the law, regardless of class, race, gender, or sexual orientation.
- Protecting the civil rights of prisoners.

Favored Policies

- Open the criminal justice process to scrutiny by the media and public.
- Abolish the death penalty.
- Limit police powers to arbitrarily search, interrogate, and seize criminal suspects.
- Limit discretion and formalize criminal justice procedures so that all suspects and convicted offenders receive the same treatment.
- Increase funding for rehabilitation and education programs in jails and prisons.

View of Criminality

- Criminal behavior can be attributed to social and biological factors.
- Criminals can be rehabilitated and returned to the community.

Case in Point

- *Mapp v. Ohio* (1961), which invalidates evidence improperly gathered by the police, even if the evidence proves the suspect's guilt.

Which Model Prevails Today?

Though both the crime control and the due process models have always been present to a certain degree, during different time periods one has taken precedence over the other. The twentieth century has seen an ebb and flow between them. The influx of immigrants and problems of urbanization in the early 1900s caused somewhat of a panic among the American upper class. Considering that most, if not all, politicians and legal theorists were members of this class, it not surprising that crime control principles prevailed during the first half of the century.

As the nation became more secure and prosperous in the 1950s and 1960s, a "due process revolution" took place. Under the leadership of Chief Justice Earl Warren, the United States Supreme Court significantly expanded the rights of the accused. Following a series of landmark cases that will be referred to throughout this textbook, suspected offenders were guaranteed, among other things, that an attorney would be provided to them by the state if they could not afford one,[28] and that they would be notified of their right to remain silent and retain counsel upon being arrested.[29] The 1960s also saw severe limits placed on the power of the police, as the Court required law enforcement officers to strictly follow specific guidelines on gathering evidence or risk having that evidence invalidated.[30]

Rising crime rates in the late 1970s and early 1980s led to increased pressure on politicians and judges to get "tough on crime." This certainly slowed down the due process revolution and perhaps returned the principles of the crime control model to our criminal justice system. In 1984, for example, three Supreme Court cases restored to police some of the freedoms they had enjoyed in the first half of the century. Even if evidence was obtained illegally, the Court ruled, it could be admitted at trial if the police officers could prove they would have obtained the evidence legally anyway.[31] Furthermore, the Court created the "good faith" exception to evidence-gathering rules, which basically allowed illegally obtained evidence to be admitted if the police officers were unaware that they were acting unconstitutionally.[32] According to Professor James P. Fleissner of Mercer University Law School, the Court's 1984 decisions resulted in the values of the crime control model gaining undue leverage. By deciding that police actions were legal as long as the officers acted in "good faith," in Fleissner's view, the Court has given the police permission to infringe upon the personal liberties of citizens in an effort to control crime.[33] (The role of the Bill of Rights in determining police power will be covered in Chapter 6.)

> "The Warren Court, after all, was not just the most liberal Supreme Court in American History, but arguably the only liberal Supreme Court in American history."
>
> —Professor David Luban, *Georgetown University Law Center* (1999)

TRENDS AND ISSUES IN CRIMINAL JUSTICE TODAY

The values of the criminal justice system are reflected not only in court decisions, but also in public policy. In the past decade, for example, the federal government and a number of states have passed tough new sentencing laws, typically called "three strikes and you're out." Discussed in detail in Chapter 11, these laws basically require judges to sentence those persons convicted of a third crime to life imprisonment, regardless of the seriousness of the offense. Such laws would have been considered unacceptably harsh thirty years ago and may be again in the future. But at the present, "three strikes and you're out" represents the will of the American public, as expressed by their elected officials.

In this textbook, we will concentrate on the structural and theoretical aspects of the criminal justice system. We cannot lose sight, however, of the system's place in the "real world"—how it affects and is affected by the citizens it serves. This final section of the introductory chapter offers a preview of the trends and issues that dominate the crime debate and thus provide the context in which the criminal justice system operates.

The Decline in Crime

Perhaps the most significant trend in criminal justice is the recent decline in crime rates. From 1984 to 1991, crime rates soared—during that time the murder rate nationwide increased by almost 25 percent. Starting in 1992, however, this trend reversed itself. In 1997, according to the FBI, the overall rate of serious crime in the United States dropped 4 percent from the year before, the sixth consecutive year of decline. Violent crimes fell by 5 percent, including a 9 percent decrease in murders and robberies. Property crimes declined by 4 percent.[34] That same year, Los Angeles reported the fewest murders since 1977 and Boston hit a thirty-six-year low.[35]

A number of explanations have been offered for this welcome situation. Some observers point to the strong economy as removing the financial incentive to commit crime. Others credit "get tough" policies that have been sending more offenders to prison for longer time periods. Improvements in policing techniques have also been cited, as has the declining popularity of crack cocaine, whose use has been linked to an upsurge in gun-related violence in the 1980s and early 1990s.[36]

Fear of Crime

Crime rates may be dropping, but fear of crime is not.[37] Polls show that over 60 percent of Americans believe that the country is not succeeding in efforts to reduce crime.[38] (See *CJ in Focus—Myth versus Reality: Are We Winning the War against Crime?*) Crime has not always been considered a crucial problem in this country. Even though Gallup polls began asking Americans their opinions on the nation's most pressing concerns in the 1930s, it was not until 1965 that crime was mentioned in the survey.[39] That year, only 4 percent of those polled considered it to be "the most important" problem in the country. Perhaps even more surprising, given that crimes per capita have tripled over the past thirty years, Americans have not consistently ranked crime as their major worry over that time period. As recently as 1990, when the violent crime rate was higher than it is today, fewer than 5 percent of Americans rated crime as the most important problem in the country; today, 20 percent do so.

Most academic discussions of the public's fear of crime begin with the role of the media. Almost half a century ago, when the modern media were in their infancy, researcher Edwin H. Sutherland noted the ability of mass communications to increase fear through the dissemination of publicity.[40] The propensity of the media—especially television—to condense any act into its most graphic aspects without providing any context has had a much-discussed effect on public perception. The media can also distort reality by the subjects they choose to cover. For example, although murder accounts for only 0.2 percent of all crimes reported to the police, it is the focus of 25 percent of all newspaper articles on crime.[41] (For a more detailed look at this subject, see the chapter-ending feature *Criminal Justice in Action—Crime and the Media*.)

Does this indicate that Americans are being manipulated into an irrational fear of crime? Not necessarily. Whether or not one follows the intense media coverage of an incident such as the bombing of the federal building in Oklahoma City in 1995, such brutality is difficult to ignore. Dramatic and violent regional crimes can menace a community—even a relatively safe one—for years. After Carl Drega killed four people one night in a remote corner of New England, a resident commented, "People are shocked that this could happen in northern New Hampshire. But I guess it can happen anywhere. I don't know that the area will ever be the same."[42]

"The fear of burglars is not only the fear of being robbed, but also the fear of a sudden and unexpected clutch out of the darkness."

—Elias Canetti, *Austrian novelist* (1962)

INFOTRAC®
COLLEGE EDITION

Walklate, Sandra. Risk and criminal victimization: a modernist dilemma?

CJ in Focus
Myth versus Reality
Are We Winning the War against Crime?

Crime is a major concern of Americans. We are indeed one of the most violent countries in the world today and will continue to be so, relatively speaking, for years to come, even if the current downward trend in violent crime continues.

THE MYTH

Most Americans, although they say that their neighborhoods are safer now than ever before, believe that we are losing ground in the war against crime. The nonpartisan Pew Research Center recently conducted a poll that asked the following question: "Is the country making progress or losing ground against crime?" Sixty-one percent of those surveyed felt that we, as a nation, were losing ground in our efforts against crime.

THE REALiTY

The reality is that crime rates have been dropping. As you can see in Figure 1.7, crime rates started dropping in 1992 and have continued to do so.

For Critical Analysis: How is it possible that the public's perception of crime rates is inconsistent with actual crime rates?

Figure 1.7 Crime in the United States, 1988 to 1998

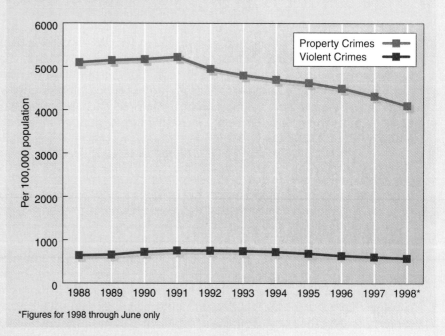

*Figures for 1998 through June only

Regardless of what the official statistics may say about crime rates, it is difficult to discount the perception that America is becoming more violent when junior high schools are installing metal detectors to find guns, and every trip to the airport is accompanied by terrorist-targeted interrogation. Professor Charles E. Silberman notes that even though walking the streets at night is statistically safer than driving a car or cleaning the house,

> it is perfectly rational for Americans to be more concerned about street crime than about accidents, or, for that matter, about white-collar crime. Violence at the hand of a stranger is far more frightening than a comparable injury incurred in an automobile accident or fall.[43]

One of the manifestations of this fear of crime is a lack of faith in the criminal justice system. A recent *U.S. News & World Report* survey found that only 8 percent of Americans had a "great deal" of confidence in the institutions we entrust to control crime.[44]

Crime as a Political Issue

Some observers feel that politicians—trying to combat the general apathy of the public—have used crime as an issue to draw the attention of voters. Though no direct correlation has been researched, the sharp increase in

Americans' professed fear of crime in the 1990s coincided with debate over the Violent Crime Control and Law Enforcement Act, which passed in 1994.[45] The stated purpose of the act was "to prevent crime, punish criminals, and restore a sense of safety and security to the American people" by increasing the number of police officers, building more prisons, and extending the reach of the death penalty for federal crimes.[46]

Because of the "tough-on-crime" aspects of the 1994 act and dozens of similar state-level bills that passed in the years that followed, politicians who favored the new laws found it necessary to focus on the most dramatic aspects of crime in the United States. The political practice of using crime as a "red flag" issue to build up support or to attack one's political opponents shows no signs of abating. It is the responsibility of the electorate to know when a politician is raising a valid point concerning criminal justice and when she or he is simply grandstanding to gain votes or more public funds.

The Growing Prison Population

One way a politician can solidify his or her anticrime credentials is to support tougher sentencing laws. As a result, many state and federal prisoners are spending more time in prison than they would have previously for the same crimes. The tougher laws are one explanation for the drastic rise in the prison population over the past twenty years, which has continued even as crime rates have dropped. According to a report by the U.S. Department of Justice, the number of Americans in local jails and state and federal prisons was over 1.8 million by the beginning of 1999.[47] (For evidence of the growth rate in our inmate population since 1985, see Figure 1.8.)

Criminal justice experts attribute the growing prison population to a number of factors besides tougher sentencing laws. With fewer crimes to solve, the police may have become more efficient in handling decreasing caseloads. Many states have abolished parole, and those that have not are more willing to send parolees back to prison for breaking the conditions of their early release. Furthermore, increased vigilance with regard to illegal drug laws has had a pronounced effect—the incarceration rate for drug arrests has increased 1,000 percent since 1980.[48]

INFOTRAC®
COLLEGE EDITION

Hannon, Lance and James Defronzo. The truly disadvantaged, public assistance, and crime.

Figure 1.8 Prison and Jail Populations in the United States, 1985–1997

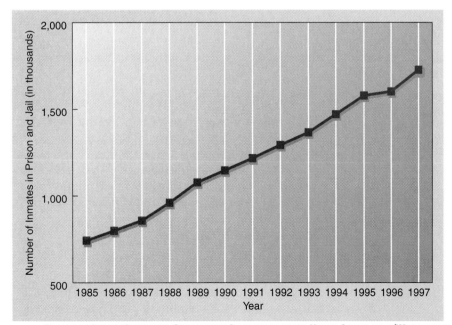

SOURCE: BUREAU OF JUSTICE STATISTICS, CORRECTIONAL POPULATIONS IN THE UNITED STATES, 1995 (WASHINGTON D.C.: U.S. DEPARTMENT OF JUSTICE, JUNE 1997), TABLE 1.1, PAGE 12; AND BUREAU OF JUSTICE STATISTICS.

Questionable police use of force can increase suspicions of a biased criminal justice system in the African American community. In the wake of one such incident, three cousins of 19-year-old Tyisha Miller comfort each other. Miller was shot to death in the early morning hours of December 29, 1998, by four Riverside City (California) police officers. The police officers (three of whom were white, one Hispanic) claimed that when they tried to wake Miller, who was sleeping in a locked car on the side of the road, she picked up a handgun from her lap and fired a shot, causing them to return fire. The victim's family questioned this account, noting that Miller's body was riddled with more than two dozen bullets. Even if Miller had fired a shot, can the police response be justified? Does it necessarily show racist intent on the part of the officers?

National concerns over violence in schools were rekindled on April 20, 1999, when two students from Columbine High School in Littleton, Colorado went on a rampage, killing 12 of their classmates and a teacher. Here, a mother and daughter are reunited after the carnage.

Race and Crime

One of the more disturbing aspects of the boom in our prison population is that it seems to be disproportionately affecting African American males. The incarceration rate for black men is eight times that of white men and twice that of Hispanic men. The lifetime likelihood of going to prison is significantly higher for African Americans (16.2 percent) and Hispanics (9.4 percent) than for whites (2.5 percent).[49] Furthermore, though blacks account for less than half of violent crime arrests, they represent 60 percent of prison admissions. Other studies show that African Americans are more likely to receive harsher penalties, including the death penalty, than other racial groups.

As we shall discuss in Chapter 18, there is significant debate as to whether these figures are proof of an inherently racist criminal justice system. That the perception of racially motivated injustice exists—especially in the African American community—is undeniable.[50] Public officials have responded by increasing the scrutiny of *hate crimes*, which can be defined as "unlawful actions designed to frighten or harm an individual because of his or her race, religion, ethnicity, or sexual orientation."[51] A number of states have implemented laws that increase the penalty for crimes that are seen to be motivated by "hate," and we shall discuss these laws at various points in the textbook.

Women and Crime

As the controversy surrounding Karla Faye Tucker's execution—discussed in the introduction to this chapter—shows, many Americans are uncertain how to react to female criminality. The criminal justice system cannot afford to be similarly uncertain. The number of women in prison is growing faster than any other significant demographic group. Though they represent only 6 percent of the nation's inmate population, the number of women in state and federal prisons is rising at a significantly faster rate than the male population of correctional facilities.[52] (See Figure 1.9.)

Many researchers see one overriding factor in this female prison population explosion: drugs. Forty-five percent of the growth in female inmates is directly attributable to breaking drug laws, and a majority of women who are arrested are charged with drug offenses or crimes committed to get money to buy drugs.[53] According to the Sentencing Project in Washington, D.C., women tend to be low-level drug dealers who receive sentences similar to those of major criminals because of tough drug laws.[54]

Drugs cannot completely explain the rise in violent crime among women, however, which has increased at more than three times the rate for men. For the most part, women commit violence crimes against someone they know—a husband, ex-husband, or boyfriend.[55] As reported incidents of rape and domestic violence are not decreasing at nearly the same rate as other serious crimes, many experts expect trends of women and violence to continue.

Children and Violence

Two incidents during the spring of 1998 drew national attention to the issue of children and violence. In late March, two young boys in Jonesboro, Arkansas, opened fire on their classmates, killing four girls and a teacher. Seven weeks later, a fifteen-year-old boy in Springfield, Oregon, murdered two classmates, wounded twenty-two others, and killed his parents. Somewhat ironically, these high-profile incidents occurred at a time when violent acts by juveniles were declining, if only slightly. From 1996 to 1997, arrests of juveniles for violent acts decreased 4 percent and the number of juveniles apprehended on murder charges dropped 16 percent. It should be noted that this has certainly not been the prevalent pattern for the past twenty years. Whereas the adult murder rate decreased 7 percent from 1978 to 1993, the juvenile murder rate rose 177 percent. During those years, the arrest rate for juveniles increased 79 percent, three times the rise for adult offenders.

As with any crime trend, a number of explanations have been offered to explain the rise in juvenile delinquency. Some observers point to the increase in gang and gun activity, spurred by the crack cocaine trade of the late 1980s and early 1990s. Others blame the environment of violence that permeates the daily life of many of our nation's youths. The Centers for Disease Control reports that Americans under the age of fifteen are murdered at a rate that is five times the combined rates of twenty-five other industrialized nations.[56] A study by Roper Starch Worldwide found that almost three-fourths of U.S. teenagers are afraid of violent crime from one of their peers.[57] Child abuse, which is difficult to measure but is believed to be widespread, can also teach a youth the values of violence, which may lead to delinquent or criminal activity later in life.

Terrorism and Civil Liberties

Many communities have instituted evening curfews to control or restrict the movement of juveniles and thereby reduce the possibility of delinquent behavior. These steps are part of a trend that worries some constitutional experts, who are concerned that Americans seem increasingly willing to sacrifice personal freedoms for enhanced safety. Residents in a high-crime housing project in Chicago, for example, willingly submit to metal detectors and random searches to keep weapons out of the buildings. The balance between civil liberty and government power seems most tenuous in the effort to combat **terrorism.**

Broadly defined as the random use of staged violence at infrequent intervals to achieve political goals, terrorism has traditionally been viewed by most Americans as an international, not a local, problem. In 1993, however, a terrorist bomb exploded in New York's World Trade Center, and two years later 168 persons were killed and hundreds injured in the bombing of the Alfred P. Murrah Federal Building in Oklahoma City.

Shocked by the graphic images of domestic terrorism, the public signified its desire for greater protections—in one poll, nearly 60 percent of those surveyed said that they would trade some civil liberties to thwart terrorism.[58]

In response, one year after the Oklahoma bombing President Bill Clinton signed the Anti-Terrorism and Effective Death Penalty Act of 1996 into law.[59] Among other measures, the antiterrorism bill made it easier to conduct surveillance operations on suspected terrorists. Combating terrorism is difficult, however, because the enemy is so invisible and because terrorist acts, by their very nature, are random and unpredictable. The possibility for state action against innocent persons is considerable. The question for Americans, which we shall examine in detail at the end of Chapter 3, is whether it is in the nation's best interest to sacrifice due process of law, freedom from improper search and seizure, and privacy rights to curb terrorism.

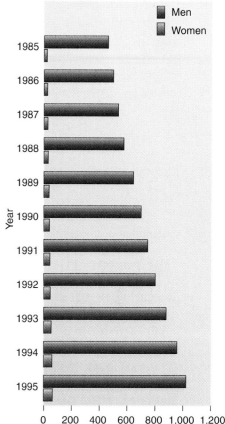

Figure 1.9 Men and Women Sentenced to Prison, 1985–1995

Men

Women

Year

Number Sentenced to Prison (in thousands)

The U.S. State Department's Office of the Coordinator for Counterterrorism hosts a Web site. Go to:

www.state.gov/www/global/terrorism/

TERRORISM
The use or threat of violence to achieve political objectives.

Criminal Justice in Action
Crime and the Media

Other than receiving a speeding ticket or some other minor communication with a police officer, most Americans will have no significant contact with the institutions that make up the criminal justice system. To a large degree, their attitudes and opinions will be shaped by the images of crime they view on television. Here we take a closer look at the presentation of crime on television news shows and other "reality-based" telecasts, and discuss how such programs affect the public's perception of the criminal justice system.

"THE CHARGE: SITTING ON A SLEEPING TODDLER!"

On an October night in 1997, the anchorman of Channel 6 in Orlando, Florida, led off the local newscast with the following story:

He tips the scale at 400 pounds, and tonight he's calling the Marion County jail his home! The charge: sitting on a sleeping toddler! Good evening. The accusations are shocking, jarring. A 22-month-old baby trapped beneath a hulk of a man.[60]

The reality of the situation was much less enticing, centering on a bizarre but minor domestic squabble. Nobody was harmed in the incident, and the local prosecutor refused to press charges.

This exaggeration by a local television station in a local market may not, in itself, be worthy of much attention. But taken as part of an increasing trend in the coverage of crime in the media, it is more troubling. As was discussed earlier, though rates of violent crime have been steadily dropping, fear of crime among the general public remains high. For many observers, the credit—or blame—for this situation lies with the media.

INCREASED CRIME COVERAGE

A recent study by eight journalism schools gave statistical credence to the common assertion that crime dominates the local news. The study showed that, on average

nationwide, local news devotes 29.3 percent of its content to crime or criminal justice, compared to 15.3 percent on politics and government, 2 percent on education, and 1.2 percent on race relations. Network news has also increased crime coverage drastically. According to the Center for Media and Public Affairs, the three major networks increased coverage of murders by 700 percent from 1993 to 1997; during that time period, one of every seven stories was dedicated to criminal justice.[61]

Several explanations are given for these statistics. In local news, deregulation in the communications industry has created greater competition, with as many as five competing local news programs in some markets. Producers have been forced to turn to sensationalistic tactics to gain and hold an audience. On the network level, observers point out that the end of the Cold War left viewers uninterested in foreign affairs. Public fascination with the O. J. Simpson trial convinced network producers to fill the gap with crime. Bill Berra, news director for the Orlando station that ran the "crushed baby" story, has a very simple explanation: "Crime is what the audience wants—all the surveys put it at the top of the list. Who am I to second-guess the audience?"[62]

THE DISTORTION OF CRIME

Is it in society's best interests to give the people what they want? The problem, say many observers, is not necessarily the quantity, but the quality, of media coverage of crime. The media are generally thought to distort the public's image of crime in three ways:

1. Media coverage conveys the false perception that America is suffering a crime epidemic.

2. The media create the perception that crime rates are rising, when in fact the opposite is true. The networks' increased coverage of homicide comes at the same time that murder rates are declining.

3. By concentrating on the most sensational and violent crimes, the media create the impression that crime equals violence. In fact, nearly nine out of every ten crimes reported to police are of the nonviolent variety.[63]

What are the consequences of these distortions? One may be the return to the crime control model of criminal justice. Vince Schiraldi of the Justice Policy Institute notes that, in late 1997, two juveniles committed homicide within one week, one in Jackson Township, New Jersey, and the other in Pearl, Mississippi. The killings were connected only by the age of the suspects, but within days *The Today Show,* Fox News, MSNBC, and CNBC had run stories linking the crimes as if they represented a trend.

Coverage of "kids who kill" and a "rising tide of superpredators" spurs viewers—and the legislators they vote into office—to demand that harsher measures be taken against juvenile criminals. But, Schiraldi remarks, the media often do not present the public with a different viewpoint. The same week as the two killings, Attorney General Janet Reno reported that violent juvenile crime had dropped by almost 10 percent over the past two years. Her press conference received little media attention.[64]

ISSUES OF CLASS AND RACE

Some observers think that media distortion of crime has had serious social consequences for America as well. Gregg Barak, a noted media and justice expert, comments that, apart from reality-based police dramas and crime reports, the working class has become almost invisible on television. As a result, the media present three classes: the upper class, the middle class, and the "criminal class."[65] American University's Jeffrey Reiman has concluded that the media-driven profile of the common criminal is that of a young, African American male. This characterization, Reiman argues, has contributed to increased *de facto* racial segregation and higher tensions in American society.[66]

Media scholar Robin Anderson has an even more cynical theory about media distortion. Anderson sees an implicit *quid pro quo* relationship between the media and law enforcement agencies in exploiting racism to build support for the "war on drugs." Statistically, Anderson points out, the typical cocaine user is a white, male, employed high school graduate living in a small metropolitan area or suburb. Recent studies have shown that nearly three out of every four Americans who use illegal drugs are Caucasians.

If one watches "reality-based" television shows such as *Cops, Night Beat,* and *America's Most Wanted,* a very different picture reveals itself. Anderson describes the effect of these shows:

> As TV cameras brought viewers dark surveillance images of black street dealers and raw video footage of police sweeps in poor neighborhoods, the drug crisis came to be defined as a black, urban problem— even though white drug use continued to predominate. The official televisual icon of the war on drugs became the young, black, street-dealer "thug."[67]

A POSSIBLE BACKLASH?

There is evidence of a backlash against the mass media's coverage of crime. The media swarm touched off by Andrew Cunanan's murder of fashion designer Gianni Versace in 1997 and his subsequent manhunt was widely viewed with distaste.[68] Americans had become so desensitized to murder, some complained, that only high-profile crimes with glamorous victims could attract national attention.

In Georgia, lawmakers have considered legislation to levy a 10 percent tax on revenue from television and radio stations and newspapers that run stories on crime. The tax revenues would go to crime victims and their families. A local television station in Texas, KBUE, has pledged to report crime more responsibly. Management of the station has set up five criteria for deciding which crime stories will be broadcast:

1. Does action need to be taken?

2. Is there an immediate threat of safety to others?

3. Is there a threat to children?

4. Does the crime have a significant community impact?

5. Does the story lend itself to a crime-prevention effort?

At least initially, KBUE's ratings did not seem to be affected by management's decision.[69]

Whether these efforts are more than incidental is doubtful, however. The "if it bleeds, it leads" approach to coverage of crime has become ingrained in many media outlets— apparently, for good reason. An Orlando station that pledged to "decriminalize" its local news as KBUE had done (it refused to run the story that opened this feature) saw itself relegated to the bottom rungs of the ratings.

Key Terms

conflict model 6

consensus model 5

crime control model 20

discretion 15

due process model 20

federalism 11

felony 18

misdemeanors 19

organized crime 9

property crime 7

public order crimes 7

terrorism 27

violent crimes 7

"wedding cake" model 18

white-collar crimes 7

Chapter Summary

1. **Describe the two most common models of how society determines which acts are criminal.** The consensus model argues that the majority of citizens will agree on which activities should be outlawed and punished as crimes; it rests on the assumption that a diverse group of people can have similar morals. In contrast, the conflict model argues that in a diverse society, the dominant groups exercise power by codifying their value systems into criminal laws.

2. **Define crime and the different types of crime.** Crime is any action punishable under criminal statutes and is considered an offense against society. Therefore, alleged criminals are prosecuted by the state rather than by victims. Crimes are punishable by sanctions that bring about a loss of personal freedom or, in some cases, fines. There are six groups of crimes: (a) violent crimes—murder, rape, assault, battery, robbery; (b) property crimes—pick-pocketing, shoplifting, larceny/theft, burglary, and arson; (c) public order crimes—public drunkenness, prostitution, gambling, and illicit drug use; (d) white-collar crime—fraud and embezzlement; (e) organized crime—crime undertaken by a number of persons who operate their activities much as legal businesses do; and (f) high-tech crime—sabotage, fraud, embezzlement, and theft of proprietary data from computer systems as well as cyber-crimes, such as selling pornographic materials to minors on the Internet.

3. **Outline the three levels of law enforcement.** Because we have a federal system of government, law enforcement occurs at both the federal and the state level and within the states at local levels. Because crime is mostly a local concern, most employees in the criminal justice system work for local governments. Agencies at the federal level include the FBI, the DEA, and the U.S. Secret Service, among others.

4. **List the essential elements of the corrections system.** Criminal offenders are placed on proba-

tion, incarcerated in a jail or prison, transferred to community-based correction facilities, or released on parole.

5. **Explain the difference between the formal and informal criminal justice processes.** The formal criminal justice process involves procedures such as booking, setting bail, and the like. For every step in the formal process, though, someone has discretion, and such discretion leads to an informal process. Even when prosecutors believe that a suspect is guilty, they have the discretion not to prosecute, for example.

6. **Describe the layers of the "wedding cake" model.** The top layer consists of celebrity cases, which are most highly publicized; the second layer involves high-profile felonies, such as rape and murder; the third layer consists of property crimes such as larcenies and burglaries; the fourth layer consists of misdemeanors.

7. **Contrast the crime control and due process models.** The crime control model assumes that the criminal justice system is designed to protect the public from criminals; thus, its most important function is to punish and repress criminal conduct. The due process model presumes that the accused are innocent and provides them with the most complete safeguards, usually within the court system.

8. **List the major issues in criminal justice today.** (a) The fear of crime; (b) the political "tough-on-crime" aspects of our system; (c) the growing prison population; (d) race and crime; (e) women and crime; (f) children and crime; and (g) terrorism.

9. **Describe how the media affect the public's view of crime.** Because crime stories dominate local news, the public is more keenly aware of crime even as it declines. Further, the media concentrate on the most sensational and violent crimes, leading to the impression that crime equals violence.

Questions for Critical Analysis

1. How is it possible to have a consensus about what should or should not be illegal in a country with several hundred million adults from all races, religions, and walks of life?

2. Why are criminals prosecuted by the state, through its public officials, rather than by the victims themselves?

3. Why are public order crimes sometimes referred to as victimless crimes?

4. At what political level is most law enforcement carried out? Relate your answer to the concept of federalism.

5. Assume that all of the officials involved in the criminal justice process were deprived of most of the discretion they now have. What might some of the results be?

6. In what way can crime be considered a political issue?

7. To what extent can terrorism be considered a criminal problem?

8. Assume that you have just taken over a local TV station. You would like to present a more realistic view of American society and hence wish to downplay violent crime coverage on the evening news. What forces would work against implementing your decision?

Selected Print and Electronic Resources

SUGGESTED READINGS

Josi, John A., et al., *The Changing Career of the Correctional Officer: Policy Implications for the 21st Century*, Boston: Butterworth-Heinemann, 1998. The authors examine the changing role of correctional officers in the twenty-first century. This is a good "read" for those contemplating such a career.

Price-Lee, Mary, et al., *100 Best Careers in Crime Fighting: Law Enforcement, Criminal Justice, Private Security, and Cyberspace Crime Detection*, New York: Macmillan General Reference, 1998. This is a relatively short (224 pages) guide to job opportunities in crime fighting from local to state to federal law enforcement positions as well as private security careers. Also presented are opportunities for women and minorities.

Zimring, Franklin E., and Gordon Hawkins, *Crime Is Not the Problem: Lethal Violence in America*, New York: Oxford University Press, 1997. This is a contemporary examination of crime and violence in America. The authors contend that America's rate of nonviolent crime is about the same as in other industrial nations. They look at the rate of lethal violence, in contrast, and find that it is way ahead of other nations. They attempt to reshape the debate about crime in the United States. They present controversial new directions for public policy in America.

MEDIA RESOURCES

The Siege (1998) A series of deadly bomb attacks have paralyzed New York City, providing FBI terrorist task force leader anthony "Hub" Hubbard (played by Denzel Washington) with the challenge of his career. With the help of CIA agent Elise Kraft (Annette Bening) and FBI agent Frank Haddad (Tony Shalhoub), Hub is able to link the attacks to an Arab terrorist group with cells in the city. When he proves unable to stop them, however, the president of the United States declares martial law and orders Gen. William Devereaux (Bruce Willis) to lead the Army into Brooklyn. Soldiers cordon off the borough and subject Arab Americans living there to highly intrusive (and unconstitutional) treatment in order to locate the terrorists.

Critically analyze this film:

1. Based on the relationship between Hub and Elise, how would you characterize the relationship between the FBI and the CIA.

2. Do you find the quick declaration of martial law by the president to be realistic? Do you think American citizens would accept the harsh restriction of civil liberties by the Army if a real American city were the target of similar terrorist attacks? Would you support a reduction of civil liberties in similar circumstances?

3. What does this film say about fear of crime in the United States?

4. When it was released, *The Siege* was the target of a number of reproaches by Arab American groups who complained that it was biased against Arab Americans. How do you feel the film represents the Arab community in the United States and abroad? Do you find it biased?

5. In the beginning of the film, President Clinton is shown commenting on a missile attack launched against terrorists. This actual footage was "borrowed" by the filmmakers to provide *The Siege* with a touch of realism. Do you think such military action is the proper response to threats of terrorism?

Bonnie and Clyde and Me: True Tales of Crime and Punishment by Floyd Hamilton, et al., Greattapes audiocassettes, 1995. These four audio tapes are enjoyable listening for anyone who wants to hear a "true" account of what it was like to go on a "job" with Bonnie and Clyde.

Using the internet for Criminal Justice Analysis

INFOTRAC®
COLLEGE EDITION

1. Log on to your InfoTrac College Edition at www.infotrac-college.com/wadsworth/access.html. Then type in the words **"Terrorism threats at home: Two years after Oklahoma City."**
   Read the entire article and answer the following questions:

   a. What groups did federal and local law enforcement agencies target after the bombing of the Oklahoma City federal building?

   b. What are the fastest growing hard-core violence-prone groups?

   c. Describe the radical right group called the Odinists.

2. Use your favorite browser to access the following URL: broadway.vera.org/pub/crimebill/legact.html Scan through the titles of the various acts included in the Violent Crime Control and Law Enforcement Act.

   a. How many separate acts were included in the House version?

   b. How many separate acts were included in the Senate version?

   c. How many separate House actions were there on the bill?

   d. How many separate Senate actions were there on the bill?

   e. When the Conference Committee of the Congress started acting on this bill, how much time elapsed from the first conference action until the last one?

3. Go to CourtTV's site where it has a summary of famous cases: www.courttv.com/famous/index.html

   a. Why do you think the Nanny Murder trial attracted international interest?

   b. Why were there two trials in the O. J. Simpson case?

   c. Why were the Menendez brothers tried more than once?

Notes

1. Beverly Lowry, "The Good Bad Girl," *New Yorker* (February 9, 1998), 63–4.

2. *Gregg v. Georgia*, 428 U.S. 153 (1976). Many United States Supreme Court decisions will be cited in this book, and it is important to understand these citations. In this citation, *Gregg v. Georgia* refers to the parties in the case that the Court is reviewing. *U.S.* is the abbreviation for *United States Reports*, the official volume of the United States Supreme Court. "428" refers to the volume of the *United States Reports* in which the citation occurs, and "153" refers to the page number. Finally, the citation ends with the year the case was decided in parentheses. Most, though not all, court citations in this book will follow this formula. For general information on how to read case decisions and find court decisions, see the appendix at the end of this chapter.

3. Charisse Jones, "For Women on Death Row, Clock Is Ticking," *USA Today* (January 16, 1997), 7A.

4. Kenneth W. Clarkson, Roger LeRoy Miller, Gaylord A. Jentz, and Frank B. Cross, *West's Business Law: Texts, Cases, Legal, Ethical. Regulatory and International Environment*, 6th ed. (Minneapolis/St. Paul, MN: West Publishing Co., 1995), 165.

5. Herman Bianchi, *Justice as Sanctuary: Toward a New System of Crime Control* (Bloomington: Indiana University Press, 1994), 72.

6. George B. Vold, *Theoretical Criminology* (New York: Oxford University Press, 1958), 203–19.

7. In 1962, the Supreme Court ruled that a person could not be criminally prosecuted because of his or her status as a homosexual. *Robinson v. California*, 376 U.S. 660.

8. Brian Dumaine, "Beating Bolder Corporate Crooks," *Fortune* (April 25, 1998), 193.

9. Bill Wallace, "Scam Artists Enjoy Economic Boom, Too," *San Francisco Chronicle* (September 8, 1997), A1.

10. Chicago Crime Commission, *The New Faces of Organized Crime* (Chicago: IL: Chicago Crime Commission, 1997).

11. John S. Kerry, *The New War* (New York: Simon & Schuster, 1997), 43–4.

12. M. J. Zuckerman, "Cybercrimes against Business Frequent, Costly," *USA Today* (November 21, 1996), 1A.

13. Tom Buerkle, "Cyberburglars Weave a Web around the Globe," *International Herald Tribune* (February 18, 1998), 1.

14. Christine Dugas, "FBI Cybercops Hunt Hackers," *USA Today* (March 3, 1998), B1.

15. President's Commission on Law Enforcement and Administration of Justice, *The Challenge of Crime in a Free Society* (Washington, D.C.: U.S. Government Printing Office, 1967), 7.

16. John Rawls, *A Theory of Justice* (Cambridge, MA: Belknap Press of Harvard University Press, 1971), 60–1.

17. President's Commission on Law Enforcement and Administration of Justice, 7.

18. John Heinz and Peter Manikas, "Networks among Elites in a Local Criminal Justice System," *Law and Society Review* 26 (1992), 831–61.

19. James Q. Wilson, "What to Do about Crime: Blaming Crime on Root Causes," *Vital Speeches* (April 1, 1995), 373.

20. Herbert Packer, *The Limits of the Criminal Sanction* (Stanford, CA: Stanford University Press, 1968), 154–73.

21. *Ibid.*

22. Daniel Givelber, "Meaningless Acquittals, Meaningful Convictions: Do We Reliably Acquit the Innocent?" *Rutgers Law Review* 49 (Summer 1997), 1317.

23. Lawrence M. Friedman and Robert V. Percival, *The Roots of Justice* (Chapel Hill, NC: University of North Carolina Press, 1981).

24. Packer, 154–73.

25. *Ibid.*

26. Givelber, 1317.

27. Guy-Uriel E. Charles, "Fourth Amendment Accommodations: (Un) Compelling Public Needs, Balancing Acts, and the Fiction of Consent," *Michigan Journal of Race and Law* (Spring 1997), 461.

28. *Gideon v. Wainwright,* 372 U.S. 335 (1963).

29. *Miranda v. Arizona,* 384 U.S. 436 (1966).

30. *Mapp v. Ohio,* 367 U.S. 643 (1961).

31. *Nix v. Williams,* 467 U.S. 431 (1984).

32. *Massachusetts v. Sheppard,* 468 U.S. 981 (1984) and *United States v. Leon,* 468 U.S. 897 (1984).

33. James P. Fleissner, "Glide Path to an 'Inclusionary Rule,'" *Mercer Law Review* 48 (Spring 1997), 1023.

34. John H. Cushman, Jr., "Serious Crime Fell in U.S. for 6th Year in a Row in '97," *New York Times* (May 18, 1998), A14.

35. Gordon Witkin, "The Crime Bust," *U.S. News & World Report* (May 25, 1998), 28.

36. James A. Inciardi and Anne E. Pottieger, "Crack-Cocaine Use and Street Crime," *Journal of Drug Issues* 24 (1984), 237.

37. Victor E. Kappeler, Mark Blumberg, and Gary W. Potter, *The Mythology of Crime and Criminal Justice,* 2d ed. (Prospect Heights, IL: Waveland Press, 1996), 43.

38. Mark Mueller, "Fear of Crime Grips Americans," *Boston Herald* (August 31, 1997), 6.

39. *The Gallup Poll,* Report 689-K (Princeton, NJ: The Gallup Poll, 1964).

40. Edwin H. Sutherland, "The Diffusion of Sexual Psychopath Laws," *American Journal of Sociology* 56 (1950), 142–8.

41. Piers Beirne and James W. Messerschmidt, *Criminology* (New York: Harcourt Brace Jovanovich, 1991), 145.

42. Mueller.

43. Charles E. Silberman, *Criminal Violence, Criminal Justice* (New York: Random House, 1978), 7.

44. Ted Guest, "The Real Problems in American Justice," *U.S. News & World Report* (October 9, 1995), 52.

45. Pub. L. No. 103-322, 108 Stat. 1796 (1994).

46. "Symposium: Violent Crime Control and Law Enforcement Act of 1994," *University of Dayton Law Review* (Winter 1995), 567.

47. Darrell K. Gilliard and Allen J. Beck, *Prison and Jail Inmates at Midyear, 1997* (Washington, D.C.: Bureau of Justice Statistics, 1998), 1.

48. Fox Butterfield, "'Defying Gravity, Inmate Population Climbs," *New York Times* (January 19, 1998), A10.

49. Thomas P. Bonczar and Allen Beck, *Lifetime Likelihood of Going to State or Federal Prison* (Washington, D.C.: Bureau of Justice Statistics, 1997), 1.

50. Bureau of Justice Statistics, *Sourcebook of Criminal Justice Statistics—1996* (Washington, D.C.: U.S. Department of Justice, 1997), 118 (table 2.10), 124 (tables 2.15 and 2.16).

51. D. W. Story, "Hate/Bias Crimes: The Need for a Planned Reaction," *Law and Order* (August 1991), 101.

52. Bureau of Justice Statistics, *Correctional Populations in the United States, 1995* (Washington, D.C.: Department of Justice, June, 1997), 15.

53. *Ibid.*

54. Mark Mauer and Tracy Huling, *Young Black Americans and the Criminal Justice System: Five Years Later* (Washington, D.C.: The Sentencing Project, 1995).

55. Coramae Richey Mann, *When Women Kill* (Albany, NY: State University of New York Press, 1996), 170–1.

56. "Reverse Violence against Youth," *Michigan Chronicle* (March 11, 1997), 6A.

57. Ira Apfel, "Teen Violence: Real or Imagined?" *American Demographics* (June 1, 1995), 22.

58. James Gerstenzang, "The Times Poll: Terrorism Fuels Fear, Support for Limits on Liberty," *Los Angeles Times* (August 8, 1996), A1.

59. Pub. L. No. 104-132, 110 Stat. 1214 (1996).

60. Michael Winerip, "Looking for an 11 O'Clock Fix," *New York Times Magazine* (January 11, 1998), 30.

61. Mark Fitzgerald, "Local TV News Lacks Substance," *Editor & Publisher* (May 24, 1997), 8–10.

62. Winerip, 31.

63. Kappeler, Blumberg, and Potter, 48.

64. Vincent Schiraldi, "The Latest Trend in Juvenile Crime: Exaggeration by the News Media," *Washington Post* (January 11, 1998), C5.

65. Gregg Barak, "Between the Waves: Mass-mediated Themes of Crime and Justice," *Social History* (Fall 1994), 133-48.

66. Jeffrey H. Reiman, ... *and the Poor Get Prison: Economic Bias in American Criminal Justice* (Boston, MA: Allyn and Bacon 1996), 42.

67. Robin Anderson, "'Reality TV and Criminal Justice," *The Humanist* (September-October 1994), 8–14.

68. Jay Weaver and Tim Collie, "Media Helped Feed Frenzy on Cunanan," *Sun-Sentinel—Ft. Lauderdale, Florida* (July 27, 1997), 1A.

69. Robert W. Winslow, "The Media's Fearmongering on Crime," *San Diego Union-Tribune* (June 1, 1997), G3.

chapter 1

How to Read Case Citations and Find Court Decisions

Many important court cases are discussed throughout this book. Every time a court case is referred to, you will be able to check its citation using the endnotes on the final pages of the chapter. Court decisions are recorded and published. When a court case is mentioned, the notation that is used to refer to, or to cite, the case denotes where the published decision can be found.

State courts of appeals decisions are usually published in two places, the state reports of that particular state and the more widely used *National Reporter System* published by West Group. Some states no longer publish their own reports. The *National Reporter System* divides the states into the following geographical areas: Atlantic (A. or A.2d, where *2d* refers to *Second Series*), South Western (S.W. or S.W.2d), North Western (N.E. or N.E.2d), Southern (So. or So.2d), and Pacific (P. or P.2d).

Federal trial court decisions are published unofficially in West's *Federal Supplement* (F.Supp.), and opinions from the circuit courts of appeals are reported unofficially in West's *Federal Reporter* (F., F2d, or F.3d). Opinions from the United States Supreme Court are reported in the *United States Reports* (U.S.), the *Lawyers' Edition of the Supreme Court Reports* (L.Ed.), West's *Supreme Court Reporter* (S.Ct.), and other publications. The *United States Reports* is the official publication of United States Supreme Court decisions. It is published by the federal government. Many early decisions are missing from these volumes. The citations of the early volumes of the *U.S. Reports* include the names of the actual reporters, such as Dallas, Cranch, or Wheaton. *McCulloch v. Maryland,* for example, is cited as 17 U.S. (4 Wheat.) 316. Only after 1874 did the present citation system, in which cases are cited based solely on their volume and page numbers in the *United States Reports,* come into being. The *Lawyers' Edition of the Supreme Court Reports* is an unofficial and more complete edition of Supreme Court decisions. West's *Supreme Court Reporter* is an unofficial edition of decisions dating from October 1882. These volumes contain headnotes and numerous brief editorial statements of the law involved in the case.

State courts of appeals decisions are cited by giving the name of the case; the volume, name, and page number of the state's official report (if the state publishes its own reports); and the volume, unit, and page number of the *National Reporter*. Federal court citations are also listed by giving the name of the case and the volume, name, and page number of the reports. In additions to the citation, this textbook lists the year of the decision in parentheses. Consider, for example, the case *Miranda v. Arizona,* 384 U.S. 436 (1966). The Supreme Court's decision in this case may be found in volume 384 of the *United States Reports* on page 436. The case was decided in 1966.

chapter

2

Measuring and Explaining Crime

Chapter Objectives

After reading this chapter, you should be able to:

1. Identify the publication in which the FBI reports crime data and list the three ways it does so.

2. Distinguish between Part I and Part II offenses as defined in the UCR.

3. Explain how the National Incident-Based Reporting System differs from the UCR.

4. Distinguish between the National Crime Victimization Survey and self-report surveys.

5. Explain why classical criminology is based on choice theory.

6. Contrast positivism with classical criminology.

7. List and describe the three theories of social structure that help explain crime.

8. List the six focal concerns that dominate disorganized community existence.

9. List and briefly explain the three branches of social process theory.

10. Indicate the ways in which victims have been given more rights.

INTRODUCTION

Looking over crime data that have been collected by the U.S. government over the past twenty years, one is struck by an interesting statistic. On average, a 1 percent increase in the number of police in any given area coincides with a 0.8 percent rise in reported violent crimes and a 0.5 percent rise in reported property crime.[1] These data seem to suggest a contradictory conclusion: police cause crime.

Such a deduction would find little support among criminal justice professionals or academics. There could be several explanations for the questionable results. The data themselves could be incorrect, in which case any conclusions drawn from them would also be flawed. Or, the relationship between the number of police and reported crime rates may not be causal, but *correlational*. That is, they may relate to each other, though one does not cause the other. Areas with high crime rates, for example, have a greater demand for protection, meaning more police will be present. Furthermore, a greater police presence in a community makes it easier for citizens to find law enforcement agents, which could lead to an increase in *reported* crimes even though the *actual* number of crimes has remained the same.[2]

This example underscores a major principle of the scientific study of crime, or **criminology:** correlation does not equal causality. Just because both ice cream sales and crime rates increase during the summer does not mean that eating more ice cream causes more crime. But, if we can agree that police do not cause crime, what does? And, considering that statistical error is always possible, how did the Department of Justice gather its data? In this chapter, the methods of collecting data on criminal offenders are reviewed. Criminologists collect and interpret these data to test their theories of crime causation. The most prominent of these theories will also be examined in the following pages. Finally, this chapter will address the question of relevance: What is the effect of data and theories on the criminal justice system's efforts to control and prevent crime?

THE UNIFORM CRIME REPORT

The Federal Bureau of Investigation posts many of its statistical findings, including the Uniform Crime Report, at
www.fbi.gov/crimestats.htm

CRIMINOLOGY
The scientific study of crime and the causes of criminal behavior.

UNIFORM CRIME REPORT (UCR)
An annual report compiled by the FBI to give an indication of criminal activity in the United States. The FBI collects data from local, state, and federal law enforcement agencies in preparing this report.

There are literally dozens of sources of crime data. The Department of Justice, however, provides the most far-reaching and oft-cited set of national crime statistics. Each year, the department releases the **Uniform Crime Report (UCR).** Since its inception in 1930, the UCR has attempted to measure the overall rate of crime in the United States by compiling "crimes known to the police."[3] To produce the UCR, the Federal Bureau of Investigation (FBI) relies on the voluntary participation of local law enforcement agencies. These agencies—approximately 16,000 in total, covering 95 percent of the population—base their information on two measurements:

1. The number of persons arrested.
2. The number of crimes reported by victims, witnesses, or the police themselves.[4]

Once this information has been sent to the FBI, the agency presents the crime data in three ways:

1. As a *rate* per 100,000 people. In 1997, for example, the crime index rate was 4,922.7. In other words, for every 100,000 inhabitants of the United States, nearly 4,923 *index crimes* (explained below) were reported to the FBI. This statistic is known as the *crime rate* and is often cited by media sources when discussing the level of crime in the United States.

2. As a *percentage* change from the previous year or other time periods. From 1996 to 1997, there was a 3.2 percent drop in the Crime Index rate.

3. As *aggregate,* or total, number of crimes. In 1997, the FBI recorded 13,175,070 index crimes.[5]

The Department of Justice annually publishes these data in *Crime in the United States.* Along with the basic statistics, this publication offers an exhaustive array of crime information, including breakdowns of crimes committed by city, county, and other geographical designations and by the demographics (gender, race, age) of the individuals who have been arrested for crimes.

The Crime Index

The UCR divides the criminal offenses it measures into two major categories: Part I and Part II offenses. Part I offenses, or **index crimes,** are those crimes that, due to their seriousness and frequency, are recorded by the FBI to give a general idea of the "crime picture" in the United States in any given year. For a description of the eight index crimes, see Figure 2.1.

The index crime rate is hardly constant. As you can see in Figure 2.2 on the following page, the last two decades have seen "peaks" (the early and late 1980s) and "valleys" (the mid-1980s and late 1990s) in the index crime rate. The reasons for these fluctuations are the matter of great debate amongst those who study crime in the United States; some point to social conditions such as poverty and education, while others see the rates as a reflection of criminal laws and the efforts of law enforcement agencies. Some claim that crime rates are directly related to the emergence and popularity of illegal drugs, such as heroin in the 1970s and crack cocaine in the 1980s. We will explore these various theories throughout the textbook.

INDEX CRIMES
Those crimes reported annually by the FBI in its Uniform Crime Report. Index crimes include murder, rape, robbery, aggravated assault, burglary, larceny, motor vehicle theft, and arson. Also known as Part I offenses.

Figure 2.1 Part I Index Crime Offenses

Every month local law enforcement agencies voluntarily provide information on serious offenses in their jurisdiction to the Federal Bureau of Investigation (FBI). These serious offenses are known as Part I offenses, or index crimes, and are defined here. The FBI collects data on Part I offenses in order to present an accurate picture of criminal activity in the United States.

Part I Offenses

Criminal homicide.—a. Murder and nonnegligent manslaughter: the willful (nonnegligent) killing of one human being by another. Deaths caused by negligence, attempts to kill, assaults to kill, suicides, accidental deaths, and justifiable homicides are excluded. Justifiable homicides are limited to: (1) the killing of a felon by a law enforcement officer in the line of duty; and (2) the killing of a felon, during the commission of a felony, by a private citizen. b. Manslaughter by negligence: the killing of another person through gross negligence. Traffic fatalities are excluded. While manslaughter by negligence is a Part I crime, it is not included in the Crime Index.

Forcible rape.—The carnal knowledge of a female forcibly and against her will. Included are rapes by force and attempts or assaults to rape. Statutory offenses (no force used—victim under age of consent) are excluded.

Robbery.—The taking or attempting to take anything of value from the care, custody, or control of a person or persons by force or threat of force or violence and/or by putting the victim in fear.

Aggravated assault.—An unlawful attack by one person upon another for the purpose of inflicting severe or aggravated bodily injury. This type of assault usually is accompanied by the use of a weapon or by means likely to produce death or great bodily harm. Simple assaults are excluded.

Burglary–breaking or entering.—The unlawful entry of a structure to commit a felony or a theft. Attempted forcible entry is included.

Larceny-theft (except motor vehicle theft).—The unlawful taking, carrying, leading, or riding away of property from the possession or constructive possession of another. Examples are thefts of bicycles or automobile accessories, shoplifting, pocket-picking, or the stealing of any property or article which is not taken by force and violence or by fraud. Attempted larcenies are included. Embezzlement, "con" games, forgery, worthless checks, etc., are excluded.

Motor vehicle theft.—The theft or attempted theft of a motor vehicle. A motor vehicle is self-propelled and runs on the surface and not on rails. Specifically excluded from this category are motorboats, construction equipment, airplanes, and farming equipment.

Arson.—Any willful or malicious burning or attempt to burn, with or without intent to defraud, a dwelling house, public building, motor vehicle or aircraft, personal property of another, etc.

SOURCE: "APPENDIX II: OFFENSES IN UNIFORM CRIME REPORTING," IN FEDERAL BUREAU OF INVESTIGATION, *CRIME IN THE UNITED STATES, 1997* (WASHINGTON, D.C.: U.S. DEPARTMENT OF JUSTICE, 1998), 407.

Figure 2.2 Index Crime Rates

These data chart the rate of index crime per 100,000 inhabitants in the United States from 1978 to 1997.

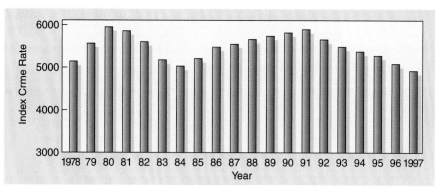

SOURCE: FEDERAL BUREAU OF INVESTIGATION, CRIME IN THE UNITED STATES, 1997 (WASHINGTON, D.C.: U.S. DEPARTMENT OF JUSTICE, 1998), TABLE 1, PAGE 66.

Index crimes are those most likely to be covered by the media and, consequently, inspire the most fear of crime in the population. These crimes have come to dominate crime coverage to such an extent that, for most Americans, the first image that comes to mind at the mention of "crime" is one person physically attacking another person or a robbery taking place with the use of threat or force.[6] Furthermore, the stereotype of crime usually involves a situation in which the offender and the victim do not know each other.

Figure 2.3 Composition of Part I Index Crimes

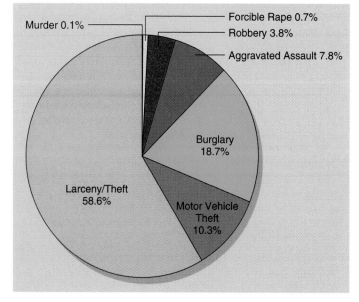

SOURCE: FEDERAL BUREAU OF INVESTIGATION, CRIME IN THE UNITED STATES, 1997 (WASHINGTON, D.C.: U.S. DEPARTMENT OF JUSTICE, 1998), CHART 2.3, PAGE 9.

Given the trauma of violent crimes, this perception is understandable. It is not, however, accurate, according to UCR statistics. A friend or acquaintance of the victim commits almost 40 percent of the homicides in the United States.[7] Furthermore, as is evident from Figure 2.3, the majority of index crimes committed are property crimes. Notice that almost 60 percent of all reported index crimes are larceny-thefts, and nearly another 20 percent are burglaries.[8]

Part II Offenses

Not only do violent crimes represent the minority of index crimes, but index crimes are far outweighed by **Part II offenses,** or those crimes that can be designated as either misdemeanors or felonies. While information gathered on index crimes reflects those offenses "known," or reported to the FBI by local agencies, Part II offenses are measured only by arrest data. In 1997, the FBI recorded slightly more than 2,700,000 arrests for index crimes in the United States. That same year, just over 12,500,000 arrests for Part II offenses took place.[9] In other words, a Part II offense was about 4.6 times more common than an index crime (for a description of Part II offenses and their rates, see Figure 2.4). Such statistics have prompted Marcus Felson, a professor at Rutgers University School of Criminal Justice, to comment that "most crime is very ordinary."[10]

The UCR: A Flawed Method?

PART II OFFENSES
All crimes recorded by the FBI that do not fall into the catergory of Part I offenses. Include both misdemeanors and felonies.

Even though the UCR is the predominant source of crime data in the country, there are numerous questions about the accuracy of its findings. These criticisms focus on the methods by which the UCR statistics are collected by local law enforcement agencies and reported to the FBI.

Offense	Estimated Annual Arrests
Other assaults	1,395,800
Forgery and counterfeiting	120,100
Fraud	414,600
Embezzlement	17,400
Stolen property	155,300
Vandalism	318,400
Weapons	218,900
Prostitution and commercialized vice	101,600
Sex offenses (except forcible rape and prostitution)	101,900
Drug abuse violations	1,583,600
Gambling	15,900
Offenses against family and children	155,800
Driving under the influence	1,477,300
Liquor laws	636,400
Drunkenness	734,800
Disorderly conduct	811,110
Vagrancy	28,800
Curfew and loitering law violations	182,700
Runaways	196,000

Figure 2.4 Part II Crime Offenses

Other assaults (simple)—Assaults and attempted assaults where no weapon is used and which do not result in serious or aggravated injury to the victim.

Forgery and counterfeiting—Making, altering, uttering, or possessing, with intent to defraud, anything false in the semblance of that which is true. Attempts are included.

Fraud—Fraudulent conversion and obtaining money or property by false pretenses. Included are confidence games and bad checks, except forgeries and counterfeiting.

Embezzlement—Misappropriation or misapplication of money or property entrusted to one's care, custody, or control.

Stolen property; buying, receiving, possessing—Buying, receiving, and possessing stolen property, including attempts.

Vandalism—Willful or malicious destruction, injury, disfigurement, or defacement of any public or private property, real or personal, without consent of the owner or persons having custody or control.

Weapons; carrying, possessing, etc.—All violations of regulations or statutes controlling the carrying, using, possessing, furnishing, and manufacturing of deadly weapons or silencers. Included are attempts.

Prostitution and commercialized vice—Sex offenses of a commercialized nature, such as prostitution, keeping a bawdy house, procuring, or transporting women for immoral purposes. Attempts are included.

Sex offenses (except forcible rape, prostitution, and commercialized vice)—Statutory rape and offenses against chastity, common decency, morals, and the like. Attempts are included.

Drug abuse violations—State and/or local offenses relating to the unlawful possession, sale, use, growing, and manufacturing of narcotic drugs. The following drug categories are specified: opium or cocaine and their derivatives (morphine, heroin, codeine); marijuana; synthetic narcotics—manufactured narcotics that can cause true addiction (demerol, methadone); and dangerous nonnarcotic drugs (barbiturates, benzedrine).

Gambling—Promoting, permitting, or engaging in illegal gambling.

Offenses against the family and children—Nonsupport, neglect, desertion, or abuse of family and children.

Driving under the influence—Driving or operating any vehicle or common carrier while drunk or under the influence of liquor or narcotics.

Liquor laws—State and/or local liquor law violations, except "drunkenness" and "driving under the influence." Federal violations are excluded.

Drunkenness—Offenses relating to drunkenness or intoxication. Excluded is "driving under the influence."

Disorderly conduct—Breach of the peace.

Vagrancy—Vagabondage, begging, loitering, etc.

Curfew and loitering laws (persons under age 18)—Offenses relating to violations of local curfew or loitering ordinances where such laws exist.

Runaways (persons under age 18)—Limited to juveniles taken into protective custody under provisions of local statutes.

SOURCE: Federal Bureau of Investigation, Crime in the United States, 1997 (Washington, D.C.: U.S. Department of Justice, 1998), Table 29, page 222; page 407.

Discretionary Distortions. For the UCR to be accurate, citizens must report criminal activity to the police, and the police must then pass this information on to the FBI. Criminologists have long been aware that neither can be expected to perform these roles with consistency.[11] Citizens may not report a crime for any number of reasons, including fear of reprisal, embarrassment, or a personal bias in favor of the offender. Many also feel that police cannot do anything to help them in the aftermath of a crime, so they do not see the point of involving law enforcement agents in their lives. Surveys of crime victims have shown that as many as 40 percent of crimes are not being reported to the police.[12] Studies have shown that police underreport crimes in certain instances, such as when the offense has occurred within a family or the victim does not wish that the offender be charged.[13]

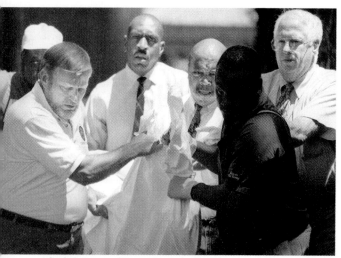

A body is removed from a home in Macon, Georgia. Many observers believe that the FBI's UCR overemphasizes violent crimes such as murder.

Former grade school teacher Mary Kay LeTourneau pled guilty in Kent, Washington, to raping a minor following her sexual relationship with a 13-year-old former student. While pregnant with the teenager's child, she was sentenced to seven years in jail in 1996. After serving part of her term, she was released in 1998 on parole, under the condition that she have no contact with her former student. Shortly after her release, however, she became pregnant for a second time by the now 15-year-old and was returned to jail to serve the remainder of her sentence. Under FBI guidelines, would LeTourneau's actions be defined as rape? How does this situation highlight inconsistencies in the Uniform Crime Reports?

Furthermore, the FBI and local law enforcement agencies do not always interpret index crimes in the same manner. FBI guidelines, for example, define forcible rape as the "carnal knowledge" of a woman "forcibly and against her will." Although some local agencies may strictly adhere to this definition, others may define rape more loosely—listing any assault on a woman as an attempted rape. Furthermore, different jurisdictions have different definitions of rape. In Alabama, rape occurs only in cases where the woman offers "earnest resistance" to sexual intercourse,[14] and in a number of other jurisdictions, the courts require proof that the victim physically opposed her attacker's advances. A number of jurisdictions have also expanded their definition of the crime to include the possibility that males can be raped.

These factors influence the arrest decision, as police officers are more likely to make arrests that can be cleared. An arrest is *cleared* when the suspect is charged with a particular crime and turned over to the court for trial. With law enforcement agents in different jurisdictions operating under different definitions of rape, or any other crime, their reports to the FBI for UCR purposes may be misleading. Indeed, when a police department in Alabama and a police department in Oregon both report a rape to the federal agency, they may not be describing the same act. Given that the UCR incorporates reports from 16,000 different local agencies, different methods of defining offenses could have a significant effect on the overall outcome.

Overreporting Violent Crime. Many observers also believe that the UCR overreports violent crime and underreports Part II offenses. This is partially due to human nature; a triple murder will certainly get more attention from a police department than the theft of a bicycle. There is evidence, however, that FBI instructions to local law enforcement agencies contribute to this situation as well. For example, if police cannot distinguish the aggressors from the victims in a multiparty physical dispute, the *Uniform Crime Reporting Handbook* advises that officers report the number of persons involved as the number of index crime offenses.[15] A barroom brawl involving five people, therefore, may be reported as five incidents of aggravated assault.

The manner of reporting multiple crimes committed by a single offender also skews results toward violent index crimes. The UCR handbook instructs local agencies to report only the most serious crime if an individual has committed a number of crimes in a single crime "spree." So, if a person steals an automobile, robs a convenience store, and then kills the store clerk, only the murder will be recorded for the UCR.[16]

Political Considerations. Finally, as with any other statistical data, crime statistics can be manipulated. For example, when President Richard Nixon instituted crime control measures in Washington, D.C., in the early 1970s, crime did go down in the city. It was later discovered, however, that this crime "reduction" occurred because local police had begun listing the value of *all* stolen property at less than $50, effectively removing the offenses from the felony category.[17] Recently, New York City forced two precinct captains and the chief of the city's Transportation Bureau into retirement after discovering that they had been underreporting crime in their jurisdictions in order to present a rosy picture of their leadership abilities.[18] When local jurisdictions place "image" concerns over those of truthful reporting, the overall trustworthiness of the UCR suffers. (See *CJ in Focus—A Question of Ethics: Tampering with Crime Statistics.*)

CJ in Focus
A Question of Ethics
Tampering with Crime Statistics

In 1997, Captain Jim Duke of the Boca Raton (Fla.) Police Department downgraded 385 felonies—11 percent of the city's total serious crimes—to misdemeanors. In one instance, he reclassified as vandalism an early morning home burglary in which the perpetrator broke a window and took a purse while the residents slept. Also downgraded to vandalism was another incident, initially labeled a burglary, during which a thief stole $5,000 in jewelry and did more than $25,000 in property damage. Duke's unethical acts had a clear purpose—he did not want to report the felonies to the FBI, which does not include misdemeanors in its Uniform Crime Reports.

Boca Raton is not the only American city that has had to face this problem. Atlanta, New York, and Philadelphia have each seen the demotion or resignation of high-ranking police officers due to falsified serious crime reports. Philadelphia was eventually forced to withdraw its figures from the UCRs of 1996, 1997, and part of 1998 because of faulty data.

In the past, most police departments saw crime statistics as having little importance beyond the need to report them to the FBI. (In fact, unethical activity in this area usually involved exaggerating violent crime in order to receive more funds from government agencies.) Because law enforcement agencies were not held responsible for the "root causes" of crime—such as poverty and illiteracy—high crime rates were not considered to reflect poorly on a local police force. As crime rates began to drop in many major cities in the 1990s, this attitude changed. Today, police officials are under pressure from politicians and citizens to produce encouraging crime-reduction statistics, and promotions and pay raises are generally tied to favorable data. Because of worries about the reliability of official crime statistics in light of these pressures, many criminologists rely on murder rates as the most accurate indicator of criminal activity. It is difficult to downgrade death.

For Critical Analysis: What steps could the FBI take to remove the incentive for police administrators to falsify crime data?

The National Incident-Based Reporting System

In the 1980s, well aware of the various criticisms of the UCR, the Department of Justice began seeking ways to revise its data-collecting system. The result was the National Incident-Based Reporting System (NIBRS). In the NIBRS, local agencies collect data on each single crime occurrence within twenty-two offense categories made up of forty-six specific crimes called Group A offenses (see Figure 2.5 for a list of NIBRS offense categories). These data are recorded on computerized record systems provided—though not completely financed—by the federal government. Though the NIBRS became available to local agencies in 1989, a decade later only fifteen states had been NIBRS cer-

Two Oakland, California, patrol officers listen to complaints from citizens during a police-community meeting. Many police departments place so much emphasis on reducing crime statistics that they spend few resources on such police-community meetings. How could an emphasis on reducing statistical crime rates limit a law enforcement agency's overall effectiveness?

1. Arson
2. Assault Offenses—Aggravated Assault, Simple Assault, Intimidation
3. Bribery
4. Burglary/Breaking and Entering
5. Counterfeiting/Forgery
6. Destruction/Damage/Vandalism of Property
7. Drug/Narcotic Offenses—Drug/Narcotic Violations, Drug Equipment Violations
8. Embezzlement
9. Extortion/Blackmail
10. Fraud Offenses—False Pretenses/Swindle/Confidence Game, Credit Card/Automatic Teller Machine Fraud, Impersonation, Welfare Fraud, Wire Fraud
11. Gambling Offenses—Betting/Wagering, Operating/Promoting/Assisting Gambling, Gambling Equipment Violations, Sports Tampering

12. Homicide Offenses—Murder and Nonnegligent Manslaughter, Negligent Manslaughter, Justifiable Homicide
13. Kidnapping/Abduction
14. Larceny/Theft Offenses—Pocket-picking, Purse-snatching, Shoplifting, Theft from Building, Theft from Coin-Operated Machine or Device, Theft from Motor Vehicle, Theft of Motor Vehicle Parts or Accessories, All Other Larceny
15. Motor Vehicle Theft
16. Pornography/Obscene Material
17. Prostitution Offenses—Prostitution, Assisting or Promoting Prostitution
18. Robbery
19. Sex Offenses, Forcible—Forcible Rape, Forcible Sodomy, Sexual Assault with an Object, Forcible Fondling
20. Sex Offenses, Nonforcible—Incest, Statutory Rape
21. Stolen Property Offenses (Receiving, etc.)
22. Weapon Law Violations

SOURCE: THE FEDERAL BUREAU OF INVESTIGATION.

Figure 2.5 NIBRS Offense Categories

The NIBRS collects data on each single incident and arrest within 22 offense categories made up of the following 46 specific crimes, called Group A offenses.

tified, with eighteen other states in the process of testing the new process.[19] Even in states that are certified, only certain jurisdictions are collecting data for the NIBRS, and as of yet no major cities are connected to the new measuring system. Many local agencies have been reluctant to switch to the NIBRS because of the costs and officer-training time involved.[20]

ALTERNATIVE MEASURING METHODS

The shortcomings of the UCR have led to other attempts to collect data that better measure crime in the United States. Two of the most highly regarded methods, along with their shortcomings, are discussed below.

Victim Surveys

One alternative source of data collecting attempts to avoid the distorting influence of the "intermediary," or the local police agencies. In **victim surveys,** criminologists or other researchers ask the victims of crime directly about their experiences, using techniques such as interviews or mail and phone surveys. The first large-scale victim survey took place in 1966, when members of 10,000 households answered questionnaires as part of the President's Commission on Law Enforcement and the Administration of Justice. The results indicated a much higher victimization rate than had been previously expected, and researchers felt the process gave them a better understanding of the **dark figure of crime,** or the actual amount of crime that occurs in the country.

The National Crime Victimization Survey. Criminologists were so encouraged by the results of the 1966 experiment that the federal government decided to institute an ongoing victim survey. The result was the National Crime Victimization Survey (NCVS), which started in 1972. Conducted by the U.S. Bureau of the Census in cooperation with the Bureau of Justice Statistics of the Justice Department, the NCVS conducts an annual survey of more than 50,000 households with nearly 120,000 occupants over twelve years of age. Participants are interviewed twice a year concerning their experiences with crimes in the prior six months. As you can see in Figure 2.6, the questions cover a wide array of possible victimization.

VICTIM SURVEYS
A method of gathering crime data that directly surveys participants to determine their experiences as victims of crime.

DARK FIGURE OF CRIME
A term used to describe the actual amount of crime that takes place. The "figure" is "dark," or impossible to detect, because a great number of crimes are never reported to the police.

Supporters of the NCVS highlight a number of aspects in which the victim survey is superior to the UCR:

1. It measures both reported and unreported crime.

2. It is unaffected by police bias and distortions in reporting crime to the FBI.

3. It does not rely on victims directly reporting crime to the police.[21]

Most important, some supporters say, is that the NCVS gives victims a voice in the criminal justice process. (For more information on victim issues, see the feature *Criminal Justice in Action—The Growing Role of the Victim* at the end of this chapter.)

Reliability of the NCVS. Even supporters of the NCVS would not, however, claim that the process is infallible. For one, there is no guarantee that those who answer the questionnaire will do so accurately. For reasons of shame, forgetfulness, or fear of reprisal, a participant may not give a completely true picture of her or his recent history. Also, as with any survey research, the manner in which the questions are asked can have a distorting effect on the answers.[22] Consider the following two questions:

1. Have you ever been the victim of a rape?

2. Were you knifed, shot, or attacked with some other weapon? Did someone try to attack you in some other way?

The second question is, in fact, one of the methods the NCVS has used in the past to measure rape. Surveyors expected, or hoped, that someone who had been raped would answer accordingly, as they had been "attacked in some other way." On the one hand, the first question was more direct and may have

Figure 2.6 Sample Questions from the NCVS

Questions Concerning Violent Crime

1. Has anyone attacked or threatened you in any of these ways:
   a. With any weapon, for instance, a gun or knife—
   b. With anything like a baseball bat, frying pan, scissors, or stick—
   c. By something thrown, such as a rock or bottle—
   d. Include any grabbing, punching, or choking,
   e. Any rape, attempted rape, or other type of sexual attack—
   f. Any face to face threats—
   OR
   g. Any attack or threat or use of force by anyone at all? Please mention it even if you are not certain it was a crime.

2. Incidents involving forced or unwanted sexual acts are often difficult to talk about. Have you been forced or coerced to engage in unwanted sexual activity by—
   a. someone you didn't know before
   b. a casual acquaintance OR
   c. someone you know well

Questions Concerning Theft and Household Larceny

1. Was something belonging to YOU stolen, such as:
   a. Things that you carry, like luggage, a wallet, purse, briefcase, book—
   b. Clothing, jewelry, or calculator—
   c. Bicycle or sports equipment—
   d. Things in your house—like a TV, stereo, or tools—
   e. Things outside your home such as a garden hose or lawn furniture—
   f. Things belonging to children in the household—
   g. Things from a vehicle, such as a package, groceries, camera, or cassette tapes—
   OR
   h. Did anyone ATTEMPT to steal anything belonging to you?

2. About your motor vehicles:
   a. Did anyone steal any parts such as a tire, tape deck, hubcap, or battery?
   b. Did anyone steal any gas from them?
   c. Did anyone ATTEMPT to steal parts attached to them?

Questions Concerning Burglary

1. Has somebody:
   a. Broken in or ATTEMPTED to break into your home by forcing a door or window, pushing past someone, jimmying a lock, cutting a screen, or entering through an open door or window?
   b. Has anyone illegally gotten in or tried to get into a garage, shed or storage room?
   OR
   c. Illegally gotten in or tried to get into a hotel or motel room or vacation home where you were staying?

SOURCE: BUREAU OF JUSTICE STATISTICS, *TECHNICAL BACKGROUND ON THE REDESIGNED NATIONAL CRIME VICTIMIZATION SURVEY* (WASHINGTON, D.C.: U.S. DEPARTMENT OF JUSTICE, 1994).

elicited more "yes" answers. On the other hand, because of the stigma attached, the word *rape,* it may have discouraged participants from answering truthfully. As a result of complaints that the vagueness of the question led rape to be seriously underreported in the NCVS (see the new version in Figure 2.6), the surveyors altered their methods of gaining information concerning sexual assaults in the early 1990s.

Victim surveys also present a number of other potential problems. Many citizens are not well versed in the terminology of criminal justice and may not know, for example, that a break-in that occurred at their home while they were at the movies is a burglary and not a robbery. (Remember that burglary refers to breaking into a structure with the intention to commit a felony, whereas robbery is the illegal taking of property using force or the threat of force.) There are also a number of crimes that victim surveys cannot record, such as drug use or gambling, for legal reasons, and murder, for more obvious ones.[23]

Furthermore, many observers still find the NCVS data on rape highly questionable. Given the emotional turmoil a victim of that crime experiences, many women are simply not willing to divulge the information. In addition, the NCVS includes only data from females aged eleven and older; yet a 1992 study by researcher Dean Kilpatrick found that in nearly one of every three rapes, the victim was under eleven years old.[24]

Self-Report Surveys

Based on many of the same principles as victim surveys, but focusing instead on offenders, **self-report surveys** are a third source of data for criminologists. In this form of data collecting, persons are asked directly—through personal interviews or questionnaires, or over the telephone—about specific criminal activity to which they may have been a party. Though not implemented on the scale of the UCR or NCVS, self-report surveys are most useful in situations in which the group to be studied is already gathered in an institutional setting, such as a juvenile facility or a prison. One of the most widespread self-report surveys in the United States, the Drug Use Forecasting Program, collects information on narcotics use from arrestees who have been brought into booking facilities.

Such studies can also be particularly helpful in finding specific information about groups of subjects. When professors Peter B. Wood, Walter R. Grove, James A. Wilson, and John K. Cochran wanted to learn how criminals "felt" when committing crimes, for example, they used self-report surveys. By comparing these results to those gathered from a group of male students at a state university, the researchers were able to draw conclusions on the "high" a criminal experiences during a crime.[25]

A "Giant" Dark Figure. Because there is no penalty for admitting to criminal activity in a self-report, subjects tend to be more forthcoming in discussing their behavior. The researchers mentioned above found that a significant number of the students interviewed admitted to committing minor crimes for which they had never been arrested. This fact points to the most striking finding of self-report surveys: the dark figure of crime, referred to earlier in the chapter as the *actual* amount of crime that takes places, appears to be much larger than the UCR or NCVS would suggest.

The first major self-report survey, conducted by James S. Wallerstein and Clement J. Wyle in 1947, queried 1,020 men and 678 women from a wide spectrum of different backgrounds on their participation in a number of crimes. Ninety-nine percent of the participants admitted to committing at least one

SELF-REPORT SURVEYS
A method of gathering crime data that relies on participants to reveal and detail their own criminal or delinquent behavior.

of the crimes referenced by Wallerstein and Wyle.[26] When factoring alcohol offenses, recreational drug use, truancy, and petty theft, self-reports consistently show that almost everybody has committed at least one crime in his or her lifetime.[27]

Besides their usefulness in determining the criminal behavior of the average American, self-reports are also valued for their ability to target specific criminological subjects. For example, to test a theory that drug use by parents leads to a greater possibility of drug use in their children, researchers can do a self-report survey with a cross section of drug users. Also, self-reports allow researchers to control aspects of the data collection themselves, thereby assuring that race, class, and gender will not bias the results.

Reliability of Self-Reports. Again, despite these advantages there are a number of perceived disadvantages with self-report surveys. The manner in which a subject answers questions often relies on his or her personality or beliefs. If a person sees criminal behavior as something to be ashamed of, he or she may downplay such behavior. In contrast, a person who sees criminal behavior as positive may exaggerate the truth to impress the questioner.

For the same reason that a participant has nothing to lose by telling the truth, she or he has nothing to gain by telling the truth, either. The effects of lying on self-report surveys can be dramatic. In a self-report survey of juveniles, researchers Thomas Gray and Eric Walsh tested their subjects with urinalysis as well as asking them about their drug use. Less than 33 percent of the juveniles who tested positive for marijuana also admitted to using the drug, and only 15 percent of those who tested positive for cocaine were truthful about their habits.[28] These types of results have led many criminologists to conclude that self-report surveys are skewed by many of the same inaccuracies that plague the other collecting methods.[29]

MISUSE OF CRIME STATISTICS

It may not be the case that, as one group of criminologists put it, "crime rates tell us virtually nothing about crime."[30] But researchers have come to understand that all measures of crime are susceptible to error and that any conclusions drawn from those measurements must account for that possibility.

Although criminologists are trained to make such adjustments, the media and their "customers" are not. Criminologist Kenneth Tunnell has argued that misuse of crime data by the media leads to unwarranted levels of concern among the public. As an example, Tunnell cites the use of the "Crime Clock," which is released every year along with the latest UCR figures (see Figure 2.7). The Crime Clock—which reported in 1997 that a homicide occurred every 27 minutes, an aggravated assault every 31 seconds, and so on—is popular among media outlets because it is easy to understand and grabs the viewer's or reader's attention. To a certain degree, the Crime Clock is misleading. The same FBI statistics also show that the chances are one in 15,000 of a person being a victim of a homicide and one in 265 of a person being the victim of an aggravated assault. Because the public does not have access to any figures other than those provided by the mass media, says Tunnell, the media can "manipulate the fear of crime."[31]

Figure 2.7 The Crime Clock

The Crime Clock is meant to convey the relative frequency of the various index crime offenses.

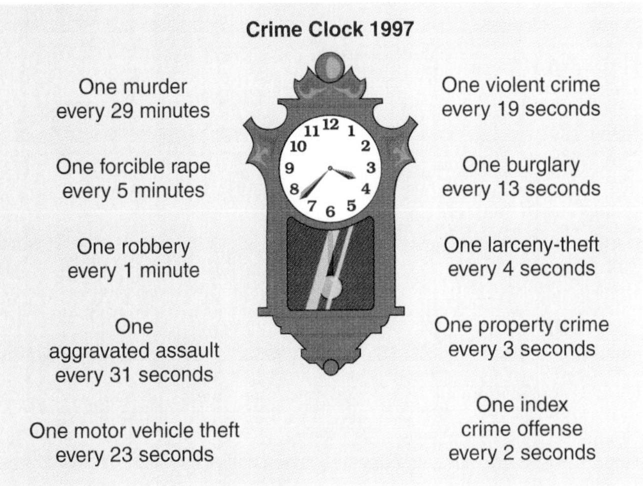

Crime Clock 1997

One murder every 29 minutes

One forcible rape every 5 minutes

One robbery every 1 minute

One aggravated assault every 31 seconds

One motor vehicle theft every 23 seconds

One violent crime every 19 seconds

One burglary every 13 seconds

One larceny-theft every 4 seconds

One property crime every 3 seconds

One index crime offense every 2 seconds

SOURCE: FEDERAL BUREAU OF INVESTIGATION, CRIME IN THE UNITED STATES, 1997 (WASHINGTON, D.C.: U.S. DEPARTMENT OF JUSTICE, 1998), CHART 2.1, PAGE 6.

Peggy Landry of New Orleans is pictured here proudly showing off her handgun and concealed-weapon license. Thanks to a new law passed by the Louisiana legislature in 1997, Landry and other citizens of the state are allowed to open fire on a person "who is reasonably believed" to be using "unlawful force" or making an "unlawful entry" into a car they happen to be driving. What might some of the drawbacks of such a law be?

CRIME TRENDS AND PATTERNS

Concoctions such as the Crime Clock may contribute to high levels of public fear of crime, as discussed in Chapter 1. But basic crime data do show that, overall, crime rates have decreased over the past two decades. Both the NCVS and the UCR show the crime rate peaking in the early 1980s, with relatively steady declines (interrupted by increases in the early 1990s) since. As can be seen in Figure 2.8, in the 1990s the NCVS and the UCR have increasingly mirrored each other in violent crime trends. The explanation for this may be that, despite the criticisms, the two measuring devices are improving. Increased willingness by victims to discuss their experiences enables the NCVS to better reflect true victimization rates, and increased police efficiency in recording incidents of crime has the same positive effect on the UCR.[32]

Place and Crime

In addition to providing the "big picture" of crime by tracking broad trends such as homicide or burglary rates, these data can also furnish "snapshots" of consistent crime patterns. By selectively applying statistics, for example, criminologists have detected definite geographical patterns to crime:

Figure 2.8 Crime Trends as Measured by the UCR and NCVS

As you can see, although the levels of violent crime reported by the Uniform Crime Reports and the National Crime Victimization Survey are different, these measuring devices both show that violent crime in the United States dropped approximately 20 percent from 1993 to 1997.

1. Urban areas have consistently higher rates of index crimes than rural or suburban areas.

2. States in the South and West have higher rates of index crimes than do those in the Midwest and the Northeast.[33] (See Figure 2.9.)

In addition, crime data also show higher rates of crime in warmer summer months than any other time of year. This information would seem to suggest that a person who wants to avoid crime should live in a small town in the upper Midwest rather than a large city on the West Coast.[34]

Furthermore, researchers have found that urban criminal activity is often concentrated in certain definable areas. Several years ago, for example, nearly 25 percent of

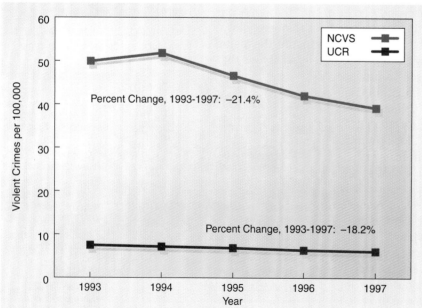

SOURCE: FEDERAL BUREAU OF INVESTIGATION, CRIME IN THE UNITED STATES, 1997 (WASHINGTON, D.C.: U.S. DEPARTMENT OF JUSTICE, 1998), TABLE 1, PAGE 66; AND BUREAU OF JUSTICE STATISTICS, CRIMINAL VICTIMIZATION, 1997 (WASHINGTON, D.C.: U.S. DEPARTMENT OF JUSTICE, 1998), TABLE 5, PAGE 9.

Boston's youth homicides, gun assaults, and drug offenses occurred in an area covering less than 4 percent of the city.[35] Due in part to the efforts of crime researchers such as Lawrence W. Sherman and David Weisburd,[36] law enforcement agencies are starting to target these high-crime settings, known as "hot spots," in intensive prevention strategies. Using computer programs that "map" patterns of crime, police departments are increasingly able to divert resources to the areas that need them the most. We will further discuss the use of this technology in police operations in Chapter 5.

Class and Crime

The general assumption that the poorest citizens are those most likely to commit serious crimes is borne out by official crime statistics. The highest crime rates in the United States are consistently recorded in low-income, urban neighborhoods. A rise of one percentage point in male unemployment appears to increase the violent crime rate by 9 percent, and a one percentage point rise in the poverty rate increases property crime by nearly 3 percent.[37]

It may seem logical that those who believe they lack a legal opportunity to gain the consumer goods and services that dominate American culture would turn to illegal methods to do so. But, logic aside, many criminologists are skeptical of such an obvious class-crime relationship. After all, poverty does not *cause* crime; the majority of residents in low-income neighborhoods are law-abiding. Furthermore, higher-income citizens are also involved in all sorts of criminal activities and are more likely to commit white-collar crimes, which are not measured by the UCR or NCVS.

Furthermore, self-report data have been used extensively in studying the crime-class relationship. The results have shown that as far as less serious crimes are concerned, lower-, middle-, and upper-class criminal behavior differ very little.[38] These findings tend to support the theory that high crime rates in low-income communities are at least partly the result of a greater willingness of police to arrest poor citizens, and of the court system to convict them.

Race and Crime

The class-crime relationship and the class-race relationship are invariably linked. Official crime data seem to indicate a strong correlation between minority status and crime: according to the UCR, African Americans—who make up 13 percent of the population—constitute 41 percent of those arrested for violent crimes and 32 percent of those arrested for property crimes.[39] Furthermore, according to the NCVS, African Americans are victims of violent crime at a rate of 49.0 per 1,000, compared to 38.3 per 1,000 for whites.[40]

The racial differences in the crime rate are one of the most controversial areas of the criminal justice system. At first glance, crime statistics seem to support the idea that the subculture of African Americans in the United States is disposed toward criminal behavior. Not all of the data, however, support that assertion. A number of crime-measuring surveys show consistent levels of crime and drug abuse across racial lines.[41] Why, then, are proportionally more minorities arrested and incarcerated than whites? This discrepancy has

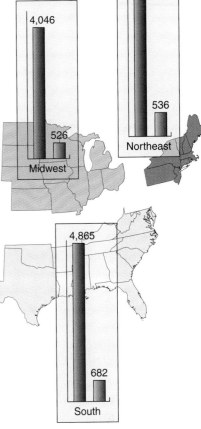

Figure 2.9 1997 Violent and Property Crime Rates, by Region, per 100,000 Inhabitants

Property Crime Rate
Violent Crime Rate

SOURCE: FEDERAL BUREAU OF INVESTIGATION, CRIME IN THE UNITED STATES, 1997 (WASHINGTON, D.C.: U.S. DEPARTMENT OF JUSTICE, 1998), CHART 2.4, PAGE 10.

been attributed to inherent racism in the criminal justice system, though criminologists are by no means of one mind regarding this possibility. A number of other factors, including poor economic and social conditions in the low-income neighborhoods where many minorities reside, have been offered to explain the complex problem of race and crime. We will address this issue throughout this textbook and focus on it in depth in Chapter 18.

Age and Crime

The strongest statistical determinant of criminal behavior appears to be age. Each of the three sources of crime data supports the hypothesis that criminal activity has been, and continues to be, most pronounced among younger citizens.[42] According to the latest UCR, 35 percent of arrests for violent crimes involve Americans 21 and younger, with the highest crime rate occurring between the ages of 16 and 19. By the same token, those aged 50 years and older are responsible for only 4.3 percent of the violent crime arrests in this country.[43] (See Figure 2.10.)

Some criminologists, notably John DiIulio of Princeton University, believe that trends of age and crime will have a dramatic influence on the criminal justice system in the near future. The number of teenage males in the United States is expected to rise sharply over the next few years, leading DiIulio to predict that the juvenile murder rate could rise 25 percent during the ten-year period ending in 2005. DiIulio also believes that society is creating "superpredators," or adolescents who have been raised in "abject moral poverty" and are "more impulsively violent and remorseless than ever."[44] DiIulio's theories, and their detractors, will be addressed in Chapter 16.

Guns and Crime

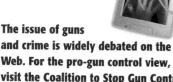

The issue of guns and crime is widely debated on the Web. For the pro-gun control view, visit the Coalition to Stop Gun Control Violence at www.gunfree.com For the anti-gun control view, go to the National Rifle Association's site at www.nra.com

Since at least the 1930s, young people have committed more violent crimes than have their elders. Since the mid-1980s, however, such rates have increased *significantly*. Between 1985 and 1992, homicide rates went up by 50 percent for white males aged fourteen to seventeen and tripled for African Americans of the same age.[45] This sharp increase has been linked to the role guns play in juvenile criminal behavior. The rise in gun ownership among gang members in high-crime urban areas has been well documented,[46] but these high rates of violence also reflect a growing pattern of gun ownership among suburban youths as well.[47]

According to the UCR, 67.8 percent of all homicides were committed with a firearm. In addition, 40 percent of all robberies and 20 percent of all aggravated assaults were carried out by someone brandishing a gun.[48] Victim's rights groups and gun control advocates argue that America's high rates of

Figure 2.10 Homicide Rates and Age

In any given year, as you can see on this graph, the number of homicides per 100,000 people is significantly higher for 18- to 24-year-olds than for any other age group.

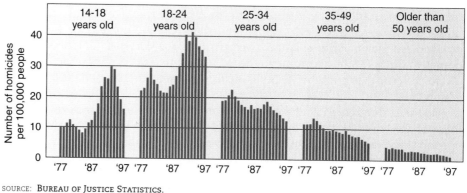

SOURCE: BUREAU OF JUSTICE STATISTICS.

Police officers gather outside Stamps High School in Stamps, Arkansas, following the early morning shooting of two students, seventeen-year-old Grover Henderson and fifteen-year-old LeTisia Finley. Henderson and Finley, who eventually recovered from their wounds, were the target of fourteen-year-old Joseph Todd, who told police that the shootings were revenge for being "picked on" by his fellow students. A spate of similar incidents in 1998 and 1999 raised fears of gun violence on campuses. Do you think measures such as police officers and metal detectors in schools could alleviate this problem? What negative consequences might result from such dramatic steps?

violence reflect the ease with which firearms are available to its citizens; hence, they push for legislation to restrict the ability to sell and purchase such weapons. (For a discussion of gun policies in other countries, see on the following page *Cross-National CJ Comparison—Armed, but Dangerous?*)

Others, however, believe that the FBI's statistics support the argument that handguns prevent crime. By comparing UCR data in communities before and after they passed "right-to-carry" gun laws (which allow an adult applicant to be granted a concealed-weapon permit unless he or she is a felon or has a history of serious mental illness), John R. Lott, Jr., of the University of Chicago Law School has estimated that such laws reduced homicide by 8 percent, rape by 5 percent, aggravated assault by 7 percent, and robbery by 3 percent. In the thirty-one states that currently have right-to-carry laws on the books, violent crime is 13 percent lower than in those states that do not.[49] Though even Lott is not willing to say that right-to-carry laws directly cause a drop in violent crime—other contributing factors could include population density and sentencing lengths—he does believe that these reductions are partly attributable to the deterrent effect of weapons on criminal behavior by reducing the number of "helpless victims" who are the main target of criminals.[50] As both supporters and opponents of stricter gun laws believe strongly in their positions, this issue promises to remain a volatile part of the nation's political dialogue.

Drugs and Alcohol and Crime

Because of methodology, neither the UCR nor the NCVS is well suited to measure the effect of drugs and alcohol on criminal behavior. The National Incident-Based Reporting System may improve official crime data in this area. Other institutions, however, have studied the role that drugs and alcohol play in crime trends. A recent report published by the National Center on Addiction and Substance Abuse at Columbia University concluded that eight out of every ten prisoners in the United States were involved with alcohol or other drugs at the time of their crimes. That is to say, 80 percent were either under the direct influence of alcohol or other drugs while committing the crime, had a history of drug abuse, committed the crime to support a drug habit, or were arrested for violating drug or alcohol laws.[51] The role of legal drugs such as alcohol and illegal drugs such as cocaine and heroin will be explored in Chapter 17.

The actor Christian Slater is led out of a West Hollywood, California, police station after being arrested for assault with a deadly weapon. Like many arrestees, Slater was under the influence of drugs and alcohol when he committed his crime.

Cross-National CJ Comparison

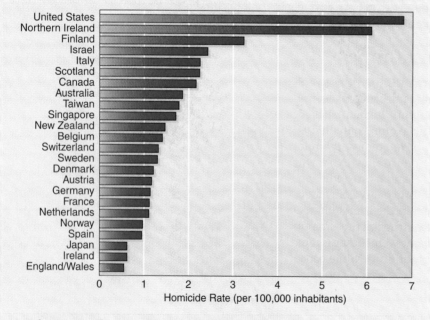

Armed, but Dangerous?

On December 11, 1998, the second part of the Brady Handgun Violence Prevention Act of 1993—commonly known as the Brady Bill—went into effect. The first part of the law required background checks on all Americans who purchase a handgun. Five years later, the law was expanded to cover those who purchase "long" guns such as shotguns and hunting rifles. The background checks, conducted by the FBI, are designed to determine whether the buyer has a criminal record. If so, she or he is not eligible to purchase the firearm. Supporters of legislative attempts to promote stricter gun control, such as the Brady Bill, believe that high rates of violence in the United States can be attributed to the widespread ownership of firearms—nearly half of American households contain at least one gun. The experiences of Japan and Switzerland, however, suggest that the issue is not so simple. These two countries have murder rates that are among the lowest in the industrialized world (see Figure 2.11) yet their gun control policies could not be more different.

JAPAN AND SWITZERLAND: OPPOSITES

Japan has a virtually gun-free society. Ownership of most firearms is almost completely outlawed; only about 15 percent of Japanese citizens are permitted to own handguns, and the weapons cannot leave the grounds of shooting ranges. Not even police officers may keep a handgun at home, and illegal possession of a handgun or ammunition is punishable by fifteen years in prison. Given the extent to which even Japanese criminals follow these laws, it is perhaps not surprising that the murder rate in the country is so low.

In Switzerland, however, most males between the ages of eighteen and forty-two possess SIG brand assault rifles—the equivalent of the M-16 rifles that American soldiers are issued. Because Switzerland does not have a standing army, the country relies on a militia consisting of most of its adult male population. These members of the "people's army" are required by the Swiss government to keep assault weapons and ammunition in their homes. The government encourages those not involved with the military to purchase firearms as well; the lenient licensing system makes it easier, according to one observer, to purchase a bazooka in Zurich than to obtain a building permit in New York City. In fact, it has been estimated that there are more firearms (7 million) in Switzerland than people (6.5 million.)

COMPARING SWITZERLAND AND THE UNITED STATES

American pro-gun ownership groups have used these figures to argue against the idea that a heavily armed society is necessarily a violent one. Any comparisons between Switzerland and the United States in this area may be misleading, however. First, gun control laws are actually much stricter in Switzerland than in the United States: every firearm is registered, and any person who misuses his or her weapon is subject to heavy penalties. Second, almost every Swiss male gun owner has been professionally trained in the use of firearms by the military, reducing many of the dangers of gun ownership. Third, there is far less poverty in Switzerland than in the United States. Those Americans most likely to use firearms to commit crimes are generally the poorest Americans.

WHAT'S THE EVIDENCE?

A number of countries besides the United States are trying to determine the extent that firearms should be available to their citizens. Determine whether Britain, Australia, and Canada are instituting policies closer to the Japanese or the Swiss model by visiting **www.health.su.oz.au/cgc/ compglawhtm.htm**.

Figure 2.11 Homicide Rates in Industrialized Nations

The following list compares homicide rates for those countries considered to be "high income" by the World Bank.

SOURCE: INTERNATIONAL JOURNAL OF EPIDEMIOLOGY 27 (1998), 216; FEDERAL BUREAU OF INVESTIGATION.

Gender and Crime

As with age patterns, UCR, self-report, and victimization data consistently show similar patterns with regard to gender and crime. That is, males commit significantly more crime than females. For example, men commit murder at almost ten times the rate of females. The male-female crime ratio does not change when other factors—such as age, race, or class—are considered. This lower female involvement in crime has been attributed to a number of reasons including the influence of gender roles, different social expectations for women and men, biology, and physical ability to commit crime; we will examine this issue in Chapter 18.

Career Criminals

A final pattern that crime data have uncovered is that of the career criminal, or **chronic offender.** The idea of the chronic offender was established by the pioneering research of Marvin Wolfgang, Robert Figlio, and Thorsten Sellin. The trio used official records to follow a **cohort** of 9,945 males born in Philadelphia in 1945 until they turned eighteen years of age in 1963. Released in 1972, the resulting study showed that 6 percent of the cohort had committed five or more offenses. Furthermore, this "chronic 6 percent" were responsible for 71 percent of the murders attributed to the cohort, 82 percent of the robberies, 69 percent of the aggravated assaults, and 73 percent of the rapes.[52] The existence of chronic offenders has been corroborated by further research, such as that done by Lawrence Sherman in Kansas City. Sherman found that although only 2.7 percent of the city's roughly 500,000 inhabitants were arrested twice or more in 1990, these offenders accounted for over 60 percent of all arrests that year.[53]

Chronic offender patterns have had a significant impact on the criminal justice system. Law enforcement agencies and district attorneys' offices have devised specific strategies to apprehend and prosecute repeat offenders. As we shall see in Chapter 11, the federal government and most states have instituted sentencing policies designed to incapacitate career criminals for long periods of time.

EXPLORING THE CAUSES OF CRIME

Why do chronic offenders persist in their criminal behavior? Criminologists have advanced a number of theories to explain this pattern, including learning disabilities or poor school performance, an unsettled home life, familial history of criminality, and hyperactivity. Some observers feel that criminal behavior is linked to certain biological or genetic traits, while others think that some people are driven to commit crimes because they like it. Serial killer John Wayne Gacy claims to have "realized that death was the ultimate thrill" after murdering the first of his more than thirty victims.[54]

Research shows at least a *correlation* between each of the above theories and the phenomenon of the chronic offender. The research community has not, however, been able to reach a consensus on the *cause* of career criminality. Such is the challenge of the criminologist. The question that is the underpinning of a career in criminology—what causes crime?—is yet to be fully answered. Many variables must be accounted for. But criminologists have uncovered a wealth of information concerning a different, and more practically applicable, inquiry: Given a certain set of circumstances, why do individuals commit certain crimes?

CHRONIC OFFENDER
A delinquent or criminal who commits multiple offenses, and is considered part of a small group of wrongdoers who are responsible for a majority of the antisocial activity in any given community.

COHORT
A group of persons gathered for study because they share a certain characteristic, such as age, income, or criminal background.

"There is no society where a more or less developed criminality is not found under different forms. No people exists whose morality is not daily infringed upon. We must therefore call crime necessary and declare that it cannot be non-existent, that the fundamental conditions of social organization, as they are understood, logically imply it."

—Emile Durkheim, *French sociologist* (1897)

CHOICE THEORY
A school of criminology that holds that wrongdoers act as if they weigh the possible benefits of criminal or delinquent activity against the costs of being apprehended. When the benefits are greater than the costs, the offender will make a rational choice to commit a crime or delinquent act.

CLASSICAL CRIMINOLOGY
A school of criminology based on the belief that individuals have free will to engage in any behavior, including criminal behavior. To deter criminal behavior, society must hold wrongdoers responsible for their actions by punishing them.

UTILITARIANISM
An approach to ethical reasoning in which the "correct" decision is the one that results in the greatest amount of good for the greatest number of people affected by that decision.

POSITIVISM
A school of social science that sees criminal and delinquent behavior as the result of biological, psychological, and social forces. Because wrongdoers are driven to deviancy by external factors, they should not be punished but treated to lessen the influence of those factors.

Various schools of criminology have developed numerous theories of crime causation. In the following sections, we will examine the most widely recognized ones: choice theories, trait theories, sociological theories, social process theories, and social conflict theories.

Crime and Free Will: Choice Theories of Crime

For the purposes of the American criminal justice system, the answer to why a person commits a crime is rather straightforward: because that person chooses to do so. This application of **choice theory** to criminal law is not absolute; if a defendant can prove that she or he lacked the ability to make a rational choice, in certain circumstances the defendant will not be punished as harshly for a crime as would normally be the case. But such allowances are relatively recent. From the early days of this country, the general presumption in criminal law has been that behavior is a consequence of free will.

Theories of Classical Criminology. This emphasis on free will and human rationality in the realm of criminal behavior has its roots in **classical criminology.** Classical theorists believed that crime was an expression of a person's rational decision-making process: before committing a crime, a person would weigh the benefits of the crime against the costs of being apprehended. Therefore, if punishments were stringent enough to outweigh the benefits of crime, they would dissuade people from committing the crime in the first place.

The earliest popular expression of classical theory came in 1764 when the Italian Cesare Beccaria (1738–1794) published his *Essays on Crime and Punishments.* Beccaria criticized existing systems of criminal law as irrational and argued that criminal procedures should be more consistent with human behavior. He believed that, to be just, criminal law should reflect three truths:

1. All decisions, including the decision to commit a crime, are the result of rational choice.

2. Fear of punishment can have a deterrent effect on the choice to commit crime.

3. The more swift and certain punishment is, the more effective it will be in controlling crime.[55]

Beccaria believed that any punishment that purported to do anything other than deter crime was cruel and arbitrary. This view was shared by his contemporary, Britain's Jeremy Bentham (1748–1832). In 1789, Bentham pronounced that "nature has placed man under the governance of two sovereign masters, *pain* and *pleasure.*" Bentham applied his theory of **utilitarianism** to the law by contending that punishment should use the threat of pain against criminal individuals to assure the pleasure of society as a whole.[56] As a result, Bentham felt that punishment should have four goals:

1. To prevent all crime.

2. When it cannot prevent crime, to assure that a criminal will commit a lesser crime to avoid a harsher punishment.

3. To give the criminal an incentive not to harm others in the pursuit of crime.

4. To prevent crime at the least possible cost to society.[57]

Positivism and Modern Rational Theory. By the end of the nineteenth century, the positivist school of criminologists had superseded classical criminology. According to **positivism,** criminal behavior is determined by biological, psychological, and social forces and is beyond the control of the individual. The Italian physician Cesare Lombroso (1835–1909), an early adherent of positivism who is known as the "father of criminology," believed that criminals were throwbacks to the savagery of early humankind and could therefore be identified by certain physical characteristics such as sharp teeth and large jaws. He also theorized that criminality was similar to mental illness and could be genetically passed down from generation to generation in families that had cases of insanity, syphilis, epilepsy, and even deafness. Such individuals, according to Lombroso and his followers, had no free choice when it came to wrongdoing—their criminality had been predetermined at birth.

Positivist theory lost credibility as crime rates began to climb in the 1970s. If crime was caused by external factors, critics asked, why had the proactive social programs of the 1960s not brought about a decrease in criminal activity? An updated version of classical criminology, known as *rational choice theory,* found renewed acceptance. James Q. Wilson, one of the most prominent critics of the positivist school, sums up rational choice theory as follows:

> At any given moment, a person can choose between committing a crime and not committing it. The consequences of committing a crime consist of rewards (what psychologists call "reinforcers") and punishments; the consequences of not committing the crime also entail gains and losses. The larger the ratio of the net rewards of crime to the net rewards of [not committing a crime], the greater the tendency to commit a crime.[58]

According to rational choice theory, we can hypothesize that criminal actions, including acts of violence and drug abuse, are committed with this ratio in mind.

The Seduction of Crime. In expanding upon rational choice theory, sociologist Jack Katz has stated that the "rewards" of crime may be sensual as well as financial. The inherent danger of criminal activity, according to Katz, increases the "rush" a criminal experiences upon successfully committing a crime. Katz labels the rewards of this "rush" the *seduction of crime.*[59] For example, a person may decide to rob a bank not just for the money, but because of the inherent excitement of the action itself. Katz believes that seemingly "senseless" crimes can only be explained by rational choice theory if the intrinsic reward of the crime itself is considered.

Choice Theory and Public Policy. The theory that wrongdoers choose to commit crimes is a cornerstone of the American criminal justice system. Because crime is seen as the end result of a series of rational choices, policymakers have reasoned that severe punishment can deter criminal activity by adding another variable to the decision-making process. Supporters of the death penalty—now used by thirty-eight states and the federal government—emphasize its deterrent effects, and legislators are increasingly using harsh mandatory sentences to control illegal drug use and trafficking.

"Born Criminal": Biological and Psychological Theories of Crime

As we have seen, Cesare Lombroso believed in the "criminal born" man and woman and was confident that he could distinguish criminals by their ape-like physical features. Such far-fetched notions have long been relegated to scientific oblivion. But many criminologists do believe that *trait theories* have validity. These theories suggest that certain biological or psychological traits in individuals could incline them toward criminal behavior given a certain set of circumstances.

"Once I've armed myself and I go in and do the robbery, my mind and my heart are racing a thousand miles an hour—yeah, I got a hell of an adrenaline rush. For me, before a crime, it's getting myself pumped up for that rush, and while committing the crime it's like being scared and excited at the same time, and it's from gaining that power over another human being. That rush gets going and doesn't stop until I succeed in whatever I am doing."

—Inmate, *interviewed by criminologist Peter B. Wood* (1997)

Biochemical Conditions and Crime. One trait theory is that biochemical conditions can influence criminal behavior. These conditions can be genetic or brought about through environmental contacts. An example of the latter occurred in 1979, when Dan White was accused of murdering San Francisco Mayor George Moscone and Supervisor Harvey Milk. White successfully pleaded the "Twinkie defense"—that he should not be held accountable for his actions because he had suffered a major "mood disturbance" caused in part by an addiction to high-sugar junk food.[60]

More recently, Ann Green was found not guilty of the attempted murder of her infant child because of postpartum psychosis. This illness, believed to be partly caused by the hormonal changes that women experience after childbirth, causes abnormal behavior in a small percentage of recent mothers.[61] Criminal activity in males has also been linked to hormones—specifically *testosterone,* which controls secondary sexual characteristics (such as the growth of facial and pubic hair and the change of voice pitch) and has been linked to traits of aggression. Testing of inmate populations has shown that those incarcerated for violent crimes have higher testosterone levels than other prisoners.[62] High testosterone levels have also been used to explain the age-crime relationship, as the average testosterone level of men under the age of twenty-eight is double that of men between thirty-one and sixty-six years old.[63]

Genetics and Crime. Some criminologists might contend that Katz's "seduction of crime" provides more support for a modern, gene-based, evolutionary theory of crime than for rational choice theory. That is, the seduction of crime represents an ancestral urge—which is stronger in some people than others—to commit acts that are considered crimes only in modern society.

Behavioral Genes. Recently, psychologist Leda Cosmides and anthropologist John Tooby have advocated a "Swiss army knife model" to explain how genetics influences brain activity. According to this model, humans have evolved special modules and networks in their brains that dispose them toward certain behavioral patterns.[64] Criminologists such as Lee Ellis and Anthony Walsh have suggested that some of these behavior patterns, which at one time were beneficial to human survival, have now become antisocial and have had sanctions imposed upon them by society. In prehistoric eras, for example, extreme sexual aggressiveness in males toward a large number of females would have diversified a community's gene pool. Now laws against sexual assault and rape restrict such behavior.[65]

Another theory suggests that personality traits associated with criminal behavior can be predicted by genetic make-up. Normally, a person has forty-six chromosomes (threadlike cellular structures that carry genetic information in the form of genes), a pair of which dictate sexual characteristics. In men, this pair of sex chromosomes is called XY, and in women XX. A number of variations in these sex chromosomes can occur, and some criminologists have focused on studies that show a correlation between the XYY chromosomal abnormality in men and criminal behavior.[66] In the 1970s, a number of defendants tried to introduce evidence of this chromosomal abnormality during criminal trials, but the courts consistently found that medical evidence could not establish a causal relationship between the XYY defect and criminal behavior.[67]

Twin Studies. Because genes are inherited, some researchers have turned to *twin studies* to determine the relationship between genetics and criminal behavior. If the two are linked, then twins should exhibit similar antisocial tendencies. The problem with twin studies is that most twins grow up in the same environment, so it is difficult to determine whether their behavior is influenced by their genes or by their surroundings. To overcome this difficulty, crim-

"Crime is a fact of the human species, a fact of that species alone, but it is above all the secret aspect, impenetrable and hidden. Crime hides, and by far the most terrifying things are those which elude us."

—Georges Bataille, *French novelist* (1965)

inologists compare identical twins, known as MZ twins, and fraternal twins of the same sex, known as DZ twins. Because MZ twins are genetically identical while DZ twins share only half of their genes, the latter should be less likely to have similar behavior patterns than the former.

Indeed, some studies seem to support this hypothesis. Researcher Karl Christiansen, for example, examined nearly four thousand male twin pairs and found that 52 percent of MZ pairs exhibited similar behavior patterns compared to only 22 percent for DZ pairs.[68] As is often the frustrating case in criminology, however, other studies seem to refute the idea that genetics is more important than environment in determining delinquent behavior. Research by criminologist David Rowe shows that nontwin siblings resemble each other in terms of delinquency to the same extent as twins do.[69] Consequently, though twin studies have contributed much to the discussion of trait theories, they have not proved conclusive in determining the effect of genetics on criminal behavior.[70]

Brain Activity and Crime. The study of brain activity, or *neurophysiology*, has also found a niche in criminology. Some criminologists hypothesize that criminal behavior can be influenced by neurological defects that are acquired early in life. Neurophysiological studies of crime have relied on *electroencephalographic (EEG)* scans of brain activity. An EEG records the series of electric oscillations, or waves, given off by the part of the brain that controls functions such as learning and memory. These brain waves are measured according to their frequency and strength, and certain patterns of brain waves can be associated with criminal behavior. (For more information on "brain mapping" procedures, see *Criminal Justice & Technology—Mapping Crime in the Brain.*) One study of a random sample of 333 subjects referred for an EEG found that those who exhibited lifelong patterns of violence had an incidence of EEG abnormality of 65 percent, three times higher than the same trait in those who had been charged with only one violent offense.[71]

Psychology and Crime. For all of his accomplishments in the field of psychology, Sigmund Freud (1856–1939) rarely turned his attention to the causes of crime. His followers, however, have proposed a *psychoanalytic theory* for criminal behavior. This theory rests on the belief that the human personality is made up of three parts:

1. The *id,* which controls sexual urges.
2. The *ego,* which controls behavior that leads to the fulfillment of the id.

Criminal Justice & Technology
Mapping Crime in the Brain

During the trial of John Hinckley, Jr., who attempted to assassinate President Ronald Reagan in 1981, the defense offered the jury a black-and-white photo of Hinckley's brain. This picture, the defense claimed, showed that Hinckley was schizophrenic and not responsible for his actions. In a controversial decision, the defendant was found not guilty by reason of insanity.

Twenty years later, "brain mapping" techniques make the black-and-white photo of Hinckley's brain look like the drawing of a child.

By placing electrodes on a subject's scalp, scientists can use computerized electroencephalography (CEEG) to measure the brain's spontaneous electrical activity, or its electrical response to visual and auditory stimuli. Using CEEG, scientists can present a color-coded display of brain activity. Other neuroimaging measures include positron emission computer tomography (PET scanning), which produces a computerized image of molecular variations in brain metabolism, and magnetic resonance imaging (MRI), which depicts the brain's form and structure by bombarding it with magnetic fields and radio waves.

Scans that measure brain activity can be particularly helpful in identifying

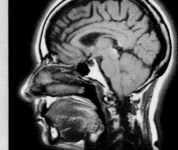
An MRI scan showing the human brain.

attention deficit/hyperactivity disorder (ADHD), a condition most commonly found in children of elementary school age. The symptoms of ADHD include an inability to concentrate and a tendency to be impulsive and hyperactive. The condition—which is believed to affect between 3 and 5 percent of the children in the United States—is associated with substance abuse, learning disabilities, and delinquency. Observers believe that because those who suffer from ADHD perform poorly in school, they are at much greater risk to develop antisocial and delinquent behavioral patterns. Brain scans can identify ADHD in "problem" children and lead to treatment that lessens the risk of future criminality.

IN THE FUTURE: The use of brain scanning to show a proclivity toward criminal behavior or as a defense strategy in criminal trials is dismissed as "junk science" by many criminologists. A number of studies, though, have established that certain brain patterns are associated with criminal behavior. As scientific methods improve, brain mapping may allow physicians to "predict" crime—with all the controversial implications that ability would bring.

WANTED BY THE FBI

Andrew Phillip Cunanan
Unlawful Flight to Avoid Prosecution - Murder

Race: White; Sex: Male; Height: 5'9" - 5'11"; Weight: 160-185 lbs
Date of Birth: 8/31/69; Hair: Brown (short); Eyes: Brown; Wears glasses and/or contact lenses
CAUTION: CONSIDER ARMED AND DANGEROUS
Please contact the nearest FBI office if you have any information
on Andrew Phillip Cunanan.

For several weeks in 1997, the nation was engrossed by the search for Andrew Cunanan, who was wanted by law enforcement agencies for five murders, including the shooting of Italian fashion designer Gianni Versace. The media storm culminated when Cunanan's body was found in a Miami Beach, Florida, houseboat after he committed suicide. Some felt, however, that Cunanan's death left unanswered questions. "I would like to know what he got out of killing all those people," said one observer. How does media coverage that portrays violent criminals as "inhuman" psychopaths lessen our understanding of why people commit violent crimes?

3 The *superego,* which is directly related to the conscience and determines which actions are right and wrong, in the context of a person's environment.

Psychoanalytic theorists contend that people who exhibit criminal behavior have an overdeveloped ego or an underdeveloped superego. A strong ego leads to such feelings of guilt that a person commits a crime in order to be punished; alternatively, a weak superego means that a person cannot control his or her violent urges.

Because these theories are based on often untestable hypotheses rather than empirical data, psychological explanations for criminal behavior are quite controversial. During the middle of the twentieth century, the concept of the criminal as *psychopath* (used interchangeably with the term *sociopath*) gained a great deal of credence. The psychopath was seen as a person who had somehow lost her or his "humanity" and was unable to experience human emotions such as love or regret, to control criminal impulses, or to understand the consequences of her or his decisions.[72] Over the past few decades, the concept of psychopathy has lost standing, as criminologists have criticized the notion that emotions can be "measured."

The Role of Intelligence. Recently, psychological studies of crime have turned toward intelligence as a determinant of crime. A study of six hundred fourth-graders by researchers from the University of Wisconsin, for example, found that low IQs were prevalent in those students who later became delinquents.[73] Again, many criminologists view such data with mistrust, as low intelligence has in no way been proved to cause deviant behavior. Even the Wisconsin researchers concluded that the delinquency of their subjects was more likely the result of a lack of respect for school as an authoritative institution, which was influenced, though not caused, by low levels of intelligence.

Trait Theory and Public Policy. Whereas choice theory justifies punishing wrongdoers, biological and psychological views of criminality suggest that antisocial behavior should be identified and treated before it manifests itself in first-time or further criminal activity. Though the focus on treatment has diminished somewhat in the past three decades, it is still evident in the criminal justice system. Some offenders are treated with mood-altering drugs to control their antisocial behavior, and nearly all corrections facilities offer group or individual therapy to help prisoners address possible root causes of their criminal predilections.

Sociological Theories of Crime

The problem with trait theory, many criminologists contend, is that it falters when confronted with certain crime patterns. Why is the crime rate in Detroit, Michigan, twenty-five times that of Sioux Falls, South Dakota? Do high levels of air pollution cause an increase in abnormal brain activity, or lower intelligence, or higher levels of testosterone? As no evidence has been found that would suggest that biological factors can be so easily influenced, several generations of criminologists have instead focused upon social and physical environmental factors in their study of criminal behavior.

The Chicago School. The importance of sociology in the study of criminal behavior was established by a group of scholars who were associated with the Sociology Department at the University of Chicago in the early 1900s. These sociologists, known collectively as the Chicago School, gathered empirical evidence from the slums of the city that showed a correlation between conditions of poverty, such as inadequate housing and poor sanitation, and high rates of

INFOTRAC ®
COLLEGE EDITION

Abbott, Andrew. Of time and space: the contemporary relevance of the Chicago School.

crime. Chicago School members Ernest Burgess (1886–1966) and Robert Ezra Park (1864–1944) argued that neighborhood conditions, be they of wealth or poverty, had a much greater determinant effect on criminal behavior than ethnicity, race, or religion.[74] The methods and theories of the Chicago School, which stressed that humans are social creatures whose behavior reflects their environment, have had a profound effect on criminology over the past century.

The study of crime as correlated to social structure revolves around three specific theories: (1) social disorganization theory, (2) strain theory, and (3) cultural deviance theory.

Social Disorganization Theory. Park and Burgess introduced an *ecological* analysis of crime to criminology. Just as ecology studies the relationships between animals and their environment, the two Chicago School members studied the relationship between inner-city residents and their environment. In addition, Clifford Shaw and Henry McKay, contemporaries of the Chicago School and researchers in juvenile crime, popularized the idea of ecology in criminology through **social disorganization theory.** This theory states that crime is largely a product of unfavorable conditions in certain communities.[75]

Studying juvenile delinquency in Chicago, Shaw and McKay discovered certain "zones" that exhibited high rates of crime. These zones were characterized by "disorganization," or a breakdown of the traditional institutions of social control such as family, school systems, and local businesses. By contrast, in the city's "organized" communities, residents had developed certain agreements about fundamental values and norms. Shaw and McKay found that residents in high-crime neighborhoods had to a large degree abandoned these fundamental values and norms. Also, a lack of social controls had led to increased levels of antisocial, or criminal, behavior.[76] According to social disorganization theory, ecological factors that lead to crime in these neighborhoods are perpetuated by continued high levels of high school dropouts, unemployment, deteriorating infrastructures, and single-parent families. (See Figure 2.12 to better understand social disorganization theory.)

Recent studies in this field have proposed that increased communication in disorganized areas can reduce crime. Studying victimization data from medium-sized cities in Florida, New York, and Missouri, Paul E. Bellair of Ohio State University found that even infrequent interaction (chatting for five minutes on the street, for example) between neighbors can lower certain types of crime. Bellair believes that such interactions strengthen community controls because neighbors who know each other will be more likely to report a burglary in progress, to give just one example.[77]

SOCIAL DISORGANIZATION THEORY
The theory that deviant behavior is more likely in communities where social institutions such as the family, schools, and criminal justice system fail to exert control over the population.

Figure 2.12 The Stages of Social Disorganization Theory

Social disorganization theory holds that crime is related to the environmental pressures that exist in certain communities or neighborhoods. These areas are marked by the desire of many of their inhabitants to "get out" at the first possible opportunity. Consequently, residents tend to ignore the important institutions in the community, such as business and education, causing further erosion and an increase in the conditions that lead to crime.

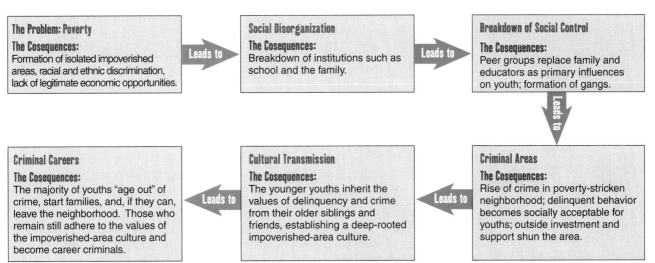

The Problem: Poverty
The Cosequences:
Formation of isolated impoverished areas, racial and ethnic discrimination, lack of legitimate economic opportunities.

Leads to

Social Disorganization
The Cosequences:
Breakdown of institutions such as school and the family.

Leads to

Breakdown of Social Control
The Cosequences:
Peer groups replace family and educators as primary influences on youth; formation of gangs.

Leads to

Criminal Areas
The Cosequences:
Rise of crime in poverty-stricken neighborhood; delinquent behavior becomes socially acceptable for youths; outside investment and support shun the area.

Leads to

Cultural Transmission
The Cosequences:
The younger youths inherit the values of delinquency and crime from their older siblings and friends, establishing a deep-rooted impoverished-area culture.

Leads to

Criminal Careers
The Cosequences:
The majority of youths "age out" of crime, start families, and, if they can, leave the neighborhood. Those who remain still adhere to the values of the impoverished-area culture and become career criminals.

SOURCE: ADAPTED FROM LARRY J. SIEGEL, CRIMINOLOGY, 6TH ED. (BELMONT, CA: WEST/WADSWORTH PUBLISHING CO., 1998), 169.

STRAIN THEORY
The assumption that crime is the result of frustration felt by individuals who cannot reach their financial and personal goals through legitimate means.

ANOMIE
A condition in which the individual suffers from the breakdown or absence of social norms. According to this theory, this condition occurs when a person is disconnected from these norms or rejects them as inconsistent with his or her personal goals.

CULTURAL DEVIANCE THEORY
A branch of social structure theory based on the assumption that members of certain subcultures reject the values of the dominant culture through deviant behavior patterns.

SUBCULTURE
A group exhibiting certain values and behavior patterns that distinguish it from the dominant culture.

INFOTRAC®
COLLEGE EDITION

Warner, Barbara and Pamela Wilcox Roundtree. Local social ties in a community and crime model: questioning the systematic nature of informal social control.

Strain Theory. Another self-perpetuating aspect of disorganized neighborhoods is that once residents gain the financial means to leave a high-crime community, they usually do so. This desire to escape the inner city is related to the second branch of social structure theory: **strain theory.** Most Americans have similar life-goals, which include gaining a certain measure of wealth and financial freedom. The means of attaining these goals, however, are not universally available. Many citizens do not have access to the education or training necessary for financial success. This often results in frustration and anger, or *strain.*

Strain theory has its roots in the works of French sociologist Emile Durkheim (1858–1917) and his concept of **anomie** (derived from the Greek word for "without norms"). Durkheim believed that *anomie* resulted when social change threw behavioral norms into a flux, leading to a weakening of social controls and an increase in deviant behavior.[78] Another sociologist, American Robert K. Merton, expanded on Durkheim's ideas in his own theory of strain. Merton believed that *anomie* was caused by a social structure in which all citizens have similar goals without equal means to achieve them.[79] One way to alleviate this strain is to gain wealth by the means that are available to the residents of disorganized communities: drug trafficking, burglary, and other criminal activities.

Cultural Deviance Theory. Combining, to a certain extent, social disorganization and strain theories, **cultural deviance theory** asserts that people adapt to the values of the subculture to which they belong. A **subculture** (a subdivision that exists within the dominant culture) has its own standards of behavior, or norms. By definition, a disorganized neighborhood is isolated from society at large, and the strain of this isolation encourages the formation of subcultures within the slum. According to cultural deviance theory, members of low-income subcultures are more likely to conform to value systems that celebrate behavior, such as violence, that directly confronts the value system of society at large and therefore draws criminal sanctions.

Sociologist Walter Miller rejected the idea that these deviant value systems were formed in protest against prevailing social norms, an idea that had gained much currency among criminologists. Instead, Miller saw the formation of a number of "homegrown" concerns that were "natural" given the context and situation of lower-class life. He identified six of these *focal concerns* that dominate the day-to-day existence of the disorganized community:

1. *Trouble.* Trouble—in the form of drinking, fighting, sexual adventures, and the like—is a mainstay of lower-class community life. The ability to "get out of trouble" lends a certain amount of prestige to a person, whereas the inability to avoid punishment for trouble can be seen as a weakness.

2. *Toughness.* Physical strength is highly valued in lower-class communities, and such toughness is more highly prized when used to show prowess in criminal acts.

3. *Smartness.* The ability to "con," or outsmart other members of the community, and particularly representatives of the dominant culture such as the police, is also appreciated. In lower-class communities; "street smarts" are often more highly prized than a formal education.

4. *Fate.* Because they do not have the means to better their financial situations, many residents of lower-class neighborhoods feel that their lives are subject to forces beyond their control.

5. *Excitement.* "Living on the edge" can be a tonic for the boredom that characterizes lower-class neighborhoods with their high rates of unemployment.

6. *Autonomy.* A common goal of individuals in lower-class neighborhoods is not to be perceived as being under the control of authority figures, such as parents, teachers, or law enforcement officers.[80]

Miller's theory has been criticized on the ground that it does not account for the many law-abiding citizens who live in lower-class neighborhoods. It has also suffered from cultural stereotyping of minority groups along the lines noted earlier when we discussed the race-crime relationship. Many criminologists have felt the need to conduct studies reinforcing the class—as opposed to the racial—aspects of social structure theories of crime.[81]

Social Structure Theory and Public Policy. If criminal behavior can be explained by the conditions in which certain groups of people live, then it stands to reason that changing those conditions can prevent crime. Indeed, government programs to decrease unemployment, reduce poverty, and improve educational facilities in low-income neighborhoods have been partly justified as part of large-scale attempts at crime prevention.

Family, Friends, and the Media: Social Processes of Crime

Some criminologists find class theories of crime overly narrow. As numerous self-report surveys have shown, the criminal instinct is pervasive in middle- and upper-class communities, even if it is expressed differently. Anybody, these criminologists argue, has the potential to act out criminal behavior, regardless of class, race, or gender.

Psychologist Philip Zimbardo conducted a well-known, if rather unscientific, experiment to make this point. Zimbardo placed an abandoned automobile with its hood up on the campus of Stanford University. The car remained in place, untouched, for a week. Then, the psychologist smashed the car's window with a sledgehammer. Within minutes, passerbys had joined in the destruction of the automobile, eventually stripping its valuable parts.[82] **Social process theories** function on the same basis as Zimbardo's "interdependence of decisions experiment": the potential for criminal behavior exists in everyone and will be realized depending on an individual's interaction with various institutions and processes of society. There are three main branches of social process theory: (1) learning theory, (2) control theory, and (3) labeling theory.

Learning Theory. Popularized by Edwin Sutherland in the 1940s, **learning theory** contends that criminal activity is a learned behavior. In other words, a criminal is taught both the practical methods of crime (such as how to pick a lock) and the psychological aspects of crime (how to deal with the guilt of wrongdoing). Sutherland's **theory of differential association** held that individuals are exposed to values from family and peers such as school friends or co-workers. If the dominant values one is exposed to favor criminal behavior, then that person is more likely to mimic such behavior.[83] Sutherland concentrated particularly on familial relations, believing that a child was more likely to commit crimes if she or he saw an older sibling or a parent doing so. Recently, learning theory has been expanded to include the growing influence of the media. Concern that high levels of televised violence are promoting aggressive behavior among American children has spurred a number of legislative actions to curb such violence.[84]

Control Theory. Criminologist Travis Hirschi focuses on the reasons why individuals *do not* engage in criminal acts, rather than why they do. According to Hirschi, social bonds promote conformity to social norms. The stronger these social bonds—which include attachment to, commitment to, involvement with, and belief in societal values—the less likely that any individual

An aerial view of the Robert Taylor Homes of Chicago, the nation's largest public housing project. Inaugurated in 1962, the Homes were envisioned as providing low-income families with affordable housing. Today, the Chicago Housing Authority would like to raze the entire community. With unemployment rates as high as 90 percent, the Homes have become a magnet for drugs and crime. The federal government pledged $716 million in grants to demolish buildings and improve social conditions in public housing areas like Robert Taylor Homes. According to social structure theories, how would these tax dollars be best spent to reduce crime?

SOCIAL PROCESS THEORIES
A school of criminology that considers criminal behavior to be the predictable result of a person's interaction with his or her environment. According to these theories, everybody has the potential for wrongdoing. Those who act upon this potential are conditioned to do so by family or peer groups, or institutions such as the media.

LEARNING THEORY
The hypothesis that delinquents and criminals must be taught both the practical and emotional skills necessary to partake in illegal activity.

THEORY OF DIFFERENTIAL ASSOCIATION
Sutherland's theory that criminality is the result of the values an individual is exposed to by family, friends, and other members of the community. When these values favor deviant behavior over conventional norms, criminal activity is more likely.

CONTROL THEORY
A series of theories that assume that all individuals have the potential for criminal behavior, but are restrained by the damage that such actions would do to their relationships with family, friends, and members of the community. Criminality occurs when these bonds are broken or nonexistent.

LABELING THEORY
The hypothesis that society creates crime and criminals by labeling certain behavior and certain people as deviant. The stigma that results from this social process excludes a person from the community, thereby increasing the chances that she or he will adopt the label as her or his identity and engage in a pattern of criminal behavior.

SOCIAL CONFLICT THEORIES
A school of criminology that views criminal behavior as the result of class conflict. Certain behavior is labeled illegal not because it is inherently criminal, but because the ruling class has an economic or social interest in restricting such behavior in order to protect the *status quo*.

"The common argument that crime is caused by poverty is a kind of slander on the poor."

—H.L. Mencken, *American journalist* (1956)

will commit a crime.[85] **Control theory** holds that although we all have the potential to commit crimes, most of us are dissuaded from doing so because we care about the opinions of our family and peers. James Q. Wilson and George Kelling describe control theory in terms of the "broken windows" effect. Neighborhoods in poor condition are filled with cues of lack of social control (for example, broken windows) that invite further vandalism and other deviant behavior.[86] If these cues are removed, according to Wilson and Kelling, so is the implied acceptance of crime within a community.

Labeling Theory. A third social process theory, **labeling theory,** focuses on perceptions of criminal behavior rather than the behavior itself. Labeling theorists study how being labeled a criminal—a "whore," or a "junkie," or a "thief"—affects that person's future behavior. Sociologist Howard Becker contends that deviance is

> a consequence of the application by others of rules and sanctions to an offender. The deviant is one to whom that label has successfully been applied; deviant behavior is behavior that people so label.[87]

Such labeling, some criminologists believe, becomes a self-fulfilling prophecy. Someone labeled a "junkie" will begin to consider himself or herself a deviant and continue the criminal behavior for which he or she has been labeled. Following this line of reasoning, the criminal justice system is engaged in artificially creating a class of criminals by labeling victimless crimes such as drug use, prostitution, and gambling as "criminal."

Social Process Theory and Public Policy. Because adult criminals are seen as too "hardened" to un-learn their criminal behavior, crime-prevention policies associated with social process theory focus on juvenile offenders. Many youths, for example, are diverted from the formal juvenile justice process to keep them from being labeled "delinquent." Furthermore, many schools have implemented programs that attempt to steer children away from crime by encouraging them to "just say no" to drugs and stay in school. As we shall see in Chapter 5, implementation of Wilson and Kelling's "broken windows" principles has been credited with lowering the violent crime rate in New York and a number of other major cities.

Social Conflict Theories

The most recent movement in criminology focuses not on psychology, biology, or sociology, but on *power*. Those who identify power—seen as the ability of one person or group of persons to control the economic and social positions of other people or groups—as the key component in explaining crime entered the mainstream of American criminology during the 1960s. These theorists saw social ills such as poverty, racism, sexism, and destruction of the environment as the "true crimes," perpetrated by the powerful, or ruling, classes. Burglary, robbery, and even violent crimes were considered reactions by the powerless against laws that were meant to repress, not protect, them. Supporters of these ideas aligned themselves with Marxist, radical, conflict, and feminist schools of criminology. Collectively, they have constructed the **social conflict theories** of crime causation.

Marxism versus Capitalism. The genesis of social conflict theory can be found in the political philosophy of Karl Marx (1818–1883). Though he did not concentrate on crime in his writings, Marx's belief that a capitalist economic system necessarily produces income inequality and leads to exploitation of the working classes has been adopted by social conflict theorists.[88] These criminologists generally hold that crime is the natural result of class inequality as identified by Marx.

For this reason, social conflict theory is often associated with a critique of our capitalist economic system. Capitalism is seen as leading to high levels of violence and crime because of the disparity of income it encourages. The poor commit property crimes for reasons of need and because, as members of a capitalist society, they desire the same financial rewards as everybody else. They commit violent crimes because of the frustration and rage they feel when these rewards seem unattainable. Laws, instead of reflecting the values of society as a whole, reflect only the values of the segment of society that has achieved power and is willing to use the criminal justice system as a tool to keep that power.[89] Thus, the harsh penalties for "lower-class" crimes such as burglary can be seen as a means of protecting the privileges of the "haves" from the aspirations of the "have-nots."

It is important to note that, according to social conflict theory, power is not synonymous with wealth. Women and members of minority groups can be wealthy and yet still be dissociated from the benefits of power in our society. We will examine the ramifications of this in Chapter 18 during our discussion of racism and sexism in the criminal justice system.

Social Conflict Theory and Public Policy. Given its radical nature, social conflict theory has had a limited impact on public policy. Even in the aftermath of situations where class conflict has had serious and obvious repercussions, such as the Los Angeles riots of 1991, few observers feel that enough has been accomplished to improve the conditions that led to the violence. As we will see in Chapter 18, many believe that the best hope for a shift in the power structure is the employment of more women and minorities in the criminal justice system itself. (See the *Concept Summary* below.)

If you want to keep updated on the hot issues in criminology, go to the homepage of the American Society of Criminology's Critical Criminology Division at sun.soci.niu.edu/~critcrim/

CONCEPT SUMMARY
The Causes of Crime

Choice Theories
Crime is the result of rational choices made by those who want to engage in criminal activity for the rewards it offers. The rewards may be financial or they may be psychological—criminals enjoy the "rush" that comes with committing a crime. According to choice theorists, the proper response to crime is harsh penalties, which force potential criminals to weigh the benefits of wrongdoing against the costs of punishment if they are apprehended.

Biological and Psychological Trait Theories
Criminal behavior is explained by biological and psychological attributes of the individual. Those who support biological theories of crime believe that the secret to crime is locked in the human body: in genes, brain disorders, reaction to improper diet or allergies, etc. Psychological attempts to explain crime are based on the study of the personality and intelligence and the development of a person's behavioral patterns during infancy.

Sociological Theories
Crime is not something a person is "born to do." Instead, it is the result of the social conditions under which a person finds him- or herself. Those who are socially disadvantaged—because of poverty or other factors such as racial discrimination—are more likely to commit crimes because other avenues to "success" have been closed off. High-crime areas will develop their own cultures that are in constant conflict with the dominant culture and create a cycle of crime that claims the youth who grow up in the area and go on to be career criminals.

Social Process Theories
The major influence on any individual is not society in general, but the interactions that dominate everyday life. Therefore, individuals are drawn to crime not by general factors such as "society" or "community," but by family, friends, and peer groups. Crime is "learned behavior"; the "teacher" is usually a family member or friend. Everybody has the potential to become a criminal. Those who form positive social relationships instead of destructive ones have a better chance of avoiding criminal activity. Furthermore, if a person is labeled "juvenile" or "criminal" by the authority figures or organizations in his or her life, there is a better chance he or she will create a personality and actions to fit that label.

Social Conflict Theories
Criminal laws are a form of social control. Through these laws, the dominant members of society control the minority members, using institutions such as the police, courts, and prisons as tools of oppression. Crime is caused by the conflict between the "haves" and "have-nots" of society. The poor commit crimes because of the anger and frustration they feel at being denied the benefits of society.

Criminal Justice in Action

The Growing Role of the Victim

Due to what one scholar calls "the prestige of evil," criminals have been and continue to be the focus of the criminal justice system.[90] The victims of crime and their families, in contrast, have not received commensurate attention, according to many observers, either in the courtrooms or in the public eye. Those who have gone through the experience of having a family member murdered speak to the difficulty of finding a sense of "closure"; the criminal justice process drags the grieving process out over a long period of time—sometimes many years. Earlier, we noted that victim surveys have given the targets of crime a greater voice in the process of measuring crime. In the following discussion, we examine the efforts of victims and victim's rights groups to become more involved in the criminal justice system.

"SECOND CLASS CITIZENS"

While David Middleton was being tried for the murders of Katherine Powell and another woman, Powell's mother and brother sat in the hallway of the courthouse in Reno, Nevada, excluded from the trial. The jury found that Middleton had locked Powell in a refrigerator, then murdered her and dumped her bound and gagged body in a trash bin.[91] During the trial, members of Middleton's family were allowed to testify as character witnesses, even though none of them had seen him for nearly a decade. When Jeff Powell, the victim's brother, told the court during sentencing that "I don't feel that any more respect, dignity, or mercy should be given to David Middleton than he gave to Kathy," the defense called for a

mistrial. After Middleton was sentenced to death, Jeff Powell commented on the experience: "Through the [trial], we the family of Kathy Powell have come to realize that our legal system has created a group of second class citizens—the victims of crime."[92]

Advocates for victim's rights contend that the system is unfairly weighted in favor of the defendant, pointing out that the Constitution extends rights to the accused fifteen times without mentioning the rights of crime's victims. After years of lobbying, these advocates are finally seeing widespread political and public support for their ultimate goal—the passage of a victim's rights amendment to the U.S. Constitution.

THE STATES RESPOND

The modern victim's rights movement began with the opening of rape-crisis centers by feminist groups in the early 1970s. Since then, hundreds of grass-roots organizations have been formed to deal with the needs of victims. Some, such as the Parents of Murdered Children,

Following the kidnapping and murder of his twelve-year-old daughter, Marc Klass, left, became an outspoken advocate for crime prevention and victim's rights.

64

Figure **2.13** The New Hampshire Victim's Bill of Rights

1. The right to be treated with fairness and respect for their dignity and privacy throughout the criminal justice process.
2. The right to be informed about the criminal justice process and how it progresses.
3. The right to be free from intimidation and to be reasonably protected from the accused throughout the criminal justice process.
4. The right to be notified of all court proceedings.
5. The right to attend trial and all other court proceedings the accused has the right to attend.
6. The right to confer with the prosecution and to be consulted about the disposition of the case, including plea bargaining.
7. The right to have inconveniences associated with participation in the criminal justice process minimized.
8. The right to be notified if presence in court is not required.
9. The right to be informed about available resources, financial assistance, and social services.
10. The right to restitution for their losses.
11. The right to be provided a secure, but not necessarily separate, waiting area during court proceedings.
12. The right to be advised of case progress and final disposition.
13. The right of confidentiality of the victim's address, place of employment, and other personal information.
14. The right to have input in the probation presentence report impact statement.
15. The right to appear and make a written or oral victim impact statement at the sentencing of the defendant.
16. The right to be notified of an appeal, an explanation of the appeal process, the time, place and result of the appeal, and the right to attend the appeal hearing.
17. The right to be notified and to attend sentence review hearings and sentence reduction hearings.
18. The right to be notified of any change of status such as prison release, permanent interstate transfer, or escape, and the date of the parole board hearing, when requested by the victim through the victim advocate.
19. The right to address or submit a written statement for consideration by the parole board on the defendant's release and to be notified of the decision of the board, when requested by the victim through the victim advocate.

SOURCE: NEW HAMPSHIRE VICTIM'S ASSISTANCE COMMISSION.

According to New Hampshire law, victims of felonies committed by an adult offender are entitled to these rights.

are primarily concerned with the emotional state of victims. Others, such as Mothers Against Drunk Driving and the National Organization of Victim Assistance, concentrate on lobbying legislators for victim's rights laws.

These advocates have had widespread influence on a state level. Between 1975 and 1987, states passed nearly 1,500 statutes pertaining to victim's rights.[93] Many states now allow victims a say in the plea bargaining and sentencing stages of trials. In a majority of states, victims can present victim impact statements to the court before sentencing or to a parole board when a prisoner is up for parole. These statements let vic-

tims describe any physical, emotional, or psychological effects caused by the crime. Currently, thirty state constitutions include victim's rights amendments, and several states have created their own Victim's Bill of Rights. (See Figure 2.13 for New Hampshire's Victim's Bill of Rights.)

Despite this flood of legislation, victim's rights advocates say that state laws are not strong enough to assure justice for victims. For example, Nevada, where David Middleton was tried for murdering Katherine Powell, has a number of state laws that give victim's rights that Powell's family was denied. The reason is that most state laws give the presiding judge control over the role of the victim, and many judges are opposed to victim participation in the criminal trial.[94]

THE McVEIGH TRIAL: A TURNING POINT

Congress has passed several federal laws in the interests of victims. For example, in 1990, the Victim's Rights and Restitution Act gave victims the right to be present at the trial and to be kept up-to-date on issues of sentencing and release.[95] But victim's rights proponents believe that only a constitutional amendment will lead to universal protection of victim's rights.

The turning point in the drive for a constitutional amendment came during the trial of Timothy McVeigh for planting the truck bomb that killed 168 people in the Alfred P. Murrah Federal Building in Oklahoma City in 1995. This act of terrorism created one of the largest united groups of victims in American history. In a series of moves that infuriated victim's rights advocates, presiding U.S. District Judge Richard Matsch barred victims from sitting in the courtroom during trial. He also disallowed the use of victim impact statements and moved the trial to Denver from Oklahoma City.[96]

Matsch made these decisions in order, in his mind, to ensure that McVeigh's right to a fair trial was not impeded by the emotionalism of victims. Congress, however, swayed by public opinion, passed a bill that overturned Matsch's ruling.[97] Within a year, President Bill Clinton and Attorney General Janet Reno were publicly supporting Senate Joint Resolution 6, the proposed Twenty-eighth Amendment that would give victims a number of rights, including the following:

1. The right to be notified of and to attend all public proceedings relating to the crime.

Yale professor David Gelernter lost the use of his right hand to one of Theodore Kaczynski's mail bombs. Gelernter expressed the frustration and helplessness many victims feel after Kaczynski was sentenced to life in prison, saying that his assailant was a "proud killer" who deserved the death penalty.

2. The right to be notified of an offender's release, parole, or escape.

3. The right to be heard during sentencing and parole hearings, through the submission of impact statements if desired.

4. The right to an order of restitution from the convicted offender (victim restitution will be discussed further in Chapter 11).

5. A conclusion to the criminal proceedings regarding the crime in question without unreasonable delay.

6. The right to have the victim's personal safety considered in determining the offender's parole or release.

7. The right to be notified of these rights.[98]

CONCERN FOR THE RiGHTS OF THE ACCUSED

Opponents of the constitutional amendment believe that it would place "enormous new burdens" on law enforcement agencies.[99] Many judges, who agreed with Matsch's decision in the McVeigh case, also feel that the increased presence of victims in the criminal trial would wrongly influence jurors and impinge upon the defendant's right to be considered innocent until proven guilty.[100] Victim's rights advocates counter that one of the main reasons many Americans have little faith in the criminal justice system stems from the lack of a victim's presence during the proceedings. A constitutional amendment, they argue, would simply give those victimized by crime equal rights to those who have been charged with committing a crime.[101]

Key Terms

Chapter Summary

1. **Identify the publication in which the FBI reports crime data and list the three ways it does so.** Every year the FBI releases the Uniform Crime Report (UCR) in which it presents different crimes as (a) a rate per 100,000 people; (b) a percentage change from the previous year; and (c) an absolute, or aggregate, number.

2. **Distinguish between Part I and Part II offenses as defined in the UCR.** Part I offenses are always felonies and include the most violent crimes. They are called index crimes and yield the index crime rate. Part II offenses can be either misdemeanors or felonies and constitute the majority of crimes committed.

3. **Explain how the National Incident-Based Reporting System differs from the UCR.** The NIBRS, yet to be widely adopted, involves collection of data on each single crime occurrence with twenty-two offense categories made up of forty-six different crimes; the data are recorded on computer systems financed in part by the federal government.

4. **Distinguish between the National Crime Victimization Survey and self-report surveys.** The NCVS involves an annual survey of about 50,000 households conducted by the Bureau of the Census along with the Bureau of Justice Statistics. The survey queries citizens on crimes that have been committed against them. As such, the NCVS includes crimes not necessarily reported to police . Self-report surveys, in contrast, involve asking individuals about criminal activity to which they may have been a party.

5. **Explain why classical criminology is based on choice theory.** Choice theory holds that those who commit crimes choose to do so. Classical criminology was based on a model of a person rationally making a choice before committing a crime—weighing the benefits against the costs.

6. **Contrast positivism with classical criminology.** Whereas classical theorists believe criminals make rational choices, those of the positivist school believe that criminal behavior is determined by psychological, biological, and social forces that the individual cannot control.

7. **List and describe the three theories of social structure that help explain crime.** Social disorganization theory states that crime is largely a product of unfavorable conditions in certain communities, or zones of disorganization. The strain theory argues that most people seek increased wealth and financial security, and the strain of not being able to achieve these goals legally leads to criminal behavior. Finally, cultural deviance theory asserts that people adapt to the values of the subculture—which has its own standards of behavior—to which they belong.

8. **List the six focal concerns that dominate disorganized community existence.** (a) Trouble, (b) toughness, (c) smartness, (d) fate, (e) excitement, and (f) autonomy.

9. **List and briefly explain the three branches of social process theory.** (a) Learning theory, which contends that people learn to be criminals from their family and peers. (b) Control theory, which holds that most of us are dissuaded from a life of crime because we place importance on the opinions of family and peers. (c) Labeling theory, which holds that a person labeled a "junkie" or a "thief" will respond by remaining whatever she or he is labeled.

10. **Indicate the ways in which victims have been given more rights.** Rape-crisis centers were initiated by feminist groups in the 1970s. Parents of Murdered Children, Mothers Against Drunk Driving, and the National Organization of Victim Assistance all help victims and lobby legislators in favor of victim's rights laws. Currently, about thirty states have victim's rights amendments in their constitutions. At the federal level, in 1990 the Victim's Rights and Restitution Act gave victims the right to be present at the trial and to be informed of sentencing and release.

Questions for Critical Analysis

1. What is the distinction between the crime rate and crime in America?

2. Although Part II offenses constitute the bulk of crimes, Part I offenses get the most publicity. Is this necessarily irrational? Why or why not?

3. Why might you consider the UCR a biased source of crime statistics?

4. What is one possible reason for higher crime rates in lower-income communities?

5. If you believe that fear of punishment can have a deterrent effect on criminal activity, to what view of human behavior are you subscribing?

6. Why might there be less criminal activity in a community where there is frequent communication among the residents?

7. If you believe that criminals learn how to be criminals, to what theory are you subscribing?

8. Why have social conflict theories had a limited impact on public policy in the United States?

9. In what ways do victims now have more rights than they did in the past?

Selected Print and Electronic Resources

SUGGESTED READINGS

Biderman, Alfred D., and James P. Lynch, *Understanding Crime Statistics: Why the UCR Diverges from the NCS*, New York: Springer-Verlag, 1991. As we pointed out in this chapter, there are conflicts between the statistics gleaned from the Uniform Crime Reports and from the National Crime Survey. These two researchers examine why. They look at the differences in procedures, definitions, counting rules, and population changes.

Flaherty, Sarah, and Austin Sarat, ed., *Victims and Victim's Rights*, New York: Chelsea House Publishers, 1998. This book of articles examines, among other things, the psychological consequences of victimization. Issues concerning emotional healing are also examined. Finally, the tension between protecting the rights of criminal defendants and granting the rights of victims is examined.

Jacoby, Joseph E., ed., *Classics of Criminology*, 2d ed., Prospect Heights, IL.: Waveland Press, 1993. This book consists of fifty-seven classic articles in criminology. It includes a well-chosen group of criminological views and theoretical issues over the past two centuries.

Wilson, Debra, *The Complete Book of Victim's Rights*, Highlands Ranch, CO.: ProSe Associates, 1996. The author examines victim assistance and compensation programs. She delves into the issues surrounding privacy rights as well as the right to be heard during the criminal justice process. Her work constitutes a thorough examination of who is actually helped by the current laws on victim's rights.

MEDIA RESOURCES

The Silence of the Lambs **(1991)** A young FBI agent, Clarice Starling (played by Jodie Foster), is assigned to help find a missing woman and save her from a psychotic serial killer who skins his victims. The FBI believes that Clarice can obtain more insight into the mind of the killer by talking to another psychopathic serial killer, Hannibal Lecter (played by Anthony Hopkins). During the movie, Dr. Lecter (who, before becoming a mass murderer, was a brilliant psychiatrist) toys with most of his inquisitors. He is finally persuaded by this female rookie FBI agent to reveal a psychological profile of the serial killer for whom the FBI is searching. As you view this movie, try to abstract from the horror and answer the following questions.

Critically analyze this film:

1. Which of the various theories or "schools" of criminology discussed in this chapter apply to the attitude the FBI takes toward finding the murderer in this film.

2. Is it reasonable for a law enforcement agent to obtain psychological information on one criminal from another criminal?

3. Why was it important that Hannibal "the Cannibal" had previously been a brilliant psychiatrist?

4. Is it reasonable that Hannibal could deduce so much about Clarice's character, life, and identity with just a cursory glance?

5. Why would Lecter develop such an intricate psychological game for FBI agent Clarice?

Logging On

You can find out a lot about victim's rights by going to the home page of the National Center for Victims of Crime at:

www.ncvc.org/

Once you are there, you have a choice of reading about information on Law and Public Policies, Civil Justice for Victims, and Safety Strategies.

Your basic source for crime statistics is the U.S. Department of Justice, Bureau of Justice Statistics. Go to its home page for "Crime and Justice Electronic Data Abstracts," at:

www.ojp.usdoj.gov/bjs/dtdata.htm

Once you are there, you can look at files on crime and arrest data and criminal justice data.

You can access the original article by James Q. Wilson and George L. Kelling on the broken windows theory by going to:

www.theatlantic.com/atlantic/election/connection/crime/windows.htm

You can obtain time-series data for criminal justice information by going to the National Archive of Criminal Justice Data at:

www.icpsr.umich.edu/NACJD/home.html

Using the internet for Criminal Justice Analysis

INFOTRAC®
COLLEGE EDITION

1. Go to your InfoTrac College Edition at **www.infotraccollege.com/wadsworth/**. After you log on, type in the words: NATIONAL CRIME CONTROL POLICIES

   This article offers a social theory of the causes of crime. Read it and answer the following questions:

   a. What is control theory and where did it have its beginnings?

   b. Why does the author make a distinction between crimes and criminals and between events and people?

   c. According to the author, what characteristic of the offender is most relevant to crime control?

   d. Why does the author believe that in criminology an increase in the seriousness of sanctions does not influence the crime rate?

   e. Why does control theory prefer local over central responsibility for crime prevention?

   f. Briefly summarize the eight rules or recommendations for crime control that control theory leads to.

   g. Which is the most important rule in your opinion and why?

2. The best way to learn about government statistics on crime is to work with those statistics. You can do this by going to: **www.albany.edu/sourcebook**

   Here you will find the Bureau of Justice Statistics Sourcebook of Criminal Statistics Online.

   Go to section three, **Nature and distribution known offenses.** Then click on **"Estimated percent distribution of violent victimizations by multiple offenders."**

   a. What percentage of the attempts at crimes of violence were completed?

   b. What percentage of crimes of violence involved robbery?

   c. Of all violent crimes, which age group of multiple offenders was most prevalent? Least prevalent?

   Now go to the section entitled **"College students experiences of violence and harassment."**

   d. What percentage of college respondents said that they suffered either threats or actual physical violence?

   e. What is the relationship between the consumption of alcohol or drugs and the experience of violence or harassment by college students?

   f. Can you think of any way in which the question asked by the interviewers (shown before the table) might elicit inaccurate responses?

3. You can find out more about the Office of Victims of Crime (OVC) by going to its home page at: www.ojp.usdoj.gov/ovc/

Once you are there, take a look through the different Web pages and answer the following questions:

a. Explain when the federal Crime Victim Assistance Fund was instituted and what it does.

b. How does the Crime Victim Assistance Fund get its funds? (HINT: Check out "OVC Partnership with United States Attorneys' Offices.")

c. What year was the Office of Victims of Crime Resource Center established?

d. When is the next national Crime Victims' Week?

e. Explain the Resources for Victims of Campus Crime. If you wanted to find out more about the program, who would be a good source?

Notes

1. William A. Niskanen, "Washington's Misdirected Efforts at Curbing Crime," *USA Today Magazine* (July 1995), 22–5.

2. *Ibid.*

3. Federal Bureau of Investigation, *Crime in the United States, 1997* (Washington, D.C.: U.S. Government Printing Office, 1998). Uniform Crime Report, or UCR, statistics cited in this chapter will reflect the latest data available.

4. *Ibid.*

5. *Ibid.*, 5.

6. Jeffrey Reiman, *The Rich Get Richer and the Poor Get Prison*, 4th ed. (Boston: Allyn & Bacon, 1995), 59–60.

7. *Crime in the United States, 1997*, 19.

8. *Ibid.*, Chart 2.3, page 9.

9. *Ibid.*

10. Marcus Felson, *Crime in Everyday Life* (Thousand Oaks, CA: Pine Forge Press, 1994), 3.

11. Donald J. Black, "Production of Crime Rates," *American Sociological Review* 35 (1970), 733–48.

12. Craig Perkins and Patsy Klaus, *Criminal Victimization, 1994* (Washington, D.C.: Bureau of Justice Statistics, 1996).

13. Victoria W. Schneider and Brian Wiersema, "Limits and Use," in Doris Layton MacKenzie, Phyllis Jo Baunach, and Roy R. Robergs, eds., *Measuring Crime: Large Scale, Long Range Efforts* (Albany, NY: State University of New York Press, 1990), 21–7.

14. Alabama Code Sections 13A-6-60(8), 13A-6-61(a)(1) (1994).

15. W. Chambliss, *Exporting Criminology* (New York: Macmillan, 1988), 30.

16. Samuel Walker, *The Police in America*, 2d ed. (New York: McGraw-Hill, 1992), 295–6.

17. David Seidman and Michael Couzens, "Getting the Crime Rate Down: Political Pressure and Crime Reporting," *Law and Society Review* 8 (1974), 457–93.

18. David Kocieniewski, "Safir Is Said to Seek to Punish a Chief over False Crime Data," *New York Times* (February 28, 1998), B1.

19. *Crime in the United States, 1997*, 3.

20. Domingo Ramirez, Jr., and Betsy Blaney, "FBI Revises Crime Log Categories," *Ft. Worth Star-Telegram* (December 1, 1996), 1.

21. Victor E. Kappeler, Mark Blumberg, and Gary W. Potter, *The Mythology of Crime and Criminal Justice*, 2d ed. (Prospect Heights, IL: Waveland Press, 1993,) 31.

22. Alfred D. Biderman and James P. Lynch, *Understanding Crime Statistics: Why the UCR Diverges from the NCS* (New York: Springer-Verlag, 1991).

23. L. Edward Vells and Joseph Rankin, "Juvenile Victimization: Convergent Validation of Alternative Measurements," *Journal of Research and Crime in Delinquency* 32 (1995), 287–307.

24. National Center for Victims of Crime and Crime Victims, *Rape in America: A Report to the Nation* (Arlington, VA: National Victim Center, 1992).

25. Peter B. Wood, Walter R. Grove, James A. Wilson, and John K. Cochran, "Nonsocial Reinforcement and Criminal Conduct: An Extension of Learning Theory," *Criminology* 35 (May 1997), 335–66.

26. James S. Wallerstein and Clement J. Wyle, "Our Law-Abiding Law Breakers," *Probation* 35 (April 1947), 107–18.

27. Michael Hindelang, "Causes of Delinquency: A Partial Replication and Extension," *Social Problems* 20 (1973), 471–87.

28. Thomas Gray and Eric Walsh, *Maryland Youth at Risk: A Study of Drug Use in Juvenile Detainees* (College Park, MD: Center for Substance Abuse Research, 1993).

29. John Braithwaite, *Inequality, Crime, and Public Policy* (London: Routledge & Kegan Paul, 1979), 21.

30. Kappeler, Blumberg, and Potter, 37.

31. Kenneth Tunnell, "Film at Eleven: Recent Developments in the Commodification of Crime," *Sociological Spectrum* 12 (1992), 293–313.

32. Robert M. O'Brien, "Police Productivity and Crime Rates: 1973–1992," *Criminology* 34 (1996), 183–207.

33. *Crime in the United States, 1997*, Chart 2.4, page 10.

34. *Ibid.*

35. David M. Kennedy, "Pulling Levers: Chronic Offenders, High-Crime Settings, and a Theory of Prevention," *Valparaiso University Law Review* 31 (Spring 1997), 449.

36. See Lawrence W. Sherman, Patrick R. Gartin, and Michael E. Buerger, "Hot Spots of Predatory Crime: Routine Activities and the Criminology of Place," *Criminology* 27 (1989), 27–55; and John Eck and David Weisburd, "Crime Place in Crime Theory," in *Crime and Place*, ed. John Eck and David Weisburd (Monsey, NY: Criminal Justice Press, 1995).

37. Niskanen.

38. Charles Tittle and Robert Meier, "Specifying the SES/Delinquency Relationship," *Criminology* 28 (1990), 270–301.

39. *Crime in the United States, 1997,* Table 43, page 240.

40. Bureau of Justice Statistics, *Criminal Victimization, 1997* (Washington, D.C.: U.S. Department of Justice, 1998), Table 2, page 4.

41. Arthur H. Garrison, "Disproportionate Minority Arrests: A Note on What Has Been Said and How It Fits Together," *New England Journal on Criminal and Civil Confinement* 23 (Winter 1997), 29.

42. Darrell Steffensmeier and Cathy Steifel, "Age, Gender, and Crime across Three Historical Periods," *Social Change* 69 (1991), 869–94.

43. *Crime in the United States, 1997,* Table 38, pages 232–3.

44. John J. DiIulio, Jr., "Fill Churches, Not Jails: Youth Crime and 'Superpredators.'" Statement before the United States Subcommittee on Youth Violence, February 28, 1996. See www.brook.edu/pa/hot/diiulio.htm.

45. James Q. Wilson, "What to Do about Crime," *Commentary* 86 (September 1994), 25–35.

46. Beth Bjerregaard and Alan J. Lizotte, "Gun Ownership and Gang Membership," *Journal of Criminal Law and Criminology* (Fall 1995), 37–58.

47. Joseph F. Sheley and Victoria E. Brewer, Public *Health Reports* (January–February 1995), 18–27.

48. *Crime in the United States, 1997,* Table 2.11, page 20 and Table 19, page 205.

49. John R. Lott, Jr., "Does Allowing Law-Abiding Citizens to Carry Concealed Handguns Save Lives?" *Valparaiso University Law Review* 31 (Spring 1997), 355.

50. John Lott and David Mustard, "Crime, Deterrence, and Right to Carry Concealed Handguns," *Journal of Legal Studies* 26 (1997), 1.

51. The National Center on Addiction and Substance Abuse at Columbia University, *Behind Bars: Substance Abuse and America's Prison Population* (New York: The National Center on Addiction and Substance Abuse at Columbia University, 1998), 6.

52. Marvin Wolfgang, Robert Figlio, and Thorsten Sellin, *Delinquency in a Birth Cohort* (Chicago: University of Chicago Press, 1972).

53. Lawrence W. Sherman, "Attacking Crime: Police and Crime Control," in *Modern Policing,* ed. Michael Tonry and Norval Morris (Chicago: University of Chicago Press, 1992), 159.

54. Tim Cahill, *Buried Dreams: Inside the Mind of a Serial Killer* (New York: Bantam Books, 1986), 349.

55. James Q. Wilson and Richard J. Hernstein, *Crime and Human Nature: The Definitive Study of the Causes of Crime* (New York: Simon & Schuster, 1985), 515.

56. *Ibid.*

57. Jeremy Bentham, *An Introduction to the Principles of Morals and Legislation,* ed. W. Harrison (Oxford: Basil Blackwell, 1948).

58. Wilson and Hernstein, 44.

59. Jack Katz, *Seductions of Crime: Moral and Sensual Attractions of Doing Evil* (New York: Basic Books, 1988).

60. "Ex-Supervisor Held Unable to Tell Right from Wrong," *New York Times* (May 8, 1979), A16.

61. Laura Mansnerus, "The Darker Side Of the 'Baby Blues,'" *New York Times* (October 12, 1988), C1.

62. L. E. Kreuz and R. M. Rose, "Assessment of Aggressive Behavior and Plasma Testosterone in a Young Criminal Population," *Psychosomatic Medicine* 34 (1972), 321–32.

63. H. Persky, K. Smith, and G. Basu, "Relation of Psychological Measures of Aggression and Hostility to Testosterone Production in Men," *Psychosomatic Medicine* 33 (1971), 265, 276.

64. Leda Cosmides and John Tooby, "Cognitive Adaptations for Social Exchange," in *The Adapted Mind: Evolutionary Psychology and the Generation of Culture,* ed. Jerome H. Berkow, Leda Cosmides, and John Tooby, (New York: Oxford University Press, 1992).

65. Lee Ellis and Anthony Walsh, "Gene-Based Evolutionary Theories in Criminology," *Criminology* 35 (May 1997), 229–76.

66. Michael Craft, "The Current Status of XYY and XXY Syndromes: A Review of Treatment Implications," in *Biology, Crime and Ethics: A Study of Biological Explanations for Criminal Behavior,* eds. Frank H. Marsh and Janet Katz (Cincinnati: Anderson Publishing Co., 1985), 113–5.

67. 14 Wash. App. 733-4, 544 P. 2d 758 (1976).

68. Sarnoff A. Mednick and Karl O. Christiansen, eds., *Biosocial Bases in Criminal Behavior* (New York: Gardner Press, 1977).

69. David C. Rowe, "Genetic and Environmental Components of Antisocial Behavior: A Study of 265 Twin Pairs," *Criminology* 24 (1986), 513–32.

70. Alison Pike and Robert Plomin, "Importance of Nonshared Environmental Factors for Childhood and Adolescent Psychopathology," *Journal of the American Academy of Child and Adolescent Psychopathology* 35 (May 1996), 560.

71. D. Williams, "Neural Factors Related to Habitual Aggression," *Brain* 92 (1969), 503.

72. Hervey M. Cleckley, *The Mask of Sanity,* 4th ed. (St. Louis: Mosby, 1964.)

73. "Delinquents as Dummies," *Psychology Today* (January-February 1994), 16.

74. Robert Park, Ernest Burgess, and Roderic McKenzie, *The City* (Chicago: University of Chicago Press, 1929).

75. Clifford R. Shaw, Henry D. McKay, and Leonard S. Cottrell, *Delinquency Areas* (Chicago: University of Chicago Press, 1929).

76. Clifford R. Shaw and Henry D. McKay, *Report on the Causes of Crime,* Vol. 2: *Social Factors in Juvenile Delinquency* (Washington, D.C.: National Commission on Law Observance and Enforcement, 1931).

77. Paul E. Bellair, "Social Interaction and Community Crime: Examining the Importance of Neighbor Networks," *Criminology* 35 (November 1997), 677.

78. Emile Durkheim, *The Rules of Sociological Method,* trans. Sarah A. Solovay and John H. Mueller (New York: Free Press, 1964).

79. Robert K. Merton, *Social Theory and Social Structure* (New York: Free Press, 1957). See chapter on "Social Structure and Anomie."

80. Walter B. Miller, "Lower Class Culture as a Generating Milieu of Gang Delinquency," *Journal of Social Issues* 14 (1958), 5–19.

81. Liqun Cao, Anthony Adams, and Vickie J. Jensen, "A Test of the Black Subculture of Violence Thesis," *Criminology* 35 (May 1997), 367–79.

82. Philip G. Zimbardo, "The Human Choice: Individuation, Reason, and Order versus Deindividuation, Impulse, and Chaos," in *Nebraska Symposium on Motivation,* ed. William J. Arnold and David Levie (Lincoln, NB: University of Nebraska Press, 1969), 287–93.

83. Edwin H. Sutherland, *Criminology,* 4th ed. (Philadelphia: Lippincott, 1947).

84. Edward Donnerstein and Daniel Linz, "The Media," in *Crime,* eds. James Q. Wilson and Joan Petersilia (San Francisco: ICS Press, 1995), 261–4.

85. Travis Hirschi, *Causes of Delinquency* (Berkeley: University of California Press, 1969).

86. James Q. Wilson and George L. Kelling, "Broken Windows," *Atlantic Monthly* (March 1982), 29.

87. Howard S. Becker, *Outsiders: Studies in the Sociology of Deviance* (New York: Free Press, 1963).

88. Lawrence L. Shornack, "Conflict Theory and the Family," *International Social Science Review* 62 (1987), 154–7.

89. Robert Meier, "The New Criminology: Continuity in Criminology Theory," *Journal of Criminal Law and Criminology* 67 (1977), 461–9.

90. Eric Schlosser, "A Grief Like No Other," *Atlantic Monthly* (September 1, 1997), 37.

91. Angela Cortex, "A Trail of Blood, Tears," *Denver Post* (July 23, 1995), A1.

92. Jeff Ashby Powell, "Victims Have Few Rights," *Las Vegas Review-Journal* (October 22, 1997), 17B.

93. Marlene A. Young, "A Constitutional Amendment for Victims of Crime: The Victim's Perspective," *Wayne Law Review* 34 (1987), 51.

94. Susan E. Gegan and Nicholas Ernesto Rodriguez, "Victims' Roles in the Criminal Justice System: A Fallacy of Victim Empowerment," *St. John's Journal of Legal Commentary* (Fall 1992), 225.

95. 2 U.S.C. Section 10606(b)(4).

96. Amanda Vogt, "Right for the Wronged," *Chicago Tribune* (April 29, 1997), 3.

97. Robert Schmidt, "Law Passed to Let Witnesses Hear Trial," *Legal Times* (March 24, 1997), 11.

98. Kelly McMurry, "Victim's Rights Movement Rises to Power," *Trial* (July 1, 1997), 12.

99. *Ibid.*

100. Dan Morales, "Ruling Dismisses Concern for Victim's Rights," *San Antonio Express-News* (February 7, 1996), 1.

101. Keith D. Nicholson, "Would You Like More Salt with That Wound? Post-Sentence Victim Allocution in Texas," *Saint Mary's Law Journal* 26 (1995), 1103.

chapter

3

Criminal Law

Chapter Objectives

After reading this chapter, you should be able to:

1. Explain precedent and the importance of the doctrine of *stare decisis*.

2. List the four written sources of American criminal law.

3. Explain the two basic functions of criminal law.

4. List and explain the six basic elements of any crime.

5. Delineate the elements required to establish *mens rea* (a guilty mental state).

6. Explain how the doctrine of strict liability applies to criminal law.

7. List and briefly define the most important excuse defenses for crimes.

8. Describe the four most important justification criminal defenses.

9. Distinguish between substantive and procedural criminal law.

10. Determine where Americans find most of their criminal procedural safeguards.

INTRODUCTION

There was little doubt in anybody's mind that Raja Chester Pinola had killed Saptal Singh. On May 16, 1997, Pinola walked into the 7-Eleven store where Singh was working, demanded money, and then shot the clerk twice in the chest. The incident was captured on videotape, and Pinola, through his lawyers, admitted that he had committed the crime. At first glance, it seemed obvious that Pinola was guilty of murder during attempted robbery, a crime that carries the penalty of life imprisonment without hope of early release.

During the trial, however, a psychiatrist testified that Pinola had exhibited many signs of alcohol "blackout" on the night of the murder. That is, the defendant was so drunk that he had an "amnesic episode" and could not remember having committed the crime. Furthermore, the specialist noted that Pinola's brain showed signs of having been damaged before he was born due to extensive alcohol and drug use by his mother during pregnancy. Given these factors, Pinola's defense lawyers claimed that their client was incapable of forming the intent to rob the store or murder the clerk and, therefore, should receive a lesser penalty.[1] Was he guilty, nonetheless?

In previous chapters, we discussed crime in relation to society. In this chapter, we will focus on the substance and procedure of criminal law, which defines those actions that are labeled crimes and sets the guidelines by which the criminal justice system determines and punishes criminal guilt. As the Pinola case suggests, criminal law must be flexible enough to allow for the intricacies of human behavior. Can Pinola, or any other person, be said to be guilty of a crime if he or she did not intend to commit the crime? In this instance, the jury rejected the "blackout" notion and sent Pinola to prison for the rest of his life. But, as we shall see in the following pages, in some situations a person is not held responsible for behavior that would otherwise be deemed criminal.

THE DEVELOPMENT OF AMERICAN CRIMINAL LAW

Given its various functions, a single definition of *law* is difficult to establish. To the Greek philosopher Aristotle (384–322 B.C.E.) law was a "pledge that citizens of a state will do justice to one another." Aristotle's mentor, Plato (427–347 B.C.E.) saw the law as primarily a form of social control. The British jurist Sir William Blackstone (1723–1780) described law as "a rule of civil conduct prescribed by the supreme power in a state, commanding what is right, and prohibiting what is wrong." In the United States, jurist Oliver Wendell Holmes, Jr. (1841–1935) contended that law was a set of rules that allowed one to predict how a court would resolve a particular dispute.

The Conception of Law

Although these definitions vary in their particulars, they are all based on the following general observation: *law* consists of enforceable rules governing relationships among individuals and between individuals and their society.[2] Searching back into history, several sources for modern American law can be found in the rules laid out by ancient societies. One of the first known sets of written law was created during the reign of Hammurabi (1792–1750 B.C.E.), the sixth king of the ancient empire of Babylon. The Code of Hammurabi set out crimes and their punishments based on *lex Talionis*, or "an eye for an eye."

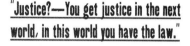

"Justice?—You get justice in the next world, in this world you have the law."

—William Gaddis, *American novelist* (1994)

For an overview of criminal law and links to an extensive number of documents relating to criminal justice, go to the Web site at Cornell University's Legal Information Institute at www.law.cornell.edu/topics/criminal.html

This concept of retribution is still important and will be discussed in Chapter 11.

Another ancient source of law can be found in the Mosaic Code of the Israelites (1200 B.C.E.). According to tradition, Moses—acting as an intermediary for God—presented the code to the tribes of Israel. The two sides entered into a covenant, or contract, in which the Israelites agreed to follow the code and God agreed to protect them as the chosen people. Besides providing the basis for Judeo-Christian teachings, the Mosaic Code is also reflected in modern American law, as evident by similar prohibitions against murder, theft, adultery, and perjury.

Modern law also owes a debt to the Twelve Tables of Roman law (451 B.C.E.). In ancient Rome, members of the lower class had become frustrated that no written law existed. They felt that without written law the ruling classes could abuse their power without being held accountable for their acts. As a result, the Twelve Tables were inscribed on bronze plaques and memorized by every adult Roman male. Though the original tables no longer exist, we know from copies that the legal code dealt with many of the day-to-day concerns of life, such as how to repay debt and questions of property.

Another important source of modern law was the Code of Justinian, promulgated throughout the Roman Empire in the sixth century. This code collected many of the laws that Western society had produced. It was influential in the development of the civil law systems of the European continent. To some extent, it influenced the common law of England, described below.

Early English Common Law

These early attempts to create formal legal codes were for the most part abandoned during the Dark Ages, a term used to describe several centuries following the fall of the Roman Empire in the fifth century. In Anglo-Saxon England, as in other European countries, the law was *decentralized*. In other words, officials were primarily responsible for keeping order in their own county. Consequently, laws tended to vary from county to county. (The specifics of Anglo-Saxon law enforcement are covered in more detail in Chapter 4.)

The beginning of the end of Anglo-Saxon law came with the Norman Conquest in 1066, when invaders from northern France took control of England. At first, William the Conqueror (1066–1087), the leader of the Normans, allowed the English counties to continue to set laws on a county-by-county basis. Eventually, however, William decided that he needed to have more control over the countryside and replaced the local courts with royal tribunals that ruled on the more important legal matters. As there were not enough royal officials to constantly oversee every English county, they would travel from county to county, spending a few days in each. In this manner, the *curia regis*, or king's court, would be presented with the legal incidents that had occurred since its last visit and make decisions based on how similar cases has previously been decided.

The English system of law as it stands today was solidified during the reign of Henry II (1154–1189). Like William the Conqueror, Henry sent judges on a specific route throughout the country known as a circuit. These circuit judges established a **common law** in England. That is, they solidified a national law in which legal principles applied to all citizens equally, no matter where they lived or what the local customs had dictated in the past. When confusion about any particular law arose, the circuit judges could refer back to Anglo-Saxon traditions, or they could borrow from legal decisions made in other European countries. Once a circuit judge made a ruling, other circuit judges faced with similar cases generally followed that ruling. Each interpretation became part of the law on the subject and served as a legal **precedent**—a decision that furnished an example or authority for deciding subsequent

INFOTRAC®
COLLEGE EDITION

Common knowledge of the common law.

COMMON LAW
The body of law developed from custom or judicial decisions in English and U.S. courts and not attributable to a legislature.

PRECEDENT
A court decision that furnishes an example of authority for deciding subsequent cases involving identical or similar facts.

STARE DECISIS
(pronounced *ster*-ay dih-si-*ses*). A common law doctrine under which judges are obligated to follow the precedents established under prior decisions.

cases involving similar legal principles or facts. Over time, a body of general rules that prescribed social conduct and that was applied throughout the entire English realm was established, and subsequently it was passed on to British colonies, including those in the New World that would eventually become the thirteen original states. (See Figure 3.1 for a list of common law crimes that were defined by common law judges in England by 1600 A.C.E. Modern criminal law has codified such crimes into state statutes.)

What is important about the formation of the common law is that it developed from the customs of the people rather than simply the will of a ruler. As such, the common law came to reflect the social, religious, economic, and cultural values of the people. All the while, a system of sheriffs, courts, juries, and lawyers accompanied the development of the common law.

INFOTRAC®
COLLEGE EDITION

Foolish consistency

Stare Decisis

The practice of deciding new cases with reference to precedents is the basis for a doctrine called ***stare decisis*** ("to stand on decided cases"). Under this doctrine, judges are obligated to follow the precedents established within their jurisdictions.[3] For example, any decision of a particular state's highest court will control the outcome of future cases on that issue brought before all of the lower courts within that same state (unless preempted by the federal Constitution). All United States Supreme Court decisions on issues interpreting the federal Constitution are binding on *all* courts.

Controlling precedents in a jurisdiction are referred to as binding authorities, as are statutes or other laws that must be followed. In civil law systems,

Figure 3.1 Common Law Crimes

Following the American Revolution, the legislatures of the new states adopted many English common law crimes into their legal codes. Thus, much of today's criminal law can be traced directly to the common law tradition. Below we present only a few examples of common law crimes.

Crimes against Persons

1. First degree murder

Definition: Unlawful killing of another person with malice aforethought and with premeditation and deliberation.

Example: A man lures his friend into the woods on the premise of a hunting trip and shoots him, attempting to make the killing look like an accident. He is motivated by the belief that his friend has discovered that he has been embezzling money from the company at which they both work.

2. Voluntary manslaughter

Definition: Intentional killing committed under extenuating circumstances that mitigate the killing, such as killing in the heat of passion or after being provoked.

Example: A woman tells her husband that she is leaving him for another man. Enraged, he chokes her to death.

3. Battery

Definition: Unlawful physical contact with another with the intent to cause injury.

Example: A man in a bar returns from a trip to the restroom to find his date conversing with someone else. He walks up to the newcomer and punches him in the face.

4. Robbery

Definition: The taking of money or personal property through the use or threat of force.

Example: A man walks into a convenience store, pulls out a handgun, and orders the clerk to hand over the contents of the cash register.

Crimes against Property

1. Burglary

Definition: Breaking and entering a dwelling of another during the nighttime with intent to commit a felony.

Example: During the night, a man picks the lock on the door of an apartment and, once inside, proceeds to take all the jewelry and other valuable items he can find.

2. Larceny

Definition: Taking and carrying away the personal property of another with the intention of stealing that property.

Example: A woman goes into a department store and, when she believes nobody is watching, slips several expensive watches into her coat pocket.

Inchoate (Not Completed) Offenses

1. Attempt

Definition: The intent to commit a crime along with an action taken toward committing that crime. The criminal act is not, however, completed.

Example: A wife intends to kill her husband by placing rat poison in his coffee. The husband, already suspicious, notices the open rat poison container before taking his first sip, and refuses to drink it.

2. Conspiracy

Definition: A voluntary agreement by two or more persons to achieve a lawful or unlawful object by unlawful means.

Example: Three adult sons plan to cause their mother to suffer a heart attack so that they may collect her life insurance.

SOURCE: BLACK'S LAW DICTIONARY AND THERESE J. LIBBY, "COMMON-LAW CRIMES" IN LARRY J. SIEGEL, CRIMINOLOGY, 6TH EDITION (BELMONT, CA: WEST/WADSWORTH PUBLISHING COMPANY, 1998), 32.

Cross-National CJ Comparison

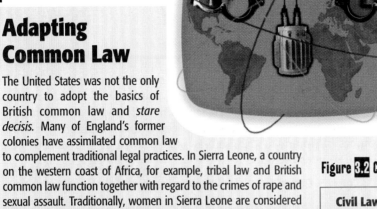

Adapting Common Law

The United States was not the only country to adopt the basics of British common law and *stare decisis*. Many of England's former colonies have assimilated common law to complement traditional legal practices. In Sierra Leone, a country on the western coast of Africa, for example, tribal law and British common law function together with regard to the crimes of rape and sexual assault. Traditionally, women in Sierra Leone are considered the property of the head of whichever family they are born or later marry into. Consequently, when a man outside the family rapes a woman, the matter is considered a property crime. The charges are brought before a tribal court, and if the offender is found guilty of sexual assault, or "woman-damage," he must pay compensation to the victim's family. If the defendant refuses to admit guilt or pay damages, the case is transferred to Sierra Leone's General Courts, which operate under the rules of British common law. If the defendant is found guilty in the General Courts, he can receive a maximum penalty of life imprisonment.

CIVIL LAW SYSTEMS

Although the influence of British common law is widespread, as Figure 3.2 shows, a number of countries operate under civil legal systems (not to be confused with the classification of civil versus criminal law, which will be explained later in this chapter). With roots in sixth-century Roman law, civil law systems rely primarily on legislation and custom rather than the doctrine of *stare decisis*. Take a hypothetical situation in which a police officer, after stopping a driver for speeding, proceeds to search the automobile and finds an unregistered handgun. In a country with a common law system, the courts will decide on the legality of the police officer's actions by reviewing statutes plus all previous court cases that cover the same topic. In a country with a civil law system, the courts will normally refer only to legislation on the subject. With their decisions, civil law judges do not necessarily set precedents for cases that follow.

WHAT'S THE EVIDENCE?

Several jurisdictions in the United States—specifically, Louisiana and Puerto Rico—have legal systems that combine aspects of both common and civil law. The French were in control of Louisiana's administration for a very short time. Go to **www.lna.org/civillaw.html**. Read through the article on the origins of Louisiana's legal system. Why did the civil law take hold there, but not in the other states?

Figure 3.2 Countries with Common and Civil Legal Systems

Civil Law	Common Law
Argentina	Australia
Austria	Bangladesh
Brazil	Canada
Chile	Ghana
China	India
Egypt	Israel
Finland	Jamaica
France	Kenya
Germany	Malaysia
Greece	New Zealand
Indonesia	Nigeria
Iran	Singapore
Italy	United Kingdom
Japan	United States
Mexico	Zambia
Poland	
South Korea	
Sweden	
Tunisia	
Venezuela	

in contrast, precedent is not binding. (But, to see the extent to which common law and the doctrine of *stare decisis* have been adopted in other countries, see *Cross-National CJ Comparison—Adapting Common Law.*)

The doctrine of *stare decisis* helps the courts to be more efficient, because if other courts have carefully examined a similar case, their legal reasoning and opinions can serve as a guide. This does not mean, however, that the system is rigid. The United States Supreme Court, for example, will sometimes rule against precedent set in a previous Court decision. It does so when there have been sufficient changes in society to warrant departing from the doctrine of *stare decisis*. In general, however, the judicial system is slow to change, and courts rarely alter major points of law. The doctrine of *stare decisis* leads to stability in the law, allowing people to predict how the law will be applied in given circumstances.

CONSTITUTIONAL LAW
Law based on the U.S. Constitution and the constitutions of the various states.

WRITTEN SOURCES OF AMERICAN CRIMINAL LAW

Originally, common law was *uncodified*. That is, it relied primarily on judges following precedents and the body of the law was not written down in any single place. Uncodified law, however, presents a number of drawbacks, not the least being that citizens have difficulty learning which acts are illegal and understanding the procedures that must be followed to establish innocence or guilt. Consequently, U.S. history has seen the development of several written sources of American criminal law, also known as "substantive" criminal law. These sources include:

1. The U.S. Constitution and the constitutions of the various states.

2. Statutes, or laws, passed by Congress and by state legislatures, plus local ordinances.

3. Regulation, created by regulatory agencies, such as the federal Food and Drug Administration.

4. Case law (court decisions).

We describe each of these important written sources of law in the following pages (see Figure 3.3).

Constitutional Law

The federal government and the states have separate written constitutions that set forth the general organization and powers of, and the limits on, their respective governments. **Constitutional law** is the law as expressed in these constitutions.

The U.S. Constitution is the supreme law of the land. As such, it is the basis of all law in the United States. Any law that violates the Constitution, as ultimately determined by the United States Supreme Court, will be declared unconstitutional and will not be enforced. The Tenth Amendment, which defines the powers and limitations of the federal government, reserves to the states all powers not granted to the federal government. Under our system of federalism (see Chapter 1), each state also has its own constitution. Unless they conflict with the U.S. Constitution or a federal law, state constitutions are supreme within their respective borders. (You will learn more about how constitutional law applies to our criminal justice system in later chapters.)

George Washington, standing, presided over the Constitutional Convention of 1787. The convention resulted in the United States Constitution, the source of a number of laws that continue to form the basis of our criminal justice system today.

Figure 3.3 Sources of American Law

1. **Constitutional law**—The law as expressed in the U.S. Constitution and the various state constitutions. The U.S. Constitution is the supreme law of the land. State constitutions are supreme within state borders to the extent that they do not violate the U.S. Constitution or a federal law.

2. **Statutory law**—Laws or ordinances created by federal, state, and local legislatures and governing bodies. None of these laws can violate the U.S. Constitution or the relevant state constitution. Uniform laws, when adopted by a state legislature, become statutory law in that state.

3. **Administrative law**—The rules, orders, and decisions of federal or state government administrative agencies. Federal administrative agencies are created by enabling legislation enacted by the U.S. Congress. Agency functions include rulemaking, investigation and enforcement, and adjudication.

4. **Case law and common law doctrines**—Judge-made law, including interpretations of constitutional provisions, of statutes enacted by legislatures, and of regulations created by administrative agencies. The common law—the doctrines and principles embodied in case law—governs all areas not covered by statutory law (or agency regulations issued to implement various statutes).

Statutory Law

Statutes enacted by legislative bodies at any level of government make up another source of law, which is generally referred to as **statutory law.** *Federal statutes* are laws that are enacted by the U.S. Congress. *State statutes* are laws enacted by state legislatures, and statutory law also includes the ordinances passed by cities and counties. A federal statute, of course, applies to all states. A state statute, in contrast, applies only within that state's borders. City or county ordinances (statutes) apply only to those jurisdictions where they are enacted. As mentioned, statutory law found by the Supreme Court to violate the U.S. Constitution will be overturned. In the late 1980s, for example, the Court ruled that any state laws banning the burning of the American flag were unconstitutional because they impinged on the individual's right to freedom of expression.

Common Law and State Statutes. Even though the body of statutory law has expanded greatly since the beginning of this nation, thus narrowing the applicability of common law doctrines, there is significant overlap between statutory law and common law. For example, many statutes essentially codify existing common law rules. Therefore, the courts, when interpreting the statutes, often rely on the common law as a guide to what the legislators intended. In some instances, statutory law has brought common law principles more in line with modern criminal theory. Under common law, for example, the law of rape applied only when the victim was a female. Today, many states recognize that both sexes may be the targets of sexual assault. Under common law, burglary was defined as the breaking and entering of a dwelling during the nighttime. State legislatures, in contrast, generally have defined burglary as occurring at any time. They have extended it to apply to structures beyond dwellings and even to automobiles.

Model Penal Code. Until the mid-twentieth century, state statutes were disorganized, inconsistent, and generally inadequate for modern society. In 1952, the American Law Institute began to draft a uniform penal code in hopes of solving this problem. The first Model Penal Code was released ten years later and has had a broad effect on state statutes.[4] Though not a law itself, the code defines the general principles of criminal responsibility and codifies specific offenses; it is the source for many of the definitions of crime in this textbook. The majority of the states have adopted parts of the Model Penal Code into their statutes, and some states, such as New York, have adopted a large portion of the Code.[5]

Administrative Law

A third source of American criminal law consists of **administrative law**—the rules, orders, and decisions of regulatory agencies. A regulatory agency is a federal, state, or local government agency established to perform a specific function. The Occupational Safety and Health Administration (OSHA), for example, oversees the safety and health of American workers; the Environmental Protection Agency (EPA) is concerned with protecting the natural environment; and the Food and Drug Administration (FDA) regulates food and drugs produced in the United States. Disregarding certain laws created by regulatory agencies can be a criminal violation. Many modern federal acts, such as the Clean Air Act, designate authority to a specific regulatory agency, such as the EPA, to promulgate regulations to which criminal sanctions are attached. The number of criminal investigators employed by the EPA has grown from six in 1982 to more than 150 at present. These investigators help the U.S. Department of Justice deliver nearly 200 environmental crime indictments each year.[6]

You can learn about some of the constitutional questions raised by various criminal laws and procedures by going to the Web site of the American Civil Liberties Union at www.aclu.org

CASE LAW
The rules of law announced in court decisions. Case law includes the aggregate of reported cases that interpret judicial precedents, statutes, regulations, and constitutional provisions.

Case Law

As is evident from the earlier discussion of the common law tradition, another basic source of American law consists of the rules of law announced in court decisions. These rules of law include interpretations of constitutional provisions, of statutes enacted by legislatures, and of regulations created by administrative agencies. Today, this body of law is referred to variously as the common law, judge-made law, or **case law.**

Case law relies to a certain extent on how courts interpret a particular statute. If you wanted to learn about the coverage and applicability of a particular statute, for example, you would need to locate the statute and study it. You would also need to see how the courts in your jurisdiction have interpreted the statute—in other words, what precedents have been established in regard to that statute. The use of precedent means that judge-made law varies from jurisdiction to jurisdiction.

THE PURPOSES OF CRIMINAL LAW

Why do societies need laws? Many criminologists believe that criminal law has two basic functions: one relates to the legal requirements of a society, and the other pertains to its need to maintain and promote social values.[7]

Protect and Punish: The Legal Function of the Law

The primary legal function of the law is to maintain social order by protecting citizens from "criminal harm." This term refers to a variety of harms that can be generalized to fit into two categories:

1. Harms to individual citizens' physical safety and property, such as the harm caused by murder, theft, or arson.

2. Harms to society's interests collectively, such as the harm caused by unsafe foods or consumer products, a polluted environment, or poorly constructed buildings.[8]

The first category is self-evident, although even murder has different degrees, or grades, of offense to which different punishments are assigned. The second, however, has proved more problematic, for it is difficult to measure society's "collective" interests. Often, laws passed to reduce such harms seem overly intrusive and marginally necessary. An extreme example would seem to be the Flammable Fabrics Act, which makes it a crime for a retailer to willfully remove a precautionary instruction label from a mattress that is protected with a chemical fire retardant.[9] Yet even in this example, a criminal harm is conceivable. Suppose a retailer removes the tags before selling a large number of mattresses to a hotel chain. Employees of the chain then unknowingly wash the mattresses with an agent that lessens their flame-resistant qualities. After the mattresses have been placed in rooms, a guest falls asleep while smoking a cigarette, starting a fire that burns down the entire hotel and causes several deaths.[10]

Maintain and Teach: The Social Function of the Law

If criminal laws against acts that cause harm or injury to others are almost universally accepted, the same cannot be said for laws that criminalize "morally" wrongful activities that may do no obvious, physical harm outside the families of those involved. Why criminalize gambling or prostitution if the participants are consenting?

"If he who breaks the law is not punished, he who obeys it is cheated. This, and this alone, is why lawbreakers ought to be punished: to authenticate as good, and to encourage as useful, law-abiding behavior. The aim of criminal law cannot be correction or deterrence, it can only be the maintenance of the legal order."

—Thomas Szasz, *American psychiatrist* (1973)

Expressing Public Morality. The answer lies in the social function of criminal law. Many observers believe that the main purpose of criminal law is to reflect the values and norms of society, or at least of those segments of society that hold power. Legal scholar Henry Hart has stated that the only justification for criminal law and punishment is "the judgment of community condemnation."[11]

Take, for example, the misdemeanor of bigamy, which occurs when someone knowingly marries a second person without terminating her or his marriage to an original husband or wife. Apart from moral considerations, there would appear to be no victims in a bigamous relationship, and indeed many societies have allowed and continue to allow bigamy to exist. In the American social tradition, however, as John L. Diamond of the University of California's Hastings College of the Law points out:

> Marriage is an institution encouraged and supported by society. The structural importance of the integrity of the family and a monogamous marriage requires unflinching enforcement of the criminal laws against bigamy. The immorality is not in choosing to do wrong, but in transgressing, even innocently, a fundamental social boundary that lies at the core of social order.[12]

When discussing the social function of criminal law, it is important to remember that a society's views of morality change over time. Puritan New England society not only had strict laws against adultery, but also considered lying and idleness criminal acts.[13] Today, such acts may carry social stigmas, but only in certain extreme circumstances do they elicit legal sanctions.

Teaching Societal Boundaries. Some scholars believe that criminal laws not only express the expectations of society, but they "teach" them as well. Professor Lawrence M. Friedman of Stanford University believes that just as parents teach children behavioral norms through punishment, criminal justice "'teaches a lesson' to the people it punishes, and to society at large." Making burglary a crime, arresting burglars, placing them in jail—each step in the criminal justice process reinforces the idea that burglary is unacceptable and is deserving of punishment.[14]

This teaching function can also be seen in traffic laws. There is nothing "natural" about most traffic laws; Americans drive on the right side of the street, the British on the left side, with no obvious difference in the results. These laws, such as stopping at intersections, using headlights at night, and following speed limits, do lead to a more orderly flow of traffic and fewer accidents—certainly socially desirable goals. Various forms of punishment for breaking traffic laws teach drivers the "social" order of the road.

CLASSIFICATION OF CRIMES

The huge body of the law may be broken down according to various classifications. Three of the most important distinctions can be made between (1) civil law and criminal law, (2) felonies and misdemeanors, and (3) crimes *mala in se* and *mala prohibita*.

Civil Law and Criminal Law

All law can be divided into two categories: civil law and criminal law. As U.S. criminal law has evolved, it has diverged from U.S. civil law. The two categories of law are distinguished by their primary goals. The criminal justice system is concerned with protecting society from harm by preventing and prosecuting crimes. A crime is an act so reprehensible that it is considered a

"Because Ste
she had been
or shot. Step
Someone mus

—C. R. Roberts, *columnist* for the (Tacoma, Washington) *Morning News Tribune*, expressing the opinion of those who felt that Brandi Blake should be prosecuted for allowing her 3-year-old daughter to ride a raft without a life-preserver, breaking a county law that requires children under the age of 12 to wear a floatation device; when the raft overturned, Blake's daughter drowned (1997)

The relatives of Ron Goldman and Nicole Brown look on during the civil trial of O. J. Simpson. Two years earlier, a criminal court found Simpson not guilty for the murders of Goldman and Brown. A civil jury, however, found that Simpson was liable for the 1994 death of Goldman and committed battery against Brown, his ex-wife, and awarded $8.5 million in compensatory damages to the Goldman and Brown families. Do you believe that defendants found innocent in criminal trials should be subject to civil trials for the same action?

wrong against society as a whole, as well as against the individual victim.[15] Therefore, the *state* prosecutes a person who commits a criminal act. If the state is able to prove that a person is guilty of a crime, the government will punish her or him with imprisonment or fines, or both.

Civil law, which includes all types of law other than criminal law, is concerned with disputes between private individuals and between entities. Proceedings in civil lawsuits are normally initiated by an individual or a corporation (in contrast to criminal proceedings, which are initiated by public prosecutors). Such disputes may involve, for example, the terms of a contract, the ownership of property, or an automobile accident. Under civil law, the government provides a forum for the resolution of *torts*, or private wrongs, in which the injured party, called the *plaintiff*, tries to prove that a wrong has been committed by the accused party, or the *defendant*. Most civil cases involve a request for monetary damages in recognition that a wrong has been committed. If, for example, a driver runs a red light and hits a pedestrian, the pedestrian could file a civil suit asking for monetary compensation for the "pain and suffering" caused by his or her injuries. (See the *Concept Summary* below for a comparison of criminal and civil law.)

Although criminal law proceedings are completely separate from civil law proceedings in the modern legal system, the two systems do have some similarities. Both attempt to control behavior by imposing sanctions on those who violate the law. Furthermore, criminal and civil law often supplement each other. In certain instances, a victim may file a civil suit against an individual who is also the target of a criminal prosecution by the government.

Because the burden of proof is much greater in criminal trials than civil ones, it is usually easier to win monetary damages than a criminal conviction.[16] After shooting sixteen-year-old exchange student Yoshihiro Hattori of Japan, for example, Rodney Pearis was acquitted of manslaughter charges by a Louisiana jury. Pearis claimed he thought Hattori—who mistook the defendant's home for the site of a Halloween party—was an intruder. After the criminal trial, however, Hattori's family brought a civil suit against Pearis and was awarded more than $650,000 in damages.[17] While the government had been unable to prove *beyond a reasonable doubt* (the burden of proof in criminal cases) that Pearis had intended to kill Hattori, the civil trial established that a *preponderance of the evidence* (the burden of proof in civil cases) showed this to be the case.

CIVIL LAW
The branch of law dealing with the definition and enforcement of all private or public rights, as opposed to criminal matters.

CONCEPT SUMMARY
Criminal Law versus Civil Law

Issue	Civil Law	Criminal Law
Area of concern	Rights and duties between individuals	Offenses against society as a whole
Wrongful act	Harm to a person	Violation of a statute that prohibits some type of activity
Party who brings suit	Person who suffered harm	The state
Standard of proof	Preponderance of the evidence	Beyond a reasonable doubt
Remedy	Damages to compensate for the harm	Punishment (fine or imprisonment)

Felonies and Misdemeanors

Depending on their degree of seriousness, crimes are classified as felonies or misdemeanors. Felonies are serious crimes punishable by death or by imprisonment in a federal or state penitentiary for one year or longer (though some states, such as North Carolina, consider felonies to be punishable by at least two years' incarceration). The Model Penal Code provides for four degrees of felony:

1. Capital offenses, for which the maximum penalty is death.

2. First degree felonies, punishable by a maximum penalty of life imprisonment.

3. Second degree felonies, punishable by a maximum of ten years' imprisonment.

4. Third degree felonies, punishable by a maximum of five years' imprisonment.[18]

Degrees of Murder. Though specifics vary from state to state, some general rules apply when grading crimes. For example, most jurisdictions punish a burglary that involves a nighttime forced entry into a home more seriously than one that takes place during the day and involves a nonresidential building or structure. Murder in the first degree occurs under two circumstances:

1. When the crime is *premeditated,* or considered beforehand by the offender, instead of being a spontaneous act of violence.

2. When the crime is *deliberate,* meaning that it was planned and decided upon after a process of decision making. Deliberation does not require a lengthy planning process; a person can be found guilty of first degree murder even if she or he made the decision to murder only seconds before committing the crime.

Second degree murder occurs when no premeditation or deliberation was present, but the offender did have *malice aforethought* toward the victim. In other words, the offender acted with wanton disregard of the consequences of his or her actions. The difference between first and second degree murder is clearly illustrated in a recent case involving a California man who beat a neighbor to death with a partially full brandy bottle. The crime took place after Ricky McDonald, the victim, complained to Kazi Cooksey, the offender, about the noise coming from a late-night barbecue Cooksey and his friends were holding. The jury could not find sufficient evidence that Cooksey's actions were premeditated, but he certainly acted with wanton disregard of his victim's safety. Therefore, the jury convicted Cooksey of second degree murder rather than first degree murder.

A homicide committed without malice toward the victim is known as *manslaughter* and is usually punishable by up to fifteen years in prison. *Voluntary manslaughter* occurs when the intent to kill may be present, but malice was lacking. Voluntary manslaughter covers crimes of passion, in which the emotion of an argument between two friends may lead to a homicide. Voluntary manslaughter can also occur when the victim provoked the offender to act violently. *Involuntary manslaughter* covers incidents in which the offender's acts were negligent, even though there was no intent to kill. When a drunk driver causes the death of another driver or a pedestrian, he or she is usually charged with involuntary manslaughter.

Degrees of Misdemeanor. Under federal law and in most states, any crime that is not a felony is considered a misdemeanor. Misdemeanors are crimes

"This woman, irrespective of whether she was guilty of anything—I don't know the answer to that question—but I know she wasn't guilty of first-degree murder. She—if she killed that child or had anything to do with it, she didn't intend to kill that child and didn't have any malice aforethought in doing it."

—Gerry Spence, *trial attorney,* commenting on the murder charges brought against *au pair* Louise Woodward after the death of an infant in her care (1997)

MALA IN SE
A descriptive term for acts that are inherently wrong, regardless of whether they are prohibited by law.

MALA PROHIBITA
A descriptive term for acts that are made illegal by criminal statute and are not necessarily wrong of themselves.

CORPUS DELICTI
The body of circumstances that must exist for a criminal act to have occurred.

punishable by a fine or by confinement for up to a year. If imprisoned, the guilty party goes to a local jail instead of a penitentiary. Disorderly conduct and trespassing are common misdemeanors. Like felonies, misdemeanors are graded by level of seriousness. In Illinois, for example, misdemeanors are either Class A (confinement for up to a year), Class B (not more than six months), or Class C (not more than thirty days).

Most states similarly distinguish between *gross misdemeanors,* which are offenses punishable by thirty days to a year in jail, and *petty misdemeanors,* or offenses punishable by fewer than thirty days in jail. The least serious form of crime is a *violation* (such as a traffic offense), which is only punishable by a small fine and does not appear on the wrongdoer's criminal record. Whether a crime is a felony or a misdemeanor can also determine whether the case is tried in a magistrate's court (for example, by a justice of the peace) or in a general trial court (e.g., superior court).

Probation and community service are often imposed on those who commit misdemeanors, especially juveniles.[19] Also, most states have decriminalized all but the most serious traffic offenses. These infractions are treated as civil proceedings, and civil fines are imposed. In many states, the violator has "points" assessed against her or his driving record.

Mala in Se and Mala Prohibita

Criminologists often express the social function of criminal law in terms of *mala in se* or *mala prohibita* crimes. A criminal act is referred to as **mala in se** if it would be considered wrong even if there were no law prohibiting it. *Mala in se* crimes are said to go against "natural laws," that is, against the "natural, moral, and public" principles of a society.[20] Examples of *mala in se* crimes are murder, rape, and theft. In contrast, the term **mala prohibita** refers to acts that are considered crimes only because they have been codified as such through statute—"human-made" laws. A *mala prohibita* crime is considered wrong only because it has been prohibited; it is not inherently a wrong, though it may reflect the moral standards of a society at any given time.[21] Bigamy, as discussed earlier, could be considered a *mala prohibita* crime.

Some observers believe that the distinction between *mala in se* and *mala prohibita* is problematic. First, it is difficult to define a "pure" *mala in se* crime; that is, it is difficult to separate a crime from the culture that has deemed it a crime.[22] Even murder, in certain cultural circumstances, is not considered a criminal act (see Cross-National CJ Comparison—"Honor Killings" in Jordan). Our own legal system excuses homicide in extreme situations, such as self-defense or when a law enforcement agent kills in the course of upholding the law. Therefore, all "natural" laws can be seen as culturally specific. Second, similar difficulties occur in trying to define a "pure" *mala prohibita* crime.[23] As already noted, an argument could be made that a law prohibiting the removal of instruction tags from a mattress could prevent the loss of human life.

THE ELEMENTS OF A CRIME

In fictional accounts of police work, the admission of guilt is often portrayed as *the* crucial element of a criminal investigation. Although an admission is certainly useful to police and prosecutors, it alone cannot establish the innocence or guilt of a suspect. Criminal law normally requires that the **corpus delicti,** a Latin phrase for "the body of the crime," be proved before a person can be convicted of wrongdoing.[24] *Corpus delicti* can be defined as "proof that a specific crime has actually been committed by someone."[25] It consists of the basic elements of any crime, which include (1) *actus reus,* or a guilty act;

Cross-National CJ Comparison

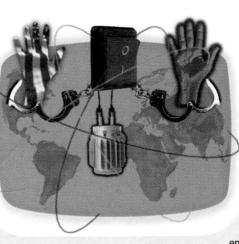

"Honor Killings" in Jordan

Twenty-one-year-old Rania Arafat was walking in a poor section of Amman, Jordan, when she was shot four times in the back of the head and once in the forehead. The gunman was her younger brother, Rami. Such "honor killings" of women suspected of sexual indiscretion, carried out by a male family member, are not uncommon in poor, traditional areas of the Middle East—more than twenty are recorded in Jordan each year. Rania's indiscretion was that she had refused an arranged marriage and eloped with her Iraqi boyfriend.

EXCUSED BY LAW AND TRADITION

In Jordan, "honor killings" are excused by law. According to Article 340 of the country's criminal code, "A husband or a close relative who kills a woman caught in a situation highly suspicious of adultery will be totally exempt from sentence." Even if the relationship in question is not consummated, under law the killer will receive a shortened sentence of three months to a year in prison. Although the Jordanian Women's Union has petitioned the Jordanian parliament to change the law, there is not widespread support for such a change. As one female politician said, "This is our tradition. We do not want to encourage women who break up the family."

WHAT'S THE EVIDENCE?

Human rights organizations are tracking "honor killings" in Jordan, Lebanon, Palestine, Pakistan, and a number of other countries. One such group is the Middle East Research and Information Project, which can be found at **www.merip.org**. Take a look at one study on honor killings in Palestine at **www.merip.org/ruggi.htm**. What is the government of that country doing to solve this problem? What is being done outside of that country?

---

(2) *mens rea*, or a guilty intent; (3) concurrence, or the coming together of the criminal act and the guilty mind; (4) a link between the act and the legal definition of the crime; (5) any attendant circumstances; and (6) the harm done, or result of the criminal act. (See the *Concept Summary* below for an example showing some of the various elements of a crime.)

INFOTRAC®
COLLEGE EDITION

Homicide Trends and Cultural Meanings

Criminal Act: *Actus Reus*

Suppose Mr. Smith walks into a police department and announces that he just killed his wife. In and of itself, the confession is insufficient for conviction unless the police find Mrs. Smith's corpse with a bullet in her brain and establish through evidence that Mr. Smith fired the gun. (This does not mean that

---

CONCEPT SUMMARY
The Elements of a Crime

On December 24, 1998, Carl Robert Winchell walked into the SunTrust Bank in Volusia County, Florida, and placed a bag containing a box on a counter. He announced that the box held a bomb, and demanded to be given an unspecified amount of money. After being provided with several thousand dollars in cash, Winchell fled, leaving the box behind. A Volusia County Sheriff's Office bomb squad subsequently determined that the box did not in fact contain any explosive device, and Winchell was eventually arrested and charged with robbery.

Winchell's actions were criminal because they satisfy the three elements of a crime:

1. Actus reus—The physical act of a crime took place. In this case, Winchell committed bank robbery.

2. Mens rea—The offender must intentionally, knowingly, or willingly commit the criminal act. In this case, Winchell obviously planned to rob the SunTrust Bank using the false threat of a bomb.

3. A **concurrence** of *actus reus* and *mens rea*—The criminal act must be the result of the offender's intention to commit that particular criminal act. In this case, the robbery was the direct result of Winchell's intent to take property using the threat of the fake bomb. If, in addition, a bank customer had died of a heart attack during the robbery attempt, Winchell could not be charged with first degree murder, because he did not intend to harm anyone.

Note that the fact that there was no bomb in the box has no direct bearing on the three elements of the crime. It could, however, lead to Winchell receiving a lighter punishment than if he had used a real bomb.

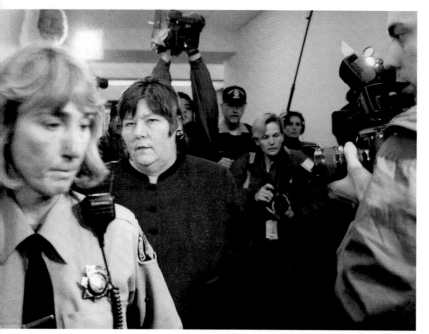

In 1996, 13-year-old Christina Corrigan of El Cerrito, California, died of heart failure. Paramedics found Christina, who weighed 680 pounds at the time of her death, covered with insect bites and lying in a pool of her own urine and feces, surrounded by empty food containers. Two years later, Christina's mother Marlene, shown above, was convicted of misdemeanor child abuse and sentenced to three years' probation and 240 hours of community service. A Contra Costa Superior Court judge refused to convict the woman of a felony, as desired by the prosecution, because there was no proof that she was aware of the harm she did her daughter by not seeking medical care for her. Describe this crime in terms of an act of omission rather than commission.

ACTUS REUS
(pronounced *ak*-tus *ray*-uhs).
A guilty (prohibited) act. The commission of a prohibited act is one of the two essential elements required for criminal liability, the other element being the intent to commit a crime.

MENS REA
(pronounced *mehns ray*-uh).
Mental state, or intent. A wrongful mental state in as necessary as a wrongful act to establish criminal liability.

NEGLIGENCE
A failure to exercise the standard of care that a reasonable person would exercise in similar circumstances.

an actual dead body has to be found in every homicide case. Rather, it is the fact of the death that must be established in such cases.)

Most crimes require an act of *commission;* that is, a person must *do* something in order to be accused of a crime. The prohibited act is referred to as the **actus reus,** or guilty act. Furthermore, the act of commission must be voluntary. For example, if Mr. Smith had an epileptic seizure while holding a hunting rifle and accidentally shot his wife, he would normally not be held criminally liable for her death. (Mr. Smith could, however, be charged with the crime if he was aware of his medical condition and had been strongly advised by his physician never to handle firearms.)

In some cases, an act of *omission* can be a crime, but only when a person has a legal duty to perform the omitted act. One such legal duty is assumed to exist based on a "special relationship" between two parties, such as a parent and child, adult children and their aged parents, and spouses.[26] For example, a Milwaukee woman was arrested for allowing her teenage daughter to be sexually assaulted and then sending her back to the scene of the assault to purchase crack cocaine.[27] Those persons involved in contractual relationships with others, such as physicians and lifeguards, must also perform legal duties to avoid criminal penalty. Some states, including Rhode Island and Vermont, have passed statutes requiring their citizens to report criminal conduct and to aid victims of such conduct if possible.[28] Another example of a criminal act of omission is failure to file a federal income tax return when required by law to do so.

The *guilty act* requirement is based on one of the premises of criminal law—that a person is punished for harm done to society. Planning to kill someone or to steal a car may be wrong, but the thoughts do no harm and are therefore not criminal until they are translated into action. Of course, a person can be punished for attempting murder or robbery, but normally only if he or she took substantial steps toward the criminal objective. Furthermore, the punishment for an *attempt* normally is less severe than if the act had succeeded.

Mental State: *Mens Rea*

A wrongful mental state—**mens rea**—is as necessary as a wrongful act in establishing guilt. The mental state, or requisite *intent*, required to establish guilt of a crime is indicated in the applicable statute or law. For theft, the wrongful act is the taking of another person's property, and the required mental state involves both the awareness that the property belongs to another and the desire to deprive the owner of it.

The Categories of *Mens Rea.* A guilty mental state includes elements of purpose, knowledge, negligence, and recklessness.[29] A defendant is said to have *purposefully* committed a criminal act when he or she desires to engage in a certain criminal conduct or to cause a certain criminal result. For a defendant to have *knowingly* committed an illegal act, he or she must be aware of the illegality, must believe that the illegality exists, or must correctly suspect that the illegality exists but fail to do anything to dispel (or confirm) his or her belief. Criminal **negligence** involves the mental state in which the defendant

CJ in Focus
Was Justice Served?
Drunk Driving and *Mens Rea*

In *People v. Brown* (1994), the Michigan Supreme Court upheld a decision that some critics believe is contrary to the *mens rea* precedent. The case concerned a man who, while legally inebriated, drove the wrong direction on an interstate highway and collided with another vehicle, killing two passengers. According to state statute, the defendant could be charged with involuntary manslaughter, which carries a possible punishment of fifteen years' incarceration, or negligent homicide, which is a misdemeanor punishable by two years in jail. Instead, the defendant was convicted of second degree murder, a crime that can bring life imprisonment. The court's ruling surprised some legal scholars, because second degree murder is defined in Michigan as killing done with malice and without provocation. How, observers asked, could intoxication be interpreted as interjecting malice into a drunk driving accident?

The Michigan Supreme Court justified its ruling based on a state law that allows the absence of "express intent" as long as "willful and wanton disregard" is proved. In other words, if the defendant acts indifferently in creating a situation in which there is a high probability of causing harm, he or she can be charged with murder in the absence of *mens rea*. Critics of the decision argue that it is impossible for a person who is mentally impaired because of intoxication to have the "state of consciousness" necessary to satisfy this requirement. Though charging drunk drivers who kill with second degree murder may satisfy public opinion, these critics say, such decisions subvert the role that intent has traditionally played in determining premeditated malice. Supporters of the decision contend that the state statute was constructed to include *implied* malice through the defendant's reckless acts.

For Critical Analysis: What precedent does the decision of the Michigan Supreme Court set? What legal consequences might this precedent have in situations other than drunk driving?

---

grossly deviates from the standard of care that a reasonable person would use under the same circumstances. The defendant is accused of taking an unjustified, substantial, and foreseeable risk that resulted in harm. In Texas, for example, a parent or handgun owner commits a felony if she or he fails to secure a loaded firearm or leaves it in such a manner that it could easily be accessed by a child.

A defendant who commits an act *recklessly* is more blameworthy than one who is criminally negligent. The Model Penal Code defines criminal recklessness as "consciously disregard[ing] a substantial and unjustifiable risk."[30] Some courts, particularly those adhering to the Model Penal Code, will not find criminal recklessness on the part of a defendant who was not subjectively aware of the risk when she or he acted. (For a case in which a questionable interpretation of *mens rea* was utilized, see *CJ in Focus—Was Justice Served?: Drunk Driving and* Mens Rea.)

Criminal Liability. Intent plays an important part in allowing the law to differentiate between varying degrees of criminal liability for similar, though not identical, guilty acts. The role of intent is clearly seen in the different classifications of homicide, defined generally as the willful killing of one human being by another. It is important to emphasize the word *willful*, as it precludes deaths caused by accident or negligence and those deemed justifiable. A death that results from negligence or accident normally is considered a private wrong and a matter for civil law, although some statutes allow for culpable negligence, which permits certain negligent homicides to be criminalized. As we saw earlier, when the act of killing is willful, deliberate, and premeditated (planned beforehand), it is considered first degree murder. When premeditation does not exist but intent does, the act is considered second degree murder. (See Figure 3.4 on the following page for an example of the different homicide statutes in Florida.)

Different degrees of criminal liability for various categories of homicide lead to different penalties. The distinction between murder and manslaugh-

You can gain some insights into criminal law and procedures, including some of the defenses that can be raised to avoid criminal liability, by looking at some of the famous criminal law cases included on Court TV's Web site. Go to www.courttv.com/index.html

Figure 3.4 Florida Homicide Statutes (Excerpts)

782.02 Justifiable use of deadly force.—The use of deadly force is justifiable when a person is resisting any attempt to murder such person or to commit any felony upon him or her or upon or in any dwelling house in which such person shall be.

782.03 Excusable homicide.—Homicide is excusable when committed by accident and misfortune in doing any lawful act by lawful means with usual ordinary caution, and without any unlawful intent, or by accident and misfortune in the heat of passion, upon any sudden and sufficient provocation, or upon a sudden combat, without any dangerous weapon being used and not done in a cruel or unusual manner.

782.04 Murder.—
(1)(a) The unlawful killing of a human being:

1. When perpetrated from a premeditated design to effect the death of the person killed or any human being;

2. When committed by a person engaged in the perpetration of, or in the attempt to perpetrate, any: [such acts as arson, robbery, burglary, etc.]; . . .

is murder in the first degree and constitutes a capital felony, ...

(2) The unlawful killing of a human being, when perpetrated by any act imminently dangerous to another and evincing a depraved mind regardless of human life, although without any premeditated design to effect the death of any particular individual, is murder in the second degree and constitutes a felony of the first degree, punishable by imprisonment for a term of years not exceeding life . . . .

782.07 Manslaughter; aggravated manslaughter of an elderly person or disabled adult; aggravated manslaughter of a child.—
(1) The killing of a human being by the act, procurement, or culpable negligence of another, without lawful justification according to the provisions of chapter 776 and in cases in which such killing shall not be excusable homicide or murder, according to the provisions of this chapter, is manslaughter, a felony of the second degree, ...

ter was evident in the punishment given to Terry Nichols, the co-conspirator in the 1995 Oklahoma City bombing. Nichols was spared the death penalty when the prosecution at his trial could not prove that the defendant had planned for the deaths of those who perished in the Alfred P. Murrah Federal Building. Nichols was acquitted of first degree murder and instead convicted of involuntary manslaughter. In a lesser known but equally demonstrative example, a judge convicted Theodore Stevens of involuntary manslaughter instead of first degree murder in the killing of Eno Bailey, his common law wife. Stevens had become convinced that Bailey was casting "evil spells" on him before he shot her in the chest, and the judge believed that this fear eliminated the intent necessary for first degree murder.[31]

Strict Liability. For certain crimes, criminal law holds the defendant to be guilty even if intent to commit the offense is lacking. These acts are known as **strict liability** crimes and generally involve endangering the public welfare in some way.[32] Drug control statutes, health and safety regulations, and traffic laws are all strict liability laws. To a certain extent, the concept of strict liability is inconsistent with the traditional principles of criminal law, which hold that *mens rea* is required for an act to be criminal. The goal of strict liability laws is to protect the public by eliminating the possibility that wrongdoers could claim ignorance or mistake to absolve themselves of criminal responsibility.[33] Thus, a person caught dumping waste in a protected pond or driving 70 miles per hour in a 55 miles-per-hour zone cannot plead a lack of intent in his or her defense.

One of the most controversial strict liability crimes is statutory rape, in which an adult engages in a sexual relationship with a minor. In most states, even if the minor consents to the sexual act, the crime still exists because being underage he or she is considered incapable of making a rational decision on the matter.[34] Therefore, statutory rape has been committed even if the adult was unaware of the minor's age or had been misled to believe that the minor was older.

STRICT LIABILITY
Certain crimes, such as traffic violations, in which the defendant is guilty regardless of her or his state of mind at the time of the act.

Concurrence

According to criminal law, there must be *concurrence* between the guilty act and the guilty intent. In other words, the guilty act and the guilty intent must occur together.[35] Suppose, for example, that a woman intends to murder her husband with poison in order to collect his life insurance. Every evening, this woman drives her husband home from work. On the night she plans to poison him, however, she swerves to avoid a cat crossing the road and runs into a tree. She survives the accident, but her husband is killed. Even though her intent was realized, the incident would be considered an accidental death because she had not planned to kill him by driving the car into a tree.

Causation

Criminal law also requires that the criminal act cause the harm suffered. In Michigan, for example, two defendants were convicted of murder even though their victim died in an unrelated basketball game several years after the initial crime.[36] In the course of that robbery, the defendants had shot the victim in the heart and abdomen and abandoned him in a sewer. Though the victim survived, his heart remained very weak. Four years later, the victim collapsed during a basketball game and died. Medical examination established that his heart failed as a direct result of the earlier injury, and the Michigan Supreme Court ruled that, despite the passing of time, the defendants' criminal act had been the cause of the man's death.[37] (It is interesting to contrast this decision with the common law rule that a victim's death must occur within a year and a day from the date of the defendant's crime.)

Attendant Circumstances

In certain crimes, attendant circumstances—also known as accompanying circumstances—are relevant to the *corpus delicti*. Most states, for example, differentiate between simple assault and the more serious offense of aggravated assault depending on whether the defendant used a weapon such as a gun or a knife while committing the crime. Criminal law also classifies degrees of property crimes based on the amount stolen. According to federal statutes, robbing a bank of less than $100 is a misdemeanor, while taking any amount over $100 results in a felony.[38]

Some states have used attendant circumstances to impose harsher penalties on hate crimes. Under Missouri's Ethnic Intimidation Law, for example, if someone commits any of a number of crimes "by reason of any motive relating to the race, color, religion, or national origin of another individual or group of individuals," she or he is guilty of the crime of "ethnic intimidation." The statute increases the penalty for certain crimes if such motives can be proved. Consequently, property damage, normally punished as a misdemeanor, is elevated to a felony when ethnic intimidation is involved.[39] Although the Supreme Court has upheld these types of laws,[40] many legal scholars believe that a court of law is ill-equipped in many cases to prove racist intent.[41]

Harm

For a crime to occur, some harm must have been done to a person or to property. A certain number of crimes are actually categorized depending on the harm done to the victim, regardless of the intent behind the criminal act. Take two offenses, both of which involve one person hitting another in the back of the head with a tire iron. In the first instance, the victim dies, and the offender is charged with murder. In the second, the victim is only knocked unconscious, and the offender is charged with battery. Because the harm in

the second instance was less severe, so was the crime with which the offender was charged, even though the act was exactly the same. Furthermore, most states have different degrees of battery depending on the extent of the injuries suffered by the victim.

Many acts are deemed criminal if they could do harm that the laws try to prevent. Such acts are called **inchoate offenses.** They exist when only an attempt at a criminal act was made. If Jenkins solicits Peterson to murder Jenkins's business partner, this is an inchoate offense on the part of Jenkins, even though Peterson fails to carry out the act. Conspiracies are also a general category of inchoate offenses.

THE LEGAL DEFINITION OF CRIME

The elements of a crime are integral to **substantive criminal law,** which is a general term that refers to the body of legislative action that defines the acts that the government will punish. In essence, substantive criminal law, in the form of penal codes, defines precisely what is illegal. The key points of most criminal laws are the *actus reus, mens rea*, attendant circumstances, and harm done to society.

Penal codes provide the framework for defining criminal acts, but they are not unchanging. Police, prosecutors, judges, and other employees of the criminal justice system must interpret the codes, and social pressures and the changing legal environment often influence these interpretations. For example, in 1998 Nushawn Williams became the first person in New York to face a felony charge of reckless endangerment on the ground that he had unprotected sex with a teenage girl months after he learned he was infected with HIV, the virus that can lead to AIDS. According to New York law:

> A person is guilty of reckless endangerment in the first degree when, under circumstances evincing a depraved indifference to human life, he recklessly engages in conduct that creates a grave risk of death to another person.[42]

The elements of reckless endangerment in New York, therefore, include engaging in conduct that creates a grave risk of death to another person (the *actus reus*) while evincing a depraved indifference to human life (the *mens rea*). The attendant circumstances are the concurrence between the guilty act and the guilty mind to create a criminal act.

The difficulty for New York prosecutors was proving that Williams was indifferent to the possibility that he was infecting his sexual partner with a deadly disease.[43] Prosecutors in other states have encountered similar problems when pressing criminal charges against HIV-infected individuals who fail to warn sexual partners that they have contracted the virus. In Maryland, officials initially succeeded in convicting Dwight Ralph Smallwood—who knew he had HIV when he raped three women—of attempted first degree murder. Maryland state law, however, holds as follows:

> All murder which shall be perpetrated by means of poison, or lying in wait, or by any kind of willful, deliberate and premeditated killing shall be murder in the first degree.[44]

Referring to this definition, a higher court overturned Smallwood's conviction. In explaining the reversal, the state judge noted that there was no medical proof that a single sexual exposure to Smallwood would necessarily result in the victim's contracting HIV. Therefore, the defendant could not have had the proper state of mind ("willful, deliberate, and premeditated") to satisfy the *mens rea* requirement for attempted murder.[45]

The concept of "harm" in criminal law does not apply only to property and violent crimes. Prostitution, for example, is illegal in almost all jurisdictions of the United States because of the perceived harm the practice causes society. This harm includes the spread of sexually transmitted diseases such as AIDS, the linkage of prostitution to illicit drug use (as many prostitutes sell their services in order to get the cash to buy drugs), and the violence done to prostitutes by customers and pimps. Under certain circumstances, however, the state of Nevada has legalized prostitution. Sweet Leif, shown above, works legally as a prostitute at the Moonlight Bunny Ranch in Carson City, Nevada. How might legalized prostitution reduce some of the social harms attributed to the practice?

Many state criminal codes are now online. To find your state's code, go to www.findlaw.com and select "State Codes."

INCHOATE OFFENSES
Conduct deemed criminal without actual harm being done, provided that the harm that would have occurred is one the law tries to prevent.

SUBSTANTIVE CRIMINAL LAW
Law that defines the rights and duties of individuals with respect to each other.

CRIMINAL RESPONSIBILITY AND THE LAW

In overturning Smallwood's conviction for attempted murder, the Maryland court was following a precedent set by the United States Supreme Court, which has held that a defendant's intent must be proved beyond a reasonable doubt.[46] The Maryland court, in essence, ruled that Smallwood could not be held responsible for a crime that he did not intend to commit. The idea of responsibility plays a significant role in criminal law. In certain circumstances, the law recognizes that a person is not responsible for wrongdoing because he or she does not meet certain mental conditions. In many jurisdictions, for example, children under a specific age are believed incapable of committing crimes because they are too young to understand the ramifications of their actions. Thus, *infancy* is an "excuse" defense, or a defense that argues that the accused's wrongdoing should be excused because he or she lacked the capacity to be held liable for the crime. Other important excuse defenses include insanity, intoxication, and mistake.

Insanity

Before Theodore J. Kaczynski, "the Unabomber," pleaded guilty to perpetrating sixteen mail-bomb attacks that left three victims dead and twenty-nine injured, his attorneys were planning to portray him as a "paranoid schizophrenic." If his defense team could have convinced a jury of Kaczynski's schizophrenia—an impaired mental state that gives rise to distortions of reality—the defendant could have been sentenced to a mental hospital rather than a prison.[47] Thus, **insanity** may be a defense to a criminal charge when the defendant's state of mind is such that she or he cannot claim legal responsibility for her or his actions.

Measuring Sanity. Although criminal law has accepted the idea that an insane person cannot be held responsible for criminal acts, society has long debated what standards should be used to measure sanity for the purposes of a criminal trial. One of the oldest tests for insanity resulted from a case in 1843 in which Daniel M'Naughten shot and killed Edward Drummond in the belief that Drummond was Sir Robert Peel, the British prime minister. At trial, M'Naughten claimed that he was suffering from delusions at the time of the murder, and he was found not guilty by reason of insanity. In response to public outcry over the decision, the British court established the **M'Naughten rule.** Also known as the right-wrong test, the *M'Naughten* rule states that a person is legally insane and therefore not criminally responsible if, at the time of the offense, he or she was not able to distinguish between right and wrong.[48]

As Figure 3.5 on the following page shows, sixteen states still use a version of the *M'Naughten* rule. Several other jurisdictions use the less restrictive **irresistible impulse test** to determine sanity. Under this test, a person may be found insane even if he or she was aware that a criminal act was wrong, providing that some "irresistible impulse" resulting from a mental deficiency drove him or her to commit the crime.[49]

Another method of determining criminal sanity—the **Durham rule**—rejects the *M'Naughten* test by focusing on the many personality factors that lead to mental instability. Under the *Durham* test, mental illness may be viewed as a permanent defect in the defendant or as a disease that can be treated. Created in New Hampshire in the nineteenth century, the *Durham* rule was adopted by the Court of Appeals for the District in Columbia in the 1954 case *Durham v. United States.*[50] Judge David Bazelon, who presided over the

INSANITY
A defense for criminal liability that asserts a lack of criminal responsibility. According to the law, a person cannot have the requisite state of mind to commit a crime if she or he did not know at the time of the act that it was wrong, or did not know the nature and quality of the act.

M'NAUGHTEN RULE
A common law test of criminal responsibility derived from *M'Naughten's case* in 1843 that relies on the defendant's inability to distinguish right from wrong.

IRRESISTIBLE IMPULSE TEST
A test for the insanity defense under which a defendant who knew his or her action was wrong may still be found insane if he or she was nonetheless unable to control the urge to complete it.

DURHAM RULE
A test of criminal responsibility adopted in a 1954 case: "an accused is not criminally responsible if his unlawful act was the product of mental disease or mental defect."

On July 24, 1998, Russell Eugene Weston, Jr., was arrested for fatally shooting Officers Jacob J. Chestnut and John M. Gibson inside the Capitol Building in Washington, D.C. A government psychologist subsequently found that Weston, who had been diagnosed as a paranoid schizophrenic, was not mentally competent to stand trial. Consequently, Weston was sent to a mental health facility to receive medical treatment until such time as he would be able to understand the charges against him. How is it in society's best interests that only mentally stable persons participate in the trial process?

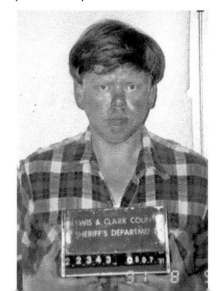

SUBSTANTIAL CAPACITY TEST
From the Model Penal Code, a test that states that a person is not responsible for criminal behavior if when committing the act "as a result of mental disease or defect he lacks substantial capacity either to appreciate the wrongfulness of his conduct or to conform his conduct to the requirements of law."

case, placed the burden on prosecutors to prove beyond a reasonable doubt that the defendant was not insane. The jury is then expected to determine whether the criminal act was the product of a mental defect or disease; for this reason the rule is referred to as the *products test.*

Today, all federal courts and nearly half the states use the **substantial capacity test** to determine sanity. Characterized as a modern improvement on the *M'Naughten* test, substantial capacity guidelines state that:

> A person is not responsible for criminal conduct if at the time of such conduct as a result of mental disease or defect he lacks substantial capacity either to appreciate the wrongfulness of his conduct or to conform his conduct to the requirements of the law.[51]

The key element of this rule is that it requires only a lack of "substantial capacity" to release a defendant from criminal responsibility. This standard is considerably easier to meet than the "right-wrong" requirements of the *M'Naughten* rule or the irresistible impulse test.

Figure 3.5 Insanity Defenses

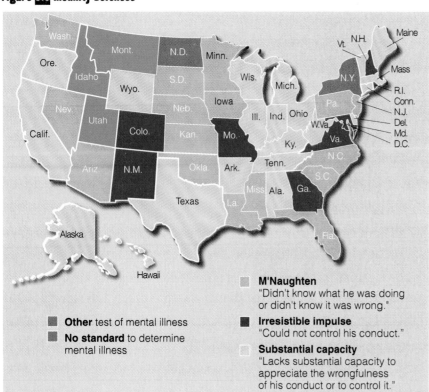

M'Naughten
"Didn't know what he was doing or didn't know it was wrong."

Other test of mental illness

No standard to determine mental illness

Irresistible impulse
"Could not control his conduct."

Substantial capacity
"Lacks substantial capacity to appreciate the wrongfulness of his conduct or to control it."

SOURCE: NATIONAL INSTITUTE OF JUSTICE, CRIME STUDY GUIDE: INSANITY DEFENSE BY NORVAL MORRIS (WASHINGTON, D.C.: U.S. DEPARTMENT OF JUSTICE, 1986), 3.

Use of the Insanity Defense. During the 1995 New Mexico legislative session, an amendment to a bill was offered to the effect that when a psychologist enters a courtroom, he or she "shall wear a cone-shaped hat that is not less than two feet tall" and the "surface of the hat shall be imprinted with stars and lightning bolts."[52] This sarcastic amendment (it did not pass) reflects the disdain with which many Americans view the insanity defense; it is seen as a method of inappropriately disguising *mens rea* as mental illness. Such perceptions are given credence by certain high-visibility cases, such as when John Hinckley was found not guilty of attempted murder of President Ronald Reagan in 1981 by reason of insanity.

In fact, the public perception is faulty. The insanity defense is rarely entered and is even less likely to result in an acquittal, as it is difficult to prove.[53] (See *CJ in Focus—Myth versus Reality: Are Too Many Criminals Found Not Guilty by Reason of Insanity?*) Psychiatry is far more commonly used in the courtroom in determining the "competency" of a defendant to stand trial. If a judge believes that the defendant is unable to understand the nature of the proceedings or to assist in his or her own defense, the trial will not take place. When competency hearings (which may also take place after the initial arrest and before sentencing) reveal that the defendant is in fact incompetent, the court may decide to place the defendant under treatment. Once competency has been restored to the defendant, the proceedings may recommence.[54]

Guilty but Mentally Ill. Partly as a response to public backlash against the insanity defense, some state legislatures have passed "guilty but mentally ill" statutes. Under these laws, a defendant is guilty but mentally ill if

CJ in Focus
Myth versus Reality
Are Too Many Criminals Found Not Guilty by Reason of Insanity?

To many Americans, it seems likely that any person who commits a gruesome murder or any other sort of violent crime has psychological problems. The question, then, is, how do we balance the need to punish such a person with the possibility that he or she may be seriously ill?

The Myth

The American system of criminal justice answers this question by stating that a person may not be tried for an offense if that person cannot be held legally responsible for her or his actions. Because of the publicity surrounding the insanity defense, many people are under the impression that it is a major loophole in our system, allowing criminals to be "let off" no matter how heinous their crimes.

The Reality

In fact, the insanity defense is raised in only about 1 percent of felony trials, and is successful only one out of every four times it is raised. The

reason: it is extremely difficult to prove insanity under the law. For example, after murdering, dismembering, and cannibalizing fifteen men in Milwaukee, Wisconsin, Jeffrey Dahmer entered a plea of not guilty by reason of insanity. There was an immediate public outcry of protest. Anyone who could do such horrible things must be insane, and many people feared that Dahmer would be acquitted. The prosecutors, however, were able to prove that Dahmer understood his actions were "wrong," and he was sentenced to fifteen consecutive life terms. Even if Dahmer had succeeded with the insanity defense, he would not have been "let off" in the sense that he would have been set free. Many defendants found not guilty by reason of insanity spend more time in mental hospitals than criminals who are convicted of similar acts spend in prison.

For Critical Analysis: What do the relatively limited use and success rate of the insanity defense indicate about the impact of public opinion on criminal law?

---

at the time of the commission of the act constituting the offense, he had the capacity to distinguish right from wrong . . . but because of mental disease or defect he lacked sufficient capacity to conform his conduct to the requirements of the law.[55]

In other words, the laws allow a jury to determine that a defendant is "mentally ill," though not insane, and therefore criminally responsible for his or her actions. Defendants found guilty but mentally ill generally spend the early years of their sentences in a psychiatric hospital and the rest of the time in prison, or they receive treatment while in prison.

Proponents of guilty but mentally ill statutes say the laws protect the public by assuring the incarceration of those who may be found not guilty by reason of insanity but still pose a threat to society.[56] Critics counter that there is virtually no difference between a guilty but mentally ill verdict and a guilty verdict, given that many "mentally ill" convicts do not receive any treatment while incarcerated. The real purpose of the laws, they say, is to provide an alternative for jurors who feel that a defendant is legally insane but would like to see her or him punished anyway.[57] Indeed, juries have embraced these statutes; between 1992 and 1997 in South Carolina, 161 persons were convicted and sentenced under the state's guilty but mentally ill law.[58]

Intoxication

The law recognizes two types of **intoxication**, whether from drugs or from alcohol: *voluntary* and *involuntary*. Involuntary intoxication occurs when a person is physically forced to ingest or is injected with an intoxicating substance, or is unaware that a substance contains drugs or alcohol. Involuntary intoxication is a viable defense to a crime if the substance leaves the person unable to form the mental state necessary to understand that the act com-

INFOTRAC®
COLLEGE EDITION

What does it take to be crazy?

INTOXICATION
A defense for criminal liability in which the defendant claims that the taking of intoxicants rendered him or her unable to form the requisite intent to commit a criminal act.

mitted while under the influence was wrong.[59] In Colorado, for example, the murder conviction of a man who shot a neighbor was overturned on the basis that the jury in the initial trial was not informed of the possibility of involuntary intoxication. At the time of the crime, the man had been taking a prescription decongestant that contained phenylpropanolamine, which has been known to cause psychotic episodes.[60]

Voluntary drug or alcohol intoxication is also used to excuse a defendant's actions, though it is not a defense in itself. Rather, it is used when the defense attorney wants to show that the defendant was so intoxicated that *mens rea* was negated. In other words, the defendant could not possibly have had the state of mind that a crime requires. Many courts are reluctant to allow voluntary intoxication arguments to be presented to juries, however. After all, the defendant, by definition, voluntarily chose to enter an intoxicated state.

Twelve states have eliminated voluntary intoxication as a possible defense, a step that has been criticized by many legal scholars but was upheld by the Supreme Court in *Montana v. Egelhoff* (1996).[61] The case concerned a double murder committed by James Allen Egelhoff, who was extremely drunk at the time of the crime. Egelhoff was convicted on two counts of deliberate homicide, which is defined by Montana law as "knowingly" or "purposefully" causing the death of another human being.[62] Egelhoff appealed his conviction, arguing that the state statute prohibiting evidence of voluntary intoxication kept his attorneys from showing the jury that he was too inebriated to "knowingly" or "purposefully" commit the murders.[63] The Court allowed Egelhoff's conviction, ruling that states were constitutionally within their rights to abolish the voluntary intoxication defense.

Mistake

Everyone has heard the saying, "Ignorance of the law is no excuse." Ordinarily, ignorance of the law or a *mistaken idea* about what the law requires is not a valid defense.[64] In 1998, for example, Gilbert A. Robinson appealed his conviction for possession of sexually explicit photographs of teenage boys, claiming he did not know that such an act had become illegal. Chief Judge Juan R. Torruella del Valle upheld Robinson's conviction, stating that child pornography is "inherently deleterious" and that the "probability of regulation is so great that anyone who is aware that he is in possession of [it] . . . must be presumed to be aware of the regulation."[65]

In some states, however, that rule has been modified. People who claim that they honestly did not know that they were breaking a law may have a valid defense if (1) the law was not published or reasonably known to the public or (2) the person relied on an official statement of the law that was erroneous.[66]

A *mistake of fact,* as opposed to a *mistake of law,* operates as a defense if it negates the mental state necessary to commit a crime. If, for example, Oliver mistakenly walks off with Julie's briefcase because he thinks it is his, there is no theft. Theft requires knowledge that the property belongs to another.

JUSTIFICATION CRIMINAL DEFENSES AND THE LAW

In certain instances, a defendant will accept responsibility for committing an illegal act, but contend that—given the circumstances—the act was justified. In other words, even though the guilty act and the guilty intent are present, the particulars of the case relieve the defendant of criminal liability. Four of the most important justification defenses are duress, self-defense, necessity, and entrapment.

Duress

Duress exists when the *wrongful* threat of one person induces another person to perform an act that she or he would otherwise not perform. In such a situation, duress is said to negate the *mens rea* necessary to commit a crime. For duress to qualify as a defense, the following requirements must be met:

1. The threat must be of serious bodily harm or death.

2. The harm threatened must be greater than the harm caused by the crime.

3. The threat must be immediate and inescapable.

4. The defendant must have been involved in the situation through no fault of his or her own.[67]

When ruling on the duress defense, courts often examine whether the defendant had the opportunity to avoid the threat in question. Two narcotics cases illustrate this point. In the first, the defendant claimed that an associate threatened to kill him and his wife unless he participated in a marijuana deal. Although this contention was proved true during the course of the trial, the court rejected the duress defense because the defendant made no apparent effort to escape, nor did he report his dilemma to the police. In sum, the drug deal was avoidable—the defendant could have made an effort to extricate himself, but he did not, therefore surrendering the protection of the duress defense.[68]

In the second case, a taxi driver in Bogotá, Colombia, was ordered by a passenger to swallow cocaine-filled balloons and take them to the United States. The taxi driver was warned that if he refused, his wife and three-year-old daughter would be killed. After a series of similar threats, the taxi driver agreed to transport the drugs. Upon arriving at customs at the Los Angeles airport, the defendant consented to have his stomach X-rayed, which led to discovery of the contraband and his arrest. During trial, the defendant told the court that he was afraid to notify the police in Colombia because he believed them to be corrupt. The court accepted his duress defense, on the grounds that it met the four requirements listed above and the defendant had notified American authorities when given the opportunity to do so.[69]

Justifiable Use of Force—Self-Defense

A person who believes he or she is in danger of being harmed by another is justified in defending him- or herself with the use of force, and any criminal act committed in such circumstances can be justified as **self-defense.** Other situations that also justify the use of force include the defense of one's dwelling, the defense of other property, and the prevention of a crime. In all these situations, it is important to distinguish between deadly and nondeadly force. Deadly force is likely to result in death or serious bodily harm.

Generally speaking, people can use the amount of nondeadly force that seems necessary to protect themselves, their dwellings, or other property or to prevent the commission of a crime. Deadly force can be used in self-defense if there is a *reasonable belief* that imminent death or bodily harm will otherwise result, if the attacker is using unlawful force (an example of lawful force is that exerted by a police officer), and if the defender has not initiated or provoked the attack.[70] In the past several years, for example, a number of states have enacted so-called battered women self-defense

DURESS
Unlawful pressure brought to bear upon a person, causing the person to perform an act that he or she would not otherwise perform.

SELF-DEFENSE
The legally recognized privilege to protect one's self or property by injury by another. The privilege of self-defense protects only acts that are reasonably necessary to protect one's self or property.

On November 25, 1998, Teresa Gaethe-Leonard was sentenced to thirty years in prison for the murder of her husband. Gaethe-Leonard's defense attorney failed in his attempt to show that his client was rendered temporarily insane by seeing her husband abusing their daughter. Gaethe-Leonard's attorney had planned to introduce evidence that his client was the victim of abuse herself and therefore was suffering from battered woman syndrome. Snohomish (Washington) County Superior Court Judge Gerald Knight refused, however, to allow testimony that Gaethe-Leonard might be suffering from the syndrome. He threatened to declare a mistrial if the subject was even mentioned. Do you agree with the judge's actions? Why or why not?

NECESSITY
A defense against criminal liability in which the defendant asserts that circumstances required her or him to commit an illegal act.

ENTRAPMENT
A defense in which the defendant claims that he or she was induced by a public official—usually an undercover agent or police officer—to commit a crime that he or she would otherwise not have committed.

statutes. These laws allow defendants charged with murder or manslaughter to present evidence that they had been the victims of repeated acts of violence by the deceased. This evidence may then be used to establish that any violent action taken by the woman against her abuser was done in self-defense.[71] In contrast, deadly force normally can be used to defend a dwelling only if the unlawful entry is violent and the person believes deadly force is necessary to prevent imminent death or great bodily harm or—in some jurisdictions—if the person believes deadly force is necessary to prevent the commission of a felony (such as arson) in the dwelling.

One of the best-known examples of justifiable self-defense occurred in 1984 when Bernhard Goetz, a thirty-seven-year-old businessman, shot four African American teenagers on a New York subway train after they asked him for $5. The focus of the subsequent trial was not whether the youths had used deadly force to threaten Goetz, but whether the defendant had a reason to believe that they were going to use deadly force. Goetz was eventually indicted and tried but not convicted of attempted murder and assault (though he was sentenced to one year in jail for an illegal weapons possession charge).

Necessity

In the case of Theodore Kaczynski referred to earlier, although his attorneys wanted him to plead not guilty by reason of insanity, Kaczynski himself wanted to raise a necessity defense. That is, he wanted to argue that the harm he did to his victims was justified as part of his campaign against the evils of technology.[72] Defendants charged with murdering physicians who perform abortions have used a similar defense—that their actions were necessary to avoid the greater evil of abortion.[73]

Though the **necessity** defense is unlikely to be accepted in such situations as these, it is a valid defense under other circumstances. According to the Model Penal Code, the necessity defense is justifiable if "the harm or evil sought to be avoided by such conduct is greater than that sought to be prevented by the law defining the offense charged."[74] For example, in one case a convicted felon was threatened by an acquaintance with a gun. The felon grabbed the gun and fled the scene, but subsequently he was arrested under a statute that prohibits convicted felons from possessing firearms. In this situation, the necessity defense was viable because the defendant's crime avoided a "greater evil."[75] The one crime for which the necessity defense is not viable is murder.[76] (For a classic case in which the necessity defense was offered for homicide, see *Landmark Cases*—Regina v. Dudley and Stephens.)

Entrapment

Entrapment is a justification defense that criminal law allows when a police officer or government agent deceives a defendant into wrongdoing. Although law enforcement agents can legitimately use various forms of subterfuge—such as informants or undercover agents—to gain information or apprehend a suspect in a criminal act, the law places limits on these strategies. Police cannot persuade an innocent person to commit a crime, nor can they coerce a suspect into doing so, even if they are certain she or he is in fact a criminal.

The guidelines for determining entrapment were established in the 1932 case of *Sorrells v. United States*.[77] The case, which took place during Prohibition when the sale of alcoholic beverages was illegal, involved a federal prohibition agent who repeatedly urged the defendant to sell him bootleg whiskey. The defendant initially rejected the agent's overtures, stating that he "did not fool with whiskey." Eventually, however, he sold the agent a half-gallon of the substance and was summarily convicted of violating the law. The Supreme

CJ in Focus
Landmark Cases
Regina v. Dudley and Stephens

Three sailors and a cabin boy were forced onto a lifeboat after their ship sank. After nearly three weeks on the open seas, they ran out of food and water, and the cabin boy was seriously ill and near death. Two of the men, Dudley and Stephens, killed the cabin boy and ate his flesh in order to survive. Four days later, the three survivors were rescued. Dudley and Stephens were prosecuted for murdering the cabin boy and raised a necessity defense. A British court found that even though the cabin boy would likely have died of natural causes, the killing was not justified.

Regina v. Dudley and Stephens
Queen's Bench Division
14 Q.B.D. 173 (1884)

In the Words of the Court . . .

LORD COLERIDGE, C.J. [chief justice]

* * * *

There remains to be considered the real question in the case whether killing under the circumstances set forth in the verdict be or be not murder. The contention that it could be anything else was, to the minds of us all, both new and strange, and we stopped the Attorney General in his negative argument in order that we might hear what could be said in Support of a proposition which appeared to us to be at once dangerous, immoral, and [opposed] to all legal principle and analogy. * * *

* * * *

Is there, then, any authority for the proposition which has been presented to us? Decided cases there are none. * * * The American case, * * * in which it was decided, correctly indeed, that sailors had no right to throw passengers overboard to save themselves, but on the somewhat strange ground that the proper mode of determining who was to be sacrificed was to vote upon the subject by ballot, can hardly * * * be an authority satisfactory to a court in this country. * * *

* * * *

Now it is admitted that the deliberate killing of this unoffending, and unresisting boy was clearly murder, unless the killing can be justified by some well-recognised, excuse admitted by the law. It is further admitted that there was in this case no such excuse, unless the killing was justified by what has been called "necessity." But the temptation to the act which existed here was not what the law has ever called necessity. Nor is this to be regretted. Though law and morality are not the same, and many things may be immoral which are not necessarily illegal, yet the absolute divorce of law from morality would be of fatal consequence; and such divorce would follow if the temptation to murder in this case were to be held by law an absolute defence of it. It is not so. To preserve one's life is generally speaking a duty, but it may be the plainest and the highest duty, to sacrifice it.

Decision: The court sentenced the two prisoners to death. The Crown later commuted the sentence to six months' imprisonment.

For Critical Analysis: Are there ever any circumstances under which sacrificing one person for the good of others is justified?

Note: Triple asterisks (* * *) indicate a few words or sentences have been deleted and quadruple asterisks (* * * *) indicate that an entire paragraph (or more) has been omitted from the opinion.

Court held that the agent had improperly induced the defendant to break the law and reversed his conviction.

In *Sorrells*, the Supreme Court set the precedent for taking a "subjective" view of entrapment. In other words, the Court decided that entrapment occurs if a defendant who is not predisposed to commit a crime is enticed to do so by an agent of the government.[78] In the 1992 case of *Jacobson v. United States*,[79] for example, the United States Postal Inspection Service targeted the defendant as a potential purchaser of child pornography. Over a period of more than two years, postal agents sent the defendant seven letters inquiring about his sexual preferences, two sex catalogues, and two sexual attitude surveys, all from fictitious persons and organizations. Eventually, the defendant ordered a publication called "Boys Who Love Boys," and was arrested and convicted for breaking child pornography laws.[80] The Court overturned the conviction, ruling that entrapment had taken place because the defendant had shown no predisposition to order the illicit publication in the absence of the government's efforts. (For an overview of justification and excuse defenses, see Figure 3.6 on the following page.)

Figure 3.6 Justification and Excuse Defenses

<u>Justification Defenses:</u> Based on a defendant admitting that he or she committed the particular criminal act, but asserting that, under the circumstances, the criminal act was justified.

1. Duress

The Defendant Must Prove That: He or she performed the criminal act under the use or threat of use of unlawful force against his or her person that a reasonable person would have been unable to resist.

Situation in Which the Defense Has Been Offered: A mother assists her boyfriend in committing a burglary after he threatens to kill her children if she refuses to do so.

2. Self-Defense

The Defendant Must Prove That: He or she acted in a manner to defend himself or herself, others, or property, or to prevent the commission of a crime.

Situation in Which the Defense Has Been Offered: A husband awakes to find his wife standing over him, pointing a shotgun at his chest. In the ensuing struggle, the firearm goes off, killing the wife.

3. Necessity

The Defendant Must Prove That: The criminal act he or she committed was necessary in order to avoid a harm to himself or herself or another that was greater than the harm caused by the act itself.

Situation in Which the Defense Has Been Attempted: Four people physically remove a friend from her residence on the property of a religious cult, arguing that the crime of kidnapping was justified in order to remove the victim from the damaging influence of cult leaders.

4. Entrapment

The Defendant Must Prove That: She or he was encouraged by agents of the state to engage in a criminal act she or he would not have engaged in otherwise.

Situation in Which the Defense Has Been Attempted: The owner of a boat marina agrees to allow three federal drug enforcement agents, posing as drug dealers, to use his dock to unload shipments of marijuana from Colombia.

<u>Excuse Defenses:</u> Based on a defendant admitting that she or he committed the criminal act, but asserting that she or he cannot be held criminally responsible for the act due to lack of criminal intent.

1. Age

The Defendant Must Prove That: Because he or she was under a statutorily determined age, he or she did not have the maturity to make the decisions necessary to commit a criminal act.

Situation in Which the Defense Has Been Attempted: A fourteen-year-old takes a handgun from his backpack at school and begins shooting at fellow students, killing three. (In such cases, the offender is often processed by the juvenile justice system rather than the criminal justice system.)

2. Insanity

The Defendant Must Prove That: At the time of the criminal act, he or she did not have the necessary mental capacity to be held responsible for his or her actions.

Situation in Which the Defense Has Been Attempted: A man with a history of mental illness pushes a woman in front of an oncoming subway train, which kills her instantly.

3. Intoxication

The Defendant Must Prove That: She or he had diminished control over her or his actions due to the influence of alcohol or drugs.

Situation in Which the Defense Has Been Attempted: A woman who had been drinking malt liquor and vodka stabs her boyfriend to death after a domestic argument. She claims to have been so drunk as to not remember the incident.

4. Mistake

The Defendant Must Prove That: He or she did not know that his or her actions violated a law (this defense is very rarely even attempted), or that he or she violated the law believing a relevant fact to be true when, in fact, it was not.

Situation in Which the Defense Has Been Attempted: A woman, thinking that her divorce in another state has been finalized when it was not, marries for a second time, placing herself in a situation in which she has committed bigamy.

PROCEDURAL SAFEGUARDS

To this point, we have focused on the substantive aspects of criminal law. We will now turn our attention to **procedural criminal law.** In the section that follows, you will be given only a short overview of criminal procedure. In later chapters, many other constitutional issues will be examined in more detail. Criminal law brings the force of the state, with all its resources, to bear against the individual. Criminal procedures, drawn from the ideals stated in the Bill of Rights, are designed to protect the constitutional rights of individuals and to prevent the arbitrary use of power by the government (see Figure 3.7).

The Bill of Rights

For various reasons, proposals related to the rights of individuals were rejected during the framing of the U.S. Constitution in 1787. Yet the importance of a written declaration of rights of individuals eventually caused the first Congress to draft ten amendments to the Constitution and submit them

PROCEDURAL CRIMINAL LAW
Rules that define the manner in which the rights and duties of individuals may be enforced.

for approval by the states. These amendments, commonly known as the **Bill of Rights**, were adopted in 1791. Since then, seventeen more amendments have been added.

The Bill of Rights, as interpreted by the United States Supreme Court, has served as the basis for procedural safeguards of the accused in this country. These safeguards include the following:

1. The Fourth Amendment protection from unreasonable searches and seizures.

2. The Fourth Amendment requirement that no warrants for a search or an arrest can be issued without probable cause.

3. The Fifth Amendment requirement that no one can be deprived of life, liberty, or property without the "due process" of law.

4. The Fifth Amendment prohibition against *double jeopardy* (trying someone twice for the same criminal offense).

5. The Fifth Amendment guarantee that no person can be required to be a witness against (incriminate) him- or herself.

6. The Sixth Amendment guarantees of a speedy trial, a trial by jury, a public trial, the right to confront witnesses, and the right to a lawyer at various stages of criminal proceedings.

7. The Eighth Amendment prohibitions against excessive bails and fines and cruel and unusual punishments.

The Bill of Rights offered citizens protection only against the federal government. Over the years, the procedural safeguards of most of the provisions of the Bill of Rights have been incorporated into the protections afforded by the Fourteenth Amendment. (And the states are free to grant even more protection than is required by the federal Constitution.) As these protections are crucial to criminal justice procedures in the United States, they will be afforded much more attention in Chapter 6, with regard to police action, and in Chapter 10, with regard to the criminal trial.

Due Process

Both the Fifth and the Fourteenth Amendments provide that no person should be deprived of "life, liberty, or property without the due process of law." This **due process clause** basically requires that any government decisions taken in the course of prosecuting a person be made fairly. For example, fair procedures must be used in determining whether a person will be subjected to punishment or have some burden imposed upon her or him. Fair procedure has been interpreted as requiring that the person have at least an opportunity to object to a proposed action before a fair, neutral decision maker (which need not be a judge). In the feature *Criminal Justice in Action—*

BILL OF RIGHTS
The first ten amendments to the U.S. Constitution.

DUE PROCESS CLAUSE
The provisions of the Fifth and Fourteenth Amendments to the Constitution that guarantee that no person shall be deprived of life, liberty, or property without due process of law. Similar clauses are found in most state constitutions.

Article I, Section 9, clause 2

The privilege of the Writ of Habeas Corpus shall not be suspended,. . .

Article I, Section 9, clause 3

No Bill of Attainder or ex post facto Law shall be passed.

Article III Section 2, clause 3

The Trial of all Crimes, . . . , shall be by Jury; and such crimes shall be held in the State where the said Crimes shall have been committed; . . .

Figure 3.7 Provisions in the Unamended United States Constitution Pertaining to Criminal Procedure

On August 7, 1998, United States embassies in the African countries of Kenya and Tanzania were the target of terrorist bombings. The blast outside the U.S. Embassy in Nairobi, pictured here, killed 213 people and injured more than 5,000, while the attack in Dar es Salaam, Tanzania, was responsible for eleven deaths. In the wake of such blatant and horrifying examples of anti-American terrorism, citizens may be willing to accept a reduction in procedural protections of their civil liberties. Recent U.S. laws geared towards fighting domestic terrorism have spurred debate over the need to curtail due process, privacy rights, and freedom from unreasonable search and seizure in the face of this threat. Do you feel that we, as a nation, would be justified in limiting the procedural safeguards discussed in this section in order to combat terrorism?

Terrorism and American Criminal Law at the end of this chapter, we examine issues of due process with regard to domestic terrorism.

The Supreme Court's Role in Due Process. The due process clause has played a defining role in the restrictions that the Supreme Court has placed on the criminal justice system in the past century. In 1936, for example, the Court ruled that a criminal confession gained through brutality was not admissible under the Fourteenth Amendment.[81] Nearly thirty years later in 1963, in *Gideon v. Wainwright*,[82] the Court held that due process requires the government to provide defendants who cannot afford to hire a defense lawyer with counsel in all felony trials, later extended to all trials resulting in a sentence of incarceration. (See Figure 3.8 for a list of important Supreme Court due process cases.)

Changes in Due Process. Some observers feel that recent due process decisions have eroded the rights of the accused. For example, two recent rulings involving the search and seizure of suspicious vehicles are seen as evidence of the Supreme Court's weakening of Fourth Amendment protections. In *Whren et al. v. United States* (1996), [83] the Court held that a police officer could stop an automobile for a traffic violation even if the officer's ultimate

Year	Issue	Amendment Involved	Court Case
1948	Right to a public trial	VI	*In re Oliver*, 333 U.S. 257
1949	No unreasonable searches and seizures	IV	*Wolf v. Colorado*, 338 U.S. 25
1961	Exclusionary rule	IV	*Mapp v. Ohio*, 367 U.S. 643
1963	Right to a lawyer in all criminal felony cases	VI	*Gideon v. Wainwright*, 372 U.S. 335
1964	No compulsory self-incrimination	V	*Malloy v. Hogan*, 378 U.S. 1
1964	Right to have counsel when taken into police custody and subject to questioning	VI	*Escobedo v. Illinois*, 378 U.S. 478
1965	Right to confront and cross-examine witnesses	VI	*Pointer v. Texas*, 379 U.S. 911
1966	Right to an impartial jury	VI	*Parker v. Gladden*, 385 U.S. 363
1966	Confessions of suspects not notified of due process rights ruled invalid	V	*Miranda v. Arizona*, 384 U.S. 436
1967	Right to a speedy trial	VI	*Klopfer v. North Carolina*, 386 U.S. 213
1967	Juveniles have due process rights, too	V	*In re Gault*, 387 U.S. 1
1968	Right to a jury trial ruled a fundamental right	VI	*Duncan v. Louisiana*, 391 U.S. 145
1969	No double jeopardy	V	*Benton v. Maryland*, 395 U.S. 784

Figure 3.8 Important United States Supreme Court Due Process Decisions

intent was to search the car for drugs. A year later, in *Maryland v. Wilson* (1997),[84] the Court ruled that an officer could order passengers, as well as the driver, out of the car during traffic stops without requiring either probable cause or reasonable suspicion. Critics of these decisions believe that the Court has severely damaged due process by giving the police too much power to stop automobiles and search their contents.[85]

Criminal Justice in Action

Terrorism and American Criminal Law

One of the strengths of both the substantive and the procedural aspects of American criminal law is that they are not set in stone. Through the efforts of judges, legislators, and criminal justice officials, the legal definition of crimes and the procedural steps needed to prevent crimes change according to the needs of society. Recently, substantive criminal law and procedural criminal law have been influenced by the American public's need to be protected from terrorism, which can be defined as "acts of violence committed against innocent persons or noncombatants that are intended to achieve political ends through fear and intimidation."[86]

New laws have been passed to counter terrorist acts, and new procedures have been established to carry out those laws. As we show below, these changes have not been universally welcomed. The problem with terrorism is that the enemy is difficult to apprehend and terrorist acts are difficult to predict. In response, to combat the terrorist threat, governments often feel pressure to take steps that curtail civil liberties (such as due process, freedom from unreasonable search and seizure, and privacy rights). Although generally accepted in other regions of the world, these steps have caused a great deal of consternation in the United States.

TERRORISM: REAL AND IMAGINED

In late February 1998, Larry Wayne Harris and William Levitt, Jr., were arrested outside Las Vegas, Nevada, by the Federal Bureau of Investigation (FBI) for possession of what was thought to be weapons-grade anthrax. A single particle of anthrax, a biological toxin that can be spread in dustlike form, can kill a human being. Local television programming around the country was interrupted for updates on Harris and Levitt—especially in New York City, which had been identified as the target of the anthrax. It seemed to many Americans that the nightmare of biological terrorism had almost come to pass.

Within days, the story evaporated. A false alarm. But Americans can hardly be blamed for their reaction. Weeks earlier, the United States was on the brink of war with Iraq over that country's refusal to allow inspections of its biological weapons industry. The past five years had seen a number of high-visibility terrorist attacks on American soil. In 1993, a bomb in a van exploded underneath the World Trade Center in New York City, killing seven and injuring more than a thousand. Two years later, a truck bomb destroyed the federal building in Oklahoma City, killing 168 and wounding over 600. In 1996, a pipe bomb exploded during Olympic festivities in Atlanta, leaving one person dead and 111 injured.

Lawmakers reacted swiftly to public fear of terrorist attack, passing laws designed to aid law enforcement agencies in their efforts to combat terrorism. The question is, have these laws gone too far?

THE ANTI-TERRORISM ACT

Almost exactly a year after the Oklahoma City bombing, President Bill Clinton signed the Anti-Terrorism and Effective Death Penalty Act of 1996[87] into law. The act included provisions to:

1. Allow victims of terrorism to sue countries sponsoring terrorism.

2. Establish the "removal court," a special court that would oversee deportation of aliens—foreign-born persons who have not qualified as citizens of the United States—suspected of terrorist activities. This court has the power to hear evidence against the suspected person without notifying or making the evidence available to that person.

3. Give immigration authorities increased power to deport aliens convicted of any crime.

4. Forbid fund-raising activities in the United States by foreign groups identified by the federal government as engaged in terrorist activity.[88]

The Clinton administration had wanted even more expansive powers, such as giving federal agents an increased ability to "bug" suspected terrorists through wiretaps and hidden microphones.

TACTICS IN ENGLAND AND FRANCE

Even with the new law, the United States does not go as far in fighting terrorism as some other Western countries do: In Great Britain, a person suspected of terrorist activity can be taken to jail and held for two days without being charged. Police in France do not have to inform arrestees of the charges against them either, and they have extensive "bugging" leeway, including the right to wiretap all of the pay phones in the neighborhood of a suspected terrorist.[89]

Such tactics are counter to the ideals of due process inherent in the United States Constitution. The Fourth Amendment protects Americans against unreasonable seizures, while the Sixth Amendment gives them the right to know the charges brought against them. Privacy protections require that law enforcement agents who want to wiretap a suspect obtain permission from a judge. Some observers feel, however, that Americans may have to give up some of these rights in the fight against terrorism. "I think that once people understand what's happening, that after the [World Trade Center bombing], Oklahoma City, and . . . Atlanta, terrorism has arrived," says a security expert from Israel.[90]

"LITTLE TO DO WITH FIGHTING TERRORISM"

Others dispute the value of tough new laws. "This bill has little to do with fighting terrorism," said Georgetown University law professor David Cole of the 1996 Anti-Terrorism Act, "and much to do with taking freedoms from citizens and aliens." Cole and many of his colleagues are particularly dismayed by the "removal court" and its infringement of alien rights. (Even though aliens are not citizens of the United States, they are guaranteed due process by the Fourteenth Amendment.[91]) "For the first time in 200 years, secret evidence will be allowed in a U.S. court," Cole said. "It is impossible to challenge or refute evidence you cannot see."[92] Furthermore, under the new law long-time legal resident aliens can be deported for minor misdemeanors. For example, Refugion Rubio, who had lived in the United States for thirty-four years, was tagged for deportation to his native Mexico because of a 1972 conviction of possession with intent to distribute marijuana.[93]

Considering that only one terrorist act on American soil since 1985 has been proved to have been committed by an alien, critics see these laws as motivated by political rather than security goals.[94] To make this point, they highlight the provision of the 1996 act that allows Americans to sue foreign countries that "sponsor" terrorism. Since American courts have no jurisdiction in foreign countries, it is virtually impossible to force them to pay any damages. For example, in 1998 a district judge in Washington, D.C., ordered Iran to pay $247.5 million to the family of Alisa Flatow, who had been killed three years earlier during a suicide bombing by a militant Palestinian in Israel. The Iranian government called the allegations unfounded and refused to pay.[95]

DANGERS IN THE FUTURE

The majority of Americans are unaffected by anti-terrorism laws, save for having to spend a few more minutes before an airline flight showing identification and having their luggage checked. If, however, the pattern of terrorism in the United States continues, the nation may have to decide whether to sacrifice some measure of due process, as has been done in Britain and France. There are signs that this decision may have to be made sooner rather than later. Even though the Las Vegas anthrax scare was unfounded, chemical weapons and biological toxins are far easier to produce and transport than traditional bombs or other weapons. A situation similar to the sarin nerve gas attack in the Tokyo, Japan, subway system, which killed ten commuters and left nearly five thousand ill in 1995, could be duplicated rather easily in the United States.[96] Such an incident would further complicate the criminal law's complex relationship with terrorism in this country.

INFOTRAC®
COLLEGE EDITION

Armed rebels are nothing new

Key Terms

Chapter Summary

1. **Explain precedent and the importance of the doctrine of *stare decisis*.** Precedent is a common law concept in which one decision becomes the example or authority for deciding future cases with similar facts. Under the doctrine of *stare decisis*, judges in a particular jurisdiction are bound to follow precedents of that same jurisdiction. The doctrine of *stare decisis* leads to efficiency in the judicial system.

2. **List the four written sources of American criminal law.** (a) The U.S. Constitution and state constitutions; (b) statutes passed by Congress and state legislatures (plus local ordinances); (c) administrative agency regulations; and (d) case law.

3. **Explain the two basic functions of criminal law.** The primary function is to protect citizens from harms to their safety and property and from harms to society's interest collectively. The second function is to maintain and teach social values as well as social boundaries, for example, laws against bigamy and speed limits.

4. **List and explain the six basic elements of any crime.** (a) The *actus reus,* or the guilty act; (b) the *mens rea,* or the proof of guilty intent by the alleged criminal; (c) a concurrence of act and intent; (d) a link between the act and the crime; (e) any attendant circumstances; and (f) the existence of harm done, or the result of a criminal act.

5. **Delineate the elements required to establish *mens rea* (a guilty mental state).** (a) Purpose, (b) knowledge, (c) negligence, or (d) recklessness.

6. **Explain how the doctrine of strict liability applies to criminal law.** Strict liability crimes are ones that do not allow the alleged wrongdoer to claim ignorance or mistake to avoid criminal responsibility, for example, exceeding the speed limit and statutory rape.

7. **List and briefly define the most important excuse defenses for crimes. Insanity**—different tests of insanity can be used including (a) the *M'Naughten* rule (right-wrong test); (b) the irresistible impulse test; (c) the *Durham* rule, also called the products test—where the criminal act was the product of a mental defect or disease; and (d) the substantial capacity test. **Intoxication**—voluntary and involuntary, the latter being a possible criminal defense. **Mistake**—sometimes valid if the law was not published or reasonably known or if the alleged offender relied on an official statement of the law that was erroneous. Also, a mistake of fact may negate the mental state necessary to commit a crime.

8. **Describe the four most important justification criminal defenses. Duress**—requires that (a) the threat is of serious bodily harm or death, (b) the harm is greater than that caused by the crime; (c) the threat is immediate and inescapable; and (d) the defendant became involved in the situation through no fault of his or her own. **Justifiable use of force**—the defense of one's person, dwelling, or property, or the prevention of a crime. **Necessity**—justifiable if the harm sought to be avoided is greater than that sought to be prevented by the law defining the offense charged. **Entrapment**—if the criminal action was induced by certain governmental persuasion or trickery.

9. **Distinguish between substantive and procedural criminal law.** The former concerns questions about what acts are actually criminal. The latter concerns procedures designed to protect the constitutional rights of individuals and to prevent the arbitrary use of power by the government.

10. **Determine where Americans find most of their criminal procedural safeguards.** Basic safeguards for the accused are found in the Bill of Rights, for example, Fourth Amendment protections from unreasonable searches and seizures, as well as the requirements that no warrants for a search or an arrest can be issued without probable cause, and the Fifth Amendment's due process requirement, prohibition against double jeopardy, and rule against self incrimination.

Questions for Critical Analysis

1. Why is the common law said to be uncodified?

2. Give an example of how the criminal justice system teaches societal boundaries.

3. Give an example of how the same person could be involved in a civil lawsuit and a criminal lawsuit for the same action.

4. What is the difficulty in defining which criminal acts are *mala in se*?

5. Many people are careless. At what point can such carelessness be deemed criminal negligence?

6. Assume you are planning to pay someone to set fire to an old barn (arson) for the insurance money. Before you get a chance to carry out your plan, you accidentally drop a tool on another metal object, creating a spark that ignites some dry hay and burns the barn down. What essential element of a crime is missing in your actions?

7. Why are accompanying, or attendant, circumstances sometimes important to alleged perpetrators of certain acts?

8. What is the most often used test for insanity, and how does it differ from the other tests?

9. Under what circumstances is the use of deadly force a justified criminal defense?

10. What trade-offs are involved in fighting terrorism?

Selected Print and Electronic Resources

SUGGESTED READINGS

Dershowitz, Alan M., *The Advocate's Devil*, New York: Warner Books, Mass Market Paperbacks, 1995. This is a work of fiction written by a well-known criminal law professor at Harvard Law School. It deals with the dilemma faced by a defense attorney who believes that his client is guilty.

Robinson, O. S., *The Criminal Law of Ancient Rome*, Baltimore: Johns Hopkins University Press, 1996. Would you like to find out how the ancient Romans dealt with muggings on the street, theft at the public bath, and assassination plots? Then read this excellent overview of criminal law in ancient Rome. The author also shows how Rome dealt with violent crimes and offenses against the public order.

Schopp, Robert F., *Justification Defenses and Just Convictions*, Cambridge, England: Cambridge University Press, 1998. The author interprets the different criminal justification defenses in such a way that he concludes that they are an integral part of the structure of criminal law. He examines both the legal and the philosophical ramifications of justification defenses.

Shute, Stephen, et al., eds., *Actions and Value in Criminal Law*, New York: Oxford University Press, 1996. This is a collection of specially commissioned essays written by leading philosophers and criminal lawyers from the United States, Britain, and Canada. The authors examine moral associations and look at luck, mistake, and mental illness in the context of criminal law.

MEDIA RESOURCES

***Anatomy of a Murder* (1959).** Based on a novel written by Judge John D. Voelker (writing under an assumed name), this courtroom drama was one of the more controversial films of its era. James Stewart received an Academy Award nomination for his portrayal of Paul Biegler, a down-on-his-luck attorney who accepts the case of Lt. Frederick Manion (Ben Gazzara). Lt. Manion has admitted to the murder of a local bar owner, claiming that the victim had raped his wife (Lee Remick). The film goes into great detail exploring the process of the trial—including the use of words such as "semen" and "panties" for the first time in mainstream American film—and virtually invented the "last minute revelation" as a cinematic device.

Critically analyze this film:

1. Biegler relies on the "irresistible impulse" theory to defend his clients action. Which of the various defense strategies discussed in this chapter most closely matches this concept of the "irresistible impulse?"

2. Does the "irresistible impulse" defense meet the legal criteria for a justification or excuse defense? Explain your answer.

3. How does the testimony provided by the various witnesses and experts suppport or reject the defense strategy?

4. Describe the relationship between Biegler, the prosecutor (played by George C. Scott), and the judge (Joseph Welch). Do they seem driven by a desire to see "justice" done?

5. Is the end of the trial realistic? Why might it not be feasible in real life.

Without Due Process by J. A. Jance, is an audiocassette, produced by Books in Motion, that presents views on due process.

Logging On

You can find a very concise summary of criminal law at the West Group's West Legal Directory Web site. Go to:

www.wld.com/conbus/weal/ wcrmlaw1.htm

At the same Web site, you can also find a great summary of the constitutional due process issue. Go to:

www.wld.com/conbus/weal/ wdueproc.htm

If you'd like to see a typical criminal law checklist of what's important in this subject, go to:

www.law.ucla.edu/Student/Outlines/crimout.html

Using the internet for Criminal Justice Analysis

INFOTRAC®
COLLEGE EDITION

1. Go to InfoTrac College Edition at **www.infotrac-college.com/wadsworth/**. After you log on, type in:

dangerous games and the criminal law

This essay concerns dangerous games such as drag racing and Russian roulette. After reading the essay, answer the following questions:

a. What movie does the author discuss when he talks about drag racing? Why?

b. Why does the author argue that such dangerous activities should be criminalized?

c. Why does he think that those who engage in dangerous games should be penalized more severely than they are today?

d. What is the maximum fine in California for drivers who exceed 100 miles an hour?

2. Go to the Web site of the Legal Information Institute at Cornell Law School at **www.law.cornell.edu/** Type in "criminal law" where it says "search." Click on U.S. criminal law. When you get to that page, scroll down on the right-hand side to "state criminal codes." Click on it. Search for your state's criminal code. Find the section on homicide. Compare it with the excerpts from the similar section on homicide in the Florida criminal code in Figure 3.4 (if you live in Florida, pick any other state).

a. What are the similarities in the two states' homicide sections? Are there any differences? What are they?

b. Why do you think the homicide sections are so similar?

Notes

1. Clark Mason, "'Blackout' Signs Detailed at Trial," *The* (Santa Rosa, Calif.) *Press Democrat* (March 19, 1998), B3.

2. Roger LeRoy Miller and Gaylord A. Jentz, *Business Law Today, Comprehensive Edition,* 5th ed. (St. Paul: West Publishing Co., 2000), 2–3.

3. *Neff v. George,* 364 Ill. 306, 4 N.E.2d 388, 390, 391 (1936).

4. Joshua Dressler, *Understanding Criminal Law,* 2d ed. (New York: Richard D. Irwin, 1995), 22–3.

5. *Ibid.,* 23.

6. Thomas R. Bartman, "High Criminal Intent Standard Needed for Complex Environmental Laws," *Legal Backgrounder* (September 15, 1995), 4.

7. *State v. Saunders,* 75 N.J. 200, 381 Atl.2d 333 (1977).

8. Joel Feinberg, *The Moral Limits of the Criminal Law: Harm to Others* (New York: Oxford University Press, 1984), 221–32.

9. Flammable Fabrics Act, 15 U.S.C. Section 1196 (1994).

10. Stuart P. Green, "Why It's a Crime to Tear the Tag Off a Mattress," *Emory Law Journal* 46 (Fall 1997), 1533–1614.

11. Henry M. Hart, Jr., "The Aims of the Criminal Law," *Law & Contemporary Problems* 23 (1958), 405–6.

12. John L. Diamond, "The Myth of Morality and Fault in Criminal Law Doctrine," *American Criminal Law Review* 34 (Fall 1996), 111.

13. Lawrence M. Friedman, *Crime and Punishments in American History* (New York: Basic Books, 1993), 34.

14. *Ibid.,* 10.

15. Robert W. Drane and David J. Neal, "On Moral Justifications for the Tort/Crime Distinction," *California Law Review* 68 (1980), 398.

16. Gail Heriot, "An Essay on the Civil-Criminal Distinction with Special Reference to Punitive Damages," *Journal of Contemporary Legal Issues* 7 (1996), 43.

17. Joan Treadway, "Judgment Against Son's Killer Applauded," *New Orleans Times-Picayune* (January 17, 1996), A1.

18. Model Penal Code 1.04 (2).

19. Advisory Task Force on the Juvenile Justice System, *Final Report* (Minneapolis, MN: Minnesota Supreme Court, 1994), 5–11.

20. *Black's Law Dictionary,* 6th ed. (St. Paul, MN: West Publishing Co., 1990), 959.

21. *Ibid.,* 960.

22. Johannes Andenaes, "The Moral or Educative Influence of Criminal Law," *Journal of Social Issues* 27 (Spring 1971), 17, 26.

23. Green, 1533–1614.

24. Thomas A. Mullen, "Rule without Reason: Requiring Independent Proof of the *Corpus Deliciti* as a Condition of Admitting Extrajudicial Confession," *University of San Francisco Law Review* 27 (1993), 385.

25. *Hawkins v. State,* 219 Ind. 116, 129, 37 N.E.2d 79 (1941).

26. David C. Biggs, "'The Good Samaritan Is Packing': An Overview of the Broadened Duty to Aid Your Fellowman, with the Modern Desire to Possess Concealed Weapons," *University of Dayton Law Review* 22 (Winter 1997), 225.

27. Jessica McBride, "Mom Accused of Not Trying to Stop Assault on Daughter," *Milwaukee Journal Sentinel* (July 31, 1997), 3.

28. Daniel B. Yeager, "A Radical Community of Aid: A Rejoinder to Opponents of Affirmative Duties to Help Strangers," *Washington University Law Quarterly* 71 (1993), 1.

29. Model Penal Code Section 2.02.

30. Model Penal Code Section 2.02 (c).

31. Marisol Bello, "Man Who Says He Feared Wife's Voodoo Acquitted of Murder," *Orange County Register* (November 27, 1997), A18.

32. *Black's Law Dictionary,* 1423.

33. *United States v. Dotterweich,* 320 U.S. 277 (1943).

34. *State v. Stiffler,* 763 P.2d 308, 311 (Idaho Ct. App. 1988).

35. *Morissette v. United States,* 342 U.S. 246, 251–52 (1952).

36. Stacey M. Studnicki, "Annual Survey of Michigan Law, June 1, 1993—May 31, 1994), *Wayne Law Review* 41 (Winter 1995), 589.

37. *People v. Harding,* 443 Mich. at 699–703, 506 N.W.2d at 486-87 (1994).

38. Federal Bank Robbery Act, 18 USCA Section 2113.

39. Missouri State Statutes 574.090 and 574.093, RSMo Supp. 1993.

40. 508 U.S. 476 (1993).

41. Sandra D. Scott and Timothy S. Wynes, "Should Missouri Retain Its 'Ethnic Intimidation' Law?" *Journal of the Missouri Bar* 49 (November/December 1993), 445.

42. New York Penal Section 120.25.

43. "Bronx D.A. Charges Nushawn Williams with Reckless Endangerment, Assault," *New York Law Journal* (August 20, 1998), 1.

44. Maryland Code 1957, Art. 27, Code 1957, Section 407.

45. *Smallwood v. State,* 680 A.2d 512 (Md. 1996).

46. *In re Winship,* 397 U.S. 358, 364 (1970).

47. Stephen Lally, "Making Sense of the Insanity Plea," *Washington Post Weekly Edition* (December 1, 1997), 23.

48. *M'Naughten's Case,* 10 Cl. & F. 200, Eng. Rep. 718 (1843). Note that the name of the rule is also spelled M'Naghten and McNaughten.

49. Jay Singer, *Understanding Criminal Law* (Boston: Little, Brown, 1981).

50. *Durham v. United States,* 214 F.2d 862 (D.C. Circuit, 1954).

51. Model Penal Code 401 (1952).

52. Bruce Wiseman, "Confronting the Breakdown of Law and Order," *USA Today Magazine* (January 1, 1997), 32.

53. Lally, 23.

54. Bruce J. Winick, "Presumptions and Burdens of Proof in Determining Competency to Stand Trial: An Analysis of *Medina v. California* and the Supreme Court's New Due Process Methodology in Criminal Cases," *University of Miami Law Review* 47 (1993), 817.

55. South Carolina Code Ann. Section 17-24-20(A) (Law. Co-op. Supp. 1997).

56. Rene J. Leblanc-Allman, "Guilty but Mentally Ill: A Poor Prognosis," *South Carolina Law Review* 49 (Summer 1998), 1095.

57. Steve Mills and Bob Kemper, "Court Rules Mentally Ill Law Unconstitutional," *Chicago Tribune* (June 24, 1997), 1.

58. Leblanc-Allman, 1095.

59. Lawrence P. Tiffany and Mary Tiffany, "Nosologic Objections to the Criminal Defense of Pathological Intoxication: What Do the Doubters Doubt?" *International Journal of Law and Psychiatry* 13 (1990), 49.

60. John Sanko, "Murder Conviction Overturned," (Denver, Colorado) *Rocky Mountain News* (April 11, 1997), 25A.

61. 116 S. Ct. 2024 (1996).

62. Mont. Code Ann. Section 45-5-102 (1997).

63. Mont. Code Ann. Section 45-2-203 (1997).

64. Kenneth W. Simons, "Mistake and Impossibility, Law and Fact, and Culpability: A Speculative Essay," *Journal of Criminal Law and Criminology* 81 (1990), 447.

65. *U.S. v. Robinson*, 119 F. 3rd 1205 (5th Circuit, 1997).

66. *Lambert v. California*, 335 U.S. 225 (1957).

67. Craig L. Carr, "Duress and Criminal Responsibility," *Law and Philosophy* 10 (1990), 161.

68. *United States v. May*, 727 F.2d 764 (1984).

69. *United States v. Contento-Pachon*, 723 F.2d 691 (1984).

70. *People v. Murillo*, 587 N.E.2d 1199, 1204 (Ill. App. Ct. 1992).

71. Michael K. Molitor, "The 'Battered Child Syndrome' As Self-Defense," *Wayne Law Review* 40 (Fall 1993), 237.

72. Michael Mello, "Unabomer Defense Should Assist and Not Resist," *National Law Journal* (January 26, 1998), A21.

73. Peter J. Howe, "Surprising Many, Abortion Issue Took Back Seat at Trial," *Boston Globe* (March 19, 1996), 22.

74. Model Penal Code Section 3.02.

75. *U.S. v. Paolello*, 951 F.2d 537 (3rd Cir. 1991).

76. *People v. Petro*, 56 P.2d 984 (Cal. Ct. App. 1936) and *Regina v. Dudley and Stephens*, 14 Q.B.D. 173 (1884).

77. 287 U.S. 435.

78. Kenneth M. Lord, "Entrapment and Due Process: Moving Toward a Dual System of Defenses," *Florida State University Law Review* 25 (Spring 1998), 463.

79. 503 U.S. 540 (1992).

80. Fred Warren Bennett, "From *Sorrells* to *Jacobson*: Reflections on Six Decades of Entrapment Law and Related Defenses in Federal Court," *Wake Forest Law Review* 27 (1992), 829

81. *Brown v. Mississippi*, 279 U.S. 278 (1936).

82. 372 U.S. 355 (1963).

83. 116 U.S. 1769 (1996).

84. 117 U.S. 882 (1997).

85. "Traffic Stops," *Harvard Law Review* 111 (November 1997), 299.

86. John Deutch, "Terrorism," *Foreign Policy* (September 22, 1997), 10.

87. Pub. L. No. 104-132, 110 Stat. 1214 (1996).

88. Roberta Smith, "America Tries to Come to Terms with Terrorism," *Cardozo Journal of International and Comparative Law* 5 (Spring 1997), 249.

89. Kyle Pope and Amy D. Marcus, "Can America Stomach a War on Terrorism?" *Wall Street Journal* (August 2, 1996), A8.

90. *Ibid.*

91. *Galvan v. Press*, 347 U.S. 522 (1954).

92. "Terrorism Bill Flaws," *Charleston Gazette & Daily Mail* (April 26, 1996), 4A.

93. Patrick J. McDonnell, "Criminal Past Comes Back to Haunt Some Immigrants," *Los Angeles Times* (January 20, 1997), A1.

94. David B. Kopel and Joseph Olson, "Preventing a Reign of Terror: Civil Liberties Implications of Terrorism Legislation," *Oklahoma City University Law Review* 21 (Summer/Fall 1996), 247.

95. "Tehran Protests Flatow Terror Ruling as Baseless," *The* (Newark, New Jersey) *Star-Ledger* (March 14, 1998), 4.

96. Deutch, "Terrorism."

part two
The Police

Chapter

4 Police: Agents of
Law and Order

5 Policing: Organization and Strategies

6 Police and the Rule of Law

7 Challenges to Effective Policing

chapter

4

Police: Agents of Law and Order

Chapter Objectives

After reading this chapter, you should be able to:

1. Describe the first systems of law enforcement in colonial America.

2. Tell how the patronage system affected policing.

3. Indicate the results of the Wickersham Commission.

4. List five main types of law enforcement agencies.

5. List some of the most important federal law enforcement agencies.

6. Identify the five investigative priorities of the FBI.

7. Analyze the importance of private security today.

8. List the four basic responsibilities of the police.

9. Indicate why patrol officers are allowed discretionary powers.

10. Explain how some states have reacted to perceived leniency to perpetrators of domestic violence.

INTRODUCTION

It was, according to some, the largest funeral gathering the state of Idaho had ever seen. Thousands of citizens and law enforcement officers lined the route from the funeral home to the cemetery to pay their last respects to Officer Mark Stall, who had been killed during a shoot-out following a routine traffic stop. Throughout the city of Boise, storefronts were plastered with signs paying tribute to Stall and donations were pouring in to several funds set up to support his wife and two young daughters.[1]

This is not to say that relations between the city's police and the community were altogether positive. At the time of Stall's funeral in the late 1990s, Boise led the nation in fatal shootings of civilians per 1,000 officers. Over the previous twenty-one months, eight people had been shot and killed by Boise police.[2] Five of the killings involved traffic violations, raising questions as to whether the use of deadly force had been justified. Public trust in the police was badly damaged. "I grew up to trust cops as my friends," one young woman said. "Now I don't know. The other night, I was pulled over for a missing headlight and I was scared. I said, 'Please don't shoot me.'"[3]

That a fallen officer could receive such an outpouring of support while many of his peers inspired suspicion, if not fear, points to the complex position of police in modern society. Police are the most visible representatives of our criminal justice system; indeed, they symbolize the system for the many Americans who may never see the inside of a courtroom or a prison cell. The police are entrusted with immense power to serve and protect the public good: the power to use weapons and the power to arrest. But that same power alarms many citizens, who fear that it may be turned arbitrarily against them.[4] The role of the police is constantly debated as well. Is their primary mission to fight crime, or should they also be concerned with the social conditions that presumably lead to crime?

This chapter will lay the foundation for our study of the police and the work that they do. A short history of policing will be followed by an examination of the many different agencies that make up American law enforcement. We will also look at the various responsibilities of police officers and discuss the crucial role of discretion in law enforcement.

> "Every society gets the kind of criminal it deserves. What is equally true is that every community gets the kind of law enforcement it insists on."
>
> —Robert Kennedy, *U.S Attorney General* (1964)

A HISTORY OF THE AMERICAN POLICE

Although modern society relies on law enforcement officers to control and prevent crime, in the early days of this country police services had little to do with crime control. The policing efforts in the first American cities were directed toward controlling certain groups of people (mostly slaves and Native Americans), delivering goods, regulating activities such as buying and selling in the town market, maintaining health and sanitation, controlling gambling and vice, and managing livestock and other animals.[5] Furthermore, these police services were for the most part performed by volunteers, as a police force was an expensive proposition. Most communities simply could not afford to pay a group of law enforcement officers.[6]

Eventually, of course, as the populations of American cities grew, so did the need for public order and the willingness to devote resources to the establishment of formal police forces. Policing in the United States and in England evolved along similar lines, and many of our policing institutions have their roots in English tradition. Consequently, we will begin our discussion of the history of American police with a look back at its English beginnings.

English Roots

Before William the Conqueror invaded the island in 1066, the dominant system of law enforcement in England was the **tithing system.** Every male was enrolled in a group of ten families, which was called a *tithing.* If one person in the tithing committed a crime, then every person in the group was responsible for paying the fine. The theory was that this obligation would be an incentive for the tithing to engage in collective community policing. Later, ten tithings were joined together to form a *hundred,* whose top law official was the *reeve.* Finally, the hundreds were consolidated into *shires* (the equivalent of modern counties), and the law enforcement official became known as the **shire-reeve.** As the phonetics suggest, this official is the earliest example of what is now the county sheriff.

Later Developments. Under William the Conqueror, the tithing system was replaced by a highly bureaucratized judicial system. Shire-reeves kept their law enforcement abilities, but the king selected his own judges who traveled across the countryside trying criminal cases. (As you recall, this system of using circuit judges is also the foundation of *stare decisis* and common law.)

In the thirteenth century, the **watch system** was introduced to protect the property of citizens in larger English towns. In theory, every male member of the community was supposed to take his turn watching the homes and property of his neighbors, and if he caught a wrongdoer, he was to turn the person over to the shire-reeve. In practice, however, many citizens did not wish to spend their nights walking the cold and quiet streets. These citizens paid others to take over their tasks, thereby introducing the concept of the deputy-for-hire into law enforcement. The paid deputies were, to a large degree, drawn from the unemployables of society. On the whole, they hardly represented ideal law enforcement officers. In fact, they were often drunkards and petty thieves themselves.[7]

In 1326, the office of the **justice of the peace** was established to replace the shire-reeve. Over the next centuries, in most English cities the justice of the peace, with the help of a constable, came to oversee various law enforcement activities, including organizing the night watch, investigating crimes, and securing criminals for trial. In the countryside, the hundred was replaced by the parish, which corresponded to the territory served by a particular church and included its members. Under the *parish constable system,* the parish hired a person to oversee criminal justice for its parishioners.

The London Experiments. By the mid-1700s, London, England—one of the largest cities in the Western world—still did not have an organized system of law enforcement. Crime was endemic to city life, and the government's only recourse was to *read the riot act* (call in the military when the lawbreaking became unbearable). Such actions were widely unpopular, as the townspeople did not appreciate being disciplined (and fired upon) by soldiers whose salaries they were paying. Furthermore, the soldiers proved unreliable peacemakers, as they were hesitant to use force against their fellow London citizens. Despite rampant crime in the city, most Londoners were not in favor of a police force under the control of the city government. English history is rife with instances in which the king or some other government official abused military power by turning it against the citizens. Therefore, the citizenry were wary of any formal, armed organization that could restrict their individual liberties.

Henry Fielding, chief magistrate of Bow Street and a novelist who is best known for his classic book *Tom Jones* (1749), reacted by forming the Bow Street Runners, also known as "Thief Takers." This amateur volunteer force focused

TITHING SYSTEM
In Anglo-Saxon England, a system of law enforcement in which groups of ten families, known as tithings, were collectively responsible for law and order within their group.

SHIRE-REEVE
The chief law enforcement officer in an early English shire, or county. The forerunner of the modern sheriff.

WATCH SYSTEM
A community law enforcement system in medieval England in which citizens were regularly required to spend a night guarding against disturbances of the peace and property crimes.

JUSTICE OF THE PEACE
Established in fourteenth-century England, a government official who oversaw various aspects of local law enforcement. The post eventually became strictly identified with judicial matters.

A satirical English cartoon depicts Sir Robert Peel fighting a group of night watchmen. The cartoon refers to the organization of the London Police Force in 1829, through which Peel tried to bring a measure of control and organization to law enforcement in the city. In doing so, Peel made obsolete the night watchmen, who were generally ineffective in preventing crime, and in many cases were themselves of questionable character. The cartoonist appears to take a slightly sarcastic view of Peel as a "savior." What attitudes in early nineteenth-century London might cause citizens to be suspicious of an organized police force?

on retrieving stolen property, but it also reflected Fielding's wish to stop violence and criminal activity before it took place.

The Bow Street Runners were highly effective in the Bow Street neighborhood and were soon being hired out all over England to prevent and solve crimes. This relatively small force, however, could do little to stem the growing problems of a city as large as London. The need for organized police became more pressing as thousands of people from the countryside streamed into the city to find employment. For several decades, the British Parliament debated what should be done to improve the situation in the poverty-stricken city. Not until Sir Robert "Bobbie" Peel took over the post of home secretary did the necessary steps begin to be taken, however.

In 1829, Peel pushed the Metropolitan Police Act through Parliament. This legislation has had lasting impact, as many of its operating goals were similar to those of modern police forces (see Figure 4.1 for a summary of the act). Under the terms of this act, the London Metropolitan Police was formed. One thousand members strong at first, the members of this police force were easily recognizable in their uniforms that included blue coats and top hats. Under Peel's direction, the "bobbies," as the police were called in honor of their founder, had four specific operating philosophies:

1. To reduce tension and conflict between law enforcement officers and the public.

2. To use nonviolent means (they did not carry firearms) in keeping the peace, with violence to be used only as a last resort. This point was crucial, because, as mentioned earlier, the English were suspicious of armed government military organizations. Being unarmed, the bobbies could hardly be confused with soldiers.

3. To relieve the military from certain duties, such as controlling urban violence. (Peel specifically hoped that his police would be less inclined to use excessive force than the military had been.)

4. To be judged on the absence of crime rather than through high-visibility police action.[8]

London's police operation was so successful that it was soon imitated in smaller towns throughout England and, eventually, in the United States.

Figure 4.1 Fundamental Principles of the Metropolitan Police Act of 1829

The first modern police force was established in London by the Metropolitan Police Act of 1829. Sir Robert Peel, the politician who pushed through the legislation, wanted a police force that would provide citizens with "the full and complete protection of the law" and "check the increase of crime." In order to fulfill these objectives, Peel's early police were guided by the basic principles listed here.

1. The police force must be organized along military lines.

2. Police administrators and officers must be under government control.

3. Emphasis must be placed on hiring qualified persons and training them properly.

4. New police officers must complete a probationary period, during which time if they fail to meet standards they will not be hired as permanent officers.

5. Police personnel should be assigned to specific areas of the city for a specific time period.

6. Police headquarters must be centrally located in the city.

7. Police officers must maintain proper appearances at all times, in order to gain and keep the respect of citizens.

8. Individual police officers should be able to control their temper and refrain from violence whenever possible.

9. Police records must be kept in order to measure police effectiveness.

The Early American Police Experience

In colonial America and immediately following the American Revolution, law enforcement virtually mirrored the English system. Constables and night watchmen were taken from the ranks of ordinary citizens. The governor of each colony hired a sheriff in each county to oversee the formal aspects of law enforcement, such as selecting juries and managing jails and prisons.[9] These colonial appointees were not always of the highest moral fiber. In 1730, the Pennsylvania colony felt the need to pass laws specifically prohibiting sheriffs from extorting money from prisoners or selling "strong liquors" to "any person under arrest."[10]

As in England, local citizens performing an early version of "community service" assisted sheriffs in their peacekeeping duties. Besides enforcing the law and keeping the peace, these citizen officers were expected to perform such duties as lighting street lamps and calling out the weather forecast.[11] The continuing American distaste for organized police structures gave rise to vigilante policing, in which groups of citizens would gather together and punish lawbreakers.

Early American Police Forces. In 1801, Boston became the first American city to acquire a formal night watch; the watchmen were paid 50 cents a night. For the next three decades, most major cities went no further than the watch system. Finally, facing the same pressures as London, major American metropolitan areas began to form "reactive patrol units" geared toward enforcing the law and preventing crime.[12] In 1833, Philadelphia became the first city to employ both day and night watchmen. Five years later, working from Sir Robert Peel's model, Boston formed the first organized police department, consisting of six full-time officers. In 1844, New York City set the foundation for the modern police department by combining its day and night watches under the control of a single police chief. By the onset of the Civil War in 1861, a number of American cities, including Boston, Baltimore, New Orleans, Philadelphia, Cincinnati, and Chicago, had similarly consolidated police departments, modeled on the Metropolitan Police of London.

Developments in City Policing. The earliest American police departments were plagued by communication problems. At first, officers and their departments could only communicate through face-to-face meetings or messages delivered by police runners. The system improved dramatically during the 1850s, when the telegraph became integrated into police operations. Now police commissioners and the captains of individual districts could communicate over telegraph lines instead of in time-consuming daily conferences.

The first revolution in city police procedure, however, came with the introduction of call boxes. Initially, these boxes, located on city street corners, contained levers that the patrol officers would use to signal the station house of their whereabouts. The call boxes were then equipped with a bell system that allowed the patrol officer to send simple signals to headquarters, such as requesting assistance or calling for an ambulance. Finally, in 1880, telephones were installed in the call boxes. At last, police officers could communicate directly with station houses.

In the post-Civil War era of increased urbanization and rapid growth of American cities, the issue of communication became increasingly important to metropolitan police work. As suburban neighborhoods were incorporated into parent cities, police departments became responsible for previously independent forces. Without effective means to integrate these additions, city police organizations suffered from inefficiency and lack of control. It was not

"You are thought here to be the most senseless and fit man for the constable of the watch, therefore bear you the lantern."

—William Shakespeare, *English playwright* (*Much Ado About Nothing*, Act 3, Scene 3.)

PATRONAGE SYSTEM
A form of corruption in which the political party in power hires and promotes police officers, receiving job-related "favors" in return.

until the advent of twentieth-century technologies such as the automobile and the two-way radio, discussed in the next chapter, that many of these problems were successfully addressed.

Politics and Early American Policing. Like their modern counterparts, many early police officers were hard working, honest, and devoted to serving and protecting the public. On the whole, however, in the words of historian Samuel Walker, "The quality of American police service in the nineteenth century could hardly have been worse."[13] This poor quality can be attributed to the fact that the recruitment and promotion of police officers were intricately tied into the politics of the day. Police officers received their jobs as a result of political connections, not because of any particular skills or knowledge. Whichever political party was in power in a given city would hire its own cronies to run the police department; consequently, the police were often more concerned with serving the interests of the political powers than with protecting the citizens.[14]

Corruption was rampant during this *political era* of policing, which lasted roughly from 1840 to 1930. (See Figure 4.2 for an overview of the three eras of policing, which are discussed in this chapter and referred to throughout the book.) Police salaries were relatively low; thus many police officers saw their positions as opportunities to make extra income through any number of illegal activities. Bribery was common, as police would use their close proximity to the people to request "favors," which went into the police officers' own pockets or into the coffers of the local political party as "contributions."[15] This was known as the **patronage system,** or the "spoils system," because to the political victors went the spoils.

Figure 4.2 The Three Eras of American Policing

George L. Kelling and Mark H. Moore have separated the history of policing in the United States into three distinct periods. Here is a brief summarization of these three eras.

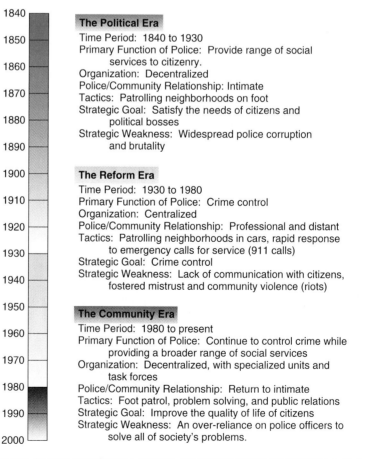

The Political Era
Time Period: 1840 to 1930
Primary Function of Police: Provide range of social services to citizenry.
Organization: Decentralized
Police/Community Relationship: Intimate
Tactics: Patrolling neighborhoods on foot
Strategic Goal: Satisfy the needs of citizens and political bosses
Strategic Weakness: Widespread police corruption and brutality

The Reform Era
Time Period: 1930 to 1980
Primary Function of Police: Crime control
Organization: Centralized
Police/Community Relationship: Professional and distant
Tactics: Patrolling neighborhoods in cars, rapid response to emergency calls for service (911 calls)
Strategic Goal: Crime control
Strategic Weakness: Lack of communication with citizens, fostered mistrust and community violence (riots)

The Community Era
Time Period: 1980 to present
Primary Function of Police: Continue to control crime while providing a broader range of social services
Organization: Decentralized, with specialized units and task forces
Police/Community Relationship: Return to intimate
Tactics: Foot patrol, problem solving, and public relations
Strategic Goal: Improve the quality of life of citizens
Strategic Weakness: An over-reliance on police officers to solve all of society's problems.

SOURCE: ADAPTED FROM GEORGE L. KELLING AND MARK H. MOORE, "FROM POLITICAL TO REFORM TO COMMUNITY: THE EVOLVING STRATEGY OF POLICE," IN COMMUNITY POLICING: RHETORIC OR REALITY, ED. JACK R. GREEN AND STEPHEN D. MASTROFSKI (NEW YORK: PRAEGER PUBLISHERS, 1991), 14–15, 22–23.

As we shall see in following chapters, two aspects of this period survive. First, corruption remains a concern in some American police forces. Second, for the most part, policing continues to be a predominantly "blue-collar, white male" profession.

The Role of Early Police. The political era also saw police officers take an active role in providing social services for their bosses' constituents. In many instances, this role even took precedence over law enforcement duties. Politicians realized that they could attract more votes by offering social services to citizens than by arresting them, and they required the police departments under their control to act accordingly.

The extent of these services is somewhat surprising, given modern expectations of a police force. In 1834, for example, the Boston Police Department emptied 3,120 privies (public toilets), removed 1,500 loads of garbage, and visited every home in the Boston area to check for cholera. In a three-month period during 1853, the number of nights of shelter for homeless people (880,161) that the New York City Police Department (NYPD) provided nearly matched the number of people they arrested (898,489).[16] The police were also heavily involved in offering services for juveniles. In 1917, the NYPD assigned "welfare officers" to ten precincts to look after wayward youths.

A horse-drawn police wagon used by the New York City Police Department, circa 1886. In the 1880s a number of American cities introduced patrol wagon services, which included transporting prisoners and drunks as well as performing ambulance duties. Along with signal service, or "call boxes," the police wagon represented a "revolution" in police methods. If a patrol officer made an arrest far from headquarters, he could now call the station and request a police wagon to pick up and deliver the arrested person (instead of having to deliver the arrestee himself).

The Modernization of the American Police

In spite of these positive activities, the abuses of the political era of policing did not go unnoticed. In 1894, the Lexow Committee of the New York legislature revealed the extent to which corruption and brutality plagued the New York City police force. In the service of Tammany Hall—the city's Democratic governing political machine—police arrested and brutalized Republican voters. The police extracted payoffs not only from the illegal businesses they "protected," such as prostitution houses, gambling dens, and abortionists, but also from fruit vendors and soda water stands. Victims of police brutality told their stories before the committee. "The eye of one man, punched out by a patrol man's club, hung on his cheek," described one observer.[17]

The Wickersham Commission. The problems brought before the Lexow Committee persisted throughout the early decades of the twentieth century. A sampling of police scandals from these years would include the following incidents:

- In 1909, Los Angeles Mayor Arthur Harper, Police Chief Edward Kern, and a local pimp attempted to monopolize the city's prostitution industry. Los Angeles police officers were ordered to arrest and harass those prostitutes not employed by their mayor and police chief.

- In 1912, several gunmen, allegedly following the orders of Lieutenant Charles Becker of the New York City Police Department, shot and killed a professional gambler who was scheduled to appear before the district attorney to accuse the department of protecting certain gambling establishments.

- In 1913, the San Francisco press reported that Frank Esola, Louis Droulette, and nearly a dozen other detectives were protecting a gang of swindlers from other police officers in return for 15 percent of the gang's estimated $300,000 annual gross income.[18]

PROFESSIONAL MODEL
A style of policing advocated by August Vollmer and O. W. Wilson that emphasizes centralized police organizations, increased use of technology, and a limitation of police discretion through regulations and guidelines.

In 1929, due in part to public outrage over these and other incidents, President Herbert Hoover appointed the national Commission on Law Observance and Enforcement to assess the American criminal justice system. The Wickersham Commission, named after its chairman, George Wickersham, focused on two areas of American policing that were in need of reform: (1) police brutality and (2) "the corrupting influence of politics." According to the commission, this reform should come about through higher personnel standards, centralized police administrations, and the increased use of technology.[19] Reformers of the time took the commission's findings as a call for the professionalization of American police and initiated the *progressive* (or *reform*) *era* in American policing.

Professionalism. In truth, the Wickersham Commission was not ground-breaking. Many of its recommendations echoed the opinions of one of its contributors—August Vollmer, the police chief of Berkeley, California, from 1905 until 1932. Known as "the Father of Modern Police Administration," Vollmer pioneered the training of potential police officers in institutions of higher learning. The first degree-granting program in law enforcement at San Jose State College (now a university) was developed under Vollmer.

Along with increased training, Vollmer also championed the use of technology in police work. His Berkeley department became the first in the nation to use automobiles to patrol city streets and to hire a forensic scientist to assist in solving crimes.[20] Furthermore, Vollmer believed that police could prevent crime by involving themselves in the lives of potential criminals, which led to his establishing the first juvenile crime unit in the nation.

Vollmer's devotion to modernism was also apparent in the career of his most successful protégé, police reformer O. W. Wilson, who promoted a style of policing known as the **professional model.** In an attempt to remove politics from police work, Wilson stressed the need for efficiency through bureaucracy and technology. After becoming police chief of Wichita, Kansas, Wilson improved the training of his officers to combat corruption and pioneered the use of one-officer patrol cars.[21] Because of his work as a consultant and the success of his textbook *Police Administration,* Wilson is recognized as one of the most influential proponents of police professionalism. In 1947, along with August Vollmer, he founded the School of Criminology at the University of California at Berkeley, the first school devoted to that subject. Wilson ended his career in the 1960s after taking over and reforming the Chicago police department. (For a recent international application of Wilson's ideals, see *Cross-National CJ Comparison—A Professional Police Force for Bosnia.*)

Administrative Reforms. As Vollmer's career shows, pressure for reform was not coming only from outside sources. Many police administrators took their jobs seriously and wanted to provide better law enforcement services for citizens. Resenting the controls placed upon them by corrupt politicians, the administrators took steps to improve the quality of the police force by removing incompetent officers who might be more easily corrupted. This internal reform focused on setting selection standards through testing and improving the training of recruits.

Police chiefs, who had been little more than figureheads during the political era, also took more control over their departments. A key to these efforts was the reorganization of police departments in many major cities. To improve their control over operations, police chiefs began to add mid-level positions to the force. These new officers, known as majors or assistant chiefs, could develop and implement crime-fighting strategies and more closely supervise individual officers. Police chiefs also tried to consolidate their power by bringing large areas of a city under their control so that no

A Professional Police Force for Bosnia

During the first half of the 1990s, the Balkan region of southeastern Europe was ravaged by a war involving Serbia, Croatia, and Bosnia-Herzegovina. After United Nations (UN) negotiators brokered an end to much of the aggression in late 1995, diplomats and citizens of the region turned to the task of keeping the peace. Maintaining order would depend heavily on local police, especially in Bosnia, which continued to be plagued by strife among the country's three main ethnic groups—the Muslims, the Serbs, and the Croats. In assessing the state of Bosnian police organizations, diplomats reached conclusions similar to those drawn by the Wickersham Commission about American law enforcers in the 1920s. The Bosnian police, outside observers said, often acted as private security forces for political parties and not only condoned but also participated in ethnic violence. To make matters worse, many Bosnian police forces had participated in the war and were still in possession of a great deal of heavy weaponry.

Two things were clear: (1) if Bosnia was to have any chance at becoming a peaceful democracy, its police would have to enforce the rule of law; and (2) the police were in no position to do so. In fact, during the first year after the end of the war, the police committed 70 percent of the country's reported human rights violations. In response, the UN, emulating police reformers of America's progressive era, decided to help Bosnia professionalize its law enforcement agencies. A UN force of more than two thousand law enforcement professionals from thirty-one countries, called the International Police Task Force (IPTF), was organized to provide training, equipment, and related assistance for local police forces in Bosnia.

Several years after its arrival, the IPTF has not been completely successful. Ethnic hatreds between rival police forces have stymied efforts to form a centralized bureaucracy, and certain areas of Bosnia remain mired in police corruption and violence. But, according to one American detective who spent nine months with the IPTF, many of the younger Bosnian officers appreciate the knowledge passed on by foreign instructors—"they soak it up like a sponge."

WHAT'S THE EVIDENCE?

To follow the efforts of the IPTF to modernize Bosnian police forces, visit the United Nations at **www.un.org/Depts/DPKO/ Missions/unmibh_p.htm**.

---

local ward, neighborhood, or politician could easily influence a single police department.

Finally, police chiefs set up special units such as criminal investigation, vice, and traffic squads with jurisdiction-wide power. Previously, all police powers within a precinct were controlled by the politicians in that precinct. By creating specialized units that worked across all precincts, the police chiefs increased their own power at the expense of the political bosses.

The Police Officer as Law Enforcer. As mentioned earlier, during the political era the social service role of the police was emphasized over the crime-fighting role. That began to change in the progressive era, spurred on by two significant events: (1) the passage of the Eighteenth Amendment to the U.S. Constitution and (2) the Great Depression.

"Prohibition," which passed in 1919, prohibited the sale, manufacture, and transportation of alcoholic beverages. In other words, it made liquor illegal. As social scientist James Q. Wilson notes, Prohibition marked the first time that police officers were placed in an adversarial law enforcement role.[22] Previously, police officers focused on maintaining order on their beats and did not risk their relationships with citizens by enforcing unpopular laws. Prohibition changed this, as police officers were charged with upholding a law that many people opposed. For the first time, police had to choose between upholding the law and maintaining a good relationship with the citizenry.

The Great Depression, which started with the crash of the stock market in 1929 and lasted through the 1930s, had a similar effect on police-citizen relations. As hundreds of thousands of Americans found themselves unemployed, broke, and homeless, they turned to crime as a means of survival. Furthermore, the "celebrity crooks" of the era—criminals such as John

Dillinger, Baby Face Nelson, Bonnie Parker and Clyde Barrow—became public heroes by taking on the establishment in the name of the common folk. In response, government officials and police administrators pressured police officers to become more stringent and effective in enforcing the law. The social services that had once been so crucial to police work were largely abandoned in favor of crime fighting.[23]

Technological innovations on all fronts—including patrol cars, radio communications, public records systems, fingerprinting, toxicology (the study of poisons), and forensics (the application of chemistry to the examination of physical evidence)—allowed police operations to move even more quickly toward O. W. Wilson's professional model. By the 1950s, America prided itself on having the most modern and professional police force in the world. As efficiency became the goal of the reform era police chief, however, relations with the community suffered. Instead of being members of the community, police officers were now seen almost as intruders, patrolling the streets in the anonymity of their automobiles. The drawbacks of this perception—and the professional model in general—would soon become evident.

Turmoil in the 1960s

The 1960s was one of the most turbulent decades in American history. The civil rights movement, though not inherently violent, intensified feelings of helplessness and impoverishment in African American communities. These frustrations resulted in civil unrest, and many major American cities experienced riots in the middle years of the decade. At the same time, the Vietnam War was generating civil disobedience on college campuses nationwide. During the first half of the 1967–1968 school year, there were 71 demonstrations on 62 college campuses. In the second half of the year, the numbers grew to 221 demonstrations on 101 campuses. Many of the students involved in the antiwar movement were also involved in other illegal activities, such as refusing to report for military service ("dodging the draft") and using illegal drugs.

Even though police brutality often provided the spark for race riots—and there is little question that police departments often overreacted to antiwar demonstrations—it would be simplistic to blame the strife of the 1960s on the police. Both the rioters and the demonstrators were reacting to social circumstances that they found unacceptable. Their clashes with the police were the result rather than the cause of these problems. Many observers, however, believed that the police *contributed* to the disorder. The National Advisory Commission on Civil Disorders stated bluntly that poor relations between the police and African American communities were partly to blame for the violence that plagued many of those communities.[24] In striving for professionalism, the police appeared to have lost touch with the citizens they were supposed to be serving. To repair their damaged relations with a large segment of the population, police would have to rediscover their community roots.

Returning to the Community

The beginning of the third era in American policing, the *community era,* may have started with several government initiatives that took place in 1968. Of primary importance was the Omnibus Crime Control and Safe Streets Act, which was passed that year.[25] Under this act, the federal government provided state and local police departments with funds to create a wide variety of police-community programs. Most large-city police departments established entire units devoted to community relations, implementing programs that ranged from summer recreation activities for inner-city youths to "officer-friendly" referral operations that encouraged citizens to come to the police with their crime concerns.

"He may be a very nice man. But I haven't got the time to figure that out. All I know is, he's got a uniform and a gun and I have to relate to him that way."

—James Baldwin, *American author* (1971)

The Law Enforcement Assistance Administration. Another critical element of the refocus on community was the formation of the Law Enforcement Assistance Administration (LEAA) in 1968. Though it came under criticism for mismanagement, the LEAA had a profound impact on police operations in the late 1960s and early 1970s. The organization awarded nearly $10 billion to state and local governments to improve police, courts, and corrections and helped fund thousands of local crime-fighting initiatives. In the wake of social unrest in many American cities, the LEAA particularly steered federal dollars to programs designed to improve relations between police officers and members of the communities in which they worked. The LEAA also created the Law Enforcement Education Program (LEEP), which provided thousands of police officers with financial assistance to further their educations.[26]

Furthermore, two events in the early 1970s paved the way for the increased presence of women and minorities in police work:

1. In 1971, the Supreme Court ruled, in *Griggs v. Duke Power Company*,[27] that tests used for employment purposes must be job related.

2. In 1972, Congress passed the Equal Employment Opportunity Act, which prohibited employment discrimination on the basis of sex, race, color, religion, or national origin.[28]

The introduction of women and minorities into the nation's police departments—which will be covered in Chapter 18—has been one of the most significant trends in law enforcement over the past thirty years.

The Advent of Community Policing. Though the civil unrest of the 1960s decreased, the 1970s did not offer any relief for America's police officers. As police departments reorganized in reaction to their past failures, a large crime wave hit the country (as we saw in Chapter 2). Consequently, police administrators were forced to combine efforts to improve community relations with aggressive and innovative crime-fighting strategies. These strategies, as we shall see in the next chapter, focused on quick response times to citizen calls for service. In other words, police departments graded their effectiveness on how quickly they were able to reach the scene of a crime or citizen complaint.

Eventually, these *reactive* strategies were supplemented with *proactive* strategies, in which police departments try to stop crimes before they are committed. (The "broken windows" theory, which was briefly touched upon in Chapter 2 and will be revisited in Chapter 5, is a proactive strategy.) Following the advice of criminologists who had been pointing to the roots of crime for decades, many police departments rededicated themselves to the concept of taking responsibility for the overall well-being of society. This led, in the late 1980s, to the adoption of community policing strategies in many jurisdictions. Community policing is based on the notion that meaningful interaction between officers and citizens will lead to a partnership in preventing and fighting crime.[29] Though the idea of involving members of the community in this manner is hardly new—a similar principle was set forth by Sir Robert Peel—innovative tactics in community policing, many of which will be discussed in Chapter 5, have had a significant impact on modern police work.

LAW ENFORCEMENT AGENCIES

Another aspect of modern police work is the fragmentation of law enforcement. When TWA Flight 800 mysteriously exploded over the Atlantic Ocean in the early evening of July 17, 1996, the first law enforcement officers on the scene were the members of Harbor Unit Launch #37 of the New York City

Police Department. As the investigation into the crash proceeded, hundreds of members of the NYPD assisted, including the department's scuba team, bomb squad, emergency services unit, aviation unit, and traffic patrol. The painstaking process of retrieving bodies and crash debris involved the further cooperation of the New York State Police, the Suffolk County Police, the Nassau County Police, the New York Air National Guard, and federal agencies such as the U.S. Coast Guard, the Federal Bureau of Investigation, the Bureau of Alcohol, Tobacco, and Firearms, and even the U.S. Navy.[30]

That disaster illustrates how many different agencies can become involved in a single incident. There are nearly 17,500 law enforcement agencies in the United States, employing over 800,000 people. The various agencies include:

- 12,502 municipal police departments.

- 3,086 sheriff's departments.

- 1,721 special police agencies, limited to policing parks, schools, airports, and so on.

- 49 state police departments, with Hawaii being the one exception.

- 50 federal law enforcement agencies.[31]

Each level has its own set of responsibilities, which we shall discuss starting with local police departments.

Municipal Law Enforcement Agencies

According to the Federal Bureau of Investigation, there are 3.3 state and local police officers for every 1,000 citizens in the United States.[32] This average somewhat masks the discrepancies between the police forces in urban and rural America. As noted in Chapter 1, the vast majority of all police officers work in small and medium-sized police departments (see Figure 4.3). While the New York City Police Department has nearly 35,000 employees, more than 850 small towns have only one police officer. Most of the nearly 2,000 "nontraditional" law enforcement agencies—those that police transit systems, schools and colleges, airports, parks, and other special jurisdictions—in the United States also operate on a local level.

Of the three levels of law enforcement, municipal agencies have the broadest authority to apprehend criminal suspects, maintain order, and provide services to the community. Whether the local officer is part of a large force or the only law enforcement officer in the community, he or she is usually responsible for a wide spectrum of duties, from responding to noise complaints to investigating homicides. Much of the criticism of local police departments is based on the belief that local police are too underpaid or poorly trained to handle these various responsibilities. Reformers have suggested that residents of smaller American towns would benefit from greater statewide coordination of local police departments, though little progress has been made in this area.[33]

Sheriffs and County Law Enforcement

A vestige of the English shire-reeve discussed earlier in the chapter, the **sheriff** is still an important figure in American law enforcement. Almost every one of the more than three thousand counties in the United States (except those in Alaska) has a sheriff. In every state except Rhode Island and Hawaii,

Figure 4.3 Full-Time Police Personnel, by Size of Population Served

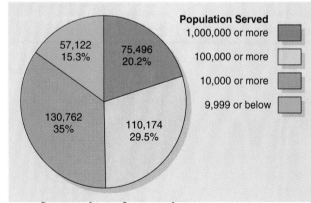

Population Served

- 1,000,000 or more
- 100,000 or more
- 10,000 or more
- 9,999 or below

57,122 15.3%
75,496 20.2%
130,762 35%
110,174 29.5%

SOURCE: BUREAU OF JUSTICE STATISTICS, LOCAL POLICE DEPARTMENTS—1993 (WASHINGTON, D.C.: U.S. DEPARTMENT OF JUSTICE, APRIL 1996), TABLE 3, PAGE 2.

SHERIFF
The primary law enforcement officer in a county, usually elected to the post by a popular vote.

sheriffs are elected by members of the community for two- or four-year terms and are paid a salary set by the state legislature or county board. As elected officials who do not necessarily need a background in law enforcement, modern sheriffs resemble their counterparts from the political era of policing in many ways. Simply stated, the sheriff is also a politician. When a new sheriff is elected, she or he will sometimes repay political debts by appointing new deputies or promoting those who have given her or him support. This high degree of instability and personnel turnover in many states is seen as one of the weaknesses of county law enforcement.[34]

Size and Responsibility of Sheriffs' Departments. Like municipal police forces, sheriffs' departments vary in size. The largest is the Los Angeles County Sheriffs' Department, with more than 11,000 full-time employees. Of the 3,086 sheriffs' departments in the country, 17 employ more than 1,000 officers, while 19 have only one.[35]

The image of the sheriff as a powerful figure patrolling vast expanses is not entirely misleading. Most sheriffs' departments are assigned their duties by state law. Almost 90 percent of all sheriffs' departments have the primary responsibility for investigating violent crimes in their jurisdictions. Other common responsibilities of a sheriff's department include:

- Protecting the public.
- Administering the county jail.
- Carrying out civil and criminal processes within county lines, such as serving eviction notices and court summonses.
- Keeping order in the county courthouse.
- Collecting taxes.
- Enforcing orders of the court, such as overseeing the sequestration of a jury during a trial.[36]

It is easy to confuse sheriffs' departments and local police departments, for good reason. As Figure 4.4 shows, both law enforcement agencies are responsible for many of the same tasks, including crime investigation and routine patrol. There are differences, however, also evident in Figure 4.4: sher-

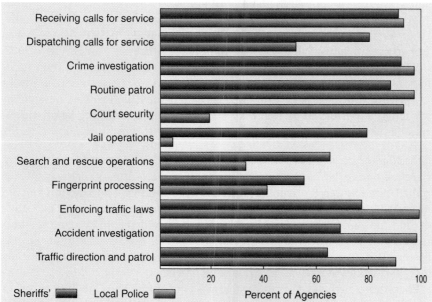

Figure 4.4 The Functions of Sheriffs' and Local Police Departments

Sheriffs' and local police departments perform many of the same functions. As you see here, however, they often emphasize the functions differently. Sheriffs' departments are much more involved in operating local jails, while police departments are more likely to deal with traffic control.

SOURCE: Bureau of Justice Statistics, Sheriffs' Departments—1993 (Washington, D.C.: U.S. Department of Justice, June 1996), iv.

CORONER
The medical examiner of a county, usually elected by popular vote.

iffs' departments are more likely to be involved in county court and jail operations and to perform certain services such as search and rescue. Local police departments, for their part, are more likely to perform traffic-related functions than are sheriffs' departments.

The County Coroner. Another elected official on the county level is the **coroner,** or medical examiner. Duties vary from county to county, but the coroner has a general mandate to investigate "all sudden, unexplained, unnatural or suspicious deaths" reported to the office. The coroner is ultimately responsible for determining the cause of death in these cases. Coroners also perform autopsies and assist other law enforcement agencies in homicide investigations.[37] In certain rare circumstances, such as when the sheriff is arrested or otherwise forced to leave his or her post, the coroner becomes the leading law enforcement officer of the county.

Nearly every state law enforcement agency hosts a Web site. To see two of the more interesting ones, go to the Pennsylvania State Police's home page at www.state.pa.us/PA Exec/State_Police **and the Washington State Patrol's home page at** www.wa.gov/wsp/wsphome.htm

State Police and Highway Patrols

The most visible state law enforcement agency is the state police or highway patrol agency. Historically, state police agencies were created for four reasons:

1. To assist local police agencies, which often did not have adequate resources or training to handle their law enforcement tasks.

2. To investigate criminal activities that crossed jurisdictional boundaries (such as when bank robbers committed a crime in one county and then fled to another part of the state).

3. To provide law enforcement in rural and other areas that did not have local or county police agencies.

4. To break strikes and control labor movements.

The first statewide police organization was the Texas Rangers. When this organization was initially created in 1835, the Rangers' primary purpose was to patrol the border with Mexico as scouts for the Republic of Texas Army. The Rangers evolved into a more general-purpose law enforcement agency, and in 1874 they were commissioned as police officers and given law enforcement duties. The Arizona Rangers (created in 1901) and the New Mexico Mounted Police (1905) were formed in a similar manner.

The first state to operate a modern state police force was Pennsylvania, which established the Pennsylvania State Police (PSP) in 1905. The PSP was formed specifically as a response to the Great Anthracite Coal Strike of 1902.

Within twenty years, state police forces were common, though their jurisdiction was limited by public mistrust. For the most part, the state police were the private tool of the governor to use when local police were unable, or unwilling, to perform a certain task, such as violently breaking labor strikes, as in Pennsylvania.

The Difference between the State Police and Highway Patrols. Today, there are twenty-three state police agencies and twenty-six highway patrols in the United States. State police agencies have statewide jurisdiction and are authorized to perform a wide variety of law enforcement tasks. Thus, they provide the same services as city or county police departments and are limited only by the boundaries of the state. Such full-service state police agencies exist in Virginia, Michigan, Texas, New Mexico, Louisiana, Oregon, New York, Kentucky, Pennsylvania, and Rhode Island.

In contrast, highway patrols have limited authority. They are limited either by their jurisdiction or by the specific types of offenses they have the authority to control. As their name suggests, most highway patrols concentrate primarily on regulating traffic; specifically, they enforce traffic laws and investigate traffic accidents. Furthermore, they usually limit their activity to patrolling state and federal highways. States such as Florida, Georgia, Ohio, Nevada, and North Carolina have highway patrols.

Trying to determine which state agency has which duties can be confusing. The Washington State Highway Patrol, despite its name, also has state police powers. In addition, thirty-five states have investigative agencies that are independent of the state police or highway patrol. Such agencies are usually found in states with highway patrols, and they have the primary responsibility of investigating criminal activities. For example, in addition to its highway patrol, Oklahoma runs a State Bureau of Investigation and a State Bureau of Narcotics and Dangerous Drugs. Each state has its own methods of determining the jurisdictions of these various organizations.

For the most part, however, state police are complementary to local law enforcement agencies. They maintain crime labs to assist in local investigations and also keep statewide intelligence files. State officers in some cases also provide training to local police and will assist local forces when needed.[38] For example, in 1997 the governor of Michigan sent state troopers into the state's murder capital: Benton Harbor, a city with a population of 12,000 that had experienced eleven homicides in ten days. These state troopers trained and supervised local officers and, under the direction of the governor's office, were given authority to enforce the law. In a one-year period, the state troopers made more than 400 arrests, captured 382 fugitives, and issued 1,835 traffic citations. Traffic accidents in Benton Harbor dropped 40 percent during the year, and only two murders were reported.[39]

Limited-Purpose Law Enforcement Agencies. Even with the agencies just discussed, a number of states have found that certain law enforcement areas need more specific attention. As a result, a wide variety of limited-purpose law enforcement agencies have sprung up in the fifty states. For example, most states have an alcoholic beverage control commission (ABC), or a similarly named organization, which monitors the sale and distribution of alcoholic beverages. The ABC monitors alcohol distributors to assure that all taxes are paid on the beverages and is responsible for revoking or suspending the liquor licenses of establishments that have broken relevant laws.

Many states have fish and game warden organizations that enforce all laws relating to hunting and fishing. Motor vehicle compliance (MVC) agencies monitor interstate carriers or trucks to make sure that they are in compliance with state and federal laws. MVC officers generally operate the weigh stations that are commonly found on interstate highways. Other limited-purpose law enforcement agencies deal with white-collar crime, regulate nursing homes, and provide training to local police departments.

Federal Law Enforcement Agencies

Statistically, employees of federal agencies do not make up a large part of the nation's law enforcement force. In fact, the New York City Police Department has nearly half as many employees as all of the federal law enforcement agencies combined.[40] The influence of these federal agencies, however, is substantial. Unlike local police departments, which must deal with all forms of crime, federal agencies have been authorized, usually by Congress, to enforce specific laws or attend to specific situations. The U.S. Coast Guard, for example, patrols the nation's waterways, while U.S. Postal Inspectors investigate and prosecute crimes perpetrated through the use of the U.S. mails.

The federal government maintains about fifty agencies that play a role in law enforcement. (See Figure 4.5 for a list of federal law enforcement agen-

INFOTRAC ®
COLLEGE EDITION

O'Toole, Mary Ellen. **Criminal profiling**: the FBI use criminal investigative analysis to solve crimes.

Figure 4.5 Federal Law Enforcement Agencies

A number of federal agencies employ law enforcement officers who are authorized to carry firearms and make arrests. The most prominent ones are under the control of either the U.S. Department of Justice or the U.S. Department of the Treasury.

Department of Justice

| Federal Bureau of Investigation (10,389 officers) | Immigration and Naturalization Service (12,403 officers) | Drug Enforcement Administration (2,946 officers) | U.S. Marshals Service (2,650 officers) |

Department of the Treasury

| U.S. Customs Service (9,746 officers) | Internal Revenue Service (3,784 officers) | U.S. Secret Service (3,185 officers) | Bureau of Alcohol, Tobacco, and Firearms (1,869 officers) |

SOURCE: BUREAU OF JUSTICE STATISTICS, *FEDERAL LAW ENFORCEMENT OFFICERS—1996* (WASHINGTON, D.C.: U.S. DEPARTMENT OF JUSTICE, DECEMBER 1997), TABLE 2, PAGE 4.

FEDERAL BUREAU OF INVESTIGATION (FBI)
The branch of the Department of Justice responsible for investigating violations of federal law. The bureau also collects national crime statistics and provides training and other forms of aid to local law enforcement agencies.

In an effort to solve the crimes that fall under its jurisdiction, the FBI often asks for help. Below, the agency's Web site provides information concerning a piece of art stolen from a church in Schenectady, New York.

cies.) We will address the most important ones here, grouping them according to the federal department or bureau to which they report.

The Department of Justice. The U.S. Department of Justice, created in 1870, is the primary federal law enforcement agency in the country. With the responsibility of enforcing criminal law and supervising the federal prisons, the Justice Department plays a leading role in the American criminal justice system. To carry out its responsibilities to prevent and control crime, the department has a number of law enforcement agencies, including the Federal Bureau of Investigation, the federal Drug Enforcement Administration, the U.S. Marshals, and the Immigration and Naturalization Service.

The Federal Bureau of Investigation (FBI). Initially created in 1908 as the Bureau of Investigation, this agency was renamed the **Federal Bureau of Investigation (FBI)** in 1935. One of the primary investigative agencies of the federal government, the FBI has jurisdiction over nearly two hundred federal crimes, including sabotage, espionage (spying), kidnapping, extortion, interstate transportation of stolen property, bank robbery, interstate gambling, and civil rights violations. (For a look at other past activities of the bureau, see *Criminal Justice & Popular Culture: Star Gazing at the FBI?*)

The FBI rose to prominence under the controversial leadership of J. Edgar Hoover from 1924 to 1972. Hoover was widely recognized for increasing the professionalism not only of FBI agents, but also of thousands of local police officers who received training at the FBI National Academy. He also instituted the national fingerprint filing system and the Uniform Crime Reports (described in Chapter 1). Furthermore, Hoover's recognition of the importance of public relations brought the bureau into the national spotlight with such devices as the FBI's Ten Most Wanted list of dangerous fugitives.[41]

For all that he was able to accomplish, Hoover's reign was also marked by a number of scandals. He constantly used illegal investigative techniques, such as unauthorized wiretaps and break-ins, to gather personal information on his "enemies," who included, most famously, the civil rights leader Martin Luther King, Jr.[42] Upon Hoover's death,

Star Gazing at the FBI?

According to the film *Men in Black,* a federal law enforcement agency exists that nobody has ever heard about. The movie stars Tommy Lee Jones (Agent K) and Will Smith (Agent J) as a pair of government officers charged with monitoring the activities of extraterrestrials who happen to live on earth. Most of these aliens are law-abiding and peaceful, but sometimes they cause trouble, which is where Agents K and J step in. To keep the citizenry from panicking, the agency shrouds itself in secrecy. Any civilian who comes in contact with the organization is zapped into forgetfulness with a special brainwashing device.

When asked to identify himself, Agent K lies, "We're with the FBI." In fact, of the dozens of federal law enforcement agencies that do exist, the Federal Bureau of Investigation (FBI) comes closest to matching the men in black. For a period of more than twenty years starting in 1947, the FBI noted nearly every purported unidentified flying object (UFO) sighting that came to its attention, investigating the more plausible or sensational ones. The agency even looked into the infamous crash of a supposed spacecraft near Roswell, New Mexico, in the late 1940s, determining that the object was actually a "high altitude weather balloon with a radar detector."

The FBI stopped investigating UFOs in 1969 after determining that they posed no threat to national security. The files of the bureau's UFO activity were kept nearly as secret as the work of Agents K and J—that is, until 1998. That year, prodded by requests made under the Freedom of Information Act, the FBI released more than 1,600 pages of information dealing with thousands of supposed flying saucer sightings and other unexplained acts. Though most of the documents (available for public viewing on the bureau's Web site at **www.fbi.gov/foipa/ufo.htm**) serve to debunk theories of an alien presence, they do show that, at least for a time, the federal government considered the topic worth examining.

efforts were made to relegitimize the FBI in the eyes of many Americans.

Today, the FBI has more than 11,000 active agents and an annual budget of over $3 billion. The agency has five investigative priorities: (1) terrorism, (2) organized crime, (3) foreign intelligence operations in the United States, (4) federal drug offenses, and (5) white-collar crime.[43] The agency also offers valuable assistance to local and state law enforcement agencies. The FBI's Identification Division maintains a huge database of fingerprint information and offers assistance in finding missing persons and identifying the victims of fires, airplane crashes, and other disfiguring disasters. The services of the FBI Laboratory, the largest crime laboratory in the world, are available at no charge to other agencies. Finally, the FBI's National Crime Information Center (NCIC) provides lists of stolen vehicles and firearms, missing license plates, vehicles used to commit crimes, and other information to local and state law enforcement officers who may access the NCIC database. (See *Careers in Criminal Justice* on the next page.)

The Drug Enforcement Administration (DEA). With a $1 billion budget and nearly 4,000 special agents, the Drug Enforcement Administration (DEA) is one of the fastest-growing law enforcement agencies in the country. The mission of the DEA is to enforce domestic drug laws and regulations and to assist other federal and foreign agencies in combating illegal drug manufacture and trade on an international level. The agency also enforces the provisions of the Controlled Substance Act, which controls the manufacture, distribution, and dispensing of legal drugs, such as prescription drugs.

As we shall see in Chapter 17, the federal government has had a role in policing the manufacture and sale of illicit drugs since 1914. The first federal drug agency, the Federal Bureau of Narcotics (FBN), was established in 1930 under President Herbert Hoover. The FBN's main priorities were cocaine and opiates such as heroin. As the level of illegal drug use expanded over the decades, and international trafficking became a more pressing problem, several more agencies were formed to deal with drug enforcement. Then, in 1970 Congress passed the comprehensive Drug Abuse Prevention and Control Act,[44] which gave Congress the authority to regulate interstate commerce of legal drugs. With the Bureau of Narcotics and Dangerous Drugs (a successor

Careers in Criminal Justice

JIM RICE, FEDERAL BUREAU OF INVESTIGATION (FBI) SUPERVISORY SPECIAL AGENT

Growing up in a small town in rural West Virginia, I always knew that I wanted to be an FBI agent. There were probably a lot of other kids in America who shared this dream, but the murder of a woman who at one time was my babysitter convinced me to do everything that I could to make my dream of becoming a law enforcement officer come true.

I received a B.S. in biology from John Marshall University in West Virginia and subsequently earned a Master's degree in biochemistry from there as well. During college, I worked at several part-time jobs, loading trucks and bagging groceries, and also served in the Coast Guard as a reservist.

Following college, I went to work for the West Virginia State Police (WVSP) as a forensic toxicologist, a job that prepared me well for my current position with the FBI. These four years were well spent, because it was an interesting and challenging job and also because the FBI seeks to attract candidates who are competitive and who bring a speciality or work experience to the job.

I joined the FBI as a Special Agent in 1988 and spent the first 16 weeks of my Bureau career at the FBI Academy in Quantico, Virginia, as do all new agents. The FBI Academy is similar to a small college campus, with classrooms, dormitories, a cafeteria, and a gymnasium, with hundreds of students in residence at any given time, including new agents, experienced agents who are back for a week or two of specialized training, and police officers from all over the country and the world.

Following graduation from the FBI Academy, agents are subject to transfer to one of the 56 field offices in the United States for their first assignment. I was sent to the Indianapolis (Indiana) Office, where I was assigned to a "reactive squad," which handled violent criminal violations, such as bank robberies, fugitives, kidnappings, and extortions.

It was during my time in Indianapolis that I worked on a case that had a major impact on me and reaffirmed that the FBI was the right career choice for me. A young boy was kidnapped by an adult family friend and driven cross-country in the subject's truck. The FBI had surveillances on a number of locations in the Midwest, including the home of the subject's relatives in Indianapolis. After many long hours of surveillance in the cold and rain, our team found a truck that matched the description of the subject's truck, parked beside a house in a desolate part

of the city. We continued the surveillance on the truck and finally, the subject and the victim emerged from the house. As they drove off in the truck, our team followed discreetly at a distance until the order came from the lead agent to move in and conduct a tactical car stop. The subject was arrested and the boy was rescued, frightened but unharmed, and reunited with his parents.

A rotational transfer brought me to Washington, D.C., field office in 1992, where I joined the SWAT team and worked on a "Safe Streets Gang Task Force" and then on a Cold Case Homicide Squad. Soon thereafter, a Joint Terrorism Task Force was formed to address domestic terrorism matters in the nation's capital, an area filled with symbolic targets for would-be terroristic activities.

I volunteered to be part of this task force in late 1992 and was promoted to the position of Supervisory Special Agent of the squad in 1998. My duties include the operational and emergency response to incidents of domestic terrorism, bombings and bomb threats, chemical, biological, and nuclear incidents, and the security for special events, like presidential inaugurations and the 50th anniversary celebration of NATO, which brought dozens of heads of state to Washington in 1999, without incident.

to the FBN), the U.S. Customs Service, the FBI, and hundreds of state and local law enforcement agencies all working to enforce drug laws—as well as the government's new responsibility with regard to legal drugs—it was evident that a new "super agency" was needed. In 1973, by order of President Richard Nixon, the DEA was formed.

How the DEA Operates. Today, DEA agents often work in conjunction with local and state authorities to prevent illicit drugs from reaching communities. The agency also uses the influence of the U.S. government to persuade the governments of drug-producing countries to take steps to fight illegal substances on their own soil. At the prodding of the DEA, for example, the Bolivian government has pledged to destroy all coca crops—used to manufacture cocaine—by the year 2002.[45] Like the FBI, the DEA operates a network of six regional laboratories used to test and categorize seized drugs. Local law enforcement agencies have access to the DEA labs and often use them to ensure that information about particular drugs that will be presented in court is accurate and up-to-date. In recent years Congress has given the FBI more authority to enforce drug laws, and the two agencies now share a number of administrative controls.

Though most of the DEA's budget goes to fighting illegal drugs, the agency increasingly has had to deal with the problem of prescription substances. According to DEA estimates, nearly $30 billion worth of prescription drugs is sold "on the streets" every year—a figure comparable to the amount Americans spend on cocaine. The DEA is also playing a larger role in political issues such as the proposed use of marijuana for medical purposes and physician-assisted suicide. The DEA has a great deal of influence over physicians because the agency is responsible for registering physicians to prescribe drugs—any doctor whose ability to do so is taken away will find it difficult to practice medicine. Therefore, when the DEA threatens to revoke prescription rights of physicians who give patients marijuana or assist in suicides, the agency is making a strong stand against more liberal drug laws.[46]

The U.S. Marshals. The oldest federal law enforcement agency is the U.S. Marshals Office. In 1789, President George Washington assigned thirteen U.S. Marshals to protect his attorney general. That same year, Congress created the Office of the U.S. Marshals. Originally, the U.S. Marshals acted as the main law enforcement officers in the western territories. Following the Civil War, when most of these territories had become states, these agents were assigned to work for the U.S. district courts, where federal crimes are tried. The relationship between the U.S. Marshals Office and the federal courts continues today and forms the basis for the officers' main duties, which include:

1. Providing security at federal courts for judges, jurors, and other courtroom participants.

2. Controlling property that has been ordered seized by federal courts.

3. Protecting government witnesses who place themselves in danger by testifying against the targets of federal criminal investigations. This protection is sometimes accomplished by relocating the witnesses and providing them with different identities.

4. Transporting federal prisoners to detention institutions.

5. Investigating violations of federal fugitive laws.[47]

The Immigration and Naturalization Service (INS). The Immigration and Naturalization Service (INS) monitors and polices the flow of immigrants into the United States. Agents of the INS patrol the borders of the continental United States and American territories to ensure that immigrants do not enter the country illegally. They also apprehend and deport *aliens* who have not complied with U.S. naturalization laws that would allow them to live within American borders.

In recent years, the United States–Mexico border has become a pressing concern because of the large number of illegal immigrants and huge amounts of illicit drugs that pass over the boundary. As a result, the U.S. Border Patrol has seen its budget rise to over $4 billion, a nearly 200 percent increase since 1993. Furthermore, the number of border patrol agents doubled to 7,000 during the same time period, with plans to add an additional 1,000 agents each year until 2008. The result has been dramatic—in the Tucson (Arizona) sector alone, agents arrested nearly 400,000 illegal aliens from October 1997 to

The Del Rio Sector of the United States Border Patrol is responsible for controling 205 miles of the Rio Grande River, the natural border between the U.S. and Mexico. Go to www.ins.usdoj.gov/delrio/dr welcome.html

Border patrol agents frisk illegal aliens captured in Nogales, Arizona. Starting in 1994, Operation Gatekeeper increased the number of border patrol agents in the southwestern United States from 800 to 2,300, resulting in a dramatic increase in the number of illegal aliens captured and returned to Mexico. The increase in agents also appears to have led to an increase in violent confrontations between agents and aliens. In four separate incidents in October 1998, border agents opened fire on rock-throwing illegal aliens. Two Mexicans were killed in the exchanges, and several agents were badly injured. Do you believe society benefits from efforts to keep illegal aliens out of the country? Is the use of force to carry out these efforts justifiable?

September 1998. According to estimates, however, at least twice that number made it safely into the United States.[48]

The Department of the Treasury. The Department of the Treasury, formed in 1789, is mainly responsible for all financial matters of the federal government. It pays all the federal government's bills, borrows money, collects taxes, mints coins, and prints paper currency. The department also has several law enforcement agencies, including the Bureau of Alcohol, Tobacco, and Firearms, the U.S. Secret Service, the Internal Revenue Service, and the Customs Service.

The Bureau of Alcohol, Tobacco, and Firearms (ATF). As its name suggests, the Bureau of Alcohol, Tobacco, and Firearms (ATF) is primarily concerned with the illegal sale, possession, and use of firearms and the control of untaxed tobacco and liquor products. The Firearms Division of the agency has the responsibility of enforcing the Gun Control Act of 1968, which sets the circumstances under which firearms may be sold and used in this country. The bureau also regulates all gun trade between the United States and foreign countries and collects taxes on all firearm importers, manufacturers, and dealers. In keeping with these duties, the ATF is also responsible for policing the illegal use and possession of explosives. Furthermore, the ATF is charged with enforcing federal wagering laws.

Because it has jurisdiction over such a wide variety of crimes, especially those involving firearms and explosives, the ATF is a constant presence in federal criminal investigations. Since 1982, for example, the agency has been working in conjunction with the FBI to prevent the bombing of abortion clinics. Technicians from the ATF linked two bombs placed in an Atlanta (Georgia) abortion clinic in 1997 to the explosive device that detonated at the Olympic Games a year earlier in that city. Recently, the agency, along with the FBI, has begun to place undercover informants inside antiabortion groups to gain information about proposed bombings. Furthermore, the ATF has been active in forming multijurisdictional drug task forces with other federal and local law enforcement agencies to investigate drug crimes involving firearms.

The U.S. Secret Service. When initially created in 1865, the Secret Service was primarily responsible for combating currency counterfeiters. In 1901, the agency was given the added responsibility of protecting the president of the United States, the president's family, the vice-president, the president-elect, and ex-presidents. These duties have remained the cornerstone of the agency, with several expansions. After a number of threats against presidential candidates in the 1960s and early 1970s, including the shootings of Robert Kennedy and Governor George Wallace of Alabama, in 1976 Secret Service agents became responsible for protecting those political figures as well.

In addition to its special plainclothes agents, the agency also directs two uniformed groups of law enforcement officers. The Secret Service Uniformed Division protects the grounds of the White House and its inhabitants, and the Treasury Police Force polices the Treasury Building in Washington, D.C. This responsibility includes investigating threats against presidents and those running for presidential office.

To aid its battle against counterfeiters and forgers of government bonds, the agency has the use of a laboratory at the Bureau of Engraving and Printing in the nation's capital.

The Internal Revenue Service (IRS). The largest bureau of the Treasury Department, the Internal Revenue Service (IRS), is concerned with violations of tax laws and regulations. The bureau has three divisions, only one of which is involved in criminal investigations. The examination branch of the IRS audits the tax returns of corporations and individuals. The collection division attempts to collect taxes from corporations or citizens who have failed to pay the taxes they owe. Finally, the criminal investigation division investigates cases of tax evasion and tax fraud. Criminal investigation agents can make arrests. The IRS has long played a role in policing criminal activities such as gambling and selling drugs for one simple reason: those who engage in such activities almost never report any illegally gained income on their tax returns. Therefore, the IRS is able to apprehend them for tax evasion. The most famous instance of this took place in the 1920s, when the IRS finally arrested crime boss Al Capone—responsible for numerous violent crimes—for not paying his taxes.

The U.S. Customs Service. The U.S. Customs Service stations agents at ports of entry and exit to the United States to police the flow of people and goods into and out of the country. A primary goal of the bureau is to prevent the smuggling of contraband (anything that is unlawful to produce or possess). Customs agents have widespread authority to investigate and search all international passengers, including those arriving on airplanes, ships, or other forms of transportation. Furthermore, the Customs Service is responsible for ensuring that proper tariffs and taxes have been paid on all goods imported into the United States. As efforts to stop the international flow of illicit drugs have become a higher priority, Customs agents are increasingly working in tandem with the federal Drug Enforcement Administration.

Private Security

Even with the increasing numbers of local, state, and federal law enforcement officers, the police do not have the ability to prevent every crime. Recognizing this, many businesses and citizens have decided to hire private security. The results of such a decision can be striking. A few years ago, residents in a six-block section of Georgetown, an upper-class neighborhood in Washington, D.C., were concerned over rising rates of auto theft. They hired a security guard from the Wells Fargo Company to patrol the area at a cost of 44 cents per household per day. After a year, burglaries had decreased by 55 percent and robberies by 50 percent. The security guard even thwarted a kidnapping attempt. Soon after, 90 percent of the entire Georgetown neighborhood was being policed by security guards.[49] This anecdote hints at the massive increase in the use of **private security** in the United States over the past three decades.

A Growing Industry. Allan Pinkerton, a Scottish immigrant, started the first private security company in the United States in 1860. Today, Pinkerton, Inc., has annual revenues of more than $600 million and is one of nearly 60,000 private security firms in the country.[50] In 1970, the ratio of private security officers to police officers paid by the government was 1.4 to 1. As Figure 4.6 shows, the discrepancy has continued to grow since then. Today, there are three times as many private police as public, and Americans are spending $90 billion a year on private security, compared to $40 billion in taxes for public police. During the 1996 Olympic Games in Atlanta, the city employed 4,800 state and local police officers and 13,000 private security guards.[51]

This increase in private security can be traced to several social and economic trends. The Hallcrest Report II, a far-reaching overview of the private

A U.S. Secret Service agent testifies during special prosecutor Kenneth Starr's investigation of President Bill Clinton for alleged misbehavior in the Monica Lewinsky affair. The Clinton administration had tried to block Starr's ability to subpoena Secret Service agents, claiming that such an action would compromise the trust between the president and those agents sworn to protect him. "If there's a moment's hesitation by the president [in providing information to a Secret Service agent], it could be the difference between life and death," said a deputy attorney general. U.S. District Judge Norma Holloway Johnson rejected this argument, holding that Secret Service agents, as officers of the law, are obligated to report wrongdoing, even if committed by the president. Do you agree with the judge's ruling? Why or why not?

PRIVATE SECURITY
The practice of private corporations or individuals offering services traditionally performed by police officers.

Figure 4.6 The Rise of Private Security in the United States

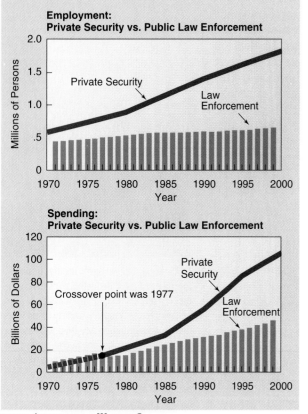

SOURCE: ADAPTED FROM WILLIAM C. CUNNINGHAM, JOHN J. STRAUCHS, AND CLIFFORD W. VAN METER, PRIVATE SECURITY TRENDS, 1970-2000: THE HALLCREST REPORT II (BOSTON: BUTTERWORTH-HEINEMANN, 1990), 237-239.

security trends funded by the National Institute of Justice, identifies four main factors in the growth of the industry:

1. An increase in fear on the part of the public triggered by the growing rate of crime, either real or perceived.

2. The problem of crime in the workplace.

3. Budget cuts in states and municipalities that have forced reductions in the number of public police, which raises the demand for private ones.

4. A rising awareness of private security products (such as home burglar alarms) and services as cost-effective protective measures.[52]

William Cunningham, the author of the report, does *not* believe that the growth of private security is a "put-down" of the police. Instead, he says, "people are taking a greater stake in protecting themselves" rather than relying on public services. (For an example of a country in which the growth of private security clearly reflects a "put-down" of the police, see *Cross-National CJ Comparison: Private Bodyguards in Mexico—Out of Control?*)

Authority of Private Police. Partly because of the speed at which the industry has grown, consensus has yet to be reached on the restrictions that should be placed on private security employees. Some courts have ruled that these personnel are not held to the same rules of action that govern public police in the use of force, interrogation, and other issues of law. Other courts have found that private police are bound by the same laws as their public counterparts because people perceive them as having the same legal authority.[53] The situation is further complicated by the fact that many members of local and state police forces **moonlight** as private security guards; that is, they work private security details during "off hours" to earn extra income.

THE RESPONSIBILITIES OF THE POLICE

Some observers, including police executives, believe that giving an increased role to private security employees—allowing them to respond to burglar alarms, for example, or handle misdemeanor reports—would free up police officers to deal with "more important" duties.[54] For the most part, the incidents that make up a police officer's daily routine would not make it onto television dramas such as *Law and Order*. Besides catching criminals, police spend a great deal of time on such mundane tasks as responding to noise complaints, confiscating firecrackers, and poring over paperwork. Sociologist Egon Bittner warned against the tendency to see the police primarily as agents of law enforcement and crime control. A more inclusive accounting of "what the police do," Bittner believed, would recognize that they provide "situationally justified force in society."[55] In other words, the function of the police is to solve any problem that may *possibly*, though not *necessarily*, require the use of force.

Within Bittner's rather broad definition of "what the police do," we can pinpoint four basic responsibilities of the police:

MOONLIGHTING
The practice of a police officer holding a second job in the private security field.

1. To enforce laws.

2. To provide services.

3. To prevent crime.

4. To preserve the peace.

Private Bodyguards in Mexico—Out of Control?

The Mexican people, it seems, have little faith in their law enforcement institutions. Weakened by decades of corruption, Mexico's police are ineffectual at best. As crime rates have been declining north of the border, they have been surging in Mexico. When police officers in Mexico City do solve a crime, it is such a rare event that it is celebrated with banner headlines in local newspapers. As a result of this situation, the number of *guaruras* (private bodyguards) roaming the streets of the country's larger cities has exploded. Some observers worry that these private bodyguards, while possibly providing security to their bosses, are increasing the dangers faced by the community as a whole.

The *guaruras* have a long tradition in Mexico; the word itself comes from the Aztecs, who flourished in the area until conquered by the Spaniards in the sixteenth century. In the past, however, only the wealthiest members of society had their own private security forces. Today, in the face of the crime wave, most office buildings and middle-class neighborhoods are guarded by *guaruras* wearing shiny black suits, black ties, and sunglasses, with handguns barely concealed under their jackets. The private bodyguards favor four-door American cars with the hubcaps removed. The cars are often equipped with a black steel grate—known as a burro-bouncer—over the front grill to clear a path should quick escape be necessary.

Nearly 200,000 Mexicans are employed by more than 3,000 private security companies. In Mexico City, the 90,000 private bodyguards outnumber police officers by more than 10,000. This proliferation has caused a number of problems. First, in their zeal-ousness to protect, the *guaruras* often exceed the boundaries of what many Mexicans regard as decent behavior. They swerve their cars from lane to lane on the highways to make sure no vehicle gets close to the luxury automobile carrying their bosses and wave their firearms menacingly at pedestrians who walk too close to the building where their bosses work or live. Second, the private security personnel appear to be adding to the crime wave instead of alleviating it. Most guards stand guard over stores or other businesses and are paid minuscule salaries, perhaps less than $50 per month. Under these circumstances, they find it more profitable to steal than protect, and police are reporting a rash of burglaries committed by security guards and night watchmen.

After Mexico City Police Chief Alejandro Gertz pulled over two private security cars painted with the colors of the official police force, he started a campaign to better supervise private security companies. Police Chief Gertz would like all private guards to pass psychological, drug, and weapons-handling tests, as well as undergo screening to ensure that their pasts are free of criminal activity. Others would simply like the *guaruras* to act more responsibly. "A professional bodyguard should be discreet," notes one observer who works in the industry. "But in this country they love to make a show of their arrogance. If there is a fight, they jump in and make it worse."

WHAT'S THE EVIDENCE?

The crime wave in Mexico has created business opportunities for private companies wishing to take advantage of the ineffectiveness of the country's law enforcement agencies. To get information on one company that is "filling the void," and to learn about the operation of an international private security firm, visit the home page of Vance International de Mexico at **www.vancesecurity.com/Mexico.htm**.

As will become evident over the next three chapters, there is a great deal of debate among legal and other scholars and law enforcement officers over which responsibilities deserve the most police attention and what methods should be employed by the police in meeting those responsibilities.

Enforcing Laws

In the public mind, the primary role of the police is to enforce society's laws—hence, the term *law enforcement officer*. In their role as "crime fighters," police officers have a clear mandate to seek out and apprehend those who have violated the law. The crime-fighting responsibility is so dominant that all police activity—from the purchase of new automobiles to a plan to hire more minority officers—must often be justified in terms of its law enforcement value.[56]

Police officers also primarily see themselves as crime fighters, or "crook catchers," a perception that often leads people into what they believe will be an exciting career in law enforcement. Although the job certainly offers challenges unlike any other, police officers do not normally spend the majority of

INFOTRAC®
COLLEGE EDITION

DiIulio, John. **Federal crime policy**: time for a moratorium.

their time in law enforcement duties. Several studies from the 1970s suggested that police officers spent a very small percentage of their workday on law enforcement matters. Both Thomas Bercal, who examined police calls in St. Louis and Detroit, and John A. Webster, who made a similar study on a wider basis, estimated that only 16 percent of those calls were related to law enforcement.[57]

More recently, police experts have come to the conclusion that these early studies of police activities were flawed in several ways, not the least of which was that they tended to focus only on general patrol officers while discounting criminal investigation units or special response units, which have heavier law enforcement duties. In 1991, Jack Greene and Carl Klockars revisited questions of police workload in Wilmington, Delaware, with the goal of improving upon the earlier research.[58] Using a more methodical set of data, they found that police officers spend about half of their time enforcing the law or dealing with crimes.

Providing Services

If Greene and Klockars are correct, what are police officers doing the other half of working hours? The emphasis on crime fighting and law enforcement tends to overshadow the fact that a great deal of a police officer's time is spent providing services for the community. The motto "To Serve and Protect" has been adopted by thousands of local police departments, and the *Law Enforcement Code of Ethics* recognizes the duty "to serve the community" in its first sentence.[59] The services that police provide are numerous—a partial list would include directing traffic, performing emergency medical procedures, counseling those involved in domestic disputes, providing directions to tourists, and finding lost children. As mentioned earlier, many police departments have adopted the strategy of community policing, and as a consequence, many officers find themselves providing assistance in areas that have not until recently been their domain.[60] For example, police are required to deal with the problems of the homeless and the mentally ill to a greater extent than in past decades.

Preventing Crime

Perhaps the most controversial responsibility of the police is to *prevent* crime. According to Jerome Skolnick of the University of California at Berkeley, there are two predictable public responses when crime rates begin to rise in a community. The first is to punish convicted criminals with stricter laws and more severe penalties. The second is to demand that the police "do something" to prevent crimes from occurring in the first place. Is it, in fact, possible for the police to "prevent" crimes? The strongest response that Professor Skolnick is willing to give to this question is "maybe."[61]

On a limited basis, police can certainly prevent some crimes. If a rapist is dissuaded from attacking a solitary woman because a patrol car is cruising the area, then that police officer behind the wheel has prevented a crime. In general, however, the deterrent effects of police presence are unclear. Carl Klockars has written that the "war on crime" is a war that the police cannot win because they cannot control the factors—such as unemployment, poverty, immorality, inequality, political change, and lack of educational opportunities—that lead to criminal behavior in the first place.[62] As we shall see in the next chapter, many police stations have adopted the idea of community policing in an attempt to better prevent crime.

INFOTRAC ®
COLLEGE EDITION

Waggoner, Kim. Focus on crime prevention: creative solutions to traditional problems.

Preserving the Peace

To a certain extent, the fourth responsibility of the police, that of preserving the peace, is related to preventing crime. Police have the legal authority to use the power of arrest, or even force, in situations in which no crime has yet occurred, but might occur in the immediate future.

In the words of James Q. Wilson, the police's peacekeeping role (which Wilson believes is the most important role of law enforcement officers) often takes on a pattern of simply "handling the situation."[63] For example, when police officers arrive on the scene of a loud late-night house party, they may feel the need to disperse the party and even arrest some of the party goers for disorderly conduct. By their actions, the officers have lessened the chances of serious and violent crimes taking place later in the evening. The same principle is often used when dealing with domestic disputes, which, if escalated, can lead to homicide. Such situations are in need of, to use Wilson's terminology again, "fixing up," and police can use the power of arrest, or threat, or coercion, or sympathy, to do just that.

The basis of Wilson and George Kelling's "broken windows" theory is similar: street disorder—such as public drunkenness, urination, and loitering—signals to both law-abiding citizens and criminals that the law is not being enforced and therefore leads to more violent crime. Hence, if police preserve the peace and "crack down" on the minor crimes that make up street disorder, they will in fact be preventing serious crimes that would otherwise occur in the future.[64]

THE ROLE OF DISCRETION IN POLICING

Though the responsibilities just discussed provide a helpful overview of "what police do," they also highlight the ambiguity of a police officer's duties. To say, for example, that highway patrol officers have a responsibility to enforce speed laws is to oversimplify their "real" job. In fact, most highway patrol officers would not find it feasible to hand out speeding tickets to every driver who exceeds the posted speed limit. Furthermore, depending on the circumstances, a patrol officer may decide not to issue a ticket to a driver who has been pulled over. Rather, most officers selectively enforce speed laws, ticketing only those who significantly exceed the limit or drive so recklessly that they endanger other drivers. As noted in Chapter 1, when police officers use their judgment in deciding which offenses to punish and which to ignore, they are said to be using *discretion*. Whether this discretion applies to speed limits or any other area of the law, it is a crucial aspect of policing.

Justification for Police Discretion

One of the ironies of law enforcement is that patrol officers—often the lowest paid members of an agency with the least amount of authority—have the greatest amount of discretionary power. Part of the explanation for this is practical. Patrol officers spend most of the day on the streets, beyond the control of their supervisors. Usually, only two people are present when a patrol officer must make a decision: the officer and the possible wrongdoer. In all cases, the law enforcement officer has a great deal of freedom to take the action that he or she feels best corresponds to the situation.[65] (For a situation in which this discretion is being taken away from many police officers, see *CJ in Focus: The Balancing Act—To Pursue or Not to Pursue?* on the following page.)

"That's the only thing that made me feel safe last night when I came home from work."

—Penny Baily, *resident of Indianapolis*, commenting on the police car patroling her neighborhood (1996)

CJ in Focus
The Balancing Act
To Pursue or Not to Pursue?

The chase began when sheriff's deputies in Martin County, Florida, were notified that Quincy Everett and two accomplices had been spotted shoplifting clothes from a department store. It ended thirty miles later, when Everett, driving at speeds of greater than 100 miles per hour, crashed into a minivan. The accident resulted in the deaths of one of Everett's accomplices and motorcyclist William Carboni, who was waiting at a traffic light when struck by the minivan.

According to the National Highway Traffic Safety Administration, approximately 400 people are killed in high-speed police pursuits each year. (Other private groups, such as Solutions to Tragedies of Police Pursuits [STOPP], claim that the number is closer to 2,500.) As Figure 4.7 shows, the potential for injury and death is quite high; the study cited shows more than four out of every ten high-speed police pursuits ending with an accident. Many observers question whether the risk created by such pursuit is greater than the need to enforce the law, especially when the initial infraction is not a serious one, as was the case in Florida. (Figure 4.7 also shows that nearly half of all pursuits are initiated by traffic offenses.) Those who believe the risk is too great favor policies to limit police discretion in deciding when to engage in a high-speed chase.

Many police departments have instituted guidelines that take the decision out of the officer's hands. The Virginia Beach (Virginia) Police

Jung Won Ko suffered serious burns when her car was hit by a drunken driver trying to outrun Los Angeles police officers.

Figure 4.7 The Causes and Consequences of High-Speed Pursuits

Over a recent five year period, Metro-Dade County (Florida) police officers engaged in 994 high speed pursuits. As you can see, most of the chases were the result of traffic violations and lasted between 5 and 10 minutes. Furthermore, one out of every five police chases in Metro-Dade County resulted in an injury.

Reason for Police Pursuit

Reason	Percentage of Total Pursuits
Traffic violation	45
BOLO*	4
Felonies or suspected felonies	35
Suspect vehicles	

Pursuit-Related Accidents and Injuries

Caused by Pursuit	Percentage of Total Pursuits
Accidents	41
Injuries	20
Property damage	25

Duration of Police Pursuit

Duration of Pursuit	Percentage of Total Pursuits
1 minute or less	3
2–4 minutes	10
5–10 minutes	59
11 minutes or more	28

*Be On Look Out situations, in which officers have been ordered to stop a certain vehicle if they happen to spot it.

SOURCE: GEOFFREY P. ALPERT, "PURSUIT DRIVING: PLANNING POLICIES AND ACTION FROM AGENCY, OFFICER, AND PUBLIC INFORMATION," POLICE FORUM 7 (JANUARY 1997), 3.

Department, for example, recently established guidelines that allow chases only when the initial crime is a violent felony or involves guns or explosives. Consequently, Virginia Beach police may no longer pursue drunk drivers, car thieves, burglars, or other nonviolent suspects. According to a recent study, nearly half of the nation's police departments have modified their pursuit policies, with 90 percent of those surveyed placing greater restrictions on their officers.

For Critical Analysis: Given that the police's primary duty is to protect the public, what might be some of the drawbacks of restrictions such as those imposed in Virginia Beach? What steps might be taken to reduce the risk of third-party deaths other than limiting police discretion?

This is not to say that police discretion is misplaced. In general, courts have recognized that a patrol officer is in a unique position to be allowed discretionary powers:

- Police officers are considered trustworthy and are therefore assumed to make honest decisions, regardless of contradictory testimony by a suspect.

- Experience and training give officers the ability to determine whether certain activity poses a threat to society, and to take any reasonable action necessary to investigate or prevent such activity.

- Due to the nature of their jobs, police officers are extremely knowledgeable in human, and by extension criminal, behavior.

- Police officers may find themselves in danger of personal, physical harm and must be allowed to take reasonable and necessary steps to protect themselves.[66]

In deciding how to apply the law to any particular situation, police officers generally consider three factors. First, and most important, is the nature of the criminal act. The less serious a crime, the more likely a police officer is to ignore it. A person driving 60 miles per hour in a 55 miles-per-hour zone, for example, is much less likely to be ticketed than someone doing 80 miles per hour. A second factor often considered is the attitude of the wrongdoer toward the officer. A motorist who is belligerent toward a highway patrol officer is much more likely to be ticketed than one who is contrite and apologetic. Third, departmental policy can place limits on discretion. If a police chief decides that all motorists who exceed the speed limit by 10 miles will be ticketed, that policy will influence the patrol officer's decisions.[67]

Police Discretion and Domestic Violence

A fourth factor that often influences police discretion is the relationship between the person committing the criminal act and the victim. The closer this relationship, the less likely some police officers are to arrest the wrongdoer.[68] This tendency is often evident in police action (or lack thereof) concerning **domestic violence.** The statistics surrounding this crime speak volumes as to the extent of the problem in the United States. An estimated three to four million American women are battered—subjected to physical, emotional, or sexual force—by their partners every year.[69] According to research cited by Congress, domestic violence is the leading cause of injury for women between the ages of fifteen and forty-four in the United States.[70] Nearly one-third of all female murder victims in the United States are killed by current or former husbands or boyfriends.[71] For most of this nation's history, the police role in domestic violence was limited to "calming" the situation, a short-term response that did little to prevent future violence. Today, more is expected.

Police Response and Leniency Theory. Many police officers see domestic violence cases as the responsibility of social service providers, not law enforcement officers. Furthermore, officers are often uncomfortable with the intensely private nature of domestic disputes.[72] Finally, even if a police officer does arrest the abuser, the victim often chooses to drop the charges.

These factors greatly influence police discretion with regard to domestic violence. Research suggests that this discretion manifests itself in what has come to be called the *leniency theory* of police response to domestic violence, which holds that police are lenient toward male batterers. Professors James J.

DOMESTIC VIOLENCE
An act of physical aggression against a spouse or intimate partner.

MANDATORY ARREST
A statutory requirement that law enforcement agents shall arrest a person suspected of committing a specific illegal act.

Fyfe of Temple University, David Klinger of the University of Houston, and Jeanne Flavin of Fordham University tested the leniency theory by studying police responses to domestic violence in the Chester (Pennsylvania) Police Department. The researchers found that Chester police were less likely to arrest male felony assailants who had attacked former or present female partners than other males who had committed similarly violent acts.[73] Among the incidents that did *not* lead to arrests were 4 attacks with guns; 38 attacks involving cutting instruments (including one with an ax); and 27 attacks with blunt instruments such as baseball bats or hammers. In one incident that did not result in an arrest, a woman was held by her feet over a second floor landing and dropped onto her head.

Mandatory Arrest. In the landmark Minneapolis Domestic Violence Experiment of 1983, the Minneapolis (Minnesota) Police Department and Professors Lawrence Sherman and Richard Berk attempted to determine the consequences of police inaction in domestic violence cases. The researchers found that the most effective deterrent to repeat episodes of battering was the arrest of the batterer.[74] Many law enforcement agencies used the results of the Minneapolis experiment to justify setting limits on police discretion in domestic violence cases.[75] Today, twenty-three states and the District of Columbia have passed **mandatory arrest** laws that require a police officer to arrest a person who has battered a spouse or domestic partner.[76] (See Figure 4.8.)

Such severe limitation of police discretion is not universally favored. In fact, additional research has showed that arrest of the batterer without subsequent conviction may actually *increase* the possibility of further violence,[77] a finding that led the authors of the Minneapolis experiment to caution that "there is a good chance that arrest works far better for some kinds of offenders than others."[78] Furthermore, some observers feel that the mandatory

Figure 4.8 Limiting Police Discretion: Mandatory Arrest for Domestic Violence

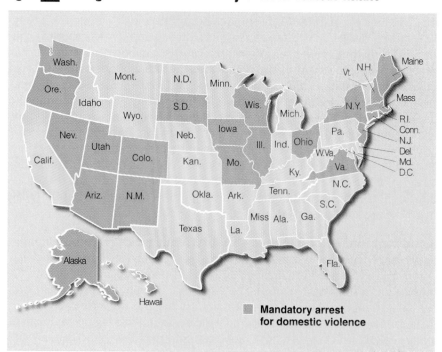

arrest laws cause police officers to focus on the batterer at the expense of the victim. In an attempt to clarify the responsibilities of a police officer responding to a domestic violence call (in effect, to reduce police discretion in favor of established procedures), the National Council of Juvenile and Family Court Judges released a Model State Code for those situations. The code states that police officers responding to domestic violence calls should use "all reasonable means to protect the victim and prevent further violence," including:

1. Confiscating any weapon involved in the alleged violence.

2. Transporting or obtaining transportation for the victim and any child to a shelter.

3. Assisting the victim in removing any personal items from the residence.

4. Assisting the victim in obtaining medical assistance, including transportation to a medical facility.

5. Giving the victim immediate and comprehensive notice of the rights of victims and of possible remedies and services available to victims of domestic or family violence.[79]

The code recognizes that policy changes with regard to domestic violence can go only so far in influencing the behavior of police officers. Regardless of the law or departmental guidelines, field officers must rely on experience and what can broadly be called "instinct" in making the split-second decisions necessary to do their job. The Model State Code for domestic violence attempts to introduce certain behaviors into the decision-making process of police officers who deal with the victims of batterers in the hope that such behaviors will eventually become instinctual.

Criminal Justice in Action
Police and Gun Control

An important aspect of police discretion, as we shall see in Chapter 7, is the decision whether to use deadly force. The deadliest weapon that a police officer owns is his or her firearm. By the same token, guns in the hands of criminals present one of the greatest risks to the well-being of a law enforcement officer. Consequently, police officers have a unique vantage point from which to consider one of the most highly charged debates in American society—gun control. Those who favor more restrictions on the ease with which citizens can purchase and own firearms point out that the United States has the most heavily armed population in the world. The result, they say, is the highest murder rate among all developed nations. Those who oppose stricter gun laws insist that Americans have a constitutional right to use firearms to protect themselves and their property. Furthermore, they say, registering and licensing guns will only keep them out of the hands of law-abiding citizens, while having no effect on wrongdoers' ability to arm themselves. In this *Criminal Justice in Action* feature, we will examine various police perspectives on these and other issues of gun control.

GUNS IN THE UNITED STATES

As Denver police officer Bruce VanderJagt started his shift at 2 P.M. on November 12, 1997, five people were in the process of committing a burglary in Buffalo Creek, a small town thirty miles away. In an effort to escape local police, one of the burglars, Matthaeus Jaehnig, drove a stolen red Trans Am into Denver. VanderJagt, along with some of his fellow officers, chased the car into a residential neighborhood, where Jaehnig fled into a condominium. As soon as VanderJagt entered the building in pursuit, a spray of bullets from an SKS Chinese semiautomatic assault rifle killed him. After taking VanderJagt's life, Jaehnig took his own.[80]

VanderJagt was one of 633 police officers murdered by firearms between 1988 and 1997. This statistic is only one measure of the violence done by guns in the United States every year. Approximately 35,000 Americans are killed each year by firearms in incidents rang-

ing from suicides to homicides to accidents. The U.S. Department of Justice estimates that one out of every three violent crimes committed annually in the country—about half a million—is done so with the use of a firearm.[81] (For a breakdown on the prevalence of firearms in criminal killing, see Figure 4.9.) Concern over the effect of guns on the safety of American citizens, as well as their own well-being, has placed police in the center of the gun control debate.

GUNS AND POLICE CULTURE

Though guns are an undeniable part of police work and culture, most officers do not like to use them. "When I used to walk into a precinct," said one Queens (New York) district attorney, "I could tell who had just shot his gun. He looked like he had a terrible disease."[82] In fact, statistically speaking, most police rarely, if ever, use their guns on the job. Nearly 95 percent of New York City police officers have never fired their weapons in the line of duty, and in a recent three-year period, the town of Madison, Wisconsin, had only five police shooting incidents.[83]

This does not mean, however, that American police agree with their British counterparts, four out of five of whom would rather not carry firearms at all.[84] Many American police officers have a psychological attachment to their weapons and would feel "exposed" working without them. Many feel that they need *more* powerful firearms to effectively fight well-armed criminals. After a bank robbery in Los Angeles during which two men armed with

Figure 4.9 The Use of Firearms in Murder and Nonnegligent Homicide

As you can see from this graph, two out of every three murders and nonnegligent manslaughters known to police are carried out with a firearm.

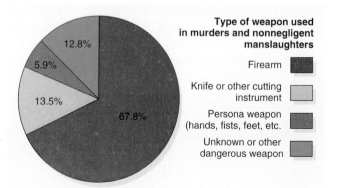

Type of weapon used in murders and nonnegligent manslaughters

- Firearm — 67.8%
- Knife or other cutting instrument — 13.5%
- Persona weapon (hands, fists, feet, etc. — 5.9%
- Unknown or other dangerous weapon — 12.8%

SOURCE: FEDERAL BUREAU OF INVESTIGATION, CRIME IN THE UNITED STATES— 1996 (WASHINGTON, D.C.: U.S. GOVERNMENT PRINTING OFFICER), TABLE 2.9, PAGE 18.

automatic rifles and wearing body armor battled police officers in broad daylight, the Los Angeles Police Department purchased 600 military surplus M-16 rifles.[85]

THE BRADY BILL

The preferred method of fighting crime, however, is not for law enforcement officers to engage in an arms race with criminals. Police associations have been instrumental in lobbying efforts to reduce the ease with which firearms are available in the United States. Their most notable success was the passage of the Brady Handgun Violence Prevention Act in 1993.[86] Commonly known as the Brady Bill, this measure requires local law enforcement agencies to conduct background checks of potential handgun purchasers. In the first twenty-eight months after the effective date of the Brady Bill, 130,200 convicted or indicted felons were prevented from buying a gun because of the new background checks.[87] Furthermore—though the causal relationship is debatable—during the same time period, murders with firearms decreased 11.6 percent, aggravated assault with firearms 5.8 percent, and armed robberies 7.6 percent.[88] Criminologists point out that other factors than the Brady Bill, such as lower poverty levels and more effective policing techniques, may be responsible for such figures.

On the whole, the Brady Bill has proved to be the exception rather than the rule when it comes to the results of police lobbying. After Officer VanderJagt's death in Denver, and despite wrenching testimony from police officers who had watched their partners killed by firearms, the Colorado legislature rejected a proposal to ban semiautomatic assault weapons in that state.[89] In 1997, the California Police Chiefs made their top legislative priority a bill to ban the manufacture and sale of cheap handguns, but the bill was vetoed by then-Governor Pete Wilson.[90]

Not all law enforcement officers agree that the Brady Bill is necessary. In fact, two sheriffs—Jay Printz of Ravali County and Richard Mack of Graham County, Arizona—dealt the legislation its most dramatic setback.[91] The two sheriffs argued that state officers could not be forced to carry out federal laws. Their case eventually reached the Supreme Court, and the Court agreed that Congress did not have the authority to enlist state law enforcement officers against their will in the effort to control firearms.[92]

GUNS AND AMERICAN CULTURE

Though many observers blame the efforts of lobbying groups such as the National Rifle Association for political reluctance to restrict firearms sales, the explanation lies more with the prominent place of the gun in American culture.[93] About 50 percent of all American households own at least one firearm.[94] Support for an outright ban on handguns decreased over the past few decades as crime rates rose; today, 40 percent of Americans are in favor of such a ban, down from 60 percent in 1959.[95] These attitudes—backed up by certain scholarly studies[96]—reflect a belief that handguns are an effective form of crime deterrence. As a sign of public support for liberal gun laws, thirty-one states have passed concealed weapons statutes that allow their citizens to carry handguns on their person and out of plain view, a situation that can prove exceedingly dangerous for police officers.

In the absence of legal protections, many municipal and state police departments are establishing special task forces to investigate and control the flow of illegal firearms into their communities. There is also hope that technology can help protect police officers. Gun manufacturers are in the process of creating "smart" guns that can be fired only by their owners. These new weapons would lessen the danger of an officer being killed by her or his own gun in someone else's hand, which happens an average of ten times a year.[97] Even more security would be provided by a new generation of security devices that will let police officers, while still at a distance, identify people who are carrying concealed guns. "If you think of the situation cops face day in and day out, the greatest risk is approaching a subject who may be armed," says Jeremy Travis of the National Institute of Justice. "So to be able to know in advance whether the individual is armed gives the officer an enormous advantage in safety and tactics."[98]

Key Terms

coroner 126

domestic violence 139

Federal Bureau of Investigation (FBI) 128

justice of the peace 115

mandatory arrest 140

moonlighting 134

patronage system 118

private security 133

professional model 120

sheriff 124

shire-reeve 115

tithing system 115

watch system 115

Chapter Summary

1. **Describe the first systems of law enforcement in colonial America.** Constables and night watchmen were drawn from the ranks of ordinary citizens. Each colony had a sheriff in each county who selected juries and managed incarcerations. Local citizens assisted sheriffs in peace-keeping duties.

2. **Tell how the patronage system affected policing.** During the political era of policing (1840–1930), bribes paid by citizens and business owners often went into the coffers of the local political party. This became known as the patronage system.

3. **Indicate the results of the Wickersham Commission.** The Wickersham Commission of 1929 called for reform to eliminate police brutality and the corrupting influence of politics. The result was the professionalization of American police, sometimes called the progressive era in American policing. Potential police officers began to be trained in institutes of higher learning. Another result was the increased use of technology in police work.

4. **List five main types of law enforcement agencies.** (a) Municipal police departments (the largest and most active); (b) sheriffs' departments; (c) special police agencies, such as those limited to school protection or airport security; (d) state police departments (in all states except Hawaii); and (e) federal law enforcement agencies.

5. **List some of the most important federal law enforcement agencies.** (a) Department of Justice—FBI, Drug Enforcement Administration, U.S. Marshals, and Immigration and Naturalization Service; and (b) Department of Treasury—Bureau of Alcohol, Tobacco, and Firearms, U.S.

Secret Service, Internal Revenue Service, and U.S. Customs Service.

6. **Identify the five investigative priorities of the FBI.** (a) Terrorism, (b) organized crime, (c) foreign intelligence operations in the United States, (d) federal drug offenses, and (e) white-collar crime.

7. **Analyze the importance of private security today.** Private security officers outnumber public police officers by a ratio of 3 to 1. Heightened fear of crime and increased crime in the workplace have led to the growth in spending on private security.

8. **List the four basic responsibilities of the police.** (a) To enforce laws, (b) to provide services, (c) to prevent crime, and (d) to preserve the peace.

9. **Indicate why patrol officers are allowed discretionary powers.** Police officers are considered trustworthy and able to make honest decisions. They have experience and training. They are knowledgeable in criminal behavior. Finally, they must be able to have the discretion to reasonably protect themselves.

10. **Explain how some states have reacted to perceived leniency to perpetrators of domestic violence.** Some states have passed mandatory arrest laws, requiring a police officer to arrest a person who has battered a spouse or domestic partner. Such laws eliminate police officers' discretion.

Questions for Critical Analysis

1. What was the major problem faced by the earliest formal American police departments? Why did it occur?

2. Increased professionalism in police forces has been made possible by two-way radios, telephones, and automobiles. In what way has society *not* benefited from this increased professionalism? Explain your answer.

3. The latest era in policing has been called the community era and dates from the 1980s. How does this "new" era differ from the era of professionalism?

4. To what extent are state police complementary to, rather than substitutes for, local law enforcement agencies?

5. Besides the FBI's five principal investigative priorities, how does that agency benefit local policing units?

6. In many neighborhoods, residents have banded together to pay for and hire private security services. What problems arise under this system?

7. Which of the four basic responsibilities of the police do you think is most important? Why?

8. Is it ever possible to completely eliminate discretion in policing? Explain.

9. What part of the Brady Bill was ultimately declared unconstitutional by the United States Supreme Court?

Selected Print and Electronic Resources

SUGGESTED READINGS

Barrett, Neil, *Digital Crime: Policing the Cybernation,* London, UK: Kogan Page Limited, 1998. The author examines what he calls digital crimes—offenses committed while using the Internet. He argues that digital crime is a growing menace to business. He examines what is necessary to catch criminals who engage in digital crime.

Douglas, John E., *Guide to Careers in the FBI,* Princeton: Kaplan, 1998. The author argues that the FBI is more selective than Harvard University. He provides tips on how to overcome the odds if you would like to become an FBI agent. He outlines the skills, volunteer experiences, and personal attributes, as well as the academic fields, that are most highly valued by FBI recruiters. He takes you through the step-by-step application process.

MacDonald, Peter, *From the Cop Shop,* North York, Ontario: Stoddart Publishing, 1997. This relatively light reading gives you some insights into what law enforcement personnel do around the world. Police officers from Australia, Canada, England, France, India, and the United States talk about their craziest experiences.

MEDIA RESOURCES

Die Hard (1988) This highly popular action movie starring Bruce Willis as John McClane spawned a series of films. McClane is a New York City policeman on his way back to Los Angeles to reconcile with his wife, Holly, played by Bonnie Bedelia. When he goes to visit her, the building in which she works is taken over by a group of terrorists led by a character played by Alan Rickman. When viewing this movie, focus on the interaction among the various law enforcement agencies.

Critically analyze this film:

1. List the different law enforcement agencies represented by the various characters in this movie.

2. What are the problems faced by the "beat" policeman in this movie, played by Reginald VelJohnson?

3. How is the chief of police portrayed in this movie and does his portrayal seem realistic?

4. What type of tension is exhibited between the FBI and the local Los Angeles Police Department?

5. How do the screenwriter and director portray the FBI agents?

6. What type of negotiating skills do these agents have?

Logging On

Visit the Federal Bureau of Investigation home page at:

www.fbi.gov/

You will be able to access mountains of information about the agency. (Perhaps that's why it takes so long to load on your computer!) To find out information about careers go to:

www.fbi.gov/employment/employ.htm

To find out about careers in the Drug Enforcement Administration, log on to:

www.usdoj.gov/dea/employ/agent/page-01.htm

If the history of the U.S. Marshals interests you, you'll find that it's the oldest federal law enforcement agency by going to:

www.usdoj.gov/marshals/usmshist.html

Using the internet for Criminal Justice Analysis

INFOTRAC ®
COLLEGE EDITION

1. Access your InfoTrac account at:

www.infoTrac.college.com/wadsworth/access/html

Once you are at the InfoTrac College Edition, type in the words "POLICE FORCES." Read the article out of the *Readers' Companion to American History*. Now answer the following questions:

a. List the three ways in which American police have always been different from the police of other Western nations.

b. When were the earliest African Americans employed as police in America?

c. How did Allan Pinkerton become well known?

2. To learn more about law enforcement agencies, go to:

www.officer.com/agencies.htm

There you can compare law enforcement agencies across states.

a. Pick a state with a large population, such as California, Texas, or New York. Determine the number of law enforcement agencies in that state.

b. Pick a sparsely populated state, such as Montana. Determine the number of agencies.

c. What are the common agencies that exist between the highly populated and sparsely populated states?

3. Go back to that same Web site:

www.officer.com/agencies.htm

You can discover information about law enforcement agencies from around the world.

a. Why do you think that certain countries have very few law enforcement agencies, even though they have tens of millions of citizens? Consider, for example, France, which lists only two agencies, compared to Japan, which has more than a dozen.

b. Choose a country. Write a short summary of the basic structure of that country's law enforcement system.

c. In what ways does the system you described above differ from what we have in the United States?

Notes

1. Quayne Kenyon, "Emotional Outpouring Shows That Police Officers Still Are Heroes," *Associated Press Online* (September 27, 1997).

2. Tom Barnes, "Nurse Doubts Boise Police," *Pittsburgh Post-Gazette* (October 20, 1997), B1.

3. Thomas Clouse, "Police Aren't Training to Avoid Danger," *Idaho Statesman* (September 7, 1997), 1A.

4. Jerome H. Skolnick and James J. Fyfe, *Above the Law: Police and the Excessive Use of Force* (New York: Free Press, 1993), 69.

5. M. K. Nalla and G. R. Newman, "Is White Collar Crime Policing, Policing?" *Policing and Society* 3 (1994), 304.

6. Richard Maxwell Brown, "Vigilante Policing" in *Thinking about Police,* ed. Carl Klockars and Stephen Mastrofski (New York: McGraw-Hill, 1990), 66.

7. Henry M. Wrobleski and Karen M. Hess, *Introduction to Law Enforcement and Criminal Justice,* 5th ed. (Minneapolis, MN: West Publishing Co., 1997), 9.

8. Peter K. Manning, *Police Work* (Cambridge, MA: MIT Press, 1977), 82.

9. Carol S. Steiker, "Second Thoughts about First Principles," *Harvard Law Review* 107 (1994), 820.

10. Lawrence M. Friedman, *Crime and Punishment in American History* (New York: Basic Books, 1993), 29.

11. Steiker, 830.

12. Mark H. Moore and George L. Kelling, "'To Serve and Protect': Learning from Police History," *Public Interest* 70 (1983), 53.

13. Samuel Walker, *The Police in America: An Introduction* (New York: McGraw-Hill, 1983), 7.

14. Moore and Kelling, 54.

15. Mark H. Haller, "Chicago Cops, 1890–1925," in *Thinking about Police,* ed. Carl Klockars and Stephen Mastrofski (New York: McGraw-Hill, 1990), 90.

16. Jack Whitehouse, "Historical Perspectives on the Police Community Service Function," *Journal of Police Science and Administration* 1 (1973), 87–92.

17. Friedman, 154.

18. Robert M. Fogelson, *Big City Police* (Cambridge, MA: Harvard University Press, 1977), 72.

19. William J. Bopp and Donald O. Shultz, *A Short History of American Law Enforcement* (Springfield, IL: Charles C. Thomas, 1977), 109–10.

20. Roger G. Dunham and Geoffrey P. Alpert, *Critical Issues in Policing: Contemporary Issues* (Prospect Heights, IL: Waveland Press, 1989).

21. Friedman, 360.

22. James Q. Wilson, "What Makes a Better Policeman," *Atlantic Monthly* (March 1969), 129–35.

23. Nathan Douthit, "August Vollmer: Berkeley's First Chief of Police and the Emergence of Police Professionalism," *California Historical Quarterly* 54 (1975), 101–24.

24. National Advisory Commission on Civil Disorders, *Report* (Washington, D.C.: U.S. Government Printing Office, 1968), 157–60.

25. 18 U.S.C.A. Sections 2510–2521.

26. Wrobleski and Hess, 50.

27. 401 U.S. 424 (1971).

28. Pub. L. No. 92-2615 8(f) 103, 109–10, codified as amended at 42 U.S.C. Section 2000e 4 (g) (6) (1994).

29. Jayne Seagrave, "Defining Community Policing," *American Journal of Police* 1 (1996), 1–22.

30. Kevin Gallagher, "TWA Flight 800—One Year Later," *Police* (July 1997), 18–24.

31. Federal Bureau of Investigation, *Crime in the United States—1995* (Washington, D.C.: Government Printing Office, 1996), 278.

32. *Ibid.*

33. G. Robert Blakey, "Federal Criminal Law," *Hastings Law Journal* 46 (April 1995), 1175.

34. Vern L. Folley, *American Law Enforcement* (Boston: Allyn & Bacon, 1980), 228.

35. Bureau of Justice Statistics, *Sheriffs' Departments 1993* (Washington, D.C.: Office of Justice Programs, 1996), 2.

36. *Ibid.,* 10–11.

37. *Black's Law Dictionary,* 982.

38. Robert Borkenstein, "Police: State Police," *Encyclopedia of Crime and Justice,* ed. Sanford H. Kadish. (New York: Free Press, 1983), 1131.

39. "Murder Capital Rescue May Become Model," *UPI Online* (March 10, 1998).

40. Bureau of Justice Statistics, *Federal Law Enforcement Officers, 1996* (Washington, D.C.: U.S. Department of Justice, January 1998), 1

41. Samuel Walker, *Popular Justice: A History of American Criminal Justice* (New York: Oxford University Press, 1980), 184.

42. Athan Theoharis and John Stuart Cox, *The Boss: J. Edgar Hoover and the Great American Inquisition* (Philadelphia: Temple University Press, 1988).

43. "Feds Have a Plan if Terrorists Strike," *UPI Online* (February 19, 1998).

44. Pub. L. No. 91-513, 84 Stat. 1242 (1970) codified as amended at 21 U.S.C. Section 801 (1994).

45. "Bolivia Goes to War against Coca," *Economist* (September 19, 1998), 43.

46. "DEA Warning Crimps Lethal Prescriptions in Oregon," *Los Angeles Times* (November 12, 1997), A21.

47. http://www.usdoj.gov/marshals/factsheets/general.htm.

48. "One Agent's Night," *Economist* (September 12, 1998), 33.

49. Tucker Carlson, "Safety Inc.," *Policy Review* (Summer 1995), 72–3.

50. *Ibid.*, 67.

51. "Policing for Profit," *Economist* (April 19, 1997), 21–24.

52. William C. Cunningham, John J. Strauchs, and Clifford W. Van Meter, *The Hallcrest Report II: Private Security Trends, 1970 to the Year 2000* (Boston: Butterworth-Heinemann, 1990), 236.

53. *People v. Zelinski*, 594 P.2d 1000 (1979).

54. Norman R. Bottom, Jr., "Privatization: Lessons of the Hallcrest Report," *Law Enforcement News* (June 23, 1986), 13.

55. Egon Bittner, *The Functions of the Police in a Modern Society*, Public Health Service Publication No. 2059 (Chevy Chase, MD: National Institute of Mental Health, 1970), 38–44.

56. Carl Klockars, "The Rhetoric of Community Policing," in *Community Policing: Rhetoric and Reality*, ed. Jack Greene and Stephen Mastrofski (New York: Praeger Publishers, 1991), 244.

57. Thomas Bercal, "Calls for Police Assistance," *American Behavioral Scientist* 13 (1970), 681–91; John A. Webster, "Police Task and Time Study," *Journal of Criminal Law, Criminology, and Police Science* 61 (1970), 94–100.

58. Jack R. Greene and Karl B. Klockars, "What Do Police Do?" in *Thinking about Police*, 2d ed., eds. Carl B. Klockars and Stephen B. Mastrofski (New York: MacGraw-Hill, 1991), 273–84.

59. Reprinted in *Police Chief* (January 1990), 18.

60. Eric J. Scott, *Calls for Service: Citizen Demand and Initial Police Response* (Washington, D.C.: U.S. Government Printing Office, 1981), 28–30.

61. Jerome H. Skolnick, "Police: The New Professionals," *New Society* (September 5, 1986), 9–11.

62. Klockars, 250.

63. James Q. Wilson, *Varieties of Police Behavior: The Management of Law and Order in Eight Communities* (Cambridge, MA: Harvard University Press, 1968).

64. James Q. Wilson and George L. Kelling, "Broken Windows," *Atlantic Monthly* (March 1982), 29.

65. A. J. Reiss, Jr., "Police Organization in the Twentieth Century," in *Modern Policing*, ed. Michael Tonry and Norval Morris (Chicago: University of Chicago Press, 1992), 51–98.

66. C. E. Pratt, "Police Discretion," *Law and Order* (March 1992), 99–100.

67. Herbert Jacob, *Urban Justice* (Boston: Little, Brown, 1973), 27.

68. *Ibid.*

69. Georgia Pabst, "Slayings Underscore Domestic Violence's Toll," *Milwaukee Journal-Sentinel* (March 4, 1998), 4.

70. Violent Crime Control and Law Enforcement Act of 1994, H.R. Conf. Rep. No. 103-711, p. 391 (1994).

71. Ronet Bachman and Linda E. Saltzman, "Violence against Women: Estimates from the Redesigned Survey," in *Bureau of Justice Statistics Special Report: National Crime Victimization Survey* (Washington, D.C.: Office of Justice Programs, 1995), 4.

72. L. Craig Parker, Robert D. Meier, and Lynn Hunt Monahan, *Interpersonal Psychology for Criminal Justice* (St. Paul, MN: West Publishing Co., 1989), 113.

73. James J. Fyfe, David A. Klinger, and Jeanne M. Flavin, "Differential Police Treatment of Male-on-Female Spousal Violence," *Criminology* 35 (August 1997), 455–473.

74. Lawrence W. Sherman and Ellen G. Cohn, "The Impact of Research on Legal Policy: The Minneapolis Domestic Violence Experiment," *Law and Society Review* 23 (1989), 261.

75. Douglas R. Marvin, "The Dynamics of Domestic Abuse," *FBI Law Enforcement Bulletin* (July 1997), 13–19.

76. Machaela M. Hoctor, "Domestic Violence as a Crime against the State: The Need for Mandatory Arrest in California," *California Law Review* 85 (May 1997), 643.

77. Virginia E. Hench, "When Less Is More—Can Reducing Penalties Reduce Household Violence?" *University of Hawaii Law Review* 19 (Spring 1997), 37.

78. Lawrence W. Sherman and Richard A. Berk, "The Specific Deterrence Effects of Arrest for Domestic Assault," *American Society Review* 49 (1984), 270.

79. *Family Violence: A Model State Code* (Reno, NV: National Council of Juvenile and Family Court Judges, 1994), 4–5.

80. Kevin Vaughan and Michael O'Keefe, "Bravery Met Madness in Firefight," (Denver) *Rocky Mountain News* (November 16, 1997), 4A.

81. Bureau of Justice Statistics, *Criminal Victimization in the United States, 1995* (Washington, D.C.: U.S. Department of Justice, 1998), Table 66.

82. Joe Sexton, "The Culture of Cops and Guns," *New York Times* (January 11, 1998), Section 4, p. 1.

83. *Ibid.*

84. Chris Oliver Wilson, "Disarming News: Why Bobbies Have No Guns," *U.S. News & World Report* (February 9, 1998), 46–7.

85. Doug Payne, "Bad Guys Outgunning Cops," *Atlanta Journal-Constitution* (October 19, 1997), H8.

86. Pub. L. No. 103-159, 107 Stat. 1536 (1993); codified as amended at 18 U.S.C. Sections 922(s)-(t) (1995).

87. Don Manson and Gene Lauver, *Presale Firearms Checks*, Bureau of Justice Statistics Bulletin (Washington, D.C.: Office of Justice Programs, February 1997), 1.

88. Darrell L. Saunders, "The Importance of the Brady Bill," *The Police Chief* (March 1997), 7.

89. Dan Luzadder, "Assault-Weapons Ban Defeated," *Rocky Mountain News* (February 4, 1998), 12A.

90. Dan Morain, "Governor Vetoes Bill to Ban Cheap Guns," *Los Angeles Times* (September 27, 1997), A1.

91. David Liechty, "*H. Jay Printz v. United States*: Supreme Court Declares Brady Act's Review of Handgun Application Requirement Unconstitutional," *Journal of Contemporary Law* 24 (1998), 178.

92. *Printz v. United States,* 117 S.Ct. 2384 (1997).

93. David E. Johnson, "Taking a Second Look at the Second Amendment and Modern Gun Control," *Kentucky Law Journal* 86 (1997–1998), 197.

94. Dennis A. Hengan, "Victims' Litigation Targets Gun Violence," *Trial* (February 1995), 50.

95. "How We Use Our Guns," *OnPatrol* (Fall 1996), 20.

96. John R. Lott, Jr., "Does Allowing Law-Abiding Citizens to Carry Concealed Handguns Save Lives?" *Valparaiso University Law Review* 31 (Spring 1997), 355.

97. Gordon Witkin, "Can 'Smart' Guns Save Many Lives?" *U.S. News & World Report* (December 2, 1996), 37–8.

98. "Highly Sensitive Gun Detectors May Soon Be in Hands of Police," (Minneapolis/St. Paul) *Star-Tribune* (April 13, 1997), 21A.

chapter

5

Policing: Organization and Strategies

Chapter Objectives

After reading this chapter, you should be able to:

1. List the three criticisms of standard bureaucratic police organization.

2. Explain the difference between arrest rates and clearance rates.

3. List the three primary purposes of police patrol.

4. Identify the different types of patrol.

5. Describe the steps that an investigator must take after a crime occurs.

6. Indicate some investigation strategies that are considered aggressive.

7. Explain community policing and its strategies.

8. Indicate the five principles of problem solving policing.

INTRODUCTION

On the evening of August 5, 1997, seven-year-old Daniel Edwards, Jr., was awakened by the sound of shattering glass.[1] Looking up, he saw the source of the noise: a smashed window. Even more upsetting, however, was the man who had climbed through the window and was standing in Daniel's room. The boy's stepfather was out of town on business, so Daniel was home alone with his mother. The boy asked the intruder what he wanted, but the man ignored his question and entered his mother's bedroom. The next noise Daniel heard was his mother's scream—the intruder had hit her in the head with a wrench.

After the man left with a microwave oven, a videocassette recorder, and car keys, Daniel wrapped a towel around his mother's head to stop the bleeding. Then he did what his parents and his teachers had taught him to do in a crisis situation: he called 911. Within four minutes, Hammond (Louisiana) Deputy Vic Ferrara, Jr., arrived on the scene, followed by an ambulance. Daniel's quick thinking probably saved his mother's life and led to the arrest of the intruder within several hours. Local police officials called the boy's actions heroic, but they were not necessarily surprising. The reflex to call 911 in emergencies is so deeply ingrained in our national consciousness that even a young child knows immediately what to do when he needs to get in touch with the police.

This was not always the case. Quick police response was not universally possible until automobile patrols replaced foot patrols—a process not completed in many rural areas until the 1960s—and the advent and proliferation of two-way radios and the telephone. Today, routine police work is dominated by answering 911 calls and other requests for service, and Americans have been socialized to "call the cops" at the first sign of trouble.[2]

Rapid response to 911 calls was indeed a benchmark of police reform in the period from the 1960s to the 1980s.[3] The system, however, is far from infallible. Miscommunication between personnel who answer 911 calls and law enforcement officers can occur, such as when Denver police were unable to find a badly beaten taxi driver in the trunk of his cab until nearly an hour after receiving the call for service. When the victim was found, he was dead.[4] Furthermore, 911 systems are being clogged by crank calls and summonses from citizens who do not understand that the service is for emergencies only. Some cities, such as Baltimore, Maryland, are implementing 311 systems to divert noncritical calls.[5] Others, such as Dayton, Ohio, are making misuse of 911 a misdemeanor, subject to a $100 fine and, after multiple infractions, jail time.[6]

Many observers are critical of the reliance on 911 for theoretical, as well as practical, reasons. Focusing on calls for service reflects a reactive rather than proactive philosophy of policing. In this chapter, we will examine a range of police strategies and discuss how the latest generation of police reformers is trying to temper professionalism with some values from the nation's law enforcement past. The chapter opens with an overview of how police departments are organized to best implement their strategies for enforcing the law and preventing crime.

POLICE ORGANIZATION

Each police department is organized according to its environment: the size of its jurisdiction, the type of crimes it must deal with, and the demographics of the population it must police. A police department in a racially diverse city often faces different challenges than a department in a homogeneous one. Geographical location also influences police organization. The make-up of the police department in Miami, Florida, for example, is partially determined by the fact that the city is a gateway for illegal drugs from Central and South America. The department directs a high percentage of its resources to special drug-fighting units and has formed cooperative partnerships with federal agencies such as the Federal Bureau of Investigation and the U.S. Customs Service in an effort to stop the flow of narcotics and weapons into the South Florida area.

The ultimate goal for any police department is to reach its maximum efficiency—to provide the best service to the community with limited resources such as staff and budget. Although some police departments are experimenting with alternative structures based on a partnership between management and the officers in the field,[7] most continue to rely on the hierarchical structure described below.

The Structure of the Police Department

One of the goals of the police reformers, especially beginning in the 1950s, was to lessen the corrupting influence of politicians. The result was a move toward a militaristic organization of police.[8] As you can seen in Figure 5.1, a typical police department is based on a chain of command that leads from the police chief down through the various levels of the department. In this formalized structure, all persons are aware of their place in the chain and of their duties and responsibilities within the organization.

Delegation of authority is a critical component of the chain of command, especially in larger departments. The chief of police delegates authority to division chiefs, who delegate authority to commanders, and so on down through the organization. This structure creates a situation in which nearly every member of a police department is directly accountable to a superior. As was the original goal of police reformers, these links encourage discipline and control and lessen the possibility that any individual police employee will have the

DELEGATION OF AUTHORITY
The principles of command on which most police departments are based; personnel take orders from and are responsible to those in positions of power directly above them.

Figure 5.1 The Command Chain of the Lombard (Illinois) Police Department

The Lombard (Illinois) Police Department is made up of 71 sworn law enforcement officers and 33 civilians. As you see, the chain of command runs from the chief of police down to crossing guards and part-time secretaries.

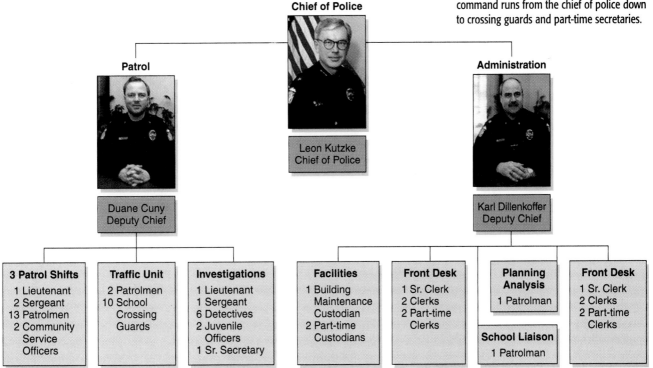

SOURCE: LOMBARD POLICE DEPARTMENT.

A lieutenant (in the white shirt) gives instructions to two sergeants. To the extreme left, a patrol officer appears to be awaiting instructions. How does the delegation of authority and the chain of command contribute to police efficiency?

unsupervised freedom to abuse her or his position.[9] In keeping with the need to delegate authority, police departments in large cities divide their jurisdictions into *precincts*. The precinct commander is then held responsible by his or her superiors at police headquarters for the performance of the officers in the precinct.

Police departments also control their officers through the use of written guidelines. These guidelines, which can be found in nearly every law enforcement organization in the country, attempt to standardize police behavior by defining what is acceptable and what is unacceptable. Written guidelines often try to limit the discretion a police officer will use in a dangerous or stressful situation. Many departments have written policies concerning high-speed automobile chases that are designed to ensure that the pursuing officers will not sacrifice public safety in their zeal to catch a suspect. Guidelines may also set out a specific procedure that must be followed under certain circumstances. When an officer handcuffs a violation suspect's hands behind his or her back, for example, the officer is placing the suspect in danger of positional asphyxia, a phenomenon that occurs when a person's body position interferes with his or her ability to breathe. To avoid positional asphyxia, some departments have procedural guidelines requiring officers to:

- Roll suspects on their backs immediately after they have been handcuffed.
- Ask suspects if they have recently ingested any drugs or have a history of respiratory problems.
- Monitor suspects carefully and have medical treatment available.
- Be trained to recognize breathing difficulties or loss of consciousness.[10]

Not only will following these procedures reduce the risk of positional asphyxia, but they may also protect the department against a civil lawsuit should a death occur after an officer failed to take the precautions.

Specialization in the Police Organization. Though personnel in smaller police departments perform a wide spectrum of duties, larger departments rely on *specialization*. Each member of the force is assigned to a specific task or unit such as investigation, patrol, juvenile, traffic, or vice. The ultimate goal of specialization is a more efficient force, in which each individual is highly skilled and experienced within the confines of her or his specialty. (See Figure 5.2 for closer look at specialization in the Tulsa [Oklahoma] Police Department.)

Criticisms of Police Organization. The model of the modern police department is bureaucratic. In a **bureaucracy,** formal rules govern an individual's actions and relationships with co-employees. Today, the word *bureaucracy* often has a negative connotation. For some, it conjures up visions of depersonalized automatons performing their chores without any sensitivity to the needs of those they serve. This stigma has not bypassed police organizations, which have been criticized for:

- *Limiting personal ingenuity.* The more rules that are placed on individuals, the less ability they have to use their particular skills in solving a problem. Many people choose police work as a career because they see it as an alternative to the desk-bound, "9 to 5" routine that seems to characterize many other occupations. Regulations add a measure of

BUREAUCRACY
A hierarchically structured administrative organization that carries out specific functions.

1. **PATROL OPERATIONS**

   Patrol officers are assigned to one of three divisions, each commanded by a major. Patrol officers work eight-hour shifts with two days off per week.

2. **SPECIAL OPERATIONS**

   The department's Special Operations Team (SOT) is made up of three teams of ten officers selected from throughout the department. SOT responds to tactical emergencies, such as armed and barricaded suspects. They also carry out search and arrest warrants for high-risk suspects. Each such incident is referred to as a "call out," and the department averages between 30 and 35 call outs a year. SOT members have special equipment, such as:

   - ARWEN kinetic baton launchers
   - body armor
   - ballistic helmets
   - H&K MP-5 Rifles

3. **NEGOTIATORS**

   The department has a negotiating team, responsible for negotiating with suspects in hostage situations.

4. **DIVE TEAM**

   The ten-member dive team recovers bodies and evidence in the waters around Tulsa.

5. **BOMB TEAM**

   The bomb team has two full-time members assigned to the Tulsa International Airport, Six additional officers with special training are available by pager to respond to bomb emergencies.

6. **K-9 UNIT**

   The department has eleven patrol K-9 units, using German shepherds to help fight and prevent crime.

7. **MOUNTED UNIT**

   The department has six officers assigned to its mounted unit, which are used in high-crime areas, primarily apartment complexes with drug problems.

8. **AIR UNIT**

   Six officers, under the direction of a sergeant, are trained to fly the two MD500 helicopters owned by the department.

SOURCE: DALE STOCKTON, "A CLOSER LOOK: TULSA (OKLA.) POLICE DEPARTMENT," POLICE (MARCH 1998), 34–35.

Figure 5.2 Specialization in the Tulsa (Oklahoma) Police Department

The Tulsa Police Department has 795 total officers. These officers are assigned to the specific operations listed here.

drudgery to the job that many officers find personally and professionally limiting. In some instances, *groupthink* can take over, as members of the police force blindly follow rules and suppress tendencies toward individual initiative.

2. *Limiting contact with the community.* One of the initial purposes of reform was to eradicate police abuse of citizens. Now, however, many departments seem to have gone too far in promoting distance between officers and "the people."[11] (As we shall see later in the chapter, the spread of community policing has lessened this problem.)

3. *Limiting contact among members of the police department.* By sharply delineating relationships within a department, the delegation of authority can limit contact among members at different ranks. The distance between a patrol officer and the police chief, as evident in Figure 5.1 on page 153, practically assures the two will have little, if any, contact.

Striving for Efficiency

If the ultimate goal of a bureaucratic organization is efficiency, have police bureaucracies made departments more efficient? This question is difficult to answer. On the whole, any bureaucracy responds best to statistical measures. In the era of professional policing, the double yardsticks of statistical efficiency for police have been (1) response time and (2) arrest rates.

INCIDENT-DRIVEN POLICING
A reactive approach to policing that emphasizes a speedy response to calls for service.

RESPONSE TIME
A measurement of police efficiency based on the rapidity with which calls for service are answered.

Police discovery of the mass suicide of 39 members of the Heaven's Gate cult in Rancho Santa Fe, California, provided an example of both the strengths and weaknesses of calls for service. Former cult member Rio DiAngelo, the first person to discover the bodies, called 911 and told the emergency dispatcher what he had found. For some undetermined reason, however, San Diego County sheriff's deputies did not respond to DiAngelo's call until two hours later. What factors might contribute to police not quickly responding to a call under such circumstances?

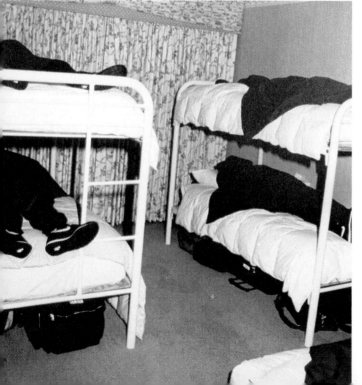

Response Time and Efficiency. Though police do not like to think of themselves as being at "the beck and call" of citizens, that is essentially the *modus operandi* of many law enforcement officers. All departments practice **incident-driven policing,** in which calls for service are the primary instigators of action. More than 85 percent of police activity is the result of 911 calls or other citizen requests, which means that a relatively small percentage of activity is initiated by a police officer in the field.[12]

The speed with which the police respond to calls for service has traditionally been seen as a crucial aspect of crime fighting and crime prevention. The ideal scenario in incident-driven policing is as follows: a citizen sees a person committing a crime and calls 911; the police arrive quickly and catch the perpetrator in the act. Or, a citizen is the victim of a crime, such as a mugging, calls 911 as soon as possible, and the police arrive to catch the mugger before she or he can flee the immediate area of the crime. Although, as we shall see, such scenarios are quite rare in real life, **response time,** or the time elapsed between the instant a call for service is received and the instant the police arrive on the scene, has become a benchmark for police efficiency.

In 1973, the U.S. National Advisory Commission on Criminal Justice Standards and Goals recommended that response time in urban areas should, under "normal circumstances," not exceed three minutes for emergency calls and twenty minutes for nonemergency calls. The commission saw a direct correlation between response time and crime rates, stating that "when the time is cut to 2 minutes, it can have a dramatic effect" on crime rates.[13] The same year, the National Commission on Productivity optimistically stated that rapid police response would accomplish three objectives:

1. It would serve as a deterrent to criminal activity because potential offenders would know that the police would arrive quickly at the scene.

2. A quicker response time would increase the apprehension rate and that in turn would serve as a deterrent.

3. A rapid response would increase citizen confidence in law enforcement, which would result in increased reporting and crime-prevention activities.[14]

Total Response Time. More recent research has shown that these early assumptions did not fully appreciate the complexity of determining *total response time*—the time from the moment the crime is committed to the moment the first police officer arrives on the scene. In essence, total response time involves three components:

- The time between the commission of the crime and the moment the victim or witness calls the police.

- The time required for the police to answer the call, gather information from the caller, and dispatch a patrol car.

- The time between the moment the patrol car receives a call from the dispatcher and the moment the car arrives at the scene.[15]

The problem, these later studies found, with grading police performance based on response time lies in the first component: citizens often wait several minutes before calling the police after a crime. This delay can be attributed to a number of factors. Often, victims of a crime are frightened, ashamed, or disoriented after the incident. Victims may call parents, friends, or even the family physician before the police. Another common reason for delay in calling 911 is even more basic: the crime has not taken place near a phone, and several minutes pass while the victim or witness looks for one. On average, between five and ten minutes elapse from the moment a serious crime is committed to the moment the police are called.[16] Under such circumstances, an emphasis on rapid response time is unlikely to have the intended effect on crime rates or give an accurate reflection of a police department's efficiency.

Differential Response. Many police departments have come to realize that overall response time is not as critical as response time for the most important calls. In Dallas, Texas, the overall response time rose from 10 minutes in 1986 to 23 minutes in 1996, drawing criticism from local politicians. The Dallas Police Department, however, pointed out that the response time for calls involving shootings, knifings, and robberies had actually dropped—from 9.7 minutes in 1986 to 7.3 minutes in 1996.[17]

The Dallas police had instituted a **differential response** strategy, in which the department distinguishes between different calls for service so that it can respond more quickly to the most serious incidents. Suppose, for example, that a police department receives two calls for service at the same time. The first caller reports that her house is in the process of being robbed, and the second says that he has returned home to find his automobile missing. If the department has instituted a differential response strategy, the robbery-in-progress—a "hot" crime—will receive immediate attention. The missing automobile—a "cold" crime that could have been committed several hours earlier—will receive attention "as time permits," and the caller may even be asked to make an appointment to come to the station. (See Figure 5.3 for possible responses to calls to a 911 operator.)

DIFFERENTIAL RESPONSE
A strategy for answering calls for service in which response time is adapted to the seriousness of the call.

"HOT" CALLS FOR SERVICE—IMMEDIATE RESPONSE

Complaint to 911 Officer	Rationale
"I just got home from work, and I can see someone in my bedroom through the window."	Possibility that the intruder is committing a crime.
"My husband has a baseball bat, and he's says he's going to kill me."	Crime in progress.
"A woman in a green jacket just grabbed my purse and ran away."	Chances of catching the suspect are increased with immediate action.

"COLD" CALLS FOR SERVICE—ALTERNATIVE RESPONSE

Complaint to 911 Officer	Rationale
"I got to my office about two hours ago, but I just noticed that the fax machine was stolen at some point during the night."	The crime occurred at least two hours earlier.
"The guy in the apartment above me has been selling pot to his hippy friends for years, and I'm sick and tired of it."	Not an emergency situation.
"My husband came home two nights ago with a black eye, and I finally got him to admit that he didn't run into a doorknob. Larry Smith smacked him."	Past crime with a known suspect who is unlikely to flee.

SOURCE: ADAPTED FROM JOHN S. DEMPSEY, AN INTRODUCTION TO POLICING, 2D ED. (BELMONT, CA: WEST/WADSWORTH COMPANY, 1999), TABLE 8.1, PAGE 175.

Figure 5.3 Putting the Theory of Differential Response into Action

Differential response strategies are based on a simple concept: treat emergencies like emergencies and nonemergencies like nonemergencies. As you see, calls for service that deal with "hot crimes" will be dealt with immediately, while those that report "cold crimes" will be dealt with at some point in the future.

Several forms of differential response have evolved. For example, many departments now take reports over the telephone rather than in person in nonemergency situations. Other departments, rather than immediately dispatching an officer to take a report, make an appointment with the citizen to take down the information at a later time. In this manner, the department is able to reschedule victim interviews to periods when the level of calls for service is not quite as heavy.

In a sense, differential response is a balancing act between improving the management of the police workload and satisfying citizens who call for service with the expectation that the police response will be timely no matter what the nature of the incident they are reporting. Different tests have shown that both these goals can be met. Several departments have diverted up to 50 percent of their calls to alternative responses without any noticeable drop-off in citizen satisfaction.[18]

Arrest Rates and Efficiency. The other measure of police efficiency, arrest rates, also seems logical. The more arrests a police department makes, the fewer the number of criminals there should be on the streets of the community.

Again, practice does not necessarily follow theory. As we saw in Chapter 2, the amount of crime is not a function of arrest rates; self-reports show that many, if not most, criminal acts do not lead to arrests. To make a generalization, police will never be able to make an arrest for *every* crime that is committed. Observers have offered other, more specific reasons for a possible disconnect between arrest rates and crime rates. One explanation is that, given the amount of paperwork each arrest forces upon a police officer, more arrests mean less time for crime prevention.[19] Perhaps arrest rates and crime rates would prove more consistent if all arrests were made for serious crimes. But, as we have discussed, this is not the case. Most arrests are for misdemeanors, not felonies. Furthermore, arrests are poor predictors of incarceration: one study found that nearly sixty times more Americans are arrested than are sent to prison each year.[20]

Perhaps a more meaningful indicator of the job a police force is doing is the *clearance rate,* or the percentage of crimes solved over any given time. This measurement allows statisticians to differentiate between types of crime. The clearance rate of violent crimes, in which the victims tend to know their assailants, are generally much higher (around 45 percent) than those for burglaries (around 17 percent), which generally are committed by strangers.[21] Low clearance rates for a certain type of crime, as compared to national averages or past performance, can indicate that police response to that crime is lacking.

Citizen Satisfaction. An additional measure of police effectiveness, which has only recently been recognized, is *citizen satisfaction.* As we saw in Chapter 1, fear of crime has risen even though violent crime rates have dropped over the past decade. Part of the reason for this seeming contradiction may be found in public attitudes toward the police. A recent poll found that one out of every two Americans had little or no confidence that the police would protect them from violent crime.[22] Many police administrators believe that this trend can be reversed if departments begin to treat citizens as "customers" who pay for the services provided by law enforcement agencies.[23]

As any businessperson knows, the customers are the most important people in any service industry (which includes police work), and the greater the effort to listen to customers' concerns, the greater their levels of satisfaction will be. In analyzing the results of a foot patrol experiment in Flint, Michigan, in which the police department made a concerted effort to forge bonds with citizens, Robert Trojanowicz of Michigan State University found a significant increase in citizen satisfaction.[24] A number of observers believe that the

INFOTRAC®
COLLEGE EDITION

Johnson, Richard. Citizen complaints: what the police should know.

strategy of increasing police presence in the community, which we will discuss later in the chapter under the heading "Community Policing," is a crucial step toward improving citizen satisfaction with police performance.

In sum, it is difficult to measure the effectiveness of the police. Even crime rates are at least partially determined by elements beyond police control, such as the sociological, biological, and psychological factors discussed in Chapter 2. Hence, crime rates cannot be relied on as definitive indicators of the job a police department is doing.

POLICE ON PATROL: THE BACKBONE OF THE DEPARTMENT

One of the great ironies of the police organization is that the people lowest on the hierarchical "stepladder"—the patrol officers—are considered the most valuable members of the force. (Many patrol officers, considering their pay and work hours, would call the situation unjust, not ironic.) As many as two-thirds of the *sworn officers,* or those officers authorized to make arrests and use force, in some large police departments are patrol officers, and every department has a patrol unit.

"Life on the street" is not easy. Patrol officers must be able to handle any given number of difficult situations, and experience is often the best, and, despite training programs, the only, teacher. As one patrol officer commented:

> You never stop learning. You never get your street degree. The person who says . . . they've learned it all is the person that's going to wind up dead or in a very compromising position. They've closed their minds.[25]

It may take a patrol officer years to learn when a gang is "false flagging" (trying to trick rival gang members into the open) or what to look for in a suspect's eyes to sense if he or she is concealing a weapon. This learning process is the backdrop to a number of different general functions that a patrol officer must perform on a daily basis.

The Los Angeles Police Department, Dallas Police Department, and New York Police Department broadcast radio reports from patrol officers live on the Web. To listen, go to www.policescanner.com/police.stm

The Purpose of Patrol

As was noted in Chapter 4, patrol officers do not spend a great deal of time chasing, catching, and handcuffing suspected criminals. The vast majority of patrol shifts are completed without a single arrest.[26] An influential study of Kansas City patrol operations—which will be discussed in detail later in this chapter—found that 60 percent of a patrol officer's time was uncommitted.[27] That is, officers spend a great deal of time meeting with other officers, taking breaks, and patrolling with the goal of preventing crime in general rather than any specific crime or criminal activity. This does not mean that the image of the patrol officer as a crime fighter is altogether incorrect. Instead, the study suggests that the activities of the patrol officer are more varied than most would expect.

As Samuel Walker noted, the basic purposes of the police patrol have changed very little since 1829, when Sir Robert Peel founded the modern police department. These purposes include:

1. The deterrence of crime by maintaining a visible police presence.

2. The maintenance of public order and a sense of security in the community.

3. The twenty-four-hour provision of services that are not crime related.[28]

Police officers spend a great deal of time performing community services such as visiting classrooms and interacting with students. Do you think that the time police officers dedicate to community services is time well spent, or should they concentrate on fighting and preventing crime?

The first two goals—deterring crime and keeping order—are generally accepted as legitimate police functions. The third, however, has been more controversial.

We saw in the last chapter that the provision of services unrelated to crime was a hallmark of police activity in the political era of policing and was discouraged in the professional era. The community era has seen a resurgence of the patrol officer as a provider of community services, many of which have little to do with crime. The extent to which noncrime incidents dominate patrol officers' time is evident in the Police Services Study, a survey of 26,000 calls to police in sixty different neighborhoods. The study found that only one out of every five calls involved the report of criminal activity.[29] (Figure 5.4 shows that calls for service concerning criminal activity are even less frequent in a small, rural town.)

There is some debate over whether community services should be allowed to dominate patrol officers' duties. The question, however, remains: If the police do not handle these problems, who will? Few cities have the financial resources to hire public servants to deal specifically with, for example, finding shelter for homeless persons. Furthermore, the police are the only public servants on call twenty-four hours a day, seven days a week, making them uniquely accessible to citizen needs.

Patrol Activities

To recap, the purposes of police patrols are to prevent and deter crime and also to provide social services. How can the police best accomplish these goals? Of course, each department has its own methods and strategies, but William Gay, Theodore Schell, and Stephen Schack are able to divide routine patrol activity into four general categories:

1. *Preventive patrol.* By maintaining a presence in a community, either in a car or on foot, patrol officers attempt to prevent crime from occurring. This strategy, which O. W. Wilson called "omnipresence," was a cornerstone of policing philosophy and still takes up roughly 40 percent of patrol time.

2. *Calls for service.* Patrol officers spend nearly a quarter of their time responding to 911 calls for emergency service or other citizen problems and complaints.

3. *Administrative duties.* Paperwork takes up nearly 20 percent of patrol time.

Figure 5.4 Calls for Service in Beaufort, South Carolina

Police officers in Beaufort, South Carolina, answered nearly 24,000 calls for service in 1997. The top five categories for which the officers answered calls do not include, as you can see here, serious crimes. In fact, serious crimes made up a minuscule percentage of calls for service in Beaufort that year.

Nonserious Crime Calls	
Description of Violation	**Percentage of Total Calls for Service**
Traffic violations	14
Security alarms/businesses	6.2
Traffic accidents	4.5
Disturbances	4.3
Petty larceny	3.6
Serious Crime Calls	
Description of Violation	**Percentage of Total Calls for Service**
Breaking and entering	1.4
Assault and battery	.009
Auto theft	.005
Rape	.0004
Murder	.00004

SOURCE: BEAUFORT POLICE DEPARTMENT.

4 *Officer-initiated activities.* Incidents in which the patrol officer initiates contact with citizens, such as stopping motorists and pedestrians and questioning them, account for 15 percent of patrol time.[30] Figure 5.5 shows a typical distribution of a patrol officer's time.

The estimates made by Gay, Schell, and Schack are not universally accepted. Professor of law enforcement Gary W. Cordner argues that administrative duties account for the largest percentage of patrol officers' time and that when these officers are not consumed with paperwork and meetings they are either answering calls for service (which takes up 67 percent of the officers' time on the street) or initiating activities themselves (the remaining 33 percent).[31]

Indeed, there are dozens of academic studies that purport to answer the question of how patrol officers spend their days and nights. Perhaps it is only fair, then, to give a police officer the chance to describe the duties patrol officers perform. In the words of Anthony Bouza, a former police chief:

[Patrol officers] hurry from call to call, bound to their crackling radios, which offer no relief—especially on summer weekend nights. . . . The cops jump from crisis to crisis, rarely having time to do more than tamp one down sufficiently and leave for the next. Gaps of boredom and inactivity fill the interims, although there aren't many of these in the hot months. Periods of boredom get increasingly longer as the nights wear on and the weather gets colder.[32]

Bouza paints a picture of a routine beat as filled with "noise, booze, violence, drugs, illness, blaring TVs, and human misery." This may describe the situation in high-crime neighborhoods, but it certainly does not represent the reality for the majority of patrol officers in the United States. Duties that all patrol officers have in common, whether they work in Bouza's rather nightmarish city streets or in the quieter environment of rural America, include controlling traffic, making preliminary investigations, making arrests, and patrolling public events.

Controlling Traffic. Enforcing traffic laws is a critical function of patrol officers. More than three times as many people lose their lives to traffic accidents than to criminal activity each year, and many more are injured in such accidents than as a result of criminal assaults.[33] Police can lessen the danger to drivers and pedestrians by facilitating an orderly flow of traffic. Patrol officers are also called upon to manage and investigate the circumstances of accidents, as well as to educate citizens on automobile and bicycle safety.

Preliminary Investigations. Because patrol officers are on duty and available for quick response, they are usually the first law enforcement officers to respond to a call for service and to reach the scene of a crime. In this capacity, they are required to secure the scene by blocking it off, interview witnesses and victims, and arrest any suspects who might still be at the scene. In smaller departments, the patrol officer may continue the investigation, but in larger ones, that task, along with the fruits of the patrol officer's initial investigations, is turned over to a detective.

Making Arrests. Making an arrest is the most dangerous duty of the patrol officer. Luckily, for most officers, an arrest is a relatively rare occurrence. According to Egon Bittner, patrol officers average about one arrest per month.[34] Furthermore, the majority of arrests do not involve violent crimes such as murder, rape, robbery, and aggravated assault. More than 15 million arrests for criminal violations (excluding traffic violations) take place in the United States each year. Eleven million of those arrests concern quality-of-life and public order crimes such as:

Figure 5.5 The Distribution of a Patrol Officer's Time on the Beat

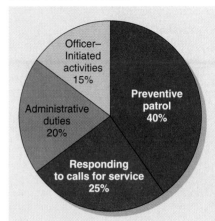

SOURCE: William G. Gay, Theodore H. Schell, and Stephen Schack, Routine Patrol: Improving Patrol Productivity, vol. 1 (Washington, D.C.: National Institute of Justice, 1977), 3–6.

DIRECTED PATROL
Patrol strategies that are designed to respond to a specific criminal activity at a specific time.

GENERAL PATROL
Patrol strategies that rely on police officers monitoring a certain area with the goal of detecting crimes in progress or preventing crime due to their presence. Also known as random or preventive patrol.

- Driving while intoxicated (DWI) or driving under the influence (DUI).
- Drug abuse violations.
- Liquor law violations, public drunkenness, and disorderly conduct.
- Misdemeanor assaults.
- Vagrancy and loitering.[35]

These arrests, though not as "flashy" as those for more violent crimes, are an important part of the patrol officer's duty as a civil servant. The power to make an arrest is a patrol officer's primary mode of law enforcement and crime control. Patrol officers are not, however, given a free rein to place citizens under the control of the state. The law heavily regulates patrol officers' actions before, during, and after arrests. At the same time, they have a great deal of discretion in whether to make arrests and how to conduct themselves during the process. The legal aspects of arrests will be discussed in Chapter 6 and police discretion in Chapter 7.

Patrolling Public Events. Uniformed police officers are a deterrent to disruptive behavior. Thus, patrol officers are often called to be present at sporting events, concerts, political rallies, and parades.

Methods of Patrol

Police administrators often give officers specific assignments such as patrolling high-crime areas or writing traffic citations at an intersection where a large number of accidents occur. These activities are considered forms of **directed patrol.** Such patrols are specifically designed to deal with crimes that commonly occur in certain locations and under circumstances that provide police with opportunity for preparation. In Chicago, for example, police recently noted a pattern of taxi holdups that took place in a single neighborhood. Officers began disguising themselves as taxi drivers in the area and were soon able to apprehend the robber. Because of their proactive nature, these police actions are also sometimes known as *aggressive patrols*.

Most police work, in contrast, is done on **general patrol,** during which officers make the rounds of a specific area with the purpose of carrying out the various patrol functions. In a sense, general patrol is random because the officers spend a substantial amount of their shift hoping to notice any crimes that may be occurring. General patrol takes place when officers are not responding to calls for service. Some observers have compared a patrol officer to a scarecrow because it is hoped that the officer's presence alone will deter any would-be criminals from attempting a crime.[36]

Patrols can be conducted by a number of different methods. For example, the Los Angeles Police Department uses sixteen patrol helicopters with 30 million candlepower searchlights to detect crimes that no land-bound patrol vehicle could hope to uncover.[37] The most common methods of patrol, however, include foot, automobile, motorcycle, mounted (on horseback), bicycle, boat, and K-9 (with the aid of a dog).

Foot Patrol. Thanks in large measure to the theories of police reformer O. W. Wilson (discussed in Chapter 4), American police departments in big cities generally abandoned foot patrol in favor of automobiles during the middle of the twentieth century. In recent years, however, the oldest form of patrolling has made a comeback. Officers on foot are now seen as more responsive to community needs and less physically separated from citizens.[38] A study done by police scholar George L. Kelling showed that increased foot patrols in Newark, New Jersey, while having no impact on crime rates, did succeed in lowering citizens' fear of crime by heightening the perception of safety in the areas patrolled.[39]

Automobile Patrols. Automobile patrols are the most common of all patrol methods. In most cases, they offer the greatest speed and flexibility. They are also the least expensive. One automobile can cover the same area as five to ten foot patrol officers. With onboard computers providing a direct link between patrol officers and criminal information databases and traffic centers, automobiles are becoming even more effective.[40] This form of patrol does have some distinct disadvantages, however; most obviously automobiles cannot pursue suspects into certain locations such as narrow alleys or buildings. Furthermore, officers in cars are less likely than those on foot patrol to notice certain "tip-off" details, such as a broken window or an open door. Finally, as noted earlier, automobiles tend to separate the police from the public they serve.

Motorcycle Patrol. The main advantage of a motorcycle over an automobile is maneuverability: a motorcycle can weave in and out of traffic and through alleys to a much greater degree than even a compact car. On the negative side, officers on motorcycles are more exposed than those riding in automobiles and are more likely to be injured in an accident. Furthermore, motorcycles cannot be used effectively in inclement weather such as heavy rain or snow.

Mounted Patrol. There are approximately two hundred mounted patrol units in the United States. Many departments have found that mounted police are useful in crowd-control situations, as the horses retain their mobility even in the midst of a riot. The elevation of an officer on horseback seems to convey the presence of authority. The officers can better scan an unruly crowd from their high perch. Furthermore, mounted patrols are useful for public relations: they can help convey a "softer" image of police to citizens, especially children.[41] Despite these advantages, mounted patrol use is on the decline in the United States, mostly due to the cost of keeping the horses.

Bicycle Patrol. Historically one of the least popular methods of patrol, at least for police officers, bicycle patrols have been gaining in popularity in recent years. As a unit, bicycle officers are the most physically fit members of any department, and they are often preferred in tourist communities that do not appreciate the severe image of police cars. Because of their mobility, bicycles are useful in areas such as beaches and parks that are inaccessible to automobiles but too vast for officers to patrol on foot. Bicycle patrols also have the advantage of being able to approach crimes in progress without making much noise. Finally, due to the speed of the bicycle, officers can more easily catch suspects who attempt to flee on foot.[42] For the most part, bicycle patrols are rendered useless in inclement weather. For that reason they are more common in warm-weather jurisdictions. (See *Careers in Criminal Justice* on the next page.)

Boat Patrol. Many departments in cities on or near large bodies of water operate boat patrols. This method of patrol is used to enforce narcotics and firearms smuggling laws, and in some areas to combat illegal immigration. Due to the expense of maintaining the type of boats required, many coastal cities have surrendered at least part of this responsibility to the U.S. Coast Guard.

K-9 Patrol. Dog units, or K-9 patrols, perform very specific tasks: detecting illegal narcotics, finding hidden bombs, assisting in searches for missing persons, and searching buildings and other areas for burglars and other suspects. With their powerful sense of smell, dogs are responsible for the seizure of millions of dollars worth of narcotics and drug-contaminated currency a year. (One legendary golden retriever sniffed out $63 million worth of drugs and was responsible for the conviction of twenty drug dealers in Miami over a two-year period.[43])

There are a number of benefits to the mounted patrol. In crowd control, the impressive stature of a horse is such that people are less likely to challenge the authority of the police officer sitting on top of it. Also, because of the positive feelings many citizens have towards horses, mounted patrols present a softer, if not "lovable," image of the patrol officer. What are some of the potential drawbacks—both strategic and economic—of mounted patrols?

Dogs can often search buildings and track down fleeing suspects more quickly and effectively than human police officers. Well-trained dogs are incredibly loyal and commonly go to great lengths to protect their handlers. When accompanying officers on foot patrol, a dog can have the double impact

Careers in Criminal Justice

LOIS PERILLO, BICYCLE COMMUNITY POLICING OFFICER

I did not always want to be a police officer. I wanted to be an astronaut. So I graduated with a B.S. in Aeronautics and promptly went to work as an accountant for the City of New York. Loving the Broadway theater and my Italian/Ukranian family, yet knowing there was something more, I emptied my bank account of its $700, bought a bike rack, packed my '76 Datsun B-210 hatchback and drove across the country to join my college roommate in San Francisco. Seventeen years later, I still live in the Bay Area, working as a police officer for fourteen of those years.

A career in law enforcement first entered my mind when I saw a recruitment poster hanging in a very bohemian San Francisco restaurant. It depicted a United Nations of women in uniform and encouraged that I join them. I did. However, the hiring process, inclusive of background checks and written, oral, physical, and polygraph testing, took two years. Concerned with my ability to scale the six-foot wall, I talked my way into a specialized physical prep class designed for female firefighter candidates. To stay motivated, I enrolled in a pre-academy study class and I hunkered down for the wait.

In late June 1994, I received a letter from the San Francisco Police Department: my academy class was to begin in four weeks. By July, my hair was significantly shorter, and I was starching a gray rookie uniform weekly and polishing my brass and shoes daily. Those of us who could write easily were forced to do pushups, and those whose pushup style was one hand behind their back were compelled to write. After three months, my star was pinned to my navy blue wool uniform by the chief of police, and I was off to four years of midnights before falling into

the daylight and community policing.

I credit my fall to Valerie, one of the very first San Francisco community officers, who was about to move to another department when she recruited me to join the Community Police Officer Program, or C.P.O.P, as her replacement. I left the darkness of Mission Police Station's midnight watch, bought a very good pair of sunglasses, and began my adjustment to days. Soon, I was investigating a stalking incident on my beat. The suspect kept eluding us, until I went undercover, riding a bicycle. We caught the guy, found he was affected by dementia, and placed him in mental health treatment. My career as S.F.P.D.'s first bicycle community officer had begun.

At first we rode our personal bicycles with rubber bands around pant legs to protect ourselves from chain death. After ten years of bicycles on the beat, we are now fully funded with departmental supplies, equipment, and uniforms.

As a bicycle community officer, I don't just lock 'em up and go to court to testify. I am charged to be a problem solver and to stem repeat calls to dispatch. For example, after catching graffiti vandals in the act, I contracted with the teens and their parents that they remove their markings in lieu of facing arrest. I managed a crime alert system that the merchants use to share information and hopefully avert criminal activity. I helped organize the community to encourage a judge to compel a once ever-present, panhandling heroin addict to choose drug treatment over jail time. And when Headquarters called me into action, I've switched into cop and robber mode to chase and catch bike thieves, shoplifters, burglars, and drug dealers on my bike.

Though it doesn't fit on my gun belt like the other tools I carry, the bicycle is an asset to my job and helps me expand my potential; it is a barrier breaker. Children and adults approach me easily, making my duties flow smoothly. My responsibilities include daily bicycle patrol, ongoing contact with the

residents and merchants, and liaison with other city departments. I frequent community meetings and crime prevention talks. I listen to neighborhood concerns and prioritize my response according to their issues, assisting in their empowerment. I maintain voice mail at the station, shortcutting community calls to dispatch for issues that are not time sensitive, yet require a police response. I share information with the community by writing the Police Beat column for the local paper, *The Noe Valley Voice,* which posts to the web. As with all police officers, I answer radio calls for service, take reports, comfort the aggrieved, bandage wounds, collect evidence, and arrest suspects. I think of myself as an old-fashioned beat officer (with the plus of my bicycle) who was fortunate enough to fall into my life's work. And while off duty, I still keep a watchful eye on the space program and the stars.

of giving the officers a sense of protection and intimidating any potential wrongdoers in the immediate area. As with horses, the primary drawback with K-9 patrols is cost. (Figure 5.6 shows that K-9 and mounted patrols are mostly used by police departments that serve large populations and have larger budgets than those that serve smaller populations.)

Preventive Patrol and the Kansas City Experiment

In theory, as has been noted, police patrol—whether it takes place on foot, in a car, on a bicycle, or with a dog—is a *preventive* measure. That is, the presence of officers on general patrol is believed to have the effect of preventing crimes before they occur. O. W. Wilson was particularly optimistic about the preventive power of automobile patrols, believing that cruising police cars would give the impression that officers could be anywhere at anytime. This impression, in

Populations Served	Percentage of Agencies Maintaining Animals for Law Enforcement Work	
	Dogs	Horses
All sizes	17	1
1,000,000 or more	92	83
500,000–999,999	96	40
250,000–499,999	89	49
100,000–249,999	90	19
50,000–99,999	64	8
25,000–49,999	45	4
10,000–24,999	26	0
2,500–9,999	17	less than .5
Under 2,500	5	less than .5

Figure 5.6 The Use of Animals by Local Police Departments

SOURCE: BUREAU OF JUSTICE STATISTICS, LOCAL POLICE DEPARTMENTS, 1993 (WASHINGTON, D.C.: U.S. DEPARTMENT OF JUSTICE, APRIL 1996), TABLE 34, PAGE 17.

turn, would keep would-be criminals from committing crimes, would-be jay-walkers from jaywalking, and would-be speeders from speeding.[44]

A number of police administrators have questioned Wilson's strong belief in preventive patrolling. On a practical level, cities simply could not afford to pay the large numbers of uniformed patrol officers who would be needed to blanket a city.[45] With existing levels of police presence, criminals still could figure that the chances of a patrol officer "catching them in the act" were slight. Furthermore, preventive patrol would have little effect on crimes committed indoors or crimes of passion committed without any thought as to whether a police officer was nearby.

The Kansas City Preventive Patrol Experiment. The suspicions of those who questioned the efficacy of preventive patrols were somewhat justified by the results of the Kansas City Preventive Patrol Experiment, conducted in 1972 and 1973. With the cooperation of the local police department, researchers chose three areas, comprised of five beats each, with similar crime statistics.[46] Over the course of one year, the police applied different patrol strategies to each designated area:

- On the *control* beats, normal preventive measures were taken, meaning that a single automobile drove the streets when not answering a call for service.
- On the *proactive* beats, the level of preventive measures was increased, with automobile patrols being doubled and tripled.
- On the *reactive* beats, preventive patrol was eliminated entirely, and patrol cars only answered calls for service.

Before, during, and after the experiments, the researchers also interviewed residents of the three designated areas to determine their opinion of police service and fear of crime.

The results of the Kansas City experiment were somewhat shocking. Researchers found that increasing or decreasing preventive police patrol had little or no impact on:

- Crime rates.
- Fear of crime.
- Public opinion on the effectiveness of police.
- Police response time.
- Traffic accidents.
- Reports of crime to the police.

Criminologists were, and continue to be, somewhat divided on how to interpret these results. For some, the Kansas City experiment and other similar data proved that patrol officers, after a certain threshold, were not effective in preventing crime, and therefore scarce law enforcement resources should be diverted to other areas. "It makes about as much sense to have police patrol routinely in cars to fight crime as it does to have firemen patrol routinely in fire trucks to fight fire," noted University of Delaware professor Carl Klockars.[47]

Others saw the experiment as proving only one conclusion in a very specific set of circumstances and were unwilling to accept the results as universal. Professor James Q. Wilson, for example, said that the study showed only that random patrols in marked automobiles were of questionable value and that it proved nothing about other types of police presence such as foot patrols or patrols in unmarked automobiles.[48]

The Lasting Effects of the Kansas City Study. Indeed, despite the Kansas City Preventive Patrol Experiment, most modern police departments continue to assign officers to random, preventive patrols. Such patrols bring local governments revenue through traffic tickets and also are believed to reassure citizens. The lasting benefit of the Kansas City study, according to researchers Robert Sheehan and Gary Cordner, seems to be that it has freed police departments from their reliance on the random patrol.[49] In light of the study, police departments realized that they could divert patrol officers from their traditional patrol duties without setting off an increase in crime. Therefore, administrators felt free to experiment with alternative strategies and tactics.

We will examine some of these more aggressive approaches—such as undercover operations, the use of informants, and police raids-—in the following section on police investigations.

POLICE INVESTIGATIONS: THE CRIME SCENE AND BEYOND

Investigation is the second main function of police, along with patrol. Whereas patrol is primarily preventive, investigation is reactive. After a crime has been committed and the patrol officer has gathered the preliminary information from the crime scene, the responsibility of finding "who dunnit" is delegated to the investigator, most commonly known as the **detective.** Today detectives make up about 15 percent of the personnel in the average mid-sized and large-city police department.[50] Detectives have not been the focus of nearly as much reform attention as their patrol counterparts, mainly because the scope of the detective's job is limited to law enforcement, with less emphasis given to social services or order maintenance.

The detective—and the work a detective does—has been romanticized to a certain degree. From Sherlock Holmes to Dirty Harry to Andy Sipowicz, the detective has been portrayed in popular culture as an anti-establishment maverick with a success rate in solving crimes close to—if not at—100 percent. There is some truth to the "maverick" characterization. Detectives, on the whole, have more room for innovation in their operations than patrol officers; their work hours are more flexible; they are not required to wear uniforms; and they are not as closely supervised.

The job is not a glamorous one, however. Detectives spend much of their time investigating common crimes such as burglaries and are more likely to be tracking down stolen property than a murderer. They must also prepare cases for trial, which involves a great deal of time-consuming paperwork. The other media-driven perception of the detective—that she or he always finds the suspect—is also somewhat exaggerated.

DETECTIVE
The primary police investigator of crimes.

Even with advances in technology such as DNA-identification methods, the clearance rate in murder cases has dropped over the past two decades, as people are committing more homicides with no traceable links to their victims.[51] Furthermore, a landmark Rand Corporation study estimated that more than 97 percent of cases that are "solved" can be attributed to a patrol officer making an arrest at the scene, witnesses or victims identifying the perpetrator, or detectives undertaking routine investigative procedures that could easily be performed by clerical personnel.[52] "There is no Sherlock Holmes," said one investigator. "The good detective on the street is the one who knows all the weasels and one of the weasels will tell him who did it."[53]

The Detection Function

A detective division in the larger police departments usually has a number of sections. These sections often include crimes-against-persons, such as homicide or sexual assault, and crimes-against-property, such as burglary and robbery. Many departments have separate detective divisions that deal exclusively with *vice,* a broad term that covers a number of public order crimes such as prostitution, gambling, and pornography. In the past, vice officers have also been primarily responsible for narcotics violations, but many departments now devote entire units to that growing social and legal problem.

The ideal case for any detective, of course, is one in which the criminal stays on the scene of the crime, has the weapon in his or her hands when apprehended, and, driven by an overriding sense of guilt, confesses immediately. Such cases are, needless to say, rare. University of Cincinnati criminal justice professor John E. Eck, in attempting to improve the understanding of the investigative process, concluded that investigators face three categories of cases:

- *Unsolvable cases,* or weak cases that cannot be solved regardless of investigative effort.
- *Solvable cases,* or cases with moderate evidence that can be solved with considerable investigative effort.
- *Already solved cases,* or cases with strong evidence that can be solved with minimum investigative effort.[54]

Eck found that the "unsolvable cases," once identified as such, should not be investigated because the effort would be wasted, and that the "already solved cases" require little additional effort or time on the part of detectives. Therefore, Eck concluded, the investigation resources of a law enforcement agency should primarily be aimed at "solvable cases." Further research by Steven G. Brandl and James Frank found that detectives had relatively high success rates in investigating burglary and robbery cases for which a moderate level of evidence was available.[55] Thus, the Rand study cited above may be somewhat misleading, in that investigators can routinely produce positive results as long as they concentrate on those cases that potentially can be solved.

The Preliminary Investigation

When police are notified of a crime, the investigation process begins. Though each investigation has its own idiosyncrasies, the steps that are taken are fairly uniform. First comes the **preliminary investigation,** which consists of the duties of the first law enforcement officer to arrive on the scene (usually a patrol officer). (See Figure 5.7 for an overview of these responsibilities.) The initial responsibility is to attend to the well-being of the victim of the crime, if there is one. Next, the investigator must secure the crime scene.

PRELIMINARY INVESTIGATION
The procedure, usually conducted by a patrol officer, that must be followed immediately upon initial arrival at a crime scene. Includes securing the crime scene, interviewing witnesses and suspects, and searching the scene for evidence.

Figure 5.7 Crime Scene Procedures

Every crime scene is different, and police officers must use discretion in determining which steps to take to best carry out their investigations. There are, however, general procedures that can be applied to crime scenes. These procedures are described here.

1. Initial Response
The first officer or officers arriving on the scene should search the area for suspects. This serves two purposes: self-protection and possible apprehension of suspects.

If injured persons are found at the scene, immediate first aid should be provided.

Any suspect found should be arrested.

Any possible witnesses should be detained.

2. Protection of the Crime Scene
Protection includes sealing off any area that may yield evidence. An area can be sealed off with banner tape or by police officers. The basic goals of protection are to prevent the destruction and contamination of evidence. Those personnel moving around within the crime scene should avoid moving items, touching surfaces, and walking about unnecessarily.

3. Obtain Briefing Information
Take statements from victims and witnesses, if possible.

Collect observations from other law enforcement agents and medical personnel present.

4. Evaluate the Crime Scene with a Walk-Through
The walk-through is a process by which the investigator tries to re-create the crime as it might have occurred. During the walk-through, the investigator:
- Determines any signs of forced entry (for indoor crime scenes).
- Notes locations of entry and exit into and out of crime scene
- Locates potential items of evidence.
- Notes the presence or absence of any signs of violence (such as blood or broken furniture).
- Evaluates the scene geometry, or special relationship of various objects (such as victim's body and a blood-stained brick).
- Evaluates the condition of any dead victims that may be present.

5. Photograph the Crime Scene

The crime scene should be photographed before any objects are removed. Photographs should be taken from a number of different angles to provide a complete "picture" of the crime scene.

Any dead victims must be thoroughly photographed, including close-ups of all visible wounds or bruises.

6. Record the Crime Scene with a Sketch

7. Process the Dead Body

This procedure should be carried out by a medical examiner/coroner, who will make an on-scene evaluation of the wounds, time and cause of death, and possible clues suggesting that the body has been moved.

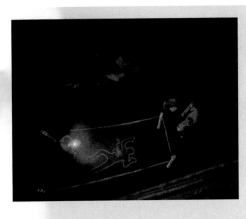

8. Collect Major Evidential Items

These items may be packaged and processed for later fingerprinting at the crime lab.

9. Search for Less Obvious Evidence, Including Trace Evidence

This includes dusting for fingerprints, and vacuum sweeps to pick up dust/hair/cloth fibers that may be of use.

10. Collection of Exemplars

For comparison purposes, samples of blood, hair, DNA, and clothing fibers must be collected from all persons with access to the crime scene, including victims, witnesses, law enforcement officers, etc.

11. Paperwork

All information concerning the crime scene should be noted in paperwork. This paperwork includes
- The assignment of a case number.
- A detailed description of the evidence.
- A detailed description of the crime scene.
- A record of to whom and when evidence is relinquished to other enforcement personnel.

12. Follow-Up Search

A final, comprehensive search of the crime scene for any evidence that may have been overlooked.

SOURCE: JEFFREY C. KERCHEVAL, HAGERSTOWN (MARYLAND) POLICE DEPARTMENT, AND SHERRY GUTIERREZ, "ESTABLISHING CRIME SCENE PROTOCOLS," POLICE (MAY 1997), 36-38.

Securing the Crime Scene. The **crime scene** is the physical area that may hold evidence that will aid in the investigation of a crime. Crime scenes contain fingerprints, bloodstains, footprints, weapons, strands of hair, and other pieces of evidence that are crucial to the investigation. The first officers to arrive at the crime scene are to protect it from being disturbed, or **contaminated,** so these clues can be effectively collected and used to solve the case.

Finding useful evidence can be a difficult task. First of all, many criminals "clean" crime scenes in an attempt to eradicate any evidence that would incriminate them; it is a foolish criminal indeed who forgets the murder weapon or leaves fingerprints.[56] Second, few crime scenes are pristine, as police are rarely the first people to reach the site. Friends and family often find victims and then effectively destroy evidence by touching and moving items. Third, the police themselves may contaminate the site. William Hagerty, a professor at the University of North Florida's Institute of Police Technology, recalled a recent murder case in Tallahassee, Florida, in which 90 of the 100 fingerprints lifted from the scene were those of police officers.[57]

Consequently, the preliminary investigator strives to keep the crime scene clear, save for the necessary law enforcement officers. In some cases, this can be done by simply closing a door, but in others police tape must be used to cordon off an area with extra officers assigned to crowd control.

Gathering Information. After the scene has been secured, the investigator's next task is to gather information that may be useful as the investigation continues or in a subsequent court case. The information may also aid the investigator's memory, should it falter further along in the process. There are a number of means of gathering information:

1. *Taking notes.* First impressions are essential to the preliminary investigation. Throughout their efforts at the crime scene, officers should take notes that address the generalities of the case, such as where and when the crime was thought to be committed, who the victims and witnesses are, and who any initial suspects might be and why.[58]

2. *Sketching.* Whatever the investigator's artistic skills, a sketch can provide a useful overall picture of the crime scene. The sketch should include details such as the position of the victim's body, possible entries to and exits from the crime scene, and the location of any relevant physical evidence. Today, several computer programs are available that assist in re-creating the crime scene. (See Figure 5.8 for a sample sketch of a crime scene.)

3. *Photography.* With the aid of police photographers, investigators can record every necessary detail of the site, from the general to the minute. The goal of the photographer is not simply to take a certain number of pictures, but to re-create the scene of the crime. Some departments now use video cameras to record crime scenes, a process that is less expensive and can provide investigators with a wider range of details.

4. *Identifying and interviewing victims (if possible) and witnesses.* One of the first crime-scene priorities is the identification of all witnesses. Given the possibility that a witness could at some point become a suspect, this step is crucial. Then, one-by-one, the victims and witnesses should be given an **interview,** or detailed questioning to determine what information each can give concerning the case.[59]

Boulder, Colorado, Sheriff's Department cadets Montez and Hill stand guard outside the home of the Ramsey family following the murder of 6 year-old Jon Benet Ramsey. The police tape is designed to keep everyone besides police investigators away from the crime scene to avoid contamination. What are some of the ways that the presence of civilians can ruin a crime scene for investigators?

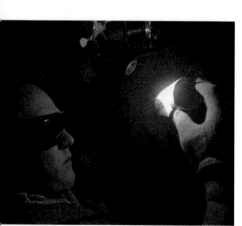

Andrew McIntyre, a technician with the Bureau of Alcohol, Tobacco and Firearms, checks a beer can for fingerprints.

CRIME SCENE
The physical area that contains or is believed to contain evidence of a crime.

CONTAMINATED
When evidence of a crime is rendered useless because of exposure to a foreign agent or improper removal from a crime scene.

INTERVIEW
The process of questioning a suspect or witness during the preliminary and follow-up investigations.

Gathering Evidence Using Forensic Techniques. Aside from information, the crime scene is also the primary source of physical evidence. An investigator must be able to locate, store, and transport the evidence without contamination. Fingerprints—the result of sweat and grease from the pores of the skin—bloodstains, footprints, tire impressions, fiber from clothing, hair and skin samples, and weapons are the primary forms of physical evidence.

Recently, technology has greatly improved law enforcement officers' ability not only to gather physical evidence, but also to use that evidence to solve crimes. The use of scientific technology in criminal investigations is known alternately as *forensic science* or *criminalistics*. The two terms are often used interchangeably, but they are not synonymous. Forensic science refers specifically to the use of science to examine, evaluate, and explain physical evidence in a court of law. Criminalistics is a branch of forensic science that deals with the collection and study of physical evidence such as fingerprints, blood, semen, hairs, clothing fibers, and firearms. To simplify matters, we will use the term *forensics* to refer to both forensic science and criminalistics.

The goal of **forensics** is to take physical evidence from the crime scene and to use that evidence either to prove that a particular person committed the crime or to clear the name of someone who did not commit the crime. (See *Criminal Justice & Technology—Putting the Finger on Unsolved Crimes*.) If, for example, forensic technicians are able to match fibers of a jacket found at the crime scene with fibers from a jacket worn by a suspect at the time of her or his arrest, then detectives have been provided with a valuable clue to use in

FORENSICS
The application of scientific methods to finding and utilizing criminal evidence.

Figure 5.8 Sketching a Crime Scene

On October 7, 1998, four law enforcement officers entered Darryl Howell's gun shop in the small town of Taft, California. Their goal: to arrest Howell for weapons violations. The attempt ended in disaster, as Howell died with four bullet wounds; one was self-inflicted and three came from the gun of Taft Police Sergeant Ed Whiting. Whiting was eventually cleared of any wrongdoing, and Howell's death was ruled a suicide. Here, you see a police sketch of the scene of the incident.

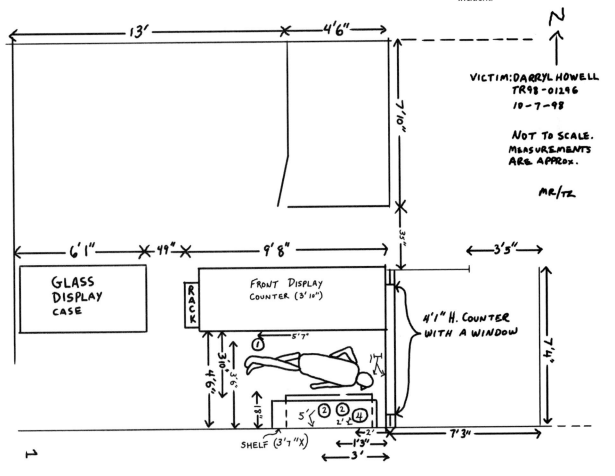

Criminal Justice & Technology

Putting the Finger on Unsolved Crimes

On February 17, 1982, Janet Nickel was raped and severely beaten in Room 121 of the Classic Inn Motel in Giddings, Texas. Her assailant managed to escape, leaving behind a pair of smudgy fingerprints, one on a light bulb and another on a doorknob. The local police unsuccessfully tried to match the prints with samples from numerous suspects, and the Nickel case became one of the thousands of violent crimes that go unsolved in the United States in the average year. Thanks to a new fingerprinting technology, however, it would not go unsolved indefinitely.

THE AUTOMATED FINGERPRINT IDENTIFICATION SYSTEM

In 1995, thirteen years later, Joe Goodson, the Lee County sheriff who worked on the Nickel case, learned about an addition to the state's technological arsenal, known as the Automated Fingerprint Identification System (AFIS). With AFIS, fingerprints are converted to algorithms—sets of mathematical equations used in problem solving. The computer compares the algorithms with other fingerprints found at crime scenes, as well with other samples recorded and stored by other law enforcement agencies. Using this program, law enforcement agencies can search and compare millions of samples in minutes. When combined with another new technology such as Live Scan—which electronically scans fingerprints instead of using black printer's ink to make a record of the

print—AFIS greatly increases the chances that fingerprints will lead to a suspect. "Fifteen years ago, I only dreamed of something like this," said one fingerprint specialist.

In the Nickel case, the old fingerprints were matched through AFIS, and the attacker, who was not considered a suspect at the time of the crime, was tried and convicted for attempted capital murder and sentenced to 99 years in prison. Other states have seen similar successes: during the first two years after installing AFIS, the Oklahoma state police resolved more than two thousand sexual assault and property crimes.

The technology will get a additional boost when the FBI launches its new Integrated Automated Fingerprint Identification System (the agency is aiming for a 2001 start date). Besides aiding the agency's own law enforcement efforts, the FBI's system will dramatically increase the speed at which state and local police departments receive fingerprint identification. AFIS technology has also been a successful export: in 1997, Great Britain established its own National Automated Fingerprint Identification System (NAFIS), which links the fingerprint-matching facilities of England, Northern Ireland, Scotland, and Wales.

In the Future: Electronic identification devices will go far beyond mere fingerprint matching. Such devices can identify individuals not only by fingerprints but also by such features as hand shape, eye characteristics, and voice timbre. The U.S. Immigration and Naturalization Service is already using rudimentary versions of these systems in airports to search for terrorist suspects.

solving the case. Most large police departments operate their own laboratories to which physical evidence can be delivered directly from the crime scene. Smaller police departments, lacking the budget to run such a facility, are usually able to use county, state, or FBI crime labs (at a price). Today there are more than three hundred crime labs in the United States, about 80 percent of which are operated by police departments.[60]

As technology advances, so does the role forensics can play in crime solving. John S. Dempsey of Suffolk County Community College has identified some of the newest techniques being used by law enforcement agencies:

- The *scanning electron microscope* can magnify material up to 100,000 times. This device is useful in distinguishing minute traces of particles such as gunpowder residue. Another device, the *gas chromatograph–mass spectrometer*, can separate and identify the components of minuscule amounts of substances. It could, for example, distinguish gunpowder residue from plain dirt.

- *Automated handwriting technology* allows forensic technicians to "fingerprint" suspects with a writing sample. The U.S. Secret Service has designed a computer program called the Forensic Information System for Handwriting (FISH) that treats handwriting samples with mathematical equations and then compares them to previously gathered samples.

- *Ultraviolet light*, also known as invisible light technology, provides forensic technicians and law enforcement officers with a "better look" at a crime scene. By flooding the scene with ultraviolet rays—which are characterized by shorter wavelengths that allow those with proper equipment to see more—investigators can pick up footprints, fingerprints, and other evidence that they missed using more traditional searching methods.

- A *computerized ballistics identification system* stores the "signatures," or distinguishing marks, that are etched on a bullet after it has been fired from a particular gun. The science of ballistics, which deals with the motion of projectiles, has traditionally been a painstaking process, as forensic technicians were forced to examine the spent bullets or shells for any telltale marks before undertaking the even more demanding task of finding the matching firearm. The new system will allow investigators to link shell casings and bullets with guns used in violent crimes across the nation.[61]

Many observers believe that the area of forensics with the greatest potential to change the criminal justice landscape involves DNA technology. As we will see in the *Criminal Justice in Action* feature at the end of the chapter, this technology, while inspiring hope in many, is also the focus of a great deal of controversy and consternation.

Errors during Preliminary Investigations. As a general rule, a homicide that is not solved within forty-eight hours of the crime is unlikely to be solved at all (though this is changing with the advent of new forensics technology).[62] Therefore, mistakes made during the preliminary investigation can cause irreparable damage. An example of this is provided by the notorious murder case of the child beauty pageant winner JonBenet Ramsey. Two years after the six-year-old girl was found strangled to death in the basement of her family's Boulder, Colorado, home, local detectives had not identified a suspect. Many observers blamed this failure on shoddy police work during the preliminary investigation.[63]

After the girl's body was discovered, the Boulder investigators' primary mistake was to treat her parents as victims instead of potential suspects. Accordingly, they did not conduct a thorough search of the home, seal the crime scene, or separate the Ramseys and interview them. Furthermore, a coroner was not called to inspect the body until seven hours after the child had been found. The absence of any signs of forcible entry into the basement and of any footprints in the melting snow around the house, as well as a ransom note that a number of experts considered phony, led many Colorado law enforcement officers to believe that JonBenet's parents "staged" a failed kidnapping to divert suspicion from themselves. The errors committed during the preliminary investigation make it unlikely that the Ramsey murder case will ever be solved.

A detailed "handbook" on the ins and outs of the crime scene investigation can be found at **police2.ucr.edu/csi.htm**

The Follow-Up Investigation

If a case is not solved—that is, if a suspect is not arrested—during the preliminary investigation, police must decide whether to pursue the matter with a **follow-up investigation.** Though the extraordinary length of the JonBenet Ramsey follow-up was driven by the publicity surrounding the case, in most instances the police will make a pragmatic decision about whether to continue the investigation based on a number of **solvability factors.** In violent crimes, these factors include the presence of a witness, useful physical evidence such as fingerprints, a possible suspect, and the amount of time between the criminal act and its discovery.[64] In burglary and robbery cases, the value of the stolen property often dictates whether an investigation will continue.[65] (See Figure 5.9 on the next page to understand how departments that operate under Managing Criminal Investigations [MCI] guidelines utilize solvability factors.) If the department decides to conduct a follow-up investigation, detectives will search for new physical evidence and re-interview witnesses.

There are three general types of follow-up investigations: (1) walkthroughs, (2) where-are-theys, and (3) whodunits.[66] Walk-throughs, comparable to Eck's "already solved cases" mentioned earlier, occur when the suspect is identified and apprehended during preliminary procedures. In where-are-

FOLLOW-UP INVESTIGATION
The steps taken by investigative personnel once it has been determined, based on the results of the preliminary investigation, that the crime is solvable.

SOLVABILITY FACTORS
Those factors that affect the probability that a case will be solved.

Figure 5.9 MCI and Solvability Factors

With the goal of helping police departments to be more effective in their investigative efforts, the Law Enforcement Assistance Administration (LEAA) funded research that led to the publication of a proposal called Managing Criminal Investigations (MCI). MCI offers a series of guidelines, including a system that grades cases according to their solvability. The solvability factors in the MCI include those listed here.

1. Is there a witness to the crime?
2. Is a suspect known or named?
3. Can a suspect be identified by a witness or some other means?
4. Will the person filing the criminal complaint cooperate in the investigation?

Each question is given a numerical weight; for every "yes" answer, the case is assigned a certain number of points. If, after all the "yes" answers have been added up, the final tally is above a certain threshold, then the department should continue investigating the case. If not, the case should be filed away until any additional information becomes available.

SOURCE: ILENE GREENBERG AND ROBERT WASSERMAN, MANAGING CRIMINAL INVESTIGATIONS (WASHINGTON, D.C.: NATIONAL INSTITUTE OF JUSTICE, 1975).

Anthony Porter celebrates his release in Chicago after spending sixteen years on death row. Porter was released when a follow-up investigation—spurred by information unearthed by a professor and five journalism students at Northwestern University—led to the taped confession of another man to the murder for which Porter was convicted.

theys, the suspect has been identified but remains at large. Finally, the whodunits are cases for which the preliminary investigation did not produce the identification of the person responsible for the crime.

If the suspect has already been arrested, a detective's primary duty in the follow-up investigation is to provide the prosecutor with all relevant material and evidence that will be needed to show the suspect's guilt in court. In some cases, the detective will gather more evidence to give the prosecutor a stronger case.

If the identity of the suspect is not known, the follow-up investigation can take several paths. Sometimes an investigator will retrace the steps already taken by patrol officers to make sure no evidence was overlooked. He or she may attempt to locate additional witnesses by contacting everybody in the area where the crime was committed. Informants can be interviewed to determine whether they have information about the crime, and attempts can be made to trace any property—such as an automobile—that was involved in the crime. Another useful tool for detectives is the *modus operandi* file, which contains descriptions of how known criminals commit specific crimes. The detective can check to see if the circumstances surrounding the crime in question match those of any crimes described in the *modus operandi* file.

Aggressive Investigation Strategies

Detective bureaus also have the option of implementing more aggressive strategies during a follow-up investigation. For example, if detectives suspect that a person was involved in the robbery of a Mercedes-Benz parts warehouse, one of them might pose as a "fence"—or purchaser of stolen goods. In what is known as a "sting" operation, the suspect is deceived into thinking that the detective (fence) wants to buy stolen car parts; after the transaction takes place, the suspect can be arrested.

Such tactics can also be used proactively; detectives can use their own initiative to apprehend wrongdoers before a crime has taken place. Besides stings, these strategies include undercover operations, the use of informants, and raids. Whether used proactively or as part of a follow-up investigation, detective initiatives are high-risk and high-reward operations. If completed successfully, the strategies can reward detectives with a large number of arrests and positive publicity for both the detective and the police department. If the plans fail, however, the risks of physical harm and negative publicity are equally great.

Furthermore, the outcome of an aggressive investigation may not always be what was expected. Researcher Robert Langworthy found that the incidence of auto theft in Birmingham, Alabama, appeared to increase after police conducted an auto theft sting. Langworthy concluded that the sting increased the market for stolen property. As soon as local car thieves learned that somebody was buying stolen autos (not realizing, of course, that the buyer was the police), they began to steal more cars to fulfill this new demand.[67]

Undercover Operations. Perhaps the most dangerous and controversial operation a detective can undertake is to go *undercover*, or to assume a different identity in order to obtain information concerning illegal activities. Though each department has its own guidelines on when undercover operations are necessary, all that is generally required is the suspicion that illegal activity is taking place.[68] (As you may recall from the discussion of entrapment in Chapter 3, police officers are limited in what they can do to convince the target of an undercover operation to participate in the illegal activity.) Today, undercover officers are most commonly used to infiltrate large-scale narcotics operations or those run by organized crime.

According to Professor John S. Dempsey, three general methods can be used for undercover drug operations.[69] In the first, the officer poses as a consumer of drugs, purchasing larger and larger amounts of the contraband so as to become an "insider" in the industry. As an insider, the officer has a better chance of making contact with and gathering information on the "kingpins" of the operation. In the second method, police "stake out" a particular location and make detailed observations of any suspected drug trafficking. The undercover officer then assumes an identity that fits in with the location and sets up a fixed surveillance team to record illegal activity, perhaps using a videotape. The third, and most dangerous, method is the "buy and bust operation," in which an undercover officer purchases drugs and, after leaving the scene, immediately contacts a backup team and identifies the seller. The backup team then makes the arrest. "Buy and bust" operations are rather large, requiring not only the buyer and the backup team, but a "ghost officer," who shadows the buyer during the deal and provides aid if needed, and a supervisor who plans and directs the operation.

The primary challenge of being an undercover officer, of course, is keeping one's identity hidden. "You've got to unlearn what you already learned," said one detective. "You gotta stop being the police. You don't want to act, walk, smell, talk or be a policeman. If you do, you tip people off."[70] There are other dangers as well. The undercover officer may become so immersed in the criminal life that she or he chooses it over the life of a law enforcement officer. Another possibility is that a patrol officer will mistake the undercover officer for a real criminal. In 1994, an NYPD undercover officer named Desmond Robinson was mistakenly shot in a New York City subway station by a transit officer.[71] Unfortunately, such errors are not uncommon.

The Use of Informants. In some cases, a detective bureau may not want to take the risk of exposing an officer to undercover work or may believe that an outsider cannot infiltrate an organized crime network. When the police need access and information, sometimes they turn to a **confidential informant (CI).** A CI is a person who is involved in criminal activity and gives information about the activity and those who engage in it to the police. The Supreme Court, in *Rovario v. United States* (1957),[72] held that the state has a *confidential informant privilege,* which means that it is not required to disclose the identity of an informant unless a court finds that such information is needed to determine the guilt or innocence of a suspect.

New York Detective Mary Glatzke, wearing a gray wig and the nonthreatening clothes of a civilian, sits on a park bench. By posing as a "Muggable Mary," Detective Glatzke is using herself as bait to lure would-be robbers. This sort of undercover strategy hopes to deter crime as well as catch criminals in the act. What might be some of the deterrent effects of Detective Glatzke's assignment?

CONFIDENTIAL INFORMANT (CI)
A human source for police who provides information concerning illegal activity in which he or she is involved.

Informants have a number of possible motivations for assisting law enforcement agencies. Most commonly, they are trying to avoid criminal charges of their own or at least receive a reduced sentence. Prisoner informants may be seeking better living conditions or some benefit to a third party. Other informants simply work for cash payments or are driven by emotional motives such as revenge.[73] In an informant-handler relationship, the law enforcement officer must be in control at all times. The officer must be sure of the informant's motives and make certain that the informant understands and agrees to the terms of the partnership. To avoid possible misunderstandings, many agencies have developed CI contracts that set out the terms agreed to by informants and the police.[74]

The mishandling of an informant can be a public relations disaster. For example, an FBI informant named Emad Salem was so intimately involved with the terrorist group responsible for the 1993 bombing of the World Trade Center in New York City that he actually purchased parts used in the explosive device.[75] In another incident with a number of ethical implications, a seventeen-year-old resident of Yorba Linda, California, was tortured and killed and his girlfriend raped and beaten ten days after the Brea Police Department dropped him as a CI. The department was harshly criticized for using someone so young in that capacity.[76] (See *CJ in Focus—A Question of Ethics: Sending Teens Undercover* for more on this case.)

Police Raids. Under many circumstances, information gathered in undercover operations and by informants is used to justify *raids,* or situations when law enforcement teams do not get permission before entering private property. Known as "booming" by police officers, raids often entail knocking down a door with specialized equipment and arresting suspects found within a dwelling. Police argue that such tactics are necessary because of the inherent element of surprise, which keeps the suspected criminals from using firearms against the police or hiding evidence.[77]

Critics of "booming" point out that it violates, if not in principle then certainly in spirit, the "knock and announce rule," which has been established by statute as upholding Fourth Amendment rights against unlawful search and seizure.[78] Also referred to as the "rule of announcement," this rule states that police officers who seek entry to a dwelling to conduct a search or make an arrest must first identify themselves and state the purpose of the proposed "visit."[79] In *Wilson v. Arkansas* (1995),[80] the Supreme Court ruled that even when officers have a search warrant and a probable cause that illegal activity is taking place in the dwelling, they must announce their presence before entering. The Court, however, noted that this rule did not apply in certain circumstances, allowing lower courts to loosely interpret the constitutional issues associated with booming. The next chapter will examine search and seizure issues in detail, as well as many other topics relating to law enforcement officers and the rule of law.

REFOCUSING ON THE COMMUNITY

While campaigning during the 1992 presidential race, President Bill Clinton promised to place 100,000 new police officers on the streets of America by the end of the decade. The Clinton administration carried out this vow by overseeing the passage of the Violent Crime Control and Law Enforcement Act of 1994 (the Crime Bill) and establishing the Office of Community Oriented Policing Services (COPS) to distribute the nearly $8 billion in federal grant money provided by the bill. Although it does provide funding for the modern policing approaches discussed in this section, to a certain extent the Crime

"The poorest man may in his cottage bid defiance to all the forces of the Crown. It may be frail; its roof may shake; the wind may blow through it; the storm may enter; the rain may enter; but the King of England cannot enter—all his force dares not cross the threshold of the ruined tenement!"

—William Pitt, *English statesman* (1913)

CJ in Focus
A Question of Ethics
Sending Teens Undercover

Though the use of confidential informants is a widespread and useful police tactic, some believe that it has important negative consequences. In a free society, these critics say, citizens should not have to fear that a friend or acquaintance is secretly working for the government. The ethical issues surrounding the practice become particularly troublesome when the informant is below the legal age of consent. The murder of a teenager who had been giving police information on drug deals has caused at least one state to restrict the freedom police agencies have in choosing and using informants.

In January 1998, seventeen-year-old Chad MacDonald of Yorba Linda, California, was arrested for possession and transportation of methamphetamine. To avoid punishment, MacDonald, with his mother's permission, took part in an undercover drug buy that led to several arrests. The teenager was eventually dropped as an informant after being arrested a second time for a drug-related infraction, but not before suspicion about his activities spread through certain segments of the Los Angeles criminal community. In March, he was killed by three men who admitted, through their lawyer, that they wanted to teach him a lesson. MacDonald's girlfriend was raped and beaten during the attack, but survived.

Many police departments see young informants as a valuable weapon—sometimes the only one available—in combating teen drug dealing and youth gangs. But some law enforcement experts question the implications of going undercover for teenagers. "The essence of being an undercover operative . . . is to win the trust of someone in order to betray it," says Eric Sterling, president of the Criminal Justice Policy Foundation in Washington. "What it teaches—to become a betrayer, to become a seducer, to become a traitor to the trust of other people—is certainly a bad thing to teach to young people." As the MacDonald case shows, it also places young people in situations of extreme danger. In the wake of MacDonald's murder, the California legislature passed a law requiring a judge's approval of the use of any informant under the age of eighteen.

For Critical Analysis: Under what circumstances, if any, do you believe the use of underage informants is justified? To what extent should the willingness of the teenager to act as an informant be considered in making the decision?

Bill was a throwback to an earlier era, reflecting the theory that more patrol officers and investigators will result in quicker response times and higher arrest rates, and thereby lower crime rates.

Many observers, however, question such conclusions. University of Arizona professors Michael Gottfredson and Travis Hirschi have found that the assumption that increasing the number of police will have a negative effect on crime rates is contrary to empirical research.[81] These researchers, along with many of their peers, believe that although incident-oriented policing—a reactive strategy—certainly has its place in law enforcement, more emphasis should be placed on proactive strategies that prevent rather than simply react to crime.[82] In other words, the number of police is often not as important as what those police are doing.

Over the past two decades, notions about what the police should be doing have experienced, in the words of George Kelling, a "quiet revolution."[83] This revolution has been fueled by the emergence of two theories of police strategy, now combined under the umbrella term of *community policing*: community-oriented policing and problem-oriented policing. Though conceptually different, both theories are based on the philosophy that to prevent and control crime effectively, police need to form partnerships with members of the community. As community policing strategies have been increasingly implemented by police departments throughout the country, many scholars have come to regard them as part of a backlash against the changes brought about by the reform era in American policing. Therefore, before we examine community policing, it will be helpful to understand the conditions from which it arose.

The Failures of Reform

As we discussed in Chapter 4, during the nineteenth century many American police departments gained a not-undeserved reputation for protecting and serving local political bosses rather than the citizenry. In response, at the end

COMMUNITY POLICING
A policing philosophy that emphasizes community support for and cooperation with the police in preventing crime. Community policing stresses a police role that is less centralized and more proactive than reform era policing strategies.

of the century reformers began to change the basics of American policing. To eliminate the influence of politicians on police officers, many jurisdictions instituted the hierarchical, militaristic chain of command referred to earlier in the chapter. The principles of professionalism—also discussed in Chapter 4—began to dominate police culture. To lessen the possibility of corruption, police officers were discouraged from establishing close ties with the community. Overall police "success" began to be determined by the rise or fall of serious crime rates as measured by the Uniform Crime Reports. Technological advances such as the patrol car and the two-way radio allowed police to become even more statistically efficient, while further alienating them from the community.

Proponents of these reforms believed that professional and well-equipped police officers could keep crime rates in control indefinitely. This belief proved false when crime rates rose dramatically in the 1960s and kept rising until the mid-1970s. As Chapter 4 described, the late 1960s were a particularly harrowing time for the nation, as many urban areas fell into disorder and were plagued by riots. One of the first hints of dissatisfaction with the philosophies of the reform era came in the wake of riots in Detroit, Michigan, in 1967. Commenting on the causes of the riots, the National Advisory Commission on Civil Disorders, also known as the Kerner Commission, cited a "deep hostility" between the police and the city's African American communities.[84]

The rising crime rates in these years predictably sparked a rise in the fear of crime. In many American cities, citizens virtually abandoned the streets at night. By the 1980s, lack of public confidence in law enforcement agencies became evident. Citizen initiatives such as block watches, foot patrols, and "Take Back the Night" rallies became common in high-crime areas.[85] The decade also saw a mushrooming of private security forces, which outnumbered their public counterparts by 2 million to 650,000 by 1990.[86] If the police can't control crime, the message seemed to be, the people will.

Community Policing

For all its negative associations, the political era of policing did have characteristics that many observers have come to see as advantageous. During the nineteenth century, police were much more involved in the community than they were after the reforms. Police officers performed many duties that today are associated with social services, such as operating soup kitchens and providing lodging for homeless people. They also played a more direct role in keeping public order by "running in" drunks and intervening in minor disturbances.[87]

To a certain extent, **community policing** advocates a return to this understanding of the police mission. In general, community policing can be defined as an approach that promotes community-police partnerships, proactive problem solving, and community engagement to address issues such as fear of crime and the causes of crime in a particular area.[88] In the reform era, the police were, in a sense, detached from the community. They did their jobs to the best of their ability, but were more concerned with making arrests or speedily answering calls for service than learning about the problems or concerns of the citizenry. In their efforts to eliminate police corruption, administrators put more emphasis on segregating the police from the public than on cooperatively working with citizens to resolve community problems. Under community policing, patrol officers have much more freedom to improvise. They are expected to develop personal relationships with resi-

Sgt. John Fontaneau does his part to promote a community policing program in Stamford, Connecticut's Vidal Court public housing project. How can establishing friendly relations with citizens help law enforcement agencies prevent crime?

dents and to encourage those residents to become involved in making the community a safer place. (See the *Concept Summary—The Professional Model of Policing and Community Policing.*)

CONCEPT SUMMARY
The Professional Model of Policing and Community Policing

The past sixty years have seen two dominant trends in the style of American policing. The first was the professional model, designed to reduce corruption and improve performance by emphasizing efficiency. The second, community policing, was a reaction against the professional model, which many thought went too far in relying on statistics and technology. The main characteristics of these two trends are summarized below.

Professional Model of Policing

- The separation of policing from politics

- Reduced emphasis on the social service function of police, with resources and strategies directed toward crime control.

- Limits placed on police discretion; emphasis placed on following guidelines and respecting the authority of the law.

- Centralized, bureaucratic police departments.

- The promotion of a certain distance between police officers and citizens, also the result of increased use of automobile patrols as opposed to foot patrols.

- Main strategies:

  1. Rapid response to calls for service, made possible by technological innovations such as the two-way radio.

  2. Preventive patrol, which attempts to use police presence to deter criminal activity.

Community Policing

- Although professionalism is still valued, it is tempered by recognition that police serve the community and its citizens, as well as the ideal of the law.

- Decentralized, less bureaucratic police departments, allowing more authority and discretion to rest in the hands of police officers.

- Recognition that crime control is only one function of law enforcement, to be included with crime prevention and the provision of social services.

- A more intimate relationship between police and citizens, which comes from an understanding that police officers can only do so much to fight crime; ultimately, they need the cooperation of the community to be successful.

- Main strategies:

  1. Return to foot patrol to "reconnect" with the community.

  2. Problem solving, which treats crimes not just as isolated incidents but as "problems" that can be "solved" with innovative, long-term approaches.

Community Policing Strategies. Thousands of local police departments have implemented community policing strategies. The following are some of the strategies that have succeeded on a nationwide basis:

- Through the *National Police Athletic League (PAL)*, police departments provide opportunities for local youths to participate in athletic events organized and officiated by officers. PAL programs reduce juvenile delinquency by giving youths something positive to do and also offer them a chance to interact with police officers in a relaxed environment.

- In *Ride-Along programs*, local citizens are allowed to ride in squad cars and watch as patrol officers go about their duties.

- In *Officer Friendly programs*, a police officer visits elementary schools to talk with the students about good citizenship and general safety issues.

- In *Citizen Crime Reporting Programs (CCRP)*, also known as Neighborhood Watch programs, local residents join together to fight crime within their neighborhoods. Typically, the residents hold meetings in which they talk about crime in their neighborhood and receive educational materials about crime prevention from the local police department. These programs also open lines of communication between citizens and the police.

Local initiatives have also played a significant role in the community era of policing. When the Bridgeport (Connecticut) Police Department decided to target a high-crime neighborhood known as the "Beirut of Bridgeport," it adopted community policing methodology. The department opened a Strategic Interventions for High-Risk Youth office in the neighborhood and invited citizens to attend meetings there to discuss their crime problems. A Neighborhood Watch Council was founded, and both police and citizens worked to improve the appearance of the area. Within four years, overall crime rates in the neighborhood dropped 75 percent.[89]

The Elgin (Illinois) Police Department has taken the idea of community involvement to the extreme with its Resident Officer's Program of Elgin (ROPE). As part of the program, police officers are offered rent-free housing in the city's high-crime neighborhoods. Prior to ROPE, the citizens in these areas had little trust in the local police. "They would say all the police do is come in here when there's a shooting and then they leave," said Elgin Police Chief Charles A. Gruber. "We needed to say we were committed to the community."[90]

These programs and others across the country typify the essence of community policing. First, they show how the police can engage in problem solving as opposed only to responding to calls for service. Second, they are examples of how the police are attempting to forge partnerships with neighborhoods or community groups. Finally, the programs illustrate how the police can engage the community by encouraging citizens' active involvement in crime and disorder problems.

Shortcomings of Community Policing. One criticism of community policing is that it can be applied to so many different strategies, rendering it rather vague as a policing philosophy. Any form of police activity that tends toward being proactive is labeled community policing. More than half of the police chiefs and sheriffs in a recent survey conducted by the National Institute of Justice were unclear about the actual meaning of "community policing,"[91] leading some observers to joke that Professor Kelling's revolution is even quieter than had been expected.[92]

Some also question whether American policing has in fact adopted new tactics and strategies. The two most frequently identified community policing programs are Drug Abuse Resistance Education (or DARE, in which specially trained police officers teach students—mostly fifth and sixth graders—about the dangers of illegal drug use, violence, and gang activity) and foot patrols, both of which existed long before the concept of community policing was introduced. Many critics wonder if community policing is more rhetoric than a "new" way of doing business for American police departments. Furthermore, much of local police agencies' motivation to reach out to citizens is financial—the 1994 Violent Crime Control and Law Enforcement Act provides federal funds for departments that embrace community policing.

Despite these possible shortcomings, the trend toward community policing is generally regarded as having a positive impact on police strategies—if for no other reason than that it forces police departments to consider the complex relationship between patrol officers and the community.

Problem-Solving Policing

Problem solving is a key component of community policing. Problem solving has its roots in **problem-solving policing,** which was introduced by Herman Goldstein of the Police Executive Research Forum in the late 1970s. Goldstein's basic premise was that police departments were devoting too many of their resources to reacting to calls for service and too few to "acting on their own initiative to prevent or reduce community problems."[93] To rec-

"We have a hard enough time dealing with real crime, let alone somebody's fantasy of it."

—Los Angles patrol officer, *complaining about the difficulty in implementing community policing programs (1998)*

PROBLEM-SOLVING POLICING
A policing philosophy that requires police to identify potential criminal activity and develop strategies to prevent or respond to that activity.

tify this situation, problem-solving policing moves beyond simply responding to incidents and attempts instead to control or even solve the root causes of criminal behavior.

Goldstein's theory was in direct contrast to the reform era theories of policing, discussed in this chapter and the previous one.[94] Goldstein was suggesting that patrol officers must become intimately involved with citizens. For example, instead of responding to a call concerning illegal drug use by simply arresting the offender—a short-term response—the patrol officers should also look at the long-term implications of the situation. They should analyze the pattern of similar arrests in the area and interview the arrestee to determine the reasons, if any, that the site had been selected for drug activity.[95] Then additional police actions should be taken to prevent further drug sales at the identified location. (See Figure 5.10 for the environmental aspects of a neighborhood that can contribute to drug activity.)

Police and "Problems." During the reform era, police officers were trained to respond to "incidents," or violations of the law. Once an incident had taken place, officers were judged by the speed at which they arrived at the scene and how quickly they were able to arrest those responsible for the incident. The introduction of problem solving represents a distinct change in strategy. Although a criminal act certainly qualifies as a "problem," the term also covers circumstances that may lead to criminal activity. To assist departments with the transformation from incident-driven policing to problem solving, the Department of Justice identified five principles of problem-solving policing:

1. A problem is something that concerns the community and its citizens, not just police officers. Issues that may be important only to police are worthy of attention, but they are not necessarily community concerns.

2. A problem is a group or pattern of incidents and therefore demands a different set of responses than does a single incident.

3. A problem must be understood in terms of the competing interests at stake. Police must be aware of these interests and respect them in dealing with the problem.

4. Responding to a problem involves more than a "quick fix," such as an arrest. Problem solving is a long-term strategy.

5. Problem solving requires a heightened level of creativity and initiative on the part of the patrol officer.[96]

---

1. Heavy traffic volume at certain hours of the night.

2. Poor street lighting, which may be the result of poor public maintenance (burned-out bulbs) or broken lights.

3. Abandoned automobiles.

4. Public property (street signs, light poles, telephone poles, statues) with graffiti.

5. Private property (homes, apartment buildings, businesses) with graffiti.

6. Large numbers of people "hanging out," that is, not working or engaging in some other obvious pursuit (such as playing street hockey or basketball).

7. An excessive amount of litter.

8. An excessive number of vacant lots in obvious disuse.

9. An excessive number of abandoned or vacant buildings.

SOURCE: "APPENDIX B: EXAMPLE OF A BLOCK ENVIRONMENTAL PROBLEM" IN BUREAU OF JUSTICE ASSISTANCE, A POLICE GUIDE TO SURVEYING CITIZENS IN THEIR ENVIRONMENT (WASHINGTON, D.C.: U.S. DEPARTMENT OF JUSTICE, OCTOBER, 1993), 69–79.

Figure 5.10 A Police Guide to Surveying Citizens in Their Environment

One of the basic truths of problem-solving policing is that crimes are not always isolated incidents, but may be part of a pattern of life in a certain neighborhood or community. Therefore, changing the environment of a high-crime area is an essential part of solving that area's crime problems. John Meeks of the Philadelphia Police Department has identified physical characteristics that may be indicative of drug activity in an area and should be "fixed" to lessen such activity.

SARA. Scanning for problems is the first step in a four-step process that problem-solving policing practitioners refer to with the acronym SARA—for scanning, analysis, response, and assessment. We will examine SARA using the example of Newport News, Virginia, the site of one of the first studies of problem-solving policing in the United States.[97]

In the early and mid-1980s, Newport News was experiencing a crime wave that was keeping businesses and citizens out of the downtown area. By *scanning* the crime reports and talking with patrol officers who worked downtown, members of the police department were able to determine that a series of prostitution-related robberies had been plaguing the area. Instead of viewing these robberies as a series of unrelated incidents, a group of Newport News police officers, led by Officer James Boswell, decided to approach them as a general problem.

To *analyze* the problem, Officer Boswell interviewed twenty-eight prostitutes who frequented the downtown area. He learned that they worked downtown because customers were easy to find and because police patrols did not notice the prostitutes soliciting in bars. Even if they were arrested, the prostitutes said, they only received a "slap on the wrist": judges generally sentenced them to probation instead of jail time, and probation was not enforced.

Based on these interviews, Officer Boswell planned a *response*. He gained the cooperation of bar owners in moving prostitutes to the street, where patrol officers could spot them more easily. He persuaded the local district attorney to ask judges to impose harsher penalties on persons convicted of prostitution. He worked with the police department's vice unit to make sure that prostitutes were arrested and that patrol officers knew which prostitutes were on probation. Finally, Officer Boswell talked with the prostitutes' customers, many of whom came from the town's naval base. He warned them that almost half the prostitutes working the streets were men posing as women. He also convinced the U.S. Navy to allow him to warn incoming sailors about the safety and health risks associated with soliciting prostitutes.

The *assessment* proved that Officer Boswell's problem-solving approach was successful. Within three months, the number of prostitutes working downtown Newport News dropped from twenty-eight to six. Robbery rates were halved. After eighteen months, neither prostitution nor robbery appeared likely to return to its previous levels.

Hot Spots. According to the tenets of reform era policing, patrol officers should be spread evenly throughout a precinct, giving each citizen the same level of service. Many observers find this shortsighted, at best. Professor Lawrence Sherman compares it to giving every citizen an equal dose of penicillin—whether that person is sick or not.[98]

MapInfo and Vertical Mapping are computer programs law enforcement agencies use to determine "hot spots." To see how this technology works, go to www.tetrad.com/crime.html

Some say a more practical response is for police to concentrate on **hot spots,** or areas of high criminal activity. Minneapolis police discovered, for example, that 100 percent of the robberies in a certain year occurred in only 2 percent of the city's zip codes.[99] Similarly, law enforcement officials in Jersey City, New Jersey, found that fifty-six hot spots of drug activity (occupying 4.4 percent of the city's street sections) accounted for 45 percent of the city's narcotics sales arrests and 46 percent of emergency calls for service.[100]

In both cases, the city's police department took part in experiments in which extra patrol coverage—in brief bursts of activity—was directed to a select number of the hot spots. In Minneapolis, robbery rates in the targeted hot spots fell by more than 20 percent, and in both cities, calls for service reporting public disorder also decreased. Neither police department, however, concluded that the hot spots experiment had decreased overall crime. Criminals had simply moved to other areas, or "scattered like cockroaches in the light," as one observer put it.[101]

HOT SPOTS
Concentrated areas of high criminal activity that draw a directed police response.

Crime Mapping. Many police departments are using *crime mapping* technology to locate and identify hot spots. A new generation of geographic information systems (GIS's) provides departments with colored maps that allow them to easily spot patterns of crime and determine where increased coverage is needed.[102] (See Figure 5.11.) With the press of a button, GIS software can find and predict crime patterns by matching variables such as time of day, type of crime, and type of weapon used. When Fontana, California, recently experienced a spate of burglaries, for example, the police department's GIS was able to direct officers to virtually the exact spot where the next attempt would take place. Deputies were able to follow the burglars into a target house, where they were arrested and confessed to more than thirty other similar crimes.[103] Crime mapping is critical to establishing police targets for directed patrols, as described earlier in the chapter.

Broken Windows: Popularizing Community Policing

If Herman Goldstein introduced the idea of problem-solving policing, James Q. Wilson and George L. Kelling brought it widespread attention. Many observers believe that Wilson and Kelling set the modern wave of community policing in motion with their 1982 article in *Atlantic Monthly* (briefly mentioned in Chapter 2) entitled "Broken Windows."[104]

The Broken Windows Theory. In "Broken Windows," Wilson and Kelling argued that reform-era police strategies focused on violent crime to the detriment of the vital police role of promoting the quality of life in neighborhoods. As a result, many American communities, particularly in large cities, had fallen into a state of disorder and disrepute, with two very important consequences. First, these neighborhoods—with their broken windows, dilapidated buildings, and lawless behavior by citizens—send out "signals" that criminal activity is tolerated. Second, this disorder promotes fear among law-abiding

INFOTRAC ®
COLLEGE EDITION

Gilchrist, Elizabeth, Jon Bannister, Jason Ditton and Stephen Farrall. Women and "fear of crime": challenging the accepted stereotype.

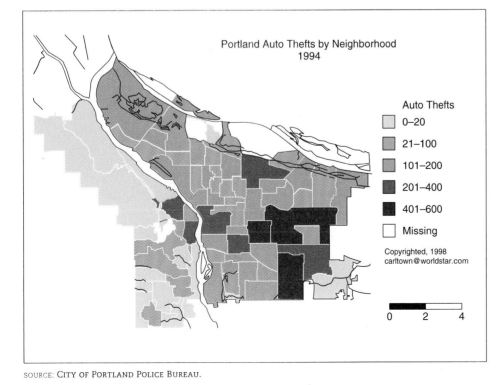

Figure 5.11 Geographic Information Systems and Auto Theft in Portland, Oregon

A geographic information system (GIS) uses digital maps to highlight areas in which crime occurs. As you can see, the Portland (Oregon) Police Department has taken advantage of GIS technology to pinpoint the incidence of auto theft in the city.

SOURCE: CITY OF PORTLAND POLICE BUREAU.

BROKEN WINDOWS THEORY

Wilson and Kelling's theory that a neighborhood in disrepair signals that criminal activity is tolerated in the area. Thus, by cracking down on quality-of-life crimes, police can reclaim the neighborhood and encourage law-abiding citizens to live and work there.

"A stable neighborhood of families who care for their homes, mind each other's children, and confidently frown on unwanted intruders can change, in a few years or even a few months, to an inhospitable and frightening jungle. A piece of property is abandoned, weeds grow up, a window is smashed. . . . Such an area is vulnerable to criminal invasion."

—James Q. Wilson and George L. Kelling, *American crime researchers* (1982)

citizens, dissuading them from leaving their homes or attempting to improve their surroundings.

The **broken windows theory,** therefore, is based on "order maintenance" of neighborhoods by cracking down on "quality-of-life" crimes such as panhandling, public drinking and urinating, loitering, and graffiti painting. Only by encouraging police diligence with regard to these quality-of-life crimes, the two professors argued, could American cities be rescued from rising crime rates.

Community policing played a prominent role in Wilson and Kelling's article. To reduce fear and crime, they insisted, police had to rely on the cooperation of the citizens. Many cities have found that a crucial step in "reconnecting" with the community has been the reintroduction of foot patrols in high-crime neighborhoods. Studies have shown that foot patrol officers pay more attention to "order maintenance crimes" such as drunkenness, vagrancy, and panhandling than do patrol officers in police cars. Although these crimes are not serious, they do increase fear of crime in a community.

Foot patrol officers are also in a better position to interact with citizens, forming relationships that allow them to deal with threatening or inappropriate behavior—such as a domestic dispute—that could eventually lead to violence.[105] After studying the reinstitution of foot patrols in Newark, New Jersey, in a study briefly mentioned earlier in the chapter, Kelling concluded that the patrols:

- Significantly reduced levels of fear.
- Improved citizen satisfaction with the police.
- Provided foot patrol officers with a greater appreciation for the values of neighborhood residents.
- Provided greater job satisfaction for the patrol officers.[106]

It is important to note that Kelling *did not* find that foot patrols affected crime rates. Instead, their primary benefits were to increase citizen satisfaction and reduce citizen fear.

Philadelphia police officers used problem-solving concepts to put the broken windows theory into effect in the high-crime neighborhood of Queen Village.[107] With a series of "Sunday Surveys" (so-called because they were conducted on Sundays when calls for service are less frequent), police identified the following problems in Queen Village:

- 20 dilapidated buildings.
- 20 abandoned cars.
- 7 blocks with serious litter problems.
- 11 blocks with serious graffiti problems.
- 5 littered vacant lots.
- 6 blocks with poor overhead lighting.

In cooperation with other city agencies, the Philadelphia police aggressively worked to alleviate these shortcomings. Although the city did not conduct a formal survey of crime rates in the neighborhood, the police department noted that residents felt a great deal safer than they had before.

Crackdowns. In many American cities, the implementation of the broken windows theory has been accompanied by aggressive patrol tactics known as

CJ in Focus

Making Waves

The Transit Cop and the New York Miracle

When Jack Maple was a lieutenant in the New York City Transit Police, he papered the walls of his office with what he called the Charts of the Future. The charts detailed each robbery and where it had been committed in the city's subway system. Maple's point was simple: figure out where the most crimes are taking place and increase the police presence in those areas. Maple had similar ideas for the entire New York City Police Department. He insisted that the city's already high crime rate would continue to rise unless the force instituted a more proactive strategy than simply responding to 911 calls. For most of his career, Maple was considered a dreamer—a transit cop with big ideas and nothing else.

Then, in 1994, new NYPD commissioner William Bratton named Maple his deputy. Maple immediately began implementing a strategy named Comstat to find out exactly where the most crimes were being committed and to stop them. Twice a week, New York City's precinct chiefs met, watched, and listened as Maple displayed dozens of maps and grids of the city. The ex-transit cop put pressure on those who presided over high-crime neighborhoods to become more proactive, and they did.

As a result of this pressure from above, patrol officers began to take a "zero tolerance" attitude toward crime on the streets. The officers cracked down on minor offenses such as loitering, public urination, loud radios, and unlicensed street vending. All minor offenders were frisked for guns and checked for outstanding warrants. Bratton and Maple also took the rather dramatic step of allowing uniformed patrol officers to make drug arrests, a practice that had been discontinued during the reform era of policing because of fear of corruption.

With these aggressive tactics, the New York City police did what many observers had thought to be impossible—they lowered crime rates in one of the most violent cities in the world. Between 1993 and 1995, homicides in New York City dropped from 1,946 to 1,170, and robberies decreased 31 percent. In 1997, the city registered its lowest homicide rate since 1968. (After a political shake-up that saw the departure of Commissioner Bratton, Maple lost his job. He was later hired as a consultant by the police department in New Orleans, Louisiana, an annual contender for the title of Murder Capital, U.S.A.)

For Critical Analysis: Do you think that Maple's tactics would automatically work in any city? Give some reasons why they might not, and research New Orleans's crime rates to see if Maple and his aggressive tactics have had similar results in that city.

"crackdowns." When police intensely focus their energies on a particular crime or set of crimes in a given area, they are said to be conducting a "crackdown." Crackdowns, which are related to the "hot spot" tactics discussed earlier, are one of the most widely used forms of directed patrol and are typically used to solve a significant crime or disorder problem in an area. New York City, which experienced a dramatic drop in violent crime in the 1990s, is often held up as the ultimate example of what can be accomplished when the broken windows theory and aggressive police actions are combined. (See *CJ in Focus—Making Waves: The Transit Cop and the New York Miracle.*)

In light of the broad acceptance of the broken windows theory, it must be noted that police abuse of their power to make "order maintenance" arrests was one of the reasons for police reform in the first place. In the 1950s and 1960s, for example, such laws were used to provide a legal shield for police harassment of civil rights and anti-Vietnam War demonstrators. During that period, courts restricted the police's freedom to make "vagrancy" arrests because such arrests were politically motivated.[108] Some scholars believe that a resurgence of police power in this area may result in similar problems in the future.[109]

Criminal Justice in Action

The DNA Revolution

As mentioned earlier in this chapter, forensics, or the application of science to criminal investigations, play a key role in police work. The development of new scientific techniques can transform criminal justice, as happened with fingerprinting. Derided as "junk science" when first introduced in the late nineteenth century, fingerprinting was eventually accepted as an important means of identifying and cataloguing criminals. The process is not, however, without its flaws. Fingerprints smudge and are often rendered useless as evidence by those who disturb a crime scene before forensics experts arrive. Furthermore, police find that children's fingerprints evaporate quickly because they contain volatile fatty acids. We look next at a relatively new technology that many law enforcement officers believe improves upon—and may eventually replace—fingerprinting.

GENETIC BLUEPRINTING

On January 13, 1998, the body of nursing administrator Sherry Crandell was found in the family practice wing of the Prince George's County (Maryland) Medical Center. Crandell had been raped and strangled. As part of his investigation, Police Chief John Farrell asked the dozens of men interviewed for information on the crime, including fifty hospital workers, to allow a cotton swab to be rubbed against the insides of their mouths. The point of this exercise was to collect skin cells, which could then be examined at a police laboratory to determine the subject's deoxyribonucleic acid (DNA).[110]

Police Chief Farrell downplayed the significance of his strategy, likening it to collecting fingerprints to rule out possible suspects. For many observers, however, this "DNA dragnet" represented the latest proof of the growing role of genetics in police investigations. In collecting the skin samples, Farrell was hoping to find a DNA match for the semen found at the scene of the crime. (He did not succeed.) DNA, which is the same in every cell of a person's body, provides a "genetic blueprint" or "code" for every living organism. DNA "profiling" is useful in criminal investigations because no two people, save for identical twins, have the same genetic code. Therefore, lab technicians, using the process described in Figure 5.12, can compare the DNA sample of a suspect to the evidence found at the crime scene. If the match is negative, it is certain that the two samples did not come from the same source. If the match is positive, the lab will determine the odds that the DNA sample at the scene of the crime could have come from somebody *other* than the suspect. These odds are so high—sometimes reaching 30 billion to one—that the match is often seen as conclusive by juries.[111]

COLD HITS

The initial use of DNA to establish criminal guilt took place in Britain in 1986; it was used for the first time in the United States by the FBI two years later. The process begins when forensics technicians gather blood, semen, skin, saliva, or hair from the scene of the crime. Sperm and blood cells are rich in DNA, making the technique particularly useful in murder and rape cases. If the victim is able to identify a suspect, that person's DNA will be tested to determine whether he or she can be placed at the crime scene. In cases of murder, or when the victim is unable to provide a suspect, police rely on DNA databases. Today, almost every state allows law enforcement agencies to collect DNA samples from wrongdoers. In South Dakota, for example, DNA samples are taken upon arrest. Virginia has the largest DNA database in the nation, with 160,000 samples.[112]

These databases can lead to what police call a **cold hit,** or the solving of a case in which there are no suspects. A typical example of a cold hit occurred in the 1997 murder case of Jamie Paine.[113] Kansas City police were able to match the DNA in a few drops of blood found near Paine's body with the DNA of Marcus L. Brummall in the state's database. Brummall was eventually convicted of first degree murder. In 1997, the first interstate cold hit took place after an Oklahoma police lab sent blood samples from the scene of an unsolved quintuple murder to a number of other jurisdictions. A match was found in the California DNA database, leading Oklahoma authorities to the felon.

COLD HIT
A term used to describe a match between a sample in a DNA database and the DNA of a suspect who was unknown to police when evidence from the crime scene was submitted to the laboratory for testing.

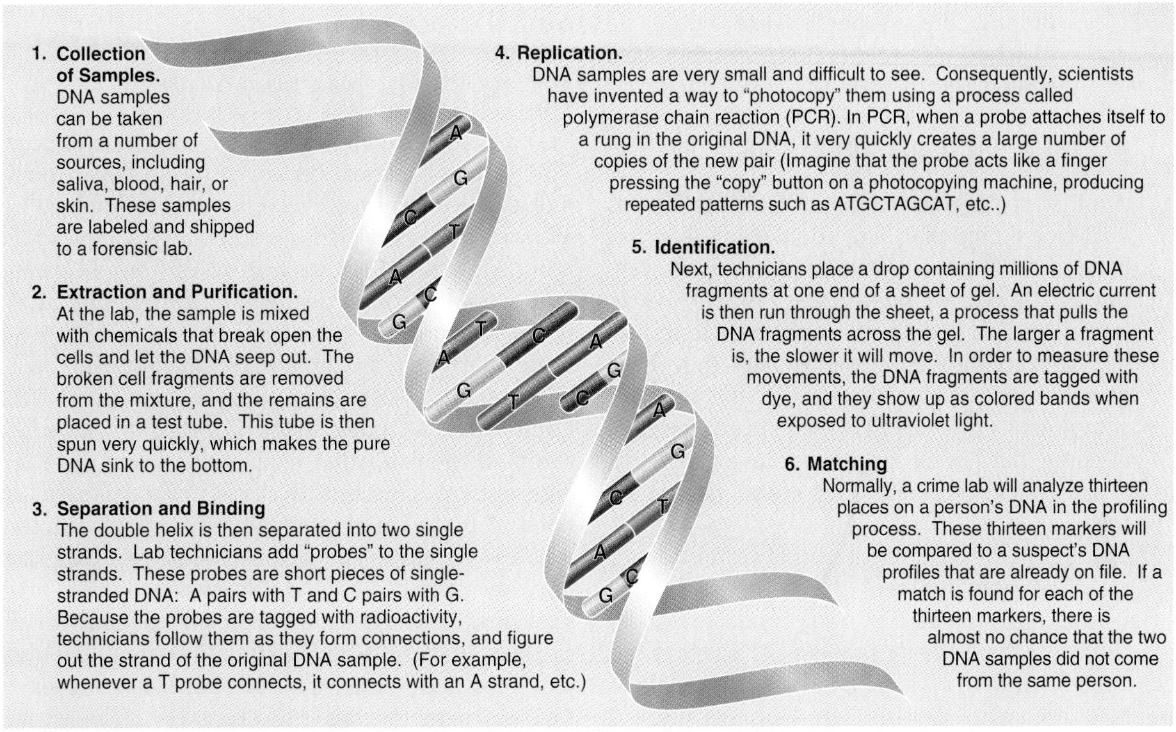

1. Collection of Samples.
DNA samples can be taken from a number of sources, including saliva, blood, hair, or skin. These samples are labeled and shipped to a forensic lab.

2. Extraction and Purification.
At the lab, the sample is mixed with chemicals that break open the cells and let the DNA seep out. The broken cell fragments are removed from the mixture, and the remains are placed in a test tube. This tube is then spun very quickly, which makes the pure DNA sink to the bottom.

3. Separation and Binding
The double helix is then separated into two single strands. Lab technicians add "probes" to the single strands. These probes are short pieces of single-stranded DNA: A pairs with T and C pairs with G. Because the probes are tagged with radioactivity, technicians follow them as they form connections, and figure out the strand of the original DNA sample. (For example, whenever a T probe connects, it connects with an A strand, etc.)

4. Replication.
DNA samples are very small and difficult to see. Consequently, scientists have invented a way to "photocopy" them using a process called polymerase chain reaction (PCR). In PCR, when a probe attaches itself to a rung in the original DNA, it very quickly creates a large number of copies of the new pair (Imagine that the probe acts like a finger pressing the "copy" button on a photocopying machine, producing repeated patterns such as ATGCTAGCAT, etc..)

5. Identification.
Next, technicians place a drop containing millions of DNA fragments at one end of a sheet of gel. An electric current is then run through the sheet, a process that pulls the DNA fragments across the gel. The larger a fragment is, the slower it will move. In order to measure these movements, the DNA fragments are tagged with dye, and they show up as colored bands when exposed to ultraviolet light.

6. Matching
Normally, a crime lab will analyze thirteen places on a person's DNA in the profiling process. These thirteen markers will be compared to a suspect's DNA profiles that are already on file. If a match is found for each of the thirteen markers, there is almost no chance that the two DNA samples did not come from the same person.

Figure 5.12 Unlocking Evidence in DNA

Deoxyribonucleic acid, or DNA, is the genetic material that carries the code for all living cells. DNA is useful to crime-solvers thanks to the discovery that the DNA of one person is different from the DNA of another person. Through DNA profiling, a process explained here, forensic scientists test DNA samples to see if they match with the DNA profile of a known criminal or other test subject.

In addition to helping police find criminals, DNA profiling also offers hope for those unjustly convicted of crimes. From 1988 to 1998, fifty-six wrongfully convicted people were exonerated after DNA testing was applied to their cases. Ten of those won release from death row.[114] One of the most celebrated reversals concerned four men who had been convicted for double murder, rape, and robbery in Ford Heights, Illinois, in 1978. When DNA evidence proved that they had not been responsible for the crimes, the so-called Ford Heights Four—one of whom had spent eleven years on death row—were released in 1996.[115]

QUESTIONS OF PRIVACY

The use of DNA profiling as evidence is not without its critics. One of the most controversial aspects of the procedure concerns the privacy rights of those tested. In the Maryland hospital case discussed earlier, legal experts complained that the police should only be allowed to take the skin tissue of those who were actual suspects in the nursing administrator's murder. A Boston judge halted the gathering of DNA samples from thousands of prisoners, probationers, and parolees in Massachusetts, ruling that the act constituted an illegal search and seizure.[116]

Furthermore, not all DNA evidence is accepted in court. Human error can render the tests useless, as occurred in *People v. Castro* (1989),[117] when the private company that conducted the DNA testing failed to inform the trial court that its sample had been contaminated with bacteria. Furthermore, sometimes the odds against a positive match are not sufficiently persuasive. In trying to build a case against one of the alleged participants in the 1993 World Trade Center bombing in New York City, prosecutors used DNA drawn from saliva found on an envelope. According to expert testimony, the suspect's DNA could be matched with that of 330,000 other New Yorkers.[118]

PASSING THE Frye TEST

Another obstacle to the use of DNA profiling as evidence during trials is a court ruling that was handed down more than three-quarters of a century ago. In *Frye v. United States* (1923),[119] a circuit court ruled that new scientific techniques will not be accepted as evidence until they have gained widespread acceptance in the scientific community. Currently, DNA evidence is accepted in some, but not all, courts: because geneticists do not agree on its reliability, it has not yet passed the *Frye* test.

A number of indicators suggest that DNA evidence will soon be able to meet this high, and rather ambiguous, legal standard. A study conducted under the banner of the National Academy of Sciences has concluded that DNA profiling is sufficiently reliable to be used in criminal courts.[120] Furthermore, the U.S. Court of Appeals for the Second Circuit in 1992 approved the use of DNA evidence in the kidnapping case of Randolph Jakobetz, who had been convicted for raping a woman in Vermont and leaving her on a New York City street. Jakobetz's conviction relied on an FBI analysis that matched semen recovered from the woman to DNA taken from the suspect's blood. Following the Jacobetz case, the Supreme Court further improved DNA pro-

filing's chances of passing the *Frye* test by ruling in two cases that it was admissible as evidence in all civil and criminal cases.[121]

THE FUTURE OF DNA PROFILING

Despite any lingering problems it may face in court, DNA testing is almost certain to play a larger role in future police investigations. Improved technology will allow police labs to extricate acceptable samples from minute traces of DNA, such as saliva from a cigarette butt or sweat from a headband. Furthermore, as the technology improves, the costs of DNA sampling will drop, making it an option for small-budget police departments. Most important, however, is the Combined DNA Index System (CODIS), a nationwide computer hook-up that enables local and state law enforcement agencies to access a single database that holds all of the country's DNA profiles of subjects convicted of homicide and sexual assault. Using this system, investigators can check evidence from their individual cases against a national file of DNA genetic markers. In 1996, Florida law enforcement investigators recorded more than 70 positive matches in CODIS, linking together 113 previously unsolved sexual assaults and homicides.[122] The reach of CODIS could become even greater, depending on the outcome of a study conducted in 1999 by the National Commission on the Future of DNA Evidence. This federal commission is examining the legality of taking DNA samples from *all persons arrested,* without waiting to determine whether they are convicted of the crime.[123]

Key Terms

Chapter Summary

1. **List the three criticisms of standard bureaucratic police organization.** (a) They limit personal ingenuity and sometimes result in groupthink; (b) they limit contact with the community; and (c) they limit contact among members of the police department.

2. **Explain the difference between arrest rates and clearance rates.** Arrest rates simply indicate the number of individuals arrested by a police department. In contrast, clearance rates show the percentage of crimes a police department has solved over any given time.

3. **List the three primary purposes of police patrol.** (a) The deterrence of crime, (b) the maintenance of public order, and (c) the provision of services that are not related to crime.

4. **Identify the different types of patrol.** Most patrols are general patrols as opposed to directed. The most common methods of general patrol include (a) foot, (b) automobile, (c) motorcycle, (d) mounted on horseback, (e) bicycle, (f) boat, and (g) K-9 (with a dog).

5. **Describe the steps that an investigator must take after a crime occurs.** The first responsibility during the preliminary investigation is to attend to the well-being of the victim. Next the crime scene must be secured so that it does not become contaminated. Then comes the information-gathering stage, which involves taking notes, sketching, taking photographs, and identifying and interviewing victims and witnesses. Then physical evidence, such as footprints and bloodstains, is collected.

6. **Indicate some investigation strategies that are considered aggressive.** Using undercover officers is considered an aggressive (and often dangerous) investigative technique. The use of informants is also aggressive, but involves danger for those who inform. Police raids without warning are also used.

7. **Explain community policing and its strategies.** Community policing involves proactive problem solving and a community-police partnership in which the community engages itself along with the police to address crime and the fear of crime in a particular geographic area. Strategies include sending police officers to schools, opening community intervention offices for high-risk youths, and encouraging police officers to live in high-crime neighborhoods.

8. **Indicate the five principles of problem-solving policing.** (a) Problems are concerns of the community, not just police officers. (b) Problems demand different sets of responses than do single incidents. (c) Competing interests are at stake in all problems. (d) Problem solving is a long-term strategy. (e) The patrol officer must become more creative and use more initiative to solve problems.

Questions for Critical Analysis

1. What type of police organization resulted from the desire to eliminate politicians' influence on the police?

2. What two criteria are most often used to measure police efficiency, and what are the weaknesses of such statistical indicators?

3. How can a differential response strategy help a police department become more effective?

4. "The number of police is often not as important as what those police are doing." Analyze this statement.

5. The Kansas City Preventive Patrol Experiment involved control beats, proactive beats, and reactive beats. Did the results of that experiment show any benefits to increasing preventive police patrol? If yes, how? If not, why not?

6. Contrast the community policing model with the professional policing model.

7. Relate the concept of "broken windows" to high-crime neighborhoods and potential ways to combat crime in such neighborhoods.

8. How effective are detectives in solving crimes? If they are not that effective, who or what is responsible for solving most crimes?

9. In what ways can crime scenes be contaminated? Who often causes the contamination?

10. How has the DNA revolution changed forensics?

Selected Print and Electronic Resources

SUGGESTED READINGS

MacKay, James A., *Allan Pinkerton and the First Private Eye*, New York: John Wiley & Sons, 1997. This is an interesting and informative full-length biography of the Scottish-born detective, Allan Pinkerton. He is credited with saving Abraham Lincoln from at least one assassination attempt. He also broke up an important Confederate conspiracy in Washington, D.C. Pinkerton had a genius for organization and attention to detail.

Peak, Kenneth J., and Ronald W. Glensor, *Community Policing and Problem Solving: Strategies and Practices*, 2d ed., Englewood Cliffs, NJ: Prentice Hall, 1998. This book looks into the processes of community policing and problem-solving policing. The authors explore the efforts of police agencies across the United States. The book shows how police are moving away from traditional methods of responding to crime.

Rosenthal, Richard, *K-9 Cops: Stories from America's Police Units*, New York: Mass Market Paperback, Pocket Books, 1997. This book gives you a sense of what K-9 police officers do with their dogs and how they feel about them. A collection of true cases from across the country, Rosenthal's work describes actual investigations in which dogs were used.

MEDIA RESOURCES

Rush (1991) This is the story of two undercover narcotics agents who find themselves hooked on the drugs that they are buying and illegally using. The experienced undercover agent, Raynor (played by Jason Patric), is helping break in the recruit, Kristen (played by Jennifer Jason Leigh). Raynor believes he is the master of the drug world. He shoots drugs himself in the presence of big-time dealers so that they cannot possibly believe he is a cop. This movie was inspired by Kim Wozencraft's book about a true story. While viewing this film, think about the different types of law enforcement agents who are involved.

Critically analyze this film:

1. In addition to narcotics agents, what other types of "workers" in this film are at least somehow connected to law enforcement?

2. Why does an undercover agent have to pretend to be the very thing that he or she has pledged to defeat?

3. Is the story believable?

4. What is the moral game that undercover agents have to play in order to bring in the dealers?

5. At any point in this film do you believe that the law enforcement officers could be accused of entrapment? Explain your answer.

Logging On

If you would like to obtain more information on forensic science resources, go to the following site:

www.tncrimlaw.com/forensic/

There you will find forensic science resources and a criminal fact investigation, including a bibliography and reference guide to the forensic sciences.

You may want to look at information on a criminal investigation developed during a class at Lake Superior State University. Check out the following web site to learn about criminal investigation, collecting information, and investigative reconstruction: **www.angelfire.com/mi/cj243/**

For more information on community policing go to: **www.communitypolicing.org/resource.html**

At that site you will find an electronic library and information-access guide, links to other community policing Web sites, and links to Popnet, for the Problem-Oriented Policing Network.

To find out about CPInet, which is a not-for-profit initiative linking lawmakers and law enforcers in different communities, go to: **www.cpinet.org/**

Using the internet for Criminal Justice Analysis

INFOTRAC® COLLEGE EDITION

1. Access your InfoTrac account at:

www.infoTrac.college.com/wadsworth/access/html

Type in "**COMMUNITY POLICING: THE PROCESS OF TRANSITIONAL CHANGE.**" This article from *The FBI Law Enforcement Bulletin* covers a study undertaken to evaluate the extent of law enforcement agencies' involvement with community policing in terms of strategies, philosophy, and officers' skills.

a. What percentage of agencies surveyed had implemented community policing?

b. Why do the authors of this article mention the Violent Crime Control and Law Enforcement Act of 1994?

c. Which of the ten principles that encompass the community-oriented policing philosophy were incorporated by the agencies surveyed in the Minneapolis–St. Paul metropolitan area?

d. What were the two most popular community policing strategies implemented by the agencies surveyed?

e. What were the three guidelines that led to successful implementation of community-oriented policing policies?

2. This question concerns the science of forensics. First go to **http://library.advanced.org/17049/gather/** Then click on "Reference."

a. Find out more about fingerprints. When were the patterns of ridges and whorls first discovered?

b. Summarize the first U.S. case in which fingerprints were used.

c. Now discover more about DNA profiling. When was the first case in which this type of profiling was used?

d. What was the first known landmark of forensic science and when did it occur?

e. When did Luigi Galvani discover that the human nervous system transmits information electronically, thereby forming a basis of lie-detection equipment?

Notes

1. Bob Anderson, "Burglar Beats Woman; Man Booked," *Baton Rouge Advocate* (August 7, 1997), 1B.
2. Samuel Walker, *The Police in America: An Introduction,* 2d ed. (New York: McGraw-Hill, 1992), 16.
3. George L. Kelling and Mark H. Moore, "From Political to Reform to Community: The Evolving Strategy of Police," in *Community Policing: Rhetoric or Reality,* ed. Jack Greene and Stephen Mastrofski (New York: Praeger Publishers, 1988), 13.
4. "Denver Cops Probe 911 Snafu," *UPI Online* (March 31, 1998).
5. Leef Smith, "Manassas Wants to Ease 911 Load," *Washington Post* (January 28, 1998), V3.
6. Laura A. Bischoff, "Abusers of 911 May Face Jail," *Dayton Daily News* (February 18, 1998), 3B.
7. H. Nees, "Policing 2001," *Law and Order* (January 1990), 257–64.
8. Walker, 14.
9. Kelling and Moore, 11–12.
10. San Diego Police Department, *Final Report of the Custody Death Task Force* (unpublished, June 1992).
11. Mark H. Moore and Robert C. Trojanowicz, *Corporate Strategies for Policing* (Washington, D.C.: National Institute of Justice, November 1988), 6.
12. Henry M. Wrobleski and Karen M. Hess, *Introduction to Law Enforcement and Criminal Justice,* 5th ed. (Minneapolis/ St. Paul, MN: West Publishing Company, 1997), 326.
13. U.S. National Advisory Commission on Criminal Justice Standards and Goals, *Police* (Washington, D.C.: U.S. Government Printing Office, 1973), 194.
14. National Commission on Productivity, *Conference on an Agenda for Economic Research on Productivity* (Washington, D.C.: U.S. Government Printing Office, 1974).
15. Samuel Walker, *The Police in America: An Introduction* (New York: McGraw-Hill, 1983), 118.
16. Kansas City Police Department, *Response Time Analysis: Executive Summary* (Washington, D.C.: U.S. Government Printing Office, 1978); and William Spellman and D. K. Brown, *Calling the Police: Citizen Reporting of Serious Crime* (Washington, D.C.: Police Executive Research Forum, 1981).
17. Lori Stahl and Stephen Power, "Response Slows on 911 Calls," *Dallas Morning News* (September 28, 1997), 1A.
18. J. Thomas McEwen, Edward F. Connors III, and Marcia J. Cohen, *Evaluation of the Differential Police Responses Field Test* (Washington, D.C.: National Institute of Justice, 1986).
19. Lawrence W. Sherman, "Attacking Crime: Police and Crime Patrol," in *Modern Policing,* ed. Michael H. Tonry and Norval Morris, vol. 16 of *Crime and Justice: A Review of Research* (Chicago: University of Chicago Press, 1992), 335.
20. *Ibid.,* 338.
21. Federal Bureau of Investigation, *Crime in the United States, 1995* (Washington, D.C.: U.S. Government Printing Office, 1996), 199.

22. Survey by the Gallup organization for *CNN/USA Today*, September 22–24, 1995.

23. David C. Couper and Sabine Lobitz, "The Customer Is Always Right," *The Police Chief* (May 1991), 17–23.

24. Robert Trojanowicz, *An Evaluation of the Neighborhood Foot Patrol Program in Flint, Michigan* (East Lansing, MI: Michigan State University, 1982), 85–87.

25. Connie Fletcher, "What Cops Know," *OnPatrol* (Summer 1996), 44–5.

26. David H. Bayley, *Police for the Future* (New York: Oxford University Press, 1994), 20.

27. George L. Kelling, Tony Pate, Duane Dieckman, and Charles Brown, *The Kansas City Preventive Patrol Experiment: A Summary Report* (Washington, D.C.: The Police Foundation, 1974), 3–4.

28. Walker, 103.

29. Eric J. Scott, *Calls for Service: Citizens Demand and Initial Police Response* (Washington, D.C.: National Institute of Justice, 1981), 28–30.

30. William G. Gay, Theodore H. Schell, and Stephen Schack, *Routine Patrol: Improving Patrol Productivity*, vol. 1 (Washington, D.C.: National Institute of Justice, 1977), 3–6.

31. Gary W. Cordner, "The Police on Patrol," in *Police and Policing: Contemporary Issues*, ed. Dennis Jay Kenney (New York: Praeger Publishers, 1989), 60–71.

32. Anthony V. Bouza, *The Police Mystique: An Insider's Look at Cops, Crime, and the Criminal Justice System* (New York: Plenum Press, 1990), 27.

33. Noel C. Bufe, "Traffic Services" in *The Encyclopedia of Police Sciences*, 2d ed., ed. William G. Bailey, (New York: Garland, 1995), 776–82.

34. Egon Bittner, *The Functions of Police in a Modern Society*, Public Health Service Publication No. 2059 (Chevy Chase, MD: National Institute of Mental Health, 1970), 127.

35. Kathleen Maguire and Ann L. Pastore, eds., *Sourcebook of Criminal Justice Statistics, 1996* (Washington, D.C.: U.S. Department of Justice, Bureau of Justice Statistics, 1997), 368.

36. Dale O. Cloninger, "Enforcement Risks and Deterrence: A Reexamination," *Journal of Socio-Economics* 23 (1994), 273.

37. Todd S. Purdum, "Vigilant Eyes Fill Skies over Los Angeles," *New York Times* (March 18, 1998), A1, A14.

38. James Q. Wilson and George L. Kelling, "Making Neighborhoods Safe," *Atlantic Monthly* (February 1989), 36–8.

39. Police Foundation, *The Newark Foot Patrol Experiment*, (1981), 122–4.

40. Tom Yates, "Magic Patrol Cars: Police Travel 'Information Superhighway,'" *Law and Order* (April 1995), 77–81.

41. Kimberly Rinker, "There's No Horsing Around in These Units," *Police* (July 1997), 26–31.

42. Bonnie Bobit, "Bicycle Patrols," *Police* (February 1998), 32–5.

43. Samuel G. Chapman, *Police Dogs in North America* (Springfield, IL: Charles C. Thomas Pub., 1990), 71.

44. Jerome H. Skolnick and James J. Fyfe, *Above the Law: Police and the Excessive Use of Force* (New York: Free Press, 1993), 251–2.

45. Andrew Halper and Richard Ku, *An Exemplary Project: New York City Police Department Street Crimes Unit* (Washington, D.C.: U.S. Government Printing Office, 1975), 1.

46. Kelling, Pate, Dieckman, and Brown.

47. Carl B. Klockars and Stephen D. Mastrofski, "The Police and Serious Crime," in *Thinking about Police*, eds. Carl Klockars and Stephen Mastrofski (New York: McGraw-Hill, 1990), 130.

48. James Q. Wilson, *Thinking about Crime* (New York: Basic Books, 1983), 65–6.

49. Robert Sheehan and Gary W. Cordner, *Introduction to Police Administration*, 2d ed. (Cincinnati, OH: Anderson, 1989), 367–8.

50. Federal Bureau of Investigation data cited in Tim McLaughlin, "Fewer Detectives Working on More Cases, Study Shows," *Capital Times (Madison, Wisconsin)* (September 5, 1997), 1A.

51. Victoria Pope and Annik Stahl, "The All-Too-Typical JonBenet Case," *U.S. News & World Report* (December 1, 1997), 32.

52. Peter W. Greenwood and Joan Petersilia, *The Criminal Investigation Process: Summary and Policy Implications* (Santa Monica, CA: Rand Corporation, 1975).

53. Fletcher, 46.

54. John E. Eck, *Solving Crimes: The Investigation of Burglary and Robbery* (Washington, D.C.: Police Executive Research Forum, 1983).

55. Steven G. Brandl and James Frank, "The Relationship Between Evidence, Detective Effort, and the Disposition of Burglary and Robbery Investigations," *American Journal of Police* 1, 149–68.

56. Sherry Gutierrez, "Establishing Crime Scene Protocol," *Police* (May 1997), 34–9.

57. Quoted in Pope and Stahl, 36.

58. Karen M. Hess and Henry M. Wrobloski, *For the Record: Report Writing in Law Enforcement*, 4th ed. (Blue Lake, CA: Innovative Systems, 1997), 24–5.

59. Gerald W. Garner, "Investigating Death," *Police* (May 1997), 26–33.

60. Joseph L. Peterson, *Use of Forensic Evidence by the Police and Courts* (Washington, D.C.: National Institute of Justice, 1987), 5.

61. John S. Dempsey, *An Introduction to Policing*, 2d ed. (Belmont, CA: West/Wadsworth Publishing Co., 1998), 353–4.

62. Pope and Stahl, 32.

63. Ann Louis Bardach, "Missing Innocence," *Vanity Fair* (October 1997), 324–30, 372–8.

64. Joel Samaha, *Criminal Justice*, 3d ed. (St. Paul, MN: West Publishing Co., 1994), 198.

65. Steven Brandl, "The Impact of Case Characteristics on Detectives' Decision Making," *Justice Quarterly* 10 (1993), 141.

66. Kuykendall, J., "The Municipal Police Detective: An Historical Analysis," *Criminology*, 24(1): 175–201.

67. Robert H. Langworthy, "Do Stings Control Crime? An Evaluation of a Police Fencing Operation," *Justice Quarterly* 6 (1989), 27.

68. *Hoffa v. United States*, 385 U.S. 293, 298 (1966).

69. Dempsey, 189–90.

70. Fletcher, 49.

71. Robert D. McFadden, "Police Cover-Up Is Asserted in Beating of Black Officer," *New York Times* (January 9, 1998), B5.

72. 353 U.S. 53 (1957).
73. Charles S. Zimmerman, "Toward a New Vision of Informants: A History of Abuses and Suggestions for Reform," *Hastings Constitutional Law Quarterly* 22 (Fall 1994), 81.
74. Dennis McCauley, "It's Not Confidential: Use Care with Informants," *Police* (May 1997), 23.
75. Ralph Blumenthal, "Tapes Show FBI Agreed to Return Timer for Bomb," *New York Times* (November 8, 1993), B3.
76. Bonnie Hayes and Scott Martelle, "Files Detail Teen's Work for Brea Police," *Los Angeles Times* (April 2, 1998), A1.
77. Todd Witten, "*Wilson v. Arkansas:* Thirty Years after *Ker* the Supreme Court Addresses the Knock and Announce Issue," *Akron Law Review* 29 (Winter 1996), 447.
78. *Miller v. United States,* 357 U.S. 301 (1958).
79. Witten, 447.
80. 514 U.S. 927 (1995).
81. Michael R. Gottfredson and Travis Hirschi, *A General Theory of Crime* (Stanford, CA: Stanford University Press, 1990), 270.
82. Sherman, 327.
83. George Kelling, "Police and Community: The Quiet Revolution," in *Perspectives on Policing* (Washington, D.C.: National Institute of Justice, 1988).
84. *Report of the National Advisory Commission on Civil Disorders* (Washington, D.C.: U.S. Government Printing Office, 1973), 157.
85. Kelling and Moore, 16–17.
86. Bayley, 10.
87. Mark H. Moore and George L. Kelling, "'To Serve and Protect': Learning from Police History," *Public Interest* (Winter 1983), 54–7.
88. A. Steven Dietz, "Evaluating Community Policing: Quality Police Service and Fear of Crime," *Policing: An International Journal of Police Strategies and Management* 20 (1997), 83–100.
89. Bureau of Justice Assistance, *Crime Prevention and Community Policing: A Vital Partnership* (Washington, D.C.: Office of Justice Programs, September 1997), 7–8.
90. Edward Walsh, "When the Force Lives with You, City's Crime Drops," *Washington Post* (March 2, 1997), A3.
91. National Institute of Justice Research Preview, *Community Policing Strategies* (Washington, D.C.: Office of Justice Programs, November 1995).
92. Jihong Zhao and Quint C. Thurman, "Community Policing: Where Are We Now?" *Crime and Delinquency* (July 1997), 345–57.
93. Herman Goldstein, "Improving Policing: A Problem-Oriented Approach," *Crime and Delinquency* 25 (1979), 236–58.
94. Kelling and Moore, 12.
95. Bureau of Justice Assistance, *Problem-Oriented Drug Enforcement: A Community-Based Approach for Effective Policing* (Washington, D.C.: Office of Justice Programs, 1993), 5.
96. *Ibid.,* 5–6.
97. John Eck et al., *Problem Solving: Problem Oriented Policing in Newport News* (Washington, D.C.: Police Executive Research Forum, 1987), 100–1.
98. Sherman, 331–2.

99. Lawrence W. Sherman, Patrick R. Gartin, and Michael E. Buerger, "Hot Spots of Predatory Crime: Routine Activities and the Criminology of Place," *Criminology* 27 (1989), 27–55.
100. *National Institute of Justice Research Preview: Policing Drug Hot Spots* (Washington, D.C.: Office of Justice Programs, January 1996).
101. Brian J. Taylor, "The Screening of America," *Reason* (May 1, 1997), 44.
102. William M. Bulkeley, "Information Age: Police Turn to Database to Link Crimes," *Wall Street Journal* (March 8, 1993), B5.
103. Elizabeth Douglass, "Crime Mapping Software Helps Officers Put Pieces Together," *Los Angeles Times* (February 16, 1998), D3.
104. James Q. Wilson and George L. Kelling, "Broken Windows," *Atlantic Monthly* (March 1982), 29–38.
105. Wilson and Kelling, "Broken Windows."
106. George L. Kelling, *Foot Patrol* (Washington, D.C.: National Institute of Justice, 1987).
107. *Problem-Oriented Drug Enforcement: A Community-Based Approach for Effective Policing*, 53–4.
108. *Coates v. City of Cincinnati*, 402 U.S. 611 (1971); *Cox v. Louisiana*, 379 U.S. 536 (1965); *Papachristou v. City of Jacksonville*, 405 U.S. 156 (1972).
109. Debra Livingston, "Police Discretion and the Quality of Life in Public Places: Courts, Communities, and the New Policing," *Columbia Law Review* (April 1997), 551.
110. Richard Willing, "Privacy Issue Is the Catch for Police DNA 'Dragnets,'" *USA Today* (September 16, 1998), 1A.
111. Judith E. Lewter, "The Use of Forensic DNA in Criminal Cases in Kentucky as Compared with Other Selected States," *Kentucky Law Journal* 86 (1997–1998), 223.
112. Carey Goldberg, "DNA Databanks Giving Police a Powerful Weapon, and Critics," *New York Times* (February 18, 1998), A12.
113. Ed Godfrey, "DNA Profiles Changing Investigations," *Sunday Oklahoman* (February 9, 1997), 1.
114. Joseph P. Shapiro, "The Wrong Men on Death Row," *U.S. News & World Report* (November 9, 1998), 22.
115. Gregory W. O'Reilly, "A Second Chance for Justice," *Judicature* (November–December 1997), 114–7.
116. "Right to Gene Privacy Protected by Massachusetts Decision," *Biotechnology Newswatch* (September 7, 1998), 4.
117. 545 N.Y.S.2d 985 (Sup. Ct. 1989).
118. Ronald S. Ostrowski, "Polymarkers: A New Generation of Forensic DNA Profiling," *Trial Briefs* (Winter 1994–1995), 24–5.
119. 293 F. 1013 (D.C. Cir. 1923).
120. "DNA Typing Endorsed By National Academy of Sciences," *CJ Update* (Fall 1992), 1.
121. *Daubert v. Merrell Dow Pharmaceuticals, Inc.*, 509 U.S. 579 (1993); and *General Electric Co. v. Joiner*, 118 S. Ct. 512 (1997).
122. Terry L. Knowles, "Meeting the Challenges of the 21st Century," *Police Chief* (June 1997), 39–43.
123. Richard Willing, "Reno: Study Broad DNA Testing," *USA Today* (March 1, 1999), 1A.

chapter

6

Police and the Rule of Law

Chapter Objectives

After reading this chapter, you should be able to:

1. Outline the four major sources that may provide probable cause.

2. Explain the exclusionary rule and the exceptions to it.

3. Distinguish between a stop and a frisk, and indicate the importance of the case *Terry v. Ohio*.

4. List the four elements that must be present for an arrest to take place.

5. Explain under what circumstances officers need not announce themselves before entering a dwelling and under what circumstances arrest warrants are not required.

6. List the four categories of items that can be seized by use of a search warrant.

7. Explain when searches can be made without a warrant.

8. Recite the *Miranda* warning.

9. Indicate situations in which a *Miranda* warning is unnecessary.

10. List the three basic types of police identification.

INTRODUCTION

Dollree Mapp was living on the second floor of a two-family brick house in Cleveland, Ohio, when, on May 23, 1957, three police officers appeared at the front door. The officers demanded entrance to the home, telling Mapp that they believed a man wanted in connection with a recent bombing was hiding inside. After consulting with her lawyer over the phone, Mapp refused the officers' request because they did not have a search warrant. Three hours later, the officers returned with reinforcements and broke down the front door. Mapp again demanded to see a search warrant. One of the officers waved a piece of paper in the air, which Mapp grabbed and shoved down the front of her blouse. After the resulting melee, which was touched off when the officer tried to retrieve the paper, Mapp was handcuffed and the police searched her house.

They did not find the bombing suspect, nor did they find any evidence that Mapp was involved in a bombing plot. The officers did, however, find four pornographic books—*Affairs of a Troubadour, Memories of a Hotel Man, London Stage Affairs,* and *Little Darlings*—as well as a hand-drawn picture of a "very obscene nature."[1] Mapp was subsequently arrested and convicted of possession of obscene materials. Her conviction was upheld by the Ohio Supreme Court, but overturned by the United States Supreme Court in *Mapp v. Ohio* in 1961.[2] As the police were never able to produce a valid search warrant for the fugitive or bomb-making components, much less for "lewd" materials, the Court ruled that any evidence gathered during the raid was inadmissible.

As this case shows, even when a law has been broken, police officers do not have absolute freedom in carrying out their duties. In delivering his majority opinion in *Mapp v. Ohio,* Justice Tom Clark wrote: "Nothing can destroy a government more quickly than its failure to observe its own laws."[3] This balance between the need for effective law enforcement and the rights of American citizens under the U.S. Constitution has been, and remains, a controversial issue. Many observers feel that courts go too far in protecting the rights of the accused, but others feel that police have been given a dangerous amount of leeway in using their powers. In this chapter we will examine the extent to which police behavior is controlled by the law, starting with a discussion of the constitutional principles on which such control is grounded.

> "A highly sophisticated set of rules, qualified by all sorts of ifs, ands, and buts and requiring the drawing of subtle nuances and hairline distinctions, may be the sort of heady stuff upon which the facile minds of lawyers and judges eagerly feed, but they may be literally impossible of application by the officer in the field."
>
> —Wayne R. LaFave, *American law professor* (1974)

THE FOURTH AMENDMENT

In *Mapp,* the Court did not address the defendant's illegal activity (possession of obscene materials). Rather, it ruled that the police officers had overstepped the boundaries of their authority in making the arrest. To understand these boundaries, law enforcement officers must understand the Fourth Amendment,[4] which reads as follows:

> The right of the people to be secure in their persons, houses, papers, and effects, against unreasonable searches and seizures, shall not be violated, and no Warrants shall issue, but upon probable cause, supported by Oath or affirmation, and particularly describing the place to be searched, and the persons or things to be seized.

SEARCHES AND SEIZURES
The legal term, as found in the Fourth Amendment of the U.S. Constitution, that generally refers to the searching for and the confiscating of evidence by law enforcement agents.

This amendment contains two critical legal concepts: a prohibition against *unreasonable* **searches and seizures** and the requirement of *probable cause* to issue a warrant (see Figure 6.1).

Figure 6.1 The Meaning of Unreasonable Searches and Seizures and Probable Cause

Unreasonable Search and Seizure

The Fourth Amendment provides that individuals have the right to be "secure in their persons" against "unreasonable searches and seizures" conducted by government agents. In practice, this means that law enforcement officers must obtain a search warrant prior to any search and seizure. Basically, the search warrant is the acknowledgment by a judge that probable cause exists for law enforcement officers to search for or take a person or property. In other words, the search and seizure must be "reasonable."

Probable Cause

Before an search can take place or an individual can be arrested, the requirement of probable cause must be met. Probable cause exists if there is a substantial likelihood that (1) a crime was committed and (2) the individual committed the crime. Note that probable cause involves a *likelihood*—not just a possibility—that the suspect committed the crime. Probable cause must exist before police can get an arrest warrant or a search warrant from a judge.

Figure 6.1 The Meaning of Unreasonable Searches and Seizures and Probable Cause

Reasonableness

Law enforcement personnel use searches and seizures to look for and collect the evidence they need to convict individuals suspected of crimes. As you have just read, when conducting a search or seizure, they must be *reasonable*. Though courts have spent innumerable hours scrutinizing the word, no specific meaning for "reasonable" exists. A thesaurus can provide useful synonyms—logical, practical, sensible, intelligent, plausible—but as each case is different, those terms are relative.

In *Mapp,* the Court found that the police officers did not use reasonable, or well-balanced, judgment in their actions toward the defendant. That does not mean that such actions would have been unreasonable under all circumstances. If the officers had suspected Dollree Mapp of being part of a pornography ring and had obtained a valid warrant to search her house, then the officers' conduct probably would have been considered reasonable.

Probable Cause

The concept of reasonableness is linked to **probable cause.** The Supreme Court has ruled, for example, that any arrest or seizure is unreasonable unless it is supported by probable cause.[5] The burden of probable cause requires more than mere suspicion on a police officer's part; that officer must know of facts and circumstances that would reasonably lead to "the belief that an offense has been or is being committed."[6]

If no probable cause existed when a police officer took a certain action, it cannot be retroactively applied. If, for example, a police officer stops a person for jaywalking and then finds several ounces of marijuana in that person's pocket, the arrest for marijuana possession would probably be disallowed. Remember, suspicion does not equal probable cause. If, however, an informant had tipped the officer off that the person was a drug dealer, probable cause might exist and the arrest could be valid. Informants are one of several sources that may provide probable cause. Others include:

1. *Personal observation.* Police officers may use their personal training, experience, and expertise to infer probable cause from situations that may not be obviously criminal. If, for example, a police officer observes several people in a car slowly circling a certain building in a high-crime area, that officer may infer that the people are "casing" the building in preparation for a robbery. Probable cause could be established for detaining the suspects.

PROBABLE CAUSE
Reasonable grounds to believe the existence of facts warranting certain actions, such as the search or arrest of a person.

Michigan state and Federal law enforcement officers take part in a pre-dawn raid of a Detroit residence. Before taking such action, the officers of the law must receive permission from a judge or magistrate in the form of a search warrant. Ideally, the judicial official will only issue such a warrant if the law enforcement agency involved can provide probable cause that an illegal activity is taking place in the dwelling. How does the need to provide probable cause in such instances limit police power?

2. *Information.* Law enforcement officers receive information from victims, eyewitnesses, informants, and official sources such as police bulletins or broadcasts. Such information, as long as it is believed to be reliable, is a basis for probable cause.

3. *Evidence.* In certain circumstances, which will be examined later in this chapter, police have probable cause for a search or seizure based on evidence—such as a shotgun—in plain view.

4. *Association.* In some circumstances, if the police see a person with a known criminal background in a place where criminal activity is openly taking place, they have probable cause to stop that person. Generally, however, association is not adequate to establish probable cause.[7]

In a sense, the concept of probable cause allows police officers to do their job effectively. Most arrests are made without a warrant because most arrests are the result of quick police reaction to the commission of a crime. Indeed, it would not be practical to expect a police officer to obtain a warrant before making an arrest on the street. Thus, probable cause provides a framework that limits the situations in which police officers can make arrests, but also gives officers the freedom to act within that framework. Once an arrest is made, however, the arresting officer must prove to a judge that probable cause existed. In *County of Riverside v. McLaughlin* (1991),[8] the Supreme Court ruled that this judicial determination of probable cause must be made within forty-eight hours after the arrest, even if this two-day period includes a weekend or holiday.

The Exclusionary Rule

Historically, the courts have looked to the Fourth Amendment for guidance in regulating the activity of law enforcement officers, as the language of the Constitution does not expressly do so. The courts' most potent legal tool in this endeavor is the **exclusionary rule,** which prohibits the use of illegally seized evidence. According to this rule, any evidence obtained by an unreasonable search or seizure is inadmissible (may not be used) against a defendant in a criminal trial.[9] Even highly incriminating evidence, such as a knife stained with the victim's blood, usually cannot be introduced at a trial if illegally obtained. Furthermore, any physical or verbal evidence police are able to acquire by using illegally obtained evidence is known as the **fruit of the poisoned tree** and is also inadmissible. For example, if the police use the existence of the bloodstained knife to get a confession out of a suspect, that confession will be excluded as well.

One of the implications of the exclusionary rule is that it forces police to gather evidence properly. If they follow appropriate procedures, they are more likely to be rewarded with a conviction. If they are careless or abuse the rights of the suspect, they are unlikely to get a conviction. Critics of the exclusionary rule, however, argue that its strict application may permit guilty people to go free because of police carelessness or innocent errors (for an example, see *CJ in Focus: The Balancing Act—Excluding Justice?*).

Establishing the Exclusionary Rule. The exclusionary rule is applied to all evidence presented in federal courts as a result of the decision in *Weeks v. United States.*[10] For almost fifty years after this 1914 case, however, state courts continued to allow illegally obtained evidence, and federal courts

EXCLUSIONARY RULE
A rule under which any evidence that is obtained in violation of the accused's rights under the Fourth, Fifth, and Sixth Amendments, as well as any evidence derived from illegally obtained evidence, will not be admissible in criminal court.

FRUIT OF THE POISONED TREE
Evidence that is acquired through the use of illegally obtained evidence and is therefore inadmissible in court.

CJ in Focus

The Balancing Act

Excluding Justice?

Early on a spring morning in Washington Heights, a drug-infested area of New York City, two detectives watched four men load a duffel bag into the trunk of a 1995 Chevrolet. When the men saw the officers, they ran, leaving only the woman who was driving the car. The detectives proceeded to find seventy-five pounds of cocaine and five pounds of heroin in the automobile. The woman admitted to being a drug courier and to making similar deliveries from Detroit twenty times for her son, a dealer.

During the woman's pretrial hearing, U.S. District Judge Harold Baer, Jr., of Manhattan ruled that the evidence the detectives had found was inadmissible. Baer's reasoning was that the officers did not have reasonable cause to stop the car and that the actions of the other four men were understandable because "residents in that neighborhood tended to regard police officers as corrupt, abusive, and violent."

The judge's decision highlighted the conflicts inherent in the exclusionary rule. On the one hand, the rule does deter police from violating an individual's constitutional rights and acts as a clear demonstration that law enforcement officers are not above the law. On the other hand, the exclusionary rule imposes costs on society. There was little doubt that the woman in this case was guilty. A number of admittedly guilty defendants have been placed back on the streets because of this rule. Furthermore, the rule weakens public confidence in American courts by giving victims and other members of society the perception that "the truth" is less important than procedure in the criminal justice system.

In this particular case, the general uproar over Baer's decision from victim's rights groups and many prominent politicians forced the judge to reconsider. Three months after his initial ruling, he reversed himself and allowed the drug evidence and a videotaped confession to be admitted at trial.

For Critical Analysis: Under what political, social, or economic conditions would you expect to see more exceptions to the exclusionary rule?

---

could do so if the evidence had been obtained by state officers. This practice was known rather sarcastically as the *silver platter doctrine*, because such evidence handed the prosecution a conviction "on a silver platter." The only exception to the silver platter doctrine was when police actions were so extreme that they "shocked the conscience" of the court.

The "shocks the conscience" standard was established in *Rochin v. California* (1952).[11] In this case, police officers entered the home of Mr. Rochin without a warrant and saw him place what they thought were narcotics in his mouth. The police tried to forcibly expel the items from Rochin. When this failed, they took him to the hospital and had his stomach pumped. This action produced two tablets of morphine. Rochin was convicted of possession of illegal drugs and sentenced to sixty days in jail. The Supreme Court overturned his conviction on the ground that the police officers' actions violated Rochin's Fourth Amendment due process rights; Justice Felix Frankfurter compared the police's methods to the "rack and screw."

Rochin did not make the exclusionary rule applicable to all state cases. Instead, the Supreme Court ruled that it applied only in cases that involved serious police misconduct. The silver platter doctrine was finally eliminated nine years later by the Court's decision in *Mapp v. Ohio* (1961).[12] This case, discussed in the opening paragraphs of this chapter, involved an illegal search and seizure conducted by Cleveland (Ohio) police officers. Whereas the Court had previously been hesitant to apply the exclusionary rule to a decision made in state courts, *Mapp* signaled a new willingness to apply the Fourth Amendment to both federal and state law enforcement officers.

Exceptions to the Exclusionary Rule. Critics of the exclusionary rule have long maintained that the costs to society of losing critical evidence were higher than the benefits of deterring police misconduct. In recent years, a number of Supreme Court decisions have mirrored this view and provided exceptions to the exclusionary rule. The **"inevitable discovery" exception** was established in the wake of the disappearance of ten-year-old Pamela Powers

"INEVITABLE DISCOVERY" EXCEPTION
The legal principle that illegally obtained evidence can be admitted in court if police using lawful means would have "inevitably" discovered it.

"GOOD FAITH" EXCEPTION
The legal principle, established through court decisions, that evidence obtained with the use of a technically faulty search warrant is admissible during trial if the police acted in good faith when they sought the warrant from a judge.

For a handy summary of the many laws regarding police procedure that can be traced to the Fourth Amendment, go to caselaw.findlaw.com/data/Constitution/amendment04/

of Des Moines, Iowa, on Christmas Eve, 1968. The police's primary suspect in the case, a religious fanatic named Robert Williams, was tricked by a detective into leading police to the site where he had buried Powers. Specifically, the detective convinced Williams that if he did not lead police to the body, he would soon forget where it was buried. This would deny his victim a "Christian burial." Initially, in *Brewer v. Williams* (1977),[13] the Court ruled that the evidence (Powers's body) had been obtained illegally because Williams's attorney had not been present during the interrogation that led to his admission. The state of Iowa appealed this decision. In *Nix v. Williams* (1984),[14] the Court reversed itself, ruling that the evidence was admissible because the body would have eventually ("inevitably") been found by lawful means.

The scope of the exclusionary rule was further diminished in the wake of the Supreme Court's ruling in *United States v. Leon* (1984).[15] The case involved evidence that had been seized by police on the authority of a search warrant that had been improperly issued by a magistrate. In allowing the evidence, the Court created a **"good faith" exception** to the exclusionary rule. Under this exception, evidence acquired by a police officer using a technically incorrect search warrant is admissible if the officer was unaware of the error. In this situation, the officer is said to have acted in "good faith." By the same token, if police officers use a search warrant that they know to be technically incorrect, the good faith exception does not apply and the evidence can be suppressed.

The Supreme Court has extended the good faith exception to cases involving computer error. In *Arizona v. Evans* (1995),[16] the defendant, after being pulled over for a traffic violation, was mistakenly identified by the data terminal in the patrol car as having a suspended driver's license. Pursuant to this information, the police officer arrested the defendant and searched his car, finding a bag of marijuana. The defendant appealed his eventual conviction for marijuana possession on the ground that the original arrest was illegally obtained. The Court upheld the conviction, ruling that the officer was acting in good faith.

Many observers believe that *Arizona v. Evans* and similar cases have weakened the exclusionary rule by corroding its very foundation: the deterrence of police misconduct. According to constitutional law professors Alan M. Dershowitz and John Hart Ely, the exclusionary rule is necessary because police officers are, for the most part, more interested in the specific goals of solving crimes and convicting criminals than the general goal of following constitutional law.[17] By providing police officers with loopholes such as the inevitable discovery and good faith exceptions, the courts have in essence given officers an incentive to use unconstitutional methods of gaining evidence. Because of these rulings, officers are aware that there is a good chance evidence will be accepted, even if their methods of obtaining it are questioned. This line of thinking reflects a rather cynical view of police motivation and behavior, but if all officers followed the laws of evidence and interrogation, the exclusionary rule would not have been necessary in the first place.[18]

STOPS AND FRISKS

In 1997, an off-duty Miami-Dade County police officer named Aaron Campbell was pulled over by two Orange County deputies while driving on the Florida turnpike, allegedly for changing lanes without properly signaling. A fistfight ensued. At the resulting trial, Campbell claimed that he was stopped because he fit a drug courier profile in use by the deputies; he was an African American and had South Florida license plates. A circuit judge agreed, ruling that Campbell had been stopped illegally.[19]

The problem was not that the deputies had stopped Campbell. Law enforcement officers are expected to stop and question people if there is a suspicion of illegal behavior. The problem was that the Orange County deputies did not have a "reasonable" suspicion that Campbell was breaking the law. Instead, they had only a "mere" suspicion based on the drug courier profile—without any other specific facts. When reasonable suspicion exists, police officers are well within their rights to *stop and frisk* a suspect. In a stop and frisk, law enforcement officers (1) briefly detain a person they reasonably believe to be suspicious, and (2) if they believe the person to be armed, proceed to pat down, or "frisk," that person's outer clothing.[20]

Miami, Florida, police officers frisk two persons who have been detained on suspicion of illegal activities. What is the main purpose behind a frisk? When are police justified in frisking someone who has been detained?

Terry v. Ohio

The precedent for the ever-elusive definition of a "reasonable" suspicion in stop-and-frisk situations was established in *Terry v. Ohio* (1968).[21] In that case, a detective named McFadden observed two men (one of whom was Terry) acting strangely in downtown Cleveland. The men would walk past a certain store, peer into the window, and then stop at a street corner and confer. While they were talking, another man joined the conversation and then left quickly. Several minutes later the three men met again at another corner a few blocks away. Detective McFadden believed the trio was planning to break into the store. He approached them, told them who he was, and asked for identification. After receiving a mumbled response, the detective frisked the three men and found handguns on two of them, who were tried and convicted of carrying concealed weapons.

The Supreme Court upheld the conviction, ruling that Detective McFadden had reasonable cause to believe that the men were armed and dangerous and that swift action was necessary to protect himself and other citizens in the area.[22] The Court accepted McFadden's interpretation of the unfolding scene as based on objective facts and practical conclusions. It therefore concluded that his suspicion was reasonable. In the Florida case described above, the deputies' reasons for stopping Campbell—his race and place of car registration—were not seen as reasonable. (For information on the role "reasonableness" plays in France's equivalent to the stop and frisk, see *Cross-National CJ Comparison—French Identity Checks*.)

For the most part, the judicial system has refrained from placing restrictions on police officers' ability to make stops. In *Terry v. Ohio*, the Supreme Court did say that the officer must have "specific and articulable facts" before making a stop, but added that the facts may be "taken together with rational inferences."[23] The Court has consistently ruled that because of their "street" experience, police officers are in a unique position to make such inferences and should be given a great deal of freedom in doing so. In *United States v. Cortez* (1981),[24] the Court augmented a police officer's discretion to stop citizens by holding that reasonable suspicion should be based on the "totality of the circumstances," which may include inferences and deductions made by a trained officer.

A Stop

The terms *stop* and *frisk* are often used in concert, but they describe two separate acts. A **stop** takes place when a law enforcement officer has reasonable

STOP
A brief detention of a person by law enforcement agents for questioning. The agents must have a reasonable suspicion of the person before making a stop.

French Identity Checks

As the Christmas holiday approached, the people of France were understandably nervous. Christmas Eve would mark the second anniversary of the hijacking of a French airplane by terrorists who accused France of supporting a repressive regime in Algeria. On December 4, 1995, four people had been killed and dozens injured when a bomb exploded on a commuter train in Paris. French law enforcement responded to the unease with a massive security operation—on December 18 alone, the police stopped and questioned six thousand people. Few, if any, of those stops would have been ruled constitutional in the United States.

French "identity checks," in which police require people to show identification, and American "stop and frisks" have similar goals. Both are tools that police officers use to detect and prevent crime. French police have much greater freedom in carrying out identity checks than do their American counterparts, though. First, French law does not require that police have a reasonable suspicion that criminal activity is about to take place. Second, a French police officer does not need to establish imminent danger to do a weapons frisk. Third, a person stopped by French police officers may be detained for up to four hours.

These conditions are the direct result of terrorist activity. For a short time before 1986, the French Procedural Code required that all identity checks be based on individualized suspicion or the threat of immediate danger. After an Iranian-backed Lebanese group carried out a bombing campaign that year, the law was changed to its present form in an attempt to better protect French citizens from terrorist acts.

WHAT'S THE EVIDENCE?

French law enforcement agencies have come under a great deal of criticism from human rights groups for the way identity checks have been used against certain groups, particularly immigrants. To learn more about the issue on the Internet, go to **www.amnesty.org/ailib/aipub/1994/EUR/210294.EUR.txt**.

---

suspicion that a criminal activity is about to take place. Because an investigatory stop is not an arrest, there are limits to the extent police can detain someone who has been stopped. For example, in one situation an airline traveler and his luggage were detained for ninety minutes while the police waited for a drug-sniffing dog to arrive. The Court ruled that the initial stop of the passenger was constitutional, but that the ninety-minute wait was excessive.[25]

A Frisk

The Supreme Court has stated that a **frisk** should be a protective measure. Police officers cannot conduct a frisk as a "fishing expedition" simply to try to find items besides weapons, such as illegal narcotics, on a suspect.[26] A frisk does not necessarily follow a stop and in fact may occur only when the officer is justified in thinking that the safety of police officers or other citizens may be endangered.

Again, the question of reasonable suspicion is at the heart of determining the legality of frisks. In *Terry*, the Court accepted that Detective McFadden reasonably believed that the three suspects posed a threat. The suspects' refusal to answer McFadden's questions, though within their rights because they had not been arrested, provided him with sufficient motive for the frisk.

ARRESTS

As in *Terry*, a stop and frisk may lead to an **arrest.** An arrest is the taking into custody of a citizen for the purpose of detaining him or her on a criminal charge.[27] It is important to understand the difference between a stop and an arrest. In the eyes of the law, a stop is a relatively brief intrusion on a citizen's rights, whereas an arrest—which involves a deprivation of liberty—is deserving of a full range of constitutional protections, which we shall discuss throughout the chapter (see the *Concept Summary—The Difference between a*

FRISK
A pat-down or minimal search by police to discover weapons; conducted for the express purpose of protecting the officer or other citizens, and not to find evidence of illegal substances for use in a trial.

ARREST
To take into custody a person suspected of criminal activity. Police may use only reasonable levels of force in making an arrest.

Stop and an Arrest). Consequently, while a stop can be made based on a reasonable suspicion, a law enforcement officer needs a probable cause, as defined earlier, to make an arrest.[28]

CONCEPT SUMMARY
The Difference between a Stop and an Arrest

Both stops and arrests are considered seizures because both police actions involve the restriction of an individual's freedom to "walk away." Both must be justified by a showing of reasonableness as well. You should be aware, however, of the important differences between a stop and an arrest:

STOP

Justification: Reasonable suspicion
Warrant: None
Intent of Officer: The investigation of suspicious activity
Search: May frisk, or "pat down," for weapons
Scope of Search: Outer clothing only

ARREST

Justification: Probable cause
Warrant: Required in some, though not all, situations
Intent of Officer: To make a formal charge against the suspect
Search: Full search for weapons and evidence
Scope of Search: Area within the suspect's immediate control, or "reach"

The stop is an important part of police activity. Police officers therefore have the right to stop and frisk a person if they suspect that a crime is about to be committed. Police may stop those who are acting strangely, do not "fit" the time or place, are known to associate with criminals, or are loitering. They may also stop a person who reasonably fits a description of a person who is wanted in conjunction with a crime. During a stop, police can interrogate the person and make a limited search of his or her outer clothing. If anything occurs during the stop, such as the discovery of an illegal weapon, then officers may arrest the person. If an arrest is made, the suspect is now in police custody and is protected by the U.S. Constitution in a number of ways that will be discussed later in the chapter.

SOURCE: ADAPTED FROM J. SCOTT HARR AND KAREN M. HESS, CRIMINAL PROCEDURE (ST. PAUL, MN: WEST PUBLISHING COMPANY, 1990), 140.

Elements of an Arrest

When is somebody under arrest? The easy—and false—answer would be whenever the police officer says so. In fact, the state of being under arrest is dependent not only on the actions of the law enforcement officers but also on the perception of the suspect. Suppose Mr. Jones is stopped by plainclothes detectives, driven to the police station, and detained for three hours for questioning. During this time, the police never tell Mr. Jones he is under arrest, and in fact, he is free to leave at any time. But if Mr. Jones or any other reasonable person *believes* he is not free to leave, then, according to the Supreme Court, that person is in fact under arrest and should receive the necessary constitutional protections.[29]

Criminal justice professor Rolando V. del Carmen of Sam Houston State University has identified four elements that must be present for an arrest to take place:

1. The *intent* to arrest. In a stop, though it may entail slight inconvenience and a short detention period, there is no intent on the part of the law enforcement officer to take the person into custody. Therefore, there is no arrest. As intent is a subjective term, it is sometimes difficult to determine whether the police officer intended to arrest. In situations when the intent is unclear, courts often rely—as in our hypothetical case of Mr. Jones—on the perception of the arrestee.[30]

2. The *authority* to arrest. State laws give police officers the authority to place citizens under custodial arrest, or take them into custody. Like other state laws, the authorization to arrest varies among the fifty states. Some states, for example, allow off-duty police officers to make arrests, while others do not.

ARREST WARRANT
A written order, based on probable cause and issued by a judge or magistrate, commanding that the person named on the warrant be arrested by the police.

EXIGENT CIRCUMSTANCES
Situations that require extralegal or exceptional actions by the police. In these circumstances, police officers are justified in not following procedural rules, such as those pertaining to search and arrest warrants.

WARRANTLESS ARREST
An arrest made without first seeking a warrant for the action; permitted under certain circumstances, such as when the arresting officer has witnessed the crime or has a reasonable belief that the suspect has committed a felony.

3. *Seizure* or *detention.* A necessary part of an arrest is the detention of the subject. Detention is considered to have occurred as soon as the arrested individual submits to the control of the officer, whether peacefully or under the threat or use of force.

4. The *understanding* of the person that she or he has been arrested. Through either words—such as "you are now under arrest"—or actions, the person taken into custody must understand that an arrest has taken place. If a subject has been forcibly subdued by the police, handcuffed, and placed in a patrol car, that subject is believed to understand that an arrest has been made. This understanding may be lacking if the person is intoxicated, insane, or unconscious.[31]

Arrests with a Warrant

When law enforcement officers have established a probable cause to arrest an individual who is not in police custody, they obtain an **arrest warrant** for that person. An arrest warrant contains information such as the name of the person suspected and the crime he or she is suspected of having committed. (See Figure 6.2 for an example of an arrest warrant.) Judges or magistrates issue arrest warrants after first determining that the law enforcement officers have indeed established probable cause.

In the last chapter, we discussed "no-knock" entries by police officers, or raids. There is a perception that an arrest warrant gives law enforcement officers the authority to enter a dwelling without first announcing themselves. This is not accurate. In *Wilson v. Arkansas* (1995),[32] the Court reiterated the common law requirement that police officers must knock and announce their identity and purpose before entering a dwelling. Under certain conditions, known as **exigent circumstances,** law enforcement officers need not announce themselves. These circumstances include situations in which the officers have a reasonable belief of any of the following:

- The suspect is armed and poses a strong threat of violence to the officers or others inside the dwelling.

- Persons inside the dwelling are in the process of destroying evidence or escaping because of the presence of the police.

- A felony is being committed at the time the officers enter.[33]

For example, in *Minnesota v. Olson* (1990),[34] the Court ruled that officers acted legally when they forcibly entered the home of an armed robber who had been fleeing arrest.

Arrests without a Warrant

Arrest warrants are not required, and in fact, most arrests are made on the scene without a warrant.[35] A law enforcement officer may make a **warrantless arrest** if:

1. The offense is committed in the presence of the officer; or

2. The officer has knowledge that a crime has been committed and a probable cause to believe the crime was committed by a particular suspect.[36]

The type of crime also comes to bear in questions of arrests without a warrant. As a general rule, officers can make a warrantless arrest for a crime they did not see if they have probable cause to believe that a felony has been committed. For misdemeanors, the crime must have been committed in the presence of the officer for a warrantless arrest to be valid.

In certain situations, warrantless arrests are unlawful even though a police officer can establish probable cause. In *Payton v. New York* (1980),[37] for example, the Supreme Court held that when exigent circumstances do not exist and the suspect does not give consent to enter a dwelling, law enforcement officers cannot force themselves in for the purpose of making a warrantless arrest. The *Payton* ruling was expanded to cover the homes of third parties when, in *Steagald v. United States* (1981),[38] the Court ruled that if the police wish to arrest a criminal suspect in another person's home, they cannot enter that home to arrest the suspect without first obtaining a search warrant, a process we will discuss in the following section.

LAWFUL SEARCHES AND SEIZURES

Like the other people on the Greyhound bus, the defendant, a woman by the name of LaShawn McDonald, got out at the Indianapolis, Indiana, stop to

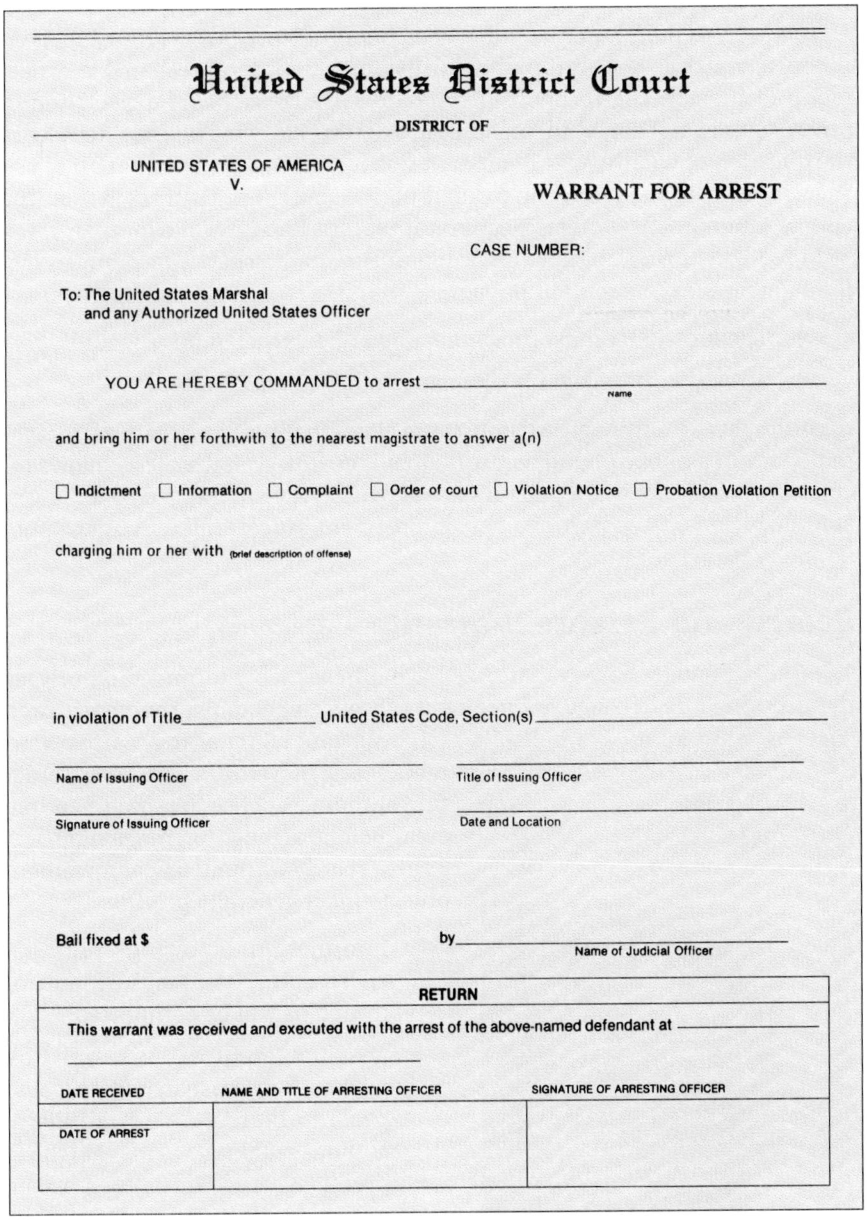

United States District Court

DISTRICT OF

UNITED STATES OF AMERICA
V.

WARRANT FOR ARREST

CASE NUMBER:

To: The United States Marshal
and any Authorized United States Officer

YOU ARE HEREBY COMMANDED to arrest ____________ Name

and bring him or her forthwith to the nearest magistrate to answer a(n)

☐ Indictment ☐ Information ☐ Complaint ☐ Order of court ☐ Violation Notice ☐ Probation Violation Petition

charging him or her with (brief description of offense)

in violation of Title ________ United States Code, Section(s) ________

Name of Issuing Officer | Title of Issuing Officer

Signature of Issuing Officer | Date and Location

Bail fixed at $ by ____________ Name of Judicial Officer

RETURN

This warrant was received and executed with the arrest of the above-named defendant at ____________

DATE RECEIVED	NAME AND TITLE OF ARRESTING OFFICER	SIGNATURE OF ARRESTING OFFICER
DATE OF ARREST		

Figure 6.2 Example of an Arrest Warrant

SEARCH
The process by which police examine a person or property to find evidence that will used to prove guilt in a criminal trial.

SEARCH WARRANT
A written order, based on probable cause and issued by a judge or magistrate, commanding that police officers or criminal investigators search a specific person, place, or property to obtain evidence.

stretch her legs and grab a bite to eat. While she and the other passengers were in the terminal, the bus driver gave permission to three Indianapolis police officers to board the vehicle and search the contents. The officers proceeded to feel the luggage in the overhead racks. When one of them came to McDonald's bag, she felt a "brick-like" object, which she suspected to be drugs. After McDonald returned to her seat, the officers confronted her. When McDonald claimed the luggage did not belong to her, as we shall see, she surrendered any privacy rights she might otherwise have had. The officers proceeded to open the bag, finding eleven kilograms of cocaine.[39]

McDonald was eventually convicted for possession with intent to distribute cocaine. Her case raises a number of questions about the lengths that law enforcement officers may go to gather evidence. The Fourth Amendment is quite specific in forbidding unreasonable searches and seizures. Was the officers' search of McDonald's luggage and seizure of its contents "unreasonable"? The U.S. Court of Appeals for the Seventh Circuit did not think so, rejecting McDonald's motion to suppress the evidence.[40]

The Role of Privacy in Searches

A crucial concept in understanding search and seizure law is *privacy*. By definition, a **search** is a governmental intrusion on a citizen's reasonable expectation of privacy. The recognized standard for a "reasonable expectation of privacy" was established in *Katz v. United States* (1967).[41] The case dealt with the question of whether the defendant was justified in his expectation of privacy in the calls he made from a public phone booth. The Court held that "the Fourth Amendment protects people, not places." Katz prevailed.

In his concurring opinion, Justice John Harlan, Jr., set a two-pronged test for a person's expectation of privacy:

1 The individual must prove that she or he expected privacy, and

2 Society must recognize that expectation as reasonable.[42]

Accordingly, the Court agreed with Katz's claim that he had a reasonable right to privacy in a public phone booth. (Remember, however, that *Terry* allows for conditions under which a person's privacy rights are submerged by a reasonable suspicion on the part of a law enforcement officer that a threat to public safety is present.)

Search and Seizure Warrants

To protect against charges that they have unreasonably infringed on privacy rights during a search, law enforcement officers can obtain a **search warrant.** (See Figure 6.3 for an example of a search warrant.) Similar to an arrest warrant, a search warrant is a court order that authorizes police to search a certain area. Before a judge or magistrate will issue a search warrant, law enforcement officers must generally provide:

In 1999, New York City implemented a new plan that allows police officers to seize the cars of people arrested for driving with blood alcohol leves of .10 or higher. As "specifically established" exceptions to search and seizure law, such seizures are considered constitutional. Are you in favor of this method of controlling drunk drivers? What might be some of the practical problems that New York police officers will encounter while enforcing this policy?

- Information showing probable cause that a crime has been committed or will be committed.

- Specific information on the premises to be searched, the suspects to be found and the illegal activities taking place at those premises, and the items to be seized.

The purpose of a search warrant is to establish, before the search takes place, that a *probable cause to search* justifies infringing upon the suspect's reasonable expectation of privacy.

Particularity of Search Warrants. The members of the First Congress specifically did not want law enforcement officers to have the freedom to make "general, exploratory" searches through a person's belongings.[43] Consequently, the Fourth Amendment requires that a warrant describe with "particularity" the place to be searched and the things—either people or objects—to be seized. (For a discussion of the effect of these warrant requirements and other legal restrictions on police procedure, see the feature *Criminal Justice in Action—Constitutional Handcuffs?* at the end of this chapter.)

This "particularity" requirement places a heavy burden on law enforcement officers. Before going to a judge to ask for a search warrant, they must prepare an **affidavit** in which they provide specific, written information on the property that they wish to search and seize. They must know the specific address of any place they wish to search; general addresses of apartment buildings or office complexes are not sufficient. Furthermore, courts gener-

AFFIDAVIT
A written statement of facts, confirmed by the oath or affirmation of the party making it and made before a person having the authority to administer the oath or affirmation.

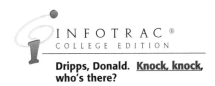

Dripps, Donald. Knock, knock, who's there?

United States District Court

_____DISTRICT OF_____

In the Matter of the Search of
(Name, address or brief description of person or property to be searched)

SEARCH WARRANT

CASE NUMBER:

TO:_____ and any Authorized Officer of the United States

Affidavit(s) having been made before me by_____ who has reason to
                                                            Affiant

believe that ☐ on the person of or ☐ on the premises known as (name, description and/or location)

in the_____District of_____there is now
concealed a certain person or property, namely (describe the person or property)

I am satisfied that the affidavit(s) and any recorded testimony establish probable cause to believe that the person or property so described is now concealed on the person or premises above-described and establish grounds for the issuance of this warrant.

YOU ARE HEREBY COMMANDED to search on or before_____
                                                                Date

(not to exceed 10 days) the person or place named above for the person or property specified, serving this warrant and making the search (in the daytime — 6:00 A.M. to 10:00 P.M.) (at any time in the day or night as I find reasonable cause has been established) and if the person or property be found there to seize same, leaving a copy of this warrant and receipt for the person or property taken, and prepare a written inventory of the person or property seized and promptly return this warrant to_____
                                                        U.S. Judge or Magistrate
as required by law.

_____ at _____
Date and Time Issued   City and State

_____   _____
Name and Title of Judicial Officer   Signature of Judicial Officer

Figure 6.3 Example of a Search Warrant

SEIZURE
The forcible taking of a person or property in response to a violation of the law.

ally frown upon vague descriptions of goods to be seized. "Stolen goods" would most likely be considered unacceptably imprecise, while "1 Optra S 1650 Lexmark Laser Printer" would be preferred.

A **seizure** is the act of taking possession of property by the government because of a (suspected) violation of the law. In general, four categories of items can be seized by use of a search warrant:

1. Items that resulted from the crime, such as stolen goods.

2. Items that are inherently illegal for anybody to possess (with certain exceptions), such as narcotics and counterfeit currency.

3. Items that can be called "evidence" of the crime, such as a blood-stained sneaker or a ski mask.

4. Items used in committing the crime, such as an ice pick or a printing press used to make counterfeit bills.[44]

Court TV hosts a useful Web site on

search and seizure law. The site offers FAQs and links to other sites that deal with this issue. Go to

www.courttv.com/legalcafe/ home/search/

Reasonableness during a Search and Seizure. No matter how "particular" a warrant is, it cannot provide for all the conditions that are bound to come up during its service. Consequently, the law gives law enforcement officers the ability to act "reasonably" during a search and seizure in the event of unforeseeable circumstances. For example, if a police officer is searching an apartment for a stolen Optra S 1650 Lexmark Laser Printer and notices a vial of crack cocaine sitting on the suspect's bed, that contraband is considered to be in "plain view" and can be seized.

Note that if law enforcement officers have a search warrant that authorizes them to search for a stolen laser printer, they would *not* be justified in opening small drawers. Because a printer could not fit in a small drawer, an officer would not have a basis for reasonably searching one. Officers are restricted in terms of where they can look by the items they are searching for.

As with arrest warrants, federal and many state statutes require that officers executing a search warrant announce themselves and state their purpose before entering a dwelling. Again, the announcement rule may be waived in exigent circumstances such as the imminent escape of the suspect. The Supreme Court has steadfastly protected the right of law enforcement officers to engage in "no-knock entries"; its latest decision upholds these rights even if the entry results in severe property damage.[45] Furthermore, courts will allow the use of trickery, such as the incident in which the Louisville-Jefferson County (Kentucky) Metro Narcotics Unit dressed an officer as a pizza delivery man to serve a search warrant. Such tactics are tolerated if there is a reasonable belief that the suspects would destroy evidence or escape if the police announced their true identity.

Searches and Seizures without a Warrant

Although the Court has established the principle that searches conducted without warrants are *per se* (by definition) unreasonable, it has set "specifically established" exceptions to the rule.[46] In fact, most searches, like most arrests, take place in the absence of a judicial order. Warrantless searches and seizures can be lawful when police are in "hot pursuit" of a subject or when they search bags of trash left at the curb for regular collection. Because of the magnitude of smuggling activities in "border areas" such as airports, seaports, and international boundaries, a warrant is normally not needed to search property in those places. The two most important circumstances in which a warrant is not needed, however, are (1) searches incidental to an arrest and (2) consensual searches.

Searches Incidental to an Arrest. The most frequent exception to the warrant requirement involves **searches incidental to arrests,** so-called because nearly every time police officers make an arrest, they also search the suspect. As long as the original arrest was based on probable cause, these searches are valid for two reasons, established by the Supreme Court in *United States v. Robinson* (1973): [47]

1. The need for a police officer to find and confiscate any weapons a suspect may be carrying.

2. The need to protect any evidence on the suspect's person from being destroyed.

Law enforcement officers are, however, limited in the searches they may make during an arrest. These limits were established by the Supreme Court in *Chimel v. California* (1969).[48] In that case, police arrived at Chimel's home with an arrest warrant but not a search warrant. Even though Chimel refused their request to "look around," the officers searched the entire three-bedroom house for nearly an hour, finding stolen coins in the process. Chimel was convicted of burglary and appealed, arguing that the evidence of the coins should have been suppressed.

The Supreme Court held that the search was unreasonable. In doing so, the Court established guidelines as to the acceptable extent of searches incidental to an arrest. Primarily, the Court ruled that police may search any area within the suspect's "immediate control" to confiscate any weapons or evidence that the suspect could destroy. The Court found, however, that there was no justification:

> for routinely searching rooms other than that in which the arrest occurs—or, for that matter, for searching through all desk drawers or other closed or concealed areas in that room itself. Such searches, in the absence of well-recognized exceptions, may be made only under the authority of a search warrant.

The exact interpretation of the "area within immediate control" has been left to individual courts, but in general it has been taken to mean the area within the reach of the arrested person. Thus, the Court is said to have established the "arm's reach doctrine" in its *Chimel* decision.

Searches with Consent. In the *McDonald* case mentioned above, Greyhound officials had given the Indianapolis Police Department permission to search for contraband in the company's terminals and buses.[49] Being a private organization, Greyhound had the right to give consent for a search.

The second most common type of warrantless searches, **consent searches,** take place when individuals give law enforcement officers permission to search their persons, homes, or belongings. (For an overview of the circumstances under which warrantless searches are allowed, see *Concept Summary—Exceptions to the Requirement That Officers Have a Search Warrant* on the next page.) The consent must, however, be *voluntary.* If a person has been physically threatened or otherwise coerced into giving consent, the search is invalid.[50] The standard for consent searches was set in *Schneckcloth v. Bustamonte* (1973),[51] in which, after being asked, the defendant told police officers to "go ahead" and search his car. A packet of stolen checks found in the trunk was ruled valid evidence because the driver consented to the search.

SEARCHES INCIDENTAL TO . Searches of persons who have been arrested for weapons and evidence. The fruit of such searches is admissible if any items found are within the immediate vicinity or control of the suspect.

CONSENT SEARCHES Searches by police that are made after the subject of the search has agreed to the action. In these situations, consent, if given of free will, validates a warrantless search.

CONCEPT SUMMARY
Exceptions to the Requirement That Officers Have a Search Warrant

In many circumstances, it would be impractical for police officers to leave a crime scene, go to a judge, and obtain a search warrant before conducting a search. Therefore, under a number of circumstances a search warrant is not required.

Exception	Circumstance Not Requiring a Warrant
Incident to Lawful Arrest	Police officers may search the area within immediate control of a person after they have arrested him or her.
Consent	Police officers may search a person without a warrant if that person agrees to be searched.
Stop and Frisk	Police officers may frisk, or "pat down," a person if they suspect that the person may be involved in criminal activity or pose a danger to those in the immediate area.
Hot Pursuit	If police officers are in "hot pursuit" or chasing a person they have probable cause to believe committed a crime, and that person enters a building, the officers may search the building without a warrant.
Automobile Exception	If police officers have probable cause that an automobile contains evidence of a crime, they may, in most instances, search the vehicle without a warrant.
Plain View	If police officers are legally engaged in police work and happen to see evidence of a crime in "plain view," they may seize it without a search warrant.
Abandoned Property	Any property, such as a hotel room that has been vacated or contraband that has been discarded, may be searched and seized by police officers without a warrant.
Border Searches	Law enforcement officers on border patrol do not need a warrant to search vehicles crossing the border.
Inevitable Discovery	Evidence that has been illegally obtained (without the necessary warrant) may be admitted as evidence if the prosecution can prove that it would have "inevitably" been found by lawful means.

Critics of consent searches hold that such searches are rarely voluntary because most citizens are intimidated by police and will react to a request for permission to make a search as if it were an order.[52] Furthermore, most citizens are unaware that they have the option *not* to comply with a request for a search. Thus, if a police officer asks to search a citizen's car after issuing a speeding ticket, the citizen is well within her or his rights to refuse. According to the Supreme Court's ruling in *Ohio v. Robinette* (1996),[53] however, the Fourth Amendment does not require a police officer to inform citizens that they are "free to go" after an initial stop when no arrest is involved. Thus, an officer can obtain consent to search from someone who is free to leave without ever informing the person that he or she is in fact free to go. The significance of this ruling is underscored by data presented by prosecutors during *Robinette*: in the two years leading up to the case, four hundred Ohio drivers were convicted of narcotics offenses that resulted directly from search requests that could have been denied but were not.[54]

Searches of Automobiles

Though *Chimel* limited the scope of searches and seizures incident to an arrest in most circumstances, the Supreme Court has not been as restrictive concerning searches in arrests involving automobile passengers. In *New York v. Belton* (1981),[55] the Court held that when police officers lawfully arrested a person driving a car, they could legally make a warrantless search of the car's entire front and back compartments. This expansive interpretation of "the area within immediate control" is indicative of the Supreme Court's lenient view of automobile searches.

CJ in Focus
Was Justice Served?
Rules of the Road

Driving down a lonely back road on a cold and rainy night, John D.–a college student with out-of-state plates–sees flashing red lights in his rearview mirror and hears the wail of a siren. Looking down at his dashboard, he realizes that he has been exceeding the speed limit by 10 miles per hour. He resignedly accepts the ticket from the police officer and is about to roll up his window when the officer asks "Sir, may I search your automobile?"

John, who knows he isn't hiding anything but is uncomfortable rejecting the request, gives his permission. While John waits outside in the cold and rain, the officer spends forty minutes going over every inch of the automobile before finally returning to her patrol car and driving off.

"LESSER EXPECTATION OF PRIVACY"

The officer did not have a warrant to search the car, nor–once she received John's permission–did she need one. Many people who have found themselves in a similar situation may ask why this is the case. Most of us would never allow police officers into our homes without a search warrant, even if they were responding to a violation similar to speeding, such as a noise complaint. Why do we have less privacy in our cars than in our homes?

The answer is certainly not found in the U.S. Constitution, which was written when the horse and buggy reigned. To find the genesis of privacy laws with regard to automobiles, one must go to the 1925 Supreme Court case of *Carroll v. United States.* The defendants, Carroll and Kiro, were stopped on a rural Michigan road by patrol officers who recognized them as "bootleggers" (the term used for those who illegally produced and transported liquor during the era of Prohibition). While searching the car, one of the officers felt something hard inside a seat and, ripping the upholstery open, found several bottles of liquor. Carroll and Kiro contested their conviction on the ground that the officers did not have a warrant to search the car.

The Supreme Court ultimately found that the search was justified, with Chief Justice William Howard Taft holding that there was a necessary difference between searching a car or any other movable vehicle and a house. It would be impractical, the Court found, to expect police officers to try to detain an automobile while a search warrant was procured. Therefore, as long as the officers had probable cause to believe that liquor was being transported, their actions satisfied constitutional privacy requirements.

Over the years since *Carroll,* the automobile has become a dominant feature of modern life. On average, Americans spend ten hours a week in their cars, and millions of commuters spend more than four hours a day behind the wheel (more time, it should be noted, than they spend awake in their homes). Yet the "lesser expectation of privacy" in the automobile has been strengthened to the point where police officers have the ability to open a container such as luggage in a car if they have probable cause to believe that it holds contraband. Although the word *automobile* is not, as one observer claimed, "a talisman in whose presence the Fourth Amendment fades away and disappears," the "automobile exception" that originated in *Carroll* has severely limited the privacy expectation of the American driver.

For Critical Analysis: Do you agree with the Supreme Court's reasoning and ruling in *Carroll v. United States*? What might the consequences be if police officers were required to obtain search warrants before searching automobiles that have been stopped for traffic violations?

The "Movable Vehicle Exception." In *Carroll v. United States* (1925),[56] the Supreme Court ruled that the law would distinguish among automobiles, homes, and persons in questions involving police searches. In the years since *Carroll,* the Court has established that the Fourth Amendment does not require police to obtain a warrant to search automobiles or other movable vehicles when they have probable cause that a vehicle contains contraband or evidence of criminal activity.[57] The reasoning behind such leniency is straightforward: requiring a warrant to search an automobile places too heavy a burden on police officers. By the time the officers could communicate with a judge and obtain the warrant, the suspects could drive away and destroy any evidence. Consequently, the Supreme Court has consistently held that someone in a vehicle does not have the same reasonable expectation of privacy as someone at home or even in a phone booth. (See *CJ in Focus— Was Justice Served?: Rules of the Road.*)

Recent rulings have increased police powers in these situations. *Mimms v. Pennsylvania* (1977)[58] established that police officers who stopped a car for a traffic violation could legally order the driver out of the vehicle. In *Whren v. United States* (1996),[59] the Supreme Court ruled that the "true" motivation of police officers in making traffic stops was irrelevant as long as they had probable cause to believe that a traffic law had been broken. In other words, police

According to the nation's highest court, the Fourth Amendment of the United States Constitution does not require police officers to obtain a warrant before searching an automobile. What is the reasoning behind this "movable vehicle exception"?

may stop a car they believe to be transporting drugs in order to issue a speeding citation. The fact that the officers are using the speeding ticket as a pretext to search for drugs (and would not have stopped the driver otherwise) does not matter, as long as the driver actually was speeding. One year later, in *Maryland v. Wilson* (1997),[60] the Court further expanded police power by ruling that an officer may order passengers as well as the driver out of a car during a traffic stop; the Court reasoned that the danger to an officer is increased when there is a passenger in the automobile.

Nevertheless, the "movable vehicle exception" has not provided police officers with complete freedom in searching automobiles. In 1998, the Supreme Court overturned a state law that would have greatly increased the ability of the police to make warrantless searches. Prior to the Court's ruling, Iowa police were allowed to conduct the same type of search after issuing a citation for a traffic violation or other minor offense as they were after making an arrest. In *Knowles v. Iowa* (1998),[61] the defendant, who had been stopped for speeding, was subsequently arrested for marijuana possession. During the trial, the arresting officer admitted that he had no basis for suspecting the defendant of committing any offense other than speeding and had conducted the search only because he was allowed to do so by the statute, which had been in effect since 1983. In a unanimous decision, the Court overturned Iowa's law, with Chief Justice William Rehnquist stating that once a driver has been issued a ticket for speeding, "all the evidence necessary to prosecute the offense has been obtained."[62]

Searches of Luggage. The legality of warrantless searches of automobiles does not, it should be noted, necessarily apply to luggage in the automobile. In *United States v. Chadwick* (1977),[63] the Supreme Court heard a case involving a warrantless search of a footlocker found in the trunk of a car. Marijuana had been found in the container. The defendants moved to suppress this evidence on the ground that it was the fruit of an improper warrantless search. The Court affirmed the suppression, rejecting the government's argument that the warrantless search was justified under the "movable vehicle exception."

Because luggage is used to store personal belongings, individuals are believed to have a reasonable expectation of privacy with regard to the contents of their luggage. In the *McDonald* case mentioned earlier, the Indianapolis detectives were justified in searching the defendant's bag because she insisted that it did not belong to her. Under those circumstances, the luggage was abandoned, and according to the **abandonment doctrine,** such property is not protected by the Fourth Amendment guarantee against unreasonable searches and seizures. The abandonment doctrine holds that once people throw something away in a public place, they no longer have any expectation of privacy with regard to the discarded objects. Accordingly, law enforcement officers can inspect the items without a search warrant.

The Plain View Doctrine

Though the contents of luggage are provided with a certain measure of protection, the same cannot be said for contraband in *plain view*. For example, suppose a traffic officer pulls over a person for speeding, looks in the driver-side window, and clearly sees a bag of heroin resting on the passenger seat. In this instance, under the **plain view doctrine,** the officer would be justified in seizing the drugs without a warrant.

ABANDONMENT DOCTRINE
The legal principle that, in cases involving searches and seizures, when a person abandons an item, he or she no longer enjoys the protection of constitutional privacy laws with regard to that item.

PLAIN VIEW DOCTRINE
The legal principle that objects in plain view of a law enforcement agent who has the right to be in a position to have that view may be seized without a warrant and introduced as evidence.

The plain view doctrine was first enunciated by the Supreme Court in *Coolidge v. New Hampshire* (1971).[64] The Court ruled that law enforcement officers may make a warrantless seizure of an item if four criteria are met:

1. The item is positioned so as to be detected easily by an officer's sight or some other sense.

2. The officer is legally in a position to notice the item in question.

3. The discovery of the item is inadvertent; that is, the officer had not intended to find the item.

4. The officer immediately recognizes the illegal nature of the item. No interrogation or further investigation is allowed under the plain view doctrine.

Contraband, such as a bag of heroin, is obviously illegal, but police officers must use greater care in seizing items that may have been illegally acquired, but are not inherently contraband. For example, a police officer who had been called to the scene of a shooting entered an apartment to search for the suspect, the weapon, and any victims. While in the run-down dwelling, he noticed some expensive stereo equipment. Because the equipment did not match its "squalid" surroundings, the officer wrote down the serial numbers of the items and determined that they had been stolen.[65] The Supreme Court ruled that because the fact that the equipment was stolen was not "immediately apparent," the officer's actions constituted a new search and were not protected by the plain view doctrine.[66] (For a discussion of how the plain view doctrine is being tested by new technology, see *Criminal Justice & Technology—X-Ray Eyes and the Fourth Amendment*.)

Electronic Surveillance

During the course of a criminal investigation, law enforcement officers may decide to use *electronic surveillance,* or electronic devices such as wiretaps or hidden microphones ("bugs"), to monitor and record conversations, observe movements, and trace or record telephone calls. Congress has passed federal legislation restricting the use of wiretapping and bugging to certain types of suspected crimes and has also limited the officials permitted to authorize such actions.[67] States may pass their own laws concerning methods of electronic surveillance, but these laws cannot be less restrictive than the federal law. That is, they cannot pro-

Criminal Justice & Technology

X-Ray Eyes and the Fourth Amendment

Suppose a detective enters a room with a warrant to search for a handgun used in a murder. The weapon is resting on a table and is immediately seized. Hidden in a closed drawer, however, is a packet of heroin. Under the plain view doctrine, the detective would most likely not have the right to search the drawer and seize the heroin. What if that detective could somehow see into the drawer without opening it? How would the plain view doctrine then apply?

A cop with X-ray eyes sounds like something out of a science fiction novel, but in fact courts around the country are already struggling with such situations. Thanks to thermal imagers, also known as forward-looking infrared devices (FLIR), law enforcement agencies now have the ability to look through walls.

THE THERMAL IMAGER AT WORK

Every object with a temperature above absolute zero emits infrared radiation, which cannot be seen by the naked eye. A thermal imager, however, can detect this radiation and project its reading onto a screen. The devices have been most commonly used in missing person searches—with our high body temperature, humans are easy targets for thermal imagers. Only recently have the devices been put to use by law enforcement agencies. Thermal imagers can be particularly effective in detecting marijuana grown indoors because marijuana plants require considerable heat to survive.

The question that courts must decide is whether, in the absence of a warrant, an infrared search of a dwelling is in violation of Fourth Amendment protections of privacy. In one marijuana case, where police used a helicopter fitted with FLIR, a Hawaii court ruled that no reasonable expectation of privacy was involved. The court held that the FLIR measured only heat emanating from the defendant's house and that this "abandoned heat" was not subject to privacy laws because the defendants had not tried to prevent its escape. A Pennsylvania court, ruling on a similar case, rejected the "abandoned heat" justification because thermal imaging allowed the police to see what otherwise would have been hidden to them. The Pennsylvania court warned that thermal imaging "can extract information from within a person's home, the place most deserving of protection from government intrusion."

IN THE FUTURE: Legal scholars expect that the Supreme Court will have the final say on the use of thermal imagers in criminal matters. If the Court rules that such devices do not constitute illegal searches, infrared measuring technology will become a mainstay of police operations—officers may be equipped with FLIR helmets, as are firefighters who use them to search for survivors in burning buildings.

INTERROGATION
The direct questioning of a suspect to gather evidence of criminal activity and try to gain a confession.

vide state law enforcement officers with more opportunities to electronically eavesdrop than does the federal statute.[68]

Given the invasiveness of electronic surveillance, the Supreme Court has generally held that the practice is prohibited by the Fourth Amendment. In *Burger v. New York* (1967),[69] however, the Court ruled that it was permissible under certain circumstances. That same year, *Katz v. United States* (discussed earlier) established that recorded conversations are inadmissible as evidence unless certain procedures are followed.

In general, law enforcement officers can use electronic surveillance only if:

1   Consent is given by one of the parties to be monitored; or

2   There is a warrant authorizing the use of the devices.[70]

Note that the consent of only one of the parties being monitored is needed to waive the reasonable expectation of privacy. The Court has ruled that people whose conversations have been recorded by supposed friends who turn out to be police informers have not been subjected to an unreasonable search.[71] Therefore, at least theoretically, a person always assumes the risk that whatever he or she says to someone else may be monitored by the police. A number of states do, however, have statutes that forbid private citizens from tape recording another person's conversation without her or his knowledge. In Maryland, for example, such an act is a felony. In 1998, Maryland state officials were contemplating charging Linda Tripp for recording phone conversations with ex-White House intern Monica Lewinsky, an act that eventually contributed to impeachment proceedings against President Bill Clinton by the U.S. Congress.

If consent exists, then law enforcement officers are not required to obtain a warrant before engaging in electronic surveillance. In most other instances, however, a warrant is required. For the warrant to be valid, it must:

1   Detail with "particularity" the conversations that are to be overheard.

2   Name the suspects and the places that will be under surveillance.

3   Show with probable cause that a specific crime has been or will be committed.[72]

"The psychological games that are played during an interrogation . . . are difficult at best to understand: assured by authorities you don't remember things, being led to doubt your own memory, having things suggested to you only to have those things pop up in a conversation a short time later but from your own lips."

—Peter Reilly, *who confessed to having murdered his mother while under police interrogation (1995)*

Once the specific information has been gathered, the law enforcement officers must end the electronic surveillance immediately.[73] In any case, the surveillance cannot last more than thirty days without a judicial extension.

THE INTERROGATION PROCESS AND *MIRANDA*

After the Pledge of Allegiance, there is perhaps no recitation that comes more readily to the American mind than the *Miranda* warning:

> You have the right to remain silent. If you give up that right, anything you say can and will be used against you in a court of law. You have the right to speak with an attorney and to have the attorney present during questioning. If you so desire and cannot afford one, an attorney will be appointed for you without charge before questioning.

The *Miranda* warning is not a mere prop. It strongly affects one of the most important aspects of any criminal investigation—the **interrogation,** or questioning of a suspect from whom the police want to get information concerning a crime and perhaps a confession.

The Legal Basis for *Miranda*

The Fifth Amendment guarantees protection against self-incrimination. A defendant's choice not to incriminate himself or herself cannot be interpreted as a sign of guilt by a jury in a criminal trial. A confession, or admission of guilt, is by definition a statement of self-incrimination. How, then, to reconcile the Fifth Amendment with the critical need of law enforcement officers to gain confessions? The answer lies in the concept of *coercion*. When torture or brutality is involved, it is relatively easy to determine that a confession was improperly coerced and is therefore invalid.

Setting the Stage for *Miranda*. The Supreme Court first recognized that a confession could not be physically coerced in a 1936 case concerning a defendant who was beaten and whipped until confessing to a murder.[74] It was not until 1964, however, that the Court specifically recognized that the accused's due process rights should be protected during interrogation. That year, the Court heard the case of *Escobedo v. Illinois*,[75] concerning a convicted murderer who claimed that police had forced incriminating statements from him during interrogation and that this evidence had been portrayed as voluntary during his trial. In *Escobedo*, the Court ruled that the defendant had been denied his Sixth Amendment right to counsel during the interrogation. He therefore had also been denied his Fifth Amendment right against self-incrimination.

Montoun T. Hart, shown above, was acquitted in 1999 of all charges in the killing a popular high school teacher in New York City. According to jury members, the verdict was a direct response to the harsh tactics used by detectives in "persuading" Hart to admit to the crime.

The *Miranda* Case. Two years later, the Supreme Court expanded upon *Escobedo* in its *Miranda* decision,[76] establishing the **Miranda rights** and introducing the concept of what University of Columbia law professor H. Richard Uviller called *inherent coercion*. That is, even if a police officer does not lay a hand on a suspect, the general atmosphere of an interrogation is in and of itself coercive.[77]

Though the *Miranda* case is best remembered for the procedural requirement it spurred, at the time the Supreme Court was more concerned about the treatment of suspects during interrogation. (See *CJ in Focus—Landmark Cases: Miranda v. Arizona* on the following page.) The Court found that routine police interrogation strategies, such as leaving suspects alone in a room for several hours before questioning them, were inherently coercive. Therefore, the Court reasoned, every suspect needed protection from coercion, not just those who had been physically abused. The *Miranda* warning is a result of this need. In theory, if the warning is not given to a suspect before an interrogation, the fruits of that interrogation, including a confession, are invalid.

When a *Miranda* Warning Is Required

As we shall see, a *Miranda* warning is not necessary under several conditions, such as when no questions are asked of the suspect. Generally, *Miranda* requirements apply *only* when a suspect is in **custody.** In a series of rulings since *Miranda*, the Supreme Court has defined custody as an arrest or a situation in which a reasonable person would not feel free to leave.[78]

MIRANDA RIGHTS
The constitutional rights of accused persons taken into custody by law enforcement officials. Following the United States Supreme Court's decision *Miranda v. Arizona,* on taking an accused person into custody, the arresting officer must inform the person of certain constitutional rights, such as the right to remain silent and the right to counsel.

CUSTODY
The forceful detention of a person, or the perception that a person is not free to leave the immediate vicinity.

CJ in Focus

Landmark Cases:

Miranda v. Arizona

Ernesto Miranda

Ernesto Miranda, a produce worker, was arrested in Phoenix, Arizona, in 1963 and charged with kidnapping and rape. After being identified by the victim in a lineup, Miranda was taken into an interrogation room and questioned for two hours by detectives. At no time was Miranda informed that he had a right to have an attorney present. When the police emerged from the session, they had a signed statement by Miranda confessing to the crimes. He was subsequently convicted and sentenced to twenty to thirty years in prison. After the conviction was confirmed by the Arizona Supreme Court, Miranda appealed to the United States Supreme Court, claiming that he had not been warned that any statement he made could be used against him, and that he had a right to counsel during the interrogation. The *Miranda* case was one of four examined by the Court that dealt with the question of coercive questioning.

Miranda v. Arizona
United States Supreme Court
384 U.S. 436 (1966)
http://laws.findlaw.com/US/384/436.html

In the Words of the Court . . .

Mr. Chief Justice WARREN, majority opinion

* * * *

The cases before us raise questions which go to the roots of our concepts of American criminal jurisprudence: the restraints society must observe consistent with the Federal Constitution in prosecuting individuals for crime. More specifically, we deal with the admissibility of statements obtained from an individual who is subjected to custodial police interrogation and the necessity for procedures which assure that the individual is accorded his privilege under the Fifth Amendment to the Constitution not to be compelled to incriminate himself.

* * * *

As for the procedural safeguards to be employed, unless other fully effective means are devised to inform accused persons of their right of silence and to assure a continuous opportunity to exercise it, the following measures are required. Prior to any questioning, the person must be warned that he has a right to remain silent, that any statement he does make may be used as evidence against him, and that he has a right to the presence of an attorney, either retained or appointed. The defendant may waive effectuation of these rights, provided the waiver is made voluntarily, knowingly and intelligently. * * * The mere fact that he may have answered some questions or volunteered some statements on his own does not deprive him of the right to refrain from answering any further inquiries until he has consulted with an attorney and thereafter consents to be questioned.

* * * *

Again we stress that the modern practice of in-custody interrogation is psychologically rather than physically oriented. * * * "[T]his Court has recognized that coercion can be mental as well as physical, and that the blood of the accused is not the only hallmark of an unconstitutional inquisition."

* * * *

[T]he very fact of custodial interrogation exacts a heavy toll on individual liberty and trades on the weakness of individuals.

* * * *

It is obvious that such an interrogation environment is created for no purpose other than to subjugate the individual to the will of his examiner. This atmosphere carries its own badge of intimidation. To be sure, this is not physical intimidation, but it is equally destructive of human dignity. The current practice of incommunicado interrogation is at odds with one of our Nation's most cherished principles—that the individual may not be compelled to incriminate himself. Unless adequate protective devices are employed to dispel the compulsion inherent in custodial surroundings, no statement obtained from the defendant can truly be the product of his free choice.

Decision: The Court overturned Miranda's conviction, stating that police interrogations are, by their very nature, coercive and therefore deny suspects their constitutional right against self-incrimination by "forcing" them to confess. Consequently, any person who has been arrested and placed in custody must be informed of his or her right to be free from self-incrimination and be represented by counsel during any interrogation. In other words, suspects must be told that they *do not have* to answer police questions. To accomplish this, the Court established the *Miranda* warning, which must be read prior to questioning of a suspect in custody.

For Critical Analysis: What is meant by the phrase "coercion can be mental as well as physical"? What role does the concept of "mental coercion" play in Chief Justice Warren's opinion?

Consequently, a **custodial interrogation** occurs when a suspect is under arrest or is deprived of her or his freedom in a significant manner. Again, a *Miranda* warning is only required before a custodial interrogation takes place.

The boundaries of custody and interrogation are not always clear. For example, *United States v. Mesa* (1980)[79] involved a situation that arose when Mesa, who was charged with shooting his common law wife and daughter, barricaded himself in a motel room. The FBI agents on the scene, aware that the suspect was armed but uncertain whether he was holding hostages, decided not to use force against him. Instead they deployed a negotiator. During a three-hour conversation with the negotiator, Mesa was persuaded to surrender peacefully; he was then arrested and read his rights. The trial court found that custodial interrogation had occurred during the conversation with the negotiator and that any statements Mesa made before leaving the hotel room could not be used against him. Although this ruling was eventually overturned, it does underscore the rather vague boundaries of being "in custody."

When a *Miranda* Warning Is Not Required

A *Miranda* warning is not necessary in a number of situations:

1. When the police do not ask any questions of the suspect.

2. When the police have not focused on a suspect and are questioning witnesses at the scene of a crime.

3. When a person volunteers information before the police have asked a question.

4. When the suspect has given a private statement to a friend or some other acquaintance. *Miranda* does not apply to these statements as long as the government did not orchestrate the situation.

5. During a stop and frisk, when no arrest has been made.

6. During a traffic stop.[80]

Furthermore, suspects can *waive* their Fifth Amendment rights and speak to a police officer, but only if the waiver is made voluntarily. Silence on the part of a suspect does not mean that his or her *Miranda* protections have been relinquished. To waive their rights, suspects must state—either in writing or orally—that they understand those rights and that they will voluntarily answer questions without the presence of counsel.

The Law Enforcement Response to *Miranda*

Many people, particularly police officials, complain that the *Miranda* ruling distorted the Constitution by placing the rights of criminal suspects above the rights of society as a whole.[81] In the more than thirty years since the decision, however, police officers seem to have adapted to the *Miranda* restrictions.

As the transcript of an interrogation in Figure 6.4 on the next page indicates, law enforcement officers have devised a number of strategies to circumvent *Miranda*. After an extensive on-site study of police interrogation tactics, Richard A. Leo, a criminologist from the University of California at Irvine, noted a pattern of maneuvers that officers would use to convince suspects to voluntarily waive their *Miranda* rights. Leo identifies three such strategies:

- The *conditioning* strategy is geared toward creating an environment in which the suspect is encouraged to think positively of the interrogator

CUSTODIAL INTERROGATION
The questioning of a suspect after that person has been taken in custody. In this situation, the suspect *must* be read his or her *Miranda* rights before interrogation can begin.

Figure 6.4 Working around *Miranda*

This exchange is taken from the transcript of a 1993 interrogation of James McNally. The detectives are employees of the Santa Monica (California) Police Department. McNally was eventually convicted of manslaughter. Notice how the detectives convince McNally that it is not in his best interests to take advantage of his constitutional right to have an attorney present during the interrogation.

McNally: How 'bout we do this?. . . Let me talk to a California lawyer and we'll get back together.

Detective: You'll what?. . . No attorney in his right mind is gonna tell you to talk with the police.

McNally: Oh, I know. . . .

Detective: You don't wanna tell us what happened. . .

McNally: Not at this time. It's, it's too scary for me right now. I'd, I'd rather talk to a lawyer.

Detective: At this point, nothing that you say can be used against you in Court . . . in California because you have invoked your right to an attorney.

McNally: Right.

Detective: I still would like to know what happened now because—well, I'll tell you where I come from. I don't trust anything that anybody tells me after they've talked to an attorney and the D.A. that will be working with us on this case doesn't either. . . . And if you were in our place, would you trust something that somebody told you after they talked to an attorney?. . .

Detective: O.K. and [expletive] your attorney. It's just—I don't care about him anymore. . . . As far as I'm concerned, you know, they really mess up the system. I wanna know now what you're gonna tell me later. It can't be used against you.

Detective: This is your opportunity. . . .

McNally: All right. I'll . . . and this can't be used against me.

Detective: No, absolutely. It's right on there. It's not—we're promising you, it's not going to be used against you—in the case in chief—against you, O.K? Just, this is for our edification of what happened.

McNally: Well, anyway, he picked me up outside, outside the Oar House, O.K.?

and thus is conditioned to cooperate. The interrogator will offer the suspect coffee or a cigarette and make pleasant small talk. These steps are intended to lower the suspect's anxiety level and generate a sense of trust that is conducive to a *Miranda* waiver and confession.

- The *de-emphasizing* strategy tries to downplay the importance of *Miranda* protections, giving the impression that the rights are unimportant and can be easily waived. For example, one officer told a suspect, "I need to advise you of your rights. It's a formality. I'm sure you've watched television with the cop shows and you hear them say their rights so you can probably recite this better than I can, but it's something I need to do and we can get this out of the way before we talk about what happened."

- When using the *persuasion* strategy, an officer will explicitly try to convince the suspect to waive her or his rights. Commonly, the detective will tell suspects that waiving the rights is the only way they will be able to get their side of the story out. Otherwise, the detective continues, only the victim's side of the story will be considered during the trial.[82]

When a suspect refuses to waive his or her *Miranda* rights, police officers know that they cannot lawfully continue the interrogation until the suspect's defense attorney arrives on the scene. In some cases, the officers will continue the interrogation, hoping that the suspect will "let the cat out of the bag."[83] This strategy has worked on numerous occasions, when courts have allowed the "fruit" of these technically illegal interrogations to be admitted as evidence, even while condemning the interrogations themselves.[84] The Supreme Court appeared to favor this approach under certain circumstances in *Harris v. New York* (1971),[85] in which the prosecutor used statements made by the defendant before the trial to show that the defendant was lying on the witness stand. The Court ruled that these statements were admissible, even though the defendant had not been read his *Miranda* warning before giving them. Thus, even though the method of obtaining these statements was faulty, the statements themselves could be used in court.

The Weakening of *Miranda*

There are no guarantees that *Miranda* will survive indefinitely. Many legal scholars see the *Harris* ruling as the first in a series of Supreme Court decisions that are slowly eroding *Miranda;* in the words of Alan M. Dershowitz, the Court has carved "out so many exceptions that [*Miranda*] is falling of its own weight."[86] Figure 6.5 provides a rundown of Court rulings that have weakened *Miranda* over the past several decades.

The Latest Challenge: Section 3501. The U.S. Appeals Court for the Fourth Circuit, based in Richmond, Virginia, may have dealt the most severe blow to *Miranda.* Ruling on *United States v. Dickerson* (1999),[87] the court effectively declared that law enforcement officers in the states over which it has jurisdiction (Maryland, North Carolina, South Carolina, Virginia, and West Virginia) would no longer be required to inform arrestees of their right to be silent.

Figure 6.5 Supreme Court Decisions Eroding *Miranda* Rights

Rhode Island v. Innis **(446 U.S. 291 [1980]).** In this case the Supreme Court clarified its definition of an interrogation, which it said could only extend to "actions or words" that the police "should have known were reasonably likely to elicit an incriminating response." In making this ruling, the Court allowed as evidence an admission made by a suspect as to where a shotgun he had used in a crime was hidden. The suspect confessed after police mentioned that there was a possibility that a handicapped child might find the firearm, given that a home for such children was nearby. This was not, the Court ruled, an interrogation and therefore *Miranda* rights were not necessary.

New York v. Quarles **(467 U.S. 649 [1984]).** This case established the "public safety" exception to the *Miranda* rule. It concerned a police officer who, after feeling an empty shoulder holster on a man he had just arrested, asked the suspect the location of the gun without informing him of his *Miranda* rights. The Court ruled that the gun was admissible as evidence and that the need for police officers to protect the public is more important than a suspect's *Miranda* rights.

Moran v. Burbine **(475 U.S. 412 [1985]).** This case established that police officers are not required to tell suspects undergoing custodial interrogation that their attorney is trying to reach them. The Court ruled that events that the suspect could have no way of knowing about have no bearing on his ability to waive his *Miranda* rights.

Illinois v. Perkins **(110 S.Ct. 2394) [1991]).** Perkins was a suspected murderer in prison on an unrelated drug charge who admitted to the murder in order to impress his cellmate, who happened to be an undercover police officer. The Court ruled that even though the undercover officer goaded Perkins into making the admission, the defendant was not being subjected to a custodial interrogation; indeed, he eagerly bragged to his cellmate, describing the murder in detail in order to impress. *Miranda* does not protect suspects from their own foolishness.

Arizona v. Fulminante **(111 S.Ct. 1246 [1991]).** In this very important ruling, the Court held that a conviction is not automatically overturned if the suspect was coerced into making a confession. If the other evidence introduced at the trial is strong enough to justify a conviction without the confession, then the fact that the confession was illegally gained can be, for all intents and purposes, ignored.

Davis v. United States **(114 S.Ct. 2359 [1994]).** This case involved a suspect who, instead of demanding that he be provided with his *Miranda* right to an attorney, said, "Maybe I should talk to a lawyer" during his custodial interrogation. The Court ruled that a suspect must unequivocally and assertively state his right to counsel in order to stop police questioning. Furthermore, police officers are not required to try and decipher the suspect's intentions in such cases.

The case involved Charles T. Dickerson, a Maryland man who voluntarily confessed to a series of bank robberies before he was read his _Miranda_ rights. In overturning a district court's ruling that the confession was inadmissible, the three-judge panel relied on a long-forgotten provision of the Omnibus Crime Control Act of 1968. In Section 3501 of that act, Congress asserted that a confession "shall be admissible in evidence if it is voluntarily given,"[88] regardless of whether suspects have received a _Miranda_ warning. Congress apparently intended to give federal judges the power to address all the circumstances surrounding a confession in deciding whether or not it was voluntary without relying primarily on the constitutional requirements set forth in _Miranda_.[89]

The Department of Justice, which dictates strategy to federal prosecutors, never used the law. In fact, a year before the _Dickerson_ ruling, U.S. Attorney General Janet Reno called Section 3501 unconstitutional. The Virginia court, therefore, acted not because of an argument made by the government, but because of information received in a "friend-of-the-court" brief provided by a private organization. The _Dickerson_ ruling applies only to federal courts in the states listed above and has no effect in state courts. Legal experts believe, however, that the decision will be reviewed again on a federal level and could lead the Supreme Court to eventually reconsider _Miranda_.[90]

The Use of Videotape. _Miranda_ may eventually find itself obsolete regardless of any decisions made in the courts. A relatively new trend in law enforcement has been for agencies to record interrogations and confessions on videotape, making it more difficult for defense attorneys to claim that their clients had been illegally coerced. In New Mexico, officers now carry tape recorders on their waist belts. State laws in Alaska and Minnesota require interrogations to be recorded.[91] Such practices can work in favor of suspects as well. In 1996, a superior court judge in San Diego threw out Delano Wright's confession to being involved in a drive-by shooting after reviewing an interview of Wright conducted by a detective. The judge ruled that Wright, who was charged with first degree murder, had been coerced into confessing by false promises on the part of the detective that Wright would be charged only as a witness.[92] Some scholars have suggested that the videotaping of _all_ custodial interrogations would satisfy the Fifth Amendment's prohibition against coercion and in the process render the _Miranda_ warning unnecessary.[93]

THE IDENTIFICATION PROCESS

A confession is a form of self-identification; the suspect has identified herself or himself as the guilty party. If police officers are unable to gain a confession, they must use other methods to link the suspect with the crime. In fact, police must do so even if the suspect confesses, as false admissions do occur. Unless police officers witness the commission of the crime themselves, they must establish the identity of the suspect using three basic types of identification procedures:

1. _Showups,_ which occur when a suspect who matches the description given by witnesses is apprehended near the scene of the crime within a reasonable amount of time after the crime has been committed. The suspect is usually returned to the crime scene for possible identification by witnesses.

2. *Photo arrays,* which occur when no suspect is in custody but the police have a general description of the person. Witnesses and victims are shown "mug shots" of people with police records that match the description. Police will also present witnesses and victims with pictures of people they believe might have committed the crime.

3. *Lineups,* which entail lining up several physically similar people, one of whom is the suspect, in front of a witness or victim. The police may have each member of the lineup wear clothing similar to that worn by the criminal and say a phrase that was used during the crime. These visual and oral cues are designed to help the witness identify the suspect.

As with the other procedures discussed in this chapter, constitutional law governs the identification process, though some aspects are more tightly restricted than others. The Sixth Amendment right to counsel, for example, does not apply during showups or photo arrays. In showups, the police often need to establish a suspect quickly, and it would be unreasonable to expect them to wait for an attorney to arrive. According to the Supreme Court in *United States v. Ash* (1973),[94] however, the police must be able to prove this need for immediate identification, perhaps by showing that it was necessary to keep the suspect from fleeing the state. As for photo arrays, courts have found that any procedure that does not require the suspect's presence does not require the presence of his or her attorney.[95] The lack of an attorney does not mean that police can "steer" a witness toward a positive identification with statements such as "Are you sure this isn't the person you saw robbing the grocery store?" Such actions would violate the suspect's due process rights.

Under certain circumstances, suspects have a right to counsel when they are placed in a lineup. A person who has been indicted—that is, formally charged with committing a crime—has a right to have an attorney present at the lineup. This right was established in *United States v. Wade* (1967),[96] which

Lineups are one of the primary means police have of identifying suspects. As you can see, in a lineup several people with similar appearances are placed so that a victim or witness can study them. The victim or witness is then asked to point out the one that most closely resembles the person who committed the crime. Lineup identifications are generally considered most valuable if they take place within several hours after the crime has been committed. Why is timing so important with regard to a lineup?

BOOKING
The process of entering a suspect's name, offense, and arrival time into the police log following her or his arrest.

concerned a bank robber who was identified by two bank employees from a lineup. The Supreme Court ruled that the lineup was a "critical stage" of the pretrial procedure and voiced concern that police officers might improperly influence a witness if the suspect did not have a lawyer present to look after his or her interests.

Five years after *Wade*, however, the Court ruled in *Kirby v. Illinois* (1972)[97] that a person who has been arrested but not yet indicted does *not* have the right to counsel if placed in a lineup. The Court drew a distinction between a suspect who has already been charged with a crime and a suspect who may be proved innocent by the lineup procedure. In the latter instance, waiting for an attorney to arrive may delay the lineup, possibly to the detriment of the investigative process if the lineup proves that the police have the wrong person in custody. Despite the *Kirby* decision, many police departments allow an attorney to be present at a pre-indictment lineup and to make reasonable suggestions, as long as this does not cause a delay. (See Figure 6.6 for an overview of identification procedures not discussed in this section.)

Some observers feel that the standard **booking** procedure—the process of recording information about the suspect immediately after arrest—infringes

Figure 6.6 Blood and Bullets: How Far Can the Police Go?

How far can the police go in identifying a suspect? They cannot, as we saw earlier when discussing *Rochin v. California,* take a suspect to the hospital and have his stomach pumped to get evidence. But what about DNA profiling? Isn't that a form of identification in which a person's DNA can be used to verify his or her guilt? Shouldn't that fall under the category of self-incrimination? After all, a person's DNA—part of him- or herself—is implicating him or her in a crime.

In fact, the Supreme Court has consistently ruled that the Fifth Amendment does not cover nontestimonial identification procedures. Oral or written communications are "testimonial," while DNA profiling is "nontestimonial." In Chapter 5 we discussed the ways in which DNA can be used to identify criminal suspects. Here are some other nontestimonial ways that suspects can be identified.

1. Blood: In *Schmerber v. California* (384 U.S. 757 [1966]), the Court ruled that blood could be forcibly extracted from a suspect to prove that he had been driving an automobile while under the influence of intoxicating liquor.

2. Voice: In *United States v. Dionisio* (410 U.S. 1 [1973]), the Court ruled that a suspect is required to provide voice samples to police if such samples can be matched with a voice spoken at the time of a crime.

3. Handwriting: In *United States v. Mara* (410 U.S. 19 [1973]), the Court ruled that police could require a suspect to provide a handwriting sample to be compared with handwriting involved in a crime.

The Court has, however, set some limits on the use of nontestimonial evidence. In the early 1980s, Ralph Watkinson of Richmond, Virginia, shot a man who had assaulted him before fleeing. Police found Rudolph Lee a few blocks from the scene of the crime bleeding from a bullet wound beneath his collarbone. Watkinson identified Lee as the assailant, and the local prosecutor tried to get a court order to remove the bullet from Lee's body in order to match it with Watkinson's gun. In *Winston v. Lee* (470 U.S. 753 [1985]), the Court ruled that the surgery required was "highly intrusive" and was offensive to the suspect's "human dignity." Therefore, the bullet was not allowed as nontestimonial evidence against the suspect.

upon a suspect's Fifth Amendment rights. During booking, the suspect is photographed and fingerprinted, and, as we saw in Chapter 5, blood samples may be taken. If these samples lead to the suspect's eventual identification, according to some, they amount to self-incrimination. In *Schmerber v. California* (1966),[98] however, the Supreme Court held that such tests are not the equivalent of *testimonial* self-incrimination (where the suspect testifies verbally against himself or herself) and therefore do not violate the Fifth Amendment.

Criminal Justice in Action
Constitutional Handcuffs?

Just as there is debate over whether the constitutional protections discussed in this chapter are necessary to protect citizens' rights from the power of the state, there is also a continuing debate over the impact constitutional law has had on police behavior. A number of studies on the exclusionary rule, for example, have found that only a minimal amount of evidence has actually been suppressed because of the rule.[99] Critics of the exclusionary rule contend, however, that the rule's ultimate impact is difficult to determine because we cannot measure actions that police officers did not take for fear of straying outside legal boundaries. As this chapter comes to a close, we will examine the arguments of those who believe that constitutional law has had a dramatic impact on police behavior—an impact that is not in society's best interest.

CONSTITUTIONAL LAW IN OREGON AND NEW YORK

On March 6, 1996, Corvallis (Oregon) police officers investigating a burglary at a nearby tire store served four search warrants for property owned by Keith Bradley, Jr., and his father, Keith Bradley, Sr. When they searched the Bradleys' barn, the Corvallis officers found an incredible array of contraband: a pipe bomb, a hand grenade, 200 pounds of Austinite 15 ammonium nitrate fertilizer mixed with fuel oil for making explosives, ammunition, 94 grams of the drug methamphetamine, a small amount of marijuana, and 29 guns, including pistols, shotguns, and assault weapons.

A few years earlier, two New York state troopers pulled over a U-Haul van going 70 miles an hour on a desolate stretch of road at 2 A.M. Hunting season had just begun. The troopers were on the lookout for hunters from New York City with illegal firearms, so they asked the driver, Leonardo Turriago, if they could check his trunk. Turriago agreed, and the troopers found a dead body, hacked into pieces and placed in several boxes. After Turriago and his two companions were arrested, investigators found that the murder was linked to illegal narcotics and that the body was being transported to the countryside for disposal.

These two cases, involving crimes committed on opposite sides of the country, would seem to have little in common, but they shared the same result—all the suspects were eventually freed. In Oregon, U.S. District Judge Malcolm F. Marsh ruled that errors in the affidavit rendered all evidence found as a result of the search warrants invalid.[100] In New York, an appellate court ruled that the police did not have a reasonable basis to suspect that a crime had taken place and that they had intimidated the defendants into agreeing to a consensual search of the trunk.[101]

THE COLLAPSE OF CRIMINAL JUSTICE?

In both cases, the court did not question the obvious guilt of the accused. Instead, it found that the police officers had infringed upon the Fourth Amendment rights of the defendants by carrying out unreasonable searches and seizures. In other words, the police did not mistakenly apprehend innocent individuals. The errors were procedural.

The purpose of criminal procedure rules is, of course, to ensure that state prosecutors do not infringe on the constitutional rights of defendants, particularly the right to due process of law. After all, a criminal prosecution brings the force of the state, with all its resources, to bear against the individual. The *Miranda* requirements, the exclusionary rule, and other procedural rules are designed to safeguard the rights of individuals against the immense power of the state.

Many contend, however, that criminal procedures are getting in the way of truth and justice. New York state trial judge Harold J. Rothwax has written that the *Miranda* requirements and court interpretations of the Fourth and Fifth Amendments have created a thicket of criminal procedures that has resulted in the "collapse of criminal justice."[102] Even defendants who confess their guilt go free if they can prove that law enforcement officers violated in some way a procedural requirement, such as failing to read the *Miranda* warning to a criminal suspect or obtaining evidence without a valid search warrant.

INFOTRAC®
COLLEGE EDITION

Cassell, Paul. <u>Protecting the innocent</u> from false confessions and lost confessionsBand from Miranda.

Furthermore, Rothwax believes the constant judicial review of criminal procedures has put law enforcement officers in the untenable position of having to keep abreast of an ever-changing set of rules:

> The problem is, the law is so muddy that the police can't find out what they are allowed to do even if they wanted to. If a street cop took a sabbatical and holed himself up in a library for six months doing nothing but studying the law on search and seizure, he wouldn't know any more than he did before he started . . . yet we expect cops to always know at every moment what the proper action is.[103]

Many police officers feel similarly. "I just don't think the Supreme Court is giving the people the protection they deserve," said one sergeant. "I mean, they've gone too far in protecting the bad guys, and the good guys are left out in the cold."[104]

INFOTRAC®
COLLEGE EDITION

Leo, Richard and Richard Ofshe. Using the innocent to scapegoat Miranda: another reply to Paul Cassell.

THE WARREN COURT AND THE EXCLUSIONARY RULE

Although the Bill of Rights spells out much of American procedural law, the country does not have a long history of judicial activism in criminal cases. Until Earl Warren's tenure as chief justice (1953–1969), the United States Supreme Court was mostly content to allow the states to set their own procedural guidelines. Under Warren, however, the Court began to significantly impact police practices on constitutional grounds. (See Figure 6.7 for a list of the cases through which the Warren Court influenced police procedure.)

For law enforcement officers, the most significant case of the Warren years was *Mapp v. Ohio,* which made the exclusionary rule binding on the states. By providing defendants with an "escape hatch"—if the evidence used to convict them was gathered in violation of the Fourth Amendment—the exclusionary rule forced police officers to readjust their on-the-job thinking. Whereas they had previously been able to

Figure 6.7 The Warren Court and Police Procedure

Chief Justice Earl Warren presided over the United States Supreme Court from 1953 to 1969. Because many of the rulings made by the Court during that period granted new rights to those accused of crimes, Warren's reign is often referred to as the "due process revolution." The Warren Court's decisions affected all areas of the criminal justice system, but in this exhibit we will concentrate on those cases that affected police procedure.

Mapp v. Ohio (1961)	Impact: Extended the exclusionary rule to the states, meaning that evidence obtained by police by an illegal search would be inadmissible in both federal and state courts.
Escobedo v. Illinois (1964)	Impact: Required police to honor the request of a suspect undergoing interrogation to consult with his or her lawyer before continuing to answer questions.
Miranda v. Arizona (1966)	Impact: In order to protect against psychological coercion of suspects during police interrogation, the Court adopted specific procedures for the interrogation of those in police custody. These procedures, called the *Miranda* warning, require police to inform suspects of their constitutional rights before a custodial interrogation can proceed.
United States v. Wade (1967)	Impact: Established that defendants have the right to be represented by counsel during police lineups.
Terry v. Ohio (1968)	Impact: Established the conditions under which it is permissible for a police officer to "stop and frisk" (though not arrest) a suspicious looking person.
Chimel v. California (1969)	Impact: Limited the search a police officer may make of a suspect at the time of arrest to the area immediately surrounding the suspect.

work according to instinct, officers now had to incorporate cerebral concepts such as "probable" and "reasonable" into their actions.

Such terms are difficult to define. For example, a Minnesota police officer was having trouble questioning a suspect for a simple reason: the suspect would not open his mouth. Noticing that the suspect was trying to swallow, the officer inferred—correctly—that he was hiding something. Upon searching the suspect's mouth, the officer found a packet of cocaine. The Supreme Court of Minnesota reversed the ensuing conviction, ruling that the police officer did not have "probable cause" to search the suspect's mouth for drugs.[105]

THE RAMIFICATIONS OF POLICE ERROR

To avoid later court reversals, officers may procure a warrant before a search or an arrest, which theoretically satisfies the need for reasonable suspicion or probable cause. Many officers disdain warrants, however, because of the time required to write up an affidavit and get judicial approval.[106] Moreover, an error on a warrant can invalidate an arrest. A drug conviction in Hartford, Connecticut, was overturned because an officer had mistakenly dated the warrant 1992 instead of 1993.[107]

The *Miranda* warning, another result of the Warren Court, is similarly disdained. Paul Cassell, a professor at the University of Utah College of Law, estimates that each year the *Miranda* requirements cause prosecutors to lose cases against 30,000 violent criminal suspects, 90,000 property offenders, 62,000 drunk drivers, 46,000 drug dealers and users, and hundreds of thousands of others accused of less serious crimes.[108]

Even though Cassell's estimates are widely disputed in the criminal justice field, arguments against the various constitutional restrictions on police are based as much on emotion as on statistics. To many people, it seems unfair and unjust that a minor error on a warrant or a debatable interpretation of the word *probable* could set a guilty person free. For supporters of these constitutional "handcuffs," however, focusing on individual cases misses the point. The exclusionary rule, warrant requirements, *Miranda* warning, and other procedural guidelines promote our society's commitment to constitutional values. In other words, the trade-off, in which some of the guilty are spared punishment to protect the rights of all citizens, is "worth it."

Key Terms

Chapter Summary

1. **Outline the four major sources that may provide probable cause.** (a) Personal observation, usually due to an officer's personal training, experience, and expertise; (b) information, gathered from informants, eyewitnesses, victims, police bulletins, and other sources; (c) evidence, which often has to be in plain view; and (d) association, which generally must concern a person with a known criminal background who is seen in a place where criminal activity is openly taking place.

2. **Explain the exclusionary rule and the exceptions to it.** This rule, established federally in *Weeks v. United States* and at the state level in *Mapp v. Ohio*, prohibits the use of illegally seized evidence, or evidence obtained by an unreasonable search and seizure in an inadmissible way. Exceptions to the exclusionary rule are the "inevitable discovery" exception established in *Nix v. Williams* and the "good faith" exception established in *United States v. Leon*.

3. **Distinguish between a stop and a frisk, and indicate the importance of the case *Terry v. Ohio*.** Though the terms *stop* and *frisk* are often used in concert, a stop is the separate act of detaining a suspect when an officer reasonably believes that a criminal activity is about to take place. A frisk is the physical "pat-down" of a suspect. In *Terry v. Ohio*, the Supreme Court ruled that an officer must have "specific and articulable" facts before making a stop, but those facts may be "taken together with rational inferences."

4. **List the four elements that must be present for an arrest to take place.** (a) Intent, (b) authority, (c) seizure or detention, and (d) the understanding of the person that he or she has been arrested.

5. **Explain under what circumstances officers need not announce themselves before entering a dwelling and under what circumstances arrest warrants are not required.** "No-knock" entries are allowed under exigent circumstances, such as when a suspect is armed and poses a threat of violence; when persons inside the dwelling are destroying evidence or escaping; and when officers believe a felony is being committed. A warrantless arrest can be made if the offense is committed in the presence of an officer or if the officer knows that a crime has been committed and has probable cause to believe that it was committed by a particular suspect.

6. **List the four categories of items that can be seized by use of a search warrant.** (a) Items resulting from a crime, such as stolen goods; (b) inherently illegal items; (c) evidence of the crime; and (d) items used in committing crimes.

7. **Explain when searches can be made without a warrant.** Searches and seizures can be made without a warrant if they are incidental to an arrest (but they must be reasonable); when they are made with voluntary consent; when they involve the "movable vehicle exception"; when property has been abandoned; and when items are in plain view, under certain restricted circumstances (see *Coolidge v. New Hampshire*).

8. **Recite the *Miranda* warning.** You have the right to remain silent. If you give up that right, anything you say can and will be used against you in a court of law. You have the right to speak with an attorney and to have the attorney present during questioning. If you so desire and cannot afford one, an attorney will be appointed for you without charge before questioning.

9. **Indicate situations in which a *Miranda* warning is unnecessary.** (a) When no questions are asked of the suspect; (b) when there is no suspect and witnesses in general are being questioned at the scene of a crime; (c) when a person volunteers information before the police ask anything; (d) when a suspect has given a private statement to a friend without the government orchestrating it; (e) during a stop and frisk when no arrests have been made; and (f) during a traffic stop.

10. **List the three basic types of police identification.** (a) Showups (b) photo arrays, and (c) lineups.

Questions for Critical Analysis

1. What are the two most significant legal concepts contained in the Fourth Amendment, and why are they important?

2. Suppose that a police officer stops a person who "looks funny." The person acts strangely, so the police officer decides to frisk him. The officer feels a bulge in the suspect's coat pocket, which turns out to be a bag of cocaine. Would the arrest for cocaine possession hold up in court? Why or why not?

3. What continues to be the best indicator of probable cause in the face of no hard and fast definitions?

4. How does the expression "fruit of the poisoned tree" relate to the issue of searches and seizures?

5. Is it possible for a person legally to be under arrest without an officer indicating to that person that she or he is in fact under arrest? Explain.

6. Are there any circumstances in which an officer can make a warrantless arrest for a crime that is a misdemeanor? Explain.

7. What is the difference between an arrest warrant and a search warrant?

8. A police officer has an arrest warrant for Jones. He enters Jones's house, presents the warrant, and handcuffs Jones. The officer then searches the house thoroughly and finds what appears to be stolen jewelry in an upstairs bedroom. If you were Jones's defense attorney, what defense would you raise?

9. "A person always assumes the risk that her or his conversation may be monitored by the police." Is there any truth to this statement? Why or why not?

10. What effect have the numerous Supreme Court rulings on the exclusionary rule had on police work?

Selected Print and Electronic Resources

SUGGESTED READINGS

Leo, Richard A., et al., eds., *The Miranda Debate: Law, Justice, and Policing*, Boston, MA: Northeastern University Press, 1998. This book presents an anthology of key writings on the 1966 *Miranda v. Arizona* ruling. The book is divided into four sections: the first reviews the pre-*Miranda* law of confessions; the second explores the legal and ethical dimensions of the *Miranda* decision; the third examines how the *Miranda* decision works in the real world; and the fourth presents a discussion of challenges to the decision.

Lewis, Anthony, *Gideon's Trumpet*, New York: Vantage Books, 1989. The author goes into the background of the landmark case created by James Earl Gideon.

Gideon was in a Florida jail for breaking and entering with intent to commit a misdemeanor. He wrote a letter in pencil to the United States Supreme Court, claiming that his constitutional rights were violated when he was denied the right to have an attorney at his trial. In the end, the Supreme Court agreed. This is the story of one man's improbable battle and the Court's ultimate decision in his favor.

McWhirter, Darien A., *Search, Seizure, and Privacy: Exploring the Constitution*, Phoenix, AZ: Oryx Press, 1994. This short book examines major privacy and search and seizure issues that the Supreme Court has addressed. It examines protecting property and privacy, searching homes and businesses, as well as the exclusionary rule. There is a glossary and a list of justices.

MEDIA RESOURCES

The Thin Blue Line (1988) This documentary painstakingly reproduces key moments in the twenty-month investigation of a wrongfully convicted young drifter named Randall Adams. Adams was wrongfully convicted of murdering a Dallas police officer named Robert Wood in 1976. The chief witness against Adams, David Harris, confesses during the last few moments of this "docudrama" to the murder of Wood. In addition to interviews, the director of this film uses staged reconstructions of the murder of Wood. Some people have called this film more like a waking nightmare than a docudrama.

Critically analyze this film:

1. Provide a general assessment of the police as portrayed in this documentary. Given what you have learned in this chapter about police procedure, do you believe that they followed the letter of the law, or did they allow discretion to supersede their constitutional obligations?

2. It is insinuated by a number of those interviewed that if Robert Wood and his partner had followed department guidelines in handling traffic violations, they would not have placed themselves in such a dangerous position. Do you agree? Why? Also, what does this particular aspect of the film seem to say about the importance of police officers following procedure as opposed to relying on discretion?

3. The Texas jury quickly sentenced Adams to death in his 1977 trial. His sentence, though, was later commuted to life in prison. How might this docudrama be used by opponents of the death penalty?

4. A staff writer for the *Washington Post*, Desson Howe, claimed that this docudrama was "an awesome indictment of America." What did he mean and do you agree with him?

Logging On

For a useful summary of the history of the exclusionary rule, you can go to a Web site developed by Edward M. Hendrie, a special agent for the Drug Enforcement Administration and a legal instructor at the FBI Academy. Go to:

www.fbi.gov/leb/sep697.htm

You can learn more about the no-knock entry standard as developed by another legal instructor at the FBI Academy, Michael J. Bulzomi: Go to:

www.fbi.gov/leb/may976.htm

You can read the dissenting opinion in *Miranda v. Arizona* by going to:

www.tourolaw.edu/patch/Miranda/White.html

You can see a debate on the *Miranda* decision by using Real Video (part of your RealPlayer). Simply go to:

www.ncpa.org/press/miranda813pr.html

When you get to that site, you can click on "See debate in Real Video."

Using the internet for Criminal Justice Analysis

INFOTRAC®
COLLEGE EDITION

1. Go to InfoTrac College Edition at www.infotrac-college.com/wadsworth/ After you log on, type in: **"COULD THIS BE THE END OF FOURTH AMENDMENT PROTECTION FOR MOTORISTS?"**

   This is an article that analyzes the Supreme Court ruling in *Whren v. United States*.

   a. What was the main ruling in *Whren v. United States*?

   b. Why are subjective intentions so important in this area of criminal procedure?

   c. What is the "pretextual" search or seizure?

   d. What other cases that the Supreme Court decided had to do with this same issue?

   e. On what basis did the defendants move to suppress the physical evidence in the case *Whren v. United States*?

   f. In the conclusion of this article, what three "problems" does the author see in the *Whren* decision?

2. In this exercise you can learn more about arrest warrants. The City of Belmont, California, police department has information about both bench and arrest warrants. Go to:

www. belmont.gov/localgov/bpd/wrnt.html

a. What is the difference between a bench warrant and an arrest warrant?

b. Are bench warrants served any differently than arrest warrants?

c. According to this home page, what must be specified in a warrant of arrest?

d. Under what circumstances will a person designated in a warrant of arrest for a misdemeanor offense be released on the issuance of a citation?

e. If a person specified in a warrant of arrest, even for a misdemeanor offense, cannot provide personal identification, will he or she be released on the issuance of such a citation?

3. Find out more about electronic surveillance by going to:

www.directhit.com

Type in the words "**ELECTRONIC SURVEILLANCE**."

a. How many sources are available for electronic surveillance devices?

b. Are there any requirements for purchasing such surveillance equipment?

c. What seems to be the most popular electronic surveillance device for which information is available on the Internet?

Notes

1. Appellee's Motion to Dismiss or Affirm at 4–5, *Mapp v. Ohio*, 367 U.S. 643 (1961).
2. 367 U.S. 643 (1961).
3. *Ibid.*, 659.
4. Jayme S. Walker, "Applying an Understanding of the Fourth Amendment," *The Police Chief* (July 1995), 44–7.
5. *Michigan v. Summers*, 452 U.S. 692 (1981).
6. *Brinegar v. United States*, 338 U.S. 160 (1949).
7. Keith Shotzberger, "Twenty-Sixth Annual Review of Criminal Procedure: Overview of the Fourth Amendment," *Georgetown Law Journal* 85 (April 1997), 821.
8. Rolando V. del Carmen, *Criminal Procedure for Law Enforcement Personnel* (Monterey, CA: Brooks/Cole Publishing Co., 1987), 63–4.
9. *United States v. Leon*, 468 U.S. 897 (1984).
10. 232 U.S. 383 (1914).
11. 342 U.S. 165 (1952).
12. Potter Stewart, "The Road to *Mapp v. Ohio* and Beyond: The Origins, Development and Future of the Exclusionary Rule in Search-and-Seizure Cases," *Columbia Law Review* 83 (October 1983), 1365.
13. 430 U.S. 387 (1977).
14. 467 U.S. 431 (1984).
15. 468 U.S. 897 (1984).
16. 115 S.Ct. 1185, 1188 (1995).
17. Alan M. Dershowitz and John Hart Ely, "*Harris v. New York*: Some Anxious Observations on the Candor and Logic of the Emerging Nixon Majority," *Yale Law Journal* 80 (1971), 1219.
18. Yale Kamisar, "On the Fruits of Miranda Violations, Coerced Confessions, and Compelled Testimony," *Michigan Law Review* 93 (March 1995), 929.
19. "Jury's Mixed Verdict in Cop Trial," *UPI Online* (April 3, 1998).
20. Karen M. Hess and Henry M. Wrobleski, *Police Operation: Theory and Practice* (St. Paul, MN: West Publishing Co., 1997), 122.
21. 392 U.S. 1 (1968).
22. *Ibid.*, 20.
23. *Ibid.*, 21.
24. 449 U.S. 418 (1981).
25. *United States v. Place*, 462 U.S. 696 (1983).
26. *Minnesota v. Dickerson*, 508 U.S. 366 (1993).
27. *Black's Law Dictionary*, 109–10.
28. Rolando V. del Carmen and Jeffrey T. Walker, *Briefs of Leading Cases in Law Enforcement* 2d ed. (Cincinnati, OH: Anderson, 1995), 38–40.
29. *Florida v. Royer*, 460 U.S. 491 (1983).
30. See also *United States v. Mendenhall*, 446 U.S. 544 (1980).
31. del Carmen, *Criminal Procedure*, 97–8.
32. 514 U.S. 927 (1995).
33. Linda J. Collier and Deborah D. Rosenbloom, *American Jurisprudence*, 2d ed. (Rochester, NY: Lawyers Cooperative Publishing, 1995), 122.
34. 495 U.S. 91 (1990).
35. Wayne R. Lefave and Jerold H. Israel, *Criminal Procedure* (St. Paul, MN: West Publishing Co., 1985), 141–4.
36. David Orlin, Jacob Thiessen, Kelli C. McTaggart, Lisa Toporek, and James Pearl, "Warrantless Searches and Seizures," in "Twenty-Sixth Annual Review of Criminal Procedure," *Georgetown Law Journal* 85 (April 1997), 847.
37. 445 U.S. 573 (1980).
38. 451 U.S. 204 (1981).
39. Andrew J. Purcell, "Feeling Violated: Seventh Circuit Puts the Squeeze on Fourth Amendment Rights of Bus Travelers," *John Marshall Law Review* 31 (Fall 1997), 245.
40. *United States v. McDonald*, 100 F.3d 1320, 1327 (7th Cir. 1996), cert. denied, 117 S.Ct. 2423 (1997).
41. 389 U.S. 347 (1967).

42. *Ibid.*, 361.

43. *Coolidge v. New Hampshire,* 403 U.S. 443, 467 (1971).

44. del Carmen, *Criminal Procedure,* 158.

45. *United States v. Ramirez,* 96 U.S. 1469 (1998).

46. *Katz v. United States,* 389 U.S. 347, 357 (1967).

47. 414 U.S. 234–235 (1973).

48. 395 U.S. 752 (1969).

49. *United States v. McDonald,* 855 F. Supp. 267, 268, n.2 (S.D. Ind. 1994).

50. *Bumper v. North Carolina,* 391 U.S. 543 (1960).

51. 412 U.S. 218 (1973).

52. Ian D. Midgley, "Just One Question before We Get to *Ohio v. Robinette:* "Are You Carrying Any Contraband . . . Weapons, Drugs, Constitutional Protections . . . Anything Like That?" *Case Western Reserve Law Review* 48 (Fall 1997), 173.

53. 117 S. Ct. 417, 419 (1996).

54. Linda Greenhouse, "Supreme Court Upholds Police Methods in Vehicle Drug Searches," *New York Times* (November 19, 1996), A23.

55. 435 U.S. 454 (1981).

56. 267 U.S. 132 (1925).

57. *United States v. Ross,* 456 U.S. 798, 804–9 (1982); and *Chambers v. Maroney,* 399 U.S. 42, 44, 52 (1970).

58. 434 U.S. 106 (1977).

59. 517 U.S. 806 (1996).

60. 519 U.S. 408 (1997).

61. 119 S.Ct. 484 (1998).

62. *Ibid.*

63. 433 U.S. 11–13 (1977).

64. 403 U.S. 443 (1971).

65. Dan Gunter, "The Plain View Doctrine and the Problem of Interpretation: The Case of *State v. Barnum,*" *Oregon Law Review* 75 (Summer 1996), 577.

66. *Arizona v. Hicks,* 480 U.S. 321 (1987).

67. 18 U.S.C. Sections 2510–2521 (1988).

68. *Commonwealth v. Vitello,* 367 Mass. 224, 327 N.E.2d 819, 833 (1975).

69. 388 U.S. 42 (1967).

70. 18 U.S.C. Sections 2510(7), 2518(1)(a), 2516 (1994).

71. *On Lee v. United States,* 343 U.S. 747 (1952).

72. Christopher K. Murphy, "Electronic Surveillance," in "Twenty-Sixth Annual Review of Criminal Procedure," *Georgetown Law Journal* (April 1997), 920.

73. *United States v. Nguyen,* 46 F.3d 781, 783 (8th Cir. 1995).

74. *Brown v. Mississippi,* 297 U.S. 278 (1936).

75. 378 U.S. 478 (1964).

76. *Miranda v. Arizona,* 384 U.S. 436 (1966).

77. H. Richard Uviller, *Tempered Zeal* (Chicago: Contemporary Books, 1988), 188–98.

78. *Orozco v. Texas,* 394 U.S. 324 (1969); *Oregon v. Mathiason,* 429 U.S. 492 (1977); *California v. Beheler,* 463 U.S. 1121 (1983).

79. 638 F.2d 582 (3d Cir. 1980).

80. del Carmen, *Criminal Procedure,* 267–8.

81. Patrick Malone, "You Have the Right to Remain Silent: *Miranda* after Twenty Years," *American Scholar* 55 (1986), 367.

82. Richard A. Leo, "The Impact of *Miranda* Revisited," *Journal of Criminal Law and Criminology* 86 (Spring 1996), 621–92.

83. Kimberly A. Crawford, "Intentional Violations of *Miranda:* A Strategy for Liability," *The FBI Law Enforcement Bulletin* (August 1997), 27–32.

84. *Michigan v. Tucker,* 417 U.S. 433 (1974); *Oregon v. Elstad,* 470 U.S. 298 (1985).

85. 401 U.S. 222 (1971).

86. Alan M. Dershowitz, "A Requiem for the Exclusionary Rule," in *Taking Liberties: A Decade of Hard Cases, Bad Laws, and Bum Raps* (Chicago: Contemporary Books, 1988), 10.

87. 97 F.2d 4750 (4th Cir. 1999).

88. 18 U.S.C. Section 3501(a).

89. William Glaberson, "*Miranda* Ruling Faces Its Most Serious Challenge," *New York Times* (February 11, 1999), A1, A25.

90. *Ibid.*

91. William A. Geller, *Videotaping Interrogations and Confessions* (Washington, D.C.: U.S. Department of Justice, March 1993), 1–11.

92. Anne Krueger, "Coerced Confession: The Law Says NO," *San Diego Union & Tribune* (April 21, 1996), A1.

93. Paul G. Cassell, "The Grand Illusion of *Miranda's* Defenders," *Northwestern University Law Review* 90 (1996), 1118–1124.

94. 413 U.S. 300 (1973).

95. *United States v. Barker,* 988 F.2d 77, 78 (9th Cir. 1993).

96. 388 U.S. 218 (1967).

97. 406 U.S. 682 (1972).

98. 384 U.S. 757 (1966).

99. See Craig J. Uchida and Timothy S. Bynum, "Search Warrants, Motions to Suppress and 'Lost Cases': The Effects of the Exclusionary Rule in Seven Jurisdictions," *Journal of Criminal Law and Criminology* 81 (1991), 1034; and Peter F. Nardulli, "The Societal Cost of the Exclusionary Rule Revisited," *University of Illinois Law Review* (1987), 223.

100. Dave Hogan, "U.S. Judge Throws Out Explosive Evidence," *Portland Oregonian* (October 25, 1996), B13.

101. *People v. Leonardo Turriago* (1997 NY Slip Opinion 4468).

102. Harold J. Rothwax, *Guilty: The Collapse of Criminal Justice* (New York: Random House, 1996).

103. *Ibid.,* 41.

104. Uviller, 119.

105. *State v. Hardy,* 96 Minn. S.Ct. 1927 (1998).

106. Carl B. Klockars, "Getting around the Fourth Amendment," in *Thinking about Police,* 2d ed., ed. Carl B. Klockars and Stephen D. Mastrofski (New York: McGraw-Hill, 1991), 434–5.

107. Matthew Kauffman, "Court Rejects Misdated Warrant," *Hartford Courant* (September 26, 1995), B7.

108. Paul G. Cassell, "*Miranda's* Social Costs: An Empirical Reassessment," *Northwestern University Law Review* 90 (1996), 387.

chapter

7

Challenges to Effective Policing

Chapter Outline

Chapter Objectives

After reading this chapter, you should be able to:

1. Explain what is involved in background checks of prospective police officers.

2. Outline how police applicants are tested.

3. Identify the five basic values of the police subculture.

4. Explain what stressors are and list some of those found in police work.

5. Indicate some of the guidelines for the use of nondeadly force in most states.

6. Identify the three traditional forms of police corruption and explain why they are less significant today.

7. Explain what an ethical dilemma is and name the four categories of ethical dilemmas typically facing a police officer.

8. List the three types of police accountability systems and indicate which one is least important.

9. Identify the four steps in a typical internal affairs unit investigation.

10. Indicate what a Section 1983 violation is and list four possible such violations.

INTRODUCTION

In many ways, being a police officer is an extremely rewarding profession, offering opportunities to serve the community and "do good" that few other occupations can match. The job is not, however, an easy one. To understand the pressures a law enforcement officer can experience, one need only consider the testimony of a metropolitan police officer. In a single three-month period, twelve children were killed during this officer's watch. They included an eight- and nine-year-old brother and sister who hanged themselves using the same rope over a door jamb; a thirteen-year-old who found her father's shotgun and shot herself in the heart; seven- and nine-year-old boys who were shot and paralyzed in a drive-by shooting while they were playing in their front yard; and a four-year-old girl who had her head "blown off" by her six-year-old sister. "After all of these incidents," the officer said, "I was ready to go running and screaming out of the division."[1]

There is an ideal image of a police officer as a person who is trustworthy and brimming with integrity; she or he is able to retrieve a kitten from a tree one instant, catch a murder suspect the next, and return home each night flush with the satisfaction of keeping the streets safe for the rest of us. Reality is not quite so tidy. Society expects law enforcement officers to uphold the law while at the same time embodying the law, but the average police officer—even in a small, rural town—faces on-the-job situations that most Americans cannot imagine. As James Fyfe of Temple University explains, by telling police officers that we expect them to eradicate crime, we are putting them in a "no win war." Like some soldiers in such combat, Fyfe adds, "they commit atrocities."[2]

In this chapter, we will examine some of these "atrocities," such as police brutality and corruption. We will also consider the possible causes of police misconduct and review the steps that are being taken to ensure that it does not characterize law enforcement officers in the future. As these issues are discussed, it is important to remember that, in the words of one police administrator, "cops are not from another planet. Their backgrounds, their weaknesses, are the same as any other human beings. They are not descended from Planet Honest. We get them from Earth."[3]

"Police officers possess awesome powers. They perform their duties under hazardous conditions and with the vigilant public eye upon them. Police officers are permitted only a margin of error in judgment under conditions that impose high degrees of physical and mental stress. Their general responsibility to preserve peace and enforce the law carries with it the power... to use force—even deadly force."

—*United States Civil Rights Comission report* (1981)

RECRUITMENT AND TRAINING: BECOMING A POLICE OFFICER

Society expects a great deal from its police officers. We expect that they will be honest, fair, and hard working. We want police officers to apply force only as a last resort, yet be prepared and able to use it when necessary. We want our law enforcement officers to be free of biases and appreciative of the diverse cultures that make up our communities. Ultimately, we expect the police to use their authority for the greater good, and not abuse it to the detriment of society.

Undoubtedly, most police officers do meet our expectations, most of the time. In fact, many observers believe that the nation's police forces are operating at the highest level of service in American history. Part of the reason for this, as we shall see later in the chapter, can be attributed to a greater emphasis on holding police officers accountable for their actions. But police organizations deserve some of the credit as well, particularly for recent improvements in attracting and training new recruits.

In 1961, police expert James H. Chenoweth commented that the methods used to hire police officers had changed little since 1829 when the Metropolitan Police of London was created.[4] The past thirty years, however, have seen a number of improvements on the original model. Efforts have been made to diversify police rolls, and recruits in most police departments undergo a substantial array of tests and screens—discussed below—to determine their aptitude. Furthermore, annual starting salaries of up to $35,000, along with the opportunities offered by an interesting profession in the public service field, have attracted a wide variety of applicants to police work.

Basic Requirements

The selection process involves a number of steps, and each police department has a different method of choosing candidates. (See Figure 7.1.) Most agencies, however, require at a minimum that a police officer:

- Be a U.S. citizen.
- Not have been convicted of a felony.
- Have or be eligible to have a driver's license in the state where the department is located.
- Be at least twenty-one years of age.

Beyond these minimum requirements, police departments usually engage in extensive background checks, including drug tests; a review of the applicant's educational, military, and driving records; credit checks; interviews with spouses, acquaintances, and previous employers; and a Federal Bureau of Investigation (FBI) search to determine whether the applicant has been convicted of any criminal acts.[5] Police agencies generally require certain physical attributes in applicants: normally, they must be able to pass a physical agility or fitness test.

Age is also a factor, as few departments will accept candidates younger than twenty-one or older than forty-five. In some departments, the applicant must take a polygraph (lie detector) exam in conjunction with the background check. The results of the polygraph exam are often compared to the information from the background check to ensure that the applicant has not been deceptive. According to one recent study, around 20 percent of the

Figure **7.1** Becoming a Police Officer

In their efforts to hire more qualified future law enforcement officers, most police departments have recruits pass through a lengthy selection process before hiring. The employment procedures of the Albuquerque (New Mexico) Police Department, left, are fairly typical of the procedures followed by law enforcement organizations across the nation.

Most police departments also have a number of factors that automatically disqualify a person from employment. The following list, provided by the Amarillo (Texas) Police Department, is also fairly representative of national trends.

1. Any felony conviction

2. Any driving-under-the-influence-of-alcohol conviction

3. Any misdemeanor conviction within the past six months

4. Any illegal possession or use of controlled substance conviction other than marijuana

5. Use of marijuana over an extended period of time within the past three years

6. Three at-fault traffic accidents within the past three years

7. Eight moving violations within the past three years, or three moving violations within the past year

8. Suspended driver's license

9. History of bad debt

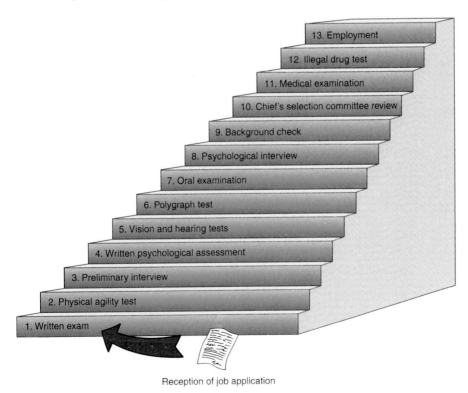

Reception of job application

13. Employment
12. Illegal drug test
11. Medical examination
10. Chief's selection committee review
9. Background check
8. Psychological interview
7. Oral examination
6. Polygraph test
5. Vision and hearing tests
4. Written psychological assessment
3. Preliminary interview
2. Physical agility test
1. Written exam

SOURCES: ALBUQUERQUE POLICE DEPARTMENT, AMARILLO POLICE DEPARTMENT.

nearly 70,000 persons who apply for police jobs annually are rejected because they lied during the screening process.[6]

Testing of Applicants

It would be difficult to find a profession that puts potential employees through a more strenuous series of tests than law enforcement. To start with, almost every police applicant must take a written examination, either the civil service examination or one designed by the department. The written exam attempts to measure the applicant's knowledge of basic information and ability to comprehend certain situations. The exam may also cover subjects such as mathematical ability and writing skills. The written examination is generally pass/fail, and the applicant must pass it to continue with the employment process.

After the written examination, the applicant usually moves on to *physical agility tests*. In the past, these tests have focused on the candidate's basic strength and endurance. In recent years, however, the tests have concentrated more on job-related physical skills that are necessary for the day-to-day work of a police officer. Consequently, many of the tests entail obstacle courses that approximate chasing after a fleeing suspect or jumping over a chain-link fence. (See Figure 7.2 for an example.)

Psychological Exams. Among the more controversial aspects of candidate testing are psychological examinations, which are used to determine whether an applicant's personality is suited to the rigors of police work. In theory, these tests help administrators gauge how a person will react to certain stressful circumstances. Although there are a number of personality tests, the Minnesota Multiphasic Personality Inventory (MMPI) is the most widely used. The MMPI asks the test taker to respond "true," "false," or "cannot say" to 550 statements. The Myers-Briggs Type Indicator uses multiple-choice questions to identify the subject as one of sixteen personality types, some of which are better suited to police work than others.

Although such tests can detect personality disorders, researchers are divided on whether they can predict that someone will make a "good" or a "bad" police officer.[7] One problem, according to critics, is that no psychological standard has been devised that can accurately predict future performance.[8] Another is that candidates may easily guess the "right" answer, even if it is not the truthful one. One personality test, for example, contains the following question:

> Today's society is a diverse one. On the job you are required to deal with people of all races, nationalities, religions and sexual orientations. Describe your ability to deal effectively with this varied group of people.[9]

If you want more information on how a police academy operates, go to the home page of the Oakland (California) Police Academy at www.occ.cc.mi.us/police/ Home.htm

Figure 7.2 The Physical Agility Exam for the Henrico County, Virginia, Division of Police

Those applying for the position of police officer at the Henrico County (Virginia) Division of Police must finish this physical agility exam within 3 minutes, 30 seconds. During the test, applicants are required to wear the equipment (with a total weight of between 9 and 13 pounds) worn by patrol officers, which includes (1) the police uniform, (2) leather gun belt, (3) firearm, (4) baton, (5) portable radio, and (6) ballistics vest.

1. Applicant begins test seated in a police vehicle, door closed, seat belt fastened.

2. Applicant must exit vehicle and jump or climb a six-foot barrier.

3. Applicant then completes a one-quarter mile run or walk, making various turns along the way (to simulate a pursuit run).

4. Applicant must jump a simulated five-foot culvert/ditch.

5. Applicant must drag a "human simulator" (dummy) weighing 175 pounds a distance of 50 feet (to simulate a situation in which an officer is required to pull or carry an injured person to safety).

6. Applicant must draw his or her weapon and fire five rounds with the strong hand and five rounds with the weak hand.

SOURCE: HENRICO COUNTY DIVISION OF POLICE.

Even an applicant with racist tendencies could easily provide an answer in keeping with the obvious spirit of the statement. Consequently, when determining a candidate's suitability for law enforcement, some police departments rely more heavily on behavioral patterns evident in the background check than on the results of personality tests.

Issues of Race and Gender. The nature of these examinations continues to generate controversy among minority communities, which claim that the tests are culturally biased in favor of white applicants. The MMPI, in particular, has been criticized for reflecting the "norms" and biases of the Anglo-Saxon dominated psychiatry profession. In the mid-1980s, the Chicago police department changed its testing process after noticing that a disproportionate number of African Americans were failing the psychological evaluation. The results changed when minority representatives were placed on the evaluating board.

Written examinations have also been criticized for discriminating against minorities. Police departments often respond by insisting that they will not lower entrance requirements to achieve racial quotas, a contention that can inflame the situation by implying that minority groups are not as qualified as whites. An official at the U.S. Department of Justice contends that it is not a question of qualification but of education and that entrance exams could be made more fair by concentrating on honesty and effective communication skills rather than reading and writing.[10]

As far as women are concerned, requirements for height, weight, and physical ability have historically been used to discourage recruitment. Following a series of court cases that successfully challenged these tests as discriminatory, most departments now measure recruits against other applicants of the same sex and general body size.[11] For example, to qualify for the Providence (Rhode Island) police department, a 25-year-old, 180-pound man must be able to bench-press 178 pounds, while a 25-year-old, 140-pound woman must be able to bench-press 83 pounds. Because women tend to be more flexible than men, a 32-year-old man must be able to reach half an inch beyond his toes in the "sit-and-reach" test, whereas a 32-year-old woman must reach 3.3 inches beyond her toes.[12] The topic of recruiting both women and minority police candidates, as well as the importance of having a diverse police force, will be discussed at length in Chapter 18.

Educational Requirements

One of the most dramatic differences between today's police recruits and those of several generations ago is their level of education. In the 1920s, when August Vollmer began promoting the need for higher education in police officers, few had attended college. By the 1990s, 65 percent of police officers had some college credits and 25 percent were college graduates.[13] Today, 95 percent of all police departments require at least a high school degree. Recruits with college or university experience are generally seen as having an advantage in hiring and promotion.[14]

The assumption in many police administrative offices is that higher education provides recruits with a number of advantages, including the following, identified by the Police Executive Research Forum:

- Greater maturity and a broad base of information to use in making decisions.
- A greater knowledge, particularly among criminal justice majors, of American history, democratic principles, and constitutional values and rights, not to mention the "big picture" of American criminal justice.

Adam Kasanof at Columbia University, where he studied Latin before becoming a New York City police officer. Although police work is still not considered an intellectual activity, the ranks of departments across the country are more highly educated than at any time in this nation's history. Many officers such as Kasanof are graduates from "elite" schools. They are sometimes considered "eggheads with a shield" by fellow officers. "If someone is overly academic," notes one police researcher, "there is an inclination to question whether they can handle themselves in a street condition." Members of academia also question the life of a cop for an Ivy Leaguer; one of Kasanof's professors called him a "saintly madman." What stereotypes of the police profession do these attitudes reflect?

FIELD TRAINING
The segment of a police recruit's training in which he or she is removed from the classroom and placed on the beat, under the supervision of a senior officer.

POLICE SUBCULTURE
The values and perceptions that are shared by members of a police department and, to a certain extent, by all law enforcement agents. These values and perceptions are shaped by the unique and isolated existence of the police officer.

INFOTRAC®
COLLEGE EDITION

Greenberg, Martin. **The model precinct**: issues involving police training.

- A greater ability to make decisions without supervision and to adapt to innovative strategies such as community policing and problem-solving policing.

- A greater understanding and tolerance of persons from different ethnic and educational backgrounds and an ability to communicate with those persons.[15]

Certain studies have also provided statistical support for the benefits of educated police officers, showing, for example, that increased education appears to lead to decreased complaint rates.[16]

Not all police observers believe, however, that education is a necessity for police officers. In the words of one police officer, "effective street cops learn their skills on the job, not in a classroom."[17] By emphasizing a college degree, say some, police departments discourage those who would make solid officers but lack the education necessary to apply for positions in law enforcement.

Training

A candidate may be in top physical condition, have a college degree and an impeccable background, and exhibit the perfect personality to be a law enforcement officer, but still be woefully unprepared for police work. Almost every state requires that police recruits pass through a training period during which they are taught the basics of police work and are under constant observation by superiors. The training period usually has two components: the police academy and field training.

The *police academy*, run by either the state or a police agency, provides recruits with a controlled, militarized environment in which they receive their introduction to the world of the police officer. They are taught the laws of search, seizure, arrest, and interrogation; how and when to use weapons; the procedures of securing a crime scene and interviewing witnesses; first aid; self-defense and other essentials of police work. Figure 7.3 shows a typical curriculum at a police academy. Academy instructors evaluate the recruits' performance and send intermittent progress reports to police administrators. (See *Careers in Criminal Justice* on the next page).

Figure 7.3 The Curriculum at the University of Maryland Police Academy

Course	Hours Required	Course	Hours Required
Accident Investigation	23.5	Defensive Tactics/Physical Training	91
Arrest Processing Procedures	4.5	DWI Enforcement	32
Arrest Practicals and Building Searches	20	Emergency/Crisis Intervention	16
Arrest/Search Warrants and Statement of Charges	8	Emergency Vehicle Operations Course	40
Automobile Theft	4	Fingerprint Practicals	6
Bloodborne Pathogens	3*	Firearms Training	80
Child Abuse/Battered Spouse	3	First Respondent/CPR	40
Civil Process	3	Hazardous Materials	4
Community Policing	8	Interview and Interrogation	4
Contemporary Issues in Law Enforcement	5	Juvenile Offenders	2.5
Copntrolled Dangerous Substances/Use of Informants	8	Maryland Correctional System	2
Courtroom Security	2	Testifying in Court	6.5
Crime Prevention	2.5	Patrol Procedures	11
Crime Scene Search	16	Police Records and Computers	2
Criminal/Constitutional Law	42.5	Radio Procedures	2.5
Criminal Investigations	14	Rape Trauma Syndrome/Sex Offenders	3.5
Crowd Control	8	Report Writing	38
Deaf Awareness	2	Traffic Arrest Practicals	20
		Stress Management	2
		Traffic Law	34

*IN THIS COURSE, THE STUDENT RECEIVES INSTRUCTION ON THE PROPER HANDLING OF BOTH INDIVIDUALS AND EQUIPMENT WITH REGARD TO HIV AND HEPATITIS B VIRUSES.

SOURCE: UNIVERSITY OF MARYLAND POLICE ACADEMY, SESSION XVI.

Field training takes place outside the confines of the police academy. A recruit is paired with an experienced police officer known as a field training officer (FTO). The goal of field training is to help rookies apply the concepts they have learned in the academy "to the streets," with the FTO playing a

Careers in Criminal Justice

PETER JOHN MANTELLO, TRAINING COORDINATOR FOR THE VERMONT CRIMINAL JUSTICE TRAINING COUNCIL

Imagine that you are a high school student and observe a "bully" who "picked" a fight with a mentally challenged person whom the bully flipped on his back. While everybody was laughing at the incident, you stood there and did absolutely nothing to help the mentally challenged person. Two years later this mentally challenged person was killed during a robbery at a gas station where he worked. This true-life incident seared my heart with the desire to serve in the police profession. I started by getting a Bachelor of Arts degree in Sociology/Criminal Justice, and I am now in the process of completing a Master's in Educational Leadership. You should never stop learning in the police profession.

My experience in the police profession has covered thirteen years. In 1986, I enlisted in the U.S. Army as a Military Policeman and spent three years stationed in the Republic of Panama. The experience of an overseas assignment really prepared me for the profession. In March 1989, I was hired as a full-time police professional for the town of Woodstock, Vermont. Because of the size of the department, my duties varied from patrol officer involved in Juvenile Services to conducting sexual abuse investigations as a Corporal. I left Woodstock in 1995 and was hired as a Training Specialist in the Vermont Criminal Justice Training Council. In 1996, I was promoted to a Training Coordinator with primary duties in basic training for full-time and part-time police professionals for certifications in the state of Vermont. Vermont is a rural state and unique because it has only one police academy that all officers

(whether they are from a municipality, county, or other state agency) attend for state certification. My primary responsibilities are coordinating, scheduling, instructing (my expertise is in Physical Training, Use of Force, and Firearms), and supervising police candidates in a thirteen-week residential program that certifies officers to enforce the law and service the community. My secondary responsibilities are working part-time in the municipality of Brandon, Vermont, as a special officer, and I am assigned to the U.S. Army Reserves in the 98th Division as a Drill Sergeant located in Manchester, NH. In those thirteen years in the police profession my heart has always been in the community that I serve. A major challenge for the police community is how to serve the local community and yet maintain a sense of security for the officer. Invariably every police officer has to develop a sense of trust. Through the process of serving the community the officer lowers his or her "defenses" in order to gain that trust. In America today the police profession needs to have that balance of community involvement and tactical awareness. Police professionals need to assume many different roles in order to be effective in the profession. Enforcing laws is just one role of the job and being tactful in enforcing those laws is very important. People who are interested in the police profession must realize that they are servants of the community and, whether they like it or not, they are role models for that community. During my years as a full-time police professional I was personally involved in mentoring young people to become responsible and accountable for their actions.

Now I train police candidates to be role models for their communities and have tactical awareness. In the past three years I have counseled many police candidates and have discovered that each candidate has a different motive for being in the

police profession. Today, if a candidate "wants in" the police profession he/she needs to have a commitment to service, a sense of humility, a disciplined lifestyle, and a proactive thinking mind. If they do not have the right attitude, then discipline and motivation are key factors that develop those attitudes in the candidates. Police professionals are leaders who need to lead by example and be genuinely concerned with the community that they serve. As one instructor once told me, "You lead people—You manage things." To teach police candidates to develop those traits trainers must challenge them mentally and physically. All police candidates should know their limitations so they can be prepared for most situations. This in turn diminishes their anxiety and makes them more effective at their jobs. My biggest challenge and fulfillment as a Training Coordinator is leading and motivating police candidates to be leaders in their community.

supervisory role to make sure that nothing goes awry. According to many, the academy introduces recruits to the formal rules of police work, but field training gives the rookies their first taste of the informal rules. In fact, the initial advice to recruits from some FTOs is along the lines of "O.K., kid. Forget everything you learned in the academy. You're in the real world now." Nonetheless, the academy is a critical component in the learning process as it provides rookies with a road map to the job.

"US VERSUS THEM": POLICE SUBCULTURE

"Us versus them": these words are often a recruit's introduction to **police subculture,** a broad term used to describe the basic assumptions and values that permeate law

SOCIALIZATION

The process through which a police officer is taught the values and expected behavior of the police subculture.

BLUE CURTAIN

A metaphorical term used to refer to the value placed on secrecy and the general mistrust of the outside world shared by many police officers.

"The police subculture permits and sometimes demands deception of courts, prosecutors, defense attorneys, and defendants."

—Jerome Skolnick, *Professor of law,* University of California at Berkeley (1966)

enforcement agencies and are taught to new members of a law enforcement agency as the proper way to think, perceive, and act.[18] Every organization has a subculture, with values shaped by the particular aspects and pressures of that organization. In the police subculture, those values are formed in an environment characterized by danger, stress, boredom, and violence.

The Core Values of Police Subculture

From the first day on the job, rookies begin the process of **socialization,** in which they are taught the values and rules of police work. This process is aided by a number of rituals that are common to the law enforcement experience. Police theorist Harry J. Mullins believes that the following rituals are critical to the police officer's acceptance, and even embrace, of police subculture.

- Attending a recruit academy.
- Working with a senior officer, who passes on the "lessons" of police work and life to the younger officer.
- Making the initial felony arrest.
- Using force to make an arrest for the first time.
- Using or witnessing deadly force for the first time.
- Witnessing major traumatic incidents for the first time.[19]

Each of these rituals makes it clear to the police officer that this is not a "normal" job. The only other people who can understand the stresses of police work are fellow officers, and consequently law enforcement officers tend to insulate themselves from civilians. Eventually, the insulation breeds mistrust, and the police officer develops an "us versus them" outlook toward those outside the force.[20]

One group of researchers described the police subculture as having five basic values:

1. Only a police officer can understand the "true" nature of police work. No one else—from lawyers to politicians to civilians—has any concept of the day-to-day challenges facing an officer.

2. The police officer is the only real crime fighter.

3. The courts have placed too many restrictions on police operations; to fight crime effectively, the police officer is forced to bend, if not break, these rules.

4. The public is fickle when it comes to police work. Civilians are quick to criticize a police officer's actions unless they need help from one themselves.

5. Loyalty is the highest virtue among police officers because everybody else is "out to get" the police and make their job more difficult.[21]

In sum, these core values create what sociologist William Westly called the **blue curtain,** also known as the "blue wall of silence" or simply "the code."[22] This curtain separates the police from the civilians they are meant to protect.

Police Cynicism

Though people become involved in police work for many different reasons, a common theme among young recruits is that they want to "serve society." This idealism tends to dissipate when the new officer is confronted with a public that seems hostile or indifferent and a justice system that appears to routinely allow criminals to go free. Slowly, the idealism is replaced with cynicism.[23]

A cynic is someone who universally distrusts human motives and expects nothing but the worst from human behavior. **Police cynicism** is characterized by a rejection of the ideals of truth and justice—the very values that an officer is sworn to uphold.[24] As cynical police officers lose respect for the law, they replace legal rules with those learned in the police subculture, which are believed to be more reflective of "reality." The implications for society can be an increase in police misconduct, corruption, and brutality.[25]

For those law enforcement officers who believe most strongly in the ideals of police work, cynicism can come as a reaction not to external forces, but to internal ones. Seeing fellow officers engage in obvious misconduct, and yet be encouraged by superiors, can quickly turn an officer into a cynic. The cynicism is exacerbated by a feeling of helplessness—to report another officer's wrong-doing is a severe breach of the blue wall of silence. As one officer said:

> If you were to challenge somebody for something that was going on, they would say: "Listen, if the supervisor isn't saying anything, what the hell are you interjecting for? What are you, a rat?" You've gotta work with a lot of these guys. You go on a gun job, the next thing you know, you got nobody following you up the stairs.[26]

The officer's statement highlights one of the reasons why police subculture resonates beyond department walls—he has basically admitted that he will not report wrongdoing by his peers. In this manner, police subculture influences the actions of police officers, sometimes to the detriment of society. In the next two sections, we will examine two areas of the law enforcement work environment that help create police subculture and must be fully understood if the cynical nature of police subculture is ever to be changed: (1) the danger of police work and (2) the need for police officers to establish and maintain authority.[27]

THE PHYSICAL AND MENTAL DANGERS OF POLICE WORK

Vincent Pupo, Jr., and his partner Robert Insalaco, members of the Erie (New York) County Sheriff's Department, knocked on the door of Paul Olson, a suspected arsonist. When the door opened, Olson stood before the officers completely naked. In a moment of shock, neither noticed that Olson was holding a .44 Magnum, which he pointed at Deputy Insalaco. Olson shot the officer in the face, killing him.[28]

Police officers face the threat of physical harm every day. According to the U.S. Department of Justice, police have one of the most dangerous jobs in the United States (along with taxi drivers, private security guards, and prison guards), with 306 of every 1,000 officers targets of nonfatal violence each year.[29] In 1997–98, more than 300 police officers were killed in the line of duty.[30] (See Figure 7.4).

POLICE CYNICISM
The suspicion that citizens are weak, corrupt, and dangerous. This outlook is the result of a police officer being constantly exposed to civilians at their worst and can negatively affect the officer's performance.

Figure 7.4 Police Officers Killed on Duty in the 1990s

The Officer Down Memorial Page (www.odmp.org) has recorded the name of every law enforcement officer killed in the United States since 1794. The site provides information such as name, city, and cause of death for all officers who died in the line of the duty in the 1990s.

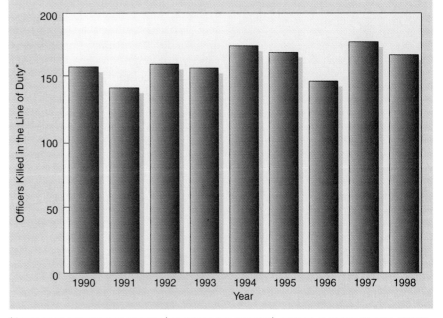

*CAUSE OF DEATH INCLUDES ASSAULT (SHOOTINGS AND STABBING), AS WELL AS HEART ATTACKS, DROWNING, AUTOMOBILE ACCIDENTS, ETC.

SOURCE: OFFICER DOWN MEMORIAL PAGE.

The casket containing the body of slain police officer Thomas A. Hamlette is carried from the Southeast Washington, D. C. church were services were held. Hamlette was one of nine D.C. police officers shot and killed from 1993 and 1998. What are some of the other occupational threats that police officers face on a daily basis?

Occupational Safety

In a sense, the greatest threat to law enforcement officers is not an armed criminal or a speeding car, but their own level of awareness, or lack thereof.[31] Police tactician Charles Remsberg believes that officers have five general states of awareness, from condition white to condition red (see Figure 7.5).[32] Condition white, in which officers have slipped into the complacency of a routine, can be fatal, as in the case of Officers Pupo and Insalaco. The ideal mental state for an officer in Remsberg's spectrum is condition yellow: alert, but relaxed.

Training is a crucial aspect of officer safety. For example, every law enforcement officer should receive specific guidance on how to handle people who are intoxicated. A recent study by the Behavioral Sciences Unit of the FBI found that more than three-fourths of those interviewed who had killed a law enforcement officer were under the influence of alcohol, drugs, or both at the time of the homicide.[33] Officers need training in how to recognize the signs of intoxication (such as slurred speech and belligerence) and the "warning flags" of when an intoxicated person is about to become violent (for example, subject's hands not visible, subject in or near a motor vehicle).[34]

In addition to training, protective equipment can improve an officer's chances in a dangerous situation. On January 3, 1997, Deputy Sheriff Henry "Bo" Huff of the Walton County (Georgia) Sheriff's Office was shot twice with a 9-mm pistol by a youth he had pulled over for a traffic violation. Huff escaped without serious injury because he was wearing a ballistic vest; he thus became the 2,000th member of the "Survivor's Club," a list of law enforcement officers from around the country who have avoided injury by wearing some sort of body armor.[35]

Stress

In the months after his partner's death, Officer Pupo continually played the "What If" Game. "What if I had been faster with my gun?" he would ask himself. "What if we had waited for more officers? What if I had been standing on his side?" Eventually, Pupo found the best way he could deal with his guilt was by drinking.

Law enforcement officers are 300 percent more likely to suffer from alcoholism than the average American.[36] The average life expectancy of a police officer is fifty-seven years, compared to seventy-one for the general public—a statistic that can be attributed to police officers' top ranking among professions in rates of heart disease, hypertension, and diabetes.[37] The social isolation police officers must deal with also leads to one of the highest divorce rates of any job, which adds to stress. According to the U.S. Bureau of Labor Statistics, policing is one of the ten most stressful occupations in the country, along with firefighting, driving a taxi, and being a surgeon.[38]

Figure 7.5 The Awareness Spectrum

As you see here, the awareness spectrum for police officers has five stages, or conditions. According to the spectrum's creator, the ideal mental state for an officer is condition yellow.

Condition Black	Condition Red	Condition Orange	Condition Yellow	Condition White
State of panic, perhaps blacked out or even dead	Continual feeling of nervous worry	State of alarm	Relaxed, but alert and aware of surroundings	Unaware of surroundings, not paying attention to environment

SOURCE: ADAPTED FROM CHARLES REMSBERG, THE TACTICAL EDGE: SURVIVING HIGH-RISK PATROL (NORTHBROOK, IL: CALIBRE PRESS, 1986), 47–51.

Police Stressors. The conditions that cause stress—such as worries over finances, relationships, and so on—are known as **stressors.** Each profession has its own set of stressors, but police are particularly vulnerable to occupational pressures and stress factors, such as the following:

1. The constant fear of becoming a victim of violent crime.

2. Exposure to violent crime and its victims.

3. The need to comply with the law in nearly every job action.

4. Lack of community support.

5. Negative media coverage.

Police face a number of internal pressures as well, such as limited opportunities for career advancement, excessive paperwork, and low wages and benefits.[39] The unconventional hours of shift work can also place pressure on an officer's private life and contribute to a lack of sleep. Each of these is a primary stressor associated with police work.[40]

The Consequences of Police Stress. Aside from the health risks already mentioned, police stress can manifest itself in different ways. If stress becomes overwhelming, an officer may suffer from **burnout,** a condition in which he or she becomes listless and ineffective due to mental and physical exhaustion. Another police problem related to stress is *post-traumatic stress disorder (PTSD)*. Often recognized in war veterans and rape victims, PTSD is a reaction to a stressor that would evoke significant distress in the average person—such stressors in police work would include a riot or a shoot-out. When experiencing PTSD, an officer will:

1. Re-experience the traumatic event through nightmares and flashbacks.

2. Become decreasingly involved with the outside world by withdrawing from others and refusing to participate in normal social interactions.

3. Experience "survival guilt," which may lead to loss of sleep and memory impairment.[41]

The effects of stress can be seen most tragically in the high rate of suicide among law enforcement officers—three times higher than that of the general population.[42]

AUTHORITY AND THE USE OF FORCE

If the police subculture is shaped by the dangers of the job, it often finds expression through authority. The various symbols of authority that decorate a police officer—including the uniform, badge, nightstick, and firearm—establish the power she or he holds over civilians. At the same time, many police officers feel that authority does not necessarily bring respect. Even though citizens may defer to the powers vested in the officer by the state, they do not respect the person who wears the uniform or carries the badge. Therefore, the manner in which police officers use their authority ultimately determines whether they are respected.

For better or for worse, both police officers and civilians tend to equate terms such as *authority* and *respect* with the ability to use force. Near the turn of the twentieth century, a police officer stated that his job was to "protect the good people and treat the crooks rough."[43] Implicit in the officer's statement is the idea that to do the protecting, he had to do some roughing up as well. This attitude toward the use of force is still with us today. Indeed, it is gener-

STRESSORS
The aspects of police work and life that lead to feelings of stress.

BURNOUT
A mental state that occurs when a person suffers from exhaustion and is incapable of maintaining acceptable standards of performance as the result of overwork and stress.

INFOTRAC ®
COLLEGE EDITION

Finn, Peter and Julie Esselman Tomz. Using peer supporters to help address law enforcement stress.

Police Stressline, which provides law enforcement officers with tips on managing stress, also offers a window into the challenges of police work. Go to www.geocities.com/HotSprings/Spa/7762/index.html

ally accepted that not only is police use of force inevitable, but that police officers who are unwilling to use force in certain circumstances cannot do their job effectively.[44] (See *CJ in Focus—The Balancing Act: Turning a Blind Eye toward Police Force.*)

The "Misuse" of Force

In the first study of its kind, the Department of Justice estimated that law enforcement officers threatened to use force or used force (including the use of handcuffs) in encounters with more than 700,000 Americans in 1996.[45] (See Figure 7.6.) Of course, police officers are often justified in using force to protect themselves or other citizens. At the same time, few observers would be naïve enough to believe that police are *always* justified in the use of force. How, then, is "misuse" of force to be defined?

One attempt to qualify excessive force that has been lauded by legal scholars, if not necessarily by police officers, was offered by the Christopher Commission. Established in Los Angeles after the beating of Rodney King in 1992, the commission advised that "an officer may resort to force only where he or she faces a credible threat, and then may only use the minimum amount necessary to control the subject."[46]

The Phoenix Study. Terms such as *credible* and *necessary* are, of course, quite subjective, rendering such definitions too vague to be practical. To better understand the subject, the Phoenix (Arizona) Police Department, in a partnership with Rutgers University and Arizona State University, implemented a study to measure how often police officers used force. The results showed that police used some form of "physical force"—defined as any "weaponless tactic" (such as kicking or shoving) or the threatened or actual use of any weapon—in 22 percent of the surveyed arrests.[47] The study also examined the predictors of force, that is, the factors that were present in the situations where force was used. As one might expect, the study found that the best predictor of police use of force was the suspect's use of force.[48]

Figure 7.6 The Use of Force by Police against Suspects

In 1996, police questioned nearly 4.5 million people who considered themselves to be suspects in a crime. About 8 percent of these self-perceived suspects were handcuffed, and about 8 percent either had force used against them or were threatened with force.

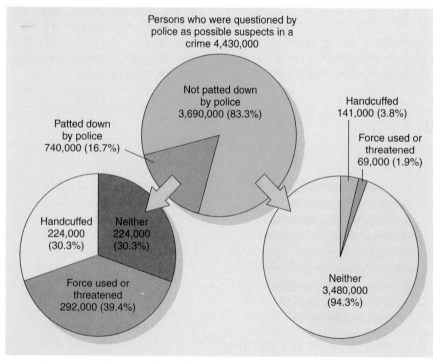

Persons who were questioned by police as possible suspects in a crime 4,430,000

Not patted down by police 3,690,000 (83.3%)

Patted down by police 740,000 (16.7%)

Handcuffed 141,000 (3.8%)

Force used or threatened 69,000 (1.9%)

Handcuffed 224,000 (30.3%)

Neither 224,000 (30.3%)

Force used or threatened 292,000 (39.4%)

Neither 3,480,000 (94.3%)

SOURCE: Adapted from Bureau of Justice Statistics, *Police Use of Force: Collection of National Data* (Washington, D.C.: U.S. Department of Justice, November 1997), Figure 8, page 13.

The Misuse of Force and Minorities. In its guidelines for the use of deadly force by undercover officers, the New York City Police Department warns its officers not to be victims of symbolic opponent syndrome, defined as a "preconceived notion that places suspects into a 'BAD GUY' category because of race, nationality, grooming or mode of dress."[49] The warning may seem self-evident, but it addresses a clear problem in law enforcement today. In the Department of Justice study mentioned earlier, African Americans and Hispanic Americans were found to be about 70 percent more likely to have contact with police than whites. Furthermore, the study revealed that those minority groups made up about half the people against whom force—being hit, pushed, choked, restrained by a police dog, or threat-

CJ in Focus
The Balancing Act
Turning a Blind Eye toward Police Force

Throughout this textbook, mention has been made of the sharp drop in violent crime in New York City over the past several years. While New York City Mayor Rudolph Giuliani and his various police commissioners basked in praise, a few observers pointed out that the statistics had a dark side. As crime rates declined, citizen complaints of excessive police force were on the rise. In 1993, the year Giuliani was elected, complaints about officer misbehavior in the city were at 3,500. By 1995, that number had surged to 5,600. In 1992, the city paid $13.5 million to those who sued the New York City Police Department (NYPD) for police brutality; three years later, such payments had more than doubled to $32 million.

Criticism of the mayor and the police department temporarily peaked in the summer of 1997, when four Brooklyn police officers were implicated in a brutal attack on a Haitian immigrant named Abner Louima. Two of the officers were charged with inserting a stick in Louima's rectum and then shoving it in his mouth. Even though it proved false, the rumor that one of the officers had said, "It's Giuliani time" while beating Louima fueled the notion that city administrators were encouraging an atmosphere in which police were out of control.

By aggressively carrying out the "broken windows" policy of cracking down on "quality-of-life" crimes such as public drunkenness and loitering (see Chapter 5), police were stretching their authority to unacceptable lengths. Furthermore, the Giuliani administration was perceived as being lenient toward problem officers. According to the American Civil Liberties Union of New York, only 1 percent of the citizen complaints lodged against city police officers since 1993 resulted in any disciplinary action. Even George Kelling, who helped develop the concept of "broken windows," disassociated himself from the NYPD's "zero tolerance" goals.

Giuliani and other city officials who are implementing similar crime-fighting programs appear to be paying more attention to voters than to criminologists. In general, Americans seem willing to tolerate excessive police force in return for lower rates of violent crimes. As arrests for misdemeanors rose 73 percent in New York City over a two-year period, 76 percent of city residents felt that Giuliani was doing a good job controlling crime.

For Critical Analysis: At what point should police authority to use force be curtailed, even if it can be proved that such force is an important factor in reducing violent crime?

---

ened by a gun—was used, even though they represented only a fifth of those surveyed.[50] The issue of police misuse of force against minorities is a significant one and will be explored in greater detail in Chapter 18.

Legal Restrictions on the Use of Force during Arrest

To comply with the various, and not always consistent, laws concerning the use of force during arrest, a police officer must first understand that there are two kinds of force: *nondeadly force* and *deadly force*. Each category has its own set of legal conditions.

Nondeadly Force. Most of the use of force by law enforcement officers comes under the category of *nondeadly force*, or force that is not likely to result in the serious injury or death of the subject. In most states, the use of nondeadly force is regulated by the concept of **reasonable force**, which holds that the use of nondeadly force is allowed when a reasonable person would assume that such force was necessary. In a recent Pennsylvania case, for example, a jury ruled that two police officers had used reasonable force in handcuffing a seventy-four-year-old disabled man. Although the incident left the man with injuries that required hospitalization, the jury agreed with the defense's argument that the police had to use force because the subject struggled to avoid being handcuffed.[51]

To provide some guidelines for nondeadly force, most states have indicated the circumstances in which such force is acceptable:

1. To prevent an escape.
2. To retake a suspect after an escape attempt.

REASONABLE FORCE
The degree of force that is appropriate to protect the police officer or other citizens and is not excessive.

Riot police in Huntington Park, California subdue one of about a dozen people arrested following a televised World Cup soccer match in 1998. Emotions from the game spilled into to streets and resulted in rock-and-bottle throwing incidents that required police intervention. Given the situation and what you can see in the photo, does the force that these police officers are using appear excessive? Explain your answer.

DEADLY FORCE
Force applied by a police officer that is likely or intended to cause death.

3. To overcome an offender's resistance to a lawful arrest.

4. To protect the officer from bodily injury.

5. To protect the suspect, other persons, or property from harm.[52]

The Supreme Court attempted to clarify the definition of "reasonable" force in *Graham v. Connor* (1989),[53] ruling that "not every push or shove" violated the suspect's Fourth Amendment rights to due process even if, in retrospect, the situation did not seem to warrant force. (See *CJ in Focus—Landmark Cases:* Graham v. Connor.)

Deadly Force. Some observers believe that the use of force should be based on the idea of a *use of force continuum* (see Figure 7.7). On one end of the continuum, cooperation by the suspect results in the officer using no force, whereas at the other end dangerous noncooperation by the suspect can bring about maximum force.[54] Otherwise known as **deadly force,** this is force that an objective officer realizes will place the subject in direct threat of serious injury or death.

Limits on the use of deadly force by law enforcement officers were set by the Supreme Court in *Tennessee v. Garner* (1985).[55] The case involved fifteen-year-old Edward Garner and Memphis, Tennessee, police officers Elton Hymon and Leslie Wright. Officers Hymon and Wright answered a call for service and were told by a woman that she had heard glass breaking in a neighboring home. While Wright radioed for back-up, Hymon went behind the home to investigate. He saw Garner running across the backyard and yelled, "Police! Halt!" Garner, unarmed with ten dollars that he had stolen from the house in his pocket, ignored the order and began to climb the backyard fence. Hymon proceeded to shoot Garner in the back of the head, killing him. Hymon testified that when he fired his weapon, he believed the boy was about to escape; Hymon said that he had been trained to shoot to keep a suspect from fleeing. At the time, Tennessee's *fleeing felon* law allowed police officers to apprehend fleeing suspects in this manner. The state appellate court ruled that Hymon's act was within the law's limits.[56]

Figure 7.7 The Use of Force Continuum

Many police departments are basing their use of force guidelines on the "use of force continuum." The concept behind this continuum is, as you can see, quite straightforward: the more resistance offered by a suspect, the more force used by the police.

Suspects	Police
0. No Response	0. No Force
1. Psychological Intimidation	1. Police Presence
2. Verbal Noncompliance	2. Verbal Comands
3. Passive Resistance	3. Control and Restraint (handcuffs)
4. Defensive Resistance	4. Chemical Agents
5. Active Agression	5. Tactics and Weapons*
6. Firearms/Deadly Force	6. Firearms/Deadly Force

*INCLUDES ALL PHYSICAL TACTICS AND WEAPONS.

SOURCE: ADAPTED FROM NATIONAL INSTITUTE OF JUSTICE, *UNDERSTANDING USE OF FORCE BY AND AGAINST THE POLICE* (WASHINGTON, D.C.: OFFICE OF JUSTICE PROGRAMS, NOVEMBER 1996), EXHIBIT 3, PAGE 5.

CJ in Focus
Landmark Cases:

Graham v. Connor

In 1984, diabetic Dethorne Graham was handcuffed and thrown against the hood of a car by Charlotte (North Carolina) Police Officer M. S. Connor and four other law enforcement officers. The vehicle carrying Graham had been pulled over for an investigative stop, and when Graham, who was having an insulin reaction, began acting strangely, Officer Connor assumed he was drunk. Graham, who was eventually released, suffered a broken foot and numerous cuts and sued the five individual officers and the city of Charlotte for depriving him of his constitutional right to be free of excessive force. Two lower courts ruled against Graham, noting that the force was "applied in good faith to maintain or restore order." The Supreme Court disagreed, in the process setting the standards that must be met in "use of force" cases.

Graham v. Connor
United States Supreme Court
490 U.S. 386 (1989)
http://laws.findlaw.com/US/490/386.html

In the Words of the Court . . .

Mr. Chief Justice Rehnquist, majority opinion

★ ★ ★ ★

Where, as here, the excessive force claim arises in the context of an arrest or investigatory stop of a free citizen, it is most properly characterized as one invoking the protections of the Fourth Amendment, which guarantees citizens the right "to be secure in their persons . . . against unreasonable . . . seizures" of the person.

★ ★ ★ ★

Determining whether the force used to effect a particular seizure is "reasonable" under the Fourth Amendment requires a careful balancing of "the nature and quality of the intrusion on the individual's Fourth Amendment interests" against the countervailing governmental interests at stake.

★ ★ ★ ★

The "reasonableness" of a particular use of force must be judged from the perspective of a reasonable officer on the scene, rather than with the 20/20 vision of hindsight. ★ ★ ★ With respect to a claim of excessive force, the same standard of reasonableness at the moment applies: "Not every push or shove, even if it may later seem unnecessary in the peace of a judge's chambers," violates the Fourth Amendment. The calculus of reasonableness must embody allowance for the fact that police officers are often forced to make split-second judgments—in circumstances that are tense, uncertain, and rapidly evolving—about the amount of force that is necessary in a particular situation.

★ ★ ★ ★

As in other Fourth Amendment contexts, however, the "reasonableness" inquiry in an excessive force case is an objective one: the question is whether the officers' actions are "objectively reasonable" in light of the facts and circumstances confronting them, without regard to their underlying intent or motivation. An officer's evil intentions will not make a Fourth Amendment violation out of an objectively reasonable use of force; nor will an officer's good intentions make an objectively unreasonable use of force constitutional.

Decision: The Court remanded the case, sending it back to the lower courts to be reconsidered. In doing so, it ended the common judicial practice of deciding excessive force cases based on whether the police officer had acted "in good faith" or "maliciously and sadistically for the very purpose of causing harm." A law officer's "evil intentions" for using force, the Court decided, were irrelevant. Instead, the Court ruled, excessive force cases should be decided by observing all the circumstances surrounding the incident, and then deciding whether the officer was "reasonable" in his or her decision to use force.

For Critical Analysis: Describe a hypothetical situation in which, in Chief Justice Rehnquist's words, an officer with "good intentions" engages in an "unreasonable use of force." Why should the officer in this situation be held liable for his actions, as they were made with good intentions?

In reviewing the case, the Supreme Court was not concerned with the actions of Officer Hymon, who had followed the law. Instead, the Court scrutinized the Tennessee statute itself, ultimately finding it unconstitutional:

> When the suspect poses no immediate threat to the officer and no threat to others, the use of deadly force is unjustified. . . . It is not better that all felony suspects die than that they escape.[57]

The Court's ruling forced twenty-three states to change their fleeing felon laws. It did not, however, completely eliminate police discretion in such situations: police officers may use deadly force if they have probable cause to believe that the fleeing suspect poses a threat of serious injury or death to the officers or others. In essence, the Court recognized the impossibility of creating guidelines to cover every eventuality. Police officers must be able to make split-second decisions without worrying about the legal ramifications. The Court tried to clarify this concept four years later in *Graham v. Connor* (discussed earlier) by stating that the deadly force should be judged by the "reasonableness of the moment." In practice, these decisions have made it difficult for police actions to be judged "unreasonable" in retrospect, unless those actions were clearly and unnecessarily violent.

Nonlethal Weapons

An important component in the use of force by police is the weapons that they use. Though no national statistics are kept, it is estimated that law enforcement officers in the nation's fifty largest cities are responsible for the combined deaths of between 200 and 300 civilians each year,[58] and police kill about 1,000 criminals or criminal suspects annually. The media often attribute these incidents to *rogue cops* (uncontrollable police officers with the same moral code as criminals), but many police departments are focusing on weaponry as much as personnel. As violent confrontations between officers and suspects are unavoidable, these departments wish to reduce the likelihood that such confrontations will lead to serious injury or death.[59] With that goal in mind, many of the 17,000 police forces in America have begun to use *nonlethal weapons,* or weapons primarily designed to subdue suspects.[60]

A wide variety of such weapons are in use. One of the most popular is Oleoresin capsicum, or OC pepper spray. An organic substance that combines ingredients such as resin and cayenne pepper, OC causes a sensation "similar to having sand or needles" in the eyes when sprayed into a suspect's face. Other common nonlethal weapons include tear gas; water cannons; 37-mm pistols that fire wood, rubber, or polyutherane bullets; and hand-held electronic "stun guns" that deliver high-voltage, low-amperage currents at ranges of up to fifteen feet.

The law enforcement community is not, however, convinced that nonlethal weapons offer the protection police officers need or significantly reduce suspect mortality. OC pepper spray, for example, is effective 85 percent of the time it is deployed—good odds, but not good enough for many police officers.[61] Furthermore, William C. Bailey of Cleveland State University conducted a study of large cities and examined the relationship between the availability of less-than-lethal weapons and rates of police-citizen killings. Bailey's data showed that the use of nonlethal weapons had little effect on the number of justifiable homicides by police, even though the author himself noted the limitations of the survey material. First, whether a police-citizen altercation results in death depends on factors other than the availability of nonlethal weapons. Second, police use of a lethal weapon such as a gun commonly does not result in a death. In fact, most weapons fired by police intentionally or unintentionally miss their target, and even when they hit their mark, the target rarely dies. Bailey believes that measuring the number of times a weapon is fired by a police officer would be more helpful than measuring police killings in determining the impact of less-than-lethal weapons. A widespread survey has yet to be done on that topic.[62]

POLICE CORRUPTION

Police corruption has been a concern since the first organized American police departments. As you recall from Chapter 4, a desire to eradicate, or at least limit, corruption was one of the motivating factors behind the reform movement of policing. For general purposes, **police corruption** can be defined as the misuse of authority by a law enforcement officer "in a manner designed to produce personal gain."[63] Corrupt police officers fall into two categories: "grass eaters" and "meat eaters." "Grass eaters" are involved in passive corruption; they simply accept the payoffs and opportunities that police work can provide. As the name implies, "meat eaters" are more aggressive in their quest for personal gain, initiating and going to great lengths to carry out corrupt schemes.[64]

Types of Corruption

Certain forms of corruption have been endemic to police work since its inception. These traditional forms of corruption include:

1. *Bribery,* in which the police officer accepts money or other forms of payment in exchange for "favors," which may include allowing a certain criminal activity to continue or misplacing a key piece of evidence before a trial. Related to bribery are *payoffs,* in which an officer demands payment from an individual or a business in return for certain services.

2. *Shakedowns,* which occur when an officer attempts to coerce money or goods from a citizen or criminal.

3. *Mooching,* in which the police officer accepts free "gifts" such as cigarettes, liquor, or services in return for favorable treatment of the gift giver.

Recent Trends in Police Corruption. The emergence of the drug trade over the past few decades, and the opportunities for corruption it provides, have made these traditional forms of corrupt activity seem almost benign. The amount of money involved in drug-related corruption can be overwhelming. When El Paso (Texas) Customs Inspector José de Jesús Ramos was arrested for his part in a scheme to traffic 2,200 pounds of cocaine across the U.S.-Mexico border, he was to be paid $1 million for simply ignoring the vehicle carrying the drugs.[65]

Between 1994 and 1998, the number of local, state, and federal law enforcement officers in federal prisons increased from 107 to 548.[66] Many of the operations, as can be seen below, involved illegal drugs.

- In Cleveland, Ohio, a federal sting operation caught forty-four officers accepting money to safeguard cocaine traffickers. According to affidavits, each officer was paid up to $3,700 to protect a single drug transaction.

- In Chicago, Illinois, ten officers were charged with robbery and extorting money and drugs from narcotics dealers.

- In Philadelphia, Pennsylvania, six officers were found to have planted illegal drugs on suspects, conducted illegal searches, and lied under oath. As a result of the investigation, 160 wrongfully convicted felons were released from prison.

- In New Orleans, Louisiana, ten officers were convicted for their role in protecting a warehouse that contained 286 pounds of cocaine.

Another aspect of police corruption concerns common crimes such as theft and burglary. The property room—where police departments store confiscated material that may be used as evidence in court—is a prime target for police theft. Sometimes, evidence such as drugs and cash will "disappear"

POLICE CORRUPTION
The abuse of authority by a law enforcement officer for personal gain.

"Who will protect the public when the police violate the law?"

—Ramsey Clark, *former U.S. Attorney General*

with no explanation—in 1997, $23,000 in cash and bonds mysteriously vanished from the New Haven (Connecticut) Police Department's property room.

Dishonest police officers often find opportunities to take advantage of "inside knowledge" of illegal dealings involving large amounts of cash or contraband. A Hartford state trooper named Ramon Valentin, for example, learned through an informant that a local drug dealer had a safe in his home that contained $100,000 in cash. Taking a sick day from work, Valentin and his partner went to the residence and, flashing their badges at the dealer's sister-in-law, confiscated the safe (which actually contained only $38,000). Later, Valentin took $7,000 and a set of keys directly off the dealer. The keys led to a storage unit, which contained a red Corvette—which Valentin also took for himself and drove to work before he was apprehended.[67]

The Three Levels of Police Corruption. According to Lawrence W. Sherman, chair of the Department of Criminology at the University of Maryland, three general types of corruption can exist within a police department.[68] The first and least pervasive is the "rotten apples and rotten pockets" level of corruption. In this case, only a single officer or a group of officers in a department or precinct are corrupt. For many, this possibility can be deceptively attractive. If only a small number of police in any given department are corrupt, then the steps that need to be taken are clear. After those officers are disciplined or removed from their posts, the problem will be solved.

If police administrators believe that there are only a few "rotten apples," they may not take the steps necessary to deal with a "rotten barrel." In Sherman's second level of corruption, the wrongdoing in a department is pervasive but not organized. That is, a majority of the officers are corrupt, but they are not working with each other in an organized manner. In contrast, in Sherman's third level of corruption, the corruption is not only pervasive, but most of the officers in the department are working together to maximize the profit from their corrupt activities. This extreme level of vice is what the Knapp Commission found while investigating police corruption in New York City in the 1970s. (See *Criminal Justice & Popular Culture—Serpico the "Rat"* for more information on this investigation.)

Corruption in Police Subculture

There is no single reason that police corruption occurs. In covering corrupt behavior by a group of Miami police officers known as the Miami River Cops, journalist John Dorschner targeted some of the factors that lead to unethical behavior, including a lack of proper training, a lack of supervision, and the fact that most officers can double or triple their salaries through corrupt activities.[69]

Lawrence Sherman identifies several stages in the moral decline of police officers.[70] In the first stage, the officers accept minor gratuities, such the occasional free meal from a restaurant on their beat. These gratuities gradually evolve into outright bribes, in which the officers receive the gratuity for overlooking some violation. For example, a law officer may accept pay from a bar owner to ensure that the establishment is not investigated for serving alcohol to minors. In the final stage, officers no longer passively accept bribes, but actively seek them out, to the point where the officers may even force the other party to pay for unwanted police services. This stage often involves large amounts of money and may entail—as we have seen—protection of or involvement in drug, gambling, or prostitution organizations.

The insulating effects of police subculture also contribute to corruption by making it difficult to uncover. The Knapp Commission highlighted the "code of silence" that exists in police departments, a code that brands anybody

ETHICS
The rules or standards of behavior governing a profession; aimed at ensuring the fairness and rightness of actions.

Serpico the "Rat"

The New York City première of the film *Cop Land* was attended by the usual Hollywood stars, industry types, and hangers-on. Also in the audience, however, were a fair number of New York City Police Department (NYPD) officials, including present and former Police Commissioners Howard Safir and

within the department who exposes corrupt behavior as a traitor. "The rookie who comes into the department," it was noted, "is faced with the situation where it is easier for him to become corrupt than to remain honest."[71]

Corruption scandals can have a long-lasting negative effect on a police department. The image of the police in the community will obviously be damaged, as citizens doubt the overall effectiveness of a department that cannot police itself. Furthermore, morale within the department is bound to suffer. Recognizing these effects, many police departments have instituted special training programs aimed at improving police ethics.

POLICE ETHICS

Police corruption is intricately connected with the ethics of law enforcement officers. **Ethics** has to do with fundamental questions of the fairness, justice, rightness, or wrongness of any action. Given the significant power that police officers hold, society expects very high standards of ethical behavior from them. These expectations are summed up in the *Police Code of Conduct*, which was developed by the International Association of Police Chiefs in 1989 (see Figure 7.8 on the following page).

To some extent, the *Police Code of Conduct* is self-evident: "A police officer will not engage in acts of corruption or bribery." In

William Bratton. The presence of law enforcement officials was fitting, given that the film told the story of Freddy Heflin (played by Sylvester Stallone), a hearing-impaired sheriff in a small New Jersey town who summons up the courage to deal with the corrupt NYPD officers who live there. Both Safir and Bratton, while noting that the film was well done, were reportedly dismissive of its premise that corruption was rife within the city's police department.

Frank Serpico testifies in 1997 at a City Council hearing on police corruption and brutality in New York City.

Another member of the audience, however, an ex-NYPD officer named Frank Serpico, felt that the true stories of corruption among the city's law enforcement officers would make *Cop Land* "sound like a kindergarten." And Frank Serpico knows something about both police corruption and movies. In the late 1960s, after being rebuffed by city officials, Serpico and detective David Durk told their story of myriad corruption within the NYPD to *New York Times* reporter David Burnham. The resulting articles caused such a public outcry that in 1970 Mayor John V. Lindsay appointed a lawyer named Whitman Knapp to head an investigatory commission on police corruption. The story of Serpico's efforts to weed out corruption were presented to the nation twice—first through the novel *Serpico,* by Peter Maas, and then by the 1973 movie of the same name starring Al Pacino.

As a star witness of the Knapp Commission, Serpico gave a chilling account of the problems facing the NYPD. He claimed that fear of retaliation kept honest cops from reporting the corruption of their fellow officers and told tales of bribery, shakedowns, and graft. The commission's final report uncovered widespread police corruption in areas such as gambling, narcotics, and prostitution and led to numerous changes in the policies of the NYPD.

Serpico left the NYPD after his testimony, convinced that he could longer operate with co-workers who considered him a "rat." (This belief was reinforced by the fact that no "officer assist" radio call was placed on his behalf when he was shot in the face during a 1971 drug bust.) Serpico has not, however, given up his efforts to fight corruption. In 1997, he appeared before the New York City Council during hearings on police practices following the beating of Haitian immigrant Abner Louima by several Brooklyn officers. He urged the council to form an independent monitoring board to investigate allegations of police brutality and repeated a warning that he had made twenty-five years earlier before the Knapp Commission: "We must create an atmosphere where the crooked cop fears the honest cop, and not the other way around."

other aspects, it is idealistic, perhaps unreasonably so: "Officers will never allow personal feelings, animosities, or friendships to influence official conduct." The police working environment—rife with lying, cheating, lawbreaking, and violence—often does not allow for such ethical absolutes.[72]

Ethical Dilemmas

Some police actions are obviously unethical, such as the behavior of a Pennsylvania officer who paid a woman he was dating $500 to pretend to be

Figure 7.8 The Police Code of Conduct

All law enforcement officers must be fully aware of the ethical responsibilities of their position and must strive constantly to live up to the highest possible standards of professional policing. The International Association of Chiefs of Police believes it important that police officers have clear advice and counsel available to assist them in performing their duties consistent with these standards, and has adopted the ethical mandates as guidelines to meet these ends.

PRIMARY RESPONSIBILITIES OF A POLICE OFFICER

A police officer acts as an official representative of government who is required and trusted to work within the law. The officer's powers and duties are conferred by statute. The fundamental duties of a police officer include serving the community, safeguarding lives and property, protecting the innocent, keeping the peace and ensuring the rights of all to liberty, equality and justice.

PERFORMANCE OF THE DUTIES OF A POLICE OFFICER

A police officer shall perform all duties impartially, without favor or affection or ill will and without regard to status, sex, race, religion, political belief or aspiration. All citizens will be treated equally with courtesy, consideration and dignity.

Officers will never allow personal feelings, animosities or friendships to influence official conduct. Laws will be enforced appropriately and courteously and, in carrying out their responsibilities, officers will strive to obtain maximum cooperation from the public. They will conduct themselves in appearance and deportment in such a manner as to inspire confidence and respect for the position of public trust they hold.

DISCRETION

A police officer will use responsibly the discretion vested in his position and exercise it within the law. The principle of reasonableness will guide the officer's determinations, and the officer will consider all surrounding circumstances in determining whether any legal action shall be taken.

Consistent and wise use of discretion, based on professional policing competence, will do much to preserve good relationships and retain the confidence of the public. There can be difficulty in choosing between conflicting courses of action. It is important to remember that a timely word of advice rather than arrest—which may be correct in appropriate circumstances—can be a more effective means of achieving a desired end.

USE OF FORCE

A police officer will never employ unnecessary force or violence and will use only such force in the discharge of duty as is reasonable in all circumstances.

The use of force should be used only with the greatest restraint and only after discussion, negotiation and persuasion have been found to be inappropriate or ineffective. While the use of force is occasionally unavoidable, every police officer will refrain from unnecessary infliction of pain or suffering and will never engage in cruel, degrading or inhuman treatment of any person.

CONFIDENTIALITY

Whatever a police officer sees, hears or learns of that is of a confidential nature will be kept secret unless the performance of duty or legal provision requires otherwise.

Members of the public have a right to security and privacy, and information obtained about them must not be improperly divulged.

INTEGRITY

A police officer will not engage in acts of corruption or bribery, nor will an officer condone such acts by other police officers.

The public demands that the integrity of police officers be above reproach. Police officers must, therefore, avoid any conduct that might compromise integrity and thus undercut the public confidence in a law enforcement agency. Officers will refuse to accept any gifts, presents, subscriptions, favors, gratuities or promises that could be interpreted as seeking to cause the officer to refrain from performing official responsibilities honestly and within the law. Police officers must not receive private or special advantage from their official status. Respect from the public cannot be bought; it can only be earned and cultivated.

COOPERATION WITH OTHER POLICE OFFICERS AND AGENCIES

Police officers will cooperate with all legally authorized agencies and their representatives in the pursuit of justice.

An officer or agency may be one among many organizations that may provide law enforcement services to a jurisdiction. It is imperative that a police officer assist colleagues fully and completely; with respect and consideration at all times.

PERSONAL-PROFESSIONAL CAPABILITIES

Police officers will be responsible for their own standard of professional-performance and will take every reasonable opportunity to enhance and improve their level of knowledge and competence.

Through study and experience, a police officer can acquire the high level of knowledge and competence that is essential for the efficient and effective performance of duty. The acquisition of knowledge is a never-ending process of personal and professional development that should be pursued constantly.

PRIVATE LIFE

Police officers will behave in a manner that does not bring discredit to their agencies or themselves.

A police officer's character and conduct while off duty must always be exemplary, thus maintaining a position of respect in the community in which he or she lives and serves. The officer's personal behavior must be beyond reproach.

SOURCE: THE INTERNATIONAL ASSOCIATION OF CHIEFS OF POLICE. WEB SITE: WWW.THEIACP.ORG/.

CJ in Focus
A Question of Ethics
The Dirty Harry Problem

Do the ends justify the means? This is one of the most difficult and complex questions of ethics, and one that is particularly crucial for police officers. Should they take steps that they know to be illegal in order to achieve a positive goal?

In addressing this moral dilemma, Carl B. Klockars turns to one of the most popular police dramas of all time, the 1971 film *Dirty Harry*. In this movie, Detective Harry Callahan, played by Clint Eastwood, faces a situation in which a young girl has been kidnapped by a psychotic killer named Scorpio. Demanding $200,000 in ransom, Scorpio has buried the girl alive, leaving her just a few hours' worth of oxygen. Callahan manages to find Scorpio, and in his efforts to learn the location of the girl, he shoots and then tortures the kidnapper. Although Callahan eventually gets the information out of Scorpio, it is too late. By the time he finds the girl, she has suffocated.

Assuming for argument's sake that Callahan was able to save the girl, would he have been justified in taking such drastic measures? After all, Callahan, like all officers, took an oath to obey the U.S. Constitution, which certainly does not permit the torture of suspects. Following proper procedure, Callahan should have arrested Scorpio and advised him of his right to an attorney. If Scorpio had exercised his right, the attorney would certainly have reminded him of his right to remain silent, and Callahan would have had no chance to save the little girl. In fact,

Callahan committed a crime himself by assaulting Scorpio. Given all these factors, was the detective justified in doing what he did in order to save a life? According to Klockars:

[The] core scene in *Dirty Harry* should only be understood as a dramatic example of a far more common problem: real, everyday, routine situations in which police officers know they can only achieve good ends by employing dirty means. Each time a police officer considers deceiving a suspect into confessing by telling him that his fingerprints were found at the scene or that a conspirator has already confessed, each time a police officer considers adding some untrue details to his account of probable cause to legitimate a crucial stop or search [he or she] faces a Dirty Harry Problem.

Klockars calls the effects of the Dirty Harry Problem on police officers "devastating." On the one hand, if the officers decide not to use dirty means, they must face the consequences: perhaps a suspect the officers know is guilty will be set free to commit further crimes. On the other hand, if the officers do abandon rules and procedures to serve the law, they are essentially breaking the very laws that they took an oath to uphold. The Dirty Harry Problem, Klockars says, makes policing the most "morally corrosive occupation."

For Critical Analysis: Are police ever justified in using unlawful methods, whatever good may be ultimately achieved? What do you believe is the proper solution to the Dirty Harry Problem?

---

an eyewitness in a murder trial. The majority of ethical dilemmas that a police officer will face are not so clear-cut. Joycelyn M. Pollock and Ronald F. Becker, both members of the Criminal Justice Department at Southwest Texas State University, define an ethical dilemma as a situation in which law enforcement officers:

- Do not know the right course of action;
- Have difficulty doing what they consider to be right; and/or
- Find the wrong choice very tempting.[73]

These ethical dilemmas are likely to occur quite often in police work, and it is how an officer deals with them that determines to what extent he or she is behaving ethically. (For further discussion of the difficult ethical situations that police officers face, see *CJ in Focus: A Question of Ethics—The Dirty Harry Problem*.)

Elements of Ethics

Pollock and Becker, both of whom have extensive experience as ethics instructors for police departments, further identify four categories of ethical dilemmas, involving discretion, duty, honesty, and loyalty.[74]

Discretion. The law provides rigid guidelines for how police officers must act and how they cannot act, but it does not offer guidelines for how officers *should* act in many circumstances.[75] It is not possible for the police to follow the exact letter of the law; if every petty crime were given the same weight as

INFOTRAC ®
COLLEGE EDITION

O'Malley, Timothy. Managing for ethics: a mandate for administrators.

DUTY
The moral sense of a police officer that she or he should apply authority in a certain manner.

"Duties are not performed for duty's sake, but because their neglect would make the man uncomfortable. A man performs but one duty—the duty of contenting his spirit, the duty of making himself agreeable to himself."

—Mark Twain, *American novelist* (1906)

more serious ones, the criminal justice system would be overwhelmed. As we saw in Chapter 4, police use discretion to alleviate this pressure. In many cases, this discretion involves an ethical dilemma. Suppose, for example, a police officer pulls over a woman with a number of outstanding traffic warrants. According to the law, the officer may be required to arrest the woman. But she has an infant child with her. Should the officer arrest the woman and call juvenile services to take the child or let the woman go with a warning? Is society best served by the police officer following legal guidelines or by using discretion concerning what is not, after all, a major crime?

Duty. The concept of discretion is linked with **duty,** or the obligation to act in a certain matter. An officer's duty is not always clear. After responding to a domestic disturbance call, a law enforcement officer must first determine whether a crime has been committed. If this is not the case, however, what is the officer's duty? The officer could stay on the scene and make sure no crime is going to be committed, or she or he could leave. Furthermore, some social problems, such as homelessness, are not technically a police concern, unless a crime is involved. Some officers may nonetheless feel a duty to assist the homeless.

Society, by passing laws, can make a police officer's duty clear and, in the process, eliminate discretion from the decision-making process. A number of communities have done this with regard to domestic violence cases. Nearly half of the nation's big city police departments now have *proarrest policies,* which require police officers to arrest the abuser in a domestic violence situation if the assault can be classified as a felony even though the victim does not want the abuser arrested. Some of these departments have adopted a policy—first used by the Seattle Police Department—that lists several factors that should *always* be considered to designate a felony assault and therefore lead to an arrest. These factors include gunshot wounds, broken bones, and intentional burns.[76]

Honesty. In their training sessions, Pollock and Becker found that issues of corruption such as bribery were rarely brought up. This could be, of course, because the trainees did not want to admit to major breaches of ethical behavior, but it also suggests that the issue of police honesty involves more mundane incidents than full-blown corruption. A common ethical dilemma, apparently, is what action to take when the officer has struck a fixed object while driving a police car. The temptation is to claim that another automobile struck the police car and then fled the scene.

Loyalty. What should a police officer do if he or she witnesses a partner using excessive force on a suspect? The choice often sets loyalty against ethics, especially if the officer does not condone the violence. The same situation occurs when a police officer is aware that one of his or her peers has committed a crime. In this situation, a police department may try to enforce ethics by disciplining officers who "cover up" corruption through their silence.

POLICE ACCOUNTABILITY

Even in a police department with excellent recruiting methods, state-of-the-art ethics and discretionary training programs, and a culturally diverse workforce that nearly matches the make-up of the community, the problems discussed earlier in this chapter are bound to occur. The question then becomes—given the inevitability of excessive force, corruption, and other misconduct—*who shall police the police?*

This is a crucial concern for a police department. Headlines such as "In Police Brutality Case, Penalty Was Lost Vacation Days" over a stark photograph of the victim's bruised and bloodied face can cause citizens to mistrust law enforcement officers, which can lead to problems on the street. Furthermore, as the feature *Criminal Justice & Technology—Telling Tales of Police Misconduct on the Internet* shows, citizens have an increasing number of outlets from which to publicize embarrassing and improper incidents. In this section, we shall examine three traditional methods of assuring police accountability for wrongdoing: (1) internal investigations, (2) civil liability, and (3) citizen oversight.

Internal Investigations

"The minute the public feels that the police department is not investigating its own alleged wrongdoing well, the police department will not be able to function credibly in even the most routine of matters" says Sheldon Greenberg, a professor of police management at Johns Hopkins University.[77] The mechanism for these investigations within a police department is the **internal affairs unit (IAU).** In many smaller police departments, the police chief conducts internal affairs investigations, while mid-size and large departments will have a team of internal affairs officers.

An IAU investigation involves four steps:

1. *Intake.* An intake officer is responsible for receiving complaints from the public and police personnel. This officer must decide if the complaint is serious enough to warrant an IAU investigation.

2. *Investigation.* The investigation into a complaint is similar to the investigation into any crime. The IAU officer gathers evidence and interviews the parties involved, including the officer against whom the complaint has been lodged.

3. *Deliberation.* When the investigation has been completed, police management reviews the case and decides what the outcome will be for the suspected officer.

4. *Disposition.* If the investigation shows that the charges against the officer were unfounded, then the matter is closed. In some cases, the investigation will **exonerate** the officer, by showing that she or he was justified in taking the scrutinized actions. When the investigation uncovers enough evidence to show that misconduct did occur, the officer will face a range of punishments, from fines to counseling to suspension. In the most egregious cases, the officer can be dismissed.[78]

Criminal Justice & Technology

Telling Tales of Police Misconduct on the Internet

After being stopped by three Colorado state troopers whom he felt harassed him and cited him for what he believed to be a baseless careless driving charge, Franklin Perez complained to a number of police administrators and wrote letters to every Colorado state legislator. Dissatisfied with the feedback he received, Perez decided to tell his story in an arena that is becoming increasingly popular with citizens wishing to highlight police misconduct—the Internet.

Perez felt justified in taking his case online for several reasons. He wanted to name the officers involved—as they had not in his opinion been sufficiently reprimanded—and to vent his anger "in a constructive manner." He also wanted to "expose an injustice" and prevent similar incidents from occurring. Indeed, the desire to change police misconduct by publicizing it is a primary motivation for these "watchdog sites." The author of the Austin (Texas) Police Department (APD) Hall of Shame site, for example, hopes that documenting abuses such as brutality and discrimination (along with publishing the names of the offending officers) will encourage the city of Austin to "hold the APD more accountable to the public."

Many of the sites are interactive. The Database of Abusive Police allows visitors to enter a particular officer's name or badge number and receive information on that officer's misconduct (or lack thereof). The site also provides visitors with an opportunity to tell their own stories of encounters with the police.

IN THE FUTURE: The Internet is a source of information, but it can also be a source of misinformation. Though much of the data on these sites are verifiable, there is no mechanism at present to identify when a claim against an officer is false or misleading. In 1997, Fairfax County (Virginia) detective William E. Baitinger filed one of the first lawsuits alleging defamation of character by an individual on the Internet. Baitinger was responding to the recounting of a traffic stop involving him that was posted on the Police Brutality Page Web site. If his suit is successful, it will have a dampening effect on the proliferation of online complaints about police.

INTERNAL AFFAIRS UNIT (IAU)
A division within a police department that receives and investigates complaints of wrongdoing by police officers.

EXONERATE
The removal of a charge of wrongdoing against a police officer by determining that the act in question was justified under the circumstances.

SECTION 1983 VIOLATIONS
Violations of a citizen's constitutional rights by a police officer or other government agent.

The internal review process has been called "the world's biggest washing machine. Everything that goes in dirty, comes out clean."[79] (See Figure 7.9.) Many observers suspect that IAU investigators have an unavoidable bias in favor of their fellow officers, and police supervisors are accused of being too lenient in their dispositions. Within a department, IAU members are also regarded with a measure of suspicion, and law enforcement officers are notoriously uncooperative during internal investigations. "Nobody who is trying to do their job likes having somebody like me looking over their shoulder," one former internal affairs chief said of his position in the department. "It is natural that when you investigate complaints against police you never quite feel a part of the group."[80]

Civil Liability

As much as police officers may resent internal affairs units, most realize that it is preferable to settle disciplinary matters in-house. The alternative can prove costly. As you recall from Chapter 3, *tort law* concerns civil wrongs in which one person causes injury to another; when the defendant is found liable in a tort case, damages usually must be paid to the plaintiff. In 1998, a Phoenix jury awarded the parents of Edward Mallet $45 million after a police officer killed their son—who had two artificial legs—while subduing him after a traffic stop.[81] In 1997 alone, the city of Detroit paid $15.7 million in damages resulting from police misconduct.[82]

The ability of citizens to sue public officials for violation of their civil rights is based on Title 42 of the United States Code, Section 1983, which states:

> Every person who, under color of any statute, ordinance, regulation, custom, or usage, of any State or Territory, subjects, or causes to be subjected, any citizen of the United States or other persons within the jurisdiction thereof to the deprivation of any rights, privileges, or immunities secured by the Constitution and laws, shall be liable to the party injured in an action at law, suit in equity, or other proper proceeding for redress.[83]

In other words, **Section 1983 violations** occur when an officer of the state violates the federal constitutional rights of an individual. Charges brought

Figure 7.9 The Internal Review Process

Like most police departments, the Tiffin, Ohio, Police Department has a formal set of steps that must be followed when a complaint is filed by a citizen against one of its officers.

STEP 1: LODGING THE COMPLAINT
All complaints made against Ohio police officers must be in writing and signed by the person making the complaint. (Recently, this has been changed to allow for email complaints, which are accepted with the proper email address of the complainant.)

STEP 2: THE COMPLAINT IS SENT TO THE INTERNAL AFFAIRS DIVISION (IAD)
When a complaint is filed, an investigator from the IAD is assigned to review and investigate the circumstances surrounding the complaint. The officer named in the complaint must also be given a copy of the complaint.

STEP 3: THE COMPLAINT IS INVESTIGATED
The Internal Affairs investigator will get statements from civilian witnesses and other police officers. Records and other evidence are collected and analyzed. When the investigation is completed, the citizen who made the complaint is notified of the results and the action taken, if any.

STEP 4A: WHEN A COMPLAINT IS FOUND TO BE TRUE
If the investigation finds that the complaint is based in fact, the Tiffin Police Department Chief of Police may take one of four possible actions against the officer, depending on the nature of the violation:

- Reprimand the officer
- Suspend the officer without pay
- Demote the officer
- Discharge the officer

STEP 4B: WHEN A COMPLAINT CANNOT BE PROVED OR IS NOT TRUE
If there is not sufficient evidence to sustain the complaint, or if the evidence shows that the complaint was incorrect, the officer is notified and continues his or her duty without further action.

STEP 5A: THE OFFICER APPEAL
As with a citizen found guilty of a criminal offense, a police officer can appeal any action taken against him or her.

STEP 5B: THE UNSATISFIED CIVILIAN
If the civilian who filed the complaint is not satisfied with the results of the investigation, he or she can contact the Captain or the Chief of Police to discuss the matter. If, following this step, the complainant is still unsatisfied, he or she can request further investigation by the local Prosecutor's Officer of the Federal Bureau of Investigation.

SOURCE: TIFFIN POLICE DEPARMENT.

under Section 1983 often contend that the police officer has inflicted physical or emotional harm on the plaintiff; the most common charges include:

- *False arrest*, which occurs when an officer makes an arrest without probable cause.
- *Assault and battery*, which covers cases of excessive use of force and police brutality.
- *Wrongful death*, which arises when the police officer's action, or inaction, leads to a death. The members of the victim's family often bring **wrongful death** cases in redress for mental anguish.
- *Negligence*, which can be defined as the failure of a statutory duty to act properly with regard to those who might be harmed by the police officer's conduct. For example, if an officer directing traffic is drunk on the job, and an accident occurs, she or he could be liable for **negligence**.[84]

Local and state law enforcement officers do have a defense against Section 1983 actions. In *Malley v. Briggs* (1986), [85] the Supreme Court ruled that police officers have **qualified immunity** in civil lawsuits. That is, if the officer can prove that his or her actions against the plaintiff were reasonable and performed in "good faith," then the officer may be found *not* to have violated Section 1983.

Some observers claim that law enforcement officers are protected from civil suits for practical reasons as well, in that most citizens who have been subjected to police abuse cannot afford to hire an attorney. Furthermore, juries are more likely to side with the officer than the plaintiff, who often has a criminal record or has committed some criminal act in the case at hand.[86] These contentions are valid, but there can be no doubt that the threat of plaintiff victories provides a strong incentive for police departments to hold their officers to high professional standards.

Citizen Oversight

In the early 1990s, the Denver Police Department had created a "gang list" of potential criminals. Much to the dismay of many community leaders, the "gang list" was composed primarily of minorities. In response to public outrage, the city's Public Safety Review Commission (PSRC) held hearings on the matter. As a result of the PSRC's actions, the Denver police eliminated nearly half the names on the list and changed their methods of labeling people gang members.[87]

The PSRC is an example of an external procedure for handling citizens' complaints known as **citizen oversight.** In this process, citizens—people who are not sworn officers and, by inference, not biased in favor of law enforcement officers—review allegations of police misconduct or brutality. The first citizen oversight bodies were civilian review boards, which appeared in the late 1950s and early 1960s in several cities, including Washington, D.C., Philadelphia, and New York City. Today, the majority of large cities utilize similar bodies, with an increasing number of smaller urban areas following suit. According to Samuel Walker, nearly 100 cities now operate some kind of review procedure by an independent body.[88]

For the most part, citizen review boards can only recommend action to the police chief or other executive. They do not have the power to discipline officers directly. Although police officers generally resent this intrusion of civilians, most studies have shown that civilian review boards are not widely successful in their efforts to convince police chiefs to take action against their subordinate officers.[89]

Michael Cox successfully sued the city of Boston following an incident in which he was mistaken for a suspect and severely beaten by members of the city's police force.

WRONGFUL DEATH
A type of civil lawsuit brought by the beneficiaries of a person who has died because of the alleged action or inaction of a police officer.

NEGLIGENCE
The failure to use the care that a reasonable person would use under the given circumstances.

QUALIFIED IMMUNITY
A defense against civil litigation used by police officers in which they try to prove that their discretionary actions fell within the boundaries of reasonable behavior.

CITIZEN OVERSIGHT
The process by which citizens review complaints brought against individual police officers or police departments. The citizens often do not have the power to discipline misconduct, but can recommend that action be taken by police administrators.

Criminal Justice in Action

Police in the Media: Good Guys or Bad?

Over the course of the past four chapters, we have discussed many aspects of police work. It would be safe to say that your knowledge of the profession surpasses that of most Americans. This is not to say that as a society, we ignore the police officer. Americans spend many hours each week reading about law enforcement officers in newspapers and magazines and watching their real-life or fictional exploits on television or in a movie theater. As we close our section on law enforcement, we will examine how the media's treatment of the police officer has influenced the public's view of the police, for better or for worse.

Two Tough Guys on the Beat

It was a hectic month for the New York City Police Department's Andy Sipowicz. During one interrogation, Sipowicz lost his temper and slapped the suspect, yelling "You shoot a girl in the head, burn her past recognition, and you're gonna crack wise with us?" His partner acted similarly when informed by a teenager that "we can file a complaint on you for violence." The detective proceeded to spell his name out loud and smash his badge in the juvenile's face, saying "Shield number thirty-one eighteen. You can get it off your forehead in the morning." The pair worked as a team as well. In a holding cell, an enraged Sipowicz throttled the neck of a suspect and bellowed, "You think I'm not going to beat you? If that lady's hurt, I'm going to throw you off the roof like the man you killed," while his partner ordered a witness in the cell to sing "Pop Goes the Weasel."

NYPD Blue, the television police drama that follows the escapades of Sipowicz and his fellow officers, is watched by millions of Americans a week. Many law enforcement officers worry that what these viewers see on *NYPD Blue* and other media portrayals of police give them a negative image. "Sipowicz is a racist brute," says one ex-cop. "People are fascinated with him, but . . . he is everything you try to get rid of."[90]

Police Subculture's Mistrust of the Media

Most police officers understand that an entertainment program cannot focus on the realities of their work, such as the piles of paperwork they must sift through. Still, many believe the images of violent television cops make their jobs more difficult by giving viewers the idea that *all* police officers act in that manner. "If I did that," one officer said, referring to an incident in which Sipowicz hit a suspect with a phone book, "I'd be looking for a job tomorrow."[91] Another problem is that jurors, whose only information about police work often comes from the media, are easily manipulated by defense attorneys who play on the notion that police routinely coerce confessions through force.[92]

Police subculture also harbors suspicions of the news media and reacts strongly to attempts by media outlets to "expose" police misconduct. When *Dateline NBC* investigated antidrug tactics in Calcasieu and Jefferson Davis parishes in Louisiana, the news show was accused of having a "chilling effect" on police efforts by turning public opinion against them. After the *Cincinnati Enquirer* ran a series of articles on police brutality, entitled "Misuse of Force," local law enforcement officers took it as a personal affront. One police psychologist wrote the newspaper, asking, "If we seek to destroy those who protect us, whom are we really hurting?"[93] Police departments are diverting an increasing amount of resources to public relations departments to combat these negative portrayals in the media.

The Public's View of the Police

Police public relations staffers may have an easier job than they expected. Despite any perceived media goal to "destroy those who protect us," law enforcement officers are actually held in high esteem by the general public (see Figure 7.10), who, according to one study, receive 95

Figure 7.10 The Public's Opinion of the Police

Every year the Gallup Organization reads its poll subjects a list of institutions in American society, and then asks, "Please tell me, how much confidence, you, yourself, have in each one—a great deal, quite a lot, some, or very little." When the institution in question is the police, more than 50 percent of nearly every demographic group say they have "a great deal" or "quite a lot" of confidence in law enforcement officers. African Americans, as you can see, are the notable exception; only 34 percent have positive feelings toward police officers.

	Great Deal/Quite a Lot	Some	Very Little	None[a]
National	58%	30%	10%	1%
Sex				
Male	59	29	11	(b)
Female	57	31	10	1
Race				
White	61	30	8	(b)
Black	34	38	25	1
Nonwhite[c]	40	33	24	1
Age				
18 to 29 years	46	34	18	(b)
30 to 49 years	59	30	10	(b)
50 to 64 years	61	29	10	1
50 years and older	64	27	6	1
65 years and older	68	26	3	1
Education				
College post graduate	55	39	6	0
College graduate	67	26	7	0
Some college	57	31	12	(b)
No college	57	28	11	1
Income				
$50,000 and over	59	33	8	0
$30,000 to $49,999	58	28	14	0
$20,000 to $29,999	65	29	6	0
Under $20,000	51	29	15	2

NOTE: THE "DONT KNOW/REFUSED" CATEGORY HAS BEEN OMITTED; THEREFORE PERCENTS MAY NOT SUM TO 100.

[a]RESPONSE VOLUNTEERED.
[b]LESS THAN 0.5%.
[c]INCLUDES BLACK RESPONDENTS.

SOURCE: ADAPTED FROM U.S. DEPARTMENT OF JUSTICE, SOURCEBOOK OF CRIMINAL JUSTICE STATISTICS, 1997 (WASHINGTON, D.C.: U.S. GOVERNMENT PRINTING OFFICE, 1998), TABLE 2.17, PAGE 107. (DATA PROVIDED BY THE GALLUP ORGANIZATION.)

percent of their information on crime from the mass media.[94] Perhaps, some observers suggest, the media's focus on the use of force by officers reassures citizens—the majority of whom have never been arrested—that the police will use any means necessary to keep the peace. Why should the public be expected to protest against police brutality, asks crime author John DeSantis, when such violence is

> glanced at with a knowing wink that says, "We know you shouldn't have done it, but we're glad to be rid of him anyway. . . ." [T]he victims of brutality are often the people whom the rest of society wishes would go away. The current social climate would seem to tend toward a secret desire for sum-

mary dispatch of felons with extreme prejudice.[95]

As for the news media, criminologist Steven M. Chermak believes that the majority of police coverage is positive for two reasons. First, reporters rely on police sources for popular crime stories and are not disposed to "bite the hand that feeds them." Second, the news media tend to cover the most newsworthy crimes (murders, kidnappings, and the like), which happen to show police in their best light: as dedicated crime fighters and investigators who "get their man" more often then not.[96]

The *Dragnet* Revolution

If any media outlet has cemented the police officer's "good guy" image in the minds of the public, it has been television. In 1947, before the first wave of successful televised police dramas, the public ranked the police fifty-fifth out of ninety professions in terms of esteem. During the 1950s—the prime years of *Dragnet,* the prototype police drama—the police's ranking increased to forty-seventh (ahead of insurance officers and traveling salesmen) and continued to rise to its now lofty level.[97]

Dragnet, starring Jack Webb as Sgt. Joe Friday, debuted in December 1951. Friday broke the mold set by private detectives such as Sam Spade, who had dominated crime television shows and movies up to that point. Whereas these "private dicks" were solitary, cynical figures who existed on the fringes of the law, Friday was a solid cop with solid law and order values. As its theme, *Dragnet* held that "the authority legally constituted with the police is the proper authority to be used in the detection of criminal action." The show was also the first to add the element of realism, having Friday speak in code: "Book him on a 358." In a 1954 cover story, *Time* magazine asserted that *Dragnet* had helped the country gain "a new appreciation of the underpaid, long-suffering, ordinary policeman" and "its first rudimentary understanding of real-life law enforcement."

COPS and Videos

Except for a brief period in the 1960s, the "reality-based" police drama has been a staple on television since *Dragnet*. Since viewers tend to equate what they see on television with reality, it can be assumed that these law and order shows offer a sense of security to those who watch them.[98]

The tradition of *Dragnet* is not carried on by contemporary offerings such as *NYPD Blue, Homicide: Life on the Street,* and *Law and Order.* These shows rely on soap-opera themes of personal trauma. The officers are too deeply troubled and introspective to be heroes in the Joe Friday mold. To find the direct descendants of *Dragnet* on television today, one must turn to "real-life" shows such as *COPS* and *Wildest Police Videos.*

Dragnet, a police drama that ruled the American airways during the 1950s, presented viewers with positive images of police officers and the work that they do.

These series have come under a great deal of criticism for their voyeurism and racist and class undertones, but there is no doubting their worshipful attitude toward the police officer. Though the show is premised on the notion of reality, officers and administrators of the police departments featured on *COPS* have a contractual right to edit the scenes to their liking.[99] The result is a slick half-hour promoting the police officer as the only thing standing between "them" and "us."

Wildest Police Videos gives the viewer an even more "realistic" idea of the life of a police officer, as the videos it features are often taken by cameras inside the patrol car. The narration provides a continuous affirmation of the police officer as hero, with commentary such as:

> Police create a thin line, a line protecting good from bad, capturing the criminals who threaten our lives and often maintaining the only hope of order against the threat of chaos.

There is no room for Sipowicz-style brutality or self-doubt on these shows about "real" cops. Interviews with the police who have been involved in the videos only serve to confirm the "good guy" image. "This is what you go into law for," says one officer, who viewers have just watched rescue a baby from being drowned by a mentally disturbed relative in an Arkansas swamp. "You see all these shows when you're a kid, where the hero goes out there and saves somebody. It feels pretty good."

Key Terms

blue curtain 240

burnout 243

citizen oversight 257

deadly force 246

duty 254

ethics 250

exonerate 255

field training 238

internal affairs unit (IAU) 255

negligence 257

police corruption 249

police cynicism 241

police subculture 238

qualified immunity 257

reasonable force 245

Section 1983 violations 256

socialization 240

stressors 243

wrongful death 257

Chapter Summary

1. **Explain what is involved in background checks of prospective police officers.** In addition to making sure that applicants meet the minimum requirements of citizenship, no prior felony record, and ability to get a driver's license, most police departments engage in checks that include drug tests; review of educational, military, and driving records; credit checks; FBI searches; and interviews with spouses and previous employers.

2. **Outline how police applicants are tested.** The testing of applicants involves (a) a written examination, which may include tests of mathematical ability and writing skills; (b) physical agility tests, such as obstacle courses; and (c) psychological tests, such as the MMPI or the Myers-Briggs Type Indicator.

3. **Identify the five basic values of the police subculture.** (a) Only a police officer can understand the "true" nature of police work; (b) she or he is the only real crime fighter; (c) to fight crime effectively, police officers must bend or break the rules imposed by the courts; (d) civilians criticize the police unless they need help; and (e) loyalty among police officers is the highest virtue because everyone else is "out to get" them.

4. **Explain what stressors are and list some of those found in police work.** Stressors are any conditions that cause stress. In police work, stressors include (a) the fear of becoming a victim of violent crime, (b) exposure to violent crimes and victims, (c) a need to comply with the law in every job action, (d) lack of community support, (e) negative media coverage, (f) excessive paperwork, and (g) unconventional hours of shift work.

5. **Indicate some of the guidelines for the use of nondeadly force in most states.** Force is acceptable in the following circumstances: (a) preventing an escape, (b) retaking a suspect after an escape attempt, (c) overcoming an offender's resistance to a lawful arrest, (d) when protecting the officer from bodily injury, and (e) when protecting the suspect, other persons, or property from harm.

6. **Identify the three traditional forms of police corruption and explain why they are less significant today.** The three traditional forms are bribery, shakedowns, and mooching. With the emergence of the drug trade and the millions upon millions of dollars involved in it, these types of corruption have been overshadowed by drug-related corruption.

7. **Explain what an ethical dilemma is and name the four categories of ethical dilemmas typically facing a police officer.** An ethical dilemma is a situation in which police officers (a) do not know the right course of action; (b) have difficulty doing what they consider to be right; and/or (c) find the wrong choice very tempting. The four types of ethical dilemmas are (a) discretion, (b) duty, (c) honesty, and (d) loyalty.

8. **List the three types of police accountability systems and indicate which one is least important.** The three ways of keeping the police accountable are (a) internal investigations, (b) civil liability, and (c) citizen oversight such as civilian review boards. Civilian review boards have been the least effective. The presence of civil liability often forces internal affairs units to act in a swift and dramatic way.

9. **Identify the four steps in a typical internal affairs unit investigation.** (a) Intake—the decision has to be made as to whether the complaint warrants an investigation. (b) The investigation—similar to the investigation of any crime. (c) Deliberation—management reviews the case. (d) Disposition—whether by exonerating the officer or punishing him or her through fines, counseling, suspension, or dismissal.

10. **Indicate what a Section 1983 violation is and list four possible such violations.** Section 1983 is part of Title 42 of the United States Code; Section 1983 violations occur when an officer violates the federal constitutional rights of an individual. The most common charges brought under Section 1983 are (a) false arrest, (b) assault and battery, (c) wrongful death, and (d) negligence.

Questions for Critical Analysis

1. In what sense have police departments' physical standards been used to discriminate against women?

2. Why do most police departments view college graduates as better candidates for their police forces than those with less education?

3. What are the various experiences that rookie police officers undergo that make them aware they are not in a "normal" job?

4. What is the end result of the police subculture on police officers?

5. What is the greatest threat to a police officer's physical safety?

6. Why is the average life expectancy of a police officer almost fifteen years less than that of the general public?

7. How can you recognize that a police officer is suffering from post-traumatic stress disorder (PTSD)?

8. Have the most recent United States Supreme Court decisions on the use of deadly force made it easier to ascertain when police actions can be judged "unreasonable"?

9. What is the basic difficulty facing the creation of an effective internal affairs unit?

10. Where does the public obtain most of its information about crime and law enforcement? What is the result?

Selected Print and Electronic Resources

SUGGESTED READINGS

Amar, Akhil Reed, *The Constitution and Criminal Procedure: First Principles,* New Haven, Conn.: Yale University Press, 1998. The author looks at the role of search warrants as well as a host of Sixth Amendment trial-related rights. He examines the status of the exclusionary rule and self-incrimination. He argues against exclusion of reliable evidence in criminal trials.

Brown, Edward S., *A Badge without Blemish: Avoiding Police Corruption,* Kearney, NE: Morris Pub., 1997. This slim volume (only 57 pages) provides some personal reflections on the author's eight years of service as a police officer for the City of Atlanta Police Department. The author contends that the greatest challenge facing law enforcement agencies is how to "resurrect" enthusiasm in their officers.

Delattre, Edwin J., and Patrick V. Murphy, *Character and Cops: Ethics in Policing,* Washington, D.C.: AEI Press, 1996. The authors examine what ethics mean in general, what they mean in a police environment, and how police personnel can adhere to them.

Manning, Peter K., *Police Work: The Social Organization of Policing,* Cambridge, MA: MIT Press, 1997. The author uses a sociological approach based on his own field work in observing, interviewing, and sharing the daily experiences of police both in the United States and the United Kingdom. The book includes an outline of technological capabilities for gathering, screening, managing, and dispatching information among police forces. It deals with the issues of deadly force and police pursuit.

MEDIA RESOURCES

Internal Affairs **(1990)** Raymond Avila (Andy Garcia) is a stock character of the "cop flick": youthful, eager, and a bit naïve. Avila's innocence does not last, however, as he and his partner Amy Wallace (Laurie Metcalf) are slowly drawn into the corrupt and disturbing world of Los Angeles police officer Dennis Peck (Richard Gere). Internal Affairs investigators Avila and Wallace start by looking into the drug-related activities of a young cop named Van Stretch (William Baldwin). The path quickly leads to Peck, who appears to be involved in a number of dubious financial schemes, besides having four families and an awesome talent for manipulation.

Critically analyze this film:

1. List the various forms of corruption in which Peck is involved. Would he be characterized as a "grass eater" or a "meat eater"?

2. Refer back to Sherman's three levels of corruption, discussed on page 250. Which level would appear to describe the situation at the Los Angeles Police Department portrayed in the film?

3. How is the "blue wall of silence" portrayed in the film?

4. Explore the general attitude in the police department towards Internal Affairs investigators. How does this impact the efforts of Avila and Wallace?

5. Starting with the film noirs of the 1940s and 1950s, American filmmakers have been fascinated by links between police officers and wrongdoers, focusing on their similarities as much as their differences. *Internal Affairs*, with an antagonist who happens to be a police officer, follows this tradition. How does the no-longer-innocent Avila begin to mirror Peck as the film progresses?

Logging On

If you want to find Web pages about police corruption, all you need to do is type into your favorite search engine the words "police corruption." Do this and then determine which of these Web pages is credible. What would make you believe that the stories presented are in fact real?

You can discover what an actual law enforcement code of ethics consists of by going to the Washington State Criminal Justice Training Commission Manual. You will find this at:

www.chelancyber-opinion.org/ethics.html

To get some of the flavor of what you might be in for if you become a new police officer, go to the following Web site:

www.officer.com/newcops.htm

To get information on the largest police union in the country, the International Brotherhood of Police Officers, go to its home page at:

www.ibpo.org/

Using the internet for Criminal Justice Analysis

INFOTRAC® COLLEGE EDITION

1. The use of deadly force by police personnel has given rise to a relatively new phenomenon called "suicide by cop." Police officers are becoming aware that they are sometimes delivering death to individuals who have suicidal tendencies. The average person, unaware of the victim's motives, blames the police for failing to make a reasonable effort to subdue the suspect without using deadly force. Read an article from the *FBI Law Enforcement Bulletin* by first accessing your InfoTrac College Edition at **www.infotrac-college.com/wadsworth/** After you log on, type in the words: **"SUICIDE BY COP."** Read the article and answer the following questions:

a. Give some examples of potential "suicide-by-cop" instances.

b. What are some hidden forms of suicide that do not involve police shootings?

c. What were the demographic characteristics of most suicide-by-cop incidents that were examined in this article?

d. Do you believe that suicide by cop constitutes a large percentage of police shootings? Why or why not?

2. You can discover a lot about employment as a police officer. First go to:
www.officer.com/jobs.htm

Survey at least three of the five sites listed under the heading "Employment in law enforcement." Do enough research to answer the following questions:

a. What is the average salary of a rookie police officer?

b. What is the average minimum age requirement to become a police officer?

c. Are there more job openings for police officers in small towns or large cities?

d. Next, check out the state in which you live. Does the information provided for the job openings for that state agree or disagree with the averages that you determined for the above questions?

Notes

1. Terri Harvey-Lintz and Romeria Tidwell, "Effect of the 1992 Los Angeles Civil Unrest: Post Traumatic Stress Disorder Symptomology among Law Enforcement Officers," *Social Science Journal* (April 1997), 171–84.

2. Gordon Witkin, "When the Bad Guys Are Cops," *U.S. News & World Report* (September 11, 1995), 22.

3. David Remnick, "The Crime Buster," *New Yorker* (February 24 and March 3, 1997), 103.

4. James H. Chenoweth, "Situational Tests: A New Attempt at Assessing Police Candidates," *Journal of Criminal Law, Criminology and Police Science* 52 (1961), 232.

5. Thomas H. Wright, "Pre-Employment Background Investigations," *FBI Law Enforcement Bulletin* 60 (1991), 16.

6. Frank Horvath, "Polygraphic Screening Candidates for Police Work in Large Police Agencies in the United States: A Survey of Practices, Policies, and Evaluative Comments," *American Journal of Police* 12 (1993), 67–86.

7. Elizabeth Burbeck and Adrian Furham, "Police Officer Selection: A Critical Review of the Literature," *Journal of Police Science and Administration* 3 (1985), 58–69.

8. James M. Poland, "Police Selection Methods and the Prediction of Police Performance," *Journal of Police Science and Administration* 6 (1988), 376.

9. Wade Lambert, "Flunking Grade: Psychological Tests Designed to Weed Out Rogue Cops Get a 'D,'" *Wall Street Journal* (September 11, 1995), A1.

10. Charles Ornstein, "Federal Probe Finds City of Garland Biased in Hiring," *Dallas Morning News* (August 21, 1997), 32A.

11. For an exhaustive overview of these cases, see Sonja A. Soehnel, "Sex Discrimination in Law Enforcement and Corrections Employment," *American Law Reports,* 1997 Supplement (Rochester: Lawyers Co-operative Publishing Company, 1997), 31.

12. Marion Davis, "They Came, They Saw and They Perspired," *Providence Journal-Bulletin* (March 31, 1998), C1.

13. David L. Carter and Allen D. Sapp, "College Education and Policing: Coming of Age," *FBI Law Enforcement Bulletin* 61 (1992), 8.

14. Alan Vodicka, "Educational Requirements for Police Recruits," *Law and Order* 42 (1994), 91.

15. David L. Carter and Allen D. Sapp, *Police Education and Minority Recruitment: The Impact of a College Requirement* (Washington, D.C.: Police Executive Research Forum, 1991), 2–4.

16. Vodicka, 91.

17. D. P. Hinkle, "College Degree: An Impractical Prerequisite for Police Work," *Law and Order* (July 1991), 105.

18. Edgar H. Schein, *Organizational Culture and Leadership* (San Francisco: Josey-Bass, 1985), 9.

19. Harry J. Mullins, "Myth, Tradition, and Ritual," *Law and Order* (September 1995), 197.

20. John Van Maanen, "Observations on the Making of a Policeman," *Human Organization* 32 (1973), 407–18.

21. Malcolm Sparrow, Mark Moore, and David Kennedy, *Beyond 911: A New Era For Policing* (New York: Basic Books, 1990), 51.

22. William Westly, *Violence and the Police: A Sociological Study of Law, Custom, and Morality* (Cambridge, MA: MIT Press, 1970).

23. Arthur Neiderhoffer, *Behind the Shield: The Police in Urban Society* (Garden City, NY: Doubleday, 1967).

24. Wallace Graves, "Police Cynicism: Causes and Cures," *FBI Law Enforcement Bulletin* (June 1996), 16–21.

25. Robert Regoli, *Police in America* (Washington, DC: R.F. Publishing, 1977).

26. Bob Herbert, "A Cop's View," *New York Times* (March 15, 1998), 17.

27. Jerome H. Skolnick, *Justice without Trial: Law Enforcement in a Democratic Society* (New York: Wiley, 1966), 44.

28. James Hibberd, "Police Psychology," *On Patrol* (Fall 1996), 26.

29. Bureau of Justice Statistics, *Workplace Violence, 1992–1996* (Washington, D.C.: U.S. Department of Justice, July 1998), 3.

30. Gary Fields, "In '98, 155 Law Officers Killed in Line of Duty," *USA Today* (December 31, 1998), 2A.

31. Greg Connor, "Improving Officer Perception," *Law and Order* (March 1992), 39–40.

32. Charles Remsberg, *The Tactical Edge: Surviving High-Risk Patrol* (Northbrook, IL: Calibre Press, 1986), 47–51.

33. Cited in Gerald W. Garner, "Drunk and Deadly," *Police* (July 1997), 50.

34. *Ibid.*

35. Anna Knight and William Brierley, "Survivors' Club," *Police Chief* (June 1997), 71.

36. Hibberd, 27.

37. "Dispatches," *On Patrol* (Summer 1996), 25.

38. Les Krantz, *Job-Rated Almanac* (New York: World Almanac, 1998).

39. Gail A. Goolsakian, et al., *Coping with Police Stress* (Washington, D.C.: National Institute of Justice, 1985).

40. J. L. O'Neil and M. A. Cushing, *The Impact of Shift Work on Police Officers* (Washington, D.C.: Police Executive Research Forum, 1991), 1.

41. M. J. Horowitz, N. Wilner, N. B. Kaltreider, and W. Alvarez. "Signs and Symptoms of Post Traumatic Stress Disorder," *Archives of General Psychiatry* 37 (1980), 85–92.

42. Thomas E. Baker and Jane P. Baker, "Preventing Police Suicide," *FBI Law Enforcement Bulletin* (October 1996), 24–8.

43. Lawrence M. Friedman, *Crime and Punishment in American History* (New York: Basic Books, 1993), 362.

44. Jerome H. Skolnick and James J. Fyfe, *Above the Law: Police and Excessive Use of Violence* (New York: Free Press, 1993), 37.

45. Bureau of Justice Statistics, *Police Use of Force: Collection of National Data* (Washington, D.C.: U.S. Department of Justice, November 1997), 13.

46. Independent Commission on the Los Angeles Police Department, *Report of the Independent Commission on the Los Angeles Police Department* (1991), ix.

47. Joel Garner, John Buchanan, Tom Schade, and John Hepburn, *Research in Brief: Understanding the Use of Force By and Against the Police* (Washington, D.C.: Office of Justice Programs, November 1996), 5.

48. *Ibid.,* 1.

49. Cited in Peter Noel, "'I Thought He Had a Gun,'" *Village Voice* (July 13, 1998), 41.

50. Bureau of Justice Statistics, *Police Use of Force: Collection of National Data.*

51. Elliot Grossman, "Officers Didn't Brutalize Disabled Vet," *Allentown Morning Call* (February 22, 1997), B11.

52. Rolando V. del Carmen, *Criminal Procedure for Law Enforcement Personnel* (Monterey, CA: Brooks/Cole Publishing Co., 1987), 107–8.

53. 490 U.S. 386 (1989).

54. Greg Connor, "Use of Force Continuum: Phase II," *Law and Order* (March 1991), 30–5.

55. 471 U.S. 1 (1985).

56. Grossman, B11.

57. 471 U.S. 11 (1985).

58. Samuel Walker, *Taming the System: The Control of Discretion in Criminal Justice, 1950–1990* (New York: Oxford University Press, 1993), 31.

59. G. Meyer, "Nonlethal Weapons vs. Conventional Police Tactics: Assessing Injuries and Liabilities," *The Police Chief* (August 1992), 10–17.

60. Warren Cohen, "When Lethal Force Won't Do," *U.S. News & World Report* (June 23, 1997), 12.

61. Brian Scott, "Heat: Deploying OC Pepper Spray," *Police* (March 1998), 40.

62. William C. Bailey, "Less-than-Lethal Weapons and Police-Citizen Killing in U.S. Urban Areas," *Crime & Delinquency* (October 1996) 535–52.

63. Herman Goldstein, *Police Corruption: A Perspective on Its Nature and Control* (Washington, D.C.: Police Foundation, 1975), 3.

64. John Kaplan, Jerome H. Skolnick, and Malcolm M. Freeley, *Criminal Justice,* 5th ed. (Westbury, NY: The Foundation Press, 1991), 205–6.

65. Dan McGraw, "The American Connection," *U.S. News & World Report* (February 24, 1997), 41.

66. Federal Bureau of Prisons, *Misconduct to Corruption* (Washington, D.C.: U.S. Department of Justice, July 1998).

67. Matthew Kauffman, "Former Trooper Pleads Guilty to Charges of Racketeering," *Hartford Courant* (May 7, 1996), A3.

68. Lawrence W. Sherman, ed., *Police Corruption: A Sociological Perspective* (Garden City, NY: Doubleday, 1974), 7.

69. J. Dorschner, "Police Deviance: Corruption and Controls," in *Critical Issues in Policing, Contemporary Readings,* eds. Roger G. Dunham and Geoffrey P. Albert (Prospect Heights, IL: Waveland Press, 1989), 249–85.

70. Lawrence W. Sherman, "Becoming Bent: Moral Careers of Corrupt Policemen," in *Police Corruption,* ed. Sherman, 191–208.

71. Knapp Commission, *Report on Police Corruption* (New York: Brazilier, 1973).

72. Jocelyn M. Pollock-Byrne, *Ethics in Crime and Justice: Dilemmas and Decisions* (Pacific Grove, CA: Brooks/Cole Publishing Co., 1989), 84–6.

73. Jocelyn M. Pollock and Ronald F. Becker, "Ethics Training Using Officers' Dilemmas," *FBI Law Enforcement Bulletin* (November 1996), 20–8.

74. *Ibid.*

75. Peter K. Manning, *Police Work: The Social Organization of Policing* (Cambridge, MA: MIT Press, 1977), 100–1.

76. National Institute of Justice, *Confronting Domestic Violence: A Guide for Criminal Justice Agencies* (Washington, D.C.: National Institute of Justice, 1986), 34.

77. Jennifer Dukes and Loren Keller, "Can Police Be Police to Selves?" *Omaha World-Herald* (February 22, 1998), 1A.

78. Lou Reiter, "How to Handle Unreasonable Force Litigation," *Law Enforcement Administrative Investigations Guide* (New York: Practicing Law Institute, 1993).

79. Lee P. Brown, "Bridge over Troubled Waters: A Perspective on Policing in the Black Community," in Robert L. Woodson, ed., *Black Perspectives on Crime and the Criminal Justice System* (Boston: G. K. Hall), 1977), 89.

80. Bob Banta, "Internal Affairs Chief: Not a Job to Win Friends," *Austin American-Statesman* (December 28, 1995), B1.

81. "$45M Awarded in Amputee Arrest Death," *Tucson Citizen* (March 13, 1998), 1C.

82. David Josar, "Cops Cost Detroit Millions in Lawsuits," *Detroit News* (March 9, 1998), A1.

83. 42 U.S.C. Section 1983 (1988), originally enacted as Section 1 of the Civil Rights Act of 1871, ch. 22, 17 Stat. 13.

84. del Carmen, 401–405.

85. 475 U.S. 335 (1986).

86. Alison L. Patton, "The Endless Cycle of Abuse: Why 42 U.S.C. Section 1983 Is Ineffective in Deterring Police Brutality," *Hastings Law Journal* 44 (March 1993), 753.

87. "Curfew Crackdown: Toughened Limits Gain Popularity, Controversy," *Denver Post* (June 26, 1994), A1.

88. Quoted in "Demands Grow for Oversight of Small-City Police by Civilians," *Grand Rapids Press* (April 5, 1998), A6.

89. Hazel Glenn Beh, "Municipal Liability for Failure to Investigate Citizen Complaints Against Police," *Fordham Urban Law Journal* 25 (Winter 1998), 209.

90. Remnick, 105.

91. Kendall Anderson, "Missing the Target?" *Dallas Morning News* (February 20, 1998), 1C.

92. *Ibid.*

93. "'Misuse of Force' Series Incited Debate," *Cincinnati Enquirer* (July 2, 1997), A11.

94. Doris A. Graber, "Evaluating Crime-Fighting Policies: Media Images and Public Perspective," in Ralph Baker and Fred A. Meyer, Jr., eds, *Evaluating Alternative Law Enforcement Policies* (Lexington, MA: D. C. Heath, 1979), 188.

95. John DeSantis, *The New Untouchables: How America Sanctions Police Violence* (Chicago: The Noble Press, 1994), 294.

96. Steven M. Chermak, "Police, Courts, and Corrections in the Media," in Frankie Bailey and Donna Hale, eds., *Popular Culture, Crime, and Justice* (Belmont, CA: West/Wadsworth Publishing Co., 1998), 87–99.

97. Information on *Dragnet* is taken from Steven D. Stark, "Perry Mason Meets Sonny Crockett: The History of Lawyers and the Police as Television Heroes," *University of Miami Law Review* 42 (September 1987), 229.

98. George Gerbner, "Trial By Television: Are We at the Point of No Return?" *Judicature* 63 (1980), 416–26.

99. Peter K. Manning, "Media Loops," in Frankie Bailey and Donna Hale, eds., *Popular Culture, Crime, and Justice* (Belmont, CA: West/Wadsworth Publishing Co., 1998), 32.

part three
Criminal Courts

chapter 8

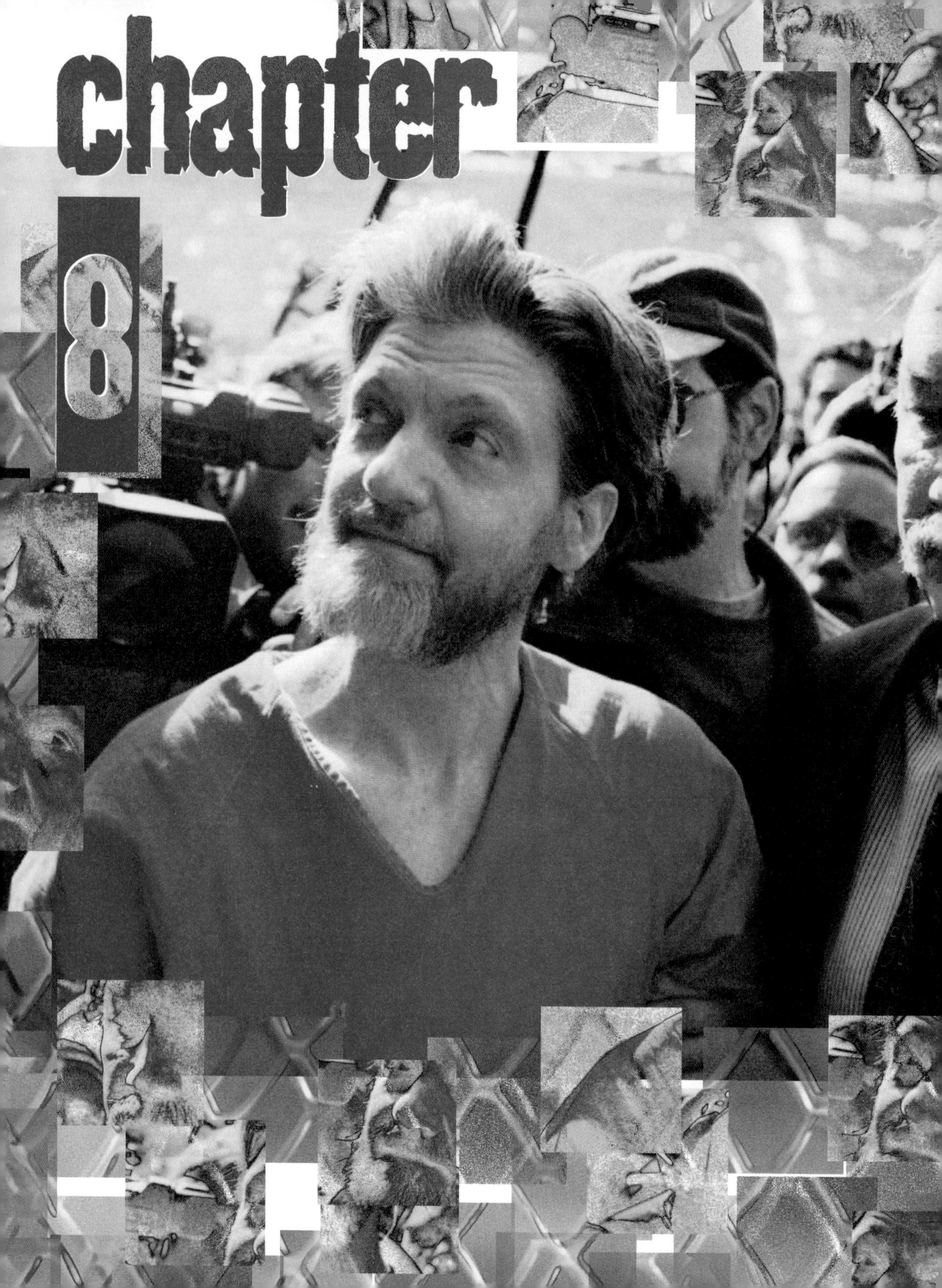

Courts and the Quest for Justice

Chapter Objectives

After reading this chapter, you should be able to:

1. Define and contrast the four functions of the courts.

2. Define jurisdiction and contrast geographical and subject-matter jurisdiction.

3. Explain the difference between trial and appellate courts.

4. Outline the several levels of a typical state court system.

5. Outline the federal court system.

6. Explain briefly how a case is brought to the Supreme Court.

7. List the actions that a judge might take prior to an actual trial.

8. Explain the difference between the selection of judges at the state level and at the federal level.

9. List and describe the members of the courtroom work group.

10. Explain the consequences of excessive caseloads.

INTRODUCTION

As Susan Mosser spoke in the federal district court in Sacramento, California, she stared straight at Ted Kaczynski. Mosser described hearing the blast of the package bomb sent by Kaczynski that, nearly four years earlier, had driven nails and razor blades through her husband's body, killing him instantly. "Please, your honor, make his sentence bullet-proof, bomb-proof, if you will," Mosser said, addressing Judge Garland E. Burrell, Jr. "Lock him so far down so that when he does die, he'll be closer to Hell. That's where the devil belongs."

Mosser's voice was not the only one heard that day as Judge Burrell considered the sentencing for Kaczynski—also known as the "Unabomber"—who had pleaded guilty to charges stemming from a seventeen-year mail bombing campaign that left three dead and twenty-two wounded. Other victims spoke, including one who said he would not "have shed a single tear" if Kaczynski, who evaded the death sentence through a plea bargain, had been executed. The federal prosecutors, representing the American people, claimed that Kaczynski was not a crusader against technology, as he had portrayed himself, but a petulant murderer driven by the desire for "personal revenge."

Theodore John Kaczynski, known to Americans as the "Unabomber," certainly fit the definition of "mentally unstable": living alone in a Montana shack, writing lengthy diatribes against the evils of modern life, and sending mail bombs to punish his victims for their worship of technology. In the end, however, Kaczynski's madness may have saved his life. In February 1998, the U.S Department of Justice accepted Kaczynski's guilty plea because it worried that a trial would dramatize his insanity and result in a less serious sentence than the life-without-parole prison term that was agreed upon. What does the Kaczynski nontrial reveal about the role of compromise in the American court system?

Judge Burrell, after sentencing the defendant to four life terms plus thirty years in prison, said Kaczynski had "committed unspeakable and monstrous crimes for which he shows utterly no remorse." Even the Unabomber himself had a chance to speak, claiming that the prosecution had improperly discredited his political beliefs and urging people to reserve judgment on him "until all the facts are available."[1]

Despite the length of the sentence, as we shall see in Chapter 9 many observers did not feel that justice had been served in Kaczynski's case. For such crimes, they argued, he should have been put to death. Others countered that, as we shall discuss in Chapter 11, no one should be executed, no matter how heinous his or her crimes. Clearly, the definition of justice is elusive. Famed jurist Roscoe Pound characterized justice as society's demand "that serious offenders be convicted and punished," while at the same time "the innocent and the unfortunate are not oppressed."[2] We can expand this noble, if idealistic, definition. Citizens expect their courts to discipline the guilty, provide deterrents for illegal activities, protect individual civil liberties, and rehabilitate criminals—all simultaneously.

Over the course of the next four chapters, we shall examine these lofty goals and the extent to which they can be reached. The Unabomber case, at the top of the wedding cake model described in Chapter 1, offered a chance for all the principal elements of the criminal justice system to participate in the quest for justice. As will become clear, the American court system does not always provide such luxuries.

FUNCTIONS OF THE COURTS

Simply stated, a court is a place where arguments are settled. The argument may be between the federal government and a corporation accused of violating environmental regulations, between business partners, between a criminal and the state, or any other number of parties. The court provides an environment in which the basis of the argument can be settled through the application of the law.

Courts have extensive powers in our criminal justice system: they can bring the authority of the state to seize property and to restrict individual liberty. Given that the rights to own private property and to enjoy personal freedom are enshrined in the U.S. Constitution, a court's *legitimacy* in taking such measures must be unquestioned by society. This legitimacy is based on two factors: impartiality and independence.[3] In theory, each party involved in a courtroom dispute must have an equal chance to present its case and must be secure in the belief that no outside factors are going to influence the decision rendered by the court. Even admitted serial murderers such as Ted Kaczynski must receive fair and impartial hearings if the court system as a whole is to retain the confidence of the public.

Due Process and Crime Control in the Courts

As mentioned in Chapter 1, the criminal justice system has two sets of underlying values: due process and crime control. Due process values focus on protecting the rights of the individual; crime control values stress the punishment and repression of criminal conduct.[4] The competing nature of these two value systems is often most evident in the nation's courts.

The Due Process Function. The primary concern of early American courts was to protect the rights of the individual against the power of the state. Memories of injustices suffered at the hands of the British monarchy were still strong, and most of the procedural rules that we have discussed in this textbook were created with the express purpose of giving the individual a "fair chance" against the government in any courtroom proceedings. Therefore, the due process function of the courts is to protect individuals from the unfair advantages that the government—with its immense resources—automatically enjoys in legal battles. Seen in this light, constitutional guarantees such as the right to counsel, the right to a jury trial, and protection from self-incrimination are equalizers in the "contest" between the state and the individual. The idea that the two sides in a courtroom dispute are adversaries is, as we shall see in the next chapter, fundamental in American courts.

The Crime Control Function. Advocates of crime control distinguish between the court's obligation to be fair to the accused and its obligation to be fair to society.[5] The crime control function of the courts emphasizes punishment and retribution—criminals must suffer for the harm done to society, and it is the courts' responsibility to see that they do so. Given this responsibility to protect the public, deter criminal behavior, and "get criminals off the streets," the courts should not be concerned solely with giving the accused a fair chance. Rather than using due process rules as "equalizers," the courts should use them as protection against blatantly unconstitutional acts. For example, a detective who beats a suspect with a tire iron to get a confession has obviously infringed upon the suspect's constitutional rights. If, however, the detective uses trickery to gain a confession, the court should allow the confession to stand because it is not in society's interest that law enforcement agents be deterred from outwitting criminals.

The Rehabilitation Function

A third view of the court's responsibility is based on the "medical model" of the criminal justice system. In this model, criminals are analogous to patients, and the courts perform the role of doctors who dispense "treatment."[6] The criminal is seen as sick, not evil, and therefore treatment is morally justified. Of course, treatment varies from case to case, and some criminals require harsh penalties such as incarceration. In other cases, how-

The architecture of courthouses reflects the mood of the societies in which they are constructed. In the past, architects have emphasized ideals of citizen participation in constructing noble yet unthreatening courthouses. Boston's new $228 million federal courthouse reflects the crime control concerns of today's society. Judging from the photo provided here, what are the values exhibited through the architectural structure of the building? Do you agree with one critic that it represents the "architecture of paranoia"?

JURISDICTION
The authority of a court to hear and decide cases within an area of the law or a geographical territory.

ever, it may not be in society's best interest for the criminal to be punished according to the formal rules of the justice system. Perhaps the criminal can be rehabilitated to become a productive member of society and thus save taxpayers the costs of incarceration or other punishment. (For information on a court system that favors rehabilitation over imprisonment, see *Cross-National CJ Comparison—Navajo Peacemaker Courts*.)

The Bureaucratic Function

To a certain extent, the crime control, due process, and rehabilitation functions of a court are secondary to its bureaucratic function. In general, a court may have the goal of protecting society or protecting the rights of the individual, but on a day-to-day basis that court has the more pressing task of dealing with the cases brought before it. Like any bureaucracy, a court is concerned with speed and efficiency, and loftier concepts such as justice can be secondary to a judge's need to wrap up a particular case before six o'clock so that administrative deadlines can be met. Indeed, many observers feel that the primary adversarial relationship in the courts is not between the two parties involved but between the ideal of justice and the reality of bureaucratic limitations.[7]

THE BASIC PRINCIPLES OF THE AMERICAN JUDICIAL SYSTEM

One of the most oft-cited limitations of the American judicial system is its complex nature. In truth, the United States does not have a single judicial system, but fifty-one different systems—one for each state and the federal government. As each state has its own unique judiciary with its own set of rules, some of which may be in conflict with the federal judiciary, it is helpful at this point to discuss the basics—jurisdiction, trial and appellate courts, and the dual court system.

Jurisdiction

In 1975, Canadian Joseph Faulder was convicted for the murder of an elderly woman in Gladewater, Texas. After his case wound its way through the appeals process, Faulder was scheduled to be put to death on December 11, 1998. Thirty minutes before the lethal injection, however, the United States Supreme Court placed a stay on his execution. According to international treaty, the Court ruled, the Canadian government should have been notified of Faulder's sentence and given the opportunity to aid him. Canadian authorities were, for their part, outraged that a citizen of Canada, which does not allow capital punishment, would be executed on American soil. How does the concept of jurisdiction apply to the Faulder case?

In Latin, *juris* means "law," and *diction* means "to speak." Thus, **jurisdiction** literally refers to the power "to speak the law." Before any court can hear a case, it must have jurisdiction over the persons involved in the case or its subject matter. The jurisdiction of every court, even the Supreme Court, is limited in some way.

Geographical Jurisdiction. One limitation is geographical. Generally, a court can exercise its authority over residents of a certain area. A state trial court, for example, normally has jurisdictional authority over crimes committed in a particular area of the state, such as a county or a district. A state's highest court (often called the state supreme court) has jurisdictional authority over the entire state, and the United States Supreme Court has jurisdiction over the entire country.

The issue of geographical jurisdiction can be complicated. Take the case in which Samuel Gonzalez and Daniel Rocha, both Texas residents, hired Joey Del Toro to drive to Sarasota, Florida, to murder Sheila Bullush. Gonzalez and Rocha were indicted in Texas for conspiracy to commit capital murder, but Florida requested that they be extradited to the state where the murder took place. *Extradition* refers to the process by which a state or country surrenders wrongdoers to the jurisdiction in which they committed a crime. In this case, Texas officials agreed to extradite Gonzalez, primarily because the penalty for his crime is harsher in Florida than in Texas.[8] States are not always so willing to

TEXAS

EX 5 8 0

1977

Cross-National CJ Comparison

Navajo Peacemaker Courts

When the Navajo returned to their native lands in 1892 after being forcibly relocated to Fort Sumner, New Mexico, by the U.S. Army during the "Long Walk" twenty-eight years earlier, the federal government operated the criminal courts on tribal property. In 1959, the Navajo Nation, which extends across several southwestern states, took control of its court system, which was still patterned after the American model and, in the words of one Navajo, had "little meaning for us in the Navajo way." Now, the tribe's judicial system is returning to the "Navajo way" in the form of Peacemaker courts. These courts reflect the traditional function of Navajo criminal law, which strives not so much to punish wrongdoers as to use community participation to resolve the issues behind the wrongdoing.

RESTORING HARMONY

The American concept of "crime" is referred to in Navajo culture as "disharmony." Disharmony is caused by *nayee,* which can be translated as "anything that gets in the way of a person living her or his life," such as depression, poverty, illness, or problems in a personal relationship. Therefore, the goal of Peacemaker courts is to restore harmony by bringing the offender back into the proper relationship with other members of the family and community who have been harmed by his or her actions. In contrast, as we shall see in upcoming chapters, American courts operate under an adversarial system that encourages conflict between the parties involved.

A Peacemaker court is "resided" over by a *naat'aani,* a respected member of the community. The *naat'aani* gathers the parties to the dispute and their relatives in a room and facilitates a process of "talking out." During the conversation, the group discusses the episode and decides what steps should be taken to resolve the problem. The *naat'aani* then gives a kind of lecture that spells out the community values that relate to the dispute. Next, the victim can request restitution or reparation. Rather than punishing the individual, a successful resolution aims at achieving *hozho nahasadli,* or a return to good relations and harmony for those involved.

In 1992, its first year, the Peacemaker court heard only forty-two cases. Today, there are more than three hundred Peacemaker courts in the seven districts of the Navajo Nation, and they hear more than two thousand cases a year. Most of these cases involve alcohol-related crimes, such as domestic violence, property damage, and child abuse, and are referred to the Peacemaker court by a Navajo district court.

WHAT'S THE EVIDENCE?

The Peacemaker courts have attracted the interest of legal scholars from many different countries. Describe the "mainstream" reaction to such courts by visiting **www.context.org/ICLIB/IC38/Yazzie.htm**

---

cooperate—in the mid-1990s, then New York Governor Mario Cuomo refused to extradite murderer Thomas Grasso to Oklahoma, where he was scheduled to be executed. Cuomo was a staunch opponent of the death penalty.[9]

Similarly, international extradition is fraught with problems. In the above case, for example, Del Toro managed to escape to Mexico, where he was apprehended. The Mexican authorities then refused to send him back to the United States unless prosecutors in Florida and Texas promised not to seek the death penalty. Similarly, France refused to extradite Ira Einhorn to Pennsylvania, where he had been convicted *in absentia* for first degree murder. French extradition policy does not recognize the results of trials in which the defendant is not present, and Einhorn was set free.[10]

Subject-Matter Jurisdiction. Jurisdiction over subject matter also acts as a limitation on the types of cases a court can hear. State court systems include courts of *general* (unlimited) *jurisdiction* and courts of *limited jurisdiction.* Courts of general jurisdiction have no restrictions on the subject matter they may address, and therefore deal with the most serious felonies and civil cases. Courts of limited jurisdictions, also known as lower courts, handle misdemeanors and civil matters under a certain amount, usually $1,000. To alleviate caseload pressures in lower courts, many states have created special subject-matter courts that only dispose of cases involving a specific crime. For example, a number of jurisdictions have established drug courts to handle an overload of illicit narcotics arrests, and California has created twelve courts that deal specifically with domestic violence offenders.

INFOTRAC® COLLEGE EDITION

Gest, Ted and Lewis Lord. The GOP's judicial freeze: a fight to see who rules over the law.

TRIAL COURTS
Courts in which most cases usually begin and in which questions of fact are examined.

APPELLATE COURTS
Courts that review decisions made by lower courts, such as trial courts. Also known as courts of appeals.

OPINION
A statement by the court expressing the reasons for its decision in a case.

DUAL COURT SYSTEM
The separate but interrelated court system of the United States, made up of the courts on the national level and the courts on the state level.

Trial and Appellate Courts

Another distinction is between courts of original jurisdiction and courts of appellate, or review, jurisdiction. Courts having *original jurisdiction* are courts of the first instance, or **trial courts.** Almost every case begins in a trial court. It is in this court that a trial (or a guilty plea) takes place, and the judge imposes a sentence if the defendant is found guilty. Trial courts are primarily concerned with *questions of fact.* That is, they are designed to determine exactly what events occurred that are relevant to questions of the defendant's guilt or innocence.

Courts having *appellate jurisdiction* act as reviewing courts, or **appellate courts.** In general, cases can be brought before appellate courts only on appeal by one of the parties in the trial court. Note that because of constitutional protections against being tried twice for the same crime, prosecutors who lose in criminal trial court *cannot* appeal the verdict. An appellate court does not use juries or witnesses to reach its decision. Instead, its judges make a decision on whether the case should be *reversed* and *remanded,* or sent back to the court of original jurisdiction for a new trial. Appellate judges present written explanations for their decisions, and these **opinions** of the court are the basis for a great deal of the precedent in the criminal justice system.

It is important to understand that appellate courts do not determine the defendant's guilt or innocence—they only make judgments on questions of procedure. In other words, they are concerned with *questions of law* and accept the facts as established by the trial court. An appeals court will rarely question a jury's decision. Instead, the appellate judges will review the manner in which the facts and evidence were provided to the jury and rule on whether errors were made in the process.

The Dual Court System

Like many other aspects of American government, the structure of the judicial system was the result of a compromise. During the framing of the U.S. Constitution, two camps emerged with different views on the courts. The Anti-Federalists, interested in limiting the power of the federal government, wanted the Supreme Court to be the only *national* court, with the states handling the majority of judicial work. The Federalists, dedicated to ensuring that the states did not have too much power, wanted all cases to be heard in federal courts. Both sides eventually made concessions, and the outcome is reflected in the **dual court system** that we have today (see Figure 8.1).[11]

Federal and state courts both have limited jurisdiction. Generally stated, federal courts deal with acts that violate federal law, and state courts deal with acts that violate state law. The distinction is not, however, always clear. A number of crimes—such as kidnaping and trans-

Figure 8.1 The Dual Court System

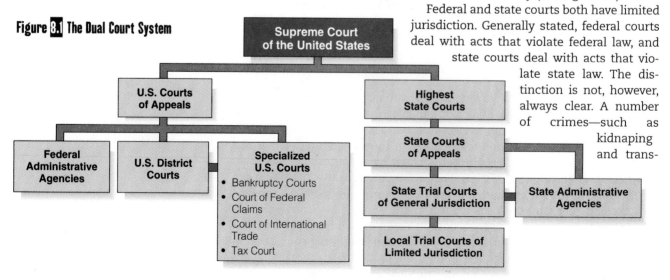

portation of narcotics—are deemed illegal by both federal and state statutes, and persons accused of such crimes can be tried in either court system. In these instances, federal and state prosecutors must decide among themselves who will handle the case—a decision based on a number of factors, including the notoriety of the crime and the relative caseloads of the respective court systems. Often, the prosecutors will "steer" a suspect toward the harsher penalty. Thus, if the punishment for a particular crime is more severe under federal law than state law, then law enforcement officials may decide to try the defendant in federal court (and vice versa).

One of the most important, and least commented upon, judicial trends of the 1990s was a strengthening of state courts vis-à-vis their federal counterparts.[12] In *United States v. Lopez* (1995),[13] for example, the Supreme Court declared unconstitutional a law that made it a *federal* crime to possess a firearm within 1,000 feet of a school. This marked the first time in nearly four decades that the Court had limited Congress's ability to pass a federal law in such a matter. The Court has also upheld state statutes concerning physician-assisted suicide—effectively preventing federal judges from changing the state law—and allowed state judicial systems wide latitude to experiment with state laws such as those designed to continue to incarcerate "sexual predators" after their normal prison terms have been served.[14]

STATE COURT SYSTEMS

Typically, a state court system includes several levels, or tiers, of courts. State courts may include (1) lower courts, or courts of limited jurisdiction, (2) trial courts of general jurisdiction, (3) appellate courts, and (4) the state's highest court. As previously mentioned, each state has a different judicial structure, in which different courts have different jurisdictions, but there are enough similarities to allow for a general discussion. Figure 8.2 shows a typical state court system.

Limited Jurisdiction Courts

Most states have local trial courts that are limited to trying cases involving minor criminal matters, such as traffic violations, prostitution, and drunk and disorderly conduct. Although these minor courts usually keep no written record of the trial

Figure 8.2 The Typical State Court System

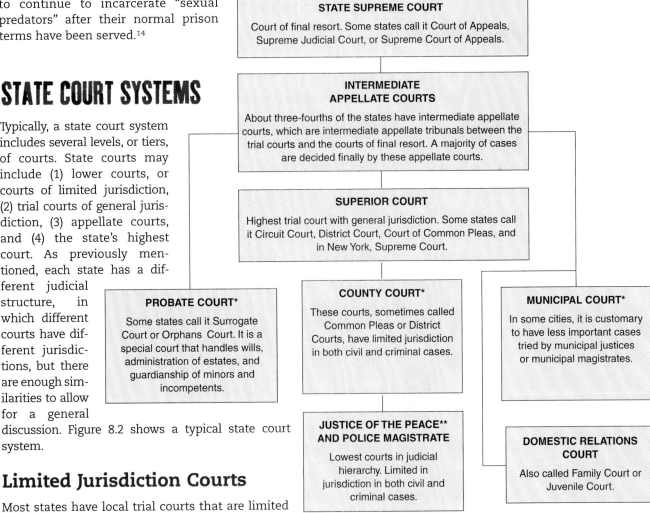

STATE SUPREME COURT

Court of final resort. Some states call it Court of Appeals, Supreme Judicial Court, or Supreme Court of Appeals.

INTERMEDIATE APPELLATE COURTS

About three-fourths of the states have intermediate appellate courts, which are intermediate appellate tribunals between the trial courts and the courts of final resort. A majority of cases are decided finally by these appellate courts.

SUPERIOR COURT

Highest trial court with general jurisdiction. Some states call it Circuit Court, District Court, Court of Common Pleas, and in New York, Supreme Court.

PROBATE COURT*

Some states call it Surrogate Court or Orphans' Court. It is a special court that handles wills, administration of estates, and guardianship of minors and incompetents.

COUNTY COURT*

These courts, sometimes called Common Pleas or District Courts, have limited jurisdiction in both civil and criminal cases.

MUNICIPAL COURT*

In some cities, it is customary to have less important cases tried by municipal justices or municipal magistrates.

JUSTICE OF THE PEACE AND POLICE MAGISTRATE**

Lowest courts in judicial hierarchy. Limited in jurisdiction in both civil and criminal cases.

DOMESTIC RELATIONS COURT

Also called Family Court or Juvenile Court.

*Courts of special jurisdiction, such as probate, family, or juvenile, and the so-called inferior courts, such as common pleas or municipal courts, may be separate courts or may be part of the trial court of general jurisdiction.

**Justices of the peace do not exist in all states. Their jurisdiction varies greatly from state to state when they do exist.

MAGISTRATE
A public civil officer or official with limited judicial authority within a particular geographical area, such as the authority to issue an arrest warrant.

proceedings and cases are decided by a judge rather than a jury, defendants have the same rights as those in other trial courts. The majority of all minor criminal cases are decided in these lower courts. Limited jurisdiction courts can also be responsible for the preliminary stages of felony cases. Arraignments, bail hearings, and preliminary hearings often take place in these lower courts.

One of the earliest courts of limited jurisdiction was the *justice court,* presided over by a *justice of the peace,* or JP. In the early days of this nation, JPs were found everywhere in the country. One of the most famous JPs was Judge Roy Bean, the "hanging judge" of Langtry, Texas, who presided over his court at the turn of the twentieth century. Today, more than half the states have abolished justice courts, though JPs still serve a useful function in some cities and rural areas, notably in Texas. The jurisdiction of justice courts is limited to minor disputes between private individuals and to crimes punishable by small fines or short jail terms. The equivalent of a county JP in a city is known as a **magistrate** or, in some states, a municipal court judge. Magistrate courts have the same limited jurisdiction as do justice courts in rural settings.

General Jurisdiction Trial Courts

The Washtenaw County (Michigan) Trial Court Web site takes you inside the operating procedure of a trial court, as well as introducing you to the people that work there. Go to www.co.washtenaw.mi.us/depts/index.htm

State trial courts that have general jurisdiction may be called county courts, district courts, superior courts, or circuit courts. In Ohio, the name is the Court of Common Pleas; in New York, it is the Supreme Court; and in Massachusetts, the Trial Court. (The name sometimes does not correspond with the court's functions. For example, in New York the trial court is called the Supreme Court, whereas in most states the supreme court is the state's highest court.) General jurisdiction courts have the authority to hear and decide cases involving many types of subject matter, and they are the setting for criminal trials (discussed in Chapter 10).

State Courts of Appeals

Every state has at least one court of appeals (known as an appellate, or reviewing, court), which may be an intermediate appellate court or the state's highest court. About half of the states have intermediate appellate courts. The highest appellate court in a state is usually called the supreme court, but in both New York and Maryland, the highest state court is called the court of appeals. The decisions of each state's highest court on all questions of state law are final. Only when issues of federal law or constitutional procedure are involved can the United States Supreme Court overrule a decision made by a state's highest court.

THE FEDERAL COURT SYSTEM

The federal court system is basically a three-tiered model consisting of (1) U.S. district courts (trial courts of general jurisdiction) and various courts of limited jurisdiction, (2) U.S. courts of appeals (intermediate courts of appeals), and (3) the United States Supreme Court.

Unlike state court judges, who are usually elected, federal court judges—including the justices of the Supreme Court—are appointed by the president of the United States, subject to the approval of the Senate. All federal judges receive lifetime appointments (because under Article III of the Constitution they "hold their offices during Good Behavior").

U.S. District Courts

On the lowest tier of the federal court system are the U.S. district courts, or federal trial courts. These are the courts in which cases involving federal laws begin, and a judge or jury decides the case (if it is a jury trial). Every state has at least one federal district court, and there is one in the District of Columbia. The number of judicial districts varies over time, primarily owing to population changes and corresponding caseloads. Currently, there are ninety-four judicial districts. The federal system also includes other limited jurisdiction trial courts, such as the Tax Court and the Court of International Trade.

U.S. Courts of Appeals

In the federal court system, there are thirteen U.S. courts of appeals—also referred to as U.S. circuit courts of appeals. The federal courts of appeals for twelve of the circuits hear appeals from the district courts located within their respective judicial circuits (see Figure 8.3). The Court of Appeals for the Thirteenth Circuit, called the Federal Circuit, has national appellate jurisdiction over certain types of cases, such as cases involving patent law and cases in which the U.S. government is a defendant. The decisions of the circuit courts of appeals are final unless a further appeal is pursued and granted; in that case, the matter is brought before the Supreme Court.

The United States Supreme Court

Alexander Hamilton, writing in *Federalist Paper* No. 78, believed that the Supreme Court would be the "least dangerous branch" of the federal government because it had neither the power of the purse nor the power of the sword

INFOTRAC®
COLLEGE EDITION

Should more limits be placed on the federal judiciary? Yes.

Figure 8.3 Geographical Boundaries of the Federal Circuit Courts of Appeals

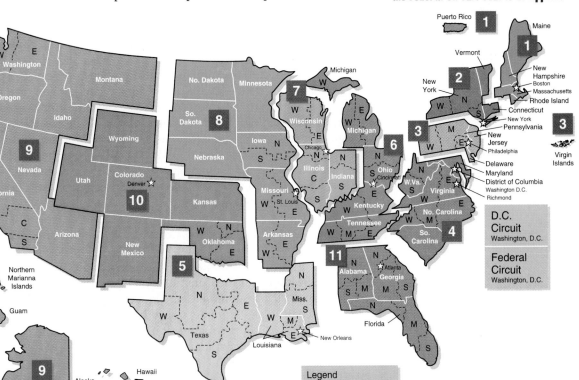

Legend
— Circuit boundaries
— State boundaries
---- District boundaries

SOURCE: Administrative Office of The United States Courts, January 1994.

The Supreme Court tends to be associated with the philosophy of its chief justice. Accordingly, since William Rehnquist (see above) took over the position in 1975, the "Rehnquist Court" is seen as adopting his conservative views. Specifically, the Rehnquist Court has voted to narrow the scope of civil rights laws and increase the powers of the states at the hands of the federal government. At the same time, however, the Rehnquist Court has championed free speech, upheld abortion rights, and protected the legal rights of homosexuals against local ordinances. Examine the record of the Rehnquist Court on criminal matters to determine whether it has followed a crime control or due process philosophy.

INFOTRAC ®
COLLEGE EDITION

Steiker, Carol. The limits of the preventive state: Supreme Court review.

(that is, it could not raise any money, nor did it have an enforcement agency).[15] The other two branches of the government—the president and Congress—would have to accept its decisions, or the Court would be superfluous.

In the Supreme Court's earliest years, it appeared that Hamilton's prediction would come true. The first chief justice of the Supreme Court, John Jay, resigned to become governor of New York because he thought the Court would never play an important role in American society. The next chief justice, Oliver Ellsworth, quit to become an envoy to France. In 1801, when the federal capital was moved to Washington, no one remembered to include the Supreme Court in the plans. It did not have its own meeting space until 1835.[16]

Interpreting and Applying the Law. Despite these early bouts of inconsequence, the Supreme Court has come to dominate the country's legal culture. Although it reviews fewer than 0.5 percent of the cases decided in the United States each year, the decisions of the Supreme Court profoundly affect our lives. The impact of Court decisions on the criminal justice system is equally far reaching: *Gideon v. Wainwright* (1963)[17] established every American's right to be represented by counsel in a criminal trial; *Miranda v. Arizona* (1966)[18] transformed pretrial interrogations; *Furman v. Georgia* (1972)[19] ruled the death penalty was unconstitutional; and *Gregg v. Georgia* (1976)[20] spelled out the conditions under which it could be allowed. As you have no doubt noticed from references in this textbook, the Court has addressed nearly every important facet of criminal law.

The Supreme Court "makes" criminal justice policy in two important ways: through judicial review and through its authority to interpret the law. *Judicial review* refers to the power of the Court to determine whether a law or action by the other branches of the government is constitutional. For example, in the late 1980s Congress and several state legislatures passed laws criminalizing the act of burning the U.S. flag. In two separate decisions—*Texas v. Johnson* (1989)[21] and *United States v. Eichman* (1990)[22]—the Court invalidated these laws as unconstitutional on the ground that they violated First Amendment protections of freedom of expression.

As the final interpreter of the Constitution, the Court must also determine the meaning of certain statutory provisions when applied to specific situations. Deciding what the framers of the Constitution or a legislative body meant by a certain phrase or provision is never easy, and inevitably, at least to some extent, the personal attributes of the justices come into play during the process. For example, those justices who oppose the death penalty for ideological reasons tend to interpret the Eighth Amendment prohibition against "cruel and unusual punishment" as sufficient constitutional justification to outlaw the execution of criminals by the state.[23]

Jurisdiction of the Supreme Court. The United States Supreme Court consists of nine justices—a chief justice and eight associate justices. The Court has original, or trial, jurisdiction only in rare instances (set forth in Article III, Section 2, of the Constitution). In other words, only rarely does a case originate at the Supreme Court level. Most of the Court's work is as an appellate court. The Supreme Court has appellate authority over cases decided by the U.S. courts of appeals, as well as over some cases decided in the state courts when federal questions are at issue.

Which Cases Reach the Supreme Court? There is no absolute right to appeal to the United States Supreme Court. Although thousands of cases are filed with the Supreme Court each year, on average the Court hears fewer than one hundred. (As Figure 8.4 shows, the number of cases the Court hears has been declining.) With a **writ of certiorari** (pronounced sur-shee-uh-*rah*-ree), the Supreme Court orders a lower court to send it the record of a case for review. A party can petition the Supreme Court to issue a writ of *certiorari,* but whether the Court will do so is entirely within its discretion.

More than 90 percent of the petitions for writs of *certiorari* (or "certs," as they are popularly called) are denied. A denial is not a decision on the merits of a case, nor does it indicate agreement with the lower court's opinion. Therefore, the denial of the writ has no value as a precedent.[24] The Court will not issue a writ unless at least four justices approve of it. This is called the **rule of four.** Although the justices are not required to give their reasons for not hearing a case, most often the discretionary decision is based on whether the legal issue involves a "substantial federal question." Political considerations aside, if the justices do not feel the case addresses an important federal law or constitutional issue, they will vote to deny the writ of *certiorari.*

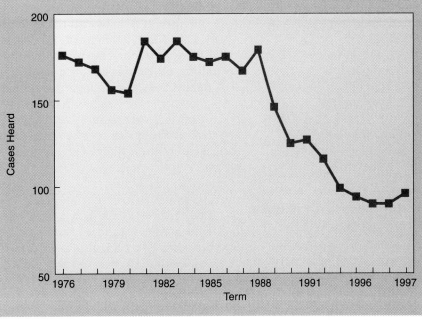

Figure 8.4 The Decline in the Number of Cases Heard by the Supreme Court

SOURCE: BUREAU OF JUSTICE STATISTICS, SOURCEBOOK OF CRIMINAL JUSTICE STATISTICS, 1997 (WASHINGTON, D.C.: U.S. DEPARTMENT OF JUSTICE, 1998), 445.

Supreme Court Decisions. Like all appellate courts, the Supreme Court normally does not hear any evidence. The Court's decision in a particular case is based on the written record of the case and the written arguments (briefs) that the attorneys submit. The attorneys also present **oral arguments**—arguments presented in person rather than on paper—to the Court, after which the justices discuss the case in *conference.* The conference is strictly private—only the justices are allowed in the room.

When the Court has reached a decision, the chief justice, if in the majority, assigns the task of writing the Court's opinion to one of the justices. When the chief justice is not in the majority, the most senior justice voting with the majority assigns the writing of the Court's opinion. The opinion outlines the reasons for the Court's decision, the rules of law that apply, and the decision.

Often, one or more justices who agree with the Court's decision may do so for different reasons than those outlined in the majority opinion. These justices may write **concurring opinions** setting forth their own legal reasoning on the issue. Frequently, one or more justices disagree with the Court's conclusion. These justices may write **dissenting opinions** outlining the reasons why they feel the majority erred. Although a dissenting opinion does not affect the outcome of the case before the Court, it may be important later. In a subsequent case concerning the same issue, a justice or attorney may use the legal reasoning in the dissenting opinion as the basis for an argument to reverse the previous decision and establish a new precedent.

JUDGES IN THE COURT SYSTEM

Supreme Court justices are the most visible and best-known American jurists, but in many ways they are unrepresentative of the profession as a

WRIT OF CERTIORARI
A request from a higher court asking a lower court for the record of a case. In essence, the request signals the higher court's willingness to review the case.

RULE OF FOUR
A rule of the United States Supreme Court that the Court will not issue a writ of *certiorari* unless at least four justices approve of the decision to hear the case.

ORAL ARGUMENTS
The verbal arguments presented in person by attorneys to an appellate court. Each attorney presents reasons why the court should rule in his or her client's favor.

CONCURRING OPINIONS
Separate opinions prepared by judges who support the decision of the majority of the court but who want to make or clarify a particular point or to voice disapproval of the grounds on which the decision was made.

DISSENTING OPINIONS
Separate opinions in which judges disagree with the conclusion reached by the majority of the court and expand on their own views about the case.

whole. Few judges enjoy three-room office suites fitted with a fireplace and a private bath, as do the Supreme Court justices. Few judges have four clerks to assist them. Few judges get a yearly vacation that stretches from July to September. Most judges, in fact, work at the lowest level of the system, in criminal trial courts, where they are burdened with overflowing caseloads and must deal daily with the detritus of society.

One thing a Supreme Court justice and a criminal trial judge in any small American city do have in common is the expectation that they will be just. Of all the participants in the criminal justice system, no single person is held to the same high standards as the judge. From her or his lofty perch in the courtroom, the judge is counted on to be "above the fray" of the bickering defense attorneys and prosecutors. When the other courtroom contestants rise at the entrance of the judge, they are placing the burden of justice squarely on the judge's shoulders.

The Roles and Responsibilities of Trial Judges

One of the reasons that judicial integrity is considered so important is the amount of discretionary power a judge has over the court proceedings. As you can see in Figure 8.5, nearly every stage of the trial process includes a decision or action to be taken by the presiding judge. (See *Careers in Criminal Justice* on page 281.)

Before the Trial. A great deal of the work done by a judge takes place before the trial even starts, free from public scrutiny. These duties, some of which you have seen from a different point of view in the section on law enforcement agents, include determining the following:

1. Whether there is sufficient probable cause to issue a search or arrest warrant.

2. Whether there is sufficient probable cause to authorize electronic surveillance of a suspect.

3. Whether enough evidence exists to justify the temporary incarceration of a suspect.

4. Whether a defendant should be released on bail, and if so, the amount of the bail.

5. Whether to accept pretrial motions by prosecutors and defense attorneys.

6. Whether to accept a plea bargain.

During these pretrial activities, the judge takes on the role of the *negotiator*.[25] As most cases are decided through plea bargains rather than through trial proceedings, the judge often

Figure 8.5 The Role of the Judge in the Criminal Trial Process

In the various stages of a felony case, judges must undertake the actions described here.

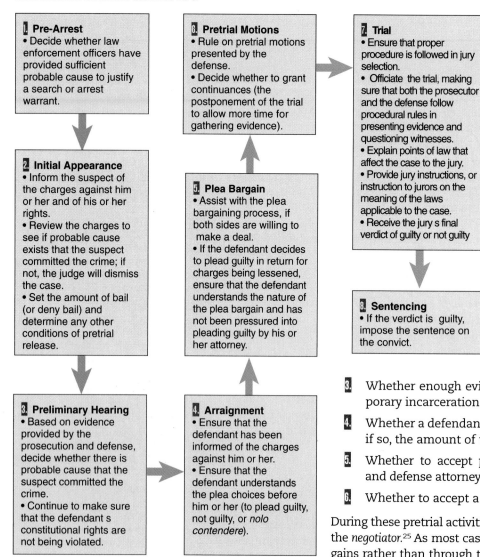

1. Pre-Arrest
• Decide whether law enforcement officers have provided sufficient probable cause to justify a search or arrest warrant.

2. Initial Appearance
• Inform the suspect of the charges against him or her and of his or her rights.
• Review the charges to see if probable cause exists that the suspect committed the crime; if not, the judge will dismiss the case.
• Set the amount of bail (or deny bail) and determine any other conditions of pretrial release.

3. Preliminary Hearing
• Based on evidence provided by the prosecution and defense, decide whether there is probable cause that the suspect committed the crime.
• Continue to make sure that the defendant s constitutional rights are not being violated.

4. Arraignment
• Ensure that the defendant has been informed of the charges against him or her.
• Ensure that the defendant understands the plea choices before him or her (to plead guilty, not guilty, or *nolo contendere*).

5. Plea Bargain
• Assist with the plea bargaining process, if both sides are willing to make a deal.
• If the defendant decides to plead guilty in return for charges being lessened, ensure that the defendant understands the nature of the plea bargain and has not been pressured into pleading guilty by his or her attorney.

6. Pretrial Motions
• Rule on pretrial motions presented by the defense.
• Decide whether to grant continuances (the postponement of the trial to allow more time for gathering evidence).

7. Trial
• Ensure that proper procedure is followed in jury selection.
• Officiate the trial, making sure that both the prosecutor and the defense follow procedural rules in presenting evidence and questioning witnesses.
• Explain points of law that affect the case to the jury.
• Provide jury instructions, or instruction to jurors on the meaning of the laws applicable to the case.
• Receive the jury s final verdict of guilty or not guilty

8. Sentencing
• If the verdict is guilty, impose the sentence on the convict.

offers his or her services as a negotiator to help the prosecution and the defense "make a deal." The amount at which bail is set is often negotiated as well. Throughout the trial process, the judge usually spends a great of time in his or her *chambers*, or office, negotiating with the prosecutors and defense attorneys.

Careers in Criminal Justice

RICHARD S. GEBELEIN, SUPERIOR COURT JUDGE

When I began my undergraduate studies, I was very much interested in sciences. Indeed, I ultimately obtained a B.S. in Mathematics, with minors in Chemistry and Physics. During college however, I began to think that I would like to work in a career where I was directly involved with people. Thus, I decided that I would attend law school. I obtained my J.D. from Villanova but was really unsure what type of law I wanted to practice.

I began my legal career as a law clerk in the Delaware Court of Chancery. Observing many good trial lawyers that year, I decided I would like to do trial practice, or litigation as it's called. My first position was as a Deputy Attorney General in Delaware's Department of Justice. There I prosecuted criminal cases as well as defending the state in civil actions. I left the Justice Department and became Delaware's Chief Deputy Public Defender. In that role, I defended serious criminal charges including murder. After a short time in private law practice I was elected Delaware Attorney General in 1978. After returning to private practice, I was appointed by the governor to my current position as a Superior Court judge. I was reappointed to a second twelve-year term in 1996.

As a Superior Court judge, I try both civil and criminal cases as well as hear appeals from administrative boards and agencies. I am currently assigned to do primarily criminal work. The large majority of all criminal cases are resolved by pleas so a large part of my work is taking those pleas, assuring that the defendant knows what he/she is doing, and then sentencing the defendant. In Superior Court these are usually serious felony charges. In those cases where there is no plea, it is my job to ensure that the defendant receives a fair trial. That means I rule on evidence issues and instruct the jury as to the law to be applied in the case. In some cases the jury will be waived, and then I must decide the facts as well as the law.

Our criminal justice system depends on the lawyers and the judge performing their different functions fairly and effectively. Thus, the responsibilities on each participant are great. Our system only works if each participant actively and aggressively fulfills the duties of his or her office.

The seriousness and reality of those duties came home to me several years ago when I was assigned to try the case of Delaware's first serial killer. The case was an extremely "high profile" case that resulted in almost daily headlines. It was not an easy case in that there were many difficult evidence issues. These included the attempt to use DNA identification for the first time in Delaware as well as an evidence suppression issue involving the key evidence that broke the case. Luckily, both the prosecutors and defense lawyers were excellent and did their jobs professionally. After a long trial and lengthy jury deliberations, the defendant was convicted of two counts of first degree murder. The jury could not reach a verdict on the third count of murder. A penalty trial was held, and the jury could not reach a unanimous recommendation of death, thereby causing a life sentence to be imposed by law.

But this was not the end of the case as evidence was developed during the trial to link the defendant directly to a fourth murder. He was re-indicted for that murder as well as the undecided murder from the first trial. The defendant waived a jury trial for this second case, and I had to try the case as to both facts and law. After conviction, I then had to hear the penalty phase. Nothing in my training prepared me to make the solitary decision that his crimes demanded the death penalty. Nothing really can prepare you to announce in front of the defendant's family, mother, wife, and child that he is to die by lethal injection.

This one hard decision, this one hard act makes it crystal clear why it is absolutely essential that good, bright, and ethical people participate as lawyers and judges in our criminal justice system. It is critical that every defendant be assured a fair trial, and that means a good, energetic effective defense lawyer, an ethical, effective prosector, and a fair judge. These are not easy jobs, but if they are done right, you can feel satisfaction that you are doing your part to ensure justice in America.

During the Trial. When the trial starts, the judge takes on the role of *referee*. In this role, she or he is responsible for seeing that the trial unfolds according to the dictates of the law and that the participants in the trial do not overstep any legal or ethical bounds. In this role, the judge is expected to be neutral, determining the admissibility of testimony and evidence on a completely objective basis. The judge also acts as a *teacher* during the trial, explaining points of law to the jury. If the trial is not a jury trial, then the judge must also make decisions concerning the guilt or innocence of the defendant. If the defendant is found guilty, the judge must decide on the length of the sentence and the type of sentence. (Different types of sentences, such as incarceration, probation, and other forms of community-based corrections, will be discussed in Chapters 12 through 15.)

DOCKET
The list of cases entered on a court's calendar and thus scheduled to be heard by the court.

The Administrative Role. Judges are also *administrators;* that is, they are responsible for the day-to-day functioning of their court. A primary administrative task of a judge is scheduling. Each courtroom has a **docket,** or calendar of cases, and it is the judge's responsibility to keep the docket current. This entails not only scheduling the trial, but also setting pretrial motion dates and deciding whether to grant attorneys' requests for *continuances,* or additional time to prepare for a case. Judges must also keep track of the immense paperwork generated by each case and manage the various employees of the court. In some instances, judges are even responsible for the budget of their courtroom.[26] In 1939, Congress, recognizing the burden of such tasks, created the Administrative Office of the United State Courts to provide administrative assistance for federal court judges.[27] Most state court judges, however, do not have the luxury of similar aid, though they are supported by a court staff.

Selection of Judges

In the federal court system, all judges are appointed by the president and confirmed by the Senate. It is difficult to make a general statement about how judges are selected in the state court system, however, because the procedure varies widely from state to state. In some states, such as Delaware, all judges are appointed by the governor and confirmed by the upper chamber of the state legislature. In other states, such as Arkansas, all judges are elected on a partisan ballot, meaning they must be affiliated with a political party and that affiliation is noted on the ballot. In still other states, such as Kentucky, all judges are elected on a nonpartisan ballot, where no party affiliation is required. Finally, some states, such as Missouri, select judges based on a subjective definition of merit. Figure 8.6 shows the variety in the procedures for selecting judges.

Figure 8.6 Methods of Judicial Selection in the Fifty States

Most states use a variety of methods to select their judges, with different procedures in different jurisdictions. The information presented here, therefore, identifies the predominant method in each state.

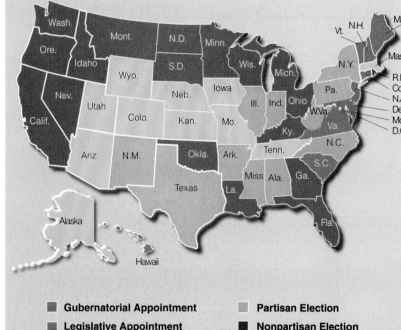

■ **Gubernatorial Appointment**
■ **Legislative Appointment**

■ **Partisan Election**
■ **Nonpartisan Election**
□ **Missouri Plan (Merit Selection)**

SOURCE: DANIEL R. DEJA, "HOW JUDGES ARE SELECTED: A SURVEY OF THE JUDICIAL SELECTION PROCESS IN THE UNITED STATES," *MICHIGAN BUSINESS JOURNAL* 75 (1996), 904–5.

The two key concepts in discussing methods of selecting judges are *independence* and *accountability.*[28] Those who feel that judicial fairness is dependent on the judges' belief that they will not be removed from office as the result of an unpopular ruling support methods of selection that include appointment.[29] In contrast, some observers feel that judges are "politicians in robes" who make policy decisions every time they step to the bench. Following this line of thought, judges should be held accountable to those who are affected by their decisions and therefore should be chosen through elections, as legislators are.[30] The most independent, and therefore least accountable, judges are those who hold lifetime appointments. They are influenced neither by the temptation to make popular decisions to impress voters nor by the need to follow the ideological or party line of the political bosses who provided them with their posts.

Appointment of Judges. Article II, Section 2, of the Constitution authorizes the president to appoint the justices of the Supreme Court with the advice and consent of the Senate. Subsequent laws enacted by Congress provide that the same procedure is used for appointing judges to the lower federal courts as well.

On paper, the appointment process is relatively simple. After selecting a nominee, the president submits the name to the Senate for approval. The Senate Judiciary Committee then holds hearings and makes its recommendation to the Senate, where a majority vote is needed to confirm the nomination. In practice, the process does not always proceed smoothly. In fact, almost 20 percent of presidential nominations to the Supreme Court have been either rejected or not acted upon by the Senate. Many bitter battles over Supreme Court appointments have ensued when the Senate and the president have disagreed on political issues. At times, the battle for nomination attracts widespread attention, as occurred when Justice Clarence Thomas faced sexual harassment charges during his confirmation process in 1991.

Eight states, as well as Puerto Rico, employ similar selection methods, with the governor offering nominees for the approval of the state legislature. Judges in these states, as would be expected, serve longer terms than their counterparts in nonappointment judicial systems.[31] They are also regarded as products of *patronage,* as are judges appointed to federal positions by the president. In other words, appointed judges often obtain their position because they belong to the same political party as the president (or governor, at the state level) and have been active in supporting the candidates and ideology of the party in power. One of the most prevalent criticisms of appointing judges is that the system is based on "having friends in high places" rather than on merit.[32]

Election of Judges. Most states moved from an appointive to an elective system for judges in the mid-nineteenth century. The reasoning behind the move was to make judges more representative of the communities in which they served. Today, elections are the dominant method of selecting judges in twenty-eight states.[33] Of these, eleven states rely primarily on **partisan elections**, in which the judicial candidate is openly supported and endorsed by a political party. The other seventeen states conduct mostly **nonpartisan elections**, in which the candidate is not affiliated with a political party.

Proponents of elections insist that unless judges are regularly forced to submit themselves to the will of the electorate, there is no way to hold them accountable for their actions. Critics, such as Judge Hans A. Linde of the Oregon Supreme Court, counter:

> "Judicial accountability" has a virtuous ring to it, until one asks, accountability for what? For judging fairly and impartially, for conscientious attention to law and facts, for staying awake, sober and courteous to the parties, witnesses, and court personnel—in short, for performing according to the classic model of judging? Or does it mean accountability for decisions in controversial cases?[34]

The answer to Judge Linde's rhetorical question, at least in his mind, is that the public will hold a judge accountable for making popular rulings, not "correct" ones. In recent years, many elected judges have felt pressure to hand out harsher sentences to convicted criminals in order to appear "tough on crime." Another problem with judicial elections is that the winning candidate does not

PARTISAN ELECTIONS
Elections in which candidates are affiliated with and receive support from political parties; the candidates are listed in conjunction with their party on the ballot.

NONPARTISAN ELECTIONS
Elections in which candidates are presented on the ballot without any party affiliation.

Judge Carol J. Vigil of Tesuque Pueblo, New Mexico, listens to the plea of a juvenile accused of violating his parole. Vigil was elected to her post in November of 1998, in the process becoming the first female Native American judge in the state's history. What are some of the benefits of electing judges? What are some of the drawbacks of this method of choosing who sits on the bench?

MISSOURI PLAN
A method of selecting judges that combines appointment and election. Under the plan, the state governor or another government official selects judges from a group of nominees chosen by a nonpartisan committee. After a year on the bench, the judges face a popular election to determine whether the public wishes to keep them in office.

always have the necessary education and experience to be a judge, and the community suffers while she or he "learns on the job."

Merit Selection. In 1940, Missouri became the first state to combine appointment and election in a single merit selection. When all jurisdiction levels are counted, thirty-four states and the District of Columbia now utilize the **Missouri Plan,** as merit selection has been labeled. The Missouri Plan consists of three basic steps:

- When a vacancy on the bench arises, candidates are nominated by a nonpartisan committee of citizens.

- The names of the three most qualified candidates are sent to the governor or executive of the state judicial system, and that person chooses who will be the judge.

- A year after the new judge has been installed, a "retention election" is held so that voters can decide whether the judge deserves to keep the post.[35]

The goal of the Missouri Plan is to eliminate partisan politics from the selection procedure, while at the same time giving the citizens a voice in the process. One noted drawback of the merit system—and indeed of any elective method of selecting judges—is that voters may lack knowledge not only of the issues of a judicial election, but of who the candidates are in the first place. A recent poll in Michigan found that nine out of ten voters could not identify any sitting state supreme court justice, and an equal number did not know how many justices served on the state's highest court or the length of their term in office.[36] (For a review of the different selection processes, see the *Concept Summary—The Selection of State and Federal Judges*.)

CONCEPT SUMMARY
The Selection of State and Federal Judges

Federal Judges

The president nominates a candidate to the U.S. Senate.

↓

The full Senate votes to confirm or reject the president's nomination.

State Judges

Partisan Elections
Judicial candidates, supported by and affiliated with political parties, place their names before the voters for consideration of a particular judicial seat.

↓

The electorate votes to decide who will retain or gain the seat.

Executive Appointment
The governor nominates a candidate to the state legislature.

↓

The legislature votes to confirm or reject the governor's nomination.

Nonpartisan Elections
Judicial candidates, not supported by or affiliated with political parties, place their names before the voters for consideration for a particular judicial seat.

↓

The electorate votes to decide who will retain or gain the seat.

Missouri Plan
A nominating commission provides a list of worthy candidates.

↓

An elected official (usually the governor) chooses from the list submitted by the commission.

↓

A year later, a "retention election" is held to allow voters to decide whether the judge will stay on the bench.

After Patrick Jeffries spent twelve years on death row for the robbery and murder of a couple in Port Angeles, Washington, his conviction was overturned by Chief U.S. District Judge Carolyn Dimmick. The judge based her decision on the finding that during the trial, one juror informed two other jurors that Jeffries had previously been convicted of armed robbery. Under federal and state law, providing information about a defendant's criminal record is considered juror misconduct because such information could prejudice the jury's verdict.

Not surprisingly, local prosecutor Christopher Melly was outraged at the judge's action. "That has got to be the most God-awful, stupid rule of law that they have come up with," he said. Judge Dimmick did not necessarily disagree. She did not believe that Jeffries was innocent. Nor did she believe that the short discussion of his prior record had any impact on the jury's guilty verdicts. Yet, given that the jurors had in fact broken the guidelines for proper conduct during a trial, she felt she had no choice but to overturn the convictions. She ordered the state to retry the defendant or set him free. (In 1998, after a second trial, Jeffries pled guilty to aggravated first degree murder and was sentenced to life in prison without parole.)

For Critical Analysis: In what ways could Judge Dimmick's decision be interpreted as furthering the interests of justice, even if it could have led to the release of a convicted murderer?

Another criticism of the Missouri Plan is that the members of the selection committees, who are mostly white, upper-class attorneys, nominate mostly white, upper-class attorneys.[37] We will discuss the issue of diversity among federal and state judges, and its impact on areas such as sentencing, in Chapter 18.

Judicial Conduct

The question of judicial accountability is further complicated by the gulf between what the public expects of judges and what the law expects of judges. The public wants judges to administer justice, while the law demands that they make sure proper legal procedures and rules have been followed. Sometimes, such as when a judge must overturn a conviction he or she knows to be justified because tainted evidence contributed to the jury's finding, proper judicial conduct leads to what we would call injustice—setting a guilty person free. In other words, for judges, proper behavior does not necessarily lead to justice, a concept many citizens have a difficult time accepting. (See CJ in Focus: A Question of Ethics—No Choice.)

Judicial Ethics. During the nineteenth century, the American public showed little enthusiasm for formal regulation of judicial conduct—as long as judges were competent, their ethics and honesty were of secondary concern.[38] It was not until the 1920s, when the entire criminal justice system was being reformed, that the American Bar Association (ABA) created the first code to regulate judicial behavior. The ABA's Canons of Judicial Ethics was updated in 1972 and 1990, and today the Model Code of Judicial Conduct forms the basis for judicial conduct codes in forty-seven states and the District of Columbia.[39]

The essence of the Code of Judicial Conduct is to prevent conduct that would "tend to reduce public confidence in the integrity and impartiality of the judiciary."[40] Consequently, the judicial ethics codes disfavor not only obviously illegal and corrupt activities such as bribery but also personal conduct that is lawful yet gives the appearance of impropriety. Rhode Island, for example, saw two successive state supreme court chief justices resign because of **judicial misconduct.** The first, Chief Justice Thomas Fay, stepped down because of allegations that he used his position to help a relative and

JUDICIAL MISCONDUCT
A general term describing behavior that diminishes public confidence in the judiciary. This behavior includes obviously illegal acts, such as bribery, and conduct that gives the appearance of impropriety, such as consorting with known felons.

IMPEACHED

As authorized by Article I of the Constitution, impeachment is voted on by the House of Representatives and then sent to the Senate for a vote to remove the president, vice-president, or civil officers (such as federal judges) of the United States.

friends, and the second, Chief Justice Joseph Bevilacqua, was under investigation for associating with organized crime figures.

Some believe that judicial ethics codes overstep the boundaries of the Constitution in their efforts to limit misconduct. Washington Supreme Court Justice Richard Sanders, for example, faced disciplinary charges from a state commission for making comments against abortion at a political rally. Canon 7 of the Code of Judicial Conduct states that judges should not announce their views on disputed political issues because doing so could give the impression that a judge's biases would affect courtroom decisions.[41] In a decision that many observers hailed for its freedom of speech implications, Sanders was eventually cleared in 1998 by a special panel of judges, who ruled that his statements did not lessen public confidence in the judiciary.[42]

The Removal of Judges. The ABA's Code of Judicial Conduct is not a binding document; it merely offers a model of judicial ethics. As the states adopted aspects of the code, however, they also developed procedures for removing those guilty of judicial misconduct from office. Nearly every state has a *judicial conduct commission,* which consists of lawyers, judges, and other prominent citizens and is often a branch of the state's highest court. This commission investigates charges of judicial misconduct and may recommend removal if warranted by the circumstances. The final decision to discipline a judge must generally be taken by the state supreme court.[43]

On average, about ten state judges are removed from office each year. Recent examples include Douglas County (Nebraska) Judge Richard Jones, who was ousted in 1998 for improper conduct that included foul language on the bench and other inappropriate behavior, such as signing court documents with the name Adolf Hitler. Such transgressions, however deplorable, would be unlikely to result in a similar outcome if committed by a federal judge. Appointed under Article II of the U.S. Constitution, federal judges can be removed from office only if found guilty of "Treason, Bribery, or other high Crimes and Misdemeanors." Before a federal judge can be **impeached,** the U.S. House of Representatives must be presented with specific charges of misconduct and vote on whether these charges merit further action. If the vote passes in the House, the U.S. Senate—presided over by the chief justice of the United States Supreme Court—holds a trial on the matter. At the conclusion of this trial, a two-thirds majority vote is required in the Senate for the removal of a federal judge.

This disciplinary action is extremely rare; only eleven federal judges have been impeached and convicted in the nation's history. Most recently, in 1989, federal judges Alcee Hastings and Walter Nixon were both removed from office—Hastings for accepting a $150,000 bribe and lying to a grand jury and Nixon for lying to a grand jury. In 1993, Judge Robert Collins resigned before he could be impeached for receiving a $100,000 bribe from a marijuana smuggler.

THE COURTROOM WORK GROUP

Television dramas often depict the courtroom as a battlefield, with prosecutors and defense attorneys spitting fire at each other over the loud and insistent protestations of a frustrated judge. Consequently, many people are somewhat disappointed when they witness a real courtroom at work. Rarely does anyone raise his or her voice, and the courtroom professionals appear—to a great extent—to be cooperating with each other. In Chapter 7, we discussed the existence of a police subculture, based on the shared values of law enforcement agents. A courtroom subculture exists as well, centered on the **courtroom work group.** The most important feature of any work group is that it is a *cooperative* unit, whose members establish shared values and methods that help the group efficiently reach its goals. Though cooperation is not a concept usually associated with criminal courts, it is in fact crucial to the adjudication process.[44]

Members of the Courtroom Work Group

The courtroom work group is made up of those individuals who are involved with the defendant from the time she or he is arrested until sentencing. The most prominent members are the judge, the prosecutor, and the defense attorney (the latter two will be discussed in detail in the next chapter). Three other court participants complete the work group:

1. The *bailiff of the court* is responsible for maintaining security and order in the judge's chambers and the courtroom. Bailiffs lead the defendant in and out of the courtroom and attend to the needs of the jurors during the trial. A bailiff, often a member of the local sheriff's department but sometimes an employee of the court, also delivers summonses in some jurisdictions.

2. The *clerk of the court* has an exhausting list of responsibilities. Any plea, motion, or other matter to be acted upon by the judge must go through the clerk. The large amount of paperwork generated during a trial, including transcripts, photographs, evidence, and any other records, is maintained by the clerk. The clerk also issues subpoenas for jury duty and coordinates the jury selection process. In the federal court system, judges select clerks, while state clerks are either appointed or, in nearly a third of the states, elected.

3. *Court reporters* record every word that is said during the course of the trial. They also record any *depositions,* or pretrial question-and-answer periods in which a party or a witness answers an attorney's questions under oath.

Formation of the Courtroom Work Group

The premise of the work group is based on constant interaction that fosters relationships among the members. As legal scholar David W. Neubauer describes:

> Every day, the same group of courthouse regulars assembles in the same courtroom, sits or stands in the same places, and performs the same tasks as the day before. The types of defendants and the nature of the crimes they are accused of committing also remain constant. Only the names of the victim, witnesses, and defendants are different.[45]

After a period of time, the members of a courtroom work group learn how the others operate. The work group establishes patterns of behavior and norms, and cooperation allows the adjudication process to function informally and smoothly.[46] In some cases, the members of the work group may even form personal relationships, which only strengthen the courtroom culture.

One way in which the courtroom work group differs from a traditional work group at a company such as Microsoft Corporation is that each member answers to a different sponsoring organization. Although the judge has ulti-

COURTROOM WORK GROUP
The social organization consisting of the judge, prosecutor, defense attorney, and other court workers. The relationships among these persons have a far-reaching impact on the day-to-day operations of any court.

"A judge is not supposed to know anything about the facts. . . until they have been presented in evidence and explained to him at least three times."

—Lord Chief Justice Parker, British judge (1961)

mate authority over a courtroom, he or she is not the "boss" of the attorneys. The prosecutor is hired by the district attorney's office; the defense attorney by a private individual or the public defender's office; the judge by the court system itself.

Each member of the work group is under pressure from his or her sponsoring organization to carry out certain tasks.[47] A judge, for example, needs to take care of the cases on her or his docket, or else a backlog will accumulate. A defense attorney—under constant pressure to attain the best results—usually has many clients and often cannot afford to spend too much time on a single case. A prosecutor must win convictions. Within the courtroom work group, each member relies on the others to help alleviate these pressures. If a defense attorney disrupts the trial routine with unnecessary motions or unreasonably rejects sentence bargains for his or her client, all members of the work group become less efficient in performing their roles. (See Figure 8.7 for an overview of the relationships among the main participants in the courtroom work group.)

The Judge in the Courtroom Work Group

The judge is the dominant figure in the courtroom and therefore exerts the most influence over the values and norms of the work group. A judge who runs a "tight ship" follows procedure and restricts the freedom of attorneys to deviate from regulations, while a *"laissez-faire"* judge allows more leeway to members of the work group. (See *CJ in Focus: Making Waves—Restoring Dignity*

Figure 8.7 The Courtroom Work Group and Incentives to Cooperate

Ideally, we like to think of the courtroom as a place where justice is served. In reality, however, the courtroom is a workplace, and each of its workers has her or his own goals, which may or may not include the accepted definition of "doing justice." Like any workplace, the courtroom functions more smoothly when workers cooperate with one another by sharing information, avoiding conflict, and reducing uncertainty. The major figures of the courtroom work group–judges, prosecutors, and defense attorneys–benefit from a certain degree of cooperation. As you can see, one of the primary considerations of each of the three principals is to dispose of cases as quickly as possible.

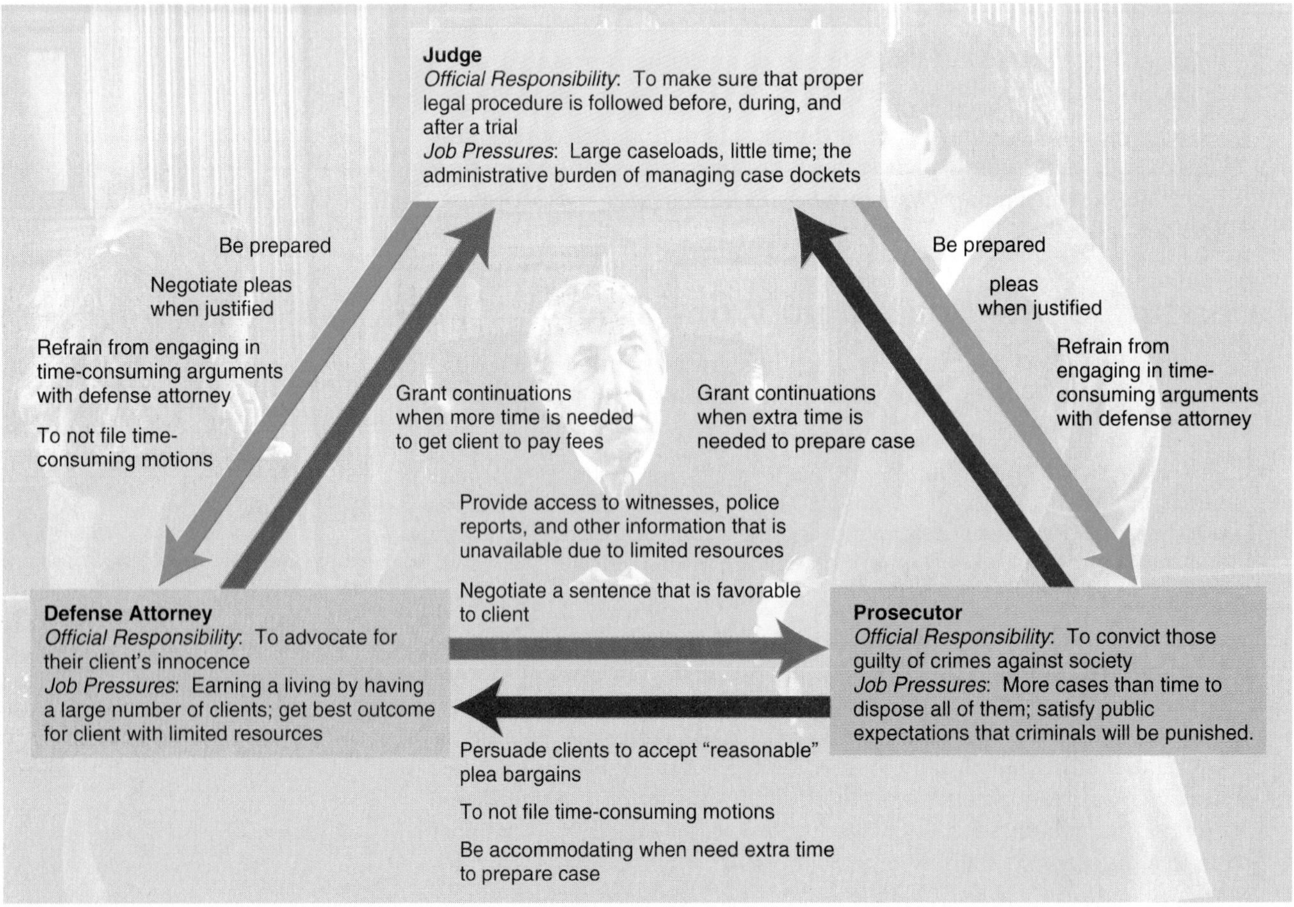

Judge
Official Responsibility: To make sure that proper legal procedure is followed before, during, and after a trial
Job Pressures: Large caseloads, little time; the administrative burden of managing case dockets

Be prepared

Negotiate pleas when justified

Refrain from engaging in time-consuming arguments with defense attorney

To not file time-consuming motions

Grant continuations when more time is needed to get client to pay fees

Grant continuations when extra time is needed to prepare case

Be prepared

pleas when justified

Refrain from engaging in time-consuming arguments with defense attorney

Provide access to witnesses, police reports, and other information that is unavailable due to limited resources

Negotiate a sentence that is favorable to client

Defense Attorney
Official Responsibility: To advocate for their client's innocence
Job Pressures: Earning a living by having a large number of clients; get best outcome for client with limited resources

Persuade clients to accept "reasonable" plea bargains

To not file time-consuming motions

Be accommodating when need extra time to prepare case

Prosecutor
Official Responsibility: To convict those guilty of crimes against society
Job Pressures: More cases than time to dispose all of them; satisfy public expectations that criminals will be punished.

CJ in Focus

Making Waves

Restoring Dignity to the Court

Stephanie Seymour, chief judge of the federal appeals court in Denver, Colorado, gave three reasons for choosing U.S. District Judge Richard Matsch to preside over the trial of accused domestic terrorist Timothy McVeigh: "he's tough, fair, and impatient." Seymour could have added a fourth reason—O. J. Simpson. The federal government did not want a repeat of the Simpson trial, which lasted eight months and degenerated into a media circus.

Judge Matsch did not disappoint. Six weeks after testimony began, McVeigh was convicted on eleven counts of murder and conspiracy tied to the bombing of the Oklahoma City Alfred P. Murrah Federal Building that killed 168 people. Besides producing a popular verdict, the trial was seen as restoring some of the dignity that had been stripped from the criminal justice system during the Simpson trial.

Before the trial even began, Judge Matsch took several steps to guarantee an efficient courtroom. He moved the trial from Oklahoma City to Denver so as to shield the proceedings from the emotional community. He imposed a gag order on the participants, forbidding them to discuss the trial with the press. Once the trial began, the judge insisted on punctuality—each morning and afternoon recess lasted precisely twenty minutes—and held hearings on weekends. Furthermore, he allowed very few "sidebar" conferences, where attorneys bicker over points of law while the jury waits.

In contrast to the Simpson trial, where jurors became minor celebrities, Judge Matsch took extreme measures to protect juror privacy. He put up a wall in the courtroom that hid the jurors from the spectators. Each morning, U.S. marshals met the jurors at a secret location and drove them to the courthouse in unmarked vans with tinted windows. Furthermore, the judge limited the evidence that both sides could bring before the jury and would remark "Let's get on with it!" if he felt testimony was wandering from the subject at hand. In contrast to the Simpson trial where a single witness sat for nine days of testimony, McVeigh's defense rested after only three and a half days.

Judge Matsch was no doubt aided by the ban on televising federal trials, but many observers feel that his methods will be carefully studied and copied by trial judges across the country. Even the defense attorney, in his closing arguments, said that the McVeigh trial "made the criminal justice system what it is supposed to be."

For Critical Analysis: What might be some of the drawbacks of taking such measures to speed up a trial?

---

to the Court.) A judge's personal philosophy also affects the court proceedings. If a judge has a reputation for being "tough on crime," both prosecutors and defense attorneys will alter their strategies accordingly. In fact, a lawyer may be able to manipulate the system to "shop" for a judge whose philosophy best fits the attorney's goals in a particular case.[48] If a lawyer is caught trying to influence the assignment of judges, she or he is said to be "corrupting judicial independence" and may face legal proceedings.

Although preeminent in the work group, a judge must still rely on other members of the group. To a certain extent, the judge is the least informed member of the trio; like a juror, the judge learns the facts of the case as they are presented by the attorneys. If the attorneys do not properly present the facts, then the judge is hampered in making rulings. Furthermore, if a judge deviates from the norms of the work group—by, for example, refusing to grant continuances—the other members of the work group can "discipline" the judge. Defense attorneys and prosecutors can request further continuances, fail to produce witnesses in a timely matter, and slow down the proceeding through a general lack of preparedness. The delays caused by such acts can ruin a judge's calendar—especially in large courts—and bring pressure from the judge's superiors.

ASSEMBLY-LINE JUSTICE AND AMERICAN COURTS

In discussing the goals of the courtroom work group, several general concepts figure prominently—efficiency, cooperation, rapidity, and socializa-

During the 1990s, thousands of new police officers were placed on the nation's streets, increasing arrest rates and lowering crime rates. A corresponding increase in district prosecuting attorneys did not follow. The result: a backlog of cases in courthouses such the one shown above. Courtroom workers say that this backlog leads to lack of preparation time for each case, which means "practicing law the way it should be practiced is sometimes not possible." Why do think that federal, state, and local governments have provided the necessary tax dollars to beef up law enforcement but have been unwilling to put significantly more money into the American courts?

tion. One aim of the work group, however, is glaring in its absence: justice. One of the main criticisms of the American court system is that it has sacrificed the goal of justice for efficiency. Some observers claim that only the wealthiest can afford to receive justice as promised by the Constitution, while the rest of society is left with a watered down version of *assembly-line justice*. (See the feature *Criminal Justice in Action—Is Justice for Sale?* at the end of the chapter.) As we discuss some of these criticisms in this section, remember that efficiency and rapidity are not seen as negatives by all segments of the criminal justice system. Indeed, proponents of the crime control model regard efficiency and rapidity as advantages rather than shortcomings.

The Impact of Excessive Caseloads

The situation in Minnesota provides a clear example of what has come to be known as assembly-line justice, in which speed is valued more highly than outcome. The average time spent by the state's district courts on misdemeanors has dropped 20 percent in the past fifteen years. Judges are spending less time dealing with orders for protection, delinquency cases, traffic cases, and even felonies. From start to finish, a drunk-driving case is disposed of in twelve minutes on average. In one county's arraignment court, the judge hears a new case every 1.9 minutes. The reason for this breakneck pace: excessive caseloads. Felony and misdemeanor filings have increased by 64 percent in Minnesota over a ten-year period with no appreciable increase in the number of the state's judges.[49]

The situation is not unique to Minnesota. As Figure 8.8 shows, caseloads in federal courts have been steadily increasing, spurred by tougher illegal narcotics laws. Approximately two out of every three states are consistently behind on their dockets. The lack of resources to deal with excessive caseloads is generally recognized as one of the most critical issues facing law enforcement agencies and courtrooms.[50]

Because a judge's worth is increasingly measured by her or his ability to keep the "assembly line" of cases moving, rather than by the quality of her or his judicial work, the judicial process is accused of being "careless and haphazard" and of routinely making decisions on the basis of incomplete information. Though definitive statistics on the subject have never been adequately gathered, many observers feel that assembly-line justice affects the actions of others in the criminal justice system as well:

Figure 8.8 Caseloads in U.S. District Courts

There are more criminal cases in federal courts today than at any time since Prohibition (1920–1933) when the consumption and sale of alcohol were illegal. As you see here, much of the growth can be attributed to drug cases.

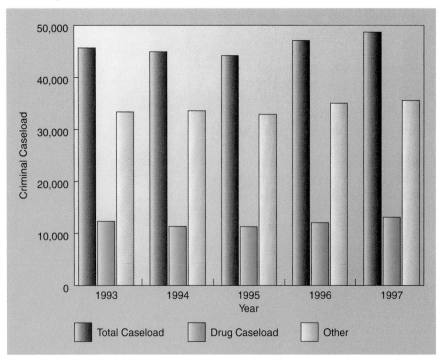

SOURCE: FEDERAL JUDICIAL CASELOAD: A FIVE YEAR RETROSPECTIVE (WASHINGTON, D.C.: ADMINISTRATIVE OFFICE OF THE UNITED STATES COURTS, 1998), 17.

- Beyond filling out a crime report, police officers often do not investigate misdemeanors and felonies unless the offender was caught in the act.

- Police officers often are encouraged to obtain confessions—using whatever means necessary—from defendants, rather than find incriminating evidence, because a confession is more likely to lead to conviction.

- Prosecutors often press charges for misdemeanors and nonviolent felonies only when the case is a "slam dunk"— that is, when conviction is certain.

- To wrap up cases quickly, prosecutors generally bargain reduced sentences for guilty verdicts; as a result, criminals spend less time in prison than is in society's best interests.[51]

If the public is under the impression that police, judges, and lawyers are more interested in speed than in justice, the pressure of caseloads may also lead to loss of respect for the criminal justice system as a whole.

Reducing Court Congestion

Community-based efforts to lessen caseloads often involve *courtroom mediation,* a method of settling disputes outside the court by using the services of a neutral third party. Traditionally, mediation has been used in civil cases, but a number of criminal courts have also adopted the method. The most common form of criminal mediation is a Victim-Offender Reconciliation Program. To understand how such programs work, let us take the hypothetical example of Ted, who hotwires his neighbor Mr. Smith's sports car for a joy ride and drives it into a telephone pole. Instead of filing a criminal complaint, Mr. Smith—who has known Ted since he was a small child and is friendly with his parents—could mediate a punishment outside the court system; in this case, Ted might be required to pay for the damage he has done to the car. Mediation programs are often affiliated with nonprofit community organizations and run by volunteers; the programs may cover a wide variety of criminal acts, from property crimes to violent ones.[52]

Some observers believe that advances in courtroom technology will eventually help clear the congested courts. (See *Criminal Justice & Technology—The*

Criminal Justice & Technology

The Electronic Courtroom

"Never forget that the human race with technology is like an alcoholic with a barrel of wine," wrote "Unabomber" Ted Kaczynski in his manifesto "Industrial Society and Its Future." Taking the analogy one step further, Kaczynski could have expected to see a great deal of "drunkenness" in the high-tech courtroom in Sacramento, California, where his trial was slated to take place. Courtrooms across the country are increasingly employing technological features with the ultimate goal of making the trial process faster and more efficient.

BEYOND THE PAPERLESS TRIAL

For several years, members of the courtroom work group have had access to technology that allows them to avoid the drawbacks of the paper-driven trial. Using digital imaging, they can store thousands of pages of testimony and evidence, photographs, blueprints, maps, and graphics on CD-ROMs and hard drives. With portable computers, attorneys can easily access these data and, in some cases, present them to judges and jurors on large screens. Even with the new tools, however, most courtrooms are not as efficient as they could be. If one side's equipment is not compatible with that of the other side or with the system used by the court, then each side must install its own apparatus, a time-consuming and expensive process. With this in mind, federal officials are experimenting with the totally media integrated courtroom.

Under the floor of this electronic courtroom, cabling connects video, audio, and real-time transcription equipment to terminals at both lawyers' work areas and the judge's bench. Branching out from a central control panel, the system converts data to a format that can be displayed on sixteen different monitors around the courtroom, including one for each juror. A special monitor on the witness stand allows the witness to use a light pen to highlight areas of a document as both the document and the additions appear on the courtroom's screens.

One of the many benefits of this integrated system is the ease with which information can be passed to the jurors, most of whom are used to receiving information from a television screen. It also helps attorneys, who can download "live" transcriptions of testimony for easy recall later in the trial without having to rely on a court reporter to find and read back certain passages. Judges benefit as well: a "kill switch" will enable them to turn off jury monitors while deciding whether evidence contested by the prosecution or defense is admissible.

IN THE FUTURE: Only five federal courtrooms in the United States can boast this level of technological integration. The cost—$100,000 for the equipment alone—assures that the electronic courtroom will not be a reality in most state courts for some years to come.

SPECIALTY COURTS
Lower courts that have jurisdiction over one specific area of criminal activity, such as illegal drugs or domestic violence.

Electronic Courtroom.) In the meantime, some states are turning to specialty courts to lessen their caseload pressures.

Specialty Courts. Many states have created **specialty courts** that have jurisdiction over very narrowly defined areas of criminal justice. Not only do these courts remove many cases from the existing court systems, but they also allow court personnel to become experts in a particular subject. Specialty courts include:

1. Drug courts, which deal only with illegal substance crimes.

2. Gun courts, which have jurisdiction over crimes that involve the illegal use of firearms.

3. Juvenile courts, which specialize in crimes committed by minors. (We will discuss juvenile courts in more detail in Chapter 16.)

4. Domestic courts, which deal with crimes of domestic violence such as child and spousal abuse.

5. Elder courts, which focus primarily on the special needs of the elderly victims rather than the offenders.

Specialty courts do have their drawbacks, primarily the difficulty of finding court space and time to set them up. Because of these limitations, most specialty courts hold session at night and therefore can be inconvenient for both court personnel and the community. Furthermore, specialty courts can inherit many of the same "assembly-line" problems as regular courts. The Cook County (Illinois) drug court, for example, handles almost 16,000 cases a year, forcing judges to complete as many as a dozen cases every half hour.[53]

Curtis Norman displays a dog bite during a session of San Francisco's Dog Court. Presided over by police Sgt. William Herndon, Dog Court provides an informal setting where citizens can resolve dog-related issues, such as minor attacks, noise complaints, and canine trespassing. San Francisco's health code gives Herndon the final word on all issues brought before the Dog Court. How do such specialty courts help alleviate some of the problems facing the American court system?

A Different Perspective. Not all observers believe that excessive caseloads are at the root of all that is wrong with the court system. After observing the lower courts in Philadelphia for several months, criminal law expert Stephen J. Schulhoffer found that each case received the amount of time necessary for its fair resolution. He reached this conclusion even though most cases were finished in twenty-five minutes on average, with many taking less than ten minutes to complete.[54] This line of reasoning suggests that cases are handled in an assembly-line fashion not because the members of the courtroom work group are rushing to fill their daily quotas, but because, in fact, most cases do not involve complicated questions of law. Most cases are routine and can be disposed of without a lengthy trial.

Furthermore, American courts have been facing large caseloads for more than a century, and the pressures experienced by the courtroom work group have not changed substantially over that time.[55] This suggests that no matter what the caseload, the courtroom work group will strive to dispose of cases as quickly as possible because that strategy offers the most benefits for all involved.

Criminal Justice in Action

Is Justice for Sale?

By connotation, "assembly-line justice" implies injustice. The term suggests that defendants are being hurried through the process, losing the safeguards built into our criminal justice system in the blur. For many observers, however, justice in the American courts is related more closely to *money* than to *speed*. As we close this chapter, we will examine the contention that, despite the stated intention of the United States Supreme Court, defendants get not the justice they deserve, but the justice they can afford.

GIDEON V. WAINWRIGHT

In the landmark case of *Gideon v. Wainwright* (1963),[56] the Supreme Court unanimously held that "any person haled into court, who is too poor to hire a lawyer, cannot be assured a fair trial unless counsel is provided for him." It seems to be "an obvious truth," wrote Justice Hugo Black, that "lawyers in criminal cases are necessities, not luxuries."[57] For the most part, the letter of *Gideon* has been followed in the almost forty years since Justice Black wrote those words. Many observers claim, however, that the spirit of the law has been abandoned in America's courts—that, in fact, a person's ability to receive justice is directly related to how much money he or she is able to spend. "If you're the average poor person, you are going to be herded through the criminal justice system about like an animal is herded through the stockyards," says Stephen Bright, the director of the Southern Center for Human Rights in Atlanta, Georgia.[58]

WORKING FOR THE MINIMUM WAGE

The Sixth Amendment of the U.S. Constitution provides that all criminal defendants have a right to the assistance of counsel for their defense. *Gideon* assured that right for indigent defendants who could not afford to hire a lawyer. Today, more than eight out of every ten Americans accused of a felony use a publicly appointed defense attorney. As spending for new prisons and law enforcement personnel has increased over the last decade, however, the budgets for public defenders are being slashed. Although Congress approved a pay hike for defense attorneys in federal courts in 1986, seventy-seven of the country's ninety-four federal districts have yet to implement the raise due to Congress's refusal to appropriate the necessary funds. Therefore, defense lawyers in those districts are still paid $45 an hour—barely enough to cover the costs of maintaining a law office. Even in the districts that have provided the extra wages, defense attorneys still receive less than half the $150–$200 rate charged by private lawyers.[59]

The contrast is even more pronounced in some states. Alabama, for example, limits compensation to court-appointed attorneys to $20 an hour for out-of-court preparation and $40 an hour for time in court.[60] In practical terms, this means that a defense attorney who spends an average amount of time preparing for a death penalty case is being paid less than the national minimum wage. Indiana spends an average of $145 for each of the 120,000 indigents it defends each year. Few states come close to matching the wages paid by those who hire attorneys for themselves.[61]

Public defenders are often overworked as well. In Jones County, Mississippi, for example, the public defender's office—which consists of two part-time attorneys—handles 450 to 500 felony cases a year, on a budget of $32,000.[62] Nationwide, the number of felony cases handled by public defenders doubled from 1986 to 1994, while their budgets remained level.[63]

Under pressure of continued budget cuts, some regions are contracting out their defense work. In this "low-bid contracting," one or more attorneys agree to represent all or a portion of a jurisdiction's caseload for a fixed price. For example, McDuffie County (Georgia) officials recently decided that the $46,000 the county was spending annually on indigent defense was too much. They allowed local attorneys to bid on the service and awarded a contract to Bill Wheeler, whose $25,000 was the lowest bid submitted. Wheeler continued to maintain a private practice as he took on the county's caseload.[64]

"YOU GET WHAT YOU PAY FOR"

Critics of low-bid contracting argue that by emphasizing price over quality, officials are sacrificing the constitutional guarantees of indigent defendants.[65] In the first three years that he held McDuffie County's contract, for example, Wheeler tried one felony case and entered 213 guilty pleas. In that time span, he entered only three pretrial motions for his defendants. This is remarkable, considering

Harvard University Law Professor Alan Dershowitz has provided high-cost counsel to some of America's best-known defendants, such as millionaire Claus von Bulow and O. J. Simpson. "If Claus von Bulow had been the Butler, he'd be in jail today," Dershowitz admits.

that pretrial motions are one of the primary weapons defense attorneys have to protect their clients. Furthermore, the quality of some public defenders is unacceptable. In a Florida murder trial, the presiding judge ordered that the defense attorney's breath be checked for alcohol each morning. During trial recesses, the defense attorney was spotted using speed, Quaaludes, alcohol, morphine, and marijuana. The defendant was eventually executed.[66]

In Texas, two defendants in murder trials had the same lawyer, who slept through a significant part of the court proceedings. In both cases, the Texas Court of Criminal Appeals found that the attorney (who claimed that sleeping was part of his strategy) was sufficient counsel under the Sixth Amendment, and one of the defendants was executed.[67] The test for sufficient counsel was established by the Supreme Court in *Strickland v. Washington* (1984).[68] Under *Strickland,* a defendant must prove that his or her counsel's conduct more likely than not altered the outcome of the case. Therefore, the fact that a public defender was drunk during a trial and entered a rehabilitation program once the proceedings had finished does not mean the defendant was denied sufficient counsel. It must be demonstrated that the lawyer's drunkenness caused the jury to return a different verdict than it would have otherwise.[69] In practice, the claim of inadequate counsel has proved almost impossible to establish on appeal.

WHO CAN AFFORD A FAIR TRIAL?

Increasingly, even those who can afford to pay for their defense in criminal cases are finding that justice has a high price tag. For example, Dale Bertsch, an anesthe-siologist living in Tucson, Arizona, was recently charged with murdering his ex-wife. Bertsch liquidated his assets— which totaled $160,000—to pay for his defense. Even with this sum, Bertsch could not afford mock-jury preparations, jury consultants, computer support, and a thorough investigation of the crime. Although there was no physical evidence linking Bertsch to the murder, he was found guilty and sentenced to life imprisonment.[70]

Attempts are being made to alleviate those costs and provide better defense service, at least for indigents. Rick Tessier, a public defender in New Orleans, Louisiana, brought suit against the state after representing 418 defendants in one seven-month period. In his lawsuit, Tessier noted that most indigent defendants did not receive investigative support because the three investigators in the public defender's office were responsible for more than 700 cases a year, and no state funds were available for expert witnesses. The state supreme court ruled that the state's indigent defendants were "not provided with the effective assistance of counsel the Constitution requires" and ordered the Louisiana legislature to provide sufficient financial support for public defense offices.[71] Similar suits have been filed in Indiana, Connecticut, and Illinois.

Federal courts are also spending greater sums to defend those charged in capital cases. The government spent more than $1 million for the defense of New Orleans police officers Len Davis, Damon Causey, and Paul Hardy in their trial for murdering a woman after she filed a brutality complaint against Davis and his partner.[72] For the most part, however, legal scholars believe the promise of "equal justice for all" inherent in the Constitution and *Gideon* is not being fulfilled. Few would dispute the assertion of one observer, who stated, "If O. J. Simpson [who spent nearly $6 million on his defense] had been a poor black man in a different part of Los Angeles County, he would be on death row now."[73]

Key Terms

Chapter Summary

1. **Define and contrast the four functions of the courts.** The four functions are (a) due process, (b) crime control, (c) rehabilitation, and (d) bureaucratic. The most obvious contrast is between the due process and crime control functions. The former is mainly concerned with the procedural rules that allow each accused individual to have a "fair chance" against the government in a criminal proceeding. For crime control, the courts are supposed to impose enough "pain" on convicted criminals to deter criminal behavior. For the rehabilitation function, the courts serve as "doctors" who dispense "treatment." In their bureaucratic function, courts are more concerned with speed and efficiency.

2. **Define jurisdiction and contrast geographical and subject-matter jurisdiction.** Jurisdiction relates to the power of a court to hear a particular case. Courts are typically limited in geographical jurisdiction, for example, to a particular state. Some courts are restricted in subject matter, such as a small claims court, which can hear only cases involving civil matters under a certain amount.

3. **Explain the difference between trial and appellate courts.** Trial courts are courts of the first instance, where a case is first heard. Appellate courts review the proceedings of a lower court. Appellate courts do not have juries.

4. **Outline the several levels of a typical state court system.** (a) At the lowest level are courts of limited jurisdiction, (b) next are trial courts of general jurisdiction, (c) then appellate courts, and (d) finally, the state's highest court.

5. **Outline the federal court system.** (a) At the lowest level are the U.S. district courts in which trials are held, as well as various minor federal courts of limited jurisdiction; (b) next are the U.S. courts of appeals, otherwise known as circuit courts of appeal; and (c) finally, the United States Supreme Court.

6. **Explain briefly how a case is brought to the Supreme Court.** Cases decided in U.S. courts of appeals, as well as cases decided in the highest state courts (when federal questions arise), can be appealed to the Supreme Court. If at least four justices approve of a case filed with the Supreme Court, the Court will issue a writ of *certiorari,* ordering the lower court to send the Supreme Court the record of the case for review.

7. **List the actions that a judge might take prior to an actual trial.** Trial judges may do the following before an actual trial: (a) issue search or arrest warrants, (b) authorize electronic surveillance of a suspect, (c) order the temporary incarceration of a suspect, (d) decide whether a suspect should be released on bail and the amount of that bail, (e) accept or reject pretrial motions by prosecutors and defense attorneys, and (f) accept or reject a plea bargain.

8. **Explain the difference between the selection of judges at the state level and at the federal level.** The president nominates all judges at the federal level, and the Senate must approve the nominations. At the state level, a similar procedure is used in some states, such as Delaware. In other states, all judges are elected on a partisan ballot, as in Arkansas, or on a nonpartisan ballot, as in Kentucky. Some states use merit selection, or the Missouri Plan, in which a citizen committee nominates judicial candidates, the governor or executive of the state judicial system chooses among the top three nominees, and a year later a "retention election" is held.

9. **List and describe the members of the courtroom work group.** (a) The judge; (b) the prosecutor, who brings charges in the name of the people (the state) against the accused; (c) the defense attorney; (d) the bailiff, who is responsible for maintaining security and order in the judge's chambers; (e) the clerk, who accepts all pleas, motions, and other matters to be acted upon by the judge; and (f) court reporters, who record what is said during a trial as well as at depositions.

10. **Explain the consequences of excessive caseloads.** Excessive caseloads have led to assembly-line justice. Such a criminal justice system increases the possibility that (a) police officers will not investigate crimes unless the offender was caught in the act; (b) officers will seek only confessions, rather than spending time finding incriminating evidence; (c) prosecutors will press charges in criminal cases only when conviction is certain; and (d) plea bargaining will be common.

Questions for Critical Analysis

1. "The primary adversarial relationship in the courts is not between the plaintiff (prosecutor, or state) and defendant, but rather between the ideal of justice and the reality of bureaucratic limitations." Explain why you agree or disagree with this statement.

2. Which court has virtually unlimited geographical and subject-matter jurisdiction? Why is this so?

3. How did we end up with a dual court system?

4. Federal judges and justices typically hold office for many years. Why is this so?

5. What effect does the Supreme Court's refusal to issue a writ of *certiorari* have on lower courts' decisions?

6. What are some of the various functions that a judge undertakes during a trial? What function does a judge assume when presiding over a trial that is not a jury trial?

7. Many states, even those using the merit system, elect their judges. What is the main drawback of using elections to select or maintain judges in office?

8. How does a courtroom work group differ from the management of a corporation?

9. Do rapid trials necessarily lead to "less justice"?

10. *Gideon v. Wainwright* guarantees that everyone has counsel in a criminal proceeding. Is this any guarantee that "justice will be served for all"?

Selected Print and Electronic Resources

SUGGESTED READINGS

Baum, Lawrence, *The Supreme Court,* 6th ed., Washington, D.C.: CQ Press, 1998. Written by a noted judicial scholar, this is a comprehensive treatment of the Supreme Court.

Howard Ball, *A Defiant Life: Thurgood Marshall and the Persistence of Racism in America,* New York: Crown Publishers, 1998. Author Ball presents Marshall's life as the "story of racism in America," starting with his childhood experiences as part of a middle-class African American family living in Baltimore, Maryland, at the dawn of the twentieth century. Ball proceeds to detail Marshall's many accomplishments in the law, from his role as a civil rights attorney in the landmark 1954 case *Brown v. Board of Education* to his struggles as a liberal on a Supreme Court dominated by a conservative majority.

Uviler, H. Richard, *Virtual Justice: The Flawed Prosecution of Crime in America,* New Haven, Conn.: Yale University Press, 1996. The author points to the ways in which our criminal justice system often goes against the public's interest in its efforts to prevent crime.

MEDIA RESOURCES

My Cousin Vinny (1992) This film stars Joe Pesci (Vinny) as a New Yorker who took six tries to pass the bar exam. He becomes the defense attorney in Alabama for his cousin, played by Ralph Macchio, and a friend, played by Mitchell Whitfield. These are two innocent college students on their way to school who have been charged with the murder of a convenience store owner. Pesci's character, Vinny, has virtually no legal experience and almost sinks his clients at every turn during the trial. As you watch this movie, concentrate on the relationship among the members of the courtroom work group.

Critically analyze this film:

1. Would you say the small-town Alabama community that acts as the setting for this film is interested in crime control, due process, or rehabilitation as the primary function of the courts? Explain your answer.

2. To the extent that the film allows, describe the court in which the action takes place. Is it a trial or appellate court? Federal or state? What is its jurisdiction?

3. How does Judge Haller exercise his discretion? Why, for example, is Vinny jailed several times?

4. How does Judge Haller fit the description of a judge as *referee* and *teacher*? What appears to be his personal philosophy—is he "big on procedures"? How does this philosophy show itself in his courtroom demeanor?

5. Describe the relationships of the courtroom work group members in this film. Do they appear to be cooperating with each other in the best interests of justice?

Logging On

If you would like to find information about your state court system, you can use the Center for Information Law. Go to:

www.clip.org/tblhome.html

Once you are at that site, click on the Policy's State Court Locator.

If you are interested in following famous cases and current controversial cases, you can access Court TV at its Web site at:

www.courttv.com

To find out more about the federal court system in general, go to the home page of the federal courts at:

www.uscourts.gov

You can hear oral arguments (in RealAudio) in cases that go before the Supreme Court by accessing the following Web site:

www.oyez.nwu.edu

Would you like to find out about procedures followed in your state courts? If so, go to the Web site of American Law Sources Online at:

www.lawsource.com/also

Using the internet for Criminal Justice Analysis

INFOTRAC®
COLLEGE EDITION

1. Go to InfoTrac College Edition at
www.infotrac-college.com/wadsworth/
Type in the words "RUNNING FOR JUDGE: HOW NON-PARTISAN?"
This article is from *Campaigns & Elections*. The author examines how to run a campaign for a judge who must run for office as would any other politician. Read the article and answer the following questions:

a. How many states have an elective system for judges?

b. How much does a campaign for a judge cost in a large city?

c. Where do judicial candidates raise the largest amount of campaign funds?

d. On what issues do judicial candidates attempt to get media attention and why?

2. In this Internet exercise you will be examining some information about drug courts. Access a "key components" site at:
www.ojp.usdoj.gov/dcpo/Design/welcome.html
Now you can access each key component in the drug court system.

a. Of the ten key components, which appears to be the most important?

b. Of the ten key components, which appears to be the most difficult to implement? Why?

c. In the preface, what aspect of the planning process is deemed most important?

Notes

1. William Booth, "Kaczynski Sentenced to Four Life Terms," *Washington Post* (May 5, 1998), A1; and Martin Kasindorf, "Bomber's Victims Have Their Say," *USA Today* (May 5, 1998), 3A.

2. Roscoe Pound, "The Administration of Justice in American Cities," *Harvard Law Review* 12 (1912).

3. Russell Wheeler and Howard Whitcomb, *Judicial Administration: Text and Readings* (Englewood Cliffs, NJ: Prentice-Hall, 1977), 3.

4. Herbert Packer, *The Limits of the Criminal Sanction* (Stanford, CA: Stanford University Press, 1968), 154–73.

5. Herbert Packer, "The Courts, the Police and the Rest of Us," *Criminal Law, Criminology & Political Science* 57 (1966), 238–9.

6. Larry J. Siegal, *Criminology: Instructor's Manual*, 6th ed. (Belmont, CA: West/Wadsworth Publishing Company, 1998), 440.

7. Gerald F. Velman, "Federal Sentencing Guidelines: A Cure Worse than the Disease," *American Criminal Law Review* 29 (Spring 1992), 904.

8. "Texan Extradited in Murder of Fla. Mom," *UPI On-Line* (February 12, 1998).

9. Carol J. Castaneda, "Texas Murderer Wins a Reprieve," *USA Today* (March 15, 1995), 2A.

10. John-Thor Dahlburg, "France Rejects U.S. Bid to Extradite Killer," *Los Angeles Times* (December 5, 1997), A12.

11. David W. Neubauer, *America's Courts and the Criminal Justice System*, 5th ed. (Belmont, CA: Wadsworth Publishing Company, 1996), 41.

12. Erwin Chemerinsky, "Restricting Federal Court Jurisdiction," *Trial* (July 1996), 18–20.

13. 115 S. Ct. 1624 (1995).

14. David Savage, "High Court Bolsters State's Rights," *State Legislatures* (September 1997), 11–14.

15. Alexander Hamilton, *The Federalist, No. 78* in Clinton Rossiter, ed., *The Federalist Papers* (New York: New American Library, 1961), 467–70.

16. G. Edward White, *History of the Supreme Court, Volumes III-IV: The Marshall Court and Cultural Change* (New York: Oxford University Press, 1988), 157–200.

17. 372 U.S. 335 (1963).

18. 384 U.S. 436 (1966).

19. 408 U.S. 238 (1972).

20. 428 U.S. 153 (1976).

21. 491 U.S. 397 (1989).

22. 496 U.S. 310 (1990).

23. *Callins v. Collins,* 510 U.S. 1141, 1159 (1994) (Blackmun, J., dissenting).

24. *Singleton v. Commissioner of Internal Revenue,* 439 U.S. 940 (1978).

25. Barry R. Schaller, *A Vision of American Law: Judging Law, Literature, and the Stories We Tell* (Westport, CT: Praeger, 1997).

26. Harlington Wood, Jr., "Judiciary Reform: Recent Improvements in Federal Judicial Administration," *American University Law Review* 44 (June 1995), 1557.

27. Pub. L. No. 76-299, 53 Stat. 1223 (codified as amended at 28 U.S.C. Sections 601–610 (1988 & Supp. V 1993)).

28. Peter D. Webster, "Selection and Retention of Judges: Is There One 'Best' Method?" *Florida State Law Review* 23 (Summer 1995), 1.

29. Irving R. Kaufman, *Chilling Judicial Independence* (New York: Association of the Bar of the City of New York, 1979).

30. Ray M. Harding, "The Case for Partisan Election of Judges," *ABA Journal* 55 (1969), 1162–3.

31. Daniel R. Deja, "How Judges Are Selected: A Survey of the Judicial Selection Process in the United States," *Michigan Bar Journal* 75 (September 1996), 904.

32. Edmund V. Ludwig, "Another Case against the Election of Trial Judges," *Pennsylvania Lawyer* 19 (May/June 1997), 33.

33. Deja, 904–5.

34. Quoted in Daniel Burke, "Code of Judicial Conduct Canon 7B(1)(c): Toward the Proper Regulation of Speech in Judicial Campaigns," *Georgetown Journal of Legal Ethics* 81 (Summer 1993), 181.

35. James E. Lozier, "The Missouri Plan a.k.a. Merit Selection Is the Best Solution for Selecting Michigan's Judges," *Michigan Bar Journal* 75 (September 1996), 918.

36. William Ballenger, "In Judicial Wilderness, Even Brickley's Not Safe," *Michigan Politics* 28 (1996), 1–3.

37. Richard A. Watson and Rondal G. Downing, *The Politics of the Bench and Bar: Judicial Selection under the Missouri Nonpartisan Court Plan* (New York: John Wiley & Sons, 1969).

38. Shirley S. Abrahamson, Foreword to *Judicial Conduct and Ethics* (Charlottesville, VA: Michie Co., 1990), vi–vii.

39. American Bar Association, *Model Code of Judicial Conduct* (Chicago: ABA, August 1990).

40. ABA Commission on Ethics and Professional Responsibility, Informal Opinion 1468 (1981).

41. Canon 7B(1)©, Model Code of Judicial Conduct.

42. Hunter T. George, "Panel Clears Washington Justice of Misconduct," *Portland Oregonian* (April 29, 1998), B7.

43. John Gardiner, "Preventing Judicial Misconduct: Defining the Role of Conduct Organizations," *Judicature* 70 (1986), 113–21.

44. Roy B. Fleming, Peter F. Nardulli, and James Eisenstein, *The Craft of Justice: Politics and Work in Criminal Court Communities* (Philadelphia: University of Pennsylvania Press, 1992).

45. Neubauer, 41.

46. Alissa P. Worden, "The Judge's Role in Plea Bargaining: An Analysis of Judges' Agreement with Prosecutors' Sentencing Recommendations," *Justice Quarterly* 10 (1995), 257–78.

47. Neubauer, 72.

48. Kimberly Jade Norwood, "Shopping for Venue: The Need for More Limits," *University of Miami Law Review* 50 (1996), 295–98.

49. "Court Costs," *Minneapolis-St. Paul Star-Tribune* (March 19, 1995), 22A.

50. Special Committee on Criminal Justice in a Free Society, *Criminal Justice in Crisis* (Washington, D.C.: American Bar Association, Criminal Justice Section 1988), 39.

51. Malcolm Feeley, *Felony Arrests: Their Prosecution and Disposition in New York Court* (New York: Vera Institute, 1981), xii.

52. Katherine L. Joseph, "Victim-Offender Mediation: What Social and Political Factors Will Affect Its Development," *Ohio State Journal on Dispute Resolution* 11 (1996), 207.

53. Gary Marx, "Swift Justice," *Chicago Tribune* (April 27, 1995), 1.

54. Stephen J. Schulhoffer, "Justice without Bargaining in Lower Criminal Courts," *American Bar Foundation Research Journal* (1985), 562.

55. Mark Haller, "Plea Bargaining: The Nineteenth-Century Context," *Law and Society Review* 13 (1979), 273–80.

56. 372 U.S. 335, 344 (1963).

57. *Ibid.*

58. Quoted in Bob Herbert, "Cheap Justice," *New York Times* (March 1, 1998), 15.

59. "Too Poor to Be Defended," *Economist* (April 11, 1998), 22.

60. Alabama Code Section 15-12-21(a) (Supp. 1992).

61. "Too Poor to Be Defended," 22.

62. Elizabeth Gleick, "Rich Justice, Poor Justice," *Time* (June 19, 1995), 39.

63. Andrew Blum, "Defense of Indigents: Crisis Spurs Lawsuits," *National Law Journal* (May 15, 1995), A1.

64. Stephen B. Bright, "Glimpses at a Dream Yet to Be Realized," *Champion* (March 1998), 12.

65. *American Bar Association Standards for Criminal Justice,* 3d ed. (Boston: Little, Brown, 1992), 46.

66. Jeffrey L. Kirchmeier, "Drink, Drugs, and Drowsiness: The Constitutional Right to Effective Assistance of Counsel and the *Strickland* Prejudice Requirement," *Nebraska Law Review* 75 (1996), 425.

67. *Ex parte Burdine,* 901 S.W.2d 456 (Tx. Crim. App. 1995); and David Dow, "The State, the Death Penalty, and Carl Johnson," *Boston College Law Review* 37 (1996), 691, 694.

68. 466 U.S. 668 (1984).

69. *Burnett v. Collins,* 982 F.2d 922, 930 (5th Cir. 1993).

70. Gleick, 41.

71. *State v. Peart,* 621 So. 2d 780, 790 (La. 1993).

72. Bill Voelker, "Killers' Attorney Costs Hit $725,000," *New Orleans Times-Picayune* (August 11, 1997), B1.

73. M. A. Stapleton, "Crisis Seen in Privatizing Public Defender Work," *Chicago Daily Law Bulletin* (October 15, 1997), 1.

chapter

9

BY·THE·PEOPLE·CITY·AND·COVNTY·OF·

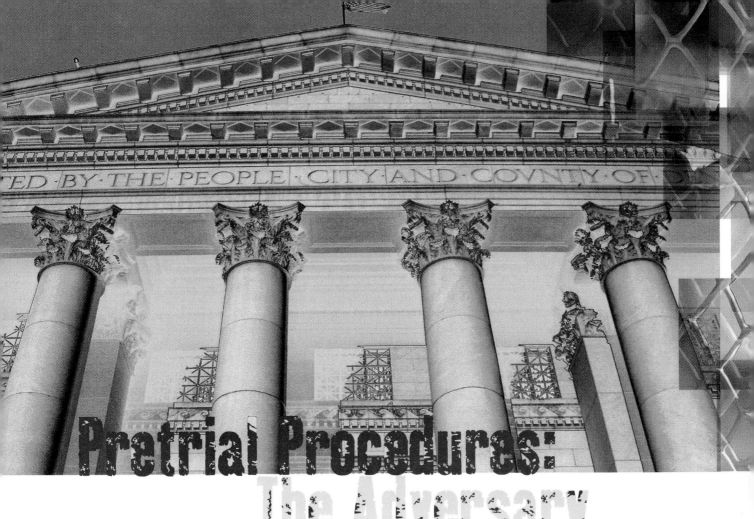

ED·BY·THE·PEOPLE·CITY·AND·COVNTY·OF

Pretrial Procedures:
The Adversary System in Action

Chapter Objectives

After reading this chapter, you should be able to:

1. List the different names given to public prosecutors and the general powers that they have.

2. Contrast the prosecutor's roles as an elected official and as a crime fighter.

3. Delineate the responsibilities of defense attorneys.

4. Indicate the three types of defense allocation programs.

5. List the three basic features of an adversary system of justice.

6. Identify the steps involved in the pretrial criminal process.

7. Indicate the three influences on a judge's decision to set bail.

8. Explain how a prosecutor screens potential cases.

9. List and briefly explain the different forms of plea bargaining agreements.

10. Indicate the ways that both defense attorneys and prosecutors can induce plea bargaining.

INTRODUCTION

At the start of the last chapter, the case of "Unabomber" Ted Kaczynski was held up as a positive example of the American court system. For many observers, however, the case raised a number of troubling issues, not the least of which was whether Kaczynski—who admitted to murdering three people and injuring twenty-eight others with his homemade bombs—deserved the right to "cop a plea" and avoid a trial that could have led to his receiving the death penalty. Governor Pete Wilson of California, where the trial would have taken place, called the federal government's decision to accept the plea bargain a "miscarriage of justice." Yale Professor David Gelernter, who lost his right hand in one of Kaczynski's attacks, said "If we can't get the death penalty in a case like this, I think this is a moral catastrophe for the country."[1]

Federal prosecutors, for their part, argued that it would have been difficult to convince a jury that Kaczynski deserved to be put to death, given that a government psychiatrist had found him to be mentally ill. Even if that were the case, said detractors, the American adversary system of justice should have been permitted to run its course. A trial should have been held in which the prosecutors and Kaczynski's defense team were given the opportunity to present their arguments under the watchful eye of a judge. For justice to "truly" have been served, said Governor Wilson, "a jury should have heard the evidence and been allowed to come to their own conclusion."[2]

In fact, the *formal* adversary process of a trial is the exception rather than the rule in American courts. Nearly 90 percent of all those charged with a felony in this country opt, like Kaczynski, for the *informal* process. That is, they plead guilty, thereby avoiding a trial and receiving, in most instances, a lighter sentence.[3] Indeed, most prosecutors, attorneys, and judges could not imagine a system in which plea bargaining was not the predominant means of resolving cases. Given that the majority of cases never go to trial, is it realistic to claim that the United States has an adversary system? In this chapter, we will attempt to answer that question by examining the actions of the courtroom work group with regard to plea bargaining, bail, and other pretrial procedures. We will start with a discussion of the two main combatants of the adversary system: the prosecutor and the defense attorney.

THE PROSECUTION

Criminal cases are tried by **public prosecutors,** who are employed by the government. The public prosecutor in federal criminal cases is called a U.S. attorney. In cases tried in state or local courts, the public prosecutor may be referred to as a *prosecuting attorney, state prosecutor, district attorney, county attorney,* or *city attorney.* Given their great autonomy, prosecutors are generally considered the most dominant figures in the American criminal justice system. In some jurisdictions, the district attorney is the chief law enforcement officer, with broad powers over police operations. Prosecutors have the power to bring the resources of the state against the individual and hold the legal keys to meting out or withholding punishment.[4] Ideally, this power is balanced by a duty of fairness and a recognition that the prosecutor's ultimate goal is not to win cases, but to see that justice is done. In *Berger v. United States* (1935), Justice George Sutherland called the prosecutor

> in a peculiar and very definite sense the servant of the law, the twofold aim of which is that guilt shall not escape or innocence suffer. He may prosecute with earnestness and vigor—indeed, he should do so. But, while he may strike

---

"If it suffices to accuse, what will become of the innocent?"

—Emperor Julian of Rome, (c 355 A.C.E.)

PUBLIC PROSECUTORS
Individuals, acting as trial lawyers, who initiate and conduct cases in the government's name and on behalf of the people.

hard blows, he is not at liberty to strike foul ones. It is as much his duty to refrain from improper methods calculated to produce a wrongful conviction as it is to use every legitimate means to bring about a just one.[5]

ATTORNEY GENERAL
The chief law officer of a state; also, the chief law officer of the nation.

The Office of the Prosecutor

When acting as an *officer of the law* during a criminal trial, there are limits on the prosecutor's conduct, as we shall see in the next chapter. During the pre-trial process, however, prosecutors hold a great deal of discretion in deciding the following:

1. Whether an individual who has been arrested by the police will be charged with a crime.

2. The level of the charges to be brought against the suspect.

3. If and when to stop the prosecution.[6]

There are more than 8,000 prosecutor's offices around the country—serving state, county, and municipal jurisdictions. Even though the **attorney general** is the chief law enforcement officer in any state, she or he has limited (and in some states, no) control of prosecutors within the state's boundaries.

Each jurisdiction has a chief prosecutor who is sometimes appointed but more often elected. As an elected official, he or she typically serves a four-year term, though in some states, such as Alabama, the term is six years. In smaller jurisdictions, the chief prosecutor has several assistants, and they work closely together. In larger ones, the chief prosecutor may administer numerous *assistant prosecutors,* many of whom he or she will rarely meet. (See *Careers in Criminal Justice* on the next page.) Assistant prosecutors—for the most part young attorneys recently graduated from law school—may be assigned to particular sections of the organization, such as criminal prosecutions in general or areas of *special prosecution,* such as narcotics or gang crimes. (See Figure 9.1 for a typical prosecutor's office.)

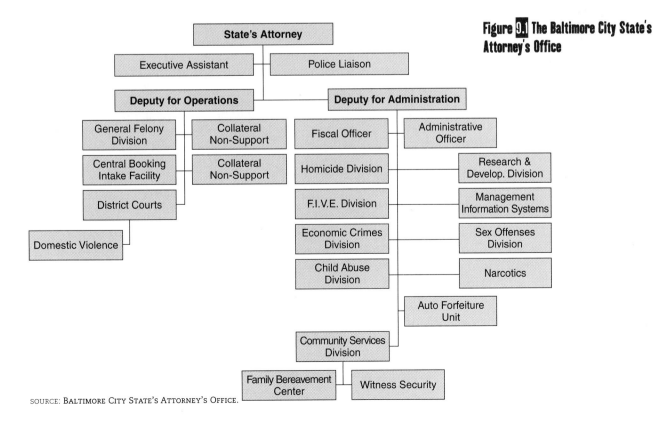

Figure 9.1 The Baltimore City State's Attorney's Office

SOURCE: BALTIMORE CITY STATE'S ATTORNEY'S OFFICE.

The Prosecutor as Elected Official

The chief prosecutor's autonomy is not complete: as an elected official, she or he must answer to the voters. (There are exceptions: U.S. attorneys are nominated by the president and approved by the Senate, and chief prosecutors in

Careers in Criminal Justice

JOHN ESMERADO, ASSISTANT PROSECUTOR

My name is John G. Esmerado. I am an assistant prosecutor in Elizabeth, New Jersey, for the County of Union. Union County is comprised of twenty-one independent townships with a population of approximately one half million. Our county lies across the river from New York City. In my office there is the prosecutor, the chief law enforcement officer of the county, and fifty-five assistant prosecutors.

I first became interested in the field of prosecution when I was in high school. In ninth grade I read Harper Lee's *To Kill a Mockingbird.* After reading the book, I wanted to be like Atticus Finch. I wanted to be a lawyer who helped people. In eleventh grade, I participated in a high school mock trial program. Our attorney adviser was a former assistant prosecutor. From her I learned for the first time the role of a prosecutor. I was intrigued. I applied to a nearby Catholic university, Seton Hall, and majored in American History. I sought to learn everything I could about the world. I took courses on a variety of liberal arts and business topics. More and more I felt drawn to being a prosecutor, to pursue the truth and to aid people in crisis. I graduated college with honors and applied to Seton Hall University Law School. After receiving early acceptance, I took all the criminal law courses offered by the school. By my third year, I secured a part-time position as a law clerk in the Union County Prosecutor's Office appellate section. I wrote and argued numerous motions.

Upon graduation and the day after I sat for the New Jersey Bar exam, I started full-time at the prosecutor's office. In March of 1993, I was sworn in as a full-time assistant prosecutor. Since then I have tried fifty-six

jury trials and worked in the appellate section, the juvenile and family court section, and pre-indictment plea screening and now work full-time on a trial team. Twice a month, I try a case. I have litigated everything from murder to robbery, sexual assault, police misconduct, drug distribution, prostitution, and aggravated assault.

My current responsibilities are two-fold. Primarily, I represent the State of New Jersey at trial. With a detective staff, I investigate crime by interviewing witnesses, searching out evidence, and asking people questions in court to establish beyond a reasonable doubt that a defendant committed a crime. Trial work is incredibly fun. It requires vast amounts of pretrial preparation. Once it starts, however, it moves at lightning speed. Trials are strategic chess games of facts and law as well as all-out mental combat, a blitzkrieg of sorts, to find the truth. My secondary responsibility is to act as legal adviser to the police. Many times during the week and periodically in the early morning hours while the world sleeps, detectives call to discuss problematic cases. They arrest someone and are not clear what the appropriate charges are. I listen to the facts and authorize certain complaints and ask the detectives to pursue additional facts to help make the case stronger for trial.

Recently, I was confronted with a moral dilemma. I was asked to participate as the second prosecutor in a death penalty trial. As a Catholic, I was ambivalent at best about the use of the death penalty by the State. I consulted the *Gospel of Life* and other Church teachings on the topic as well as my own conscience. The defendant was charged with hiring a hit man to kill his longtime girlfriend. The defendant had served a previous state prison sentence for threatening the same woman in the past. The defendant was no angel and had a lengthy criminal record. After much soul searching, I consented to work on the case with the premier assistant prosecutor in the office, Regina Caulfield. We worked day

and night six days a week for over four months. Due to the lengthy juror interviews necessary for a capital case, jury selection took eight weeks. After a three-week trial, we secured a conviction for first degree murder for hire. The guilt phase of the trial was over. We had one week off to prepare for the penalty phase. I began to have doubts about the whole process. Was this really fair to both the defendant and the victim's family? Is death a legitimate tool in the prosecutor's arsenal of justice? The volume of work I had at the time prevented further moral exploration. After a four-day hearing and a day and a half of deliberation, the jury returned a verdict for life and not for death. The victim's family was disappointed. I was relieved.

As a prosecutor, I have always sought to do what is right and just. Incoming data support the conclusion that the current system with all its byzantine rules cannot function properly. Jurors disregard legal instructions, while defense attorneys engender emotional sympathy for the defendant's upbringing, and victims are offered little if any opportunity to place their loss before the jury. Death must be reevaluated by the entire criminal justice community.

Immediately after this trial, I took some time off, grew a beard, and gained weight. I was depressed. For the first time in my career I had participated in something I did not wholly believe in. Since that time, I found my razor, exercise consistently, and have firmly resolved not to participate in another capital case.

In summary, I am glad to have a job that provides an outlet for my desire to do good. Sometimes, when I am working late at night, for free, on a case, I say to myself, this is the greatest job in the world. I receive a salary to find the truth. I help people in crisis, people subject to violence, confront their attackers and ultimately bring some form of closure. Truth, justice, and the American way, a job far too important to leave to Superman cartoons, is the job of the prosecutor every day in and out of court.

Alaska, Connecticut, Rhode Island, New Jersey, and the District of Columbia are either appointed or hired as members of the attorney general's office.) The prosecutor may be part of the political machine; in many jurisdictions the prosecutor must declare a party affiliation and is expected to reward fellow party members with positions in the district attorney's office if elected. The post is often seen as a "stepping stone" to higher political office, and many prosecutors have gone on to serve in legislatures or as judges. Arlen Specter, a Republican senator from Pennsylvania, Ron Castille, who sits on the state's supreme court, and Philadelphia mayor Ed Rendell all served as Philadelphia district attorneys early in their careers.

Prosecutors are also subject to community pressures. As antidrug sentiment becomes more prevalent around the country, for example, many prosecutors feel obliged to aggressively prosecute and charge narcotics law offenders.[7] A prosecutor whose personal philosophy conflicts with public opinion can find himself or herself in a difficult political position. In 1998, New York Governor George Pataki removed Bronx District Attorney Robert T. Johnson from trying the case of an ex-convict accused of killing a police officer. New York voters had just voted to reinstate capital punishment, much to the chagrin of Johnson, who opposed the practice. Pataki, a supporter of capital punishment, suspected correctly that the district attorney would not seek the death penalty in the politically charged case of the cop murderer and replaced him with somebody who would.[8]

Representative Bob Barr, right, a Republican from Georgia's 7th district, was the U.S. attorney for the Northern District of Georgia before being elected to his present post in 1995. Give several reasons why ex-prosecutors are often attractive candidates for positions in the state and federal government.

The Prosecutor as Crime Fighter

One of the reasons the prosecutor's post is a useful first step in a political career is that it is linked to crime fighting. Thanks to savvy public relations efforts and television police dramas such as *Law and Order*—with its opening line "In the criminal justice system, the people are represented by two separate yet equally important groups: the police who investigate crime and the district attorneys who prosecute the offenders"—prosecutors are generally seen as law enforcement agents. Indeed, the prosecutors and the police do have a symbiotic relationship. Prosecutors rely on police to arrest suspects and gather sufficient evidence, and police rely on prosecutors to convict those who have been apprehended.

Police-Prosecutor Conflict. Despite, or perhaps because of, this mutual dependency, the relationship between the two branches of law enforcement is often strained. Part of this can be attributed to background. Most prosecutors come from middle- or upper-class families, while police are often recruited from the working class. Furthermore, prosecutors are required to have a certain level of education that is not achieved by most police officers.

More important, however, is a basic divergence in the concept of guilt. For a police officer, a suspect is guilty if he or she has in fact committed a crime. For a prosecutor, a suspect is guilty if enough evidence can be legally gathered to prove such guilt in a court of law.[9] In other words, police officers often focus on *factual guilt,* whereas prosecutors are ultimately concerned with *legal guilt.*[10] Thus, police officers will feel a great deal of frustration when a suspect they "know" to be guilty is set free. Similarly, a prosecutor may become annoyed when police officers do not follow the letter of the law in gathering evidence, thereby effectively ruining the chances of conviction.

DEFENSE ATTORNEY
The lawyer representing the defendant.

PUBLIC DEFENDERS
Court-appointed attorneys who are paid by the state to represent defendants who are unable to hire private counsel.

Attempts at Cooperation. Tension arising from these grievances can hamper crime control efforts. As a result, a number of jurisdictions are trying to better police-prosecutor relations. A key step in the process seems to be improving communications between the two groups. In San Diego, for example, the district attorney has a permanent office in the police department for the express purpose of counseling officers on legal questions. From the office, a deputy district attorney (DDA) acts as a human legal reference book, advising the police on how to write a search warrant, what steps they can take to help solidify a prosecutor's case, and other issues. The DDA will even sit in on morning briefings, giving updates on how changes in the law may affect police work.[11]

THE DEFENSE ATTORNEY

The media provide most people's perception of defense counsel: the idealistic public defender who nobly serves the poor; the "ambulance chaser"; or the celebrity attorney in the $3,000 suit. These stereotypes, though not entirely fictional, tend to obscure the crucial role that the **defense attorney** plays in the criminal justice system. Most persons charged with crimes have little or no knowledge of criminal procedure. Without assistance, they would be helpless against a government prosecutor. By acting as a staunch advocate for her or his client, the defense attorney (ideally) assures that the government prove every point against that client beyond a reasonable doubt, even for cases that do not go to trial. In sum, the defense attorney provides a counterweight against the state in our adversary system.

The Responsibilities of the Defense Attorney

The Sixth Amendment right to counsel is not limited to the actual criminal trial. In a number of instances, the Supreme Court has held that defendants are entitled to representation as soon as their rights may be denied, which, as we have seen, includes the custodial interrogation and line-up identification procedures.[12] Therefore, the primary responsibility of the defense attorney is to represent the defendant at the various stages of the custodial process, such as arrest, interrogation, line-up, and arraignment. Other responsibilities include:

Leavitt, Michele. Defending the guilty.

- Investigating the incident for which the defendant has been charged.
- Communicating with the prosecutor, which includes negotiating plea bargains.
- Preparing the case for trial.
- Submitting defense motions, including motions to suppress evidence.
- Representing the defendant at trial.
- Negotiating a sentence, if the client has been convicted.
- Determining whether to appeal a guilty verdict.[13]

One question that has troubled defense attorneys and legal ethicists is whether a lawyer has a duty to defend a client he or she knows to be guilty. This debate is addressed in the feature *Criminal Justice in Action—Legal Ethics on Trial: Defending the Guilty* at the end of this chapter.

The Public Defender

Generally speaking, there are two different types of defense attorneys: (1) private attorneys, who are hired by individuals, and (2) **public defenders,** who work for the government. The distinction is not absolute, as many private attorneys hire out as public defenders, too. The modern role of the public defender was established by the Supreme Court's interpretation of the Sixth Amendment in *Gideon v. Wainwright* (1963).[14] The Court ruled that no defendant can be "assured a fair trial unless counsel is provided for him," and therefore the state must provide a public defender to those who cannot afford to hire one for themselves. Subsequently, the Court extended this protection to juveniles in *In re Gault* (1967)[15] and those suspected of committing misdemeanors in *Argersinger v. Hamlin* (1972).[16] The impact of these decisions is substantial: approximately three out of every four inmates in state prisons and jails had been represented by publicly paid counsel.[17]

In most areas, the county government is responsible for providing indigent defendants with attorneys. Three basic types of programs are used to allocate defense counsel:

1. *Assigned counsel programs*, in which local private attorneys are assigned clients on a case-by-case basis by the county.

2. *Contracting attorney programs*, in which a particular law firm or group of attorneys is hired to regularly assume the representative and administrative tasks of indigent defense (see Chapter 8).

3. *Public defender programs*, in which the county assembles a salaried staff of full-time or part-time attorneys and creates a public (taxpayer-funded) agency to provide the service.[18]

Jurisdictions can use several of these programs concurrently. In the most recent published survey, 58 percent of state court prosecutors' offices used assigned counsel, 25 percent contracted out their defense counsel, and 64 percent had public defender programs.[19] An alarming trend in the eyes of some observers is the increasing number of counties contracting out their indigent defense programs in order to cut costs. As we saw in the last chapter, some observers believe that contracted law firms do not provide an acceptable level of defense to indigents.

The Attorney-Client Relationship

To defend a client effectively, a defense attorney must have access to all the facts concerning the case, including those that may be harmful to the defense. To promote the unrestrained flow of information between the two parties, laws of **attorney-client privilege** have been constructed. These laws require that communications between a client and his or her attorney be kept confidential, unless the client consents to disclosure. The scope of this privilege is not all encompassing, however. In *United States v. Zolin* (1989),[20] the Supreme Court ruled that attorneys may disclose the contents of a conversation with a client if the client has provided information concerning a crime that has yet to be committed.

The implied trust between an attorney and her or his client is not usually in question when the attorney has been hired directly by the defendant—as an "employee," the attorney well understands her or his duties. Relationships between public defenders and their clients, however, are often marred by suspicion on both sides. As Northwestern University's Jonathan D. Casper discovered while interviewing indigent defendants, many of them feel a certain

Defense attorney William G. Kelley, clapping, during a pretrial competency hearing for his client, accused serial killer Charles Ng, left. After the prosecution showed home videos of Ng threatening two of his alleged victims with rape and death, Kelley told the jury, "there's one thing you never see: that's someone getting murdered." In 1999, Ng was convicted on eleven counts of murder.

ATTORNEY-CLIENT PRIVILEGE
A rule of evidence requiring that communications between a client and his or her attorney be kept confidential, unless the client consents to disclosure.

Playing the Fool

In *Primal Fear*, Richard Gere plays Martin Vail, a suave, high-profile defense attorney who decides to defend Aaron Stampler—a.k.a "the Butcher Boy of St. Mike's"—against charges of stabbing a Chicago archbishop seventy-eight times. Although Stampler is apprehended fleeing the crime and found with the victim's blood smeared all over his body, he proclaims his innocence. Vail, eager to work a high-profile murder case, offers to represent the suspect *pro bono* (without charge). As the trial progresses, Vail and the audience learn that altar boy Stampler is a schizophrenic with a psychotic alter ego named Roy. It is obvious, Vail thinks, that Roy committed the murder, and he sets out to prove that his client needs to receive psychiatric care instead of a prison sentence or capital punishment.

The strategy is successful. Vail's period of self-congratulation, however, is short-lived. In the film's final scene, we learn that the multiple personalities were an act on Aaron's part to escape conviction. It is difficult to determine how often such a ploy has been successful in the real world. Defense attorneys are loath to admit that they have been made to look foolish and insist that they could not be taken in by such deception.

This does not mean that prosecutors are shy about claiming that a defendant is faking mental illness. One example of

Vincent "Chin" Gigante, looking disheveled and disoriented, is escorted to a New York court by his son.

this involves Richard "the Chin" Gigante, alleged head of the Genovese crime family. For years, Gigante has wandered the streets of Greenwich Village in a bathrobe, mumbling to himself. Federal agents once found the "Oddfather" standing in a shower beneath an open umbrella. Gigante's family and attorneys have asserted that he is mentally unfit to be a Mafia boss, while U.S. attorneys claim he has hidden behind a "shameless camouflage" to avoid conviction. In 1997, a federal judge agreed with the prosecutors, and Gigante went to trial to face charges for

six murders, three attempted murders, conspiracy, and extortion.

Although the public seems to believe that defendants often fake mental illness, empirical studies show that it is almost impossible for a sane person to keep up an insanity act for any length of time. More commonly, legal scholars say, mentally disabled criminals try to act sane, even when their disabilities would help them in court.

amount of respect for the prosecutor. Like police officers, prosecutors are just "doing their job" by trying to convict the defendant. In contrast, the defendants' view of their own attorneys can be summed up in the following exchange between Casper and a defendant:

> *Did you have a lawyer when you went to court the next morning? No, I had a public defender.*[21]

This attitude is somewhat understandable. Given the caseloads that most public defenders carry, they may have as little as five or ten minutes to spend with a client before appearing in front of a judge. How much, realistically, can a public defender learn about the defendant in that time?[22] Furthermore, the defendant is well aware that the public defender is being paid by the same source as the prosecutor and the judge. Ted Kaczynski acted on impulses felt by many defendants when he requested the right to defend himself, complaining that his public counsel was "supping from the same trough" as the prosecution.[23]

The situation handcuffs the public defenders as well. With so little time to spend on each case, they cannot validate the information provided by their clients. If the defendant says he or she has no prior offenses, the public defender often has no choice but to believe the client. Consequently, many public defenders find themselves in positions where their clients have deceived them. (For an extreme example, see *Criminal Justice & Popular Culture—Playing the Fool.*) In addition to the low pay and high pressures of the job, a client's lack of cooperation and disrespect can limit whatever satisfaction a public defender may find in the profession.[24]

TRUTH, VICTORY, AND THE ADVERSARY SYSTEM

In strictly legal terms, three basic features characterize the **adversary system:**

1. A neutral and passive decision maker, either the judge or the jury.

2. The presentation of evidence from both parties.

3. A highly structured set of procedures (in the form of constitutional safeguards) that must be followed in the presentation of that evidence.[25]

Some critics of the American court system believe that it has been tainted by overzealous prosecutors and defense attorneys. Gordon Van Kessel, a professor at Hastings College of Law in California, complains that American lawyers see themselves as "prize fighters, gladiators, or, more accurately, semantic warriors in a verbal battle," and bemoans the atmosphere of "ritualized aggression" that is endemic to the courts.[26]

Our discussion of the courtroom work group in the last chapter, however, seems to belie this image of "ritualized aggression." As political scientists Herbert Jacob and James Eisenstein have written, "pervasive conflict is not only unpleasant; it also makes work more difficult."[27] The image of the courtroom work group as "negotiators" rather than "prize fighters" seems to be supported by the fact that nine out of every ten cases conclude with negotiated "deals" rather than trials. Jerome Skolnick of the University of California at Berkeley has found that work group members grade each other according to "reasonableness"[28]—a concept criminal justice scholar Abraham S. Blumberg has embellished by labeling the defense attorney a "double agent." Because a defense attorney's main object is, Blumberg believes, to finish the case quickly so as to collect the fee and move on, these lawyers are likely to cooperate with the prosecutor in convincing a client to accept a negotiated plea of guilty.[29]

Perhaps, then, the most useful definition of the adversary process tempers Professor Van Kessel's criticism with the realities of the courtroom work group. University of California at Berkeley law professor Malcolm Feeley observes:

> In the adversary system the goal of the advocate is not to determine truth but to win, to maximize the interests of his or her side within the confines of the norms governing the proceedings. This is not to imply that the theory of the adversary process has no concern for the truth. Rather, the underlying assumption of the adversary process is that truth is most likely to emerge as a by-product of vigorous conflict between intensely partisan advocates, each of whose goal is to win.[30]

Blumberg takes a more cynical view when he calls the court process a "confidence game" in which "victory" is achieved when a defense attorney—with the implicit aid of the prosecutor and judge—is able to persuade the defendant to plead guilty.[31] As you read the rest of the chapter, which deals with pretrial procedures, keep in mind Feeley's and Blumberg's contentions concerning "truth" and "victory" in the American courts.

PRETRIAL DETENTION

After an arrest has been made, the first step toward determining the suspect's guilt or innocence is the **initial appearance.** During this brief proceeding, a magistrate (see Chapter 8) informs the defendant of the charges that have been brought against him or her and explains his or her constitutional

ADVERSARY SYSTEM
A legal system in which the prosecution and defense are opponents, or adversaries, and present their cases in the light most favorable to themselves. The court arrives at a just solution based on the evidence presented by the contestants and determines who wins and who loses.

INITIAL APPEARANCE
An accused's first appearance before a judge or magistrate following arrest; during the appearance, the defendant is informed of the charges, advised of the right to counsel, told the amount of bail, and given a date for the preliminary hearing.

Using the O. J. Simpson criminal trial as an example, England's David Newlyn compares and contrasts the adversary system with the inquisitorial system used in many European countries. To access this site, go to
www.ozemail.com.au/~ dtebbut/oj/ojeurope1/html

BAIL
The amount or conditions set by the court to ensure that an individual accused of a crime will appear for further criminal proceedings. If the accused person provides bail, whether in cash or by means of a bail bond, then she or he is released from jail.

rights—particularly, the right to remain silent (under the Fifth Amendment) and the right to be represented by counsel (under the Sixth Amendment). At this point, if the defendant cannot afford to hire a private attorney, a public defender may be appointed, or private counsel may be hired by the state to represent the defendant. As the U.S. Constitution does not specify how soon a defendant must be brought before a magistrate after arrest, it has been left to the judicial branch to determine the timing of the initial appearance. Figure 9.2 gives a summary of those decisions.

In misdemeanor cases, a defendant may decide to plead guilty and be sentenced during the initial appearance. Otherwise, the magistrate will usually release those charged with misdemeanors on their promise to return at a later date for further proceedings. For felony cases, however, the defendant is not permitted to make a plea at the initial appearance, because a magistrate's court does not have jurisdiction to decide felonies. Furthermore, in most cases the defendant will be released only if she or he posts **bail**—an amount of money paid by the defendant to the court and retained by the court until the defendant returns for further proceedings. Defendants who cannot afford bail are generally kept in a local jail or lockup until the date of their trial, though many jurisdictions are searching for alternatives to this practice because of overcrowded incarceration facilities.

The Purpose of Bail

Historically, the main purpose of bail has been to ensure the appearance of the defendant at trial without detention. The bail system developed as part of the common law of Great Britain, where judges traveled on circuits and might visit a town once every several years. Instead of holding a suspect until the judge's return, local sheriffs would allow another person to guarantee the appearance of the suspect at trial. If the suspect failed to show up, then his or her guarantor was tried instead. Eventually, the guarantor was allowed to offer a sum of money as *surety* instead of his or her person.[32]

Figure 9.2 Notable U.S. Supreme Court Decisions Regarding the Initial Appearance

McNabb v. United States **(318 U.S. 322 [1943]).** This case concerned the fate of Benjamin McNabb, who had been held for six days before his initial appearance before the court. During this time, he confessed to the crime for which he was being held, and this confession was the main factor in his conviction. The Court ruled that confessions gained during an unnecessary delay before the initial appearance could not be used in federal court.

Mallory v. United States **(354 U.S. 449 [1957]).** Expanding on *McNabb,* in this case the Court ruled that unnecessary delays before the initial appearance violated the suspect's due process rights. The case concerned a defendant who confessed during an 18-hour delay before he was brought before a magistrate, and subsequently convicted and sentenced to death.

Gerstein v. Pugh **(420 U.S. 103 [1975]).** Included in this decision was the ruling that defendants must have their initial appearance in court "promptly" following arrest. The Court did not, to the chagrin of many police officers and prosecutors, define "promptly."

Riverside County, California v. McLaughlin **(500 U.S. 44 [1991]).** In order to clarify the *Gerstein* decision, this case saw the Court provide more a more specific definition of "promptly." In what is known as the "48-hour rule," the Court specified that a delay of up to two days between booking and initial appearance could be considered "prompt." The 48-hour rule is not, however, absolute. Defendants can challenge a 48-hour delay on constitutional grounds if they can prove that the delay was unreasonable. Furthermore, delays can exceed two days if it can be proved that such a delay was unavoidable. Consequently, appeals courts are often called upon to decide the constitutionality of pre-initial appearance delay and can interpret the Court's decision according to their own discretion.

In the United States, bail is provided for under the Eighth Amendment. The amendment does not, however, guarantee the right to bail. Instead, it states that "excessive bail shall not be required." This has come to mean that in all cases except those involving a capital crime (where bail is prohibited), the amount of bail required must be reasonable compared with the seriousness of the wrongdoing. It *does not* mean that the amount of bail must be within the defendant's ability to pay.

The vagueness of the Eighth Amendment has encouraged a second purpose of bail: to protect the community from a defendant's committing another crime before trial. To achieve this purpose, a judge can simply set bail at a level the suspect cannot possibly afford. As we shall see, several states and the federal government have passed laws that allow judges to detain suspects deemed a threat to the community without going through the motions of setting relatively high bail.

Setting Bail

There is no uniform system for pretrial detention; each jurisdiction has its own *bail tariffs,* or general guidelines concerning the proper amount of bail. For misdemeanors, the police usually follow a pre-approved bail schedule created by local judicial authorities. In felony cases, the primary responsibility to set bail lies with the judge. Figure 9.3 shows typical bail amounts for various offenses.

The Judge and Bail Setting. Bail tariffs can be quite extensive. In Illinois, for example, a judge is required to take thirty-eight different factors into account when setting bail: fourteen involve the crime itself, two refer to the evidence gathered, four to the defendant's record, nine to the defendant's flight risk and immigration status, and nine to the defendant's general character.[33] For the most part, however, judges are free to use such tariffs as loose guidelines, and they have a great deal of discretion in setting bail according to the circumstances in each case.

Extralegal factors may also play a part in bail setting. University of New Orleans political scientist David W. Neubauer has identified three contexts that may influence a judge's decision-making process:[34]

> 1 *Uncertainty.* To a certain extent, predetermined bail tariffs are unrealistic, given that judges are required to set bail within forty-eight hours of arrest. It is often difficult to get information on the defendant in that period of time, and even if a judge can obtain a "rap sheet," or list of prior arrests ("priors"), she or he will probably not have an opportunity to verify its accuracy. Due to this uncertainty, most judges have no choice but to focus primarily on the seriousness of the crime in setting bail.

"Unless th[e] right to bail before trial is preserved, the presumption of innocence, secured only after centuries of struggle, would lose its meaning."

—Fred M. Vinson, *U.S. Supreme Court Chief Justice* (1951)

Offense	Median Bail Amount
Murder	$75,000
Rape	$23,500
Robbery	$10,000
Assault	$5,000
Burglary	$5,000
Theft	$4,000
Drug offense	$5,000
Weapons offense	$3,000

Figure 9.3 Average Bail Amounts for Various Misdemeanors and Felonies

These figures represent the median bail figures for the 75 largest counties in the nation.

SOURCE: ADAPTED FROM BUREAU OF JUSTICE STATISTICS, PRETRIAL RELEASE OF FELONY DEFENDANTS, 1992 (WASHINGTON, D.C.: U.S. DEPARTMENT OF JUSTICE, NOVEMBER 1994), TABLE 5, PAGE 5.

Figure 9.4 The Likelihood of Pretrial Release

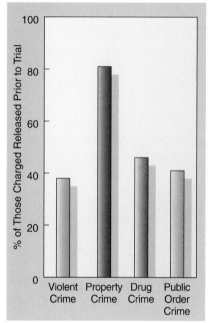

SOURCE: ADAPTED FROM BUREAU OF JUSTICE STATISTICS, COMPENDIUM OF FEDERAL JUSTICE STATISTICS, 1996 (WASHINGTON, D.C.: U.S. DEPARTMENT OF JUSTICE, NOVEMBER 1998), FIGURE 2.1, PAGE 24.

2 *Risk.* There is no way of knowing for certain whether a defendant released on bail will return for his or her court date, or whether he or she will commit a crime while free. Judges are aware of the criticism they will come under from police groups, prosecutors, the press, and the public if a crime is committed during that time. Consequently, especially if she or he is up for reelection, a judge may prefer to "play it safe" and set a high bail to detain a suspect or refuse outright to offer bail when legally able to do so. In general, risk aversion also dictates why those who have committed violent crimes are less likely to be released prior to trial than those who have committed property crimes (see Figure 9.4). In the minds of many judges, someone who is under suspicion of stealing a television is much less of a risk than someone who is under suspicion of murder.

3 *Overcrowded jails.* As we will discuss in detail in Chapter 13, many of the nation's jails are overcrowded. This may force a judge to make a difficult distinction between those suspects she or he believes *must* be detained and those who *might* need to be detained. To save jail space, a judge might be more lenient in setting bail for members of the latter group.[35]

Prosecutors, Defense Attorneys, and Bail Setting. Though the judge has ultimate discretion in setting bail, the prosecutor and, to a lesser extent, the defense attorney can influence his or her decision. If the two sides disagree on the question of bail, a judge will usually side with the prosecutor. In many cases, given the uncertainty mentioned above, a trusted prosecutor can be a useful source of information for the judge. A hearing in Brigham City, Utah, provides a fairly typical example of the extent of the adversary process in determining pretrial detention. The defense attorney for a man charged with rape and sexual abuse asserted that his client was not a risk to the community. The prosecutor countered that the defendant had been accused of an average of one sexual offense every ten days over a three-month period. Not surprisingly, the judge denied bail.[36]

Defense attorneys have a number of incentives for wanting their clients to be free on bail before a trial. A defendant who shows that she or he can function in the community without committing any further crimes may reduce the chances of conviction or at least impress upon the judge the feasibility of a lighter sentence. Furthermore, a defendant on bail is able to assist in the preparation for her or his defense by helping to gather evidence and personally steering the defense attorney toward favorable witnesses. Finally, a client free on bail is more likely to be able to earn income to pay legal bills.

In a classic study of Philadelphia conviction rates, legal scholar Caleb Foote found that 67 percent of those suspected of violent crimes who had been released on bail were acquitted, compared to 25 percent of those who had been jailed before their trial.[37] Additional research in Philadelphia by Temple University professor of criminal justice John Goldkamp showed that convicted offenders who had been denied bail were more likely to go to prison than to receive a less severe sentence.[38] (Critics of these studies point out, though, that none of them controlled completely for the fact that most accused *not* released on bail were likely to be more violent and to have more extensive prior criminal records than those granted bail.)

Given these benefits, one would think that defense attorneys would fight vigorously for low bail for their clients. This is not the case, however. Most courtroom work groups establish "rules of the game" that determine the levels at which bail will be set for particular crimes, and judges, prosecutors, and defense attorneys do not spend a great deal of time contesting the matter.[39]

Gaining Pretrial Release

Earlier, we mentioned that many jurisdictions are looking for alternatives to the bail system. One of the most popular options is **release on recognizance (ROR).** This is used when the judge, based on the advice of trained personnel, decides that the defendant is not at risk to "jump" bail and does not pose a threat to the community. The defendant is then released with the understanding that he or she will return at the time of the trial. The Vera Institute, a nonprofit organization in New York City, introduced the concept of ROR as part of the Manhattan Bail Project in the 1960s, and such programs are now found in nearly every jurisdiction. When properly administered, ROR programs seem to be successful, with less than 5 percent of the participants failing to show for trial.[40]

Posting Bail. Those suspected of committing a felony are, however, rarely released on recognizance. These defendants may post, or pay, the full amount of the bail in cash to the court. The money will be returned when the suspect appears for trial. Given the large sums involved, and the relative lack of wealth of many criminal defendants, a defendant can rarely post bail in cash. Another option is to use personal property as collateral. These *property bonds* are also rare because most courts require property valued at double the bail amount. Thus, if bail is set at $5,000, the defendant (or the defendant's family and friends) will have to produce a piece of property valued at $10,000.

Bail Bondspersons. If unable to post bail with cash or property, a defendant may arrange for a **bail bondsperson** to post a bail bond on the defendant's behalf. The bondsperson, in effect, promises the court that he or she will turn over to the court the full amount of bail if the defendant fails to return for further proceedings. The defendant usually must give the bondsperson a certain percentage of the bail (often 10 percent) in cash. This amount, which is often not returned to the defendant later, is considered payment for the bondsperson's assistance and assumption of risk. Depending on the amount of the bail bond, the defendant may also be required to sign over to the bondsperson rights to certain property (such as a car, a valuable watch, or other asset) as security for the bond.

Although bail bondspersons obviously provide a service for which there is demand, several states—including Oregon, Kentucky, Wisconsin, Nebraska, and Illinois—have abolished bail bonding for profit. The rationale for such reform focuses on two perceived problems with the practice.

1 Bail bondspersons provide opportunities for corruption, as they may bribe officials who set bail (police, etc.) to inflate the bail.

2 Because they can refuse to post a bail bond, bail bondspersons are, in essence, making a business decision concerning a suspect's pretrial release. This is considered the responsibility of a judge, not a private individual with a profit motive.[41]

The states that have banned bail bondspersons have established an alternative known as **ten percent cash bail.** This process, pioneered in Chicago in the early 1960s, requires the court, in effect, to take the place of the bondsperson. An officer of the court will accept a deposit of 10 percent of the bail amount, refundable when the defendant appears at the assigned time.[42] A

RELEASE ON RECOGNIZANCE (ROR)
A judge's order that releases an accused from jail with the understanding that he or she will return for further proceedings of his or her own will; used instead of setting a monetary bond.

BAIL BONDSPERSON
An businessperson who agrees, for a fee, to pay the bail amount if the accused fails to appear in court as ordered.

TEN PERCENT CASH BAIL
An alternative to traditional bail in which defendants may gain pretrial release by posting 10 percent of their bond amount to the court instead of seeking a bail bondsperson.

I N F O T R A C ®
COLLEGE EDITION

Parenti, Christian. 'I hunt men': meet the self-ordained officers of the bail-bond industry

In Macon, Georgia, bounty hunter Cedric Miller takes aim at Stan Bernard Rouse. Miller, a former Macon narcotics cop, is often paid substantial sums by bail bondspeople to capture bond-jumping clients.

PREVENTIVE DETENTION
The retention of an accused person in custody due to fears that she or he will commit a crime if released before a trial.

The Professional Bail Agents of the United States Web site is designed to help bail bondspersons to be more competent and effective. You can visit the site at www.pbus.com/pba2.htm **Or, if you want to understand how a bail bond agency operates, go to Action Bail Bond's home page at** www.actionbail.com

number of jurisdictions allow for both bail bondspersons and ten percent cash bail, with the judge deciding whether a defendant is eligible for the latter.

Bail Reform

Release on recognizance programs and ten percent cash bail were the result of a movement in the 1960s to reform the bail system. As various researchers produced empirical proof that pretrial detention increased the odds of conviction and led to longer sentences, reformers began to point out that this created an imbalance of justice between the wealthy and the poor.[43] Those who could afford to post bail were convicted less frequently and spent less time in jail than those who could not. Furthermore, the conditions in pretrial detention centers were considerably worse than the conditions in prison, and the cost of maintaining these centers was becoming prohibitive.

In response to these concerns, Congress passed the Bail Reform Act of 1966.[44] Though the new law did not place statutory restrictions on the discretionary powers of federal judges, it did strongly suggest that judges implement a wide range of "conditions of release" for suspects who qualified.[45]

A 1994 amendment to the Bail Reform Act of 1966 requires that judges also consider patterns of illegal narcotics use in determining whether to grant pretrial release.[46] Given the findings of some studies that African American and Hispanic American suspects already suffer discrimination in bail settings,[47] and the fact that these minority groups are more likely to be arrested on drug charges, some observers are worried that the amendment will lead to increased pressure on the pretrial detention infrastructure.

Preventive Detention

The Bail Reform Act of 1966 was criticized for concentrating on ways of increasing pretrial release, while failing to give judges the ability to detain suspects who posed a danger to the community.[48] Although judges have always had the *de facto* power to do just that by setting prohibitively high bails for dangerous defendants, thirty states have passed **preventive detention** laws that allow judges to deny bail to suspects with prior records of violence or nonappearance for trial. The Bail Reform Act of 1984 similarly states that federal offenders can be held without bail to assure "the safety of any other person and the community."[49]

Critics of the 1984 act believe that it violates the U.S. Constitution by allowing the freedom of a citizen to be restricted before he or she has been proved guilty in a court of law. For many, the act also brings up the troubling issue of *false positives*—erroneous predictions that defendants, if given pretrial release, would commit a crime, when in fact they would not.[50] (See *CJ in Focus—The Balancing Act—Innocent on Bail?*) In *United States v. Salerno* (1987),[51] however, the Supreme Court upheld the act's premise. Chief Justice William Rehnquist wrote that preventive detention was not a "punishment for dangerous individuals" but a "potential solution to a pressing social problem." Therefore, "there is no doubt that preventing danger to the community is a legitimate . . . goal."

ESTABLISHING PROBABLE CAUSE

Once the initial appearance has been completed and bail has been set, the prosecutor must establish *probable cause*. That is, the prosecutor must prove that a crime was committed and link the defendant to that crime. There are two formal procedures for establishing probable cause at this stage of the pretrial process: preliminary hearings and grand juries.

CJ in Focus
The Balancing Act
Innocent on Bail?

On April 4, 1998, Sylvia Hernandez was stabbed to death in Austin, Texas, by Leonard Saldana, her common law husband. Saldana, it turned out, had been arrested a month earlier for violating a court order to keep away from Hernandez. He had been jailed nineteen times in ten years, including four times for assaults involving domestic violence and once for violating a protective court order concerning a different woman. When he murdered Hernandez, Saldana was free on $4,000 bail.

In retrospect, Saldana should not have been released for such a small amount, given his background. Concern over such situations has convinced three-fifths of the states and the federal government to pass laws that allow judges to confine suspects before trial without bail if there is a threat of harm to the community. Civil libertarians, however, believe such preventive detention laws unjustly sacrifice the individual's right to be presumed innocent to a generally unsubstantiated government interest in pretrial detention. Supreme Court Justice Thurgood Marshall, in his dissent in the case in which the Bail Reform Act of 1984 was upheld, wrote that the denial of due process in such judicial decisions was "consistent with the usage of tyranny and the excesses of what bitter experience teaches us to call the police state."

The main criticism of preventive detention is that it presumes a certain ability to predict future criminal activity on the basis of past activity (a presumption that is usually not allowed in criminal trials). Criminologist Charles Ewing has concluded that statistical predictions about violent criminal behavior are "much more likely to be wrong than right." Some observers believe preventive detention will be used indiscriminately by judges who do not want to risk being criticized for freeing a suspect who goes on to commit a crime while out on bail. Furthermore, though it is possible to measure how many suspects eligible to be detained under these laws committed violent crimes after being released (between 5 and 10 percent, according to recent studies), it is not possible to determine how many of those who *were* detained would *not* have committed crimes if freed.

For Critical Analysis: Given the relatively low rate of criminal activity by suspects who have been released pending trial, are preventive detention laws justified?

The Preliminary Hearing

During the **preliminary hearing,** the defendant appears before a judge or magistrate who decides whether the evidence presented is sufficient for the case to proceed to trial. Legally, a suspect has a right to this hearing within a reasonable amount of time after his or her initial arrest[52]—typically, no later than ten days if the defendant is in custody or twenty days if he or she has gained pretrial release.

The preliminary hearing is conducted in the manner of a minitrial. Typically, a police report of the arrest is presented by a law enforcement officer, supplemented with evidence provided by the prosecutor. Because the burden of proving probable cause is relatively light (compared to proving guilt beyond a reasonable doubt), prosecutors rarely call witnesses during the preliminary hearing, saving them for the trial. During this hearing, the defendant has a right to be represented by counsel, who may cross-examine witnesses and challenge any evidence offered by the prosecutor. In most states, defense attorneys can take advantage of the preliminary hearing to begin the process of **discovery,** in which they are entitled to have access to any evidence in the possession of the prosecution relating to the case. Discovery is considered a keystone in the adversary process, as it allows the defense to see the evidence against the defendant prior to making a plea.

The preliminary hearing often seems rather perfunctory. It usually lasts no longer than five minutes, and the judge or magistrate rarely finds that probable cause does not exist. In one study, only 2 percent of the cases were dismissed by the judicial official at this stage in the process.[53] For this reason, defense attorneys commonly advise their clients to waive their right to a preliminary hearing. Once a judge has ruled that probable cause has been established, the prosecutor issues an **information,** which replaces the police complaint as the formal charge against the defendant for the purposes of a trial.

PRELIMINARY HEARING
An initial hearing in which a magistrate decides if there is probable cause to believe that the defendant committed the crime with which he or she is charged.

DISCOVERY
Formal investigation prior to trial. During discovery, the defense uses various methods to obtain information from the prosecution to prepare for trial.

INFORMATION
The formal charge against the accused issued by the prosecutor after a preliminary hearing has found probable cause.

GRAND JURY
The group of citizens called to decide whether probable cause exists to believe that a suspect committed the crime with which she or he has been charged.

INDICTMENT
A charge or written accusation, issued by a grand jury, that probable cause exists to believe that a named person has committed a crime.

The Grand Jury

The federal government and about half of the states require a grand jury to make the decision as to whether a case should go to trial. A **grand jury** is a group of citizens called to decide whether probable cause exists. Grand juries are *impaneled,* or created, for a period of time usually not exceeding three months. During that time, the grand jury sits in closed (secret) session and hears only evidence presented by the prosecutor—the defendant cannot present evidence at this hearing. The prosecutor presents to the grand jury whatever evidence the state has against the defendant, including photographs, documents, tangible objects, the testimony of witnesses, and other items. If the grand jury finds that probable cause exists, it issues an **indictment** against the defendant. Like an information in a preliminary hearing, the indictment becomes the formal charge against the defendant. As Figure 9.5 shows, some states require a grand jury to indict for certain crimes, while in other states a grand jury indictment is optional.

The grand jury has a long history in the United States, having been brought over from England by the colonists and codified in the Fifth Amendment of the U.S. Constitution. Historically, it has been seen to act as both a "shield" and a "sword" in the criminal justice process. By giving citizens the chance to review government charges of wrongdoing, it "shields" the individual from the power of the state. At the same time, the grand jury offers the government a "sword"—the opportunity to provide evidence against the accused—in its efforts to fight crime and protect society.[54]

Today, this function of the grand jury is in doubt—critics say that the "sword" aspect works too well and the "shield" aspect not at all. Statistically, the grand jury is even more prosecutor-friendly than the preliminary hearing. Defendants are indicted at a rate of nearly 99.5 percent,[55] leading to the common characterization of the grand jury as little more than a "rubber stamp" for the prosecution. Certainly, the procedural rules of the grand jury favor prosecutors. The exclusionary rule (see Chapter 6) does not apply in grand jury investigations, so prosecutors can present evidence that would be disallowed at any subsequent trial. Furthermore, because the grand jury is given only one version of the facts—the prosecution's—it is likely to find probable cause. In the words of one observer, a grand jury would indict a "ham sandwich" if the government asked it to do so.[56] As a result of these concerns, more than half of the jurisdictions have abolished grand juries.

Figure 9.5 State Grand Jury Requirements

As you can see, in some states a grand jury indictment is required to charge an individual with a crime, while in others it is either optional or prohibited. When a grand jury is not used, the discretion of whether to charge or not is left to the prosecutor, who must then present his or her argument at the preliminary hearing (discussed earlier in the chapter).

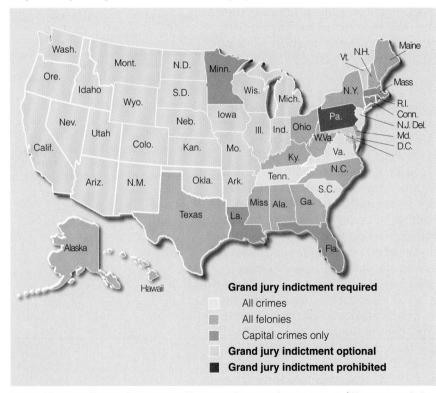

Grand jury indictment required
All crimes
All felonies
Capital crimes only
Grand jury indictment optional
Grand jury indictment prohibited

SOURCE: Marianne Zawitz, Report to the Nation on Crime and Justice, 2nd ed. (Washington, D.C.: U.S. Government Printing Office, 1988), 72.

Cross-National CJ Comparison

Japan's All-Powerful Prosecutors

Prosecutors in the United States are generally believed to have a great deal of charging discretion. The discretionary power of American prosecutors, however, does not equal that of their Japanese counterparts. With the ability to "cherry pick" their cases, prosecutors in Japan routinely have annual conviction rates of over 99.9 percent.

THE "CONFESSION MILL"

One observer described the Japanese courts as a "confession mill." Unlike the American system, Japan has no arraignment procedure during which the accused can plead guilty or innocent. Instead, the focus of the Japanese criminal justice system is on extracting confessions of guilt: police can hold and question suspects for up to twenty-three days without pressing charges. Furthermore, the suspect has no absolute right to counsel during the interrogation, and police are often able to get confessions that make for open-and-shut convictions. The prosecutor also has the "benevolent" discretion to drop the case altogether if the suspect expresses remorse.

The extraordinarily high conviction rate is also a product of Japanese culture. To fail in an attempt to convict results in a loss of face, not only for the individual prosecutor but also for the court system as a whole. The Japanese Justice Ministry estimates that, to avoid the risk of losing, prosecutors decline to press charges against 35 percent of indictable suspects each year. Japanese judges—there are no juries—contribute to the high conviction rate by rarely questioning the manner in which prosecutors obtain confessions.

NO PLEA BARGAINING

Interestingly, given the amount of prosecutorial discretion, the Japanese criminal justice system does *not* allow for plea bargaining. The Japanese see the practice of "trading" a guilty plea for a lesser sentence as counterproductive, as a defendant may be tempted to confess to crimes she or he did not commit if the prosecution has a strong case. For the Japanese, a confession extracted after twenty-three days of interrogation may be "voluntary," but a confession gained through a promise of leniency is "forced" and therefore in conflict with the system's goals of truth seeking and accuracy.

WHAT'S THE EVIDENCE?

The Japan Criminal Policy Society (JCPS) offers a wealth of information on all aspects of Japan's criminal justice system. To learn more about Japanese prosecutors, visit the JCPS at **www.tokyoweb.or.jp/JCPS/sc2.htm**

THE PROSECUTORIAL SCREENING PROCESS

Some observers see the high government success rates in pretrial proceedings as proof that prosecutors successfully screen out weak cases before they get to a grand jury or preliminary hearing. If, however, grand juries have indeed abandoned their traditional duties in favor of "rubber stamping" most cases set in front of them, and preliminary hearings are little better, what is to keep prosecutors from using their charging powers indiscriminately? Nothing, say many observers. Once the police have initially charged a defendant with committing a crime, the prosecutor can prosecute the case as it stands, reduce or increase the initial charge, file additional charges, or dismiss the case. In a system of government and law that relies on checks and balances, asked legal expert Kenneth Culp Davis, why should the prosecutor be "immune to review by other officials and immune to review by the courts?"[57] (For even more powerful prosecutors, see *Cross-National CJ Comparison—Japan's All-Powerful Prosecutors*.)

Though American prosecutors have far-ranging discretionary charging powers, it is not entirely correct to say that they are unrestricted. Controls are indirect and informal, but they do exist.[58]

CASE ATTRITION
The process through which prosecutors, by deciding whether or not to prosecute each person arrested, effect an overall reduction in the number of persons prosecuted. As a result, the number of persons convicted and sentenced is much smaller than the number of persons arrested.

Case Attrition

Prosecutorial discretion includes the power *not* to prosecute cases. Figure 9.6 depicts the average outcomes of one hundred felony arrests in the United States. As you can see, of the sixty-five arrestees brought before the district attorney, only fifty-five were prosecuted, and only thirty-two of these prosecutions led to incarceration. Consequently, only one in five adults arrested for a felony sees the inside of a prison or jail cell. This phenomenon is known as **case attrition,** and it is explained in part by prosecutorial discretion.

According to Figure 9.6, about five-eighths of felony cases that fail to end in conviction are dismissed by the prosecutor through a *nolle prosequi.* Why are these cases "nolled," or not prosecuted by the district attorney? In the section on law enforcement, you learned that the police do not have the resources to arrest every lawbreaker in the nation. Similarly, district attorneys do not have the resources to prosecute every arrest. They must choose how to distribute their scarce resources. In some cases, the decision is made for them, such as when police break procedural law and negate important evidence. This happens rarely—less than 1 percent of felony arrests are dropped because of the exclusionary rule, and almost all of these are the result of illegal drug searches.[59]

Most prosecutors have a *screening process* for deciding when to prosecute and when to "noll." This process varies a bit from jurisdiction to jurisdiction, but most prosecutors consider several factors in making the decision:

- The most important factor in deciding whether to prosecute is not the prosecutor's belief in the guilt of the suspect, but whether there is

Figure 9.6 Following One Hundred Felony Arrests: The Criminal Justice Funnel

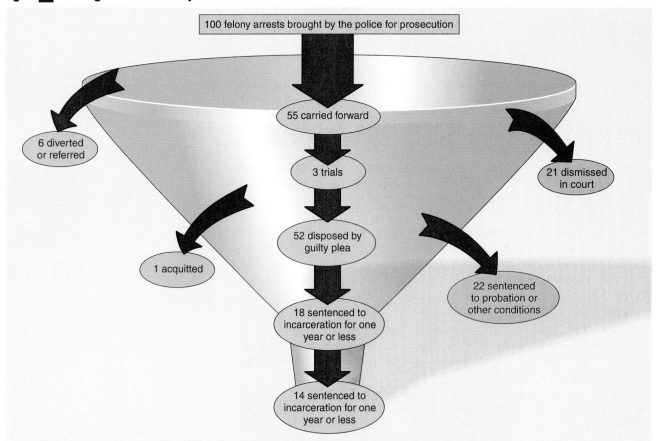

100 felony arrests brought by the police for prosecution

55 carried forward

6 diverted or referred

3 trials

21 dismissed in court

52 disposed by guilty plea

1 acquitted

22 sentenced to probation or other conditions

18 sentenced to incarceration for one year or less

14 sentenced to incarceration for one year or less

SOURCE: BUREAU OF JUSTICE STATISTICS, THE PROSECUTION OF FELONY ARRESTS (WASHINGTON D.C., 1989)

sufficient evidence for conviction.[60] If prosecutors have strong physical evidence and a number of reliable and believable witnesses, they are quite likely to prosecute.

- Prosecutors also tend to establish *case priorities.* In other words, everything else being equal, a district attorney will prosecute a rapist instead of a jaywalker because the former presents a greater threat to society than does the latter. A prosecutor will also be more likely to prosecute someone with an extensive record of wrongdoing than a first-time offender. Often, in coordination with the police, a district attorney's office will target a single area of crime, such as drug use or drunk driving.

- Sometimes a case is dropped even when it involves a serious crime and a wealth of evidence exists against the suspect. These situations usually involve *uncooperative victims.* For example, violent offenses committed by one member of a family against another member are difficult to prosecute because the victim is often unwilling to cooperate. Despite legislative and law enforcement attempts to protect victims of domestic violence (discussed at more length in Chapter 18), prosecutors are three times more likely to drop charges after arrests for intrafamily violence than for violence between strangers.[61]

- *Unreliability of victims* can also affect a charging decision. If the victim in a rape case is a crack addict and a prostitute, while the defendant is the chief executive officer of a large corporation, prosecutors may be hesitant to have a jury decide which one is more trustworthy.

- A prosecutor may be willing to drop a case, or reduce the charges, against a *defendant who is willing to testify against other offenders.* In New Jersey, for example, prosecutors are allowed to waive mandatory sentencing laws for low-level drug traffickers who agree to "snitch," or give the police information on major narcotics suppliers.[62]

Furthermore, in certain situations the "interests of justice" do not seem to warrant aggressive prosecutorial action. For example, pop singer George Michael was arrested for committing an unspecified "lewd act" in a park in Beverly Hills, California. The crime carries a penalty of up to six months in jail, but the district attorney's office instead fined Michael $810, ordered him to perform eighty hours of community service, and forbade him to return to the park.

Managing the Charging Decision

According to criminologist Joan Jacoby, prosecutor's offices develop certain policies that determine their charging decisions. These policies take into account the factors mentioned in the prior section and are molded according to the ideology and strategy goals of the lead officials in any given prosecutorial organization. Jacoby's management policies, or models, include the following:

- The *transfer model,* in which very little screening take place, and prosecutors charge most cases transferred to them by the police. The transfer model is only feasible where the prosecutor's office has enough resources to try to convict most suspects arrested by law enforcement officers.

- The *unit model,* in which individual assistant prosecutors are given the authority to make charging decisions without much organizational guidance. In essence, the unit model describes a prosecutor's office that has no overriding policy.

- The *legal sufficiency model,* which relies on the elements of a crime (criminal act and criminal intent) that were discussed in Chapter 2. If these

> "Let me tell you, you can paint pictures and get people indicted for just about anything."
>
> —Alfonse D'Amato, *former U.S. Senator from New York* (1996)

elements are present, then the prosecutors will feel obliged to bring charges in the case.

- The *system efficiency model,* which emphasizes the quickest possible disposition of the most possible cases. The prosecutor's office will choose to prosecute only those cases that have a high probability of success and will reject those time-consuming cases that, although they may ultimately lead to conviction, will use up too many scarce resources.

- The *trial sufficiency model,* in which charges are filed only if conviction is very likely. The amount of resources that will be expended on the case is a secondary consideration if the prosecutor is confident of conviction. (Obviously, a prosecutor's office with a large budget and staff will be more likely to follow the trial sufficiency model.)

- The *defendant rehabilitation model,* which relies on the prosecutor's assessment of the possibility that the defendant can be rehabilitated. If the prosecutor believes rehabilitation is possible, he or she will find alternatives to charging or charge and accept a plea to a lesser charge to help the defendant receive treatment outside the criminal justice system.[63]

The wedding cake model of criminal justice, discussed in Chapter 1, suggests a more cynical view of how the decision to prosecute is made. As you recall, in this model Samuel Walker compares the various cases that come before prosecutors to layers on a wedding cake. On the top layer are the few celebrity cases that draw the most public attention, while the many misdemeanors and minor crimes that make up the bottom layer are generally ignored. According to Walker, the decision to prosecute is determined by the social importance of the offender and the victim and the amount of media attention given the crime, as well as the seriousness of the crime.[64]

Prosecutorial Charging and the Defense Attorney

For the most part, there is little the defense attorney can do when the prosecutor decides to charge a client. If a defense attorney feels strongly that the charge has been made in violation of the defendant's rights, he or she can, however, submit *pretrial motions* to the court requesting that a particular action be taken to protect his or her client. Pretrial motions include the following:

1. Motions to suppress evidence gained illegally.

2. Motions for a change of venue because the defendant cannot receive a fair trial in the original jurisdiction.

3. Motions to invalidate a search warrant.

4. Motions to dismiss the case because of a delay in bringing it to trial.

5. Motions to obtain evidence that the prosecution may be withholding.

As we shall soon see, defense attorneys sometimes use these pretrial motions to pressure the prosecution into offering a favorable deal for their client.

Rolando Cruz, right, spent 12 years in prison for a rape/murder he did not commit. When he was released by a judge's order in 1995, attention turned towards the efforts made by Illinois state prosecutors to see that Cruz died in the electric chair. Following an official investigation, three of the prosecutors in the Cruz case were indicted for conspiracy and obstruction of justice. A grand jury decided that three prosecutors had purposefully lied and fabricated evidence in their zealous advocacy of Cruz's guilt.

PLEADING GUILTY

Based on the information (delivered during the preliminary hearing) or indictment (handed down by the grand jury), the prosecutor submits a motion to the court to order the defendant to appear before the trial court for an **arraignment.** Due process of law, as guaranteed by the Fifth Amendment, requires that a criminal defendant be informed of the charges brought against her or him and be offered an opportunity to respond to those charges. The arraignment is one of the ways in which due process requirements are satisfied by criminal procedure law.

At the arraignment, the defendant is informed of the charges and must respond by pleading not guilty or guilty. In some but not all states, the defendant may also enter a plea of **nolo contendere,** which is Latin for "I will not contest it." The plea of *nolo contendere* is neither an admission nor a denial of guilt. (The consequences for someone who pleads guilty and for someone who pleads *nolo contendere* are the same in a criminal trial, but the latter plea cannot be used in a subsequent civil trial as an admission of guilt.) Most frequently, the defendant pleads guilty to the initial charge or to a lesser charge that has been agreed on through *plea bargaining* between the prosecutor and defendant. If the defendant pleads guilty, no trial is necessary, and the defendant is sentenced based on the crime he or she has admitted committing.

Plea Bargaining in the Criminal Justice System

Plea bargaining usually takes place after the arraignment and before the beginning of the trial. In its simplest terms, it is a process by which the accused, represented by the defense counsel, and the prosecutor work out a mutually satisfactory disposition of the case, subject to court approval. Plea bargaining agreements can have several different forms:

- *Charge bargaining.* In charge bargaining, the defendant pleads guilty in exchange for a reduction of the charges. A felony burglary charge, for example, could be reduced to the lesser offense of breaking and entering. The more serious the initial charge, the more an accused has to gain by bargaining: pleading guilty to second degree murder can save the defendant from the risk of being convicted of first degree murder, which carries the death penalty in some states.

- *Sentence bargaining.* In sentence bargaining, the defendant pleads guilty in exchange for a lighter sentence, which may include a shorter prison term or probation. In most jurisdictions, the judge makes the final decision on whether to accept this agreement; the prosecutor can only recommend a lighter sentence. The prosecutor may also suggest that the defendant be placed in a counseling program, such as a drug rehabilitation center, in return for the guilty plea.

- *Count bargaining.* A person can be charged with multiple counts, either for committing multiple crimes or from different aspects of a single incident. A person who goes on a killing spree that results in seven deaths, for example, would be charged with seven counts of first degree murder. A person who breaks into a home, sexually assaults the inhabitants, and then takes their credit cards could be charged with counts of rape, aggravated burglary, misdemeanor theft, felony theft, and criminal use of a credit card. In count bargaining, a defendant pleads guilty in exchange for a reduction in the counts against him or her.

  In a sense, count bargaining is a form of sentence bargaining. If a person is convicted of multiple counts, her or his prison time is calculated

---

ARRAIGNMENT
A court proceeding in which the suspect is formally charged with the criminal offense stated in the indictment. The suspect enters a plea (guilty, not guilty, *nolo contendere*) in response.

NOLO CONTENDERE
Latin for "I will not contest it." A criminal defendant's plea, in which he or she chooses not to challenge, or contest, the charges brought by the government. Although the defendant may still be sentenced or fined, the plea neither admits nor denies guilt.

PLEA BARGAINING
The process by which the accused and the prosecutor work out a mutually satisfactory conclusion to the case, subject to court approval. Usually, plea bargaining involves the defendant's pleading guilty to a lesser offense in return for a lighter sentence.

On September 9, 1998, Jeremy Strohmeyer pleaded guilty to kidnapping, molesting, and strangling a seven-year-old girl in the Primadonna casino. The plea bargain was made with the express purpose of avoiding the death penalty. "For the sake of his parents, he chose to be assured he would live," said Leslie Abramson, Strohmeyer's attorney. Cases such as this one invariably lead to criticism of plea bargaining as a means for criminals to "get off" with light sentences. In contrast, how does the practice benefit the criminal justice system?

by combining the attendant sentence of each count (which is why some criminals are sentenced to a seemingly ridiculously long prison term, way past their life expectancy). If a count is dropped, so is the prison time that goes with it.

In *Santobello v. New York* (1971),[65] the Supreme Court held that plea bargaining "is not only an essential part of the process but a highly desirable part for many reasons." Many observers would agree, but with ambivalence. They understand that plea bargaining offers the practical benefit of saving court resources, but question whether it is the best way to achieve justice.[66] Given the pressures placed on the court system, many participants conclude that plea bargaining is, in fact, an ethically acceptable means of determining the defendant's fate.

Motivations for Plea Bargaining

Given the high rate of plea bargaining—see Figure 9.7—it follows that the prosecutor, defense attorney, and defendant each have strong reasons to engage in the practice.

Prosecutors and Plea Bargaining. In most cases, a prosecutor has a single goal after charging a defendant with a crime: conviction. If a case goes to trial, no matter how certain a prosecutor may be that a defendant is guilty, there is always a chance that a jury or judge will disagree. Plea bargaining removes this risk. Furthermore, the prosecutorial screening process described earlier in the chapter is not infallible. Sometimes, a prosecutor will find that the evidence against the accused is weaker than first thought or will uncover new information that changes the complexion of the case. In these situations, the prosecutor may decide to drop the charges or, if he or she still feels that the defendant is guilty, turn to plea bargaining to "save" a questionable case.

The prosecutor's role as an administrator also comes into play. She or he may be interested in the quickest, most efficient manner to dispose of caseloads, and plea bargains reduce the time and money spent on each case. Personal philosophy can affect the proceedings as well. A prosecutor who feels that a mandatory minimum sentence for a particular crime, such as marijuana possession, is too strict may plea bargain in order to lessen the penalty. Similarly, some prosecutors will consider plea bargaining only in certain instances—for burglary and theft, for example, but not for more serious felonies such as rape and murder.[67]

Figure 9.7 Rates of Plea Bargaining

As you can see, most convictions are gained when the defendant pleads guilty. The numbers used here refer to convictions in cases terminating in federal courts between October 1, 1995, and September 30, 1996.

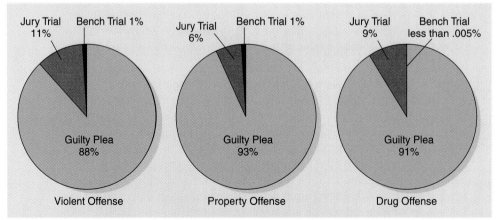

SOURCE: ADAPTED FROM BUREAU OF JUSTICE STATISTICS, *COMPENDIUM OF FEDERAL JUSTICE STATISTICS, 1996* (WASHINGTON, D.C.: U.S. DEPARTMENT OF JUSTICE, NOVEMBER 1998), TABLE 3.2, PAGE 42.

Defense Attorneys and Plea Bargaining. Political scientist Milton Heumann has said that the most important thing that a defense attorney learns is that "most of his clients are guilty."[68] Given this stark reality, favorable plea bargains are often the best a defense attorney can do for clients, aside from helping them to gain acquittals. Some have suggested that defense attorneys have other, less savory motives for convincing a client to plead guilty such as a desire to increase profit margins by quickly disposing of cases[69] or wish to ingratiate themselves with the other members of the courtroom work group by showing their "reasonableness."[70] In other cases, a defense attorney may want to go to trial when it is *not* in the client's best interest to win publicity or gain work experience.[71]

Defendants and Plea Bargaining. The plea bargain allows the defendant a measure of control over his or her fate. When Unabomber Ted Kaczynski accepted the government's plea bargain for life imprisonment, against the wishes of his defense counsel, he did so because he wanted to spare himself a trial that would have focused on his mental health.[72] The benefits of plea bargaining are tangible. As Figure 9.8 shows, defendants who plea bargain receive significantly lighter sentences on average than those who are found guilty at trial.

Plea Bargaining and the Adversary System

One criticism of plea bargaining is that it subverts the adversary system, the goal of which is to determine innocence or guilt. Although plea bargaining does value negotiation over conflict, it is important to remember that it does so in a context in which legal guilt has already been established. Even within this context, plea bargaining is not completely divorced from the adversary process.

Strategies to Induce a Plea Bargain. Earlier, we pointed out that the most likely reason why a prosecutor does not bring charges is the lack of a strong case. This is also the most common reason why a prosecutor agrees to a plea bargain once charges have been brought. Defense attorneys are well aware of

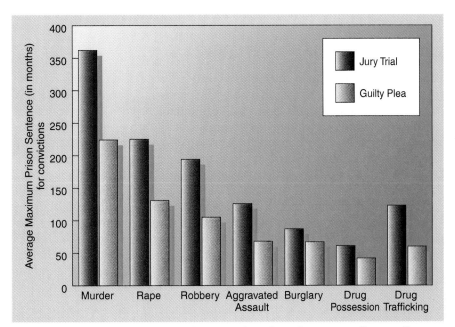

Figure 9.8 Sentencing Outcomes for Guilty Pleas

SOURCE: ADAPTED FROM BUREAU OF JUSTICE STATISTICS, STATE COURT SENTENCING OF CONVICTED FELONS, 1994 (WASHINGTON, D.C.: U.S. DEPARTMENT OF JUSTICE, MARCH 1998), TABLE 4.5, PAGE 48.

BOYKIN FORM
A form that must be completed by a defendant who pleads guilty; the defendant states that she or he has done so voluntarily and with full comprehension of the consequences.

this fact and often file numerous pretrial motions in an effort to weaken the state's case. Even if the judge does not accept the motions, the defense may hope that the time required to process them will wear on the prosecutor's patience. As one district attorney has said, "the usual defense strategy today is to bring in a stack of motions as thick as a Sunday newspaper; defense attorneys hope that we won't have the patience to ride them out."[73]

Prosecutors have their own methods of inducing a plea bargain. The most common is the ethically questionable practice of *overcharging,* that is, charging the defendant with more counts than may be appropriate. There are two types of overcharging:

1. In *horizontal overcharging,* the prosecutor brings a number of different counts for a single criminal incident.

2. In *vertical overcharging,* the prosecutor raises the level of a charge above its proper place. For example, the facts of the case warrant a charge of battery, but the prosecutor charges the defendant with attempted murder.

After overcharging, prosecutors allow themselves to be "bargained down" to the correct charge, giving the defense attorney and the defendant the impression that they have achieved victory.

Protecting the Defendant. Watching the defense attorney and the prosecutor maneuver in this manner, the defendant often comes to the conclusion that the plea bargaining process is a sort of game with sometimes incomprehensible rules.[74] The Supreme Court is also aware of the potential for taking advantage of the defendant in plea bargaining and has taken steps to protect the accused. Until *Boykin v. Alabama* (1969),[75] judges would often accept the defense counsel's word that the defendant wanted to plead guilty. In that case, the Court held that the defendant must make a clear statement that he or she accepts the plea bargain. As a result, many jurisdictions now ask the accused to sign a **Boykin form** waiving his or her right to a trial. A statement in which the defendant admits exactly what crime he or she committed must accompany this guilty plea. (For other important cases protecting the defendant during plea bargaining, see Figure 9.9.)

"I pleaded guilty on second degree murder because they said there is too much evidence, but I ain't shot no man, but I take the fault for the other man. . . . I just pleaded guilty because they said if I didn't they would gas me for it, and that is all."

—Henry Alford, who claimed that he pled guilty to a murder charge only because he faced the threat of the death penalty if the case went to trial (1970)

Is Plea Bargaining Inevitable?

Observers on both sides of the criminal justice "fence" feel that the compromises inherent in plea bargaining make the process unjust. Those interested in protecting due process believe that negotiated pleas deny defendants the stricter procedural protections of a criminal trial.[76] Furthermore, the practice gives innocent people an incentive to plead guilty if they feel that the evidence is against them. For their part, those committed to crime control believe that plea bargaining allows dangerous criminals to "beat the system" by negotiating for lighter sentences than they deserve; consequently, these observers feel that it undermines the deterrent effects of punishment.[77]

It is not easy to combat these criticisms. Instead, proponents of plea bargaining argue that although it may not be the ideal solution to problems such as overwhelming caseloads, it is the best one available under the circumstances. In a 1970 speech to the American Bar Association, then Supreme Court Chief Justice Warren Burger said:

> The consequences of what might seem on its face a small percentage change in the rate of guilty pleas can be tremendous. A reduction from 90 percent to

Boykin v. Alabama **(395 U.S. 238 [1969]).** This case established the formal procedures that must be followed when a plea bargain is agreed upon, with the goal of ensuring that the defendant has voluntarily agreed to the plea bargain and understands the consequences of entering a guilty plea.

Brady v. United States **(397 U.S. 742 [1970]).** In this case, the defendant entered a guilty plea in order to avoid the death penalty. In allowing this action, the Court ruled that plea bargains are a legitimate part of the adjudication process as long as they are entered into voluntarily and the defendant has full knowledge of the consequences of pleading guilty.

North Carolina v. Alford **(400 U.S. 25 [1970]).** Although maintaining he was innocent of the first degree murder for which he was charged, Alford pleaded guilty to second degree murder in order to avoid the possibility of the death penalty that came with the original charges. After being sentenced to thirty years in prison, Alford argued that he was forced to plea bargain because of the threat of the death penalty. The Court refused to invalidate Alford's guilty plea, stating that plea bargains are valid even if the defendant claims innocence, as long as the plea was entered into voluntarily.

Santobello v. New York **(404 U.S. 257 [1971]).** This case focused on the prosecutor's role in the plea bargain process. The Court ruled that if a prosecutor promises a more lenient sentence in return for the defendant's guilty plea, the promise must be kept.

Bordenkircher v. Hayes **(434 U.S. 357 [1978]).** A Kentucky prosecutor told Hayes that if he entered a guilty plea, he would recommend a light sentence. If not, he would indict Hayes under the state's habitual offender act, which carried the possibility of life imprisonment. The Court ruled that prosecutors are within their rights to threaten defendants with harsher sentences in order to induce a guilty plea.

Ricketts v. Adamson **(483 U.S. 1 [1987]).** In return for a reduction of charges, Ricketts agreed to plead guilty and to testify against a codefendant in a murder case. When the codefendant's conviction was reversed on appeal, Ricketts refused to testify a second time. Therefore, the prosecutor rescinded his offer of leniency. The Court ruled that the prosecutor's action was justified, and that defendants must uphold their side of the plea bargain in order to receive its benefits.

United States v. Mezzanatto **(513 U.S. 196 [1995]).** The Court ruled that a prosecutor can refuse to plea bargain with a defendant unless the defendant agrees that any statements made by him or her during the bargaining process can be used against him or her in a possible trial. In other words, if the defendant admits to committing the crime during plea bargain negotiations, and then decides to plead not guilty, the prosecution can use the admission as evidence during the trial.

Figure 9.9 Notable United States Supreme Court Decisions on Plea Bargaining

The constitutional justification of the plea bargain as an accepted part of the criminal justice process has been fortified by these Supreme Court rulings.

80 percent in guilty pleas requires the assignment of twice the judicial manpower and facilities—judges, court reporters, bailiffs, clerks, jurors and courtrooms. A reduction to 70 percent trebles this demand.[78]

Abolishing Plea Bargaining. Was Chief Justice Burger correct in stating, essentially, that the court system could not function without plea bargaining? Skeptics point out that rates of guilty pleas in felony cases vary from jurisdiction to jurisdiction, implying that some court systems have managed to reduce the practice without collapsing.[79] The main body of research, however, implies the opposite: that, regardless of regulations governing plea bargaining from jurisdiction to jurisdiction, the rate of guilty pleas remains stable (see Figure 9.10 on the following page).

Perhaps more to the point, certain jurisdictions have provided case studies for Chief Justice Burger's assumption by abolishing plea bargaining. In 1975, prosecutors and defense attorneys in El Paso, Texas, were prohibited from negotiating the sentencing of a guilty party. Instead, punishment was determined by a "point system" that would base probation or imprisonment

Figure 9.10 Holding Steady: Guilty Plea Rates in Five Jurisdictions

The five jurisdictions compared here are dissimilar in many ways, save for one: their rates of guilty pleas for burglaries and robberies are virtually the same. This seems to lend credence to the theory that the guilty plea is entrenched as a necessary aspect of the criminal justice process.

Tucson, AZ	New Orleans, LA	Norfolk, VA	Delaware County, PA	Seattle, WA
Population: 500,000	Population: 562,000	Population: 285,500	Population: 600,000	Population: 1,157,000
Number of indictments and informations filed each year: 2,309	Number of indictments and informations filed each year: 5,063	Number of indictments and informations filed each year: 2,800	Number of indictments and informations filed each year: 3,000	Number of indictments and informations filed each year: 4,500
Number of public prosecutors: 30	Number of public prosecutors: 63	Number of public prosecutors: 15	Number of public prosecutors: 30	Number of public prosecutors: 69
Annual number of felony trials: 270	Annual number of felony trials: 1,069	Annual number of felony trials: 648	Annual number of felony trials: 491	Annual number of felony trials: 4,567
Restrictions placed on prosecutor's ability to plea bargain: Not allowed for career criminals	Restrictions placed on prosecutor's ability to plea bargain: Limited to charge bargaining	Restrictions placed on prosecutor's ability to plea bargain: Low	Restrictions placed on prosecutor's ability to plea bargain: Low	Restrictions placed on prosecutor's ability to plea bargain: Not allowed for high-impact cases
Percentage of robbery and burglary convictions resulting from guilty pleas: 87	Percentage of robbery and burglary convictions resulting from guilty pleas: 81	Percentage of robbery and burglary convictions resulting from guilty pleas: 78	Percentage of robbery and burglary convictions resulting from guilty pleas: 80	Percentage of robbery and burglary convictions resulting from guilty pleas: 86

SOURCE: WILLIAM F. MCDONALD, PLEA BARGAINING: CRITICAL ISSUES AND COMMON PRACTICES (WASHINGTON, D.C.: NATIONAL INSTITUTE OF JUSTICE, 1985), 7.

on a set of guidelines. This removed the incentive for either side to plea bargain, and most cases went to trial. Within three years, the county's caseload increased by 250 percent, and the prohibition was eventually rescinded.[80]

In other areas that have implemented similar policies, the results suggest that the court system will naturally change its procedures to keep caseloads from growing excessively. In the early 1970s, when New York passed stringent drug control laws that prohibited plea bargaining in narcotics cases, total convictions for drug offenses actually dropped, as prosecutors used their screening discretion to dismiss cases that were not "slam dunks."[81] Similarly, after California banned plea bargaining for a number of "serious felonies," researchers found that the practice continued surreptitiously with the aid of sympathetic judges.[82] It seems that even when steps are taken to eliminate plea bargaining, the practice continues in different forms.

GOING TO TRIAL

The pretrial process does not inexorably lead to a guilty plea. (For a review of these different procedures, see Figure 9.11.) Just as prosecutors, defense attorneys, and defendants have reasons to negotiate, they may also be motivated to take a case to trial. If either side is confident in the strength of its arguments and evidence, it will obviously be less likely to accept a plea bargain. Both prosecutors and defense attorneys may favor a trial to gain publicity, and sometimes public pressure after an extremely violent or high-profile crime will force a chief prosecutor (who is, remember, normally an elected official) to take a weak case to trial. Also, some defendants may insist on their right to a trial, regardless of their attorney's advice. In the next chapter, we will examine what happens to the 10 percent of indictments that do lead to the courtroom.

Booking

After arrest, at the police station, the suspect is searched, photographed, fingerprinted, and allowed at least one telephone call. After the booking, charges are reviewed, and if they are not dropped, a complaint is filed and a judge or magistrate examines the case for probable cause.

Initial Appearance

The suspect appears before the judge, who informs the suspect of the charges and of his or her rights. If the suspect requests a lawyer, one is appointed. The judge sets bail (conditions under which a suspect can obtain release pending disposition of the case).

Preliminary Hearing

In a proceeding in which both sides are represented by counsel, the judge determines whether there is probable cause to believe that the suspect committed the crime, based on the evidence.

Grand Jury Review

The federal government and about half of the states require grand jury indictments for at least some felonies. In those states, a grand jury determines whether the evidence justifies a trial on the charges sought by the prosecutor.

Prosecutorial Review

In jurisdictions that do not require grand jury indictments, a prosecutor issues an information. An information is similar to an indictment: both are charging instruments that replace the complaint.

Arraignment

The suspect is brought before the trial court, informed of the charges, and asked to enter a plea.

Plea Bargain

A plea bargain is a prosecutor's promise of concessions (or promise to seek concessions) in return for the defendant's guilty plea. Concessions include a reduced charge and/or a lesser sentence.

Guilty Plea

In more jurisdictions, most cases that reach the arraignment stage do not go to trial but are resolved by a guilty plea, often as the result of a plea bargain. The judge sets the case for sentencing.

Trial

If the defendant refuses to plead guilty, he or she proceeds to either a jury trial (in most instances) or a bench trial.

Figure 9.11 The Steps Leading to a Trial

Legal Ethics on Trial: Defending the Guilty

One of the most prominent aspects of the adversary system described in this chapter and the next is the amount of power it places in the hands of lawyers. They decide the course of the trial, which evidence to provide, what witnesses to call, whether to plea bargain, and so on. In countries that favor an "inquisitorial system," including most European nations, this is not the case. The inquisitorial system places power with judges; they decide what evidence will be admitted to court and who will interview witnesses. Lawyers, for the most part, act as investigators and provide information for the judge. These differing roles for lawyers seem to breed different perspectives on the legal profession. French *avocats*, for example, are generally held in high esteem, while in the United States, lawyer bashing can get so fierce that the president of the California Bar Association demanded that lawyer jokes be considered hate crimes.[83] In this *Criminal Justice in Action* feature, we examine one attribute of the adversary system that seems to inspire a great deal of mistrust toward lawyers, particularly defense attorneys.

Jim Carrey in *Liar, Liar*

STRONG FEELINGS AGAINST LAWYERS HAVE LONG HISTORY

Disdain for the members of the legal profession is nothing if not enduring. At the end of the sixteenth century, Shakespeare wrote a play in which a character exhorted his colleagues to "kill all the lawyers." Four hundred years later, the very same words were used as the title of a film. This general enmity seems to be based on the perception that legal practitioners are deeply dishonest. The plot to another movie, *Liar Liar*, revolves around the difficulties an attorney has when he is forced to tell the truth.

A great deal of this mistrust is based on the presumption that lawyers will do anything in the interests of their clients. To a certain extent, the ideals of the adversary system promote this view. In a classic statement, the British attorney Lord Brougham asserted:

[A]n advocate, in the discharge of his duty, knows but one person in all the world, and that person is his client. To save the client by all means and expedients, and at all hazards and costs to other persons, and among them, himself, is his first and only duty; and in performing this duty he must not regard the alarm, the torments, the destruction which he may bring upon others.[84]

When Lord Brougham made this statement in 1820, he was serving as defense attorney to the very popular Queen Caroline, who was charged with having engaged in an adulterous relationship with a courtier before ascending to the throne. The ethical issues he raises may not be so clear to a defense attorney today, especially one who is working on behalf of a client she or he suspects, or knows, is guilty.

THE "TRUTH" OF THE COURTROOM

It is a question many defense attorneys come to dread: How can you defend a client you know is guilty? Many non-lawyers seem to sympathize with the premise of the film *Devil's Advocate*, in which Satan is a senior partner in a law firm that specializes in representing the rich and the guilty. If defense attorneys are not doing the "devil's work" in defending the guilty, the popular line of thought goes, then certainly they are breaking some moral or legal rule.

Many legal scholars disagree. Just as a physician is morally obliged to treat a patient even if that patient may go on to do harm, they say, a defense attorney is morally obliged to represent a client who may have committed or will possibly commit a crime. This obligation is based on every American citizen's constitutional right to counsel, protection against self-incrimination, and, most importantly, presumption of innocence. Because the burden of proof is on the government, the framers of the Constitution saw fit to provide the accused with an ally. Indeed, as legal expert Murray L. Schwartz noted, "If lawyers refuse to represent defendants who they believe are guilty, the right of a defendant to be represented by counsel is eliminated and with it the entire traditional criminal trial."[85]

Furthermore, defense attorneys, as advocates, have a responsibility *not* to interject their own personal opinions into the process. Theoretically, no absolute "truth" exists in a courtroom. Instead, "truth" emerges through a process in which the prosecution and defense present their cases and a judge or jury decides questions of guilt and innocence.[86]

PRIVILEGED CONFESSIONS

Practical reasons also compel an attorney to defend a client who may be guilty. Attorney-client privilege, for example, rests on the assumption that a free flow of information between the two parties is crucial to providing a solid defense. This privilege must cover all attorney-client communications, including those that suggest the client's guilt, as well as confessions. If, upon hearing any statement that points toward guilt, the defense lawyer either uses the statement to help the prosecution convict the client or tries to resign from the case, the attorney-client privilege is rendered meaningless.[87]

If such behavior on the part of defense attorneys became commonplace, notes legal expert John Kaplan, lawyers would be forced to give their clients the equivalent of *Miranda* warnings before representing them.[88] That is, lawyers would have to make clear what clients could or could not say in the course of preparing for trial, because any incriminatory statements might be used against them in court. Such a development would have serious ramifications for the criminal justice system.

ON A PERSONAL LEVEL

Although most defense lawyers are aware of constitutional, theoretical, and practical arguments in favor of defending guilty clients, it can be a difficult task. In the words of one prominent defense attorney:

> [I]f you're a decent human being and you've been a victim of crime yourself and you have family members that have been victims of crime, you feel tremendous turmoil. We're supposed to say, "It's not our job to worry about society, and everyone is entitled to a defense." That's all true, at an intellectual level, but at an emotional level, this takes a terrible toll, which is why some lawyers don't want to know if their clients are guilty.[89]

Sometimes, the decision to uphold client confidentiality can have tragic results, as in the situation surrounding the case of *Frank v. Magnum* (1915).[90] In that trial, Leo Frank had been convicted of murder and sentenced to life in prison. After Frank had been imprisoned, a client of attorney Arthur Powell admitted to Powell that he, and not Frank, had committed the murder in question. Powell decided not to divulge this information, and other inmates eventually lynched Frank in prison. Afterward, an anguished Powell said, "I could not have revealed the information the client had given me in the confidential relationship, without violating my oath as an attorney. . . . Such is the law; I did not make the law; but it is my duty and the court's duty to obey the law, so long as it stands."[91]

Key Terms

adversary system   309

arraignment   321

attorney general   303

attorney-client privilege   307

bail   310

bail bondsperson   313

Boykin form   324

case attrition   318

defense attorney   306

discovery   315

grand jury   316

indictment   316

information   315

initial appearance   309

nolo contendere   321

plea bargaining   321

preliminary hearing   315

preventive detention   314

public defenders   306

public prosecutors   302

release on recognizance (ROR)   313

ten percent cash bail   313

Chapter Summary

1. **List the different names given to public prosecutors and the general powers that they have.** At the federal level, the prosecutor is called the U.S. attorney. In state and local courts, the prosecutor may be referred to as the prosecuting attorney, state prosecutor, district attorney, county attorney, or city attorney. Prosecutors in general have the power to decide when and how the state will pursue an individual suspected of criminal wrongdoing. In some jurisdictions, the district attorney is also the chief law enforcement officer, holding broad powers over police operations.

2. **Contrast the prosecutor's roles as an elected official and as a crime fighter.** In most instances, the prosecutor is elected and therefore may feel obliged to reward members of her or his party with jobs. To win reelection or higher political office, the prosecutor may feel a need to bow to community pressures. As a crime fighter, the prosecutor is dependent on the police, and indeed prosecutors are generally seen as law enforcement agents. Prosecutors, however, generally only pursue cases when they believe there is sufficient legal guilt to obtain a conviction.

3. **Delineate the responsibilities of defense attorneys.** (a) The investigation of the supposed criminal incident; (b) communication with the prosecutor (including plea bargaining); (c) preparation of the case for trial; (d) submission of defense motions; (e) representation of the defendant at trial; (f) negotiation of a sentence after conviction; and (g) appeal of a guilty verdict.

4. **Indicate the three types of defense allocation programs.** (a) Assigned counsel programs, which use local private attorneys; (b) contracting attorney programs; and (c) public defender programs.

5. **List the three basic features of an adversary system of justice.** (a) A neutral decision maker (judge or jury); (b) presentation of evidence from both parties; and (c) a highly structured set of procedures that must be used when evidence is presented.

6. **Identify the steps involved in the pretrial criminal process.** (a) Suspect taken into custody or arrested; (b) initial appearance before a magistrate, at which time the defendant is informed of his or her constitutional rights and a public defender may be appointed or private counsel may be hired by the state to represent the defendant; (c) the posting of bail or release on recognizance; (d) preventive detention, if deemed necessary to ensure the safety of other persons or the community, or regular detention, if the defendant is unable to post bail; (e) preliminary hearing (minitrial), at which the judge rules on whether there is probable cause and the prosecutor issues an information; or in the alternative (f) grand jury hearings, after which an indictment is issued against the defendant if the grand jury finds probable cause; (g) arraignment, in which the defendant is informed of the charges and must respond by pleading not guilty or guilty (or in some cases *nolo contendere*); and (h) plea bargaining.

7. **Indicate the three influences on a judge's decision to set bail.** (a) Uncertainty about the character and past criminal history of the defendant; (b) the risk that the defendant will commit another crime if out on bail; and (c) overcrowded jails, which may influence a judge to release a defendant on bail.

8. **Explain how a prosecutor screens potential cases.** (a) Is there sufficient evidence for conviction? (b) What is the priority of the case? The more serious the alleged crime, the higher the priority. The more extensive the defendant's criminal record, the higher the priority. (c) Are the victims cooperative? Violence against family members often yields uncooperative victims; therefore, these cases are rarely prosecuted. (d) Are the victims reliable? (e) Might the defendant be willing to testify against other offenders?

9. **List and briefly explain the different forms of plea bargaining agreements.** (a) Charge bargaining, in which the charge is reduced to a lesser crime; (b) sentence bargaining, in which a lighter sentence is obtained; (c) count bargaining, in which a certain number or most of the multiple counts are eliminated.

10. **Indicate the ways that both defense attorneys and prosecutors can induce plea bargaining.** Defense attorneys can file numerous pretrial motions in an effort to weaken the state's case. Prosecutors can engage in horizontal or vertical overcharging, so they can be "bargained down" in the process of plea bargaining.

Questions for Critical Analysis

1. Why are public prosecutors considered the most dominant figures in the American criminal justice system?

2. Which of the three basic types of programs used to allocate defense counsel in criminal cases has aroused the most criticism recently?

3. Is it true that there is no concern for truth in our adversary system of justice? Explain your answer.

4. During an initial appearance, can defendants plead guilty of having committed a felony? Why or why not?

5. What are the arguments against preventive detention?

6. What is the distinction between a preliminary hearing and an initial appearance?

7. If grand juries indict almost all criminal defendants brought before them, why do we use grand juries?

8. What is case attrition, and why does it occur?

9. Is plea bargaining inevitable?

10. Do defense attorneys have an obligation to defend a client they know is guilty? Why or why not?

Selected Print and Electronic Resources

SUGGESTED READINGS

Burton, Bob, *Bail Enforcer: The Advanced Bounty Hunter*, Boulder, CO.: Paladin Press, 1990. This book contains stories about bounty hunting that the author personally undertook.

Heumann, Milton, *Plea Bargaining: The Experiences of Prosecutors, Judges, and Defense Attorneys*, Chicago: University of Chicago Press, Reprint Edition, 1981. This classic treatise on plea bargaining is both amusing and informative. It gives realistic accounts of the institutional roles and norms that are relevant to the plea bargaining universe. Lawyers and judges speak their piece about this necessary aspect of the criminal justice system.

Hewett, Joan, *Public Defender: Lawyer for the People*, New York: LoneStar Books, 1991. This book describes the day-to-day life of a public defender for Los Angeles County. It also includes black-and-white photos taken in the courtroom, hallways, and lockup. Hewett provides a good overview of the criminal justice system.

Saltzburg, Stephen A., et al., *Basic Criminal Procedure*, Eagan, MN: West/Wadsworth, 1997. This is a basic handbook, which is part of the Black Letter Series published by West Publishing Company. It provides all of the necessary details on pretrial procedure.

MEDIA RESOURCES

The Hunter **(1980)** Steve McQueen's last movie focuses on Ralph "Papa" Thorson, a veteran bounty hunter who works for a bail bondsman. We follow Thorson as he goes on a series of routine and not-so-routine searches. At times he is forced to use extreme measures. He even ends up killing some of the lawbreakers. Although some critics believe that this was McQueen's worst film, it does show the ways in which a real-life bounty hunter may be forced to operate.

Critically analyze this film:

1. To what extent does McQueen's character act as a private law enforcer?

2. Does the movie make the institution of the bail bondsman seem reasonable? Why or why not?

3. Does McQueen do anything illegal to capture his "prey"?

4. Does McQueen act differently than a uniformed (or undercover) police officer could legally act?

Logging On

To find out about a typical state attorney's office, visit Florida's at:

www.jud13.flcourts.org/sao/vap.html

For information on the criminal prosecution system in Korea, go to:

www.sppo.go.kr/

When you get there, click on the word "English."

You can find more about public defenders by accessing the National Legal Aid & Defender Association (NLADA) at:

www.nlada.org/index.htm

Using the internet for Criminal Justice Analysis

INFOTRAC®
COLLEGE EDITION

1. Go to your InfoTrac College Edition at **www.infotrac-college.com/wadsworth/**. After you log on, type in the words: **"COMMUNITY PROSECUTION: COMMUNITY POLICING'S LEGAL PARTNER"**

Here you will find an article from *The FBI Law Enforcement Bulletin*. It concerns the concept of a proactive partnership involving law enforcement agencies, the community, the district attorney's office, and public and private groups. It argues that an ideal community justice movement will arise from the combination of community prosecution and community policing. Read the article and answer the following questions:

a. What is the difference between community prosecution and the traditional method of setting prosecutorial priorities?

b. What are the geographic limitations of a community prosecution strategy?

c. How is there community input into the process?

d. What are the eight steps in instituting a community prosecution program?

e. Of the nine components of community prosecution, list the three that you think are the most important. Explain why.

2. Learn about the District of Columbia criminal justice system by accessing:

www.ojp.usdoj.gov/BJA/html/victsguide.htm

Once you are at the home page of the District of Columbia criminal justice system, scroll down until you find the information on the system itself, which is presented after the map. Answer the following questions:

a. What does the word "papering" mean in the context of this explanation of the D.C. criminal justice system?

b. Who handles the prosecution of most cases in the District of Columbia?

c. Where does the arrestee first appear?

d. What is the longest time that an arrestee has to wait until there is a preliminary hearing?

e. Within what time frame is an arrestee informed of the charges against him or her, advised of his or her constitutional rights, and asked to enter a plea of guilty or not guilty?

f. When does plea bargaining occur in this process in the District of Columbia?

g. Under what law are victims of crimes provided compensation?

Notes

1. Paul Van Slambrouck, "Kaczynski Trial Ended before Questions Could Be Answered," *Christian Science Monitor* (January 26, 1998), 3.

2. *Ibid.*

3. Bureau of Justice Statistics, *Sourcebook of Criminal Justice Statistics, 1995* (Washington, D.C.: U.S. Department of Justice, 1996), 489, 498.

4. Bennett L. Gershman, "Abuse of Power in the Prosecutor's Office," in *Criminal Justice 92/93*, ed. John J. Sullivan and Joseph L. Victor (Guilford, CT: The Dushkin Publishing Group, 1991), 117–23.

5. 295 U.S. 78 (1935).

6. Celesta Albonetti, "Prosecutorial Discretion: The Effects of Uncertainty," *Law and Society Review* 21 (1987), 291–313.

7. Harry T. Edwards, "To Err Is Human, But Not Always Harmless," *New York University Law Review* 70 (1995), 1191.

8. Michael Cooper, "Slaying Puts Prosecutor on Spot Again over Death Penalty," *New York Times* (January 23, 1998), B3.

9. Malcolm M. Feeley and Mark H. Lazerson, "Police-Prosecutor Relationships: An Interorganizational Perspective," in *Empirical Theories about Court*, eds. Keith O. Boyum and Lynn Mather (New York: Longman, 1983), 229–32.

10. Herbert Packer, *Limits of the Criminal Sanction* (Stanford, CA: Stanford University Press, 1968), 166–7.

11. Mark Platte, "Building Relations Pays Off," *Los Angeles Times* (July 31, 1995), 10.

12. *Gideon v. Wainwright*, 372 U.S. 335 (1963); *Massiah v. United States*, 377 U.S. 201 (1964); *United States v. Wade*, 388 U.S. 218 (1967); *Argersinger v. Hamlin*, 407 U.S. 25 (1972); *Brewer v. Williams*, 430 U.S. 387 (1977).

13. Larry Siegel, *Criminology*, 6th ed. (Belmont, CA: West/Wadsworth Publishing Company, 1998), 487–8.

14. 372 U.S. 335 (1963).

15. 387 U.S. 1 (1967).

16. 407 U.S. 25 (1972).

17. Bureau of Justice Statistics, *Indigent Defense* (Washington, D.C.: U.S. Department of Justice, 1996), 3.

18. "Criminal Justice for the Poor, 1986," *Bureau of Justice Statistics Bulletin* (Washington, D.C.: U.S. Department of Justice, 1988).

19. Bureau of Justice Statistics, *Indigent Defense*, 2.

20. 491 U.S. 554 (1989).

21. Jonathan D. Casper, *American Criminal Justice: The Defendant's Perspective* (Englewood Cliffs, NJ: Prentice-Hall, 1972), 101.

22. *Ibid.*, 106.

23. William Finnegan, "Defending the Unabomber," *New Yorker* (March 16, 1998), 61.

24. Anthony Platt and Randi Pollock, "Channeling Lawyers: The Careers of Public Defenders," in *The Potential for Reform in Criminal Justice*, ed. Herbert Jacob (Newbury Park, CA: Sage, 1974).

25. Johannes F. Nijboer, "The American Adversary System in Criminal Cases: Between Ideology and Reality," *Cardozo Journal of International and Comparative Law* 5 (Spring 1997), 79.

26. Gordon Van Kessel, "Adversary Excesses in the American Criminal Trial," *Notre Dame Law Review* 67 (1992), 403.

27. James Eisenstein and Herbert Jacob, *Felony Justice* (Boston: Little, Brown, 1977), 24.

28. Jerome Skolnick, "Social Control in the Adversary System," *Journal of Conflict Resolution* 11 (1967), 52–70.

29. Abraham S. Blumberg, "The Practice of Law as Confidence Game: Organizational Cooption of a Profession," *Law and Society Review* 4 (June 1967), 115–39.

30. Malcolm Feeley, "The Adversary System," in *Encyclopedia of the American Judicial System*, ed. Robert J. Janosik (New York: Scribners, 1987), 753.

31. Blumberg, 115.

32. "Law and Order Reconsidered," Report of the Task Force on Law and Law Enforcement to the National Commission on the Causes and Prevention of Violence (Washington, D.C.: General Publishing Office, 1968), 427–30.

33. Illinois Ann. Stat. ch. 725, para. 5/110-5.

34. David W. Neubauer, *America's Courts and the Criminal Justice System*, 5th ed. (Belmont, CA: Wadsworth Publishing Company, 1996), 179–81.

35. Roy Flemming, C. Kohfeld, and Thomas Uhlman, "The Limits of Bail Reform: A Quasi Experimental Analysis," *Law and Society Review* 14 (1980), 947–76.

36. Jacob Santini, "Accused Rapist Denied Bail before 2nd Trial," *Salt Lake City Tribune* (February 12, 1998), B2.

37. Caleb Foote, "Compelling Appearance in Court: Administration of Bail in Philadelphia," *University of Pennsylvania Law Review* 102 (1954), 1031–52.

38. John Goldkamp, *Two Classes of Accused* (Cambridge, MA: Ballinger, 1979).

39. Frederic Suffet, "Bail Setting: A Study of Courtroom Interaction," *Crime and Delinquency* 12 (1966), 318.

40. Wayne H. Thomas, Jr., *Bail Reform in America* (Berkeley, CA: University of California Press, 1976), 4.

41. John S. Goldkamp and Michael R. Gottfredson, *Policy Guidelines for Bail: An Experiment in Court Reform* (Philadephia: Temple University Press, 1985), 18.

42. Thomas, 7.

43. Esmond Harmsworth, "Bail and Detention: An Assessment and Critique of the Federal and Massachusetts Systems," *New England Journal on Criminal and Civil Confinement* 22 (Spring 1996), 213.

44. 18 U.S.C. Section 3146(b) (1966).

45. Harmsworth, 213.

46. 18 U.S.C. Section 3142(g) (1994).

47. Ian Ayres and Joel Waldfogel, "A Market Test for Race Discrimination in Bail Setting," *Stanford Law Review* 46 (May 1994), 987.

48. Thomas C. French, "Is It Punitive or Is It Regulatory?" *University of Toledo Law Review* 20 (Fall 1988), 189.

49. 18 U.S.C. Sections 3141–3150 (Supp. III 1985).

50. Douglas Mossman, "Assessing Predictions of Violence: Being Accurate about Accuracy," *Journal of Consulting and Clinical Psychology* 62 (1994), 783.

51. 481 U.S. 739 (1987).

52. *Gerstein v. Pugh*, 420 U.S. 103 (1975).

53. David W. Neubauer, *Criminal Justice in Middle America* (Morristown, NJ: General Learning Press, 1974).

54. Andrew D. Leipold, "Why Grand Juries Do Not (and Cannot) Protect the Accused," *Cornell Law Review* 80 (January 1995), 260.

55. Thomas P. Sullivan and Robert D. Nachman, "If It Ain't Broke, Don't Fix It: Why the Grand Jury's Accusatory Function Should Not Be Changed," *Journal of Criminal Law and Criminology* 75 (1984), 1050, citing *Statistical Report of U.S. Attorney's Offices, Fiscal Year 1984*, 2.

56. New York Court of Appeals Judge Sol Wachtler, quoted in David Margolik, "Law Professor to Administer Courts in State, *New York Times* (February 1, 1985), B2.

57. Kenneth C. Davis, *Discretionary Justice: A Preliminary Inquiry* (Baton Rouge, LA: Louisiana State University Press, 1969), 189.

58. Mirjan R. Damaska, *The Faces of Justice and State Authority* (New Haven, CT: Yale University Press, 1986), 483–7.

59. Barbara Boland, Paul Mahanna, and Ronald Scones, *The Prosecution of Felony Arrests, 1988* (Washington, D.C.: Bureau of Justice Statistics, 1992).

60. *Ibid.*

61. Brian Forst, Frank Leahy, Jean Shirhall, Herbert Tyson, Eric Wish, and John Bartolemo, *Arrest Convictability as a Measure of Police Performance* (Washington, D.C.: Institute for Law and Social Research, 1981).

62. Kathy B. Carter, "Court Orders Statewide Drug Penalties, Ending County Disparities," *Newark Star-Ledger* (February 20, 1998), 46.

63. Joan Jacoby, *Basic Issues in Prosecution and Public Defender Performance* (Washington, D.C.: U.S. Department of Justice/National Institute of Justice, 1982), 24–32; and Joan Jacoby, "The Changing Policies of Prosecutors," in *The Prosecutor*, ed. William McDonald (Beverly Hills, CA: Sage Publications, 1979), 75–97.

64. Samuel Walker, *Sense and Nonsense about Crime: A Policy Guide*, 2nd ed. (Monterey, CA: Brooks/Cole Publishing, 1989), 22–27.

65. 404 U.S. 257 (1971).

66. Fred C. Zacharias, "Justice in Plea Bargaining," *William and Mary Law Review* 39 (March 1998), 1121.

67. Albert W. Alschuler, "The Prosecutor's Role in Plea Bargaining," *University of Chicago Law Review* 36 (1968), 52.

68. Milton Heumann, *Plea Bargaining: The Experiences of Prosecutors, Judges, and Defense Attorneys* (Chicago: University of Chicago Press, 1978), 58.

69. Albert W. Alschuler, "The Defense Attorney's Role in Plea Bargaining," *Yale Law Journal* 84 (1975), 1200.

70. Stephen J. Schulhofer, "Plea Bargaining as Disaster," *Yale Law Journal* 101 (1992), 1987.

71. Kevin Cole and Fred C. Zacharias, "The Agony of Victory and the Ethics of Lawyer Speech," *South California Law Review* 69 (1996), 1660–3.

72. William Glaberson, "Kaczynski Avoids a Death Sentence with Guilty Plea," *New York Times* (January 23, 1998), A1.

73. Alschuler, "The Prosecutor's Role in Plea Bargaining," 53.

74. Casper, 77–81.

75. 395 U.S. 238 (1969).

76. Stephen A. Saltzburg, "Lawyers, Clients, and the Adversary System," *Mercer Law Review* 37 (1986), 651–5.

77. Douglas A. Smith, "The Plea Bargaining Controversy," *Journal of Criminal Law and Criminology* 77 (1986), 949.

78. Warren Burger, "Address to the American Bar Association Annual Convention," *New York Times* (August 11, 1970), 24.

79. Stephen J. Schulhofer, "Is Plea Bargaining Inevitable," *Harvard Law Review* 97 (March 1984), 1037.

80. Robert A. Weninger, "The Abolition of Plea Bargaining: A Case Study of El Paso County, Texas," *UCLA Law Review* 35 (December 1987), 265.

81. Stephen J. Schulhofer, "Rethinking Mandatory Minimums," *Wake Forest Law Review* 28 (1993), 207–8.

82. Jeff Brown, "Proposition 8: Origins and Impact—A Public Defender's Perspective," *Pacific Law Journal* 23 (April 1992), 881.

83. Vicki Torres, "Chief of Bar Association Asks End to Lawyer-Bashing," *Los Angeles Times* (July 6, 1993), A1.

84. Quoted in Charles Fried, "The Lawyer as Friend: The Moral Foundations of the Lawyer-Client Relation," *Yale Law Journal* 85 (1976), 1060.

85. Murray L. Schwartz, *Cases and Materials on Professional Responsibility and the Administration of Criminal Justice* (New York: Council on Legal Education for Professional Responsibility, 1961), 115.

86. David Luban, "The Adversary System Excuse," in *The Good Lawyer: Lawyers' Roles and Lawyers' Ethics*, ed. David Luban (Totowa, NJ: Rowman & Allanheld, 1983), 83.

87. David Rosenthal, "The Criminal Defense Attorney, Ethics and Maintaining Client Confidentiality: A Proposal to Amend Rule 1.6 of the Model Rules of Professional Conduct," *St. Thomas Law Review* 6 (Fall 1993), 153.

88. John Kaplan, "Defending Guilty People," *University of Bridgeport Law Review* 7 (1986), 223.

89. Cheryl Lavin, "Alan Dershowitz Defends Attorneys," *Fort Worth Star-Telegram* (April 4, 1995), 1.

90. 237 U.S. 309 (1915).

91. Quoted in Rosenthal, 153.

chapter

10

The Criminal Trial

Chapter Objectives

After reading this chapter, you should be able to:

1. Identify the basic protections enjoyed by criminal defendants in the United States.

2. List the three requirements of the Speedy Trial Act of 1974.

3. Explain what "taking the Fifth" really means.

4. List the requirements normally imposed on potential jurors.

5. Contrast challenges for cause and peremptory challenges during *voir dire*.

6. List the standard steps in a criminal jury trial.

7. Explain the difference between testimony and real evidence; between lay witnesses and expert witnesses; and between direct and circumstantial evidence.

8. List possible affirmative defenses.

9. Delineate circumstances in which a criminal defendant may in fact be tried a second time for the same act.

10. List the six basic steps of an appeal.

INTRODUCTION

The criminal trial receives more scrutiny than any other aspect of the criminal justice system. This is due, in part, to the obviously dramatic nature of a trial. When viewed through the lenses of the ever-attentive media, trials can appear to be gripping confrontations between good and evil (though reasonable persons may disagree as to which side is which). The film industry's propensity to mass-produce courtroom dramas is also understandable. Few screenplays could match the plot and characters of the 1995 O. J. Simpson criminal trial or the theatrics of its conclusion. It is not surprising that the American public is infatuated with a "trial of the century" seemingly once every decade.

At the same time, the criminal trial is a statistically rare event. Only a small percentage of those arrested for crimes ever wind up in front of a judge and jury. Furthermore, as we know from the wedding cake model (see Chapter 1), most trials that do take place are ignored by the media and, hence, the public.

Neither the distortion of the criminal trial by the media, nor its relative rarity, should be seen to lessen the importance of the trial. Protection against the arbitrary abuse of power is at the heart of the U.S. Constitution. In the criminal justice system, the right to a criminal trial before a jury is one means of assuring this protection. For many, the fairness exhibited in criminal trials inspires faith in the system as a whole.[1]

Fairness, however, is not easily defined. The criminal trial is basically a fact-finding process, but how those facts are presented by the prosecution and defense and then deciphered by the jury adds a measure of uncertainty to the process. For example, in 1984 Curtis Kyles was arrested in connection with the murder of Delores Dye. New Orleans police found Dye's purse in the front seat of Kyles's car, the murder weapon behind Kyles's stove, and ammunition that matched the bullet that killed Dye in his car and in his dresser.

Fourteen years later, after five criminal trials, Kyles was released. Kyles's attorneys had been able to produce enough evidence of the *possibility* that their client was framed to cause three hung juries (in which a verdict could not be reached) and one Supreme Court reversal. After the final trial, prosecutors insinuated that the trial process had been *too* fair to Dye, placing procedural and legal concerns above those of justice for his victim and society at large.[2]

In this chapter, we will examine the fairness of the criminal trial in the context of the current legal environment. Because "fairness" can only be defined subjectively, we will also make an effort to look into what effect human nature has on the adversary process. Trials may be based on fact finding, but, as Judge Jerome Frank once sardonically asserted, when it comes to a jury, "facts are guesses."[3]

"[O]ur fundamental principles of justice declare that the defendant is as innocent on the day before his trial as he is on the morning after his acquittal."

—Thurgood Marshall,
U.S. Supreme Court Associate Justice (1987)

SPECIAL FEATURES OF CRIMINAL TRIALS

Civil trials (see Chapter 3) and criminal trials have many similar features. In both types of trials, attorneys from each side select a jury, make their opening statements to the court, examine and cross-examine witnesses, and summarize their positions in closing arguments. The jury is charged (instructed), and if it reaches a verdict, the trial comes to an end.

The principal difference is that in civil trials, the adversaries are persons (including corporations, which are legal persons, and businesses), one of whom often is seeking a remedy in the form of damages from the other. In a criminal trial, it is the state, not the victim of the crime, that brings the action against an alleged wrongdoer.[4] Criminal trial procedures reflect the need to protect criminal defendants against the power of the state by providing them with a number of rights. Many of the significant rights of the accused are spelled out in the Sixth Amendment, which reads, in part, as follows:

> In all criminal prosecutions, the accused shall enjoy the right to a speedy and public trial, by an impartial jury of the State and the district wherein the crime shall have been committed, . . . and to be informed of the nature and cause of the accusation; to be confronted with the witnesses against him; to have compulsory process for obtaining witnesses in his favor; and to have the Assistance of Counsel for his defense.

In this section, we will examine the aspects of the criminal trial that make it unique, beginning with two protections explicitly stated in the Sixth Amendment: the right to a speedy trial by an impartial jury. (For a discussion on how televising trials might affect a defendant's Sixth Amendment rights, see the feature *Criminal Justice in Action—Cameras in the Courtroom: Is Justice Served?* at the end of this chapter.)

A "Speedy" Trial

As you have just read, the Sixth Amendment requires a speedy trial for those accused of a criminal act. The reason for this requirement is obvious: depending on various factors, the defendant may lose his or her right to move freely and may be incarcerated prior to trial. Also, the accusation that a person has committed a crime jeopardizes that person's reputation in the community. If the defendant is innocent, the sooner the trial is held, the sooner his or her innocence can be established in the eyes of the court and the public.

A group of college students has put together a Web site that addresses the most important aspects of the criminal trial in the United States. To visit this highly informative site, go to **tqd.advanced.org/2760/ homep.htm**

Reasons for Delay. As the preceding chapter made clear, there are numerous reasons for delay in bringing a defendant to trial. In defending the rights of the accused, a defense attorney may use a number of legal tactics, including pretrial motions and plea negotiations. Court congestion also contributes to the problem; many jurisdictions do not have enough judges and courtroom space to meet the needs of the system. This situation has been aggravated by the recent increase in drug-related arrests, which threatens to create judicial "gridlock" in certain metropolitan courthouses.[5]

The Definition of a Speedy Trial. The Sixth Amendment does not specify what is meant by the term *speedy*. The Supreme Court has refused to quantify "speedy" as well, ruling instead in *Barker v. Wingo* (1972)[6] that only in situations in which the delay is unwarranted and proved to be prejudicial can the accused claim a violation of Sixth Amendment rights.

As a result, all fifty states have their own speedy-trial statutes.[7] For example, the Illinois Speedy Trial Act states that a defendant must be tried within 120 days of arrest unless both the prosecution and the defense agree otherwise. States can also decide what constitutes the "go point" of a particular case. The Tennessee Supreme Court recently ruled that a five-year period between the issuance of an arrest warrant and the actual arrest of the defendant did not deny the accused his right to a speedy trial. The decision was based on the court's belief that the clock does not begin to run until the defendant is arrested or is indicted by a grand jury.[8]

At the national level, the Speedy Trial Act of 1974[9] (amended in 1979) specifies time limits for those in the federal court system. This act requires:

1. No more than thirty days between arrest and indictment.

2. No more than ten days between indictment and arraignment.

3. No more than sixty days between arraignment and trial.

JURY TRIAL
A trial before a judge and a jury.

BENCH TRIAL
A trial conducted without a jury, in which a judge makes the determination of the defendant's guilt or innocence.

ACQUITTAL
A declaration following a trial that the individual accused of the crime is innocent in the eyes of the law and thus absolved from the charges.

Federal law allows extra time for hearings on pretrial motions, mental competency examinations, and other procedural actions.

Note that when discussing issues of a "speedy trial," the primary issue is the time period between the arrest and the beginning of the actual trial, not the length of the trial itself. Indeed, most trials are completed relatively quickly, as you can see in Figure 10.1.

The Role of the Jury

The Sixth Amendment also states that anyone accused of a crime shall be judged by "an impartial jury." In *Duncan v. Louisiana* (1968),[10] the Supreme Court solidified this right by ruling that in all felony cases, the defendant is entitled to a **jury trial.** The Court has, however, left it to the individual states to decide whether juries are required for misdemeanor cases.[11] If the defendant waives her or his right to trial by jury, a **bench trial** takes place in which a judge decides questions of legality and fact, and no jury is involved.

Jury Size. The predominant American twelve-person jury is not the result of any one law—the Constitution does not require that the jury be a particular size. Historically, the number was inherited from the size of English juries, which was fixed at twelve during the fourteenth century.

In 1970, responding to a case that challenged Florida's practice of using a six-person jury in all but capital cases, the Supreme Court ruled that the accused did not have the right to be heard by a twelve-person jury. Indeed, the Court labeled the number twelve "a historical accident, wholly without significance except to mystics."[12] In *Ballew v. Georgia* (1968),[13] however, the Court did strike down attempts to use juries with fewer than six members, stating that a jury's effectiveness was severely hampered below that limit. About half the states allow fewer than twelve persons on criminal juries, though only for misdemeanor cases. In federal courts, defendants are entitled to have the case heard by a twelve-member jury unless both parties agree in writing to a smaller jury.

Unanimity. In most jurisdictions, jury verdicts in criminal cases must be *unanimous* for **acquittal** or conviction. As will be explained in more detail later, if the jury cannot reach unanimous agreement on whether to acquit or convict the defendant, the result is a hung jury, and the judge may order a new trial.

Again, the Supreme Court has not held unanimity to be a rigid requirement. It has declared that jury verdicts must be unanimous in federal criminal trials, but has given states leeway to set their own rules.[14] Five states—Oklahoma, Texas, Oregon, Montana, and Louisiana—permit nonunanimous trial verdicts, though none allow more than three dissenting votes for convictions by twelve-person juries.

The Privilege against Self-Incrimination

In addition to the Sixth Amendment, which specifies the protections we have just discussed, the Fifth Amendment of the Constitution also provides important safeguards for the defendant. The Fifth Amendment states that no person "shall be compelled in any criminal case to be a witness against himself." Therefore, a defendant has the right *not* to testify at a trial if to do so would implicate him or her in the crime. Witnesses may also refuse to testify on this ground. For example, if a witness, while testifying, is asked a question and the answer would reveal her or his own criminal wrongdoing, the witness may "take the Fifth." In other words, she or he can refuse to testify on the ground that such testimony may be self-incriminating. This rarely occurs, however,

Figure 10.1 The Length of Criminal Trials in U.S. District Courts

Because many of the trials in the public eye last for weeks, one could easily get the impression that trials are lengthy undertakings. As you see here, that is not true in most cases.

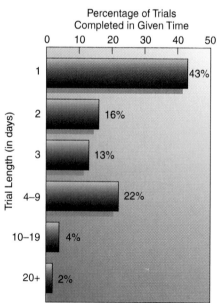

Percentage of Trials Completed in Given Time

Trial Length (in days)

1: 43%
2: 16%
3: 13%
4–9: 22%
10–19: 4%
20+: 2%

SOURCE: BUREAU OF JUSTICE STATISTICS, SOURCEBOOK OF CRIMINAL JUSTICE STATISTICS, 1997 (WASHINGTON, D.C.: U.S. DEPARTMENT OF JUSTICE, 1998), 417–8.

The British Right to Remain Silent

Under current court interpretations of the Fifth Amendment and because of the *Miranda* ruling, when police officers question a suspect, the suspect can remain silent. No adverse inference may be drawn from the suspect's refusal to speak to police or to testify at trial. Thus, under current law, O. J. Simpson's refusal to take the stand could be interpreted negatively by everyone in the country—except by the twelve jurors.

Great Britain has had its own version of the Fifth Amendment (no person "shall be compelled in any criminal case to be a witness against himself"). Since a 1994 act of Parliament, however, at trial an adverse inference *may* be drawn from the defendant's refusal to speak when questioned by the police. In Britain, at each arrest, the arresting officer tells the suspect that he or she need not say anything, but "it may harm your defense if you do not mention when questioned something which you later rely on in court." In plain words, silence may be used as evidence of guilt in Britain.

WHAT'S THE EVIDENCE?

Great Britain has come under a great deal of criticism from human rights organizations in Europe for its lack of a privilege against self-incrimination. For an informed look at this issue, go to **http://mishpatim.huji.ac.il/ilr/ilr3l_1c.htm**

---

as witnesses are often granted immunity before testifying, meaning that no information they disclose can be used to bring criminal charges against them. Witnesses who have been granted immunity cannot refuse to answer questions on the basis of self-incrimination.

It is important to note that not only does the defendant have the right to "take the Fifth," but also that the decision to do so should not prejudice the jury in the prosecution's favor. The Supreme Court came to this controversial decision while reviewing *Adamson v. California* (1947),[15] a case involving the convictions of two defendants who had declined to testify in their own defense against charges of robbery, kidnapping, and murder. The prosecutor in *Adamson* frequently and insistently brought this silence to the notice of the jury in his closing argument, insinuating that if the pair had been innocent, they would not have been afraid to testify. The Court ruled that such tactics effectively invalidated the Fifth Amendment by using the defendants' refusal to testify against them. Now judges are required to inform the jury that an accused's decision to remain silent cannot be held against him or her. (For a look at the right to remain silent in Great Britain, see *Cross-National CJ Comparison: The British Right to Remain Silent.*)

The Presumption of a Defendant's Innocence

A presumption in criminal law is that a defendant is innocent until proved guilty. The burden of proving guilt falls on the state (the public prosecutor). Even if a defendant did in fact commit the crime, she or he will be "innocent" in the eyes of the law unless the prosecutor can substantiate the charge with sufficient evidence to convince a jury (or judge in a bench trial) of the defendant's guilt.[16]

A Strict Standard of Proof

In a criminal trial, the defendant is not required to prove his or her innocence. As mentioned, the burden of proving the defendant's guilt lies entirely with the state. Furthermore, the state must prove the defendant's guilt **beyond a reasonable doubt.** That is, the prosecution must show that, based on all the evidence, the defendant's guilt is clear and unquestionable. In *In re Winship* (1970),[17] a case involving the due process rights of juveniles, the Supreme

BEYOND A REASONABLE DOUBT
The standard used to determine the guilt or innocence of a person charged with a crime. To be guilty of a crime, a suspect must be proved guilty "beyond and to the exclusion of a reasonable doubt."

Court ruled that the Constitution requires the reasonable doubt standard because it reduces the risk of convicting innocent people and therefore reassures Americans of the law's moral force and legitimacy.

This high standard of proof in criminal cases reflects a fundamental social value—the belief that it is worse to convict an innocent individual than to let a guilty one go free. The consequences to the life, liberty, and reputation of an accused person from an erroneous conviction for a crime are enormous, and this has been factored into the process. Placing a high standard of proof on the prosecutor reduces the margin of error in criminal cases (at least in one direction).

JURY SELECTION

The initial step in a criminal trial involves choosing the jury. The framers of the Constitution ensured that the importance of the jury would not easily be overlooked. The right to a trial by jury is explicitly mentioned no fewer than three times in the Constitution: in Article III, Section 2; in the Sixth Amendment; and again in the Seventh Amendment. The use of a peer jury not only provided safeguards against the abuses of state power that the framers feared, but also gave Americans a chance—and a duty—to participate in the criminal justice system.[18]

In the early years of the country, a jury "of one's peers" meant a jury limited to white, landowning males. Now, as the process has become fully democratized, there are still questions about what "a jury of one's peers" actually means and how effective the system has been in providing the necessary diversity in juries.

Initial Steps: The Master Jury List and *Venire*

The main goal of jury selection is to produce a cross section of the population in the jurisdiction where the crime was committed. Sometimes, a defense attorney may argue that his or her client's trial should be moved to another community to protect against undue prejudice. Judges, mindful of the intent of the Constitution, are hesitant to grant such pretrial motions.

This belief that trials should take place in the community where the crime was committed is central to the purpose of selecting a jury of the defendant's "peers." The United States is a large, diverse nation, and the outlook of its citizens varies accordingly. Two very different recent cases, one tried in rural Maine and the other in San Francisco, illustrate this point.[19] In Maine, the defendant had accidentally shot and killed a woman standing in her back yard; he had mistaken her white mittens for a deer's tail. His attorney argued that it was the responsibility of the victim to wear bright colored clothing in the vicinity of hunters during hunting season. The jury agreed, and the defendant was acquitted of manslaughter. In the San Francisco case, two people were charged with distributing sterile needles to intravenous drug users. Rather than denying that the defendants had distributed the needles, the defense admitted the act but insisted that it was necessary to stem the transmission of AIDS and, thus, to save lives. The jury voted 11–1 to acquit, causing a mistrial.

These two outcomes may surprise or even anger people in other parts of the country, but they reflect the values of the regions where the alleged crimes were committed. Thus, a primary goal of the jury selection process is to ensure that the defendant is judged by members of her or his community—peers in the true sense of the word.

The Master Jury List. Besides having to live in the jurisdiction where the case is being tried, there are very few restrictions on eligibility to serve on a

When juries are presented with compelling evidence, they can make their decision quickly. The photo below was shown as an exhibit in the 1999 murder trial of John William King, who was charged with dragging an African American named James Byrd, Jr., to his death behind a pickup truck. Jurors were shown a number of photos of images tattooed on King's body, including one that showed a black man hanging from a tree. The jury found King guilty after deliberating for only 150 minutes. Do you agree with prosecutors that the intricate racist, satanic, and neo-Nazi tattoos covering King's body helped prove motive, intent, and state of mind? Or do you agree with the defense attorney who said that the tattoos do not necessarily make King a racist?

jury. State legislatures generally set the requirements, and they are similar in most states. For the most part, jurors must be

1. Citizens of the United States.
2. Over eighteen years of age.
3. Free of felony convictions.
4. Of the necessary good health to function in a jury setting.
5. Sufficiently intelligent to understand the issues of a trial.
6. Able to read, write, and comprehend the English language.

The **master jury list,** sometimes called the *jury pool*, is made up of all the eligible jurors in a community. This list is usually drawn from voter registration lists or driver's license rolls, which have the benefit of being easily available and timely.

Increasing Jury List Diversity. The drawback of tying master jury lists to voter registration lists is that the practice has tended historically to exclude the poor, racial minorities, the young, and the uneducated (in other words, the same groups who are less likely to vote). Also, it has been surmised that some people don't vote for the express reason of keeping their names off the master jury list.[20] These people may not be able to afford to miss work at the low pay offered jurors—less than $30 per day on average—or simply may not want to deal with the inconvenience.

A number of states have taken steps to increase the diversity of the master jury list.[21] Both Arizona and New York access welfare and unemployment rolls to find potential jurors, and Arizona also canvasses phone books and water service customer lists for that purpose. California uses Social Security rolls and tax returns as sources of names. In Florida and elsewhere, lists of persons with driver's licenses are also consulted.

Venire. The next step in gathering a jury is to draw together the **venire** (Latin for "to come"). The *venire* is composed of all those people who are notified by the clerk of the court that they have been selected for jury duty. Those selected to be part of the *venire* are ordered to report to the courthouse on the date specified by the notice.

Some people are excused from answering this summons. Persons who do not meet the qualifications listed earlier in this section either need not appear in court or, in some states, must appear only in order to be officially dismissed. Also, people in some professions, including teachers, physicians, and judges, can receive exemptions due to the nature of their work. Each court sets its own guidelines for the circumstances under which it will excuse jurors from service, and these guidelines can be as strict or as lenient as the court desires.

Voir Dire

At the courthouse, prospective jurors are gathered, and the process of selecting those who will actually hear the case begins. This selection process is not haphazard. The court ultimately seeks jurors who are free of any biases that may affect their willingness to listen to the facts of the case impartially. To this end, both the prosecutor and the defense attorney have some input into the ultimate make-up of the jury. Each attorney questions prospective jurors in a proceeding known as **voir dire** (French for "to tell the truth").[22] During *voir dire*, jurors are required to provide the court with a significant amount of personal information, including their home address, marital status, employment status, arrest record, and life experiences (see Figure 10.2).

MASTER JURY LIST
The list of citizens in a court's district from which a jury can be selected; often compiled from voter registration lists, driver's license lists, and other sources.

VENIRE
The group of citizens from which the jury is selected.

VOIR DIRE
The preliminary questions that the trial attorneys ask prospective jurors to determine whether they are biased or have any connection with the defendant or a witness.

INFOTRAC®
COLLEGE EDITION

Herman, Russ. Jury selection.

Figure 10.2 Sample Juror Questionnaire

PANEL: JUROR NUMBER

To facilitate the jury selection process, the court requires that you provide the information requested below under penalty of perjury. The completed questionnaire will be a public record and open to public inspection. If you feel that any question requires an answer which is too sensitive (personal or private) to be included in a public record, you have the right to request a private hearing rather than filling out the answer in writing. If you prefer to have a private hearing for a sensitive question, write "P" (for "private") in the space provided for the answer.

QUALIFICATIONS

I am able to read and understand English.   Yes   No

I am now serving as a grand juror in a court in this state.   Yes   No

I am a citizen of the United States.   Yes   No

I am under a court appointed conservatorship.   Yes   No

I am eighteen years of age or older.   Yes   No

I am a peace officer pursuant to 830.1 or 830.2c PC.   Yes   No

I am a resident of Sacramento County.   Yes   No

I have been convicted of a felony.   Yes   No

If so, answer yes unless you have received a full pardon.

1. Marital Status: Married   Single   Divorced   Widowed

2. Education: Completed Degrees: _____ Highest grade level _____

3. Occupation: Previous Occupation:

   Employer: Previous Employer:

4. Information regarding spouse or other adults with whom you reside:

   Occupation: Previous Occupation:

   Employer: Previous Employer:

5. Information about your children or step-children:

   [ ] I have no children or step-children.

AGE	SEX	OCCUPATION	AGE	SEX	OCCUPATION
___	___	_____	___	___	_____
___	___	_____	___	___	_____
___	___	_____	___	___	_____

6. Military service: Branch _____

   Highest Rank _____

   Specialty _____

   Did you have any involvement with the military criminal justice system? If yes, explain.

7. Prior jury service: (For each case, without disclosing the results, indicate yes or no, did the case end in a verdict?)

YEAR	TYPE OF CASE	YES/NO	YEAR	TYPE OF CASE	YES/NO
___	_____	___	___	_____	___
___	_____	___	___	_____	___

8. In what area of Sacramento do you live (neighborhood)?

9. Have you, a close friend or relative ever been employed by a law enforcement agency (federal, state, or local)? If yes, what agency?

10. Have you, a close friend or relative ever been a victim of crime? If yes, state the nature of the crime(s).

11. Have you, a close friend or relative ever been arrested for a crime (including driving under the influence)? If yes, state the nature of the crime(s).

12. Except as revealed in question 10 or 11 above, have you, a close friend or relative, ever been witness to a crime? If yes, state the nature of the crime(s).

I hereby declare under penalty of perjury that the foregoing is true and correct. (2015.5 CCP) Executed at Sacramento, County of Sacramento, California.

Date _____ Signature _____

SOURCE: THIS IS A MODEL BASED ON THE QUESTIONNAIRE IN USE AT SACRAMENTO (CALIFORNIA) SUPERIOR AND MUNICIPAL COURTS.

The *voir dire* process involves both written and oral questioning of potential jurors. Attorneys fashion their inquiries in such a manner as to uncover any biases on the parts of prospective jurors and to find persons who might identify with the plights of their respective sides. As one attorney noted, though a lawyer will have many chances to talk to a jury as a whole, *voir dire* is his only chance to talk with the individual jurors.[23]

Challenges for Cause. During *voir dire,* the attorney for each side may exercise a certain number of challenges to prevent particular persons from serving on the jury. Both sides can exercise two types of challenges: challenges "for cause" and peremptory challenges.

If a defense attorney concludes that a prospective juror is unfit to serve, the attorney may exercise a **challenge for cause** and request that that person not be included on the jury. Attorneys must provide the court with a sound, legally justifiable reason for why potential jurors are "unfit" to serve. For example, jurors can be challenged for cause if they are mentally incompetent, do not speak English, or are proved to have a prior link—be it personal or financial—with the defendant or victim. (As Figure 10.3 shows, jurors can also be dismissed after the trial has started if they have not been truthful in the *voir dire* process.)

Jurors can also be challenged if they are outwardly biased in some way that would prejudice them for or against the defendant. The Supreme Court has ruled that individuals may be legally excluded from a jury in a capital case if they would under no circumstances vote for a guilty verdict if it carried the death penalty.[24] At the same time, potential jurors cannot be challenged for

CHALLENGE FOR CAUSE
A *voir dire* challenge for which an attorney states the reason why a prospective juror should not be included on the jury.

JUROR 228

Juror 228 was an employee of the Hertz Corporation, a leading car rental agency. O. J. Simpson had been a celebrity spokesperson for Hertz. During *voir dire,* Juror 228 stated that he had never met the defendant. Later, the prosecution discovered that, in fact, Juror 228 had been a member of a Hertz Corporation Committee that planned and attended a social event that involved Simpson, and had most certainly met him.

Reason for dismissal: A juror who conceals relevant facts or gives false answers during the *voir dire* examination thus undermines the jury selection process and commits misconduct.

JUROR 620

The court received information that Juror 620 had indicated to friends and co-workers that he would never vote to find the defendant guilty. Furthermore, investigation by the prosecution revealed that during Juror 620's first marriage he had been arrested for domestic violence. These allegations had not been disclosed during *voir dire,* and certainly would have eliminated Juror 620 from the proceedings, given that domestic violence was a major issue in the case.

Reason for dismissal: The failure to candidly answer questions during *voir dire* deprives the parties of their right to intelligently exercise their peremptory challenges. Failure to disclose a criminal arrest involving allegations of domestic violence constitutes juror misconduct.

JUROR 1489

The other jurors had several complaints concerning the behavior of Juror 1489, a 54-year-old male weighing nearly 200 pounds. Juror 1427, a 28-year-old female, complained that Juror 1489 bumped her several times in an elevator, making sexually suggestive facial gestures to the other jurors in the elevator. Later, court bailiffs noted that Juror 1427 was upset to the point of crying because Juror 1489 had offensively brushed up against her in the jurors' lounge. Both Juror 1427 and Juror 1290 also complained that Juror 1489 stared at them in an unpleasant manner in the jury room. Finally, Juror 353 reported that Juror 1489 physically threatened her after she accidentally stepped on his foot.

Reason for dismissal: Juror 1489's conduct was found to be disruptive of the truth-finding process.

SOURCE: Defendant's Motion for an Evidentiary Hearing, People v. Orenthal James Simpson, Superior Court of the State of California In and For the County of Los Angeles (July 15, 1995), Case #BA097211.

Figure 10.3 Jurors Dismissed from the O. J. Simpson Criminal Trial
A jury trial starts with twelve jurors and several alternate jurors. In some instances, the prosecution, defense, or court receives information that requires one or more of these jurors to be excused from the trial. In the O. J. Simpson trial, the adversarial nature of the trial extended to the jury box, with both sides demanding the removal of various jurors. The reasons for some of these removals are given here.

PEREMPTORY CHALLENGES
Voir dire challenges to exclude potential jurors from serving on the jury without any supporting reason or cause.

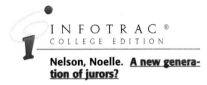

INFOTRAC®
COLLEGE EDITION

Nelson, Noelle. A new generation of jurors?

cause if they have "general objections" or have "expressed conscientious or religious scruples" against capital punishment.[25] The final responsibility for deciding whether a potential juror should be excluded rests with the judge, who may choose not to act on an attorney's request.

Peremptory Challenges. Each attorney may also exercise a limited number of **peremptory challenges.** These challenges are based *solely* on an attorney's subjective reasoning; that is, the attorney is usually not required to give any legally justifiable reason for wanting to exclude a particular person from the jury. Because of the rather random nature of peremptory challenges, each state limits the number that an attorney may utilize: between five and ten for felony trials (depending on the state) and ten and twenty for capital trials (also depending on the state). Once an attorney's peremptory challenges are used up, he or she must accept forthcoming jurors, unless a challenge for cause can be used.

An attorney's decision to exclude a juror may sometimes seem whimsical. One state prosecutor who litigated drug cases was known to use a peremptory challenge whenever he saw a potential juror with a coffee mug or backpack bearing the insignia of the local public broadcasting station. The attorney presumed that this was evidence that the potential juror had donated money to the public station, and that anybody who would do so would be too "liberal" to give the government's case against a drug offender a favorable hearing.[26] Lawyers have been known to similarly reject potential jurors for reasons of demeanor, dress, and posture.

Jury Science. A great deal of what has been called "jury folklore" has come to surround the use of peremptory challenges. According to this folklore, defense attorneys favor Jewish people, who are seen to have played the historical role of victims. Some prosecutors see jurors of Scandinavian or German descent as more willing to punish a perceived wrongdoer. Stockbrokers are considered useful for the prosecutors, musicians are not, and so on.[27]

Though this folklore still exists, it is increasingly being accompanied by the phenomenon of *jury science,* which replaces guesses and intuition with a "scientific process" for determining the biases—conscious or subconscious—of the members of the jury pool. Generally, this science is carried out by consultants who determine the "ideal" juror profile for their client and direct the attorney to use peremptory or for-cause challenges to shape the jury accordingly.[28]

Applying jury science is quite expensive, costing hundreds of thousands of dollars in some cases. For this reason, many critics believe it should be disallowed, as it gives wealthy or high-profile defendants an advantage that is not available to most Americans.[29]

Race and Gender Issues in Jury Selection

The Sixth Amendment guarantees the right to an *impartial* jury. But, as researcher Jeremy W. Barber notes, it is in the best interests of neither the defense nor the prosecution attorneys to seek an impartial jury.[30] In fact, the goal of their peremptory challenges is to create a *partial* jury—partial, that is, toward or against the defendant. If the jury turns out to be impartial, it may be that the efforts of each side have balanced each other out.

For many years, prosecutors used their peremptory challenges as an instrument of *de facto* segregation in juries. Prosecutors were able to keep African Americans off juries in cases in which an African American was the defendant. The argument that African Americans—or members of any other minority group—would be impartially disposed toward one of their own was tacitly supported by the Supreme Court. Despite its own assertion, made in *Swain v. Alabama* (1965),[31] that blacks have the same right to appear on a jury as whites, the Court mirrored the apparent racism of society as a whole by protecting the actions of many prosecutors.

The *Batson* Reversal. The Supreme Court reversed this policy in 1986 with *Batson v. Kentucky*.[32] In this case, the Court declared that the equal protection clause prohibits prosecutors from using peremptory challenges to strike possible jurors on the basis of race. Under *Batson*, the defendant must prove that the prosecution's use of a peremptory challenge was racially motivated. Doing so requires a number of legal steps.[33]

1. First, the defendant must make a *prima facie* case that there has been discrimination during *venire*. (*Prima facie* is Latin for "at first sight"; legally, it refers to a fact that is presumed to be true unless contradicted by evidence.)

2. To do so, the defendant must show that he or she is a member of a recognizable racial group and that the prosecutor has used peremptory challenges to remove members of this group from the jury pool.

3. Then, the defendant must show that these facts and other relevant circumstances raise the possibility that the prosecutor removed the perspective jurors solely because of their race.

4. If the court accepts the defendant's charges, the burden shifts to the prosecution to prove that its peremptory challenges were race neutral. If the court finds against the prosecution, it rules that a *Batson* violation has occurred. (For a closer look at the *Batson* decision, see *CJ in Focus: Landmark Cases*—Batson v. Kentucky on the next page.)

The Court has revisited the issue of race a number of times in the years since *Batson*. In *Powers v. Ohio* (1991),[34] it ruled that a defendant may contest race-based peremptory challenges even if the defendant is not of the same race as the excluded jurors. In *Georgia v. McCollum* (1992),[35] the Court placed defense attorneys under the same restrictions as prosecutors when making race-based peremptory challenges.

Women on the Jury. Given the *Batson* precedent, it seemed inevitable that the Supreme Court would eventually address another issue: whether women were constitutionally protected from peremptory challenges based on their gender.[36] The exclusion of women has been more codified than the exclusion of racial groups. At the end of World War II, twenty-one states still prohibited women jurors, and the last state to end this practice—Alabama—did not do so until 1966.

In *J.E.B. v. Alabama* (1994),[37] the Supreme Court extended *Batson* to cover gender bias in jury selection. The case was a civil suit for paternity and child support brought by the state of Alabama. Prosecutors used nine of their ten challenges to remove men from the jury, while the defense made similar efforts to remove women. When challenged, the state defended its actions on what it called the rational belief that men and women might have different views on the issues of paternity and child support. The Court held this to be unconstitutional under the equal protection clause.

Alternate Jurors

Because unforeseeable circumstances or illness may necessitate that one or more of the sitting jurors be dismissed, the court also seats several *alternate jurors* who will hear the entire trial. Depending on the rules of the particular

> "A jury consists of twelve persons chosen to decide who has the better lawyer."
>
> —Robert Frost,
> *American poet (1874–1963)*

CJ in Focus

Landmark Cases:

Batson v. Kentucky

James Kirkland Batson, an African American, had been charged with second degree burglary and receipt of stolen goods. In the jury selection process for Batson's trial, the prosecutor used his peremptory challenges to strike the only four African Americans in the *venire,* resulting in an all white jury. Batson was convicted. In appealing his conviction, Batson claimed that by removing the potential jurors on the basis of their race, the prosecution had denied him his right to a jury drawn from a cross section of the community. Previously, the Supreme Court had ruled that racially discriminatory peremptory challenges could not be proved in a single case, but had to be shown as a pattern over a period of time. With *Batson,* however, the Court would reject this ruling.

Batson v. Kentucky
United States Supreme Court
476 U.S. 79 (1986)
http://laws.findlaw.com/US/476/79.html

In the Words of the Court . . .

Mr. Justice POWELL, majority opinion

* * * *

More than a century ago, the Court decided that the State denies a black defendant equal protection of the laws when it puts him on trial before a jury from which members of his race have been purposefully excluded. [*Strauder v. West Virginia*, 100 U.S. 303 (1880).] That decision laid the foundation for the Court's unceasing efforts to eradicate racial discrimination in the procedures used to select the venire from which individual jurors are drawn.

* * * *

Purposeful racial discrimination in selection of the venire violates a defendant's right to equal protection because it denies him the protection that a trial by jury is intended to secure. "The very idea of a jury is a body . . . composed of the peers or equals of the person whose rights it is selected or summoned to determine; that is, of his neighbors, fellows, associates, persons having the same

legal status in society as that which he holds."

* * * *

The harm from discriminatory jury selection extends beyond that inflicted on the defendant and the excluded juror to touch the entire community. Selection procedures that purposefully exclude black persons from juries undermine public confidence in the fairness of our system of justice.

* * * *

The reality of [peremptory challenges], amply reflected in many state- and federal-court opinions, shows that the challenge may be, and unfortunately at times has been, used to discriminate against black jurors. By requiring trial courts to be sensitive to the racially discriminatory use of peremptory challenges, our decision enforces the mandate of equal protection and furthers the ends of justice. In view of the heterogeneous population of our Nation, public respect for our criminal justice system and the rule of law will be strengthened if we ensure that no citizen is disqualified from jury service because of his race.

Decision: The Court overturned Batson's conviction and remanded the case, holding that prosecutors could not constitutionally use peremptory challenges to strike potential jurors based solely on their race. It also rejected the notion that African American jurors, as a whole, are unable to impartially consider a case against an African American defendant. To protect against discrimination, the Court set standards by which a defendant could prove that the jury in his or her trial had been tainted by racially motivated peremptory challenges.

For Critical Analysis: In this ruling, the Court (a) states a belief that diverse juries are necessary to ensure fair trials and (b) rejects the notion that a juror's race will influence his or her judgment. Some observers, while noting the obvious drawbacks of discrimination in jury selection, have labeled this the "*Batson* Paradox." How could these two opinions contradict each other when applied to a potential *Batson* violation?

Note: Triple asterisks (* * *) indicate that a few words or sentences have been deleted, and quadruple asterisks (* * * *) indicate that an entire paragraph (or more) has been omitted from the opinion.

jurisdiction, two or three alternate jurors may be present throughout the trial. If a juror has to be excused in the middle of the trial, an alternate may take his or her place without disrupting the proceedings.

THE TRIAL

Once the jury members are seated, the judge swears in the jury and the trial itself can begin. A rather pessimistic truism among attorneys is that every case "has been won or lost when the jury is sworn." This reflects the belief that a juror's values are the major, if not dominant, factor in the decision of guilt or innocence.[38]

Specific cases have shown, however, that the attorney who takes such a mantra as truth is not giving proper credit to the trial process. For example, when an obscenity charge was brought against the rap group 2 Live Crew in Broward County, Florida, the defense claimed it could not get a fair hearing in that community. This feeling was only strengthened when the jury was chosen: of the six jurors, only one was African American and three were elderly white women. Luther Campbell, the leader of the group, insisted that the jury was too Caucasian and too middle class to understand the values behind his music.

In fact, the jury quickly acquitted Campbell and his bandmates of all charges.[39] In the process of the trial, the jurors were convinced that protecting the First Amendment right of free speech was in society's best interests, whatever their private misgivings about 2 Live Crew's means of expression. Ideally, then, the purpose of a trial is not to separate the jurors from their values, but to provide a forum in which they can apply those values to the law.

Opening Statements

Attorneys may choose to open the trial with a statement to the jury, though they are not required to do so. In these **opening statements,** the attorneys give a brief version of the facts and the supporting evidence that they will present during the trial. Because some trials can drag on for weeks or even months, it is extremely helpful for jurors to hear a summary of what will unfold. In short, the opening statement is a kind of "road map" that describes the destination that each attorney hopes to reach and outlines how she or he plans to reach it. The danger for attorneys is that they will offer evidence during the trial that might contradict an assertion made during the opening statement. This may cause jurors to disregard the evidence or shift their own narrative further away from the narrative being offered by the attorney.[40] In *United States v. Dinitz* (1976),[41] the Supreme Court ruled that attorneys are limited in the opening statements to subjects they believe will be presented in the trial itself.

The opening statement is also the first opportunity for the prosecution and defense to put their "spin" on the events being addressed in trial. As you can see in Figure 10.4, the attorneys will often employ dramatic language in an immediate attempt to win the jury over to their side.

The Role of Evidence

Once the opening statements have been made, the prosecutor begins the trial proceedings by presenting the state's evidence against the defendant. Courts

OPENING STATEMENTS
The attorneys' statements to the jury at the beginning of the trial. Each side briefly outlines the evidence that will be offered during the trial and the legal theory that will be pursued.

MR. FRAWLEY: I would like to start by showing you a photograph so that you can have a face to go with some of the names that you're going to be hearing throughout this trial.

This photograph is of Sherri Dally and her family. That's Michael Dally, the other adult in the picture, and Max and Devon. Max is the younger one. On the date that Sherri was killed, May 6, 1996, Max was six. And Devon, he had just turned eight a couple months before.

You will learn that children were Sherri's life.

Aside from her own, she ran a day care center out of her home.

And beyond that, the other focus of Sherri's life was Michael Dally. They had been married for 14 years.

Michael Dally was the only male that Sherri had ever dated.

And what the evidence is going to show is that the defendant, Diana Haun, wanted to take Sherri Dally's place.

Figure 10.4 The Opening Statement
On May 6, 1996, Sherri Dally of Ventura, California, was kidnapped from a parking lot and later killed. Prosecutors charged Diana Haun with the murder, alleging that she was in love with Dally's husband and wanted to "replace" her. In his opening statements, Deputy District Attorney Michael Frawley immediately attempts to humanize Dally for the jury, with the ultimate purpose of making her murder all the more worthy of harsh punishment.

EVIDENCE
Anything that is used to prove the existence or nonexistence of a fact.

TESTIMONY
Verbal evidence given by witnesses under oath.

REAL EVIDENCE
Evidence that is brought into court and seen by the jury, as opposed to evidence that is described for a jury.

LAY WITNESS
A witness who can truthfully and accurately testify on a fact in question without having specialized training or knowledge; an ordinary witness.

EXPERT WITNESS
A witness with professional training or substantial experience qualifying her or him to testify on a certain subject.

DIRECT EVIDENCE
Evidence that establishes the existence of a fact that is in question without relying on inference.

CIRCUMSTANTIAL EVIDENCE
Indirect evidence that is offered to establish, by inference, the likelihood of a fact that is in question.

have complex rules about what types of evidence may be presented and how the evidence may be brought out during the trial. **Evidence** is anything that is used to prove the existence or nonexistence of a fact. For the most part, evidence can be broken down into two categories: testimony and real evidence. **Testimony** consists of statements by competent witnesses. **Real evidence,** presented to the court in the form of exhibits, includes any physical items—such as the murder weapon or a bloodstained piece of clothing—that affect the case.

Rules of evidence are designed to ensure that testimony and exhibits presented to the jury are relevant, reliable, and not unfairly prejudicial against the defendant. One of the tasks of the defense attorney is to challenge evidence presented by the prosecution by establishing that the evidence is not reliable. Of course, the prosecutor also tries to demonstrate the irrelevance or unreliability of evidence presented by the defense. The final decision on whether evidence is allowed before the jury rests with the judge, in keeping with his or her role as the "referee" of the adversary system.

Testimonial Evidence. A person who is called to testify on factual matters that would be understood by the average citizen is referred to as a **lay witness.** If asked about the condition of a victim of an assault, for example, a lay witness could relate certain facts, such as "she was bleeding from her forehead" or "she lay unconscious on the ground for several minutes." A lay witness could not, however, give information about the medical extent of the victim's injuries, such as whether she suffered from a fractured skull or internal bleeding. Coming from a lay witness, such testimony would be inadmissible. When the matter in question requires scientific, medical, or technical skill beyond the scope of the average person, prosecutors and defense attorneys may call an **expert witness** to the stand. The expert witness is an individual who has professional training, advanced knowledge, or substantial experience in a specialized area, such as medicine, computer technology, or ballistics. The rules of evidence state that expert witnesses may base their opinions on three types of information:

1 Facts or data of which they have personal knowledge.

2 Material presented at trial.

3 Secondhand information given to the expert outside the courtroom.[42]

Expert witnesses are considered somewhat problematic for two reasons. First, they may be chosen for their "court presence"—whether they speak well or will appear sympathetic to the jury—rather than their expertise. Second, attorneys pay expert witnesses for their services. Given human nature, the attorneys expect a certain measure of cooperation from an expert they have hired, and an expert witness has an interest in satisfying the attorneys so that he or she will be hired again.[43] Under these circumstances, some have questioned whether the courts can rely on the professional nonpartisanship of expert witnesses.[44]

Direct versus Circumstantial Evidence. Two types of testimonial evidence may be brought into court: direct evidence and circumstantial evidence. **Direct evidence** is evidence that has been witnessed by the person giving testimony. "I saw Bill shoot Chris" is an example of direct evidence. **Circumstantial evidence** is indirect evidence that, even if believed, does not establish the fact in question but only the degree of likelihood of the fact. In other words, circumstantial evidence can create an inference that a fact exists.

Suppose, for example, that the defendant owns a gun that shoots bullets of the type found in the victim's body. This circumstantial evidence, by itself, does not establish that the defendant committed the crime. Combined with other circumstantial evidence, however, it may do just that. For instance, if other circumstantial evidence indicates that the defendant had a motive for harming the victim and was at the scene of the crime when the shooting occurred, the jury might conclude that the defendant committed the crime.

Relevance. Evidence will not be admitted in court unless it is relevant to the case being considered. **Relevant evidence** is evidence that tends to prove or disprove a fact in question. Forensic proof that the bullets found in a victim's body were fired from a gun discovered in the suspect's pocket at the time of arrest, for example, is certainly relevant. The suspect's prior record, showing a conviction for armed robbery ten years earlier, is, as we shall see in the next section, irrelevant to the case at hand and in most instances will be ruled inadmissible by the judge.

Prejudicial Evidence. Evidence may be excluded if it would tend to distract the jury from the main issues of the case, mislead the jury, or cause jurors to decide the issue on an emotional basis. In American trial courts, this rule precludes prosecutors from using prior purported criminal activities or actual convictions to show that the defendant has criminal propensities or an "evil character."[45]

This concept is codified in the Federal Rules of Evidence, which state that evidence of "other crimes, wrongs, or acts is not admissible to prove the character of a person in order to show action in conformity therewith." Such evidence is allowed only when it does not apply to character construction and focuses instead on "motive, opportunity, intent, preparation, plan, knowledge, identity, or absence of mistake or accident."[46]

Though this legal concept has come under a great deal of criticism, it is consistent with the presumption of innocence standards discussed earlier. Presumably, if a prosecutor is allowed to establish that the defendant has shown antisocial or even violent character traits, this will prejudice the jury against the defendant. (For a discussion of similar rules that protect the victim, see *CJ in Focus: The Balancing Act—Rape Shield Laws* on the next page.) While discussing a 1930 murder case, New York Supreme Court Chief Justice Benjamin Cardozo addressed the issue thusly:

> With only the rough and ready tests supplied by their experience of life, the jurors were to look into the workings of another's mind, and discover its capacities and disabilities, its urges and inhibitions, in moments of intense excitement. Delicate enough and subtle is the inquiry, even in the most favorable conditions, with every warping influence excluded. There must be no blurring of the issues by evidence illegally admitted and carrying with it in its admission an appeal to prejudice and passion.[47]

Authentication of Evidence. At trial, an attorney must lay the proper foundation for the introduction of certain evidence, such as documents, exhibits, and other objects, and must demonstrate to the court that the evidence is what the attorney claims. The process by which this is accomplished is referred to as **authentication.** The authentication requirement relates to relevance because something offered in evidence is relevant to the case only if it is authentic, or genuine.

Commonly, evidence is authenticated by the testimony of witnesses. For example, if an attorney wants to introduce an autopsy report as evidence in a case, he or she can have the report authenticated by the testimony of the medical examiner who signed it. By the same token, before drugs taken from a crime scene can be admitted as evidence, the law enforcement agent who collected them will be required to testify that they are in fact the same drugs.

It is extremely rare for a defendant to be convicted of first degree, or premeditated, murder in a case in which the body of a victim or a murder weapon cannot be found. About sixty people have been convicted for murder without the body of the victim, including Thomas Capano, above, who was found guilty in 1999 of killing his lover. The circumstantial evidence in the case, including an admission by Capano's brother that the two had dumped a body seventy miles off the New Jersey coast on the night of the murder, was sufficient for the jury to deliver a guilty verdict and recommend the death penalty. Why do you think the body of the victim has proven to be so important in establishing that a defendant is guilty beyond a reasonable doubt?

RELEVANT EVIDENCE
Evidence tending to make a fact in question more or less probable than it would be without the evidence. Only relevant evidence is admissible in court.

AUTHENTICATION
Establishing the genuineness of an item that is to be introduced as evidence in a trial.

CJ in Focus
The Balancing Act
Rape Shield Laws

During the rape trial of University of Akron freshman Nathaniel Lewis, the defense offered as evidence a passage from the accuser's diary. "I think I pounced on Nate because he was the last straw," the diary read. "I'm sick of men taking advantage of me and I'm sick of myself for giving in to them. I'm not a nympho like all of those guys think. I'm just not strong enough to say no to them."

The defense wanted to present the diary passage as evidence that the accuser had engaged in sex willingly with the defendant and may have fabricated the rape charge because she was ashamed of her behavior. The Summit County (Ohio) Court, however, ruled that the diary was inadmissible as evidence because it introduced prejudicial information about the accuser's past sexual history.

PROTECTING THE VICTIM

Ohio, like many other states, has enacted so-called rape shield laws in the past decade to right what had been seen as a social wrong—a woman who brought a rape charge was likely to have her sexual history dragged into the courtroom. The defense used such evidence to place doubt in the jurors' minds, insinuating that the alleged victim could have "asked for it" because she might have been promiscuous in the past. Rape shield laws specifically protect rape victims from having their prior sexual history used against them in court. These laws make the presumption that past history generally has no relevance to whether the woman consented to have sex with the accused rapist in the situation under question.

PROTECTING THE ACCUSED

The law protects those charged with sexual assault in a similar manner. The Federal Rules of Evidence permit testimony of prior sexual assault "on any matter for which it is relevant," but impose the condition that the value of the evidence not be "substantially outweighed by the danger of unfair prejudice." Similar language is written into many state laws.

For Critical Analysis: Do rape shield laws infringe upon the rights of the accused? When would past sexual history be "relevant" in a courtroom?

The rules of evidence require authentication because certain types of evidence, such as exhibits and objects, cannot be cross-examined by opposing counsel, as witnesses can, yet such evidence may have a significant effect on the jury. (The cross-examination process will be examined later in the chapter.) The authentication requirement provides a safeguard against the introduction of nonverified evidence that may strongly influence the outcome of the case.

The Prosecution's Case

Because the burden of proof is on the state, the prosecution is generally considered to have a more difficult task than the defense. The prosecutor attempts to establish guilt beyond a reasonable doubt by presenting the *corpus delicti* ("body of the offense" in Latin) of the crime to the jury. The *corpus delicti* is simply a legal term that refers to the substantial facts that show a crime has been committed. By establishing such facts through the presentation of evidence, the prosecutor hopes to convince the jury of the defendant's guilt.

As was mentioned earlier, this evidence must be relevant and nonprejudicial. For example, a prosecutor might not be allowed to show the jury graphic photographs of a victim in a murder trial. Such photographs could elicit emotional responses from jurors and prejudice them against a defendant who is to be presumed innocent.[48] This is not to say, however, that evidence is never used for emotional effect. A prosecutor may, for example, place the murder weapon on a table in plain view of the jury, forcing the jurors to consider that a violent crime has in fact taken place and focus on their duty to ensure that the guilty party is punished.

Direct Examination of Witnesses. Witnesses are crucial to establishing the prosecutor's case against the defendant. The prosecutor will call witnesses to the stand and ask them questions pertaining to the sequence of events that the trial is addressing. This form of questioning is known as **direct examina-**

tion. During direct examination, the prosecutor will usually not be allowed to ask *leading questions*—questions that might suggest to the witness a particular desired response. A leading question might be something like "So, Mrs. Williams, you noticed the defendant threatening the victim with a broken beer bottle?" If Mrs. Williams answers "yes" to this question, she has in effect, been "led" to the conclusion that the defendant was, in fact, threatening with a broken beer bottle. (A properly worded query would be, "Mrs. Williams, please describe the defendant's manner toward the victim during the incident.") The fundamental purpose behind testimony is to establish what actually happened, not what the trial attorneys would like the jury to believe happened.

Hearsay. When interviewing a witness, both the prosecutor and the defense attorney will make sure that the witness's statements are based on the witness's own knowledge and not hearsay. **Hearsay** can be defined as any testimony given in court about a statement made by someone else.[49] Literally, it is what someone heard someone else say. For the most part, hearsay is not admissible as evidence.[50] It is excluded because the listener may have misunderstood what the other person said, and without the opportunity of cross-examining the originator of the statement, the misconception cannot be challenged.

Exceptions to the hearsay rule are made in certain circumstances. Generally, these exceptions allow for hearsay to be considered as evidence when it consists of statements that are highly reliable or believable.[51] Recordings of 911 tapes, for example, have traditionally not been allowed as evidence in New York state courts. Such tapes were considered hearsay because they consisted of statements made outside the trial proceedings. But the New York Court of Appeals recently ruled that 911 recordings are sufficiently reliable to warrant inclusion in the trial process, and they have been recognized as an exception to the hearsay rule.[52] Furthermore, courts will sometimes allow secondhand statements attributed to the defendant because he or she is in the courtroom and able to refute or verify the statements.

Competence and Reliability of Witnesses. The rules of evidence include certain restrictions and qualifications pertaining to witnesses. Witnesses must have sufficient mental competence to understand the significance of testifying under oath. They must also be reliable in the sense that they are able to give a clear and unadulterated description of the events in question. For example, attorneys for Mir Aimal Kasi, who was convicted of murdering two CIA agents, challenged his conviction on the basis that prosecution witness Judy Becker-Darling was under medical treatment for traumatic stress disorder during her testimony. Becker-Darling's medical condition, the defense argued, made her an unreliable witness.[53] (The judge denied the motion.)

Cross-Examination

After the prosecutor has directly examined her or his witnesses, the defense attorney is given the chance to question the same witnesses. The Sixth Amendment states that "In all criminal prosecutions, the accused shall enjoy the right . . . to be confronted with witnesses against him." In practical terms, this gives the accused, through his or her attorneys, the right to cross-examine witnesses. **Cross-examination** refers to the questioning of an opposing witness during trial, and both sides of a case are allowed to do so (see Figure 10.5 on the next page).

Cross-examination allows the attorneys to test the truthfulness of opposing witnesses and usually entails efforts to create doubt in the jurors' minds that the witness is reliable.[54] (In theory, the veracity of witnesses—and the defendant—could be tested by polygraphs. For a discussion of this controver-

The job of the prosecution is to remove any traces of doubt concerning the defendant's innocence. This task can prove more difficult when the defendant is a respected member of the community, as was the case in the trial of the Rev. Henry H. Lyons, the president of the National Baptist Convention, U.S.A. During the 1999 trial of Lyons, prosecutors described how he pocketed more than $200,000 of church contributions and took millions more from companies wishing to be on the religious group's mailing list. They also showed how he used the money to finance a "lavish" lifestyle that included two vacation homes and a Rolls Royce. Lyons was eventually found guilty of grand theft and racketeering. What was the *corpus delicti* in this case?

DIRECT EXAMINATION
The examination of a witness by the attorney who calls the witness to the stand to testify.

HEARSAY
An oral or written statement made by an out-of-court declarant that is later offered in court by a witness (not the declarant) concerning a matter before the court. Hearsay is not usually admissible as evidence.

CROSS-EXAMINATION
The questioning of an opposing witness during the trial.

Figure 10.5 The Cross-Examination

In the so-called Boston Nanny case, 19-year-old British *au pair* Louise Woodward was charged with second degree murder of an infant left in her care. Prosecutors tried to convince the jury that Woodward was a temperamental teenager who became frustrated with caring for a sick child and "snapped." The defense claimed that the brain hemorrhage that killed the child was actually the delayed result of another accident that had occurred several weeks earlier.

Detective Sergeant William Byrne, who interviewed Woodward following the boy's death, testified that she claimed to have dropped the infant on a towel on the bathroom floor, and that the infant "may have banged his head on the floor where it meets the tub." On cross-examination, defense counsel tried to clarify exactly what Woodward, who denied making such statements, had told the police officer.

Defense: You asked her, "What do you mean by 'drop him on the floor,'" and her answer was, "I was angry."

Detective Sergeant Byrne: Yes, sir.

Defense: So she wasn't telling you, according to your testimony, that "I dropped him by accident."

Detective Sergeant Byrne: No, sir.

Defense: She wasn't saying, "I tripped and he fell."

Detective Sergeant Byrne: No, sir.

Defense: She wasn't saying, "He slipped out of my hands."

Detective Sergeant Byrne: No, sir.

Defense: You're saying that she told you that she did this on purpose.

Detective Sergeant Byrne: She was angry, sir.

Defense: Okay. That's what she meant by "angry," according to you, right, that she did this on purpose.

Detective Sergeant Byrne: She didn't say that she did it on purpose.

Defense: But you understood that to mean that she did it on purpose.

Detective Sergeant Byrne: That was my feeling.

In this case, the cross-examination may have hurt the defendant, as Detective Sergeant Byrne was able to reassert his belief that Woodward was responsible for the death. In fact, the Boston jury did convict Woodward, though the trial judge later overturned the conviction.

sial subject, see *Criminal Justice & Technology—The Polygraph Problem: How to Tell a Lie.*) Cross-examination is also linked to the problems presented by hearsay evidence. When a witness offers hearsay, the person making the original remarks is not in the court, and therefore cannot be cross-examined. If such testimony were allowed, the defendant's Sixth Amendment right to confront witnesses against him or her would be violated.

After the defense has cross-examined a prosecution witness, the prosecutor may want to reestablish any reliability that might have been lost. The prosecutor can do so by again questioning the witness, a process known as *redirect examination.* Following the redirect examination, the defense attorney will be given the opportunity for *recross-examination,* or to ask further questions of prosecution witnesses. Thus, each side has two opportunities to question a witness. The attorneys need not do so, but only after each side has been offered the opportunity will the trial move on to the next witness or the next stage.

Motion for a Directed Verdict

After the prosecutor has finished presenting evidence against the defendant, the government will inform the court that it has rested the people's case. At this point, the defense may make a **motion for a directed verdict** (now also known as a *motion for judgment as a matter of law* in federal courts). Through this motion, the defense is basically saying that the prosecution has not offered enough evidence to prove that the accused is guilty beyond a reasonable doubt. If the judge grants this motion, which rarely occurs, then a judgment will be entered in favor of the defendant, and the trial is over.

The Defendant's Case

Assuming that the motion for a directed verdict is denied, the defense attorney may offer the defendant's case. Because the burden is on the state to prove the accused's guilt, the defense is not required to offer any case at all. It can simply "rest" without calling any witnesses or producing any real evidence and ask the jury to judge the merits of the case on what it has seen and heard from the prosecution.

MOTION FOR A DIRECTED VERDICT A motion requesting that the court grant judgment in favor of the defense on the ground that the prosecution has not produced sufficient evidence to support the state's claim.

Placing the Defendant on the Stand. If the defense does present a case, its first—and often most important—decision is whether the defendant will take the stand in her or his own defense. Because of the Fifth Amendment protection against self-incrimination, the defendant is not required to testify. Therefore, the defense attorney must make a judgment call. He or she may want to place the defendant on the stand if the defendant is likely to appear sympathetic to the jury or is well spoken and able to aid the defense's case. With a less sympathetic or less effective defendant, the defense attorney may decide that exposing the defendant before the jury presents too large a risk. Also, if the defendant testifies, she or he is open to cross-examination under oath from the prosecutor. In any case, remember that the prosecution cannot comment on a defendant's refusal to testify.[55]

It is not uncommon for a defendant to take the stand against the advice of his or her attorney. Sometimes, defendants feel frustrated by the enforced silence of the courtroom and relish the chance to give their "side of the story." In other instances, they may simply want to vent anger—one murder suspect took advantage of his time before the court to call the jurors "scumbags."[56] Given that all Americans have a constitutional right to testify in their own defense, lawyers can do little when a client insists on taking the stand. When this does occur, the defense attorney is best served by notifying the court that the defendant is testifying against the advice of counsel—a step that protects the attorney from facing charges of ineffective representation later in the appeals process.

Criminal Justice & Technology

The Polygraph Problem: How to Tell a Lie

The history of polygraph, or lie detector, tests in the courtroom is a long one. More than four thousand years ago, the Chinese are believed to have used physicians at trial to determine whether a defendant was telling the truth based on his or her heartbeat. Today, however, polygraph technology is rare in American courtrooms. A Supreme Court ruling more than seventy years ago barred new types of scientific evidence from federal courts until they were judged reliable by a consensus of the scientific community. For the polygraph, this consensus has proved hard to come by. Though the tests are thought to be accurate 90 percent of the time, at least one observer feels that "you might as well have a witch look at chicken bones at the bottom of a pot."

MEASURING A LIE

The operating principle of the polygraph machine is that certain bodily activities change when a person tells a lie—the person sweats more and her or his heartbeat increases. During the test, rubber tubes are strapped over the subject's chest and abdomen to monitor respiratory rates, and two small metal plates are attached to the fingers to record sweat gland changes. Blood pressure is measured by a cuff on the arm. Criticism of the polygraph centers on the fact, admitted even by its supporters, that it is not completely reliable.

IN THE FUTURE: Until recently, polygraph evidence was admissible only when both the prosecution and the defense agreed—a rare occurrence indeed. A 1993 Supreme Court decision eased restrictions by giving judges more discretion in admitting scientific evidence, a ruling that has allowed several state courts to lift the ban on lie detector evidence. It seems likely that science and technology, not the law, will decide the ultimate fate of the polygraph. Researchers have hypothesized that a neurotransmitter is secreted in the brain when a person consciously tells a lie. The ability to detect and measure such a secretion would alter the courtroom profoundly.

Creating a Reasonable Doubt. Defense lawyers most commonly defend their clients by attempting to expose weaknesses in the prosecutor's case. Remember that if the defense attorney can create reasonable doubt concerning the client's guilt in the mind of just a single juror, the defendant has a good chance of gaining an acquittal or at least a hung jury. Even in cases in which the defendant's guilt seems obvious, the defense may be able to create doubt through cross-examination, calling its own witnesses, and attacking the prosecution's evidence. Defense lawyers for Theodore J. Kaczynski, the Unabomber, were faced with a daunting task: a great deal of evidence in their client's Montana cabin pointed to his sending mail bombs to sixteen targets. Nevertheless, they were still confident that they could induce reasonable doubt. There were no eyewitnesses to any of the attacks and no known accomplices—all of the evidence against the defendant was circumstantial. The prosecution could prove without a doubt that Kaczynski made bombs, but that did not necessarily make him the Unabomber.

REBUTTAL
Evidence given to counteract or disprove evidence presented by the opposing party.

Even if the prosecution can present seemingly strong evidence, a defense attorney may succeed by creating reasonable doubt. In a 1998 case, Jason Korey bragged to his friends that he had shot and killed Joseph Brucker in Pittsburgh, Pennsylvania, and a great deal of circumstantial evidence linked Korey to the killing. Again, however, police could find no direct evidence: they could not link Korey to the murder weapon, nor could they match his footprints to those found at the crime scene. Michael Foglia, Korey's defense attorney, explained his client's bragging as a ploy to gain attention from his friends. Though this explanation may strike some as unlikely, in the absence of physical evidence it did create doubt in the jurors' minds, and Korey was acquitted.[57]

This strategy is also very effective in cases that essentially rely on the word of the defendant against the word of the victim. In sexual assault cases, for example, if the defense attorneys can create doubt about the victim's credibility—in other words, raise the possibility that he or she is lying—then they may prevail at trial. Not all observers, however, feel that this strategy is always in the client's best interests. Prosecutor Herbert J. Stern says, "nothing pleases me more" than to hear his opponent focus squarely on weaknesses in the state's case. "It tells the jury nothing but that your defendant is likely guilty," notes Stern, "although the prosecution may have its difficulties proving it."[58]

Other Defense Strategies. The defense can choose among a number of strategies to generate reasonable doubt in the jurors' minds. It can present an *alibi defense,* by submitting evidence that the accused was not at or near the scene of the crime at the time the crime was committed. Another option is to attempt an *affirmative defense,* by presenting additional facts to the ones offered by the prosecution. Possible affirmative defenses, which we discussed in detail in Chapter 2, include the following:

1. Self-defense
2. Insanity
3. Duress
4. Entrapment[59]

> "I'm trusting in the Lord and a good lawyer."
>
> —Oliver North, *U.S. marine officer, after being indicted for obstruction of justice* (1986)

With an affirmative defense strategy, the defense attempts to prove that the defendant should be found not guilty because of extenuating circumstances surrounding the crime. An affirmative strategy can be difficult to carry out because it forces the defense to prove the veracity of its own evidence, not simply disprove the evidence offered by the prosecution.

The defense is often willing to admit that a certain criminal act took place, especially if the defendant has already confessed. In this case, the primary question of the trial becomes not whether the defendant is guilty, but what the defendant is guilty of. In these situations, the defense strategy focuses on obtaining the lightest possible penalty for the defendant. As we saw in the last chapter, this strategy is responsible for the high percentage of proceedings that end in plea bargains.

Rebuttal and Surrebuttal

After the defense closes its case, the prosecution is permitted to bring new evidence forward that was not used during its initial presentation to the jury. This is called the **rebuttal** stage of the trial. When the rebuttal stage is finished, the defense is given the opportunity to cross-examine the prosecution's new witnesses and introduce new witnesses of its own. This final act is part of the *surrebuttal*. After these stages have been completed, the defense may offer another motion for a directed verdict, asking the judge summarily to find in the defendant's favor. If this motion is rejected, and it almost always is, the case is closed, and the opposing sides offer their closing arguments.

Closing Arguments

In their **closing arguments,** the attorneys summarize their presentations and argue one final time for their respective cases. In most states, the defense attorney goes first, and then the prosecutor. (In Kentucky, Colorado, and Missouri the order is reversed.) An effective closing argument includes all of the major points that support the government's or the defense's case. It also emphasizes the shortcomings of the opposing party's case. Jurors will view a closing argument with some skepticism if it merely recites the central points of a party's claim or defense without also responding to the unfavorable facts or issues raised by the other side. Of course, neither attorney wants to focus too much on the other side's position, but the elements of the opposing position do need to be acknowledged and their flaws highlighted.

One danger in the closing arguments is that an attorney will become too emotional and make remarks that are later deemed by appellate courts to be prejudicial. Once both attorneys have completed their remarks, the case is submitted to the jury, and the attorneys' role in the trial is, for the moment, complete.

THE FINAL STEPS OF THE TRIAL AND POSTCONVICTION PROCEDURES

After closing arguments, the outcome of the trial is in the hands of the jury. Due to a few highly publicized jury decisions, the effectiveness of jury verdicts has come under increasing scrutiny. Many Americans who saw videotape of Rodney King's 1991 beating by Los Angeles policemen were stunned when a Simi Valley (California) jury acquitted the officers. Similarly, there was consternation when two men who participated in the ensuing riots were convicted of only mayhem and misdemeanor assault after attacking truck driver Reginald Denny. A videotape of the attack, which showed the defendants beating Denny in the head with bricks after dragging him out of his truck, caused many to ask: If such actions are not attempted murder, what is?[60] And, four years later, the O. J. Simpson verdict incited intense debate on a nationwide scale.

Whether or not these verdicts were in keeping with the law, they instigated calls for jury reform. Among the proposed reforms were to allow jurors to take notes and to ask questions during the trial proceedings.[61] Both suggestions emanated from a growing belief that long, complex trials were taxing the patience and abilities of jurors.

Others argue that uncertainty cannot be reformed out of the jury system. Political scientist Jeffrey Abramson commented:

> The direct and raw character of jury democracy makes it our most honest mirror, reflecting both the good and the bad that ordinary people are capable of when called upon to do justice.[62]

In this section, we examine the efforts to give jurors the means necessary to make informed decisions about the guilt or innocence of the accused. We will also look at the post-trial motions that can occur when the defense feels that the jurors, prosecution, or trial judge made errors that necessitate remedial legal action.

Jury Instructions

Before the jurors begin their deliberations, the judge gives the jury a **charge,** summing up the case and instructing the jurors on the rules of law that apply to the issues in the case. These charges, also called jury instructions, are usu-

CLOSING ARGUMENTS
Arguments made by each side's attorney after the cases for the plaintiff and defendant have been presented.

CHARGE
The judge's instructions to the jury following the attorneys' closing arguments; the charge sets forth the rules of law that the jury must apply in reaching its decision, or verdict.

Terry Nichols was convicted on December 23, 1997, of conspiracy and eight counts of involuntary manslaughter in the 1995 bombing of the Oklahoma City Federal Building. When the twelve jurors began deliberating Nichols's fate, however, their first vote was 10–2 for acquittal. "I couldn't believe it," recalled juror Tim Burge, who initially voted to convict. "I was like, man, did I miss something here or what." It took six days of heated arguments, which left some of the jurors in tears, before a compromise verdict was worked out in which the defendant was acquitted of more serious murder- and weapons-related counts. How does this case show the strengths and/or weaknesses of the jury system?

ally prepared during a special *charging conference* involving the judge and the trial attorneys. In this conference, the attorneys suggest the instructions they would like to see be sent to the jurors, but the judge makes the final decision as to the charges submitted.[63] If the defense attorney disagrees with the charges sent to the jury, he or she can enter an objection, thereby setting the stage for a possible appeal.

The judge usually begins by explaining basic legal principles such as the need to find the defendant guilty beyond a reasonable doubt. Then, the jury instructions narrow to the specifics of the case at hand, and the judge explains to the jurors what facts the prosecution must have proved in order to convict. (See Figure 10.6.) If the defense strategy centers on an affirmative defense such as insanity or entrapment, the judge will discuss the relevant legal principles that the defense must have proved to obtain an acquittal. The final segment of the charges discusses possible verdicts. These always include "guilty" and "not guilty," but some cases also allow for the jury to find "guilt by reason of insanity" or "guilty but mentally ill." Juries are often charged with determining the seriousness of the crime as well, such as deciding whether a homicide is murder in the first degree, murder in the second degree, or manslaughter.

A serious problem with jury instructions is that jurors often do not seem to understand them.[64] This is hardly surprising, as most average Americans do not have the education or legal background to understand the somewhat unfathomable jargon of the law. One study came to the unfortunate conclusion that juries that received no instructions whatsoever were basically as well equipped—or poorly equipped, as the case may be—as juries that did receive instructions.[65]

One solution is to simplify the language of the jury instructions. This idea, however, has met resistance among legal professionals, who are accustomed to "legal speak" and do not wish to change. Another suggestion is for the judge to give the jury its instructions before *and* after the trial. In this way, some of the legal concepts would be introduced before the evidence and narratives are established, giving jurors a chance to comprehend the issues involved before they are overwhelmed by the evidence in a complicated case.

Jury Deliberation

After receiving the charge, the jury begins its deliberations. Jury deliberation is a somewhat mysterious process, as it takes place in complete seclusion. In

---

Figure **10.6** Jury Instructions

These are model jury instructions for cases where the charge is involuntary manslaughter.

The defendant is charged in [Count _____ of] the indictment with involuntary manslaughter in violation of Section 1112 of Title 18 of the United States Code. [Involuntary manslaughter is the unlawful killing of a human being without malice aforethought and without an intent to kill.] In order for the defendant to be found guilty of that charge, the government must prove each of the following elements beyond a reasonable doubt.

- First, the defendant committed an unlawful act not amounting to a felony, or a lawful act, done either in an unlawful manner or with wanton or reckless disregard for human life, which might produce death;

- Second, the defendant's act was the proximate cause of the death of the victim. A proximate cause is one which played a substantial part in bringing about the death so that the death was the direct result or a reasonably probable consequence of the defendant's act;

- Third, the killing was unlawful; and

- Fourth, the defendant either knew that such conduct was a threat to the lives of others or knew of circumstances that would reasonably cause the defendant to foresee that such conduct might be a threat to the lives of others.

SOURCE: OFFICE OF THE CIRCUIT EXECUTIVE, NINTH CIRCUIT.

extreme cases, the judge will order that the jury be *sequestered*, or isolated from the public, during the trial and deliberation stages of the proceedings. Sequestion is used when deliberations are expected to be lengthy, or the trial is attracting a high amount of interest and the judge wants to keep the jury

Careers in Criminal Justice

COLLINS E. IJOMA, TRIAL COURT ADMINISTRATOR

I moved to the United States from Nigeria in 1976 to complete my college education majoring in Accounting and Business Administration. I earned a Master's Degree in Public Administration from Seton Hall University in 1982 with a concentration in Public Budgeting and Finance. I was immensely interested in public service but was not particularly aware of the judiciary as a potential employer. My first job in the court system was by accident rather than design. After completing a graduate internship with the Essex County government, I had the opportunity to seek permanent employment with the county-funded judiciary. I was first employed in the Trial Court Administrator's Office in Newark, New Jersey, as the Court Finance Officer in 1983. Much of my education in court administration was gained through the Institute for Court Management of the National Center for State Courts. I pursued this program of professional development from 1984 through 1991 when I graduated as a Fellow of ICM.

My initial position offered many opportunities to learn about court management and the workings of a large urban court system. My primary concentration was in human resources, budget, and finance. As a state court, funded by the county, we had to continually justify and fight for positions, space, and equipment. Our court was growing rapidly, and we needed additional resources to allow for an effective and efficient operation. In 1985, I was promoted to Director of Personnel. I had direct responsibility for all personnel programs, policies, and practices. My association with professional organizations including the National Association for Court Administration, the American Judicature Society, the Mid-Atlantic Association for Court Administration, and the American Society for Public Administration was critical to my professional development. The knowledge gained combined with experience helped me to successfully seek the position of Assistant Trial Court Administrator and my present position as Trial Court Administrator.

As the Trial Court Administrator, I serve principally as the Chief Administrative Officer to the largest trial and municipal court system in New Jersey. We provide technical and managerial support to the court (over 60 Superior Court Judges and 36 Municipal Court Judges) on such matters as personnel, program development, caseflow, resources, and facilities management. This description may sound highfalutin considering that most people can only describe a court in terms of a judge, one or two courtroom staff, and a few other employees associated with the visible activities in the courthouse. Obviously, there is a lot more going on behind the scenes that the average citizen is not aware of. For example, besides directing caseflow for the four major divisions (criminal, civil, family, and probation) the work involved in managing personnel programs for more than 1,200 employees, information systems and technology infrastructure, maintaining records of proceedings, coordination of transcription, grand and petit jury operations, and court interpreting to mention but a few examples is enormous. The modern court needs dedicated professionals in each of these areas.

One thing that keeps me going and enthused about this profession is the resolve and dedication of our judges and staff. We know that this is an important job no matter which division we serve. Criminal division seeks justice with those accused of committing crimes. In civil court people seek relief for injuries and when they have been wronged by others. The family division embraces a host of issues, and in some cases those who seek help are hurting and desperate. The court may be their only hope. We are also actively engaged in pursuing new ways to offer and manage dispute resolution. Some of these include drug courts to give nonviolent drug offenders a chance at rehabilitation rather than going to jail, complimentary dispute resolution to reach more satisfactory conclusions in less time and at a lower cost to litigants, and creative uses of volunteers to assist in the work of the court and create a positive connection to the community. So the challenge and excitement escalate as we look forward to the new millennium and further advances in court administration.

from being unduly influenced. Juries are usually sequestered in hotels and kept under the watch and guard of officers of the court. (For information on a courtroom participant who oversees sequestering and many other aspects of the trial, see *Careers in Criminal Justice*.)

Most of what is known about how a jury deliberates comes from mock trials or interviews with jurors after the verdict has been reached. A general picture of the deliberation process can be constructed from this research. It shows that the romantic notion of jurors with high-minded ideals of justice making eloquent speeches is, for the most part, not the reality. In approximately three out of every ten cases, the initial vote by the jury led to a unanimous decision. In 90 percent of the remaining cases, the majority eventually dictated the decision.[66] Furthermore, the idea of a lone juror holding out against his or her eleven peers—as shown in the classic film *Twelve*

VERDICT
A formal decision made by the jury.

HUNG JURY
A jury whose members are so irreconcilably divided in their opinions that they cannot reach a verdict. In this situation, the judge may order a new trial.

ALLEN CHARGE
An instruction by a judge to a deadlocked jury with only a few dissenters that asks the jurors in the minority to reconsider the majority opinion.

JURY NULLIFICATION
An acquittal of a defendant by a jury even though the evidence presented and the judge's instructions indicate that the defendant is guilty.

Angry Men—is somewhat of an anomaly. The peer pressure inherent in small-group situations is usually too great for dissenters to resist.[67]

The Verdict

Once it has reached a decision, the jury issues a **verdict.** The most common verdicts are guilty and not guilty, though as we have seen, juries may signify different degrees of guilt if instructed to do so. Following the announcement of a guilty or not guilty verdict, the jurors are discharged, and the jury trial proceedings are finished. (See Figure 10.7 for a review of the steps of a jury trial.)

The Hung Jury. When a jury in a criminal trial is unable to agree on a unanimous verdict—or a majority in certain states—it returns with no decision. This is known as a **hung jury.** After the trauma of a trial, a hung jury is often unsatisfactory to the participants of the trial. When a high-profile case ends with a hung jury, as occurred in the trial of Oklahoma City bombing co-conspirator Terry Nichols, there is a predictably high level of disapproval in the press concerning the jury's inability to come to a decision.

A judge can do little to reverse a hung jury, considering that "no decision" is just as legitimate a verdict as guilty or not guilty. In some states, if there are only a few dissenters to the majority view, a judge can send the jury back to the jury room under a set of rules set forth more than a century ago by the Supreme Court in *Allen v. United States* (1896).[68] The **Allen Charge,** as this instruction is called, asks the jurors in the minority to reconsider the majority opinion. Many jurisdictions do not allow *Allen* Charges on the ground that they improperly coerce jurors with the minority opinion to change their minds.[69]

For all of the attention they receive, hung juries are relatively rare. Juries are unable to come to a decision in only about 13 percent of all cases.[70] Furthermore, juries may be more lenient (or easy to "trick") than is generally perceived; one study found that juries were six times more likely than judges (in bench trials) to acquit a person who turns out to be guilty.[71]

Jury Nullification. The last statistic points to a growing concern of a number of criminal justice observers: the question of whether the jury's verdict is always based on the proper legal principles. This question deals with the controversial subject of **jury nullification,** which occurs when jurors "nullify" the law by acquitting a defendant who may be guilty according to the instruction given to them by the court. In other words, the jury acquits *in spite* of the evidence, rather than *because* of the evidence.[72] The specter of jury nullification is most often raised in cases that involve issues on which jurors may have

INFOTRAC ®
COLLEGE EDITION

Haynie, Erick. Populism, free speech and the rule of law: the fully informed jury movement and its implications.

Figure 10.7 The Steps of a Jury Trial

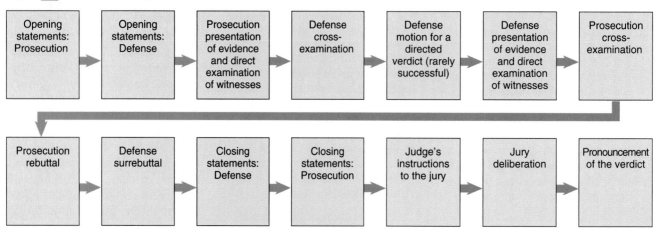

Opening statements: Prosecution → Opening statements: Defense → Prosecution presentation of evidence and direct examination of witnesses → Defense cross-examination → Defense motion for a directed verdict (rarely successful) → Defense presentation of evidence and direct examination of witnesses → Prosecution cross-examination → Prosecution rebuttal → Defense surrebuttal → Closing statements: Defense → Closing statements: Prosecution → Judge's instructions to the jury → Jury deliberation → Pronouncement of the verdict

CJ in Focus
A Question of Ethics
The Nullifying Juror

Imagine that you are a juror in the following case. The victim, Mr. Hampton, was an elderly gentleman in advance stages of terminal lung cancer. The defendant, Mrs. Hampton, disconnected her husband's life support system to put him out of his misery. During the trial, you hear that Mr. Hampton's every breath was made in agony and that a nurse overheard him ask his wife to end his life. You also hear Mrs. Hampton freely admit that she "killed" her husband. The facts are clear: Mrs. Hampton broke the law.

Even if you believe that Mrs. Hampton was justified in her actions, regardless of any law against them, would you be willing to vote for her acquittal? In a somewhat similar situation, Laura J. Kriho did. A juror on a felony drug possession trial in Gilpin County, Kriho caused a mistrial when she refused to convict the defendant, saying that "I'm against the drug laws and won't vote for guilty" and "drug cases should be handled by families and the community."

Paul Butler, an associate professor at George Washington Law School, takes the idea of jury nullification a step further, suggesting that it should be common practice for all African American jurors in cases involving African American defendants. Butler's "framework for criminal justice in the black community" includes the following points:

- In cases involving violent crimes, jurors should consider the evidence and acquit only if they have reasonable doubt that the defendant is guilty.

- In cases involving nonviolent crimes (such as theft), jury nullification is an option to be used at the juror's discretion. If, for example, a poor African American is on trial for stealing from a wealthy person, the juror should acquit, but if the victim is also poor, the juror should convict.

- In cases involving victimless crimes such as prostitution or drug violations, the juror should nullify as a matter of course. An African American charged with cocaine possession, for example, should be automatically acquitted.

Butler believes that he is calling on African American jurors to, in his words, "serve a higher calling than the law: justice." His critics point out that different people have different concepts of what "justice" is, and that such broad-based jury nullification has its own dangers. These dangers were shown in a very clear and dramatic way in the South, where, until the 1960s, white juries virtually never found another white person guilty of a crime committed against an African American.

For Critical Analysis: Do you agree with the stand taken by Kriho and Butler? Should laws be held accountable to the people that they serve? How might widespread jury nullification affect the criminal justice system?

---

strong ideological opinions, such as race, the death penalty, assisted suicide, or drug offenses. The not guilty verdict in O. J. Simpson's criminal trial was widely seen as an example of jury nullification, with jurors swayed by the racially based arguments of the defense rather than the facts of the case.

Many observers believe jury nullification is counter to the principles of American law because it allows a jury to "play by its own rules." Others, however, feel that jurors are within their rights when they question not only the facts in the case before them, but also the merits of the laws that the court is asking them to enforce. This argument has been made since the earliest days of the American legal system, when John Adams (1735–1826) said that a juror has not only a right, but a duty, "to find the verdict according to his own best understanding, judgment, and conscience, though in direct opposition to the direction of the court."[73] By this reasoning, jurors who feel that a particular law is unjust, or that the penalty for a law is too severe, are justified in nullifying a guilty verdict. (See *CJ in Focus: A Question of Ethics—The Nullifying Juror* for other arguments in favor of jury nullification.)

Once a trial has begun, it is quite difficult for a court to remove a juror because of fears of jury nullification. In *United States v. Thomas* (1997),[74] the Second Circuit Court of Appeals found that nullification violated a juror's oath and is counter to the rule of law; at the same time, the court set a very high standard of proof before a judge can remove a juror. The case involved the removal of an African American juror who had said in the course of deliberation that he would not convict the black defendants (on drug charges) because they were "his people." Despite these views, the appeals court found

Many Americans, including those pictured here, were quite unhappy with the decision of a California jury to acquit O. J. Simpson of murder charges. Why did some observers view the Simpson verdict as an example of jury nullification?

APPEAL
The process of seeking a higher court's review of a lower court's decision for the purpose of correcting or changing the lower court's judgment or decision.

DOUBLE JEOPARDY
To twice place at risk (jeopardize) a person's life or liberty. The Fifth Amendment to the U.S. Constitution prohibits a second prosecution for the same criminal offense.

"Appeal: In law, to put the dice into the box for another throw."

—Ambrose Bierce,
American author (c. 1900)

that the trial judge had erred in removing the juror, because there was no proof that he would *not* have voted to acquit the defendants regardless of his personal opinions.[75]

Appeals

Even if a defendant is found guilty, the trial process is not necessarily over. In our criminal justice system, a person convicted of a crime has a right to appeal. An **appeal** is the process of seeking a higher court's review of a lower court's decision for the purpose of correcting or changing the lower court's judgment. Any defendant who loses a case in a trial court cannot automatically appeal the conviction. The defendant normally must first be able to show that the trial court acted improperly on a question of law. Common reasons for appeals include the introduction of tainted evidence by the prosecution or faulty jury instructions delivered by the trial judge.

Double Jeopardy. The appeals process is available only to the defense. If a jury finds the accused not guilty, the prosecution cannot appeal to have the decision reversed. To do so would infringe upon the defendant's Fifth Amendment rights against multiple trials for the same offense. This guarantee against being tried a second time for the same crime is known as protection from **double jeopardy.**

The basic idea of the double jeopardy clause, in the words of Supreme Court Justice Hugo Black, is that the state should not be allowed to

> make repeated attempts to convict an individual for an alleged offense, thereby subjecting him to embarrassment, expense and ordeal and compelling him to live in a continuing state of anxiety and insecurity, as well as enhancing the possibility that even though innocent he may be found guilty.[76]

Today, some observers are arguing that certain defendants are being unfairly subjected to the embarrassment, expense, ordeal, and anxiety that Justice Black warned against.[77] Though it remains true that a defendant may not be retried on the same criminal charge, that person can be the target of a civil suit following participation in a criminal trial. For example, in 1995, after a criminal trial, a jury acquitted O. J. Simpson of the murders of his ex-wife Nicole Brown Simpson and Ron Goldman. Sixteen months later, however, Simpson lost a civil wrongful death suit brought by the families of the victims, was found *liable* for the murders, and was ordered to pay damages of $33.5 million. This is not considered double jeopardy because the second suit involved a civil claim, not a criminal one. Therefore, Simpson, or anybody else in the same situation, has not been charged with committing the same *crime* twice.

Note also that a defendant may be acquitted of violating a state criminal law and then be tried for violating a federal law. Both trials may relate to the same act. Sometimes, for example, the federal government decides to charge a person with having violated the civil rights of the purported victim, after a state jury has acquitted the defendant of having committed a crime against that person.

The Appeal Process. There are two basic reasons for the appeals process. The first is to correct an error made during the initial trial. The second is to review policy. Because of this second function, the appellate courts are an important part of the flexible nature of the criminal justice system. When existing law has ceased to be effective or no longer reflects the values of society, an appellate court can effectively change the law through its decisions and the precedents that it sets.[78] A classic example was the *Miranda v. Arizona* decision, which, although it failed to change the fate of the defendant (he was found guilty on retrial), had a far-reaching impact on custodial interrogation of suspects.

It is also important to understand that once the appeal process begins, the defendant is no longer presumed innocent. The burden of proof has shifted, and the defendant is obligated to prove that her or his conviction should be overturned. The method of filing an appeal differs slightly among the fifty states and the federal government, but the six basic steps are similar enough for summarization in Figure 10.8.

For the most part, defendants are not required to exercise their right to appeal. The one exception is in the case of the death sentence. Given the seriousness of capital punishment, the defendant is required to appeal the case, regardless of his or her wishes.

The Increase in Appeals. The appeal process is quite expensive. The legal help in an appeal must be of the highest quality because relatively little time is allowed for a number of complex procedures.[79] Until relatively recently, appeals were severely limited by their cost. This changed in the late 1950s and early 1960s due to a number of Supreme Court decisions that held that defendants could not be denied their Fourteenth Amendment right of equal protection because of lack of financial resources.[80] As Figure 10.9 shows, the result has been a sharp rise in the number of appeals since the early 1980s.

Habeas Corpus

The 1980s and early 1990s saw a similar rise in a postconviction process known as **habeas corpus** (Latin for "you have the body"). *Habeas corpus* is a judicial order that literally commands a corrections official to bring a prisoner before a federal court so that the court can hear the person's claim that he or she is being held illegally. A writ of *habeas corpus* differs from an appeal

HABEAS CORPUS
An order that requires correctional officials to bring an inmate before a court or a judge and explain why he or she is being held in prison.

---

1. Within a specific period of time—usually between thirty and ninety days—the defendant must file a *notice of appeal*. This is a short written statement outlining the basis of the appeal.

2. The appellant, or losing party in the lower court, must then transfer the trial court record to the appellate court. This record includes items of the case file, including exhibits, and a transcript of the testimony.

3. Next, the briefs must be filed. A *brief* is a written argument that presents the party's legal arguments and precedents to support these arguments. Both the appellant and the winning prosecutorial team must submit briefs to the appellate court.

4. The briefs are followed by *oral arguments,* in which attorneys from both sides appear before the appellate court panel to state their positions. In oral arguments, the judge or judges ask questions of the attorneys to clarify certain points or voice a particular disagreement.

5. After the oral arguments, the judges retire to deliberate the case. After a decision has been made, one or more of the judges prepare the *written opinion.* (This process is described in Chapter 8 in more detail.) A judge who disagrees with the majority opinion may write a *dissenting opinion.*

6. Finally, the court holds a disposition in which it announces the next step for the case. The court can *uphold* the decision of the lower court, or it can *modify* the lower court decision by changing a part of it but not the whole. The lower court's decision can be *reversed,* or set aside, or the appellate court can *reverse and remand* the case, meaning that the lower court's decision is overturned and the matter is sent back for further proceedings. Or, the appellate court may simply *remand* the case without overturning it.

Figure 10.8 The Steps of an Appeal

Figure 10.9 Appeals in U.S. Courts of Appeals

As you can see, the number of cases addressed by U.S. courts of appeals almost doubled between 1982 and 1997.

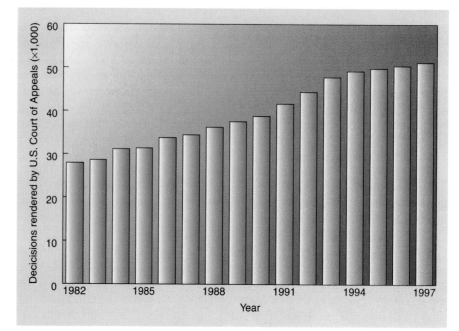

SOURCE: Administrative Office of the United States Courts, Annual Report to the Director, 1997 (Washington, D.C.: U.S. Government Printing Office, 1998), Table 1, page 14.

In 1998, attorneys for convicted murder Karla Faye Tucker filed a last-minute writ of *habeas corpus* in an attempt to save their client from her scheduled execution. To view a copy of this writ, go to www.courttv.com/legaldocs/ newsmakers/tucker

in several respects. First, it can be filed only by someone who is imprisoned. Second, it can address only constitutional issues, not technical errors. Thus, an inmate can file a *habeas corpus* petition claiming that the conditions of her or his imprisonment constitute cruel and unusual punishment, but not that the judge provided the jury with improper instructions during the trial.

Habeas Corpus in the Courts. For most of the nation's history, convicts had a difficult time gaining writs of *habeas corpus* because they first had to exhaust all appellate avenues on a state level before applying for review to the United States Supreme Court. In *Fay v. Noia* (1963),[81] the Court reversed this trend by ruling that federal courts were required to hear all *habeas corpus* petitions from state prisoners, even if the prisoner had failed to appeal the case properly on the state level. Writing for the majority in *Fay*, Justice William Brennan stated that *habeas corpus* was an important, and vastly underused, means to restrain the powers of the government to detain citizens illegally.[82] The result: a rise in the annual number of *habeas corpus* hearings from around 2,000 at the time of *Fay* to nearly 25,000 in the 1980s. These petitions were rarely successful (less than 2 percent saw the inmates released), and critics complained that they were clogging federal court dockets and allowing death-row inmates to avoid execution by filing numerous *habeas corpus* requests.

In the early 1990s, a more conservative Supreme Court made several rulings that limited *habeas corpus* avenues. In *McClesky v. Zant* (1991),[83] the Court ruled that a death-row inmate is limited to filing one petition, unless solid constitutional reasons exist for additional ones. *Keeney v. Tamayo-Reyes* (1992)[84] saw the Court eliminate a federal court's obligation to hear a *habeas corpus* petition from a state prisoner, even if the facts suggest that a review might be warranted. Furthermore, in *Herrera v. Collins* (1993),[85] the Court upheld a state's right to limit the amount of time inmates have to file a claim after their final appeal has been rejected.

***Habeas Corpus* in Congress.** The most aggressive move to limit *habeas corpus* review in recent years has come not from the Supreme Court, but from Congress. In 1996, motivated by the politically popular goal of shortening the time between conviction and execution in death penalty cases, Congress passed the Anti-Terrorism and Effective Death Penalty Act, which placed a one-year time limit on filing a *habeas corpus* petition and restricted a federal court's ability to overturn a state court's criminal conviction.[86] Many observers felt that the Court would uphold this legislation in the event that it was challenged on the basis that Article I of the Constitution limits Congress's ability to suspend *habeas corpus*.[87]

The Supreme Court was given the chance to do so almost immediately when Georgia inmate Ellis Wayne Felker challenged the new law, claiming it unconstitutionally limited the appeals of convicted murderers. Felker had been found guilty of rape and murder in 1983 and sentenced to die, but he had managed to elude the death penalty through *habeas corpus* petitions. In a unanimous decision, the Court rejected Felker's claim and upheld the act,[88] setting the stage for further erosion of *habeas corpus* in the future.

Criminal Justice in Action

Cameras in the Courtroom: Is Justice Served?

German physicist Werner Heisenberg once commented that the act of observation changes the thing that is being observed. Heisenberg was referring to Albert Einstein's theories of space and time, but this principle may also be applied to the criminal trial. In this chapter, we have discussed many of the guidelines to the trial process contained in the U.S. Constitution. The framers, however, would have been hard pressed to envision Court TV and the modern media storm that surrounds high-profile cases. Consequently, the decision to televise or not to televise rests with individual judges. As we close this chapter, we will examine two crucial questions: (1) Does the act of televising trials change them? (2) Even if it does, should the practice continue to be allowed?

A RIGHT OR A WRONG?

The issue of media in the courtroom has been debated since the 1935 trial of Bruno Hauptman, who was charged with kidnapping and murdering the baby of aeronautic pioneer Charles Lindbergh. After the disruption caused by 120 photographers at the trial, the presiding judge banned all cameras from the courtroom, and the American Bar Association moved to remove permanently journalists from court proceedings. In the 1981 case of *Chandler v. Florida*,[89] the Supreme Court ruled that states had free rein to set their own regulations concerning cameras in the courtroom. Today, only Mississippi and South Dakota have total bans on televising trials. (Federal courts, including the Supreme Court, generally do not allow their proceedings to be televised, though some are doing so on an experimental basis.)

Those who favor cameras in the courtroom point to the First Amendment's guarantee of freedom of the press. They argue that viewers have a right of access to the trial process and that this scrutiny will make the system more accountable to the public. Also, a televised trial is, in the words of one proponent, "the ultimate civics lesson" and contributes to Americans' overall understanding of the criminal justice system.[90]

Opponents of televised trials counter that the presence of cameras infringes upon the defendant's right to a fair trial. The participants in a trial, they claim, will modify their behavior if they are aware that they are on television. These opponents insist that even the slightest change in behavior by a judge, attorney, witness, or juror damages the entire process of justice.[91]

THE SIMPSON SHADOW

As in so many areas of the criminal justice system, the example of the O. J. Simpson trial has come to dominate the debate on televised trials. Attorneys from both sides came under criticism for grandstanding before the cameras, as did Los Angeles Superior Court Judge Lance Ito. Yet in the years prior to the Simpson trial, sensational court proceedings were routinely televised. It is estimated that 62 percent of the public watched some part of the trial of Lorena Bobbit for mutilating her husband in 1994. Similar ratings were garnered for the Menendez brothers trial for killing their parents (53 percent), the Rodney King police brutality trial (81 percent), and the William Kennedy Smith rape trial (55 percent).[92]

The decision of whether a trial will be televised is, for the most part, the domain of the presiding judge. Since the Simpson experience, judges have been much more reluctant to allow the trial proceedings to be televised. In fact, for Simpson's civil trial, Judge Hiroshi Fujisaki placed a blanket gag order on all participants in the proceedings (meaning they could not speak to the press) and banned television cameras, photographers, and even sketch artists from the courtroom. The second Menendez murder trial, the trial of Susan Smith for murdering her children, and Yolanda Salvidar's trial for the homicide of pop singer Selena were also kept off the airwaves by wary judges. Other members of the courtroom work group have

The trial of Lyle Menendez, pictured, and his brother Erik for the murder of their parents was watched by millions of Americans on television.

been similarly troubled by the Simpson example. The prosecutor in the Selena trial said that he did not want to become "the Marcia Clark of Texas," referring to the prosecutor in the Simpson case who became a media target during and following that trial, and who later became a television host and commentator.[93]

THE EFFECTS OF PUBLIC OPINION

On the first day of their initial trial, the Menendez brothers arrived at the proceedings dressed in double-breasted suits. Soon after, under instructions from their attorney, the brothers appeared in soft-toned sweaters. The reason for this change of dress was that the suits made the defendants look too stiff in the eyes of the public.

Such effects of public opinion on the behavior of trial participants are often cited as a reason that cameras should be kept out of the courtroom.[94] In televised trials, participants lose their anonymity and often act accordingly. Witnesses may alter their stories to appeal to the television audience, thereby introducing improper or inaccurate testimony into the proceedings. Simpson witness Kato Kaelin, who in post-trial interviews contradicted statements he made from the witness stand, is often cited as an example of this problem.

Attorneys may also modify their actions to appeal to a wider audience, and some observers have contended that an attorney will use a televised trial as a free personal advertisement. A further worry is that jurors, knowing the trial is gaining public exposure, will be contaminated by a desire to satisfy the wishes of the public rather than the demands of the law. Supreme Court Justice David H. Souter, in arguing against the presence of cameras in the Court, attested to television's effect on the judge. As a state judge in New Hampshire, Souter admitted, he altered his behavior when he knew he was going to appear on the evening news.[95]

TWO RIGHTS IN CONFLICT?

Many see the issue of televised trials as a conflict between the media's right to freedom of the press and the defendant's right to a fair trial. In 1941, Justice Hugo Black commented that "free speech and fair trials are two of the most cherished policies of our civilization, and it would be a trying task to choose between them."[96]

If such a choice must be made, argues legal scholar Taffiny L. Smith, the right to a fair trial must carry more weight.[97] Smith points out that the Supreme Court, in *Richmond Newspapers, Inc. v. Virginia* (1980),[98] ruled that the media's right of access to trials is not absolute and may be subject to reasonable limitations. These lim-

itations come in the form of judicial discretion. Furthermore, though a judge has an inherent right to set the courtroom off-limits to television cameras, she or he may not exclude the print media from the proceedings. That *would* deny the media freedom of the press.

Proponents of televised trials argue that it is precisely this judicial discretion that allows the rights of the press and the trial to coexist. If a judge sees media coverage contaminating the trial, he or she can take several steps to remedy it, including the following:

- Sequestering the jurors, or isolating them from contact with the public or the media during the course of the trial. Officers of the court control the flow of information to jurors while they are sequestered, keeping them from being unduly influenced by media reports on the trial.

- Ordering a *change of venue,* in which the trial is transferred to a new location. A judge will take this step if the publicity and interest in a case in its original jurisdiction are so intense that the judge believes the defendant cannot receive a fair trial in that area.

- Placing a *gag order* on the participants in the trial.

If a judge believes any of these efforts to secure a fair trial has been compromised, she or he can take dramatic action. For example, in DeKalb County, Georgia, a judge declared a mistrial after one of the witnesses violated a direct order by watching testimony on television.[99]

Just because the O. J. Simpson case was handled poorly, the proponents contend, the public should not be denied the benefits of seeing a criminal trial in progress. The Massachusetts murder trial of British *au pair* Louise Woodward—which was televised—is held up as an example of a judge (Hiller B. Zobel) successfully keeping the media frenzy outside the courtroom. "The legal system is the public's legal system," said one of Zobel's peers. "Who are we to say that we can work in an isolated little courtroom with a select few people who can stand in line to get in? If 100 people can see it, then why can't the rest of the world see it? The public should have access. Simple as that."[100]

Key Terms

Chapter Summary

1. **Identify the basic protections enjoyed by criminal defendants in the United States.** According to the Sixth Amendment, a criminal defendant has the right to a speedy and public trial by an impartial jury in the physical location where the crime was committed. Additionally, a person accused of a crime must be informed of the nature of the crime and be confronted with the witnesses against him or her. Further, the accused must be able to summon witnesses in her or his favor and have the assistance of counsel.

2. **List the three requirements of the Speedy Trial Act of 1974.** In federal court, those accused of crimes must experience (a) no more than thirty days between arrest and indictment; (b) no more than ten days between indictment and arraignment; and (c) no more than sixty days between arraignment and trial. Of course, extra time is allowed for hearings on pretrial motions, mental competency examinations, and other procedural actions.

3. **Explain what "taking the Fifth" really means.** The Fifth Amendment states that no person "shall be compelled in any criminal case to be a witness against himself." Thus, defendants do not have to testify if their testimony would implicate them in the crime. Witnesses may refuse to tes-

tify on this same ground. (Witnesses, though, are often granted immunity and thereafter can no longer take the Fifth.) In the United States, silence on the part of a defendant cannot be used by the jury in forming its opinion about guilt or innocence.

4. **List the requirements normally imposed on potential jurors.** They must be (a) citizens of the United States; (b) over eighteen years of age; (c) free of felony convictions; (d) of the necessary health to function on a jury; (e) sufficiently intelligent to understand the issues at trial; and (f) able to read, write, and comprehend the English language.

5. **Contrast challenges for cause and peremptory challenges during *voir dire*.** A challenge for cause occurs when an attorney provides the court with a legally justifiable reason why a potential juror should be excluded, for example, because the juror does not speak English. In contrast, peremptory challenges do not require any justification by the attorney and are usually limited to a small number. They cannot, however, be based, even implicitly, on race or gender.

6. **List the standard steps in a criminal jury trial.** (a) Opening statements by the prosecutor and the defense attorney; (b) presentation of evidence, usually in the form of questioning by the prosecutor, known as direct examination; (c) cross-examination by the defense attorney of the same witnesses; (d) motion for a directed verdict by the defense at the end of the prosecutor's presentation of evidence (also called a motion for judgment as a matter of law in the federal courts), which is normally denied by the judge; (e) presentation of the defendant's case, which may include placing the defendant on the stand and direct examination of the defense's witnesses; (f) cross-examination by the prosecutor; (g) rebuttal by the prosecution after the defense closes its case, which may involve new evidence that was not used initially by the prosecution; (h) cross-examination of the prosecution's new witnesses by the defense and introduction of new witnesses of its own, called the surrebuttal; (i) closing arguments by both the defense and the prosecution; (j) the charging of the jury by the judge, during which the judge sums up the case and instructs the jurors on the rules of law that apply; (k) jury deliberations; and (l) presentation of the verdict.

7. **Explain the difference between testimony and real evidence; between lay witnesses and expert witnesses; and between direct and circumstantial evidence.** Testimony consists of statements by competent witnesses, whereas real evidence includes physical items that affect the case; a lay witness is an "average person," whereas an expert witness speaks with the authority of one who has had professional training, advanced knowledge, or substantial experience in a specialized area; direct evidence is evidence presented by witnesses as opposed to circumstantial evidence, which can create an inference that a fact exists, but does not directly establish the fact.

8. **List possible affirmative defenses.** (a) Self-defense, (b) insanity, (c) duress, and (d) entrapment.

9. **Delineate circumstances in which a criminal defendant may in fact be tried a second time for the same act.** When the defendant is acquitted in a criminal trial but is sued in a civil case for essentially the same act.

10. **List the six basic steps of an appeal.** (a) The filing of a notice of appeal; (b) the transfer of the trial court records to the appellate court; (c) the filing of briefs; (d) the presentation of oral arguments; (e) the deliberation of the appellate judges who then prepare a written opinion; and (f) the announcement of the judges—upholding the decision of the lower court, modifying part of the decision, reversing the decision, or reversing and remanding the decision to the trial court.

Questions for Critical Analysis

1. If a defendant waives his or her right to a jury trial, what type of trial then takes place?

2. Why is there a higher standard of proof in criminal cases than in civil cases?

3. Why is the phenomenon of jury science not significant for most criminal defendants?

4. What danger lies in a defense attorney's or prosecutor's decision to present an opening statement to the jury?

5. Under what circumstances may evidence be excluded?

6. How does an attorney authenticate evidence presented?

7. Are there exceptions to the hearsay rule, and if so, what are they?

8. Why might a defense attorney not want to call the defendant to the stand to testify?

9. What is the major problem with the jury instructions that judges usually present prior to jury deliberations?

10. What are the arguments for and against televising criminal trials?

Using the internet for Criminal Justice Analysis

I N F O T R A C ®
COLLEGE EDITION

1. Go to your InfoTrac College Edition at www.infotrac-college.com/wadsworth/. After you log on, type in the words: "HIDING THE IDENTITY OF POTENTIAL JURORS"

In highly charged criminal cases, the identity of jurors is kept secret. Jurors are hidden from the press and no cameras are allowed in the court. This is what occurred during the case of *United States v. McVeigh* in April of 1997.

a. What did the case concern? Why was it so important to the media?

b. What does it mean when a case is tried by an "anonymous" jury?

c. What does it mean when a judge "seals all records"?

d. What was the two-part type of *voir dire*? Is such a two-part *voir dire* common?

e. What is the historical basis of public jury selection in the United States?

f. In what case did the United States Supreme Court rule that *voir dire* normally has to be open to the public?

g. Why is the author of this article presumably so concerned about anonymous juries?

2. You can learn a lot about criminal appeals by examining at least one home page of a criminal appeals court in the United States. Go to the following site:
www.occa.state.ok.us/occaon.htm

This is the home page of the Oklahoma Court of Criminal Appeals. Click on OCCAOnline. Then click on "Court Rules." Take a look at some of the rules in "Section 1, General Rules of the Court and Definitions."

a. What is a *Forma Pauperis*?

b. How many rules apply to the initiation of an appeal from the trial court?

c. Which rules apply to death penalty cases?

Now try to find jury instructions. Once you are there, answer the following questions:

d. Which "chapter" of jury instructions involves drug offenses?

e. List the affirmative defenses that are given in Chapter 8 of jury instructions.

f. Where can you find information on grand juries?

3. Go to the following Web site, which shows a federal court's "Change of Venue Order" in a criminal case:
www.courttv.com/casefiles/oklahoma/documents/venue.html

Read through the order, and answer the following questions:

a. Who were the defendants in this case, and with what crimes were they charged?

b. What was the original venue for the trial?

c. Who requested a change of venue, and why?

d. What constitutional provisions did the court cite as relevant to the request for a change of venue?

e. According to the federal procedural rule that is based on these constitutional provisions, in what circumstances will a change of venue be permitted?

f. Why did the court grant a change of venue?

Selected Print and Electronic Resources

SUGGESTED READINGS

Freedman, Warren, *The Constitutional Right to a Speedy and Fair Criminal Trial*, New York: Quorum Books, 1989. The author is a seasoned criminal trial attorney. He examines the constitutional guarantee of a speedy and fair criminal trial. He looks first at the historical background of this constitutional right and then at excessive trial delays and unfair trial situations. He reviews

the Sixth and Fourteenth Amendments and their interpretations by the courts.

Gist, Gilbert, and Leigh B. Bienen, *Crimes of the Century*, Evanston, IL: Northwestern University Press, 1998. These authors recount five important trials, including O. J. Simpson's. They examine whether successful trials are overly dependent on skilled, high-priced lawyers. They examine the inadequacies and underlying processes of our criminal justice system.

Holmes, Burnham, *The Fifth Amendment,* Morristown, N.J.: Silver Burdette Press, 1991. The author traces the history of the right to a grand jury, the right to due process, and the prohibition against double jeopardy and self-incrimination.

Kurland, Michael, *How to Try a Murder: The Handbook for Armchair Lawyers,* New York: Macmillan General Reference, 1998. In spite of its title, this book explains the details of a criminal trial. The author examines the powers of judges and juries. He looks at defense strategies as well as prosecutors' tactics. He examines each stage of the criminal trial.

MEDIA RESOURCES

12 *Angry Men* (1957) This classic movie is a primer on what *not* to do when deliberating as a juror, but it is great to watch. One juror (Henry Fonda) applies the correct legal standard of requiring proof beyond a reasonable doubt. He is the only juror who will not accept the prosecution's case. He continues questioning the rest of the jurors during deliberations and one by one causes them to examine the facts presented at the trial. The jurors show their prejudices and weaknesses throughout the movie.

Critically analyze this film:

1. The jury is all male? Why?

2. Why did the jurors want a quick decision?

3. Is juror #8, Davis (played by Henry Fonda), truly certain of the boy's innocence?

4. Explore some of the prejudices of the jurors. Do you think any of them could have been excluded by for-cause exemptions?

5. Do you see any evidence of jury nullification in this film? If so, is it justified?

Logging On

An excellent cite for information on the criminal justice system is:

www.tqd.advanced.org/2760/homep.htm

Here, you can follow a fictional criminal case through the courts, find a glossary of terms used in criminal law, view actual forms that are filled out during the course of an arrest, locate landmark Supreme Court cases in criminal law, and learn about some controversial issues in criminal law. The American Civil Liberties Union (ACLU) has long acted as a guardian of Americans' civil liberties. You can learn about some of the constitutional questions raised by various criminal laws and procedures by going to the ACLU's Web site at:

www.aclu.org.

For an example of an appeal petition in an actual criminal case, go to:

www.courttv.com/trials/woodward/appeal.html

You can find summaries of famous criminal cases and sometimes related pleadings and other documents at the Web site of Court TV. Go to:

www.courttv.com/trials

Many state criminal codes are now online. To find your state's code, go to:

www.findlaw.com

and select "State Codes."

Notes

1. National Advisory Commission on Criminal Justice Standards and Goals, *Courts* (Washington, D.C.: U.S. Government Printing Office, 1973), 66.

2. Pamela Coyles, "Fifth Murder Trial a Mistrial," *New Orleans Times-Picayune* (February 18, 1998), A1.

3. Jerome Frank, *Courts on Trial: Myth and Reality in American Justice* (New York: Atheneum, 1969), 14–33.

4. William L. Prosser, *Handbook of the Law of Torts,* 2d ed. (St. Paul, MN: West Publishing Co., 1955), 7.

5. David L. Cook, Steven R. Schlesinger, Thomas J. Bak, and William T. Rule II, "Criminal Caseload in U.S. District Courts: More than Meets the Eye," *American University Law Review* 44 (June 1995), 44.

6. 407 U.S. 514 (1972).

7. Roger Misner, *Speedy Trials: Federal and State Practice* (Charlottesville, VA: The Michie Co., 1983).

8. *State v. Utley*, 956 S.W.2d 489 (Tenn. 1997).

9. 18 U.S.C. Section 3161.

10. 391 U.S. 145 (1968).

11. *Blanton v. Las Vegas*, 489 U.S. 538 (1989).

12. *Williams v. Florida*, 399 U.S. 102 (1970).

13. 435 U.S. 223 (1968).

14. *Johnson v. Louisiana*, 406 U.S. 356 (1972); *Apodaca v. Oregon*, 406 U.S. 404 (1972).

15. 332 U.S. 46 (1947).

16. Barton L. Ingraham, "The Right of Silence, the Presumption of Innocence, the Burden of Proof, and a Modest Proposal," *Journal of Criminal Law and Criminology* 85 (1994), 559–95.

17. 397 U.S. 358 (1970).

18. Akhil Reed Amar and Vikram David Amar, "Unlocking the Jury Box," *Policy Review* (May–June 1996), 38.

19. James P. Levine, "The Impact of Local Political Cultures on Jury Verdicts," *Criminal Justice Journal* 14 (1992), 163–4.

20. John Kaplan, Jerome H. Skolnick, and Malcolm M. Freeley, *Criminal Justice*, 5th ed. (Westbury, NY: The Foundation Press, 1991), 410–1.

21. Jeff Herman, "Ending the U.S. Jury System Circus," *USA Today Magazine* (September 1997,) 26–9.

22. John Kaplan and Jon R. Waltz, *The Trial of Jack Ruby* (New York: Macmillan, 1965), 91–4.

23. James L. Gilbert, Stuart A. Ollanik, and David A. Wenner, "Overcoming Juror Bias in Voir Dire," *Trial* (July 1997), 42–6.

24. *Lockhart v. McCree*, 476 U.S. 162 (1986).

25. *Witherspoon v. Illinois*, 391 U.S. 510 (1968).

26. Kaplan and Waltz, 91–4.

27. Jeremy W. Barber, "The Jury Is Still Out," *American Criminal Law Review* 31 (Summer 1994) 1225–52.

28. Diane Burch Beckham, "The Art of the *Voir Dire*: Is It Really a Science?" *New Jersey Law Journal* (July 5, 1990), 5.

29. Barber, "The Jury Is Still Out."

30. *Ibid.*

31. 380 U.S. 224 (1965).

32. 476 U.S. 79 (1986).

33. Eric L. Muller, "Solving the *Batson* Paradox: Harmless Error, Jury Representation, and the Sixth Amendment," *Yale Law Journal* 106 (October 1996), 93.

34. 499 U.S. 400 (1991).

35. 502 U.S. 1056 (1992).

36. Karen L. Cipriani, "The Numbers Don't Add Up: Challenging the Premise of *J.E.B. v. Alabama*," *American Criminal Law Review* 31 (Summer 1994) 1253–77.

37. *J.E.B. v. Alabama ex rel T.B.*, 511 U.S. 127 (1994).

38. Harry Kalven and Hans Zeisel, *The American Jury* (Boston: Little, Brown, 1966), 163–7.

39. Sara Rimer, "In 2 Live Crew Trial, Cultures Didn't Clash," *New York Times* (October 22, 1990), B1.

40. Nancy Pennington and Reid Hastie, "The Story Model for Juror Decision Making," in *Inside the Juror: The Psychology of Juror Decision Making* (Cambridge, MA: Harvard University Press, 1983), 192, 194–5.

41. 424 U.S. 600 (1976).

42. Federal Rule of Evidence 703.

43. Richard A. Epstein, "Judicial Control over Expert Testimony: Of Deference and Education," *Northwestern University Law Review* 87 (1993), 1156.

44. L. Timothy Perrin, "Expert Witnesses under Rules 703 and 803(4) of the Federal Rules of Evidence: Separating the Wheat from the Chaff," *Indiana Law Journal* 72 (Fall 1997), 939.

45. Thomas J. Reed, "Trial by Propensity: Admission of Other Criminal Acts Evidenced in Federal Criminal Trials," *University of Cincinnati Law Review* 50 (1981), 713.

46. *Ibid.*

47. *People v. Zackowitz*, 254 N.Y. 192 (1930).

48. Charles McCormick, *Handbook on Evidence* (St. Paul, MN: West Publishing Co., 1987), Chapter One.

49. Jay L. Hack, "Declaration against Penal Interest: Standards of Admissibility under an Emerging Majority Rule," *Boston University Law Review* 56 (1976), 148.

50. Emily F. Duck, "The Williamson Standard for the Exception to the Rule against Hearsay for Statements against Penal Interest," *Journal of Criminal Law and Criminology* 85 (Spring 1995), 1084–113.

51. Hack, 148.

52. *People v. Brown*, 80 N.Y.2d 729 (1993) and *People v. Buie*, 86 N.Y.2d 501 (1995).

53. Wendy Melillo, "Judge Rejects Kasi's Request for a New Trial," *Washington Post* (February 5, 1998), D1.

54. Leonard E. Davies, *Anatomy of Cross-Examination* (Englewood Cliffs, NJ: Prentice-Hall Law & Business, 1994).

55. *Griffin v. California*, 380 U.S. 609 (1965).

56. Hilary E. MacGregor, "Shopper's Murderer Receives Life Term," *Los Angeles Times* (March 20, 1998), B1.

57. John M. R. Bull, "Knoxville Teen Acquitted in Youth's Shooting Death," *Pittsburgh Post-Gazette* (January 12, 1999), B4.

58. Herbert J. Stern, *Trying Cases to Win* (New York: Wiley Law Publications, 1991), 151.

59. David W. Neubauer, *America's Courts and the Criminal Justice System*, 5th ed. (Belmont, CA: Wadsworth Publishing Co. 1996), 254.

60. James P. Levine, "Jury Wisdom," *Criminal Justice Ethics* (Winter/Spring 1997), 53.

61. Herman.

62. Jeffrey Abramson, *We, the Jury: The Jury System and the Ideal of Democracy* (New York: Basic Books, 1994), 250.

63. Roger LeRoy Miller and Mary S. Urisko, *West's Paralegal Today* (St. Paul, MN: West Publishing Co., 1995), 443.

64. Firoz Dattu, "Illustrated Jury Instructions," *Judicature* 82 (September/October 1998), 79.

65. Walter J. Steele, Jr. and Elizabeth Thornburg, "Jury Instructions: A Persistent Failure to Communicate," *Judicature* 74 (1991), 249–54.

66. David W. Broeder, "The University of Chicago Jury Project," *Nebraska Law Review* 38 (1959), 744–60.

67 Harold J. Rothwax, *Guilty: The Collapse of the Criminal Justice System* (New York: Random House, 1996), 214.

68. 164 U.S. 492 (1896).

69. *United States v. Fioravanti*, 412 F.2d 407 (3d Cir. 1969).

70. Jeffrey Rosen, "One Angry Woman," *New Yorker* (February 24 and March 3, 1997), 55.

71. Joseph L. Gastwirth and Michael D. Sinclair, "Diagnostic Test Methodology in the Design and Analysis of Judge-Jury Agreement Studies," *Jurimetrics Journal* 39 (Fall 1998), 59.

72. Peter Western, "The Three Faces of Double Jeopardy: Reflections on Government Appeals of Criminal Sentences," *Michigan Law Review* 78 (1980), 1001–2.

73. Quoted in Abramson, *We, The Jury,* 30.

74. 116 F.3d 606 (2d Cir. 1997).

75. Lawrence Fleischer, "Does Jury Nullification Subvert Rule of Law? Yes," *New York Law Journal* (June 25, 1997), 121.

76. *Green v. United States,* 355 U.S. 184 (1957).

77. Donald A. Dripps, "The Continuing Decline in Finality in Criminal Law," *Trial* (April 1997), 78–9.

78. Neubauer, 331.

79. David T. Wasserman, *A Sword for the Convicted: Representing Indigent Defendants on Appeal* (New York: Greenwood Press, 1990).

80. *Griffin v. Illinois,* 351 U.S. 12 (1956); *Douglas v. California,* 372 U.S. 353 (1963).

81. 372 U.S. 391 (1963).

82. *Ibid.,* 402–3.

83. 499 U.S. 467 (1991).

84. 504 U.S. 1 (1992).

85. 506 U.S. 390 (1993).

86. 28 U.S.C. Section 2254(d)(1).

87. F. Martin Tieber, "Federal Habeas Corpus Law and Practice—The Antiterrorism and Effective Death Penalty Act of 1996," *Michigan Bar Journal* 77 (January 1998), 50.

88. *Felker v. Turpin,* 116 S.Ct. 2333 (1996).

89. 949 U.S. 560 (1981).

90. Claire Papanastasiou, "Cameras in the Courtroom," *The Massachusetts Lawyer* (December 15, 1997), B1.

91. Taffiny L. Smith, "The Distortion of Criminal Trials through Televised Proceedings," *Law and Psychology Review* 21 (Spring 1997), 257.

92. Dan Trigoboff, "Court Coverage Hindered by O. J. Backlash?" *Broadcasting & Cable* (June 23, 1997), 24.

93. *Ibid.*

94. Smith, 257.

95. Jim Gordon, "No Camera Fans Here," *News Photographer* (May 1, 1996), 4.

96. *Bridges v. California,* 314 U.S. 252 (1941).

97. Smith, 257.

98. 448 U.S. 555 (1980).

99. Celia Sibley, "Sandlin Ruling: Eye Is on Courtroom Cameras," *Atlanta Journal and Atlanta Constitution* (July 19, 1997), B2.

100. Papanastasiou, B1.

chapter

11

Punishment and Sentencing

Chapter Objectives

After reading this chapter, you should be able to:

1. List and contrast the four basic philosophical reasons for sentencing criminals.

2. Contrast indeterminate with determinate sentencing.

3. Explain why there is a difference between a sentence imposed by a judge and the actual sentence carried out by the prisoner.

4. List the five forms of punishment.

5. State who has input into the sentencing decision and list the factors that determine a sentence.

6. Explain some of the reasons why sentencing reform has occurred.

7. Contrast sentencing guidelines with mandatory sentencing guidelines.

8. Outline the Supreme Court rulings on capital punishment.

INTRODUCTION

Consider the case of Marcos Mascarenas of Questa, New Mexico. Several years ago, Mascarenas was responsible for the death of his six-month-old son by "shaken baby syndrome." In other words, Mascarenas shook the child so hard that his retinas became detached, causing severe hemorrhaging and eventually killing him.

How should Mascarenas have been punished? The crime of infanticide is so horrific that the government would have been justified in seeking the severest possible penalty for Mascarenas. It may be a surprise, then, to learn that the judge who presided over the case was distraught at having to sentence the defendant to twelve years in prison. Eighth Judicial District Judge Peggy Nelson said she would have given Mascarenas an even lighter sentence, except that twelve years was the minimum allowed by state law. The reason: Mascarenas had an intelligence quotient (IQ) of 90 and purportedly was not aware of what he was doing. When he realized that his son had been injured, he rushed the infant to a hospital and remained by the child's side until life support was discontinued. After the trial, Mascarenas's defense attorney worried that by going to prison, his client was being sent into "an eternal howling wilderness" that would expose him to "danger and abuse."[1]

Some of the citizens of New Mexico, if asked, might have agreed that Mascarenas was sentenced too harshly. Yet, it was the public's discontent with "lenient" judges that led to the restrictions that kept Judge Nelson from easing the penalty. As this isolated case shows, sentencing presents some of the most complex issues of the criminal justice system. One scholar has even asserted that:

> There is no such thing as "accurate" sentencing; there are only sentences that are more or less just, more or less effective. Nothing in the recent or distant history of sentencing reform suggests that anything approaching perfection is attainable.[2]

In this chapter, we will discuss the various attempts to "perfect" the practice of sentencing over the past century and explore the ramifications of these efforts for the American criminal justice system. Whereas previous chapters have concentrated on the prosecutor and defense attorney, this one will spotlight the judge and his or her role in making the sentencing decision. We will particularly focus on recent national and state efforts to limit judicial discretion in this area, a trend that has had the overall effect of producing harsher sentences for many offenders. Finally, we will examine the issues surrounding the death penalty, a controversial subject that forces us to confront the basic truth of sentencing: the way we punish criminals says a great deal about the kind of people we are.[3]

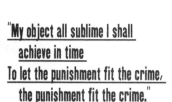

"My object all sublime I shall achieve in time
To let the punishment fit the crime,
the punishment fit the crime."

—Gilbert and Sullivan,
The Mikado (1885)

INFOTRAC ®
COLLEGE EDITION

For Shame: Paying for Crime Without Serving Time

THE PURPOSE OF SENTENCING

Professor Herbert Packer has said that punishing criminals serves two ultimate purposes: the "deserved infliction of suffering on evil doers" and "the prevention of crime."[4] Even this straightforward assessment raises several questions. How does one determine the sort of punishment that is "deserved"? How can we be sure that certain penalties "prevent" crime? Should criminals be punished solely for the good of society, or should their well-being also be taken into consideration? Sentencing laws indicate how any given group of people has answered these questions, but does not tell us *why* they were answered in that manner. To understand why, we must first consider the four basic philosophical reasons for sentencing—retribution, deterrence, incapacitation, and rehabilitation.

Retribution

The oldest and most common justification for punishing someone is that he or she "deserved it"—as the Old Testament states, "an eye for an eye and a tooth for a tooth." Under a system of justice that favors **retribution,** a wrongdoer who has freely chosen to violate society's rules must be punished for the infraction. Retribution relies on the principle of **just deserts,** which holds that the severity of the punishment must be in proportion to the severity of the crime. Retributive justice is not the same as *revenge.* Whereas revenge implies that the wrongdoer is punished only with the aim of satisfying a victim or victims, retribution is more concerned with the needs of society as a whole. (Retribution is discussed in more detail in the feature *Criminal Justice in Action—Victims and Retribution* at the end of this chapter.)

The *principle of willful wrongdoing* is central to the idea of retribution. That is, society is only morally justified in punishing someone if that person was aware that he or she had committed a crime. Therefore, animals, children, and the mentally incapacitated are not responsible for criminal action, even though they may be a threat to the community.[5] Furthermore, the principles of retribution reject any wide-reaching social benefit as a goal of punishment. The philosopher Immanuel Kant, an early proponent of retributivism, believed that punishment by a court:

> can never be inflicted merely as a means to promote some other good for the criminal himself or for civil society. It must always be inflicted upon him only because he has committed a crime. For a man can never be treated merely as a means to the purposes of another.[6]

In other words, punishment is an end in itself and cannot be justified by any future good that may result from a criminal's suffering.

One problem with retributive ideas of justice lies in proportionality. Whether or not one agrees with the death penalty, the principle behind it is easy to fathom: the punishment (death) fits the crime (death). But what about the theft of an automobile? How does one fairly determine the amount of time the thief must spend in prison? Should the type of car matter or the wealth of the car owner? Theories of retribution often have a difficult time providing answers to such questions.[7]

Deterrence

The concept of **deterrence** (as well as incapacitation and rehabilitation) takes the opposite approach: rather than seeking only to punish the wrongdoer, the goal of sentencing should be to prevent future crimes. By "setting an example," society is sending a message to potential criminals that certain actions will not be tolerated. Jeremy Bentham, a nineteenth-century British reformer who first articulated the principles of deterrence, felt that retribution was counterproductive because it does not serve the community. (See Chapter 2 to review Bentham's utilitarian theories.) He believed that a person should be punished only when doing so was in society's best interests and that the severity of the punishment should be based on its deterrent value, not on the severity of the crime.[8] (See *Cross-National CJ Comparison—Singapore: A Utilitarian Oasis* on the next page.)

State-sanctioned executions continue to be controversial. These protesters, who swelled to over 300, demonstrate against the death penalty at San Quentin Prison on February 8, 1999. California Governor Gray Davis refused to spare convicted double murderer Jay Siripongs, in spite of an eleventh-hour plea by Pope John Paul II. The accused's lawyers had unsuccessfully appealed to the U.S. Court of Appeals in San Francisco and the United States Supreme Court.

RETRIBUTION
The philosophy that those who commit criminal acts should be punished based on the severity of the crime, and no other factors need be considered.

JUST DESERTS
A sanctioning philosophy based on the assertion that criminals deserve to be punished for breaking society's rules. The severity of the punishment should be determined by no other factor than the severity of the crime.

DETERRENCE
The strategy of preventing crime through the threat of punishment. Assumes that potential criminals will weigh the costs of punishments versus the benefits of the criminal act; therefore, punishments should be severe.

Cross-National CJ Comparison

Singapore—A Utilitarian Oasis

Suppose one were to ask Immanuel Kant and Jeremy Bentham the following question: Is the death penalty a justifiable punishment for illegally selling marijuana? Kant, a proponent of the "principle of equity," would answer no; such a punishment would be too harsh for the crime. Bentham, however, might not agree. If the ultimate goal of punishment is to deter people from committing future crimes, then a literal reading of Bentham's utilitarian theory would seem to support severe penalties for seemingly minor criminal behavior.

Singapore, a nation-city of three million people in Southeast Asia, leans toward Bentham rather than Kant in its sentencing theories. According to Singapore law, the selling of any drug—including marijuana—carries a mandatory death sentence by hanging, as do murder and the use of a firearm in committing or attempting to commit a crime. Someone caught smoking marijuana is sentenced to a ten-year prison term. Citizens who litter are fined the equivalent of $1,000, with similar penalties imposed for chewing gum and failing to flush a public toilet. Vandals are sentenced to up to three years in prison and (as American teenager Michael Fay learned in the mid-1990s) are subject to caning.

Many observers criticize Singapore, claiming its strict laws violate human rights. But Singaporeans point to one of the world's lowest crime rates as justification for their system. The year after robbery with a firearm was deemed punishable by death, for example, not one such incident took place in the city. Singapore officials also point out that the United States—which consistently criticizes human rights abuses in other nations—has the highest violent crime rate and the most citizens in prison of any country in the West.

WHAT'S THE EVIDENCE?

To better understand the historical and social forces that shape criminal justice in Singapore, as well as visit links that allow discussion of the country's policies, go to **www.gov.sg/agc.** For discussion on how Singapore's restrictive laws impact the country's democratic principles, visit the homepage of the Socratic Circle at **web.signet.com.sg/~greenliz/socratic.**

"Men are not hanged for stealing horses, but that horses may not be stolen."

—Marquis de Halifax, *Political Thoughts and Reflections* (1750)

Deterrence can take two forms: general and specific. The basic idea of *general deterrence* is that by punishing one person, others will be dissuaded from committing a similar crime. *Specific deterrence* assumes that an individual, after being punished once for a certain act, will be less likely to repeat that act because she or he does not want to be punished again.[9] Both forms of deterrence have proved problematic in practice. General deterrence assumes that a person commits a crime only after a rational decision-making process, in which he or she implicitly weighs the benefits of the crime against the possible costs of the punishment. This is not necessarily the case, especially for young offenders who tend to value the immediate rewards of crime over the possible future consequences.[10] Specific deterrence, for its part, seems to be contradicted by the fact that a relatively small number of habitual offenders are responsible for the majority of certain criminal acts.[11]

Another criticism of deterrence is that for most crimes, wrongdoers are unlikely to be caught, sentenced, and imprisoned. As Figure 11.1 shows, the majority of all crimes go unpunished. A study by Texas A&M economist Morgan Reynolds found that, after factoring in the low likelihood of capture and imprisonment, the average statistically expected stay in prison is only 4.8 days for an act of burglary, 60.5 days for rape, and 1.8 years for murder.[12] Thus, in general, potential criminals have less to fear from the criminal justice system than one might expect. Professors Paul H. Robinson of Northwestern University School of Law and John M. Darley of Princeton University note that this low probability of punishment could be offset by making the punishment so severe that even the slightest chance of apprehension could act as a deterrent—for example, a 250-year prison term for shoplifting or the loss of a hand for burglary.[13] Our society is, however, unwilling to allow for this possibility.

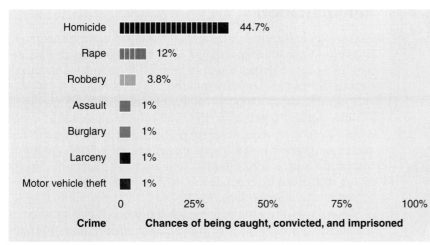

Figure 11.1 Risk of Punishment

SOURCE: PAUL H. ROBINSON AND JOHN M. DARLEY, "THE UTILITY OF DESERT," NORTHWESTERN LAW REVIEW 91 (WINTER 1997), 453. TABLE I.

Incapacitation

"Wicked people exist," said James Q. Wilson. "Nothing avails except to set them apart from innocent people."[14] Wilson's blunt statement summarizes the justification for **incapacitation** as a form of punishment. As a purely practical matter, incarcerating criminals guarantees that they will not be a danger to society, at least for the length of their prison terms. To a certain extent, the death penalty is justified in terms of incapacitation, as it prevents the offender from committing any future crimes.

Several studies have pointed to the effectiveness of incapacitation as a crime prevention tool. Criminologist Isaac Ehrlich of the University of Chicago estimated that a 1 percent increase in sentence length will produce a 1 percent decrease in crime rates.[15] Another Chicago professor, Steve Levitt, has noticed a trend that further supports incapacitation: violent crimes rates rise in communities where inmate litigation over prison overcrowding has forced the early release of some inmates and a subsequent drop in the prison population.[16]

Incapacitation as a theory of punishment suffers from several weaknesses, however. Unlike retribution, it offers no proportionality with regard to a particular crime. Giving a burglar a life sentence would certainly assure that she or he would not commit another burglary; does that justify such a severe penalty? Furthermore, incarceration only protects society until the criminal is freed. Many studies have shown that, upon release, offenders may actually be more likely to commit crimes than before they were imprisoned.[17] In that case, incapacitation may increase the likelihood of crime, rather than diminishing it.

Some observers believe that strategies of *selective incapacitation* should be favored over strategies of collective incapacitation to solve this problem. With *collective incapacitation*, all offenders who have committed a similar crime are imprisoned for the same time period, whereas selective incapacitation provides longer sentences for individuals, such as career criminals, who are judged more likely to commit further crimes if and when they are released.[18] The problem with selective incapacitation, however, lies in the difficulty of predicting just who is the greatest risk to commit future crimes. Studies have shown that with even the most effective methods the predictions are correct only 47 percent of the time.[19]

INCAPACITATION
A strategy for preventing crime by detaining wrongdoers in prison, thereby separating them from the community and reducing criminal opportunities.

Much of the human carnage occurring on the nation's highways is due to drunk drivers, often repeat offenders. This accident occurred in Waukesha County in Wisconsin. Several counties in that state now order repeat drunk drivers into alcohol abuse treatment programs. In many counties, these programs are not voluntary. Such mandatory programs offer an example of the rehabilitation rationale for punishment. In counties in which such programs are voluntary, those repeat drunk drivers who choose not to participate are twice as likely to be rearrested for drunk driving. What other types of programs might fit the rehabilitation rationale for punishment?

REHABILITATION
The philosophy that society is best served when wrongdoers are not simply punished, but provided the resources needed to eliminate criminality from their behavioral pattern.

INDETERMINATE SENTENCING
An indeterminate term of incarceration in which a judge determines the minimum and maximum terms of imprisonment. When the minimum term is reached, the prisoner becomes eligible to be paroled.

Rehabilitation

The fourth, and most controversial, justification for punishment is an outgrowth of incapacitation theories. Beginning in the nineteenth century, prisons began to be seen as places where criminals would not only be incarcerated but rehabilitated as well. In 1870, the National Congress of Prisons set forth the theory of punitive rehabilitation in a Declaration of Principles that called crime "a moral disease, of which punishment is the remedy." The declaration went on to state that punishment is "directed not to the crime but to the criminal" and that the "supreme aim of prison discipline is the reformation of criminals and not the infliction of vindictive suffering."[20]

For most of the past century, **rehabilitation** has been seen as the most "humane" goal of punishment. This line of thinking reflects the view that crime is a "social phenomenon" caused not by the inherent criminality of a person, but by factors in that person's surroundings. By removing wrongdoers from their environment and intervening to change their values and personalities, the rehabilitative model suggests, criminals can be "treated" and possibly even "cured" of their proclivities toward crime.

As will become clear over the course of this chapter, the American criminal justice system is currently in the process of rejecting many of the precepts of rehabilitation in favor of "get tough" retributive, deterrent, and incapacitating sentencing strategies. It would be a mistake, however, to separate these four philosophies. For the most part, a society's overall sentencing direction is influenced by all four theories, with political and social factors determining which one is predominant at any given time.

THE STRUCTURE OF SENTENCING

Philosophy not only is integral to explaining *why* we punish criminals, but also influences *how* we do so. The history of criminal sentencing in the United States has been characterized by shifts in institutional power among the three branches of the government. When public opinion moves toward more severe strategies of retribution, deterrence, and incapacitation, *legislatures* have responded by asserting their power over determining sentencing guidelines. In contrast, periods of rehabilitative justice are marked by a transfer of this power to the *judicial* and *administrative* branches.

Legislative Sentencing Authority

Because legislatures are responsible for making law, these bodies are also initially responsible for passing the criminal codes that determine the length of sentences.

Indeterminate Sentencing. For most of the twentieth century, goals of rehabilitation dominated the criminal justice system, and legislatures were more likely to enact **indeterminate sentencing** policies. Penal codes with indeterminate sentences set a minimum and maximum amount of time that a person must spend in prison. For example, the indeterminate sentence for aggravated assault could be three to nine years, or six to twelve years, or twenty years to life. Within these parameters, a judge can prescribe a particular term, after which an administrative body known as the *parole board* decides at what point the offender is to be released. A prisoner is aware that he or she is eligible for *parole* as soon as the minimum time has been served and that good behavior can further shorten the sentence.

Determinate Sentencing. Disillusionment with the ideals of rehabilitation has led to **determinate sentencing**, or fixed sentencing. As the name implies, in determinate sentencing an offender serves exactly the amount of time to which she or he is sentenced (minus "good time," described below). For example, if the legislature deems that the punishment for a first-time armed robber is ten years, then the judge has no choice but to impose a sentence of ten years, and the criminal will serve ten years before being freed.

"Good Time" and Truth-in-Sentencing. Often, the amount of time prescribed by a judge bears little relation to the amount of time the offender actually spends behind bars. In states with indeterminate sentencing, parole boards have broad powers to release prisoners once they have served the minimum portion of their sentence. Furthermore, all but four states offer prisoners the opportunity to reduce their sentences by doing **"good time"**— or behaving well—as determined by prison administrators. (See Figure 11.2 for an idea of the effects of good time regulations and other early-release programs.)

Sentence-reduction programs promote discipline within a correctional institution and reduce overcrowding; therefore, many prison officials welcome them. The public, however, may react negatively to news that a violent criminal has served a shorter term than ordered by a judge and pressure elected officials to "do something." In Illinois, for example, some inmates were serving less than half their sentences by receiving a one-day reduction in their term for each day of "good time." Under pressure from victims' groups, the state legislature passed a **truth-in-sentencing law** that requires murderers and others convicted of serious crimes to complete at least 85 percent of their sentences with no time off for good behavior.[21] Today, forty states have instituted some form of truth-in-sentencing laws, though the future of such statutes is in doubt due to numerous challenges on constitutional grounds and the pressure of overflowing prisons.

Judicial Sentencing Authority

Determinate sentencing is a direct encroachment on the long-recognized power of judges to make the final decision on sentencing. Historically, the judge bore most of the responsibility for choosing the proper sentence within

DETERMINATE SENTENCING
A period of incarceration that is fixed by a sentencing authority and cannot be reduced by judges or other corrections officials.

"GOOD TIME"
A reduction in time served of prisoners based on good behavior, conformity to rules, and other positive actions.

TRUTH-IN-SENTENCING LAWS
Legislative attempts to assure that convicts will serve approximately the terms to which they were initially sentenced.

Most Serious Conviction Offense	Average Prison Sentence (in months)	Estimated Time in Prison (in months)	% Expected to Be Served
Murder/manslaughter	269	126	47
Rape	158	87	55
Robbery	116	53	46
Aggravated assault	79	39	49
Burglary	69	27	39
Drug trafficking	66	25	38

SOURCE: BUREAU OF JUSTICE STATISTICS, SOURCEBOOK OF CRIMINAL JUSTICE STATISTICS 1977 (WASHINGTON, DC, 1998), TABLE 5.58.

Figure 11.2 Average Sentence Length and Estimated Time to Be Served in State Prison

the guidelines set by the legislature.[22] In the twentieth century, this power was reinforced by the rehabilitative ethic. Each offender, it was believed, has a different set of problems and should, therefore, receive a sentence tailored to her or his particular circumstances. Legislators have generally accepted a judge as the most qualified person to choose the proper punishment.

Between 1880 and 1899, seven states passed indeterminate sentencing laws, and in the next dozen years, another twenty-one followed suit. By the 1960s, every state in the nation allowed its judges the freedom of operating under an indeterminate sentencing system.[23] In the 1970s, however, criticism of indeterminate sentencing began to grow. Marvin E. Frankel, a former federal district judge in New York, gained a great deal of attention when he described sentencing authority as "unchecked" and "terrifying and intolerable for a society that professes devotion to a rule of law."[24] As we shall see, the 1980s and 1990s saw numerous attempts on both the state and federal level to limit this judicial discretion.

Administrative Sentencing Authority

Parole is a condition of early release in which a prisoner is released from a correctional facility but is not freed from the legal custody and supervision of the state. Generally, after an inmate has been released on parole, he or she is supervised by a parole officer for a specified amount of time. The decision of whether or not to parole an inmate lies with a body called the parole board. Parole is a crucial aspect of the criminal justice system and will be discussed in detail in Chapter 15.

For now, it is important to understand the role rehabilitation theories play in *administrative sentencing authority*. The formation in 1910 of the U.S. Parole Commission and similar commissions in the fifty states implied that the judge, though a legal expert, was not trained to determine when an inmate had been rehabilitated. Therefore, the sentencing power should be given to experts in human behavior, who were qualified to determine whether or not a convict was fit to return to society.[25] The recent repudiation of rehabilitation principles has not spared these administrative bodies; since 1976, 14 states and the federal government have abolished traditional parole for their prisoners.[26] (See *Concept Summary—Who Has the Responsibility to Determine Sentences?*)

> During a guilty-plea colloquy, a defendant was asked by the judge if he understood all the rights he was waiving by pleading guilty. "Judge," the man responded, "the only right I'm interested in is the right sentence."
>
> —David Racher, *Philadelphia Daily News* (1990)

CONCEPT SUMMARY
Who Has the Responsibility to Determine Sentences?

Three different sentencing authorities determine the amount of time a person who has been convicted of a felony will spend in prison: legislatures, judges, and officials of the executive branch. The process through which these three groups influence the sentencing process is summarized below.

First Step: Legislators Pass Laws

Federal and state legislators are responsible for creating and updating the criminal codes that define how the law will punish those who commit crimes. Legislatures specify the terms of imprisonment in two different ways:

- By passing *indeterminate sentencing laws.* These laws designate a maximum and minimum amount of time that a person who commits a specific crime must spend in prison—one to three years, five to ten years, etc.

- By passing *determinate sentencing laws.* These laws designate a fixed amount of time that a person who commits a specific crime must spend in prison—seven years, for example, instead of five to ten.

If lawmakers feel that the other two bodies—judges and officials of the executive branch—are being too lenient in their sentencing decisions, they can pass truth-in-sentencing laws that require convicts to serve the amount of time indicated in criminal codes.

Second Step: Judges impose Sentences

Judges have the authority to choose among the sentencing

INDIVIDUALIZED JUSTICE AND THE JUDGE

During the pretrial procedures and the trial itself, the judge's role is somewhat passive and reactive. She or he is a primarily a "procedural watchdog," assuring that the rights of the defendant are not infringed upon while the prosecutor and defense attorney dictate the course of action.

At a traditional sentencing hearing, however, the judge is no longer an arbiter between parties; she or he is now called upon to exercise the ultimate authority of the state in determining the defendant's fate.

From the 1930s to the 1970s, when theories of rehabilitation held sway over the criminal justice system, indeterminate sentencing practices were guided by the theory of "individualized justice." Just as a physician gives specific treatment to individual patients depending on their particular health needs, the hypothesis goes, a judge needs to consider the specific circumstances of each individual offender in choosing the best form of punishment. Taking the analogy one step further, just as the diagnosis of a qualified physician should not be questioned, a qualified judge should have absolute discretion in making the sentencing decision. *Judicial discretion* rests on the assumption that a judge should be given ample leeway in determining punishments that fit both the crime and the criminal.[27] As we shall see later in the chapter, the growth of determinate sentencing has severely restricted judicial discretion in many jurisdictions.

Forms of Punishment

Within whatever legislative restrictions apply, the sentencing judge has a number of options when it comes to choosing the proper form of punishment. These sentences, or *dispositions*, include:

1. *Capital punishment.* Reserved normally for those who commit first degree murder under aggravated circumstances, capital punishment, or the death penalty, is a sentencing option in thirty-eight states and in federal courts.

2. *Imprisonment.* Whether for the purpose of retribution, deterrence, incapacitation, or rehabilitation, a common form of punishment in American history has been imprisonment. In fact, it is currently so

This is a photo of Luis Felipe, who was sentenced to life in solitary confinement by federal Judge John S. Martin, Jr., in the fall of 1997. Such individualized justice was based on Felipe's role as founder of the New York chapter of the Almighty Latin Kings and Queens Nation. Felipe, already in jail, had ordered murders by writing to his lieutenants on the outside. Judge Martin even forbade Felipe to be visited by anyone except his lawyers and close relatives. Because Felipe has no close relatives, only his lawyers can visit. What legal arguments might Felipe's lawyers use to appeal his harsh sentence?

PRESENTENCE INVESTIGATIVE REPORT
An investigative report on an offender's background that assists a judge in determining the proper sentence.

common that judges—and legislators—are having to take factors such as prison overcrowding into consideration when making sentencing decisions. The issues surrounding imprisonment will be discussed in Chapters 13 and 14.

3. *Probation.* One of the effects of prison overcrowding has been a sharp rise in the use of probation, in which an offender is permitted to live in the community under supervision and is not incarcerated. Probation is covered in Chapter 12. *Alternative sanctions* (also discussed in Chapter 12) combine probation with other dispositions such as electronic monitoring, house arrests, boot camps, and shock incarceration.

4. *Fines.* Fines can be levied by judges in addition to incarceration and probation or independently of other forms of punishment. When a fine is the full extent of the punishment, it usually reflects the judge's belief that the offender is not a threat to the community and does not need to be imprisoned or supervised. In some instances, mostly involving drug offenders, a judge can order the seizure of an offender's property, such as his or her home.

5. *Restitution and community service.* Whereas fines are payable to the government, restitution and community service are seen as reparations to the injured party. *Restitution* is a direct payment to the victim or victims of a crime; community service consists of "good works"—such as cleaning up highway litter or tutoring disadvantaged youths—that benefit the entire community.

In some jurisdictions, judges have a great deal of discretionary power and can impose sentences that do not fall into any of these categories (see *CJ in Focus—Making Waves: The Shaming Judge*). In Illinois, for example, Kane County Judge Donald Hudson agreed to a convicted child molester's request to undergo surgical castration in penance for his crime.[28] Though a number of state legislatures are considering making this punishment mandatory for certain sex offenders, it is still considered cruel and unusual punishment in most jurisdictions.

The Sentencing Process

The decision of how to punish a wrongdoer is the end result of what Yale Law School Professor Kate Stith and U.S. Court of Appeals Judge José A. Cabranes call the "sentencing ritual."[29] The two main participants in this ritual are the judge and the defendant, but prosecutors, defense attorneys, and probation officers also play a role in the proceedings. Individualized justice requires that the judge consider all the relevant circumstances in his or her sentencing decisions. Therefore, judicial discretion is often tantamount to *informed* discretion—without the aid of the other members of the courtroom work group, the judge would not have sufficient information to make the proper sentencing choice.

The Presentence Investigative Report. For judges operating under various states' indeterminate sentencing guidelines, information in the **presentence investigative report** is a valuable component of the sentencing ritual. Compiled by a probation officer, the report describes the crime in question, notes the suffering of any victims, and lists the defendant's prior offenses (as well as any alleged but uncharged criminal activity). The report also contains a range of personal data such as family background, work history, education, and com-

CJ in Focus
Making Waves
The Shaming Judge

In colonial times, shame played a large role in punishment. A baker who cheated customers would be placed in the pillory with dough piled on his head; a first-time thief was "burnt in the hand with the letter T," while repeat offenders had an "R" branded on their forehead. Such tactics largely disappeared from the criminal justice system until recently, when high numbers of repeat offenders have driven some judges to search for alternative sentencing measures. Led by Judge Ted Poe of Houston, Texas, shame has made a comeback.

"Most people care what others think of them," explains Poe, "and if they are embarrassed publicly, they probably won't do the crime again." In one case, Poe ordered a man found guilty of interfering with child custody to spend 600 hours shoveling manure from the police department's stables; in another case the judge required a music teacher convicted of molesting two of his students to give away his $16,000 piano, refrain from playing any piano for twenty years, and post a sign on his front door warning anybody under eighteen years old of his crime. Poe has also sentenced wife-beaters to apologize to their spouses in front of women's groups.

The judge believes that shame sentences work. After Poe ordered a man to stand outside a store from which he had shoplifted wearing a sign that listed the items he had stolen, incidents of shoplifting in the area dropped sharply. Of the past fifty-nine humiliation sentences he has passed down, Poe notes that only two of the offenders have been rearrested. Other judges are starting to follow Poe's lead: the idea of shame has become particularly popular in dealing with persons who solicit prostitutes. Some cities are even posting photos of these "johns" on special Internet sites.

For Critical Analysis: Some states have expressly prohibited sentences devised to shame offenders. Is there anything "cruel and unusual" about this form of punishment? Are there any other reasons that such sentences might be ineffective?

---

munity activities, information that is not admissible as evidence during trial. In putting together the presentence investigative report, the probation officer is supposed to gain a "feel" for the defendant and communicate these impressions of the offender to the judge.[30]

The report also includes a sentencing recommendation. In the past, this aspect has been criticized as giving probation officers too much power in the sentencing process, because lazy judges would simply rely on the recommendation in determining punishment.[31] Consequently, as we shall see, many jurisdictions have moved to limit the influence of the presentence investigative report.

The Prosecutor and Defense Attorney. To a certain extent, the adversary process does not end when the guilt of the defendant has been established. Both the prosecutor and the defense attorney are interviewed in the process of preparing the presentence investigative report, and both will try to present a version of the facts consistent with their own sentencing goals. The defense attorney in particular has a duty to make sure that the information contained in the report is accurate and not prejudicial toward his or her client. Depending on the norms of any particular courtroom work group, prosecutors and defense attorneys may petition the judge directly for certain sentences. Note that this process is not always adversarial. As we saw in Chapter 9, in some instances the prosecutor will advocate leniency and may join the defense attorney in requesting a short term of imprisonment, probation, or some form of intermediate sanction.[32]

Factors of Sentencing

The sentencing ritual strongly lends itself to the concept of individualized justice.[33] With inputs—sometimes conflicting—from the prosecutor, attorney, and probation officer, the judge can be reasonably sure of getting the

Figure 11.3 Average Sentences for Selected Crimes

Crime	Average Sentence (in months)	Median Sentence (in months)
Murder	263	300
Rape	159	120
Robbery	114	84
Aggravated assault	78	49
Burglary	69	60
Larceny	43	36
Drug trafficking	65	48

SOURCE: U.S. DEPARTMENT OF JUSTICE, BUREAU OF JUSTICE STATISTICS, STATE COURT SENTENCING OF CONVICTED FELONS, 1994, NCJ-164614 (WASHINGTON, D.C.: U.S. DEPARTMENT OF JUSTICE, 1998), 48–49.

"REAL OFFENSE"
The actual offense committed, as opposed to the charge levied by a prosecutor as the result of a plea bargain. Judges who make sentencing decisions based on the real offense are often seen as undermining the plea bargain process.

MITIGATING CIRCUMSTANCES
Any circumstances accompanying the commission of a crime that may justify a lighter sentence.

AGGRAVATING CIRCUMSTANCES
Any circumstances accompanying the commission of a crime that may justify a harsher sentence.

SENTENCING DISPARITY
A situation in which those convicted of similar crimes do not receive similar sentences.

"full picture" of the crime and the criminal. In making the final decision, however, most judges consider two factors above all others: the seriousness of the crime and any mitigating or aggravating circumstances.

The Seriousness of the Crime. As would be expected, the seriousness of the crime is the primary factor in a judge's sentencing decisions. The more serious the crime, the harsher the punishment, for society demands no less. (See Figure 11.3.) Each judge has his or her own methods of determining the seriousness of the offense. Many judges simply consider the "conviction offense"; that is, they base their sentence on the crime for which the defendant was convicted.

Other judges—some mandated by statute—focus instead on the **"real offense"** in determining the punishment. The "real offense" is based on the actual behavior of the defendant, regardless of the official conviction. For example, through a plea bargain, a defendant may plead guilty to simple assault when in fact he hit his victim in the face with a baseball bat. A judge, after reading the presentence investigative report, could decide to sentence the defendant as if he had committed aggravated assault, which is the "real" offense. Though many prosecutors and defense attorneys are opposed to "real offense" procedures, which can render a plea bargain meaningless, there is a growing belief in criminal justice circles that they bring a measure of fairness to the sentencing decision.[34]

Mitigating and Aggravating Circumstances. In the case of Marcos Mascarenas that opened this chapter, Judge Peggy Nelson expressed frustration that she was forced to sentence the defendant to prison. Because of his lack of mental capacity, the judge felt that Mascarenas did not deserve the punishment he received. In many situations, circumstances surrounding the crime may prompt a judge to adjust a sentence so that it more accurately reflects the totality of the crime. Judge Nelson considered Mascarenas's lack of mental capacity a mitigating circumstance, and given the opportunity, she would have given him a lesser punishment. There are other **mitigating circumstances**, or those circumstances that allow a lighter sentence to be handed down. They can be defined to include a defendant's youth or the fact that the defendant was coerced into committing the crime. In contrast, **aggravating circumstances** such as a prior record, blatant disregard for safety, or the use of a weapon can lead a judge to inflict a harsher penalty than otherwise might be the case (see Figure 11.4).

Judicial Philosophy. Most states spell out mitigating and aggravating circumstances in statutes, but there is room for judicial discretion in applying the law to particular cases. Judges are not uniform, or even consistent, in their opinions concerning which circumstances are mitigating or aggravating. One judge may believe a fourteen-year-old is not fully responsible for his or her actions, while another may believe teenagers should be treated as adults. Those judges who support rehabilitative theories of criminal justice have been found to give more lenient sentences than those who are governed by goals of deterrence and incapacitation.[35] Furthermore, judges can have different philosophies with regard to different crimes, handing down, for example, harsh penalties for domestic abusers while showing leniency toward drug offenders.

Aggravating Circumstances

- An offense involved multiple participants and the offender was the leader of the group.
- A victim was particularly vulnerable.
- A victim was treated with particular cruelty for which an offender should be held responsible.
- The offense involved injury or threatened violence to others committed to gratify an offender's desire for pleasure or excitement.
- The degree of bodily harm caused, attempted, threatened, or foreseen by an offender was substantially greater than average for the given offense.
- The degree of economic harm caused, attempted, threatened, or foreseen by an offender was substantially greater than average for the given offense.
- The amount of contraband materials possessed by the offender or under the offender's control was substantially greater than average for the given offense.

Mitigating Circumstances

- An offender acted under strong provocation, or other circumstances in the relationship between the offender and the victim were extenuating.
- An offender played a minor or passive role in the offense or participated under circumstances of coercion or duress.
- An offender, because of youth or physical or mental impairment, lacked substantial capacity for judgment when the offense was committed.

SOURCE: AMERICAN BAR ASSOCIATION (1994). ABA STANDARDS FOR CRIMINAL JUSTICE SENTENCING. (WASHINGTON, D.C.: ABA.) 47, 52–53.

Figure 11.4 Aggravating and Mitigating Circumstances

INCONSISTENCIES IN SENTENCING

For some, the natural differences in judicial philosophies, when combined with a lack of institutional control, raise important questions. Why should a bank robber in South Carolina receive a different sentence than a bank robber in Michigan? Even federal indeterminate sentencing guidelines seem overly vague: a bank robber can receive a prison term from one day to twenty years, depending almost entirely on the judge.[36] Furthermore, if judges have freedom to use their discretion, do they not also have the freedom to misuse it?

Purported improper judicial discretion is often the first reason given for two phenomena that plague the criminal justice system: sentencing disparity and sentencing discrimination. Though the two terms are often used interchangeably, they describe different statistical occurrences—the causes of which are debatable.

Sentencing Disparity

Justice would seem to demand that those who commit similar crimes should receive similar punishments. **Sentencing disparity** occurs when this expectation is not met in one of three ways:

1. Criminals receive similar sentences for different crimes of unequal seriousness.

2. Criminals receive different sentences for similar crimes.

3. Mitigating or aggravating circumstances have a disproportionate effect on sentences. Prosecutors, for example, reward drug dealers who inform on their associates with lesser sentences. As a result, low-level drug sellers, who have no information to trade for reduced sentences, often spend more time in prison than their better-informed employers.[37]

A number of different explanations have been offered to explain sentencing disparity. Two of these involve geography and courtroom norms.

This police photograph shows Brian Stewart, who was charged with injecting his son with blood infected with the AIDS virus because Stewart allegedly wanted to avoid paying child support. To make the punishment fit the crime, Circuit Judge Ellsworth Cundiff on January 8, 1999, imposed the maximum sentence that he could: life in prison. The judge then told Stewart that such a sentence was "far too lenient." Will Stewart necessarily spend his entire life behind bars?

Multiple Choice Question 30

Geographical Disparities. For wrongdoers, the amount of time spent in prison often depends as much on where the crime was committed as on the crime itself. A study of the lengths of sentences for robbery revealed that whereas the national average was 120 months of incarceration, a robber in the Northern District of Texas faced 220 months in prison, while a similar offender in the Central District of California could expect 96 months.[38] As Figure 11.5 shows, the South is characterized by longer prison terms than other regions of the United States. Such disparities can be attributed to a number of different factors, including local attitudes toward crime and available financial resources to cover the expenses of incarceration. Geographical disparities between urban and rural areas are also evident; urban courts are more likely to make use of probation and issue shorter sentences than those in rural jurisdictions.[39] Even within a single state with uniform laws, the differences between counties can be striking. Georgia provides numerous examples:

- Cocaine dealers sentenced in Henry and Butts Counties receive an average sentence of nearly eighteen years, while their counterparts in Fulton, DeKalb, Douglas, and Clayton Counties usually get six years or less.

- Aggravated assault in Rockdale or Paulding County leads to an average prison term of six years or less, about half the typical 11.3-year sentence in the Augusta Judicial Circuit.

- Child molestation in Americas County draws only a third of the prison time in Tifton, part of an adjacent judicial circuit.[40]

Offenders can take advantage of these inconsistencies. When John Harris, an Atlanta-based office manager, was charged with embezzlement, he learned that four different counties could claim jurisdiction for his crime. Harris chose to plead guilty in DeKalb County, where he was given probation and ordered to pay $200,000 restitution. In the nearby Griffin Judicial Circuit, Harris likely would have been sentenced to prison for up to ten years.[41]

Courthouse Norms. The norms established by individual courtroom work groups can also lead to sentencing disparities. Since the 1930s, scholars have been producing studies that point to different sentencing tendencies of different judges for similar crimes.[42] A Department of Justice survey concluded that more than 20 percent of sentencing disparities can be directly attributed to the propensity of a particular judge to give harsh or lenient sentences.[43]

Sentencing Discrimination

Sentencing discrimination occurs when disparities can be attributed to extralegal variables such as the defendant's gender, race, or economic standing. At first glance, racial discrimination would seem to be rampant in sentencing practices. In 1998, nearly half of all inmates in state and federal prisons in the United States were African American, even though that minority group makes up only 13 percent of the country's population.[44] We will discuss the ramifications of these statistics, as well as other issues of race and gender in sentencing, in Chapter 18.

Figure 11.5 Regional Sentencing Differences

Crime	Mean Prison Sentence South (in months)	Mean Prison Sentence Outside South (in months)
Rape	183	142
Robbery	130	96
Burglary	84	53

SOURCE: JODI M. BROWN AND PATRICK A LANGAN, BUREAU OF JUSTICE STATISTICS (1998) STATES COURT SENTENCING OF CONVICTED FELONS, 1994. WASHINGTON, D.C.: U.S. DEPT. OF JUSTICE, 56-57. TABLES 5.2 AND 5.3.

SENTENCING DISCRIMINATION A situation in which the length of a sentence appears to be influenced by a defendant's race, gender, economic status, or other factor not directly related to the crime he or she committed.

SENTENCING REFORM

Judicial discretion, then, appears to be a double-edged sword. Although it allows judges to impose a wide variety of sentences to fit specific criminal situations, it appears to fail to rein in a judge's subjective biases, which leads to disparity and perhaps discrimination. Critics of judicial discretion believe that its costs (the lack of equality) outweigh its benefits (providing individualized justice). As Columbia law professor John C. Coffee noted:

> If we wish the sentencing judge to treat "like cases alike," a more inappropriate technique for the presentation could hardly be found than one that stresses a novelistic portrayal of each offender and thereby overloads the decisionmaker in a welter of detail.[45]

In other words, Professor Coffee feels that judges are given *too much* information in the sentencing process, making it impossible for them to be consistent in their decisions. It follows that limiting judicial discretion would not only simplify the process but lessen the opportunity for disparity or discrimination. Since the 1970s, this attitude has spread through state and federal legislatures, causing more extensive changes in sentencing procedures than in any other area of the American criminal justice system over that time period.

Beginnings of Reform

Research efforts in the mid-1970s laid the groundwork for sentencing reform. Particularly influential was the Twentieth Century Fund report developed by a task force of twelve criminal justice experts. The task force introduced the idea of **presumptive sentencing.** Revising ideas of determinate sentencing, the report urged lawmakers to legislate sentences that were "presumed" to be fair for any given crime category, restricting the court's discretion to finding aggravating or mitigating circumstances.[46]

Around the same time, Dr. Robert Martinson and several colleagues released an exhaustive study that seemed to prove that efforts to rehabilitate prisoners were generally unsuccessful.[47] Politicians on both sides seized on Martinson's report as an excuse to reject the idea of rehabilitating criminals and reestablish the ideals of determinate sentencing. Conservatives, believing judges, on the whole, to be too lenient, wished to limit their discretionary powers. Liberals—led by Senator Edward Kennedy (D-Mass.), who called sentencing a "national scandal" that leads to "massive injustice"[48]—felt the only way to eliminate the evils of sentencing disparity was to remove judicial bias from the process. Supported by a public alarmed by dramatic increases in violent crime, politicians moved sharply away from the notion of "treating" prisoners toward the goal of punishing them.

Sentencing Guidelines

As the rehabilitative model came under criticism, so did its manifestations; indeterminate sentencing discretion, parole, probation, and "good-time" credit became scapegoats for a failed system.[49] In an effort to reinstate determinacy into the sentencing process, many states and the federal government turned to **sentencing guidelines,** which require judges to dispense legislatively determined sentences based on factors such as the seriousness of the crime and the offender's prior record.

Daniel Leroy Crocker is shown here at his sentencing at the Johnson County Court House in Olathe, Kansas. Crocker had confessed to smothering 19-year-old Tracy Fesquez in 1979 after sexually assaulting the sleeping woman. Crocker was sentenced in January 1999 to only 20 years in prison, and will be eligible for parole in just ten years. This lenient sentence was based on the fact that he was never a suspect in the case. Rather, he eventually admitted to the murder, based on his religious faith. Three members of the victim's family urged in court that Crocker be given a life sentence.

PRESUMPTIVE SENTENCING
A sentencing strategy in which legislators set the average sentence that should be served for any particular crime, leaving judges with the ability to shorten or lengthen the sentence based on the circumstances of each case.

SENTENCING GUIDELINES
Legislatively determined guidelines that judges are required to follow when sentencing those convicted of specific crimes. These guidelines limit judicial discretion.

State Sentencing Guidelines. In 1978, Minnesota became the first state to create a Sentencing Guidelines Commission with a mandate to construct and monitor the use of a determinate sentencing structure. The Minnesota Commission left no doubt as to the philosophical justification for the new sentencing statutes, stating unconditionally that retribution was its primary goal.[50] Today, seventeen states employ some form of sentencing guidelines with similar goals.

In general, these guidelines remove discretionary power from state judges by turning sentencing into a mathematical exercise. Members of the courtroom work group are guided by a *grid,* which helps them determine the proper sentence. Figure 11.6 shows the grid established by the Oregon Sentencing Commission. As with the grids used by most states, one axis ranks the type of crime, while the other refers to the offender's criminal history. In Oregon, each of roughly fifty felonies is ranked in seriousness for use with the grid.

For example, Burglary I is assigned a crime seriousness level of 9 if it involves the use of a deadly weapon, level 8 if the dwelling was occupied at the time of the crime, and so on. The state's crime history grid ranks the offender based on prior felonies and misdemeanors, with various points accrued on the basis of the seriousness of the prior crime. Of the ninety-nine cells in Oregon's grid, fifty-three "presume" prison terms and forty-six "presume" probationary sentences. The judge cannot deviate from these guidelines except under certain circumstances, which we will explore shortly.

Go to
www.ussc.gov/general.htm
to find out information about the U.S.
Sentencing Commission.

Federal Sentencing Guidelines. In 1984, Congress passed the Sentencing Reform Act (SRA),[51] paving the way for federal sentencing guidelines that went into effect in 1987. Similar in many respects to the state guidelines, the SRA also eliminated parole for federal prisoners and severely limited early release from prison due to good behavior.[52] Furthermore, the act changed the sentencing role of U.S. probation officers. No longer would they be allowed to "suggest" the terms of punishment in presentence investigative reports. Instead, they are simply called upon to calculate the presumptive sentence based on the federal sentencing guidelines grid.[53]

Judicial Departures. Even in their haste to limit a judge's power, legislators realized that sentencing guidelines could not be expected to cover every possible criminal situation. Therefore, both state and federal sentencing guidelines allow an "escape hatch" of limited judicial discretion known as a **departure.** The SRA has a proviso that a judge may "depart" from the presumptive sentencing range if there are aggravating or mitigating circumstances present that are not adequately covered in the guidelines. For example, suppose two men are involved in the robbery of a liquor store, and during court proceedings it becomes clear that one of them forced his partner to take part in the crime by threatening physical harm. In this case, a federal judge could reduce the accomplice's sentence because he committed the crime under "duress," a factor that is not accounted for in the sentencing guidelines.[54]

Judges do not, however, have unlimited access to departures. Any such decision must be justified in writing, and both the prosecution and the defense may appeal a judicial departure. In 1989, the Court of Appeals for the First Circuit ruled that departures must be measured on the basis of the circumstances and facts of the case and the reasonableness of the judge's decision.[55] (See *CJ in Focus: Was Justice Served?—The "Good" Defendant* on page 392.)

DEPARTURE
A stipulation in many federal and state sentencing guidelines that allows a judge to adjust his or her sentencing decision based on the special circumstances of particular cases.

Figure 11.6
Oregon's Sentencing Guidelines

Post-Prison Supervision			Multiple (3+) felony person offender	Repeat (2) felony person offender	Single (1) felony person with felony non-person offender	Single (1) felony person offender	Multiple (4+) felony non-person offender	Repeat (2-3) felony non-person offender	Significant minor criminal record	Minor criminal record	Minor misdemeanor or no criminal record	Probation Term
			A	B	C	D	E	F	G	H	I	
3 years	Murder	11	225–269	196–224	178–194	149–177	149–177	135–148	129–134	122–128	120–121	5 years
	Manslaughter I, Assault I, Rape I, Arson I	10	121–130	116–120	111–115	91–110	81–90	71–80	66–70	61–65	58–60	
	Rape I, Assault I, Kidnapping II, Arson I, Burglary I, Robbery I	9	66–72	61–65	56–60	51–55	46–50	41–45	39–40	37–38	34–36	
	Manslaughter II, Sexual Abuse I, Assault II, Rape II, Using Child in Display of Sexual Conduct, Drugs-Minors, Cult/Mftr/Delivery, Compelling Prostitution, Negligent Homicide	8	41–45	35–40	29–34	27–28	25–26	23–24	21–22	19–20	16–18	Opt probation
	Extortion, Coercion, Supplying Contraband, Escape I	7	31–36	25–30	21–24	19–20	16–18	180 90	180 90	180 90	180 90	3 years
2 years	Robbery II, Assault III, Rape III, Bribe Receiving, Intimidation, Property Crimes (more than $50,000), Drug Possession	6	25–30	19–24	15–18	13–14	10–12	180 90	180 90	180 90	180 90	
	Robbery II, Theft by Receiving, Trafficking Stolen Vehicles, Property Crimes ($10,000–$49,999)	5	15–16	13–14	11–12	9–10	6–8	180 90	120 60	120 60	120 60	2 years
	FTA I, Custodial Interference II, Property Crimes ($5,000–$9,999), Drugs-Cult/Mftr/Delivery	4	10 10	8–9	120 60	120 60	120 60	120 60	120 60	120 60	120 60	
1 year	Abandon Child, Abuse of Corpse, Criminal Nonsupport, Property Crimes, ($1,000–$4,999)	3	120 60	120 60	120 60	120 60	120 60	120 60	90 30	90 30	90 30	
	Dealing Child Pornography, Violation of Wildlife Laws, Welfare Fraud, Property Crimes (less than $1,000)	2	90 30	90 30	90 30	90 30	90 30	90 30	90 30	90 30	90 30	18 mos.
	Altering Research, Habitual Offender Violation, Bigamy, Paramilitary Activity, Drugs–Possession	1	90 30	90 30	90 30	90 30	90 30	90 30	90 30	90 30	90 30	

Column headers (top, left to right):
- Three or more person felonies
- Two person felonies, adult or juvenile
- One person felony, plus one or more adult or juvenile non-person felony
- One adult or juvenile person felony and no other felony
- Four or more adult non-person felonies
- Two or three adult non-person felonies
- 4 or more adult A misdo's, or 1 adult non-person felony, or 3 or more juvenile non-person felonies
- No more than 3 adult A misdo's, or no more than 2 juvenile non-person felonies
- No juvenile felony or adult A misdemeanors

• In green blocks, numbers are presumptive prison sentences expressed as a range of months.

• In blue blocks, upper number is the maximum number of custody units which may be imposed; lower number is the maximum number of jail days which may be imposed.

SOURCE: BUREAU OF JUSTICE STATISTICS, SOURCEBOOK OF CRIMINAL JUSTICE STATISTICS 1997 (WASHINGTON D.C., 1998), TABLE 5.58.

CJ in Focus

Was Justice Served?

The "Good" Defendant

When twenty-three-year-old law school student Angela Freitag attended the rehearsal dinner for a friend's wedding, she did what most people do on these occasions: she took part in a series of toasts. Driving back to her home in Seattle, Washington, early that morning in an uninsured Porsche, Freitag ran a red light and collided with another vehicle. The occupant of the other car suffered a broken neck. Freitag, who had a blood alcohol level of 0.16 percent (the legal limit was 0.10 percent at the time, and has since been lowered to .08 percent), pleaded guilty to a charge of vehicular assault.

THE ONE-DAY SENTENCE

According to the dictates of Washington State's Sentencing Reform Act (SRA), vehicular assault is considered a "violent offense" and categorized as a "most serious" Level IV felony. Under the SRA presumptive sentencing guidelines, Freitag, who had no prior offenses, could be sen-

tenced to between three and nine months in jail. The trial court chose the low end of the spectrum for Freitag's sentence—90 days incarceration and restitution—and then converted 89 of those days to community service, leaving the defendant with a one-day jail term.

Under the SRA, jail time cannot be converted to community service in sentences for "violent" crimes. The trial court, however, cited "substantial and compelling" reasons to supersede the law, including the defendant's lack of prior record, her history of charitable work, a sincere sense of regret, and a family background that made it unlikely she would commit any further crimes. The state appellate court agreed, determining that because of the defendant's family background, her charity work, and her great remorse, Freitag indeed deserved a lighter sentence than other offenders guilty of the same crime.

For Critical Analysis: What problems arise when a court bases its sentences on subjective factors?

INFOTRAC®
COLLEGE EDITION

A New "Sliding Scale of Deference" Approach to Abuse of Discretion

Sentencing Guidelines Examined. Although guidelines have diminished the ability of judges to use unbridled discretion in their sentencing decisions, ample evidence shows that the guidelines have not eliminated disparities to the extent that reformers may have hoped. According to the U.S. Sentencing Commission, a decade after passage of the SRA, a person convicted in Arizona was twenty times more likely to have his or her sentence reduced by a federal judge than a person convicted of the same crime in the Western District of Oklahoma. By the same token, a person convicted in Southern Georgia was ten times more likely to receive a harsher penalty than the guidelines suggest than a person convicted in twenty-four other federal districts.[56] The results have been similar with regard to racial disparities in sentencing: one study found that African Americans received 28 percent higher sentences for similar crimes than whites in federal courts.[57]

Observers say that these continuing disparities reflect a lack of willingness among judges to accept the guidelines' restrictions. Not only can judges use departure to circumvent the guidelines, they can also engage in "hidden" plea bargaining by allowing defendants to plead to lesser charges that the judge (and the prosecutor) believe to be more fair. As a number of Supreme Court cases—most recently, *Koon v. United States* (1996)[58]—have given judges even more leeway in departing from federal and state sentencing guidelines, this trend will probably continue.

Mandatory Sentencing Guidelines

In response, politicians (urged on by their constituents) have passed sentencing laws even more contrary to the idea of individualized justice. These **mandatory** (minimum) **sentencing guidelines** further limit a judge's power to deviate from determinate sentencing laws by setting firm standards for certain crimes. Forty-six states have mandatory sentencing laws for crimes such as selling drugs, driving under the influence of alcohol, and committing any crime with a dangerous weapon. In Alabama, for example, any person

MANDATORY SENTENCING GUIDELINES
Statutorily determined punishments that must be applied to those who are convicted of specific crimes.

caught selling drugs must spend at least two years in prison, with five years added to the sentence if the sale takes place within three miles of a school or housing project.[59] Similarly, Congress has set mandatory minimum sentences for more than one hundred crimes, mostly drug offenses.

Habitual Offender Laws. **Habitual offender laws** are a form of mandatory sentencing that have proved increasingly popular over the past decade. Also known as "three strikes and you're out" laws, these statutes require that any person convicted of a third felony must serve a lengthy prison sentence. The crime does not have to be of a violent or dangerous nature. Under Washington's habitual offender law, for example, a "persistent offender" is automatically sentenced to life if the third felony offense happens to be "vehicular assault" (a automobile accident that causes injury), unarmed robbery, or attempted arson, among other lesser felonies.[60] Today, twenty-two states and the federal government employ "three strikes" statutes, with varying degrees of severity.

The Supreme Court paved the way for these "three strikes" laws when it ruled in *Rummel v. Estelle* (1980)[61] that Texas's habitual offender statute did not constitute "cruel and unusual punishment." Basically, the Court gave each state the freedom to legislate such laws in the manner that it deems proper. This had led to some "fine-tuning" of state statutes. California, for example, had a strict "three strikes" law that in its first two years saw more than 15,000 felony offenders receive sentences of between twenty-five years and life. Eighty percent of the criminals sentenced under this law had committed nonviolent crimes such as drug use and petty thievery.[62] In one celebrated case, Jerry Dewayne Williams was sentenced to twenty-five years in state prison for committing his third crime, which happened to be stealing a slice of pizza. In *People v. Superior Court (Romero)* (1996),[63] the California Supreme Court changed the law to allow judges to use discretion in its application. (After this decision, Williams's sentence was reduced to four years.)

Mandatory Sentences Examined. Mandatory sentences are quite popular with the public. One national poll found that more than eight out of ten Americans supported life sentences for three-time convicted felons.[64] Furthermore, the laws do appear to have the desired result. According to the Justice Department, the average time served in state prisons by violent prisoners rose from forty-three months in 1993 to forty-nine months in 1997.[65]

Criminologists point out, however, that such laws may not ultimately have the effect that politicians promise and citizens expect. When prisons reach their capacities, legislatures, judges, and parole officers must find a way to free up space. Because felons imprisoned under mandatory sentences—the majority of whom are nonviolent drug offenders—cannot be released, administrators are forced to place *violent* offenders, who have committed crimes that do not carry mandatory sentences, back on the streets.[66] Furthermore, because African Americans and Hispanic Americans are more likely to be arrested on drug charges, the mandatory sentences contribute greatly to the higher proportion of minorities in prison, in direct contrast to the antidiscrimination aims of some sentencing reformers.[67]

Opposition to Determinate Sentencing

Just as indeterminate sentencing produced outrageous examples of judicial discretion, so determinate sentencing has given its opponents fodder for criticism. Examples of mandatory sentencing "gone wild" usually involve situations such as the one in which a teenager was sentenced to life in prison for

HABITUAL OFFENDER LAWS
Statutes that require lengthy prison sentences for those who are convicted of multiple felonies.

"Those who repeatedly assault our citizens, terrorize our elderly, and prey upon our children must pay a severe price."

—former California Governor Pete Wilson (1996)

The Sentencing Project has news publications and a search engine. Go to: **www.sentencingproject.org/**

stealing a cell phone.[68] Determinate sentencing, complained one observer, has "shown that there are things worse than disparity: rigidity, extreme severity, irrationality."[69] Among the staunchest opponents of the new sentencing measures have been members of the courtroom work group, who have seen the laws transform their well-established procedural norms.

Judges and Determinate Sentencing. As might be expected, judges, for the most part, have not welcomed the reduction in their discretionary powers. University of Minnesota law professor Michael Tonry has written that sentencing guidelines are the most "disliked sentencing reform initiative in the history of the United States" among judges.[70] U.S. District Judge Vincent Broderick exhorted his colleagues to "Depart! Depart! Depart!" to circumnavigate the guideline restrictions.[71] According to a study conducted by researchers Michael S. Gelacak, Ilene H. Nagel, and Barry L. Johnson, federal jurists have responded to Broderick's call. Of the thirty U.S. district courts Gelacak, Nagel, and Johnson examined over a two-year period, twenty-four were characterized as deviating from federal sentencing guidelines to a significant degree. Furthermore, the researchers found that in many of the cases in which judges departed, they did so because they disagreed with the sentences required by the guidelines, not because the guidelines failed to cover the circumstances of the case.[72]

A Transfer of Power. Despite these efforts, determinate sentencing has led to a transfer of power in the sentencing process from the judge to another member of the courtroom work group. Prosecutors can evade mandatory minimums by plea bargaining or charging offenders with lesser crimes than the "real offense." If a person with a limited criminal history commits aggravated robbery, for example, and the prosecutor decides to charge him or her with simple robbery, the prosecutor has effectively reduced the offender's presumptive prison sentence. Evidence from Minnesota shows that nearly half of all defendants with no prior record who had been alleged to commit aggravated robbery were convicted of charges that did not carry presumptive prison terms.[73] Federal law also allows prosecutors to request sentences below the mandatory minimum for defendants who have cooperated by giving evidence against other wrongdoers.[74]

A California prison requires that male inmates sleep on bunk beds and on the floor, because of overcrowding. This current overcrowding is due in part to California's three strikes and you're out law, under which a trial judge must treat a defendant's third offense, even if a petty crime, as if it were a felony for purposes of applying the law's mandatory sentencing provisions. In January 1999, the United States Supreme Court rejected a challenge to California's three strikes law by Michael Riggs, who was sentenced to 25 years to life in prison after stealing a bottle of vitamins from a grocery store. How do states, in response, deal with the prison overcrowding issue?

Sentencing Reform and Prison Overcrowding

While passing "get tough" sentencing legislation, many lawmakers seemed to forget, or conveniently ignore, a predictable result: increased prison populations. As we will see in Chapter 13, the number of convictions in federal courts and, consequently, the number of inmates in federal prisons rose dramatically after the Sentencing Reform Act went into effect. After establishing sentencing guidelines in 1983, Florida experienced an equally dramatic rise that forced the state to abolish its guidelines fifteen years later. States such as Michigan, Minnesota, and North Carolina have addressed this problem by taking prison capacity into consideration as part of their sentencing guidelines. In North Carolina, for instance, the state's guidelines are tied into a computer simulation model that calculates the number of prison cells that will be needed. Before any new crime legislation can be enacted, the computer program must determine whether existing prison budgets and available space are sufficient to handle the influx of prisoners.[75]

CAPITAL PUNISHMENT— THE ULTIMATE SENTENCE

"You do not know how hard it is to let a human being die," Abraham Lincoln (1809–1865) once said, "when you feel that a stroke of your pen will save him." Despite these misgivings, during his four years in office Lincoln approved the execution of 267 soldiers, including those who had slept at their post.[76] Our sixteenth president's ambivalence toward **capital punishment** is reflected in America's continuing struggle to reconcile the penalty of death with the morals and values of society. Capital punishment has played a role in sentencing since the earliest days of the Republic and—having survived a brief period of abolition between 1972 and 1976—continues to enjoy public support.

Still, few topics in the criminal justice system inspire such heated debate. Death penalty opponents such as legal expert Stephen Bright wonder if "there comes a time when a society gets beyond some of the more primitive forms of punishment?"[77] They point out that two dozen countries have abolished the death penalty since 1985, and the United States is the only Western democracy that continues the practice. Critics also claim that a process whose subjects are chosen by "luck and money and race" cannot serve the interests of justice.[78] Proponents believe that the death penalty serves as the ultimate deterrent for violent criminal behavior and that the criminals who are put to death are the "worst of the worst" and deserve their fate.

Today, more than 3,000 convicts are living on "death row" in American prisons. In 1997 and 1998, 142 were executed, a number that pales in comparison to execution rates from earlier in the century, but represents a high point over the past twenty-five years (see Figure 11.7). As legislators pass laws that increase the circumstances under which death can be sentenced, and prosecutors become more aggressive in seeking the harshest penalty, capital punishment appears likely to play a larger role in the sentencing process in the

CAPITAL PUNISHMENT
The use of the death penalty to punish wrongdoers for certain crimes.

Sentencing Guidelines and Prison Population Growth

Figure 11.7 Executions in the United States, 1930 to Present

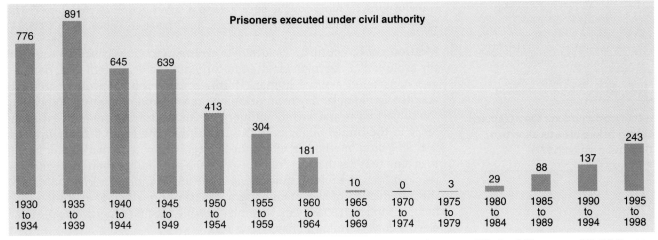

SOURCE: U.S. DEPARTMENT OF JUSTICE, BUREAU OF JUSTICE STATISTICS, CORRECTIONAL POPULATIONS IN THE UNITED STATES, 1995, NCJ-163916 (WASHINGTON, D.C.: U.S. DEPARTMENT OF JUSTICE, 1997).

future. Thus, the questions that surround the death penalty—Is it fair? Is it humane? Does it deter crime?—will continue to inflame both its supporters and its detractors.

The American Tradition of Capital Punishment

"Before there were prisons" in the American tradition, points out social psychologist Mark Costanzo, "there was the penalty of death."[79] Indeed, traces of capital punishment are as old as written law itself. The Code of Hammurabi (see Chapter 3) provides for the death sentence for the fraudulent sale of beer, among other crimes, and the Bible marks twenty-five separate crimes, from fornication to murder, as punishable by death. The first person executed by an American colonial government—taking its cue from the homeland of England, where capital punishment was widespread—was George Kendall, who was placed before a firing squad in Virginia for spying for Spain.[80] Since Kendall, more than 18,000 Americans have been legally executed as punishment for crimes.

Capital Punishment in the Seventeenth and Eighteenth Centuries. In studying capital punishment in the colonies and the early days of the United States, one is struck by two aspects of the practice: the variety of crimes that were punished by death, and the public execution of the sentence. During the 1600s, colonists were put to death for the crime of murder, but also for witchcraft, blasphemy, sodomy, and adultery. In the 1700s, citizens were executed for robbery, forgery, and illegally cutting down a tree.[81] These executions by hanging, beheading, or firing squad regularly took place in the town square or common area and were attended by the public. In fact, by modern standards the death penalty was often carried out in an overly gruesome manner in an attempt to deter criminal behavior by members of the audience. In 1710, a Virginia court ordered the bodies of two slaves who had been hanged for inciting rebellion to be cut up and displayed in various parts of the colony to keep "other Slaves from entering into such dangerous Conspiracys."[82]

The practice of public executions continued unabated until the 1830s, when reformers instigated the first widespread movement to abolish capital punishment. Government officials in northeastern states, aware that public executions provided death penalty opponents with opportunities to protest, passed a number of laws limiting the number of witnesses at an execution and requiring law enforcement officers to set up enclosures for the event. Furthermore, a desire to "civilize" the execution process moved it indoors, transforming it from a public spectacle to a sober action of the state.[83] The last public execution in the United States took place in Kentucky in 1936.

Methods of Execution. The desire to civilize executions can also be seen in the evolution of the methods used to carry out the death sentence. Hanging was considered a more humane form of execution than other methods adopted from England, which including drawing and quartering and boiling the subject alive, and was the primary means of carrying out the death sentence in the United States until the end of the nineteenth century. (Indeed, the "long drop" method, in which the subject was hung from a greater height to ensure that death came from breaking the neck rather than strangulation, resulted from the reform movement in the 1830s and 1840s.) The 1890s saw the introduction of electrocution as a less painful method of execution than hanging, and in 1890 William Kemmler became the first American to die in an electric chair in Auburn Prison, New York.

"Let's do it ."

—convicted murderer Gary Gilmore shortly before his execution by a Utah firing squad (1977)

Even though Nevada introduced lethal gas as an even more humane method of capital punishment in 1924, the "chair" remained the primary form of execution until the 1980s. In 1982, Texas became the first state to use lethal injection, and today this method dominates executions in the United States.[84] In this process, the condemned convict is usually given a sedative, followed by a combination of lethal drugs administered intravenously. Lethal injection is widely recognized as causing the least amount of pain and suffering to the subject, though, as we shall see, the method is not perfect.

The Death Penalty and the Supreme Court

In 1890, William Kemmler challenged his sentence to die in New York's new electric chair (for murdering his mistress) on the grounds that electrocution infringed upon his Eighth Amendment rights against cruel and unusual punishment.[85] Kemmler's challenge is historically significant in that it did not challenge the death penalty *itself* as being cruel and unusual, but only the method by which it was carried out. Many constitutional scholars believe that the framers never questioned the necessity of capital punishment, as long as due process is followed in determining the guilt of the suspect.[86] Accordingly, the Supreme Court rejected Kemmler's challenge, stating that:

> Punishments are cruel when they involve torture or a lingering death; but the punishment of death is not cruel, within the meaning of that word as used in the Constitution. It implies there something inhuman and barbarous, something more than the mere extinguishment of life.[87]

Thus, the Court set a standard that it has followed to this day. No *method* of execution has ever been found to be unconstitutional by the Supreme Court.

Weems v. United States. For nearly eight decades following its decision regarding Kemmler, the Supreme Court was silent on the question of whether capital punishment was constitutional or not. In *Weems v. United States* (1910),[88] however, the Court did make a ruling that would significantly affect debate on the death penalty. *Weems* concerned a defendant who had been sentenced to fifteen years of hard labor, a heavy fine, and a number of other penalties for the relatively minor crime of falsifying official records. The Court overturned the sentence, ruling that the penalty was too harsh considering the nature of the offense. Ultimately, in the *Weems* decision, the Court set three important precedents concerning sentencing:

1. Cruel and unusual punishment is defined by the changing norms and standards of society and so is not based on historical interpretations.

2. Courts may decide whether a punishment is unnecessarily cruel with regard to physical pain.

3. Courts may decide whether a punishment is unnecessarily cruel with regard to psychological pain.[89]

The first hint that the "changing norms and standards of society" would lead to a reassessment of the constitutionality of capital punishment came in the Supreme Court's ruling in *Witherspoon v. Illinois* (1968).[90] The case concerned an Illinois court that had permitted a sentence of death delivered by a jury from which any person who philosophically disagreed with capital punishment had been deliberately excluded by the prosecution. The Court ruled that such "death-qualified" juries were unconstitutional.

Any hopes that *Witherspoon* signified the beginning of the end for the death penalty were disappointed three years later, when the Court ruled in

A general information center on the death penalty can be found at: www.essential.org/dpic/

If you want information on the National Association of Sentencing Advocates, go to: www.sproject.com/nasa.htm

McGautha v. California (1971)[91] that, in general, juries were constitutionally qualified to sentence a convict to death. Though many observers saw *McGautha* as the Court's final word on capital punishment, in reality it merely set the stage for the Court's landmark ruling a year later.

Furman v. Georgia. In 1971, three cases challenging the death penalty as "cruel and unusual" were brought before the Supreme Court. Again, these cases did not question the death penalty itself as cruel and unusual. Instead, they raised the argument that capital punishment was imposed arbitrarily; that is, the death penalty was unconstitutional because there were no recognizable standards under which it could or could not be imposed.

In *Furman v. Georgia* (1972),[92] the lead case, the Supreme Court issued a very complex ruling on this issue. By a 5–4 margin, the Court essentially agreed that the death penalty violated the Eighth Amendment. Only two of those in the majority (Justices Marshall and Brennan), however, were willing to state that capital punishment was blatantly unconstitutional. The other three (Justices Douglas, Stewart, and White) took the narrower view that the sentence was unconstitutional as practiced by the states. Justice Stewart was particularly eloquent on the subject, stating that the sentence of death was so arbitrary as to be comparable to "being struck by lightning."[93] (See *CJ in Focus: Landmark Cases*—Furman v. Georgia.) In its decision, therefore, the Court did not rule that the death penalty inherently violated the Eighth Amendment's protection against cruel and unusual punishment or the Fourteenth Amendment's guarantee of due process, only that it did so as practiced by the states. So, although *Furman* invalidated the death penalty for over six hundred offenders on death row at the time, it also provided the states with a window of opportunity to bring their death penalty statutes up to constitutional standards.

Gregg v. Georgia. By 1976, thirty-five states had done just that, attempting to comply with *Furman* by either making the death penalty mandatory for certain offenses or adopting elaborate procedures to ensure that standards of due process were upheld during the sentencing process. The ten states that attempted the mandatory route found their statutes invalidated for a second time in 1976, when, in *Woodson v. North Carolina,*[94] the Supreme Court ruled that such laws failed to allow for different circumstances in different cases.

The remaining twenty-five states adopted a different means of satisfying the questions raised in *Furman* by establishing a two-stage, or *bifurcated,* procedure for capital cases. In the first stage, a jury determines the guilt or innocence of the defendant for a crime that has statutorily been determined to be punishable by death. If the defendant is found guilty, the jury reconvenes in the second stage and considers all relevant evidence to decide whether the death sentence is in fact warranted. Therefore, even if a jury were to find the defendant guilty of a crime, such as first degree murder, that *may be* punishable by death, in the second stage it could decide that the circumstances surrounding the crime only justified a punishment of life in prison. (See *Concept Summary: The Bifurcated Death Penalty Process* on page 400.)

In *Gregg v. Georgia* (1976),[95] the Supreme Court ruled in favor of Georgia's new bifurcated process, stating that the state's legislative guidelines removed the ability of a jury to "wantonly and freakishly impose the death penalty." The Court upheld similar procedures in Texas and Florida, establishing a "road map" for all states to follow that would assure them protection from lawsuits based on Eighth Amendment grounds. On January 17, 1977, Gary Mark Gilmore became the first American executed (by Utah) under the new

CJ in Focus

Landmark Cases:

Furman v. Georgia

Three cases were brought before the Supreme Court regarding the death penalty and the assertion that racial biases inherent in the system rendered the practice "cruel and unusual." The lead case concerned William Henry Furman, who was sentenced to death for killing a man during a burglary in Savannah, Georgia. For the first time, in *Furman v. Georgia,* the Supreme Court in a 5–4 vote ruled that all existing death penalty statutes were unconstitutional under the Eighth Amendment because they were being applied arbitrarily and inconsistently.

Furman v. Georgia
United States Supreme Court
408 U.S. 238 (1972)
http://laws.findlaw.com/US/408/238.html

In the Words of the Court . . .

Mr. Justice BRENNAN, concurring

* * * *

At bottom, then, the Cruel and Unusual Punishments Clause prohibits the infliction of uncivilized and inhuman punishments. The State, even as it punishes, must treat its members with respect for their intrinsic worth as human beings. A punishment is "cruel and unusual," therefore, if it does not comport with human dignity.

* * * *

In determining whether a punishment comports with human dignity, we are aided also by a * * * principle inherent in the Clause—that the State must not arbitrarily inflict a severe punishment. This principle derives from the notion that the State does not respect human dignity when, without reason, it inflicts upon some people a severe punishment that it does not inflict upon others.* * * Although there are no exact figures available, we know that thousands of murders and rapes are committed annually in States where death is an authorized punishment for those crimes. However the rate of infliction is characterized—as "freakishly" or "spectacularly" rare, or simply as rare—it would take the purest

sophistry to deny that death is inflicted in only a minute fraction of these cases. * * * When the punishment of death is inflicted in a trivial number of the cases in which it is legally available, the conclusion is virtually inescapable that it is being inflicted arbitrarily.

Indeed, it smacks of little more than a lottery system. * * * No one has yet suggested a rational basis that could differentiate in those terms the few who die from the many who go to prison. Crimes and criminals simply do not admit of a distinction that can be drawn so finely as to explain, on that ground, the execution of such a tiny sample of those eligible. * * * In other words, our procedures are not constructed to guard against the totally capricious selection of criminals for the punishment of death.

* * * *

When an unusually severe punishment is authorized for wide-scale application but not, because of society's refusal, inflicted save in a few instances, the inference is compelling that there is a deep-seated reluctance to inflict it. Indeed, the likelihood is great that the punishment is tolerated only because of its disuse.

* * * *

Death is an unusually severe and degrading punishment; there is a strong probability that it is inflicted arbitrarily; its rejection by contemporary society is virtually total; and there is no reason to believe that it serves any penal purpose more effectively than the less severe punishment of imprisonment.

Decision: The Court held that the death penalty, as carried out by the states, was cruel and unusual punishment and therefore violated the Eighth Amendment. The Court did, however, later reinstate capital punishment in *Gregg v. Georgia,* ruling that by following certain procedures the states could satisfy Eighth Amendment requirements when sentencing a convict to be executed.

For Critical Analysis: How does the fact that the death penalty is rarely carried out lend itself to Justice Brennan's argument that it is arbitrary and therefore cruel and unusual punishment?

Note: Triple asterisks (* * *) indicate that a few words or sentences have been deleted and quadruple asterisks (* * * *) indicate that an entire paragraph (or more) has been omitted from the opinion.

laws, and today thirty-eight states and the federal government have capital punishment laws based on the guidelines established by *Gregg.*

Mitigating Circumstances. Several mitigating circumstances will prevent a defendant found guilty of first degree murder from receiving the death penalty. In 1986, the Supreme Court ruled that the execution of a mentally incompetent defendant violated the Eighth Amendment.[96] This ruling, however, has been rendered practically meaningless by a subsequent Court decision that set a standard of competence so low that few convicted murderers

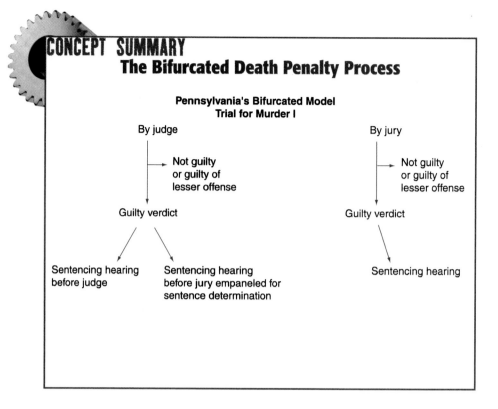

CONCEPT SUMMARY
The Bifurcated Death Penalty Process

Pennsylvania's Bifurcated Model
Trial for Murder I

By judge → Not guilty or guilty of lesser offense
Guilty verdict → Sentencing hearing before judge / Sentencing hearing before jury empaneled for sentence determination

By jury → Not guilty or guilty of lesser offense
Guilty verdict → Sentencing hearing

have been spared the death sentence because of mental incapacity.[97] The Court has also held that age can be a mitigating factor: in *Thompson v. Oklahoma* (1988),[98] it halted the execution of fifteen-year-old William Wayne Thompson, stating that capital punishment for juveniles did not meet the "evolving standards of decency" for a "maturing society." Within a year, however, the Court upheld death sentences for a sixteen-year-old and a seventeen-year-old,[99] and it appears to be willing to allow each state to set its own age limits for capital punishment.

Debating the Sentence of Death

Indeed, in the years since *Gregg* the Supreme Court has rarely agreed to hear cases involving capital punishment. When it has done so, its main goal has been to support the right of each state to set its own laws. In 1998, the Court scolded a federal appeals court for halting a scheduled execution in California; in his majority opinion, Justice Kennedy said that federal courts should reverse a state's decision to execute only in "the most rare and extraordinary case[s]."[100]

With the nation's highest court relatively quiet on the issue, the debate over capital punishment is found in the public forum. Few topics seem to inspire such strongly held views among Americans, and those on both sides use a variety of arguments to support their positions. The key points of the capital punishment debate—discussed below—include morality, retribution, deterrence, incapacitation, arbitrariness, fallibility, and constitutionality.

Morality. Both advocates and opponents of the death penalty support their position on moral grounds. Some advocates point to several passages from the Old Testament, including "eye for eye, tooth for tooth . . ." and "Whoever sheds the blood of man, by man shall his blood be shed," as providing moral justification for the death penalty. Others contend that capital punishment makes a moral statement concerning the value of a human life, which should be valued so highly that any person who takes it must forfeit his or her own.

Those who are morally opposed to capital punishment also cite the Bible, particularly the passages of the New Testament that suggest that only God can punish wrongdoers and that human beings should not presume to make decisions concerning life and death. Using the language of the U.S. Constitution, a number of human rights groups such as Amnesty International argue that the death penalty violates the right to life under any circumstances and therefore is always cruel and unusual punishment.[101] Another opposition argument holds that the death penalty sends the wrong moral message to members of a society by showing them that the only way to protect human life is by taking it.

Retribution. The "eye for an eye" argument mentioned earlier is also the basis for the argument that execution is "just deserts" for those who commit heinous crimes. In the words of Ernest van den Haag, death is the "only fitting retribution for murder that I can think of."[102] Opponents worry that retribution is simply another word for vengeance and that "the use of the death penalty by the state will increase the acceptance of revenge in our society and will give official sanction to a climate of violence."[103] Like the arguments based on morality, arguments based on retribution, whether in favor or opposed to capital punishment, are more emotional than logical. They reflect individual value systems, which explains to a large degree why people rarely change their stand on the death penalty.

Deterrence. Those advocates of the death penalty who wish to show that the practice benefits society often turn to the idea of deterrence. In other words, they believe that by executing convicted criminals, the criminal justice system discourages potential criminals from committing similar violent acts. Deterrence was the primary justification for the frequent public executions carried out in this country before the 1830s and for the brutality of those events. Many social scientists claim that there is little valid statistical proof of the deterrent effect of capital punishment. Nonetheless, in 1975, Isaac Ehrlich, an economist at the University of Chicago, attempted to find some by focusing on the relationship between different jurisdictions' homicide rates and the percentage of those convicted of murder who were actually executed. According to Ehrlich, each additional execution that would have taken place between 1933 and 1967 could have saved the lives of as many as eight murder victims.[104] Ehrlich's results, though widely hailed at the time of their release, remain controversial; they have not been duplicated to the satisfaction of some scholars, and numerous subsequent studies have found that execution rates appear to have little effect on homicide rates.

In the end, the deterrence debate follows a familiar pattern. Opponents of the death penalty claim that murderers rarely consider the consequences of their act, and therefore it makes no difference whether capital punishment exists or not. Proponents counter that this proves the death penalty's deterrent value, because if the murderers *had* considered the possibility of execution, they would *not have* committed the crime.

Incapacitation. In one sense, capital punishment acts as the ultimate deterrent by rendering those executed incapable of committing further crimes. A study done by Paul Cassell and Stephen Markman analyzed the records of 52,000 state inmates doing time for murder and found that 810 of them had been previously convicted for the same crime. These 810 recidivists had killed

"We didn't feel she should get the death penalty. When you're on Death Row, you're there so long with nothing to bother you. In jail, she'll be with murderers and rapists. We thought the death penalty would be too easy for her."

—Jodi Dotts, explaining her decision to ask the prosecutor not to seek capital punishment for her daughter's killer (1999)

Prizefighter Rubin "Hurricane" Carter was convicted in 1966 of a triple murder in New Jersey and sentenced to life. In 1985 he was exonerated. Today he heads the Association in Defense of the Wrongly Convicted. At one conference he stated that "There is no separation between being on death row or being held unjustly for the rest of your life. Prison is death." What might be the cost to society if no sentences of life imprisonment were ever handed out?

821 people after being released from prison the first time.[105] If, hypothetically, the death penalty was mandatory for those convicted of murder, then 821 innocent lives would have been saved in Cassell and Markman's example, and thousands of others among the general population. Such projections seem to show that by incapacitating dangerous criminals, capital punishment could provide society with measurable benefits.

Fallibility. The incapacitation justification for capital punishment, however, rests on two questionable assumptions: (1) every convicted murderer is likely to recidivate; and (2) the criminal justice system is *infallible*. That is, the system never convicts someone who is actually not guilty. In fact, between 1976, when the Supreme Court reinstated capital punishment, and 1998, seventy-five American men and women who had been convicted of capital crimes and sentenced to death were later found to be innocent. Over that same time period, 486 executions took place, meaning that for every seven convicts put to death since *Gregg,* one death row inmate has been found innocent.[106]

There are several explanations for this relatively high ratio of error in capital cases. First, police and prosecutors are often under a great deal of public pressure to solve violent crimes and may be overzealous in arresting and prosecuting suspects. Such was the case with Rolando Cruz, who spent a decade on Illinois's death row for the rape and murder of a ten-year-old girl. Even after another man named Brian Dugan confessed to the crime and DNA testing linked Dugan to the crime scene, prosecutors still insisted that Cruz was the culprit. Only after a police officer admitted that he lied under oath concerning Cruz's "confession" was Cruz declared not guilty.[107]

Outright lying by persons involved in capital cases contributes to false convictions. Professors Hugo Bedau of Tufts University and Michael Radelet of the University of Florida found that one-third of wrongful capital convictions resulted from "jailhouse snitches" who perjured themselves by telling the court that they overhead a confession by the defendant. In addition, false confessions and faulty eyewitness identifications were found to be responsible for two of every seven wrongful convictions.[108] The single factor that contributes the most to the criminal justice system's fallibility, however, is widely believed to be unsatisfactory legal representation. Many states refuse to allocate adequate funds for public defenders, meaning that poor capital defendants are often provided with inexperienced or incompetent counsel. Alabama, for example, pays its lawyers just $20 an hour, with a cap of $1,000, to prepare for a capital trial and $40 an hour for work in court.[109] (By comparison, private lawyers receive as much as $500 an hour.)

Arbitrariness. One of the reasons it is so difficult to determine the deterrent effect of the death penalty is that it is rarely meted out. Despite the bifurcated process required by *Furman,* a certain amount of arbitrariness appears to remain in the system. Comparing the number of murders known by police to the number of executions carried out between 1979 and 1996, the chances of a murderer being executed were approximately 1,000 to 1.[110]

The chances of a defendant in a capital trial being sentenced to death seem to depend heavily on, as we have just seen, the quality of the defense counsel and the jurisdiction where the crime was committed. Of the 5,000 death sentences imposed in the United States since 1977, 2,000 have been overturned because the original defense counsel was found by an appellate court to be incompetent.[111] Furthermore, as Figure 11.8 shows, a convict's chances of being executed are strongly influenced by geography. Six southern states (Texas, Georgia, Virginia, Florida, Louisiana, and Missouri) account for nearly two-thirds of all death sentences, while twelve states and the District of Columbia do not provide for capital punishment within their borders. Therefore, a person on trial for first degree murder in New Mexico has a much better chance of avoiding execution than someone who has committed the same crime in Texas. Accordingly, Professor Hugo Bedau compares those who are executed to "losers in an arbitrary lottery."[112]

Not all observers of the criminal justice system agree with Professor Bedau's assessment. Walter Berns of the American Enterprise Institute and Joseph Bessette of Claremont McKenna College point out that 37 percent of inmates on Illinois's death row committed murders involving more than one victim, compared to 4 percent of murderers in the state's prisons but not on death row. Similarly, 20 percent of those on Illinois's death row committed murder during rape or sexual assault, compared to less than 1 percent of murderers in the general prison population. Berns and Bessette interpret these statistics as showing that "the worst of the worst" are most likely to be sentenced to death.[113]

Figure 11.8 Number of Executions by State since 1976

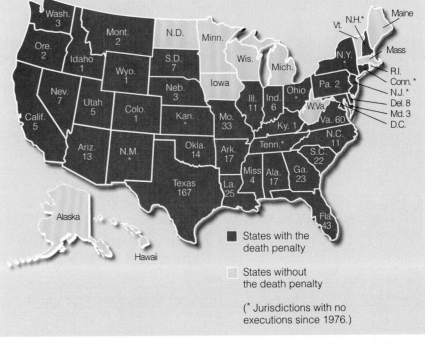

- States with the death penalty
- States without the death penalty

(* Jurisdictions with no executions since 1976.)

SOURCE: DEATH PENALTY INFORMATION CENTER

Whether or not capital punishment is imposed arbitrarily, claim some observers, it is not done without bias. Between 1930 and 1996, of the 4,220 prisoners executed in the United States, 53 percent were African American, even though that minority group made up between 10 and 15 percent of the national population during that time span.[114] Along with other issues of race in the criminal justice system, we will discuss the possibility of a bias in death penalty sentences in Chapter 18.

Still Cruel and Unusual. Finally, many observers believe that the Supreme Court should revisit the idea of the death penalty as cruel and unusual punishment, given the changing standards of society provided for in the *Weems* decision discussed earlier. Even lethal injection, critics point out, may cause undue suffering to the condemned. Texas, in particular, has experienced trouble with that method, taking more than forty minutes to insert the IV in Stephen Morin's vein in one instance and having to repair the equipment while Raymond Landry lay half dead on the gurney in another. The Court, however, has remained unwilling to rule on the constitutionality of methods of execution, even for the four states (Washington, Montana, Delaware, and New Hampshire) that still allow convicts to be hanged.

Another Eighth Amendment issue regarding capital punishment today concerns the psychological pain associated with spending a long period on death row awaiting execution. In *Gregg*, the Supreme Court interpreted the Fourteenth Amendment as requiring "meaningful appellate review" for anybody found guilty of a capital crime.[115] In other words, the case of any defendent sentenced to death must automatically be reviewed by a higher court. Although this requirement decreases the chances that the death sentence will be imposed "in a freakish manner," to use the Court's phrase, it also adds to the procedural requirements of capital punishment.

Not surprisingly, the average length of time an inmate spends on death row has doubled to nearly eleven years since the *Gregg* decision. (For example, twelve years passed between the conviction and execution of Charles Rodman Campbell for aggravated first degree murder. See Figure 11.9 for a rundown of the legal procedures that contributed to Campbell's time on death row.) A number of legal scholars have argued that the stress of living for long periods on death row as the appeals process advances (as required by the Fourteenth Amendment) represents cruel and unusual punishment (as defined by the Eighth Amendment). Some see this apparent contradiction between the two amendments as evidence that the death penalty cannot be fairly administered and should be discarded.[116]

Public Opinion and the Expansion of the Death Penalty

Today, the capital punishment debate appears to be dominated by one factor: public support. Throughout the past decade, polls have consistently shown that 70 to 80 percent or more of Americans are in favor of the death penalty.[117] Though some question whether these polls truly reflect the will of the people, their effect on public policy has been, and will continue to be, significant.

Public Ambivalence? When addressing the subject of public support, many opponents of capital punishment claim that the poll results are misleading. The problem, they say, rests in the "standard polling question" on the death

Figure 11.9 Charles Rodman Campbell: From Conviction to Execution

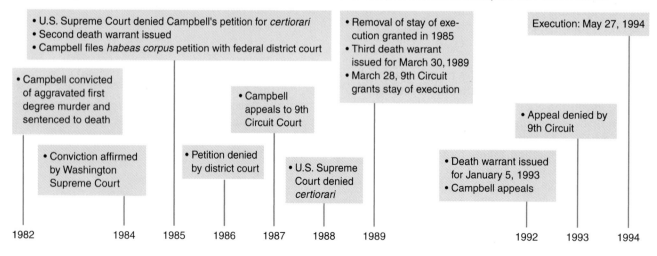

Charles Rodman Campbell was convicted of killing Renae Wicklund, her neighbor Barbara, and Renae's nine-year-old daughter. Charles committed these murders while serving a prison sentence for the sexual assault of Renae Wicklund. At the time of the murders, he was in work release. The sequence of the time from the commission of the offense to Charles Campbell's execution on May 27, 1994 was as follows:

- U.S. Supreme Court denied Campbell's petition for *certiorari*
- Second death warrant issued
- Campbell files *habeas corpus* petition with federal district court

- Removal of stay of execution granted in 1985
- Third death warrant issued for March 30, 1989
- March 28, 9th Circuit grants stay of execution

Execution: May 27, 1994

- Campbell convicted of aggravated first degree murder and sentenced to death

- Campbell appeals to 9th Circuit Court

- Appeal denied by 9th Circuit

- Conviction affirmed by Washington Supreme Court

- Petition denied by district court

- U.S. Supreme Court denied *certiorari*

- Death warrant issued for January 5, 1993
- Campbell appeals

1982   1984   1985   1986   1987   1988   1989   1992   1993   1994

penalty, which is often framed along these lines: "Do you favor or oppose the death penalty for persons convicted of murder?" or "Are you in favor of the death penalty for persons convicted of murder?"[118] Although a majority of respondents answer "yes" to these kinds of questions, they are more likely to temper this opinion when provided with other options. According to a study conducted by the Death Penalty Information Center (which opposes capital punishment), support for the death penalty falls to 41 percent when those surveyed are given the alternative of life imprisonment without parole for a wrongdoer.[119]

Proportionality. Subtleties of polling techniques aside, many prosecutors and legislators have taken high levels of support for capital punishment as a public mandate to expand the role of the death penalty in the criminal justice system. In general, prosecutors have become more aggressive in seeking the death penalty, and their success rate is reflected in a nationwide death row population that is growing by 100 to 150 people a year (see Figure 11.10). For their part, lawmakers in some states have responded to voters' demands with legislation that challenges one of the foundations of post-*Gregg* capital punishment law: proportionality.

Figure **11.10** The Death Row Population, 1967 to Present

The concept of *proportionality* in sentencing is fairly simple: the punishment a person receives for breaking the law should be in keeping with the seriousness of the crime has committed. A shoplifter, for example, will not be punished as harshly as will a bank robber. With regard to capital punishment in the twentieth century, proportionality generally dictated that to receive the death sentence, a defendant had to have been involved in a crime that involved homicide. This was not, to be sure, a strict rule; between 1930 and 1982, 455 Americans were executed for rape and 70 for various crimes such as armed robbery, kidnapping, and espionage.[120]

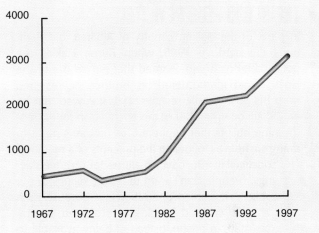

SOURCE: DEATH PENALTY INFORMATION CENTER.

By ruling that it was unconstitutional to sentence a defendant to death for the crime of rape in *Coker v. Georgia* (1977),[121] the Supreme Court virtually eliminated capital punishment for nonhomicide crimes since then. The Court did not, however, rule that the death penalty is *automatically* unconstitutional in cases where no person was killed. Consequently, thirteen states and the federal government have passed laws that allow for capital punishment for crimes other than murder. In Missouri, for example, a prosecutor can seek the death penalty against a defendant who sold drugs near a school or planted a bomb near a bus terminal.[122]

Although nobody is currently on death row for committing a crime that did not involve homicide, legal experts do not expect that these new statutes will remain untested for long. One of the cases will undoubtedly find its way to the Supreme Court, where its fate will determine the direction of capital punishment in the immediate future.[123]

Criminal Justice in Action
Victims and Retribution

In this chapter, we have discussed the various authorities that influence sentencing decisions—legislators, judges, prosecutors, defense attorneys, and parole officers. One group of unwilling participants in the legal system that is notable in its absence are the victims of crimes and their families. Over the past decade, however, victims have begun to gain a place in the sentencing process. As the following discussion shows, this newfound clout of victims and victim's rights groups is a subject of great debate within the criminal justice system.

THE BLOOD FEUD REVISITED

In parts of the Balkan country of Albania, old traditions die hard. In 1998, when Fatmir Haklaj, the police chief of Tropjo, learned that a member of the Hoxe clan had murdered his brother, he resigned from his post to take revenge. Haklaj vowed that he would kill one member of the enemy clan for each of the nine bullets that peppered his brother's body. In doing so, he was following the precepts of a medieval code, still in effect, which allows for revenge slayings. "People don't want to report killings to the police," remarked one Albanian, "because then the accused would be protected by the state in prison instead of being available to kill."[124]

This form of retributive justice, known as a "blood feud," is based on the concept that the punishment for a crime should be determined by the "worth" of the victim. Based on class structure, the more important the person killed, the higher the price to be paid by the murderer and his or her family.[125] Though this variation of retribution does appear in the Anglo-American legal tradition, today our criminal justice system is based not on the victim's need for vengeance, but on society's need to protect citizens and control crime. Since the 1980s, however, as the victim's rights movement gained a stronger voice (see Chapter 2), the practice of victim retribution has returned. The methods of restitution have been mostly financial, but some observers worry that in giving victims more power, we are moving closer to the Albanian system than the U.S. Constitution allows.

THE "SOCIAL CONTRACT"

Restitution has long played a role in legal codes. A requirement of restitution to compensate the victim of crime for resulting loss, damage, or injury can be found in the 4,000-year-old Code of Hammurabi. The ancient Greeks instituted a "death fine" to mandate payment to the family of a crime victim, and the "composition" system of the Middle Ages, in which the injured party received damages from the wrongdoer, was similar to the modern civil law.[126]

In this country, prior to the American Revolution, a crime was still considered an affront to the individual rather than the state, and the victim played a considerable role in the criminal justice system.[127] This began to change with the drafting of the U.S. Constitution. The Bill of Rights does not provide any special protections for victims of crime, and legal precedent subsequently moved the United States toward the theory of the "social contract." Based on the theories of Cesare Beccaria (see Chapter 2), this implied "contract" held that a criminal justice system should serve society's interests, not those of the individual. Therefore, the state should not seek private retribution on behalf of any individual, but rather should protect the rights of all by treating crimes as offenses against the state.[128]

In the 1960s and early 1970s, grass-roots efforts to increase the visibility of crime victims led to a reconsideration of victim retribution. In particular, attention was focused on the economic suffering of victims, which can include medical expenses and lost wages in addition to any monies taken during the crime. One study estimated that the victim of a shotgun assault can lose up to $5 million in lost income and medical expenses over a thirty-five-year working life.[129] As the avenue of a civil suit against the offender is not an option for many low-income victims unable to afford legal aid, federal and state legislatures began to pass laws providing for economic damages to be paid to victims.

RESTITUTION

All fifty states have enacted statutes to provide restitution for crime victims. **Restitution,** which has its roots in the older legal systems mentioned above, requires offenders to compensate their victims for damages suffered in the criminal act. In most cases, the court has the discretion to set the terms of the payment. Restitution is not seen as a form of "revenge," because the losses can only be levied to cover the actual costs of the crime, not to provide remuneration for pain and suffering.[130]

The main problem with restitution is the difficulty in collecting the payments. The U.S. Attorney's Office in Chicago, for example, recovers just four cents on every restitution dollar owed.[131] Sometimes, judges aggravate the problem by setting unreasonable levels of restitution. For example, a U.S. district judge in San Jose ordered an equipment leasing company operator named Jeffrey Avila to pay $8 million for starting a fire that destroyed 25,000 acres of national forest and five private homes.[132]

Another form of restitution has evolved through the emergence of **victim compensation programs**. The Federal Victims of Crime Act of 1984 set the guidelines for these programs, in which state governments directly compensate victims of violent crime.[133] Under funding requirements, the federal government reimburses each state for 40 percent of the amount it pays to victims each year. The fund is financed through fines and penalties assessed on convicted federal criminals. The federal government pays out more than $500 million to state victim compensation programs each year.

GOING TOO FAR?

Critics of restitution and compensation programs claim that they contradict the idea that a criminal is being prosecuted for a crime against society and not the individual.[134] Even more insidious, suggest some, is the newly won right of "allocution," or the right of the victim to make an oral statement to the sentencing court to influence the terms of punishment. In *Payne v. Tennessee* (1991),[135] the Supreme Court upheld the use of victim impact statements in capital sentencing hearings by reasoning that they demonstrated the harm of the crime and therefore could be considered in setting the punishment. Today, Indiana is the only state that excludes these statements from death penalty procedures.

The problem with victim impact statements, say some scholars, is that they resurrect the "blood feud" notion of a victim's life having a relative worth. When, for example, one victim's mother testifies that her son wanted to be president of the United States, or another talks about her daughter's "dance recitals, swim team competitions and church and youth group plays," the implied point is that because the victim was a worthy person, the killer should receive a harsher sentence.[136] In certain instances, the victim impact statement directly asks for the death penalty; one Arizona victim said that it was "ridiculous to keep a murderer alive," and that he "should suffer as Irene did."[137] The situation, in certain aspects, is similar to the one described in Albania—a vengeful family seeking the life of the offender. In his dissent in *Payne*, Justice John Paul Stevens argued that because the victim is not on trial, her or his "character, whether good or bad, cannot therefore constitute either an aggravating or a mitigating circumstance."[138]

RESTITUTION
A sanction that requires the wrongdoer to compensate for the financial, physical, or emotional harm done through a direct payment to the victim or a form of service to the community as a whole.

VICTIM COMPENSATION PROGRAMS
Government-operated restitution programs that collect fines from criminals for distribution among victims and their families.

Key Terms

Chapter Summary

1. **List and contrast the four basic philosophical reasons for sentencing criminals.** (a) Retribution, (b) deterrence, (c) incapacitation, and (d) rehabilitation. Under the principle of retributive justice, the severity of the punishment is in proportion to the severity of the crime. Punishment is an end in itself. In contrast, the deterrence approach seeks to prevent future crimes by setting an example. Such punishment is based on its deterrent value and not necessarily on the severity of the crime. The incapacitation theory of punishment simply argues that a criminal in jail cannot impose further harm on society. In contrast, the rehabilitation theory believes that criminals can be rehabilitated in the appropriate prison environment.

2. **Contrast indeterminate with determinate sentencing.** Indeterminate sentencing follows from legislative penal codes that set minimum and maximum amounts of incarceration time; determinate sentencing carries a fixed amount of time, although this may be reduced for "good time."

3. **Explain why there is a difference between a sentence imposed by a judge and the actual sentence carried out by the prisoner.** Although judges may decide on indeterminate sentencing, thereafter it is parole boards that decide when prisoners will be released after the minimum sentence is served.

4. **List the five forms of punishment.** (a) Capital (death sentence), (b) imprisonment, (c) probation, (d) fines, and (e) restitution and community service.

5. **State who has input into the sentencing decision and list the factors that determine a sentence.** The prosecutor, defense attorney, probation officer, and judge provide inputs. The factors considered in sentencing are (a) seriousness of the crime, (b) mitigating circumstances, (c) aggravating circumstances, and (d) judicial philosophy.

6. **Explain some of the reasons why sentencing reform has occurred.** One reason is because of sentencing disparity, which has been seen on a geographical basis and on a courtroom basis (due to a particular judge's philosophy). Sentencing discrimination has also occurred on the basis of defendants' gender, race, or economic standing. An additional reason for sentencing reform has been a general desire to "get tough on crime."

7. **Contrast sentencing guidelines with mandatory sentencing guidelines.** At the state level, courtroom work groups are guided by a grid, which determines the proper sentence. The grid uses the type of crime, the seriousness of the crime, and other factors to generate a "presumed" prison term. Starting in 1987, a similar grid system was put into place at the federal level. In response to judges' continued departures from such sentencing guidelines, federal and state legislatures have instituted mandatory (minimum) sentencing guidelines, which limit a judge's discretion for certain classes of crimes, such as selling drugs. The most stringent guideline is represented by "three strikes and you're out" laws, which require any person convicted of a third felony to serve a lengthy prison sentence without the possibility of parole.

8. **Outline the Supreme Court rulings on capital punishment.** In 1967, the Supreme Court placed a hold on all scheduled executions. In 1972, the Court invalidated the death penalty in states that imposed it because the way it was practiced violated the Eighth and Fourteenth Amendments. By 1976, thirty-five states had changed their death penalty statutes to comply with the Supreme Court ruling. The Supreme Court then declared mandatory death penalty statutes invalid, but established a bifurcated process that involved two steps. Today, thirty-eight states have adopted this process and provide for legally acceptable capital punishment.

(Questions for Critical Analysis

1. How can punishing a wrongdoer be reconciled with the concept of rehabilitation?

2. How does the limitation of "good time" along with fixed sentencing make a prison warden's job more difficult?

3. What single fact will probably lead to a reduction in truth-in-sentencing laws as well as a reduction in mandatory minimum sentencing laws?

4. What restricts judicial discretion in sentencing in many jurisdictions?

5. What has caused the gradual disappearance of presentence investigative reports in some jurisdictions?

6. How do "real offense" procedures effectively render plea bargains without much meaning?

7. What happens to the concept of parole under a system of mandatory sentencing guidelines?

8. How do mandatory sentences lead to a disproportionate number of persons from minority groups in prison?

9. What are some of the arguments that proponents of the death penalty offer in its favor? What are some of the arguments that opponents offer against it?

10. Some people believe that giving victims more power brings us closer to the concept of vengeance. Why?

(Selected Print and Electronic Resources

SUGGESTED READINGS

Bedau, Hugo Adam, ed., *The Death Penalty in America: Current Controversies*, New York: Oxford University Press, 1998. This collection of forty original essays is actually a comprehensive reference book. It also includes statistical and research data and recent Supreme Court decisions.

Latzer, Barry, *Death Penalty Cases: Leading U.S. Supreme Court Cases on Capital Punishment.* Stoneham, MA: Butterworth-Heinemann, 1997. This book presents a detailed analysis of the major cases on capital punishment that have been heard by the Supreme Court in modern times. All important cases are examined.

Lovegrove, Austin, *The Framework of Judicial Sentencing: A Study in Legal Decision Making.* Cambridge: Cambridge University Press, 1997. This book looks at how judges think when they sentence multiple offenders. The author tries to determine the strategies that judges develop to help them apply sentencing law in each case. From interviews with judges, the author tries to develop a standardized framework of judicial sentencing.

Stith, Kate, José A. Caranes, and José A. Cabranes, *Fear of Judging: Sentencing Guidelines in the Federal Courts,* Chicago: University of Chicago Press, 1998. This book presents an accessible explanation of how federal sentencing guidelines work. The authors argue against such guidelines. They would prefer that a common law of sentencing be used instead. They point out that federal judges exercised wide discretion in criminal sentencing for more than two centuries. All this changed in 1987 when federal sentencing guidelines went into effect. The authors believe that the sentencing guidelines have failed to address inequities in sentencing.

Vila, Bryan, and Cynthia Morris, eds., *Capital Punishment in the United States: A Documentary History,* Westport, CT: Greenwood Publishing Group, 1997. This book contains 112 key documents on the political, social, and legal aspects of capital punishment, arranged by historical period. The documents include records of congressional hearings, Supreme Court cases, biographical accounts, and news stories. Each document is preceded by an explanatory introduction.

MEDIA RESOURCES

Dead Man Walking (1995) This film is about a religious woman who becomes the spiritual adviser of a convicted murderer on death row. Sister Helen (Susan Sarandon) faces an angry community and the victims'

anguished parents. The film examines the challenge of bringing fairness, honor, and a voice from the victims' families to the process.

Critically analyze this film:

1. Both those in favor and those against the death penalty have said that this film supports their views. How is this possible?

2. In the film, Susan Sarandon's character, Sister Helen Prejean, visits the parents of the two teenagers who allegedly were murdered by Sean Penn's character, Matthew Poncelet. The movie viewer sees that at least one couple seeks retribution. What do these scenes indicate to you about the interjection of victim's rights into the sentencing process?

Logging On

If you want to find out more about truth-in-sentencing laws, you can go to:

www.klaaskids.org/v1n1truth.htm

There you will find the Klaas Action Review, which is the newsletter of the Mark Klaas Foundation for Children. The article is called "The Truth about Truth-in-Sentencing," by Jim Wooton, who is the founder and president of the Safe Streets Alliance in Washington, D.C.

You can visit the Bureau of Justice Statistics home page at:

www.ojp.usdoj.gov/bjs/welcome.html

To find out information on sentencing, click that phrase and you will find the latest information on courts and sentencing statistics in the federal court system as well as in the state court systems.

Using the internet for Criminal Justice Analysis

INFOTRAC ®
COLLEGE EDITION

1. Go to InfoTrac College Edition at
www.infotrac-college.com/wadsworth/
After you log on, go to the article entitled:
"INDIVIDUAL AND CONTEXTUAL INFLUENCES ON SENTENCING LENGTHS"
Then go to:
"THOU SHALL NOT KILL ANY NICE PEOPLE:"
This article, from the *American Criminal Law Review,* examines the problems associated with victim impact statements in capital sentencing.

a. Summarize the Supreme Court decision in *Payne v. Tennessee.*

b. How did the Supreme Court's decisions in *Booth v. Maryland* and *South Carolina v. Gathers* differ from its decision in *Payne v. Tennessee?*

c. In *Payne v. Tennessee,* did all of the Supreme Court justices agree with the opinion?

d. According to the article, how many states utilize victim impact statements in their capital sentencing hearings?

2. Use your favorite Internet browser to go to **www.ussc.gov/guidelin.htm.** There you will find the U.S. Sentencing Commission guidelines, manuals, and amendments. Briefly examine parts of both the oldest *Federal Sentencing Guidelines Manual* and the latest. Describe at least two differences that you can find between these two sets of guidelines.

3. Now go to **www.ussc.gov/meeting.htm.** There you will find information about the U.S. Sentencing Commission meetings.

a. How often does the commission appear to meet?

b. Describe in your own words at least one important area in which the commission wanted to amend the sentencing guidelines.

Notes

1. Dick Behnke, "Dad Sentenced in Baby's Death," *Albuquerque Journal* (July 30, 1997), 6.

2. David Yellen, "Just Deserts and Lenient Prosecutors: The Flawed Case for Real Offense Sentencing," *Northwestern University Law Review* 91 (Summer 1997), 1434.

3. Brian Forst, "Prosecution and Sentencing," in *Crime*, ed. James Q. Wilson and Joan Petersilia (San Francisco: ICS Press, 1995), 386.

4. Herbert L. Packer, "Justification for Criminal Punishment," in *The Limits of Criminal Sanction* (Palo Alto, CA: Stanford University Press, 1968), 36–37.

5. Jami L. Anderson, "Reciprocity as a Justification for Retributivism," *Criminal Justice Ethics* (Winter/Spring 1997), 13–14.

6. Immanuel Kant, *Metaphysical First Principles of the Doctrine of Right,* translated by Mary Gregor (Cambridge, UK: Cambridge University Press, 1991), 331.

7. Harold Pepinsky and Paul Jesilow, *Myths That Cause Crime* (Cabin John, MD: Seven Locks Press, 1984).

8. Jeremy Bentham, *An Introduction to the Principles of Morals and Legislation,* 1789 (New York: Hafner Publishing Corp., 1961).

9. Forst, 376.

10. John J. DiIulio, Jr., "Help Wanted: Economists, Crime and Public Policy," *Journal of Economic Perspectives* 10 (1996), 3, 16–17.

11. Sue T. Reid, *Crime and Criminology,* 7th ed. (New York: Holt, Rinehart, and Winston, 1995), 352.

12. Morgan O. Reynolds, *Why Does Crime Pay?* (Dallas, TX: National Center for Policy Analysis Backgrounder #110, 1990), 5.

13. Paul H. Robinson and John M. Darley, "The Utility of Desert," *Northwestern University Law Review* 91 (Winter 1997), 453.

14. James Q. Wilson, *Thinking about Crime* (New York: Basic Books, 1975), 235.

15. Isaac Ehrlich, "Participation in Illegitimate Activities: A Theoretical and Empirical Investigation," *Journal of Political Economy* 81 (May/June 1973), 521–64.

16. Steve Levitt, "The Effect of Prison Population Size on Crime Rates," *Quarterly Journal of Economics* 111 (May 1996), 319.

17. Todd Clear, *Harm in Punishment* (Boston: Northeastern University Press, 1980).

18. Richard Hawkins and Geoffrey P. Albert, *American Prison Systems* (Englewood Cliff, NJ: Prentice Hall, 1989), 141–62.

19. Peter Schmidt and Ann Witte, *Predicting Recidivism Using Survival Methods* (New York: Springer-Verlag, 1988), 158.

20. Quoted in Ilene H. Nagel, "Structuring Sentencing Discretion: The New Federal Sentencing Guidelines," *Journal of Criminal Law and Criminology* 80 (Winter 1990), 883.

21. Gregory W. O'Reilly, "Truth-in-Sentencing, Illinois Adds Yet Another Later of 'Reform' to Its Complicated Code of Corrections," *Loyola University of Chicago Law Journal* (Summer 1996), 986, 999–100.

22. Arthur W. Campbell, *Law of Sentencing* (Rochester, NY: Lawyers Co-operative Publishing Co., 1978), 9.

23. Marvin Zalman, "The Rise and Fall of the Indeterminate Sentence," *Wayne Law Review* 24 (1977), 45, 52.

24. Marvin E. Frankel, *Criminal Sentences: Law without Order* (New York: Hill and Wang, 1972), 5.

25. Jessica Mitford, *Kind and Usual Punishment* (New York: Alfred A. Knopf, 1973), 80–83.

26. Bureau of Justice Statistics, *Truth in Sentencing in State Prisons,* (Washington, DC: Department of Justice, 1999).

27. Paul W. Keve, *Crime Control and Justice in America: Searching for Facts and Answers* (Chicago: American Library Association, 1995), 77.

28. Gary Wisby, "Child Molester Has Castration Surgery," *Chicago Sun-Times* (January 21, 1998), 9.

29. Kate Stith and José A. Cabranes, "Judging under the Federal Sentencing Guidelines," *Northwestern University Law Review* 91 (Summer 1997), 1247.

30. Stephen A. Fennell and William N. Hall, "Due Process at Sentencing: An Empirical and Legal Analysis of the Disclosure of Presentence Reports in Federal Courts," *Harvard Law Review* 93 (1980), 1666–8.

31. Mark M. Lanier and Claud H. Miller III, "Attitudes and Practices of Federal Probation Officers towards Pre-Plea/Trial Investigative Report Policy," *Crime & Delinquency* 41 (July 1995), 365–6.

32. Stith and Cabranes, 1247.

33. Andrew Von Hirsch, *Doing Justice: The Choice of Punishments* (New York: Hill and Wang, 1976), 98.

34. Julie R. O'Sullivan, "In Defense of the U.S. Sentencing Guidelines Modified Real-Offense System," *Northwestern University Law Review* 91 (1997), 1342.

35. Brian Forst and Charles Wellford, "Punishment and Sentencing: Developing Sentencing Guidelines Empirically from Principles of Punishment," *Rutgers Law Review* 33 (1981).

36. 18 U.S.C. Section 2113(a) (1994).

37. Alfred Blumstein, Jacqueline Cohen, Susan Martin, and Michael Tonry, *Research on Sentencing: The Search for Reform*, Volume 1 (Washington, D.C.: National Academy Press, 1983), 7–8.

38. U.S.C.C.A.N. 3182, 3228 (1984).

39. Thomas Austin, "The Influence of Court Location on Types of Criminal Sentences: The Rural-Urban Factor," *Journal of Criminal Justice* 9 (1981), 305.

40. Bill Rankin, "Special Report: Unequal Justice," *Atlanta Journal & Constitution* (January 25, 1998), A1.

41. *Ibid.*

42. Frederick J. Gaudet, et al., "Individual Differences in the Sentencing Tendencies of Judges," *Journal of Criminal Law and Criminology* 23 (1933), 811–8.

43. U.S.C.C.A.N. 3182, 3227 (1984).

44. David L. Evans, "Lost Behind Prison Bars," *Newsweek* (September 7, 1998), 20.

45. John C. Coffee, "Repressed Issues of Sentencing," *Georgetown Law Journal* 66 (1978), 987.

46. Twentieth Century Fund Task Force on Criminal Sentencing, *Fair and Certain Punishment* (New York: McGraw-Hill, 1976).

47. Robert Martinson, "What Works?—Questions and Answers about Prison Reform," *Public Interest* 35 (Spring 1974), 22.

48. Edward Kennedy, "Introduction to Symposium on Sentencing," *Hofstra Law Review* 1 (1978), 1.

49. Francis A. Allen, *The Decline of the Rehabilitative Ideal* (New Haven, CT: Yale University Press, 1981), 8.

50. J. S. Bainbridge Jr., "The Return of Retribution," *ABA Journal* (May 1985), 63.

51. Sentencing Reform Act of 1984, Pub. L. No. 98–473, 98 Stat. 1987 [codified as amended at 18 U.S.C. Sections 3551–3742 and 28 U.S.C. Sections 991–998 (1988)].

52. Julia L. Black, "The Constitutionality of Federal Sentences Imposed under the Sentencing Reform Act of 1984 after Mistretta v. United States," *Iowa Law Review* 75 (March 1990), 767.

53. Roger Haines, Kevin Cole, and Jennifer Wole, *Federal Sentencing Guidelines Handbook* (New York: McGraw-Hill, 1994), 3.

54. Michael S. Gelacak, Ilene H. Nagel, and Barry L. Johnson, "Departures under the Federal Sentencing Guidelines: An Empirical and Jurisprudential Analysis," *Minnesota Law Review* 81 (December 1996), 299.

55. *United States v. Diaz-Villafane*, 874 F.2d 43, 49 (1st Cir. 1989).

56. *1996 Annual Report* (Washington, D.C.: U.S. Sentencing Commission, 1997).

57. Barbara S. Meierhoefer, *The General Effect of Mandatory Minimum Prison Terms: A Longitudinal Study of Federal Sentences Imposed* (Washington, D.C.: Federal Judicial Center, 1992), 20.

58. 116 S. Ct. 2035 (1996).

59. Alabama Code 1975 Section 20–2–79.

60. Washington Rev. Code Ann. Sections 9.94A.030.

61. 445 U.S. 263 (1980).

62. California Department of Corrections study, cited in Carl Ingram, "Serious Crime Falls in State's Major Cities," *Los Angeles Times* (March 13, 1996), A3.

63. 13 Cal. 4th 497, 917 P.2d 628, 53 Cal. Rptr. 2d 789 (1996).

64. Brandon K. Applegate, Francis T. Cullen, Michael G. Turner, and Jody L. Sundt, "Assessing Public Support for Three-Strikes-and-You're-Out Laws: Global versus Specifics Attitudes," *Crime & Delinquency* 42 (October 1996), 518.

65. Bureau of Justice Statistics, *Truth in Sentencing in State Prisons*, (Washington, DC: Department of Justice, 1999).

66. Keve, 93.

67. Meierhoefer, 3.

68. Joe Domanick, "Dumb Kid, Petty Crimes: A Life Term?" *Los Angeles Times* (July 24, 1998), B9.

69. Yellen, 1434.

70. Michael Tonry, "The Failure of the U.S. Sentencing Commission's Guidelines," *Crime & Delinquency* 39 (1993), 131–49.

71. Comments by Judge Vincent L. Broderick, United States District Court for the Southern District of New York, "Conference on the Federal Sentencing Guidelines: Summary of Proceedings," *Yale Law Journal* 101 (1992), 2053.

72. Michael S. Gelacak, Ilene N. Nagel, and Barry L. Johnson, "Departures Under the Federal Sentencing Guidelines: An Empirical and Jurisprudential Analysis," *Minnesota Law Review* 81 (1996), 299.

73. Kay A. Knapp, "Impact of Minnesota Sentencing Guidelines on Sentencing Practices," *Hamline Law Review* 5 (1982), 255.

74. 18 U.S.C. Section 3553(e) (1991).

75. Bill Rankin, "Sentencing Guidelines: N.C. Offers Model for States," *Atlanta Journal & Constitution* (January 25, 1998), A9.

76. Walter Berns, "Abraham Lincoln (book review)," *Commentary* (January 1, 1996), 70.

77. Comments made at the Georgetown Law Center, "The Modern View of Capital Punishment," *American Criminal Law Review* 34 (Summer 1997), 1353.

78. David Bruck quoted in Bill Rankin, "Fairness of the Death Penalty Is Still on Trial," *Atlanta Constitution & Journal* (July 29, 1997), A13.

79. Mark Costanzo, *Just Revenge: Costs and Consequences of the Death Penalty* (New York: St. Martin's Press, 1997), 11.

80. Randall Coyne and Lyn Entzeroth, *Capital Punishment and the Judicial Process* (Durham, NC: Carolina Academic Press, 1994), 2.

81. Jeffrey C. Matura, "When Will It Stop? The Use of the Death Penalty for Non-Homicide Crimes," *Journal of Legislation* 24 (1998), 249.

82. Thorsten Sellin, "The Philadelphia Gibbet Iron," *Journal of Criminal Law, Criminology, and Police Science* 46 (1955), 19.

83. G. Mark Mamantov, "The Executioner's Song: Is There a Right to Listen?" *Virginia Law Review* 69 (March 1983), 373.

84. Stephen Trombley, *The Execution Protocol: Inside America's Capital Punishment Industry* (New York: Crown Publishers, 1992), 73.

85. Larry C. Berkson, *The Concept of Cruel and Unusual Punishment* (Lexington, MA: Lexington Books, 1975), 43.

86. John P. Cunningham, "Death in the Federal Courts: Expectations and Realities of the Federal Death Penalty Act of 1994," *University of Richmond Law Review* 32 (May 1998), 939.

87. *In re Kemmler*, 136 U.S. 447 (1890).

88. 217 U.S. 349 (1910).

89. Pamela S. Nagy, "Hang by the Neck until Dead: The Resurgence of Cruel and Unusual Punishment in the 1990s," *Pacific Law Journal* 26 (October 1994), 85.

90. 391 U.S. 510 (1968).

91. 402 U.S. 183 (1971).

92. 408 U.S. 238 (1972).

93. 408 U.S. 309 (1972), (Stewart, concurring).

94. 428 U.S. 280 (1976).

95. 428 U.S. 153 (1976).

96. *Ford v. Wainwright*, 477 U.S. 409 (1986).

97. *Penry v. Lynaugh*, 109 S. Ct. 2934 (1989).

98. 108 S.Ct. 1687 (1988).

99. *Stanford v. Kentucky* 492 U.S. 361 (1989); *Wilkins v. Missouri* 492 U.S. 361 (1989).

100. *Calderon v. Thompson*, 97 U.S. 215 (1998).

101. *United States of America: The Death Penalty and Juvenile Offenders* (New York: Amnesty International (USA), 1991), 1.

102. Ernest van den Haag, "The Ultimate Punishment: A Defense," *Harvard Law Review* 99 (1986), 1669.

103. *The Death Penalty: The Religious Community Calls for Abolition* (pamphlet published by the National Coalition to Abolish the Death Penalty and the National Interreligious Task Force on Criminal Justice, 1988), 48.

104. Isaac Ehrlich, "The Deterrent Effect of Capital Punishment: A Question of Life and Death," *American Economic Review* 65 (June 1975), 397–417.

105. Stephen Markman and Paul Cassell, "Protecting the Innocent: A Response to the Bedau-Radelet Study," *Stanford Law Review* 41 (1988), 153.

106. "The Death Penalty: One in Seven Isn't Guilty," *Economist* (November 28, 1998), 29–30.

107. Joseph F. Shapiro, "The Wrong Men on Death Row," *U.S. News and World Report* (November 9, 1998), 26.

108. Hugo Adam Bedau and Michael L. Radelet, "Miscarriages of Justice in Potentially Capital Cases," *Stanford Law Review* 40 (1987), 21–23.

109. John McCormick, "The Wrongly Condemned," *Newsweek* (November 9, 1998), 64.

110. John J. DiIulio, "Abolish the Death Penalty, Officially," *Wall Street Journal* (December 15, 1997), A23.

111. "Cruel and Even More Unusual," *Economist* (February 14, 1998), 3.

112. Quoted in Walter Berns and Joseph Bessette, "Why the Death Penalty Is Fair," *Wall Street Journal* (January 9, 1998), A16.

113. *Ibid.*

114. Scott Shepherd, "More Blacks Agreeing with Death Penalty, Data Show," *Fresno Bee* (April 18, 1998), A6.

115. *Gregg v. Georgia*, 428 U.S. 153, 195 (1976).

116. Dan Crocker, "Extended Stays: Does Lengthy Imprisonment on Death Row Undermine the Goals of Capital Punishment?" *Journal of Gender, Race and Justice* (Spring 1998), 555.

117. National Opinion Research Center, University of Chicago.

118. William J. Bowers, Margaret Vandiver and Patricia H. Dugan, "A New Look at Public Opinion on Capital Punishment: What Citizens and Legislators Prefer," *American Journal of Criminal Law* 22 (1994), 79.

119. John A. MacArthur, "The Death Penalty and the Decline of Liberalism," *John Marshall Law Review* 30 (Winter 1997), 321.

120. Faye A. Silas, "America's 14,000 Executions," *ABA Journal* 71 (April 1985), 53.

121. 433 U.S. 584 (1977).

122. Missouri Ann. Stat. Section 578.310 (West 1996).

123. Matura, 249.

124. Jane Perlez, "Feuds Rack Albania, Loosed from Communism," *New York Times* (April 14, 1998), A1.

125. Lynne N. Henderson, "The Wrongs of Victim's Rights," *Stanford Law Review* 37 (1985), 949–50.

126. Stephen Schafer, *Victimology: The Victim and His Criminal* (Reston, VA: Reston Publishing Company, 1977), 6–10.

127. William F. McDonald, "Towards a Bicentennial Revolution in Criminal Justice: The Return of the Victim," *American Criminal Law Review* 13 (1976), 650.

128. Mario M. Cuomo, "The Crime Victim in a System of Criminal Justice," *St. Johns Journal of Legal Commentary* 8 (Fall 1992), 1.

129. Jeremy Rankin, "Sue the Government," *New Republic* (May 8, 1995), 19.

130. James H. Stark and Howard W. Goldstein, *The Rights of Crime Victims* (Carbondale, Ill: Southern Illinois University Press, 1985), 154.

131. Deborah Nelson, "Uncollected Fines Leave Shelters Out in Cold," *Chicago Sun-Times* (January 2, 1995), 11.

132. "5-Year Prison Term for Setting Big Sur Fire," *San Francisco Chronicle* (May 21, 1998), A22.

133. 42 U.S.C. Section 10601–10605 (1984).

134. Henderson, 1008–9.

135. 501 U.S. 808 (1991).

136. Amy K. Phillips, "Thou Shalt Not Kill Any Nice People: The Problem of Victim Impact Statements in Capital Sentencing," *American Criminal Law Review* (Fall 1997), 93.

137. Quoted in Phillips, 95.

138. *Payne*, 501 U.S. 859 (Stevens, dissenting).

part four
Corrections

Chapter

12 Probation and Community Corrections

13 Prisons and Jails

14 Life Behind Bars

15 Reentry into Society

chapter

12

Probation and Community Corrections

Chapter Outline

- The Justification for Community Corrections

- Probation: Doing Time in the Community

- Intermediate Sanctions

- The Future of Community Corrections

- Criminal Justice in Action—Boot Camps: Do They Work?

Chapter Objectives

After reading this chapter, you should be able to:

1. Explain the justifications for community-based corrections programs.

2. Indicate when probation started to fall out of favor and explain why.

3. List and explain several alternative sentencing arrangements.

4. Specify the conditions under which an offender is most likely to be denied probation.

5. Describe the three general categories of conditions placed on a probationer.

6. Explain why probation officers' work has become more dangerous.

7. List and explain the three stages of probation revocation.

8. List the five sentencing options for a judge besides imprisonment and probation.

9. Contrast day reporting centers with intensive supervision probation.

10. List the three levels of home monitoring.

INTRODUCTION

In 1997, twenty-one-year-old Michael Angel Sierra shot Michael McDonald five times with a .22 caliber pistol in a dispute over a woman, killing the man. During his trial in Bell County, Texas, witnesses described Sierra as a "good boy caught in a bad situation," and his defense lawyer hammered home the point that his client had no prior criminal record. Despite these mitigating circumstances, Sierra was convicted of murder. The verdict was expected— after all, Sierra had committed homicide. The sentence, however, came as a shock to local citizens and criminal justice officials alike. Instead of putting Sierra behind bars, the jury decided to grant him five years' probation.[1]

In fact, the Bell County jury was not breaking new ground. A system that initially gave judges the discretion to show leniency to first-time, minor offenders increasingly allows those who have committed serious crimes to serve their time in the community rather than in a prison or jail. Nearly one of every five probationers in the United States has been convicted of a violent felony such as homicide, rape, or assault.[2] Ironically, this increase can be partly attributed to the "get tough" approach to crime that has emerged in public policy. Campaigns to crack down on drunk drivers, the "war on drugs," harsher sentencing statutes, and severe limitations on judicial discretion have placed a great amount of pressure on the American corrections infrastructure. Even with unprecedented rates of prison and jail construction, there is simply not enough space to incarcerate all of the new criminals. The result: more than 3 million adults are under the supervision of state and federal probation organizations—a figure growing at a rate of 3 percent each year.[3]

There is little question that our corrections system is suffering from "probation overload." Today in Los Angeles, for example, 900 probation officers are responsible for supervising 88,000 offenders.[4] Consequently, judges and correctional officials are increasingly turning to intermediate sanctions such as intensive supervision programs, fines, boot camps, electronic monitoring, and home confinement to alleviate the pressure on both incarceration facilities and probation rolls. As widespread as these community-based punishments have become, however, they have not been completely accepted by the public. Numerous opinion polls show that a majority of Americans consider any punishment besides imprisonment a "slap on the wrist."

In this chapter, we will discuss the strengths and weaknesses of probation and other community sanctions, as well as efforts to make these sentencing alternatives more efficient and more palatable to the electorate. Given the scarcity of prison resources, decisions made today concerning community-based punishment will affect the criminal justice system for decades to come.

THE JUSTIFICATION FOR COMMUNITY CORRECTIONS

In the court of popular opinion, retribution and crime control take precedence over community-based correctional programs. America, says University of Minnesota law professor Michael Tonry, is preoccupied with the "absolute severity of punishment" and the "widespread view that only imprisonment counts."[5] Mandatory sentencing guidelines and "three strikes" laws are theoretically opposed to community-based corrections.[6] To a certain degree correctional programs that are administered in the community are considered a less severe, and therefore less worthy, alternative to imprisonment.

CJ in Focus

The Balancing Act

"Jason's Law" and Compromised Justice

When the Roberts family learned that a man named Callahan had been released from a Massachusetts county jail after only three months, under the condition that he wear an electronic monitoring bracelet, they were outraged. A year earlier, a drunk Callahan had killed twenty-one-year-old Jason Roberts in an automobile accident. Callahan had been sentenced to thirty months in jail, with eighteen months suspended. The Roberts family felt that Sheriff John Flood, who made the decision to release Callahan, had betrayed their trust and the trust of the community.

Community-based corrections represent a compromise society makes with certain wrongdoers. Theoretically, society benefits by saving scarce incarceration space for truly dangerous criminals and by giving supposedly low-risk offenders the opportunity to reintegrate into the community. These utilitarian justifications, however, often fail to counterbalance the cold, hard facts of an incident such as Jason Roberts's death. Given that we cannot predict criminal activity, inevitably some convicts being supervised outside prison or jail will commit crimes, and some of those crimes will be violent. In any given year, offenders in community corrections programs are responsible for more than 10,000 murders and nearly 40,000 robberies, along with tens of thousands of other crimes. For the victims of these acts, the scales of justice appear to be heavily weighted in favor of the individual offender and against the best interests of society.

In response to the Callahan incident, the Massachusetts legislature is considering "Jason's Law," which would prohibit sheriffs from transferring inmates sentenced to prisons or jails into programs such as house arrest and electronic monitoring. The Massachusetts Sheriff's Association strongly protested the bill, arguing that its members use an objective classification system to determine who is eligible for community supervision. Furthermore, noted critics of the bill, existing local corrections facilities were already overcrowded, and the county in question did not have the financial resources to incarcerate all convicts: the cost of keeping an inmate in jail for a year is $35,000, compared to only $6,000 for electronic monitoring.

For Critical Analysis: Should victims and victims' families such as the Roberts family have a say in whether criminals are sentenced to community-based corrections?

Reintegration

Supporters of probation and intermediate sanctions reject such views as not only shortsighted, but also contradictory to the aims of the corrections system. A very small percentage of all convicted offenders have committed crimes that warrant capital punishment or life imprisonment—most, at some point, will return to the community. Consequently, according to one group of experts, the task of the corrections system:

> includes building or rebuilding solid ties between the offender and the community, integrating or reintegrating the offender into community life—restoring family ties, obtaining employment and an education, securing in the larger sense a place for the offender in the routine functioning of society.[7]

Considering that some studies have shown higher recidivism rates for offenders who are subjected to prison culture, a frequent justification of community-based corrections is that they attempt to reintegrate the offender into society.

Reintegration has a strong theoretical basis in rehabilitative theories of punishment. An offender is generally considered to be "rehabilitated" when he or she no longer represents a threat to other members of the community and therefore is believed to be fit to live in that community. In the context of the next four chapters, it will also be helpful to see reintegration as a process through which corrections officials such as probation and parole officers provide the offender with incentives to follow the rules of society. In doing so, the corrections system must constantly balance the rights of the individual offender against the rights of law-abiding members of the community. (See *CJ in Focus—The Balancing Act: "Jason's Law" and Compromised Justice*.)

REINTEGRATION
A goal of corrections that focuses on preparing the offender for a return to the community unmarred by further criminal behavior.

DIVERSION
In the context of corrections, a strategy to divert those offenders who qualify away from prison and jail and toward community-based and intermediate sanctions.

PROBATION
A criminal sanction in which a convict is allowed to remain in the community rather than be imprisoned as long as she or he follows certain conditions set by the court.

Diversion

Another justification for community-based corrections, based on practical considerations, is **diversion.** As you are already aware, most criminal offenses fall into the category of "petty," and it is practically impossible, as well as unnecessary, to imprison every offender for every offense. Community-based corrections are an important means of diverting criminals to alternative modes of punishment so that scarce incarceration resources are consumed by only the most dangerous criminals. In his "strainer" analogy, corrections expert Paul H. Hahn likens this process to the workings of a kitchen strainer. With each "shake" of the corrections "strainer," the less serious offenders are diverted from incarceration. At the end, only the most serious convicts remain to be sent to prison.[8] (The concept of diversion is closely linked to that of selective incapacitation, mentioned in Chapter 11.)

The diversionary role of community-based punishments has become more pronounced as prisons and jails have filled up over the past three decades. In fact, probationers now account for nearly two-thirds of all adults in the American corrections systems (see Figure 12.1). According to the U.S. Department of Justice, on any single day, nearly 2 percent of all adult citizens are under probation supervision.[9]

PROBATION: DOING TIME IN THE COMMUNITY

As Figure 12.1 shows, **probation** is the most common form of punishment in the United States. Although it is administered differently in various jurisdictions, probation can be generally defined as

> the legal status of an offender who, after being convicted of a crime, has been directed by the sentencing court to remain in the community under the supervision of a probation service for a designated period of time and subject to certain conditions imposed by the court or by law.[10]

The theory behind probation is that certain offenders, having been found guilty of a crime, can be more economically and humanely treated by placing

Figure 12.1 Probation in American Corrections

As you can see, the number of Americans on probation almost tripled between 1980 and 1997 (matching the growth rate of prison and jail populations.)

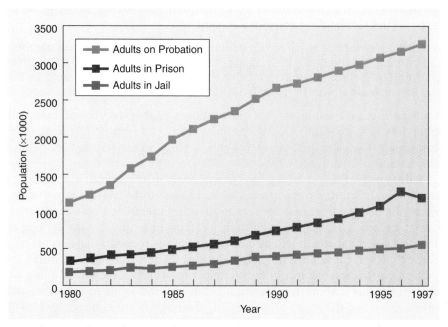

SOURCE: BUREAU OF JUSTICE STATISTICS, SOURCEBOOK OF CRIMINAL JUSTICE STATISTICS, 1997 (WASHINGTON, D.C.: U.S. DEPARTMENT OF JUSTICE, 1998), 464.

them under controls while still allowing them to live in the community. One of the advantages of probation has been that it provides for the rehabilitation of the offender while saving society the costs of incarceration. Despite probation's widespread use, certain participants in the criminal justice system question its ability to reach its rehabilitative goals. Critics point to the immense number of probationers and the fact that many of them are violent felons as evidence that the system is "out of control." Supporters contend that nothing is wrong with probation in principle, but admit that its execution must be adjusted to meet the goals of modern corrections.[11]

The Roots of Probation

In its earliest forms, probation was based on a desire to inject leniency into an often harsh criminal justice system. Nineteenth-century English judges had the power to issue **judicial reprieves,** or to suspend sentences for a certain amount of time, on the condition of continued good behavior on the part of the defendant. This practice was adopted in the United States, albeit in a different form. American judges used their reprieve power to suspend the imposition of a penalty indefinitely, so long as the offender committed no second crime. If another crime was committed, the offender could be punished for both crimes.

In *Ex parte United States* (1916),[12] the Supreme Court ruled that such indefinite reprieves were unconstitutional because they limited the ability of the legislative and administrative branches to make and enforce sentencing laws. With this diversion option removed, judges increasingly turned to the model of probation first established in Massachusetts eighty years earlier.

John Augustus and the Origins of Probation. The roots of probation can be directly traced to a Boston shoemaker named John Augustus. In 1841, Augustus, a religious man with considerable wealth, offered to post bail for a man charged with drunkenness. Augustus persuaded the judge to defer sentencing for three weeks, during which time the offender would be in his custody. At the end of this probationary period, the offender was able to convince the judge that he had been reformed and received a fine instead of incarceration.

During the next eighteen years until his death, Augustus bailed out and supervised nearly 1,800 persons in lieu of confinement in the Boston House of Corrections. He carefully screened potential probationers, researching their personal backgrounds before deciding whether to include them on his caseload. Generally, Augustus accepted only first offenders of otherwise good character. During the probationary period, he helped his charges find employment and lodging and aided them in obtaining an education.[13] Augustus can be credited with nearly every aspect of modern probation, from the name itself (from the Latin term *probatio,* or a "period of governing or trial") to presentence investigations to supervision to revocation.

Augustus's work was continued by a group of volunteer "probation officers" who worked to rescue youths from the dangers of imprisonment. In 1869, the state of Massachusetts passed a law that allowed for probation of juveniles and, nine years later, provided for paid probation officers to be hired by Boston's criminal courts. The law limited probation to "such persons as may reasonably be expected to be reformed without punishment." By 1891, Massachusetts had established the first statewide probation program.[14]

Mohammed Haroon Ali, pictured above, was arrested for the murder of his girlfriend Tracey Biletnikoff on February 16, 1999. Three years earlier, Ali plead guilty to felony kidnapping and threatening bodily injury in an incident involving a former girlfriend. Instead of being sent to prison for his crimes, however, Ali was sentenced to probation. How does a case like Ali's leave the probation system open to criticism?

JUDICIAL REPRIEVE
Temporary relief or the postponement of a sentence on the authority of a judge. In the United States, the judicial power to offer a reprieve has been limited by the Supreme Court.

The Evolution of Probation. Even as probation systems have been adopted in each of the fifty states and the federal government, the basic conflict between "help" and "punishment" has dominated the context of probation. When both criminal justice practitioners and the public hold the rehabilitative model in favor, as was the case for most of the first half of the twentieth century, probation is generally considered a valuable aspect of treatment. When, however, retributive goals come to the fore, probation is seen as being in need of reform, as has been the case in the United States since the mid-1970s. (It should be noted, though, that the number of Americans on probation has continued to grow even as its theoretical underpinnings are being challenged.)

The Modern Mission of Probation

DiIulio, John. Reinventing parole and probation.

In the 1930s, Harvard University criminologist Sheldon Glueck warned that probation (and other forms of community-based corrections) were overly reliant on the goodwill of the public at large.[15] Today, Glueck's warning still seems relevant, as American attitudes toward probation are tending toward the negative. One survey, conducted by Professor Timothy J. Flanagan of the College of Criminal Justice at Sam Houston State University found that only 26 percent of the participants had a "great deal" or "quite a lot" of confidence in probation.[16] Many observers believe that the probation system has left itself open to criticism by failing to establish a distinct mission and to define the methods of accomplishing that mission. In other words, the public does not understand exactly what probation is meant to do. Is its primary mission to punish wrongdoers, while also saving scarce corrections resources, or to rehabilitate offenders so as to reintegrate them into society?

Given this lack of an overriding institutional philosophy, these questions are often answered by individual probation officers. Researchers Marylouise E. Jones and Arthur J. Lurigio of Loyola University in Chicago have identified four types of probation officers, each characterized by a particular view of the officer's role in the corrections process:

1. *The punitive officer.* The punitive probation officer constructs a relationship with the probationer that is built entirely on the conditions of the sentence. Any violations (discussed in detail later in the chapter), no matter how minor, will be duly reported, even if this results in the probationer being incarcerated. The punitive officer is primarily concerned with preserving community safety and takes a "tail 'em, nail 'em, jail 'em" attitude toward controlling probationers.

2. *The therapeutic officer.* The therapeutic, or welfare, probation officer follows the values introduced by John Augustus. She or he focuses primarily on the needs of the offender and the goal of rehabilitation. Even if the probationer violates the terms of the sentence, the therapeutic officer may be willing to "look the other way" to help the client's reintegration into society.

3. *The bureaucratic officer.* This type of probation officer is not interested in the welfare of the community or of the client. Instead, he or she aims to lessen the workload and takes no initiative beyond the basic requirements of the job. Because the bureaucratic officer values time-saving above all else, such civil servants are accepted and even welcomed in probation agencies with overwhelming caseloads.

4. *The mediator.* Probation officers who focus on mediation try to reconcile the contradictory goals of treatment and control in their work. They try to balance the needs of the community with those of the client and make decisions on a case-by-case basis.[17]

To a certain extent, the existence of these various types is a reflection of the discretion that has traditionally been allowed to probation officers. The 1990s, however, saw a movement to limit probation officers' discretion, similar to the campaign to limit judicial discretion that we discussed in the last chapter. Through sentencing reform, legislative bodies on both the national and state level have steered probation away from principles of rehabilitation and toward principles of punishment, hoping to provide the practice with a mission that they find more in keeping with the public's desire to be tough on criminals.

Sentencing Choices and Probation

Probation is basically an "arrangement" between sentencing authorities and the offender. In traditional probation, the offender agrees to follow certain terms for a specified amount of time in return for serving the sentence in the community. One of the primary benefits for the offender, besides not getting sent to a correctional facility, is that the length of the probationary period is usually considerably shorter than the length of a prison term (see Figure 12.2).

The "traditional" form of probation is not, however, the only arrangement that can be made. A judge can forgo probation altogether by handing down a **suspended sentence.** A descendant of the judicial reprieve discussed earlier, a suspended sentence places no conditions or supervision on the offender. He or she remains free for a certain length of time, but the judge keeps the option of revoking the suspended sentence and remanding the offender to prison or jail if circumstances call for such action.

Alternative Sentencing Arrangements. Judges can also combine probation with incarceration. Such sentencing arrangements include:

- *Split sentences.* In **split sentence probation,** also known as *shock probation,* the offender is sentenced to a specific amount of time in prison or jail, to be followed by a period of probation.

- *Shock incarceration.* In this arrangement, an offender is sentenced to prison or jail with the understanding that after a period of time, she or

SUSPENDED SENTENCE
A judicially imposed condition in which an offender is sentenced after being convicted of a crime, but is not required to begin the sentence immediately. The judge may revoke the suspended sentence and remit the offender to prison or jail if he or she does not follow certain conditions.

SPLIT SENTENCE PROBATION
A sentence that consists of incarceration in a prison or jail, followed by a probationary period in the community.

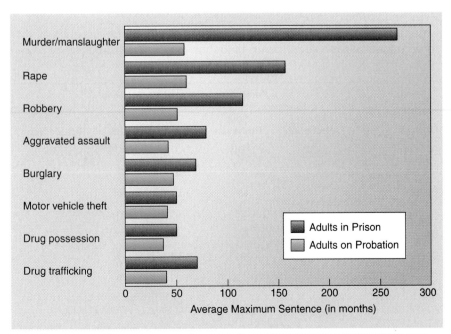

SOURCE: ADAPTED FROM BUREAU OF JUSTICE STATISTICS, *FELONY SENTENCES IN THE UNTIED STATES, 1994* (WASHINGTON, D.C.: U.S. DEPARTMENT OF JUSTICE, JULY 1997), 8.

Figure 12.2 Average Length of Sentence: Prison versus Probation
As you can see, the average probation sentence is much shorter than the average prison sentence for most crimes.

he may petition the court to be released on probation. Shock incarceration is discussed more fully later in the chapter.

- *Intermittent incarceration.* Intermittent incarceration requires that the offender spend a certain amount of time each week, usually during the weekend, in a jail, workhouse, or other government institution.

Such arrangements have become more popular with judges, as they combine the "treatment" aspects of probation with the "punishment" aspects of incarceration. According to the Department of Justice, nearly one-quarter of all convicted felons receive split sentences.[18] (See Figure 12.3.)

Eligibility for Probation. Not every offender is eligible for probation. In Bell County, Texas, the setting for the homicide case that opened this chapter, juries can recommend probation only for assessed prison sentences of ten years or less. Generally, research has shown that offenders are most likely to be denied probation if they:

- Are convicted on multiple charges.

- Were on probation or parole at the time of the arrest.

- Have two or more prior convictions.

- Are addicted to narcotics.

- Seriously injured the victim of the crime.

- Used a weapon during the commission of the crime.[19]

As might be expected, the chances of a felon being sentenced to probation are highly dependent on the seriousness of the crime he or she has committed (see Figure 12.4).

Differences in Probation Rates. Even though eligibility requirements for probation are generally uniform, the use of probation can vary greatly from jurisdiction to jurisdiction. One recent study found only 30 percent of offenders received probation in New York City compared to 75 percent in Minneapolis, Minnesota.[20]

Certain statistics seem to show that other, extralegal factors such as race and economic class also influence probation decisions. An analysis of proba-

Figure 12.3 Felony Sentences Imposed by State Courts

As you can see, about half of all felony sentences handed out by state courts involve probation.

Offense	Percentage of Felony Convictions				
	Straight Probation	Split Probation	Prison	Jail	No Incarceration
All offenses	26%	24%	37%	10%	3%
Murder	3	7	89	1	0
Rape	11	24	59	4	2
Aggravated assault	21	26	40	10	3
Burglary	21	23	45	7	4
Drug possession	32	30	27	9	2
Drug trafficking	23	23	39	9	6

SOURCE: ADAPTED FROM BUREAU OF JUSTICE STATISTICS, *STATE COURT SENTENCING OF CONVICTED FELONS, 1994* (WASHINGTON, D.C.: U.S. DEPARTMENT OF JUSTICE, MARCH 1998), TABLE 3.2, PAGE 31.

tion in Georgia from 1990 to 1997 showed that white criminals were 30 to 60 percent more likely to get probation than African Americans committing similar crimes.[21] Nationwide, even though African Americans make up approximately half of all federal and state prison inmates, they only account for 28 percent of probation rolls.[22] We will address the possibility of discrimination in probation and other community corrections in Chapter 18.

Conditions of Probation

As part of the decision to sentence an offender to probation, a judge may also set conditions of probation. These conditions represent a "contract" between the judge and the offender, in which the latter agrees that if she or he does not follow certain rules, probation may be revoked (see Figure 12.5). The probation officer usually recommends the conditions of probation, but judges also have the power to set any terms they believe to be necessary.

Figure 12.4 Adults on Probation by Felony Conviction Type

As you see here, the majority of adults on probation were convicted of property crimes or drug offenses.

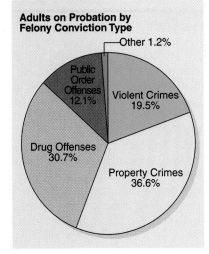

Adults on Probation by Felony Conviction Type

- Other 1.2%
- Violent Crimes 19.5%
- Property Crimes 36.6%
- Drug Offenses 30.7%
- Public Order Offenses 12.1%

SOURCE: ADAPTED FROM BUREAU OF JUSTICE STATISTICS, CHARACTERISTICS OF ADULTS ON PROBATION, 1995 (WASHINGTON, D.C.: U.S. DEPARTMENT OF JUSTICE, DECEMBER 1997), TABLE 1, PAGE 3.

Figure 12.5 Conditions of Probation

Conditions of Probation
UNITED STATES DISTRICT COURT
FOR THE DISTRICT OF COLUMBIA

To _____ No. 84-417
Address: 1440 N St., N.W., #10, Wash., D.C.

In accordance With authority conferred by the United States Probation Law, you have been placed on probation this date, January 25, 2000 for a period of one year by the Hon. Louis F. Oberdorfer United States District Judge, sitting in and for this District Court at Washington, D.C.

CONDITIONS OF PROBATION

It is the order of the Court that you shall comply with the following conditions of probation:

(1) You shall refrain from violation of any law (federal, state, and local). You shall get in touch immediately with your probation officer if arrested or questioned by a law-enforcement officer.

(2) You shall associate only with law-abiding persons and maintain reasonable hours.

(3) You shall work regularly at a lawful occupation and support your legal dependents, if any, to the best of your ability. When out of work you shall notify your probation officer at once. You shall consult him prior to job changes.

(4) You shall not leave the judicial district without permission of the probation officer.

(5) You shall notify your probation officer immediately of any change in your place of residence.

(6) You shall follow the probation officer's instructions.

(7) You shall report to the probation officer as directed.

(8) You shall not possess a firearm (handgun or rifle) for any reason.

The special conditions ordered by the Court are as follows:

Imposition of sentence suspended, one year probation, Fine of $75 on each count.

I understand that the Court may change the conditions of probation, reduce or extend the period of probation, and at any time during the probation period or within the maximum probation period of 5 years permitted by law, may issue a warrant and revoke probation for a violation occurring during the probation period.

I have read or had read to me the above conditions of probation. I fully understand them and I will abide by them.

(Signed)   1/25/00
You will report as follows: Probationer Date

As directed by your Probation Officer

(Signed)   1/5/00
U.S. Probation Officer Date

CJ in Focus

Was Justice Served?

Probation and the Scarlet Letter

The Scarlet Letter (1850), a novel by Nathaniel Hawthorne, tells the story of Hester Prynne, a woman in seventeenth-century New England who is convicted of adultery. As part of her punishment, Prynne is required to wear a scarlet letter "A" on her dress to remind herself and others of her shame. Many modern judges are including "scarlet-letter" provisions as conditions of probation, raising questions of whether society's interests are served by the public shaming of a convict.

As the Supreme Court has yet to rule on the constitutionality of scarlet-letter probation conditions, the issue has been decided on a state-by-state basis. Consequently, similar conditions can inspire different interpretations of the limitations placed on trial judges in setting the terms of probation. Take, for example, two cases with a number of similarities but different outcomes: one took place in Georgia, the other in North Carolina.

THE REHABILITATIVE EFFECTS OF SHAME

The Georgia case concerned Mr. Ballenger, who had been convicted of the felony of driving under the influence (DUI). As a condition of his probation, Ballenger was ordered by the trial court to wear a fluorescent pink plastic bracelet on which was written "DUI Convict." In North Carolina, Mr. Mewborn pleaded guilty to possession with intent to sell and deliver cocaine. In his case, the judge mandated as a condition of probation that, as long as Mewborn resided in North Carolina, he must wear each day a black sweatshirt or a black T-shirt bearing the words "Convicted Drug Dealer" in orange letters.

Ballenger argued before the Georgia Court of Appeals that having to wear the pink bracelet violated his equal protection rights and constituted cruel and unusual punishment because it fell outside the standard probation conditions. In 1993, the court rejected this argument and let the scarlet-letter probation condition stand. Stating that the two goals of probation are rehabilitation and the protection of society, the court decided that it could *not* say with certainty that wearing the pink bracelet would not further these goals: "Being jurists rather than psychologists, we cannot say that the stigmatizing effect of wearing the bracelet may not have a rehabilitative, deterrent effect on Ballenger." In other words, the court left open the possibility that the "stigmatizing effects" of the bracelet could shame Ballenger into not committing future crimes, therefore rehabilitating (or at least deterring) him.

In contrast, a three-judge panel of the North Carolina Court of Appeals held in 1998 that forcing Mewborn to wear the shaming sweatshirts and T-shirts did not meet reasonable conditions of probation. The panel agreed with the defendant's argument that the condition violated a state law that probation conditions must be "reasonably necessary to insure that the defendant will lead a law-abiding life or assist him to do so." In fact, stated the panel, the emblazoned shirts would hinder Mewborn's efforts to "lead a law-abiding life," because they would make it practically impossible for him to get a job (another condition of his probation).

For Critical Analysis: Do you believe the interests of justice were better served by the decision of the appeals court in Georgia or the one in North Carolina? Depending on your point of view, make the argument that the public humiliation of probationers satisfies (or does not satisfy) the dual purposes of probation.

This power is far-reaching, and a judge's personal philosophy is often reflected in the probation conditions that are set. In *In re Quirk* (1998),[23] for example, the Supreme Court upheld the ability of a Louisiana trial judge to impose church attendance as a condition of probation. Though judges have a great deal of discretion in setting the conditions of probation, they do operate under several guiding principles. First, the conditions must be related to the dual purposes of probation, which most federal and state courts define as (1) the rehabilitation of the probationer and (2) the protection of the community. (See *CJ in Focus—Was Justice Served?: Probation and the Scarlet Letter.*) Second, the conditions must not violate the U.S. Constitution. That is, probationers are generally entitled to the same constitutional rights as other prisoners.[24] Of course, probationers do give up certain constitutional rights when they consent to the terms of probation; most probationers, for example, agree to spot checks of their homes for contraband such as drugs or weapons, and they therefore have a diminished expectation of privacy.

Obviously, probationers who break the law are very likely to have their probation revoked. Other, less serious infractions may also result in revocation. The conditions placed upon a probationer fall into three general categories:

▎ *Standard conditions*, which are imposed on all probationers. These include reporting regularly to the probation office, notifying the agency of any change of address, not leaving the jurisdiction without permission, and remaining employed.

▌ *Punitive conditions,* which usually reflect the seriousness of the offense and are intended to increase the punishment of the offender. Such conditions include fines, community service, restitution, drug testing, and home confinement (discussed later).

▌ *Treatment conditions,* which are imposed with the goal of helping the offender with a condition that may contribute to his or her criminal activity. Recent data show that more than 40 percent of probationers were required to seek drug or alcohol treatment as part of their sentence, and an additional 18 percent were ordered to seek other kinds of treatment such as anger-control therapy.[25] (Figure 12.6 shows the most common conditions for adult felony probationers.)

Some observers feel that judges have too much discretion in imposing overly restrictive conditions that no person, much less one who has exhibited antisocial tendencies, could meet. Citing prohibitions on drinking liquor, gambling, and associating with "undesirables," as well as requirements such as meeting early curfews, University of Delaware professor Carl B. Klockars claims that if probation rules were taken seriously, "very few probationers would complete their terms without violation."[26] As more than eight out of ten federal probationers do complete their terms successfully, Klockars's statement leads to several assumptions. Either probation officers are unable to determine that violations are taking place, or many of them are following the therapeutic model discussed earlier and use a great deal of discretion in reporting minor probation violations. Or, perhaps, the officers realize that violating probationers for every single "slip-up" is unrealistic, and would add to the already immense problem of jail and prison overcrowding.

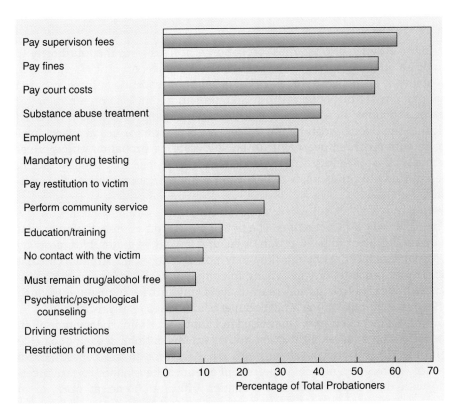

Figure 12.6 Special Conditions Imposed on Probationers

SOURCE: Bureau of Justice Statistics, Characteristics of Adults on Probation, 1995 (Washington, D.C.: U.S. Department of Justice, December 1997), 7.

AUTHORITY
The power designated to an agent of the law over a person who has broken the law.

The Supervisory Role of the Probation Officer

The probation officer has two basic roles. The first is investigative and consists of conducting the presentence investigation (PSI), which was discussed in Chapter 11. The second is supervisory and begins as soon as the offender has been sentenced to probation. In smaller probation agencies, individual officers perform both tasks. In larger jurisdictions, the trend has been toward separating the responsibilities, with investigating officers handling the PSI and *line officers* concentrating on supervision. (For insight into this role, see *Careers in Criminal Justice—The Probation Officer.*)

Supervisory policies vary and are often a reflection of whether the authority to administer probation services is *decentralized* (under local, judicial control) or *centralized* (under state, administrative control). In any circumstance, however, certain basic principles of supervision apply. Starting with a preliminary interview, the probation officer establishes a relationship with the offender. This relationship is based on the mutual goal of both parties: the successful completion of the probationary period. Just because the line officer and the offender have the same goal, however, does not mean that probation is necessarily marked by excessive cooperation.

The Use of Authority. The ideal probation officer–offender relationship is based on trust. In reality, this trust does not often exist. Any incentive an offender might have to be completely truthful with a line officer is marred by one simple fact: self-reported wrongdoing can be used to revoke probation. Even probation officers whose primary mission is to rehabilitate are under institutional pressure to punish their clients for violating conditions of probation. One officer deals with this situation by telling his clients

> that I'm here to help them, to get them a job, and whatever else I can do. But I tell them too that I have a family to support and that if they get too far off track, I can't afford to put my job on the line for them. I'm going to have to violate them.[27]

In the absence of trust, most probation officers rely on their **authority** to guide an offender successfully through the sentence. An officer's authority, or ability to influence a person's actions without resorting to force, is based not only on her or his power to revoke probation, but also on a number of lesser sanctions. For example, if a probationer fails to attend a required alcohol treatment program, the officer can place him or her in a "lock-up," or detention center, overnight. To be successful, a probation officer must establish this authority early in the relationship; it is the primary tool in persuading the probationer to behave in a manner acceptable to the community.[28]

The Offender's Perspective. The public perception of probationers is that they are lucky not to be in prison or jail and should be grateful for receiving a "second chance." Although they may not describe their situation in that way, many probationers are willing to comply with the terms of their sentence, if for no other reason than to avoid any further punishments. Such offenders can make a line officer's supervision duties relatively simple.

By the same token, as we discussed in Chapter 2, criminal behavior is often predicated on a lack of respect for authority. This outlook does not coincide with the supervisory aspects of probation. According to the Department of Justice, in any given month, 61 percent of offenders have a face-to-face meeting with their supervisors in a probation office, at home, at work, or in another setting. Another 25 percent were in contact through the mail or over the phone.[29] Furthermore, to follow the conditions of probation, convicts may

> "I've had a lot of people come up to me from the past, asking me to do things. When I see them, it's like, no can't do that, don't talk to me no more because my PO (probation officer) is shadowing me. Look, I don't like police officers or probation officers, I do what I got to do and that's all."
>
> —Vanessa Martinez, *probationer convicted of attempted murder (1997)*

have to discontinue activity that they find enjoyable, such as going to a bar for a drink on Saturday night. Consequently, some probationers consider supervision as akin to "baby-sitting" and resist the strict controls placed on them by the government.

Careers in Criminal Justice

SCOTT T. BALLOCK, U.S. PROBATION OFFICER

Uncertain about my future at the beginning of my sophomore year, I stumbled into an Introduction to Criminal Justice course at Indiana University and quickly became fascinated with the work of professionals in this field. The only difficulty was deciding which route to go; there were so many possibilities and they all seemed fun and interesting. Throughout the rest of my undergraduate and graduate programs, I set out to get a closer look at each career path and volunteered variously at the local jail, probation office, police department, courthouse, and different social services agencies. I rode along with police officers, interviewed prison administrators, and met with attorneys and judges. My time spent with these people provided me with a more realistic picture of each profession than I had received through my education. Ultimately, the field of probation and parole appeared to provide the best fit for my interests and goals.

As a Federal Probation Officer, I work for the United States District Court in the District of Nevada (Las Vegas Office). U.S. Probation Officers serve as officers of the court and as agents of the U.S. Parole Commission. We are responsible for the supervision of all persons conditionally released to the community by the courts, the Parole Commission, the Federal Bureau of Prisons, and military authorities. Being released "conditionally" to the community means that in exchange for allowing an offender to remain in the community, the court expects them to meet certain standards and goals. These include remaining law-abiding and drug-free, working, supporting family, repaying victims, perhaps performing volunteer work for the community, and making other improvements in their lives.

Supervising offenders in the community, our mission is to execute the court's sentence, control risk, and promote law-abiding behavior. In order to meet these goals, probation officers must become very knowledgeable about an offender's activities and lifestyle. We do so by meeting with them on a regular basis in the community, conducting unannounced home inspections, speaking regularly with their family, friends, neighbors, and employers, and—when necessary—conducting surveillance or warrantless searches of their homes and vehicles.

I am often asked whether probation officers are law enforcement officers or social workers. We are both. Responsible for protecting the public, we are also charged with promoting positive change among our probationers and parolees. Half of our day may be spent following an offender through the city to learn if he is engaged in illegal activities, while the second half is spent counseling offenders, helping them prepare a resume, or referring them to local social service agencies for further assistance. Our dual role is an especially challenging aspect of the job. I struggle daily with whether to continue to help someone who is unable to comply with the court's orders, or whether it's time to ask the court to send them to prison. It's often a difficult choice to make, particularly after having invested so much time and energy in attempting to turn an individual's life around.

Fortunately, we have the guidance of our boss, the sentencing judge. I used to think that justice was dispensed routinely and methodically with little consideration given to the impact of a sentence. Having worked for several judges, however, I have learned that sentences are carefully crafted and well thought out. Probation officers and judges are genuinely concerned about the welfare of the people who appear before them. If offenders have a substance abuse problem they'll be offered treatment. If they are lacking in job skills, a judge may order successful completion of a vocational training program. There seems to be no end to our creativity when imposing a sentence.

We recognize that a prison sentence is a very costly proposition, to both the offender and the community. A decision to send or return a person to a prison setting is a serious matter, and great lengths are taken to first effect positive change. I think even those we supervise come to realize this. It's not infrequent that a person I've spent months trying to help, and who ultimately fails and is sent back to prison, extends his hand to thank me for trying—even as he's being led away by the U.S. Marshals.

Probation officers come from a variety of fields and bring wide-ranging experiences to the job. Such diversity is necessary for the type of work we do. We have so many responsibilities, ranging from conducting financial investigations to investigating evidence of new criminal activity, and this requires that we develop a working knowledge of many different areas of criminal justice. Probation officers are filled with officers who have backgrounds in financial matters, counseling, law enforcement, and social service work. I would strongly recommend students consider probation and parole as an option for employment. It's a good feeling to know that each day, simply by going to work, you've made a difference for the community.

The Changing Environment of the Probation Officer. To some extent, today's probation officers function similarly to John Augustus's volunteers. They spend a great deal of time in the community, working with businesses, churches, schools, and neighborhood groups on behalf of their charges. The probation officer's work environment has not, however, remained static.[30]

During the 1970s and 1980s, various court decisions established a precedent that probation officers could be held responsible

The Corrections Connections acts as a clearinghouse for information concerning the corrections industry. It offers links to about 20 community corrections sites at www.correction.com/links/communty.html

for failing to take sufficient care in their duties.[31] Although the number of civil lawsuits filed against probation officers has climbed accordingly, these actions are rarely successful.[32] In 1997, for example, the Supreme Court refused to consider a request to hold Donna Chester, the Milwaukee (Wisconsin) probation officer of serial killer Jeffrey Dahmer, responsible for his murders.[33] The father of one of Dahmer's victims claimed that Chester had failed to make a single home visit to Dahmer's apartment, where all seventeen of his murders took place. Even under such circumstances, most courts recognize that poor decision making does not equal negligence, especially given the demanding workload of most probation officers. In fact, Chester had been given permission *not* to visit Dahmer because of her heavy caseload.

Some observers are also questioning another traditional aspect of probation: the separation of police and probation officers. Due to interdepartmental rivalries, and perhaps a lack of communication, few police and probation departments have taken advantage of the resources offered by the other agency.[34] This lack of cooperation is somewhat shortsighted, given that both sides have knowledge and expertise that could be helpful in reaching the overall goal of crime prevention. The state of Maryland, for example, has begun stationing probation officers in high-crime neighborhoods, the assumption being that patrol officers, not knowing the identity of probationers, will not recognize probation violations in progress.[35]

As far as the probation officers themselves are concerned, the major change in their work is that it is getting progressively more dangerous.[36] This can be attributed to two factors:

- *The demographics of probation.* As probation is increasingly offered to felons, probation officers find themselves dealing with a higher percentage of violent offenders.

- *The proliferation of firearms.* With more guns on the streets, the likelihood that a probationer is armed has increased significantly.[37]

One recent study found that more than 60 percent of probation officers had been the victims of a physical attack at some point in their careers.[38] In response, many districts are rethinking the long-held opinion that probation officers—given the "social work" aspects of their jobs—should not be allowed to carry firearms for protection. Following a congressional order in 1996 that gave each federal district the ability to make the decision for itself,[39] 87 percent of these districts have allowed federal probation officers to choose whether to carry a firearm, and 83 percent of those officers have opted to do so.[40]

Revocation of Probation

The probation period can end in one of two ways. Either the probationer successfully fulfills the conditions of the sentence or the probationer misbehaves and probation is revoked, resulting in a prison or jail term. The decision of whether to revoke after a **technical violation**—such as failing to report a change of address or testing positive for drug use—is often a "judgment call" by the probation officer and therefore the focus of controversy.

Revocation Trends. In the past, a technical violation almost always led to revocation. Today, many probation officers will only take that step if they believe the technical violation in question represents a danger to the community. At the same time, the public's more punitive attitude, along with improved drug testing methods, has increased the number of conditions that probationers are placed under, and consequently the odds that they will violate one of those conditions. To a certain extent, these two trends have

TECHNICAL VIOLATION
An action taken by a probationer that, although not criminal, breaks the terms of probation as designated by the court; can result in the revocation of probation and a return to prison or jail.

negated each other: since 1987 there has been almost no change in the percentage (between 75 and 80 percent) of offenders who successfully complete their probation terms.[41]

The reasons why probationers do not successfully complete their terms, have, however, shifted. As Figure 12.7 shows, the percentage of probationers with special conditions related to drug abuse has more than doubled since 1987. Not surprisingly, as the data in Figure 12.7 also indicate, the number of probationers caught and punished for using drugs has risen as well.

The Revocation Process. Probationers do not enjoy the same rights as other members of society. In *Griffin v. Wisconsin* (1987),[42] the Supreme Court ruled that probationers have only "conditional liberty" that is dependent "on observance of special restrictions." As long as the restrictions assure that a probationer works toward rehabilitation and does not harm the community, the Court allows the probationer's privacy to be restricted in a manner it would not accept otherwise.

The Supreme Court has not stripped probationers of all due process rights. In *Mempa v. Rhay* (1967),[43] the Court ruled that probationers were entitled to an attorney during the revocation process. Then, in *Morrissey v. Brewer* (1972) and *Gagnon v. Scarpelli* (1973),[44] the Court established a three-stage procedure by which the "limited" due process rights of probationers must be protected in potential revocation situations:

▌ *The preliminary hearing.* In this appearance before a "disinterested person" (often a judge), the facts of the violation or arrest are presented, and it is determined whether probable cause for revoking probation exists. This hearing can be waived by the probationer.

▌ *The revocation hearing.* During this hearing, the probation agency presents evidence to support its claim of violation, and the probationer can attempt to refute this evidence. The probationer has the right to know the charges being brought against him or her. Furthermore, probationers can testify on their own behalf and present witnesses in their favor, as well as confront and cross-examine adverse witnesses. A "neutral and

INFOTRAC®
COLLEGE EDITION

Albonetti, Celesta and John Hepburn. Probation revocation: a proportional hazards model of the conditioning effects of social disadvantage.

Figure 12.7 Drug Use and Probation Revocation

Given the increased number of drug offenders in our corrections system, it is not surprising that judges are increasingly making drug treatment a condition of probation. Nor is it surprising, given improved methods of drug testing, that the proportion of probation terminations for drug use has increased as well.

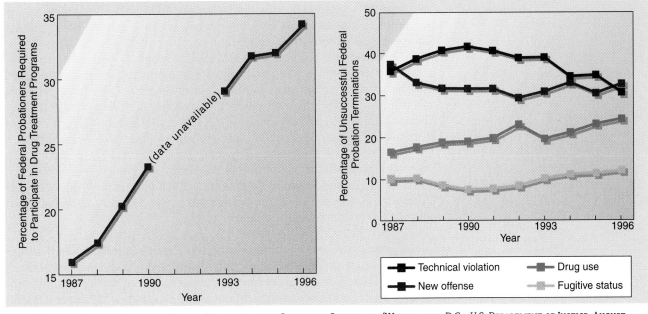

SOURCE: BUREAU OF JUSTICE STATISTICS, FEDERAL OFFENDERS UNDER COMMUNITY SUPERVISION (WASHINGTON, D.C.: U.S. DEPARTMENT OF JUSTICE, AUGUST 1998), TABLE 3, PAGE 4; TABLE 7, PAGE 6.

detached" body must hear the evidence and rule in favor of the probation agency or the offender.

▎ *Revocation sentencing.* If the presiding body rules against the probationer,
then the judge must decide whether to impose incarceration and for
what length of time. In a revocation hearing dealing with technical violations, the judge will often reimpose probation with stricter terms or
intermediate sanctions.

In effect, this is a "bare-bones" approach to due process. Most of the rules
of evidence that govern regular trials do not play a role in revocation hearings. Probation officers are not, for example, required to read offenders
Miranda rights when questioning them about crimes that may have been
committed during probation. In *Minnesota v. Murphy* (1984),[45] the Supreme
Court ruled that a meeting between probation officer and client does not
equal custody, and therefore the Fifth Amendment protection against self-
incrimination does not apply.

Does Probation Work?

To address the question of whether probation is effective, one must first
establish its purpose. Should the probation system be designed to rehabilitate
offenders? Is it primarily a method of surveillance and control? Should probation's role in the criminal justice system be to reduce pressure on prison
and jail populations? Each of these aspects of probation has its supporters
and critics. Indeed, the only consensus among supporters of probation is that
the system is severely underfunded. Even though two of every three
Americans in the corrections system are on probation, only one-tenth of the
corrections budget is allocated to probation agencies.[46] Furthermore, probation populations have tripled since 1977, yet spending for probation (after
correcting for inflation) remains unchanged.[47]

The Caseload Dilemma. As a result of these low budgets, say observers,
probation agencies do not have the resources to provide full services to all
offenders. Patrick A. Langan of the U.S. Department of Justice estimates that
fully half of this country's probationers do not comply with the conditions of
their sentence. The problem, contends Langan and many of his colleagues, is
that probation officers have such large caseloads that they cannot rigorously
enforce the conditions imposed on many of their clients.[48]

Unlike a prison cell, a probation officer can always take on "just one more"
offender/client. As there is no accepted standard for determining optimal
caseloads, probation officers can find themselves responsible for supervising
an extremely large number of convicts. One official interviewed by Professors
Charles Linder and Robert L. Bonn at John Jay College of Criminal Justice
admitted to having 6,500 clients supervised by four probation officers.[49]
Though data vary from state to state, Professor Joan Petersilia of the
University of California at Irvine estimates that, on average, each probation
officer in the United States has a caseload of 258 offenders.[50] Another study
found that 20 percent of adult *felony* probationers had no personal contact
with their probation officers whatsoever.[51]

Recidivism and Probation. Such statistics fuel the popular belief that probation allows dangerous felons to roam the streets and commit new crimes
at will. This perception is not entirely accurate. In fact, up to 80 percent of probationers complete their terms without being arrested (which does not necessarily mean that they did not commit a new offense).[52] Many criminologists

"I try to get in the field two to three nights
a week to see my offenders. It's really the
only way to stop trouble before it happens.
Otherwise, it's a free-for-all."

—Kevin Dudley, *Salt Lake City
probation officer* (1997)

are not surprised by this high percentage, given that many of those on probation are first-time, low-risk offenders. Furthermore, a controlled comparison of the recidivism rates of 511 probationers and 511 offenders released from prison found that probation can be at least as effective as incarceration, if not more so. Seventy-two percent of the prisoners were rearrested and 47 percent were imprisoned, while only 38 percent of the probationers were rearrested and 31 percent incarcerated.[53]

It is difficult to make general assumptions about recidivism rates. A Rand Corporation study of two California counties garnered a great deal of national attention by showing that 65 percent of felons on probation were rearrested for crimes such as assault, robbery, and burglary.[54] A subsequent study using the same methodology but based in Kentucky, however, found felony rearrest rates to be only 22 percent.[55] While recognizing that these differences may be influenced by factors such as sentencing guidelines and incarceration practices, the two studies do point to the regional differences in recidivism rates that can occur.

Not surprisingly, there seems to be a positive correlation between probationary success and the completion of treatment and education programs. In Arizona, for example, the state supreme court ordered adult education programs for its county probation departments.[56] The results, exhibited in Figure 12.8, have been encouraging.

Risk Assessment Management. Many reformers reject the notion that large caseloads are to blame for the inadequacies of the supervision system. These critics believe that probation agencies have failed to direct their limited resources efficiently. That is, they have failed to devote more supervisory controls to the relatively small percentage of offenders who run the highest risk of recidivism and pose the greatest threat to the community.

In 1981, the National Institute of Corrections developed a "model system" of case management to address these concerns. Based on the notion that some offenders require more attention than others, the model provides probation officers with statistical methods—based on the type of crime committed—to identify these offenders.[57] Within a decade, nearly every probation system in the nation was using similar classification devices to determine the level of supervision based on *risk assessment*.[58]

Basically, risk assessment management strategies determine the offender's threat to the community and the level of supervision required to lessen that threat.[59] In doing so, the probation officer or other officer of the court considers several factors, such as the offender's record of committing violent crimes; previous performance in probation, parole, or other community-based corrections programs; previous experience in jail or prison; and substance abuse or anger-management problems. In general, those offenders who are believed to pose the greatest threat to the community are labeled "maximum" risk and subjected to the highest level of supervision. Offenders who have not committed violent crimes or are deemed "medium" or "minimum" risks for other reasons are subjected to less supervision, thus freeing probation officers to deal with their most dangerous clients. This risk assessment model has two benefits: (1) in keeping with "just deserts," those who have committed more serious crimes are subject to more restrictive probationary terms, and (2) it prioritizes community protection.

Figure 12.8 Literacy Programs, Successful Probation Completion, and Recidivism

The Principle of Alphabet Literacy System (PALS) is a part of Pima County, Arizona's Adult Probation Department's Literacy, Education and Reading Network. PALS targets those probationers who read below a sixth-grade level and have difficulty writing complete sentences. Upon finishing 80 to 100 hours of instruction, PALS graduates are able to write complete sentences and fill out job applications. In a study comparing those probationers who completed PALS to those who did not, Arizona correctional officials found a correlation between literacy and positive results. As you can see, PALS graduates are more likely to complete their probation period without revocation and less likely to recidivate.

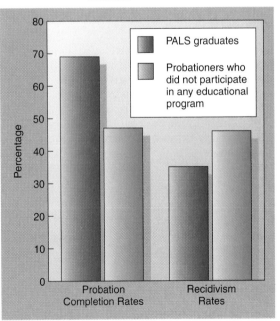

SOURCE: ADAPTED FROM GAYLE R. SEIGEL AND JOANNE BASTA, "THE EFFECT OF ADULT EDUCATION PROGRAMS ON PROBATIONERS," PERSPECTIVES (SPRING 1998), 42–44.

INTERMEDIATE SANCTIONS
Sanctions that are more restrictive
than probation and less restrictive
than imprisonment. Intended to
alleviate pressure on overcrowded
corrections facilities and understaffed
probation departments.

INTERMEDIATE SANCTIONS

During the 1960s and 1970s, many probation departments experimented with smaller caseloads under a management program known as *intensive supervision probation (ISP)*. These programs were discontinued when research showed that offenders in ISP had similar rearrest rates and more technical violations than those under regular supervision.[60] ISP was resurrected by the state of Georgia in 1982, however, with a different mandate. The state, experiencing prison crowding and a limited corrections budget, saw ISP as an alternative sanction for offenders who would have otherwise gone to prison. Georgia's version of ISP has been adopted in some measure by all fifty states, and it is at the vanguard of a movement to use **intermediate sanctions** to a greater degree in the American corrections system.

Many observers feel that the most widely used sentencing options—imprisonment or probation—fail to reflect the immense diversity of crimes and criminals. Intermediate sanctions provide a number of additional sentencing options for those wrongdoers who require stricter supervision than that supplied by probation, but for whom imprisonment would be unduly harsh and counterproductive.[61] The intermediate sanctions discussed in this section are designed to match the specific punishment and treatment of an individual offender with a corrections program that reflects that offender's situation.

Dozens of different variations of intermediate sanctions are handed down each year. To cover the spectrum succinctly, two general categories of such sanctions will be discussed in this section: those administered primarily by the courts and those administered primarily by probation departments, including day reporting centers, ISP programs, shock incarceration, and home confinement. Remember that none of these sanctions are exclusive: they are often combined with imprisonment and probation, and with each other.

Judicially Administered Intermediate Sanctions

The lack of sentencing options is most frustrating for the person who, in most cases, does the sentencing: the judge. Consequently, when judges are given the discretion to "color" a punishment with intermediate sanctions, they will often do so. Besides imprisonment and probation (and, to a lesser extent, other intermediate sanctions), a judge has five sentencing options:

1. Fines
2. Community service
3. Restitution
4. Forfeiture
5. Pretrial diversion programs

Fines, community service, and restitution were discussed in Chapter 11. In the context of intermediate sanctions, it is important to remember that these punishments are generally combined with incarceration or probation. For that reason, some critics feel the retributive or deterrent impact of such punishments is severely limited. Many European countries, in contrast, rely heavily on fines as the sole sanctions for a variety of crimes. (See *Cross-National CJ Comparison—Swedish Day-Fines.*)

Forfeiture. In 1970, Congress passed the Racketeer Influenced and Corrupt Organizations Act (RICO) in an attempt to prevent the use of legitimate business enter-

Two gang members perform their court-ordered community service under the watchful eye of a supervisor. Community service is one of a number of intermediate sanctions used to punish offenders instead of probation or incarceration. Why might corrections officials support the increased use of intermediate sanctions?

Swedish Day-Fines

Few ideals are cherished as highly in our criminal justice system as equality. Most Americans take it for granted that individuals guilty of identical crimes should face identical punishments. From an economic perspective, however, this emphasis on equality renders our system decidedly *unequal.* Take two citizens, one a millionaire investment banker and the other a checkout clerk earning the minimum wage. Driving home from work one afternoon, each is caught by a traffic officer doing 80 miles-per-hour in a 55-mile-per-hour zone. The fine for this offense is $150. This amount, though equal for both, has different consequences: it represents mere pocket change for the investment banker, but a significant chunk out of the checkout clerk's weekly paycheck.

Restricted by a "tariff system" that sets specific amounts for specific crimes, regardless of the financial situation of the convict, American judges often refrain from using fines as a primary sanction. They either assume that poor offenders cannot afford the fine or worry that a fine will allow wealthier offenders to "buy" their way out of a punishment.

PAYING FOR CRIME

In searching for a way to make fines more effective sanctions, many reformers have seized on the concept of the "day-fine," as practiced in Sweden and several other European countries. In this system, which was established in the 1920s and 1930s, the fine amount is linked to the monetary value of the offender's daily income. Depending on the seriousness of the crime, a Swedish wrongdoer will be sentenced to between 30 and 150 days or, as combined punishment for multiple crimes, up to 200 days. Each day, the offender is required to pay the equivalent of one-third of her or his daily discretionary income (as established by the Prosecutor General's Office) to the court. Consequently, the day-fine system not only reflects the degree of the crime, but ensures that the economic burden will be equal for those with different means.

Swedish police and prosecutors can levy day-fines without court involvement. Consequently, plea bargaining is nonexistent, and more than 80 percent of all offenders are sentenced to intermediate sanctions without a trial. The remaining cases receive full trials, with an acquittal rate of only 6 percent, compared to roughly 30 percent in the United States.

WHAT'S THE EVIDENCE?

A number of American jurisdictions have experimented with day-fines. To learn more about these efforts, and for information on how day-fine programs are planned and organized, go to **www.ncjrs.org/txtfiles/156242.txt**. Or, to download this report prepared by the Bureau of Justice Programs and the Vera Institute of Justice, go to **www.ncjrs.org.pdffiles/156242.pdf**.

---

prises as shields for organized crime.[62] As amended, RICO and other statutes give judges the ability to implement forfeiture proceedings in certain criminal cases. **Forfeiture** refers to a process by which the government seizes property gained from or used in criminal activity. For example, if a person is convicted for smuggling cocaine into the United States from South America, a judge can order the seizure of not only the narcotics, but also the speedboat the offender used to deliver the drugs to a pickup point off the coast of South Florida. In *Bennis v. Michigan* (1996),[63] the Supreme Court ruled that a person's home or car could be forfeited even if the owner was unaware that it was connected to illegal activity.

Once property is forfeited, the government has several options. It can sell the property, with the profits going to the state and/or federal government law enforcement agencies involved in the seizure. Alternatively, the government agency can use the property directly in further crime-fighting efforts or award it to a third party, such as an informant. Forfeiture has proven highly profitable: federal law enforcement agencies impound close to $2 billion worth of contraband and property from alleged criminals each year.[64]

Pretrial Diversion Programs. Not every criminal violation requires the courtroom process. Consequently, some judges have the discretion to order an offender into a **pretrial diversion program** during the preliminary hearing. (Prosecutors can also offer an offender the opportunity to join such a program in return for reducing or dropping the initial charges.) These programs represent an "interruption" of the criminal proceedings and are generally reserved

FORFEITURE
The seizure of private property attached to criminal activity by the government.

PRETRIAL DIVERSION PROGRAM
An alternative to trial offered by a judge or prosecutor, in which the offender agrees to participate in a specified counseling or treatment program in return for withdrawal of the charges.

Judges and prosecutors may, in certain cases, give offenders the chance to attend pretrial diversion programs. Offered by care giving facilities such as the community substance abuse center pictured above, these programs provide a chance to treat the causes behind criminal behavior without sending the offender to prison or jail. Do pretrial diversion programs "punish" offenders? If not, can they be justified as part of the corrections system?

DAY REPORTING CENTER
A community-based corrections center to which offenders report on a daily basis for purposes of treatment, education, and incapacitation.

INTENSIVE SUPERVISION PROBATION
A punishment-oriented form of probation in which the offender is placed under stricter and more frequent surveillance and control by probation officers with limited caseloads.

for young or first-time offenders who have been arrested on charges of illegal drug use, child or spousal abuse, or sexual misconduct. Pretrial diversion programs usually include extensive counseling, often in a treatment center. If the offender successfully follows the conditions of the program, the criminal charges are dropped.

Like other intermediate sanctions, pretrial diversion programs are not risk-free. In Jacksonville, Florida, for example, those arrested for sexually assaulting children were indiscriminately placed in counseling programs. The practice led to a public scandal when a man who had already completed two diversion programs for molesting children murdered a third victim. He was eventually sentenced to die in the state's electric chair.[65]

Day Reporting Centers

First used in Great Britain, **day reporting centers** are mainly tools to reduce jail and prison overcrowding. Although the offenders are allowed to remain in the community, they must spend all or part of each day at a reporting center. To a certain extent, being sentenced to a day reporting center is an extreme form of supervision. With offenders under a single roof, they are much more easily controlled and supervised.

Day reporting centers are also instruments of rehabilitation. Many house treatment programs for drug and alcohol abusers and provide counseling for a number of psychological problems, such as depression and anger management. Many of those found guilty in the Roanoke (Virginia) Drug Court, for example, are ordered to participate in a year-long day reporting program. At the center, offenders meet with probation officers, submit to urine tests, and attend counseling and education programs, such as parenting and life-skills classes. After the year has passed, if the offender has completed the program to the satisfaction of the judge and found employment, the charges will be dropped.[66]

Given that each day reporting center is unique, it is difficult to evaluate the success of this particular intermediate sanction. One survey of six Massachusetts day reporting centers, however, did find that nearly 80 percent of the participants completed the programs successfully, with only 5 percent being returned to jail or prison for having committing further crimes over a five-year period.[67]

Intensive Supervision Probation

As stated previously, **intensive supervision probation (ISP)** offers a more restrictive alternative to regular probation, with higher levels of face-to-face contact between offenders and officers, drug testing, and electronic surveillance (see Figure 12.9). Different jurisdictions have different methods of determining who is eligible for ISP. In New Jersey, for example, violent offenders may not be placed in the program, while a majority of states limit ISP to those who do not have prior probation violations. The frequency of officer-client contact also varies widely. A Rand study of fourteen ISP sites found that offenders in Contra Costa County, California, had 2.7 contacts per month, compared to 22.8 contacts per month in Waycross, Georgia.[68]

Intensive supervision has two primary functions: (1) to *divert* offenders from overcrowded prisons or jails, and (2) to place these offenders under higher levels of *control*, as befits the risk they pose to the community. Researchers have had difficulty, however, in determining whether ISP is succeeding in these two areas. Any diversion benefits of ISP programs have tended to be offset by the stricter sentencing guidelines discussed in Chapter 11.[69] Furthermore, a number of studies have found that ISP clients have higher violation rates than traditional probationers.[70] One theory is that ISP "causes" these high failure rates—greater supervision increases the chances that an offender will be caught breaking conditions of probation. Despite its questionable performance, ISP is viable in today's political landscape because it satisfies the public's desire for stricter controls on convicts, while providing intermediate sanctions options for judges, prosecutors, and corrections administrators.

Shock Incarceration

Before the concept of intermediate sanctions was widely recognized in the criminal justice community, "Scared Straight" programs were used by some jurisdictions with the express purpose of deterring further criminal activity by juveniles and first-time offenders. The original Scared Straight was developed by the Lifers Group at Rahway State Prison (now East Jersey State Prison) in New Jersey in the mid-1970s. Consisting of about forty inmates serving sentences from twenty-five years to life, the Lifers Group would oversee juvenile offenders who had not yet been incarcerated but were considered "at risk" during a short stint (between 30 and 120 days) in the prison. The hope, as the program's name indicates, was that by getting a taste of the brutalities of daily prison life, the offender would be shocked into a crime-free existence.

A form of **shock incarceration,** Scared Straight programs generally fell out of favor in the 1980s, though several states, including Nevada, still employ them. Critics contended that the programs seemed to have no discernible effect on recidivism rates and thus needlessly exposed minor offenders to mental and physical cruelties from hardened criminals.[71]

Today, corrections officials are turning toward programs such as Colorado's "Shape-Up" and Idaho's DETOUR. These programs assign a juvenile offender to an adult "partner" who is serving a prison term. The juvenile spends a day in prison with the partner, followed by a meeting among the adult offender, the juvenile offender, and the juvenile's family. A coordinator of DETOUR believes that these programs are more effective because they are not merely trying to scare already hardened juvenile offenders. Instead, he sees DETOUR as an educational program.[72] The concept appears to work; Colorado's juvenile corrections department reports an 86 percent success rate for Shape-Up.[73]

The precepts of shock incarceration have not disappeared, however. In fact, this particular form of intermediate sanctioning has prospered with the rapid, and controversial, proliferation of boot camps. (For an in-depth discussion of the controversy surrounding this form of shock incarceration, see the feature *Criminal Justice in Action—Boot Camps: Do They Work?* at the end of the chapter.)

Figure **12.9** Supervision Levels

As you can see, intensive supervision dictates more contact between the probationer and his or her probation officer.

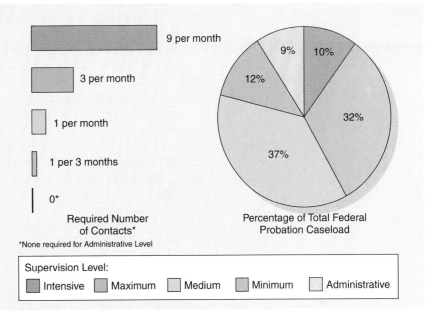

Required Number of Contacts*
*None required for Administrative Level

Percentage of Total Federal Probation Caseload

Supervision Level:
■ Intensive ■ Maximum ■ Medium ■ Minimum ■ Administrative

SOURCE: BUREAU OF JUSTICE STATISTICS, *RECIDIVISM OF FELONS ON PROBATION, 1986–89* (WASHINGTON, D.C.: U.S. DEPARTMENT OF JUSTICE, 1992).

SHOCK INCARCERATION
A short period of incarceration that is designed to deter further criminal activity by "shocking" the offender with the hardships of imprisonment.

HOME CONFINEMENT
A community-based sanction in which offenders serve their terms of incarceration in their homes.

ELECTRONIC MONITORING
A technique of probation supervision in which the offender's whereabouts, though not his or her actions, are kept under surveillance by an electronic device; often used in conjunction with home confinement.

Offenders who are confined to their homes are often monitored by an electronic device that fits around their ankle. A transmitter in the device sends a continuous signal to a receiver, also located within the home. If this signal is broken—that is, the offender moves outside the range of the device—the police are automatically notified. What are some of the drawbacks of this form of electronic monitoring?

Home Confinement and Electronic Monitoring

Various forms of **home confinement**—in which offenders serve their sentence not in a government institution but at home—have existed for centuries. It has often served, and continues to do so, as a method of political control, used by totalitarian regimes to isolate and silence dissidents. Today, for example, the military government of Myanmar (Burma) has confined Nobel Peace laureate Aung San Suu Kyi to her home since she won an election for leadership of that county in 1990.

For purposes of general law enforcement, home confinement was impractical until relatively recently. After all, one could not expect offenders to "promise" to stay at home, and the manpower costs of guarding them were prohibitive. In the 1980s, however, with the advent of **electronic monitoring,** or using technology to "guard" the prisoner, home confinement became more viable. Today, all fifty states and the federal government have home monitoring programs.

The Levels of Home Monitoring and Their Benefits. Home monitoring has three general levels of restriction:

1. *Curfew,* which requires offenders to be in their homes at specific hours each day, usually at night.

2. *Home detention,* which requires that offenders remain home at all times, with exceptions being made for education, employment, counseling, or other specified activities such as the purchase of food or, in some instances, attendance at religious ceremonies.

3. *Home incarceration,* which requires the offender to remain home at all times, save for medical emergencies.

Under ideal circumstances, home confinement serves many of the goals of intermediate sanctions. It protects the community. It saves public funds and space in correctional facilities by keeping convicts out of institutional incarceration. It meets public expectations of punishment for criminals. Uniquely, home confinement also recognizes that convicts, despite their crimes, play important roles in the community, and allows them to continue in those roles. An offender, for example, may be given permission to leave confinement to care for elderly parents.

Home confinement is also lauded for giving sentencing officials the freedom to match the punishment with the needs of the offender. In Missouri, for instance, the conditions of detention for a musician required him to remain at home during the day, but allowed him to continue his career at night. In addition, he was obliged to make antidrug statements before each performance, to be verified by the manager at whichever club he appeared.[74]

Types of Electronic Monitoring. According to some reports, the inspiration for electronic monitoring was a *Spiderman* comic book in which the hero was trailed by the use of an electronic device on his arm. In 1979, a New Mexico judge named Jack Love, having read the comic, convinced an executive at Honeywell, Inc., to begin developing similar technology to supervise convicts.[75]

Two major types of electronic monitoring have grown out of Love's initial concept. The first is a "programmed contact" program, in which the offender is contacted periodically by telephone or beeper to verify his or her whereabouts. Verification is obtained via a computer that uses voice or visual identification techniques or by requiring the offender to enter a code in an electronic box when called. The second is a "continuously signaling" device, worn around the convict's wrist, ankle, or neck. A transmitter in the device sends out a continuous signal to a "receiver-dialer" device located in the offender's dwelling. If the receiver device does not detect a signal from the transmitter, it informs a central computer, and the police are notified.[76] (For the latest advances in this field, see *Criminal Justice & Technology—Satellite Tracking: The Next Step in Electronic Monitoring.*)

Effectiveness of Home Confinement. As might be expected, technical problems can limit the effectiveness of an electronic monitoring device. So can tampering by the offender. In Washington, D.C., for example, a participant in a home monitoring program was caught on the street holding eighty small bags of cocaine. His continuous signal device was still at his home, transmitting the "all is well" signal. The possibility of such problems will decrease as tamper-resistant monitoring devices are perfected. One such device reacts to the application of heat, which normally loosens some transmitters, by contracting; if enough heat is applied, the offender's circulation will be cut off.[77]

Because most participants in home confinement programs are low-risk offenders, their recidivism rates are quite low. Joan Petersilia found that most home confinement programs report rearrest rates of less than 5 percent.[78] The data are less supportive when measuring how many offenders broke the conditions of confinement. In Indiana, over 40 percent of participants had at least one violation, and between one-third and one-half failed to complete the program.[79]

One concern about home confinement is that offenders are often required to defray program costs, which can be as high as $100 per week (see Figure 12.10 on the next page). Consequently, those who cannot afford to pay for electronic monitoring may not be eligible. Furthermore, families of offenders confined to the home can experience high levels of stress and a loss of privacy.[80] In general, however, those who successfully complete a home confinement term seem to benefit in areas such as obtaining and holding employment.[81]

Criminal Justice & Technology

Satellite Tracking: The Next Step in Electronic Monitoring

As we have already discussed, all intermediate sanctions entail a certain amount of risk. In electronic monitoring, as with other sanctions, this risk is compounded by the fact that the success of the program depends on the offender's commitment to "play by the rules." If the offender decides to leave the area of confinement, the signaling device will emit an alarm, alerting the police of the infraction but giving them no clues as to where the person is going.

A new breakthrough in electronic monitoring may provide the solution to this problem. Pro Tech Monitoring, Inc., a Palm Harbor (Florida) company, has developed a system that uses federal government satellites to monitor an offender's movements from above. Under this system, each subject will carry a "smart box" along with an ankle bracelet. The "smart box" contains a tracking device and is programmed with information about the offender's geographical restrictions. A satellite monitors the offender's movements and notifies the police if she or he violates conditional boundaries. So, for example, if a pedophile approaches an "off limits" junior high school, the satellite warning system would alert police of the person's present location.

IN THE FUTURE: As satellite tracking technology becomes more advanced, corrections agencies will have the ability to keep an "electronic eye" on convicts at all times, calling up a visual image whenever necessary.

Widening the Net

As mentioned above, most of the convicts chosen for intermediate sanctions are low-risk offenders. From the point of view of the corrections official doing the choosing, this makes sense. Such offenders are less likely to commit crimes and attract negative publicity. This selection strategy, however, appears to invalidate one of the primary reasons intermediate sanctions exist: to reduce prison and jail populations. If most of the offenders in intermediate sanctions programs would otherwise have received probation, then the effect on these populations is nullified. Indeed, studies have shown this to be the case.[82]

Figure 12.10 Supervision Fees

One of the most popular aspects of intermediate sanctions is that convicts must often pay for the programs themselves. Here you can see listed the fees for various forms of court-ordered community supervision in Marin County, California.

Form of Supervision	Fee
Community service	$27
House arrest	$13 per day
Anger management	$50
Domestic violence program	$20 per visit
Drug education	$410
First offender DUI counseling program	$516

SOURCE: MARIN COUNTY PROBATION DEPARTMENT.

INFOTRAC®
COLLEGE EDITION

Whitman, James. What is wrong with **inflicting shame** sanctions?

WIDEN THE NET
The criticism that intermediate sanctions designed to divert offenders from prison actually increase the number of citizens who are under the control and surveillance of the American corrections system.

CONTINUUM-OF-SANCTIONS
A corrections strategy in which offenders are not assigned a single punishment, but rather are initially sentenced based on their criminal act and then moved toward harsher or more lenient forms of sanction depending on their behavior within the corrections system.

At the same time, such selection processes broaden the reach of the corrections system. In other words, they increase rather than decrease the amount of control the state exerts over the individual. Suppose a person is arrested for a misdemeanor such as shoplifting and, under normal circumstances, would receive probation. With access to intermediate sanctions, the judge may add a period of home confinement to the sentence. Critics contend that such practices **widen the net** of the corrections system by augmenting the number of citizens who are under the control and surveillance of the state and also *strengthen the net* by increasing the government's power to intervene in the lives of its citizens.[83]

THE FUTURE OF COMMUNITY CORRECTIONS

It should be noted that although the theoretical basis for intermediate sanctions is widely recognized, relatively few offenders have been sentenced to such programs. Researchers Norval Morris and Michael Tonry believe that this is attributable to the prominence of retribution and incapacitation in our corrections system. Regardless of the scope of the crime, imprisonment is regarded as "just deserts" for criminal behavior. Furthermore, even if a judge believes that a crime is not serious enough to warrant imprisonment, he or she can be certain of one thing: an incarcerated offender, being locked up, is in no position to harm the general community (and the judge is not at risk of being blamed for releasing a repeat offender). Morris and Tonry believe these two modes of thinking will have to be overcome if intermediate sanctions are to play a more prominent role in criminal justice.[84]

As in other areas of the corrections system, efforts to reform community-based corrections have concentrated on making sentencing procedures more standardized. **Continuum-of-sanctions** strategies envision a corrections system in which an offender is not sentenced to a single sanction, but moves from different levels of punishment depending on behavior. Each crime is assigned an "accountability rating" that determines the initial sanction; the convict's compliance with the conditions of that sanction then determine whether she or he will move to more or less restrictive punishment. Continuum-of-sanctions strategies are attractive because they can be codified, reducing the discretion of sentencing officials. (See Figure 12.11 for an example of how a continuum-of-sanctions strategy might be carried out.)

Another innovation is the idea of *exchange rates,* where a certain number of days of community supervision would be equated to a single day of incarceration in a prison or jail. For example, authorities might determine that five days of house detention equal one day in prison or jail and structure the length of community-based supervision accordingly. Such exchanges would be made after the offender has been sentenced to prison or jail, hopefully reducing the net-widening effect of intermediate sanctions.[85]

The problem with such strategies, say some observers, is that they fail to address the basic paradox of community-based corrections: the more effectively offenders are controlled, the more likely they are to be caught violating the terms of their conditional release. As you may have noticed, the community supervision programs discussed in this chapter are "graded" according to rates of recidivism and revocation, with low levels of each reflecting a successful program. Increased control and surveillance, however, will necessarily raise the level of violations, thus increasing the probability that any single violation will be discovered. Therefore, as factors such as the number of conditions placed on probationers and the technological proficiency of electronic monitoring devices increase, so, too, will the number of offenders who fail to meet the conditions of their community-based punishment.

Initial Accountability Level: 850
Status: Incarcerated in medium-security prison
Mobility in the Community: 0%
Amount of Supervision: 24 hours/day

(After one year of good behavior)

New Accountability Level: 550
Status: Work-release program, spends nights and weekends at minimum-security prison.
Mobility in the Community: 30% (restricted 40–50 hours/week)
Amount of Supervision: Daily phone contact, daily face-to-face

(After one year, no further violations)

New Accountability Level: 250
Status: On probation, weekly community service, no drinking allowed
Mobility in Community: 90% (restricted 0–10 hours/week)
Amount of Supervision: 1–2 face-to-face/month, 1–2 phone contact/week

(After two months misses scheduled meeting with probation officer following a night of drinking with friends)

New Accountability Level: 450
Status: Mandatory alcohol treatment program, confined to home at nights and on weekends
Mobility in the Community: 60% (restricted 30–40 hours/week)
Amount of Supervision: 2–6 face-to-face/week, daily phone)

(After four months without any further violations, John X. is returned to Accountability Level 250. Three more months of good behavior follow, and John X. is reclassified at Level 50 for the remainder of his term.)

New Accountability Level: 50
Status: Unsupervised probation
Mobility in the Community: 100%
Amount of Supervision: None

Such a system benefits both John X. and the correctional system. John X. has an incentive to behave because he knows that if he does, the circumstances of his sentence will be more pleasant. The correctional system is able to move John X.—a nonviolent felon—out of a crowded prison into less restrictive options.

SOURCE: ADAPTED FROM NORVAL MORRIS AND MICHAEL TONRY, BETWEEN PRISON AND PROBATION: INTERMEDIATE PUNISHMENTS IN A RATIONAL SENTENCING SYSTEM (NEW YORK: OXFORD UNIVERSITY PRESS, 1990), 66–67.

Figure 12.11 Continuum-of-Sanctions: From Theory to Action

John X. has been convicted of forging checks. It is his second conviction for this crime in a two-year period, and he is sentenced to three years under correctional supervision. He will start his term in a medium-security prison, but, under a continuum-of-sanctions strategy employed by the county, he will not necessarily stay there.

One observer calls this the "quicksand" effect of increased surveillance. Instead of helping offenders leave the corrections system, increased surveillance pulls them more deeply into it.[86] The quicksand effect can be quite strong, according to researchers Barbara Sims of Sam Houston State University and Mark Jones of East Carolina University. In a study of North Carolina corrections data, Sims and Jones found that 26 percent of the probationers whose probation terms were revoked had been guilty of violations such as failing a single drug test. The researchers believe this strategy is overly punitive—anybody who has tried to quit smoking is aware of the difficulties of breaking an addiction.[87] (Remember from Figure 12.7 on page 431, however, that as revocation rates for drug use have risen, revocation rates for other violations have dropped, causing overall revocation rates to remain steady. Thus, while the quicksand effect may be relevant in individual cases, it may be more of a potential concern than an actual one.)

Many criminal justice experts are calling for the focus of community-based sanctions to be shifted more toward rehabilitation and away from punishment and supervision.[88] Furthermore, these experts have drawn attention to a number of public opinion polls that show support for sentencing options that rehabilitate a wide range of serious but *nonviolent* offenders. These data prove, they argue, that a shift in the orientation of community-based corrections is politically feasible.[89]

Boot Camps: Do They Work?

One might say that the American corrections system is "between a rock and a hard place." On the one hand, prisons and jails do not have enough space for all the offenders being arrested by law enforcement agencies. On the other hand, as noted throughout this chapter, community corrections and intermediate sanctions, while lessening the pressure on prisons and jails, are regarded as insufficiently "tough" by many citizens and public officials. In this *Criminal Justice in Action* feature, we will examine what would seem to be the perfect corrections option—a "tough" intermediate sanction known as the boot camp.

BEYOND PUNISHMENT

You are nothing and nobody, fools, maggots, dummies, mothers, and you have just walked into the worst nightmare you ever dreamed. I don't like you. I have no use for you, and I don't give a f** who you are on the street. This is my acre, hell's half acre, and it matters not one damn to me whether you make it here or get tossed out into the general prison population, where, I promise you, you won't last three minutes before you're somebody's wife. Do you know what that means, tough guys?[90]

Such was the welcome a group of inmates received upon arriving at **boot camp.** A form of shock incarceration, boot camp programs are modeled after military basic training, emphasizing strict discipline, manual labor, and physical training. Boot camps provide a short term of incarceration—usually between three and six months—for young, first-time offenders. The idea is that the program's intense nature makes it as punitive as a longer prison term. But boot camps promise more than punishment. They are designed to instill self-discipline, self-responsibility, and self-respect, thereby lessening the chances that the offender will return to crime upon release.

The first boot camp program appeared in Georgia in 1983. Within ten years, fifty-nine similar programs were operating in

Boot camps rely on tough, militaristic discipline to steer young and first-time offenders away from a criminal lifestyle.

twenty-nine states.[91] An important reason for this rapid growth has been public acceptance of boot camps.[92] In contrast to generally negative feelings about probation, a recent survey found that 78 percent of the respondents had a positive impression of boot camps as a form of alternative sanctioning. Boot camps seem to reflect commonly held beliefs that offenders should receive strict punishment, while also offering the chance of rehabilitation within a confined space. Politicians, not wanting to appear soft on crime, have reacted to this support by earmarking funds to construct new camps. After a two-decade-long honeymoon period, however, many criminal justice participants are questioning whether boot camps deliver on all of their promises.

BOOT CAMP
A correctional facility based on militaristic principles of discipline and physical conditioning; reserved primarily for juvenile and first-time offenders serving terms of less than six months, with the ultimate goal of deterring further criminal behavior.

Figure 12.12 Eligibility Requirements of Boot Camps in the United States

1. **Offender Status**

   Boot camps are for the most part limited to first-time, nonviolent offenders.

2. **Age**

   States differ in their age requirements, as these examples show:

   - Oklahoma: Under 25 years
   - Illinois: Ages 17 to 29
   - New York: Age 30 or under
   - Kansas: Ages 18 to 25
   - Maryland: Under 32 years
   - California: Age 40 or under
   - Tennessee: Ages 17 to 29

3. **Sentence Length**

   As one of the primary goals of boot camps is to reduce prison overcrowding, those who are sent to boot camps are generally diverted from prison. Consequently, many states have specific requirements concerning the prison sentences that boot "campers" must have received. In Maryland, for example, boot camps are restricted to offenders who have been sentenced for no longer than 10 years and who have at least 9 months remaining on their sentences. Illinois requires offenders to have been sentenced for up to 5 years and Tennessee for up to 6 years.

SOURCE: JOHN K. ZACHARIAH, "CORRECTIONAL BOOT CAMPS: A TOUGH INTERMEDIATE SANCTION—CHAPTER 2," IN AN OVERVIEW OF BOOT CAMP GOALS, COMPONENTS, AND RESULTS (WASHINGTON, D.C.: NATIONAL INSTITUTE OF JUSTICE, 1996).

THE BENEFITS OF BOOT CAMPS

Offenders are sent to boot camps either by the sentencing judge or by an official within the corrections agency. (In four states, the decision is made by a probation or parole officer.)[93] Though eligibility varies across jurisdictions (see Figure 12.12), most boot camps are restricted to young (though not necessarily juvenile) first offenders. In most cases, attending a boot camp is a voluntary decision, and the offender can leave at any time and finish the sentence in a jail or prison.

The McNeil Island camp in Washington State is typical of such programs. Approximately 125 inmates, aged eighteen to twenty-eight, spend eight hours a day doing menial labor such as pulling weeds and painting the ferries that travel to and from the island. This work is supplemented by a number of seminars, including adult education, anger management, planning for life after prison, and victim awareness. Inmates also receive drug abuse counseling and other treatments. The dropout rate from McNeil Island is 30 percent, even though completion of the four-month program can reduce a prison term by as much as a year.[94]

Besides the benefits for individual inmates, supporters of boot camps believe the programs are advantageous to society in three ways:

1. By reducing prison and jail overcrowding.

2. By saving costs associated with prison and jail terms.

3. By lowering recidivism rates among offenders.

The explanations behind these three supposed benefits are fairly straightforward. First, inmates placed in boot camps do not take up space in prisons and jails. Second, even though the average yearly costs of housing an inmate in a boot camp and in a prison are comparable, the term of a boot camp is much shorter and therefore less costly. Third, through improved self-discipline and treatment programs, inmates will change their behavior and therefore be less likely to commit further crimes upon release from the camp.

EVIDENCE TO THE CONTRARY

Few observers doubt that the boot camp experience is a positive one for those who complete it—inmates learn valuable life skills and receive treatment, options often not available in prisons and jails.[95] Statistical benefits have also been reported: the state of Illinois estimates that boot camp graduates have a recidivism rate of 21 percent, as compared to 34 percent for those on probation or those who have served time behind bars.[96]

Criminologists, however, are wary of claims that boot camps are fulfilling their mandates. A number of long-term studies seem to show that although boot camps do not have a negative impact, they are not a panacea for the ills of the corrections system. One of the earliest surveys of boot camp graduates, compiled in Louisiana, found no difference in recidivism rates between boot campers and convicts who were confined in traditional correctional facilities.[97] More recently, the Juvenile Justice Advisory Board in Florida found rearrest rates of 45 percent for attendees of the state's six boot camps.[98] The most extensive study of boot camps, evaluating programs in seven states, concluded that the overall effect of boot camps on recidivism was negligible.[99]

Similar doubts are raised concerning boot camps' ability to reduce costs and prison overcrowding. Researcher Dale G. Parent notes that when calculating the amount saved by sending inmates to boot camps instead of to prison, officials tend to account only for the goods consumed by offenders, such as food, clothing, and health care. These short-term savings amount to only a few dollars a day. To achieve substantial, long-term savings, prison populations must be reduced to the point where a cellblock or even an entire facility can be closed.[100] This has yet to occur.

Parent uses similar arguments to counteract claims that boot camps reduce prison and jail overcrowding. First of all, boot camps suffer from the net-widening effect discussed earlier in the chapter. That is, the offenders sent to boot camps would most likely have been given probation if intermediate sanctions did not exist. Even when specific steps are taken to avoid "net widening," the results are negligible. When the New York State Department of Correctional Services designed its boot camps, all inmates were chosen from incoming prison populations—no net widening was possible. In its first five years, the department estimated that it had reduced the state's prison rolls by 1,540 inmates. During that same period, however, the prison rolls grew from 41,000 to 58,000, overwhelming the small gains made by the boot camps. To have an effect on either costs or overcrowding, Parent concludes, boot camp populations would have to be increased significantly, which would lessen their ability to treat individual offenders.[101]

THE FUTURE OF BOOT CAMPS

Boot camps have raised other concerns. Working in a boot camp can be a demanding task, and some observers believe staff stress and burnout contribute to verbal and physical intimidation of offenders.[102] Sometimes, these intimidation tactics break the bounds of legality. In Houston, for example, five drill instructors were indicted on felony charges after choking and beating inmates with their fists, feet, and broomsticks. After her daughter died of dehydration in a Florida boot camp, one woman echoed the thoughts of many observers: "either regulate this industry or abolish it."[103]

Given the continued popular support for boot camps, it seems highly unlikely that they will be abolished. As long as the media portray these programs as "tough on prisoners," the political appeal of boot camps will continue to be high.[104] Some observers have gone as far as to suggest that corrections officials are aware of the drawbacks of boot camps, but are willing to take advantage of their popularity in order to receive government funding for these operations.[105] If this is indeed the strategy, it appears to be working. California alone received more than $1 billion in federal funds between 1995 and 2000 for alternative sentencing programs such as boot camps.

Key Terms

authority 428

boot camp 442

continuum-of-sanctions 440

day reporting centers 436

diversion 420

electronic monitoring 438

forfeiture 435

home confinement 438

intensive supervision probation (ISP) 436

intermediate sanctions 434

judicial reprieve 421

pretrial diversion program 435

probation 420

reintegration 419

shock incarceration 437

split sentence probation 423

suspended sentence 423

technical violation 430

widen the net 440

Chapter Summary

1. **Explain the justifications for community-based corrections programs.** The first justification involves reintegration of the offender into society. Reintegration restores family ties, encourages employment and education, and secures a place for the offender in the routine functioning of society. The other justification involves diversion; by diverting criminals to alternative modes of punishment, further overcrowding of jail and prison facilities can be avoided.

2. **Indicate when probation started to fall out of favor and explain why.** When both criminal justice practitioners and the public held the rehabilitative model in favor, probation was generally considered a valuable aspect of this treatment. Since about the 1950s and more seriously since the mid-1970s, retributive goals have become more important, and probation has fallen out of favor in some criminal justice circles. Nonetheless, two-thirds of those involved in the American corrections system are on probation at any given time.

3. **List and explain several alternative sentencing arrangements.** In addition to a suspended sentence, which is in fact a judicial reprieve, there are three general types of sentencing arrangements: (a) split sentence probation, in which the judge specifies a certain time in jail or prison followed by a certain time on probation; (b) shock incarceration, in which a judge sentences an offender to be incarcerated, but allows that person to petition the court to be released on proba-

tion; and (c) intermittent incarceration, in which an offender spends a certain amount of time each week in jail or in a halfway house or another government institution.

4. **Specify the conditions under which an offender is most likely to be denied probation.** The offender (a) has been convicted of multiple charges, (b) was on probation or parole when arrested, (c) has two or more prior convictions, (d) is addicted to narcotics, (e) seriously injured the victim of the crime, or (f) used a weapon while committing the crime.

5. **Describe the three general categories of conditions placed on a probationer.** (a) Standard conditions, such as requiring that the probationer notify the agency of a change of address, not leave the jurisdiction without permission, and remain employed; (b) punitive conditions, such as restitution, community service, and home confinement; and (c) treatment conditions, such as required drug or alcohol treatment.

6. **Explain why probation officers' work has become more dangerous.** One reason is that probation is increasingly offered to felons, even those who have committed violent crimes. Additionally, because there are more guns on the streets, a probationer is more likely to be armed.

7. **List and explain the three stages of probation revocation.** (a) The preliminary hearing, which usually takes place before a judge, during which the facts of the probation violation are presented;

(b) the revocation hearing, during which the claims of the violation are presented as well as any refutation by the probationer; and (c) revocation sentencing, during which a judge decides what to do with the probationer convicted of violating the terms of probation.

8. **List the five sentencing options for a judge besides imprisonment and probation.** (a) Fines, (b) community service, (c) restitution, (d) forfeiture, and (e) pretrial diversion programs.

9. **Contrast day reporting centers with intensive supervision probation.** In a day reporting center, the offender is allowed to remain in the community, but must spend all or part of each day at the reporting center. While at the center, offenders meet with probation officers, submit to drug tests, and attend counseling and education programs. In contrast, with intensive supervision probation (ISP), more restrictions are imposed, and there is more face-to-face contact between offenders and probation officers. ISP may also include electronic surveillance.

10. **List the three levels of home monitoring.** (a) Curfew, which requires that the offender be at home during specified hours; (b) home detention, which requires that the offender be at home except for education, employment, and counseling; and (c) home incarceration, which requires that the offender be at home at all times except for medical emergencies.

Questions for Critical Analysis

1. What is the major reason that probationers account for nearly two-thirds of all adults in the American corrections system?

2. Why did the Supreme Court rule against indefinite reprieves?

3. What benefit might arise from more coordination between police and probation officers?

4. Why don't probationers have all constitutionally defined due process rights during revocation procedures?

5. Is the small number of probation officers a reason that recidivism is high?

6. What happens to property that is forfeited by a convicted criminal?

7. What is the purpose of day reporting centers?

8. "Home confinement is only for rich criminals." Comment.

9. What does the term "widening the net" mean, and why is it important today?

10. What benefits are attributed to boot camps, and what is the evidence to support these proposed benefits?

Selected Print and Electronic Resources

SUGGESTED READINGS

Anderson, David C., *Sensible Justice: Alternatives to Prison*, New York: New Press, 1998. The author examines a range of probation-based supervision and rehabilitation programs, all of which involve no time in prison. He goes through the options in ascending order of severity. They range from community service to daily reporting, all the way to boot camps. He examines the various options in the context of how different jurisdictions have applied them.

Anderson, James F., et al., *Boot Camps: An Intermediate Sanction*, Lanham, MD: University Press of America, 1999. The authors examine the theory and practice of boot camps throughout the United States. They offer criticisms of the concept as well as suggestions on how it might be applied for better results.

Ellsworth, Thomas, ed., *Contemporary Community Corrections,* Prospect Heights, IL: Waveland Press, 1996. This collection of articles discusses the evolution of intermediate sanctions. Some of the articles question the traditional practices of community corrections.

Hamai, Koichi, et al., eds., *Probation Round the World: A Comparative Study,* New York: Routledge, 1995. This appears to be the first book that compares probation throughout many criminal justice systems in different countries. The book deals with conceptual issues. It also describes how different probation systems operate.

Hammer, Hy, *Probation Officer, Parole Officer,* 5th ed., New York: Macmillan General Reference, 1996. This is a guide to applying and qualifying for the position of either parole or probation officer. It includes several full-length sample examinations. It also lists the eligibility requirements for most states.

MEDIA RESOURCES

Good Will Hunting (1997) Will Hunting, played by Matt Damon, is a complex character. On the one hand, he is a tough kid from Boston who regularly finds himself in trouble with the law. On the other hand, he is a genius with a photographic memory. His mental capacity is uncovered by Professor Lambeau (Stellan Skargard), a professor at the Massachusetts Institute of Technology, where Hunting works as a janitor. Lambeau offers Hunting a path out of his blue-collar existence but the genius janitor, scared of the challenges a new life might present, refuses. Then, fate steps in. Hunting is involved in a street brawl and faces serious prison time for striking a police officer. Lambeau makes a deal with the criminal justice system, persuading the judge to give Hunting probation if he agrees to attend therapy sessions with counselor Sean McGuire (Robin Williams).

Critically analyze this film:

1. Describe how Professor Lambeau takes advantage of the probation system.

2. What are some of the reasons that a real judge might not consider probation given the circumstances surrounding Will Hunting's arrest?

3. What are the conditions of Hunting's probation?

4. Given what you've read in this chapter, how realistic is Hunting's probationary situation?

5. At what points in the film could Hunting's probation be revoked?

Logging On

You can learn about the technology of home detention systems by going to the web page of a private company called PHD:

http://homedetention.com/

Once on the homepage click on "Technology."

You can find out about boot camps from the National Criminal Justice Information Center. Go to:

http://ncjrs.org/bcamps.htm

You can find out more about alternative sentencing by examining the web pages of Laramie County in Colorado. Go to:

www.co.larimer.co.us/depts/sherif/depctr1.htm

There you can look at community services information and electronic home detention information, as well as "workender" and work-release programs.

For more information on alternative sentencing, go to the home page of the National Center on Institutions and Alternatives at:

www.ncianet.org/ncia/index.html

Once you are at that site, click on Community Based Alternatives Initiative.

Using the internet for Criminal Justice Analysis

INFOTRAC® COLLEGE EDITION

1. Go to your InfoTrac College Edition at www.infotrac-college.com/wadsworth/. After you log on, type in the words: FORGING A POLICE-PROBATION ALLIANCE

Probation officers can work with police officers, even though there often seem to be rivalries between the two agencies. In this article you will read about a number of police departments that have established collaboration with local probation officers. Read the article and answer the following questions:

a. Why does the author believe that the police cannot solve numerous crime and public order problems without forming partnerships with other resources?

b. What did the ride-a-long program in Greenville, Texas, involve?

c. How is a bulletin board utilized in such a partnership arrangement?

d. What benefits did the Greenville Police Department realize from the partnership with probation officers?

e. List the five suggested improvements in a police-probation partnership. In your mind, which is the most important and why?

2. You can learn about a private organization that helps the criminal justice system institute intermediate sanctions. Go to the home page of the American Community Corrections Institute (ACCI) at: www.accilifeskils.com

Once you are there, click on **"Cognitive Formats."** Then click on "cognitive therapy."

a. What is the theory behind cognitive therapy?

b. Why does it apply to intermediate sanctions?

Now go back to the ACCI home page. Click on **"Products and Services."** Click on *Life Skills WorkBooks*.

c. What is the basis of the ACCI's program?

d. Approximately how many hours of counseling are recommended for those committing misdemeanors? For those committing felonies who are adults?

Now go to the *"Adult Probation Services."* Click on *"Testimonials."*

e. Are the testimonials convincing?

f. Is there any way to substantiate whether these testimonials are in fact real or at least have not been modified from what was originally written?

Now find out about *"Alternative Probation."*

g. What is it?

h. How does it differ from normal probation programs?

Notes

1. "Man Gets Probation for Murder," *Dallas Morning News* (May 3, 1997), 39A.
2. Bureau of Justice Statistics, *Characteristics of Adults on Probation, 1995* (Washington, D.C.: U.S. Department of Justice, December 1997), 1.
3. *Ibid.*
4. Joan Petersilia, "Probation in the United States," *Perspectives* (Spring 1998), 37.
5. Michael Tonry, *Sentencing Matters* (New York: Oxford Press, 1996), 28.
6. Todd Clear and Anthony Braga, "Community Corrections," in *Crime*, eds. James Q. Wilson and Joan Petersilia (San Francisco: ICS Press, 1995), 444.
7. Corrections Task Force of the President's Commission on Law Enforcement and Administration of Justice (1967).
8. Paul H. Hahn, *Emerging Criminal Justice: Three Pillars for a Proactive Justice System* (Thousand Oaks, CA: Sage Publications, 1998), 106–8.
9. Bureau of Justice Statistics, *Characteristics of Adults on Probation, 1995*, 1.
10. Paul W. Keve, *Crime Control and Justice in America* (Chicago: American Library Association, 1995), 183.
11. Andrew R. Klein, *Alternative Sentencing, Intermediate Sanctions and Probation*, 2d ed. (Cincinnati: Anderson Publishing Co., 1997), 72.
12. 242 U.S. 27 (1916).

13. Petersilia, 32–3.

14. Barry A. Krisberg and James F. Austin, "The Unmet Promise of Alternatives to Incarceration," in John Kaplan, Jerome H. Skolnick, and Malcolm M. Freeley, *Criminal Justice*, 5th ed. (Westbury, NY: The Foundation Press, 1991), 537.

15. Sheldon Glueck, "The Significance and Promise of Probation," in *Probation and Criminal Justice; Essays in Honor of Herbert C. Parson* (New York: Macmillan, 1933).

16. Timothy J. Flanagan, "Community Corrections in the Public Mind," *Federal Probation* 60 (September 1996), 3.

17. Marylouise E. Jones and Arthur J. Lurigio, "Ethical Considerations in Probation Practice," *Perspectives* (Summer 1997), 29–31.

18. "National Report on Probationers Says Half Got Split Sentences," *Corrections Journal* (December 22, 1997), 7.

19. Joan Petersilia and Susan Turner, *Prison versus Probation in California: Implications for Crime and Offender Recidivism* (Santa Monica, CA: Rand Corporation, 1986).

20. Mark A. Cunniff and Mary Shilton, *Variations on Felony Probation: Persons under Supervision in 32 Urban and Suburban Counties* (Washington, D.C.: U.S. Department of Justice, 1991).

21. Bill Rankin, "Unequal Justice: White More Apt to Get Probation," *Atlanta Journal-Constitution* (February 8, 1998), A1.

22. Bureau of Justice Statistics, *Characteristics of Adults on Probation, 1995*, Table 2, page 2.

23. 97 U.S. 1143 (1998).

24. Neil P. Cohen and James J. Gobert, *The Law of Probation and Parole* (Colorado Springs, CO: Shepard's/McGraw-Hill, 1983), Section 5.01, at 183–4; Section 5.03, at 191–2.

25. "National Report on Probationers Says Half Got Split Sentences."

26. Carl B. Klockars, Jr., "A Theory of Probation Supervision," *Journal of Criminal Law, Criminology, and Police Science* 63 (1972), 550–7.

27. *Ibid.*, 551.

28. Hahn, 116–8.

29. "Most Probationers Have Contact with Probation Officers," *Crime and Justice International* (March 1998), 23.

30. Richard J. Maher, "Variety on the Job: Special Skills, Special Duties in Federal Probation," *Federal Probation* (March 1997), 26.

31. *Rieser v. District of Columbia*, 21 Cr.L. 2503 (1977); *Acevedo v. Pima County Adult Probation Department*, 142 Ariz. 319, 690 P.2d 38, 44 ALR4th 631 (1984).

32. David N. Adair, "Civil Liability of Probation and Pretrial Services Officers," *Federal Probation* (June 1995), 62.

33. *Weinberger v. State of Wisconsin*, 105 F.3d 1182 (7th Cir. 1997).

34. Brian McKay and Barry Paris, "Forging a Police-Probation Alliance," *The FBI Law Enforcement Bulletin* 67 (November 1, 1998), 27.

35. "Maryland Puts Probation Officers on Patrol in Neighborhoods," *Corrections Journal* (July 22, 1997), 5–6.

36. Merril A. Smith, "That Way It Was," *Federal Probation* (March 1997), 76.

37. Charles Linder and Robert L. Bonn, "Probation Officer Victimization and Fieldwork Practices: Results of a National Study," *Federal Probation* (June 1996), 16.

38. W. H. Parsonage and J. A. Miller, *A Study of Probation and Parole Worker Safety in the Middle Atlantic Region*, Middle Atlantic States Corrections Association, 1990.

39. Public Law No. 104-317, 110 Stat. 3847 (October 19, 1996).

40. Paul W. Brown, "The Evolution of the Federal Probation and Pretrial Service System's National Firearms Program," *Federal Probation* (December 1996), 27.

41. Bureau of Justice Statistics, Special Report, *Federal Offenders under Community Supervisions, 1987–1996* (Washington, D.C.: U.S. Department of Justice, August 1998), Table 6, page 5.

42. 483 U.S. 868, 874 (1987).

43. 389 U.S. 128 (1967).

44. *Morrissey v. Brewer*, 408 U.S. 471 (1972); *Gagnon v. Scarpelli*, 411 U.S. 778 (1973).

45. 465 U.S. 420 (1984).

46. Petersilia, 39.

47. Patrick Langan, "Between Prison and Probation: Intermediate Sanctions," *Science* 264 (1994), 791–3

48. Quoted in John J. DiIulio, Jr., "Reinventing Parole and Probation," *Brookings Review* 5 (Spring 1997), 43.

49. Linder and Bonn, 16.

50. Petersilia, 37.

51. Patrick Langan and M. Cunniff, "Recidivism of Felons on Probation, 1986–89," *Special Report* (Washington, D.C.: U.S. Department of Justice, 1992).

52. Bureau of Justice Statistics, *Bulletin* (Washington, D.C.: U.S. Department of Justice, 1991).

53. Petersilia and Turner, vii.

54. Joan Petersilia, Susan Turner, James Kahan, and Joyce Peterson, *Granting Felons Probation: Public Risks and Alternatives* (Santa Monica, CA: Rand Corporation, 1985).

55. Gennaro F. Vito, "Felony Probation and Recidivism: Replication and Response," *Federal Probation* 50 (1986), 17–25.

56. Gayle R. Seigel and Joanne Basta, "The Effect of Adult Education Programs on Probationers," *Perspectives* (Spring 1998), 42–44.

57. James M. Byrne and Linda M. Kelly, *Restructuring Probation as an Intermediate Sanction: An Evaluation of the Massachusetts Intensive Probation Supervision Program* (Washington, D.C.: National Institute of Justice, 1989).

58. Todd R. Clear and George F. Cole, *American Corrections*, 4th ed. (Belmont, CA: Wadsworth Publishing Co., 1997), 179.

59. John P. Storm, "What United States Probation Officers Do," *Federal Probation* (March 1997), 13.

60. Robert M. Carter and Leslie T. Wilkins, "Caseloads: Some Conceptual Models," in *Probation, Parole, and Community Corrections,* eds. Robert M. Carter and Leslie T. Wilkins (New York: Wiley & Sons, 1976), 391–401.

61. Norval Morris and Michael Tonry, *Between Prison and Probation: Intermediate Punishments in a Rational Sentencing System* (Oxford, UK: Oxford University Press, 1990).

62. 18 U.S.C. Sections 1961–1968.

63. 516 U.S. 442 (1996).

64. "The Supreme Court: Recent Cases," *Harvard Law Review* 110 (1996), 215.

65. "Duval's Counseling Progam for Sex Offenders under Attack," *Tampa Tribune* (June 24, 1996), 2.

66. Laurence Hammck, "Drug Court to Recognize Those Who've Stayed Clean," *Roanoke Times & World News* (May 31, 1998), B1.

67. Jack McDevitt and Robin Miliano, "Day Reporting: An Innovative Concept in Intermediate Sanctions," in *Smart Sentencing: The Emergence of Intermediate Sanctions,* eds. James M. Byrne, Arthur Lurigio, and Joan Petersilia (Newbury Park, CA: Sage, 1992), 160.

68. Joan Petersilia and Susan Turner, *Intensive Supervision for High-Risk Probationers: Findings from Three California Experiments* (Santa Monica, CA: Rand Corporation, 1990).

69. Betsy Fulton, Edward J. Latessa, Amy Stichman, and Lawrence F. Travis, "The State of ISP: Research and Policy Implications," *Federal Probation* (December 1997), 65.

70. See Peter Jones, "Expanding the Use of Non-Custodial Sentencing Options: An Evaluation of the Kansas Community Corrections Act," *Howard Journal* 29 (1990), 114–29.

71. Dale Parent, *Shock Incarceration: An Overview of Existing Programs* (Washington, D.C.: U.S. Department of Justice, 1989).

72. Candice Chung, "Cigarette Money Will Fund Juvenile Program," *Idaho Statesman* (May 9, 1997), 2B.

73. Ibid.

74. Paul J. Hofer and Barbara S. Meierhoefer, *Home Confinement: An Evolving Sanction in the Federal Criminal Justice System* (Washington, D.C.: Federal Judicial Center, 1987).

75. Josh Kurtz, "New Growth in a Captive Market," *New York Times* (December 31, 1989), 12.

76. Jeff Potts, "American Penal Institutions and Two Alternative Proposals for Punishment," *South Texas Law Review* (October 1993), 443.

77. Russell Carlisle, "Electronic Monitoring as an Alternative Sentencing Tool, *Georgia State Bar Journal* 24 (1988), 132.

78. Joan Petersilia, *Expanding Options for Criminal Sentencing* (Santa Monica, CA: Rand Corporation, 1987).

79. Terry Baumer and Robert Mendelsohn, "Electronically Monitored Home Confinement: Does It Work?" in *Smart Sentencing: The Emergence of Intermediate Sanctions,* eds.

James M. Byrne, Arthur Lurigio, and Joan Petersilia. (Newbury Park, CA: Sage, 1992).

80. Joseph B. Vaughn, "Planning for Change: The Use of Electronic Monitoring as a Correctional Alternative," in *Intermediate Punishments: Intensive Supervision, Home Confinement, and Electronic Surveillance,* ed. Belinda R. McCarthy (Monsey, NY: Criminal Justice Press, 1987), 158.

81. Terry Baumer and Robert Mendelsohn, *The Electronic Monitoring of Nonviolent Convicted Felons* (Washington, D.C.: National Institute of Justice, 1992).

82. Michael Tonry and Mary Lynch, "Intermediate Sanctions" in *Crime and Justice,* vol. 20, ed. Michael Tonry (Chicago: Unversity of Chicago Press, 1996), 99.

83. Dennis Palumbo, Mary Clifford, and Zoann K. Snyder-Joy, "From Net Widening to Intermediate Sanctions: The Transformation of Alternatives to Incarceration from Benevolence to Malevolence," in *Smart Sentencing: The Emergence of Intermediate Sanctions,* eds. James M. Byrne, Arthur Lurigio, and Joan Petersilia. (Newbury Park, CA: Sage, 1992), 231.

84. Morris and Tonry.

85. James M. Byrne and Mary Brewster, "Choosing the Future of American Corrections: Punishment or Reform," *Federal Probation* 57 (1993), 3–9.

86. Keve, 207.

87. Barbara Sims and Mark Jones, "Predicting Success or Failure on Probation: Factors Associated with Felony Probation Outcomes," *Crime & Delinquency* 43 (July 1997), 314–27.

88. Edward E. Rhine, "Probation and Parole Supervision: In Need of a New Narrative," *Corrections Management Quarterly* (Spring 1997), 71–5.

89. Richard D. Sluder, Allen D. Sapp, and Denny C. Langston, "Guiding Philosophies for Probation in the 21st Century," *Federal Probation* (June 1994), 3.

90. Quoted in Doris L. Mackenzie and Claire Souryal, "A 'Machiavellian' Perspective on the Development of Boot-Camp Prison: A Debate," *University of Chicago Roundtable* 2 (1995), 435.

91. "A Tough Intermediate Sanction," in *Correctional Boot Camps: A Tough Intermediate Sanction,* eds. Doris L. MacKenzie and Eugene E. Hebert (Washington, D.C.: National Institute for Justice, 1996).

92. Sarah Glazer, "Juvenile Justice," *CQ Researcher* 4 (1994), 180.

93. United States General Accounting Office, "Prison Boot Camps: Short-Term Prison Costs Reduced, but Long-Term Impact Uncertain," (Washington, D.C.: U.S. General Accounting Office, 1993), 16.

94. Deborah Sharp, "Boot Camps—Punishment and Treatment," *Corrections Today* (June 1, 1995), 81.

95. "A Tough Intermediate Sanction."

96. Sharp, 81.

97. Doris L. MacKenzie and Dale Parent, "Shock Incarceration and Prison Crowding in Louisiana," *Journal of Criminal Justice* 19 (1991), 231.

98. "Boot Camps' Success Questioned as 45 Percent Rearrest Rate for Recruits Raises Eyebrows," *Florida Today* (June 22, 1997), 8B.

99. Doris L. MacKenzie and Claire Souryal, *Multisite Evaluation of Shock Incarceration, Evaluation Report* (Washington, D.C.: National Institute of Justice, 1994).

100. Dale G. Parent, "Boot Camps and Prison Crowding," in *Correctional Boot Camps: A Tough Intermediate Sanction,* eds. Doris L. MacKenzie and Eugene E. Hebert (Washington, D.C.: National Institute for Justice, 1996).

101. *Ibid.*

102. L. R. Acorn, "Working in a Boot Camp," *Corrections Today* (October 1991), 110.

103. Mareva Brown, "4 Moms Rip Youth Boot Camps," *Sacramento Bee* (March 18, 1998), A1.

104. Adam Nossiter, "As Boot Camps for Criminals Multiply, Skepticism Grows," *New York Times* (December 18, 1993), 37.

105. Mackenzie and Souryal, "A 'Machiavellian' Perspective."

chapter

13

Prisons and Jails

Chapter Outline

Chapter Objectives

After reading this chapter, you should be able to:

1. Contrast the Pennsylvania and the New York penitentiary theories of the 1800s.

2. List the factors that have caused the prison population to grow dramatically in the last several decades.

3. Explain the three general models of prisons.

4. List and briefly explain the four types of prisons.

5. Contrast formal with informal prison management systems.

6. List the reasons why private prisons can be run more cheaply than public ones.

7. Summarize the distinction between jails and prisons, and indicate the importance of jails in the American correctional system.

8. Explain how jails are administered.

9. Indicate the difference between traditional jail design and new generation jail design.

10. Indicate some of the consequences of our high rates of incarceration.

INTRODUCTION

Sir Henry Alfred McCardie, the famed English jurist, once said, "Trying a man is easy, as easy as falling off a log, compared with deciding what to do with him when he has been found guilty."[1] In the American criminal justice system, to a certain extent, the decision has been simplified: many of the guilty go behind bars. The United States has the largest corrections system in the world. More than 1.2 million convicts are locked up in our 1,500 state and federal prisons. Another 592,000 reside in the nation's 3,300 jails. Of every 100,000 Americans, 668 are in a federal or state prison or in a local jail.[2] Despite comparable crime rates, the United States incarcerates five times as many of its citizens as Canada does, and seven times as many as most European democracies.[3] In fact, the United States has one of the highest incarceration rates in the world (see Figure 13.1).

For the most part, this high rate is a product of the past thirty years. From the 1920s until 1970, America's incarceration rates remained fairly stable at 110 per 100,000. Throughout the course of this textbook, we have discussed many of the social and political factors that help explain the nearly 600 percent increase in the jail and prison population since 1970. In this chapter and the next, we turn our attention to the incarceration system itself. This chapter focuses on the history and organizational structures of prisons (which generally hold those who have committed serious felonies for long periods of time) and jails (which generally hold those who have committed less serious felonies and misdemeanors, and those awaiting trial, for short periods of time). Though the two terms are often used interchangeably, they refer to two very different institutions, each with its own responsibilities and its own set of seemingly unsolvable problems.

A SHORT HISTORY OF AMERICAN PRISONS

Today, we view prisons as instruments of punishment; the loss of freedom imposed on inmates is society's retribution for the crimes they have committed. This has not always been the function of incarceration. The prisons of eighteenth-century England, known as "bridewells" after London's Bridewell Palace, actually had little to do with punishment. These facilities were mainly used to hold debtors or those awaiting trial, execution, or banishment from the community.[4] (In many ways, as shall be made clear, these facilities resemble the modern jail.) Prisoners rarely spent a great deal of time in confinement. Indeed, given the filthy conditions of early prisons, they could not have survived long-term imprisonment without succumbing to disease.

Given the practices of the time, the English did not particularly need prisons. English courts generally imposed one of two sanctions on convicted felons: they turned them loose or they executed them.[5] (To be

Figure 13.1 Incarceration Rates of Selected Nations

Only Russia incarcerates its citizens at a higher rate than the United States.

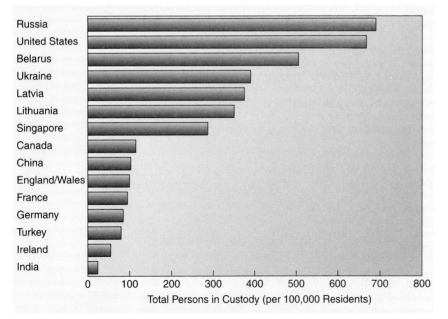

Total Persons in Custody (per 100,000 Residents)

SOURCE: THE SENTENCING PROJECT, BUREAU OF JUSTICE STATISTICS.

sure, most felons were released, pardoned either by the court or the clergy after receiving a whipping or a branding.) Consequently, when a series of sturdy, clean prisons began springing up in the last quarter of the eighteenth century, they were seen as part of a large-scale reform of the English criminal justice system. Believing that "small crimes lead to great," the reformers wanted to rehabilitate wrongdoers as well as punish them and urged the use of prisons as places where inmates could be "cured" of their evil ways through religious instruction and the discipline of hard labor.[6]

The correctional system in the American colonies differed very little from that of their motherland. If anything, colonial administrators were more likely to use corporal punishment than their English counterparts, and the death penalty was not uncommon in early America. The one exception was William Penn, who adopted the "Great Law" in Pennsylvania in 1682. Based on Quaker ideals of humanity and rehabilitation, this criminal code forbade the use of torture and mutilation as forms of punishment; instead, felons were ordered to pay restitution of property or goods to their victims. If the felons did not have sufficient property to make restitution, they were placed in a prison, which was primarily a "workhouse."[7] The death penalty was still allowed under the "Great Law," but only in cases of premeditated murder. Penn proved to be an exception, however, and the path to reform was much slower in the colonies than in England.

Walnut Street Prison: The First Penitentiary

Upon Penn's death in 1718, the "Great Law" was rescinded in favor of a harsher criminal code, similar to those of the other colonies. At the time of the American Revolution, however, the Quakers were instrumental in the first wide swing of the incarceration pendulum from punishment to rehabilitation. In 1776, Pennsylvania passed legislation ordering that offenders be reformed through treatment and discipline rather than simply beaten or executed.[8] Several states, including Massachusetts and New York, quickly followed Pennsylvania's example.

Under pressure from the renowned Quaker Dr. Benjamin Rush, Pennsylvania continued its reformist ways by opening the country's first **penitentiary** in a wing of Philadelphia's Walnut Street Jail in 1790. Based on the ideas of the British reformer John Howard, the penitentiary operated on the assumption that silence and labor provided the best hope of rehabilitating the criminal spirit. Remaining silent would force the prisoners to think about their crimes, and eventually the weight of conscience would lead to repentance. At the same time, enforced labor would attack the problem of idleness—regarded as the main cause of crime by penologists of the time.[9] Consequently, inmates at Walnut Street were isolated from one another in solitary rooms and kept busy with constant menial chores.

Eventually, the penitentiary at Walnut Street succumbed to the same problems that continue to plague institutions of confinement: overcrowding and excessive costs. As an influx of inmates forced more than one person to be housed in a room, silence became a nearly impossible condition. By the early 1800s, officials could not find work for all of the convicts, so many were left idle.

The Great Penitentiary Rivalry: Pennsylvania versus New York

The apparent lack of success at Walnut Street did little to dampen enthusiasm for the penitentiary concept. Throughout the first half of the nineteenth century, a number of states reacted to prison overcrowding by constructing new penitentiaries. Each state tended to have its own peculiar twist on the roles of

PENITENTIARY
An early form of correctional facility that emphasized separating inmates from society and from each other so that they would have an environment in which to reflect on their wrongdoing and ponder their reformation.

"In one corrupt and corrupting assemblage were to be found the disgusting objects of popular contempt, besmeared with filth from the pillory—the unhappy victim of the lash . . . the half naked vagrant—the loathsome drunkard—the sick suffering from various bodily pains, and too often the unaneled malefactor."

—Robert Vaux, *describing Pennsylvania jails* (1776)

Figure **13.2** The Eastern Penitentiary

The Eastern Penitentiary opened in 1829 with the controversial goal of changing the behavior of inmates instead of merely punishing them. An important component of this goal was the layout of the facility. As you can see, the Eastern Penitentiary was designed in the form of a "wagon wheel," known today as the radial style. The back-to-back cells in each "spoke" of the wheel faced outward from the center to limit contact between inmates. About 300 prisons worldwide have been built based on this design.

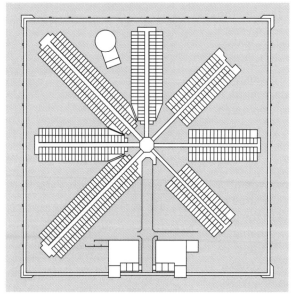

silence and labor, and two such systems—those of Pennsylvania and New York—emerged to shape the debate over the most effective way to run a prison.

The Pennsylvania System. After the failure of Walnut Street, Pennsylvania constructed two new prisons: the Western Penitentiary near Pittsburgh (opened in 1826) and the Eastern Penitentiary in Cherry Hill, near Philadelphia (1829). The Pennsylvania system took the concept of silence as a virtue to new extremes. Based on the idea of **separate confinement,** these penitentiaries were constructed with back-to-back cells facing both outward and inward. (See Figure 13.2 for the layout of the original Eastern Penitentiary.) To spare each inmate from the corrupting influence of the others, prisoners worked, slept, and ate alone in their cells. Their only contact with other human beings came in the form of religious instruction from a visiting clergyman or prison official.[10]

The New York System. If Pennsylvania's prisons were designed to transform wrongdoers into honest citizens, those in New York focused on obedience. When New York's Newgate Prison (built in 1791) became overcrowded, the state authorized the construction of Auburn Prison, which opened in 1816. Auburn initially operated under many of the same assumptions that guided the penitentiary at Walnut Street. Solitary confinement, however, seemed to lead to an inordinate amount of sickness, insanity, and even suicide among inmates, and it was abandoned in 1822. Nine years later, Elam Lynds became warden at Auburn and instilled the **congregate system,** also known as the Auburn system. Like Pennsylvania's separate confinement system, the congregate system was based on silence and labor. At Auburn, however, inmates worked and ate together, with silence enforced by prison guards.[11]

If either state can be said to have "won" the debate, it was New York. The Auburn system proved more popular, and a majority of the new prisons built during the first half of the nineteenth century followed New York's lead, though mainly for economic reasons rather than philosophical ones. New York's penitentiaries were cheaper to build because they did not require so much space. Furthermore, inmates in New York were employed in workshops, whereas those in Pennsylvania toiled alone in their cells. Consequently, the Auburn system was better positioned to exploit prison labor in the early years of widespread factory production.

The Reformers and the Progressives

The Auburn system did not go unchallenged. During the landmark 1870 meeting of the National Prison Association (forerunner of today's American Correctional Association) in Cincinnati, Ohio, a group of penal reformers contended that existing prisons did not provide sufficient incentive for inmate reformation. Arguing that fixed sentences, imposed silence, and isolation did nothing to improve the prisoners, the reformers proposed that instead penal institutions should offer the "carrot" of early release as a prime tool for rehabilitation. Echoing the views of the Quakers a century earlier, the reformers presented an ideology that would heavily influence American corrections for the next century.

The Elmira Reformatory. Upon his appointment as superintendent at New York's Elmira Reformatory in 1876, Zebulon Brockway put the concepts of this

SEPARATE CONFINEMENT
A nineteenth-century penitentiary system developed in Pennsylvania in which inmates were kept separate from each other at all times, with daily activities taking place in individual cells.

CONGREGATE SYSTEM
A nineteenth-century penitentiary system developed in New York in which inmates were kept in separate cells during the night but worked together in the daytime under a code of enforced silence.

"new penology" into practice. "It cannot be too often stated," Brockway insisted, "that prisoners are of inferior class and that our prison system is intended for treatment of defectives." These defectives, he felt, could be cured through "scientifically directed bodily and mental exercises."[12] Designed for first-time felons between the ages of sixteen and thirty, the Elmira Reformatory had no fixed sentences. The institution's administrators had the final say on when an inmate could be released, so long as the time served did not exceed the maximum sentence prescribed by law.[13]

At Elmira, good behavior was rewarded by early release, and misbehavior was punished with extended time under a three-grade system of classification. Upon entering the institution, a wrongdoer was assigned a grade of 2. If the inmate followed the rules and completed work and school assignments, after six months he would be moved up to grade 1, the necessary grade for release. If, however, the inmate broke institutional rules or otherwise failed to cooperate, he would be lowered to grade 3. A grade 3 inmate needed to behave properly for three months before he could return to grade 2 and begin to work toward grade 1 and eventual release.[14] (You will learn more on the "marks system" in Chapter 15.)

The Progressives. Although Brockway and his reforming peers had largely disappeared by 1900, their theories had a great influence on the Progressive movement that came into prominence in the first two decades of the twentieth century. The Progressive movement was linked to the positivist school, which was discussed in Chapter 2. The Progressives believed criminal behavior was caused by social, economic, and biological reasons, and therefore a corrections system should have a goal of treatment, not punishment. The Progressives were greatly responsible for the spread of indeterminate sentences, probation, community sanctions, and parole in the first half of the twentieth century.

They also trumpeted the **medical model** of prisons, which held that institutions should offer a variety of programs and therapies to cure inmates of their "ills," whatever the root causes. The "glory years" of the medical model and the ideals of rehabilitation came in the decade after the end of World War II in 1945. The general postwar optimism applied to the nation's criminals as well—a society that had defeated the Axis powers in Europe and the Pacific could certainly "cure" the "disease" of criminality.[15] At the forefront of the rehabilitation movement in these years was a commitment to behavior modification programs ranging from group therapy to shock therapy to psychotherapy. Holding out the possibility of a "cure" for inmates, the American corrections system eased its more punitive aspects. Capital punishment, for example, dropped significantly from prewar levels.[16]

The Reassertion of Punishment

Even though the Progressives had a great influence on the corrections system as a whole, their theories had little impact on the prisons themselves, many of which had been constructed in the nineteenth century and were impervious to change. More importantly, prison administrators usually did not agree with the Progressives and their followers, so the day-to-day lives of most inmates varied little from the congregate system of Auburn Prison.

Inmates of Elmira State Prison in New York attend a presentation at the prison auditorium. Zebulon Brockway, the superintendent at Elmira, believed that criminals were an "inferior class" of human being and should be treated as society's defectives. Thus, mental exercises designed to improve the inmates' minds were part of the prison routine at Elmira. To what extent do you believe that treatment should be a part of the incarceration of criminals?

MEDICAL MODEL
A model of corrections in which the psychological and biological roots of an inmate's criminal behavior are identified and treated.

Academic attitudes began to shift toward the prison administrators in the mid-1960s. As we saw in Chapter 11, the publication of Robert Martinson's famous "What Works?" essay in 1974 provided critics of the medical model with statistical evidence that rehabilitation efforts did nothing to lower recidivism rates.[17] This is not to say that Martinson's findings went unchallenged. A number of rebuttals arguing that rehabilitative programs could be successful appeared immediately after the publication of "What Works?"[18] In fact, Martinson himself retracted most of his claims in a little noticed article published five years after his initial report.[19] Attempts by Martinson and others to "set the record straight" went largely unnoticed, however, as a sharp rise in crime in the early 1970s led many criminologists and politicians to champion "get tough" measures to deal with criminals they now considered "incurable." By the end of the 1980s, the legislative, judicial, and administrative strategies that we have discussed throughout this text had positioned the United States for an explosion in inmate populations and prison construction unparalleled in the nation's history.

THE PRISON POPULATION BOMB

The number of Americans in prison or jail has doubled since 1985 and continues to rise at an annual rate of between 5 and 7 percent (see Figure 13.3). These numbers are not only dramatic, but also, say some observers, inexplicable, given the overall crime picture in the United States. In the 1990s, violent and property crime rates dropped; yet the number of inmates continued to rise. According to accepted theory, rising incarceration rates should be the result of a rise in crime, leaving one expert to comment that America's prison population is "defying gravity."[20] (See *CJ in Focus—Myth versus Reality: Does Placing Criminals in Prison Reduce Crime?*)

Factors in Prison Population Growth

Alfred Blumstein of Carnegie Mellon University attributes much of the growth in the number of Americans behind bars to the enhancement and

INFOTRAC®
COLLEGE EDITION

Rentschler, William. Lock-em up and <u>throw away the key</u>: a policy that won't work.

Figure 13.3 The Inmate Population of the United States

The total number of inmates in custody in the United States has risen from 744,208 in 1985 to 1,802,496 in 1998.

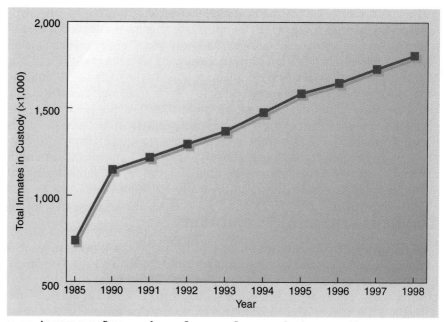

SOURCE: ADAPTED FROM BUREAU OF JUSTICE STATISTICS, *PRISON AND JAIL INMATES AT MIDYEAR 1998* (WASHINGTON, D.C.: U.S. DEPARTMENT OF JUSTICE, MARCH 1999), TABLE 1, PAGE 2.

CJ in Focus

Myth versus Reality

Does Placing Criminals in Prison Reduce Crime?

Violent crime rates in the United States have been stable or declining in recent years. At the same time, as Figure 13.4 shows, the rate at which Americans have been imprisoned has climbed precipitously. The correlation between these two trends has become a subject of much discussion among crime experts.

THE MYTH

A popular view of incarceration is that "a thug in jail can't shoot your sister." Obviously, a prison inmate is incapable of doing any further harm to the community. By extension, then, as the number of criminals behind bars increases, the crime rate should drop accordingly.

THE REALITY

Numerous studies have shown that this is not always the case. Prison population rates in Texas and Michigan, for example, increased by nearly the same amount over a recent ten-year period. During that time, however, Texas experienced a much sharper increase in violent crime rates than did Michigan. Louisiana has had the highest incarceration rates in the nation and also one of the highest rates of violent crime. At the other extreme, North Dakota has had both the lowest incarceration rates and the lowest crime rates. Such statistics may show that other factors (particularly the social factors discussed in Chapter 2) play a more significant role in crime rates than the number of criminals who are incapacitated.

One theory offered to explain the apparent lack of positive correlation between rates of imprisonment and crime in general is the "replacement" hypothesis. Most crimes, especially those related to drug sales, are committed by groups of co-offenders, not by a single criminal. Consequently, when one member of the group is arrested, the criminal activity does not stop. Instead, the group merely recruits somebody else to take his or her place. Furthermore, there is widespread support for the idea that some inmates become hard-core criminals only after being exposed to prison culture and commit more crimes after being released from prison than they would have if they had never gone there in the first place.

Few observers would suggest that imprisonment rates have *no* effect on crime rates. Instead, criminologists seem to be cautioning that the relationship between the prison population and crime rates is not fully understood, and that public policymakers should not make laws on the assumption that more prisoners equals less crime.

For Critical Analysis: What other factors could explain the lack of positive correlation between incarceration rates and crime rates?

Figure 13.4 Comparing Crime Rates and Incarceration Rates

As you can see, the crime rate in the United States has been going down while the number of inmates in federal and state prisons and jails has been rising.

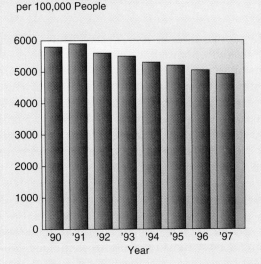

Violent and Property Crimes per 100,000 People

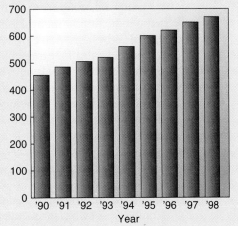

Inmates in Federal and State Prisons and Local Jails per 100,000 People on July 1 Each Year

SOURCE: FEDERAL BUREAU OF INVESTIGATION AND BUREAU OF JUSTICE STATISTICS.

stricter enforcement of the nation's drug laws. Since 1980, he points out, the rate of incarceration for drug arrests in the United States has risen 1,000 percent, and there are more Americans in prison or jail for drug offenses today than there were for *all* offenses in the early 1970s.[21] We will explore the background and ramifications of this situation in detail in Chapter 17.

With the prison population boom has come a rapid increase in the corporate and industrial aspects of the correctional system. At trade shows, like the 1997 American Correctional Association Convention shown above, businesses hock their wares to public and private prison administrators. There is, for example, heated competition between telephone companies to place pay phones in prisons. Such phones, which are an inmate's only link to the outside world, can generate $15,000 a year—about five times the revenue of a normal pay phone. MCI went so far as to install phones in California prisons at no cost and offer the California Department of Corrections 32 percent of all revenues from inmates' phone calls. Do you think it is ethical for private corporations to profit from the incarceration of criminals?

Other reasons for the growth in incarceration populations include:

Increased probability of incarceration. Simply stated, the chance of someone who is arrested going to prison today is much greater than it was twenty years ago. Most of this growth took place in the 1980s, when the likelihood of incarceration after arrest increased fivefold for drug offenses, threefold for weapons offenses, and twofold for crimes such as sexual assault, burglary, auto theft, and larceny. These trends leveled off in the 1990s, though those arrested for murder, sexual assault, and weapons offenses still have a greater chance of going to prison or jail today than they did a decade ago.[22]

Inmates serving more time for each crime. After the Sentencing Reform Act of 1984 (see Chapter 11), the length of time served by federal convicts for their crimes rose significantly. Since the law went into effect, the average time served by inmates in federal prisons has climbed from 15 months to 25 months—a 67 percent increase.[23] State sentencing reform statutes and "truth-in-sentencing" laws have had similar consequences. In Michigan, for example, the average minimum term for a prisoner grew a full year between 1989 and 1995.[24]

Revocation of community-based sanctions. As we discussed in Chapter 12, increased control over offenders supervised in the community has led to increased rates of their rearrest. From 1977 to 1994—a period in which the corrections system readjusted its sights from rehabilitation to punishment, deterrence, and incapacitation—the rate of probationer and parolee recidivism grew 600 percent.[25]

Rising incarceration rates of women. In 1981, 14,000 women were prisoners in federal and state institutions; by 1997, the number had grown to 78,067. Women still account for only 6.4 percent of all prisoners nationwide, but their rates of imprisonment are growing more rapidly than those of men.[26] We will discuss some of the possible reasons for this phenomenon in Chapter 18.

Though exact figures are difficult to establish, many observers also believe that a reduction in mental health services has led to an injection of the mentally ill into the nation's prisons and jails. No longer provided with free care in mental health institutes by state or federal governments, these people are increasingly being dealt with by the criminal justice system. According to one estimate, on any given day 200,000 people behind bars are known to suffer from schizophrenia—a thought disorder often characterized by intellectual deterioration, disorganized speech and behavior, and hallucinations—or some form of severe depression.[27]

The Prison Construction Boom

The escalation in the prisoner population has brought with it an increased demand for new prisons. One out of every three federal correctional facilities and one of every eight state facilities were built in the 1990s.[28] In 1971, total corrections construction spending was $2.3 billion; today, it is nearly $40 billion.[29] These costs have pushed corrections' budgets to unprecedented levels. Seven states spend in excess of $1 billion each year on corrections-related services.[30] (See Figure 13.5.) Indeed, for many states, the single largest item on their budgets is correctional expenditures. In the absence of politically unpopular tax increases, legislators are thereby forced to find another revenue source to pay for the new prisons. Thus, the opportunity cost of prison construction can be great—every dollar that goes to build a prison is a dollar

State	Total Corrections Budget (Approximate)	Incarceration Rate*
California	$3,900,000,000	477
Texas	1,900,000,000	700
New York	1,500,000,000	384
Florida	1,320,000,000	445
Michigan	1,315,000,000	453
Pennsylvania	1,240,000,000	297
Ohio	1,145,000,000	440
Illinois	785,000,000	353
Wisconsin	660,000,000	321
New Jersey	605,000,000	367

*The number of prisoners with a sentence of more than 1 year per 100,000 state residents.

SOURCE: BUREAU OF JUSTICE STATISTICS, SOURCEBOOK OF CRIMINAL JUSTICE STATISTICS, 1997 (WASHINGTON, D.C.: U.S. DEPARTMENT OF JUSTICE, 1998), TABLE 11, PAGE 13; BUREAU OF JUSTICE STATISTICS, PRISON AND JAIL INMATES AT MIDYEAR 1998 (WASHINGTON, D.C.: U.S. DEPARTMENT OF JUSTICE, MARCH 1999), TABLE 2, PAGE 3.

Figure 13.5 State Corrections Budgets

Seven states have corrections budgets that exceed $1 billion. The ten states with the highest corrections budgets are listed here, along with their incarceration rates.

that cannot be used to fund education programs, health care, and other social programs.[31]

Legislative efforts have kept prison construction well financed. The 1994 Crime Bill allocated $10 billion in grants for the construction of new incarceration facilities through 2000.[32] Forty-five states are required by law and/or court order to keep crowding in prisons and jails below a certain level; therefore, as the number of inmates continues to increase, state corrections agencies are forced to build new facilities or find alternative forms of punishment such as the community-based sanctions discussed in Chapter 12.

As we shall see, this infusion of government funds has convinced a number of private firms to enter the corrections market. It has also forced many communities to reconsider their NIMBY (Not In My Back Yard) attitude toward prisons and jails. Small towns can no longer afford to reject corrections industry dollars. In Florida, for example, fifteen communities went so far as to offer the state government free land for the construction of a new prison within their boundaries. The benefits are tangible: the $67 million prison being built in Bowling Green, Missouri, will bring the town $150,000 a year in taxes and has provided the impetus for the construction of a new housing project, a fast-food restaurant, and a hotel.[33]

On average, one new jail or prison is completed every week in the United States. The federal prison being built in the Mojave Desert near Victorville, California, was to be filled to capacity when it opened in late 1999.

Spending on prisons has grown 60 percent since 1990 in order to house an inmate population that has nearly doubled over that time period. What are some of the drawbacks of the boom in prison construction? What are some of the benefits?

THE ROLE OF PRISONS IN SOCIETY

The demands placed upon penal institutions are hardly limited to providing tax and job benefits for the communities in which they are located. As University of Connecticut sociologist Charles Logan once noted, Americans expect prisons to "correct the incorrigible, rehabilitate the wretched . . . restrain the dangerous, and punish the wicked."[34] Basically, prisons exist to make society a safer place. Whether this is to be achieved through retribution, deterrence, incapacitation, or rehabilitation—the four justifications of corrections introduced in Chapter 11—depends on the operating philosophy of the individual penal institution.

Three general models of prisons have emerged to describe the different schools of thought behind prison organization:

- The *custodial model* is based on the assumption that prisoners are incarcerated for reasons of incapacitation, deterrence, and retribution. All decisions within the prison—such as what form of recreation to provide the inmates—are made with an eye toward security and discipline, and the daily routine of the inmates is highly controlled. The custodial model has dominated the most restrictive prisons in the United States since the 1930s.

- The *rehabilitation model* stresses the ideals of individualized treatment that we discussed in Chapter 11. Security concerns are often secondary to the well-being of the individual inmate, and a number of treatment programs are offered to aid prisoners in changing their criminal and antisocial behavior. The rehabilitation model came into prominence during the 1950s and enjoyed widespread popularity until it began to lose general acceptance in the 1970s and 1980s.

- In the *reintegration model,* the correctional institution serves as a training ground for the inmate to prepare for existence in the community. Prisons that have adopted this model give the prisoners more responsibility during incarceration and offer halfway houses and work programs (both discussed in Chapter 15) to help them reintegrate into society. This model is becoming more influential, as corrections officials react to problems such as prison overcrowding.[35]

Alternative views of the prison's role in society are at odds with these three "ideal" perspectives. Professor Blumstein argues that prisons *create* new criminals, especially with regard to nonviolent drug offenders. Not only do these nonviolent felons become socialized to the criminal lifestyle while in prison, but the stigma of incarceration makes it more difficult for them to obtain employment upon release. Their only means of sustenance "on the outside" is to apply the criminal methods they learned in prison.[36]

TYPES OF PRISONS

Prison administrators have long been aware of the need to separate different kinds of offenders. In federal prisons, this led to a system with six levels based on the security needs of the inmates, from level 1 facilities with the lowest amount of security to level 6 with the harshest security measures. (Many states also use the six-level system, an example of which can be seen in Figure 13.6.) To simplify matters, most observers refer to correctional facilities as being one of three levels—minimum, medium, and maximum. A fourth level—the supermaximum-security prison—is relatively rare and extremely controversial due to its hyper-harsh methods of punishing and controlling the most dangerous prisoners. (See the feature *Criminal Justice in Action—The End of the Line: Supermax Prisons* at the end of the chapter.)

Maximum-Security Prisons

MAXIMUM-SECURITY PRISON
A correctional institution designed and organized to control and discipline dangerous felons, as well as prevent escape with intense supervision, cement walls, and electronic, barbed wire fences.

In a certain sense, the classification of prisoners today owes a debt to the three-grade system developed by Zebulon Brockway at the Elmira Penitentiary, discussed earlier in the chapter. Once wrongdoers enter a corrections facility, they are constantly graded on behavior. Those who serve good time, as we have seen, are often rewarded with early release. Those who compile extensive misconduct records are usually housed, along with violent

Level	Restrictions
Level 1-Low	No Murder I or II, Robbery, Sex-Related crime, Kidnapping/abduction, Felonious Assult (current or prior), Flight/Escape, Carjacking, Malicious Wounding, No Escape Risk, No Disruptive Behavior
Level 1-High	No Murder I or II, Sex offense, Kidnap/Abduction, Escape history. No Disruptive Behavior for at least past 24 months.
Level 2	For initial assignment only. No escape history for past 5 years. No disruptive behavior for at least past 24 months prior to transfer to any less secure facility.
Level 3	Single, Multiple and Life + sentences. Must have served 20 consecutive years on sentence. No disruptive behavior for past 24 months for a transfer to any less secure facility.
Level 4	Single, Multiple and Life + sentences. No disruptive behavior for past 24 months for a transfer to any less secure facility.
Level 5	Same as level 4.
Level 6	Single, Multiple and Life + sentences. PROFILE OF INMATES: Disruptive, Assaultive, Severe Behavior Problems; Predatory-type behavior; Escape Risks; No disruptive behavior for past 24 months for a transfer to any less secure facility.

SOURCE: VIRGINIA DEPARTMENT OF CORRECTIONS.

Figure 13.6 Security Levels in Virginia

The security levels of correctional facilities in Virginia are graded from Level 1 to Level 6. As you can see, Level 1 facilities are for those inmates who pose the least amount of risk to fellow inmates, staff members, and themselves. Level 6 facilities are for those who are considered the most dangerous by the Virginia Department of Corrections.

and repeat offenders, in **maximum-security prisons.** The names of these institutions—Folsom, San Quentin, Sing Sing, Attica—conjure up foreboding images of concrete and steel jungles, with good reason.

Maximum-security prisons are designed with full attention to security and surveillance. In these institutions, inmates' lives are programmed in a militaristic fashion to keep them from escaping or from harming themselves or the prison staff. About a quarter of the prisons in the United States are classified as maximum security, and these institutions house about 16 percent of the country's prisoners.

The Design. Maximum-security prisons tend to be large—holding more than a thousand inmates—and they have similar features. The entire operation is usually surrounded by concrete walls that stand 20 to 30 feet high and have also been sunk deep into the ground to deter tunnel escapes; fences reinforced with razor-ribbon barbed wire that can be electrically charged may supplement or replace the walls. The prison walls are studded with watchtowers, from which guards armed with shotguns and rifles survey the movement of prisoners below. The designs of these facilities, though similar, are not uniform. Though correctional facilities built using the radial design pioneered by Eastern State Penitentiary still exist, several other designs have become prominent in more recently constructed institutions. For an overview of the these designs, including the radial design, see Figure 13.7 on the next page.

Inmates live in cells, most of them with similar dimensions to those found in the I-Max maximum-security prison for women in Topeka, Kansas: 8 feet by 14 feet with cinder block walls.[37] The space contains bunks, a toilet, a sink, and possibly a cabinet or closet. Cells

This photograph shows the stark and austere quality of the Condemned Inmates Housing Adjustment Center (death row) at California's San Quentin Prison. Maximum-security prisons such as San Quentin are designed with one overriding concern in mind: control of inmates. Examine the photo and identify the various features of this area of San Quentin that show the facility's emphasis on security.

Figure **13.7** Prison Designs

The Radial Design

The radial design has been utilized since the early nineteenth century. The "wagon wheel"–like form of the structure was created with the dual goals of separation and control. Inmates are separated from each other in their cells on the "spokes" of the wheel, and prison officials can control the activities of the inmates from the control center in the "hub" of the wheel.

The Courtyard Style

In the courtyard-style prison, a courtyard replaces the transportation function of the "pole" in the telephone-pole prison. That is, the prison buildings form a square around a courtyard, and to get from one part of the facility to another, the inmates go across the courtyard. In a number of these facilities, the recreational area, mess hall, and school are located in the courtyard.

The Telephone-Pole Design

The main feature of the telephone-pole design is a long central corridor that serves as a means for transporting inmates from one part of the facility to another. Branching off from this main corridor are the functional areas of the facility: housing, food services, workshops, treatment program rooms, etc. Prison officials survey the entire facility from the central "pole" and can shut off the various "arms" when necessary for security reasons. The majority of maximum-security prisons in the United States were constructed using this design blueprint.

The Campus Style

Some of the newer maximum-security prisons have adopted the campus style, a style that had previously been used in correctional facilities for women and juveniles. Like a college campus, housing units are scattered among functional units such as the dining room, recreation area, and treatment centers. The benefit of the campus style is that individual buildings can be used for different functions, making the operation more flexible. Due to concerns that the campus style provides less security than the other designs discussed, it remains for the most part the design of choice for medium- and minimum-security prisons.

SOURCE: TEXT ADAPTED FROM TODD R. CLEAR AND GEORGE F. COLE, AMERICAN CORRECTIONS, 4TH ED. (BELMONT, CA: WADSWORTH PUBLISHING COMPANY, 1997), 255–6.

are located in rows of *cell blocks*, each of which forms its own security unit, set off by a series of gates and bars. A maximum-security institution is essentially a collection of numerous cell blocks, each constituting its own prison within a prison.

Inmates' lives are dominated by security measures. Whenever they move from one area of the prison to another, they do so in groups and under the watchful eye of armed correctional guards. Television surveillance cameras may be used to monitor their every move, even when sleeping, showering, or using the toilet. They are subject to frequent pat-downs or strip searches at the guards' discretion. Constant "head counts" assure that every inmate is where he or she should be. Tower guards—many of whom have orders to shoot to kill in the case of a disturbance or escape attempt—constantly look down on the inmates as they move around outdoor areas of the facility.

Technology has added significantly to the power an institution holds over the individual prisoner. Walk-through metal detectors and X-ray body scanners can detect weapons or other contraband hidden on the body of an inmate. Ground-penetrating radar allows the correctional staff to search courtyards for buried items. Prison officials expect that within the next decade, electronic eye scans and noninvasive skin patches will be available to determine whether a prisoner has been using drugs.

Aging Foundations. The advancing age of many maximum-security prisons is a major concern today. Given their size and the expense involved in their construction, these institutions were built to last, and many have achieved that goal. Fifty-four prisons constructed before 1900 are still in use.[38] Illinois's Menard Correctional Center, for example, began operating in 1878 and experiences constant difficulties with outdated electric and plumbing systems.

Besides being inconvenient for staff and inmates, aging penal institutions increase the possibility of the most dangerous of all security situations: the escape. Recently, six prisoners were able to tunnel out of the century-old State Correctional Institution near Pittsburgh, Pennsylvania, by drilling through the prison wall with a hydraulic jack. Though the escapees were eventually recaptured, state officials immediately budgeted $135.5 million for a new maximum-security prison that would have better sight lines from guard towers and enable corrections officers to exact more control over the inmates.[39]

Medium- and Minimum-Security Prisons

Medium-security prisons hold about 35 percent of the prison population and minimum-security prisons 49 percent. Inmates at **medium-security prisons** have for the most part committed less serious crimes than those housed in maximum-security prisons and are not considered high risks to escape or to cause harm. Consequently, medium-security institutions are not designed for control to the same extent as maximum-security prisons and have a more relaxed atmosphere. These facilities also offer more educational and treatment programs and allow for more contact between inmates. Medium-security prisons are rarely walled, relying instead on high fences. Prisoners have more freedom of movement within the structures, and the levels of surveillance are much lower. Living quarters are less restrictive as well—many of the newer medium-security prisons provide dormitory housing.

A **minimum-security prison** seems at first glance to be more like a college campus than an incarceration facility. Most of the inmates at these institutions are nonviolent and well behaved and include a high percentage of white-collar criminals. Indeed, inmates are often transferred to minimum-security prisons as a reward for good behavior in other facilities. Therefore, security measures are lax compared even to medium-security prisons. Unlike medium-security institutions, minimum-security prisons do not have armed guards. Prisoners are allowed amenities such as television sets and computers in their rooms, they enjoy freedom of movement, and they are allowed off prison grounds for educational or employment purposes to a much greater extent than those held in more restrictive facilities. Some critics have likened minimum-security prisons to "country clubs," but in the corrections system, everything is relative. A minimum-security prison may seem like a vacation spot when compared to the horrors of Sing Sing, but it still represents a restriction of personal freedom and separates the inmate from the outside world.

Security measures—including television surveillance, pat downs, and the constant attention of correctional officers in towers (pictured above)—dominate the lives of inmates in maximum-security prisons. How do guard towers contribute to the overall security of a prison facility? What might be some of the limitations of the guard tower as a security device?

MEDIUM-SECURITY PRISON
A correctional institution that houses less dangerous inmates, and therefore uses less restrictive measures to avoid violence and escapes.

MINIMUM-SECURITY PRISON
A correctional institution designed to allow inmates, most of whom pose low security risks, a great deal of freedom of movement and contact with the outside world.

PRISON ADMINISTRATION

The security level of the institution generally determines the specific methods by which a prison is managed. There are, however, general goals of prison administration, summarized by Charles Logan as follows:

> The mission of a prison is to keep prisoners—to keep them in, keep them safe, keep them in line, keep them healthy, and keep them busy—and to do it with fairness, without undue suffering and as efficiently as possible.[40]

Considering the environment of a prison—an enclosed world inhabited by people who are generally violent, angry, and would rather be anywhere else—Logan's mission statement may be slightly Utopian. A prison staff must supervise the daily routines of hundreds or thousands of inmates, a duty that includes providing them with meals, education, vocational programs, and different forms of leisure. The smooth operation of this supervision is made more difficult—if not, at times, impossible—by budgetary restrictions, overcrowding, and continual inmate turnover.

The implications of mismanagement are severe. While studying a series of prison riots, sociologists Bert Useem and Peter Kimball found that breakdowns in managerial control commonly preceded such acts of mass violence.[41] During the 1970s, for example, conditions in the State Penitentiary in New Mexico deteriorated significantly; inmates who had become well organized and comfortable with their daily routines increasingly became the targets of harsh treatment from the prison staff, while at the same time a reduction in structured activities left prison life "painfully boring."[42] The result, in 1980, was one of the most violent prison riots in the nation's history.

Formal Prison Management

In some respects, the management structure of a prison is similar to that of a police department, as discussed in Chapter 5. Both systems rely on a hierarchical (top-down) *chain of command* to increase personal responsibility. Both assign different employees to specific tasks, though prison managers have much more direct control over their subordinates than do police managers. The main difference is that police departments have a *continuity of purpose* that is sometimes lacking in prison organizations. All members of a police force are, at least theoretically, working to reduce crime and apprehend criminals. In a prison, this continuity is less evident. An employee in the prison laundry service and one who works in the visiting center have little in common. In some cases, employees may even have cross-purposes: a prison guard may want to punish an inmate, while a counselor in the treatment center may want to rehabilitate her or him.

Consequently, a strong hierarchy is crucial for any prison management team that hopes to meet Logan's expectations. As Figure 13.8 shows, the **warden** (also known as a superintendent) is ultimately responsible for the operation of a prison. He or she oversees deputy wardens, who in turn manage the various organizational lines of the institution. The custodial employees, who deal directly with the inmates and make up more than half of a prison's staff, operate under a militaristic hierarchy, with a line of command passing from the deputy warden to the captain to the corrections officer.

Informal Prison Management

Within the confines of the management structure, the personal philosophy of an administrator plays a significant role in prison management. Tara Gray and Jon'a F. Meyer of New Mexico State University illustrate this point by con-

WARDEN
The prison official who is ultimately responsible for the organization and performance of a correctional facility.

Figure **13.8** Organizational Chart for a Typical Correctional Facility

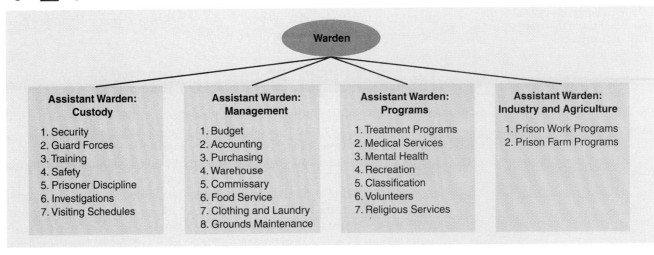

Warden

Assistant Warden: Custody	**Assistant Warden: Management**	**Assistant Warden: Programs**	**Assistant Warden: Industry and Agriculture**
1. Security	1. Budget	1. Treatment Programs	1. Prison Work Programs
2. Guard Forces	2. Accounting	2. Medical Services	2. Prison Farm Programs
3. Training	3. Purchasing	3. Mental Health	
4. Safety	4. Warehouse	4. Recreation	
5. Prisoner Discipline	5. Commissary	5. Classification	
6. Investigations	6. Food Service	6. Volunteers	
7. Visiting Schedules	7. Clothing and Laundry	7. Religious Services	
	8. Grounds Maintenance		

trasting two influential prison administrators of the 1960s and 1970s.[43] George Beto, director of corrections in Texas for ten years, espoused the *control model* of administration, and Tom Murton, an Arkansas warden depicted in the 1980 film *Brubaker,* preferred the *participation model.*

Beto felt that by forcing inmates to abide by stringent prison rules, he was preparing them to follow the rules of society when they were released. Consequently, Texas prisons under Beto were tightly controlled. Infractions such as talking in a loud voice were summarily—and, some said, cruelly—punished. Because Texas had only about half as many prison guards per convict as other states, Beto made widespread use of a practice in which selected inmates known as "building tenders" were given the status of guards or overseers in return for certain privileges. Building tenders had been employed in the South for nearly fifty years, and in many cases these inmate guards were more brutal than their state-employed counterparts.

In contrast, Murton felt that

> Inmates cannot learn to dance by having their legs tied together. The only way to prepare them for life in a democracy is to expose them to democracy while they are incarcerated.[44]

In keeping with this philosophy, Murton allowed the inmates to govern some aspects of their prison lives. For example, he established inmate councils whose leaders were elected by the prisoners themselves. These councils were responsible for controlling inmate violence and making decisions such as who would be allowed to leave the prison on furlough. One criminologist, after visiting Murton's prison, stated that his theories would lead to a "renaissance in corrections."

The prediction failed to come true, not necessarily because Murton's ideas were invalid, but because the philosophy was rejected. Contemporary management practices frown on giving such power to inmates. As for Beto's system, building tenders were discontinued following the Texas prison reform lawsuit *Ruiz v. Estelle* (1977).[45] The fact that neither Beto's inmate guards nor Murton's inmate councils have sur-

In the 1980 film, *Brubaker,* Robert Redford, right, played Henry Brubaker, the new warden at an Arkansas prison. In order to get a first-hand view of how the prison is run, Brubaker disguises himself as an inmate. Brubaker tries to put an end to the corruption and violence he witnessed on the inside, only to be thwarted by the deep-seated resistance of prison officials and the local business community. Brubaker was loosely based on the real-life experiences of Tom Murton.

PRIVATE PRISONS
Correctional facilities operated by private corporations instead of the government, and therefore reliant on profit for survival.

vived suggests that prison management is an inherently conservative field. Most wardens have their hands full simply trying to run the prison, without attempting to "change the system"—even if the courts would let them. (See *Careers in Criminal Justice—The Prison Warden.*)

THE EMERGENCE OF PRIVATE PRISONS

In addition to all the other pressures placed on wardens and other prison administrators, they must operate within a budget assigned to them by an overseeing governmental agency. The great majority of all prisons are under the control of federal and state governments. The Federal Bureau of Prisons (BOP), part of the U.S. Department of Justice, operates nearly 100 prisons. The executive branch of each state is responsible for state prisons and, in some instances, jails. In the nineteenth century, not all correctional facilities were under the control of the state. In fact, the entire Texas prison system was privately operated from 1872 to the late 1880s. For most of the twentieth century, however, **private prisons,** or prisons run by private business firms to make a profit, could not be found in the United States.

That is certainly not the case today. With corrections exhibiting all appearances of, in the words of one observer, "a recession-proof industry," the American business community eagerly entered the market in the late 1980s and 1990s.[46] (See Figure 13.9.) Thirteen private corrections firms operate nearly 200 facilities across the United States. The two largest corrections companies, Corrections Corporation of America (CCA) and Wackenhut Corrections Corp., are contracted to supervise nearly 85,000 inmates. In 1997 the BOP awarded the first contract paying a private company to operate one of its prisons—Wackenhut received $88 million to run the Taft Correctional Institution in Taft, California.[47] Some industry experts are predicting annual growth of 25 percent for private prisons in the first five years of the new millennium.[48]

Figure 13.9 The Growth of Private Prisons in the United States

The number of adult prison beds operated by private management companies has shown a marked increase since the late 1980s.

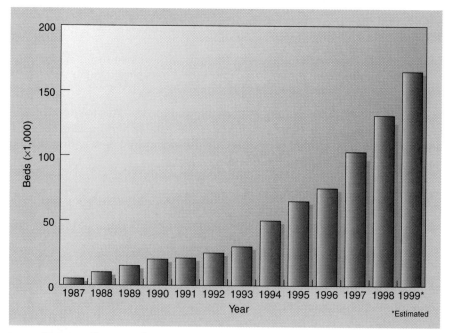

SOURCE: CENTER FOR STUDIES IN CRIMINOLOGY AND LAW, UNIVERSITY OF FLORIDA, AND BUREAU OF JUSTICE STATISTICS, *SOURCEBOOK OF CRIMINAL JUSTICE STATISTICS, 1997* (WASHINGTON, D.C.: U.S. DEPARTMENT OF JUSTICE, 1998), 83.

Why Privatize?

It would be a mistake to automatically assume that private prisons are less expensive to run than public ones.[49] The incentive to privatize is, however, primarily financial. In the 1980s and 1990s, a number of states and cities saved operating costs by converting government-run services such as garbage col-

Careers in Criminal Justice

PENNY LUCERO, WARDEN

As Warden of the New Mexico Women's Correctional Facility, I have executive oversight of the management and operation of the nation's first privately managed, multi-custody state prison. I became interested in corrections as a result of the employment opportunities made available with the state. When I entered the job market, I had received my undergraduate degree in psychology and completed work toward my graduate degree from New Mexico State University.

My corrections career began in 1981 with the New Mexico Department of Corrections, where I held a series of progressively more responsible positions, including training officer, ACA accreditation manager and chief classification officer. In 1985, I became the first woman to be promoted to the rank of Assistant Warden at a male prison in New Mexico. In order to expand my experience to include juvenile corrections, I took the position of Deputy Superintendent at the Youth Diagnostic Center and New Mexico Girls' School.

Although I left corrections for a while to manage my own business, I realized that my true career had become corrections. Being my own boss had its "pros," but the "cons" had won my heart; I wanted to dedicate my energy, expertise, and leadership to corrections. Fortunately, Corrections Corporation of America was opening the new women's prison in Grants, and I was quickly recruited as a member of the management team. Joining this team of experi-

enced corrections professionals is what I claim to be the catalyst that propelled me to the highest executive level of institutional leadership. The management team included three well-established professionals: two retired wardens from the New Mexico system and one nationally recognized warden of a female prison. All three became friends and mentors, always encouraging me to excel.

Working with the adult female offenders and for a private company were both new experiences for me. The opening of New Mexico Women's Correctional Facility was the first time the state had provided a purpose-built staffed and programmed facility specifically for female offenders. As Program Director, I had the opportunity to develop a wide array of state-of-the-art programs and services that would help prepare the women for a successful return to their communities.

As Warden, I consider my major responsibilities to be maintaining a healthful, positive, safe, and mutually respectful environment for staff and inmates; establishing a working relationship with outside communities in order to assist with public education about offenders and the mutual benefit of working with them upon release; participating in civic and professional organizations and encouraging the staff to do so; ensuring that New Mexico Women's Correctional Facility meets established national correctional standards; and, staying current on new management, program, and technology trends that can assist me in maintaining the standards of excellence established at the facility.

Prisons have changed dramatically over the past two decades. No longer "closed" communities where "outsiders" are unwelcome, they have become an extension of society, welcoming daily

interaction with local citizens, elected officials, researchers, student interns, and volunteers in order to create a more normalized environment. Equally important is the commitment to assist offenders in preparing for a lawful return to society. To that end, correctional administrators are eager to recruit and retain creative, thoughtful, and industrious employees for rewarding careers in a lifetime of service to society.

lection and road maintenance to the private sector. Similarly, private prisons can be run more cheaply and efficiently than public ones for the following reasons:

- *Labor costs.* The wages of public employees account for nearly two-thirds of a prison's operating expenses. Although private corrections firms pay base salaries comparable to those enjoyed by public prison employees, their nonunionized staffs receive lower levels of overtime payments, workers' compensation claims, sick leave, and health care insurance.

- *Competitive bidding.* Because of the profit motive, private corrections firms have an incentive to buy goods and services at the lowest possible price.

- *Less red tape.* Private corrections firms are not part of the government bureaucracy and therefore do not have to contend with the massive amount of paperwork that can clog government organizations.[50]

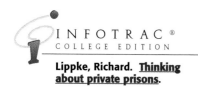

When CCA built a detention center for the Immigration and Naturalization Service (INS), it completed the project in less than six months at a cost of $14,000 per bed. The INS estimated that federal contractors would have taken two-and-a-half years to complete the center, at a cost of $26,000 per bed.[51] In Louisiana, a study showed that the state pays 14 to 16 percent more per day to house a prisoner than CCA and Wackenhut cost the state.[52]

Executives at corrections firms claim that, because their contracts can be canceled for poor performance, private prisons have a greater incentive to provide higher-quality service than their public counterparts. At least one study, conducted by Charles Logan, supports this contention. Logan found that, according to statistical data and staff surveys, a private women's prison in New Mexico outperformed a state prison and a federal prison in a number of areas such as security, safety, living conditions, and management.[53] One reason a private prison might be expected to perform better than a public one is that the latter enjoys some immunity from civil liability suits. In other words, an aggrieved inmate can more easily sue a private prison in a civil court.[54]

The Argument against Private Prisons

Significantly, in Logan's study mentioned above, the inmates themselves gave the private prison lower scores than did the staff members. Opponents of private prisons worry that, despite the assurances of corporate executives, private corrections companies will "cut corners" to save costs, denying inmates important security guarantees in the process.

Financial Concerns. These criticisms find some support in the anecdotal evidence. U.S. District Judge Sam Bell of the Northern District of Ohio, for example, recently ordered CCA to devise a classification system to divert dangerous offenders after two inmates were killed and eleven others injured in a spate of stabbings at the company's medium-security facility in Youngstown, Ohio.[55] The state of Colorado closed a private teen detention center after one inmate committed suicide and others reported being abused by the staff. In response to such incidents, in 1998 the state of Tennessee indefinitely postponed plans to privatize most of its prison system.[56]

Furthermore, some observers note, if a private corrections firm receives a fee from the state for each inmate housed in its facility, would that not give management an incentive to increase the amount of time each prisoner serves? Though government parole boards make the final decision on an inmate's release from private prisons, the company could manipulate misconduct and good behavior reports to maximize time served and, by extension, profits.[57]

Philosophical Concerns. Other critics see private prisons as inherently unjust, even if they do save tax dollars or provide enhanced services. These observers believe that corrections is not simply another industry, like garbage collection or road maintenance, and that only the government has the authority to punish. In the words of Princeton University criminologist John DiIulio:

> It is precisely because corrections involves the deprivation of liberty, precisely because it involves the legally sanctioned exercise of coercion by some citizens over others, that it must remain wholly within public hands.[58]

The Future of Privatization in the Corrections Industry

Critics of private correctional facilities still hope to slow, and eventually stop, their growth. They believe that private prisons are constitutional contradictions and offer Article I of the U.S. Constitution as support. That passage states that "legislative powers herein granted shall be vested in a Congress of the United States." These powers include the authority to define penal codes and to determine the punishments that will be handed out for breaking the law. Therefore, a strict interpretation of the Constitution appears to prohibit the passing of this authority from the government to a private company.[59]

Critics also anticipate that the benefits of privatization will prove illusory. They believe that the facilities will not save as many tax dollars as expected, that prison corporations will act in their own interests rather than those of society, and that the government will be unable to properly monitor abuses of inmates in private institutions.[60] Rising costs of incarceration and the rapid growth of the prison population have placed a great deal of pressure on government agencies to find space for inmates, however. Thus, it appears that the demand for private prisons will outweigh any reservations about their constitutionality or operating practices.[61] Indeed, supporters see private prisons and jails as the only viable option to solve many of the problems that modern corrections officials face.

JAILS

Although prisons and prison issues dominate the public discourse on corrections, there is an argument to be made that jails are the dominant penal institutions in the United States. In general, a prison is a facility designed to house people convicted of felonies for lengthy periods of time, while a **jail** is authorized to hold pretrial detainees and offenders who have committed misdemeanors. Approximately 7 million Americans spend time in jail each year—annual admissions are nearly 14 million, but many people are admitted more than once. With an annual growth rate of nearly 10 percent in the late 1990s, jail populations are growing more rapidly than prison populations.[62] Yet jail funding is often the lowest priority for the tight budgets of local governments, leading to severe overcrowding and other dismal conditions.[63]

Many observers see this negligence as having far-reaching consequences for criminal justice. Jail is often the first contact that citizens have with the corrections system. It is at this point that treatment and counseling have the best chance to deter future criminal behavior.[64] By failing to take advantage of this opportunity, says Professor Frank Zimring of the Earl Warren Legal Institute at the University of California at Berkeley, corrections officials have created a situation in which "today's jail folk are tomorrow's prisoners."[65]

The Function of Jails

Until the eighteenth century, all penal institutions existed primarily to hold those charged with a crime until their trial. Although jails still serve this purpose, they have evolved to play a number of different roles in the corrections system. According to the Department of Justice, these roles include the following:

- Holding those convicted of misdemeanors.
- Receiving individuals pending arraignment and holding them while awaiting trial (if they cannot post bail), conviction, or sentencing.
- Temporarily detaining juveniles pending transfer to juvenile authorities.
- Holding the mentally ill pending transfer to health facilities.
- Detaining those who have violated conditions of probation or parole and those who have "jumped" bail.
- Housing inmates awaiting transfer to federal or state prisons.

JAIL
A facility, usually operated by county government, used to hold persons awaiting trial or those who have been found guilty of misdemeanors.

Salvatore Gemelli, a guard at the Nassau County (New York) Correctional Center, holds a photograph of an inmate he supposedly beat with a metal cooking utensil. Violence is only one of the problems that plague the nation's jails, others being poor living conditions and inadequate health care facilities. Yet jail issues do not receive nearly the same attention as prison issues. Why is this the case?

▮ Operating community-based corrections programs such as home confinement and electronic monitoring.

Increasingly, jails are also called on to handle the overflow from saturated state and federal prisons. In Texas, for example, corrections officials were recently forced to rent a thousand county jail cells to house inmates for whom no space was available in state prisons.[66]

According to sociologist John Irwin, the unofficial purpose of the jail is to manage society's "rabble," so-called because

> [they] are not well integrated into conventional society, they are not members of conventional social organizations, they have few ties to conventional social networks, and they are carriers of unconventional values and beliefs.[67]

In Irwin's opinion, "rabble" who act violently are arrested and sent to prison. The jail is reserved for merely offensive rabble, whose primary threat to society lies in their failure to conform to its behavioral norms. This concept has been used by some critics of American corrections to explain the disproportionate number of poor and minority groups who may be found in the nation's jails at any time.

The Jail Population

Almost 90 percent of the nearly 600,000 jail inmates in the United States are male. As in other areas of corrections, however, women are becoming more numerous. Since 1985, the adult female jail population has grown at an annual rate of 9.9 percent, compared to 6.4 percent for males.[68] Jails also follow the general corrections pattern in that a disproportionate number of their inmates are members of minority groups. (For an overview of the characteristics of the jail population, see Figure 13.10.)

Figure 13.10 The Characteristics of America's Jail Population

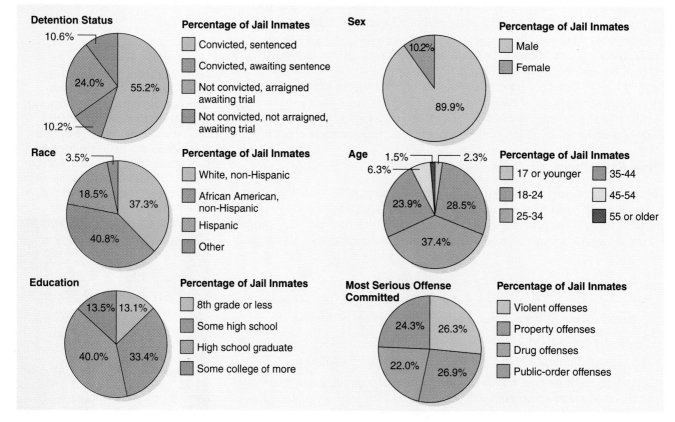

SOURCE: BUREAU OF JUSTICE STATISTICS, PROFILE OF JAIL INMATES 1996 (WASHINGTON, D.C.: U.S. DEPARTMENT OF JUSTICE, APRIL 1998), 1–4.

CJ in Focus

Landmark Cases:

Bell v. Wolfish

In a class action suit, several pretrial detainees in the Metropolitan Corrections Center in New York City challenged the constitutionality of the conditions under which they were being held. The practices under dispute include placing two inmates in cells designed for one ("double-bunking"), restricting books and magazines, and intrusive body searches. The basis of the plaintiffs' argument was that, as pretrial detainees, they should not be subjected to the same terms of confinement as those persons in the jail who had been convicted of crimes. Both the district court and the court of appeals agreed with the plaintiffs. In addressing the case, the Supreme Court focused on whether the Constitution indeed could be seen to require different treatment of those who were awaiting trial and those who had been convicted.

Bell v. Wolfish
United States Supreme Court
441 U.S. 520 (1979)
http://laws.findlaw.com/US/441/520.html

In the Words of the Court . . .

Mr. Chief Justice REHNQUIST, majority opinion

* * * *

The presumption of innocence is a doctrine that allocates the burden of proof in criminal trials; * * * But it has no application to a determination of the rights of a pretrial detainee during confinement before his trial has even begun.

* * * *

[T]he Government concededly may detain [a person] to ensure his presence at trial and may subject him to the restrictions and conditions of the detention facility so long as those conditions and restrictions do not amount to punishment, or otherwise violate the Constitution.* * * Whether it be called a jail, a prison, or a custodial center, the purpose of the facility is to detain. Loss of freedom of choice and privacy are inherent incidents of confinement in such a facility. And the fact that such detention interferes with the detainee's understandable desire to live as comfortably as possible and with as little restraint as possible during confinement does not convert the conditions or restrictions of detention into "punishment."

* * * *

[M]aintaining institutional security and preserving internal order and discipline are essential goals that may require limitation or retraction of the retained constitutional rights of both convicted prisoners and pretrial detainees. * * * Prison officials must be free to take appropriate action to ensure the safety of inmates and corrections personnel and to prevent escape or unauthorized entry. Accordingly, we have held that even when an institutional restriction infringes a specific constitutional guarantee, such as the First Amendment, the practice must be evaluated in the light of the central objective of prison administration, safeguarding institutional security.

* * * *

Judges, after all, are human. They, no less than others in our society, have a natural tendency to believe that their individual solutions to often intractable problems are better and more workable than those of the persons who are actually charged with and trained in the running of the particular institution under examination. But under the Constitution, the first question to be answered is not whose plan is best, but in what branch of the Government is lodged the authority to initially devise the plan. This does not mean that constitutional rights are not to be scrupulously observed. It does mean, however, that the inquiry of federal courts into prison management must be limited to the issue of whether a particular system violates any prohibition of the Constitution or, in the case of a federal prison, a statute. The wide range of "judgment calls" that meet constitutional and statutory requirements are confided to officials outside of the Judicial Branch of Government.

Decision: The Court reversed the court of appeals's ruling, holding that the possible innocence of pretrial detainees does not prevent corrections officials from taking any steps necessary to manage jails and maintain security. In a larger sense, the *Bell* decision is seen as giving corrections officials a great deal of freedom in making decisions without interference from the courts.

For Critical Analysis: Which constitutional principles apply to the arguments being made in *Bell v. Wolfish*? How much weight does the Court give these principles in light of the need to maintain security in correctional facilities?

Pretrial Detainees. As you can see in Figure 13.10, a significant number of those detained in jails technically are not prisoners. They are **pretrial detainees** who have been arrested by the police and, for a variety of reasons that we discussed in Chapter 9, are unable to post bail. Pretrial detainees are, in many ways, walking legal contradictions. According to the U.S. Constitution, they are innocent until proven guilty. At the same time, by being incarcerated while awaiting trial, they are denied a number of personal freedoms and are subjected to the poor conditions of many jails. In 1979, the Supreme Court rejected the notion that this situation is inherently unfair by refusing to give pretrial detainees greater legal protections than sentenced jail inmates have.[69] (See *CJ in Focus—Landmark Cases:* Bell v. Wolfish.)

PRETRIAL DETAINEES
Individuals who cannot post bail after arrest and are therefore forced to spend the time prior to their trial incarcerated in jail.

TIME SERVED
The period of time a person denied bail has spent in jail prior to his or her trial. If the suspect is found guilty and sentenced to a jail or prison term, the judge will often lessen the duration of the sentence based on the amount of time served as a pretrial detainee.

Sentenced Jail Inmates. According to the Department of Justice, 42 percent of those in jail have been convicted of their current charge.[70] That is, they have been found guilty of a crime, usually a misdemeanor, and sentenced. The typical jail term lasts between thirty and ninety days, and rarely does a prisoner spend more than one year in jail for any single crime. Often, a judge will credit the length of time the convict has spent in detention waiting for trial—known as **time served**—toward his or her sentence. This practice acknowledges two realities of jails:

1. Terms are generally too short to allow the prisoner to gain any benefit (that is, rehabilitation) from the jail's often limited or nonexistent treatment facilities. Therefore, the jail term can serve no other purpose than to punish the wrongdoer. (Judges who believe jail time can serve purposes of deterrence and incapacitation may not follow this line of reasoning.)

2. Jails are chronically overcrowded, and judges need to clear space for new offenders.

Other Jail Inmates. Pretrial detainees and misdemeanants make up the vast majority of the jail population. As mentioned earlier, jail inmates also include felons either waiting for transfer or assigned to jails because of prison overcrowding, probation and parole violators, the mentally ill, and juveniles. In addition, jails can hold those who require incarceration but do not "fit" anywhere else. A material witness or an attorney in a trial who refuses to follow the judge's instructions may, for example, be held in contempt of court and sent to jail.

Jail Administration

Of the nearly 3,300 jails in the United States, more than 2,700 are operated on a county level by an elected sheriff. Most of the remaining 600 are under the control of municipalities, although eight states (Alaska, Connecticut, Delaware, Hawaii, Maine, Rhode Island, Texas, and Vermont) manage jails.

Given that the public's opinion of jails ranges from negative to indifferent, many sheriffs neglect their jail management duties.[71] Instead, they focus on high-visibility issues such as placing more law enforcement officers on the streets and improving security in schools. In fact, a jail usually receives publicity only after an escape or an incident in which inmates are abused by jailers.

Despite most sheriffs' general apathy toward jails, not many would be willing to give up their management duties. As troublesome as they may be, jails can be useful in other ways. The sheriff appoints a jail administrator, or deputy sheriff, to oversee the day-to-day operations of the facility. The sheriff also has the power to hire other staff members such as deputy jailers. The sheriff may award these jobs to people who helped her or him get elected, and, in return, jail staffers can prove helpful to the sheriff in future elections.

The Challenges of Overcrowding

In many ways, the sheriff is placed in an untenable position when it comes to jail overcrowding. He or she has little control over the number of people who are sent to jail; that power resides with prosecutors and judges. Yet the jail is expected to find space to hold all comers, regardless of its capacity. A sheriff from Kane County, Utah, describes the situation:

> We have people who should get 60 or 90 days, and they just do a weekend and we kick them out. Unless we get a real habitual abuser, we have no choice but to set them free. Most of the time we're pretty sure they will be back in a couple of days with a new offense.[72]

INFOTRAC ®
COLLEGE EDITION

Greene, Judith. Controlling prison crowding.

CJ in Focus

Making Waves

Roughing It with America's Toughest Sheriff

Sheriff Joe Arpaio of Maricopa County, Arizona, is not a popular figure among the inmates in his jails. He forces them to wear pink underwear and work on chain gangs. He has banned hot lunches, cigarettes, and coffee and serves such delicacies as green baloney for dinner. Recently, he launched a program called "Scared Stiff," in which inmates bury the bodies of indigents at local cemeteries.

"America's Toughest Sheriff," as Arpaio's autobiography is entitled, is widely regarded as a publicity-seeking maverick by his fellow law enforcers. But, as cities find themselves hard pressed to build jails quickly enough to house everyone sent to them by the courts, one of Arpaio's ideas is being taken seriously. Arpaio has constructed a "Tent City," using surplus Army tents from the Korean War, to house nearly 1,600 inmates on county property. The program resulted from a campaign promise to lock up every convict placed in his control. Given the costs of constructing new jails, which can reach $120 million, the only way for Arpaio to keep his word was to find a cheaper alternative. A tent jail for 600 inmates costs the county between $80,000 and $100,000 a year.

Human rights groups complain that Arpaio's tents constitute cruel and unusual punishment. In the Arizona summer, temperatures under the canvas flaps can reach 130 degrees. Any breeze that does reach inmates comes from a nearby dump, a dog pound, and a waste-disposal plant. A U.S. Department of Justice investigation found excessive use of restraint chairs, pepper spray, and "unprovoked" and "unjustified" violence against inmates. Three years after the tents were constructed, convicts rioted for three hours in protest against the conditions. The inmates, most of whom are either awaiting trial or serving a sentence of a year or less for a misdemeanor, say they would receive better treatment if they had committed a more serious crime and been incarcerated in the state prison.

Despite the criticisms, other jurisdictions pressed for jail space are following Arpaio's lead. After county voters rejected a plan to build a new jail, Butler County (Ohio) Sheriff Harold Don Gabbard decided to construct a system modeled after Tent City. Jurisdictions in Florida and Louisiana have tested their own tent cities, and counties in Nevada and Arizona are considering the idea.

For Critical Analysis: Consider the four justifications for corrections—retribution, incapacitation, deterrence, and rehabilitation. Which of these, if any, can be applied to Arpaio's Tent City?

One way to alleviate overcrowding is to build more jails. Currently, the United States is adding nearly 30,000 new jail beds each year in an effort to keep pace with demand. The problem, however, is what economists call supply creating its own demand. That is, the number of jail inmates seems to expand to meet the number of available beds. Today, the nation's jails are filled to 97 percent of their capacity, and the occupancy rate for facilities with 1,000 or more inmates is 100 percent.[73]

Furthermore, most counties do not have the economic resources to construct new jails. In these jurisdictions, criminal justice officials can turn to community corrections programs such as those discussed in Chapter 12 to alleviate the pressure. Or, they can house prisoners in various forms of "makeshift" jails such as hotels or converted gas stations. The state of New York moored decommissioned ferry boats at its Riker's Island jail to provide additional capacity.[74] Counties are even considering setting up tent jails after a model devised by a sheriff in Arizona (see *CJ in Focus—Making Waves: Roughing It with America's Toughest Sheriff*). We will discuss the effects of overcrowding on the living conditions in prisons and jails in the following chapter.

New Generation Jails

The boom in jail construction has been accompanied by a growing realization that simply adding bed space is not sufficient to deal with the problems endemic to the facilities. These problems include high suicide rates, an influx of mentally ill inmates, high drug use, and violence and rape. In other words, *how* the jail is built is just as important as *why* it is built. Over the past thirty years, the trend in jail construction has moved away from a traditional design toward a structure known as the new generation jail.

The linear design is similar to that of a hospital in which long rows of rooms are placed along a corridor. To carry out her or his surveillance duties, the custodial officer must either look down the corridor, or walk down it and peer into the windows of the individual cells. What sorts of risks are inherent in this type of jail design?

The Traditional Design. For most of the nation's history, the architecture of a jail was secondary to its purpose of keeping inmates safely locked away. Consequently, most jails in the United States continue to resemble those from the days of the Walnut Street Jail in Philadelphia. In this *traditional*, or *linear*, *design*, jail cells are located along a corridor (see the photo on this page). To supervise the inmates while they are in their cells, correctional staff members must walk up and down the corridor; thus, the number of prisoners they can see at any one time is severely limited. With this limited supervision, inmates can more easily misbehave.

The harsh environment and lack of supervision inherent in the traditional design have been found to contribute to inmates' antisocial behavior. The prisoners spend most of their free time isolated and devoid of social control, and they have a tendency to respond with hostility.[75] Given that most jail inmates are released after a short period of confinement, many observers feel that the traditional design can pose a threat to the community by "creating" citizens who are more disposed toward violence upon release than when they entered the jail.

Podular Design. In the 1970s, the Federal Bureau of Prisons (BOP) decided to upgrade the traditional design based on the motto "If you can't rehabilitate, at least do no harm."[76] The BOP implemented a new management philosophy in designing three Metropolitan Correctional Centers in San Diego, Chicago, and New York. The National Institute of Corrections designated these three facilities **new generation jails** to distinguish them from the older models.[77]

The new generation jails differ significantly from their predecessors. The layout of the new facilities makes it easier for the staff to monitor cell-confined inmates. The basic structure of the new generation jail is based on a **podular design**. Each "pod" contains "living units" for individual prisoners. These units, instead of lining up along a straight corridor, are often situated in a triangle so that a staff member in the center of the triangle has visual access to nearly all the cells. Daily activities such as eating and showering take place in the pod, which also has an outdoor exercise area. Treatment facilities are also located in the pod, allowing greater access for the inmates. Furthermore, the surroundings are not as harsh as in the older jails. Cells have comfortable furniture, rugs, and windows, and a communal "day-room" has televisions, radios, and telephones.[78]

In a direct supervision jail, the custodial officer is stationed at an in-pod control terminal. From this point, he or she has visual contact with all inmates and can communicate with inmates quickly and easily. During the day, inmates stay in the open area and are only allowed in their cells when given permission. The officer locks the door to the cells from his or her control terminal. How would the behavior of inmates in a direct supervision jail differ from that of inmates in a traditional, linear jail?

Direct Supervision Approach. The podular design also enables a new generation jail to be managed using a **direct supervision approach**.[79] One or more jail officers are stationed in the living area of the pod and are therefore in constant interaction with all prisoners in that particular pod (see the photo on this page). Some new generation jails even provide a desk in the center of the living area, which sends a very different message to the prisoners than the traditional control booth. Theoretically, jail officials who have constant contact with inmates will be able to stem misconduct quickly and efficiently and will also be able to recognize "danger signs" of individual inmates and stop outbursts before they occur.

Overcoming Initial Apprehension. At first, the new generation jails provoked a great deal of skepticism, as they were seen as inherently "soft" on criminals. A number of empirical results, however, seem to speak to the success of podular design and direct supervision. One study measured inmate behavior in an adult detention facility before and after it was converted to a direct supervision jail. The researchers found a "dramatic reduction" in the number of assaults, batteries, attempted suicides, sex offenses, possession of weapons, and escapees.[80] Today, nearly 200 new generation jails are in operation or under construction.

THE CONSEQUENCES OF OUR HIGH RATES OF INCARCERATION

For many observers, especially those who support the crime control theory of criminal justice, America's high rate of incarceration has contributed significantly to the drop in the country's crime rates.[81] At the heart of this belief is the fact, which we covered in Chapter 2, that most crimes are committed by a relatively small number of repeat offenders. A number of studies have corroborated this belief, including a Rand Corporation survey that concluded that each repeat offender commits between 187 and 287 crimes a year.[82] By this calculation, each year a repeat offender spends in prison prevents a significant number of criminal acts.

Criminologists, however, note the negative consequences of America's growing prison and jail population. For one, incarceration can have severe social consequences for communities and the families that make up those communities. When a parent is imprisoned, her or his children will often suffer financial hardships, reduced supervision and discipline, and a general deterioration of the family structure.[83] These factors are used to explain the fact that children of convicts are more likely to become involved in delinquent behavior. Our high rates of incarceration also deny one of the basic rights of American democracy—the right to vote—to a large segment of the citizenry. (A number of states and the federal government disfranchise, or take away the ability to vote, from those convicted of felonies.) This has a disproportionate impact on minority groups who are disproportionately imprisoned, weakening their voice in the democratic debate.[84]

The prison boom has economic consequences as well. Every dollar that is spent on corrections is a dollar that is unavailable for other public services. Several states are funding corrections at the expense of public education. California is hiring prison guards at the same time it is laying off college professors,[85] and Florida provides more funds for nearly 60,000 prisoners than it does for over 200,000 university students.[86] Idaho spends five times more on a prisoner than for a child on welfare.[87]

Whether the American incarceration situation is "good" or "bad" depends to a large extent on one's personal philosophy. In the end, it is difficult to do a definitive cost-benefit analysis for each person incarcerated, weighing the benefits of preventing crimes that might (or might not) have been committed by an inmate against the costs to the convict's family and society. One thing that can be stated with some certainty is that, given the present political and social atmosphere, the increase in correctional facilities and inmates will continue in the foreseeable future.

NEW GENERATION JAIL
A type of jail that is distinguished architecturally from its predecessors by a design that encourages interaction between inmates and jailers and that offers greater opportunities for treatment.

PODULAR DESIGN
The architectural style of the new generation jail. Each "pod" consists of between twelve and twenty-four one-person cells and a communal "day room" to allow for social interaction.

DIRECT SUPERVISION APPROACH
A process of prison and jail administration in which correctional officers are in continuous physical contact with inmates during the day.

Criminal Justice in Action

The End of the Line: Supermax Prisons

On Easter Sunday, 1993, inmates at a maximum-security prison in Lucasville, Ohio, seized control of an entire cell block and held it for eleven days. During the extended rioting, one correctional officer and nine inmates were killed; afterward the state spent nearly $80 million on prison repairs, investigations, and lawsuits. The Easter riot had a profound effect on the state's prison system. Within five years, Ohio had added seven new penal institutions and doubled the budget of the Department of Rehabilitation and Corrections. The centerpiece of the new efforts was the Ohio State Penitentiary in Youngstown. At its opening in the spring of 1998, the Youngstown facility was celebrated by officials as the nation's latest **supermax** (short for supermaximum-security) **prison.** In this *Criminal Justice in Action* feature, we will examine these "intense" corrections facilities, condemned by critics as inhuman and lauded by supporters as the ultimate in "get tough" incarceration.

"THE WORST OF THE WORST"

Supermax prisons are reserved for the "worst of the worst." Inmates generally are not sent to such facilities by a court; instead, commitment to a supermax prison is usually the result of misbehavior within a penal institution. As Figure 13.11 shows, the murder or attempted murder of a fellow inmate was the most common reason for commitment to the BOP's U.S. Penitentiary Administrative Maximum (ADX) in Florence, Colorado.

The main purpose of a supermax prison is to strictly control the inmates' movement, thereby limiting (or eliminating) situations that could lead to breakdowns in discipline. The conditions in California's Security Housing Unit (SHU) at Pelican Bay State Prison are representative of most supermax institutions. Prisoners are confined to their one-person cells for twenty-two and a half hours each day under video camera surveillance; they receive meals through a slot in the door. The cells measure 8 by 10 feet in size and are windowless. No decorations of any kind are permitted on the white walls.[88]

For the ninety minutes each day the inmates are allowed out of their cells (compared to twelve to sixteen hours in regular maximum-security prisons), they may either shower or exercise in an enclosed, concrete "yard" covered by plastic mesh. Prisoners are strip-searched before and after leaving their cells, and placed in waist restraints and handcuffs on their way to and from the "yard" and showers. They can have a limited number of books or magazines in their cell and, if they can afford it, a television or radio.[89]

Removing the most violent and problematic inmates from the general prison population is seen as a key to modern prison management. Because those inmates transferred to supermax facilities are more likely to be impulsive

SUPERMAX PRISON
A correctional facility reserved for those inmates who have extensive records of misconduct in maximum-security prisons; characterized by extremely strict control and supervision over the inmates, including extensive use of solitary confinement.

Figure 13.11 Reasons for Transfer to a Supermax Prison

Rarely are offenders sent directly to a supermax facility by a court. For the most part, they are transferred there because of misbehavior in another correctional facility. This figure shows the reason inmates were transferred to the most secure facility operated by the Federal Bureau of Prisons: the U.S. Penitentiary Administrative Maximum (ADX) in Florence, Colorado.

Reason for Transfer	Percent
Murder or attempted murder of a fellow inmate	20
Assault of a fellow inmate with a weapon	18
Assault of a staff member	16
Escape attempt	10
Involved in riot	5
Judicial order	3
Other*	28

*Includes attempted murder of a staff member, involvement in a work or food strike, taking a staff member hostage, introducing drugs into a correctional facility, involvement in gang activity.
SOURCE: GREGORY L. HERSHBERGER, "TO THE MAX: SUPERMAX FACILITIES PROVIDE PRISON ADMINISTRATORS WITH MORE SECURITY OPTIONS," CORRECTIONS TODAY 60 (FEBRUARY 1, 1998), 54.

A typical supermax prison cell at the ADX outside Florence, Colorado. The cell is 8 ft. 8 in. x 12 ft. 3 in., and contains a stainless steel mirror and a 12-inch black-and-white television set, as well as a concrete desk, stool, and bed, that are permanently fixed to the floor. The small window has no view.

and unpredictable and to have a gang affiliation, their absence is believed to create a safer environment for other inmates and the correctional staff. Furthermore, prison administrators use the supermax as a disciplinary tool—problematic inmates may change their behavior if they fear being transferred.[90]

MARION—THE FIRST SUPERMAX

The precursor of today's supermax was San Francisco's Alcatraz Prison. Opening in 1932 on Alcatraz Island in San Francisco Bay, the maximum-security prison was populated by the most dangerous and disruptive federal convicts. Alcatraz was closed in 1963—mainly due to the expense of operating an island prison. For most of the next two decades, the BOP used the **dispersion** model for placing the most hazardous inmates. That is, the department dispersed its "hard-core" offenders to various federal prisons around the country, hoping the general inmate population would assimilate them.[91]

By the late 1970s, it became apparent that this strategy was not functioning as planned. The "hard-cores" continued to act violently, endangering other inmates and correctional employees. Then, in October 1983, two staff members and an inmate were murdered within a week at the federal prison in Marion,

Illinois. Prison officials instituted a **lock-down,** in which all inmates are confined to their cells, and social activities such as meals, recreational sports, and treatment programs are canceled. Lockdowns are considered temporary, "cooling off" measures, but officials at Marion decided to leave the conditions in effect indefinitely, creating the first supermax prison. The supermax is based on the model of **consolidation:** all high-risk inmates are placed in a single institution, which is administered with a focus on complete control.[92]

THE NEW GENERATION SUPERMAX

At first, the consolidation model led federal and state officials to construct supermax facilities on existing prison grounds. Over the past decade, however, the trend has been toward building new penal institutions, expressly designed with the goals of the supermax in mind. The Closed Maximum Security Correctional Center (CMAX) in Tamms, Illinois, for example, is designed around inmate housing pods (much like the new generation jails mentioned earlier in the chapter). Each pod contains sixty cells on two levels, arranged around a control station with complete visual access. CMAX is designed so that an inmate never leaves his pod; medical facilities, library cells, and recreational areas are located within its boundaries.

All inmate movement in the pod takes place on the lower level, while armed security staff patrol the upper level. These guards can see through the upper-level flooring grid, allowing them to closely monitor any activity below. Furthermore, officials can control circulation by sealing off portions of the facility at will.[93] These new generation supermax prisons also strive to limit contact between staff and

DISPERSION
A corrections model in which high-risk inmates are spread throughout the general prison population, in the hopes that they will be absorbed without causing misconduct problems.

LOCKDOWN
A disciplinary action taken by prison officials in which all inmates are ordered to their quarters and nonessential prison activities are suspended.

CONSOLIDATION
A corrections model in which the inmates who pose the highest security risk are housed in a single facility to separate them from the general prison population.

inmates through technology. Automatic doors, intercoms, and electronic surveillance cameras have reduced the exposure of guards to inmates at most of the new facilities.

SENSELESS SUFFERING?

Many prison officials support the proliferation of supermax prisons because they provide increased security for the most dangerous inmates. Observers believe that as the inmate population becomes aware of these new facilities, their harsh reputation will deter convicts from misbehaving for fear of transfer to a supermax.

The supermax has aroused a number of criticisms, however. Amnesty International and other human rights groups assert that the facilities violate international standards of proper treatment for prisoners. Other opponents point out that inmates are provided minimal due process protections during the transfer process. An inmate has no right to an attorney while being considered for a transfer, and the decision to send someone to a supermax cannot be appealed. Because this decision is made by an administrative—and not a judicial or legislative—body, in *Sandin v. Conner* (1995),[94] the Supreme Court ruled only that such a move must not impose an "atypical and significant hardship on the inmate in relation to the ordinary incidents of prison life." As of yet, no court has found that the conditions in a supermax constitute such a hardship.[95]

Other observers believe not only that those conditions are atypical and significant, but that they violate Eighth Amendment protections against cruel and unusual punishment. The negative effects of solitary confinement on a prisoner's psyche are considerable, and supermax facilities are structured to keep their inmates isolated at all times. After studying inmates at California's Pelican Bay, a Harvard University psychiatrist found that 80 percent suffered from what he called "SHU [security housing unit] syndrome"; after spending a certain amount of time at the facility, the inmates either exhibited new signs of mental instability, or their existing conditions were exacerbated.[96] In *Madrid v. Gomez* (1995),[97] U.S. District Judge Thelton Henderson found that Pelican Bay violated its inmates' Eighth Amendment rights, writing that "dry words on paper cannot adequately capture the senseless suffering" of the convicts.

Despite his harsh sentiments, Judge Henderson's ruling only forced the supermax to improve medical care and had no discernible effect on the operation of the facility. Indeed, it does not appear that the American courts will pose a threat to the operation of these institutions. According to the National Institute of Corrections, supermax prisons are the fasting growing type of prison in the United States, and house more than 16,000 inmates.[98]

Key Terms

Chapter Summary

1. **Contrast the Pennsylvania and the New York penitentiary theories of the 1800s.** Basically, the Pennsylvania system imposed total silence on its prisoners. Based on the concept of separate confinement, penitentiaries were constructed with back-to-back cells facing both outward and inward. Prisoners worked, slept, and ate alone in their cells. In contrast, New York used the congregate system; silence was imposed, but inmates worked and ate together.

2. **List the factors that have caused the prison population to grow dramatically in the last several decades.** (a) The enhancement and stricter enforcement of the nation's drug laws; (b) increased probability of incarceration; (c) inmates serving more time for each crime; (d) revocation of community-based sanctions; and (e) rising incarceration rates for women.

3. **Explain the three general models of prisons.** (a) The custodial model assumes the prisoner is incarcerated for reasons of incapacitation, deterrence, and retribution. (b) The rehabilitation model puts security concerns second and the well-being of the individual inmate first. As a consequence, treatment programs are offered to prisoners. (c) The reintegration model sees the correctional institution as a training ground for preparing convicts to reenter society.

4. **List and briefly explain the four types of prisons.** (a) Maximum-security prisons, which are designed mainly with security and surveillance in mind. Such prisons are usually large and consist of cell blocks, each of which is set off by a series of gates and bars. (b) Medium-security prisons, which offer considerably more educational and treatment programs and allow more contact between inmates. Such prisons are rarely walled, but rather are surrounded by high fences. (c) Minimum-security prisons, which permit prisoners to have television sets and computers and often allow them to leave the grounds for educational and employment purposes. (d) Supermaximum-security (supermax) prisons, in which prisoners are confined to one-person cells for up to twenty-two and a half hours per day under constant video camera surveillance.

5. **Contrast formal with informal prison management systems.** A formal system is militaristic with a hierarchical (top-down) chain of command; the warden (or superintendent) is on top, then deputy wardens, and lastly custodial employees. The informal prison management system depends on the philosophy of the warden, or superintendent, and may even allow for inmate councils and inmate "guards."

6. **List the reasons why private prisons can be run more cheaply than public ones.** (a) Labor costs are lower because private prison employees are nonunionized and receive lower levels of overtime payments, sick leave, and health care. (b) Competitive bidding requires the operators of private prisons to buy goods and services at the lowest possible prices. (c) There is less red tape in a private prison facility.

7. **Summarize the distinction between jails and prisons, and indicate the importance of jails in the American correctional system.** Generally, a prison is for those convicted of felonies who will serve lengthy periods of incarceration, whereas a jail is for those who have been convicted of misdemeanors and will serve less than a year of incarceration. A jail also (a) receives individuals pending arraignment and holds them while awaiting trial, conviction, or sentencing; (b) temporarily holds juveniles pending transfer to juvenile authorities; (c) holds the mentally ill pending transfer to health facilities; (d) detains those who have violated probation or parole and those who have "jumped" bail; and (e) houses those awaiting transfer to federal or state prisons. Approximately seven million Americans spend time in jail each year, and jail populations are growing at about 10 percent per year.

8. **Explain how jails are administered.** Most jails are operated at the county level by an elected sheriff, although about 20 percent are under the control of municipalities and eight states manage jails themselves. Sheriffs appoint jail administrators (deputy sheriffs) as well as deputy jailers.

9. **Indicate the difference between traditional jail design and new generation jail design.** A traditional design is linear with jail cells located along a corridor. Such a physical structure is rather cold with an emphasis on iron and steel fixtures that are not easily broken. New generation jails, in contrast, use a podular design, with the "pods" often arranged in a triangle. Each cell has furniture, rugs, and windows, and there are communal "day-rooms" with televisions, radios, and telephones.

10. **Indicate some of the consequences of our high rates of incarceration.** (a) Some people believe that the reduction in the country's crime rate is a direct result of increased incarceration rates; (b) others believe that high incarceration rates are having increasing negative social consequences, such as financial hardships, reduced supervision and discipline of children, and a general deterioration of the family structure when one parent is in prison; and (c) more money spent on prisons has taken away money for other public services, such as education.

Questions for Critical Analysis

1. Explain the benefit of nonfixed sentences coupled with the possibility of early release.

2. How did the Elmira Reformatory classify prisoners? How did the system work?

3. Crime rates are falling, yet prison rates are rising rapidly. Why?

4. What are several reasons why prison construction continues to increase?

5. The chain of command in prisons and police departments appears quite similar, yet there is a big difference. What is it?

6. Why are private prisons growing so rapidly today?

7. Why are jails so important in the American corrections system?

8. There are 14 million admissions to jails annually, yet only about 7 million Americans spend time in jail each year. Why the discrepancy?

9. Most sheriffs are quite apathetic toward the job of running jails, yet they do not want to give up their management duties. Why not?

10. In the first two decades after the closing of Alcatraz, what method did the Bureau of Prisons use in dealing with its most dangerous inmates? Was the method successful?

Selected Print and Electronic Resources

SUGGESTED READINGS

Kerle, Kenneth E., *American Jails: Looking to the Future*, Boston: Butterworth-Heinemann, 1998. The author is the cofounder of the American Jail Association and editor of the magazine *American Jails*. He looks at the jail system and contrasts it with the prison system. He examines overcrowding and other issues. He also predicts what will happen to prisons in the future.

Keve, Paul W., *Prisons and the American Conscience: A History of U.S. Federal Corrections*, Carbondale, IL: Southern Illinois University Press, 1995. The authors look at the political and cultural factors that determined federal imprisonment practices in the 1800s. They then examine the differences between the federal prison system and prisons at the state and local levels.

McShan, Marilyn D., and Frank P. Williams, eds., *Encyclopedia of American Prisons*, New York: Garland Publishers, 1996. This complete analysis of the American prison system consists of 160 essays written by corrections experts. Of interest is the brief "chronology of American prison history," which starts in 1773. The articles include numerous statistics about prisons and imprisonment.

MEDIA RESOURCES

Escape from Alcatraz **(1979)** According to legend, Alcatraz Prison, located on Alcatraz Island in San Francisco Bay, was escape proof. Indeed, during the 31 years that Alcatraz was operational, nobody did manage to escape. That is, most people are pretty sure that nobody managed to escape. This film tells the story of Frank Morris (played by Clint Eastwood), a bank robber who may have indeed been able to find his way out of the prison and off the island. Shot on location, the film strives to give a realistic picture of life at Alcatraz while at the same time providing a dramatic setting for Morris's efforts at escape.

Critically analyze this film:

1. Why was Alcatraz called "The Rock"?

2. How would you describe the prison environment within Alcatraz?

3. The prison was built to hold really dangerous prisoners. Does the film give the impression that those are the only types of prisoners there? Why or why not?

4. What kind of tight security at Alcatraz was evident in the movie?

5. Describe the use of solitary confinement in Alcatraz, both as a punishment and as a way of life.

6. Did prisoners share cells at Alcatraz?

7. How much privacy was available for prisoners in their cells?

8. What percentage of a day were prisoners monitored and regulated at Alcatraz?

Logging On

If you want to get information on the corrections industry, go to:

www.corrections.com/

In 1829, Eastern State Penitentiary was opened as a place for "confinement and solitude with labor." It quickly became the most expensive and most copied building in the U.S. correctional system. Go to the following web site:

www.EasternState.com/

Once at the site, click on the *History of the Penitentiary*. After you have read it, click on the *Virtual Reality Tour*. Using *QuickTime* you can look at various views of this famous penal institution.

If you would like information on another famous penal institution, Alcatraz, you can go to the official U.S. government site at:

www.nps.gov/alcatraz/

Once there, click on "Penitentiary" at the top of the page. You will read about the history of Alcatraz from 1934 to 1963.

Using the internet for Criminal Justice Analysis

INFOTRAC®
COLLEGE EDITION

1. Go to your InfoTrac College Edition at **www.infotrac-college.com/wadsworth/**. After you log on, type in the words:

TO THE MAX: SUPERMAX FACILITIES PROVIDE PRISON ADMINISTRATORS WITH MORE OPTIONS.

This is an article about the design and administration of supermax facilities. Read the article and answer the following questions:

a. When you click on the photo on the left-hand margin about halfway down the article, what are some of the characteristics that you see from the aerial view of the Florence, Colorado, supermax prison?

b. Why is it misleading to label supermax facilities as "lockdown" institutions?

c. What is the distinction between dispersion and the consolidation model of handling extremely dangerous inmates?

d. What are the benefits of the disperson model?

e. What are the benefits of the consolidation model?

f. What was the best-known consolidation model institution at the federal level and why?

g. What do the initials "ADX" stand for?

h. Are inmates in supermax prisons, such as in Florence, Colorado, given any choice in programs and services?

2. You can find out a lot about the corrections industry on the Internet. One private site is called "the official site" of the corrections industry. It is at: **www.corrections.com/**
Once you are there, go to the "News Center."

a. What is the most common subject discussed in "This Week in the News"?

Click on "Students." Then click on the "Resume Database of Recent College Graduates."

b. Examine five resumes. What is the most common background of these potential corrections officer candidates?

c. Check through all of the resumes. What is the most common position desired? Why?

Within that site, visit the "Student Question Board."

d. Browse through the questions. What is the most common type of question?

e. Do the questions seem reasonable?

Notes

1. Quoted in Claud Mullins, *Crime and Psychology* (London: Methuen, 1943), 142.

2. Bureau of Justice Statistics, *Prison and Jail Inmates at Midyear 1998* (Washington, D.C.: U.S. Department of Justice, March 1999), 1–2.

3. Kenneth F. Schoen and Julie Peterson, "How Powerful Is Prison as a Crime Fighting Tool," *Perspectives* (Summer 1996), 32.

4. Joanna Innes, "Prisons for the Poor: English Bridewells, 1555–1800," in *Labour, Law, and Crime: A Historical Perspective*, eds. Francis Snyder and Douglas Hay (London: Tavistock Publications, 1987), 42–3.

5. James M. Beattie, *Crime and the Courts in England 1660–1800* (Princeton, NJ: Princeton University Press, 1986), 506–7.

6. George Fisher, "The Birth of the Prison Retold," *Yale Law Journal* 104 (April 1995), 1235.

7. Samuel Walker, *Popular Justice* (New York: Oxford University Press, 1980), 11.

8. Michael Meranze, *Laboratories of Virtue: Punishment, Revolution, and Authority in Philadelphia, 1760–1835* (Chapel Hill, NC: University of North Carolina Press, 1996), 55.

9. Negley K. Teeters, *The Cradle of the Penitentiary: The Walnut Street Jail at Philadelphia, 1773–1835* (Philadelphia: 1955), 30.

10. Negley K. Teeters and John D. Shearer, *The Prison at Philadelphia's Cherry Hill* (New York: Columbia University Press, 1957), 142–3.

11. Henry Calvin Mohler, "Convict Labor Policies," *Journal of the American Institute of Criminal Law and Criminology* 15 (1925), 556–7.

12. Zebulon R. Brockway, "The American Reformatory," in *Correction Contexts: Contemporary and Classical Readings*, eds. James W. Marquart and Jonathan R. Sorenson (Los Angeles: Roxbury Publishing Co., 1997), 68.

13. Alan H. Dershowitz, "Indeterminate Sentencing: Letting the Therapy Fit the Crime," *University of Pennsylvania Law Review* 123 (1974), 313–4.

14. Zebulon Brockway, *Fifty Years of Prison Service* (Montclair, NJ: Patterson Smith, 1969), 400–1.

15. American Correctional Association, *The American Prison: From the Beginning* (College Park, MD: American Correctional Association, 1983), 279.

16. Lawrence Friedman, *Crime and Punishment in American History* (New York: Basic Books, 1993), 316.

17. Robert Martinson, "What Works? Questions and Answers about Prison Reform," *Public Interest* 35 (Spring 1974), 22.

18. See Ted Palmer, "Martinson Revisited," *Journal of Research on Crime and Delinquency* (1975), 133; and Paul Gendreau and Bob Ross, "Effective Correctional Treatment: Bibliotherapy for Cynics," *Crime & Delinquency* 25 (1979), 499.

19. Robert Martinson, "New Findings, New Views: A Note of Caution Regarding Sentencing Reform," *Hofstra Law Review* 7 (1979), 243.

20. Fox Butterfield, "'Defying Gravity,' Inmate Population Climbs," *New York Times* (January 19, 1998), A10.

21. Ibid.

22. Allen J. Beck, "Growth, Change, and Stability in the U.S. Prison Population, 1980–1995," *Corrections Management Quarterly* (Spring 1997), 9–10.

23. Ibid., 12.

24. Office of Planning, Research and Management Information Services, *Trends in Prison Intake, Population Growth and Population Projections* (Lansing, MI: Michigan Department of Corrections, December 6, 1996), 18.

25. Beck, 10.

26. U.S. Department of Justice, Bureau of Justice Statistics, *Prison and Jail Inmates at Midyear 1997* (Washington, D.C.: U.S. Department of Justice, January 1998), 4.

27. Fox Butterfield, "Prisons Replace Hospitals for the Nation's Mentally Ill," *New York Times* (March 5, 1998), A1, A26.

28. "Number of Prison Beds Grew by 41 Percent in Five Years," *Corrections Journal* (August 22, 1997), 5.

29. The National Center on Addiction and Substance Abuse at Columbia University, *Behind Bars: Substance Abuse and America's Prison Population* (New York: The National Center on Addiction and Substance Abuse at Columbia University, 1998), 1.

30. Bureau of Justice Statistics, *Sourcebook of Criminal Justice Statistics, 1997* (Washington, D.C.: U.S. Department of Justice, 1998), Table 11, page 13.

31. Corina L. Eckl, Karen C. Hayes, and Artura Perez, *State Budget Actions 1993* (Denver, CO: National Conference of State Legislatures, 1993), 32.

32. Holly Idelson, "Republican Crime Bills Take a 'Get Tougher' Approach," *Congressional Quarterly Weekly Report* 53 (1995), 211.

33. David Lamb, "Jails Give a Life to Rural Economies," *The Guardian* (October 15, 1996), 14.

34. Charles H. Logan, *Criminal Justice Performance Measures in Prisons* (Washington, D.C.: U.S. Department of Justice, 1993), 5.

35. Todd R. Clear and George F. Cole, *American Corrections*, 4th ed. (Belmont, CA: Wadsworth Publishing Co., 1997), 245–6.

36. Alfred Blumstein, "Prisons," in *Crime*, eds. James Q. Wilson and Joan Petersilia, (San Francisco: ICS Press, 1995), 392.

37. Tony Izzo, "I-Max Awaits Green," *Kansas City Star* (May 26, 196), A1.

38. Cited in Joe Hallinan, "Old Prisons Locked in the Past," *The (Newark, NJ) Star-Ledger* (June 9, 1996), 1.

39. "Pennsylvania Plans New Prison to Replace Site of Tunnel Escape," *Corrections Journal* (February 9, 1998), 6.

40. Charles H. Logan, "Well Kept: Comparing Quality of Confinement in a Public and Private Prison," *Journal of Criminal Law and Criminology* 83 (1992), 580.

41. Bert Useem and Peter Kimball, *Stages of Siege: U.S. Prison Riots, 1971–1986* (New York: Oxford University Press, 1989).

42. Bert Useem, "Disorganization and the New Mexico Prison Riot of 1980," *American Sociology Review* 50 (1985), 685.

43. Tara Gray and Jon'a F. Meyer, *Prison Administration: Inmate Participation versus the Control Model* in *Correction Contexts: Contemporary and Classical Readings*, eds. James W. Marquart and Jonathan R. Sorenson (Los Angeles: Roxbury Publishing Co., 1997), 203–11.

44. Ibid., 208.

45. 550 F.2d 238 (5th Cir. 1977), cert. denied, 460 U.S. 1042 (1983).

46. "A Recession-Proof Industry," *Economist* (November 15, 1997), 28.

47. "BOP Awards First Contract for a Privatized Prison," *Corrections Journal* (August 7, 1997), 3.

48. Gail DeGeorge, "Go Directly to Jail," *Business Week* (December 15, 1997), 139.

49. G. Larry Mays and Tara Gray, *Privatization of Correctional Services* (Cincinnati, OH: Anderson Publishing Co., 1997).

50. Alex Singal, "The Private Prison Industry," *Corrections Compendium* (January 1998), 16–17.

51. David Yarden, "Prisons, Profits, and the Private Sector Solution," *American Journal of Criminal Law* 21 (1994), 325–34.

52. William G. Archambeault and Donald R. Deis, *Cost-Effectiveness Comparisons of Private versus Public Prisons in Louisiana* (Baton Rouge, LA: Louisiana State University, 1996).

53. Charles Logan, "Well Kept: Comparing Quality of Confinement in Private and Public Prisons," *Journal of Criminal Law and Criminology* 83 (1992), 577.

54. Richard C. Brister, "Changing of the Guard: A Case for Privatization of Texas Prisons," *The Prison Journal* 76 (September 1996), 322–3.

55. "Private Prison Is Ordered to Screen Dangerous Inmates," *Corrections Journal* (March 9, 1998), 5.

56. Ted Gest, "Private Prisons, Public Concerns," *U.S. News & World Report* (May 18, 1998), 37.

57. Richard L. Lippke, "Thinking about Private Prisons," *Criminal Justice Ethics* (Winter/Spring 1997), 32.

58. John DiIulio, "Prisons, Profits, and the Public Good: The Privatization of Corrections," in *Criminal Justice Center Bulletin* (Huntsville, TX: Sam Houston State University, 1986).

59. Ira P. Robbins, "Privatization of Prisons, Privatization of Corrections: Defining the Issues," *Vanderbilt Law Review* 40 (1987), 823.

60. *Ibid.*, 813.

61. Stephen D. Gottfredson and Sean McConville, Introduction to *America's Correctional Crisis: Prison Populations and Public Policy*, eds. Stephen D. Gottfredson and Ralph B. Taylor (Washington, D.C.: U.S. Department of Justice, 1987).

62. U.S. Department of Justice, *Prison and Jail Inmates at Midyear 1997*, 5.

63. Paul Katsampes, "Jail Megatrends," *Corrections Management Quarterly* (Winter 1997), 64–6.

64. Arthur Wallenstein, "Jail Crowding: Bringing the Issue to the Corrections Center Stage," *Corrections Today* (December 1996), 76–81.

65. Quoted in Butterfield, "Defying Gravity."

66. "State to Rent County Jails for Inmates," *UPI Online* (February 5, 1998).

67. John Irwin, *The Jail: Managing the Underclass in American Society* (Berkeley, CA: University of California Press, 1985), 2.

68. U.S. Department of Justice, *Prison and Jail Inmates at Midyear 1997*, 6.

69. 441 U.S. 520 (1979).

70. U.S. Department of Justice, *Prison and Jail Inmates at Midyear 1997*, 7.

71. G. Larry Mays and Joel A. Thompson, "The Political and Organizational Context of American Jails," in *American Jails: Public Policy Issues*, eds. Joel A. Thompson and G. Larry Mays (Chicago: Nelson-Hall, 1991), 10.

72. Quoted in Greg Burton, "Jail Builders Race to Keep Up with Demand," *Salt Lake City Tribune* (May 6, 1998), N31.

73. U.S. Department of Justice, *Prison and Jail Inmates at Midyear 1997*, 7.

74. M. Welch, "The Expansion of Jail Capacity: Makeshift Jails and Public Policy," in *American Jails: Public Policy Issues*, eds. Joel A. Thompson and G. Larry Mays (Chicago: Nelson-Hall, 1991), 151.

75. John J. Gibbs, "Environmental Congruence and Symptoms of Psychopathology: A Further Exploration of the Effects of Exposure to the Jail Environment," *Criminal Justice and Behavior* 18 (1991), 351–74.

76. Richard Weiner, William Frazier, and Jay Farbstein, "Building Better Jails," *Psychology Today* (June 1987), 40.

77. R. L. Miller, "New Generation Justice Facilities: The Case for Direct Supervision," *Architectural Technology* 12 (1985), 6–7.

78. Gerald J. Bayens, Jimmy J. Williams, and John Ortiz Smyka, "Jail Type and Inmate Behavior: A Longitudinal Analysis," *Federal Probation* (September 1997), 54.

79. Linda L. Zupan, *Jails: Reform and the New Generation Philosophy* (Cincinnati, OH: Anderson Publishing Co., 1991).

80. Gerald J. Bayens, Jimmy J. Williams, and John Ortiz Smykla, "Jail Type and Inmate Behavior: A Longitudinal Analysis," *Federal Probation* 61 (September, 1997), 54.

81. John DiIulio and Charles Logan, "Ten Deadly Myths about Crime and Punishment," in *Restoring Responsibility in Criminal Justice*, 2d ed., ed. Robert J. Bidinotto (Irvington-on-Hudson, NY: Foundation for Economic Education, 1996).

82. Peter Greenwood and Allan Abrahamse, *Selective Incapacitation* (Santa Monica, CA: The Rand Corporation, 1982).

83. Todd R. Clear and Dina R. Rose, "A Thug in Jail Can't Shoot Your Sister: The Unintended Consequences of Incarceration," A paper presented to the American Sociological Association (August 18, 1996).

84. Alice E. Harvey, "Ex-Felon Disenfranchisement and Its Influence on the Black Vote: The Need for a Second Look," *University of Pennsylvania Law Review* 142 (January 1994), 1145.

85. Fox Butterfield, "Crime Keeps on Falling, but Prisons Keep on Filling," *New York Times* (September 28, 1997), Section 4, 1.

86. Tara-Jen Ambrosio and Vincent Schiraldi, *From Classrooms to Cell Blocks: A National Perspective* (Washington, D.C.: Justice Policy Institute, February 1997).

87. Timothy Egan, "As Idaho Booms, Prisons Fill and Spending on Poor Lags," *New York Times* (April 16, 1998), A1.

88. Scott N. Tachiki, "Intermediate Sentences in Supermax Prisons Based on Alleged Gang Affiliations," *California Law Review* (July 1995), 1115.

89. "Facts about Pelican Bay's SHU," *California Prisoner* (December 1991).

90. Jeffrey Endicott, Jerry Berge, and Gary McCaughtry, "Prison Wardens Push for 'Supermax' Prison," *Wisconsin State Journal* (February 12, 1996), 5A.

91. Gregory L. Hershberger, "To the Max," *Corrections Today* (February 1998), 55.

92. *Ibid.*, 55–6.

93. Robert A. Sheppard, Jeffrey G. Geiger, and George Welborn, "Closed Maximum Security: The Illinois Supermax," *Corrections Today* (July 1996), 4.

94. 515 U.S. 472 (1995).

95. "Supermax Placement Raises New Concerns about Due Process," *Correctional Law Reporter* (October/November 1997), 1–2, 45–6.

96. Robert Perkinson, "Shackled Justice: Florence Federal Penitentiary and the New Politics of Punishment," *Social Justice* 21 (Fall 1994), 117–23.

97. 889 F.Supp. 1146 (1995).

98. National Institute of Corrections, *Supermax Housing: A Survey of Current Practice* (Longmont, CO: National Institute of Corrections Information Center, March 1997), 4–7.

chapter
14

Life Behind Bars

Chapter Objectives

After reading this chapter, you should be able to:

1. Explain the concept of prison as a total institution.

2. Contrast the indigenous model of prison behavior with the importation model.

3. List and briefly describe the possible patterns of inmate behavior, which are driven by the inmate's personality and values.

4. Indicate some of the reasons for violent behavior in prisons.

5. List and briefly explain the six general job categories among correctional officers.

6. List the five types of correctional officers.

7. Contrast the hands-off doctrine of prisoner law with the hands-on approach.

8. Describe the procedural safeguards for a prisoner subjected to disciplinary measures.

9. List and explain three strategies being used to avoid prison overcrowding.

10. Indicate two major problems prisons face besides overcrowding.

INTRODUCTION

For inmates at New York's Auburn Prison, the lockstep shuffle was an integral part of daily life. In keeping with nineteenth-century ideals of silence and order, the shuffle was designed to produce such a state of mind-numbing drudgery that the prisoners would have no choice but to ponder their evil ways. The choreography of the lockstep was simple: inmates formed a line; each stood with his right foot slightly behind the left and his right arm outstretched with the hand resting on the right shoulder of the man in front of him. To move, each man would slide his left foot forward, then bring his right foot back to its original position. Repeating this awkward motion, inmates would slowly shuffle across the prison grounds.

The spirit of the lockstep shuffle, if not its actual practice, still permeates modern prison life. One observer notes that today's penal institutions are characterized by "grindingly dull routine interrupted by occasional flashes of violence and brutality."[1] A "no frills" movement in political thought and prison management has moved to eliminate comforts from inmates' existence.[2] Five states have banned weightlifting in their prisons, and others have barred televisions, radios, adult magazines, hot pots, and, to the chagrin of correctional officers, cigarettes. The pleasures, as they were, of food and dress are also under attack: Texas prisoners have dined on "vita-pro," a tasteless soybean-based meat product, while Mississippi inmates are required to wear color-coded, zebra-striped uniforms.[3]

Life behind bars has long been predicated on the **principle of least eligibility,** which holds that the least advantaged members of outside society should lead a better existence than any person living in prison or jail.[4] As the "no frills" movement shows, the idea that incarceration is not punishment enough, and that daily life itself must be an arduous trial for prisoners, is particularly popular at the moment. In recent polls, as many as 82 percent of Americans believe life in prison is too easy. Many critics, however, feel that the treatment of prisoners has become increasingly inhumane and, indeed, unconstitutional. During the 1990s, forty states were legally required to improve living conditions in their penal institutions.[5]

In this chapter, we look at these living conditions and the factors that influence the quality of life in America's prisons and jails. To that end, we will discuss the ramifications of violence in prison, the role played by correctional officers, efforts by prisoners and prisoners' rights advocates to improve the conditions, and several other issues that are at the forefront of prison debate today. To start, we must understand the forces that shape prison culture and how those forces affect the overall operation of the correctional facility.

PRISON CULTURE

Any institution—whether a school, a bank, or a police department—has an organizational culture, that is, a set of values that help the people in the organization understand what actions are acceptable and what actions are unacceptable.[6] According to a theory put forth by the influential sociologist Erving Goffman, prison cultures are unique because prisons are **total institutions** that encompass every aspect of an inmate's life. Unlike a student or a bank teller, a prisoner cannot leave the institution, nor have any meaningful interaction with outside communities. Others arrange every aspect of daily life, and all prisoners are required to follow this schedule in exactly the same manner.[7]

Inmates develop their own *argot*, or language (see Figure 14.1). They create their own economy, which, in the absence of currency, is based on the barter

"I know not whether Laws be right
Or whether Laws be wrong;
All that we know who live in gaol
Is that the wall is strong;
And that each day is like a year,
A year whose days are long."

—Oscar Wilde, *Irish playwright, author* (1898)

PRINCIPLE OF LEAST ELIGIBILITY
The belief that, as part of their punishment, prisoners should not have access to any goods or services that are not available to citizens who have not broken the law.

TOTAL INSTITUTION
An institution, such as a prison, that provides all of the necessities for existence to those who live within its boundaries.

Figure 14.1 Prison Slang

Ace-duce. Best friend.

All day. Life sentence, as in "he's doing all day."

Big bitch. A felon who has been convicted under habitual criminal laws that carry a mandatory life sentence.

Catch a ride. To ask a friend with drugs to get you high, as in "Hey, man, can I catch a ride?"

Catch a square. To prepare to fight, as in "you'd better catch a square."

Chi-mo, also *chester, baby-raper, short eyes.* Child molester.

Click up. To join a gang.

Deck. Pack of cigarettes.

Ding. A term of derision for a mentally deranged prisoner.

Fish. A new arrival who does not yet know the rules of the prison culture.

Gangster, or *monster.* HIV/AIDS. As in "watch out for that guy, he's got the gangster."

Hacks, also *hogs, snouts, pigs, cops, bulls, screws.* Correctional officers.

Herb. Weak inmate.

The hole. Solitary confinement.

Jigger. An inmate who stands watch while an illegal act is taking place.

Luv, luv. Doing well, as in "living luv, luv."

Mule. A person who smuggles drugs into the correctional facility.

Nazi low rider. A member of a white prison gang.

Old school. A prisoner who is seen as having values from the "old days" in prisons, when more respect was given to fellow prisoners.

On the leg. A prisoner who is seen as being overly friendly with prison staff.

Pepsi generation. The newer, younger inmates who are seen as having no respect for the old school ways of the prison.

Pitcher. A sexually aggressive, dominant inmate.

Playing on ass. Gambling without having any cash, as in "if you lose, it's your ass."

Punk. A derogatory term referring to a homosexual or weak-willed person.

Rapo. Anyone imprisoned on a sex offense.

Riding leg. An inmate who is friendly with staff in order to receive preferential treatment.

Split your wig. A quick punch to the head.

Stick. A marijuana joint.

T-jones. An inmate's mother or parents, as in "I got a letter from my T-jones."

Wolf ticket. To "talk tough" without the will to back it up, as in, "he's selling wolf tickets," or "he's making a lot of noise but doesn't have the guts to stand up for himself."

Prisoners also use rhyming slang in order to make their conversations confusing to newcomers or outsiders. In rhyming slang, "bees and money" could mean "honey," "oh my dear" could mean "beer," and so on.

SOURCE: ADAPTED FROM MUCH LARGER GLOSSARIES FOUND AT WWW.HALCYON.COM/SCRIPTS/DANTE/ CGI-PVT AND WWW.WCO.COM/~AERICK/LINGO.HTM.

of valued items such as food, contraband, and sexual favors. They establish methods of determining power, many of which, as we shall see, involve violence. Isolated and heavily regulated, prisoners create a social world that is, out of both necessity and design, separate from the outside world.[8]

Who Is in Prison?

The culture of any prison is heavily influenced by its inmates; their values, beliefs, and experiences in the outside world will be reflected in the social order that exists behind bars. In Chapter 2, we noted that a majority of Americans commit at least one crime that could technically send them to prison. In reality, slightly more than 5 percent will be confined in a state or federal prison during their lifetimes. That percentage is considerably higher for male members of minority groups: statistically, nearly 30 percent of African American males and 16 percent of Hispanic males will be imprisoned at one point in their lives.[9]

The prison population is not static. As we will discuss in Chapter 18, the past two decades have seen the incarceration rates of women and minority groups rise sharply. Furthermore, the crimes of inmates have changed over that period. Figure 14.2 shows that inmates are increasingly likely to have been convicted on drug charges, and less likely to have been convicted of a violent or property crime.

Figure 14.2 Offenders in Prison

These figures show the changing proportion of inmates, based on crimes committed, in state correctional facilities in the United States between 1985 and 1996.

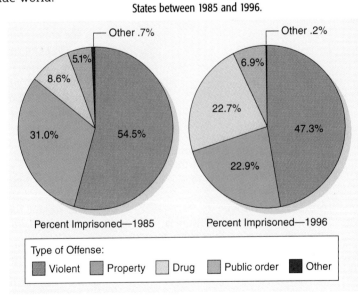

Other .7%
5.1%
8.6%
31.0%
54.5%
Percent Imprisoned—1985

Other .2%
6.9%
22.7%
22.9%
47.3%
Percent Imprisoned—1996

Type of Offense:
■ Violent ■ Property □ Drug ■ Public order ■ Other

SOURCE: BUREAU OF JUSTICE STATISTICS, CORRECTIONAL POPULATION IN THE UNITED STATES, 1995 (WASHINGTON, D.C.: U.S. DEPARTMENT OF JUSTICE, JUNE 1997), TABLE 1.2, PAGE 10; AND BUREAU OF JUSTICE STATISTICS, PRISONERS IN 1997 (WASHINGTON, D.C.: U.S. DEPARTMENT OF JUSTICE, JUNE 1997), TABLE 15, PAGE 10.

Among age groups, persons aged eighteen to twenty-four account for the highest percentage of new admissions to prison, approximately 30 percent.[10] The median age of the prison population is twenty-nine, though that number is expected to rise in the near future. Because of determinate sentences, long terms, and more restrictive release policies, criminal justice experts are predicting that inmates over the age of fifty will comprise 33 percent of the total prison population by 2010, compared to just under 10 percent today.[11]

Education also appears to be a determinant in who goes to prison. Over 60 percent of inmates failed to earn a high school diploma, and fewer than one in ten have attended college.[12] As lack of education is often connected with criminal activity, however, it is important to distinguish between its importance as a causative factor and as a correlative factor. On the one hand, when judges impose lighter sentences on those with more formal education, years of schooling are a causative factor. On the other hand, when those who commit crimes are, as a group, also those who tend to quit school early, then years of schooling and imprisonment rates are simply correlated.

Adapting to Prison Society

Upon arriving at prison, each convict attends an orientation session and receives a "Resident's Handbook." The handbook provides information such as meal and official count times, disciplinary regulations, and visitation guidelines. The norms and values of the prison society, however, cannot be communicated by the staff or learned from a handbook. As first described by Donald Clemmer in his classic 1940 work, *The Prison Community*, the process of **prisonization**—or adaptation to the prison culture—advances as the inmate gradually understands what constitutes acceptable behavior in the institution, as defined not by the prison officials but by other inmates.[13]

In studying prisonization, criminologists have focused on one crucial point: What is the basis for acceptable behavior in the prison environment? Two models have been formulated to answer this question—the indigenous model and the importation model.

Response to Captivity. Clemmer and his followers support the **indigenous model** of prisonization. Sociologist Gresham M. Sykes provided the groundwork for this model by asserting that the conditions of incarceration are so painful that the prisoner must create an entirely new social outlook in order to deal with them. In particular, the prisoner is deprived of liberty, autonomy, material goods and services, heterosexual relationships, and security. In response, each inmate organizes his or her life with the primary goal of alleviating the hardships of deprivation. Therefore, the prison culture evolves from within the institution.[14] Various levels of deprivation have also been used to explain levels of prison violence, as we shall see later in the chapter.

Individual Characteristics. The **importation model,** in contrast, argues that offenders bring their own individual cultural attitudes and behaviors into the prison from their lives on the outside. (For some examples of the opposite process, see *Criminal Justice & Popular Culture—Prison Chic*.) Sociologists John Irwin and Donald Cressey have described three types of prisoners whose personalities strongly influence prison culture:

- *The Thief,* who mistrusts all authority and forms a philosophy based on an "us versus them" solidarity among inmates.

- *The Convict,* who has spent many years in penal institutions and is fairly comfortable in the prison setting. This person will try to use the prison system for personal gain.

PRISONIZATION
The socialization process through which a new inmate learns the accepted norms and values of the prison population.

INDIGENOUS MODEL
The theory that prison culture is primarily formed by the environment of deprivation that inmates experience after they have been incarcerated.

IMPORTATION MODEL
The theory that prison culture is primarily formed by the values inmates bring into the institution from their outside lives.

Prison Chic

If inmates import cultural attitudes from outside life into the prison, there is mounting evidence that they are in the export business as well. According to Richard Stratton, the editor of *Prison Life,* "the prison culture [is] spilling out and becoming the popular culture." Stratton offers the examples of rap music and tattoos, both of which are rooted in prison communities and have been adopted by the culture at large. Another popular export has been the fashion statement known as "sagging," in which adolescent boys wear baggy pants slung low around their hips, intentionally exposing their underwear and covering their shoes.

The origins of sagging can be found in the common prison policy of denying inmates the use of belts, which can be used either as a weapon or as a means to commit suicide by hanging. Without belts, the prisoners' pants tend to sag. The style first caught on among rap musicians, whose exposure through MTV and other media outlets brought the practice to a wider audience. "Sagging" holds an obvious appeal for youths—"If it will upset [adults], they'll wear it," says a psychologist who specializes in adolescent behavior.

Many adults who are offended by the fashion sit on school boards, and baggy pants have been banned in numerous districts because of gang associations. The issue has even led to a lawsuit. In *Bivens v. Albuquerque* (1995), the plaintiff tried to overturn such a ban by arguing that by wearing baggy pants he was expressing his African American urban identity. The judge ruled in favor of the New Mexico school district, reasoning that sagging was a widespread trend followed by hundreds of thousands of young men across the nation; therefore, the plaintiff could not be sending a particularized message that deserved constitutional protection.

Baggy pants may not be the last prison fashion trend. When Alabama recently brought back chain gangs, the state corrections department began receiving outside requests for the white pants, shirt, and caps worn by inmates on the gangs.

The Square, who lacks a criminal background and feels "out of place" in the prison environment. Such persons will tend to disassociate themselves from the general prison community.[15]

Irwin also identifies several patterns of inmate behavior, each one driven by the inmate's personality and values:

1. Professional criminals adapt to prison by "doing time." In other words, they follow the rules and generally do whatever is necessary to speed up their release so they can continue their chosen careers.

2. Some convicts, mostly state-raised youths or veterans of juvenile detention centers, are more comfortable inside prison than outside. These inmates serve time by "jailing," or establishing themselves in the power structure of prison culture.

3. Other inmates take advantage of prison resources such as libraries or drug treatment programs by "gleaning," or working to improve themselves to prepare for a return to society.

4. Finally, "disorganized" criminals exist on the fringes of prison society. These inmates may have mental impairments or low levels of intelligence and find it impossible to adapt to prison culture on any level.[16]

The process of categorizing prisoners has a theoretical basis, but it serves a practical purpose as well, allowing administrators to reasonably predict how different inmates will act in certain situations. An inmate who is "doing time" generally does not present the same security risk as one who is "jailing."

The Changing Inmate Code

Though both models have aspects to recommend them, recent changes in the traditional **inmate code** point to the practical relevance of the importa-

INMATE CODE
A system of social norms and values established by inmates to regulate behavior within the correctional institution.

Gangs such as the Crips (a member of which is shown above), the Aryan Brotherhood, the Bloods, and Barrio Azteca function within prison walls and add to the overall levels of violence in correctional facilities. What factors make prisons susceptible to gang activity?

tion model. In the early studies of prisoner culture, researchers found that an unwritten set of rules guided inmate conduct. A prisoner's standing among his or her peers was determined by whether he or she followed the inmate code; those who failed to do so were rejected by the institutional society. The two most important tenets of the code were "never rat on a con" and "do your own time"—in other words, never inform on another inmate and don't interfere in another inmate's affairs (see Figure 14.3). [17]

During the era when the code dominated prison culture (generally encompassing the three decades following World War II), prisons were repressive but relatively safe. In contrast, one observer calls the modern institution an "unstable and violent social jungle."[18] There has been an influx of youthful inmates and drug offenders who are seen as being only "out for themselves" and unwilling to follow any code that preaches collective values. With the formation of racial gangs in prison, the inmate code has been replaced by one in which the shared values of gang loyalties are preeminent; as we shall see, inmate-on-inmate violence has risen accordingly.[19]

PRISON VIOLENCE

A prison is a dangerous place to live. Although homicide rates in prison are about half the civilian homicide rate,[20] the prison culture is predicated on violence. Prison guards use the threat of violence (and, at times, its reality) to control the inmate population. Among the prisoners, violence is used to establish power and dominance. Often, this violence leads to death. About 100 inmates are murdered by fellow inmates each year, and about 26,000 inmate-on-inmate assaults take place annually.

The worry among prisoners' rights advocates is that inmate violence has become so common that Americans—especially American judges—will come to see it as inevitable. This line of thinking would practically absolve prison officials from the responsibility to take measures to limit violent behavior.[21] In *Farmer v. Brennan* (1994),[22] the Supreme Court stated that being assaulted in prison is not "part of the penalty criminal offenders pay for their offenses against society." Increasingly, however, the reality of prison life suggests otherwise.

INFOTRAC®
COLLEGE EDITION

Danitz, Tiffany. The gangs behind bars.

Figure 14.3 The Inmate Code

According to many studies of prison life done from the 1940s to the 1970s, inmates lived by an unwritten code. The tenets of the code, which are listed here, stressed reliability, toughness, and a social structure in which individual inmates avoided conflict with each other.

- Never rat on a con.
- Do your own time.
- Don't interfere with the interests of other inmates.
- Mind your own business.
- Don't have a loose lip.
- Be tough.

- Be a man.
- Don't exploit inmates.
- Be sharp.
- Keep off a man's back.
- Don't put a guy on the spot.
- Be loyal to your class.
- Be cool.

SOURCE: GRESHAM SYKES AND SHELDON MESSINGER, "THE INMATE SOCIAL SYSTEM" IN THEORETICAL STUDIES IN THE SOCIAL ORGANIZATION OF THE PRISON, ED. R. CLOWARD ET AL. (NEW YORK: SOCIAL SCIENCE RESEARCH COUNCIL, 1960), 6–10.

Violence in Prison Culture

In the inmate code era, with its emphasis on "noninterference," the prison culture did not support inmate-on-inmate violence. Prison "elders" would themselves punish any of their peers who showed a proclivity toward assaulting fellow inmates. Today, in contrast, violence is used to establish the prisoner hierarchy by separating the powerful from the weak. Humboldt State University's Lee H. Bowker has identified several other reasons for violent behavior:

▌ It provides a deterrent against being victimized, as a reputation for violence may eliminate an inmate as a target of assault.

▌ It enhances self-image in an environment that does not respect other attributes, such as intelligence.

▌ In the case of rape, it gives sexual relief.

▌ It serves as a means of acquiring material goods through extortion or outright robbery.[23]

The **deprivation model** can be used to explain the high level of prison violence. According to this model, the stressful and oppressive conditions of prison life lead to aggressive behavior on the part of inmates. When conditions such as overcrowding worsen, prison researcher Stephen C. Light found that inmate misconduct often increases.[24] In these circumstances, the violent behavior may not have any express purpose—it may just be a means of relieving tension.[25]

Riots

The deprivation model is helpful, though less convincing, in searching for the roots of collective violence. As far back as the 1930s, Frank Tannenbaum noted that harsh prison conditions can cause tension to build among inmates until it eventually explodes in the form of mass violence.[26] Living conditions in prisons are fairly constant, however, so how can the seemingly spontaneous outbreak of prison riots be explained?

Researchers have addressed these inconsistencies with the concept of **relative deprivation,** a theory that focuses on the gap between what is expected in certain situation and what is achieved. Peter C. Kratcoski has argued that because prisoners enjoy such meager privileges to begin with, any further deprivation can spark disorder.[27] A number of criminologists, including Bert Useem in his studies made in the wake of the riot at the Penitentiary of New Mexico in 1980, have noted that collective violence occurs in response to heightened measures of security at corrections facilities.[28] Thus, the violence occurs in response to an additional reduction in freedom for inmates, who enjoy very little freedom to begin with.

Riots, which have been defined as situations in which a number of prisoners are beyond institutional control for a significant amount of time,[29] are relatively rare. Because of their explosive nature and potential for high casualties, however, riots have a unique ability to focus public attention on prison conditions (see Figure 14.4 on the next page). The collective violence at Attica Prison in upstate New York has been described as a turning point in the history of American corrections by alerting citizens to the situation in correctional facilities and spurring the prisoners' rights movement.[30]

Attica: Organized Violence. The Attica Prison riot lasted five days in September 1971. Nearly half of the institution's 2,500 inmates seized control

DEPRIVATION MODEL
A theory that inmate aggression is the result of the frustration inmates feel at being deprived of freedom, consumer goods, sex, and other staples of life outside the institution.

RELATIVE DEPRIVATION
The theory that inmate aggression is caused when freedoms and services that the inmate has come to accept as normal are decreased or eliminated.

Figure 14.4 Prison Riots in the 1990s

Any number of circumstances or incidents can cause prison riots. The incidents described here offer a few examples of situations that became violent in the 1990s.

Facility: Southport Correctional Facility, Elmira, New York.
Year: 1991
What Happened: Fifty-two inmates escaped from exercise pens in A Block yard. Six correctional officers taken hostage, stripped, chained about the neck, and paraded around the prison grounds.
Cause: Inmate dissatisfaction with food service, ventilation in cells, and medical care.
Aftermath: Five of the hostages received hospital care.

Facility: Southern Ohio Correctional Facility, Lucasville, Ohio.
Year: 1993
What Happened: More than 400 inmates occupied Cell Block L at the prison for eleven days, holding twelve correctional officers hostage. Nearly 2,000 law enforcement officers and National Guard members were involved in the effort to end the occupation.
Cause: Overcrowding. Inmate dissatisfaction with living conditions.
Aftermath: One guard and nine inmates killed.

Facility: Carl Robinson Correctional Institution, Enfield, Connecticut.
Year: 1994
What Happened: Inmates broke into a maintenance building and gathered rakes, shovels, and screwdrivers to be used as weapons. Fighting spread from the exercise yard into individual cells, where gang members apparently targeted certain inmates for attack.
Cause: A disagreement over the use of a clothes dryer set off gang tensions that, according to prison officials, had been building for months.
Aftermath: Two correctional officers and 35 inmates injured. Two inmates killed. $300,000 worth of damage.

Facility: Five federal prisons in Alabama, Pennsylvania, Illinois, Tennessee, and Oklahoma.
Year: 1995
What Happened: Hundreds of inmates set fire to mattresses, broke windows, threw chairs, and caused destruction with baseball bats. Prison officials do not believe the disturbances, which happened simultaneously, were coordinated, though some inmates may have been incited by reports of violence at other facilities.

Cause: Reaction to vote by the U.S. House of Representatives to end a disparity in sentences for those convicted of crimes involving powder cocaine and crack cocaine.
Aftermath: Several million dollars in damages and 25 injured inmates and prison staff.

Facility: California State Prison, Sacramento, California.
Year: 1996
What Happened: Clusters of African American and Hispanic gang members fought each other and staff members for nearly half an hour in an exercise yard, medical clinic, and work center.
Cause: Racial tensions.
Aftermath: Fifteen correctional officers and 60 inmates were injured. One inmate bled to death after being shot in the buttocks by a correctional guard.

Facility: Mohawk Correctional Facility, Rome, New York.
Year: 1997
What Happened: Inmates used recreational equipment, such as weights, aluminum baseball bats, and horseshoes to attack guards and try to break open prison gates.
Cause: After an inmate hung himself, rumors spread among the inmate population to the effect that he had been killed by correctional officers who were trying to cover up the death by calling it a suicide.
Aftermath: Ten correctional officers injured.

Facility: Crowley County Correctional Center, Pueblo, Colorado.
Year: 1999
What Happened: An inmate, upset over the quality of his food, hit a correctional guard in the face with his tray. Close to 100 inmates began rioting, flooding cell blocks by clogging toilets, setting fires, and smashing furniture.
Cause: Many of the inmates involved had just been transferred to the private facility in Colorado from public facilities in Washington State, which needed to alleviate overcrowding. The inmates were unhappy about being taken away from their families.
Aftermath: Inmates subdued with OC spray, minor injuries.

of most of the prison. They took thirty-eight prison guards as hostages. The riot leaders, mostly members of the Black Muslims, presented prison administrators with a list of demands—modeled after the United Nations' Standards for Imprisoned Persons—that included better food, more programs, and due process for disciplinary action. In general, the riot appeared to be a reaction to the punitive atmosphere in Attica; one of its leaders complained to his lawyer that he had been beaten for walking with his hands in his pockets. During negotiations, another prisoner read the following statement:

> We are men, we are not beasts and we will not be beaten or driven as such. What has happened here is but the sound before the fury of those who are oppressed.[31]

The negotiations ended abruptly when New York state troopers raided the prison grounds, killing thirty-nine inmates and wounding eighty-eight others. In the wake of the riot, however, New York Governor Nelson Rockefeller called for "radical reforms" in the state's corrections system, and twenty-four of the Attica prisoners' twenty-eight original demands were met.

Santa Fe: Disorganized Violence. The Attica riot has proved to be the exception rather than the rule. Most riots are disorganized and have no political agenda. They are marked by extreme levels of inmate-on-inmate violence. In a disturbance that broke out at the Penitentiary of New Mexico at Santa Fe in 1980, prisoners killed thirty-three of their fellow inmates, and nearly two hundred others were tortured, beaten, and raped. The riot was used as an excuse to take revenge for personal grievances, and the levels of violence—including the use of blowtorches on genitals—shocked the public.[32]

During the postriot investigations, prison administrators were strongly criticized for their lack of control over the Santa Fe institution. Two weeks before the riot, an outside consultant warned that New Mexico prison officials were playing "Russian roulette with the lives of inmates" by failing to properly staff and train the personnel at the state's penal institutions.[33] Some observers see poor management, rather than levels of deprivation, as the primary cause of riots.[34]

Issues of Race and Ethnicity. The night before the Attica riot erupted, inmates yelled "[g]et a good night's sleep, whitey. Sleep tight, because tomorrow's the day." Officers in the prison were known to refer to their batons as "nigger sticks."[35] Race plays a major role in prison life, and prison violence is often an outlet for racial tension. As prison populations have changed over the past three decades, with African Americans and Hispanics becoming the majority in many penal institutions, issues of race and ethnicity have become increasingly important to prison administrators and researchers. We will examine these issues in detail in Chapter 18, including a discussion of the growing problem of prison gangs.

Rape

In contrast to riots, the problem of sexual assault in prisons receives very little attention from media sources. This can be partly attributed to the ambiguity of the subject: that rape occurs in prisons and jails is undisputed, but determining exactly how widespread the problem is has proved difficult. Prison officials, aware that any sexual contact is prohibited in most penal institutions, are often unwilling to provide realistic figures for fear of negative publicity. Even when they are willing they may be unable to do so. Most inmates are ashamed of being rape victims and refuse to report instances of sexual assault. Consequently, it has been difficult to come up with consistent statistics for sexual assault in prison. One source estimated that 22 percent of male inmates are raped while incarcerated,[36] but another found evidence that only 2 percent suffer this fate.[37]

Whatever the figures, prison rape, like all rape, is considered primarily an act of violence rather than sex. Inmates subject to rape ("punks") are near the bottom of the prison power structure and, in some instances, may accept rape by one particularly powerful inmate in return for protection from others.[38] Raped inmates often suffer from rape trauma syndrome and a host of other psychological ailments including suicidal tendencies. Many prisons do not offer sufficient medical treatment for rape victims, nor does the prison staff take the necessary measures to protect obvious targets of rape—young, slightly built, nonviolent offenders. (See *CJ in Focus—Making Waves: Stop Prisoner Rape* on the next page.) Furthermore, as we will see, corrections officials are rarely held liable for inmate-on-inmate violence.

"I've seen seven stabbings, about six bashings and three self-mutilations. Two hangings, one attempted hanging, any number of overdoses. And that's only me, in just 70 days."

—Anonymous jail inmate (1998)

CJ in Focus
Making Waves
Stop Prisoner Rape

Nearly three decades ago, Stephen Donaldson was arrested for taking part in a pray-in at the White House marking the twenty-eighth anniversary of the atomic bombing of Nagasaki, Japan, during World War II. Taken to the Washington, D.C., jail, Donaldson refused to pay the $10 bail on moral grounds. As punishment for his stubbornness, the Navy veteran was transferred into the jail's general population. Almost immediately, an inmate approached Donaldson and said that he and a group of his friends wanted to discuss politics. After following nine prisoners into a cell, Donaldson was forced to perform oral sex on one of them. Then, the gang leader dragged Donaldson from cell to cell for four hours, and he was raped at each visit.

"After I was raped, my life was totally disrupted," Donaldson remembered. Following the initial jailing, he was imprisoned four more times and sexually assaulted on each occasion. In the wake of the last imprisonment, Donaldson received counseling for rape trauma syndrome and eventually became a rape counselor himself. He went on to form the New York–based advocacy group Stop Prisoner Rape to try to bring the issue of inmate sexual assault to the public eye. The group lobbies state legislatures to pass laws that require prison officials to counsel new pris- oners on the dangers of rape and how to avoid it and to allow rape crisis counselors into prisons to treat victimized inmates.

"Hooking Up: Protective Pairing for Punks," a pamphlet written and distributed by Donaldson, provides frank advice to inmates on the best way to survive the sexually predatory nature of prison life. One passage reads:

> If you want to be able to choose your daddy, tell the other prisoners that you want to hook up. The word will get around fast, and guys will start to talk to you about it. This has to be done quickly, otherwise events will overwhelm you and you may get gang-raped or forced to hook up before you can make a choice.

Donaldson described his advocacy work as a "mission" that "has allowed me to interpret a devastating experience as something that had meaning." He recently died from AIDS, having contracted HIV as a result of being raped while in jail.

For Critical Analysis: No inmate has ever been criminally charged for sexually assaulting a male prisoner in the United States. How do you think a "crackdown" on prison rape would affect the prison culture? What sort of reaction would such a policy draw from the public?

CORRECTIONAL OFFICERS AND DISCIPLINE

Under model circumstances, the presence of correctional officers—the standard term used to describe prison guards—would mitigate the levels of violence in American correctional institutions. To large extent, this is indeed the case; without correctional officers, the prison would be a place of anarchy. But in the highly regulated, oppressive environment of the prison, correctional officers must use the threat of violence, if not actual violence, to instill discipline and keep order. Thus, the relationship between prison staff and inmates is marked by mutual distrust. Consider the two following statements, the first made by a correctional officer and the second by a prisoner:

> [My job is to] protect, feed, and try to educate scum who raped and brutalized women and children . . . who, if I turn my back, will go into their cell, wrap a blanket around their cellmate's legs, and threaten to beat or rape him if he doesn't give sex, carry contraband, or fork over radios, money, or other goods willingly. And they'll stick a shank in me tomorrow if they think they can get away with it.[39]

> The pigs in the state and federal prisons . . . treat me so violently, I cannot possibly imagine a time I could ever have anything but the deepest, aching, searing hatred for them. I can't begin to tell you what they do to me. If I were weaker by a hair, they would destroy me.[40]

It may be difficult for an outsider to understand the emotions that fuel such sentiments. French philosopher Michael Foucault points out that discipline, both in prison and in the general community, is a means of social organization as well as punishment.[41] Discipline is imposed when a person behaves in a manner that is contrary to the values of the dominant social group.

Correctional officers and inmates have different concepts of the ideal structure of prison society, and, as the two quotations above demonstrate, this conflict generates intense feelings of fear and hatred, which often lead to violence.

Rank and Duties of Correctional Officers

The custodial staff at most prisons is organized according to four general ranks—captain, lieutenant, sergeant, and officer. In keeping with the militaristic model, captains are primarily administrators who deal directly with the warden on custodial issues. Lieutenants are the disciplinarians of the prison, responsible for policing and transporting the inmates. Sergeants oversee platoons of officers in specific parts of the prison, such as various cell blocks or workspaces.

Lucien X. Lombardo, professor of sociology and criminal justice at Old Dominion University, has identified six general job categories among correctional officers.[42]

Block Officers. In Lombardo's opinion, the most demanding job assignment is that of the block officer. This employee may supervise the cell blocks of as many as 400 inmates, as well as the correctional officers on block guard duty. During the day, the job is a hectic combination of security, housekeeping, and human services. At night, when the convicts are confined to their cells, block officers must maintain continuous inspections in order to assure that no self-destructive behavior is taking place.

In general, the block officer is responsible for the "well-being" of the inmates. In addition to making sure that inmates do not harm themselves or other prisoners, the block officer also acts as somewhat of a camp counselor, dispensing advice and seeing that inmates understand and follow the rules of the facility. Finally, because the block officer comes in daily close contact with prisoners, she or he is most likely to be the target of inmate violence when it erupts.

Work Detail Supervisors. In many penal institutions, the inmates work in the cafeteria, the prison store, the laundry, or other areas. Work detail supervisors oversee small groups of inmates as they perform their jobs. In general, the atmosphere in these work groups is more relaxed than in the cell blocks. The inmates and their supervisor are actively working toward the same goal—to complete the assignment—and therefore can develop a solidarity that does not exist in the cell blocks. If an inmate and work supervisor find themselves on the same detail for an extended period of time, they may even develop a friendly personal relationship, though it would be based on the parent-child model rather than a relationship of two equals.[43]

Industrial Shop and School Officers. These officers perform maintenance and security functions in educational and workshop programs. Their primary responsibility is to make sure that inmates are on time for these programs and that attendance requirements are followed. The officers must also make sure that the inmates are not disruptive during the sessions and that they do not steal items from the workshop or classroom.

Yard Officers. Officers who work the prison yard usually have the least seniority, befitting the assignment's reputation as dangerous and stressful. Unlike the cell blocks, programs, and work details, which are strictly organized, the prison yard is a place of relative freedom for the inmates. Consequently, yard officers must be constantly on alert for breaches in prison discipline or regulations. If collective violence occurs, yard officers run the highest chance of being injured, taken hostage, or even killed.

One benefit of the prison boom has been economic, as prisons infuse money and jobs into the regions where they are located. These regions are often rural and poor. In upstate New York's North County, for example, the average worker earns about $18,000 a year; the correctional officers at North County's Clinton Prison, shown below, earn an average of $36,000. Working as a correctional officer is one of the few ways that residents of North County who do not have a college degree can enjoy a middle-class life. Furthermore, as prisons are recession-proof, job security among correctional officers is higher than in most other local industries. Why, despite these benefits, does the profession of correctional officer continue to have a negative image?

Tower Guards. Previously, a wall post was considered the worst assignment in the prison. Tower guards spend their entire shifts, which usually last eight hours, in their isolated, silent posts high above the grounds of the facility. While keeping watch with a high-powered rifle, they communicate only through walkie-talkies. As prison violence has become more commonplace, however, the tower guard, being "above" any real danger, has become a more coveted position. Correctional officers now feel the benefits of safety outweigh the loneliness that comes with the job.

Administrative Building Assignments. Officers who hold administrative building assignments are in even less personal danger than tower guards and therefore hold the most desired job assignments. These officers provide security at prison gates, oversee visitation procedures, act as liaisons for civilians, and handle administrative tasks such as processing the paperwork when an inmate is transferred from another institution. Because such assignments involve contact with the public, the officers are often chosen for their public relation skills as well as any other talents they may have.

Characteristics of Correctional Officers

Media portrayals of correctional officers as unintelligent, racist, and violent have, to a certain extent, scared off those who might otherwise be interested in such a career. A recent Harris poll showed that only 1 percent of all teenagers interested in a security career wished to become a correctional officer. Prison administrators are trying to change this situation by offering more competitive salaries, with extra pay for added levels of education. One aspect of this recruiting effort is to attract qualified women correctional officers, a subject that we will discuss in Chapter 18. (See *Careers in Criminal Justice—The Correctional Officer.*)

To visit the Correctional Officers Development Center, go to codc.nmu.edu/sites/scoa.htm

The importance of having highly qualified correctional officers is difficult to overstate. In the isolated environment of the prison, the attitude and competency of these employees are crucial to the day-to-day operations of the institution, not to mention the obvious fact that prisoners greatly outnumber correctional officers. To a certain degree, any particular prison culture is determined by the relationship between custodial staff and inmates. A strict regime in which misconduct is harshly and quickly punished may lead to a well-run prison, but may also cause resentment and anger to build up among the inmate population. A more lenient administration that gives prisoners more leeway may be less stressful for all involved, but may also lead to a lack of discipline and the problems that follow.

A recent study categorized five types of correctional officers and their different attitudes toward their charges:

- The *punitive officer* demands total submission from inmates and harshly punishes the slightest misbehavior.

- The *custodial officer* is less interested in punishment than in efficiency, and he or she expects inmates to follow rules so as to create a secure environment.

- The *patronage officer* is interested in establishing lines of communication with the inmates and forms a protective relationship with them.

- The *therapist officer* sees inmates as patients and works to rehabilitate them.

- The *integrative officer* regards each inmate as an individual and combines the previous four types depending on situational conditions.[44]

Not every correctional officer fits one of these prototypes, though most can be loosely defined by them. The most important personality traits for officers, no matter what their personalities, are consistency and fairness. Situations in which an officer does not act as expected, favors one inmate over the others,

Careers in Criminal Justice

ROBERT M. LUCAS
CORRECTIONS FACILITY COMMANDER

My interest in the corrections field grew out of the need to be involved in solving problems associated with crime and punishment. I began my career as a law enforcement deputy. Upon completion of my undergraduate studies I sought experience in the counseling and programs aspect of detention. Ultimately I became interested in the management of jails and decided to become a sworn detention officer. My career path has given me a unique perspective from having experience in three major components of criminal justice: law enforcement, detention, and programs. Throughout my career I have continued my education as a corrections professional, and my accomplishments include a Master of Arts degree in criminal justice from the University of South Florida, and I am a graduate of the Southern Police Institute's Administrative Officers Course.

I am currently assigned as a facility commander in a 1,714 bed direct supervision jail. The facility is divided into two factions: housing and central intake. Central intake encompasses all facets of booking as well as the classification and records bureau. There is a combined total of approximately 300 sworn and civilian employees assigned to this multidimensional command and responsible for the processing and booking of over 62,000 inmates in 1998. Additionally, my command must ensure that inmates make all required court appearances and that all transfers or releases are proper and within established releasing standards. My most important duties are ensuring that staff are properly trained, that they are assigned to functions which guarantee security is maintained at the highest level, and which all inmates are treated in accordance with local, state, and federal standards.

A defining incident in my career was being involved in the mass arrest of 186 individuals as a result of a demonstration. As an assistant tactical commander, I was responsible for remote booking, security, crowd control, and the coordination of inmate transportation to the central jail facility. The incident was significant from two aspects: 1) the dynamics and logistics involved in the arrest, detainment, and booking of a large number of individuals in a short period of time; and 2) the awareness of the importance of a cooperative effort between law enforcement and detention. A number of problems were immediately evident in the arrest and processing of this large number of inmates, including security, site location, feeding, sanitation, and medical care for those in need. As is typical with most agencies, the booking process was normally accomplished in a secure facility separate from any outside disruptive factors. The remote booking exposed the staff to dissidents and necessitated the initial processing of the inmates in a temporary booking area without normal security.

This incident clearly displayed the talents and abilities of the detention staff assigned to the tactical unit. The members functioned as a disciplined team and demonstrated to law enforcement peers that the detention staff was capable and anxious to work together towards common goals. Subsequent to that mass arrest, the detention tactical unit has worked in tandem with law enforcement in training exercises, support for crowd control during a Super Bowl game, preparation for natural emergencies, search for missing persons, and the development of a honor guard in which representatives from detention and law enforcement routinely perform together in funerals, civic events, dedications, and public demonstrations.

I feel the qualities essential to the corrections field are those common to most fields such as a desire to perform at a high level of standards, a commitment to personal growth through change and development, and facing each task as a challenge as opposed to a problem. The management and operation of any detention facility is taxing, and it challenges the abilities, knowledge, and experience of those in supervisory roles. Staff are expected to fulfill a number of roles and encounter any number of problems or emergencies daily. The jail practitioner of today must be well-versed in all aspects of the jail operation, applicable laws and standards, and be able to address problems associated with expanding inmate populations, construction needs, and specialized inmate categories.

or is perceived as being racist can prove inflammatory. Inmates may respond with blatant misconduct or by subtle tactics such as loitering in the prison yard and holding up head counts. These tactics make it difficult for the correctional officer to do her or his job and can result in administrative action against the officer.[45]

Discipline and Brutality

As Erving Goffman noted in his essay on the "total institution," in the general society adults are rarely placed in a position where they are "punished" as a child would be.[46] Therefore, the strict disciplinary measures imposed on prisoners come as something of a shock and can provoke strong defensive reactions. Correctional officers who must deal with these responses often find that disciplining inmates is the most difficult and stressful aspect of their job.

The prisoners' manual lists the types of behavior that can result in disciplinary action. An institutional disciplinary committee decides the sanctions for specific types of misconduct. These sanctions include loss of privileges such as visiting and recreational opportunities for minor infractions, as well as more serious punishments for major infractions. The most severe sanction is punitive segregation, also known as solitary confinement or sensory deprivation, in which the inmate is isolated in a cell known as "the hole." This punishment is considered so debilitating that most facilities—initially fearful that the courts would find long periods of total deprivation "cruel and unusual" under the Eighth Amendment—have placed a twenty-day limit on the length of the confinement. Prison officials can, if they so choose, remove the inmate for a short period of time and then return him or her to the hole, effectively sidestepping the restrictions.

Use of Force. This is not to say that the judicial system has greatly restricted disciplinary actions in prison. For the most part, correctional officers are given the same discretionary powers as police officers (discussed in Chapter 5) to use their experience to determine when force is warranted. In *Whitney v. Albers* (1986),[47] the Supreme Court held that the use of force by prison officials violates an inmate's Eighth Amendment protections only if the force amounts to "the unnecessary and wanton infliction of pain." Excessive force can be considered "necessary" if the legitimate security interests of the penal institution are at stake. Consequently, an appeals court ruled that when officers at a Maryland prison formed an "extraction team" to remove the leader of a riot from his cell, beating him in the process, the use of force was justified given the situation.[48]

In contrast, in *Hudson v. McMillan* (1992)[49] the Supreme Court ruled that minor injuries suffered by a convict at the hands of a correctional officer following an argument did violate the inmate's rights, because there was no security concern at the time of the incident. To protect themselves from lawsuits, many corrections departments have developed codes to help guide correctional officers in the proper use of force (see Figure 14.5).

Brutality. In addition to the formal system of discipline, in which a correctional officer writes the equivalent of a "ticket" for inmates who have broken

Figure 14.5 Use of Force Guidelines

Between 1994 and 1998, twelve inmates in California's maximum-security prisons were killed and thirty-two more were injured by correctional officers using firearms to break up fights. During that same time period, in all of the other states combined only six inmates were shot and killed by correctional officers. In response to public pressure over what was seen as overly brutal control tactics, the California Department of Corrections issued these use of force guidelines, which went into effect in 1999.

1. Deadly force, defined as "any use of force that is likely to result in death," will only be used when it is reasonably needed to:
   - Defend the employee or other persons from an immediate threat of death or great bodily injury.
   - Prevent an escape.
   - Stop acts such as riots or arson that constitute an immediate jeopardy to institutional security and, because of their magnitude, are likely to result in escapees or the death of other persons.

2. A firearm shall not be discharged if there is reason to believe that persons other than the intended target may be injured.

3. Deadly force is not intended to stop fist fights.

SOURCE: CALIFORNIA DEPARTMENT OF CORRECTIONS.

institutional rules, a prison will have an informal disciplinary system as well. In this system, correctional guards handle misconduct on their own without notifying the administration. Informal discipline is often a response to the personal danger and stress felt by correctional officers. It almost certainly contributes to instances of brutality by corrections staff.

The legal line between proper use of force and brutality is rather subjective, but in many cases a correctional officer who reacts violently to an inmate is *retaliating*. After fifteen prisoners attacked staff in the courtyard of the Terrell Prison Unit outside Livingston, Texas, breaking an officer's nose, the officers reacted in a retaliatory manner. They beat several prisoners severely, killing one of them.[50] Prison administrators, recognizing that due process must be followed in enforcing discipline, do not officially condone this type of action. Nevertheless, staff members, who face the daily pressure of keeping order in the violent prison culture, feel they must establish their authority when it is directly threatened. It may be said that correctional officers have their own unwritten code of prison behavior, and in this code inmate-on-officer violence is rarely tolerated.

PROTECTING PRISONERS' RIGHTS

Legally, correctional officers do not have the right to retaliate in the manner described above. In fact, the officers in the Terrell Prison Unit incident were convicted of manslaughter; one received an eight-year sentence and the other a ten-year sentence. Such punishment is generally reserved for the most heinous of prison officer misconduct, such as homicide. The general attitude of the law toward inmates is summed up by the Thirteenth Amendment to the U.S. Constitution:

> Neither slavery not involuntary servitude, except as a punishment for crime whereof the party shall have been duly convicted, shall exist within the United States.

In other words, inmates do not have the same guaranteed rights as other Americans. For most of the nation's history, courts have followed the spirit of this amendment by applying the **"hands-off" doctrine** of prisoner law. This (unwritten) doctrine assumes that the care of inmates should be left to prison officials and that it is not the place of judges to intervene in penal administrative matters.

The inmate code flourished during the "hands-off" period; prisoners, unable to count on any outside forces to protect their rights, needed an internal social structure that would allow them to do so themselves. In the 1960s, as disfranchised groups from all parts of society began to insist on their constitutional rights, prisoners did so as well. The prisoners' rights movement demanded, and received, fuller recognition of prisoners' rights and greater access to American courts. It would be difficult, however, to label the movement a complete success. As one observer notes, "conditions of confinement in many American prisons have deteriorated during the same time period in which judicial recognition and concern for prisoners' legal rights dramatically increased."[51]

The "Hands-On" Approach

The end of the "hands-off" period can be dated to the Supreme Court's decision in *Cooper v. Pate* (1964).[52] In this case, Cooper, an inmate at the Illinois State Penitentiary, filed a petition for relief under the Civil Rights Act of 1871, stating that he had a First Amendment right to purchase reading material

"HANDS-OFF" DOCTRINE
The unwritten judicial policy that favors noninterference by the courts in the administration of prisons and jails.

"[C]ourts are ill equipped to deal with the increasingly urgent problems of prison administration and reform. Judicial recognition of that fact reflects no more than a healthy sense of realism."

—Lewis Powell, *U.S. Supreme Court Associate Justice* (1974)

"DELIBERATE INDIFFERENCE"
A standard that must be met by inmates trying to prove that their Eighth Amendment rights were violated by a correctional facility. It occurs when prison officials are aware of harmful conditions of confinement but fail to take steps to remedy those conditions.

about the Black Muslim movement. The Court, overturning rulings of several lower courts, held that the act did protect the constitutional rights of prisoners. This decision effectively allowed inmates to file civil lawsuits under Title 42 of the United States Code, Section 1983—known simply as Section 1983—if they felt that a prison or jail was denying their civil rights. (For a review of Section 1983, see Chapter 7.) An inmate who has been beaten by a correctional officer, for example, can bring a Section 1983 suit against the penal institution for denial of Eighth Amendment protection from cruel and unusual punishment.

Symbolically, the Supreme Court's declaration in *Wolff v. McDonnell* (1974)[53] that "[t]here is no iron curtain drawn between the Constitution and the prisons of this country" was just as significant as the *Cooper* ruling. It signified to civil rights lawyers that the Court would no longer follow the "hands-off" doctrine. The case had practical overtones as well, establishing that prisoners have a right to the following basic due process procedures when being disciplined by a penal institution:

- A fair hearing.
- Written notice at least twenty-four hours in advance of the hearing.
- An opportunity to speak at the hearing (though not to be represented by counsel during the hearing).
- An opportunity to call witnesses (unless doing so jeopardizes prison security).
- A written statement detailing the final decision and reasons for that decision.

Indeed, the prisoners' rights movement can count to its credit a number of legal decisions that have increased protection of inmates' constitutional rights. (See Figure 14.6 for a summary of the key Supreme Court decisions.)

Limiting Prisoners' Rights

Despite these successes, not all proponents of prisoners' rights feel that the courts have entirely abandoned the "hands-off" doctrine. Instead, they believe that by establishing standards of "deliberate indifference" and "identifiable human needs," court rulings have merely provided penal institutions with legally acceptable methods of denying prisoners' constitutional protections.

"Deliberate Indifference." In the 1976 case *Estelle v. Gamble*,[54] the Supreme Court established the **"deliberate indifference"** standard. Specifically, Justice Thurgood Marshall wrote that prison officials violated a convict's Eighth

Figure 14.6 The Supreme Court in the 1970s: Expanding Prisoners' Rights

In these cases, the Supreme Court recognized inmates' rights to freedom of religion, freedom of expression, due process, and protection from cruel and unusual punishment.

Cruz v. Beto (405 U.S. 319 [1972]). Prisoners cannot be denied the right to practice their religion, even if that religion is not one of the "standard" belief systems in the United States. In this case, the inmate who had been denied the opportunity to practice was a Buddhist.

Procunier v. Martinez (416 U.S. 396 [1974]). Correctional officials can censor an inmate's mail only when such censorship is necessary to maintain prison security.

Wolff v. McDonnell (418 U.S. 539 [1974]). Prisoners have due process rights when they are faced with disciplinary action that may place them in segregation or add time to their sentences. The rights include the right to a hearing, an opportunity to speak at the hearing, and an opportunity to call witnesses (unless doing so would threaten prison security).

Hutto v. Finney (437 U.S. 678 [1978]). Solitary confinement that lasts for more than thirty days is cruel and unusual punishment.

Amendment rights if they deliberately failed to provide him or her with necessary medical care. At the time, the decision was hailed as a victory for prisoners' rights. Defining the term "deliberate" has proved difficult, however. Does it mean that prison officials "should have known" that an inmate was placed in harm's way, or does it mean that prison officials purposefully placed the inmate in harm's way?

In recent decisions, the Supreme Court appears to have accepted the latter interpretation. In ruling on two separate 1986 cases, for example, the Court held that "simple negligence" was not acceptable grounds for a Section 1983 civil suit, and that a prison official's behavior was actionable only if it was done "maliciously or sadistically for the very purpose of causing harm."[55] Since it is quite difficult to prove in court a person's state of mind, the "deliberate negligence" standard has become a formidable one for prisoners to meet.

In *Wilson v. Seiter* (1991),[56] for example, Pearly L. Wilson filed a Section 1983 suit alleging that certain conditions of his confinement—including overcrowding, excessive noise, inadequate heating, cooling, and ventilation, and unsanitary bathroom and dining facilities—were cruel and unusual. The Supreme Court ruled against Wilson, stating that he had failed to prove that these conditions, even if they existed, were the result of "deliberate indifference" on the part of prison officials. Three years later, in a case concerning a transsexual inmate who was placed in the general population of a federal prison and subsequently beaten and raped, the Court narrowed the definition of "deliberate" even further. Though ruling in favor of the inmate, it held that the prison official must both be *aware* of the facts that create a potential for harm and also *draw the conclusion* that those facts will lead to harm.

"Identifiable Human Needs." The *Wilson* decision created another standard for determining Eighth Amendment violations that has drawn criticism from civil rights lawyers. It asserted that a prisoner must show that the institution has denied her or him a basic human need such as food, warmth, or exercise.[57] The Court failed, however, to mention any other needs besides these three, forcing other courts to interpret **"identifiable human needs"** for themselves. Taking a similar slant, in *Sandin v. Conner* (1995),[58] the Court ruled that inmates have rights to due process in disciplinary matters only when the punishment imposes "atypical or significant hardships in relation to ordinary incidents of prison life." Using this standard, inmates transferred to supermax prisons do not have the right to a hearing because the conditions in a supermax (discussed in Chapter 13) are not atypical. They are merely extreme.

Limiting Prisoner Litigation

The prisoners' rights movement has also been slowed by federal and state legislation to limit the number of Section 1983 lawsuits inmates can file. During the early 1990s, politicians and the media took up the issue of "frivolous prison lawsuits." Though a small percentage of these lawsuits are valid, the majority cannot be defended on constitutional grounds. One Colorado inmate, for example, claimed that by confiscating his pornographic mail, prison officials were denying him his right to "obtain a doctorate in obstetrics-gynecology."[59] Such cases invariably found their way into the media, angering the public.

As most prisoner lawsuits are filed *pro se*—without the aid of an attorney—they are subject to screening by judges (or, often, their law clerks), who can dismiss a case if they feel it is frivolous. Of the nearly 40,000 prisoner lawsuits filed annually in the early 1990s, 95 percent were found to be "without merit" and never even reached the preliminary trial stage.[60] Mindful of the enor-

Michael Blucker filed a court suit, charging that prison officials at the Menard Correctional Center in Illinois failed to protect him from being sexually assaulted while he was an inmate at the facility. A jury found that five members of the prison staff were not liable for the pain and suffering of Blucker. How would the concepts of "simple negligence" and "deliberate indifference" apply to Blucker's case and its outcome?

"IDENTIFIABLE HUMAN NEEDS"
The basic human necessities that correctional facilities are required by the Constitution to provide to inmates. Beyond food, warmth, and exercise, the court system has been unable to establish exactly what these needs are.

mous toll this screening process took on the courts, Congress passed the Prison Litigation Reform Act (1996), which, among other things, placed strict limits on the number of cases an inmate can file in federal court. It also forced prisoners to pay their own court costs.[61] Within a year after the act was passed, Section 1983 cases filed by inmates in federal courts dropped 90 percent.[62] Prisoners began to file their claims in state courts, providing many states with an incentive to adopt laws similar to the federal statute. As a result, the broad issue of prisoners' rights has faded somewhat into the background, replaced in the mind of the public and many corrections officials by the issues discussed in the following section.

CONTEMPORARY DILEMMAS IN CORRECTIONS

One of the earliest references to a prison on what is now American soil appears in the records of the colony of Massachusetts, circa 1629. In this document, the colony leadership ordered that "there shall be a sufficient fence erected about the common prison, in Boston, [and] house of correction such as may debar persons from conversing with the prisoners." Different though they are in other respects, this early house of correction and the new maximum-security penitentiary in Florence, Colorado, both have the same primary goal: to erect a "fence" between "prisoners" and "persons" to make the community a safer place.

As we have seen in the past two chapters, however, this fence—whether made of wood, barbed wire, or reinforced concrete—cannot completely separate the prison community from society at large or its problems. Every era has its "prison crises," and in most cases the crises reflect social and political conditions outside the prison walls. In this section, we will discuss three issues that are confronting the American corrections system at the dawn of the twenty-first century, as well as the conditions that have fostered them: overcrowding, the spread of acquired immune deficiency syndrome (AIDS) among the prison population, and the questions surrounding prisoners who work for pay behind bars.

Figure 14.7 State-by-State Prison Overcrowding

In 1998, a group of corrections planners and researchers set out to project the extent of the prison overcrowding problem in each of the fifty states. According to their study, which relied heavily on information provided by state corrections departments, forty states believed that inmate population growth would continue to such an extent in their jurisdiction that the problem was "critical," "very serious," or "serious." (Note that two states—New Hampshire and North Carolina—did not respond to the researchers' request for information.)

Overcrowding

American prisons have had to deal with the problem of crowding since the earliest model penitentiaries in New York and Pennsylvania. For reasons discussed in Chapter 13, however, the past three decades have seen a particular spurt in the number of incarcerated Americans. Today, state prisons are operating at 115 percent capacity, meaning that these institutions are holding 115 inmates for every 100 that they were designed to house. (See Figure 14.7 to get an idea of the prevalence of the prison overcrowding problem.) Federal prisons are currently operating at 119 percent of capacity.

When we say that these numbers reflect "overcrowding," we are

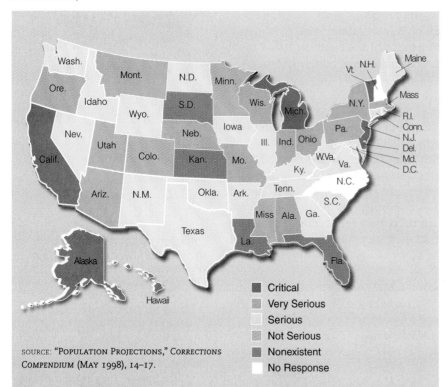

Critical
Very Serious
Serious
Not Serious
Nonexistent
No Response

SOURCE: "POPULATION PROJECTIONS," CORRECTIONS COMPENDIUM (MAY 1998), 14–17.

not referring to an established standard. No such standard exists, though different organizations do have opinions about how many prisoners are too many. The American Correctional Association Commission on Accreditation for Corrections, for example, has stated that prisoners who spend less than ten hours a day in their room or cell should have a floor area of at least 60 square feet. For those who are confined more than ten hours a day, the personal floor area should be at least 80 square feet.[63] Such conditions would, in fact, be sheer luxury in many facilities. On a practical level, overcrowding has come to refer to an environment in which the number of inmates compromises the effective operation of the institution.

The Consequences of Overcrowding. As the inmate-to-staff ratio increases, more pressure is placed on correctional officers to supervise larger populations of convicts. Security procedures such as taking head counts and routine procedures such as meals become more difficult. The amount of resources, such as library and recreational space, is limited, leaving prisoners restless and discontented. All these factors create a less manageable environment, which can increase inmate-inmate and inmate-staff violence. To control a large, unruly population, correctional officials must invariably employ harsher methods of discipline, only worsening the situation.[64] Overcrowding caused the first outbreak of prison riots in this country, in the 1920s. At the time of the Lucasville prison riot in 1993, in which nine inmates were killed, the Ohio prison system was operating at 175 percent of prisoner capacity.

In 1998, thirty-nine of the fifty states had, by their own estimation, "serious," "very serious," or "critical" overcrowding problems.[65] Corrections officials have generally reacted to this crisis by employing three strategies: front-door reduction, back-door reduction, and capacity expansion.[66] *Front-door reduction* strategies are designed to reduce the number of inmates admitted to prison, shorten the length of sentences, or divert wrongdoers to the community-based sanctions discussed in Chapter 12. *Back-door reduction* strategies, in contrast, focus on increasing the number of inmates released from prison. These programs include sentence reductions for "good time" (also discussed in Chapter 12) and parole (which will be addressed in Chapter 15). Some states use *trap door reductions* when severe overcrowding requires the emergency releases of groups of inmates with less than six months to serve. As we saw in the last chapter, many jurisdictions are reacting to the crisis by building new prisons and jails, or *increasing capacity*, a solution that has limited prospects for alleviating the problem in the long run.[67]

Overcrowding and the Courts. Some corrections systems have taken the opposite approach: instead of creating more space, they are attempting to fit more inmates into the existing space. One such strategy is known as **double-celling,** because officials place two prisoners in a cell designed for one. Double-celling was given the judicial stamp of approval in two separate cases. The first, *Bell v. Wolfish* (1979),[68] which we discussed in this last chapter, saw the Supreme Court rule that double-bunking and other restrictions placed on pretrial detainees were acceptable, given the security concerns of prison officials. In the second, *Rhodes v. Chapman* (1981),[69] the Supreme Court ruled that the practice does not automatically violate an inmate's Eighth Amendment rights—"the Constitution does not mandate comfortable prisons," wrote Justice Lewis Powell in the majority opinion. (See *CJ in Focus— Landmark Cases: Rhodes v. Chapman on the next page.*) A number of lower courts have followed the *Rhodes* precedent in approving double-bunking, most recently in New York State.[70]

DOUBLE-CELLING
The practice of placing two inmates in a cell that is designed for one, usually occurs in facilities with prison populations that exceed the institution's capacity.

"It isn't true that convicts live like animals: animals have more room to move around."

—Mario Vargas Llosa,
Peruvian author (1984)

CJ in Focus

Landmark Cases:

Rhodes v. Chapman

Kelly Chapman and Richard Jaworski, roommates at the Southern Ohio Correctional Facility (SOCF) in Lucasville, Ohio, filed a complaint against the facility seeking the end of the practice of "double-celling," in which two inmates were placed in a cell designed for one. Chapman and Jaworski claimed that the practice violated the Constitution by confining cellmates too closely together, which led to overcrowding, which in turn led to increased tensions and hostilities among inmates. The District Court found that double-celling was indeed "cruel and unusual punishment" as prohibited by the Eighth Amendment, a ruling that the Supreme Court addressed in its consideration of the case.

Rhodes v. Chapman
United States Supreme Court
452 U.S. 337 (1981)
http://laws.findlaw.com/US/452/337.html

In the Words of the Court . . .

Mr. Justice POWELL, majority opinion

* * * *

The Eighth Amendment, in only three words, imposes the constitutional limitation upon punishments: they cannot be "cruel and unusual." * * * No static "test" can exist by which courts determine whether conditions of confinement are cruel and unusual, for the Eighth Amendment "must draw its meaning from the evolving standards of decency that mark the progress of a maturing society."

* * * *

But conditions that cannot be said to be cruel and unusual under contemporary standards are not unconstitutional. To the extent that such conditions are restrictive and even harsh, they are part of the penalty that criminal offenders pay for their offenses against society.

* * * *

The double celling made necessary by the unanticipated increase in prison population did not lead to deprivations of essential food, medical care, or sanitation. Nor did it increase violence among inmates or create other conditions intolerable for prison confinement. Although job and educational opportunities diminished marginally as a result of double celling, limited work hours and delay before receiving education do not inflict pain, much less unnecessary and wanton pain; deprivations of this kind simply are not punishments. We would have to wrench the Eighth Amendment from its language and history to hold that delay of these desirable aids to rehabilitation violates the Constitution.

* * * *

[T]here is no evidence that double-celling under these circumstances either inflicts unnecessary or wanton pain or is grossly disproportionate to the severity of crimes warranting imprisonment. At most, these considerations amount to a theory that double celling inflicts pain. Perhaps they reflect an aspiration toward an ideal environment for long-term confinement. But the Constitution does not mandate comfortable prisons, and prisons of SOCF's type, which house persons convicted of serious crimes, cannot be free of discomfort.

* * * *

Decision: The Court agreed that the practice of double celling could cause the inmates pain. It would not go so far as to say, however, that double celling "unnecessarily and wantonly" caused pain, and therefore reversed the lower court's decision, ruling that the practice did not violate the Eighth Amendment. The Court's *Chapman* decision set a high standard for those who wished to show that the conditions of their confinement are cruel and unusual. Unless the conditions are obviously "sordid," the Court seemed to be saying, courts should not infringe upon the ability of correctional authorities to run prisons.

For Critical Analysis: In an earlier case, the Court ruled that "deliberate indifference" to an inmate's medical needs does constitute "cruel and unusual punishment." How does that situation differ from the one described in this case? What would have to be the effects of double-celling for it to be considered cruel and unusual?

Note: Triple asterisks (* * *) indicate that a few words or sentences have been deleted and quadruple asterisks (* * * *) indicate that an entire paragraph (or more) has been omitted from the opinion.

This does not mean, however, that "anything goes" as far as overcrowding is concerned. In 1992, the U.S. District Court for Utah ruled that shelter was a "basic human need," and that if officials at the Utah State Prison double-bunked prisoners in 44-square-foot cells, they would be guilty of "deliberate indifference" because the negative consequences of such a move for the well-being of the inmates were obvious.[71] Officials of the Harris County Jail in Texas, which was overcrowded to the extent that 2,700 inmates were sleeping on the floor, were also found to be deliberately indifferent to the suffering such conditions could cause.[72] In 1997, for the first time, the U.S. Department of Justice signed an agreement with local corrections officials to alleviate conditions of overcrowding. The agreement requires jails in Clay County, Georgia, to provide each inmate with more space and a mattress, mattress cover, sheets, pillow, blanket, washcloth, and towel as well.[73]

Health Care in Prison and Inmates with AIDS

Space is not the only scarce resource affected by overcrowding. Correctional budgets are also feeling the strain of the increased number of inmates in American prisons and jails. Health-care services, in particular, have become an area of grave concern for correctional officials. According to a report commissioned by the Department of Justice, the increase in spending on correctional health-care services over the past two decades has been greater than that of all other correctional services combined.[74]

Today, the federal government spends $9.70 a day to provide health care for each of its 120,000 inmates, and state systems spend a daily average of $6.59 for each of their charges. These average costs per inmate are expected to grow even more quickly as the prison population ages because older prisoners require far more medical services than younger ones. Nationwide, the average cost of housing a prisoner for a year is about $20,000, compared to $67,000 for inmates over fifty-five years of age; nearly 100 percent of the extra cost is attributable to medical expenses.[75]

Cutting Costs. As prison administrators attempt to cut their health-care bills, they cannot lose sight of their constitutional requirements to care for prisoners. The boundaries of these requirements were established by the Supreme Court in *Estelle v. Gamble* (1976).[76] As was noted in the section on prisoners' rights earlier in this chapter, the Court stated that "deliberate indifference to serious medical needs of prisoners constitutes the 'unnecessary and wanton infliction of pain'" as determined by the Eighth Amendment. Furthermore, in *City of Revere v. Massachusetts General Hospital* (1983),[77] the Court held that government entities must take all reasonable steps to make sure that medical care needed by those in prisons or jails is provided.

Both rulings provide prison administrators with a great deal of "wiggle room" in the level of health care. Under *Estelle,* it is quite difficult to prove that a facility "deliberately" provided substandard levels of health care, and *Revere* simply states that the government must see that the medical care is provided without specifying *who* must provide it. Consequently, a number of jurisdictions have implemented programs that require inmates who can afford to pay for at least part of their medical expenses to do so.[78] In Oklahoma County,

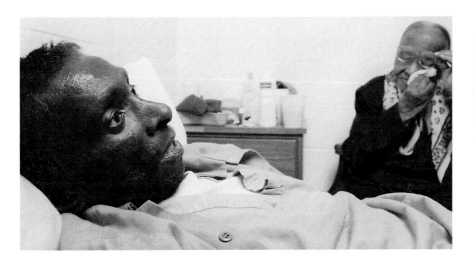

Clifford Williams, an inmate at Piedmond Correctional Center in Salisbury, North Carolina, is shown here in the facility's health care unit, suffering from AIDS. Williams asked prison officials to commute his sentence so that he could die at home, but his request was denied. Do you think there are any circumstances when such a request could be granted? Explain your answer.

for example, jail inmates must pay an $8 fee each time they visit the facility's medical center.

Besides fee systems, prison administrators are turning to a number of other strategies to cut expenses. In 1997, the Colorado Department of Corrections was able to cut medical costs at its nineteen facilities by 27.5 percent in seven months by turning its services over to a health-maintenance organization (HMO). Furthermore, jails—lacking the on-site medical facilities available in most prisons—often contract with nearby hospitals to provide health-care services. To save money, some city and county governments are paying these hospitals an annual lump sum per inmate, instead of being charged separately for each visit. Although this practice may reduce medical costs by millions of dollars a year, it also gives the hospitals an incentive to cut corners on service, as they have been paid for a service before it is provided.

In 1998, such concerns prompted the New York State attorney general's office to investigate St. Barnabas Hospital, which had just received a $342 million contract to prove health care for New York City jails. Inmate complaints about medical service increased 404 percent in the first ten months of the contract, and the hospital was charged with, among other things, ignoring a sore on an AIDS patient's upper arm until most of the limb had to be cut away to prevent further infection.[79]

AIDS and the Correctional Institution. Managing inmates with AIDS is one of the greatest economic, administrative, and humanitarian challenges facing prison officials today. Caused by the human immunodeficiency virus (HIV), AIDS attacks the bloodstream and destroys the body's ability to protect itself against a wide variety of diseases. The two main groups at risk to contract AIDS through the transmission of bodily fluids such as semen or blood are intravenous drug users and those who engage in unprotected anal sex. As both groups are overrepresented among inmates, it is not surprising that HIV and AIDS are relatively widespread in correctional facilities.[80] In fact, the incidence of AIDS among the prison population is six times that of the general population. In 1995, the latest year for which reliable statistics are available, 2.3 percent of the federal and state male prison population was HIV-positive, while 4.0 percent of female inmates in state and federal prisons were infected with the disease. Furthermore 104 out of every 10,000 prisoners died from AIDS-related causes that year.[81] (See Figure 14.8 for a list of the states where the disease is most prominent in the prison population.)

Prison administrators have several incentives to reduce AIDS in the prison population. On a practical level, caring for AIDS patients is extremely expensive, costing from $70,000 to $100,000 per year, compared to $22,000 for a healthy inmate. More important, however, is the fact that an inmate who contracts HIV while in prison and is then is returned to society poses a threat to other citizens. Because the disease can remain dormant for long periods of time, freed prisoners might not even be aware that they are carrying the disease.

Figure 14.8 Highest Incidences of HIV

According to the Department of Justice, HIV infection is most prominent among the inmate populations of correctional facilities in the Northeast. As you can see, five of the seven states with HIV-positive rates over the national average of 2.3 percent for male inmates and 4.0 percent for female inmates are located in the Northeast.

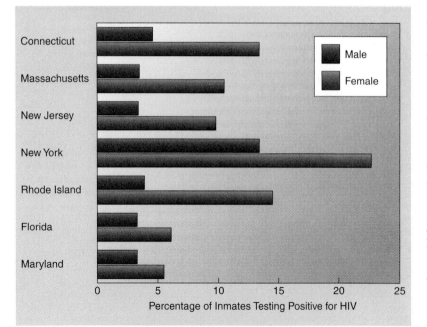

SOURCE: BUREAU OF JUSTICE STATISTICS, *HIV IN PRISONS AND JAILS, 1995* (WASHINGTON, D.C.: U.S. DEPARTMENT OF JUSTICE, AUGUST 1997), 6.

CJ in Focus

A Question of Ethics

Should Inmates Be Tested for HIV?

When an inmate bit Martin Nowak, an officer at the Wende Correctional Facility in upstate New York, on the hand, the guard was terrified. The bite had broken Nowak's skin, and the inmate's bleeding gums and open sores were signs that he was possibly infected with HIV. Nowak immediately began taking medical precautions in case the prisoner was infected, but he could never be sure. In New York, inmates enjoy the same right to keep their HIV status confidential, as do all citizens.

Since the issue first arose in the early 1980s, many prisons have refused to institute mandatory testing policies or to disclose the identity of inmates who are infected with HIV or AIDS. First of all, the activities that carry the highest risk for contracting the disease—intravenous drug use and sexual activity—are prohibited by prison rules. Second, HIV confidentiality has generally been considered important in all segments of society because of potential discrimination and violence against carriers. A number of corrections systems, however, have decided that mandatory testing of prisoners is necessary to protect against situations such as the one in which Martin Nowak finds himself. To date, seventeen states have implemented such programs in their prisons, and two states—Mississippi and Alabama—completely segregate inmates with HIV from the rest of the prison population.

Proponents of HIV testing see it as a "win-win" proposition. Inmates who test positive are able to receive the treatment they need, while other inmates and prison staff members are protected by the knowledge. Many prisoners' rights advocates, however, point out that a person who has committed a crime does not surrender all privacy rights. This is a concern because an inmate with HIV/AIDS often becomes the target of violence and harassment from other inmates and correctional officers. One Texas prisoner, who hides his HIV-positive status by saying he suffers from sclerosis of the liver, describes the general reaction by fellow inmates to those who are infected: "They'll burn up your room or stick a knife under your bed or plant some marijuana so the guards can find it and put you in the hole. It's a dirty business in here." This kind of treatment can be partly explained by negative attitudes toward those with HIV/AIDS, which exist in the general population as well as the prison population. Furthermore, in the highly competitive and predatory arena of prison culture, certain inmates will take advantage of any perceived weakness.

For Critical Analysis: Under what circumstances, if any, do you believe prisons are justified in forcing inmates to undergo HIV tests, and segregating them if they have the disease?

Reducing AIDS. Correctional administrators have turned to several different strategies to reduce HIV/AIDS rates in prisons and jails. In a short-term solution known as *compassionate release*, terminally ill inmates are allowed to leave the institution before the end of their terms. This option has humanitarian benefits—it gives the inmate a chance to die outside prison walls—but does little to limit the risk for other prisoners. Furthermore, some question whether illness is sufficient grounds for early release under any circumstances.[82]

Many prison officials see the twin strategies of education and prevention as the best hope of significantly reducing HIV/AIDS rates in prison. To this end, they are turning to outside help. According to research done by the National Institute of Justice (NIJ) and the Centers for Disease Control and Prevention (CDC), virtually every correctional facility collaborates with public health agencies on some level. These collaborations include disease surveillance, testing and screening, staff training, and education and prevention programs.[83]

Education provided through instructor- and peer-led counseling programs can make sure that inmates are aware of the ways HIV is transmitted. Prevention programs such as giving drug-addicted inmates clean needles and dispensing free condoms are less common, mostly due to political opposition from those who believe such programs would "send the wrong message" that drug use and sex between prisoners are acceptable behaviors. Since 1990, seventeen states have passed laws that allow corrections departments to test inmates for HIV/AIDS without the inmates' permission in order to protect prison employees and other prisoners. As the feature *CJ in Focus—A Question of Ethics: Should Inmates Be Tested for HIV?* shows, these programs are extremely controversial because of their confidentiality implications.

WAREHOUSE PRISONS
A perception of modern prisons as institutions that subject inmates to an idle and regimented existence while providing few opportunities for rehabilitation.

CONTRACT LABOR SYSTEM
The system in which a correctional facility would sell inmate labor to a private employer, who would provide the inmates with the raw materials to produce goods for sale.

LEASE SYSTEM
A variation of the contract system in which the private employer not only oversaw inmate labor but also took responsibility for the food, shelter, and discipline of the inmate laborers.

The Prison Workforce

Many observers find the prison living conditions we have discussed in this chapter disheartening. James E. Robertson, a professor of sociology and corrections at Mankato State University, sums up life behind bars in maximum- and supermaximum-security prisons thusly:

> Offenders are largely idle, and live in a divided inmate subculture weakened by [internal] conflict. Prison authorities provide them with little more than the necessities of daily survival—food, shelter, clothing, medical care, and exercise.[84]

Critics have labeled institutions where such conditions exist **warehouse prisons** because they "offer an existence, not a life" and "their inhabitants survive rather than live."[85] Proponents of the "no frills movement," believing that inmates should not have the opportunity to live a fulfilling life, find the concept of warehouse prisons laudatory. Opponents believe, however, that such conditions are unhealthful not only for prisoners, but for society as a whole. Warehouse prisons, they warn, dehumanize inmates to the point that they are unfit to return to society, even though 95 percent of them will eventually do so. To remedy the situation, some are calling for a large-scale return to an idea from America's corrections past—putting the prison force to work.

The History of Prison Work in the United States. As we saw in Chapter 13, America's earliest prison experts saw work as a centerpiece of both the primary and the rehabilitative function of incarceration. When prison officials realized that the new penitentiaries would be quite costly to maintain and operate, they created the **contract labor system.** In this system, the state sold the labor of its inmates to private firms, which provided raw materials and oversaw the production of convict-made goods for the open market. Massachusetts began contracting its prison labor in 1807, and the system was widespread in the North by the mid-1800s. In the South, inmate labor was available under the **lease system,** which was similar to the contract system, but gave the leasing firm more responsibility for the inmates. The company would provide the prisoners with food, clothes, and shelter, as well as discipline, in return for their labor. In essence, under the lease system the private firm acted as a penal institution.

By the end of the nineteenth century, organized labor unions had begun to protest the use of prison labor; the unions feared that in a shrinking job market low-priced prison workers would "steal" work from their members. Both the contract and the lease system were easy targets as they were rife with corruption, with prison officials receiving kickbacks from private corporations in return for cheap labor. Treatment of the inmates, especially in the South, was sometimes atrocious. In 1885, for example, twenty-year-old Martin Tabert was arrested for vagrancy in Florida and sentenced to ninety days in jail. Tabert was subsequently leased to the Putnam Lumber Company for $20, and after two months of shoveling mud in "hip-deep water for fifteen hours a day,"

Inmates at the Correctional Facility at Putnamaville, Indiana, assemble Hoosier Hickory Historic Furniture chairs, earning up to $7.95 an hour. What are the arguments for and against prison labor?

he died. Negative publicity surrounding the incident helped end inmate leasing in Florida.[86]

As the contract and lease systems gradually disappeared, they were replaced by the **state use system.** As the name suggests, goods produced by prison labor in the state use system are purchased only by other state institutions and never entered the free market. Furthermore, private firms were no longer involved; the entire operation was run by government agencies. In the North, prisoners labored on prison property, and in the South, chain gangs and work farms were the norm. (For a discussion of the return of the chain gang, see the feature *Criminal Justice in Action—Back on the Chain Gang* at the end of this chapter.)

Prison Work Today. Following the Great Depression of 1929, Congress passed a number of laws that made the interstate transportation and sale of prison-made goods a federal crime. These restrictions were not lifted until the Prison Industry Enhancement Act (PIE) of 1979,[87] and it is only since then that prison industry has begun to recover. Still, in 1997, only 6.2 percent of the prison population were working, compared to 90 percent in 1885.[88]

The largest employer of inmates is the federal government. Federal Prisons Industries, Inc. (FPI), often referred to by its trade name UNICOR, manages the work of nearly 20,000 federal convicts. FPI operates on the state use system, meaning that only other agencies of the federal government can purchase its products. In addition, the language of PIE allows private firms to employ prison labor and sell the resulting goods on the open market under certain circumstances. To qualify for a PIE program, the private firm must agree to pay inmates the prevailing wage for the particular job, and it must prove that convict labor does not displace free labor in the area. (See Figure 14.9 for some items made by prison labor.)

Opponents of prison labor raise the same objections as did their forerunners a century ago. They see the programs as exploitive (prisoners earn between $0.23 and $1.15 an hour for regular prison jobs, although inmate employees of UNICOR earn wages that are closer to those earned by civilians in similar jobs), and they believe inmate workers are used as cheaper replacements for civilian workers. Furthermore, "no frills" advocates do not believe prisoners deserve the "right" to work or to receive pay for their efforts.

Those who support inmate labor programs, however, point to their benefits:

- They reduce inmate idleness and consequently promote order within the prisons, reducing incidents of inmate-inmate and inmate-staff violence.

- Profits from inmate industries reduce the cost to taxpayers of supporting penal institutions.

- Wages are earmarked to support the inmate's family and to provide restitution for victims of her or his crime.

The most important goal of prison work, however, is to rehabilitate the inmates and reduce their chances of recidivism.[89] Most felons are poorly educated and, with a prison record, are unlikely to find a good-paying job when released from incarceration. As a result, they have an incentive to return to crime. Many reformers believe that prison employment systems can provide inmates with skills and a proper work ethic and can help them find a job that provides adequate wages. As nearly every inmate is eventually returned to the community, prison work programs are one means of trying to ensure that he or she will not pose a threat to fellow citizens.

Figure 14.9 Items Produced by Prison Labor

The old stereotype of prisoner workers churning out license plates has become quite outdated. Although license plates are still manufactured in prisons, the industry has become significantly more diverse. The items listed here are only a few of those offered to government agencies by UNICOR (Federal Prison Industries, Inc.) in 1999.

- Guided missile propulsion equipment
- Fire control radar equipment
- Vehicular brake, steering components
- Water purification equipment
- Night vision equipment, emitted and reflected radiation
- Prescription eyeglasses
- Sofas
- Ergonomic seating
- Draperies, awnings, and shades
- Paints and artists' brushes
- Men's underwear and nightwear

SOURCE: UNICOR, SCHEDULE OF PRODUCTS, 1999 (WASHINGTON, D.C.: U.S. DEPARTMENT OF JUSTICE, 1999).

"Number one, a prison needs to be a place they want to get out of and don't want to come back to. If it's not more difficult in prison than it is out, you're beating your head against the wall in the effort against [repeat offenders]."

—Wayne Garner, *Commissioner of the Georgia Department of Corrections (1998)*

STATE USE SYSTEM
A system of using inmate labor under which the goods produced by such labor can only be sold to other government industries or organizations and cannot compete on the free market.

Criminal Justice in Action

Back on the Chain Gang

Prison work is not always something that an inmate would desire or that a proponent of "no frills" institutions would dislike. In his 1932 autobiography, Robert Burns described the physical and psychological effects of serving on a chain gang:

Torture every day. Any idea of reformation, any idea of trying to inoculate ideas of decency, manners or good and right thinking in the convict, is prohibited. All the convicts get is abuse, curses, punishment, and filth. In a few weeks all are reduced to the same level, just animals, and treated worse than animals.[90]

During the 1930s and 1940s, such descriptions were instrumental in the banning of chain gangs—a term used to describe small groups of convicts who are chained to each other with heavy steel or iron shackles while doing hard labor outside prison walls. Today, as chain gangs are returning to the corrections landscape, Burns's description—given current public opinion—would probably serve as a testimonial in favor of the practice.

Though opponents call chain gangs degrading, cruel, humiliating, and uncivilized, they seem to have captured the imagination of many Americans who feel that life behind bars is too easy, replete with cable television, steak dinners, and elaborate gyms.[91] Speaking for many politicians who have worked to reinstate chain gangs, a Mississippi state representative said, "We want a prisoner to look like a prisoner, to smell like a prisoner. When you see [a prisoner working on a chain gang dressed in a striped uniform], you'll say, 'I didn't know we had zebras in Mississippi.'"[92]

FOLLOWING ALABAMA'S LEAD

On May 3, 1995, Alabama became the first state since Georgia in the 1960s to place its prisoners on chain gangs. The Alabama Department of Corrections referred to them as "Alternative Thinking Units," and they were primarily reserved for male inmates who had misbehaved while in prison. After being assigned to one of these units, prisoners worked 180 days, twelve to thirteen hours a day, six days a week, cleaning debris and overgrown grass from state roadsides.[93]

Three other states soon followed Alabama's lead. The Arizona legislature mandated the use of chain gangs for jail inmates, who are paid ten cents an hour to clean up litter, control weeds, cut railroad ties, and perform other menial tasks. The Florida statute refers to chain gangs as "restricted labor squads" and only allows chained maximum-security prisoners to work on prison grounds. Iowa's "highly secured work groups" are comprised of randomly chosen low- to medium-risk prisoners who have violated disciplinary rules. Eligible Iowa prisoners can volunteer for chain gangs and are rewarded by having time taken off their sentence.[94] Today, Wisconsin, Indiana, and Oklahoma also use chain gangs, and a number of state legislatures are considering adding the practice to their correctional systems.

FROM LEASING TO SHAMING

The original justification for chain gangs was economic. After the Civil War, the South lost its primary source of cheap labor: slaves. To replenish the workforce, southern landowners would lease inmates from local prisons and jails. In 1871, Virginia's Supreme Court upheld convict leasing by ruling that a prisoner is essentially a "slave of the state."[95]

Today, proponents offer a number of penal goals for chain gangs: (1) they save the state money by having convicts perform public works at low or nonexistent wages; (2) they provide a general and specific deterrent to crime; and (3) they aid in rehabilitation by offering the inmates a constructive outlet for their energies.[96] These claims have, however, proved difficult to back up with factual evidence. The primary, if often unstated, motivations behind chain gangs appear instead to be shame and humiliation. Combining elements of punishment and deterrence, the theory of "shaming" holds that being chained by the ankles and forced to work in public will humiliate inmates to the point where they will not want to repeat the experience. Members of Arizona chain gangs operate in the middle of large cities such as Phoenix, and other states have reported that drivers shout insults at the inmates or stop by the side of the highway to watch the spectacle.[97] "It's embarrassing and degrading," said one prisoner of the ordeal. "I hate to think of my people seeing me this way."[98]

CHAIN GANG LITE

Legal opposition to chain gangs has primarily focused on Eighth Amendment protections against cruel and unusual punishment. In the early days of chain gangs, such punishment was often barbarous. Inmates were overworked, beaten and whipped, and subjected to poor living conditions. The death rates in some of the chain gangs were as high as 45 percent.[99] Using the Eighth Amendment and the standard set in *Weems v. United States* (1910)[100]—that the level of punishment should fit the level of the crime—state courts were able to place a number of restrictions on chain gang operations.[101]

Modern chain gangs are not as susceptible to legal challenges. In *Trop v. Dulles* (1957),[102] the Supreme Court confirmed that the Eighth Amendment derives its meaning "from the evolving standards of decency that mark the progress of a maturing society." In other words, the definition of "cruel and unusual punishment" is not static, but changes with the values of society. As polls show Americans overwhelmingly in favor of chain gangs, legal experts believe the practice falls within the bounds of acceptable forms of punishment.[103]

The Supreme Court further established the standards for determining Eighth Amendment violations in *Gregg v. Georgia* (1976),[104] stating that a punishment must not "involve the unnecessary and wanton infliction of pain." Whatever their hardships, today's chain gangs generally do not meet these criteria. Indeed, they have been dubbed "Chain Gang Lite" in comparison with earlier practices.[105] The chains are lighter (some counties use plastic instead of metal), the hours are shorter, and the sanitary conditions of the work are better than those suffered by earlier inmates.

ALABAMA BOWS OUT

Some legal experts believe the best way to attack chain gangs is through the "deliberate indifference" standard established in *Wilson v. Seiter* (discussed earlier in the chapter). Evidence could easily suggest, they say, that prison officials are aware of the physical risk to inmate safety posed by the conditions under which chain gangs operate.[106] In fact, when Alabama abandoned its chain gang policy only one year after its installation, state officials blamed the "public relations disaster" that followed an incident in which a correctional officer shot and killed an inmate involved in a fight. (Convicts in Alabama continue to work on state highways. Although their feet are still in chains, they are no longer chained to one another.)

Inmates on a chain gang near Prattville, Alabama.

Chain gangs have presented other problems to prison administrators. The costs of providing extra supervision and equipment to prisoners appear to outweigh any savings realized in other areas. Iowa's Department of Correction, for example, needs nearly $3 million to create the necessary work projects for inmates.[107] Furthermore, many convicts are oblivious to the supposed "shaming" effects of the punishment—they actually prefer chain gangs to the monotony of prison.

In the immediate future, it seems unlikely that these drawbacks will cause other states to follow Alabama's lead and scale back their chain gang programs. The enduring image of the chain gang as harsh punishment for violent criminals has made it popular with the voting public and therefore ensured its continued existence in those jurisdictions where it already exists. The only threat to chain gangs would be, it appears, a challenge to the practice on Eighth Amendment grounds that reaches the Supreme Court, an event that has not as yet taken place.

Key Terms

contract labor system   512

"deliberate indifference"   504

deprivation model   495

double-celling   507

"hands-off" doctrine   503

"identifiable human needs"   505

importation model   492

indigenous model   492

inmate code   493

lease system   512

principle of least eligibility   490

prisonization   492

relative deprivation   495

state use system   513

total institutions   490

warehouse prisons   512

Chapter Summary

1. **Explain the concept of prison as a total institution.** Though many people spend time in partial institutions—schools, companies where they work, and religious organizations—only in prison is every aspect of an inmate's life controlled, and that is why prisons are called total institutions. Every detail for every prisoner is fully prescribed and managed.

2. **Contrast the indigenous model of prison behavior with the importation model.** According to the indigenous model, because prisoners are deprived of liberty, autonomy, material goods and services, among other things, they must create a new social outlook. Hence the prison culture evolves from within the institution. In contrast, those who subscribe to the importation model argue that offenders bring their own individual cultural attitudes to prison, including the "us versus them" attitude.

3. **List and briefly describe the possible patterns of inmate behavior, which are driven by the inmate's personality and values.** (a) Professional criminals adapt to prison by "doing time" and follow the rules in order to get out quickly. (b) Those who are "jailing" establish themselves within the power structure of prison culture. These are often veterans of juvenile detention centers and other prisons. (c) Those who are "gleaning" are working to improve themselves for return to society. (d) "Disorganized" criminals have mental impairments or low IQs and therefore are unable to adapt to prison culture.

4. **Indicate some of the reasons for violent behavior in prisons.** (a) To separate the powerful from the weak and to establish a prisoner hierarchy; (b) to minimize one's own probability of being a target of assault; (c) to enhance one's self-image; (d) to obtain sexual relief; and (e) to obtain material goods through extortion or robbery.

5. **List and briefly explain the six general job categories among correctional officers.** (a) Block officers, who supervise cell blocks or are on block guard duty; (b) work detail supervisors, who oversee the cafeteria, prison store, and laundry, for example; (c) industrial shop and school officers, who generally oversee workshop and educational programs; (d) yard officers, who patrol the prison yard when prisoners are allowed there; (e) tower guards, who work in isolation; and (f) those who hold administrative building assignments, such as prison gate guards, overseers of visitation procedures, and so on.

6. **List the five types of correctional officers.** (a) Punitive, (b) custodial, (c) patronage, (d) therapist, and (e) integrative.

7. **Contrast the hands-off doctrine of prisoner law with the hands-on approach.** The hands-off doctrine assumes that the care of prisoners should be left entirely to prison officials and that it is not the place of judges to intervene. In contrast, the hands-on philosophy started in 1964 after the Supreme Court decision *Cooper v. Pate*. Prisoners have been able to file civil lawsuits, called Section 1983 petitions, when they felt their civil rights had been violated.

8. **Describe the procedural safeguards for a prisoner subjected to disciplinary measures.** (a) A fair hearing, (b) written notice at least twenty-four hours in advance of the hearing, (c) an opportunity to speak at the hearing, (d) an opportunity to call witnesses, and (e) the right to a written statement detailing the final decision and the reasons for that decision.

9. **List and explain three strategies being used to avoid prison overcrowding.** (a) Front-door strategies—reducing the number of prisoners admitted, reducing the length of sentences, or diverting wrongdoers to community-based sanctions;

(b) back-door strategies—increasing the number of prisoners released for "good time" and parole; and (c) increasing capacity—building new prisons and jails.

10. **Indicate two major problems prisons face besides overcrowding.** (a) Increased medical expenses, due in part to the increased number of prisoners who have AIDS or are HIV-positive; and (b) the attempt to change prisons from warehouse institutions into places where prisoners work.

Questions for Critical Analysis

1. Why is the principle of least eligibility relevant in today's political environment?

2. What is the major implication of the increasing median age of the prison population?

3. How does the deprivation model seek to explain prison violence?

4. What is the most demanding job assignment in the correctional institution hierarchy?

5. Why are so few Section 1983 petitions being made by prisoners today?

6. Why don't inmates who are transferred to super-max prisons have a right to a hearing?

7. Why is it often difficult for prisons to find out whether prisoners are HIV-positive?

8. Contrast the contract labor system with the lease system and with the state use system for prison workforces.

9. What are some of the reasons for the reimposition of chain gangs in the American corrections system?

10. What are some of the problems chain gangs present to prison administrators?

Selected Print and Electronic Resources

SUGGESTED READINGS

Burns, Robert E., and Matthew J. Manchini, *I Am a Fugitive from a Georgia Chain Gang!* Athens, GA: University of Georgia Press, 1997. This book chronicles the true saga of Robert E. Burns. After World War I he was a shell-shocked and penniless veteran. For a small transgression, he ended up in Georgia's penal system. His brutal treatment on the Georgia chain gang is intense reading.

Burton-Rose, Daniel, et al., eds., *The Celling of America: An Inside Look at the U.S. Prison Industry,* Monroe, ME: Common Courage Press, 1998. This book is an edited collection of articles written by criminals in prison as well as interviews with them. Two of the coeditors were in prison while the book was being put together. Their message is that the United States seems to be in an era of social vengeance. They describe the prison system as a bleak environment where brutality, substandard medical care, racism, and extremely crowded conditions are common. Many of the prisoners contend that conditions are getting worse each year.

Hassine, Victor, et al., *Life Without Parole: Living In Prison Today,* 2d ed., Los Angeles: Roxbury Publishing Company, 1999. These authors capture the essence of what it is like to be an inmate in prison with seemingly no chance for parole. The authors give a balanced view of day-to-day life in prison. The overwhelming impression is of constant boredom with a heavy overlay of barely suppressed violence.

Lichtenstein, Alexander C., *Twice the Work of Free Labor: The Political Economy of Convict Labor in the New South,* New York: Varso Books, 1997. The author examines prison industries in the southern part of the United States. He examines what prisoners do, how they are supervised, and how much they are paid. He analyzes why such a system is allowed to continue.

Palmer, John W., *Constitutional Rights of Prisoners,* 5th ed., Cincinnati, OH: Anderson Publishing Company, 1996. The author examines the basic constitutional underpinning of prisoners' rights. He examines how prisoners may file civil lawsuits under Section 1983 when they feel that their civil rights have been violated. He looks at the procedural safeguards available for prisoners subjected to discipline.

Zehr, Howard, ed., *Doing Life: Reflections of Men and Women Serving Life Sentences,* Intercourse, PA: Good Books, 1996. This is a collection of photos and edited interviews with almost sixty "lifers" in Pennsylvania prisons. The prisoners typically talk about their loneliness as well as how they cope with prison life.

MEDIA RESOURCES

The Farm: Angola, U.S.A. (1998) This is a black-and-white documentary depicting the day-to-day life in the

Louisiana State Penitentiary at Angola, the largest maximum-security prison in the country. Angola is a former slave plantation turned into a maximum-security "lifer" penitentiary. The facility houses almost 5,000 inmates. More than 85 percent of those who enter Angola will never leave. *The Farm* was nominated for an Oscar for best feature documentary in 1999.

Critically analyze this film:

1. Do you see evidence of any sort of "inmate code" at Angola? What aspects of "prisonization" (page 492) are evident?

2. How does the prospect of spending one's life behind bars color virtually every scene in the film?

3. Of the six inmates who are chronicled in different stages of their life sentences, how many believe they stand a good chance of making it out of Angola?

4. Warden Burl Cain said "If we keep their despair down and their hopes up, they won't try to escape." How can the inmates' hopes be kept up?

5.. The Italian newspaper *Corriere della Sera* describes Angola as "America's Gulag." Why do you think the paper refers to Angola this way, and what does the term mean?

Logging On

If you would like to find out how the federal government uses UNICOR—Federal Prison Industries, Inc.—to shop for affordable, high-quality goods and services, go to the homepage of UNICOR at:

www.unicor.gov/

When you are there, you can look at all of the products that are made by prisoners and get more information on UNICOR itself. Click on FAQs (frequently asked questions)

to find out everything you wanted to know about UNICOR.

You can link to all federal and state prison agencies by going to:

www.stadtcorrections.com/links/

If you want to know more about prisoners' slang, go to:

www.wco.com/~aerick/lingo.htm

Using the internet for Criminal Justice Analysis

INFOTRAC®
COLLEGE EDITION

1. Go to your InfoTrac College Edition at **www.infotrac-college.com/wadsworth/**. After you log on, type in the words:

Inmates, Inc.: In favor of prison labor

This article examines a study for the National Center for Policy Analysis called "Factories Behind Bars." Read the article and answer the following questions:

a. What are the benefits of increasing the number of prison employment programs?

b. What is the connection between prison employment and restitution for victims, if any?

c. By how much does the author of this study argue that the taxpayer cost of imprisonment would be reduced if 25 percent of prisoners worked for private enterprise over the next five to ten years?

d. Can prisoner employment be increased without heavy private sector involvement?

e. The study argues that eight steps must be taken to increase prisoner employment. Of the eight steps, which appears to be the most important and why?

f. This article presents only the positive side of increased prisoner employment. Can you think of any negative aspects of increased prisoner employment? What are they?

2. Prison gangs are an important part of prison life. The Florida Department of Corrections maintains a Security Threat Group Intelligence Unit (STGIU) that

has obtained detailed information on major prison gangs. Go to:

www.dc.state.fl.us/security/reports/gangs/prison.html

Once you are there, read the information on the six major prison gangs.

a. Which appears to be the most violent?

b. What is the predominant racial or ethnic make-up of prison gangs?

c. Which is the oldest prison gang?

d. Which prison gang has the most rivals or enemies?

e. Which gangs have a "kill on sight" relationship with each other?

f. What are the distinctions among the three gangs whose members are mostly Mexican Americans?

g. Why do you think tattoos are so popular among prison gang members?

h. Which gang members are the most secretive about admitting their membership in the gang?

Notes

1. Norval Morris, "The Contemporary Prison: 1965–Present," in *The Oxford History of Prisons: The Practice of Punishment in Western Society*, ed. Norval Morris and David J. Rothman (New York: Oxford University Press, 1995), 227.

2. Peter Finn, "No-Frills Prisons and Jails: A Movement in Flux," *Federal Probation* (September 1996), 35.

3. Kenneth Adams, "A Bull Market in Corrections," *The Prison Journal* (December 1996), 465, 467.

4. Edward W. Sieh, "Less Eligibility: The Upper Limits of Penal Policy," *Criminal Justice Policy Review* 3 (1989), 159.

5. Edward I. Koren, "Status Report: State Prisons and the Courts," *National Prison Project Journal* 13 (1992), 7.

6. Gregory Moorhead and Ricky W. Griffin, *Organizational Behavior*, 2d ed. (Boston: Houghton Mifflin, 1989), 497.

7. Erving Goffman, "On the Characteristics of Total Institutions," in *Asylums: Essays on the Social Situation of Mental Patients and Other Inmates* (New York: Doubleday, 1961), 6.

8. Justin Brooks, "How Can We Sleep While the Beds Are Burning: The Tumultuous Prison Culture of Attica Flourishes in American Prisons Twenty-Five Years Later," *Syracuse Law Journal* 47 (1996), 159.

9. Bureau of Justice Statistics, *Lifetime Likelihood of Going to State or Federal Prison* (Washington, D.C.: U.S. Department of Justice, March 1997), 1.

10. Craig Perkins, *National Corrections Reporting Program 1992* (Washington, D.C.: U.S. Department of Justice, 1994).

11. Connie L. Neeley, Laura Addison, and Delores Craig-Moreland, "Addressing the Needs of Elderly Offenders," *Corrections Today* (August 1997), 120.

12. Perkins, *National Corrections Reporting Program 1992.*

13. Donald Clemmer, *The Prison Community* (Boston: Christopher, 1940).

14. Gresham M. Sykes, *The Society of Captives: A Study of a Maximum Security Prison* (Princeton, NJ: Princeton University Press, 1958).

15. John Irwin and Donald R. Cressey, "Thieves, Convicts, and the Inmate Culture," *Social Problems* 10 (Fall, 1962), 142–55.

16. John Irwin, *Prisons in Turmoil* (Boston: Little, Brown, 1980), 67.

17. Gresham M. Sykes and Sheldon Messinger, "The Inmate Social System," in *Theoretical Studies in the Social Organization of the Prison,* ed. Richard A. Cloward (New York: Social Science Research Council, 1960), 6–10.

18. Robert Johnson, *Hard Time: Understanding and Reforming the Prison,* 2d ed. (Belmont, CA: Wadsworth Publishing Company, 1996), 133.

19. Jocelyn Pollock, "The Social World of the Prisoner," in *Prisons: Today and Tomorrow,* ed. Jocelyn Pollock (Gaithersburg, MD: Aspen Publishers, 1997), 246–59.

20. Michael Puisis, "Update on Public Health in Correctional Facilities," *Western Journal of Medicine* (December 1, 1998).

21. Anders Kaye, "Dangerous Places: The Right to Self-Defense in Prison and Prison Conditions," *University of Chicago Law Review* 63 (Spring 1996), 693.

22. 511 U.S. 825 (1994).

23. Lee H. Bowker, *Prison Victimization* (New York: Elsevier, 1981), 31–3.

24. Stephen C. Light, "The Severity of Assaults on Prison Officers: A Contextual Analysis," *Social Science Quarterly* 71 (1990), 267–84.

25. Lee H. Bowker, "An Essay on Prison Violence," in *Prison Violence in America,* ed. Michael Braswell, Steven Dillingham, and Reid Montgomery, Jr. (Cincinnati, OH: Anderson Publishing Co., 1985), 7–18.

26. Frank Tannenbaum, *Crime and Community* (Boston: Ginn & Co., 1938).

27. Randy Martin and Sherwood Zimmerman, "A Typology of the Causes of Prison Riots and an Analytical Extension to the 1986 Virginia Riot, *Justice Quarterly* 7 (1990), 711–37.

28. Bert Useem, "Disorganization and the New Mexico Prison Riot of 1980," *American Sociological Review* 50 (1985), 677–88.

29. Bert Useem and Peter Kimball, *State of Siege: U.S. Prison Riots 1971–1984* (New York: Oxford University Press, 1989), 4.

30. Stuart B. Klein, "Prisoners' Rights to Physical and Mental Health Care: A Modern Expansion of the Eighth Amendment's Cruel and Unusual Punishment Clause," *Fordham University Law Journal* 7 (1978), 1.

31. Herman Badillo and Milton Haynes, *A Bill of No Rights: Attica and the American Prison System* (New York: Outerbridge & Lazard, 1972), 42.

32. Mark Colvin, *The Penitentiary in Crisis: From Accommodation to Crisis in New Mexico* (Albany, NY: SUNY Press, 1992).

33. Michael S. Serrill and Peter Katel, "New Mexico: The Anatomy of a Riot," *Corrections Magazine* (April 1980), 6–7.

34. Useem and Kimball; and John J. DiIulio, *Governing Prisons* (New York: Free Press, 1987).

35. Badillo and Haynes, 26.

36. Cindy Struckman-Johnson, David Struckman-Johnson, Lila Rucker, Kurt Bumby, and Stephen Donaldson, "Sexual Coercion Reported by Men and Women in Prison," *Journal of Sex Research* 33 (1996), 67–74.

37. Christine A. Saum, Hilary L. Surratt, James A. Inciardi, and Rachael E. Bennett, "Sex in Prison: Exploring the Myths and Realities," *The Prison Journal* (December 1995), 413–30.

38. Mary Dallao, "How to Make Your Facility Safer," *Corrections Today* (December 1996), 101.

39. John J. DiIulio, Jr., No Escape: *The Future of American Corrections* (New York: BasicBooks, 1991), 268.

40. Jack Henry Abbott, *In the Belly of the Beast* (New York: Vintage Books, 1991), 54.

41. Michael Foucault, *Discipline and Punish: The Birth of the Prison* (New York: Pantheon Books, 1977), 128.

42. Lucien X. Lombardo, *Guards Imprisoned: Correctional Officers at Work* (Cincinnati, OH: Anderson Publishing Co., 1989), 51–71.

43. Ben M. Crouch, "The Book vs. the Boot: Two Styles of Guarding in a Southern Prison," in *The Keepers*, ed. Ben M. Couch (Springfield, IL: Thomas, 1980), 207–24.

44. Sarah Ben-David, "Staff-to-Inmate Relations in a Total Institution: A Model of Five Modes of Association," *International Journal of Offender Therapy and Comparative Criminology* 36 (1992), 213–5.

45. Gordon Hawkins, *The Prison: Policy and Practice* (Chicago: University of Chicago Press, 1976), 105.

46. Goffman, "Characteristics of Total Institutions," 7.

47. 5 U.S. 312 (1986).

48. *Stanley v. Hejirika* (U.S. Court of Appeals for the 4th Circuit, No. 97-62124, 1998).

49. 503 U.S. 1 (1992).

50. Kathy Walt, "Less-Experienced Guards Fall Victim to Prison Tensions," *Houston Chronicle* (October 16, 1994), 1.

51. Craig Haney, "Psychology and the Limits to Prison Pain," *Psychology, Public Policy, and Law* 3 (December 1997), 499.

52. 378 U.S. 546 (1964).

53. 418 U.S. 539 (1974).

54. 429 U.S. 97 (1976).

55. *Daniels v. Williams*, 474 U.S. 327 (1986); and *Whitley v. Albers*, 475 U.S. 312 (1986).

56. 501 U.S. 296 (1991).

57. *Ibid.*, 294, 304.

58. 515 U.S. 472 (1995).

59. Genevieve Anton, "Lawmakers Seek to Halt Silly Lawsuits by Prisoners," *Colorado Springs Gazette-Telegraph* (March 22, 1998), NEWS1.

60. Andrew Peyton Thomas, "Rule of Law: Congress Revokes Prisoners' Access to Frivolous Appeals," *Wall Street Journal* (July 3, 1996), A11.

61. Public Law Number 104-34 110 Stat. 1321 (1996).

62. Anton, NEWS1.

63. American Correctional Association, *Standards for Adult Correctional Institutions*, 2d ed. (Laurel, MD: American Correctional Association, 1981), 2.

64. Susan P. Sturm, "The Legacy and Future of Corrections Litigation," *University of Pennsylvania Law Review* 142 (1993), 687–8.

65. "Survey Summary: Population Projections," *Corrections Compendium* (May 1998), 14–17.

66. Sandra Evans Skovron, "Prison Crowding: The Dimensions of the Problem and Strategies of Population Control," in *Controversial Issues in Crime and Justice*, ed. Joseph E. Scott and Travis Hirschi (Newbury Park, CA: Sage Publications, 1988), 192.

67. Sheldon Ekland-Olson, William R. Kelly et al., *Justice under Pressure: A Comparison of Recidivism Patterns among Four Successive Parolee Cohorts* (New York: Springer-Verlag, 1993), 126.

68. 441 U.S. 520 (1979).

69. 452 U.S. 337 (1981).

70. "Court Decisions," *New York Law Journal* (December 21, 1998), 32.

71. *Baker v. Holden*, 787 F. Supp. 1008 (D. Utah 1992).

72. *Alberti v. Sheriff of Harris County, Texas*, 937 F.2d 984 (5th Cir. 1991).

73. U.S. Department of Justice, Press Release, "Justice Department Reaches Agreement with Georgia County Jail," August 21, 1997.

74. Douglas C. McDonald, *Managing Prison Health Care and Costs* (Washington, D.C.: National Institute of Justice, 1995), 1.

75. Marjorie P. Russell, "Too Little, Too Late, Too Slow: Compassionate Release of Terminally Ill Prisoners—Is the Cure Worse Than the Disease?" *Widener Journal of Public Law* 3 (1994), 799.

76. 429 U.S. 97 (1976).

77. 463 U.S. 239 (1983).

78. Wesley P. Shields, "Prisoner Health Care: Is It Proper to Charge Inmates for Health Services?" *Houston Law Review* 32 (1995), 280.

79. Marty Rosen, "State Joins Inmate Hospital Probe," *New York Daily News* (October 16, 1998), 8.

80. Theodore M. Hammet, *1994 Update: HIV/AIDS and STDS in Correctional Facilities* (Washington, D.C.: National Institute of Justice, 1995), 17.

81. Peter M. Brien and Allen J. Beck, *HIV in Prisons 1994* (Washington, D.C.: National Institute of Justice, 1996), 1–5.

82. Russell, 799–808.

83. National Institute of Justice, *Public Health/Corrections Collaborations: Prevention and Treatment of HIV/AIDS, STDs, and TB* (Washington, D.C.: U.S. Department of Justice, 1998).

84. James E. Robertson, "Houses of the Dead: Warehouse Prisons, Paradigm Change, and the Supreme Court," *Houston Law Review* (Winter 1997), 1003.

85. Johnson, *Hard Time*, 7–8.

86. N. Gordon Carper, "Martin Tabert: Martyr of an Era," *Florida History Quarterly* 52 (1972), 115.

87. Justice System Improvement Act of 1979, Pub. L. No. 96-157, Section 827, 93 Stat. 1167, 1215, (codified as amended at 18 U.S.C. Section 1761 (1994)).

88. Greg Wees, "Prison Industries 1997," *Corrections Compendium* (June 1997), 10.

89. Kerry L. Pyle, "Prison Employment: A Long-Term Solution to the Overcrowding Crisis," Boston *University Law Review* 77 (February 1997), 151.

90. Robert E. Burns, *I Am a Fugitive from a Georgia Chain Gang* (New York: Vanguard Press, 1932), 56.

91. Sander Jacobowitz, "Rattling Chains and Smashing Rocks: Testing the Boundaries of the Eighth Amendment," *Rutgers Law Journal* 28 (Winter 1997), 519.

92. Quoted in "Back to the Chain Gang," *Newsweek* (October 17, 1994), 87.

93. Rick Bragg, "Chain Gangs to Return to Roads of Alabama," *New York Times* (March 26, 1995), 16.

94. Wendy Imatani Peloso, "Les Miserables: Chain Gangs and the Cruel and Unusual Punishments Clause, *Southern California Law Review* 70 (July 1997), 1459.

95. *Ruffin v. Commonwealth*, 62 Va. (21 Gratt.) 790, 796 (1871).

96. Peloso, 1459.

97. Adam Cohen, "Back on the Chain Gang," *Time* (May 15, 1995) 26.

98. William Booth, "The Return of the Chain Gangs," *Washington Post* (May 4, 1995), A1.

99. Cohen, 26.

100. 217 U.S. 349 (1910).

101. *Harper v. Wall*, 85 F.Supp. 783 (D.N.J. 1949); *Johnson v. Dye*, 175 F.2d 250 (3d Cir. 1949).

102. 356 U.S. 86, 101 (1957).

103. Jacobowitz, 522.

104. 428 U.S. 153 (1976).

105. "Alabama: Chained to the Past," *Economist* (May 13, 1995), 26.

106. Peloso, 1452.

107. Holli Hartman, "Iowa Slow to Put Inmates to Work," *Des Moines Register* (February 1, 1996), 4.

chapter

15

Reentry into Society

Chapter Objectives

After reading this chapter, you should be able to:

1. List the types of assessments that jails or prisons might use with new prisoners.

2. Describe four types of psychological treatment programs for prisoners.

3. List the concepts on which parole is based.

4. Contrast probation, parole, mandatory release, pardon, and furlough.

5. List the four basic roles of a typical parole board.

6. Explain what truth-in-sentencing laws are and describe their goals.

7. Describe typical conditions of parole.

8. Contrast a probation officer with a parole officer and indicate some of the problems facing parole officers.

9. Explain whether the exclusionary rule applies to events that lead to parole revocation.

10. Indicate typical conditions for release for a paroled child molester.

INTRODUCTION

The scene has been replayed countless times in films and television shows. A convict, having completed his or her sentence, is taken to the prison entrance in handcuffs. The guard opens the gate, undoes the cuffs, and leaves the former prisoner standing alone in a strange, new world.

This is not pure fantasy. A number of inmates do leave incarceration in this manner and, depending on the penal institution, may even get a little help. Most inmates receive *gate pay* upon release, ranging from $10 (from the state of Alabama) to $500 (from the Federal Bureau of Prisons). The majority of jurisdictions also provide ex-cons with complimentary transportation to their hometowns, and nearly half throw in free clothing as well.

The majority of prisoners, however, are not "left at the curb" by the correctional system, discharged after having fully paid their "debt to society." Of the roughly 460,000 prisoners released from prison in the average year, nearly 333,000 will be placed under some form of community supervision, or parole.[1] One of the basic assumptions of the parole system is that prisoners are generally ill equipped to deal with a sudden transfer from incarceration to freedom. The skills necessary to survive in prison—where violence is the primary means of resolving conflict and independent thought is counterproductive—are often diametrically opposed to those needed in the "real world." A study done by the Vera Institute of Justice showed that inmates coming out of prison have four choices:

1. They can get a job.
2. They can go on welfare.
3. They can return to criminal behavior.
4. They can die (by their own hands).[2]

Aside from the rather dramatic fourth option, the first three choices underline the dilemma for released inmates. Finding a job is often difficult, as few employers are eager to hire someone with a criminal record. Many prisoners find welfare demeaning. They not eager to return to being dependent on an agency or institution. Committing further crimes holds the same risks that led to the inmate's arrest in the first place. Regardless, many prisoners do return to crime. Research conducted by statistician Allen J. Beck for the U.S. Department of Justice found that more than 60 percent of all released state prisoners were rearrested for a felony or a serious misdemeanor within three years, with 41 percent finding their way back to prison or jail.[3]

Postrelease programs such as parole are designed to lower these rates of recidivism. The fact that they are commonly unable to do so has opened them to a great deal of criticism and, as with other areas of the American corrections system, reform. In this chapter, we will explore the methods by which the state returns lawbreakers to the community and the efforts being made to protect both the lawbreaker and the community in the process. First, we will examine various in-prison and in-jail programs designed to prepare the inmates for this transition period, not to mention for the remainder of their lives on the outside.

PREPARING FOR RELEASE

J. Michael Self, serving a thirty-three-and-a-half-year sentence in Virginia for second degree homicide, has a blunt assessment of the current state of the corrections system: "Prisons don't need reform, people do."[4] Though Self may

> "Probably the only place where a man can feel really secure is in a maximum security prison, except for the imminent threat of release."
>
> —Germain Greer,
> *Australian writer* (1998)

be correct that prisoners need help, the more pertinent question in the context of present-day criminal justice is whether they deserve it. Following a precedent set by the Supreme Court in *San Antonio Independent School District v. Rodriguez* (1973),[5] lower courts have consistently ruled that there is "no constitutional mandate to provide educational, rehabilitative, or vocational programs" to prisoners.[6] According to the tenets of punishment and incapacitation, even if such programs could be proved to have positive results, they are inappropriate—a "slap in the face" to the victims of crime, who, as taxpayers, must support the costs of rehabilitation.[7]

While this view may be prevalent among correctional officials, it is not universal. There is a feeling in some quarters that, contrary to the conclusions drawn from Robert Martinson's early 1970s research that "nothing works"[8] (though this was not Martinson's intent as we saw in Chapter 13), certain programs can succeed in rehabilitating inmates. The operating strategies of some penal institutions such as the Orange County Jail in Florida are, as we shall see, based on the assumption that "some things work." Inmates themselves certainly want access to self-improvement programs; they rate such support as their highest priority, above privacy, safety, and even freedom.[9] For many of them, given their weak social and financial circumstances, prison offers their best chance at improving their lives. The first step in the process is classification.

Classification

Upon entering a penal institution, new inmates undergo **classification,** a series of evaluations primarily designed to establish the level of security risk that each new offender poses. In most prisons, classification lasts between three and six weeks. During this process, prison officials evaluate the inmate's personal characteristics and criminal record to try to determine the probability that he or she will engage in future criminal conduct, attempt to escape, or become involved in other disruptive activity. The inmate is assigned to living quarters accordingly. In some institutions, classification extends beyond security considerations and also evaluates the inmate's needs for rehabilitative programs.

Classification at the Orange County Jail. Florida's Orange County Jail, the ninth largest in the nation with 3,300 beds, is administered according to the precepts of direct supervision (discussed in Chapter 13). Somewhat of a rarity among American jails, the entire institution is organized with the goal of offering inmates treatment and counseling (see Figure 15.1).

After initial booking at the jail, inmates go through classification to determine the form of custody they will require and the programs that will best serve their needs. At the Orange County Jail, classification takes five days to complete and, along with security-risk evaluations, includes the following three tests:

1. The Test of Adult Basic Education, to determine the inmate's grade level.

2. The Substance Abuse/Life Circumstances Evaluation, to determine whether the inmate needs treatment for drug or alcohol abuse.

3. A vocational needs and interests assessment, to identify suitable job options upon release.[10]

After orientation, the inmate is transferred to one of four facilities based on his or her program needs. Not all inmates will live in the rehabilitative areas of the jail—those who are security risks, mentally ill, serving sentences of less than

CLASSIFICATION
The process that determines the security and treatment needs of an inmate upon her or his initial contact with the correctional system.

Figure 15.1 Rehabilitation at the Orange County (Florida) Jail

As you can see, the operation of the Orange County Jail revolves around its educational and vocational programs. From intake to release, the inmate is given a number of opportunities at self-improvement.

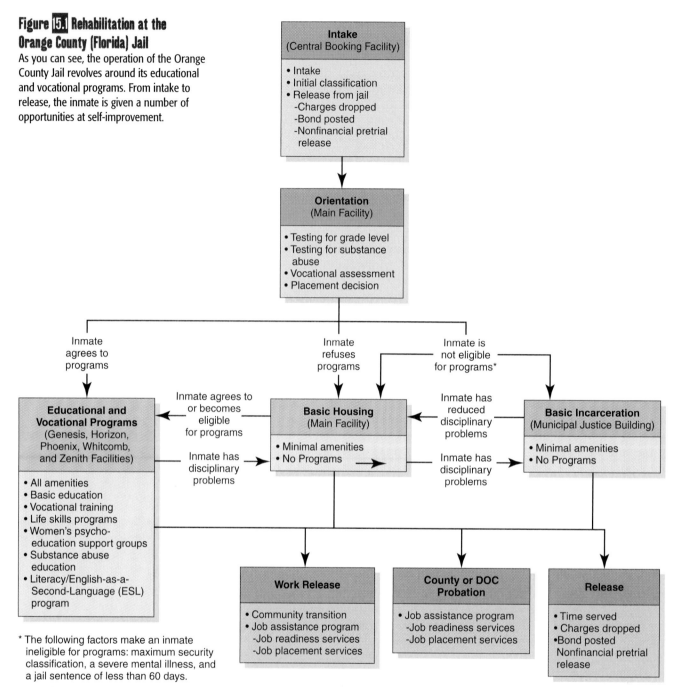

* The following factors make an inmate ineligible for programs: maximum security classification, a severe mental illness, and a jail sentence of less than 60 days.

SOURCE: ADAPTED FROM PETER FINN, THE ORANGE COUNTY, FLORIDA, JAIL EDUCATIONAL AND VOCATIONAL PROGRAMS (WASHINGTON, D.C.: NATIONAL INSTITUTE OF JUSTICE, 1997), EXHIBIT 1, PAGE 2.

sixty days, or refuse to take part in the programs are assigned to the main facility of the jail and its less amenable living conditions. Furthermore, inmates can be removed from a program facility as a punishment for misconduct.

Classification Standards. Objective classification systems such as the one in use at the Orange County Jail were not widespread until the mid-1970s, when the Federal Bureau of Prisons (BOP) established criteria for classifying inmates. The BOP's classification system focused on six factors to establish a prisoner's security risk:

▌ History of escape or attempted escape from correctional facilities.

▌ History of behavior during prior prison or jail terms.

| Type of prior crime for which the inmate has been imprisoned.
| History of violence.
| Severity of offense.
| Length of sentence.[11]

PSYCHOTHERAPY
The treatment of psychological disorders in order to determine the causes of and rehabilitate criminal behavior.

Today, the American Correctional Association (ACA) maintains uniformity in classification standards. The ACA, a semipublic organization that is not directly affiliated with the BOP, sets standards of classification similar to those listed above. Those correctional facilities that follow these standards (along with hundreds of others ranging from safety codes to inmate recreation opportunities to the quality of food) are accredited by the ACA, much as universities are accredited by outside organizations.[12] The ACA has played an important role in making sure that private prisons and jails are organized and run properly. A number of state governments, when contracting with companies to provide corrections services, require that the private facilities be accredited by the ACA.

Psychological Treatment

As we saw in Chapter 2, many criminologists believe that psychological traits influence criminal behavior. That belief is reflected in psychological treatment programs run by penal institutions to address the emotional or mental problems of their inmates. For example, under the supervision of a professor of social work, students from the University of Central Florida conduct small group sessions three times a week at the Orange County Jail, in which inmates discuss the reasons for their criminal behavior. This is one form of **psychotherapy,** a general term that refers to the treatment of the mind. Although psychotherapy is widespread in the corrections system, no empirical evidence of its effectiveness has been established. The best that can be said of these programs is that they may have a positive effect on inmates, though it is difficult to determine whether this effect can be attributed to the programs themselves or to other factors.[13] The most common forms of psychotherapy in prisons and jails are social therapy programs.

Group therapy sessions such as the one pictured above are commonplace in today's prison and jails. What are some of the goals of group therapy, and why has it proved so popular with prison administrators?

Social Therapy Programs. The problems of many criminals can be traced to an inability to function in a social setting. Social therapy programs concentrate on improving the inmate's ability to interact with other people. *Group therapy* gathers people with similar problems into a group. The program consists of several stages, starting with exercises to break down a common unwillingness to discuss personal problems in a group setting and ending with each member of the group helping the others to recognize and change their harmful behavioral traits. In theory, patients are better able to accept criticism if it comes from someone who has experienced many of the same problems they have. For most penal institutions, group therapy is preferable to individual therapy because it requires fewer financial and human resources.

REALITY THERAPY
A form of social therapy that encourages inmates to take responsibility for their actions and for the consequences of those actions.

BEHAVIOR THERAPY
Treatment programs that attempt to change an inmate's behavior patterns to eliminate or lessen criminal tendencies.

TOKEN ECONOMY
A form of behavior therapy that offers inmates incentives (in the form of tokens that can be used to purchase desired goods or services) to abide by the rules of the institution.

GENERAL EQUIVALENCY DEGREE (GED)
Considered the equivalent of a high school diploma and required for many forms of nonprofessional employment in the United States; the focus of many educational programs in correctional facilities.

Another form of social therapy is **reality therapy.** Developed by psychologist William Glasser in the 1960s, reality therapy is based on the simple premise that behavior has consequences.[14] According to Glasser, those who exhibit criminal behavior do so because they were never taught by parents or other authority figures to deal with reality responsibly. This form of therapy focuses on teaching the inmate to behave more "realistically," that is, in a manner that will be accepted by society and will allow the inmate to be an accepted member of society. Reality therapy attempts to accomplish this by having the inmate set and reach a series of goals for her or his behavior.

Behavior Modification. A second branch of prison psychotherapy concentrates on behavior rather than self-knowledge. **Behavior therapy** rests on the assumption that behavior is learned and can therefore be unlearned with the proper stimuli. This therapy usually does not target the criminal act itself, but instead tries to eliminate problem behaviors that lead to criminality. For example, an inmate who has been convicted of aggravated assault will undergo anger management treatment to learn how to control violent outbursts and react differently to confrontational situations. Drugs can also play a part in behavior therapy. Alcoholics are given anectine and antabuse, for example, because these drugs cause nausea and vomiting when any alcohol is consumed.[15] The goal is not for the inmate to understand fully the roots of the problem, but to end the alcohol abuse by associating it with an unpleasant experience.

The **token economy** is another, more general form of behavior therapy. In this system, inmates are given plastic chips or some other form of tokens upon achieving a certain goal, such as attending class or finishing a work project. The token can be used to purchase library privileges, recreation time, a television or radio, items from the canteen, and other amenities. The goal of the token economy is to condition the inmate to positive behavior by rewarding that behavior. The long-term effects of such programs are questionable, however. Although they may produce desired behavior within the institution, it would not seem to transfer to life outside prison. In the real world, after all, ex-cons can earn "tokens" by getting a job *or* by robbing a convenience store.

Vocational Programs

For many inmates, a successful transition following release is predicated upon finding and keeping steady employment. Two main obstacles to achieving this goal are a lack of education and a lack of employable skills. Consequently, many penal institutions offer programs in these areas.

Educational Programs. Only about 40 percent of jail and prison inmates have a high school diploma, compared to 85 percent of the general population.[16] Illiteracy is also a major problem among prisoners. In response, the BOP mandates that all inmates be able to read at a high school equivalency level and requires a ninety-day Adult Basic Education (ABE) program for any who cannot. In addition, every state has its own ABE program.

Like the programs at most correctional institutions, the ABE program at Florida's Orange County Jail focuses on helping inmates earn their **general equivalency degree (GED).** The GED is a written test that evaluates general comprehension and knowledge of science, math, writing, and reading. It is considered to be the equivalent of a high school degree. Earning a GED is a practical benefit for most inmates, as it is the standard requirement for nonprofessional employment in the United States. Furthermore, several studies have shown that prisoners who have received their GED are less likely to recidivate upon release.[17] In one study, 557 Louisiana inmates who earned the degree had a recidivism rate of only 4 percent.[18] At the Orange County Jail, as in many penal institutions, educational programs are supervised by employees of local public school systems.

All but four states also offer their inmates access to some form of college education, and more than 35,000 inmates are enrolled in secondary education programs. The number of inmates taking college courses has dropped precipitously since 1994, however. That year, Congress barred inmates from receiving federal loans, known as Pell Grants, for low-income students.[19] The program was not discontinued due to a lack of results. In one study in New Mexico, inmates who attended college for one or more years had a 15 percent recidivism rate compared to 68 percent for the general prison population.[20] Instead, Congress was acting on the principle of least eligibility, which, as we saw in Chapter 14, holds that prisoners should not have the same opportunities as other citizens.

Vocational Programs. At the Phoenix facility of the Orange County Jail, inmates spend six hours a day attending classes on desktop publishing, auto maintenance, carpentry, cooking, and other trades and occupations. These vocational programs are designed to give the inmate a marketable skill. In many correctional facilities, these programs suffer a number of shortcomings. The equipment used to train the prisoners is often obsolete, and the training facilities are handicapped by a lack of funds. One exemplary tale concerns a large state prison that provided inmates with a print shop apprenticeship program, using a printing press donated by a local newspaper. When the inmates, upon release, tried to get jobs in the printing business, they learned that the type of printing press on which they had been tutored was no longer in use due to its inefficiency, which explained why the local newspaper had donated it in the first place.[21]

More importantly, however, the menial job skills taught in most vocational programs place the inmate in direct competition with a large labor pool upon release. Given the disadvantage of a criminal record, prisoners tend to fare poorly in such job markets. In order to alleviate this problem, correctional officials often rely on employment-counseling organizations to help inmates find work after release.[22]

"Life Skills" Programs

Even when inmates are able to pass the GED and learn a vocation, many lack the basic disposition needed to keep a job. They have difficulty arriving on time, taking orders, and communicating with co-workers. In the last few decades, penal institutions have devised **"life skills" programs** to deal with these and other issues of day-to-day living. At Florida's Orange County Jail, for example, a program addresses employability, as well as money management techniques and parenting and relationship skills. An increasingly popular component of life skills programs is Moral Recognition Therapy (MRT). This program treats the ability to make moral choices as a skill that is necessary for a crime-free life. Starting with the assumption that inmates have limited moral development, MRT tries to restructure their goals and values and instill a sense of right and wrong that is more in keeping with that of society.[23]

No large-scale academic or correctional studies have been attempted to determine the effect of life skills programs on recidivism. Individual facilities, however, have measured the incidence of criminal activity of those inmates participating in the programs and have found positive results. The one-year

"LIFE SKILLS" PROGRAMS
Institutional programs that attempt to teach inmates the practical skills necessary to function and prosper in the community.

To visit the home page of Better People, a Portland, Oregon, non-profit, volunteer employment and counseling program dedicated to finding employment for ex-inmates, go to betterpeople.org/

Figure 15.2 Meeting Treatment Needs

The National Center on Addiction and Substance Abuse at Columbia University estimates that 75 percent of state prison inmates and 31 percent of federal prison inmates suffer from substance abuse and would benefit from correctional treatment programs. As you see, a relatively small amount of these inmates are receiving the treatment many believe they need.

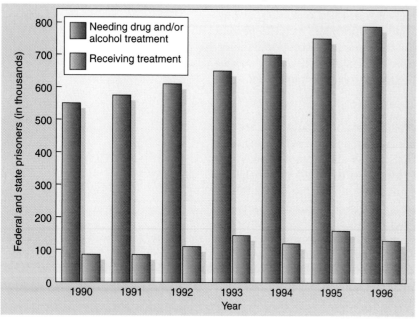

SOURCE: BEHIND BARS: SUBSTANCE ABUSE AND AMERICA'S PRISON POPULATION (NEW YORK: NATIONAL CENTER ON ADDICTION AND SUBSTANCE ABUSE AT COLUMBIA UNIVERSITY, 1998).

INFOTRAC®
COLLEGE EDITION

Editor. Federal study touts effectiveness of prison-based treatment.

recidivism rate for participants in the life skills program at the four major prisons in Delaware, for example, was 8.1 percent, compared to 34.9 percent for a comparison group that did not participate.[24]

Substance Abuse Programs

A 1998 report by the National Center on Addiction and Substance Abuse at Columbia University stated that of the 1.8 million inmates in America's prisons and jails, 1.4 million could attribute their crimes to drugs or alcohol. The same report found that of the 840,000 federal prisoners who needed drug treatment, only 150,000 received any care before being released (see Figure 15.2).[25] These numbers suggest that by failing to treat addicts, correctional facilities fail to address one of the basic causes of criminal behavior and therefore invite recidivism.

The main problem faced by substance abuse programs, both inside prison and out, is that science still has an incomplete understanding of what causes addiction. Traditionally, prison programs have followed the principles of Alcoholics Anonymous and Narcotics Anonymous, which see addiction as a disease that can be treated only by rigorous self-examination and sacrifice. In recent years, addiction specialists have increasingly turned to drugs such as Prozac to treat the symptoms that lead to substance abuse, and this attitude has filtered into prison programs.[26]

If substance abuse programs are measured by their effectiveness in "curing" inmates of addiction, their performance will generally be found lacking. As we will see in Chapter 17, the scientific community is still learning a great deal about the mechanics of addiction, and even without the pressures of prison life, fewer than one-third of all Alcoholics Anonymous members stay sober during the first five years of the program.[27] Numerous studies have shown, however, that prison-based alcohol and drug programs can reduce recidivism.[28] Researchers recently found that prisoners who had participated in the Ozarks Correctional Center Drug Treatment Program in Missouri were half as likely to be arrested or convicted a year after release than other prisoners with substance abuse problems.[29]

PAROLE AND RELEASE FROM PRISON

Though little empirical research exists to support the claim, many criminal justice experts suspect that inmates attend prison programs not for self-improvement but to secure an early release.[30] This can be accomplished in two ways. First, many penal institutions, following the rules of behavior therapy, offer prisoners incentives to take part in the programs. Inmates in the Orange County Jail, for example, earn eleven days of *good-time credit* for every month they successfully complete a program. As was discussed in Chapter 11, inmates receive these credits—which allow time to be subtracted from their terms—for obeying prison rules, working within the prison, and other laudable activities.

Second, inmates believe that by participating in prison programs, they can impress parole boards and increase their chances of early release by **parole,** or the *conditional* release of a prisoner after a portion of his or her sentence has been served. Parole allows the corrections system to continue to supervise an offender who is no longer incarcerated. As long as parolees follow the conditions of their parole, they are allowed to finish their terms outside the prison. If parolees break the terms of their early release, however, they face the risk of being returned to a penal institution.

According to Todd Clear and George F. Cole, parole is based on three concepts:

1. *Grace:* The prisoner has no right to be given an early release, but the government has granted her or him that privilege.

2. *Contract of consent:* The government and the parolee enter into an agreement whereby the latter agrees to abide by certain conditions in return for continued freedom.

3. *Custody:* Technically, though no longer incarcerated, the parolee is still the responsibility of the state. Parole is an extension of corrections.[31] (The phonetic and administrative similarities between probation and parole can be confusing. See *Concept Summary—Probation versus Parole* for clarification.)

PAROLE
The conditional release of an inmate before his or her sentence has expired. The remainder of the sentence is served in the community under the supervision of correctional officers, and the offender can be returned to incarceration if he or she breaks the conditions of parole, as determined by a parole board.

CONCEPT SUMMARY
Probation versus Parole

Probation and parole have many aspects in common. In fact, probation and parole are so similar that many jurisdictions combine them into a single agency. There are, however, some important distinctions between the two systems, as noted below.

	Probation	Parole
Basic Definition	An alternative to imprisonment in which a person who has been convicted of a crime is allowed to serve his or her sentence in the community subject to certain conditions and supervision by a probation officer.	An early release from a correctional facility as determined by an administrative body (the parole board), in which the convicted offender is given the chance to spend the remainder of his or her sentence under supervision in the community.
Timing	The offender is sentenced to a probationary term in place of a prison or jail term. If the offender breaks the conditions of probation, he or she is sent to prison or jail. Therefore, probation occurs *before* imprisonment.	Parole is a form of early release. Therefore, parole occurs *after* an offender has spent time behind bars.
Authority	Probation falls under the domain of the judiciary. In other words, judges make the decision whether to send a convicted offender to prison or jail or to give her or him a sentence of probation. If a person violates the terms of probation, a judge ultimately decides whether she or he should be sent to a correctional facility as punishment.	Parole falls under the domain of an administrative body (often appointed by an executive such as a state governor) known as the parole board. The parole board determines whether or not the prisoner is qualified for early release, and under which conditions he or she will be allowed to remain in the community. When a parolee violates the conditions of parole, the parole board must decide whether to send him or her back to prison. (Although they can be asked to make recommendations to the parole board, judges generally *are not* involved in the parole decision.)
Characteristics of Offenders	As Todd R. Clear and George F. Cole point out, probationers are normally less involved in the criminal lifestyle. Most of them are first-time offenders who have committed nonviolent crimes.	Many parolees, Clear and Cole note, have spent many months or even years in prison and, besides abiding by conditions of parole, must make the difficult transition to "life on the outside."

Because of these differences, many observers believe that probation and parole should not be combined in the same agency, though limited financial resources will assure that many jurisdictions will continue to do so.

MANDATORY RELEASE
Release from prison that occurs when an offender has served the length of his or her sentence, with time taken off for good behavior.

PARDON
An act of executive clemency that overturns a conviction and erases mention of the crime from the person's criminal record.

FURLOUGH
Temporary release from a prison for purposes of vocational or educational training, to ease the shock of release, or for personal reasons.

Because of good-time credits and parole, most prisoners do not serve their entire sentence in prison. In fact, the average felon serves only about half of the term handed down by the court.

Other Types of Prison Release

Parole, a conditional release, is the most common form of release, but it is not the only one (see Figure 15.3). Prisoners receive an unconditional release when they have completed the terms of their sentence and no longer require incarceration or supervision. One form of unconditional release is **mandatory release** (also known as "maxing out"), which occurs when an inmate has served the maximum amount of time on the initial sentence, minus reductions for good-time credits.

Another, quite rare unconditional release is a **pardon,** a form of executive clemency. The president (on the federal level) and the governor (on the state level) can grant pardon, or forgive, a convict's criminal punishment. Most states have a board of pardons—affiliated with the parole board—which makes recommendations to the governor in cases where it believes a pardon is warranted. Most pardons involve obvious miscarriages of justice, though sometimes a governor will pardon an individual to remove the stain of conviction from his or her criminal record.

Certain *temporary releases* also exist. Some inmates, who qualify by exhibiting good behavior and generally proving that they do not represent a risk to society, are allowed to leave the prison on **furlough** for a certain amount of time, usually between a day and a week. At times, a furlough is granted because of a family emergency, such as a funeral. Furloughs can be particularly helpful for an inmate who is nearing release and can use them to ease the readjustment period. Though most furloughed inmates return to the correctional facility without incident, the program is under constant scrutiny. When Willie Horton, who committed a rape while on his tenth furlough from a life sentence, became a political issue during the 1988 presidential elections, many states placed their furlough programs on hold in response to public outcry. Other temporary releases, such as work release programs, are often used in conjunction with parole and will be discussed later in the chapter.

The Evolution of Parole

Parole comes from the French phrase *libération sur parole,* which means regaining one's freedom by giving one's word (*parole*). The concept comes from the practice of releasing captured prisoners of war if they promised not to fight again (on the condition that they would be executed if recaptured).

Maconochie and the "Marks" System. England's Alexander Maconochie first gave voice to the idea, crucial to modern parole, that prisoners could be released before serving their full sentences. In 1840, Maconochie, a retired naval captain, was made superintendent of Norfolk Island, a penal colony off the coast of Australia. Norfolk Island was designed

Figure 15.3 Release from State and Federal Correctional Facilities

Type of Release	Percentage of All Releases
Parole/Mandatory Supervision	71
Expiration of Sentence	18
Probation*	6
Other	5

*AS THE SECOND STEP IN A SPLIT SENTENCE.

SOURCE: ADAPTED FROM BUREAU OF JUSTICE STATISTICS, *CORRECTIONAL POPULATIONS IN THE UNITED STATES, 1995* (WASHINGTON, D.C.: U.S. DEPARTMENT OF JUSTICE, 1997), TABLE 5.13.

to be a "hell on earth" for Britain's worst convicts, but when Maconochie arrived, he changed the operating procedure at the institution. Maconochie thought that imprisonment was punishment enough and felt no need to torture and degrade the inmates as had his predecessors.

The ex-captain's most revolutionary innovation was the "marks system."[32] Under this system, the convict would be given a certain number of marks when he landed on Norfolk Island. He could then reduce his store of marks by participating in religious and educational programs, volunteering for labor, and behaving well. For every ten marks earned, inmates would shorten their sentence by one day.

In Boston, Massachusetts, parole board members watch convicted drug courier Walter O. Victoria testify on video. What factors do these boards consider when making the parole decision?

The marks system appeared to be a success. Only 3 percent of the 450 convicts discharged during Maconochie's tenure are known to have been reconvicted.[33] Despite claims of miraculous behavioral changes in once- ungovernable inmates, his ideas did not find favor among correction officials in England who viewed imprisonment as a punishment rather than an opportunity for rehabilitation. Maconochie was removed four years after taking the position, and his marks system was never implemented in mainland England. In 1854, however, Sir Walter Crofton did import the marks system to Ireland with several adjustments. Crofton's main contribution to today's parole system was the *ticket-of-leave*, which provided inmates with a conditional release from prison.[34]

Parole in the United States. In its present form, parole was introduced in the United States in the late 1800s by Zebulon Brockway at the Elmira Reformatory.[35] Brockway, a student of Maconochie and Crofton, was given the opportunity to release his prisoners on parole because New York had adopted indeterminate sentencing; with these less restrictive guidelines, prison officials had the freedom to choose the departure dates of inmates. As indeterminate sentencing spread, so did parole, and by 1942 all of the states were using this system of early release.[36]

In 1930, the federal government created the U.S. Board of Parole, consolidating a number of separate parole systems under one organization that released and supervised federal prisoners. Parole has generally been popular with correctional administrators, who have found it to be an effective means of controlling prison populations. It has also been praised for its cost-cutting propensities (though, as we shall see, recent studies show that it may actually be cheaper to keep certain offenders incarcerated than to set them free).

> "I can't believe that someone who's a convicted murderer and has a life sentence comes up for parole in 25 years. Vivian has no chance to live again. She didn't get her death sentence shortened."
>
> —Karla Cooper, *commenting on the parole eligibility of the man who murdered her godmother (1997)*

Reshaping Parole. This is not to say, however, that parole has remained above criticism. Since the 1920s, political movements to abolish the system have been nearly continuous. The reason is not hard to fathom—to a certain extent, parole represents a "guess" on the part of the parole board that a convict poses no threat to the community. Sometimes, the guess will be incorrect, leaving the parole board in particular and the system in general open for criticism. Consequently, political pressures have been a powerful force in reshaping parole over the past sixty years. The three-stage evolution of the Oregon Board of Parole, which was created in 1939, mirrors the changes in parole policies as a whole during that time period:

Stage One: Until 1977, the Oregon Board of Parole operated under a *discretionary* method of determining early release; during this time, the board had almost unlimited power in making parole decisions.

Stage Two: From 1977 until 1989, the board set prison terms using matrix ranges based on the type of crime committed and the offender's prior criminal history.

Stage Three: Since 1989, when the state legislature adopted *mandatory* sentencing guidelines, the board's discretion in determining release dates has been, for the most part, annulled.[37]

Discretionary release and mandatory parole are the two prevailing methods of determining conditional release in the United States today. The contrasts between the two systems dominate the debate over the practice's future.

DISCRETIONARY RELEASE

As you may recall from Chapter 11, corrections systems are classified by sentencing procedure—indeterminate or determinate. Indeterminate sentencing occurs when the legislature sets a range of punishments for particular crimes, and the judge and the parole board exercise discretion in determining the actual length of the prison term. For that reason, states with indeterminate sentencing are said to have systems of **discretionary release.** Until the mid-1970s, all states and the federal government operated in this manner.

Eligibility for Parole

Under indeterminate sentencing, parole is not a right but a privilege. This is a crucial point, as it establishes the terms of the relationship between the inmate and the corrections authorities during the parole process. In *Greenholtz v. Inmates of the Nebraska Penal and Correctional Complex* (1979),[38] the Supreme Court ruled that inmates did not have a constitutionally protected right to expect parole, thereby giving states the freedom to set their own standards for determining parole eligibility. In most states that have retained indeterminate sentencing, a prisoner is eligible to be considered for parole release after serving a legislatively determined percentage of the minimum sentence—usually one-half or two-thirds—less any good time or other credits.

Peter "Commando Pedro" Langan, shown here as he is escorted by Franklin County (Ohio) sheriff's deputies from the county jail, was found guilty in 1998 of participating in twenty-two bank robberies over a two-year period. Langan was the leader of the Midwestern Bank Bandits, a white separatist gang that decreed itself in opposition to the government. U.S. District Judge John D. Holschuh sentenced Langan to a life sentence without possibility of parole. Do you agree with some observers who believe that life-without-parole is a harsher sentence than the death penalty? Or do you believe that life-without-parole is a humane alternative to the death penalty?

Contrary to what is depicted in many films and television shows, a convict does not "apply" for parole. An inmate's case automatically comes up before the parole board a certain number of days—often ninety—before she or he is eligible for parole. The date of eligibility depends on statutory requirements, the terms of the sentence, and the behavior of the inmate in prison. The board has an eligibility report prepared, which provides information on the various factors that must be taken into consideration in making the decision. The board also reviews the case file to acquaint itself with the original crime and conducts an interview with the

CJ in Focus
Was Justice Served?
A Matter of Life and Death Sentences

On a hot day in July, Jonathan Dale Simmons entered the South Carolina residence of seventy-nine-year-old Josie Lamb. Finding Lamb alone in the bathroom, Simmons proceeded to bludgeon her to death with a toilet lid. By the next day, Simmons was in custody and charged with murder. The suspect also confessed to beating and sexually assaulting three other elderly women, including his grandmother. Three weeks before his capital trial, he pleaded guilty to first degree burglary and two counts of criminal sexual assault in connection with the prior attacks. Under South Carolina law, this meant that Simmons—if convicted of Lamb's murder—would be ineligible for parole.

A jury found Simmons guilty after a three-day trial. During sentencing, the trial judge refused a request by the defense to instruct the jury that Simmons would be legally ineligible for parole if he was sentenced to life imprisonment instead of the death penalty. Then, after ninety minutes of deliberation, the jury sent a note to the trial judge, asking if "the imposition of a life sentence" would carry with it the "possibility of parole."

THE PREFERRED ALTERNATIVE

The question was crucial for Simmons. Studies have shown that if a jury believes that a "life sentence" carries the possibility of parole, it is more likely to sentence the defendant to death. In the two years before Indiana introduced life-without-parole, for example, ten death sentences were imposed. In a two-year period after passage of the new law, that number dropped to one. Support for the death penalty nationwide falls from 77 percent to 41 percent if the alternative is life-without-parole.

In reply to the jury's question, the trial judge in Simmons's case charged that the jury was not to "consider parole or parole eligibility" in setting the sentence. Within twenty-five minutes, the jury sentenced Simmons to be executed.

For Critical Analysis: Eventually, the Supreme Court overturned the trial court's conviction, ruling that Simmons had been denied due process by the trial judge's actions. Why should sentencing juries be given the option of life-without-parole in capital cases?

---

inmate. At some point before the eligibility date, the entire board, or a subcommittee of the board, votes on whether parole will be granted.

Not all convicts are eligible for parole. Many states have a sentencing system in which offenders who have committed the most serious crimes receive life terms without the possibility of early release. In general, life-without-parole is reserved for those offenders who have

- committed capital, or first degree, murder;
- committed serious offenses other than murder; or
- been defined by statute as habitual, or repeat, offenders, such as those sentenced under "three strikes" laws.[39]

Besides murder, drug offenders and sex offenders are most commonly targeted for life-without-parole. The sentence is fraught with controversy, as many observers, including inmates, feel serving life-without-parole is a crueler punishment than the death penalty.[40] Furthermore, there are questions as to whether juries should be informed of a defendant's parole opportunities. (See CJ in Focus—Was Justice Served?: A Matter of Life and Death Sentences.)

The Parole Board

The cumulated efforts of the police, the courtroom work group, and correctional officials lead to a single question in most cases: When should an offender be released?[41] This is a difficult question and is often left to **parole boards** to answer. When members of the parole board make what in retrospect was a mistake, they quickly draw the attention of the media, the public, and the courts.

According to the American Correctional Association, the parole board has four basic roles:

- To decide which offenders should be placed on parole.

PAROLE BOARD
A body of appointed civilians that decides whether a convict should be granted conditional release before the end of his or her sentence.

535

PAROLE GRANT HEARING
A hearing in which the entire parole board or a subcommittee reviews information, meets the offender, and hears testimony from relevant witnesses to determine whether to grant parole.

2. To determine the conditions of parole and aid in the continuing supervision of the parolee.

3. To discharge the offender when the conditions of parole have been met.

4. If a violation occurs, to determine whether parole privileges should be revoked.[42]

Most parole boards are small, made up of five to seven members. In many jurisdictions, board members' terms are limited to between four and six years. The requirements for board members vary. Nearly half the states have no prerequisites, while others require a bachelor's degree or some expertise in the field of criminal justice.

Parole boards are either affiliated with government agencies or act as independent bodies. In the first instance, board members are usually members of the correctional staff appointed by the state department of corrections. In contrast, independent parole boards are made up of citizens from the community who have been chosen for the post by a government official, usually the governor. Because most states with independent boards have no specific criteria for the members, critics believe that these boards tend to be "politicized" by the appointment of members—who have limited knowledge of the criminal justice system—as a return for political favors.[43]

The Parole Hearing

In a system that uses discretionary parole, the actual release decision is made at a **parole grant hearing.** During this hearing, the entire board or a subcommittee reviews relevant information on the convict. Sometimes, but not always, the offender is interviewed. Because the board members have only limited knowledge of each offender, key players in the case are often notified in advance of the parole hearing and asked to provide comments and recommendations. These participants include the sentencing judge, the attorneys at the trial, the victims, and any law enforcement officers who may be involved.[44] After these preparations, the typical parole hearing itself is *very* short—usually lasting just a few minutes.

In May 1999, boxer Mike Tyson was released on parole after serving about a third of a one-year prison sentence he had received following a plea of no contest to misdemeanor assault charges stemming from a minor traffic accident. The Maryland Parole Commission voted 5-1 to grant Tyson parole, under the condition that he pass two drug tests a week and undergo anger management treatment for the balance of his sentence.

Due Process at Parole Hearings. Due process rights for offenders during parole hearings vary from state to state. By deciding in the *Greenholtz* case that parole is a privilege rather than a right, the Supreme Court basically allowed each state to decide on its own to what degree inmates would enjoy due process rights during the parole hearing. Therefore, if state statutes only offer "hope" for parole, due process protection is not necessary. If the state, however, creates "expectancy" for parole, then inmates do have a right to counsel, cross-examination, and presentation of witnesses at the hearing.[45] An expectancy is created if, for example, state law holds that all felons serving life sentences are to be granted parole after thirty years if they have not broken any prison regulations.

The Parole Decision. Again, the actual decision-making process varies. In Pennsylvania, two members of the five-member board form

Figure 15.4 The Parole Explosion

Both the number of adults on parole and the percentage of prisoners granted parole have grown dramatically in recent years. As the number of adults in jail or prison has increased, so too has the pressure on prison administrators to release prisoners early (through parole) in order to relieve overcrowding.

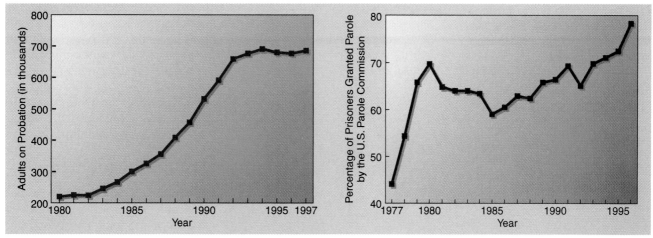

SOURCE: ADAPTED FROM BUREAU OF JUSTICE STATISTICS, SOURCEBOOK OF CRIMINAL JUSTICE STATISTICS, 1997 (WASHINGTON, D.C.: U.S. DEPARTMENT OF JUSTICE, 1998), TABLE 6.1 AT PAGE 464 AND TABLE 6.69 AT PAGE 521.

a panel to make the release decision. If these two cannot agree, the chair of the board appoints a third member to render a decision. When the offender has committed a violent crime, three members of the Pennsylvania board must vote in favor of granting parole.[46] As Figure 15.4 shows, both the number of Americans on parole and the rate at which parole is granted by parole boards nationwide have risen dramatically over the past two decades.

If parole is denied, the entire process is replayed at the next "action date," which depends on the nature of the offender's crimes and all relevant laws. In 1998, for example, Leslie Van Houten was denied parole for the twelfth time. Van Houten was convicted of murder in 1969 for the role she played in the gruesome Beverly Hills killing of pregnant actress Sharon Tate and six others under the direction of Charles Manson. While in prison, Van Houten— who claims that she played a minimal role in the murders—has earned bachelor's and master's degrees and has never had a disciplinary report filed against her. Families of the victims continue to petition the California Board of Prison Terms to keep her incarcerated, and although the board has said Van Houten's chances improve with each hearing, most observers believe she will never be released. (Manson himself has been denied parole nine times and stated during his last hearing in 1997 that he did not want to be released.) In some states, the parole board is required to give written reasons for denying parole, and some jurisdictions give the inmate, prosecution, or victims the option to appeal the board's decision. Many states provide parole boards with legal requirements for parole, designed to give some structure to a process that relies to a great extent on personal discretion (see Figure 15.5).

THE EMERGENCE OF MANDATORY RELEASE

The legitimacy of discretionary release relies to a certain extent on the perception of parole decisions by offenders, victims, and the general public. Like judicial discretion (as we discussed in Chapter 11), parole board discretion is criticized when the decisions are seen as arbitrary and unfair and lead to rampant disparity in the release dates of similar offenders.[47] Proponents of discretionary release argue that parole boards must tailor their decisions to the individual case, but such protestations seem to be undermined by the raw

Figure 15.5 Legal Requirements for Parole

Although parole boards have a great deal of discretion in granting or denying parole, many states have passed laws that provide specific, if somewhat minimal, guidelines for the parole decision. In Nebraska, for example, state law provides that the parole board should consider these factors in deciding whether to authorize the release of a prisoner.

1. Whether there is substantial risk that the parolee will violate parole conditions.
2. Whether the release would depreciate the seriousness of the offense or promote disrespect for the law.
3. Whether the release would have a substantial, adverse effect on prison discipline.
4. Whether continued prison treatment, medical care, or vocational training will substantially affect the parolee's capacity to become a law-abiding citizen if released at a later time.

SOURCE: NEBRASKA REVISED STATUTE, SECTION 83-1, 114(1).

Figure 15.6 State Truth-in-Sentencing Requirements

Twenty-nine states and the District of Columbia have adopted federal truth-in-sentencing laws that require convicts to serve at least 85 percent of their sentence before being released.

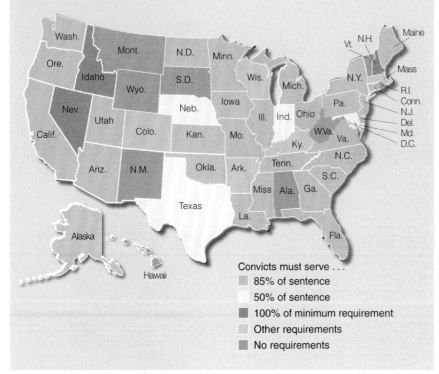

Convicts must serve . . .
- 85% of sentence
- 50% of sentence
- 100% of minimum requirement
- Other requirements
- No requirements

SOURCE: ADAPTED FROM BUREAU OF JUSTICE STATISTICS, TRUTH IN SENTENCING IN STATE PRISONS (WASHINGTON, D.C.: U.S. DEPARTMENT OF JUSTICE, 1999), TABLE 1.

data: research done by the Bureau of Justice Statistics has found that most offenders were serving less than a third of their sentences in the early 1990s.[48]

As Michael Tonry noted, such statistics gave the impression that parole board members "tossed darts at a dartboard" to determine who should be released and when.[49] As a result of this criticism, twenty-seven states have now implemented determinate sentencing systems, which set minimum mandatory terms without possibility of parole. These systems provide for *mandatory release,* in which offenders leave incarceration when their sentences have expired, minus adjustments made for good time.

Truth in Sentencing

The move toward mandatory release has come partly at the urging of the federal government. The federal sentencing guidelines that went into effect in 1987 required those who were convicted in federal courts to serve at least 85 percent of their term.[50] Federal crime bills in 1994 and 1995 encouraged states to adopt this *truth-in-sentencing* (mentioned previously in Chapter 11) approach by making federal aid for prison construction conditional on the passage of such laws.[51] Many have done just that (see Figure 15.6.)

"Truth in sentencing" is an umbrella term that covers a number of different state and federal statutes. In general, these laws have the following goals:

- To restore "truth" to the sentencing process by eliminating situations in which offenders are released by a parole board after serving less than the minimum term to which they were sentenced.

- To increase the percentage of the term that is actually served in prison, with the purpose of reducing crime by keeping convicts imprisoned for a longer period.

- To control the use of prison space by giving corrections officials the benefit of predictable terms and policymakers advance notice of the impact that sentencing statutes will have on prison populations.[52]

The decision to switch from indeterminate to determinate sentencing is for the most part a political, one often made after a parolee commits a violent crime. New Jersey, for example, saw a number of these incidents in the mid-1990s. In one, a seven-year-old girl was raped and murdered by a parolee who had been released six weeks earlier. In another, motorcycle gang member Robert "Mudman" Simon, who had been paroled in Pennsylvania several months earlier, shot and killed a New Jersey police officer during a routine traffic stop.[53] As a result, the New Jersey legislature passed the No Early Release Act. Under this new law, criminals convicted of first and second degree violent crimes must complete 85 percent of their sentences before becoming eligible for parole.[54]

Parole Guidelines

One of the most popular methods of ensuring truth in sentencing is the use of **parole guidelines.** Similar to sentencing guidelines (see Chapter 11), parole guidelines attempt to measure a potential parolee's risk of recidivism by considering factors such as the original offense, criminal history, behavior in prison, past employment, substance abuse, and performance under any previous periods of parole or probation. Inmates who score positively in these areas are considered less likely to pose a danger to society and have a better chance of obtaining an early release date.

Risk Assessments. Because of this emphasis on risk, many jurisdictions essentially use their guidelines as risk assessment devices. Colorado ranks its convicts as high risk, high-medium risk, medium risk, or low risk. When Colorado prisoners become eligible for parole (after serving half of their sentences), the parole board is required to base its decision on the inmate's risk level. High-risk offenders cannot receive parole until their sentence has expired. For high-medium and medium risks, the parole decision is contingent on an acceptable parole plan (discussed later in the chapter).[55] In general, low-risk offenders can expect to be paroled upon becoming eligible. As this example shows, many states have mixed aspects of mandatory and discretionary release into their parole procedures.

One problem with using risk assessment as a tool to determine parole is that, as we have seen when discussing bail and sentencing, future human behavior is difficult to predict based on past human behavior. Furthermore, it is not clear that complex, multifaceted methods of determining risk are necessarily superior to simpler methods. After studying the outcomes of 4,500 released prisoners, Stephen D. Gottfredson and Don M. Gottfredson found little difference among them based on the complexity of the guidelines used to determine whether they posed a risk to the community.[56]

Presumptive Parole Dates. Parole guidelines and other forms of mandatory release allow authorities to determine the **presumptive parole date,** or the presumed time at which an inmate will be paroled, based on the decision-making criteria. Ohio's latest parole guidelines, which went into effect in 1998, require inmates (excluding those who committed sex crimes or have received life sentences) to be informed of their expected release date the first time they appear before the parole board, which is usually within the first few weeks of imprisonment.[57] The presumptive parole date is not final—an inmate's good or bad behavior can shift the release date in either direction.

The Inmate's View of Parole

In 1998, Katherine Ann Power, who had been imprisoned for her role in a bank robbery that resulted in the death of a police officer, used her parole hearing to withdraw a request for early release and to apologize to the officer's family.[58] This is, needless to say, not normal inmate behavior. Many prisoners focus on their parole possibilities to the point of obsession. Inmates put a great deal of effort into convincing parole boards that they deserve early release. This effort can manifest itself in a genuine desire for self-improvement, or it can result in a series of manipulations, as prisoners try to "scam" the parole board into letting them out early.[59] (See *Popular Culture & Criminal Justice—Playing the Parole Game* on the next page.)

For some inmates, aspects of mandatory release such as presumptive parole dates offer a welcome change from the uncertainties of indeterminate sen-

---

PAROLE GUIDELINES
Employed to remove discretion from the parole process, these guidelines attempt to measure the risks of an offender recidivating, and then use these measurements to determine whether early release will be granted and under what conditions.

PRESUMPTIVE PAROLE DATE
The date, provided to a convict at the time of sentencing, at which he or she will be eligible for parole.

"Johnny plus alcohol plus women equals trouble."

—*Excerpt from 1976 parole report on Johnny Robert Eggers, who was released on parole five different times before stabbing a female teenager to death in 1994*

Playing the Parole Game

"They got a name for people like you. That name is called recidivism," one of the parole board members tells Hi, a repeat offender played by Nicholas Cage in the comedy *Raising Arizona*. "Not a pretty name, is it?"

"No sir," replies Hi dutifully. "That's one bonehead name, but that ain't me any more."

"You're not just telling us what we want to hear?" the board member asks, over Hi's protestations. "We just want to hear the truth."

"Well," says Hi, momentarily confused. "I guess I am telling you what you want to hear."

"Boy, didn't we just tell you not to do that!" comes back the reply.

This scene, without the comic touch, is replayed every day in thousands of parole boards around the country. And, like Hi, many of the parolees—nearly half—do recidivate. Although the simple Hi could not be accused of manipulat-

ing the system, many observers believe that in the real world, some convicts are expert at "playing the parole game." They know how to tell the board exactly what it wants to hear in order to get an early release.

"Some of your repeat offenders . . . can pick up on the answers they're supposed to give," said one corrections psychiatrist. "The more intelligent they are, the more they can literally read the system." In some instances, observers suggest, taking part in prison treatment programs actually increases the chances that an inmate will be able to successfully manipulate a parole board. By participating in the programs, the inmates learn the jargon of rehabilitation from staff members and are consequently better prepared to play, and win, the game.

When asked, the inmates themselves will sometimes admit to ulterior motives. Seventy-one percent of the

convicts polled at the U.S. Federal Penitentiary at Terre Haute, Indiana, agreed or strongly agreed with the following statement: "Inmates should look for activities that will show the parole board that they have used their time constructively."

known.[60] Others have reacted bitterly to the "get tough" atmosphere that has led to mandatory release policies. According to one felon,

> Were it not for the political climate, I would be home with my family, paying taxes, and starting over. Instead, I am being turned down for parole over and over again, because it is politically popular to do so.[61]

Indeed, some correctional officials have argued against limiting parole opportunities by raising the specter of inmate violence. During debate over whether to abolish parole in Georgia, a representative of the state prison guards' union warned that the hope of parole is the "only element that prevents riots and chaos."[62]

PAROLE CONTRACT
An agreement between the state and the offender that establishes the conditions under which the latter will be allowed to serve the remainder of her or his prison term in the community.

PAROLE SUPERVISION

The term *parole* has two meanings. The first, as we have seen, refers to the establishment of a release date. The second relates to the continuing supervision of convicted felons after they have been released from prison.

Conditions of Parole

Many of the procedures and issues of parole supervision are similar to those of probation supervision. Like probationers, when parolees are granted parole, they are placed under the supervision of correctional officers and required to follow certain conditions. Some of these conditions are fairly uniform. All parolees, for example, must comply with the law, and they are generally responsible for reporting to their parole officer at certain intervals. The frequency of these visits, along with the other terms of parole, are spelled out in the **parole contract,** which sets out the agreement between the state and the paroled offender. Under the terms of the contract, the state agrees to release the inmate under certain conditions, and the future parolee agrees to follow these conditions.

Each jurisdiction has its own standard parole contract, although the parole board can add specific provisions if it sees the need (see Figure 15.7). Besides common restrictions, such as no drug use, no association with known felons, and no change of address without notifying authorities, parolees have on occasion been ordered to lose weight and even to undergo chemical castration.

Recently, the U.S. Parole Commission began restricting high-risk federal parolees' ability to use the Internet. The new rules allow parole officers to make unannounced examinations of a parolee's computer and to check the required daily log of computer use. This move came as a result of the increase in online services that provide "how-to" instructions and other information in areas such as the illegal use of explosives, child pornography, and hate crimes.[63] Some precedents, however, suggest that parolees could argue that the restriction violates their constitutional rights. In 1971, a New York court struck down a condition that prohibited a parolee from making antiwar speeches, ruling that it impinged upon his right to freedom of speech.[64]

Work Release

Parole plans are not always one-sided. In some instances, prison authorities will agree to help the parolee find employment and a place to live during the supervision period.

Work Release Programs. These efforts reflect two realities of the release process:

1. Most inmates do not have the skills necessary to find a job and a home on their own.

INFOTRAC®
COLLEGE EDITION

Kuzma, Susan. **Civil disabilities of convicted felons.**

Figure 15.7 Standard Conditions of Parole

1. Upon my release I will report to my parole officer as directed and follow the parole officer's instructions.

2. I will report to my parole officer in person and in writing whenever and wherever the parole officer directs.

3. I agree that the parole officer has the right to visit my residence or place of employment at any reasonable time.

4. I will seek, obtain and maintain employment throughout my parole term, or perform community service as directed by my parole officer.

5. I will notify my parole officer prior to any changes in my place of residence, in my place of employment, or of any change in my marital status.

6. I will notify my parole officer within 48 hours if at any time I am arrested for any offense.

7. I will not at any time have firearms, ammunition, or any other weapon in my possession or under my control.

8. I will obey all laws, and to the best of my ability, fulfill all my legal obligations, including payment of all applicable child support and alimony orders.

9. I will not leave the state of _____ without prior permission of my parole officer.

10. I will not at any time, use, or have in my possession or control, any illegal drug or narcotic.

11. I will not at any time have contact or affiliation with any street gangs or with any members thereof.

12. Your release on parole is based upon the conclusion of the parole panel that there is a reasonable probability that you will live and remain at liberty without violating the law and that your release is not incompatible with the welfare of society. In the event that you engage in conduct in the future which renders this conclusion no longer valid, then your parole will be revoked or modified accordingly.

SOURCE: CONNECTICUT BOARD OF PAROLE.

WORK RELEASE PROGRAM
Temporary release of convicts from prison for purposes of employment. The offenders may spend their days on the job, but must return to the correctional facility at night and during the weekend.

HALFWAY HOUSE
A community-based form of early release that places inmates in residential centers and allows them to reintegrate with society.

The Delancey Street residential facility for drug offenders in San Francisco offers nearly 500 male and female residents the opportunity to kick their habits. What are some of the benefits of these facilities, both for the residents and for society?

2 A successful transition from prison life to life in the "real world" is often dependent on the personal stability that a job and a home can offer.

Work release programs are usually available for low-risk prisoners nearing the end of their sentences. In some cases, the employment opportunities are offered directly by government agencies or funded by tax dollars. In New York, for example, nonviolent parolees are hired as part of work crews that perform short-term, low-skilled, minimum-wage day labor, such as cleaning roadside areas for the State Department of Transportation.

These programs are relatively rare: less than 3 percent of American inmates participate in them.[65] The reason for this is twofold. First, many state corrections systems do not have the funds to pay for the programs. Second, prison authorities are very selective in choosing which inmates may participate. Those selected must not pose a threat to fellow workers. They also must be stable enough to handle the responsibility of employment.[66]

Halfway Houses. Inmates on work release either return to the correctional facility in the evening or live in community residential facilities, known as **halfway houses.** These facilities, also available to other parolees and those who have finished their sentences, are often remodeled hotels or private homes. They provide a less institutional living environment than a prison or jail for small numbers of inmates (usually between ten and twenty-five).

Despite the more congenial setting, halfway houses are strictly regulated. Depending on their status, some residents are not permitted to leave the facility except for purposes of employment and education. Most are held to a curfew that requires them to return at night. Normally, visits from family and friends are forbidden except during certain predetermined times. In addition, many of these homes offer a continuation of rehabilitative services such as substance abuse and life skills programs. Despite these precautions, halfway houses face major opposition in the community. Many citizens are not open to the idea of having convicts living in their midst and will often place pressure on local politicians to make sure that these residential centers are not located in their neighborhoods. This phenomenon is known as NIMBY, an acronym for "Not In My Back Yard."

Parole Officers

The correctional agent given the responsibility to supervise parolees is the parole officer. In many respects, the parole officer's relationship with the parolee mirrors that of the probation officer and the probationer (see Chapter 12); in fact, many municipal and state departments of corrections combine the two posts to create probation/parole officers. Parole officers are required to enforce the conditions of parole and initiate revocation hearings when these conditions are not met. Furthermore, a parole officer is expected to help the parolee readjust to life outside the correctional institution by helping her or him find a place to live and a job, and seeing that she or he receives any treatment or rehabilitation that may be necessary.

A Greater Challenge. The major difference between the work of a probation officer and that of a parole officer reflects the differences between probationers and parolees. The community supervision of probationers, as will be recalled from Chapter 12, serves as an alternative to incarceration; these individuals generally have not been sent to prison and thus do not suffer from the effects of incarceration. In contrast, parolees have been separated from the outside community—sometimes for many years—and may retain many of the values of prison life. Furthermore, a parolee carries the stigma of being an "ex-con," which makes reintegration (finding employment and housing) even more difficult. The parolee is literally in a strange new world, where even family members or friends may be unable to offer useful assistance.

Consequently, a parole officer usually has to take a much more active role in supervising a parolee than a probation officer does with a probationer.

Careers in Criminal Justice

REBECCA ANN PASTRANA, THE PAROLE OFFICER

My name is Rebecca Ann Pastrana. I obtained my Bachelor of Science in Criminal Justice from the University of Texas at El Paso in May 1982. Currently, I'm attending the Master's Program at New Mexico State Univeristy in Criminal Justice. While obtaining my degree, I did an internship at Juvenile Probation and became interested in probation/parole work. At that time I thought that because of my degree and all of my college hours in sociology and psychology, I would solve all of my clients' problems and make them productive citizens. After briefly living outside the country, I finally decided to work in my chosen career and found a job as a parole officer in Houston, Texas for an agency known at that time as the Board of Pardons and Parole. During my interview, they asked only one question, did I speak Spanish? I do and so I was hired. In October of 1986, I moved to another job in Houston and naively believed I was going to make a difference. Imagine a middle-class 27 year old woman who had yet to work a 40 hour job, moving from El Paso, a pre-dominantly conservative Hispanic city to Houston, a huge, fast-paced, cosmopolitan city. I had never even been to a bad neighborhood in El Paso. I had never experienced being poor or any form of violence. At the university I was taught, simply stated, that being poor was a factor in becoming a criminal. Being as naive as I was, I believed I was going to conquer the world and rid it of crime. Then I woke up abruptly.

At the moment, I'm in charge of the Electronic Monitoring Program for approximately 30 releasees. In my program, I'm responsible for the equipment, billing, inventory, and especially my clients. The other 20 officers in the El Paso office use E.M. as a sanction, which means I am responsible for correcting negative behaviors such as not obtaining employment, using drugs, or not attending substance abuse classes. E.M. is a form of house arrest and if the offender is not home at the commencement of his curfew a pre-revocation warrant will be issued. Most releasees have a pre-conceived notion that I am setting them up to return to the Texas Department of Corrections, and therefore my success rate is only about 10%. These aren't good odds and most releasees are very reluctant to go on my caseload. I try to help releasees by making referrals to different agencies such as the Texas Workforce Commission to obtain employment, Aliviane Drug Program, Life Management, or GED classes. My job primarily consists of making sure they attend their counseling sessions, that they report on time, and reside at the correct address. My co-workers sometimes joke that we are simply glorified baby-sitters.

During my first few months on the job in Houston, I had a life altering experience that probably happened because I was not properly trained by my department. I had scheduled a home visit to verify a new address for a client who had moved to the Third Ward of Houston. This was out of my district, and I wanted to verify that I could transfer the case. I had been told never to visit the Third Ward alone, and that not even the Houston Police Department went alone. So I asked a co-worker to go with me. To enter the apartment complex, we had to climb up a stairwell where the front doors opened inside into the hall way. There was only one way in and out. I completed my contact with the releasee and proceeded to leave. On the stairs three men were waiting. In a flash, I was shoved up against the wall, thrown again, and fell down the remaining stairs. They robbed me of a chain with a cross. My glasses were broken and gone was my naïve belief that all people are good. Unfortunately, I had ignored my instinct to ask the parolee to walk me down the stairs. Subsequently, I have learned to listen to those instincts. The worst part was returning to the office and telling my immediate supervisor and the parole supervisor. They began to yell at me and told me that I was going to face disciplinary action for taking another officer with me. I could only imagine what might have happened had she not been there. I thought my supervisors treated me unfairly, especially since I had never received formal training, and I realized that the agency's support of employees was not always what they claimed it to be. Ten years later I eventually received some verbal-judo training, which seemed a little late in retrospect.

This difficult incident made me realize the dangers and the law enforcement aspects of the job. As a profession we are becoming more law enforcement oriented, and we are now being allowed to carry firearms. We are hoping to become commissioned officers in the very near future. Being a parole officer is a challenge and every work day is different. I enjoy my job and hope that in some way I am making a small contribution, even if I can't change the world, as I had originally planned.

Given the lack of rehabilitation services in most correctional facilities, the parole officer cannot assume that the paroled offender has "learned his or her lesson" and hence must be vigilant in reporting any violations. Furthermore, parolees, having been subjected to the violence of prison culture, are considered more dangerous than probationers. For this reason, parole officers are generally armed, and in some jurisdictions they wear bulletproof vests when they make their rounds. (See *Careers in Criminal Justice—The Parloe Officer*.)

PAROLE REVOCATION
When a parolee breaks the conditions of parole, the process of withdrawing parole and returning the person to prison.

"Change" Agents. According to Todd Clear of Florida State University and Edward Latessa of the University of Cincinnati, the major role conflict for parole officers is whether to be a law enforcement officer or a social worker.[67] That is, parole officers are constantly required to choose between the good of the community and the good of the paroled offender. In one study of parole officer stress and burnout, researchers found that more than 60 percent of the officers interviewed felt uncertain about how to balance these two requirements.[68] To be sure, some parole officers focus entirely on protecting the community and see the welfare of the client as a secondary concern. (For an example of this conflict, see *CJ in Focus—The Balancing Act: Cop or Caretaker?*)

A growing number of parole experts, however, believe that parole officers should act as agents of change, meaning that they should try not simply to control the offender's behavior but also to change it. This entails that the parole officer establish strong bonds of trust and commitment with the parolee by taking what could be called a parental attitude to the officer-client relationship.[69]

Many parole officers react to the idea of being "change" agents by asking, "Where do I find the time?" Besides role conflict, stress is also caused by heavy caseloads. Jurisdictions from metro Denver to rural New Hampshire report more than a hundred parolees assigned to each officer, a situation that seriously compromises an officer's ability to supervise individual offenders. In 1998, veteran Tacoma (Washington) parole officer Barbara Nelson was fired after three offenders under her supervision committed murder. The offenders had exhibited signs of criminal behavior, including one who was fired from his job for violent outbursts, but Nelson insisted she had done everything within her power to supervise the men. The problem, she said, was that she and her colleagues were "swamped" with cases, with individual officers being responsible for as many as 160 offenders.

Following Nelson's firing, outside consultants found that morale among Tacoma parole officers was extremely low; the agents worried that, any day, they might be "the last person holding the dynamite."[70] Some observers believe that technology may offer relief for the stressed-out, overburdened parole officer. The GENIE (Graphically Enhanced Network Information Enterprise) System, for example, gives nonviolent parolees the opportunity to fulfill their "meeting" requirement by answering questions presented by computer monitors at electronic kiosks.[71] The reporting centers, not unlike ATMs in appearance, would free parole officers to concentrate on high-risk offenders who pose the greatest threat to the community.

Parole Revocation

If convicts follow the conditions of their parole until the *maximum expiration date,* or the date on which their sentence ends, then they are discharged from supervision. A large number—about 40 percent, according to the latest research—return to incarceration before their maximum expiration date, most because they were convicted of a new offense or had their parole revoked (see Figure 15.8). **Parole revocation** is similar in many aspects to probation revocation. If the parolee commits a new crime, then a return to prison is very likely. If, however, the individual breaks a condition of parole, known as a technical violation, the parole authorities have discretion as to whether revocation proceedings should be initiated. An example of a technical viola-

Figure 15.8 Terminating Parole

As you can see, nearly half of all parolees successfully complete their terms of parole. The rest are either returned to incarceration, transferred, or die while on parole.

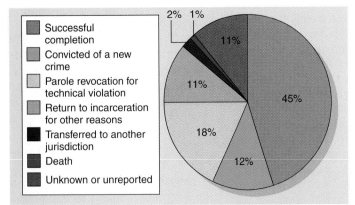

- Successful completion
- Convicted of a new crime
- Parole revocation for technical violation
- Return to incarceration for other reasons
- Transferred to another jurisdiction
- Death
- Unknown or unreported

2% 1%
11%
11%
45%
18%
12%

SOURCE: ADAPTED FROM BUREAU OF JUSTICE STATISTICS, *CORRECTIONAL POPULATIONS IN THE UNITED STATES, 1995* (WASHINGTON, D.C.: U.S. DEPARTMENT OF JUSTICE, 1997), TABLE 6.5, PAGE 130.

CJ in Focus

The Balancing Act:

Cop or Caretaker?

When five parole officers burst into the residence in Noble, Oklahoma, they expected to find one Ned Snow, parolee. Snow was wanted for alleged parole violations. Even though Snow did not happen to be at the residence at the time of the "visit," the parole officers, who were accompanied by two local deputies, proceeded to search the house and seize prescription drugs from the women who lived there. Several days later, the parole officers returned to the dwelling, once again to find that Snow was not at home. Snow's wife and mother, to their misfortune, were present. The parole officers proceeded to handcuff the two women and place them in a state vehicle. At this point, Snow arrived in another car, but fled as soon as he saw what was taking place. One of the parole officers commandeered the women's pickup truck and chased Snow at a high speed until the truck's engine blew.

In the aftermath of these events, one of the parole officers involved lost her job and three others were suspended. This was not, however, an isolated incident. To the chagrin of many Oklahoma corrections and law enforcement officials, it represented an internal philosophical debate over the proper role of the state's parole officers. Was their primary purpose to act as surrogate police officers or as social workers concerned mainly with the well-being of their clients?

The parole officers involved in the Snow debacle, along with a number of their colleagues, leaned toward assuming the role of law enforcement officer. In the words of one insider, these officers felt that their job was "to take names and kick asses." According to another officer, "These few guys want to be 120 percent law enforcement and they don't want to do any of the social-work part of it."

A further worry was that this aggressive attitude was denying parolees their constitutional rights. Although parole officers are allowed to conduct unannounced "visits" at the homes and workplaces of parolees, they do not have the authority to conduct searches without a warrant. In the words of one parole officer, parolees "have a right to a search warrant just like everybody else does." In several Oklahoma counties, parole and probation officers have an understanding with local police agencies: if the police suspect a parolee of illegal activity but do not have a warrant to search his or her abode, they will call on the parolee's parole officer to make an unannounced visit and search.

Supporters of "John Wayne-style" parole officers argue that such tactics are needed to protect citizens. Senior Oklahoma probation and parole officer Kris Evans disagrees. "We do have a law enforcement component to our job, but we're not supposed to be out there playing detective," Evans says. "We supervise people on probation or parole, and that's the scope of our employment." He adds, "If you want to go kick in doors, go apply to the OSBI (Oklahoma State Bureau of Investigation) or a local law enforcement agency."

For Critical Analysis: What would be some of the consequences if all parole officers focused on the law enforcement aspects of their job rather than its social service responsibilities?

---

tion would be failure to report a change in address to parole authorities. As with probation revocation, many observers believe that those who commit technical violations should not be imprisoned, as they have not committed a crime.

Due Process and Parole Revocation. Until 1972, parole officers had the power to arbitrarily revoke parole status for technical violations. A parolee who was returned to prison had little or no recourse. In *Morrissey v. Brewer* (1972),[72] the Supreme Court changed this by deciding that a parolee has a "liberty interest" in remaining on parole. (See *CJ in Focus—Landmark Cases: Morrissey v. Brewer.*) In other words, before parolees can be deprived of their liberty, they must be afforded a measure of due process at a parole revocation hearing.

Although this hearing does not provide the same due process protections as a criminal trial, the parolee does have the right to be notified of the charges, to present witnesses, to speak in his or her defense, and to question any hostile witnesses (as long as such questioning would not place them in danger). In the first stage of the hearing, the parole board determines whether there is probable cause that a violation occurred. Then, the board decides whether to return the parolee to prison.

The Exclusionary Rule and Parole Revocation. The Fourth Amendment guarantee against unreasonable searches is protected by the exclusionary rule, which provides a disincentive for such searches by excluding illegally

CJ in Focus

Landmark Cases:

Morrissey v. Brewer

Morrissey was paroled from the Iowa State Penitentiary in 1967, having served one year of a seven-year sentence for forging checks. Seven months later, his parole officer ordered his arrest based on a number of alleged violations, including buying a car under a false name and failing to report his place of residence to his parole officer. After reading the parole officer's written report, the Iowa Board of Parole revoked Morrissey's parole and returned him to the penitentiary. Morrissey filed a *habeas corpus* petition claiming that he had been denied his Fourteenth Amendment right to due process because his parole had been revoked without a hearing. The Court of Appeals held that parole was a privilege, not a right, and therefore due process is not applicable to revocation proceedings. The Supreme Court agreed to hear Morrissey's appeal in order to decide whether due process applies to the parole system.

Morrissey v. Brewer
United States Supreme Court
408 U.S. 471 (1972)
http://laws.findlaw.com/US/408/471.html

In the Words of the Court . . .

Mr. Chief Justice BURGER, majority opinion

* * * *

We begin with the proposition that the revocation of parole is not part of a criminal prosecution and thus the full panoply of rights due a defendant in such a proceeding does not apply to parole revocations. * * * Revocation deprives an individual, not of the absolute liberty to which every citizen is entitled, but only of the conditional liberty properly dependent on observance of special parole restrictions. We turn, therefore, to the question whether the requirements of due process in general apply to parole revocations. * * * Whether any procedural protections are due depends on the extent to which an individual will be "condemned to suffer grievous loss."

* * * *

[T]he liberty of a parolee, although indeterminate, includes many of the core values of unqualified liberty and its termination inflicts a "grievous loss" on the parolee and often on others. It is hardly useful any longer to try to deal with this problem in terms of whether the parolee's liberty is a "right" or a "privilege." By whatever name, the liberty is valuable and must be seen as within the protection of the Fourteenth Amendment. Its termination calls for some orderly process, however informal.

* * * *

Given the previous conviction and the proper imposition of conditions, the State has an overwhelming interest in being able to return the individual to imprisonment without the burden of a new adversary criminal trial if in fact he has failed to abide by the conditions of his parole. Yet, the State has no interest in revoking parole without some informal procedural guarantees. * * * A simple factual hearing will not interfere with the exercise of discretion. Serious studies have suggested that fair treatment on parole revocation will not result in fewer grants of parole.

* * * *

Society has a stake in whatever may be the chance of restoring [the parolee] to normal and useful life within the law. Society thus has an interest in not having parole revoked because of erroneous information or because of an erroneous evaluation of the need to revoke parole, given the breach of parole conditions. And society has a further interest in treating the parolee with basic fairness: fair treatment in parole revocations will enhance the chance of rehabilitation by avoiding reactions to arbitrariness. Given these factors, most States have recognized that there is no interest on the part of the State in revoking parole without any procedural guarantees at all. What is needed is an informal hearing structured to assure that the finding of a parole violation will be based on verified facts and that the exercise of discretion will be informed by an accurate knowledge of the parolee's behavior.

Decision: The Court held that the Fourteenth Amendment requirement of due process of law applied to the parole process. In other words, it ruled that even though parolees are restricted to a much greater degree than the average citizen, they still enjoyed a measure of freedom that could not be taken away arbitrarily. The Court moved to enforce this ruling by adding two steps to the revocation process. First, an informal inquiry conducted by an impartial probation official must determine if there is reasonable grounds to believe that the parolee has violated his or her conditions of parole. Second, a revocation hearing must be held in which the parolee has basic due process rights, such as a chance to hear the charges, speak in his or her defense, and present witnesses in his or her favor.

For Critical Analysis: Many parole officers disagreed with Chief Justice Burger's assertion that "a simple factual hearing" would "not interfere with the exercise" of their discretion. What are some of the ways in which this decision does interfere with a parole officer's discretion, and how do you feel the *Morrissey* ruling strengthened or weakened the parole process?

Note: Triple asterisks (***) indicate a few words or sentences have been deleted and quadruple asterisks (****) indicate that an entire paragraph (or more has been omitted from the opinion.

obtained evidence from criminal proceedings. (See Chapter 5 to review the exclusionary rule.) Many jurisdictions have traditionally allowed evidence from searches that would otherwise be found unconstitutional to be presented at parole revocation hearings. In *Pennsylvania Board of Probation v. Scott* (1998),[73] the Supreme Court validated this practice in a case involving the search of a murderer's home that uncovered guns and other weapons that he possessed in violation of his parole conditions. In his opinion, Justice Clarence Thomas justified the practice by noting that parolees "are more likely to commit future criminal offenses than are average citizens."[74]

The lack of strong due process and exclusionary rule protection adds to the number of parole revocations. Police officers and prosecutors find it far simpler to process arrestees by charging them with violating their conditions of parole than by charging them with a new offense. The result has been a new form of plea bargaining, in which the defendant waives her or his right to a parole hearing and returns to custody in exchange for the prosecutor dropping any new charges.

TOO DANGEROUS FOR RELEASE?

In a letter to the Pennsylvania Board of Pardons, Reginald McFadden asked for a chance to show that he could "function normally" among law-abiding citizens. "You have given me these years to reassess my life's values," McFadden wrote, "and as a result, I am a better person." Three months after being granted parole, McFadden was arrested on three charges of murder and suspected of a fourth.[75] Such incidents, rare though they may be, not only lead to questions about the parole system, but also heighten fears of releasing *any* violent criminal.[76]

Citizens in Limbo

This mistrust manifests itself in the legal restrictions faced by all convicts, even those who were model prisoners or parolees. Figure 15.9 provides a list of rights that are currently or have in the past been denied to convicts once they return to the community. Perhaps no statutory restrictions better represent society's feeling toward the "dangerous" ex-prisoner than sex offender notification laws, known as "Megan's Laws." (See the feature *Criminal Justice in Action—Protecting the Community from Sex Offenders* at the end of this chapter.)

For many released inmates, however, the inability to serve on a jury or other civil rights restrictions are the least of their worries. For all the hardships of incarceration, it does offer a haven from the day-to-day decisions that characterize life on the outside. Furthermore, the prison environment insulates inmates; a convict released after a long prison term may find common acts such as using an ATM or pumping his or her gas completely alien.

High-profile cases such as that of Richard Allen Davis (pictured), who was sentenced to death in 1993 for the kidnapping and murder of 12-year-old Polly Klaas, have led many communities to limit the rights and freedoms of released sex offenders.

In many jurisdictions, convicts do not have the right to:

- Hold public office.
- Be employed by the public sector. (This restriction is gradually being removed.)
- Own firearms.
- Serve on a jury.
- Have automobile and life insurance.
- Adopt children.

SOURCE: GEORGE KILLINGER, PROBATION AND PAROLE IN THE CRIMINAL JUSTICE SYSTEM (ST. PAUL, MN: WEST PUBLISHING COMPANY, 1976), 126–144.

Figure 15.9 The Limited Rights of Convicts

At one time, convicted offenders were denied the right to vote, the reasoning being that they did not have the required honesty and proper values to be allowed to participate in the voting process. Such restrictions have been lifted, but the rights of convicted offenders are still limited in other areas.

In prison, according to one inmate, the "rules" of daily life followed by citizens on the outside are turned upside-down:

> An unexpected smile could mean trouble. A man in uniform was not a friend. Being kind was a weakness. Viciousness and recklessness were to be respected and admired.[77]

Consequently, inmates experience a shift in reality while behind bars. In other words, they live differently than do those on the outside. As another long-term inmate commented:

> For most, the prison experience is a one-way ride on a psychological roller coaster—downhill. And the easiest thing to do, in a world where almost everything is an assault against you, is to permit yourself to be defeated by the overwhelming indifference and sense of hopelessness that steals into your daily existence, slowly, almost unnoticeably sapping your drive, your dreams, your ambition, evoking cries from the soul to surrender.[78]

It is understandably difficult for many inmates to readjust to life on the outside after feeling such pressures. A friend of Reginald McFadden's blamed his recidivism on the fact that he "could not handle any of the emotions that come with being set free."[79]

The Move to Abolish Parole

The concept of parole strikes many observers as problematic. Why go through the considerable effort of arrest and trial to incarcerate a dangerous individual, only to release him or her before the date legally mandated? Furthermore, logic seems to dictate that if the average violent criminal serves only half of his or her sentence, then the crimes that these offenders might commit would be reduced substantially if they were forced to serve their full time.[80]

Indeed, using these justifications, fourteen states and the federal government have "abolished" parole since Maine first took the step in 1975 (see Figure 15.10). In many of these jurisdictions, however, the emphasis is on prison terms that are "truthful," not necessarily "longer." Therefore, in Louisiana—noted for its harsh sentencing practices—violent offenders who serve only 50 percent of their term spend more time in prison than do offenders in states that have "abolished" parole.[81] Virginia is one state that has tried to address these inconsistencies through reform.

The Virginia Model. Between 1985 and 1991, nearly 80 percent of Virginia felons arrested for violent crimes served fewer than three years in prison.[82] In light of these statistics, Governor George Allen ordered the implementation of a release system that would

- Abolish parole and overly generous good-time credits.

- Ensure that violent criminals serve significantly longer prison terms.

- Divert nonviolent offenders to alternative forms of punishment to free bed space for violent criminals.

The resulting reform was based on two assumptions: (1) offenders who had a violent crime in their past were more likely to recidivate than those who did not; and (2) the peak age for violence was between eighteen and twenty-four years. The new sentencing guidelines reflected these assumptions by dramatically increasing the minimum sentences for certain crimes. For example, whereas armed robbers committing a first offense served an average of 2.7

Figure 15.10 Abolishing Parole

Since 1975, fourteen states have abolished early release by the discretion of a parole board.

State	Year
Maine	1975
Indiana	1977
Illinois	1978
Minnesota	1980
Florida	1983
Washington	1984
Oregon	1989
Delaware	1990
Kansas	1993
Arizona	1994
North Carolina	1994
Mississippi	1995
Ohio	1996
Wisconsin	1999

SOURCE: Bureau of Justice Statistics, Truth in Sentencing in State Prisons (Washington, D.C.: U.S. Department of Justice, 1999), 3.

years under the old parole system, the new guidelines demanded that they serve 5.4 years. A convicted armed robber with a prior record would be required to serve at least 10.8 years.[83] As a result, violent criminals would be more likely to spend their peak "violent years" in prison,

Blueprint for the Future? Virginia's reform plan has been the target of criticism. Primarily, opponents say it will be prohibitively expensive because it will force correctional facilities to continue paying incarceration costs of prisoners who would otherwise be living in the community.[84]

Initially, however, this does not seem to be the case. Although violent offenders are serving longer terms, nonviolent offenders—who make up the majority of prison populations—are not, so the number of people incarcerated has been reduced.[85] People convicted of first degree murder are slated to serve an average of nearly 46 years under the new laws, compared to just over 12 years prior to reform. The incarceration length for those convicted of forcible rape has risen from 5.6 years to 11 years.[86] Furthermore, the system appears to be less expensive, lending credence to a Department of Justice study that stated that it costs the government nine times more to prosecute crimes committed by repeat offenders each year than it does to keep them in prison (mainly due to the attorney's fees and other expenses connected with a trial).[87] It should be noted that Virginia has not abolished the supervisory aspects of early release, which still exists on a limited scale because of good-time credits.

Although it is too early to determine the effect of Virginia's reform on its overall crime rates, the state would seem to have found a blueprint for the future: a system that reduces overcrowding and cuts costs by keeping violent offenders imprisoned while finding alternative sanctions for nonviolent ones. The solutions for the problems that plague the American corrections system are not so simple, however. In the final three chapters of this text, we will examine subjects, such as juvenile crime and the spread of illegal drugs, which can frustrate even the most optimistic reformers.

Victims' rights groups have become more and more vocal in trying to keep violent criminals from receiving parole. Go to www.parolewatch.org/ welcome.htm and home.sprynet.com/ ~statnisle/clemency.htm to see the tactics favored by these groups.

Criminal Justice in Action

Protecting the Community from Sex Offenders

In the summer of 1994, seven-year-old Megan Kanka of Hamilton Township, New Jersey, was raped and murdered by a twice-convicted pedophile (an adult sexually attracted to children) who had moved into her neighborhood after being released from prison on parole. As we have seen in this chapter, the actions of one released offender can have far-reaching consequences. The next year, the state passed a series of laws known collectively as the New Jersey Sexual Offender Registration Act, or "Megan's Law."[88] Today, forty-seven states and the federal government have passed their own versions of Megan's Law, which require local law authorities to alert the public when a sex offender has been released in the community. Hailed by victim's rights groups and reviled by civil libertarians, these laws—which are the focus of this *Criminal Justice in Action* feature—have been the topic of much controversy.

ACTIVE AND PASSIVE NOTIFICATION

No two of these laws have exactly the same provisions, but all are designed with the goal of allowing the public to learn the identities of convicted sex offenders living in their midst. The incentive to institute such laws was enhanced in 1996 when Congress passed its own Megan's Law, which requires a state to provide communities with relevant information on sex offenders as a condition of receiving federal anticrime funds.[89]

In general, these laws demand that a paroled sexual offender notify local law enforcement authorities upon taking up residence in a state. This registration process must be renewed every time the parolee changes address. The process of community notification by the authorities has two models. The "active" model requires that they directly notify the community or community representatives. This often takes the form of bulletins or flyers, distributed and posted within a certain distance from the offender's home. In the "passive" model, informa-

tion on sex offenders must be open and available for public scrutiny. In California, for example, the state has created a CD-ROM that provides the names, photos, and Zip Codes of nearly 64,000 of the state's released sex offenders.[90]

In some instances, convicts must notify authorities themselves. Paroled sex offenders in Georgia are required to present themselves to both the sheriff and the superintendent of the public school district where they plan to reside.[91] Generally, sex offenders are supervised by parole officers and are subject to the same threat of revocation as other parolees. Paroled child molesters usually have the following conditions of release:

- Must have no contact with children under the age of sixteen.
- Must continue psychiatric treatment.
- Must receive permission from their parole officer to change residence.
- Must stay a certain distance from schools or parks where children are present.
- Cannot own toys that may be used to lure children.
- Cannot have a job or participate in any activity that involves children.

In some cases, after release from incarceration, sex offenders must return to the county where they committed their crime.

LEGAL ISSUES

In nearly every jurisdiction, Megan's Laws have been challenged as unconstitutional. The common theme among these court cases is that Megan's Laws represent a form of "punishment" and as such violate state and federal constitutional prohibitions against double jeopardy and cruel and unusual punishment. In other words, by forcing sex offenders to register in expectation of a crime they have yet to commit, these laws operate in opposition to the principle that persons are innocent until proven guilty. Furthermore, because of the scrutiny that is certain to fall upon a pedophile whose past crimes have been broadcast to the community, offenders have filed suit claiming that the laws unconstitutionally invade their privacy.[92]

Most courts have ruled that the notification process in Megan's Laws does not, in fact, constitute "punishment." The Supreme Court of New Jersey, for example, found that although some of the ramifications of the law may indeed be punitive, its intent was remedial and consequently did not violate the state or federal constitution.[93] The New Jersey court also found that the law did infringe upon offenders' privacy rights, but held that the need to protect those rights was outweighed by the strong state interest of disclosure.[94] In other words, the offender's right to privacy was not as strong as the public's right to be informed of his or her presence.

Many legal experts are awaiting a Supreme Court ruling on notification laws, hoping that it would eliminate some of the confusion and inconsistency that plague the many different state statutes. In 1998, however, the Court refused to hear challenges to the Megan's Laws of New York and New Jersey, effectively allowing individual jurisdictions to continue setting their own notification policies.[95]

GETTING TOUGHER WITH SEX OFFENDERS

Megan's Laws have increased community awareness of the danger of sex offenders—one in twelve of the 24,000 Californians who accessed the sex offender CD-ROM recognized a registrant. Furthermore, notification policies have no doubt forced some offenders

to confront their psychological problems and driven them to participate more actively in their own rehabilitation.

Even some supporters are beginning to question the laws, however. Identified offenders often become targets of vigilante action, and sometimes that action is misguided. In New Jersey, for example, a man broke into an apartment and severely beat its occupant after finding the address on the state's sex offender computer bank. The convict had moved, however, and the beating victim was not a former criminal.

Such cases are rare, but they have been more effective than the constitutional challenges in raising questions in the public mind about Megan's Laws. Why, observers are beginning to ask, is the government releasing people from prison when the state itself considers them so likely to re-offend that the community must be warned of their very presence? As a result, state legislators are calling for harsher mandatory

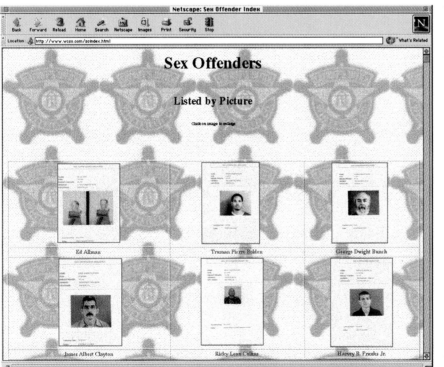

Several states and hundreds of communities post lists of convicted sex offenders and their addresses on the Internet as a public service. How does posting information on a Web site differ from other forms of notification? Do such sites unfairly infringe upon the privacy rights of the offenders?

sentences for sex crimes, which would reduce the number of sex offenders on parole and reduce the need for Megan's Laws in the first place.

The Supreme Court opened the door for this type of state action and provided what many legal experts saw as tacit approval of Megan's Laws in *Hendricks v. Kansas* (1997).[96] The case involved a challenge to Kansas's Sexually Violent Predator Act, which allows the state to commit to a mental institution any inmate with a "personality disorder" or "mental abnormality" who is likely to engage in "predatory acts of sexual violence."[97] Practically, this allows prosecutors to send convicted sex offenders to mental institutions after they have served the term of their original sentence. The Court's favorable ruling bolstered similar laws in Arizona, California, Minnesota, New Jersey, Washington, and Wisconsin, and provided a legal opening for nearly thirty other states considering such statutes.

IS THERE ANOTHER WAY?

The spread of sex offender laws reflects a dual need among citizens: notification and prevention. In the case of notification, it would appear that these laws can be effective. That is, they can help answer the question: Is my neighbor a sex offender?

As for preventing further sex offenses, the new laws may not be as effective as citizens and politicians may hope. The problem is that sex offenders have a high rate of recidivism; according to the Bureau of Justice Statistics, they are "substantially more likely" than other violent criminals to be rearrested for a new violent offense.[98] Megan's Laws represent an attempt to prevent further crimes by supervising and controlling the movement of sex offenders. There are alternatives.[99]

A number of jurisdictions are leaning toward civil commitment, in which sex offenders are sent to another, noncorrectional facility (such as a psychiatric hospital) after serving their prison or jail terms. Some observers have proposed the additional options of "banishment," in which sex offenders are sent to restricted communities in remote areas, and castration. There is also a movement to increase the penalties for sex offenders. As one New Jersey judge commented, "Why doesn't Congress, or why don't the states, pass an act [requiring that] if you commit a sex offense against a child you never get out of jail—you never get off probation and you lock them up forever?"[100]

Certainly, it would be simple if society could just send all sex offenders to an island and forget about them—simple, but unconstitutional and, ultimately, impossible. Megan's Law and similar legislation, for all the criticism they receive, may represent the best way to protect communities from sex offenders by providing citizens with the means to protect themselves.

Key Terms

behavior therapy 528

classification 525

discretionary release 534

furlough 532

general equivalency degree (GED) 528

halfway house 542

"life skills" programs 529

mandatory release 532

pardon 532

parole 531

parole board 535

parole contract 540

parole grant hearing 536

parole guidelines 539

parole revocation 544

presumptive parole date 539

psychotherapy 527

reality therapy 528

token economy 528

work release programs 542

Chapter Summary

1. List the types of assessments that jails or prisons might use with new prisoners. (a) Give a test of adult basic education; (b) make a substance abuse and/or life circumstances evaluation; and (c) assess the new prisoner's vocational needs and interests.

2. Describe four types of psychological treatment programs for prisoners. (a) Social therapy, and in particular group therapy. These include exercises to break down prisoners' unwillingness to discuss their personal problems. (b) Reality therapy, which involves teaching the inmate to reject irresponsible behavior. (c) Behavior therapy, which attempts to eliminate problem behaviors that lead to criminality and which may involve the use of drugs to control or eliminate certain behaviors, such as alcoholism. (d) Token economy programs, which condition the inmate to positive behavior by rewarding that behavior with tokens that can be used to purchase certain privileges.

3. List the concepts on which parole is based. (a) Grace, (b) contract of consent, and (c) custody.

4. Contrast probation, parole, mandatory release, pardon, and furlough. Probation is an alternative to incarceration. Parole is an early release program for those incarcerated. Mandatory release occurs when the inmate has served the maximum time for her or his initial sentence minus good-time credits. A pardon can only be given by the president or one of the fifty governors. Furlough is a temporary release while in jail or prison.

5. List the four basic roles of a typical parole board. (a) To decide which inmates should be given parole; (b) to determine the conditions of parole;

(c) to discharge the offender when the conditions of parole have been met; and (d) to determine whether parole privileges should be revoked when a violation of parole occurs.

6. Explain what truth-in-sentencing laws are and describe their goals. Such laws make more transparent the actual time that a convicted criminal will serve in jail or prison. The goals are (a) to restore "truth" to the sentencing process; (b) to increase the percentage of the term that is actually served in prison in order to reduce crime by keeping convicts "off the streets" for a longer period; and (c) to better control the use of prison space by giving corrections officials predictable terms and policymakers advanced notice of potential overcrowding.

7. Describe typical conditions of parole. Parolees must not use drugs, not associate with known felons, not change their addresses without notifying authorities, and report to their parole officer at specified intervals. (The latter is usually specified in the parole contract.)

8. Contrast a probation officer with a parole officer and indicate some of the problems facing parole officers. A probation officer deals with those convicted of a crime but not sentenced to be incarcerated. A parole officer deals with those who have spent time behind bars. Because parolees have been subjected to the violence of prison culture, they are more dangerous than probationers, and therefore parole officers feel in more danger. Many such officers carry guns. Parole officers face excessive caseloads (as do many probation officers).

9. Explain whether the exclusionary rule applies to events that lead to parole revocation. In general, the exclusionary rule does not apply to evidence that may be presented in parole revocation hearing. A parolee does not have the same rights to due process as does the average citizen.

10. **Indicate typical conditions for release for a paroled child molester.** (a) Have no contact with children under the age of sixteen; (b) continue psychiatric treatment; (c) obtain permission from a parole officer to change residence; (d) keep away from schools or parks where children are present; (e) cannot own toys that may be used to lure children; and (f) cannot have a job or participate in any activity that involves children.

Questions for Critical Analysis

1. Do prisoners have a constitutional right to any type of educational, rehabilitative, or vocational programs? If yes, what right? If no, why not?

2. What is the purpose of assessing prisoners at the beginning of their stay in prison?

3. What is one of the main reasons inmates attend prison educational and vocational programs?

4. What has caused a reduction in the amount of discretion that parole boards have?

5. Who are some of the individuals who are asked to provide comments and recommendations for a parole grant hearing?

6. What can affect the actual date parole is granted compared to the presumptive parole date?

7. For whom are work release programs usually created, and do a large percentage of prisoners participate?

8. When a parolee is caught committing a crime, what typically tends to happen and why?

9. During the 1990s, Virginia changed its prisoner release system. Among other things, it abolished parole, yet incarceration costs have not skyrocketed. Why not?

10. Why do civil libertarians criticize Megan's Laws?

Selected Print and Electronic Resources

SUGGESTED READINGS

Michaud, Stephen G., and Roy Hazelwood, *The Evil That Men Do: FBI Profiler Ray Hazelwood's Journey into the Minds of Sexual Predators*, New York: St. Martins Press, 1999. This book is written by one of the world's leading experts on the sexual criminal. He has developed accurate profiles and can predict criminal behavior of this type using his logical reasoning. He offers a disturbing glimpse at some of the most deranged violent people modern society has produced. Though essentially a textbook for the law enforcement and forensic science professional, this book makes fascinating reading for just about anyone.

Moore, Kathleen, *Pardons: Justice, Mercy, and the Public Interest*, New York: Oxford University Press, 1997. The author discusses what justifies pardoning power, who is to be pardoned, and which crimes should never be pardoned. She includes an interesting historical analysis of the pardon.

Petersilia, Joan, ed., *Community Corrections: Probation, Parole, and Intermediate Sanctions*, New York: Oxford University Press, 1997. This book evaluates the effectiveness of parole and other sanctions. It provides a detailed examination of total quality management.

Rios, Mrs., *Me . . . Teach Criminals?: The True Adventures of a Prison Teacher*, Burlington, VT: Vantage Press, 1996. Mrs. Rios describes her eight years as a teacher in a Texas prison. This is the true story of a correctional educator who sincerely believes that there is hope for inmates. She depicts brief episodes, some of them with great humor.

MEDIA RESOURCES

Straight Time (1978) This is one of Dustin Hoffman's less well-known movies, in which he plays a parolee, Max Dembo, who has a difficult time handling "life on the outside." He establishes a tense relationship with his power-hungry parole officer. Indeed, for a technical violation, his parole officer returns him to incarceration. When Max is released, he assaults the parole officer, steals his car, and returns to a life of crime. Max has spent most of his juvenile life in prisons. He has a very difficult time accepting "straight time"— life on the outside.

Critically analyze this film:

1. Does the film capture the alienation and exploitation that ex-convicts have to deal with after being in prison for so long? Why or why not?

2. Does Max's unsympathetic parole officer exaggerate his official duties?

3. Why would most parole officers not be so fanatical?

4. What does Max do to construct a "normal" life for himself?

5. Was Max's return to prison on a technical violation fair?

Logging On

Many groups are active in trying to change prison conditions. One group has a web page at:

www.prisonactivists.org/

When you are there, you will be welcomed to the Prison Issues Desk, which is a project of the Prison Activists Resource Center (PARC). This site includes such departments as *Prison Issues*, *Prison News*, and *Activist/Advocacy Groups*.

Some individuals feel so strongly about violent offenders being paroled that they have established Web sites where the public can find information about when such offenders are up for parole. One such organization is Parole Watch. Go to:

www.parolewatch.org/

If you want more information about a typical set of community release programs, go to:

www.ctrenaissance.com/programs_comm_release.htm

Once there you can examine the Waterbury, Connecticut, Community Release Program as well as the Bridgeport Community Release Program.

Using the internet for Criminal Justice Analysis

INFOTRAC® COLLEGE EDITION

1. Go to your InfoTrac College Edition at www.infotrac-college.com/wadsworth/. After you log on, type the words: "MODERATING PROBATION AND PAROLE OFFICER ATTITUDES TO ACHIEVE DESIRED OUTCOMES."
This is an article from *Prison Journal*. It is based on a study of how to moderate parole officer attitudes to improve effective correctional intervention. Basically, the conclusion is that a comprehensive training and development program must be instituted to instill in parole officers the supervision attitudes that are most conducive to promoting offender change. After you read the article, answer the following questions:

a. What is the "seemingly inherent conflict between treatment and control"?

b. Of the eight principles of effective intervention for parole officers, which one appears to be the most important and why?

c. How did the study find out about parole officers' attitudes?

Read Table 1, which gives "The Subjective Role Scale."

d. Which questions seem most important and why?

2. To find out more about federal parole, go to the homepage of the U.S. Parole Commission at: www.usdoj.gov/uspc/parole.htm
Once you are there, click on *An Overview of the U.S. Parole Commission* and answer the following questions:

a. When was the U.S. Board of Parole created by Congress?

b. When was the U.S. Parole Commission named as such?

c. Over which type of prisoners does the U.S. Parole Commission have jurisdiction?

Read the conditions of parole and mandatory release supervision.

d. Under what circumstances does a parolee *not* have to work?

e. Under what circumstances can a parolee associate with persons who have a criminal record?

f. Under what circumstances can a probation officer require a federal parolee to submit to a drug test?

g. How many days after a change in residence does a federal parolee have to notify his or her probation officer?

h. When does parole eligibility occur for federal prisoners not serving a specified minimum time?

Notes

1. Bureau of Justice Statistics, *Correctional Populations in the United States, 1995* (Washington, D.C.: U.S. Department of Justice, 1997), Table 5.13.
2. Michele Sviridoff and James W. Thompson, "Links between Employment and Crime: A Qualitative Study of Rikers Island Releases," *Crime and Delinquency* 29 (1983), 195–212.
3. Allen J. Beck, *Special Report: Recidivism of Prisoners Released in 1983* (Washington, D.C.: U.S. Department of Justice, 1989), 1.
4. J. Michael Self, "Tomorrow's Neighbors," *Virginia Journal of Social Policy and the Law* 2 (Spring 1995), 401.
5. 411 U.S. 1 (1973).
6. *Garza v. Miller*, 688 F.2d 480 (7th Cir. 1982).
7. Michael K. Greene, "'Show Me the Money!': Should Taxpayer Funds Be Used to Educate Prisoners under the Guise of Reducing Recidivism?" *New England Journal on Criminal and Civil Confinement* 24 (Winter 1998), 173.
8. Robert Martinson, "What Works? Questions and Answers about Prison Reform," *Public Interest* (Spring 1974), 22.
9. K. Wright, "Race and Economic Marginality in Explaining Prison Adjustment, *Journal of Crime and Justice* 26 (1989), 67–89.
10. Peter Finn, *The Orange County, Florida, Jail Educational and Vocational Programs* (Washington, D.C.: U.S. Department of Justice, National Institute of Justice, 1997), 2.
11. Mary Dallao, "Keeping Classification Current," *Corrections Today* (July 1, 1997), 86.
12. American Correctional Association (ACA), *Standards for Adult Correctional Institutions*, 3d ed. (Laurel, MD: ACA, 1990).
13. Allen E. Bergin, "The Evaluation of Therapeutic Outcomes," in *Handbook of Psychotherapy and Behavior Change*, ed. Allen E. Bergin and Sol L. Garfield (New York: Wiley, 1971), 263–4.
14. William Glasser, *Reality Therapy: A New Approach to Psychiatry* (New York: Harper & Row, 1965.)
15. Jocelyn Pollock, "Rehabilitation Revisited," in *Prisons: Today and Tomorrow*, ed. Jocelyn Pollock (Gaithersburg, MD: Aspen Publishers, 1997), 179.
16. Bureau of Justice Statistics, *Survey of State Prison Inmates* (Washington, D.C.: U.S. Department of Justice, 1993), 2.
17. R. E. Schumacker, D. B. Anders, and S. L. Anderson, "Vocational and Academic Indicators of Parole Success, *Journal of Correctional Education* 41 (1990), 8-13.
18. Russell G. Dugas, "An Education Program That Lowers Recidivism," *American Jails* (July/August 1990), 64.
19. Violent Crime Control and Law Enforcement Act of 1994, Pub. L. No. 103-322, Section 20411, 108 Stat. 1797 (1994).
20. Sylvia G. McCollum, "Prison College Programs," *Prison Journal* 74 (1994), 58–59.
21. Todd R. Clear and George F. Cole, *American Corrections*, 4th ed. (Belmont, CA: Wadsworth Publishing Co., 1997), 371.
22. Peter Finn, *Successful Job Placement for Ex-Offenders: The Center for Employment Opportunities* (Washington, D.C.: National Institute of Justice, 1997).
23. Marsha L. Miller and Bruce Hobler, "Delaware's Life Skills Program Reduces Inmate Recidivism," *Corrections Today* (August 1996), 116.
24. *Ibid.*, 143.
25. *Behind Bars: Substance Abuse and America's Prison Population* (New York: National Center on Addiction and Substance Abuse at Columbia University, 1998).
26. Jami Floyd, "The Administration of Psychotropic Drugs to Prisoners: State of the Law and Beyond," *California Law Review* 78 (1990), 1243.
27. Ethan G. Kalett, "Twelve Steps, You're Out (of Prison): An Evaluation of 'Anonymous Programs' as Alternative Sentences," *Hastings Law Journal* 48 (November 1996), 129.
28. See Harry K. Wexler, Gregory P. Falkin, Douglas S. Lipton, and A. B. Rosenbaum, "Outcome Evaluation of a Prison Therapeutic Community for Substance Abuse Treatment," in *Drug Abuse Treatment in Prisons in Jails*, ed. Carl G. Leukfeld and Frank M. Tims (Washington, D.C.: U.S. Government Printing Office, 1992), 156–75.
29. David J. Hartmann, James L. Wolk, J. Scott Johnston, and Corey J. Coyler, "Recidivism and Substance Abuse Outcomes in a Prison Based Therapeutic Community," *Federal Probation* (December 1997), 18.
30. Ted Palmer, "The Effectiveness of Intervention: Recent Trends and Current Issues," *Crime & Delinquency* 37 (1991), 34.
31. Clear and Cole, 416.
32. Christopher Hibbert, *The Roots of Evil* (Boston: Little, Brown, 1963), 148–9.
33. *Ibid.*, 149.
34. Elizabeth Eileen Dooley, "Sir Walter Crofton and the Irish or Intermediate System of Prison Discipline," *New England Journal of Prison Law* 575 (Winter 1981), 55.
35. Paul F. Cromwell, *Probation and Parole in the Criminal Justice System*, 2nd ed. (St. Paul, MN: West Publishing Company, 1985), 158.
36. *Ibid.*
37. Michael E. Pacheco, "The Educational Role of the Board of Parole," *Federal Probation* (December 1994), 38.
38. 442 U.S. 1 (1979).
39. Danya W. Blair, "A Matter of Life and Death: Why Life without Parole Should Be a Sentencing Option in Texas," *American Journal of Criminal Law* 22 (Fall 1994), 191.
40. Julian H. Wright, Jr., "Life-without-Parole: An Alternative to Death or Not Much of a Life at All?" *Vanderbilt Law Review* 43 (March 1990), 529.
41. Victoria J. Palacios, "Go and Sin No More: Rationality and Release Decisions by Parole Boards," *South Carolina Law Review* 45 (Spring 1994), 567.

42. William Parker, *Parole: Origins, Development, Current Practices, and Statutes* (College Park, MD: American Correctional Association, 1972), 26.

43. Susan Blaustein, "Witness to Another Execution," *Harper's Magazine* (May 1994), 57.

44. Mike A. Cable, "Limiting Parole: Required Consideration of Statements and Recommendations Received by the Parole Board," *Pacific Law Journal* 28 (Spring 1997), 778.

45. 442 U.S. 12 (1979).

46. D. Michael Fisher, "Changing Pennsylvania's Sentencing Philosophy through the Elimination of Parole for Violent Offenders," *Widener Journal of Public Law* 5 (1996), 269.

47. Andrew Von Hirsch and Kathleen J. Hanrahan, *The Question of Parole: Retention, Reform, or Abolition* (Cambridge, MA: Ballinger Publishing Company, 1979), 4.

48. Bureau of Justice Statistics, *Bulletin* (Washington, D.C.: U.S. Department of Justice, January 1995), 2.

49. Michael Tonry, "Twenty Years of Sentencing Reform: Steps Forward, Steps Backward," *Judicature* 78 (January/February 1995), 169.

50. Comprehensive Crime Control Act of 1984, Pub. L. No. 98-473, Section 217(a), 98 Stat. 1837, 2017 (1984), codified as amended at 28 U.S.C. Sections 991-98 (1988).

51. 42 U.S.C.A. Sections 13701-09.

52. Marc Mauer, "The Truth about Truth in Sentencing," *Corrections Today* (February 1, 1996), S1.

53. Stacey L. Pilato, "New Jersey's No Early Release Act: A Band-Aid Approach to Victims' Pain and Recidivism?" *Seton Hall Legislative Journal* 25 (1997), 357.

54. 1997 New Jersey Sess. Law Serv. 117.

55. Kim English, *Colorado Parole Guidelines Handbook* (Denver: Colorado Division of Criminal Justice, 1990), 20.

56. Stephen P. Gottfredson and Don M. Gottfredson, "Screening for Risk among Parolees: Policy, Practice, and Method," in *Prediction in Criminology,* ed. David P. Farrington and Roger Tarling (Albany, NY: State University of New York Press, 1985).

57. "Ohio Revises Parole Guidelines for More Consistent Prison Terms," *Corrections Journal* (February 23, 1998), 1, 6–7.

58. Carey Goldberg, "Sorrowful Outlaw Radical Abandons Bid for Parole," *New York Times* (March 7, 1998), A6.

59. Robert W. Kastenmeier and Howard G. Eglit, "Parole Release Decision-Making," in *Parole: Legal Issues, Decision Making, Research,* ed. William E. Amos and Charles L. Newman (New York: Federal Legal Publications, 1975), 76.

60. Andrew Von Hirsch, *Doing Justice: The Choice of Punishments* (New York: Hill and Wang, 1976), 31.

61. Self, 402.

62. Quoted in Rhonda Cook, "No Parole Could Be Risky, Officials Say," *Atlanta Journal & Constitution* (February 17, 1998), D5.

63. "USPC Approves New Parole Conditions for Restricting Ex-Inmates' Computer Use," *M2 Presswire* (December 24, 1996).

64. *Sobell v. Reed,* 327 F.Supp. 1294 (S.D. N.Y., 1971).

65. Bureau of Justice Statistics, *Census of State and Federal Correctional Facilities* (Washington, D.C.: U.S. Department of Justice, Bureau of Justice Statistics, 1990), 1.

66. Susan Turner and Joan Petersilia, *Work Release: Recidivism and Corrections Costs in Washington State* (Washington, D.C.: National Institute of Justice, December 1996), 2.

67. Todd R. Clear and Edward Latessa, "Probation Officer Roles in Intensive Supervision: Surveillance versus Treatment," *Justice Quarterly* 10 (1993), 441–62.

68. J. T. Whitehead and C. A. Lindquist, "Job Stress and Burnout among Probation/Parole Officers: Perceptions and Causal Factors," *International Journal of Offender Therapy and Comparative Criminology* 29 (1985), 109–19.

69. Betsy Fulton, Amy Stichman, Lawrence Travis, and Edward Latessa, "Moderating Probation and Parole Officers' Attitudes to Achieve Desired Outcomes," *Prison Journal* (September 1, 1997), 295.

70. Julie Sullivan, "City of Second Chances," *Spokesman Review* (Spokane, WA) (June 19, 1998), 3.

71. Doreen Geiger and Mark Shea, "The GENIE System," *Corrections Today* (July 1997), 72-5.

72. 408 U.S. 471 (1972).

73. 118 S.Ct. 2014 (1998).

74. Ibid.

75. "Deadly Spree Followed Vote to Give Killer '2nd Chance,'" *Buffalo News* (July 2, 1996), A12.

76. Tim Landis, "Real Time: Truth-in-Sentencing Law Changes Plea Negotiations, *St. Louis Dispatch* (July 11, 1996), 1.

77. Victor Hassine, *Life without Parole: Living in Prison Today,* ed. Thomas J. Bernard and Richard McCleary (Los Angeles: Roxbury Publishing Company, 1996), 12.

78. Wilbert Rideau and Ron Wikberg, *Life Sentences: Rage and Survival behind Bars* (New York: Times Books, 1992), 59–60.

79. "Deadly Spree Followed Vote to Give Killer '2nd Chance,'" A12.

80. James Wooten, *Truth in Sentencing: Why States Should Make Violent Criminals Do Their Time* (Washington, D.C.: The Heritage Foundation, 1993).

81. Mauer.

82. Richard Kern, "Sentencing Reform in Virginia," *Federal Sentencing Reporter* 8 (September/October 1995), 84.

83. Ibid.

84. Jenni Gainsborough, "Eliminating Parole Is a Dangerous and Expensive Proposition," *Corrections Today* (July 1997), 23.

85. Richard Perez-Pena, "Pataki's Plan to End Parole is Tougher Than Other States' Moves," *New York Times* (January 26, 1998), B6.

86. Jon Frank, "Number of Parolees Up in Va.; Get-Tough Law Slow to Have Effect," *Virginia Pilot & Ledger Star* (August 24, 1998), A1.

87. National Institute of Justice, *Research in Brief: Making Confinement Decisions* (Washington, D.C.: U.S. Department of Justice, July 1987).

88. NJ.REV.STAT. Section 2C:7-8(c) (1995).

89. Megan's Law, Pub. L. No. 104-145, 110 Stat. 1345 (1996).

90. Carl Ingram, "Megan's Law Works Well to Protect Public, Lungren Says," *Los Angeles Times* (June 13, 1998), A15.

91. Ga. Code Ann. Section 42-9-44.1(b)(1).

92. Tara L. Wayt, "Megan's Law: A Violation of the Right to Privacy?" *Temple Political and Civil Rights Law Review* 6 (Fall 1996-Spring 1997), 139.

93. *Doe v. Poritz*, 662 A.2d 405 (N.J. 1995).

94. *Ibid.*, at 411.

95. Linda Greenhouse, "High Court Refuses to Hear Challenges to Megan's Laws," *New York Times* (February 24, 1998), A1.

96. 521 U.S. 346 (1997).

97. Kan. Stat. Ann. Section 59-29a03.

98. Lawrence A. Greenfeld, "Sixty Percent of Convicted Sex Offenders Are on Parole or Probation," *Bureau of Justice Statistics News Release,* February 2, 1997.

99. Brian D. Gallagher, "Now That We Know Where They Are, What Do We Do with Them? The Placement of Sex Offenders in the Age of Megan's Law," *Widener Journal of Public Law* 7 (1997), 39.

100. Quoted in Sheila A. Campbell, "Battling Sex Offender: Is Megan's Law an Effective Means of Achieving Public Safety?" *Seton Hall Legislative Journal* 19 (1995), 562.

part five
Special Issues

chapter

16

The Juvenile Justice System

Chapter Objectives

After reading this chapter, you should be able to:

1. Describe the child saving movement and its relationship to the doctrine of *parens patriae*.

2. List the four major differences between juvenile courts and adult courts.

3. Identify and briefly describe the single most important Supreme Court case with respect to juvenile justice.

4. List the factors that normally determine what police do with juvenile offenders.

5. Describe the four primary stages of pretrial juvenile justice procedure.

6. Explain the distinction between an adjudicatory hearing and a disposition hearing.

7. List the four categories of residential treatment programs.

8. Describe the one variable that always correlates highly with juvenile crime rates.

9. Indicate some of the reasons why youths join gangs.

INTRODUCTION

In March of 1998, eleven-year-old Andrew Golden and thirteen-year-old Mitchell Johnson shot and killed four fellow students and a teacher at Westside Middle School in Jonesboro, Arkansas. Three months later, Kipland Kinkel, a fifteen-year-old, went on a rampage with a firearm at Thurston High School in Springfield, Oregon, killing two students and wounding twenty others. Because the Oregon incident closely followed the one in Arkansas, the two shootings became linked in the public's mind, setting off a national furor on the subject of violent children. Although the two situations were similar, the punishments for the young wrongdoers could not have been more different. In keeping with Arkansas's sentencing laws, neither Golden nor Johnson could be tried as an adult for their actions. They will most likely be released from a juvenile detention center when they reach the age of eighteen. Under Oregon's stricter statutes, Kinkel (who had also killed his parents) was tried as an adult for four counts of aggravated murder, twenty-five counts of attempted aggravated murder with a firearm, and numerous counts of assault. He faced a lifetime in prison.[1]

The different sentencing approaches in Arkansas and Oregon highlight the contradictions inherent to the American juvenile justice system, which, in the words of one observer, "has been both hailed as one of the greatest social inventions of modern times and attacked for failing to protect either the legal rights of the juvenile offenders or the public on whom they prey."[2] Should criminal acts by youths be given the same weight as those committed by adults or should they be seen as "mistakes" that can be "corrected" by the state?

For most of its century-long history, the system was dominated by the latter philosophy; only recently have political trends summarized by the sound bite "old enough to do the crime, old enough to do the time" gained widespread credibility. Since 1994, forty-three states have changed their laws to make it easier to try juveniles as adults. In the wake of the Arkansas shootings, Texas legislator Jim Pitts proposed changing that state's law to allow for the execution of murderers as young as eleven years old, and a Michigan prosecutor sought a life sentence for an eleven-year-old who had killed a teenager. These legislative and legal moves represent a shift toward harsher measures in a juvenile justice system that generally acts as a "compromise between rehabilitation and punishment, treatment and custody."[3]

In this chapter, we will discuss the successes and failures of this compromise and examine the aspects of the juvenile justice system that differentiate it from the criminal justice system. As you will see, observers on both sides of the "rehabilitation versus punishment" debate find many flaws with the present system; some have even begun to argue for its complete dismantling. Others blame social problems such as poverty, racism, and a culture dominated by images of violence for creating a situation that no government agency or policy can effectively control. To add to the urgency of the issue, research data predict a sharp upswing in youth crime in the next decade, raising the level of fear in a society that is increasingly scared of its own children.[4]

THE EVOLUTION OF AMERICAN JUVENILE JUSTICE

In a recent poll, more than seven in ten Americans indicated that they favored trying violent youths in adult criminal court instead of juvenile courts, which were perceived as too lenient.[5] To a certain degree, such opinions reflect a desire to return the focus of the American juvenile justice system toward punishment and incapacitation, as was the case at the beginning of the nineteenth century. At that time, juvenile offenders were treated the same as adult offenders—they were judged by the same courts and sentenced to the same severe penalties. This situation began to change in the early 1800s, as urbanization and industrialization created an immigrant underclass that was, at least in the eyes of certain reformers, predisposed to deviant activity. Certain members of the Progressive movement, known as the *child savers*, began to take steps to "save" children from these circumstances, introducing the idea of rehabilitating delinquents in the process.

The Child Saving Movement

In general, the child savers favored the doctrine of **parens patriae,** which holds that the state has not only a right but a duty to care for children who are neglected, delinquent, or in some other way disadvantaged. Juvenile offenders, the child savers believed, required treatment, not punishment, and they were horrified at the thought of placing children in prisons with hardened adult criminals. Supreme Court Justice Abe Fortas said of the child savers:

> They believed that society's role was not to ascertain whether the child was "guilty" or "innocent," but "What is he, how has he become what he is, and what had best be done in his interest and in the interest of the state to save him from a downward career." The child—essentially good, as they saw it—was made "to feel that he is the object of [the government's] care and solicitude," not that he was under arrest or on trial.[6]

Child saving organizations convinced local legislatures to pass laws that allowed them to take control of children who exhibited criminal tendencies or had been neglected by their parents. To separate these children from the environment in which they were raised, the organizations created a number of institutions, the best known of which was New York's House of Refuge. Opening in 1825, the House of Refuge implemented many of the same reformist measures popular in the penitentiaries of the time, meaning that its charges were subjected to the healthful influences of hard study and labor. Although the House of Refuge was criticized for its harsh discipline (which caused many boys to run away), similar institutions sprang up throughout the Northeast during the middle part of the nineteenth century.

The Illinois Juvenile Court

The efforts of the child savers culminated with the passage of the **Illinois Juvenile Court Act** in 1899. The Illinois legislature created the first court specifically for juveniles, guided by the principles of *parens patriae* and based on the concepts that children are not fully responsible for criminal conduct and are capable of being rehabilitated.[7]

The Illinois Juvenile Court and those from other states that followed in its path were (and, in many cases, remain) drastically different from adult courts:

- *No juries.* The matter was decided by judges who wore regular clothes instead of black robes and sat at a table with the other principals rather than behind a

PARENS PATRIAE
A doctrine that holds that the state has a responsibility to look after the well-being of children and to assume the role of parent if necessary.

ILLINOIS JUVENILE COURT ACT
The 1899 statute under which the nation's first juvenile court was established, laying the groundwork for the modern juvenile justice system.

An illustration detailing the daily activities in the New York House of Refuge that appeared in *Harper's Weekly* in 1868. The House of Refuge was created in 1825 as a result of reformers' outrage that children who broke the law were treated the same as adults. The purpose of the House was to receive "all such children as shall be taken up or committed as vagrants, or convicted of criminal offenses." As you can see, the children were put to work at a number of different tasks, such as making shoes and hoop skirts. They also attended four hours of school every day. Judging from this illustration, how would you characterize the philosophy behind the House of Refuge?

STATUS OFFENDER
A juvenile who has been found to have engaged in behavior deemed unacceptable for those under a certain, statutorily determined age.

JUVENILE DELINQUENCY
Behavior that is illegal under federal or state law that has been committed by a person who is under an age limit specified by statute.

bench. Because the primary focus of the court was on the child and not the crime, the judge had wide discretion in disposing of each case.

- *Different terminology.* To reduce the stigma of criminal proceedings, "petitions" were issued instead of "warrants"; the children were not "defendants," but "respondents"; they were not "found guilty" but "adjudicated delinquent."

- *No adversarial relationship.* Instead of trying to determine guilt or innocence, the parties involved in the juvenile court worked together in the best interests of the child, with the emphasis on rehabilitation rather than punishment.

- *Confidentiality.* To avoid "saddling" the child with a criminal past, juvenile court hearings and records were kept sealed, and the proceedings were closed to the public.

By 1945, every state had a juvenile court system modeled after the first Illinois court. For the most part, these courts were able to operate without interference until the 1960s and the onset of the juvenile rights movement.

After the first juvenile court was established in Illinois, the Chicago Bar Association described its purpose as, in part, to "exercise the same tender solicitude and care over its neglected wards that a wise and loving parent would exercise with reference to his own children under similar circumstances."[8] In other words, the state was given the responsibility of caring for those minors whose behavior seemed to show that they could not be controlled by their parents. As a result, many **status offenders** found themselves in the early houses of refuge and continue to be placed in state-run facilities today. Also known as "children (or minors, youths, etc.) in need of supervision," status offenders have exhibited behavior—such as violating curfew, truancy (skipping school), and alcohol consumption—that is considered illegal only if an offender is below a specified age (see Figure 16.1). In contrast, **juvenile delinquency** refers to conduct that would be criminal if committed by an adult.

INFOTRAC ®
COLLEGE EDITION

Jenson, J. and M. Howard. Youth crime, public policy and practice in the juvenile justice system: recent trends and needed reform.

Figure 16.1 Status Offenses

A status offense is an act that, if committed by a juvenile, is considered grounds for apprehension and perhaps state custody. The same act, if committed by an adult, does not warrant law enforcement action.

Status Offenses

1. Smoking cigarettes
2. Drinking alcohol
3. Being truant (skipping school)
4. Disobeying teachers
5. Running away from home
6. Violating curfew
7. Participating in sexual activity
8. Using profane language

Constitutional Protections and the Juvenile Court

Though the ideal of the juvenile court seemed to offer the "best of both worlds" for juvenile offenders, in reality the lack of procedural protections led to many children being arbitrarily punished not only for crimes, but for status offenses. Juvenile judges were treating all respondents similarly, which led to many status offenders being incarcerated in the same institutions as violent delinquents. In response to a wave of lawsuits demanding due process rights for juveniles, the Supreme Court issued several rulings in the 1960s and 1970s that significantly changed the juvenile justice system.

Kent v. United States. The first decision to extend due process rights to children in juvenile courts was *Kent v. United States* (1966).[9] The case concerned sixteen-year-old Morris Kent, who had been arrested for breaking into a woman's house, stealing her purse, and raping her. Because Kent was on juvenile probation, the state sought to transfer his trial for the crime to an adult court (a process to be discussed later in the chapter). Without giving any reasons for his decision, the juvenile judge consented to this judicial waiver, and Kent was sentenced in the adult court to a thirty- to ninety-year prison term. The Supreme Court overturned the sentence, ruling that juveniles have a right to counsel and a hearing in any instance in which the juvenile judge is considering sending the case to an adult court. The Court stated that, in jurisdiction waiver cases, a child receives "the worst of both worlds," getting neither the "protections accorded to adults" nor the "solicitous care and regenerative treatment" offered in the juvenile system.[10]

CJ in Focus
Landmark Cases:
In re Gault

In 1964, fifteen-year-old Gerald Gault and a friend were arrested for making lewd telephone calls to a neighbor in Gila County, Arizona. Gault, who was on probation, was placed under custody with no notice given to his parents. The juvenile court in his district held a series of informal hearings to determine Gault's punishment. During these hearings, no records were kept, Gault was not afforded the right to counsel, and the complaining witness was never made available for questioning. At the close of the hearing, the judge sentenced Gault to remain in Arizona's State Industrial School until the age of twenty-one. The defendant filed a writ of *habeas corpus*, claiming that he had been denied due process rights at his hearing. The Arizona Supreme Court affirmed the dismissal of this writ, ruling that the proceedings did not infringe upon Gault's due process rights, a matter eventually taken up by the United States Supreme Court.

In re Gault
United States Supreme Court
387 U.S. 1 (1967)
http://laws.findlaw.com/US/387/1.html

In the Words of the Court . . .

Mr. Justice FORTAS, majority opinion

* * * *

From the inception of the juvenile court system, wide differences have been tolerated—indeed insisted upon—between the procedural rights accorded to adults and those of juveniles. In practically all jurisdictions, there are rights granted to adults which are withheld from juveniles.

* * * *

Accordingly, the highest motives and most enlightened impulses led to a peculiar system for juveniles, unknown to our law in any comparable context. The constitutional and theoretical basis for this peculiar system is—to say the least—debatable. And in practice, as we remarked in the Kent case, the results have not been entirely satisfactory. * * * The absence of substantive standards has not necessarily meant that children receive careful, compassionate, individualized treatment. The absence of procedural rules based upon constitutional principle has not always produced fair, efficient, and effective procedures. Departures from established principles of due process have frequently resulted not in enlightened procedure, but in arbitrariness.

* * * *

Ultimately, however, we confront the reality of that portion of the Juvenile Court process with which we deal in this case. A boy is charged with misconduct. The boy is committed to an institution where he may be restrained of liberty for years. It is of no constitutional consequence—and of limited practical meaning—that the institution to which he is committed is called an Industrial School. The fact of the matter is that, however euphemistic the title, a "receiving home" or an "industrial school" for juveniles is an institution of confinement in which the child is incarcerated for a greater or lesser time. His world becomes "a building with white-washed walls, regimented routine and institutional hours . . . ." Instead of mother and father and sisters and brothers and friends and classmates, his world is peopled by guards, custodians, state employees, and "delinquents" confined with him for anything from waywardness to rape and homicide. In view of this, it would be extraordinary if our Constitution did not require the procedural regularity and the exercise of care implied in the phrase "due process." Under our Constitution, the condition of being a boy does not justify a kangaroo court.

* * * *

Decision: The Court held that juveniles were entitled to the basic procedural safeguards afforded by the Fourteenth Amendment, including the right to advance notice of charges, the right to counsel, the right to confront and cross-examine witnesses, and the privilege against self-incrimination. The decision marked a turning point in juvenile justice in this country: no longer would informality and paternalism be the guiding principles of juvenile courts. Instead, due process would dictate the adjudication process, much as in an adult court.

For Critical Analysis: What might be some of the negative consequences of the *In re Gault* decision for juveniles charged with committing delinquent acts?

In re Gault. Kent provided the groundwork for *In re Gault* one year later. Considered by many the single most important case concerning juvenile justice, *In re Gault* involved a young offender who was arrested for allegedly making a lewd phone call while on probation.[11] (See *CJ in Focus—Landmark Cases:* In re Gault.) In its decision, the Supreme Court held that juveniles are entitled to many of the same due process rights granted to adult offenders, including notice of charges, the right to counsel, the privilege against self-incrimination, and the right to confront and cross-examine witnesses.

Other Important Court Decisions. Over the next ten years, the Supreme Court handed down three more important rulings on juvenile court proce-

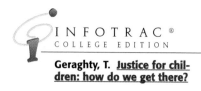
dure. *In re Winship* (1970)[12] required the government to prove "beyond a reasonable doubt" that a juvenile had committed an act of delinquency, raising the burden of proof from a "preponderance of the evidence." In *Breed v. Jones* (1975),[13] the Court held that the Fifth Amendment's double jeopardy clause prevented a juvenile from being tried in an adult court for a crime that had already been adjudicated in juvenile court. In contrast, *McKeiver v. Pennsylvania* (1971)[14] represented the one instance in which the Court did not move the juvenile court further toward the adult model. It ruled that the Constitution did *not* give juveniles the right to a jury trial.

DETERMINING DELINQUENCY TODAY

In the eyes of many observers, the net effect of the Supreme Court decisions during the 1966–1975 period was to move juvenile justice away from the ideals of the child savers and toward a formalized system that is often indistinguishable from its adult counterpart. But, though the Court has recognized that minors possess certain constitutional rights, it has failed to dictate at what age these rights should be granted and at what age minors are to be held criminally responsible for delinquent actions. Consequently, the legal status of children in the United States varies depending on where they live, with each state making its own policy decisions on the crucial questions of age and competency.

The Age Question

Under common law, a child under the age of seven was considered to lack the requisite *mens rea* to commit a crime. (That is, he or she did not possess the mental capacity to understand the consequences of his or her action.) Also under common law, a child between the age of seven and fourteen could use the defense of infancy (being a minor) to plead innocent. On attaining fourteen years of age, the youth was considered an adult and treated accordingly.[15]

Today, as Figure 16.2 shows, twenty-six states and the District of Columbia do not have age restrictions in prosecuting juveniles as adults. Indeed, many states require juveniles who commit violent felonies such as murder, rape, or armed robbery to be waived to adult courts. When juveniles in a state without such a requirement commit a serious crime, they are given a "limited" sentence, usually meaning they cannot remain incarcerated in juvenile detention centers past their eighteenth or twenty-first birthday.

Figure 16.2 The Minimum Age at Which a Juvenile Can Be Tried as an Adult

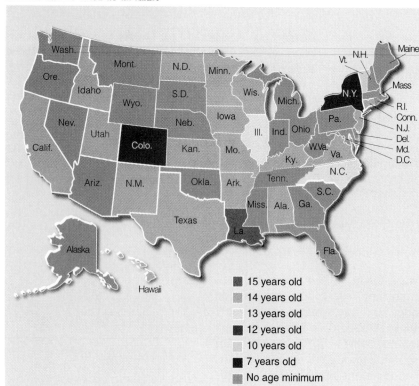

- ■ 15 years old
- 14 years old
- 13 years old
- ■ 12 years old
- 10 years old
- ■ 7 years old
- No age minimum

SOURCE: NATIONAL CENTER FOR JUVENILE JUSTICE.

The Competency Question

One of the precepts of *parens patriae* was the assumption that children are not legally competent and must, in the absence of parental care, be protected by the state. In today's juvenile justice environment, however, the question of a minor's competency to make informed decisions about criminal actions is far more complicated.

Psychological Competency. Most researchers believe that by the age of fourteen, an adolescent has the same ability to make a competent decision as does an adult.[16] Nevertheless, according to some observers, a juvenile's ability to theoretically understand the difference between "right" and "wrong" does not mean that she or he should be held to the same standards of competency as an adult. Legal psychologist Richard E. Redding believes that:

> adolescents' lack of life experience may limit their real-world decision-making ability. Whether we call it wisdom, judgment, or common sense, adolescents may not have nearly enough.[17]

Juveniles are generally more impulsive, more likely to engage in risky behavior, and less likely to calculate the long-term consequences of any particular action. Furthermore, adolescents are far more likely to respond to peer pressure than are adults. The desire for acceptance and approval may drive them to commit crimes; juveniles are arrested as part of a group at much higher rates than adults.[18]

Legal Competency. In *Thompson v. Oklahoma* (1988),[19] the Supreme Court overturned the death penalty for a juvenile who was fifteen at the time he committed his capital crime. In ruling that such a punishment violated the Eighth Amendment's prohibition against "cruel and unusual punishment," the Court stated that a defendant that young "is not capable of acting with the degree of culpability that can justify the ultimate penalty."[20] One year later, however, the Court upheld the death penalty for sixteen- and seventeen-year-olds in *Stanford v. Kentucky* (1989).[21] Though the Court continued to hold that juveniles were less culpable than adults committing the same crime, it reversed its prior finding that capital punishment for juveniles *always* violates the Constitution. The Court basically gave states permission to determine their own age limits for executions. (See *Cross-National CJ Comparison—U.S. against the World* on the next page.)

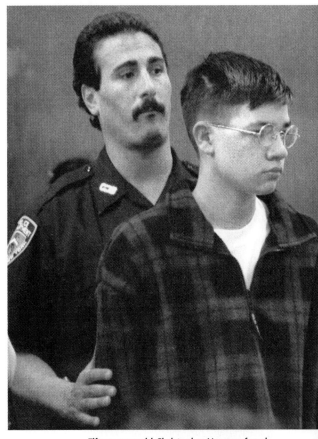

Fifteen-year-old Christopher Vasquez faced murder charges for stabbing Michael McMorrow, a forty-four-year-old man, in New York City's Central Park. The case attracted a great deal of interest because of Vasquez's age and the brutality of the crime—McMorrow was stabbed more than thirty times. Many observers felt that, despite his age, Vasquez should have received the same harsh punishment as would an adult who committed the same crime. In fact, the jury acquitted Vasquez of second degree murder, which would have carried a lifetime prison sentence. Instead he was found guilty of the less serious charge of manslaughter. Do you believe that a wrongdoer's age should be a consideration in determining punishment?

FIRST CONTACT: DELINQUENTS AND THE POLICE

Until recently, most police departments allocated few resources to dealing with juvenile crime. The rise in violent crimes committed by citizens under the age of eighteen has, however, provided a strong incentive for departments to set up special services for children. The standard bearer for these operations is the *juvenile officer*, who operates either alone or as part of a juvenile

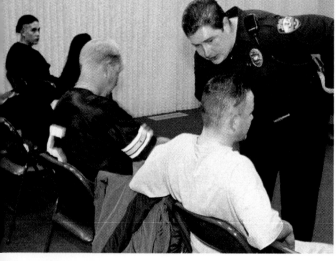

U.S. against the World

In the late 1980s, the General Assembly of the United Nations adopted the Convention on the Rights of the Child. Article 37 of the Convention states: "Neither capital punishment nor life imprisonment without possibility of release shall be imposed for offenses committed by a person below eighteen years of age." The United States is one of only two countries, the other being Somalia, that has not signed this convention. Three other international treaties—two of which the United States has signed but not ratified—obligate participants to abolish the death penalty for juveniles. In the past three years, China, South Africa, and Russia have taken steps to eliminate capital punishment for juvenile offenders, leaving the United States as one of only six countries that are known to execute juvenile offenders; the others are Pakistan, Saudi Arabia, Iran, Nigeria, and Yemen.

THE SOVEREIGN POWER OF THE STATES

"We should be embarrassed to find ourselves in that company," says one observer. "Every one of those other countries is known for human-rights violations." Opponents of the death penalty for juveniles hope that shame will work to reverse American policy on the subject. Organizations such as Amnesty International and influential individuals such as the pope have been outspoken in criticizing the U.S. stance.

Others argue that prohibition of the juvenile death penalty has reached the status of *jus cogens;* that is, it has become a principle of international law binding on all nations. The Supreme Court, however, even while noting international disapproval of American practice, has held that each state has the sovereign power to decide the question of juvenile execution for itself.

Indeed, the public and political tides in the United States seem to favor an extension of the death penalty for juveniles. In the 1990s, the United States executed six juvenile offenders, more than any other country. As noted earlier, a legislator in Texas—which contains forty of the seventy Americans on death row for crimes they committed as juveniles—has introduced legislation that would lower the age at which a minor can be sentenced to death from fourteen to eleven.

WHAT'S THE EVIDENCE?

A number of human rights groups believe that the United States has a moral obligation to follow the example of the rest of the world. To explore their arguments on the Internet, go to **www.amnesty.it/ailib/aipub/1998/AMR/25105898.htm** and **www.omct.woa-tusa/ Default.htm**.

---

unit within a department. The initial contact between a juvenile and the criminal justice system is usually handled by a regular police officer on patrol who either apprehends the juvenile while he or she is committing a crime or answers a call for service. (See Figure 16.3 for an overview of the juvenile justice process.) The youth is then passed on to a juvenile officer, who must decide how to handle the case.[22]

Although a certain stigma is attached to working with youths (juvenile officers have been referred to as the "lollipop squad"), juvenile officers have a level of expertise comparable to other police officers. The Los Angeles Unified School District Police Department requires that all of its officers undergo the same state-mandated training as personnel from other police agencies, and there is little "lollipop" about the work that these officers do. The district recently purchased seventy-five 12-gauge Remington shotguns to help the school police deal with the criminal behavior of their young charges.[23]

In Fort Lupton, Colorado, police officers punish juveniles who have broken the city's noise laws by forcing them to listen to music "that kids would hate."

Police Discretion and Juvenile Crime

Police arrest about two million youths under the age of eighteen each year, 30 percent for serious crimes. In most states, police officers must have a probable cause to believe that the minor has committed an offense, as they would if the suspect was an adult. Police power with regard to juveniles is greater than with adults, however, because police can take youths into custody for status offenses such as possession of

Figure **16.3** The Juvenile Justice Process

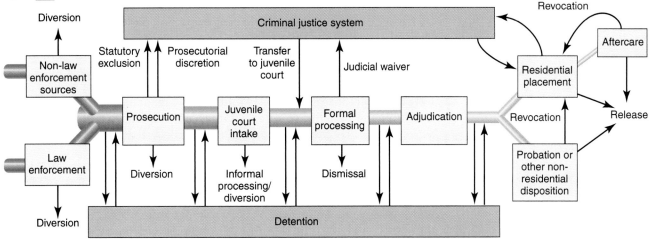

SOURCE: OFFICE OF JUVENILE JUSTICE AND DELINQUENCY PREVENTION.

alcohol or truancy. In these cases, the officer is acting *in loco parentis*, or in the place of the parent. The officer's role is not necessarily to punish the youths, but to protect them from harmful behavior.

Low-Visibility Decision Making. Police officers also have a great deal of discretion in deciding what to do with juveniles who have committed crimes or status offenses. Juvenile justice expert Joseph Goldstein labels this discretionary power **low-visibility decision making** because it relies on factors that the public is generally not in a position to understand or criticize.[24] When a grave offense has taken place, a police officer may decide to formally arrest the juvenile, send him or her to juvenile court, or place the youth under the care of a social service organization. In less serious situations, the officer may decide simply to issue a warning or to take the offender to the police station and release the child into the custody of her or his parents (see Figure 16.4).

In making these discretionary decisions, police generally consider the following factors:

- The nature of the child's offense.
- The offender's past history of involvement with the juvenile justice system.
- The setting in which the offense took place.
- The ability and willingness of the child's parents to take disciplinary action.
- The attitude of the offender.
- The offender's race and sex (discussed in Chapter 18).

Following the seriousness of the offense and past history, the most important factor in the police officer's decision on whether to arrest or release appears to be the offender's attitude toward the police. An offender who is polite and apologetic generally has a better chance of being released. If the juvenile is hostile or unresponsive, then police are more likely to place him or her in custody for even a minor offense.[25]

LOW-VISIBILITY DECISION MAKING
A term used to describe the discretionary power police have in determining what to do with misbehaving juveniles. For the most part, this power goes unchallenged and unnoticed by citizens.

Figure **16.4** Police Disposition of Juveniles Taken into Custody

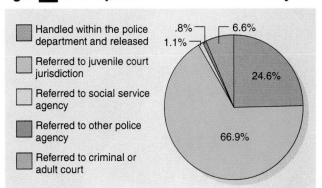

- Handled within the police department and released
- Referred to juvenile court jurisdiction
- Referred to social service agency
- Referred to other police agency
- Referred to criminal or adult court

.8%
1.1%
6.6%
24.6%
66.9%

SOURCE: FEDERAL BUREAU OF INVESTIGATION, *CRIME IN THE UNITED STATES, 1997* (WASHINGTON, D.C.: U.S. DEPARTMENT OF JUSTICE, 1998), TABLE 68 AT PAGE 279.

The Need for More Arrests. Some observers believe that police officers are too hesitant to arrest juveniles, preferring other, less time-consuming options such as issuing warnings and releasing the young offenders to their parents. Steven D. Levitt of the University of Chicago believes that the rise in juvenile crime since the mid-1980s can be partly attributed to the relative leniency of the juvenile justice system compared to the adult system. Levitt found that the chances of a juvenile being arrested and incarcerated for a serious crime were only half those of an adult committing a similar offense.[26] Not only does this limit the benefits of incapacitation, but it undermines the deterrent aspects of police work—juveniles do not believe they will be arrested for delinquent acts.

Levitt's assertion seems to be supported by actions taken in Boston, Massachusetts, to reduce juvenile crime. Spurred by crack cocaine and youth gangs, the city's murder count reached a record 152 in 1990. In 1993 alone, sixteen Boston youths under the age of seventeen were killed. As part of a coalition with federal and local law enforcement agencies and social organizations, Boston police agreed to increase efforts to get known juvenile delinquents and gang members off city streets. Members of a Youth Violence Strike Force began to arrest and rearrest these offenders, with the goal of "building up such an arrest record that finally [the district attorney's office] will direct-indict them and put them away." By 1997, the city's murder rate had dropped by nearly 40 percent, and not one youth under the age of seventeen had been killed by a firearm in twenty-five months.[27]

Juveniles and the Constitution

The privacy and *Miranda* rights of juveniles are protected during contact with law enforcement officers, though not to the same extent as for adults. In most jurisdictions, the Fourth Amendment ban against unreasonable searches and seizures and Fifth Amendment safeguards against custodial self-incrimination apply to juveniles. That is, juvenile court judges cannot use illegally seized evidence in juvenile hearings, and police must read youths their *Miranda* rights after arrest.

Such rights are not absolute, however. In *New Jersey v. T.L.O.* (1985),[28] the Supreme Court held that school officials may search a student on mere "reasonable suspicion" that he or she has violated school regulations or laws. The Court justified this lower standard—most searches require probable cause—on the grounds of maintaining school discipline and the *in loco parentis* doctrine.[29] In 1995, the Court further strengthened school officials' ability to search students by upholding a random drug-testing policy for high school athletes.[30]

In *Fare v. Michael C.* (1979),[31] the Supreme Court clarified law enforcement officials' responsibilities with regard to *Miranda* warnings and juveniles. The case involved a boy who had been arrested on suspicion of murder. After being read his rights, the youth asked to speak to his probation officer. The request was denied. The boy eventually confessed to the crime. The Court ruled that juveniles may waive their

As second-grader Ejuanda Fields exits the school bus that takes her to Indianapolis Public School 84, Indianapolis Public Schools Police Sgt. Kelly Browning checks her backpack for weapons and drugs. Similar searches are being conducted with regularity at schools across the United States. The Supreme Court has upheld such searches based on two legal concepts. First, students on school grounds do not enjoy the same constitutional rights to privacy as does the general population. Second, the legality of a search of a student depends simply on the reasonableness, under all the circumstances, of the search. Do you believe that students should have the same privacy protections against searches as everybody else? What reasons can be given for denying them those protections?

CJ in Focus
A Question of Ethics
Interrogating Children

The seven-year-old boy had been brought to the Wentworth Area police headquarters in Chicago for questioning in connection with the murder of Ryan Harris. Two weeks earlier, on July 27, 1998, the beaten and sexually assaulted body of the eleven-year-old girl had been found lying in a lot behind an abandoned building. Two Chicago detectives took the boy into an empty room and asked him if he knew what a lie was. "You should never lie," he answered. Each detective took one of the boy's hands and then asked him about Harris. The seven-year-old admitted throwing a brick at the girl and knocking her off her bicycle, and then dragging her body into the weeds with the help of an eight-year-old friend. After checking the story with the friend, the police detained the boys and classified the case of Ryan Harris as "Cleared/Closed by Arrest."

Because of the age of the assailants and the brutality of the murder, the case immediately attracted the attention of the national media. Consequently, the spotlight was just as bright several weeks later, when the police abruptly released the two suspects. A forensic examination had found semen—that boys so young could not have produced—on the girl's torn underwear. Questions immediately arose concerning the Chicago police's interrogation techniques. Why had both boys been questioned at various times without the presence of counsel or even

their parents? Both boys had waived their *Miranda* rights, but how could those so young understand the concept or consequences of such an act? Why weren't obvious disparities between the two boys' stories given more attention, such as the contention by the eight-year-old that Harris was dead before she was hit in the head with the brick?

The Chicago police denied that they had bent any rules in gaining the confessions. In fact, a parent or guardian is not required by law to be present when police advise juvenile suspects of their constitutional rights—police must only make a "reasonable attempt" to contact parents, after which they can question the child. *Miranda* rights must only be read if the youth is "in custody," meaning that he or she does not feel free to leave. Finally, if a child "spontaneously confesses," as did the seven-year-old, *Miranda* warnings are not required.

To avoid situations such as occurred in Chicago, many police departments are considering videotaping all interrogations of juveniles. Some observers are even suggesting that *all* interrogations of juveniles *must* take place in the presence of a parent or counsel.

For Critical Analysis: How reliable are the statements of juveniles, especially those as young as the boys in the Harris case? Regardless of the law, how should police approach the interrogation of children who may not fully understand the concept of constitutional rights?

right to protection against self-incrimination and that admissions made to the police in the absence of counsel are admissible. The Court did, however, order juvenile courts to study the "totality of circumstances" to determine whether a child had been coerced into making a confession.

In other instances, the question is not whether the juvenile was coerced, but whether she or he can comprehend *Miranda* warnings or many other aspects of the interrogation process. As can be seen in the feature *CJ in Focus—A Question of Ethics: Interrogating Children*, police can be taking a chance by relying on the testimony of young suspects and witnesses.

PRETRIAL PROCEDURES IN JUVENILE JUSTICE

After arrest and before the start of the trial, various decision makers are provided the opportunity to determine how the juvenile justice system will dispose of each case. The offender may be diverted to a social services program or detained in a juvenile lockup facility. In the most serious cases, the youth may even be transferred to adult court. To ensure due process during pretrial procedures, offenders and their families may retain an attorney or have one appointed by the court. The four primary stages of this critical period—intake, diversion, waiver, and detention—are discussed below.

Intake

If, following arrest, a police officer feels the offender warrants the attention of the juvenile justice process, the officer will refer the youth to juvenile court. The court receives the majority of its respondents from the police, though parents, relatives, welfare agencies, and school officials may also refer

INTAKE
Following referral of a juvenile to juvenile court by a police officer or other concerned party, the process by which an official of the court must decide whether to file a petition, release the juvenile, or place the juvenile under some other form of supervision.

PETITION
The document filed with a juvenile court alleging that the juvenile is a delinquent or a status offender, and asking the court to either hear the case itself or transfer it to an adult court.

DIVERSION
The removal of an alleged juvenile delinquent from the formal criminal or juvenile justice system and the referral of that person to a treatment or rehabilitation program.

The Juvenile Justice Center is a valuable source for juvenile justice information and data. Go to www.abanet.org/crimjust/ juvjust/homt.html

juveniles. Once this step has been taken, a complaint is filed with a special division of the juvenile court, and the **intake** process begins. During intake, an official of the juvenile court—usually a probation officer, but sometimes a judge—must decide, in effect, what to do with the offender. The screening official has several options during intake.

1. Simply dismiss the case, releasing the offender without taking any further action.

2. Divert the offender to a social services program, such as drug rehabilitation and anger management.

3. File a **petition** for a formal court hearing.

4. Transfer the case to an adult court where the offender will be tried as an adult.

The intake process is changing in several very important ways. In particular, the influence of prosecutors on the fate of the juvenile wrongdoer is growing significantly. In the past, the primary responsibility for providing a juvenile judge with a recommendation on how the case should be handled was left to probation personnel. Even though the judge handed down the final decision, in most cases she or he followed the recommendation of a probation officer as to whether the juvenile should take part in a formal court hearing. This approach, indicative of a system that favors rehabilitation, is being replaced in some jurisdictions.

The new processes give more power to the prosecutor, who is seen as being more interested in protecting the public than rehabilitating the offender. Some states now require the prosecutor to approve decisions by intake officers, while others eliminate the role of probation personnel entirely.[32] Furthermore, an increasing number of states are allowing the victims of wrongdoing by juveniles the chance to appeal an intake officer's decision not to file a petition for a formal court hearing.[33] Prosecutors play a major role in this process as well, as they are often charged with the responsibility of filing the appeal on behalf of the victim.

Pretrial Diversion

To a certain extent, the juvenile justice system started as a diversionary program with the goal of diverting children from the punitive adult court to the more rehabilitative juvenile court.[34] By the 1960s, many observers felt that juvenile courts had lost sight of this early mandate and were badly in need of reform. One specific target for criticism was the growing number of status offenders—40 percent of all children in the system—who were being punished even though they had not committed a delinquent act.

The idea of diverting certain children, including status and first-time offenders, from the juvenile court system to nonjudicial community agencies was encouraged by the President's Commission on Law Enforcement and Administration of Justice in 1967.[35] Seven years later, Congress passed the Juvenile Justice and Delinquency Prevention (JJDP) Act, which ordered the development of methods "to divert juveniles from the traditional juvenile justice system."[36] Within a few years, hundreds of diversion programs had been put into effect. Today, **diversion** refers to the process of removing low-risk offenders from the formal juvenile justice system by placing them in community-based rehabilitation programs.

Diversion programs vary widely, but fall into three general categories:

1. *Probation.* In this program, the juvenile is returned to the community, but placed under the supervision of a juvenile probation officer. If the

youth breaks the conditions of probation, he or she can be returned to the formal juvenile system.

2. *Treatment and aid.* Many juveniles have behavioral or medical conditions that contribute to their delinquent behavior, and many diversion programs offer remedial education, drug and alcohol treatment, and other forms of counseling to alleviate these problems.

3. *Restitution.* In these programs, the offender "repays" her or his victim, either directly or, in the case of community service, symbolically.[37]

Proponents of diversion programs include many labeling theorists (see Chapter 2), who believe that contact with the formal juvenile justice system "labels" the youth a delinquent, which leads to further delinquent behavior.

Transfer to Adult Court

One side effect of diversionary programs is that the youths who remain in the juvenile courts are more likely to be seen as "hardened" and less amenable to rehabilitation.[38] This, in turn, increases the likelihood that the offender will be transferred to an adult court, a process in which the juvenile court waives jurisdiction over the youth. As the American juvenile justice system has shifted away from ideals of treatment and toward punishment, transfer to adult court has been one of the most popular means of "getting tough" on delinquents.

Juveniles are most commonly transferred to adult court through **judicial waiver.** In forty-eight states (excluding New York and Nebraska), the juvenile judge is the official who determines whether jurisdiction over a minor offender should be waived to adult court. The judge formulates this ruling by taking into consideration the offender's age, the nature of the offense, and any criminal history.

Thirty-four states have taken the waiver responsibility out of judicial hands through **automatic transfer,** also known as legislative waiver. In these states, the legislatures have designated certain conditions—usually involving serious crimes such as murder and rape—under which a juvenile case is automatically "kicked up" to adult court. In Rhode Island, for example, a juvenile sixteen or older with two prior felony adjudications will automatically be transferred upon being accused of a third felony.[39] Ten states allow for **prosecutorial waiver,** in which juvenile court judges are allowed to waive jurisdiction when certain age and offense conditions are met. In general, no matter what the process, those juveniles who commit violent felonies are most likely to be transferred to an adult court (see Figure 16.5).

Juvenile jurisdiction waiver is often criticized for not giving sufficient protection to the community. Apparently, judges in adult courts are disposed to give juveniles more lenient sentences than they would adults who had committed the same crime, meaning that juvenile courts actually provide harsher punishments.[40] Furthermore, research has shown that juveniles tried in adult courts have higher recidivism rates than those who are tried in juvenile courts.

A joint study by the University of Florida and the University of Central Florida found that 30 percent of

JUDICIAL WAIVER
The process in which the juvenile judge, based on the facts of the case at hand, decides that the alleged offender should be transferred to adult court.

AUTOMATIC TRANSFER
The process by which a juvenile is transferred to adult court as a matter of state law. In some states, for example, a juvenile who is suspected of murder is automatically transferred to adult court.

PROSECUTORIAL WAIVER
A procedure in which juvenile court judges have the discretion to transfer a juvenile case to adult court, when certain predetermined conditions as to the seriousness of the offense and the age of the offender are met.

Figure 16.5 Felony Arrest Charge for Juveniles Transferred to Adult Criminal Courts

Two out of every three juveniles transferred to adult criminal court under suspicion of committing a felony were charged with a violent offense. The data shown here were collected in criminal courts located in the 75 largest counties in the United States.

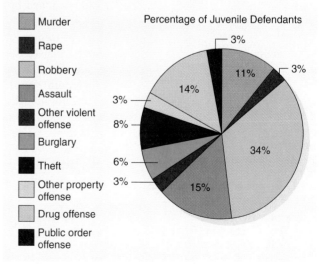

Murder
Rape
Robbery
Assault
Other violent offense
Burglary
Theft
Other property offense
Drug offense
Public order offense

Percentage of Juvenile Defendants

3%
11%
3%
14%
3%
8%
6%
3%
34%
15%

SOURCE: BUREAU OF JUSTICE STATISTICS, *JUVENILE FELONY DEFENDANTS IN CRIMINAL COURTS* (WASHINGTON, D.C.: U.S. DEPARTMENT OF JUSTICE, SEPTEMBER 1998), TABLE 2 AT PAGE 2.

those juveniles who had been transferred to adult court were rearrested, compared to 19 percent of those who remained in the juvenile justice system. Those who passed through the adult system were also rearrested more quickly (after an average of 135 days) than those who had not been transferred (an average of 277 days).[41] After doing a similar study, Jeffrey Fagan, director of the Center for Violence Research and Prevention at Columbia University, concluded that "increasing the severity of criminal court sanctions [for juveniles] may actually enhance the likelihood of recidivism."[42] These conclusions support the theory that prison life socializes younger offenders to a career in crime.

Detention

Once the decision has been made that the offender will face adjudication in a juvenile court, the intake official must decide what to do with him or her until the start of the trial. Generally, the juvenile is released into the custody of parents or a guardian—most jurisdictions favor this practice in lieu of setting money bail for youths. The intake officer may also place the offender in **detention,** or temporary custody in a secure facility, until the disposition process begins. Once a juvenile has been detained, most jurisdictions require that a **detention hearing** be held within twenty-four hours. During this hearing, the offender has several due process safeguards, including the right to counsel, the right against self-incrimination, and the right to cross-examine and confront witnesses.

In justifying its decision to detain, the court will usually address one of three issues:

1 Whether the child poses a danger to the community.

2 Whether the child will return for the adjudication process.

3 Whether detention will provide protection for the child.

The Supreme Court upheld the practice of preventive detention (see Chapter 8) for juveniles in *Schall v. Martin* (1984)[43] by ruling that youths can be detained if they are deemed a "risk" to the safety of the community, or to their own welfare.

On any given day, approximately 250,000 juveniles are held in detention facilities. A continuing concern for juvenile justice experts is that close to 9,000 of these youths are kept in adult jails, where they face dangerous situations caused by overcrowding and the violent and predatory nature of the adult inmates.[44] Because of the poor conditions in these jails and the exposure of minors to physical and sexual abuse from other inmates, reformers have consistently lobbied for separate adult and juvenile detention facilities. Under the JJDP Act, the federal government mandated that any state receiving federal funds must attempt to remove juveniles from adult jails.[45] If this is not possible, then "sight and sound separation" between adult and juvenile offenders must be established. In other words, juvenile offenders must not be able to see or hear the adult inmates. The data show, however, that a significant number of juveniles are still being placed in adult jails and are in contact with adult inmates, mostly in rural areas where no other facilities exist or officials do not have the resources to separate the two groups.

JUVENILES ON TRIAL

Over the past thirty years, the one constant in the juvenile justice system has been change. Supreme Court rulings in the wake of *In re Gault* (1967) have increased the procedural formality and the overriding punitive philosophy of the juvenile court. Diversion policies have worked to remove many status

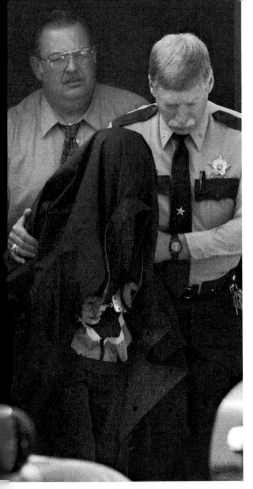

Vance County Deputies lead one of two 11-year-old identical twins from a courtroom in Henderson, North Carolina, following an appearance in which the boys faced charges of killing their father. Had the boys been 13, they could have been charged as adults under state law for murder.

DETENTION
The temporary custody of a juvenile in a state facility after a petition has been filed and before the adjudicatory process begins.

DETENTION HEARING
A hearing to determine whether a juvenile should be detained, or remain detained, while waiting for the adjudicatory process to begin.

offenders from the juvenile court's jurisdiction, and waiver policies assure that the most violent juveniles are tried as adults. Some observers feel these adjustments have "criminalized" the juvenile court, effectively rendering it indistinguishable both theoretically and practically from adult courts.[46]

Along with a number of his colleagues, law professor Barry C. Feld thinks that the juvenile court has become obsolete and should be abolished. Feld believes the changes noted above have "transformed the juvenile court from its original model as a social service agency into a deficient second-rate criminal court that provides young people with neither positive treatment nor criminal procedural justice."[47] Indeed, juvenile hearings do proceed along many of the same lines as the adult criminal court, with similar due process protections and rules of evidence (though minors do not enjoy the right to a jury trial). As the *Concept Summary* on this page explains, however, juvenile justice proceedings may still be distinguished from the adult system of criminal justice, and these differences are evident in the adjudication and disposition of the juvenile trial.

CONCEPT SUMMARY
The Criminal Justice System versus the Juvenile Justice System

When the juvenile justice system first began in the United States, its participants saw it as being separate from the adult criminal justice system. Indeed, the two systems remain separate in many ways. There are, however, a number of similarities between juvenile and adult justice. In this *Concept Summary*, we summarize both the similarities and the differences.

Similarities between Juvenile and Adult Justice Systems

- The right to receive the *Miranda* warning applies to both juveniles and adults.
- Juveniles and adults enjoy similar procedural protection when making the admission of guilt.
- Prosecutors and defense attorneys play equally important roles in the adjudication of adults and juveniles.
- Juvenile and adults have the right to be represented by counsel at the crucial stages of the trial process.
- Juveniles and adults have access to plea bargains.
- Juveniles and adults have the right to a hearing and an appeal.
- The standard of evidence in adult criminal trials and the juvenile delinquency process is proof beyond a reasonable doubt.
- Juveniles and adults can be placed on probation by the judge.
- Juveniles and adults can be held before adjudication if the judge believes them to be a threat to the community.
- Following trial, juveniles and adults can be sentenced to community supervision.

Differences between Juvenile and Adult Justice Systems

- The overriding theoretical purpose behind juvenile justice is the rehabilitation of the offender, while the adult justice system is more concerned with punishment.

- Juveniles can be apprehended by law enforcement officers for acts (status offenses) that are not criminal for adults.
- Juvenile wrongdoing is considered a "delinquent act"; adult wrongdoing is considered a "crime."
- Adult criminal proceedings are more formal and regimented than juvenile proceedings.
- Juvenile court proceedings are closed to the public. Adult criminal trials are open to the public.
- Courts may not release identifying information about a juvenile facing delinquency charges to the press, while courts must release information about adults facing criminal charges.
- Parents play a significant role in the juvenile justice process. This is not the case in the criminal justice process.
- Juvenile are released into parental custody, while adults are given the opportunity to post bail when justified.
- In most, but not all, states, juveniles do not have the right to a jury trial. All adults have this right.
- Juveniles can be searched in school without probable cause. No adult can be searched without probable cause.
- A juvenile's delinquency record is sealed when the age of majority is reached. An adult's criminal record is permanent.
- Juveniles cannot be sentenced to county jails or state prisons, institutions that are reserved for adults.
- The juvenile justice system does not have a death penalty. The Supreme Court has ruled, however, that the Constitution does not prohibit states from punishing crimes committed by juveniles aged 16 and 17 with execution. Capital punishment is not allowed for those under 16.

SOURCE: LARRY SIEGEL AND JOSEPH SENNA, JUVENILE DELINQUENCY: THEORY, PRACTICE AND LAW 6TH ED. (ST. PAUL, MN: WEST PUBLISHING COMPANY, 1997), 446.

ADJUDICATORY HEARING
The process through which a juvenile court determines whether there is sufficient evidence to support the initial petition.

DISPOSITION HEARING
Similar to the sentencing hearing for adults, a hearing in which the juvenile judge or officer decides the appropriate punishment for a youth found to be delinquent or a status offender.

PREDISPOSITION REPORT
A report prepared during the disposition process that provides the judge with relevant background material to aid in the disposition decision.

Adjudication

During the adjudication stage of the juvenile justice process, a hearing is held to determine whether or not the offender is delinquent or in need of some form of court supervision. Most state juvenile codes dictate a specific set of procedures that must be followed during the **adjudicatory hearing,** with the goal of providing the respondent with "the essentials of due process and fair treatment." Consequently, the respondent in an adjudicatory hearing has the right to notice of charges, counsel, confrontation and cross-examination, and the privilege against self-incrimination.[48] Furthermore, "proof beyond a reasonable doubt" must be established to find the child delinquent. When the child admits guilt—that is, admits to the charges of the initial petition—the judge must ensure that the admission was voluntary.

The increased presence of defense attorneys in juvenile courts has had a significant impact on juvenile adjudication. (See *Careers in Criminal Justice— The Juvenile Public Defender.*) Aspects of the adversarial system have become increasingly apparent in juvenile courts, as has the practice of plea bargaining. To a certain extent, however, juvenile trials have retained the informal atmosphere that characterized pre-*In re Gault* proceedings. Respondents and their families often waive the due process rights provided by the Supreme Court at the suggestion of a juvenile probation officer or judge. One study of Minnesota juvenile courts found that no counsel was present in 50 percent of that state's adjudicatory hearings.[49]

At the close of the adjudicatory hearing, the judge is generally required to rule on the legal issues and evidence that have been presented. Based on this ruling, the judge determines whether or not the respondent is delinquent or in need of court supervision. Alternatively, the judge can dismiss the case based on a lack of evidence. It is important to remember that finding a child to be delinquent is *not* the same as convicting an adult of a crime. A delinquent does not face the same restrictions, such as those concerning the right to vote and to run for political office, as do adult convicts (discussed in Chapter 15).

Disposition

Once a juvenile has been adjudicated delinquent, the judge must decide what steps will be taken toward treatment and/or punishment. Most states provide for a *bifurcated process* in which a separate **disposition hearing** follows the adjudicatory hearing. Depending on state law, the juvenile may be entitled to counsel at the disposition hearing.

In an adult trial, the sentencing phase is primarily concerned with the "needs" of the community to be protected from the convict. In contrast, a juvenile judge uses the disposition hearing to determine a sentence that will serve the "needs" of the child.[50] For assistance in this crucial process, the judge will order the probation department to gather information on the juvenile and present it in the form of a **predisposition report.** The report usually contains information concerning the respondent's family background, the facts surrounding the delinquent act, and interviews with social workers, teachers, and other important figures in the child's life.

In keeping with the rehabilitative tradition of the juvenile justice system, many judges have a great deal of discretion in choosing one of several disposition possibilities. Generally, the choice is among incarceration in a juvenile correctional facility, probation, or community treatment. In most cases seriousness of the offense is the primary factor used in determining whether to incarcerate a juvenile, though history of delinquency, family situation, and the offender's attitude are all relevant.[51] Further research suggests that race plays a significant role in disposition—that minority delinquents are more likely to be incarcerated than their white counterparts. We will discuss the ramifications of this practice in Chapter 18.

Careers in Criminal Justice

CATHY WASSERMAN, PUBLIC DEFENDER: JUVENILE COURTS

Grandpa had always said I could talk my way out of the electric chair. So when a friend in college suggested applying to law school, I thought, yes, why not. I attended Seton Hall Law In Newark, New Jersey, where I participated in the Juvenile Justice Clinic for two and a half semesters. This experience representing delinquents, coupled with a childhood of being raised on Perry Mason, as well as a law clerkship with a Superior Court judge, helped me to recognize my strong interest in criminal law. The forum of pleading my case in open court seemed like the only place to be.

Following my clerkship, I was hired by the Office of the Public Defender. Working for the P.D. is the fastest way to be in command of your own cases and to appear in court on all kinds of matters, particularly trials. My caseload consisted of clients charged with everything from fourth degree theft to armed robbery. The first year and a half, I represented adults. Then I went to the Appellate Section where I wrote briefs for two and a half years. I enjoyed the treasure hunt of looking for the cases to support my arguments. I also enjoyed presenting those arguments to the Appellate Division panels. However, I found I missed being in court on a daily basis and dealing with clients in person. Thus, when the opportunity to transfer to another trial region arose, I grabbed it and began representing juveniles once again.

Every day I enter court prepared to do battle for a youngster who in all likelihood is not cognizant of how at risk his or her freedom is. Initially, my most

important responsibility is to interview my client and his family to gain their trust, obtain information about the child, and learn their version of the facts in the case. I gather all the evidence provided by the State, review it carefully and conduct my own investigations. Following a careful review of all the evidence available, weighing all the strengths and weaknesses in the case, and considering whether any trial would be before a judge rather than a jury, I discuss the options, risks, and penalties with my client. Whether we go to trial or negotiate a plea agreement, my duties are to be an effective attorney for the child. However, once we face a sentence, I must also become a social worker as I attempt to fashion the least restrictive disposition from the myriad of sentencing alternatives. It is this array of options and the court's discretion to impose them which most clearly distinguishes the juvenile system from its adult counterpart.

Some of the most challenging cases of my career have involved representing children the State is seeking to have referred to adult court. In New Jersey, there is a presumption of referral where a juvenile is charged with the most serious offenses and is fourteen years or older. The discretion to file for referral lies solely in the hands of the prosecutor. There are few tasks more difficult than having to tell a fourteen year old, who had a fight in which someone died, that he could be spending the next thirty years of his life in an adult jail. I faced this very scenario a number of years ago. In that particular case, H. T. had no prior involvement with the system and did not inflict the fatal wound. Worse, the confession he gave to the police to "help" himself was the main evidence against him. Although the State's psychiatrist agreed with the defense expert that the boy could be rehabilitated in the

juvenile system, the State pressed on. The pressure and emotional toll on me as counsel was enormous. I struggled to construct arguments out of the jigsaw puzzle of facts and the kid's life. I was confidante, commander, and advisor to not only my client in custody but also to his family. Contrary to the norm in waiver cases, H. T. prevailed. This case helped me to recognize how important my role can be in the life of a child.

I am an impassioned advocate for children because I believe most offenders should be allowed to survive childhood and adolescence without permanently damaging their prospects for a positive future. My skills as an attorney and negotiator give my clients the opportunity to rise above their acts, often committed through poor judgment, inexperience, or by succumbing to peer pressure. Occasionally, I make a significant difference in the life of a youngster.

Further indication of the treatment goals of juvenile courts can be found in the indeterminate sentencing practices that, until recently, dominated disposition. Under indeterminate sentencing, correctional administrators were given the freedom to decide when a delinquent had been sufficiently rehabilitated and could be released. In a clear indication of the shift toward the crime control model, today nearly half of the states have enacted determinate or minimum mandatory sentencing laws that cover convicted juvenile offenders. Such statutes shift the focus of disposition from the treatment needs of the delinquent to society's desire to punish and incapacitate.[52]

GRADUATED SANCTIONS
The practical theory in juvenile corrections that a delinquent or status offender should receive a punishment that matches in seriousness the severity of the wrongdoing.

RESIDENTIAL TREATMENT PROGRAMS
Government-run facilities for juveniles whose offenses are not deemed serious enough to warrant incarceration in a training school.

JUVENILE CORRECTIONS

In general, juvenile corrections is based on the concept of **graduated sanctions**—that is, the severity of the punishment should fit the crime. Consequently, status and first-time offenders are diverted or placed on probation, repeat offenders find themselves in intensive community supervision or treatment programs, and serious and violent offenders are placed in correctional facilities.[53] As society's expectations of the juvenile justice system have changed, so have the characteristics of its corrections programs. In some cities, for example, juvenile probation officers join police officers on the beat. Because the former are not bound by the same search and seizure restrictions as other law enforcement officials, this interdepartmental teamwork provides more opportunities to fight youth crime aggressively. Juvenile correctional facilities are also changing their operations to reflect public mandates that they both reform *and* punish. (See *CJ in Focus—Making Waves: Tough Love in Texas.*)

Probation and Residential Treatment Programs

The most common form of juvenile corrections is probation—35 percent of all delinquency cases disposed of by juvenile courts result in conditional diversion. The majority of all adjudicated delinquents (nearly 55 percent) will never receive a disposition more severe than being placed on probation.[54] These statistics reflect a general understanding among juvenile court judges and other officials that removing a child from her or his home should be considered primarily as a last resort.

The organization of juvenile probation is very similar to adult probation (see Chapter 12), and juvenile probationers are increasingly subjected to electronic monitoring and other supervisory tactics. The main difference between the two programs lies in the attitude toward the offender. Adult probation officers have an overriding responsibility to protect the community from the probationer, while juvenile probation officers are expected to take the role of a mentor or a concerned relative in looking after the needs of the child.[55]

When intensive supervision must be instituted, youths can be placed in **residential treatment programs.** These programs, run by either probation departments or social service organizations, provide treatment in a nonsecure living facility. Residential treatment programs can be divided into four categories:

1. *Foster care programs*, in which the juvenile lives with a couple who act as surrogate parents.

2. *Group homes*, which generally house between twelve and fifteen youths and provide treatment, counseling, and educational services by a professional staff.

3. *Family group homes*, which combine aspects of foster care and group homes, meaning that a single family, rather than a group of professionals, looks after the needs of the offenders.

4. *Rural programs*, which include wilderness camps, farms, and ranches where between thirty and fifty children are placed in an environment that provides recreational activities and treatment programs.[56]

The Arizona Boys Ranch, which housed 200 troubled youths, lost its license to operate in 1999 after mistreatment by staff members led to the death of 14-year-old Nicholaus Contreraz. While this example is extreme, residential facilities for juveniles often struggle to balance attempts to rehabilitate their charges with the need to keep discipline.

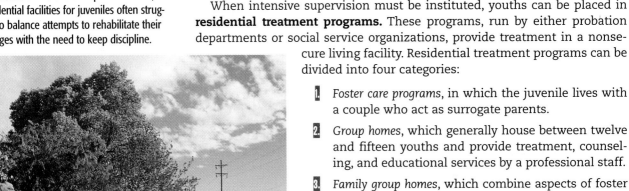

CJ in Focus

Making Waves

Tough Love in Texas

Before Steve Robinson was named director of the Texas Youth Commission (TYC), juvenile offenders incarcerated at the agency's fourteen detention centers wore their own clothing and spent a great deal of time watching television. Punishment for misbehavior was rare. Since Robinson took over the helm of TYC in the early 1990s, the institution has changed dramatically. Inmates now wear bright orange uniforms and march in a straight line with their hands behind their backs. From the time they arise at 5 A.M. until lights out at 9 P.M., nearly every moment in the offenders' day is strictly planned. With only eight (silent) minutes allotted for each meal, plenty of time is left for "resocialization" programs such as group therapy and education. When the juveniles break institutional rules, they are sent to Security and restricted in a single cell with a toilet and a steel bunk bed, similar to "the hole" in adult prisons. "I always felt like the only way you can deal with kids and help kids is to hold them accountable," says Robinson of his policies.

For the 4,300 minors housed at TYC, representing some of the state's most violent juvenile offenders, progress is based on a phase system. New arrivals begin at phase zero, and they must reach phase four before release. Phase zero offenders must memorize a personal "layout," a recital that describes their situation and goals. "I am sixteen years old," says one inmate:

I have caused serious pain and injury to my family by selling drugs. . . . I need help, I want help. I'm willing to accept help to become a person who no longer hurts others. To become a person who no longer hurts others, I need to . . . start going to school more, stop selling drugs, and start spending more time with my family.

In group therapy sessions, offenders revisit traumatic moments in their lives to better understand the roots of their behavior. In one session, for example, a group of inmates reenact a scene in which one of them is beaten with a wooden board by his father, while his mother stands mutely in an adjoining room.

Does Robinson's "tough love" program work? According to 1998 data, 48.9 percent of the juveniles released from TYC were rearrested within one year, with 9.2 percent facing charges of a violent offense. Five years earlier, when Robinson took over the institution, 59.6 percent of those released from TYC were rearrested within a year, with 12.2 percent of them apprehended for violent acts.

For Critical Analysis: What are the drawbacks of judging institutions such as TYC solely on recidivism rates? What further statistics would you need to fully understand the implications of the rearrest rates?

Institutionalizing Juveniles

More than 100,000 American youths (up from 30,000 at the end of the 1970s) are incarcerated in public and private juvenile correctional facilities in the United States.[57] Most of these juveniles have committed crimes against people or property, but a significant number (about 16 percent) have been incarcerated because of other factors, such as familial neglect or mental incapacity.

Deterioration of Services. The most restrictive of these facilities—referred to as **training schools**—are similar in many aspects to adult prisons and jails. In theory, training schools differ from adult prisons and jails in their efforts to treat and rehabilitate young offenders. And although many juvenile facilities do uphold this traditional justification for incarcerating children, a number do not.

Corrections officials contend that the institutionalization of increasing numbers of mentally ill youths, along with decreasing appropriations for educational and psychiatric programs as funds are instead used to construct new facilities, has led to widespread deterioration in the nation's juvenile corrections facilities.[58] Recognizing the problem, in the late 1990s the U.S. Department of Justice began a series of investigations into juvenile facilities in Louisiana, Kentucky, Georgia, and Puerto Rico.

Aftercare. Most juveniles leave corrections facilities through an early release program or because they have served the length of their sentence. Juvenile corrections officials recognize that many of these children, like adults, need

TRAINING SCHOOLS
Correctional institutions for juveniles found to be delinquent or status offenders.

assistance readjusting to the outside world. Consequently, released juveniles are often placed in *aftercare* programs. Similar to adult parole, an aftercare program is designed to offer services for the juvenile, while at the same time supervising him or her to reduce the chances of recidivism. The ideal aftercare program includes community support groups, aid in finding and keeping employment, and continued monitoring to assure that the juvenile is able to deal with the demands of freedom.[59]

RECENT TRENDS IN JUVENILE DELINQUENCY

When asked, juveniles will admit to a wide range of illegal or dangerous behavior (see Figure 16.6). Have juvenile law enforcement efforts, juvenile courts, and juvenile corrections been effective in controlling and preventing this kind of misbehavior, as well as more serious acts?

To answer this question, many observers turn to the Federal Bureau of Investigation's Uniform Crime Report (UCR), initially covered in Chapter 2. Because the UCR breaks down arrest statistics by age of the arrestee, it has been considered the primary source of information on the presence of juveniles in America's justice system. This does not mean, however, that the UCR is completely reliable when it comes to measuring juvenile delinquency. The process measures only those juveniles who were caught and therefore does not accurately reflect all delinquent acts in any given year. Furthermore, it measures the number of arrests but not the number of arrestees, meaning that—due to repeat offenders—the number of actual juveniles could be below the number of juvenile arrests.

Figure 16.6 Delinquent and Risky Behavior by High School Students

As you can see, a self-report survey of high school students reveals a wide array of delinquent and dangerous behavior.

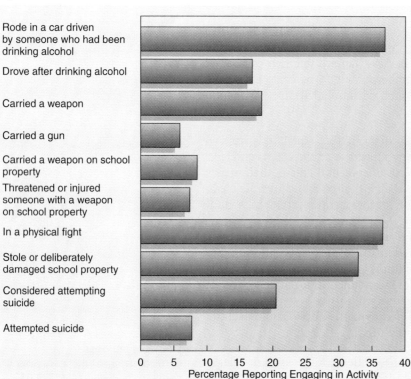

Ten Years of Delinquency: 1985 to 1994

With these cautions in mind, UCR findings are quite clear as to the extent of the juvenile delinquency problem in the United States today. In 1997, juveniles accounted for 17.2 percent of violent crime and 18.7 percent of criminal activity in general.[60] According to the 1997 UCR, juveniles were responsible for

- 14 percent of all murder arrests;
- 14 percent of all aggravated assault arrests;
- 17 percent of all forcible rapes;
- 24 percent of all weapons arrests;
- 30 percent of all robbery arrests;
- 35 percent of all property crimes; and
- 14 percent of all drug offenses.

SOURCE: ADAPTED FROM LAURA KANN, "YOUTH RISK BEHAVIOR SURVEILLANCE—UNITED STATES, 1997," IN *MORBIDITY AND MORTALITY WEEKLY REPORT* 47 (WASHINGTON, D.C.: U.S. GOVERNMENT PRINTING OFFICE, AUGUST 14, 1998), 35–47.

Furthermore, although girls cannot compare with their male counterparts in the number of crimes they commit each year, between 1992 and 1996 the number of female juveniles arrested for violent crimes rose at a rate 25 percent higher than for male juveniles.[61]

The impact of juvenile delinquency on America's overall crime rate cannot be overstated. As Figure 16.7 shows, the ten-year period between 1985 and 1994 saw a drastic rise in the rate of juvenile arrests. Especially distressing were juvenile violent crime arrest trends: murder arrests alone rose 150 percent over that decade. Further scrutiny of UCR research, also evident in Figure 16.7, reveals an especially disturbing trend: the juvenile crime rate rose faster than the overall crime rate. Violent crimes committed by youths rose by over 60 percent in the 1990s, even as the overall violent crime rate dropped.

Is Juvenile Crime Leveling Off?

Just as Figure 16.7 paints a bleak picture of the years between 1985 and 1994, it also shows that arrest rates for juveniles have leveled off, and even fallen in many categories, since then. Arrest rates dropped for juveniles involved in violent crimes (3 percent) and property crimes (2 percent) between 1994 and 1995 and have as yet failed to resume their climb. (It must be noted, however, that the rates are still relatively high.)

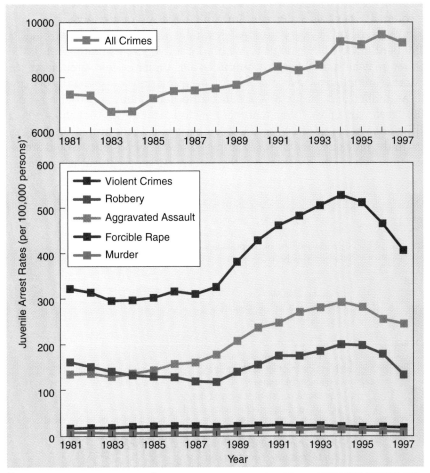

Figure 16.7 Arrest Rates of Juveniles, 1981–1997

After rising dramatically from 1985 to 1994, arrest rates for juveniles began to level off.

*ARRESTS OF PERSONS UNDER AGE 18 PER 100,000 PERSONS AGES 10 TO 17 IN THE POPULATION OF THE UNITED STATES.

SOURCE: HOWARD SNYDER, *JUVENILE ARRESTS 1997* (WASHINGTON, D.C.: OFFICE OF JUVENILE JUSTICE AND DELINQUENCY PREVENTION, 1998).

Although the theory is not universally accepted, many observers see the rise and decline of juvenile arrests as mirroring the rise and decline of crack cocaine.[62] When inner-city youths took advantage of the economic opportunities offered by the crack trade in the 1980s, they found they needed to protect themselves against rival dealers. This led to the proliferation of firearms among juveniles, as well as the formation of violent youth gangs. As the crack "epidemic" has slowed in recent years, so have arrest and violent crime rates for juveniles.

Even before juvenile crime rates began to taper off, the threat to public safety from youths was not as widespread as the yearly UCRs might have indicated. In 1994, for example, 92 percent of the counties in the United States experienced one or zero youth homicides. Four cities—Chicago, New York, Los Angeles, and Detroit—accounted for 5 percent of the country's juvenile population and nearly one-third of its juvenile murders.

FACTORS IN JUVENILE DELINQUENCY

In one of the most influential studies in the field of criminology, Professor Marvin Wolfgang found that 6 percent of all boys in any given cohort (group of persons who share similar characteristics) will become chronic offenders, defined as someone who is arrested five or more times before his eighteenth birthday. Furthermore, Wolfgang found that these chronic offenders were responsible for half of all crimes and two-thirds of all violent crimes within the cohort.[63] Does this Six Percent Rule mean that no matter what steps society takes, six out of every hundred juveniles are "bad seeds" and will act delinquently? Or does it point to a situation in which a small percentage of children may be more likely to commit crimes under certain circumstances?

Most criminologists favor the second interpretation. It is generally believed that a number of "risk factors" are linked to delinquent activity (see Figure 16.8). Researchers have found a number of statistical trends that show certain youths to be at higher risk for antisocial behavior. According to the last statistic in the previous section, for example, juvenile delinquency would appear to be somewhat site-specific—youths in certain geographical areas have a

> "Good kids have guns .... Good kids who want to go to school and do the right thing—they're afraid of the gangs and the drug dealers; they want to protect themselves and their families. Good kids, bad kids—the categories don't apply anymore."
>
> —John Silva, *director of safety and security for the Cambridge, Massachusetts public schools (1994)*

Figure 16.8 Risk Factors for Juvenile Delinquency

The characteristics listed here are generally accepted as "risk factors" for juvenile delinquency. In other words, if one or more of these factors are present in a juvenile's life, he or she has a greater chance of exhibiting delinquent behavior—though such behavior is by no means a certainty.

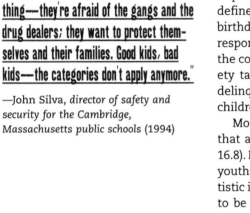

Family	Broken home/lack of parental role model
	Parental or sibling drug/alcohol abuse
	Extreme economic deprivation
	Family members in a gang
School	Academic frustration/failure
	Learning disability
	Negative labeling by teachers
	Disciplinary problems
Community	Social disorganization (refer to Chapter 2)
	Presence of gangs in the community
	Presence of obvious drug use in the community
	Availability of firearms
	High crime/constant feeling of danger
	Lack of social and economic opportunities
Peers	Delinquent friends
	Friends who use drugs or are members of gangs
	Lack of "positive" peer pressure
Individual	Tendency toward aggressive behavior
	Inability to concentrate or focus/easily bored/hyperactive
	Alcohol or drug use
	Fatalistic/pessimistic viewpoint

higher chance of being perpetrators or victims of murder. High school dropouts also seem to be at greater risk of becoming part of Wolfgang's 6 percent; a recent study shows that about 70 percent of all adults in prison in the United States failed to complete the twelfth grade.[64] In this section, we will discuss the four factors that are most commonly used to explain juvenile criminal behavior and violent crime rates: age, substance abuse, family problems, and gangs.

The Age-Crime Relationship

Crime statistics are fairly conclusive on one point: the older a person is, the less likely he or she will exhibit criminal behavior. According to many criminologists, particularly Travis Hirschi and Michael Gottfredson, age is the one constant factor in criminal behavior, more important than sex, race, intelligence, or class.[65] Any group of at-risk persons—whether they be high school dropouts or (as we shall see) the children of abusive parents—will commit fewer crimes as they grow older. This process is known as **aging out.**

Another view sees the **age of onset,** or the age at which the youth begins delinquent behavior, as a consistent predictor of future criminal behavior. One study compared recidivism rates between juveniles first judged to be delinquent before the age of fifteen and those first adjudicated delinquent after the age of fifteen. Of the seventy-one subjects who made up the first group, 32 percent became chronic offenders. Of the sixty-five who made up the second group, none became chronic offenders.[66] This research suggests that juvenile justice resources should be concentrated on the youngest offenders, with the goal of preventing crime and reducing the long-term risks for society.

Substance Abuse

As we have seen throughout this textbook and will see again in the next chapter, substance abuse plays a strong role in criminal behavior for adults. The same can certainly be said for juveniles. According to the Office of National Drug Control Policy, nearly 10 million Americans under the age of twenty consume alcohol each year, increasing the probability that they will experience academic problems, drop out of school, or commit acts of vandalism (the willful destruction of property).[67] The health consequences of this level of underage drinking are staggering: alcohol is a factor in between 50 and 65 percent of all teenage suicides, and nearly 2,500 youths are killed each year in alcohol-related automobile crashes.

Arrests for alcohol-related incidents, however, have recently declined. From 1987 to 1996, for example, juvenile arrests for driving under the influence declined 27.6 percent, while arrests for drunkenness declined 10.6 percent.[68] Over that same time period, juvenile arrests for drug abuse violations *increased* 132.9 percent (see Figure 16.9 on the next page).[69] A male between the ages of twelve and seventeen who uses drugs is eight times more likely to be arrested for any offense, and a female in that age range who uses drugs is eleven time more likely to be arrested.[70] In fact, many criminologists point out that increases in juvenile violence began in 1985, the same year that marked the start of the recent rise in juvenile arrests for drug use and trafficking.[71]

Child Abuse and Neglect

Substance abuse by parents also plays a substantial role in juvenile delinquency. In 1997, 1,054,000 (15 out of every 1,000) American children were confirmed by child protective services as having been abused or neglected by their parents. **Child abuse** can be broadly defined as the infliction of physical

AGING OUT
A term used to explain the fact that criminal activity declines with age.

AGE OF ONSET
The age at which a juvenile first exhibits delinquent behavior. The earlier the age of onset, according to some observers, the greater the chance a person will become a career offender.

CHILD ABUSE
Mistreatment of children by causing physical, emotional, or sexual damage without any plausible explanation, such as an accident.

Figure **16.9** Juvenile Arrest Rates for Drug Abuse Violations

Although juvenile arrest rates for violent crimes have leveled off and even declined since 1994 (refer back to Figure 16.7 on page 581), juvenile arrest rates for drug abuse violations have continued to climb.

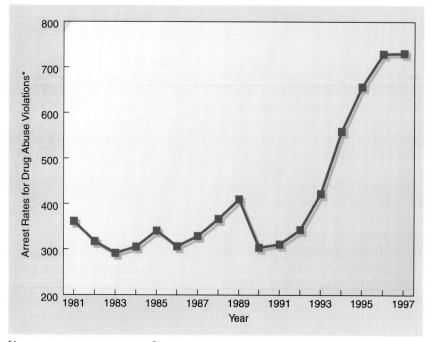

*ARRESTS OF PERSONS UNDER AGE 18 PER 100,000 PERSONS AGES 10 TO 17 IN THE POPULATION OF THE UNITED STATES.

SOURCE: HOWARD SYNDER, "JUVENILE ARREST RATES FOR DRUG ABUSE VIOLATIONS, 1981–1997," IN JUVENILE ARRESTS 1997 (WASHINGTON, D.C.: OFFICE OF JUVENILE JUSTICE AND DELINQUENCY PREVENTION, 1998).

CHILD NEGLECT
A form of child abuse in which the child is denied certain necessities such as shelter, food, care, and love. Neglect is justification for a government agency to assume responsibility for a child in place of the parents or legal guardian.

YOUTH GANGS
Self-formed groups of youths with several identifiable characteristics, including a gang name and other recognizable symbols, a geographic territory, a leadership structure, a meeting pattern, and participation in illegal activities.

or emotional damage on a child, while **child neglect** refers to deprivations—of love, shelter, food, proper care—children undergo by their parents. A significant portion (estimates can range from 40 percent[72] to 88 percent[73]) of parents who mistreat their children are believed to be under the influence of illegal drugs or alcohol.

Children in homes characterized by violence or neglect suffer from a variety of physical, emotional, and mental health problems at a much greater rate than their peers.[74] This, in turn, increases their chances of engaging in delinquent behavior. Research done for the Office of Juvenile Justice and Delinquency Prevention by David Huizinga, Rolf Loeber, and Terence Thornberry, for example, recently found that a history of maltreatment increases the chances of a youth being violent by 24 percent.[75] Another survey of violent juveniles showed that 75 percent had suffered severe abuse by a family member, 80 percent had witnessed violence in their home, 33 percent had a sibling with a criminal record, and 25 percent had at least one parent who abused drugs or alcohol.[76]

Cathy Spatz Widom, a professor of criminal justice and psychology at the State University of New York at Albany, compared the arrest records of two groups of subjects—one made up of 908 cases of substantiated parental abuse and neglect and the other made up of 667 children who had not been abused or neglected. Widom found that those who had been abused or neglected were 53 percent more likely to be arrested as juveniles than those who had not.[77]

Gangs

When youths cannot find the stability and support they require in the family structure, they will often turn to their peers. This is just one explanation for why juveniles join **youth gangs.** Although jurisdictions may have varying definitions, for general purposes a youth gang is viewed as a group of three or more persons who (1) self-identify themselves as an entity separate from the community by special clothing, vocabulary, hand signals, and names and (2) engage in criminal activity. Although the first gangs may have appeared at the time of the American Revolution in the 1780s, there have been four periods of major gang activity in American history: the late 1800s, the 1920s, the 1960s, and the 1990s. According to an exhaustive survey of law enforcement agencies, there are probably close to 650,000 juvenile gang members in the United States. As Figure 16.10 shows, nearly 60 percent of these gang members can be found in California, Illinois, and Texas.

Who Joins Gangs? The average gang member is seventeen to eighteen years old, though members tend to be older in cities with longer traditions of gang activity such as Chicago and Los Angeles.[78] In a student survey of nearly 6,000 eighth-graders at eleven different sites, 31 percent of those who said they were gang members were African American, 25 percent were white, 25 percent were Hispanic, 5 percent were Asian, and 14 percent were from other ethnic or racial backgrounds.[79] Though gangs tend to have racial or ethnic characteristics—that is, one group predominates in each gang—many researchers do not believe that race or ethnicity is the dominant factor in gang membership. Instead, gang members seem to come from lower-class or working-class communities, mostly in urban areas but with an increasing number from the suburbs and rural counties.

Female Gangs. Females are also increasingly associated with gangs. According to criminologist Walter B. Miller, girls and women are involved in three different types of gangs:

- A female auxiliary group to an existing male gang. The Los Angeles–based Crips, for example, have a female auxiliary group known as the Crippettes. In most cases, these auxiliary groups are subordinate to the main male gang and are involved in the same illegitimate activities.

- Sexually integrated gangs, where male and female members operate under the same gang name and have the same gang leadership. The female gang members are often seen as the "property" of the male gang members.

- Independent, autonomous female gangs, characterized by all-female membership.[80]

Most female gang members belong to auxiliary groups. Researchers are finding, however, that the number of autonomous female gangs, though still relatively small, is growing.[81] Meda Chesney-Lind of the University of Hawaii has suggested that the "liberation hypothesis" helps to explain this rise in all-female gangs as well as why girls initially join gangs.[82] This theory holds that for many girls, an independent gang offers a refuge of female solidarity and diminishes the importance of relationships with males. One reformed female gang member said of her gang membership: "It made me feel good, high and powerful—visible when for the most part I felt very invisible and very powerless."[83]

Estimates of female gang activity tend to vary depending on the source. In 1975, after consulting data from six cities, Walter Miller estimated that gang membership was 90 percent male.[84] Although this "90 percent" figure is still taken as a general rule, further studies have claimed that it both overestimates and underestimates female gang activity. A 1992 survey by the National Institute of Justice found that females made up only 3.65 percent of the nation's gang members,[85] but sociologist Joan W. Moore estimates that one-third of all gang members are female.[86] This discrepancy may be partly explained by research methods. Surveys that rely on official law enforcement data tend to uncover low levels of female gang activity because girls are less likely to be identified as gang members than boys. In contrast, research that relies on fieldwork and interviews with juveniles may exaggerate the percentage of female gang members, as girls who are not gang affiliated will claim affiliation in an attempt to impress the interviewer.[87]

Why Do Youths Join Gangs? Aside from the "liberation hypothesis," gang membership often appears to be linked with status in the community.[88] This tends to be true of males as well as females.

Figure 16.10 Top Ten States by Number of Gang Members

California	254,618
Illinois	75,226
Texas	57,060
Ohio	17,025
Indiana	17,005
New Mexico	16,910
Arizona	16,291
Florida	15,247
Nevada	12,525
Minnesota	12,382

SOURCE: OFFICE OF JUVENILE JUSTICE AND DELINQUENCY PREVENTION, 1995 YOUTH GANG SURVEY (WASHINGTON, D.C.: U.S. DEPARTMENT OF JUSTICE, AUGUST 1997), FIGURE 16 AT PAGE 16.

Along with wearing "colors," speaking in code, and marking their turf with graffiti, gangs use hand signals to differentiate themselves from other gangs and to strengthen the social bonds between gang members (such as the Crips of San Fernando Valley, California, pictured here). A number of communities have tried to limit gang activity by forbidding such expressions of unity, including barring gang members from appearing in public together.

Figure **16.11** Comparison of Gang and At-Risk Youth Criminal Behavior

Matching gang and nongang youths for age, race, education, and other personal characteristics, C. Ronald Huff found that the gang members were much more likely to commit violent and property offenses.

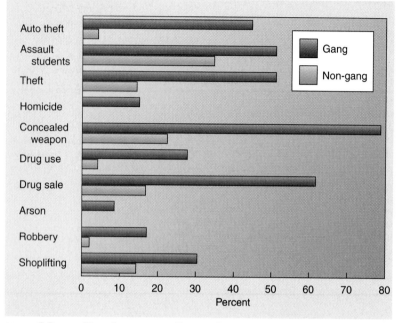

SOURCE: C. RONALD HUFF, COMPARING THE CRIMINAL BEHAVIOR OF YOUTH GANGS AND AT-RISK YOUTHS (WASHINGTON, D.C.: U.S. DEPARTMENT OF JUSTICE, OCTOBER 1998), 4.

"My homeboys became my family—the older ones were father figures. Each time I shot someone, each time I put another gun on the set, each time I successfully recruited a combat soldier, I was congratulated by my older homeboys."

—Sanyka Shakur, *former gang member* (1993)

Many teenagers, feeling alienated from their families and communities, join gangs for the social relationships and the sense of identity a gang can provide.[89]

Gang membership is seen as a necessity for a number of youths, especially those who live in high-crime neighborhoods—joining a gang is a form of protection against violence from other gangs. Excitement is another attraction of the gang life, as is the economic incentive of enjoying the profits from illegal gang activities such as dealing drugs or robbery.[90] Finally, some teenagers are literally forced to join gangs by the threat of violence from gang members.

Gangs and Crime. To a certain extent, the violent and criminal behavior of youths has been exaggerated by information sources such as the media. In proportion to all gang activities, violence is a rare event; gang members spend most of their time "hanging out" and taking part in other normal adolescent behavior.[91] That having been said, gang members are responsible for a disproportionate amount of violent and nonviolent criminal acts by juveniles. Traditional gang activities such as using and trafficking drugs, protecting their territory in "turf battles," and graffiti/vandalism all contribute to high crime rates among members.

According to estimates, the nearly half a million gang members in the United States commit more than 600,000 crimes a year. Furthermore, a recent study of criminal behavior among juveniles in Cleveland found that gang members were considerably more likely to commit crimes than at-risk youths who shared many characteristics with gang members but were not affiliated with any gang (see Figure 16.11).[92] With regard to a crucial subject that we will cover in the feature *Criminal Justice in Action—Gangs and Guns* at the end of this chapter, the gang members in Cleveland were also much more likely to own firearms or have friends who owned firearms.

JUVENILE DELINQUENCY AND THE "TIME BOMB"

Though the slight decrease in some juvenile crime statistics over the past few years has been welcome, many criminologists and law enforcement officials have expressed concern that this recent drop in youth crime will lead to a sense of complacency among their colleagues. Any such decline, they believe, should be seen in the context of the immense growth in delinquency since 1985. Furthermore, the factors we have just discussed—substance abuse by adults and adolescents, child abuse and neglect, gang membership—are on the upswing.

The most pessimistic predictions concerning the immediate future for juvenile delinquency are based on the age-crime relationship. Princeton University's John DiIulio, Jr., and many of his colleagues are predicting that a "time bomb" of juvenile crime is set to detonate in the next ten years. This prediction is based on the fact that 40 million American adolescents—the largest such group since the 1950s—will reach their most crime-prone age between 2003 and 2005.[93] Many of these children have been exposed to broken homes, poor schools, inadequate housing, and other social and economic factors that contribute to criminality, and the concern is that the juvenile justice system will not be prepared to handle the influx of delinquency that this group will present.

Three general strategies are being put in place to deal with juvenile delinquency—and its possible increase—in the near future. The first, transfer to adult court, was discussed earlier in the chapter and is based on the notion that harsher punishments will deter juvenile crime. The second, known as *social control regulation*, aims to prevent crime by changing behavior without addressing underlying causes. Examples of social control regulation would be

- *Juvenile curfews*, which restrict the movements of minors during certain hours, usually after dark.

- *Parental responsibility statutes*, which make parents responsible in some way for the offenses of their children. At present, forty-two states have enacted these statutes; seventeen of these states hold the parents *criminally* liable for their child's actions, punishing them with fines, community service, and even jail time.

The third method of juvenile prevention can be found in community-based programs that attempt to improve the chances that at-risk youth will not turn to crime. These programs may try to educate children about the dangers of drugs and crime or they may counsel parents who abuse their children. Today, nearly a thousand private and public groups hold afterschool workshops to prevent youth violence. Though the results of community-based efforts are difficult, if not impossible, to measure—it cannot be assumed that children would have become delinquent if they did not participate—they are generally considered a crucial element in defusing the possible "time bomb" of youth crime.

For more information on gangs and crime, visit the National Youth Gang Centers home page at <u>www.iir.com/nygc/</u> To learn about the issues surrounding school violence, go to the Center for the Prevention of School Violence's Web site at <u>www.ncsu.edu/cpsu/</u>

Criminal Justice in Action
Gangs and Guns

In several places in this textbook (particularly Chapters 2 and 4), we have discussed the impact of firearms on the American criminal justice landscape. Guns are an issue for our juvenile justice system as well, and in this *Criminal Justice in Action* feature, we will discuss the effects of firearms on juvenile violence, especially violence associated with youth gangs.

ADDING DANGER TO VIOLENCE

At the time he was murdered, seventeen-year-old Anthony Burgos was not in a gang. Nevertheless, his killing was gang related. Burgos had been confronted on a Chicago street by two sixteen-year-olds who demanded to know his gang affiliation. When Burgos answered truthfully that he did not have one, one of the boys drew a pistol and shot him in the temple. Burgos died the next day.[94]

At first glance, Burgos's death offers further testimony to the violence of modern youth—yet another warning of the rise of a generation of young "superpredators." Not all criminologists, however, agree with the theory that cultural and social changes have conspired to create a new breed of violent juveniles.[95] Instead, these observers point to the unprecedented access minors have to lethal weapons. According to Carnegie Mellon University's Alfred Blumstein:

[Y]outh have always fought with each other. But when it's a battle with fists, the dynamics run much more slowly. With a gun it evolves very rapidly, too fast for a third party to intervene. That also raises the stakes and encourages others to arm themselves, thereby triggering a pre-emptive strike: "I better get him before he gets me."[96]

One of the most extensive surveys of gun use by minors shows just how accessible such weapons are. Nearly 15 percent of the 2,508 adolescents surveyed claimed to have carried a firearm within the past thirty days, and 59 percent said they could get a handgun if they so desired.[97]

Research done for the National Institute of Justice showed that 50 percent of gang members who have been arrested admit to using a gun while committing a crime, which is double the average for all arrestees.[98] As a result, many criminologists and law enforcement officials have concluded that to have a positive impact on juvenile crime rates, they must better understand the correlation between the two factors that combined to end Anthony Burgos's life: gangs and guns.

"NO TROUBLE AT ALL"

According to a series of interviews conducted by researchers Joseph Sheley and James Wright, urban youths have "no trouble at all" obtaining guns. Indeed, the high supply of stolen firearms on the black market keeps their street costs well below the average retail price.[99] Not surprisingly, self-report surveys show that between 50 and 70 percent of gang members own or have access to firearms. Furthermore, the weapons are increasingly sophisticated. Law enforcement officials in Dade County, Florida, for example, regularly confiscate semiautomatic weapons such as AK-47s and MAC-10s from gang members.[100]

As might be expected, the proliferation of armed gang members leads to an increase in juvenile violent crime. In the 1970s and early 1980s, when youth gang activity was minimal, youth homicide rates remained stable, and in about half of the offenses, a weapon other than a firearm was used. In 1987, when gang activity began to increase, so did the number of juvenile homicides involving guns. By 1994, nearly 80 percent of youth homicides were committed with a firearm, and four times as many minors were killed with guns that year than a decade earlier.[101] In homicides that are specifically attributed to gang members, the percentages are even higher. Chicago police report that a gun is the murder weapon in nearly 96 percent of all youth gang-related murders in that city.[102]

THE LINKS AMONG DRUGS, GUNS, AND GANGS

Because the appearance of crack cocaine in the inner city coincided with the surge in gang activity in the late 1980s, many observers linked youth gun violence to illegal drug dealing. More recent research shows, however, that youth gangs are more likely to use firearms in "turf battles" than in drug deals and that the recent decline in crack use has *not* led to a similar reduction in youth gang and gun activity. To explain this phenomenon, researchers David M. Kennedy, Anne M. Piehl, and Anthony A. Braga of Harvard University have hypothesized that the impact of drug trafficking on inner-city communities occurs in two stages.[103]

In the first stage, competition between drug traffickers causes high levels of violence. To protect themselves and their markets, drug dealers—many of whom are young and aggressive—purchase and carry firearms. Because the "place of business" for these dealers is the street corner, "business" disputes are settled through public gun battles, which place innocent bystanders in harm's way. Furthermore, crime increases in communities with high levels of drug dealing, as addicts turn to robbery and burglary to get the funds needed to purchase illegal drugs.

In the second stage, the level of fear rises for all members of the community—not just those involved in the drug trade. Juveniles begin arming themselves and joining gangs not because they want to become drug traffickers, but because they want protection from the increasing violence of their daily lives. One sixteen-year-old gang member explained, "I joined the Fultons because there are a lot of people out there who are trying to get you and if you don't got protec-

tion [you will find yourself] in trouble."[104] For youths living in the community of Anthony Burgos, his death (discussed at the beginning of this feature) may have been an incentive to become a gang member. Paradoxically, joining a gang for protection also means that the juvenile will be targeted by rival gangs, increasing his or her chances of being victimized and creating a cycle of violence.[105]

"DECOUPLING" FROM DRUGS

Thus, according to researchers Kennedy, Piehl, and Braga, in the second stage guns and gangs have become "decoupled" from the drug problem. That is, the youth violence and crime endemic to certain neighborhoods may continue regardless of any decrease in drug trafficking. Indeed, the spread of gang-related gun violence to remote, rural areas often has little to do with illegal narcotics operations or any other form of criminal activity. It appears that small-town teenage "wannabees" are simply fascinated with the mystique of the gang lifestyle and see it as a tonic for what they consider the boredom of rural life.

Key Terms

adjudicatory hearing 576

age of onset 583

aging out 583

automatic transfer 573

child abuse 583

child neglect 584

detention 574

detention hearing 574

disposition hearing 576

diversion 572

graduated sanctions 578

Illinois Juvenile Court Act 563

intake 572

judicial waiver 573

juvenile delinquency 564

low-visibility decision making 569

parens patriae 563

petition 572

predisposition report 576

prosecutorial waiver 573

residential treatment programs 578

status offenders 564

training schools 579

youth gangs 584

Chapter Summary

1. **Describe the child saving movement and its relationship to the doctrine of *parens patriae*.** Under the doctrine of *parens patriae,* the state has a right and a duty to care for neglected, delinquent, or disadvantaged children. The child saving movement, based on the doctrine of *parens patriae,* started in the 1800s. Its followers believed that juvenile offenders require treatment rather than punishment.

2. **List the four major differences between juvenile courts and adult courts.** (a) No juries, (b) different terminology, (c) limited adversarial relationship, and (d) confidentiality.

3. **Identify and briefly describe the single most important Supreme Court case with respect to juvenile justice.** The case was *In re Gault*, decided by the Supreme Court in 1967. In this case a minor was arrested for allegedly making an obscene phone call. His parents were not notified. They were not present during the juvenile court judge's decision-making process. In this case, the Supreme Court held that juveniles are entitled to many of the same due process rights granted to adult offenders, including notice of charges, the right to counsel, the privilege against self-incrimination, and the right to confront and cross-examine witnesses.

4. **List the factors that normally determine what police do with juvenile offenders.** The arresting police officers consider (a) the nature of the offense, (b) the youthful offender's past criminal history, (c) the setting in which the offense took place, (d) whether the parents can take disciplinary action, (e) the attitude of the offender, and (f) the offender's race and sex.

5. **Describe the four primary stages of pretrial juvenile justice procedure.** (a) Intake—when an official of the juvenile court engages in a screening process to determine what to do with the youthful offender; (b) pretrial diversion—which may consist of probation, treatment and aid, and/or restitution; (c) jurisdictional waiver to an adult court—in which case the youth leaves the juvenile justice system; and (d) some type of detention in which the youth is held until the disposition process begins.

6. **Explain the distinction between an adjudicatory hearing and a disposition hearing.** An adjudicatory hearing is essentially the "trial." There may be defense attorneys present during the adjudicatory hearing in juvenile courts in some states. In many states, once adjudication has occurred, there is a separate disposition hearing that is similar to the sentencing phase in an adult court. At this point, the court, often aided by a predisposition report, determines the sentence that serves the "needs" of the child.

7. **List the four categories of residential treatment programs.** Foster care, group homes, family group homes, and rural programs such as wilderness camps, farms, and ranches.

8. **Describe the one variable that always correlates highly with juvenile crime rates.** The older a person is, the less likely he or she will exhibit criminal behavior. This process is known as aging out. Thus, any group of at-risk persons will commit fewer crimes as they get older.

9. **Indicate some of the reasons why youths join gangs.** Some alienated teenagers join gangs for the social relationships and the sense of identity that gangs can provide. Youths living in high-crime neighborhoods join gangs as a form of protection. The excitement of belonging to a gang is another reason to join.

Questions for Critical Analysis

1. In spite of the constitutional safeguards given to juvenile defendants by the Supreme Court decision *In re Gault*, only 50 percent of juvenile defendants have lawyers. Why?

2. Why is the discretion given to police officers over juveniles called low-visibility decision making?

3. Is probable cause necessary before a search can legally be conducted in a school setting? Why or why not?

4. Under what conditions in certain states is a juvenile automatically transferred to the adult court system?

5. The presence of defense attorneys in juvenile courts has led to what changes? In what way have these changes made juvenile courts resemble adult courts?

6. What distinguishes the sentencing phase in juvenile versus adult courts?

7. Why is the age of onset an important factor in predicting juvenile criminal behavior?

8. What has been the relationship between alcohol and drug abuse and juvenile offenders?

9. Why might juvenile delinquency increase starting in the year 2003?

10. What has been the statistical relationship between armed gang members and juvenile violent crime?

Selected Print and Electronic Resources

SUGGESTED READINGS

Ayers, Williams, *A Kind and Just Parent: The Children of Juvenile Court,* Boston: Beacon Press, 1997. The author teaches juvenile offenders in the Chicago juvenile court system. He examines the lives of many of his students, who are often from the juvenile temporary detention center, as well as others who are in custody for a longer time. He uses a single school year to structure his portrait of the teenage residents and those teachers who help them. He offers a sympathetic portrait of those caught up in the juvenile justice system. He claims that society has failed to nurture them.

Clement, Mary, *The Juvenile Justice System: Law and Process,* Boston: Butterworth-Heinemann, 1996. This professor of criminal justice looks at the inner workings of the juvenile justice system. While presenting a complete history of the system, she examines case law as well as research and theories derived from the behavioral sciences. She also examines the constitutional issues of search, seizure, investigation, and interrogation of juveniles.

Hawkins, J. David, *Delinquency and Crime: Current Theories,* New York: Cambridge University Press, 1996. This book contains nine essays by leading criminologists. They seek to answer the question of what determines crime by describing the relationship between delinquency and crime. They explore the practical implications of their theoretical work.

Knox, Mike, *Gangsta in the House,* Troy, MI: Momentum Books, 1995. Author Mike Knox looks at how kids change the way they think and are recruited into gangs. He examines the nature of gang uniforms, the purpose of graffiti, and numerous gang myths. He even offers diagrams outlining the genealogy of America's youth gang "families."

Rodriguez, Joseph, et al., *East Side Stories: Gang Life in East LA,* New York: Powerhouse Cultural Entertainment, 1998. This book presents a collection of essays and photographs, as well as an interview with ex-gang member Luis J. Rodriguez, who is now the author of five books. The rules and codes of gang life are examined and explained. Some have called this the definitive work on the gangs of East Los Angeles.

Sikes, Gini, *8 Ball Chicks: A Year in the Violent World of Girl Gangsters,* New York: Doubleday, 1998. This book presents a riveting account of female gangs in Los Angeles, San Antonio, and Milwaukee. According to the author: "In a world of second-class citizens, they remain third-class." Many of the girl gang members were mothers themselves.

MEDIA RESOURCES

***Bad Boys* (1983)** In one of his first roles, Sean Penn plays Mick O'Brien, a "young punk" looking for trouble. He finds it when he and a buddy attempt to rip off a cache of drugs from a gang headed by Paco Moreno (Esai Morales). The scam goes wrong, and after the dust has settled, Moreno's younger brother is dead. Charged with the boy's murder, O'Brien is sent to a juvenile correctional facility. In order to get revenge,

Moreno rapes O'Brien's girlfriend and winds up in the same facility. Though the inevitable showdown between the two is somewhat forced, the film paints an impressively horrific portrait of life in a juvenile correctional facility.

Critically analyze this film:

1. Describe the juvenile correctional facility in which O'Brien is incarcerated. Is there any evidence of *parens patriae* in its operating philosophy?

2. What treatment programs do exist in the facility? Do they seem to have any impact on the juvenile inmates?

3. What values appear to dominate the society within the facility? What implications does this have for the juveniles once they are released?

4. Does this film offer any arguments *against* the idea of treating juvenile offenders as adults?

Logging On

You can read articles out of the bimonthly online magazine *Juvenilejustice.com:* It targets those involved in youth services, human services, law enforcement, probation, parole, court administration, and staff training. Go to:

www.juvenilejustice.com/

You can find a lot of information at the home page of the Office of Juvenile Justice and Delinquency Prevention. This is part of the U.S. Department of Justice, Office of Justice Programs. Go to:

http://ojjpd. ncjrs.org/

Florida State University and Florida A&M University have a Web site providing information on the Juvenile Justice Role Model Program. Go to:

www.fsu.edu/~crimdo/jjclearinghouse.html

A very useful site is from the Koch Crime Institute. This is an independent group that promotes the dissemination of information about effective solutions for juvenile offenders. Go to:

www.kci.org/

Using the internet for Criminal Justice Analysis

I N F O T R A C ®
COLLEGE EDITION

1. Go to your InfoTrac College Edition at **www. infotrac-college.com/wadsworth/**. After you log on, type in the words: **Breaking the Cycle of Juvenile Crime.**

   This article examines research pursuant to actions by the Office of Juvenile Justice and Delinquency Prevention (OJJDP). The article claims that the rates of juvenile offending and victimization are of "crisis" proportion. Specifically, the author believes that there have been failures by neglectful families, schools, communities, and social systems for which adults are responsible. Read the article and answer the following questions:

   a. Do the statistics in the first part of the article indicate that juvenile crime is on the rise and is in fact overwhelming the country? Why or why not?

   b. What are the key risk factors for becoming a juvenile offender? Which one is most important?

   c. This article lists six OJJDP programs and strategies. Which two are the most important and why?

   d. What is the role of the criminal court in this system, according to the author?

2. You can find out facts about children and the law by going to the Web site offered by the American Bar Association. First go to: **www.abanet.org/media/ factsbook/**. When you are there, click on **Facts about Children and the Law.** Now answer the following questions:

   a. What do the words "guardian *ad litem*" mean?

   b. Are curfews legal?

   c. During a juvenile delinquency hearing, are juveniles afforded all constitutional due process protections?

   d. Under what circumstances are children sent to adult criminal court?

   e. What percentage of American juveniles is arrest-free?

Notes

1. Maxine Bernstein, "Videotape Might Hold Kinkel Confession," *Portland Oregonian* (June 27, 1998), A1.

2. Peter W. Greenwood, "Juvenile Crime and Juvenile Justice," in *Crime*, eds. James Q. Wilson and Joan Petersilia, (San Francisco: ICS Press, 1995), 91.

3. Jennifer M. O'Connor and Lucinda K. Treat, "Getting Smart about Getting Tough: Juvenile Justice and the Possibility of Progressive Reform," *American Criminal Law Review* 33 (Summer 1996), 1299.

4. Eric K. Klein, "Dennis the Menace or Billy the Kid: An Analysis of the Role of Transfer to Criminal Court in Juvenile Justice," *American Criminal Law Review* 35 (Winter 1998), 371

5. Sam Vincent Meddis, "Poll: Treat Juveniles the Same as Adult Offenders," *USA Today* (October 29, 1993), 1A.

6. *In re Gault*, 387 U.S. 15 (1967).

7. Samuel Davis, *The Rights of Juveniles: The Juvenile Justice System*, 2d ed. (New York: C. Boardman Company, 1995), Section 1.2.

8. Cited in Anthony Platt, *The Child Savers* (Chicago: University of Chicago Press, 1969), 119.

9. 383 U.S. 541 (1966).

10. *Ibid.*, 556.

11. 387 U.S. 1 (1967).

12. 397 U.S. 358 (1970).

13. 421 U.S. 519 (1975).

14. 403 U.S. 528 (1971).

15. Andrew Walkover, "The Infancy Defense in the New Juvenile Court," *UCLA Law Review* 31 (1984), 509–13.

16. Gary B. Melton, "Toward 'Personhood' for Adolescents: Autonomy and Privacy as Values in Public Policy," *American Psychology* 38 (1983), 99–100.

17. Richard E. Redding, "Juveniles Transferred to Criminal Court: Legal Reform Proposals Based on Social Science Research," *Utah Law Review* (1997), 709.

18. Howard N. Snyder and Melissa Sickmund, *Juvenile Offenders and Victims: A National Report* (Washington, D.C.: U.S. Department of Justice, 1995), 47.

19. 487 U.S. 815 (1988).

20. *Ibid.*, at 822–23.

21. 492 U.S. 361, 371 (1989).

22. Larry Siegel and Joseph Senna, *Juvenile Delinquency*, 6th ed. (St. Paul, MN: West Publishing Co., 1997), 470–1.

23. Duke Helfand, "Board Approves Shotguns for L.A. School Police Campuses," *Los Angeles Times* (February 24, 1998), A15.

24. Joseph Goldstein, "Police Discretion Not to Invoke the Criminal Process: Low-Visibility Decisions in the Administration of Justice," *Yale Law Journal* 69 (1960), 544.

25. William T. Rusinko, "The Importance of Police Contact in the Formulation of Youth's Attitudes Toward Police," *Journal of Criminal Justice* 6 (1978), 53–4.

26. Cited in "Why Juvenile Crime Exploded," *Business Week* (November 24, 1997), 32.

27. Maria Elena Fernandez, "The Boston Miracle: How They Stopped the Shooting," *The Atlanta Journal-Constitution* (August 24, 1997), C4.

28. 469 U.S. 325 (1985).

29. *Ibid.*, at 348.

30. *Vernonia School District v. Acton*, 515 U.S. 646 (1995).

31. 442 U.S. 23 (1979).

32. Ted Rubin, "The Emerging Prosecutor Dominance of the Juvenile Court Intake Process," *Crime and Delinquency* 26 (1980), 299–318.

33. Robert E. Shepherd, Jr., "Victims in the Juvenile Court Process," *Criminal Justice* 13 (Fall 1998), 27.

34. Frederick Ward, Jr., "Prevention and Diversion in the United States," in *The Changing Faces of Juvenile Justice*, ed. V. Lorne Stewart (New York: New York University Press, 1978), 43.

35. President's Commission on Law Enforcement and Administration of Justice, *Task Force Report: Juvenile Delinquency and Youth Crime* (Washington, D.C.: U.S. Government Printing Office, 1967).

36. 42 U.S.C. Sections 5601-5778 (1974).

37. S'Lee Arthur Hinshaw II, "Juvenile Diversion: An Alternative to Juvenile Court," *Journal of Dispute Resolution* (1993), 305.

38. Eric L. Jensen, "The Waiver of Juveniles to Criminal Court: Policy Goals, Empirical Realities, and Suggestions for Change," *Idaho Law Review* 21 (1994), 180.

39. Rhode Island Gen. Laws Section 14-1-7.1 (1994 & Supp. 1996).

40. Margaret A. Bortner, "Traditional Rhetoric, Organizational Realities: Remand of Juveniles to Adult Court," *Crime and Delinquency* 32 (1996), 56–7.

41. Donna M. Bishop and Charles E. Frazier, "Transfer of Juveniles to Criminal Court: A Case Study and Analysis of Prosecutorial Waiver," *Notre Dame Journal of Legal Ethics and Public Policy* 5 (1991), 281–4.

42. Jeffrey Fagan, *The Comparative Impacts of Juvenile and Criminal Court Sanctions on Adolescent Felony Offenders* (Washington, D.C.: National Institute of Justice, 1991).

43. 467 U.S. 253 (1984).

44. Patricia Purtitz, "Seeking Better Representation for Young Offenders," *Criminal Justice* 10 (1996), 14–5.

45. 42. U.S.C. Section 5633 (1974).

46. Barry C. Feld, "Criminalizing the American Juvenile Court," *Crime and Justice* 17 (1993), 227–54.

47. Barry C. Feld, "Abolish the Juvenile Court," *Journal of Criminal Law and Criminology* 88 (Fall 1997), 68.

48. *In re Gault* 387 U.S. 1 (1967).

49. Barry C. Feld, "Violent Youth and Public Policy: A Case Study of Juvenile Justice Law Reform," *Minnesota Law Review* 79 (May 1995), 965.

50. Barry C. Feld, "The Juvenile Court Meets the Principle of Offense: Punishment, Treatment, and the Difference It Makes," *Boston University Law Review* 68 (1988), 848–9.

51. Lawrence E. Cohen, *Delinquency Dispositions: An Empirical Analysis of Processing Decisions in Three Juvenile Courts* (Washington, D.C.: U.S. Government Printing Office, 1975).

52. Jullianne P. Sheffer, "Serious and Habitual Juvenile Offender Statutes: Reconciling Punishment and Rehabilitation within the Juvenile Justice System," *Vanderbilt Law Review* 48 (1995), 500–6.

53. Eric R. Lotke, "Youth Homicide: Keeping Perspective on How Many Children Kill," *Valparaiso University Law Review* 31 (Spring 1997), 395.

54. Bureau of Justice Statistics, *Sourcebook of Criminal Justice Statistics, 1997* (Washington, D.C.: U.S. Department of Justice, 1998), Table 5.76 at page 441.

55. Charles E. Springer, "Rehabilitating the Juvenile Court," *Notre Dame Journal of Law, Ethics, and Public Policy* 5 (1991), 397.

56. Siegel and Senna, 602–4.

57. Melissa Sickmund, Howard N. Snyder, and Eileen Poe-Yamagata, *Juvenile Offenders and Victims: 1997 Update on Violence* (Washington, D.C.: Office of Juvenile Justice and Delinquency Prevention, 1998).

58. Fox Butterfield, "Profits at a Juvenile Prison Come with a Chilling Cost," *New York Times* (July 15, 1998), A1, A14.

59. Troy L. Armstrong and David M. Altschuler, "Recent Developments in Programming of High-Risk Juvenile Parolees," in *Critical Issues in Crime and Justice*, ed. Albert Roberts (San Francisco: Sage Publications, 1994).

60. Federal Bureau of Investigation, *Crime in the United States, 1997* (Washington, D.C.: U.S. Department of Justice, 1998), Table 38 at page 232.

61. Howard N. Synder, *Juvenile Arrests 1996* (Washington, D.C.: Office of Juvenile Justice and Delinquency Prevention, November 1997).

62. Alfred Blumstein, "Youth Violence, Guns, and Illicit Drug Markets," *NIJ Research Journal* (Washington, D.C.: National Institute of Justice, 1995).

63. Marvin E. Wolfgang, *From Boy to Man, From Delinquency to Crime* (Chicago: University of Chicago Press, 1987).

64. Susan Gaertner, "Three Strikes Against Juvenile Crime: Prevention, Intervention, and Detention, *Prosecutor* (November/December 1996), 18.

65. Travis Hirschi and Michael Gottfredson, "Age and the Explanation of Crime," *American Journal of Sociology* 89 (1982), 552–84.

66. David P. Farrington, "Offending from 10 to 25 Years of Age," in *Prospective Studies of Crime and Delinquency*, ed. Katherine Teilmann Van Dusen and Sarnoff A. Mednick (Boston: Kluwer-Nijhoff Publishers, 1983), 17.

67. *Combating Underage Drinking, Fact Sheet #75* (Washington, D.C.: Office of Juvenile Justice and Delinquency Prevention, February 1998).

68. Federal Bureau of Investigation, *Crime in the United States, 1996* (Washington, D.C.: U.S. Government Publishing Office, 1997), 218.

69. *Ibid.*

70. U.S. Department of Health and Human Services, Substance Abuse and Mental Health Services Administration, *Substance Use among Women in the United States, Analytic Series A-3* (Rockville, MD: U.S. Department of Health and Human Services, 1997), 8–18.

71. Alfred Blumstein, "Violence by Young People: Why the Deadly Nexus," *National Institute of Justice Journal* 229, (1995), 2–9.

72. *Collaboration, Coordination, and Cooperation: Helping Children Affected by Parental Addiction and Family Violence* (New York: Children of Alcoholics Foundation, 1996).

73. Ching-Tung Lung and Deborah Daro, *Current Trends in Child Abuse Reporting and Fatalities: The Results of the 1997 Annual Fifty State Survey* (Chicago: National Committee to Prevent Child Abuse, 1998).

74. Polly E. Bijur, Matthew Kurzon, Mary Overpeck, and Peter C. Scheidt, "Parental Alcohol Use, Problem Drinking and Child Injuries," *Journal of the American Medical Association* 267 (1992), 3166–3171.

75. David Huizinga, Rolf Loeber, and Terence Thornberry, *Urban Delinquency and Substance Abuse* (Washington, D.C.: Office of Juvenile Justice and Delinquency Prevention, 1993).

76. Grover Trask, "Defusing the Teenage Time Bomb," *Prosecutor* (March/April 1997), 29.

77. Cathy Spatz Widom, *The Cycle of Violence* (Washington, D.C.: National Institute of Justice, October 1992).

78. G. David Curry and Scott H. Decker, *Confronting Gangs: Crime and the Community* (Los Angeles: Roxbury, 1998).

79. Finn-Aage Esbensen and D. Wayne Osgood, *National Evaluation of G.R.E.A.T.,* (Washington, D.C.: National Institute of Justice Research in Brief, 1997).

80. Walter B. Miller, *Violence by Youth Gangs and Youth Groups as a Crime Problem in Major American Cities* (Washington, D.C.: U.S. Government Printing Office, 1975), 23.

81. G. David Curry, Richard A. Ball, and Robert J. Fox, *Gang Crime and Law Enforcement Recordkeeping* (Washington, D.C.: National Institute of Justice Research in Brief, August 1994), 8.

82. Meda Chesney-Lind, "Girls, Gangs, and Violence: Reinventing the Liberated Female Crook," *Humanity and Society* 17 (1993), 321–44.

83. Quoted in Alexandra Marks, "Crusade to Curb Girl Gangs Subway Savvy," *Christian Science Monitor* (November 12, 1998), 1.

84. Miller, 23.

85. Curry, Ball, and Fox, 8.

86. Joan W. Moore, *Going Down to the Barrio: Homeboys and Homegirls in Charge* (Philadelphia: Temple University Press, 1991).

87. G. David Curry, "Female Gang Involvement," *Journal of Research in Crime and Delinquency* (February 1, 1998), 100.

88. John C. Quicker, *Homegirls: Characterizing Female Gangs* (San Pedro, CA: International University Press, 1983).

89. Martin Sanchez Jankowski, *Islands in the Street: Gangs and American Urban Society* (Berkeley: University of California Press, 1991), 37–47.

90. Scott H. Decker and B. Van Winkle, *Life in the Gang: Family, Friends, and Violence* (New York: Cambridge University Press, 1996).

91. Sara R. Battin, Karl G. Hill, Robert D. Abbott, Richard F. Catalano, and J. David Hawkins, "The Contribution of Gang Membership to Delinquency beyond Delinquent Friends," *Criminology* 36 (1998), 93–115.

92. C. Ronald Huff, *Comparing the Criminal Behavior of Youth Gangs and At-Risk Youths* (Washington, D.C.: U.S. Department of Justice, October 1998).

93. John J. DiIulio, Jr., "Moral Poverty: The Coming of the Super-Predators Should Scare Us into Wanting to Get to the Roots Causes of Crime a Lot Faster," *Chicago Tribune* (December 15, 1995), 31.

94. Larry Hartstein, "Turning Back on Gangs Didn't Save Teen's Life; He Was in Wrong Place at Wrong Time, Cops Say," *Chicago Tribune* (December 1, 1994), N3.

95. John J. DiIulio, Jr., "Fill Churches, Not Jails: Youth Crime and 'Superpredators,'" statement before the U.S. Senate Subcommittee on Youth Violence, February 28, 1996.

96. Quoted in Gracie Bonds Staples, "Guns in School," *Fort Worth Star-Telegram* (June 3, 1998), 1.

97. *A Survey of Experiences, Perceptions, and Apprehensions about Guns among Young People in America* (New York: LH Research, 1993), iii.

98. Scott H. Decker, Susan Pennell, and Ami Caldwell, *Illegal Firearms: Access and Use by Arrestees* (Washington, D.C.: National Institute of Justice, January 1997), 3.

99. Joseph F. Sheley and James D. Wright, *Gun Acquisition and Possession in Selected Juvenile Samples* (Washington, D.C.: National Institute of Justice, December 1993), 5–6.

100. Dan Bryant, "Communitywide Responses Crucial for Dealing with Youth Gangs," *Juvenile Justice Bulletin* 2 (1989), 4.

101. Lotke, 395.

102. Carolyn R. Block and Richard Block, *Street Gang Crime in Chicago* (Washington, D.C.: National Institute of Justice, 1993), 7.

103. David M. Kennedy, Anne M. Piehl, and Anthony A. Braga, "Youth Violence in Boston," *Law and Contemporary Problems* 59 (Winter 1996), 147.

104. Jankowski, 45.

105. G. David Curry and Scott H. Decker, "Understanding and Responding to Gangs in an Emerging Gang Problem Context," *Valparaiso University Law Review* 31 (Spring 1997), 523.

chapter

17

The Ongoing War against Illegal Drugs

Chapter Objectives

After reading this chapter, you should be able to:

1. Explain why the criminal law concepts of *mala in se* and *mala prohibita* are necessary to understand drug laws.

2. Tell what happened to alcohol use and murder rates during Prohibition.

3. List the three factors in the learning process that cause first-time drug users to become multiple users.

4. Explain the 20-80 Rule as it applies to the use of psychoactives.

5. Contrast the medical model of addiction with the criminal model of addiction.

6. Present the federal agencies that are involved in drug law enforcement.

7. Explain the importance of High Intensity Drug Trafficking Areas (HIDTAs).

8. Summarize the use of asset forfeiture laws.

9. Explain the *iron law of substitution.*

10. Outline the three major arguments against legalization.

INTRODUCTION

The awesome impact of drugs on the criminal justice system has been evident throughout this textbook. Illegal drug and alcohol abuse and addiction played a role in the crimes committed by 80 percent of the 1.8 million Americans behind bars.[1] Nearly half a million of those inmates were arrested for selling or using a banned drug substance. The illegal drug trade in the United States has reached $150 billion per year, part of an annual $400 billion worldwide industry. The federal government spends over $17 billion a year for drug control, yet two leading indicators of law enforcement success—illegal drug price and availability—show little improvement. The effects of drugs on society as a whole are also apparent. Three-fourths of all foster children in the United States are from families with drug- or alcohol-addicted parents. The nation's businesses lose 500 million workdays a year to alcoholism, and half of all workplace fatalities are linked to drugs and alcohol. Nearly half of all high school seniors reported using an illegal drug within the past year.

For many Americans, these numbers call for greater drug enforcement efforts. They believe illegal drugs are an insidious presence on the country's social and cultural landscape. They support drastic measures to attempt to eradicate drugs. A growing number of observers, in contrast, contend that drug policies have caused most of the violence and crime associated with drug use and that further "get tough" measures will only exacerbate the problem.

In 1988, Congress passed a resolution proclaiming the goal of "a drug-free America by 1995."[2] Perhaps chastened by the obvious implausibility of such a claim, ten years later the Clinton administration proposed only to halve drug use and availability by 2007.[3] Contrast this with the attitude of a New York

Figure 17.1 Psychoactive Use and Abuse

Listed here are the important features of some of the drugs that we will be discussing in this chapter.

Drug: Opium
Medical use: Relieves pain, diarrhea
Slang names: Opium
Dependence potential: High
Administrative methods: Oral, smoked
Possible effects: Euphoria, drowsiness, nausea
Effects of overdose: Slow and shallow breathing, clammy skin, convulsions, coma, possible death
Withdrawal syndrome: Watery eyes and runny nose, loss of appetite, irritability, tremors ("the shakes"), panic, chills and sweating

Drug: Morphine
Medical use: Relieves pain, suppresses coughing
Slang names: White, Emma, monkey
Dependence potential: High
Administrative methods: Oral, smoked, injected
Possible effects: Same as opium
Effects of overdose: Same as opium
Withdrawal syndrome: Same as opium

Drug: Heroin
Medical use: None
Slang names: Horse, smack, junk, H
Dependence potential: High
Administrative methods: Injected, sniffed, smoked
Possible effects: Same as opium
Effects of overdose: Same as opium
Withdrawal syndrome: Same as opium

Drug: Benzodiazepines
Medical use: Reduce anxiety and convulsions, act as a sedative
Slang names: Downers, sleeping pills, candy
Dependence potential: Low
Administrative methods: Oral

Possible effects: Slurred speech, appearance of being drunk
Effects of overdose: Shallow breathing, dilated pupils, weak and rapid pulse, coma, possible death
Withdrawal syndrome: Anxiety, insomnia, tremors, delirium, possible death

Drug: Barbiturates
Medical use: Reduce anxiety and convulsions, act as a sedative, agents for veterinary euthanasia
Slang names: Yellows, reds, barbs, phennies
Dependence potential: Moderate to high
Administrative methods: Oral
Possible effects: Same as benzodiazepines
Effects of overdose: Same as benzodiazepines
Withdrawal syndrome: Same as benzodiazepines

Drug: Cocaine
Medical use: Relieves pain
Slang names: Coke, toot, flake, snow, crack
Dependence potential: Low-medium physical, high psychological
Administrative methods: Sniffed, smoked, injected
Possible effects: Increased alertness and excitation, euphoria, insomnia, loss of appetite, increased pulse rate and blood pressure
Effects of overdose: Increase in body temperature, hallucinations, agitation, convulsions, possible death
Withdrawal syndrome: Long periods of sleep, depression, disorientation

narcotics officer, who said of law enforcement efforts to counter the drug trade: "We're like a gnat biting on a horse's behind."[4] In this chapter, we will try to determine whether the officer's pessimism is warranted by examining the United States's century-long struggle against illicit drug substances. We will also discuss the tactics of the continuing "war on drugs," as well as assertions that such a war should never have been declared and can never be won. We will start, however, by asking a deceptively simple question that rests at the center of the debate: What is a drug?

DRUG
Any substance that modifies behavior; in particular, an illegal substance with those properties.

PSYCHOACTIVE DRUGS
Chemicals that affect the brain, causing changes in emotions, perceptions, and behavior.

DRUGS DEFINED

To use the broadest possible definition, a **drug** is any substance that modifies biological, psychological, or social behavior.[5] In popular terminology, however, the word *drug* has a more specific connotation. When people speak of the "drug" problem, or the war on "drugs," or "drug" abuse, they are referring specifically to illegal drugs. To be even more precise, they are referring to illegal **psychoactive drugs,** which affect the brain and alter consciousness or perception.[6] Almost all the drugs that concern the criminal justice system are psychoactive.

Types of Psychoactives

Psychoactives can be classified by their effects on the central nervous system. The different types of psychoactives are summarized in Figure 17.1 and explained in the following overview.[7]

Figure 17.1 Continued

Drug: Amphetamine
Medical use: Weight control, attention deficit disorders
Slang names: Bennies, uppers, black beauties, speed, crank, scoobie snacks
Dependence potential: Low-medium physical, high psychological
Administrative methods: Oral, injected
Possible effects: Same as cocaine
Effects of overdose: Same as cocaine
Withdrawal syndrome: Same as cocaine

Drug: LSD
Medical use: None
Slang names: Acid, cubes, windowpane,
Dependence potential: None physical, unknown psychological
Administrative methods: Oral
Possible effects: Hallucinations, poor perception of time and space
Effects of overdose: Long, intense "trips," psychosis
Withdrawal syndrome: Not relevant

Drug: Phencyclidine
Medical use: None
Slang names: PCP, angel dust
Dependence potential: Unknown physical, high psychological
Administrative methods: Smoked, oral, injected
Possible effects: Same as LSD
Effects of overdose: Same as LSD
Withdrawal syndrome: Same as LSD

Drug: Marijuana
Medical use: Debated, many say it suppresses nausea and pain
Slang names: Pot, grass, weed, reefer, joint, bud, Mary Jane
Dependence potential: Moderate
Administrative methods: Smoked, oral
Possible effects: Euphoria, relaxed inhibitions, increased appetite,

disoriented behavior
Effects of overdose: Fatigue, paranoia
Withdrawal syndrome: Insomnia, hyperactivity, decreased appetite

Drug: Nicotine
Medical use: None
Slang names: Chew (chewing tobacco), coffin nails (cigarettes)
Dependence potential: High
Administrative methods: Smoked, oral
Possible effects: Calm nerves, slight euphoria, lack of appetite
Effects of overdose: Not applicable
Withdrawal syndrome: Headaches, rapid pulse, irritability, nausea

Drug: Alcohol
Medical use: None
Slang names: Booze, juice
Dependence potential: Moderate to high
Administrative methods: Oral
Possible effects: Relaxed inhibitions, slurred speech, decreased motor skills, possible increase in aggressive behavior, depression
Effects of overdose: Unconsciousness, coma, possible death
Withdrawal syndrome: Convulsions, rapid heartbeat, sweating, severe vomiting

Drug: Caffeine
Medical use: None
Slang names: Joe, java, mud, battery juice (coffee)
Dependence potential: Low to high
Administrative methods: Oral
Possible effects: Difficulty falling asleep, increased energy, slight euphoria
Effects of overdose: Anxiety, insomnia, restlessness, difficulty concentrating
Withdrawal syndrome: Headaches, drowsiness, fatigue, slowing of motor functions

SOURCE: ADAPTED FROM WELDON WITTERS, PETER VENTURELLI, AND GLEN HANSON, *DRUGS AND SOCIETY*, 3D ED. (BOSTON: JONES & BARTLETT, 1992), 24–7.

OPIATES
Drugs containing opium or its derivatives; have the effects of dulling sensations including pain and anxiety, producing a feeling of euphoria, and causing general inaction.

STIMULANTS
Drugs such as cocaine or amphetamine that stimulate the central nervous system, thereby quickening motor functions of the body.

HALLUCINOGENS
Drugs that cause the user to experience alterations in sensory experiences, or hallucinations.

Opiates. For more than six thousand years, humans have extracted **opiates** from the seed pod of the opium poppy. In harvesting the substance, the pod is sliced open, releasing a milky sap. The sap dries to form a resin called *opium*. Opium and its derivatives have the ability to block pain receptors in the brain and therefore have a variety of medical uses. The substance also produces a feeling of euphoria and reduction of anxiety, which explains its popularity as a pleasure drug.

Opiates may be ingested orally, smoked, sniffed, or injected. It is generally believed that opium smoking was brought to the United States in the mid-nineteenth century by Chinese laborers. The opium derivatives *morphine* and *codeine* were not taken full advantage of for their medicinal uses until 1853, when the perfection of the hypodermic syringe allowed delivery of the drugs directly into the bloodstream. Morphine was so widely used as a painkiller in the American Civil War (1861–1865) that many infantrymen became addicted—morphine addiction became known as the "soldier's disease." *Heroin,* a substitute for codeine and morphine, was created and marketed by Bayer Laboratories following the war as nonaddictive. In fact, heroin—more fat soluble and therefore able to reach the brain more quickly—was two to three times more potent than morphine.

Stimulants. Acting on both the central nervous system (the spinal cord and the brain) and the peripheral nervous system (the muscles, glands, organs, and fibers that carry sensory information to the brain), **stimulants** produce feelings of well-being and mood elevation. The stimulant *cocaine* is the active ingredient in the South American coca plant. It is isolated from the leaves by soaking them in a mixture of water, potassium carbonate, and a petroleum product such as kerosene. The resulting paste is then dried and purified into a white powder, which can be snorted, or the paste itself can be smoked. In the 1970s, "freebasing"—a process in which the drug is vaporized and inhaled—became popular among cocaine users because it produced a more intense high. A cheaper, less complex method of freebasing led to the production of *crack cocaine* in the 1980s. (The impact of crack on the criminal justice system was discussed in Chapter 2.)

Amphetamine, originally developed in the 1920s to treat asthma sufferers, was found to be a stimulant in the 1930s and prescribed to narcoleptics, or individuals who involuntarily fall asleep. The drug was dispensed to soldiers in World War II to keep them alert during combat, which led to its popularization as a nonmedical substance that could be taken in pill form, via inhalants, or intravenously. *Nicotine,* a naturally occurring substance in the tobacco plant, and *caffeine,* found in coffee, tea, and soft drinks, are also stimulants.

Marijuana. The cannabis plant is the source of *marijuana,* the most widely used illegal drug in the United States today. Marijuana is a mixture produced by grinding the leaves and stem of the plant. Delta-9-tetrahydrocannabinol (THC), the active ingredient in marijuana, is rapidly absorbed from the surface of the lungs when the mixture is smoked, producing effects of mild sedation, euphoria, and, in rare cases, hallucination in the user. The Spanish probably imported cannabis to Central and South America in the sixteenth century because its strong fibers can be used to make rope. The plant is easily grown and cultivated (to the point where it has been called a weed), which has contributed to its widespread use.

Hallucinogens. A wide variety of plants and other natural products can be classified as **hallucinogens,** or substances that intensify sensory perception and in the process bring about hallucinations. The best-known hallucinogen is called *LSD,* after the substance lysergic acid diethylamide from which it is made. Synthesized in 1938, LSD rose in popularity during the 1960s as part of the then-prevailing youth culture. Only minuscule amounts of LSD (less than two-thousandths of a gram per kilogram of body weight) are needed to induce a hallucinatory state. Other hallucinogens include PCP *(phencyclidine)*, *mescaline* (taken from the peyote cactus), and *psilocybin* (taken from wild mushrooms). In the 1980s, new forms of hallucinogens known as *designer drugs* arrived. Produced by modifying the chemical structure of amphetamines, these drugs, such as Ecstasy, take on hallucinogenic properties.

Sedatives. Sedatives are able to reduce anxiety or induce sleep by depressing functions of the brain. Also known as "sleeping pills," the most popular form of sedatives in the first half of the twentieth century were *barbiturates*. Today, a different class of sedative, the *benzodiazepines*, has captured the market, with millions of prescriptions for Valium and Xanax being dispensed every year.

Alcohol. The most widely used drug in the United States, *alcohol*, in the form of alcoholic beverages, is consumed at least occasionally by over two-thirds of adult Americans.[8] Alcohol is unique in the sense that it acts as both a stimulant and a sedative, initially giving the user a feeling of euphoria before beginning to act as a depressant.

Illicit and Licit Drugs

Most people do not consider alcohol—or nicotine or caffeine, for that matter—to be a drug. In one survey, for example, 95 percent of adults recognized heroin as a drug, but only 39 percent and 29 percent identified alcohol and nicotine, respectively, as drugs.[9] To a certain extent, then, the definition of drugs has been equated with **illicit drugs**, or those drugs whose sale and use have been made illegal. **Licit** (legal) **drugs** such as alcohol, caffeine, and nicotine are not seen as drugs, but as socially acceptable substances, if used in moderation and not by children. Furthermore, the common use of drugs for medical purposes—Americans spend approximately $80 billion for prescription drugs and $16.6 billion for over-the-counter drugs each year—is seen as enhancing our quality of life.[10]

Distinguishing between Licit and Illicit Drugs. Why has society prohibited the use of certain drugs, while allowing the use of others? The answer cannot be found in measuring the risk of harm caused by the substances. As we saw in Figure 17.1, both licit and illicit drugs, if abused, can have serious consequences for the health of the user. Nor is illegality linked to the addictive quality of the drug. According to the American Medical Associaton, nicotine is the most addictive substance, with over two-thirds of people who smoke cigarettes becoming addicted.[11] The next most addictive drug is heroin, followed by cocaine, alcohol, amphetamines, and marijuana, in that order. The drug most widely associated with violent behavior, especially domestic violence, is alcohol.[12] One professor of preventive medicine has concluded that "there are no scientific . . . or medical bases on which the legal distinctions between various drugs are made."[13]

Society and the Law. If drug laws are not based on science or medicine, on what are they based? To understand in part how the distinctions are made between illegal and legal drugs, we must

SEDATIVES
Drugs that slow the signals sent from the brain to other parts of the body, thereby inducing sleep or reducing anxiety.

ILLICIT DRUGS
Certain drugs or substances whose use or sale has been declared illegal.

LICIT DRUGS
Legal drugs or substances, such as alcohol, coffee, and tobacco.

In 1999, after the death of one user, the Food and Drug Administration issued a strong warning against ingesting GBL, also known as Blue Nitro. The chemical is believed by some to reduce stress, increase muscle mass, and improve sexual performance when taken orally. GBL is one of many substances that has a viable use (as a paint thinner) and can also be taken as a psychoactive drug.

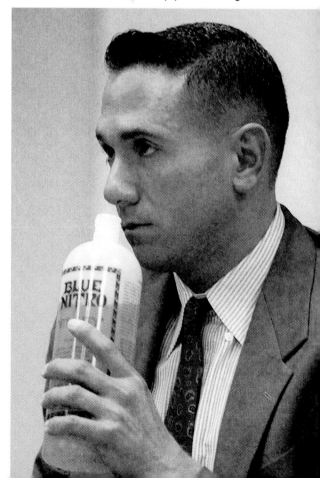

turn to the concepts of criminal acts that are considered *mala in se,* or inherently evil, and *mala prohibita,* or deemed evil by the laws of society. From our discussion in Chapter 3, you will recall that acts such as murder and rape are *mala in se,* whereas those such as prostitution and gambling are *mala prohibita.* Taking a *mala prohibitum* view, certain drugs are characterized as illicit while others are not because of the presiding societal norms and values.

Society's norms and values are reflected in its laws, and the primary law for determining illicit drugs in the United States is the Controlled Substances Act (CSA), which is part of the Comprehensive Drug Abuse Prevention and Control Act of 1970.[14] The CSA specifies five hierarchical categories for drugs and the penalties for the manufacture, sale distribution, possession, or consumption of these drugs, based on the substances' medical use, potential for abuse, and addictive qualities (see Figure 17.2). The CSA explicitly excludes "distilled spirits, wine, malt beverages, and tobacco" from the legal definition of a "controlled substance."[15] Therefore, alcohol and tobacco are legal not because they have pharmacological effects that are considerably different, or safer, than those of illicit drugs, but rather because the law, as supported by society, says so.[16]

PROHIBITION IN THE UNITED STATES

Government policies to limit and outlaw narcotics have a long and varied history, both in the United States and other parts of the world (see Figure 17.3). Drugs were not always, however, regulated in this country to the extent that they are today. The general attitude of American society toward drugs has changed over the past century. With the notable exception of alcohol, many drugs were considered useful, medicinal substances in the 1800s. Cocaine was promoted as a remedy for tuberculosis, whooping cough, and asthma. Coca-Cola, introduced in 1886, was marketed as providing the benefits of coca without the dangers of alcohol. Opium was labeled "God's Own Medicine,"

Figure 17.2 Schedules of Narcotics as Defined by the Federal Controlled Substances Act

The Comprehensive Drug Abuse Prevention Act of 1970 continues to be the basis for the regulation of drugs in the United States. Substances named by the act were placed under direct regulation of the Drug Enforcement Administration (DEA). The act "ranks" drugs from I to IV, with Schedule I drugs being the most heavily controlled and carrying the most severe penalties for abuse.

	Criteria	Examples
SCHEDULE: I	Drugs with high abuse potential that are lacking therapeutic utility or adequate safety for use under medical supervision.	Marijuana, heroin, LSD, peyote, PCP, mescaline
SCHEDULE: II	Drugs with high abuse potential that are currently accepted in medical practice despite high physical and psychological dependence potential.	Opium, cocaine, morphine, Benzedrine, methadone, methamphetamine
SCHEDULE: III	Drugs with moderate abuse potential that are currently utilized in medical practice, despite dependence potential.	Barbiturates, amphetamine
SCHEDULE: IV	Drugs with low abuse potential that are currently accepted in medical practice despite limited dependence potential.	Valium, Darvon, Phenobarbital
SCHEDULE: V	Drugs with minimal abuse potential that are currently used in medical practice despite limited dependence potential.	Cough medicine with small amounts of narcotic

SOURCE: The Comprehensive Drug Abuse Prevention Act of 1970; James E. Royce and David Scratchley, Alcoholism and Other Drug Problems (New York: Free Press, 1996), Table 3 at page 80.

and opiates were prescribed for a number of different ailments, including rheumatism, food poisoning, dysentery, and lockjaw.[17]

Under the U.S. Constitution, the states assumed responsibility for regulating and controlling the health profession, including pharmacological products. For most of the nineteenth century, the states chose to impose no controls whatsoever in this area.[18] As a result, the United States led the

Figure **17.3** Attempts to Limit Drug Use and Abuse

This time line indicates only a handful of the many attempts to limit narcotic use and abuse in the United States and other countries.

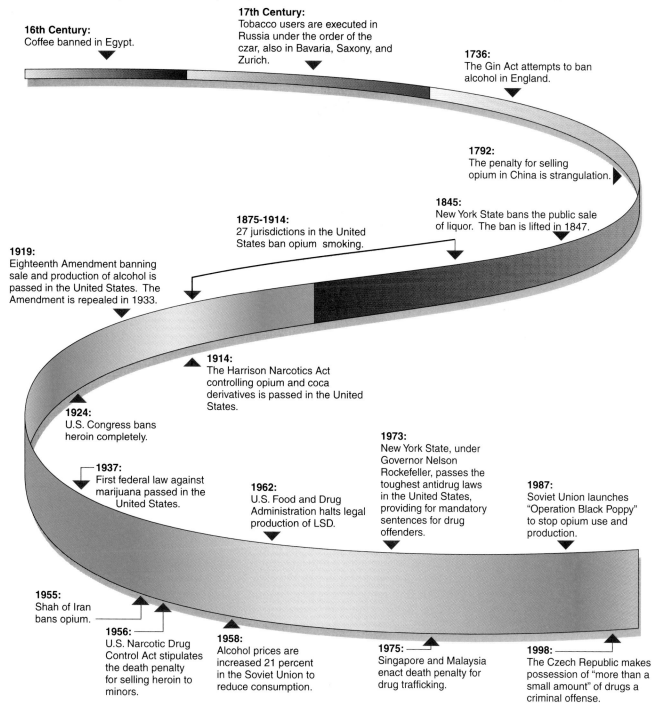

16th Century:
Coffee banned in Egypt.

17th Century:
Tobacco users are executed in Russia under the order of the czar, also in Bavaria, Saxony, and Zurich.

1736:
The Gin Act attempts to ban alcohol in England.

1792:
The penalty for selling opium in China is strangulation.

1845:
New York State bans the public sale of liquor. The ban is lifted in 1847.

1875-1914:
27 jurisdictions in the United States ban opium smoking.

1919:
Eighteenth Amendment banning sale and production of alcohol is passed in the United States. The Amendment is repealed in 1933.

1914:
The Harrison Narcotics Act controlling opium and coca derivatives is passed in the United States.

1924:
U.S. Congress bans heroin completely.

1937:
First federal law against marijuana passed in the United States.

1962:
U.S. Food and Drug Administration halts legal production of LSD.

1973:
New York State, under Governor Nelson Rockefeller, passes the toughest antidrug laws in the United States, providing for mandatory sentences for drug offenders.

1987:
Soviet Union launches "Operation Black Poppy" to stop opium use and production.

1955:
Shah of Iran bans opium.

1956:
U.S. Narcotic Drug Control Act stipulates the death penalty for selling heroin to minors.

1958:
Alcohol prices are increased 21 percent in the Soviet Union to reduce consumption.

1975:
Singapore and Malaysia enact death penalty for drug trafficking.

1998:
The Czech Republic makes possession of "more than a small amount" of drugs a criminal offense.

SOURCE: ADAPTED IN PART FROM JAMES OSTROWSKI, "THINKING ABOUT DRUG LEGALIZATION," POLICY ANALYSIS 121 (MAY 25, 1989).

Western world in opium and morphine consumption and was, in Edward Brecher's words, a "dope fiend's paradise."[19] To the extent that addiction was seen as a problem, concern was primarily focused on drug use by middle-class housewives, who were prohibited from drinking alcohol by the social customs of the day.

The Harrison Act

America's first comprehensive antidrug legislation, the Harrison Narcotic Drug Act of 1914,[20] was primarily a political act, driven by foreign policy concerns rather than by medical or criminal ones. The United States had recently colonized the Philippines, an island-nation with a considerable opium-smuggling problem. At the same time, China had started a campaign against opium use in an attempt to modernize and wean its citizens off the drug. This campaign relied a great deal on limiting the drug supply in outside markets, which included the Philippines. Partly to control rampant opium smuggling in its new territory and partly to appease the Chinese government, which had been complaining about treatment of Chinese nationals in America, the United States led an international effort to combat *narcotics* trafficking.[21] (Narcotics are a class of drugs derived from the opium poppy and include opium, heroin, and morphine.)

These efforts culminated in the Hague Convention of 1912, in which twelve countries, including the United States, agreed to outlaw the international nonmedical opium trade. Certain American politicians—embarrassed that the United States was a signatory to an international trafficking ban without having a similar domestic law—urged Congress to pass legislation prohibiting the nonmedical use of narcotics. The resulting Harrison Act of 1914 banned the importation, sale, or possession of narcotics outside proper medical channels. To accomplish this goal, the act empowered the Internal Revenue Service to strictly control the sale of narcotics by placing a tax on such transfers—any such transfer that did not result in the tax being paid and was not authorized by an accredited physician became *de facto* illegal.

Interestingly, cocaine was included in the substances covered by the Harrison Act, even though it is not a narcotic (that is, it derives from the coca plant, not from opium poppies). Some historians believe that cocaine was willfully misclassified because of its usefulness as a propaganda tool to combat the apathetic views on drug criminalization held by many legislators.[22] The antidrug reformer Dr. Hamilton Wright, for example, informed Congress that "cocaine is often the direct incentive to the crime of rape . . . [in] the South and other sections of the country."[23]

The National Prohibition Act

In contrast to the *laissez-faire* attitude toward most drugs, the nineteenth century saw an active anti-alcohol movement. Between 1850 and 1855, thirteen states passed statutes prohibiting alcohol within their borders. Though all but five had repealed such legislation within a decade, public sentiment against the evils of alcohol remained strong. Finally, in 1919, the passage of the National Prohibition Act (also known as the Volstead Act), which became our Eighteenth Amendment, made it illegal to manufacture, sell, and transport alcoholic beverages in the United States.

This period of **Prohibition** remains a crucial component in the debate over a society's proper response to the problem of addictive substances. For almost fourteen years until the Eighteenth Amendment was repealed by the Twenty-first Amendment, both the costs and benefits of prohibition policies were evident. Alcoholism and health problems attendant to alcohol use—such as

"An evil grips America, a life-sapping, drug-related habit. It beclouds reason and corrodes the spirit .... It's the habit of drug prohibition ... [which is] right up there with heroin and nicotine among the habits that are hell to kick."

—Barbara Ehrenreich, *American writer* (1994)

PROHIBITION
A period in American history, lasting from the passage of the Eighteenth Amendment in 1919 until its repeal in 1933, during which the production and consumption of alcohol were prohibited by federal law.

death from cirrhosis of the liver—declined during Prohibition.[24] At the same time, the enormous profits to be made from illegally transporting and selling alcoholic beverages—a bottle of gin that sold for $1 in Ontario, Canada, was worth $6 across the border in Detroit—provided gangsters such as Al Capone sufficient incentive to use violent measures to protect their underground markets. Nationwide, the murder rate reached record levels.

The spread of lawlessness and corruption eventually turned public opinion against Prohibition, and the law was repealed in 1933. As might be predicted, alcoholism and alcohol-related abuses rose, while violent crime rates dropped. In fact, the country's murder rate declined eleven consecutive years after the repeal of Prohibition.[25]

The Marijuana Tax Act

Four years after Prohibition ended, Congress passed the Marijuana Tax Act, which outlawed the sale, possession, and use of marijuana.[26] The new law effectively added marijuana to the Harrison Act's list of illicit drugs. The timing of the law was not a coincidence. Though its euphoria-inducing effects were well known during the nineteenth century and the early part of the twentieth century, marijuana was primarily used as a remedy for ailments such as asthma.[27]

It was not until the 1920s that marijuana (still legal) began to be widely used for recreational purposes, in many cases as a replacement for criminalized alcoholic beverages.[28] During the decade, a number of states began to pass laws prohibiting the sale or use of marijuana, based primarily on concerns that the drug caused users to commit violent crimes. This worry was also the basis for the passage of the national law, and the image of the violent "dope fiend" dominated government efforts to increase restrictions on marijuana use into the 1950s.[29]

The Gateway Drug

Few people still believe that marijuana leads to violence; all available evidence shows that marijuana inhibits, rather than causes, aggressive behavior. Yet more people are arrested for marijuana-related crimes today than for those associated with any other drug (see Figure 17.4). The reason for restrictions against marijuana use is fairly straightforward: although marijuana does not directly lead to violence, use of the drug may have serious repercussions. First of all, those who smoke marijuana may suffer negative health consequences. Heavy marijuana use can damage the part of the brain that is crucial for learning and memory, and smoked marijuana contains twice as many carcinogens (agents that lead to cancer) as does smoked tobacco.[30]

Second, many members of the criminal justice system, as well as the scientific community, regard marijuana as a "gateway" drug that leads the user to experiment with, and possibly become addicted to, "harder" illegal substances. These observers feel that a person who uses marijuana will become socialized to the drug culture and more readily use cocaine and heroin.[31] A 1997 study financed by the National Institute on Drug Abuse provided further evidence of the "gateway effect" by showing that heavy marijuana use changes the makeup of the brain, making the user more likely to become addicted to other drugs.[32] According to Columbia University's Center on Addiction and Substance Abuse, an adolescent who uses marijuana is eighty-five times more likely to use cocaine than one who has not.[33] Such findings are particularly notable when combined with further research showing that nearly 45 percent of all American high school seniors have experimented with marijuana.[34]

Figure 17.4 Distribution of Arrests by Drug Violation

Approximately 1.6 million arrests for drug abuse violations were made in the United States in 1997. As you can see, more of these arrests concerned marijuana than any other illegal drug.

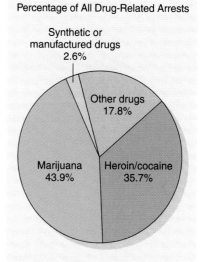

Percentage of All Drug-Related Arrests

Synthetic or manufactured drugs
2.6%

Other drugs
17.8%

Marijuana
43.9%

Heroin/cocaine
35.7%

SOURCE: FEDERAL BUREAU OF INVESTIGATION, *CRIME IN THE UNITED STATES, 1997* (WASHINGTON, D.C.: U.S. DEPARTMENT OF JUSTICE, 1998), TABLE 4.1 AT PAGE 221.

This is not to say that all segments of American society are steadfastly against any shift in current marijuana laws. In the late 1990s, a movement to legalize marijuana for medical purposes gained widespread support, and a number of states, including California, Arizona, Alaska, Nebraska, Oregon, and Washington, passed medical marijuana initiatives allowing doctors to prescribe the drug to patients under certain circumstances. Indeed, drug liberalization referenda passed in seven states in the 1998 elections. The federal government, however, has taken legal action against these state initiatives, claiming that state laws cannot supersede the federal Controlled Substances Act, which designates marijuana as a Schedule I illicit drug.[35]

THE ABUSE OF DRUGS

Do we need the federal government to be so vigilant in enforcing drug laws? How you answer the question probably depends on how widespread you believe the problem of illicit drug use is. When a major political figure announces, as President Bill Clinton did in a policy speech, that "roughly one in three Americans has used an illicit drug in his or her lifetime," it brings to mind images of a nation with almost 90 million lawbreakers.[36] To be fully understood, however, the "one in three" statistic demands further investigation. What does it mean to "use" and, by extension, "abuse" a drug? What are the ramifications of individual drug use for society as a whole?

Drug Use Examined

The source of President Clinton's data is the National Household Survey on Drug Abuse, conducted annually by the National Institute on Drug Abuse. Though the president's statement was factually correct, its connotation is misleading. As can be seen in Figure 17.5, only 6.4 percent of those surveyed had used an illicit drug in the past month. Even so, this means that a significant number of Americans—13.9 million—are regularly using illegal drugs, and the figure mushrooms when one considers licit substances such as alcohol and tobacco.[37]

At first glance, the reason people use psychoactive drugs is obvious: such drugs give the user pleasure and provide a temporary escape for those who may feel tension or anxiety. Ultimately, however, such explanations are unsatisfactory because they fail to explain why some people use drugs while others do not. Several theories, some of which were discussed in Chapter 2, have been formulated to explain drug use. *Social disorganization theory* holds that rapid social change can cause people to become disaffiliated from mainstream society, causing them to turn to drugs. *Subculture theory*, particularly as applied to adolescents, sees drug use as the result of peer pressure. *Control theory* hypothesizes that a lack of social control, as provided by units such as the family or school, can lead to antisocial activity such as drug use.

Focusing on the question of why first-time drug users become multiple users (especially given that the

Figure 17.5 Drug Use in the United States

According to the National Household Survey on Drug Abuse, approximately 13.9 million Americans can be considered "illicit drug users." As you can see, most of these people used marijuana instead of other, stronger, drugs. Furthermore, 16- and 17-year-olds were more likely to have used drugs than any other age segment.

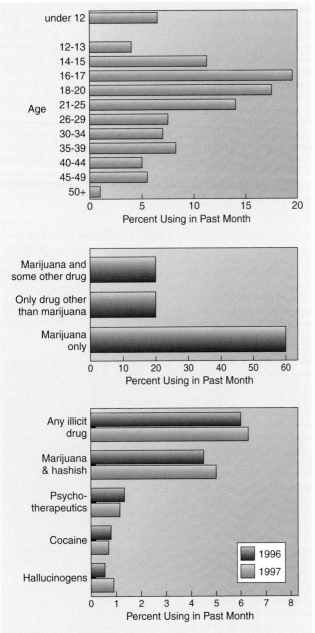

SOURCE: NATIONAL HOUSEHOLD SURVEY ON DRUG ABUSE, 1997. GO TO WWW.HEALTH.ORG/PUBS/97HHS.

Heroin Chic

One of the most alarming illicit drug trends of the 1990s was increased heroin use among Americans, particularly young ones. Approximately 600,000 people in the United States are addicted to heroin, a 50 percent increase over the estimates for the 1970s and 1980s. According to a Monitoring the Future Survey by the Institute for Social Research at the University of Michigan, the number of high school seniors who had tried the drug doubled between 1991 and 1996. Researchers also found a 60 percent higher rate of heroin use among eighth-graders (1.6 percent) than among twelfth-graders (1.0 percent). On the whole, heroin-related emergency room admissions rose nearly 70 percent between 1988 and 1994—from 38,063 to 64,103.

These statistics can be attributed to several factors. The price of heroin fell precipitously, with one-eighth to one-tenth of a gram selling for $10 to $20 on

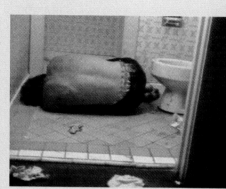

The gaunt and glamorous supermodel Kate Moss, accused of promoting "heroin chic," left, and the harsh reality of addiction as seen in a public service announcement, above.

city streets. In addition, higher-potency heroin allows users to smoke or inhale the drug, thus avoiding the need to inject it with a hypodermic needle. But many observers attribute the rise in heroin use to the emergence of "heroin chic"—a term used to describe the glamorization of heroin use in popular culture.

The primary purveyors of heroin chic are believed to be the film and fashion industries. Movies such as *Pulp Fiction, Drugstore Cowboy,* and, specifically, *Trainspotting* have been targeted for offering tantalizing images of heroin use. "People think [heroin is] all about misery and desperation and death," says the narrator in *Trainspotting,* "but what they forget is the pleasure of it. . . . Take the best orgasm you ever had, multiply it by a thousand, and you're

still nowhere near it." Similarly, the fashion industry is criticized for magazine ads that feature models with pale, gaunt faces, dark eye sockets, and sunken cheeks—supposedly the "heroin chic" look.

The net effect of these popular images, say teen counselors, is to remove the social stigma that had previously surrounded heroin use. Now, in the words of Robert Taylor of the University of North Texas, "It's a social drug." Others feel that popular culture is being made an easy scapegoat for a societal problem. "I don't think someone gets interested in taking heroin because there's a picture of a junkie in a magazine," says one member of the fashion industry.

first experience is often a negative one), sociologist Howard Becker sees three factors in the "learning process." He believes first-time users:

1. Learn the techniques of drug use.
2. Learn to perceive the pleasurable effects of drug use.
3. Learn to enjoy the social experience of taking drugs.[38]

Becker's assumptions are evident in a growing belief that positive images of drug use in popular culture "teach" adolescents that such behavior is not only acceptable but desirable. The film and fashion industries, in particular, have been criticized for glamorizing various forms of drug use (see *Criminal Justice & Popular Culture—Heroin Chic*).

Drug Addiction and Dependency

Another theory rests on the assumption that some people possess overly sensitive drug receptors in their brains and are therefore biologically dis-

DRUG ABUSE
The use of drugs that results in physical or psychological problems for the user, as well as disruption of personal relationships and employment.

MEDICAL MODEL OF ADDICTION
An approach to drug addiction that treats drug abuse as a mental illness and focuses on treating and rehabilitating offenders rather than punishing them.

CRIMINAL MODEL OF ADDICTION
An approach to drug abuse that holds that drug offenders harm society by their actions to the same extent as other criminals and should face the same punitive sanctions.

"Drug misuse is not a disease, it is a decision, like the decision to step out in front of a moving car. You would call that not a disease but an error of judgment."

—Philip K. Dick, *American author* (1977)

posed toward drug use.[39] Though there is little conclusive evidence that biological factors can explain initial drug experimentation, science has provided a great deal of insight into patterns of drug use. In particular, it has aided in understanding the difference between drug *use* and drug *abuse*. **Drug abuse** can be defined as the use of any drug—licit or illicit—that causes either physiological or psychological harm to the abuser or to third parties. Just as most people who drink beer or wine avoid abusing that drug, most users of controlled substances are not abusers. For most drugs, only between 7 and 20 percent of all users suffer from compulsive abuse.[40]

Despite their small numbers, drug abusers have a disparate impact on the drug market. The 20 percent of Americans, for example, who drink the most consume more than 80 percent of all alcoholic beverages sold in the United States.[41] The data are similar for illicit substance abusers, leading to the conclusion that, to a large extent, abusers and addicts sustain the market for drugs.

Addiction Basics. The most extreme abusers are addicted, or physically dependent on a drug. To understand the basics of addiction and physical dependence, one must understand the role of *dopamine* in the brain.[42] Dopamine is responsible for delivering pleasure signals to brain nerve endings in response to behavior—such as eating good food or engaging in sex—that makes us feel good. The bloodstream delivers drugs to the area of the brain that produces dopamine, thereby triggering a large amount of the neurotransmitter. Over time, the continued use of drugs physically changes the nerve endings, called receptors. To continue operating in the presence of large amounts of dopamine, the receptors become less sensitive, meaning that greater amounts of any particular drug are required to create the amount of dopamine needed for the same level of pleasure. When the supply of the drug is cut off, the brain strongly feels the lack of dopamine stimulation, and the abuser will suffer symptoms of withdrawal until the receptors readjust.

Addiction and physical dependence are interrelated, though not exactly the same. Those who are physically dependent on a drug suffer withdrawal symptoms when they stop using it, but after a certain time period they are generally able to emerge without further craving. Addicts, in contrast, continue to feel a need for the drug long after withdrawal symptoms have passed. Though some evidence suggests that certain people are genetically predisposed to alcoholism,[43] researchers are still striving to determine whether some people are more likely to become addicts than others for biological reasons.

The Medical Model of Addiction. Since the late nineteenth century, the treatment and rehabilitation of addiction have played a role in determining the attitude society takes toward criminal drug abusers. Those who followed, and follow, the **medical model of addiction** believe that addicts are not criminals, but mentally or physically ill individuals who are forced into acts of petty crime to "feed their habit." Those who believe in the "enslavement theory of addiction" advocate treating addiction as a disease and hold that society should not punish addicts but attempt to rehabilitate them, as would be done for any other patients.[44]

The Drug-Crime Relationship

Although a number of organizations, including the American Medical Association, recognize alcoholism and other forms of drug dependence as diseases, the criminal justice system has tended to favor the **criminal model of addiction** over the medical model. The criminal model holds that drug abusers and addicts endanger society with their behavior and should be treated the same as any other citizens who commit crimes.[45] (See Figure 17.6 for the latest research on drug and alcohol use by criminals.)

Research Efforts. The argument that drug use is an intricate part of criminal culture has been made since the 1920s. In the mid-1970s, the newly created National Institute of Drug Abuse (NIDA) and the National Institute of Justice estimated the number of arrestees and prisoners who used illicit drugs (mostly heroin and marijuana) at between 15 percent and 40 percent.[46] Later studies further cemented the drug-crime relationship. In the early 1990s, a team of researchers in Miami, Florida, interviewed 699 cocaine users and found that nearly 92 percent had criminal histories and 41.5 percent had participated in robberies. Furthermore, each member of the test group had committed hundreds of crimes in the ninety days before being interviewed (nearly 93 percent of which involved retail drug sales).[47] The opening paragraph of this chapter cited a study by Columbia University's National Center on Addiction and Substance Abuse that links 80 percent of the nation's criminal activity to drug and alcohol abuse and addiction.

Figure **17.6** Committing Crime under the Influence of Drugs and Alcohol

For most crime categories more than half of state prisoners and about one-third of federal prisoners said that they were under the influence of either drugs or alcohol when they committed the crime for which they were arrested.

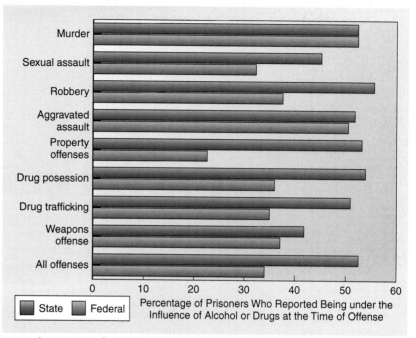

SOURCE: ADAPTED FROM BUREAU OF JUSTICE STATISTICS, SUBSTANCE ABUSE AND TREATMENT, STATE AND FEDERAL PRISONERS, 1997 (WASHINGTON, D.C.: U.S. DEPARTMENT OF JUSTICE, JANUARY 1999), TABLE 1 AT PAGE 3.

Epidemiologist Paul Goldstein has devised three models to explain the relationship between drugs and crime:

- The *psychopharmacological model* holds that individuals act violently or criminally as a direct result of the drugs they have ingested.

- The *economically impulsive model* holds that drug abusers commit crimes to get the money to purchase drugs. According to the U.S. Department of Justice, 19 percent of state prisoners and 16 percent of federal prisoners said that they committed the crimes for which they were incarcerated in order to get money to buy drugs.[48]

- The *systemic model* suggests that violence is a by-product of the interpersonal relationships within the drug-using community, such as when a dealer is assaulted by a buyer for selling "bad" drugs.[49]

The strength of the drug-crime relationship has provided justification for increased law enforcement efforts to criminalize drug use and punish offenders of controlled substance laws. Indeed, the connection was cited as the reason overall crime rates fell in the mid-1990s, in conjunction with a similar downturn in the use of crack cocaine.[50]

Other Explanations. Some observers, however, have questioned the conclusion that drug use causes crime. Instead, they contend, drug use and criminal activity both reflect the same willingness to deviate from established

SUPPLY-SIDE ENFORCEMENT
The law enforcement strategy of combating the use of illegal drugs by concentrating on the suppliers of the drugs rather than the buyers. Thus, agents will focus on a single drug dealer rather than on his or her many clients.

norms among certain members of society, labeled by sociologists as the *criminal subculture*.[51]

Furthermore, many believe that the violent and property crimes associated with illicit drugs take place "not because the drugs are drugs [but because] the drugs are illegal."[52] Seventy years ago, when alcohol was illegal in this country, the criminal gangs that controlled the alcohol trade used methods of violence similar to those associated with today's drug gangs. The fact that we

> no longer have drive-by shooting, turf wars and "cement shoes" in the alcohol business [is due to the fact that] alcohol today is legal—not because alcohol no longer intoxicates people, not because alcohol is no longer addicting, and not because alcohol dealers have suddenly developed a social conscience.[53]

FIGHTING THE WAR ON DRUGS

The consumption of most illicit drugs is preceded by an act of voluntary exchange: a willing seller provides a willing buyer with the drug of choice. When a government decides to prohibit voluntary exchange, its officials must decide whether to target the seller or the buyer. For the past four decades, the American government has decided to focus on the seller, or supplier; therefore, the "war on drugs" is generally predicated on the idea of **supply-side enforcement.** As Figure 17.7 shows, the largest portion of the 1998 federal drug control budget went to law enforcement agencies, which are primarily concerned with reducing the supply of illegal drugs in this country.[54] Only 34 percent (an increase from prior budgets) was appropriated for treatment and prevention programs, which target the buyer by trying to reduce demand for illegal drugs.

Law Enforcement Efforts

Federal, state, and local law agencies share responsibility for carrying out supply-side enforcement. In 1973, the federal Drug Enforcement Administration (DEA) was formed to restrict the supply of controlled substances through coordination with state and local agencies. Today, the DEA has nearly 3,000 officers. The Controlled Substances Act gave the Federal Bureau of Investigation (FBI) concurrent jurisdiction with the DEA for domestic drug law enforcement. Along with the DEA and FBI, the Immigration and Naturalization Services, U.S. Customs, U.S. Coast Guard, U.S. Border Patrol, and branches of the U.S. military work to stem the flow of illegal drugs from other countries into the United States. Called *interdiction*, this process is discussed at length in the feature *Criminal Justice in Action—The Global Drug War* at the end of this chapter.

Local Police Efforts. Most arrests for drug law violations take place at the local and state level. In general, the goals of local police with regard to illegal drug activity are as follows:

I N F O T R A C ®
COLLEGE EDITION

Souder, Mark and Lynn **Zimmer. Q: Is the government's war against marijuana justified as public policy?**

Figure 17.7 Federal Drug Control Budget, 1998

The federal drug control budget for 1998 was six times larger than the federal drug control budget of 1986. As you can see, the single largest item on the budget is domestic law enforcement.

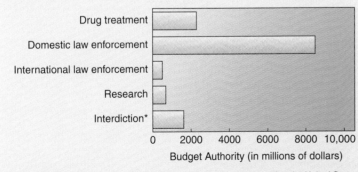

*Law enforcement efforts to reduce the supply of illegal drugs entering the United States.

SOURCE: HTTP://WWW.WHITEHOUSEDRUGPOLICY.GOV/POLICY/BUDGET99/BUDGET-3.HTML.

- To reduce the gang violence associated with the illegal drug trade.
- To control the street crimes committed by illegal drug users.
- To improve the quality of life in communities plagued by illegal drug use.
- To deter minors from using illegal drugs.
- To improve the physical, social, and economic well-being of illegal drug users.[55]

To accomplish these goals, police use tactics such as crackdowns, raids, and surveillance, discussed in Chapter 5. In some areas, concerted police activity has had a marked impact on drug abuse. As part of Tampa, Florida's Quick Uniformed Action against Drugs (QUAD) program, police constantly pressured sellers to change their sales venues, and posed as buyers in "reverse sting" operations to confiscate illegal drugs. Six months after QUAD was initiated, street-corner drug dealing had been virtually eliminated in the targeted areas.[56]

There is evidence, however, that drug dealers have begun to adjust to aggressive police tactics. In New York City, for example, dealers have responded to "reverse sting" operations by moving their transactions from the street corner into apartment buildings. Within the confines of the closed space, the sellers frisk potential buyers to make sure they are not wearing a bulletproof vest or a hidden recording device. New York undercover officers have also reported an increase in "forced ingestions," in which the dealers force buyers to sample the drugs before finishing the deal.[57]

Federal Aid to Local Drug Law Enforcement. Recognizing that local police agencies are often restricted by lack of resources, the federal government has increased its funding for local supply-side enforcement over the past twenty years. In 1986, Congress established the Edward Byrne Memorial State and Local Law Enforcement Assistance Program, named after a New York City police officer who was shot during a drug arrest.[58] Recipients of Byrne grants must use the funds specifically on programs or technology designed to enforce drug laws.

The Office of National Drug Control Policy also supports local drug law enforcement by funding High Intensity Drug Trafficking Areas (HIDTAs). An HIDTA is an area that has been designated as a primary entry point for illicit drugs into the United States, or as a primary distribution center, or as a high-density manufacturing site for a specific drug. Within the HIDTA, law enforcement agents from various state, county, and city narcotics squads combine their resources to form a multijurisdictional drug task force. Twenty HIDTAs are currently operational in the United States, including one that covers Puerto Rico and the U.S. Virgin Islands.[59]

Legislative Efforts

Given public approval of increased sanctions against those who commit drug offenses, federal and state legislators have generally been willing, if not eager, to fortify existing drug laws. One Texas politician recently proposed cutting off a finger for each drug conviction. A peer from Delaware suggested flogging for drug felons, and William Bennett, former National Drug Policy director (or "drug czar"), voiced the opinion that drug dealers should be beheaded.[60] Though none of these propositions was taken seriously, recent legislation has provided law enforcement officers, prosecutors, and judges with a more varied array of "weapons" to combat drug offenses, including mandatory minimum sentencing laws, asset forfeiture laws, and child protection statutes.

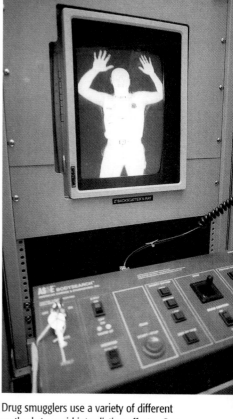

Drug smugglers use a variety of different methods to avoid interdiction efforts. One that is becoming more popular is paying poor men and women to swallow thumb sized pellets of heroin wrapped in the cut-off fingers of surgical gloves. While this strategy makes it more difficult to find the drugs, it is also more dangerous for the "mule," or carrier. If the thin plastic of the pellet ruptures, the heroin will spill into the carrier's stomach and can result in death. The body scanner shown above is being used in many international airports to stop this form of smuggling. Customs officers use it as an alternative to pat-down searches. According to one customs official, these searches focus on "high-risk flights" from "high-risk countries." How can such an attitude lead to complaints of racial and ethnic bias?

ASSET FORFEITURE LAW
A statute that allows law enforcement agents to seize any equipment used in manufacturing, storing or transporting illicit drugs and any profits or property gained from the sale of the drugs, as well as the drugs themselves.

Mandatory Minimum Sentencing Laws. As we discussed in Chapter 11, mandatory minimum sentencing laws remove discretion from judges by predetermining the prison term for a crime depending on the circumstances surrounding that crime. The Anti-Drug Abuse Act of 1986 established two levels of mandatory prison terms for first-time drug traffickers: a five-year term and a ten-year term.[61] The level at which an offender will be sentenced depends on the quantity and the type of drug involved. If a defendant is found guilty of the sale of one kilogram of heroin, five kilograms of powder cocaine, or fifty grams of crack cocaine, he or she will be sentenced to the ten-year term. Lesser amounts will trigger the five-year term.

Passed during the period in which the effects of crack cocaine were beginning to be seen in the nation's cities, the 1986 law provided for a 100:1 quantity ratio in punishing crimes involving crack versus powder cocaine. That is, the Federal Sentencing Guidelines provide the same punishment for someone convicted of possessing or distributing 1 gram of crack cocaine as for someone possessing or distributing 100 grams of powder cocaine.[62]

Thirty-two states have enacted similar mandatory minimum sentences for drug offenses. New York's "Rockefeller" drug laws, for example, passed by Governor Nelson A. Rockefeller in 1973, require state judges to dispense a sentence of fifteen years to life for any person convicted of selling two ounces or possessing four ounces of illicit drugs such as heroin or cocaine.[63] The state of Michigan imposed a mandatory life sentence on anyone convicted of selling 650 or more grams of cocaine, a law that was so heavily criticized for sending harmless offenders to a life in prison that it was partially repealed in August of 1998.[64] The effects of these state and federal laws can be seen in the sentences being handed down to first-time drug offenders compared to first-time offenders convicted of other crimes (see Figure 17.8).

Asset Forfeiture Laws. The first **asset forfeiture law** was included in the Comprehensive Drug Abuse Prevention and Control Act of 1970.[65] The act authorized the government to seize and forfeit contraband, drug manufacturing and storage equipment, and any item used to transport drugs.[66] The goal of the act was to combat the spread of drugs not only by arresting the traffickers, but also by confiscating the material used in the illegal operation. In the three decades since the initial law, Congress has expanded the forfeiture law to include all assets purportedly *traceable* to drug transactions[67] and real property.[68] In 1984, Congress enacted the Asset Forfeiture Program, which allows the U.S. Department of Justice to share seized assets such as cash, bank accounts, cars, boats, houses, and land with state and local law enforcement agencies that contributed to the investigation and arrests.

For prosecutors, forfeiture offers certain advantages over criminal prosecution of drug offenders. First, in legal terms, during a forfeiture action it is the property, not the individual, that is "on trial." Therefore, forfeiture can be used if there is insufficient evidence for a criminal trial or if the defendant who owns the property is a fugitive. Second, because forfeiture proceedings are civil and not criminal, none of the constitutional safeguards of criminal proceedings apply. Consequently, there is no presumption of innocence, no right to an attorney, and no hearsay objection for the property as a "defendant." Forfeiture can occur even if the owner is acquitted.[69] In 1997, the Drug Enforcement Administration seized more than $550,000,000 worth of cash and property under forfeiture statutes (see Figure 17.9).

Figure 17.8 Punishment for First-Time Offenders

With mandatory minimum sentencing laws in effect, judges do not have the discretionary ability to give offenders shorter sentences if they believe such leniency is warranted by the circumstances. Consequently, mandatory minimum laws have tended to push drug sentences to greater lengths compared to those associated with other crimes.

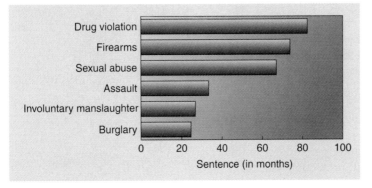

SOURCE: FEDERAL BUREAU OF PRISONS, "QUICK FACTS," SEPTEMBER 1996.

Asset Seized	Number of Seizures	Total Value
Currency	8,123	$284,680,029
Other financial instruments	507	$73,602,029
Real property	748	$108,833,498
Vehicles	3,695	$47,379,874
Vessels	111	$5,884,754
Aircraft	24	$8,945,000
Other conveyance instruments	172	$1,734,731
Other	2,480	$20,620,172
Total	15,860	$551,680,150

SOURCE: Bureau of Justice Statistics, Sourcebook of Criminal Justice Statistics, 1997 (Washington, D.C.: U.S. Department of Justice, 1998), Table 4.39.

Figure 17.9 Asset Seizures by the Drug Enforcement Administration, 1997

Child Protection Laws. To protect children from drug use and drug users, many legislatures have increased the penalties for drug offenses that involve minors. Under federal law, for example, any person convicted of selling a controlled substance to a person under eighteen years of age is subject to a sentence of up to twice the term and fine that would otherwise be authorized. At least ten states have passed **schoolyard statutes,** which specify a minimum term ranging from three years to life or up to three times the term and fine that would otherwise be authorized for any person distributing illicit drugs on or within 1,000 feet of school property. Congress passed a similar federal law, but it was declared unconstitutional by the Supreme Court in *United States v. Lopez* (1995).[70] Finally, a person who uses, hires, or coerces a minor to violate any federal drug laws faces a doubled prison sentence and fine.[71]

Prospects for Success

A recent study of homicides in New York offered the following breakdown of drug-related murders: they were overwhelmingly the result of the drug trade (74 percent), not of someone acting violently while under the influence of drugs nor of someone killing to get the money to purchase drugs.[72] Such data raise a central question about the nation's current illegal drug policy: Do drugs laws cause more harm than illegal drugs?[73]

Critics of American drug policy believe the answer is yes—that the "cure" of enforcement is worse than the "disease" of drug use. They offer a number of reasons for their stand, as summarized by professor of philosophy and law at Rutgers University Douglas N. Husak:

- The drug trade has created opportunities for a black market to flourish, which has greatly benefited organized crime. By keeping the prices of illegal drugs higher than they would be otherwise, law enforcement has provided a "subsidy" for drug dealers.

- The enormous profits have made corruption of law enforcement officials inevitable.

- Because the quality of illegal drugs is not regulated, consumers face risks of medical complications from "bad" drugs.

- Drugs are expensive not because of their production costs, but because of their illegality. Heroin is approximately 100 times more expensive and cocaine 20 times more expensive than they would be if the drugs were legal. As a result, users commit property crimes to obtain the funds necessary to purchase the drugs.

- Millions of otherwise law-abiding Americans have been labeled "criminals" because of drug use, with consequences throughout the criminal justice system.[74]

SCHOOLYARD STATUTES
Laws that intensify the penalties for drug offenses if they occur on or near school property.

If this list represents some of the drawbacks of America's drug policy, what have been its benefits? Have supply-side enforcement tactics been successful? To answer that question, we must turn to the issue of illicit drug supply and price.

Reducing the Supply of Illegal Drugs

It is very difficult to "measure" the success of drug enforcement policies. After all, neither the sellers nor the buyers are eager to report their activities to official sources. If authorities are not certain of the total amount of drugs being manufactured and sold, then they can only guess as to the overall effect of their efforts. There is, however, a way to gauge these efforts: the price of illegal drugs on the street. This measurement is based on two assumptions:

1. If law enforcement agents are successful in incapacitating those who grow, refine, transport, and sell drugs, the amount of drugs available should drop. When the supply of a resource that many people want—whether it be diamonds, baseball cards, or drugs—decreases, the price should rise.

2. When authorities seize drugs and destroy the means of manufacturing and distributing them by arresting people in the drug business and confiscating equipment, drug lords must spend resources to rebuild their operations. If it become more expensive to make and distribute drugs, the dealers will pass these costs on to their customers, and the price should rise.

Therefore, if the price of illegal drugs is rising, then law enforcement agents know that they are having an impact. In reality, the opposite is taking place. According to many observers, the street price of illegal drugs has dropped dramatically since the beginning of the "war on drugs." Mark Kleiman, a professor of drug policy at the University of California at Los Angeles, believes that the real, or inflation-corrected, price of a gram of cocaine today is one-eighth of its price in 1979.[75]

The Substitution Effect. Further complicating supply-side enforcement is the *iron law of substitution,* which holds that successful efforts to restrict the supply of one drug will lead to increased production and consumption of a substitute. As a corollary of this "law," whenever a drug is made illegal, more potent forms of the drug will drive less potent forms out of the market. Producers have a profit incentive to provide consumers with "more bang for the buck."[76] The smaller the "package," the less risk involved for both suppliers and consumers. Hence, it did not make economic sense to ship and sell beer when all alcohol was illegal.[77] During Prohibition, for example, America changed from a predominantly beer-drinking society to a hard-liquor one. Hard liquor can be more easily concealed because it has a greater potency and thus smaller quantities are needed for the same effect.

The same process has been played out with cocaine replacing marijuana in the 1970s and crack replacing powder cocaine in the 1980s.[78] Today, successful law enforcement efforts to reduce crack production have led to a resurgence in the use of methamphetamine, otherwise known as crank.[79] The consequence of this substitution effect is that although law enforcement efforts may reduce the supply of a particular illicit drug in a particular place, they have been unsuccessful in reducing the supply of *all* illicit drugs on the national market.

"Coke is just a way for me to make some money and do some of the things I would otherwise not have the chance of doing. . . . [S]elling coke is just like any other business—you gotta work hard, stay on your toes, protect what's yours. . . ."

—Drug dealer from New York City's Washington Heights, (1993)

The Darwinian Trafficker. The substitution effect applies to drug suppliers as well as the illegal drugs themselves. For every "drug kingpin" or dealer that law enforcement manages to incarcerate, others are willing to take his or her place. The reason: few industries can match the profit incentive of the illegal drug market. In fact, successful apprehension of drug dealers may lead to what Jerome H. Skolnick calls "the Darwinian trafficker dilemma." According to Skolnick, law enforcement efforts succeed in capturing the marginal traffickers and dealers, leaving the most violent and efficient ones to dominate the market.[80] (The term *Darwinian* refers to the doctrine of English naturalist Charles Darwin [1809–1882]. Darwin believed that living things change and adapt to their environment. Consequently, any characteristic of an individual that allows it to better adapt to its environment will increase its chances of survival, as well as the chances of its offspring.)

Illegal Drugs and America's Inner Cities

For many, the negative consequences of our drug policy are most evident in low-income neighborhoods across the United States. The social and economic conditions of the inner cities seem designed to foster both illegal drug sellers and drug buyers. For those inner-city residents with ambition, mainstream educational and employment opportunities are less available. The only way to gain wealth and status seems to be through the drug trade. "Ambitious, energetic, inner-city youth are attracted to the underground economy precisely because they believe in the rags-to-riches American dream," notes anthropologist Phillipe Bourgeois.[81] Other residents of poor neighborhoods may react to their surrounding with despair, indifference, and a sense that the future holds no hope. (See the discussion of anomie theory in Chapter 2.) Such people are at high risk of turning to the induced euphoria of drug use to escape their surroundings.

To a certain extent, then, inner cities are ideal environments for illegal drug activity and risky behavior.[82] Law enforcement officers often react to this by converging on poor neighborhoods, where they make a disproportionate number of drug-related arrests.[83] Because statistics tend to show that the majority of American drug users do not live in poor neighborhoods (see *CJ in Focus—Myth versus Reality: Who Is Using Drugs?* on the following page) critics see these arrest rates as evidence of police bias.

It is true that African Americans make up a high proportion of those charged and incarcerated for drug offenses, a phenomenon we will discuss in Chapter 18. The targeting of inner cities for drug arrests may, however, be the result of selective enforcement rather than overt racism. Because of the low-income levels of those areas, residents are unlikely to hire expensive legal help to contest police action. A faulty drug arrest in a middle-class or wealthy neighborhood

> is apt to earn the police an expensive and embarrassing lawsuit by the wronged individual. The same mistake inflicted on the resident of an inner city will likely produce little more than a futile voice complaint. Quite simply, the inner city is an expedient locale for police to rack up impressive arrest numbers, with little fear for consequences if mistakes are made.[84]

Furthermore, because inner-city residents are often disconnected from the political process, elected officials will not suffer any negative consequences if they single out such areas for "get tough" police action.

Ruben Ortega, the chief of police in Salt Lake City, Utah, caused a stir in 1998 when he asserted that illegal immigrants from Mexico were the main cause of the city's illegal drug problems. Ortega's plan to give local police officers the power to enforce federal immigration laws enraged the local Latino community, and it was voted down by the City Council.

CJ in Focus
Myth versus Reality
Who Is Using Drugs?

Illegal drug abuse in the United States follows certain demographic patterns. In other words, people are more or less likely to abuse illegal drugs depending on factors such as their age, sex, race, or economic status. These patterns, however, do not necessarily match the expectations of many Americans.

THE MYTH

The stereotypical drug abuser is an uneducated, unemployed minority male living in a large city. This image is perpetuated by media coverage of drug use, which focuses on America's inner cities.

THE REALITY

The only aspect of the stereotype that is clearly supported by statistics is that drug abusers tend to be male. In 1997, according to the National Household Survey on Drug Abuse, 8.5 percent of American men, compared to 4.5 percent of women, were users of illicit drugs. As for race, the study found that 74 percent of all users were white, 13 percent African American, and 9 percent Hispanic. These findings closely resem-

ble those of prior years; in fact, the only significant change between 1996 and 1997 was the rate among white youths between the ages of twelve and seventeen, which rose 2.6 percent. Furthermore, seven of every ten illegal drug users are employed, and 75 percent of the demand for illegal drugs comes from middle-class users living in the suburbs.

As with many statistics, however, these do not tell the entire story of drug use. Though the overall number of white drug users dwarfs black users, the percentage of all African Americans who use drugs (7.5 percent) is slightly higher than for whites (6.4 percent). Furthermore, the negative consequences of drug use—loss of employment, family dislocation, overdose, death—are much greater for minorities than for whites. Researcher Jeffrey Kallan found that black males were almost twice as likely to die from illegal drug-related causes than whites.

You Be the Judge: Kallan also found that people who have never been married have a significantly higher chance of dying from illegal drug use than those who have been married. What conclusion concerning illegal drug use and risky behavior can you draw from this finding? Also, what factors could explain higher mortality rates among African American users than white users?

Turning to Prevention

Not all law enforcement officials engaged in efforts to reduce illegal drug use in the United States agree with the connotation of the phrase "war on drugs." In 1998, General Barry R. McCaffrey, director of the federal government's Office of National Drug Control Policy (ONDCP), suggested that the metaphor of "cancer" more appropriately described the Clinton administration's long-term strategy of using education and treatment to prevent Americans—especially young ones—from succumbing to drug use. To this end, in 1997 the Drug-Free Communities Support Program was created under the Drug-Free Communities Act.[85] Administered through the ONDCP, the act authorizes between $10 million and $43 million in federal funds each year until 2002 to be distributed to community-based, grass-roots antidrug coalitions that generally do one of three things:

1. Provide factual information about the dangers of drug use.
2. Provide counseling to address the attitudes that lead to drug use.
3. Strive to change drug use behavior.[86]

These programs, often run with the help of citizen volunteers, operate out of churches, schools, community groups, police departments, and local government organizations.

Target Groups. Two groups appear to be primary targets for prevention efforts: prisoners and youths. As we discussed in Chapter 12, substance abuse is widespread among our growing prison population. Yet only about 20 percent of those inmates with a history of drug use are attending a drug treatment program in prison.[87] According to the Rand Drug Policy Research Center, such programs are more cost-efficient than traditional "warlike" strategies against illegal drugs. The study calculated the impact of spending

$1 million on three different methods of fighting cocaine abuse: increased law enforcement through additional police officers, prosecutors, and seizure of contraband; mandatory minimum sentences; and treatment programs. The treatment programs were found to be 7.7 times more effective than law enforcement and 3.7 times more effective than harsher sentences in reducing cocaine use.[88]

Nevertheless, these programs are becoming less and less available. The proportion of inmates in state prisons who received treatment for their drug abuse fell from 24.5 percent in 1991 to 9.7 percent in 1997. The number receiving drug treatment in federal prisons also declined, from 15.7 percent to 9.2 percent over the same time period.[89]

Not surprisingly, programs to educate young people are more popular with the public than those to treat prisoners. In 1998, to great fanfare, the federal government announced a five-year $2 billion advertising campaign to warn teenagers about the dangers of alcohol and drug use. Programs such as the nationwide Red Ribbon Week, in which high school students participate in a variety of activities to highlight the dangers of substance abuse, have been popular since the 1980s. Such programs often include symbolic gestures such as placing a car destroyed in a drunk driving accident on campus grounds, as southern California's Moorpark High School did in 1998. The effectiveness of programs aimed at children and teenagers is debatable, however. By refusing to acknowledge the pleasurable aspects of drug use and—in some cases—overstating the risks, the educational efforts may alienate the teenagers they are trying to help.

Drug Courts. One of the successes of the prevention movement has been the proliferation of **drug courts** across the country. Following the lead of the first such court, which appeared in Dade County, Florida, in the late 1980s, these programs are based on the idea that treatment will do more to lower recidivism rates of drug offenders than will incarceration.[90]

Though each of the nearly 300 drug courts in operation today (up from 2 in 1989) has its own specific operational strategies, the general model is universal. Nonviolent offenders whose involvement in the criminal justice system is a direct result of drug abuse are diverted from general criminal court to the drug court. On waiving the right to a speedy trial, the defendant is immediately placed in a drug treatment program. This program includes frequent meetings with the presiding judge, treatment at a rehabilitation center, and constant monitoring through status hearings, urinalysis, and reports from the treatment providers. If the defendant completes the program, the initial charges are dismissed. If not, the charges are reinstated and the defendant must go through the normal adjudication system.

Aside from the benefits to drug law offenders, drug courts also represent significant savings for taxpayers. The cost of such programs is approximately $4,000 a year, compared to $30,000 for a year of incarceration. Furthermore, those who successfully complete the program have been found to have significantly lower rates of recidivism—dropping from 45 percent for all defendants charged with illegal drug possession to between 5 and 28 percent for drug-court participants, according to American University's Drug Court Clearinghouse and Technical Assistance Project.[91]

ALTERNATIVES TO PROHIBITION

Considering the economic and social costs of "zero-tolerance" drug policies, many observers have called for liberalization of the nation's controlled substances laws. In general, these alternatives to prohibition fall into three broad categories: legalization, decriminalization, and harm reduction.

DRUG COURTS
Courts whose jurisdiction is limited to drug offenses. Offenders are offered treatment as an alternative to incarceration.

INFOTRAC®
COLLEGE EDITION

Field, Gary. From the institution to the community: studies show benefits of continuity of care in reduced recidivism, relapse rates.

The Office of Justice Program's Drug Court Clearinghouse and Technical Assistance Project offers information, FAQs, and sample materials for those interested in drug courts. Go to gurukul.ucc.american.edu /justice/dcclear.htm

LEGALIZATION
The elimination or modification of federal and state laws that prohibit the manufacture, use, and sale of illegal drugs.

Legalization

Believing that drug laws create worse evils than they solve, and that these same laws can never reduce illicit drug demand, some observers believe that illicit drugs should be made legal. In its most extreme form, **legalization** refers to the removal of all criminal sanctions on the sale and production of all psychoactive substances—with the exception of restrictions on sales to children.[92] Some see such a move as a panacea for many of the problems of the criminal justice system. Others, however, believe legalization is a risky proposition with consequences that cannot be predicted.

The Benefits of Legalization. Certain proponents of legalization cite the "peace dividend" that would come with the end of the "war on drugs." On the one hand, law enforcement agencies could eliminate costly drug enforcement programs. On the other hand, the state would reap a windfall in taxes on the controlled sale of substances previously available only on the black market. One expert concluded that the net economic gain for the United States would be $75 billion a year.[93] Other predicted benefits of legalization include:

- The reduction in drug prices to competitive levels, which means drug abusers and addicts would no longer require large sums of money to finance their drug use. This would reduce, if not eliminate (given the examples of alcohol and cigarettes), the need to steal money or engage in prostitution to acquire sufficient funds to cover one's habit.

- The end of violent crime associated with drug dealing, as black market organizations would be put out of business or forced to rely on less profitable criminal activities.

- A more efficient criminal justice system, as scarce law enforcement resources would be diverted away from drug offenses toward violent crimes, and the pressure on both overloaded court dockets and overcrowded prisons would be alleviated.[94]

Furthermore, as economist Milton Friedman has observed, legalization would improve the living conditions both in American inner cities and in drug-producing nations, whose corrupt political and law enforcement systems and high levels of violence can be attributed, at least in part, to America's demand for illicit drugs.[95]

Arguments against Legalization. Many observers insist that such a policy would cause more problems than it would solve. Given what we know about the "gateway effect," discussed earlier, they ask, how could we as a society justify making it *easier* for young people to obtain drugs? As an example, they point to cigarettes. Although tobacco products are generally prohibited to those under eighteen years of age, most teenagers find little to stop them from smoking if they so desire. Furthermore, a gateway effect is evident with tobacco as well. Those between twelve and seventeen who smoke cigarettes are 23 times more likely to use marijuana, 12 times more likely to use heroin, and 51 times more likely to use cocaine than those who do not.[96]

In general, opponents of legalization rely on three arguments, summarized by drug abuse researchers James A. Inciardi and Duane C. McBride:

- *The public health and behavioral consequences argument.* If drugs such as marijuana, cocaine, and heroin were legalized, more people would use and abuse them. The abuse of

In Amsterdam, a customer smokes a marijuana cigarette in a coffee house. Law enforcement agencies generally turn a blind eye to cannabis use in these establishments, of which some 2,000 are in operation in the city. This lax attitude encourages marijuana users from countries with harsher laws to flock to Amsterdam, and has caused many of the Netherlands' neighbors to criticize its policies as contributing to drug use throughout northern Europe. What do you think would be the consequences if an American city or state took a similar stance on marijuana use?

these and other illicit drugs does negatively affect users' health, and the consequences could be significant. It is estimated that cigarette- and alcohol-related illnesses cause the death of 400,000 and 100,000 Americans each year, respectively.

▌ *The expanded-market argument.* Even with the restrictions imposed by government regulations, American alcohol and tobacco companies spend $7 billion a year on advertising. The goal of this advertising is to expand the market for their products, and one could assume the same would occur with legalized drugs. Furthermore, just as minors can often obtain cigarettes or alcoholic beverages, they are likely to have access to other legalized drugs.

▌ *The drugs and violence argument.* The United States already has a problem with alcohol-related violence. Although some drugs, notably marijuana, do not provoke aggressive behavior, others such as cocaine and certain hallucinogens do.[97]

Another argument against legalization warns that we do not know what the exact consequence of such an action would be. What happens if drugs are legalized and the results are unacceptable? Once instituted, legalization would be difficult to rescind. Finally, it would be a mistake to say that antidrug efforts have been a complete failure. Between 1977 and 1994 the number of drug users is believed to have dropped by 13.1 million people.[98]

Decriminalization

"It would be strange," writes UCLA policy studies professor Mark Kleiman, "if one could not devise a set of laws and programs tighter than the light taxes and poorly enforced age restrictions to alcohol, yet much looser than the virtually total prohibition now applied to marijuana."[99] Kleiman, along with many other observers, advocates a middle ground between legalization and prohibition, generally known as **decriminalization.** In general, a decriminalization policy would:

▌ Place high taxes on the substance in question.

▌ Severely limit promotion of the substance, while using tax proceeds to finance public relations campaigns warning of its health risks.

▌ Restrict the sellers of the substance through governmental licensing.

▌ Restrict buyers by age and through strict sanctions for any public harm caused by abuse of the substance.[100]

At times, decriminalization has had political support in the United States. In 1972, for example, the Presidential Commission on Marijuana and Drug Abuse recommended the decriminalization of marijuana. A number of Western European countries have adopted this policy, most notably the Netherlands, which has decriminalized "soft drugs" such as marijuana and hashish. A comparison of the similarly sized cities of Amsterdam (the capital of the Netherlands) and Baltimore, Maryland, can provide insight on the possible benefits of decriminalization. Whereas Baltimore has approximately 6,100 addicts per 100,000 citizens, Amsterdam has 1,000. Furthermore, in 1991 Amsterdam reported 20 deaths from drug-related causes, compared to 269 in Baltimore.[101]

Harm Reduction

A third alternative accepts that a certain amount of drug use is inevitable and would focus drug policies on minimizing the harms for both the user

DECRIMINALIZATION
A policy that combines the elimination of criminal penalties on drug use with restrictions to discourage use such as high taxes and limitations on advertising of drugs.

The Internet hosts a number of organizations involved in the debate on drug policy. Drug Watch International's home page at www.DrugWatch.org **provides arguments against the legalization of drugs. The Drug Reform Coordination Network, in contrast, supports drastic changes in our drug laws. Visit its Web site at** www.drcnet.org/

Cross-National CJ Comparison

Prescribing Heroin in Switzerland

Over the past fifteen years, Switzerland has implemented two dramatic programs to combat the country's narcotic addiction rate, which at 30,000 addicts among a population of seven million is one of the highest in Europe. The first program—setting aside Platspitz (Needle) Park in the capital of Zurich as a police-free zone where junkies could buy, sell, and use heroin at will—lasted from 1986 until 1992. After crime and overdose rates skyrocketed in the area, Needle Park was closed down. The second, a program in which narcotics are provided without charge to addicts by the government, has had more success.

The Medical Prescription of Narcotics Programme was devised to determine whether prescribing heroin, morphine, or injectable methadone could reduce crime and other drug-related antisocial behavior. Beginning in 1994, more than 1,000 volunteer long-term heroin addicts began receiving their daily doses of the drug at one of eighteen clinics around the country. (Most participants preferred heroin, which is illegal in Switzerland, to morphine or

methadone.) After nearly three years, the Swiss government released the results of the trial: criminal offenses among the test group dropped by nearly 60 percent; illegal heroin and cocaine use declined substantially; the percentage of income from illegal activities fell from 69 percent to 10 percent; and stable employment increased from 14 percent to 32 percent. There were only eleven new cases of hepatitis and HIV infection (all from outside drug use) among the test group, and 83 participants began abstinence therapy after quitting heroin use.

In a referendum, 70 percent of the Swiss voters approved the program's renewal. Its success has also spurred interest in other countries. The Netherlands and Spain have begun their own narcotics prescription trials, and health officials in Baltimore, Maryland, are preparing to petition the federal government for permission to do likewise.

WHAT'S THE EVIDENCE?

To follow the Swiss experience with heroin prescription, as well as those in other countries including the United States, go to the home page of the Lindesmith Center at **www.lindesmith.org**. Then click on "subject index" from the menu on the left, and choose "maintenance-heroin" from the options that follow.

INFOTRAC ®
COLLEGE EDITION

Kleiman, Mark. Drugs and drug policy: the case for a slow fix.

and society that result from the activity. Ethan A. Nadelmann, director of the Lindesmith Center, a drug policy research institute, summarizes **harm reduction** strategy as follows:

> Rather than attempt to wean all illicit drug addicts off drugs by punitive means, harm reduction policies begin with the acknowledgement that some users cannot be persuaded to quit. These policies then seek to reduce the likelihood that they will contract or spread diseases such as hepatitis and AIDS, overdose on drugs of unknown purity and potency, or otherwise harm themselves or others.[102]

Again, harm reduction policies have gained support in Western Europe (see *Cross-National CJ Comparison—Prescribing Heroin in Switzerland*). In the United States, they tend to be quite controversial, as opponents see them as "sending the wrong message" to potential drug users. In 1998, for example, despite findings by the U.S. Department of Health and Human Services that free needle exchange programs reduced the transmission of HIV among intravenous drug users, the Clinton administration refused to lift a ban on federal funding for such programs. At the time of the decision, studies had found that 40 percent of new HIV infections in the United States were attributable to contaminated needles.[103]

Another controversial harm reduction program involves *methadone maintenance treatment*. Methadone is a synthetic narcotic that has some of the same physiological effects on the brain as heroin. Many physicians believe that it can be used to lessen the trauma of heroin withdrawal when administered at decreasing doses over a certain time period. Although methadone maintenance has been found to have the highest probability of treating heroin addiction among available methods,[104] its designation as a Schedule II controlled substance under the CSA has greatly limited its use in the United States. Methadone was not created as a treatment method, and many health care offi-

HARM REDUCTION
A drug policy based not on reducing use of illicit drugs but on reducing the crime and health problems associated with drug use.

cials continue to question its use in this manner. A frequently cited concern is that methadone maintenance treatment simply replaces dependence on one addictive substance (heroin) for dependence on another (methadone).[105]

PUBLIC SUPPORT FOR THE WAR ON DRUGS

In certain countries such as Singapore and Vietnam, the sale of minuscule amounts of illicit drugs—as little as half an ounce of heroin or 100 grams of marijuana—carries the death penalty. Though there is no evidence that a majority of Americans would favor such strict penalties (though they would certainly lessen the sale of drugs if applied uniformly), public opinion polls show that we would rather continue the "war on drugs" than liberalize drug policy. A recent poll conducted by the Harvard School of Public Health shows that although most Americans agree that U.S. antidrug efforts have failed, they support the continuation and expansion of such efforts.[106] Only 14 percent of those surveyed supported legalization, and, more revealingly, 76 percent said they would not favor legalization of heroin and cocaine even if doing so would lead to less crime (see Figure 17.10).

These survey results show that most Americans view the war on drugs as a moral issue rather than a legal, economic, or health-related issue. Some observers blame this on the media, which they say overplay issues of crime and violence instead of addiction and treatment when dealing with the drug issue.[107] Others point out that, having started a "war" on drugs, to reduce law enforcement efforts would constitute a "surrender," an act with which Americans have never been comfortable. Whatever the reason, it seems clear that as long as our society considers illegal drugs a major danger to community values, the government will continue to take great efforts to eradicate them.

Figure 17.10 Public Support for Drug Control Policies

The American public is not convinced that the "war on drugs" is working. According to the Harvard School of Public Health, 94 percent of those surveyed felt that the illegal drug problem is not under control, and 58 percent felt that the problem would get worse over time. This pessimism has not, however, translated into disfavor with the country's policies. As you can see, the public generally supports "get tough" government action when it comes to enforcing drug laws.

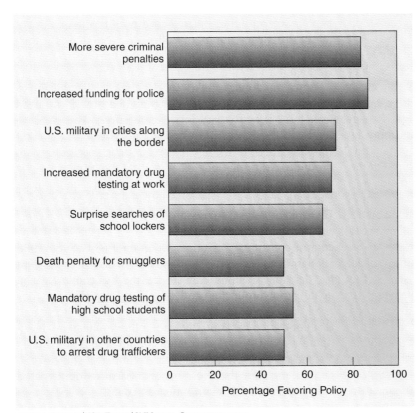

Percentage Favoring Policy

SOURCE: GALLUP/USA TODAY/CNN POLL, SEPTEMBER 1995.

In this chapter, we have focused mostly on domestic efforts to stop the consumption and sale of illegal drugs. The problem, however, is hardly limited to our national boundaries. A high percentage of the heroin, cocaine, marijuana, and amphetamines seized in the United States was smuggled across the Mexican border, mostly coming from sources in Central and South America. Southeast Asia has been a major source of illegal drugs in the past, and Africa is expected to be one in the future. The international illegal drug trade has been infiltrated by *narcoterrorists,* who finance their terrorist activities by participating in the drug trade. The ease with which funds can be transferred from country to country has contributed to *money laundering,* in which drug dealers convert illegally gained profits to cash using foreign businesses and banks. As we close this chapter, we will take a closer look at the challenges presented by the globalization of the illegal drug trade.

THE BALLOON PRINCIPLE

In the spring of 1998, federal officials in South Florida found 4,000 pounds of cocaine, with a street value of $34 million, hidden in a 62-foot-long luxury yacht at a private Fort Lauderdale dock. The seizure, thought to be the largest confiscation ever from a pleasure boat, was not in itself extraordinary. In 1997, the Texas Border Patrol alone seized $765 million worth of illegal drugs. The significance of the incident was the route by which the boat entered American territory: from the Bahamian island of Bimini. For the past two decades, South American drug trafficking organizations have primarily smuggled their contraband into the United States across the Mexican border, a reaction to law enforcement efforts to close the Bahamas/South Florida route in the 1970s. Now that attention is being focused on the overland route, the traffickers have begun to revert to their old habits. In 1996, 2,000 pounds of cocaine were seized in the Bahamas. During the first five months of 1998, 14,000 pounds of the drug were confiscated in the same area.

When you press your finger on a balloon, the air inside pushes the balloon outward somewhere else. This *balloon principle* applies to the "war on drugs" as well. As can be seen from the above example, when law enforcement agents place pressure on one segment of the illicit drug trade, the market shifts to compensate. Given the overall scope of the international illegal drug market—estimated by the United Nations to have $400 billion in annual revenues, or 8 percent of total international trade—the balloon principle represents the single largest impediment to efforts to stop, or even slow, the flow of illegal drugs into the United States.

INTERDICTION EFFORTS

These efforts are extensive. Each year, $2 billion of federal funds go to **interdiction** programs. In the early 1980s, Vice President George Bush coordinated the National Narcotics Border Interdiction System, which linked the four military branches (Air Force, Navy, Army, and Marines) with local and federal law enforcement agencies to combat drug trafficking.[108] The "militarization" of interdiction can be seen in efforts such as Operation Blast Furnace, during which U.S. Army Blackhawk helicopters attempted to destroy coca production labs in the South American country of Bolivia. In 1989, the U.S. military invaded Panama to arrest its president, Manuel Noriega, for violating federal drug trafficking laws.

INTERDICTION
Law enforcement efforts to restrict the flow of illicit drugs over national borders.

American foreign policy is also heavily influenced by interdiction goals. In 1998, Congress allocated $2.6 billion over three years toward interdiction efforts. Part of these funds, in the form of foreign aid, are directed at *source-zone* countries, or those countries in which illicit drugs are produced, with the understanding that the money is to be used to enhance local law enforcement efforts and provide alternative sources of income for drug-producing citizens. The United States also uses the *certification system* to pressure foreign governments to establish domestic illegal drug control measures. Passed as an amendment to the 1986 Foreign Assistance Act,[109] this statute allows the president to "decertify" nations that are deemed uncooperative in fighting drug production and trafficking. Decertification may result in the end of direct aid from the United States and U.S. opposition to World Bank and other multilateral developmental loan programs for that country. The United States also has extradition treaties with a number of source-zone nations, meaning that these nations will surrender targeted drug offenders for trial on American soil.

Workers tend to an opium field in Myanmar (Burma).

GREATER SUPPLY, LOW PRICES

The goal of interdiction is to reduce the supply of illegal drugs entering the United States, thereby raising the prices of the substances that do reach American streets. In fact, as noted earlier in the chapter, illegal drug prices have dropped as interdiction efforts have increased. In Miami, for example, a kilo (2.2 pounds) of cocaine that sold for up to $38,000 in 1984 can be bought for as little as $12,500 today, without correcting for inflation or increased potency.[110]

Figure 17.11 Global Illicit Drug Production

According to the U.S. State Department, the countries indicated below are the world's major producers, for export, of opium, coca, and marijuana. Consequently, they are the focus of American interdiction efforts.

Opium	Coca
Myanmar	Colombia
Laos	Brazil
Thailand	Peru
Vietnam	Ecuador
Afghanistan	
Pakistan	**Marijuana**
India	Mexico
Iran	Colombia
Colombia	Jamaica
Mexico	

SOURCE: U.S. DEPARTMENT OF STATE.

There are a number of reasons for this phenomenon. First, law enforcement agents seize only a small percentage of the illegal drugs that enter this country—10 percent, according to the DEA.[111] Second, the supply of drugs is expanding rapidly; estimates are that the world production of cocaine has more than doubled and the supply of heroin has more than tripled over the past decade. In other words, while the finger pressure on the balloon remains weak, the size of the balloon is rapidly expanding.[112]

Two factors seem to predict that the balloon principle will continue to hamper interdiction efforts: (1) the plants from which illegal drugs derive are easy to grow; and (2) the profits to be made from illegal drug sales are substantial.

A MATTER OF CLIMATE AND ECONOMY

The coca bush, whose leaves provide the raw material for cocaine, is averse to below-freezing temperatures, but otherwise it will flourish in any climate that receives between 40 and 240 inches of rain annually. The opium poppy requires mild, sunny, and drier conditions, but the marijuana plant literally grows like a weed and can be found on every continent except Antarctica. Figure 17.11 lists the countries that are primarily responsible for producing and exporting the drugs that can be made using these three plants.

Illegal drug production depends on more than climate, however. As Figure 17.11 also shows, the major producers of coca, opium, and cannabis are among the world's materially poorer nations. As a result, the people who live in these countries have an economic incentive to grow illicit crops, and their governments do not have the resources to restrict the practice. In the Southeast Asian country of Myanmar (formerly Burma), for example, farmers earn ten times more growing opium poppies than they could producing soybeans.[113] This general poverty restricts the United States's ability to offer foreign aid as an inducement to reduce production of illicit crops. In the early 1990s, when the United States was providing Bolivia with $100 million in annual economic aid, cocaine was adding billions of dollars to the country's economy each year. Finally, because law enforcement agents and government officials earn such low wages in these countries, they are more susceptible to corruption: according to Mexican authorities, major drug cartels in their country pay as much as $1 million a week in bribes.[114]

THE WAR ON DRUGS: A CONTINUING CHESS GAME

The combination of these conditions has thwarted even the most successful American efforts at interdiction. The virtual elimination of the Medellin and Cali cartels, which were responsible for much of Colombia's cocaine production and distribution in the 1980s and 1990s, did not significantly reduce drug trafficking in that country. Instead, several dozen smaller organizations turned their attention to heroin, which is easier to smuggle, more addictive, and more profitable. Now, the Colombians operate nearly 60 percent of the American heroin market.

In 1997, nearly 70 percent of the cocaine in the United States had come across the Mexican border. By 1998, as a result of increased border patrols, that number dropped to 53 percent. Over the same time period, however, the amount of cocaine being smuggled into America through the Caribbean increased by a third.[115]

Some observers feel that U.S. policymakers still see the illegal drug problem as an essentially domestic problem. They are not willing to divert the resources necessary to improve interdiction performance.[116] Of the $125 billion spent by the federal government between 1981 and 1995 on illegal drug control programs, only 4 percent was devoted to interdiction efforts.[117] In 1998, interdiction accounted for 11 percent of the federal drug control budget. At present, one DEA agent compares the situation to a chess game: "[The drug traffickers] figure out a way to do it, we figure out a way to stop them [and then] they figure out a way to do it again."[118]

Key Terms

Chapter Summary

1. **Explain why the criminal law concepts of *mala in se* and *mala prohibita* are necessary to understand drug laws.** Because there are no clear-cut differences in risk of harm among certain psychoactives, to understand which are legal and which are illegal one must look to which drugs are considered *mala prohibita*, or inherently evil, depending on presiding societal norms and values. Basically, whatever psychoactives are deemed illegal by the Controlled Substances Act of 1970 and its amendments are therefore prohibited.

2. **Tell what happened to alcohol use and murder rates during Prohibition.** Alcohol abuse fell during most of the almost fourteen years of Prohibition, whereas violent crime and especially murder rates increased dramatically. After Prohibition was repealed, these two trends reversed themselves.

3. **List the three factors in the learning process that cause first-time drug users to become multiple users.** (a) They learn the techniques of drug use, (b) they learn to perceive the pleasurable effects of drug use, and (c) they learn to enjoy the social experience of taking drugs.

4. **Explain the 20-80 Rule as it applies to the use of psychoactives.** For most psychoactives, 20 percent of users consume about 80 percent of the total amount used.

5. **Contrast the medical model of addiction with the criminal model of addiction.** Those who support the former believe that addicts are not criminals but rather are mentally or physically ill individuals who are forced into acts of petty crime to "feed their habit." Those in favor of the criminal model of addiction believe that abusers and addicts endanger society with their behavior and should be treated like any other citizens who commit crimes.

6. **Present the federal agencies that are involved in drug law enforcement.** The Drug Enforcement Administration (DEA), Federal Bureau of Investigation (FBI), Immigration and Naturalization Service (INS), U.S. Customs, U.S. Coast Guard, U.S. Border Patrol, and branches of the U.S. military.

7. **Explain the importance of High Intensity Drug Trafficking Areas (HIDTAs).** An HIDTA is an area designated as a primary entry point for illicit drugs into this country or as a primary distribution or manufacturing center for a specific drug. The Office of National Drug Control Policy supports funding of HIDTAs in which multijurisdictional drug task forces combine efforts.

8. **Summarize the use of asset forfeiture laws.** Governments can seize and keep contraband, drug manufacturing and storage equipment, and any item used to transport drugs. Currently, forfeiture laws cover all assets purportedly traceable to drug transactions as well as real property purportedly obtained or used in the illegal drug trade. These include cash, bank accounts, cars, boats, houses, and land. Because forfeiture proceedings are civil, few of the constitutional safeguards of the criminal justice process, such as presumption of innocence, right to an attorney, and hearsay objections, apply.

9. **Explain the *iron law of substitution*.** Successful efforts to restrict the supply of one drug will lead to increased production and consumption of substitutes. The corollary to this "law" is that when a drug is made illegal, more potent forms of the drug drive less potent forms out of the market.

10. **Outline the three major arguments against legalization.** (a) Legalization would lead to increased use and abuse of the newly legalized drugs; (b) the market for newly legalized drugs would expand through advertising and word of mouth; and (c) violence would increase with the use of newly legalized drugs.

Questions for Critical Analysis

1. On what basis is a distinction made between licit and illicit drugs?

2. Why did the murder rate rise during Prohibition and fall thereafter?

3. Why is it relatively easy for authorities to confiscate assets purportedly traceable to drug transactions?

4. What are some of the reasons that illegal drug trafficking has grown so consistently?

5. What should happen to the price of successfully interdicted drugs and why?

6. Why have we observed a resurgence in the use of methamphetamines ("crank")?

7. When are arrestees diverted from general criminal courts to so-called drug courts?

8. What is the distinction between legalization of illicit drugs and decriminalization?

9. How does the balloon principle apply to the war on drugs?

10. Why are the major illegal drug production areas found in the world's materially poorer nations?

Selected Print and Electronic Resources

SUGGESTED READINGS

Behr, Edward, *Prohibition: 13 Years to Change America*, New York: Arcade Publishers, 1997. This is a comprehensive history of the thirteen years of alcohol prohibition. The author shows that this period was one of rampant corruption maintained by vicious violence and widespread dishonesty throughout government. He examines how the social movements and forces converged at this time. He also describes various personalities of the era, including Al Capone.

Burnham, John C., *Bad Habits: Drinking, Smoking, Taking Drugs, Gambling, Sexual Misbehavior, and Swearing in American History*, New York: New York University Press, 1994. This historian looks at the social aspects of so-called minor vices in nineteenth- and twentieth-century America. He argues that mass media advertising with a strong economic interest and the entertainment industry have worked together to make "bad habits" a big business.

Drug Enforcement Agency, *DEA Classified Intelligence Reports: Inside Secrets of the Smuggling Trade*, Boulder, CO.: Paladin Press, 1988. The title of this book tells it all. The narcotics smuggling trade is big business and you find out all about it in these reports.

Reinarman, Craig, and Harry Gene Levine, eds., *Crack in America: Demon Drugs and Social Justice*, Berkeley: University of California Press, 1997. Numerous papers in this work look at the crack cocaine problem in America. Some view it from a medical perspective, others from a legal perspective, and yet others from a social sciences perspective.

Stares, Paul B., *Global Habit: The Drug Problem in a Borderless World*, Washington, D.C.: The Brookings Institute, 1996. The author lays out all sides of this complex issue. He argues that revenues generated by the retail sales of illegal drugs exceed the total national yearly income of three-fourths of the world's economies. He points out that the world's appetite for dangerous drugs shows no signs of diminishing. He gives a strong argument in favor of increased sanctions against drug trafficking. He also says that we must spend more resources on treatment and prevention.

MEDIA RESOURCES

***Drugstore Cowboy* (1989)** The tale of four junkies in Portland, Oregon, in the early 1970s, *Drugstore Cowboy* is not a "just say no" indictment of drug culture. It does not glamorize the lifestyle either. Led by Bob (Matt Dillon), the quartet spends most of their time either doing drugs or stealing them. After the inevitable overdose of one of the characters, Bob decides that the junkie lifestyle is a dead end street, and he kicks his habit. In the end, however, the habit kicks him.

Critically analyze this film:

1. Explore the crime-drug relationship in this film. Which of Paul Goldstein's three models, listed on page 609, does the film most closely resemble?

2. What kind of drugs are Bob and his gang most interested in? Are these drugs licit or illicit?

3. Describe Bob's efforts to end his addiction. What aspects of the drug subculture appear to make it difficult for an addict to quit the lifestyle?

4. What is this film's political outlook regarding drug abuse, if it has one? Do you think Gus Van Zant, the filmmaker, would support decriminalization, legalization, or harm reduction? Explain your answer.

5. This film was criticized for its neutral tone regarding drug abuse. Do you feel the movie is too "soft" on drugs? Why or why not?

Logging On

You can get current information on the funds spent on the war on drugs as well as the number of people arrested for drug offenses by going to the "drug war clock" at:

www.drugsense.org/
wodclock.htm

Find out about the Office of National Drug Control Policy by accessing its home page at:

www.whitehousedrugpolicy.
gov/

There you can find out about this organization, as well as enforcement, prevention, education, and our national drug control policy.

You can get more information about statistics on drugs and crimes by going to the U.S. Department of Justice, Bureau of Justice Statistics at:

www.ojp.usdoj.gov/bjs/drugs.htm

Learn about the National Institute of Justice's Arrestee Drug Abuse Monitoring (ADAM) program by going to its home page at:

www.adam-nij-net/adam/

To learn more about the Drug Enforcement Administration (DEA) of the U.S. Department of Justice, go to its web page at:

www.usdoj.gov/dea/

Businesses and law enforcement agencies have developed a Partnership for a Drug-Free America. At the Drug-Free Resource Net, sponsored by this group, you are welcomed to "the most complete and accurate compilation of information of drugs on the Web." Go to:

www.drugfreeamerica.org/

Using the internet for Criminal Justice Analysis

INFOTRAC®
COLLEGE EDITION

1. Go to your InfoTrac College Edition at www.infotrac-college.com/wadsworth/. After you log on, type in the words: **BEYOND THE WAR ON DRUGS: HARM REDUCTION AND CORRECTIONS.**

This article out of *Corrections Today* examines harm reduction techniques in the rehabilitation of substance abusers. The author argues that a gradual approach to reducing substance abuse may benefit some users. He looks at the war on drugs' mixed effects on corrections. On the one hand, the corrections industry has experienced a boom in construction because of mandatory minimum sentencing for drug traffickers and users. On the other hand, correctional administrators have more problems because of the war on drugs. Prisons and jails must deal with an increasingly high concentration of offenders who are infected with HIV, hepatitis A, B, and C, and other infectious diseases associated with injection drug use. Read the article and answer the following questions:

a. Does the author appear to be "soft on drugs"? Why or why not?

b. What does the author mean when he talks about "supply-side" approaches to injection drug users (IDUs)?

c. How does the author use the example of Prohibition?

d. About what percentage of drug users under correctional supervision have participated in substance abuse treatment using reliable treatment methods?

e. When did harm reduction as an approach to substance abuse problems begin? Where did it begin?

f. What is the ultimate goal of harm reduction?

g. What is the difference between contextual and cognitive approaches to harm reduction?

2. The war on marijuana has been waged for many years. The public broadcasting station in Boston, WGBH, has created a *Frontline* program online. To learn about it go to:

www.pbs.org/wgbh/pages/frontline/shows/dope/

Once you are there, answer the following questions:

a. Make a line graph of the prices of commercial-grade marijuana.

b. Find the Federal Sentencing Guidelines. What is the recommended sentence in months for possession of less than one kilogram, but more than 250 grams of marijuana? What level offense is this?

c. According to the marijuana time line, when did the government actually encourage the production of hemp, from which marijuana can be obtained?

d. According to the time line, when and by whom was marijuana introduced in the United States as a recreational drug?

e. By 1931, how many states had outlawed marijuana?

Notes

1. *Behind Bars: Substance Abuse and America's Prison Population* (New York: National Center on Addiction and Substance Abuse at Columbia University, 1998).

2. Anti-Drug Abuse Act of 1988, Public Law No. 100-690, Section 5011, 102 Stat. 4181.

3. Pete Yost, "Accountability Promised for Drug Effort," *Pittsburgh Post-Gazette* (February 8, 1999), A6.

4. Quoted in Jerome H. Skolnick, "Rethinking the Drug Problem," in *Drugs, Crime, and Justice*, ed. Larry K. Gaines and Peter B. Kraska (Prospect Heights, IL: Waveland Press, 1997), 404.

5. Weldon Witters, Peter Venturelli, and Glen Hanson, *Drugs and Society*, 3d ed. (Boston: Jones & Bartlett, 1992), 4.

6. Ibid., 5.

7. James E. Royce and David Scratchley, *Alcoholism and Other Drug Problems* (New York: Free Press, 1996), Chapters 1, 2, and 5.

8. National Institute on Alcohol Abuse and Alcoholism, Surveillance Report #35, *Apparent Per Capita Alcohol Consumption: National, State, and Regional Trends, 1977–93* (Washington, D.C.: U.S. Department of Health and Human Services, 1993).

9. Referred to in Douglas N. Husak, *Drugs and Rights* (New York: Cambridge University Press, 1992), 21.

10. "Give Them Their Pills, the Fuddled Masses," *Economist* (May 2, 1998), 23–4.

11. John Slade, "Health Consequences of Smoking: Nicotine Addiction," *Hearings before the Subcommittee on Health and the Environment of the House Committee on Energy and Commerce* (Washington, D.C.: U.S. Government Printing Office, 1988), 163–4.

12. Ethan Nadelmann, "Should We Legalize Drugs? History Answers: Yes," *American Heritage* (February/March 1993), 41.

13. Steven Jonas, "Solving the Drug Problem: A Public Health Approach to the Reduction of the Use and Abuse of Both Legal and Illegal Recreational Drugs," *Hofstra Law Review* 18 (1990), 753.

14. Codified as amended at 21 U.S.C. Sections 801-966 (1994).

15. Uniform Controlled Substances Act (1994) Section 201(h).

16. Husak, 25.

17. David F. Musto, *The American Disease: Origins of Narcotic Control* (New York: Oxford University Press, 1987), 1.

18. David F. Musto, "Opium, Cocaine and Marijuana in American History," in *Drugs, Crime, and Justice*, ed. Larry K.

19. Edward M. Brecher, *Licit and Illicit Drugs* (Boston: Little, Brown, 1972), 3.

20. 38 Stat. 785 (1923).

21. Musto, 28–35.

22. Franklin E. Zimring and Gordon Hawkins, *The Search for Rational Drug Control* (New York: Cambridge University Press, 1992), 58–61.

23. Quoted in Erik Grant Luna, "Our Vietnam: The Prohibition Apocalypse," *DePaul Law Review* 46 (Winter 1997), 483.

24. P. Aaron and David F. Musto, "Temperance and Prohibition in America: A Historical Overview," in *Alcohol and Public Policy: Beyond the Shadow of Prohibition*, ed. Mark H. Moore and Dean R. Gerstein (Washington, D.C.: National Academy Press, 1981), 165.

25. Daniel K. Benjamin and Roger L. Miller, *Undoing Drugs: Beyond Legalization* (New York: Basic Books, 1991), 21.

26. 26 U.S.C.A. Section 4742(a)(2) (1937).

27. Zimring and Hawkins, 70.

28. Brecher, 409.

29. Duane C. McBride and Clyde B. McCoy, "The Drugs-Crime Relationship: An Analytical Framework," in *Drugs, Crime, and Justice*, ed. Larry K. Gaines and Peter B. Kraska (Prospect Heights, IL: Waveland Press, 1997), 91–2.

30. Gabriel G. Nahas and Nicholas A. Pace, "Marijuana as Chemotherapy Aid Poses Hazards," *New York Times* (December 4, 1993), 20.

31. Richard R. Clayton and Harwin W. Voss, *Young Men and Drugs in Manhattan: A Causal Analysis* (Rockville, MD: Alcohol, Drug Abuse, and Mental Health Administration, 1981).

32. Sandra Blakeslee, "Study: Pot 'Gateway to Other Drugs,'" *Dayton Daily News* (June 27, 1997), 3A.

33. Cited in Linda Bayer, "A Drug-Free Open Society," *Washington Post* (March 12, 1997), A19.

34. Bureau of Justice Statistics, *Sourcebook of Criminal Justice Statistics, 1997* (Washington, D.C.: U.S. Department of Justice, 1998), Table 3.71 at page 236.

35. Mary Curtius and Maria La Ganga, "U.S. Launches Drive to Close Marijuana Clubs," *Los Angeles Times* (January 10, 1998), A1.

36. Quoted in Larry K. Gaines and Peter B. Kraska, "Introduction," in *Drugs, Crime, and Justice*, ed. Larry K.

Gaines and Peter B. Kraska (Prospect Heights, IL: Waveland Press, 1997), 1.

37. Preliminary results from the 1997 National Household Survey on Drug Use.

38. Howard S. Becker, *Outsiders: Studies in the Sociology of Deviance* (New York: Free Press, 1966).

39. Meyer Glantz and Roy Pickens, "Introduction and Overview," in *Vulnerability to Drug Abuse,* ed. Meyer Glantz and Roy Pickens (Washington, D.C.: American Psychological Association, 1992), 29–32.

40. Peter B. Kraska, "The Unmentionable Alternative: The Need for and the Argument Against the Decriminalization of Drug Laws," in *Drugs, Crime, and the Criminal Justice System,* ed. Ralph Weisheit (Cincinnati, OH: Anderson Publishing, 1990).

41. Dean R. Gerstein, "Alcohol Use and Consequences," in *Alcohol and Public Policy; Beyond the Shadow of Prohibition,* ed. Mark H. Moore and Dean R. Gernstein (Washington, D.C.: National Academy Press, 1981).

42. Anthony A. Grace, "The Tonic/Phasal Model of Dopamine System Regulation," *Drug & Alcohol Dependence* 37 (1995), 111.

43. Lawrence K. Altman, "Scientists See a Link Between Alcoholism and a Specific Gene," *New York Times* (April 18, 1990), A1.

44. James A. Inciardi, *The War on Drugs: Heroin, Cocaine, and Public Policy* (Palo Alto, CA: Mayfield, 1986), 148.

45. *Ibid.,* 106.

46. Duane C. McBride, "The Relationship between Type of Drug Use and Arrest Change in an Arrested Populations," in *Drug Use and Crime* (Springfield, VA: National Technical Information Service, 1976), 409–18.

47. James A. Inciardi, Duane C. McBride, H. Virginia McCoy, and Dale D. Chitwood, "Recent Research on the Crack-Cocaine/Crime Connection," in *Studies in Crime and Crime Prevention* (Stockholm, Sweden: National Council for Crime Prevention), 63–82.

48. Bureau of Justice *Statistics, Substance Abuse and Treatment, State and Federal Prisoners, 1997* (Washington, D.C.: U.S. Department of Justice, January 1999), 5.

49. Paul J. Goldstein, "The Drugs/Violence Nexus: A Tripartite Conceptual Framework," *Journal of Drug Issues* 15 (1985), 493–506.

50. Gordon Witkin, "The Crime Bust: What's behind the Dramatic Drop in Crime," *U.S. News & World Report* (May 25, 1998), 28–33, 36–7.

51. McBride and McCoy, 99.

52. Benjamin and Miller, 110.

53. *Ibid.,* 110–1.

54. Nancy Mathis, "Record Budget Sought to Carry Out Drug War," *Houston Chronicle* (February 14, 1998), 6A.

55. Mark H. Moore and Mark A. R. Kleiman, " The Police and Drugs," in *Drugs, Crime, and Justice,* ed. Larry K. Gaines and Peter B. Kraska (Prospect Heights, IL: Waveland Press, 1997), 229.

56. David M. Kennedy, "Closing the Market: Controlling the Drug Trade in Tampa, Florida," *National Institute of Justice Program Focus* (Washington, D.C.: U.S. Department of Justice, April 1993).

57. David Kocieniewski, "In New York City Drug War, Risky Tactics and Casualties," *New York Times* (January 21, 1998), A1, B3.

58. Pub. L. No. 100-690, 102 Stat. 4329, codified at 42 U.S.C. Sections 3750-55 (1994).

59. "Central Florida Anti-Drug Assault," *The NarcOfficer* (March/April 1998), 9-13.

60 Quoted in Husak, 13.

61. Pub. L. No. 99-570, 100 Stat. 3207 (1986).

62. United States Sentencing Common Guidelines Manual Section 2D1. (c) (1994).

63. David Shribman, "Bush's Get Tough Drug Plan Shares Philosophy That Didn't Work for Rockefeller 20 Years Ago," *Wall Street Journal* (September 7, 1989), A16.

64. Upheld by U.S. Supreme Court in *Harmelin v. Michigan,* 501 U.S. 957 (1991).

65. Pub. L. No. 91-513, 84 Stat 1242 (1970), codified at 21 U.S.C. Sections 801 et seq. (1994).

66. 21 U.S.C. Section 881.

67. Psychotropic Substances Act of 1978, Pub. L. No. 95-633, 92 Stat. 3768, codified at 21 U.S.C. Section 881(a)(6) (1994).

68. Pub. L. No. 98-473, 98 Stat. 2050 (1984), codified at 21 U.S.C. Section 881(a)(7) (1994).

69. Pub. L. No. 98-473, 98 Stat. 2050 (1984), codified at 21 U.S.C. Section 881(a)(7) (1994).

70. 514 U.S. 549 (1995).

71. Comment, "'Possessing with Intent to Distribute' Under the Schoolyard Statute," *Chicago Law Review* 64 (1997), 1399–1424.

72. Paul J. Goldstein, "Crack and Homicide in New York City, 1988: A Conceptually Based Event Analysis," *Contemporary Drug Problems* 16 (1989), 662.

73. Husak, 18.

74. *Ibid.,* 53–8.

75. Cited in " 'Drug Czar's' Plan To Shore Up Leaky Border Meets with Skepticism," *Christian Science Monitor* (August 27, 1998), 3.

76. Steven B. Duke, "Drug Prohibition: An Unnatural Disaster," *Connecticut Law Review* 27 (Winter 1995), 571.

77. Skolnick, 414.

78. Joseph L. Galiber, "A Bill to Repeal Criminal Drug Laws: Replacing Prohibition with Regulation," *Hofstra Law Review* 18 (1990), 831.

79. Edwin Chen, "Meth Use on Rise in West as Cocaine Rates Fall," *Los Angeles Times* (July 12, 1998), A1.

80. Skolnick, 412.

81. Phillipe Bourgeois, "Just Another Night on Crack Street," *New York Times Magazine* (November 12, 1989), 63.

82. Jeanette Covington, "The Social Construction of the Minority Drug Problem," *Social Justice* (December 22, 1997), 117.

83. Sam Meddis, "Stereotypes Fuel Cycle of Suspicion, Arrest," *USA Today* (July 23, 1993), 6A.

84. Benjamin and Miller, 66.

85. 21 U.S.C.A. Sections 1521 et seq.

86. Michael S. Goodstadt, *Drug Education,* National Institute of Justice Crime File Study Guide (Washington, D.C.: U.S. Government Printing Office, 1988), 1.

87. *Behind Bars: Substance Abuse and America's Prison Population* (New York: National Center on Addiction and Substance Abuse at Columbia University, 1998).

88. Jonathan Caulkins, *Mandatory Minimum Drug Sentences: Throwing Away the Key or the Taxpayers Money* (Santa Monica, CA: Rand, 1997).

89. Bureau of Justice Statistics, *Substance Abuse and Treatment, State and Federal Prisoners, 1997,* Table 9 at page 10.

90. Peter Finn and Andrea Newlyn, "Miami Drug Court Gives Drug Defendants a Second Chance," *Judicature* 77 (1994), 268.

91. Drug Court Clearinghouse and Technical Assistance Project, *Drug Court Activity: Summary Information* (Washington, D.C.: U.S. Department of Justice, May 1997), 1.

92. Ethan A. Nadelmann, "The Case for Legalization," *Public Interest* (Summer 1992), 5.

93. James Ostrowski, "The Moral and Practical Case for Drug Legalization," *Hofstra Law Review* 18 (1990), 670.

94. James A. Inciardi and Duane C. McBride, "Debating the Legalization of Drugs," in *Handbook of Drug Control in the United States,* ed. James A. Inciardi (New York: Greenwood Press, 1990), 285–9.

95. Milton Friedman, "A Quarter-Century Later, 'War on Drugs' Is Still Misguided," *Seattle Post-Intelligencer* (January 15, 1998), A11.

96. *National Household Study on Drug Abuse, 1995* (Bethesda, MD: National Institute on Drug Abuse, 1996).

97. Inciardi and McBride, 289-94.

98. Center for Substance Abuse Prevention, *Drug Free for a New Century* (Washington, D.C.: U.S. Department of Health and Human Services, September 1995), 17.

99. Mark A. R. Kleiman, "Neither Probation Nor Legalization: Grudging Toleration in Drug Control Policy," in *Drug Use and Drug Policy,* ed. Marilyn McShane and Frank P. Williams III (New York: Garland Publishing, 1997), 180.

100. *Ibid.,* 186–90.

101. Rob A. Stewart, "Surgical Strikes, Not Carpet Bombing: The Dutch Approach to Drug Enforcement," *Drug Policy Letter* (November/December 1993), 13.

102. Ethan A. Nadelmann, "Thinking Seriously about Alternatives to Drug Prohibition," *Daedalus* 121 (1992), 88.

103. Donna Shalala, "Report to the Committee on Appropriations of the Department of Labor, Health and Human Services, Education and Related Agencies," *Needle Exchange Programs in America: A Review of Published Studies and On-going Research* (Washington, D.C.: U.S. Department of Health and Human Services, 1997), 11.

104. "Program and Abstracts: National Institute of Health Consensus Development Conference on Effective Medical Treatment of Heroin Addiction," Officer of the Director, National Institutes of Health, November 17–19, 1997.

105. Joyce H. Lowinson, Pedro Ruiz, and Robert B. Millman eds. *Substance Abuse: A Comprehensive Textbook,* 2d ed. (Baltimore: Williams & Wilkins, 1992), 550.

106. Robert J. Blendon and John T. Young, "The Public and the War on Illicit Drugs," *Journal of the American Medical Association* (March 18, 1998), 287.

107. Peter Reuter, "Hawks Ascendant: The Punitive Trend of American Drug Policy," in *Drug Use and Drug Policy,* ed. Marilyn McShane and Frank P. Williams III (New York: Garland Publishing, 1997), 394.

108. R. Moore, "Posse Comitatus Revisited: The Use of Military in Civilian Law Enforcement," *Journal of Criminal Justice* 15 (1987), 375–86.

109. 22 U.S.C. Section 2291 (1988), as amended by the Anti-Drug Abuse Act of 1986, Pub. L. No. 99-570, Section 2005, 100 Stat. 3207-61 to -62 (1986).

110. Mireya Navarro, "Upgraded Drug Traffic Flourishes on Old Route," *New York Times* (May 31, 1998), 12.

111. *Drug Smuggling: Large Amounts of Illegal Drugs Not Seized by Federal Authorities* (Washington, D.C.: U.S. General Accounting Office, 1987).

112. Murray E. Jarvik, "The Drug Dilemma: Manipulating the Demand," *Science* (October 19, 1990), 389.

113. Christopher S. Wren, "Where Opium Reigned, Burmese Claim Inroads," *New York Times* (April 19, 1998), 3.

114. "Mexico's Drug Menace," *Economist* (November 15, 1997), 38.

115. Douglas Farah and Serge F. Kovaleski, "Cartels Make Puerto Rico a Major Gateway to the U.S.," *Washington Post* (February 16, 1998), A1.

116. Robert B. Charles, "Back to the Future: The Collapse of National Drug Control Policy and a Blueprint for Revitalizing the Nation's Counternarcotics Effort," *Harvard Journal on Legislation* (Summer 1996), 339.

117. Patrick Clawson and Renssalaer Lee, *The Andean Cocaine Industry* (New York: St. Martin's Press, 1966), 12.

118. Navarro, 12.

chapter

18

Diversity Issues in the Criminal Justice System

Chapter Objectives

After reading this chapter, you should be able to:

1. Indicate the two reasons why it is important to study diversity in the criminal justice system.

2. Outline the basic racial, ethnic, and gender trends in crime.

3. Briefly describe the social reality of crime theory.

4. Trace the progression of theories about the causes of female criminality from the late 1800s until today.

5. Contrast the disparity view with the discrimination view of disproportionate crime statistics for minorities.

6. Explain why crack sentencing laws have been viewed as racist.

7. Outline the reasons why female offenders are less likely to go to prison than male offenders or, if sent to prison, why they receive shorter sentences.

8. Define balkanization as it relates to prisons.

9. Explain why the presence of female custodial employees in jails and prisons has instigated inmate Section 1983 lawsuits.

10. List some of the purported consequences of the lack of diversity in state trial courts.

INTRODUCTION

In many African American families, when a son is on the cusp of adolescence he receives a piece of wisdom known as "The Lesson" from his father. This advice does not concern the best way to hit a baseball or the facts of life. Instead, the son is told what to do when stopped by the police: "keep your hands visible, don't argue, get a badge number, and never, *never* try to run."[1] Fathers do not give "The Lesson" because they expect their sons to break the law; instead, it reflects their belief that the odds are that any young African American male will be stopped by the police at least once, whether or not he has done anything wrong. "The Lesson," they hope, will allow their sons to escape the stop without being harmed.

Such negative perceptions of law enforcement appear to be widely held in America's minority communities. In a recent national poll of African Americans, 87 percent indicated that they felt the criminal justice system does not treat all people equally, with 61 percent saying specifically that minorities do not get a "fair shake."[2] According to Harvard Law professor Randall Kennedy, such high levels of mistrust can wreak havoc on minority/law enforcement relations, causing citizens

> who might otherwise be of assistance to police to avoid them, to decline to cooperate with police investigations, to assume bad faith or dishonesty on the part of police officers, and to teach others that such reactions are prudent lessons of survival on the streets.[3]

In this chapter, we will examine perhaps the most controversial question in the study of the criminal justice system: Does the system discriminate against people on the basis of race, ethnicity, gender, or any other personal characteristic? We will dissect the facts, which show that (1) minorities are more involved in criminal activities than European Americans based on their respective populations, and (2) women commit fewer crimes than do men. We will also study the theories that attempt to account for these statistical anomalies and discuss efforts by the criminal justice system to increase employee diversity. At the close of the chapter, we will look at the debate surrounding hate crime laws. We begin, however, with an overview of race and gender issues in the criminal justice system and how these issues affect our basic notions of fairness, justice, and equality.

RACE, GENDER, AND CRIMINAL JUSTICE

Why do criminologists and other members of the criminal justice system care about the particular characteristics of the perpetrators and victims of crime? Should it matter that the person robbed was an African American, or that the rapist was white, or that the murderer was a woman? After all, all crimes are equally unacceptable and undesirable no matter who is involved. Indeed, labeling crimes by race or gender can sometimes have the negative effect of reinforcing stereotypes, especially when those labels are communicated through popular media.[4]

In general, two reasons can be given for studying the characteristics of offenders and victims. The first is practical. By observing patterns of criminality and victimization, participants in the criminal justice system can adjust crime-fighting strategies accordingly. The knowledge, for example, that the victims of women who kill are likely to be abusive partners has changed law enforcement attitudes toward domestic violence. The second justification for this kind of research is idealistic. Our concept of "justice" is partly based on the idea that the criminal justice system will not treat anyone differently on the

"There is dignity and security in the assurance that each of us—plain or beautiful, rich or poor, black, white, tall, curly, whatever—is promised treatment as bland, fungible, 'equal' before the law."

—Marvin E. Frankel, *American jurist* (1973)

basis of race, gender, ethnicity, or sexual orientation. If African Americans are being arrested for acts that are routinely ignored when committed by other racial groups, or if homosexuals are targeted as victims of violence, then the system must adjust its methods to correct these inconsistencies.

Measuring Diversity in Crime

The three primary sources of data for statistics on criminals and victims are the Federal Bureau of Investigation's Uniform Crime Reports (UCR), victim surveys, and self-reports. The strengths and weaknesses of each method in general were discussed at length in Chapter 2, but they also have specific implications for the subject at hand. The UCR, which is the main source of official statistics, measures arrests but not convictions.[5] Victim surveys have tended to underreport the most common crimes against women such as domestic violence and sexual assault because victims are often reluctant to admit that such acts have taken place.[6]

Another significant aspect of statistical studies of minority offenders and victims is that they tend to focus on *race*, which distinguishes groups based on physical characteristics such as skin color, rather than *ethnicity*, which denotes similar national or cultural backgrounds. Thus, the bulk of criminological research in this area has focused on the differences between European Americans and African Americans, both because the latter have been the largest minority group in the United States for most of its history and because the racial differences between the two groups are easily identifiable. Americans of Hispanic descent—who number close to 30 million—have either been excluded from many crime studies or been linked with whites based on racial characteristics.[7] Other minority groups, such as Asian Americans, Native Americans, and immigrants from the South Pacific or Eastern Europe, have been similarly underreported in crime studies.

INFOTRAC®
COLLEGE EDITION

Barlow, Melissa Hickman.
Race and the problem of crime in *Time* and *Newsweek* cover stories, 1946-1995.

Racial and Ethnic Trends in Crime

According to the University of Maryland's Katheryn K. Russell, the best-kept secret in criminology is that the United States has a "white crime" problem.[8] Whites, Russell points out, are the subject of 67 percent of the arrests in this country each year and represent a majority of those Americans in prison or jail. Russell's point is that public and academic obsession with minority crime, particularly "black crime," has severely limited discussion of "white crime." This fascination can be understood, at least from a criminological standpoint, as a result of the different *proportional* involvement of racial minorities in crime. As Figure 18.1 shows, although white involvement in crime is high, it is relatively low given the percentage of the American population that is of European descent. In contrast, minorities have a disproportionate involvement in crime based on their population statistics.

Figure **18.1** Crime and Race in the United States

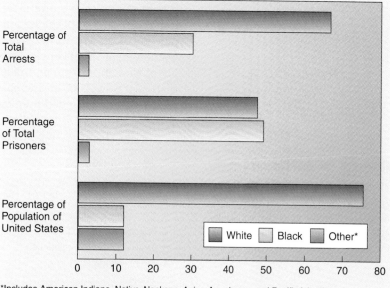

*Includes American Indians, Native Alaskans, Asian Americans, and Pacific Islanders

Note: For purposes of crime statistics, government agencies distinguish between race and ethnicity. Hispanic Americans are seem a separate ethnicity, not a separate race. Therefore, most crime statistics will make a distinction between "white non-Hispanic" and "black non-Hispanic" if they aim to draw conclusions about ethnicity in the criminal justice system.

SOURCE: U.S. CENSUS, U.S. DEPARTMENT OF JUSTICE, FEDERAL BUREAU OF INVESTIGATION.

> "**Racism in the criminal justice system hides behind discretion.**"
>
> —Susan N. Herman, *professor of law, Brooklyn Law School* (1993)

Minorities and Arrests. Keeping its shortcomings in mind, the UCR provides a stark picture of the overrepresentation of minorities, particularly African Americans, in arrest statistics. In 1997, 30 percent of those Americans arrested were black, more than double their population percentage. Long-term studies have come up with similar results: tracing arrest records of minority males in California over a fourteen-year period, Robert Tillman of St. John's University found that two-thirds had been arrested and jailed at least once between their eighteenth and thirtieth birthdays.[9] These statistics, however, should not lead to the conclusion that the patterns of minority and white crime are different. In fact, as Professor Marvin D. Free, Jr., points out, they are quite similar.[10] Eight of the top ten most common offenses resulting in arrest for whites match those for African Americans (see Figure 18.2).

Minorities in Prison. The percentage of minorities in American prisons is also disproportionate (refer back to Figure 18.1 on page 635). Relative to their populations, there are more than seven times as many minorities in prison as whites. Nearly one in every three African American males between the ages of twenty and twenty-nine is either in prison, in jail, or involved in some form of community supervision. The percentage of Hispanics in the prison population doubled between 1980 and 1993 to nearly 15 percent.[11] If incarceration rates for both groups continue to grow at the present pace, by 2020 two-thirds of all African American men and one-fourth of all Hispanic men will be in prison, in jail, or involved in some form of community supervision.[12]

The rise in minority prison populations can be attributed to drug offenses rather than increased rates of violent or property crimes. From 1986 to 1991, for example, inmates serving time in state prisons for violent crimes dropped 20 percent while those sentenced for drug offenses rose 447 percent.[13]

Gender Trends in Crime

Patterns of criminal involvement along racial lines are found among women as well as men. A black woman is 20 percent more likely to be imprisoned than a white woman. In general, however, women account for a small fraction of this country's offenders. Only 11 percent of the national jail population and 6 percent of the national prison population are female, and only 21.6 percent of all arrests involve women. This does not mean, however, that women are insignificant in the criminal justice system. Nationally, the number of women in state and federal prisons grew from 21,345 in 1995 to more than 78,000 in 1997, an increase of 265 percent (compared to a 148 percent increase for imprisoned men over that period).[14]

Figure 18.2 Ten Most Common Arrests, African Americans and Whites

Of the ten most common offenses resulting in arrests for African Americans and whites, only weapons offenses and liquor laws do not appear on both lists.

African Americans	Whites
1. Drug abuse violations	Driving under the influence
2. Larceny-theft	Drug abuse violations
3. Disorderly conduct	Larceny-theft
4. Aggravated assault	Drunkenness
5. Driving under the influence	Liquor laws
6. Drunkenness	Disorderly conduct
7. Fraud	Aggravated assault
8. Burglary	Fraud
9. Weapons offense	Burglary
10. Vandalism	Vandalism

SOURCE: FEDERAL BUREAU OF INVESTIGATION, CRIME IN THE UNITED STATES, 1997 (WASHINGTON, D.C.: U.S. DEPARTMENT OF JUSTICE, 1998), TABLE 43 AT PAGE 240.

Female Offending. In addition to committing far fewer crimes than their male counterparts (at least judging by official statistics), women also become involved in different types of crimes (see Figure 18.3). Criminologists who reject the idea that the explosion in female arrests and incarceration signifies a change in female criminality over the past twenty years point to changes in criminal justice policy concerning crimes that women are most likely to commit. The popularity of mandatory minimum sentences (discussed in Chapter 8), in particular, has been credited with much of the rise in female incarceration. In 1986, one in eight women in prison had been convicted of a drug crime. Within five years, the ratio was one in three, where it remains today.[15]

Women and Violent Crime. At the same time that the overall female crime rate has been increasing, the female rate for the most serious crimes has been falling. Between 1980 and 1995, for example, convictions of women for murder and manslaughter dropped 48 percent.[16] As we will see later in the chapter, some observers see this as proof that the criminal justice system treats violent women more leniently than violent men. Others see the trend as a reflection of the fact that women and men tend to act violently under very different circumstances.

Research conducted by social psychologists Angela Browne and Kirk R. Williams showed that when women do kill, the victim is usually an intimate male partner. Moreover, a woman is likely to kill in response to physical aggression or threats of physical aggression by her partner.[17] Consequently, women may receive lesser sentences because their actions were spontaneous reactions to male violence or were committed in self-defense. (To learn how the boundaries of self-defense are expanding for women in domestic violence situations, see *CJ in Focus—Was Justice Served? The Battered Woman Defense* on the next page.)

Women in prison and jails bring their own set of challenges to correctional officials, including issues of sexual abuse by correctional officers, medical aid, pregnancy, and motherhood. (Approximately 200,000 American children have a mother behind bars.) What are some of the explanations for the increase in female criminality and incarceration?

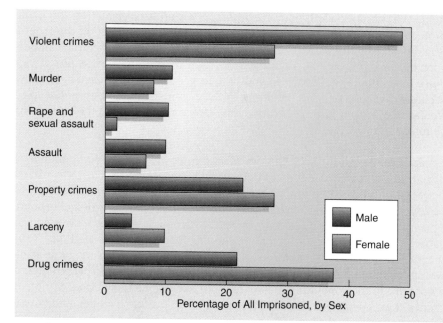

Percentage of All Imprisoned, by Sex

Figure 18.3 Prisoners by Sex and Offense

As you can see, women are more likely than men to be incarcerated in state prison for nonviolent crimes such as drug offenses and larceny whereas men are more likely to be imprisoned for violent crimes such as murder or assault.

SOURCE: BUREAU OF JUSTICE STATISTICS, PRISONERS IN 1997 (WASHINGTON, D.C.: U.S. DEPARTMENT OF JUSTICE, AUGUST 1998), TABLE 15 AT PAGE 11.

CJ in Focus
Was Justice Served?
The Battered Woman Defense

When Albert Hampton beat his companion Evelyn Humphrey, he tried to hit her in the back of the head, where, he told her, "it won't leave bruises." Driving back from a 1992 camping trip to their home in Fresno, California, Albert told Evelyn that the mountains would be a good place to kill her because nobody would find the body. The next day, he started hitting her again and went to grab his gun. Evelyn got the gun first, said "you're not going to hit me anymore," and shot him. Evelyn waited outside the home for the police. She was charged with murder.

During her trial, Dr. Lee Bowker testified that Evelyn suffered from "Battered Woman's Syndrome (BWS)," a term that has come to describe the psychological state a person descends into following a lengthy period of battering. Experts say that those suffering from BWS lose self-esteem and feel helpless, trapped in the relationship because of a lack of money, socially isolated, and fearful of reprisals. Evelyn's lawyers tried to use BWS as a defense on two levels. First, they used the "partial responsibility" defense, claiming that although Evelyn's actions were wrong, she was not in a mental state to comprehend what she was doing. Second, they presented the justification defense, admitting to killing Albert, but saying that the act was justified as self-defense.

These defenses were difficult to prove, given that Albert had acted violently before without causing Evelyn to fear for her life. Furthermore, the trial judge ordered that the jury not consider the BWS testimony when deciding whether Evelyn's actions were reasonably justified. Evelyn was found guilty of voluntary manslaughter and sentenced to eight years in prison. On appeal, however, the California Supreme Court ruled that the trial judge erred in his jury instructions and that BWS should be considered when trying to determine a woman's belief that her life is in danger. The court's ruling set an important precedent by allowing a jury to consider whether a "reasonable battered woman" would feel life-threatening danger. If the jurors do find this, they can decide that the homicide was justifiable and, as happened with Evelyn Humphrey on retrial, set the defendant free.

For Critical Analysis: In another case, a woman was pardoned after she shot her batterer-husband while he was sleeping. Under what circumstances do you believe such an act would be considered justifiable homicide? What might be some unexpected implications of allowing BWS to be used as a defense for justifiable homicide?

Victimization

The fact that a woman would be a victim of a crime simply because she is a woman, or that any person would be targeted due to sex, race, ethnicity, religion, or sexual orientation, is judged by many to be contrary to the language of the U.S. Constitution. Specifically, Section 1 of the Fourteenth Amendment holds that no state shall deny "any person within its jurisdiction the equal protection of the laws." In 1994, Congress applied this concept on the federal level by passing the Violence Against Woman Act, which states that "all persons in the United States shall have the right to be free from crimes of violence motivated by gender."[18] In addition, forty states have passed hate crime statutes that increase the penalties for crimes instigated by prejudice. (See the feature *Criminal Justice in Action—Hate Crimes and the Law* at the end of this chapter.)

Minorities as Victims of Crime. Most crimes are not driven by prejudice or hatred of a particular type of person. Instead, crimes appear to be driven by geography. If you live in a high-crime neighborhood, you are more likely to be a victim of crime than is someone who lives in a low-crime neighborhood. This seemingly straightforward assertion does have some controversial aspects, however, because "high-crime neighborhood," as well as "low-income neighborhood," "inner city," and "slum," are seen by many as code words for "black." And, in fact, African Americans—a greater percentage of whom live in metropolitan areas—are more likely to be the victims of violent crimes than are whites. This is particularly true for for juveniles and young adults; homicide is the leading cause of death for African Americans between the ages of 15 and 24.[19]

Such statistics have led some criminologists to conclude, as has John DiIulio, Jr., that "America does not have a crime problem; inner-city America does."[20] This suggests that minority victimization rates would decrease if more minorities would move out of high-crime areas. To a certain extent, there is statistical proof for this assertion. Research done by the U.S. Department of Justice found that African Americans of both sexes living in nonmetropolitan areas are *less* likely to be victims of personal crimes and theft than their white counterparts.[21] In spite of such findings, a number of criminologists find the ramifications of DiIulio's statement disturbing. If crime is "written off" as an "inner-city" problem, they fear, efforts to improve the crime situation in metropolitan areas will be abandoned in favor of increased migration to the suburbs and rural areas by those minorities who can afford to do so.[22]

The minority group with the highest victimization rates, as shown in Figure 18.4, are Native Americans. This can be attributed primarily to alcohol and drug use. Fifty-five percent of Native American victims of violent crime reported that their assailant was under the influence of drugs or alcohol, compared to 44 percent of white victims and 35 percent of African American victims. Furthermore, the arrest rates for alcohol abuse violations such as drunk driving and public drunkenness among Native Americans are more than double the national rate. As a result, leaders in Native American communities are striving to change the social conditions that lead to this alcohol and drug abuse.

Figure 18.4 Victimization by Race

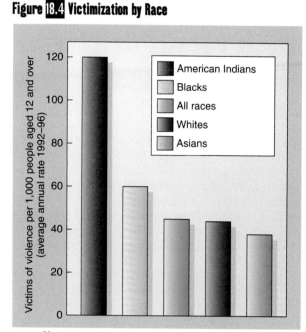

SOURCE: Various research by the U.S. Department of Justice.

Fear and Racism. In a sense, fear of victimization can play a more significant role in public perception of crime than actual victimization. Consider the following statistic: more than 80 percent of all crime is *intraracial*.[23] That is, most crime is "white on white," "black on black," "Hispanic on Hispanic," and so on. This is to be expected, as a majority of Americans live in communities with other citizens who are racially and ethnically similar. Yet the public perception of crime seems to focus on what Katheryn Russell calls the *criminalblackman,* a "mythical criminal" figure that has no counterpart among other races or ethnic groups.[24] The strength of this perception is underlined by a recent poll that showed that 56 percent of Americans believe African Americans are violence prone.[25] This fear and its consequences manifest themselves in incidents such as that involving Susan Smith, who explained the disappearance of her two young children by claiming that a black man wearing a wool cap had stolen her car with the children in it. In response, the Union County (South Carolina) police detained nearly thirty men from the town's African American community before Smith admitted that she had drowned her children by driving the car into a lake with them inside.[26]

James Q. Wilson of the University of California at Los Angeles believes that this fear has reached such proportions that it is indistinguishable from racism. Wilson says:

> [It is not racism] that keeps whites from exploring black [and Latino] neighborhoods, it is fear. It is not racism that makes whites uneasy about blacks moving into their neighborhoods, it is fear. . . . Fear of crime, of drugs, of gangs, of violence.[27]

Wilson believes that this fear is understandable, given the statistical evidence that minorities are more likely to commit crimes than whites. The best way to reduce racism, therefore, would be to reduce the minority crime rate.

CJ in Focus
Myth versus Reality
Race Stereotyping and Crime

In an effort to study the effect of race on perception, Birt Duncan gathered 104 white undergraduate students at the University of California and had them observe an argument between two people in which one person shoved the other. The undergraduates were randomly assigned to view one of four different conditions: (1) white shover/African American victim, (2) white shover/white victim, (3) African American shover/white victim, and (4) African American shover/African American victim. The students were then asked to rate the behavior of the person who did the shoving.

Duncan found that when the shover was African American and the victim was white, 75 percent of the students considered the shove to be "violent behavior" and 6 percent saw it as "playing around." In contrast, when the shover was white and the victim black, only 17 percent characterized the shove as violent while 42 percent saw it as playful.

THE MYTH

The results of Duncan's study are not, in the end, surprising. Racial stereotyping is not an aberration in our society. Negative stereotypes of African Americans label them as prone to violence and more likely to be criminals or members of gangs than others. Stereotyping can work in the other direction as well. Asian Americans, for example, are perceived as hard-working, intelligent, respectful of authority, and law-abiding. Indeed, Asian Americans are often seen as the "model" minority, leading many observers to believe that blacks are regarded as the "nonmodel" minority.

THE REALITY

A quick glance at Figure 18.1 on page 635 would seem to support these stereotypes: African Americans are responsible for 30.3 percent of arrests and 49.4 percent of prisoners in the United States, compared to percentages of 1.3 and 1.8 for Asian Americans. These statistics can be misleading. When the number of African Americans arrested for violent offenses is compared to the total number of African Americans in the United States, a different picture emerges. In fact, less than 1 percent of the African American population and only 1.86 percent of the African American male population have been arrested for violent crimes. Furthermore, large Asian American communities face many of the same crime problems as any other communities. In California, where nearly one-third of the more than 9 million Asian Americans live, law enforcement agencies have been setting up Asian gang units to deal with this growing problem.

Racial stereotyping has more than just social or theoretical ramifications. Take, for example, self-defense laws. How should judges and juries react when defendants claim they are acting in self-defense based on the race of the alleged attacker? There have been cases where race was obviously a factor in self-defense claims. Technically, Bernhard Goetz should not have been able to plead self-defense after shooting four African American youths in a New York City subway in 1984. Although one of the youths asked him for five dollars, none of them had threatened Goetz with a weapon or other bodily harm. Stereotypes can work in the same manner for Asian Americans as well. After Anthony Simon shot Steffen Wong, his Chinese American neighbor, after an argument, he claimed that he felt threatened by Wong. Simon explained to the jury that he felt the need to defend himself because he thought Wong, because of his racial heritage, was an expert in martial arts. A jury acquitted Simon of two counts of aggravated assault.

You Be the Judge: According to Figure 18.1, although African Americans are arrested at less than half the rate of whites, they comprise more of the prison population. Also, Asian Americans are much more likely to be arrested for gambling offenses than for any other crime. How can these statistical anomalies be explained?

Critics of Wilson, and of this concept in general, point out that this "fear/racism" is based on a false premise because whites are in fact more likely to be the victims of white crime. Hence, Wilson's theory only serves to strengthen the stereotype of Russell's *criminalblackman* and increases levels of fear. (See *CJ in Focus—Myth versus Reality: Race Stereotyping and Crime*.)

The Female Victim. A number of researchers have shown that, in general, women have a greater fear of being the victims of crime than men do.[28] Other studies have shown that men are more likely to be victims of crime, leading some criminologists to conclude that women are under the false impression that they are more likely to be victims.[29] Joanne Belknap of the University of Cincinnati, however, attributes this discrepancy to the fact that the violence that women are most susceptible to has traditionally been seen as a "family" or "private" matter and has therefore remained "invisible" to the criminal justice system.[30] In the early 1990s, under pressure from the U.S. Congress, the National Crime Victimization Survey (NCVS) was revised in order to better understand this aspect of female victimization. The redesigned survey showed that crime against women was indeed a more personal matter than crime against men: women were approximately six times more likely than men to experience violence at the hands of someone they knew (see Figure 18.5.)

In an example of how crime statistics can provide insight on "why" crimes are committed, research on the abuse of female prisoners seems to draw a correlation between such victimization and criminality. A recent study shows that 43 percent of female inmates have reported physical or sexual abuse prior to their current incarceration.[31] Women tend to react to such abuse with self-blame and victimization (whereas men are more likely to become aggressive and violent) and to turn to drugs and alcohol to deaden those unpleasant emotions.[32] Drug offenses are generally considered the greatest single contributing factor to the rapid increase in female arrest and incarceration rates over the past several decades. Thus, one might surmise that law enforcement efforts to lessen sexual abuse and battering could reduce the crime levels of women.

RACE, GENDER, AND CRIMINOLOGY

An overview of the available statistics (with all of their shortcomings duly noted) suggests that two generalizations can be made about crime in the United States: (1) women commit fewer crimes than men, and (2) minorities have a rate of offending that is higher than their populations would suggest. The obvious question is *why*, but the answer is not so obvious.

In Chapter 2, we explored the five main theories criminologists use to explain patterns of criminality—choice theory, trait (biological and psychological) theory, social structure theory, social process theory, and social conflict theory. Aside from the final one, for the most part these theories do not

Figure 18.5 Victim–Offender Relationship and Sex of Victim

As you can see, women are significantly more likely than men to know their victimizer.

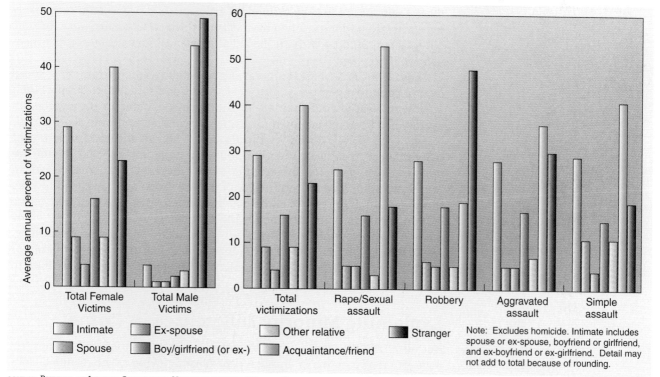

Intimate   Ex-spouse
Spouse   Boy/girlfriend (or ex-)
Other relative   Stranger
Acquaintance/friend

Note: Excludes homicide. Intimate includes spouse or ex-spouse, boyfriend or girlfriend, and ex-boyfriend or ex-girlfriend. Detail may not add to total because of rounding.

SOURCE: BUREAU OF JUSTICE STATISTICS, VIOLENCE AGAINST WOMEN: ESTIMATES FROM THE REDESIGNED SURVEY (WASHINGTON, D.C.: U.S. DEPARTMENT OF JUSTICE, 1995), TABLE 4 AT PAGE 3.

SOCIAL REALITY OF CRIME
The theory that criminal laws are designed by those in power (the rich) to help them keep power at the expense of those who do not have power (the poor). This would explain, for example, why the punishment for white-collar crime, mostly committed by members of the upper and middle classes, is less severe than the punishment for property and violent crimes, mostly committed by members of the lower class.

look specifically at race, ethnicity, or gender in explaining crime; they may apply to African Americans or women, but they do not start with the idea that these groups are, as a result of their social conditions, predisposed toward or away from criminal behavior. In contrast, social conflict theory is based on the existence of struggle among social classes. Minorities and women have historically had less collective power than European males in the United States, and social conflict theory attempts to show that criminal behavior is intricately linked to this "power gap."

The Social Reality of Crime

Richard Quinney, one of the most influential social conflict theorists of the past thirty years, encompasses issues of race, gender, power, and crime in a theory known as the **social reality of crime**.[33] Quinney, along with many of his intellectual peers, sees the criminal justice system as essentially the tool of society's most powerful classes. Criminal law does not reflect a universal moral code, but instead is a set of "rules" through which those who hold power can control and subdue those who do not. Any conflict between the "haves" and the "have-nots," therefore, is bound to be decided in favor of the "haves," who make the law and control the criminal justice system. Following this reasoning, Quinney sees violations of the law not as inherently criminal acts, but rather as political ones—as revolutionary acts against the power of the state.

Thinking along racial lines, many observers would assert that African Americans as a group have been "have-nots" since the colonial period. Today, the median income of an African American male is nearly $15,000, compared to $24,000 for a white male. In addition, African Americans do not seem to have the same access to positions of power as whites; in 1990, only one of the nation's 500 most profitable companies had a black chief executive.[34] Similarly, women have run up against what has been called the "glass ceiling" as they attempt to assume positions of power in corporations; only two of these positions are held by women.[35] Furthermore, those women most likely to be arrested and imprisoned have exactly the characteristics—low income, often raising children without the aid of a partner—that social conflict theorists would predict.

Those who perceive the criminal justice system as an instrument of social control point to a number of historical studies and statistics to support their argument. Nearly three-quarters of the female inmates in the nineteenth century had been incarcerated for sexual misconduct and were sent to institutions such as New York's Western House of Refuge at Albion to be taught the virtues of "true" womanhood.[36] Today, approximately 45,000 women are arrested each year for prostitution. After the Civil War, many African Americans were driven from the South by "Jim Crow laws" designed to keep them from attaining power in the postwar period. Today, the criminal justice system performs a similar function; on any given day in the early 1990s, 42 percent of African American males between the ages of eighteen and thirty-five in Washington, D.C., were either in prison, in jail, on probation/parole, or being sought for arrest.[37] Social conflict theorists have used these data to support their theories.

Explaining Minority Differences in Crime

Not all of the statistical evidence supports the contention that minorities have different patterns of criminal behavior than whites. The results of self-report studies, in particular, have contradicted the findings of the UCR. One such study, conducted at the Behavioral Science Institute, found little or no difference in criminal activity by minority and white youths nationwide, though these social scientists did find that black juveniles were more likely to be arrested and taken into custody than their white counterparts.[38]

The Effect of Social Inequality. Those criminologists who subscribe to the notion that minorities are more likely to commit crimes often use inequality to explain why. Structure theorists believe that those who are disconnected from mainstream culture reject the law-abiding values of that culture. Strain theorists contend that the disadvantaged must turn to illegitimate methods to gain material success. Conflict theorists hold that the poor use violent and property crime to resist the oppression of the rich. (To review these theories, return to Chapter 2, pages 62–63.)

Willie Dantzler, Jr., does not belong to any school of criminology, but his views provide a unique perspective on minority criminality. Dantzler, an African American prisoner in Illinois, focuses primarily on the culture of the inner city in identifying several factors that lead to male criminality in minority areas.[39] He believes this culture provides black males with a distorted concept of manhood, one that glorifies sex, violence, and athletics over intelligence and compassion. The culture of the inner city also breeds mistrust of American institutions such as the criminal justice system and corporations and in turn convinces many young African American males that opportunities for economic and social advancement are closed to them. Finally, Dantzler notes the lack of positive male role models for many black youths. Specifically, a high percentage of these youths are raised without fathers to teach them discipline, cooperation, and respect for education.

Frustration-Aggression Theory. A psychological explanation for African American criminality is offered by **frustration-aggression theory,** which holds that violent acts result from an individual's frustration at not being able to achieve a goal.[40] Psychiatrist James P. Comer links this frustration and anger to African Americans' historical experience in this country, first as slaves and subsequently as the targets of racism and limited opportunity.[41] The effects of this history—the destruction of the black family and black culture—have been, according to Comer, so complete that recovery may be impossible. Violence in general and intraracial violence in particular are a reaction to an "inability to cope with the larger society" that effectively shuts African Americans out of the major institutions of power.

Explaining Gender Differences in Crime

Most early criminologists thought that female criminals could be explained quite simply: they were not "real" women. In his 1885 book *The Female Offender*, Cesare Lombroso upheld this **masculinity hypothesis** by concluding that female criminals were not only abnormal women, but were biologically more like men.[42] This line of thinking eventually fell into disfavor, and by the middle of the twentieth century most criminologists focused on *socialization* to explain gender differences in crime. The low rates of female criminality compared to male criminality were due to different levels of parental control asserted over boys and girls. This theory was updated in the early 1970s by Dale Hoffman-Bustamante, who saw the childhood of most boys as a virtual training ground for delinquency, at least in contrast to the childhood of girls.[43] Boys were given the freedom to develop physical skills such as running and jumping and to take part in male rituals such as hunting (using firearms) or mechanical problem solving (working on automobiles, watches, etc.). Girls were expected to be "ladylike" and had more restrictive responsibilities in the home.

FRUSTRATION-AGGRESSION THEORY
The theory that aggression is the result of an individual's inability to reach his or her goals. In the context of minority offending, this theory holds that the social, political, and economic restrictions historically placed on African Americans result in a higher rate of African American offending.

MASCULINITY HYPOTHESIS
The theory that women who commit crimes are biologically and psychologically similar to men.

LIBERAL FEMINIST THEORY
A theory of female criminality that concentrates on the economic and social disparities between women and men. Liberal feminist criminologists predicted that as women gained more financial and social power, male and female rates of criminality would become more similar.

Feminist Theories of Female Criminality. The types of crime women engage in most often—consumer crimes such as check forgery and shoplifting and sex-related crimes such as prostitution—seemed to support Hoffman-Bustamante's theory. Around the time these ideas were published, however, the field was coming to be dominated by the **liberal feminist theory** of female criminality. Feminist theory, as popularized by Rita James Simon's *Women and Crime* (1975)[44] and Freda Adler's *Sisters in Crime* (1975),[45] sees crime in terms of the power relationship between men and women. Both Simon and Adler believed that as this power relationship became more even, female crime patterns would become more like male crime patterns.

When female crime rates did begin to turn upward in the 1970s, in tandem with the feminist movement and greater workplace opportunities for women, many observers felt that Simon and Adler had accurately predicted the appearance of a "new female criminal." It quickly became clear, however, that the "new" female criminal was very similar to the old one, committing the same crimes, albeit in greater numbers, as before. It appeared that women who were able to take advantage of the greater opportunities had improved their social status to the point where, as a social conflict theorist would say, they had become part of the ruling class.

Postfeminist Theories. According to Jane Roberts Chapman, the "new female criminal" is in fact a single mother with children, who commits property crimes out of need or abuses drugs as an avenue of escape from her difficult situation.[46] In fact, four-fifths of all female prisoners are mothers, and nearly 30 percent describe themselves as the "primary caregiver" of their children (meaning that they do not have a partner to share the responsibility).[47] Chapman predicts that if the number of single mothers below the poverty line increases, so will female crime rates.

Using information found in presentencing investigation reports (discussed in Chapter 8), feminist criminologist Kathleen Daly has identified several distinct pathways to crime that women follow.[48] The *harmed-and-harming woman*, for example, suffered from abuse and neglect as a child, which in turn led her to "act out" and be labeled a "problem child." As an adult, this woman reacts to difficult situations with violence. The *battered woman*, in contrast, does not necessarily have a history of childhood abuse, but used violence to defend herself against an abusive partner. Similarly, the *drug-connected woman* does not have a criminal past, but has become involved in a relationship—either with a partner or with a child—characterized by drug use. A drug-connected woman might, for example, let her son use their home as a place to sell drugs, or she might turn to street crime to support a boyfriend or husband's drug habit.

MINORITIES AND THE CRIMINAL JUSTICE SYSTEM: DISPARITY OR DISCRIMINATION?

Another opinion, held by labeling theorists (see Chapter 2), is that the criminal justice system creates high rates of criminality because its unfair treatment of the minority community convinces minorities that they are indeed criminals. Those who take this view can produce a large amount of data to support their thesis. As already noted, though African Americans make up roughly 12 percent of the country's population, they account for 30 percent of its arrests. In Massachusetts, African Americans and Hispanics are imprisoned for drug offenses at rates that are, respectively, 39 and 81 times higher than for whites.[49] Prosecutors in King County, Washington, are more likely to bring charges against minorities than whites for similar crimes.[50] An analysis of more than 1,100 arrests in New Haven, Connecticut, showed that bail amounts were set at levels 35 percent higher for African Americans than for whites.[51] Nationwide, as Figure 18.6 shows, a higher percentage of African Americans and Hispanics are likely to be imprisoned for drug offenses than whites.

The pressing question for many observers is whether these statistics represent disparity or discrimination. **Disparity** refers to inconsistencies that result from legitimate factors in the decision-making process of judges, prosecutors, police officers, and other authority figures in the criminal justice system. **Discrimination,** in contrast, reflects illegitimate influences (such as the suspect's race) that may affect this decision-making process. A great deal of research has been done on the treatment of minorities by the criminal justice system, but no simple answers to the question of disparity versus discrimination have emerged.

Selective Law Enforcement

In looking for answers, however, many suggest that the actions of police may play a role in disparities in minority-white arrest rates. In a recent Department of Justice study (noted in Chapter 7), African Americans and Hispanics were found to be about 70 percent more likely to have contact with police than whites. Furthermore, the study revealed that those minority groups made up about half the people against whom force—being hit, pushed, choked, restrained by a police dog, or threatened by a gun—was used, even though they represented only a fifth of those surveyed.[52]

The "Just Us" System. These experiences have led some to believe that the United States has, in practice, not a justice system but a "just us" system. For example, African Americans speak of a particular law that police officers seem to apply selectively—DWB, or "driving while black." This perception is supported by empirical evidence from Florida, Maryland, and New Jersey that African American drivers are targeted more often for traffic violations than other racial groups.[53] The Maryland data, collected by the American Civil Liberties Union and Temple University, revealed that although blacks constituted only 17 percent of all motorists and 17.5 percent of all traffic violators

DISPARITY
Inconsistencies between the treatment of minorities and nonminorities that result from legitimate factors in the decision-making process of the criminal justice system.

DISCRIMINATION
Inconsistencies in the treatment of an individual that can be attributed to extralegal variables such as the defendant's race, ethnicity, gender, sexual orientation, or economic standing.

Figure 18.6 Prisoners by Race/ Ethnicity and Offense

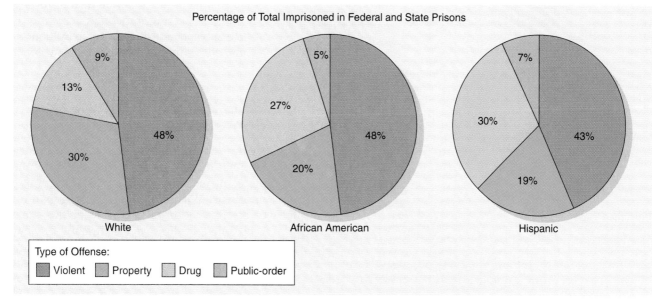

Percentage of Total Imprisoned in Federal and State Prisons

White

African American

Hispanic

Type of Offense:
Violent Property Drug Public-order

SOURCE: BUREAU OF JUSTICE STATISTICS, PRISONERS IN 1997 (WASHINGTON, D.C.: U.S. DEPARTMENT OF JUSTICE, AUGUST 1998), TABLE 16 AT PAGE 12.

According to a lawsuit filed by the American Civil Liberties Union, college student Mecca Agunabo I was a victim of "racial profiling" by Maryland state troopers who detained him for two hours while searching his car for contraband. "Racial profiling" refers to the police practice of choosing suspects based on their race.

on a section of highway I-95 near Baltimore, they made up nearly 73 percent of all motorists pulled over and subjected to searches by police.[54]

William Chambliss of George Washington University also noted this phenomenon while spending several years riding with the rapid deployment unit (RDU) of the Washington, D.C., metropolitan police.[55] Chambliss observed that RDU patrols ignored the city's white neighborhoods, but used any excuse (including having an item hanging from the rearview mirror) to stop cars driven by young black males. According to one RDU officer:

> This is the jungle . . . we rewrite the Constitution every day down here. . . . If we pull everyone over, they will eventually learn that we aren't playing games any more.[56]

It is this sort of attitude, say critics of such tactics, that leads to unnecessary harassment of minorities by police and instills feelings of ill will toward law enforcement in many minority neighborhoods.

Police Attitudes and Discretion. A greater police presence in minority neighborhoods is not necessarily evidence of law enforcement bias. As we learned in Chapter 5, the primary operational tactic of all metropolitan police forces is returning calls for service. According to research done by law enforcement expert Richard J. Ludman, greater police presence in these communities is mainly the result of calls for service from residents, which, in turn, are caused by higher local crime rates. Indeed, Randall Kennedy believes that such "selective law enforcement" should be and, for the most part, is welcomed by those who live in high-crime areas and who appreciate the added protection.[57]

Furthermore, as several experts point out, cultural differences often exist between police officers and the residents of the neighborhoods they patrol. One recent survey found that police working in minority areas perceived higher levels of abuse and less respect from citizens than those working in nonminority areas.[58] Though the same study found that such attitudes were unlikely to affect police performance, other evidence suggests that cultural differences can influence police discretion. Another survey, for example, found that the most important factor in a police officer's decision to arrest a juvenile (the major determinant in 50 to 60 percent of all arrests) was not the youth's prior record, but his or her demeanor toward the officer.[59] Judging someone's demeanor is often a subjective task and can be influenced by lack of communication between two people from different backgrounds.

Selective Prosecution and Sentencing

Racial and ethnic differences in sentence lengths focus attention on the possible biases of judges (see Figure 18.7). According to ethicist Willard Gaylin, a certain amount of discrimination is inevitable in this area. Each judge, Gaylin says, has "a point of view, a set of standards and values, a bias, if you will, which will color, influence, and direct the nature of his verdicts independently of the specific condition of the criminal being charged." Therefore, even though this "bias"

Figure 18.7 Sentence Lengths by Race

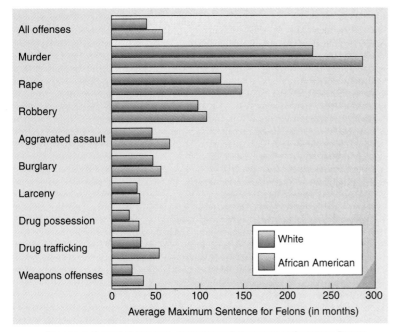

SOURCE: BUREAU OF JUSTICE STATISTICS, *STATE COURT SENTENCING OF CONVICTED FELONS, 1994* (WASHINGTON, D.C.: U.S. DEPARTMENT OF JUSTICE, 1998), 21.

may not be intentional, it "will influence equity and fairness in exactly the same way as naked bigotry does."[60] To avoid such unintentional inclinations, many jurisdictions have limited judicial discretion by law, as we saw in Chapter 8. In a number of instances, particularly regarding crack cocaine, the law is seen as more discriminatory than any judge's action.

Crack Sentencing Laws. The Omnibus Crime Prevention Act of 1986 established a ratio of 100:1 for the punishment for selling or using crack cocaine as compared to powdered cocaine.[61] Therefore, if one person is caught selling 5 grams of crack cocaine and another is caught selling 500 grams of powder cocaine, they will both receive the same five-year minimum sentence. The reasoning behind the 100:1 ratio centered on the perceived higher addictive qualities of crack cocaine and studies that showed higher crime rates surrounding its use.[62] Whatever the law's intentions, say its many critics, its actual effect has been to disproportionately punish African Americans. About half of all crack users are white, yet they make up only 4 percent of all federal convictions on crack-related charges. African Americans, who represent 38 percent of all crack users, account for 85 percent of federal crack convictions.[63]

The federal crack law provides for much harsher penalties than do the majority of state laws. For this reason, defendants tried in federal courts are likely to spend more time in prison than those tried in state courts. In *United States v. Armstrong* (1996),[64] the Supreme Court considered this disparity. Nine African Americans who had been tried by the U.S. Attorney in California for intent to distribute crack argued that their indictment should have been dismissed on the ground that they had been selected for prosecution because of their race. The defendants showed that of the twenty-four defendants charged with similar crimes under federal instead of state law, all were black. The Court ruled against the defendants, holding that they had not proved that the U.S. Attorney would not similarly charge suspects of other races under the same circumstances. By ruling that disparate results do not equate to discriminatory intent, the Court in *Armstrong* made it difficult for future defendants to prove a racial bias in prosecutorial decisions.[65]

Discriminatory Intent and the Death Penalty. Many observers also see evidence of prosecutorial and judicial bias in the use of the death penalty in this country. Of the 4,220 prisoners executed in the United States between 1930 and 1996, 53 percent were African American, even though that minority group made up between 10 and 15 percent of the national population during that time span.[66] Of the 415 convicts executed since 1972, 235 have been white, compared with 152 African Americans. Although the continued discrepancy with regard to overall population percentages may be explained by the factors discussed earlier in the chapter, another set of statistics continues to be problematic. African Americans are approximately four times more likely to receive the death penalty if their victim is white than if she or he is black. In contrast, only two white men have been executed since 1976 for murdering African Americans.[67]

In *McCleskey v. Kemp* (1987),[68] the defense attorney of an African American sentenced to death for killing a white police officer used similar statistics to challenge Georgia's death penalty law. A study of 2,000 Georgia murder cases showed that although African Americans were the victims of six out of every ten murders in the state, over 80 percent of the cases in which death was imposed involved murders of whites.[69] In a 5–4 decision, the Supreme Court rejected the defense's claims. (See *CJ in Focus—Landmark Cases: McCleskey v. Kemp* on the next page.)

In 1982, former Black Panther activist Mumia Abu-Jamal was convicted of killing a Philadelphia police officer. Abu-Jamal, who has consistently proclaimed his innocence, remains on death row and has become a focal point in the debate over discrimination and the death penalty in the United States. In Philadelphia, the defendant's lawyers point out, of the 126 persons sentenced to death, all but 14 were minorities, and 80 percent of those living on death row are African American. Do these kinds of statistics prove discriminatory intent in the criminal justice system?

CJ in Focus
Landmark Cases:
McCleskey v. Kemp

Warren McCleskey, an African American, had been convicted in Georgia in 1978 of murdering a white police officer. He challenged his conviction and his subsequent death sentence based on a highly complex study of capital punishment in Georgia. Known as the Baldus study, the research showed that defendants charged with killing white victims were 4.3 times more likely to receive the death penalty as those who murdered African Americans. Also, the study claimed that black defendants were 1.1 times as likely to receive the death penalty as other defendants. Based on the Baldus study, McCleskey asserted that Georgia had denied him equal protection of the law as guaranteed under the Fourteenth Amendment by discriminating against him based on his race and the race of his victim. The Supreme Court did not find fault with the Baldus study, but questioned its relevance to the matter at hand.

McCleskey v. Kemp
United States Supreme Court
481 U.S. 279 (1987)
http://laws.findlaw.com/US/481/279.html

In the Words of the Court . . .

Mr. Justice POWELL, majority opinion

* * * *

Our analysis begins with the basic principle that a defendant who alleges an equal protection violation has the burden of proving "the existence of purposeful discrimination." A corollary to this principle is that a criminal defendant must prove that the purposeful discrimination "had a discriminatory effect" on him. Thus, to prevail under the Equal Protection Clause, McCleskey must prove that the decisionmakers in his case acted with discriminatory purpose. He offers no evidence specific to his own case that would support an inference that racial considerations played a part in his sentence. Instead, he relies solely on the Baldus study.

* * * *

Even Professor Baldus does not contend that his statistics prove that race enters into any capital sentencing decisions or that race was a factor in McCleskey's particular case. Statistics at most may show only a likelihood that a particular factor entered into some decisions. There is, of course, some risk of racial prejudice influencing a jury's decision in a criminal case. There are similar risks that other kinds of prejudice will influence other criminal trials. The question "is at what point that risk becomes constitutionally unacceptable". McCleskey asks us to accept the likelihood allegedly shown by the Baldus study as the constitutional measure of an unacceptable risk of racial prejudice influencing capital sentencing decisions. This we decline to do.

* * * *

At most, the Baldus study indicates a discrepancy that appears to correlate with race. Apparent disparities in sentencing are an inevitable part of our criminal justice system.* * * In light of the safeguards designed to minimize racial bias in the process, the fundamental value of jury trial in our criminal justice system, and the benefits that discretion provides to criminal defendants, we hold that the Baldus study does not demonstrate a constitutionally significant risk of racial bias affecting the Georgia capital sentencing process.

* * * *

The Baldus study seeks to deduce a state "policy" by studying the combined effects of the decisions of hundreds of juries that are unique in their composition. It is incomparably more difficult to deduce a consistent policy by studying the decisions of these many unique entities. It is also questionable whether any consistent policy can be derived by studying the decisions of prosecutors. * * * Even assuming the statistical validity of the Baldus study as a whole, the weight to be given the results gleaned from this small sample is limited.

Decision: The Court accepted the accuracy of the Baldus study but ultimately rejected McCleskey's claims. The information contained in the Baldus study, the Court held, was insufficient to overturn a death sentence delivered by a jury. In a wider sense, the decision made it more difficult for defendants to challenge death penalty verdicts.

For Critical Analysis: In dissenting from the opinion, Justice Brennan complained that the Court appeared to be "fearful of too much justice." Do you agree with Justice Powell that, even though a certain amount of racial bias is inevitable, the "fundamental value" of the jury trial is sufficient to safeguard against widespread discrimination? Explain your answer.

Note: Triple asterisks (* * *) indicate that a few words or sentences have been deleted and quadruple asterisks (* * * *) indicate that an entire paragraph (or more) has been omitted from the opinion.

The Racist Criminal Justice System: A Myth?

In the end, the question of whether the criminal justice system suffers from discrimination comes down to two explanations for the disproportionate number of minority offenders in the system: either (1) the system is biased, or (2) the system is reacting to higher levels of minority criminality. The latter opinion is held by many members of the criminal justice community, who maintain that when statistics are *controlled*, evidence for racial discrimination is weakened.

Earlier in the chapter, for instance, we noted that African Americans are incarcerated at a rate seven times that of whites. Alfred Blumstein of Carnegie-Mellon University believes that most of this disparity can be attributed to the fact that African Americans are more likely to be arrested than whites and are therefore more likely to be put in prison.[70] To use another example from earlier in the chapter, the discrepancy in bail settings for whites and blacks in New Haven can be explained by factors besides discrimination. The African American defendants may have had more significant criminal records or may have been less likely to be employed, variables that would lead to higher bail.[71]

For those who find little proof of a discriminatory criminal justice system, the reasons for disproportionate minority involvement can also be found in social indicators. When compared with whites, minorities have higher instances of living conditions that can be correlated with crimes. Research done in Massachusetts shows that a person of any race who lives in a neighborhood designated as an "extreme poverty" area is nineteen times more likely to be arrested for a drug offense than someone who lives in a non-poverty area.[72] Furthermore, minorities are generally less likely than whites to be represented by a private attorney, which lessens their chances of receiving a favorable plea bargain and increases their conviction rates and sentence lengths.[73]

The funeral of Amadou Diallo in the village of Hollande Bourou, Guinea. Diallo was killed in New York City on February 4, 1999, when plainclothes police officers searching for a rapist fired 41 bullets at him, 19 of which found their mark. As Diallo was unarmed and innocent, the incident raised serious questions of racism in the NYPD.

FEMALE OFFENDERS AND THE CHIVALRY EFFECT

Few people would argue that race or ethnicity should be a factor in criminal justice decisions. The system should be "color blind." But what about women—should the system be "gender blind" as well? Until recently, the question has not received much attention from criminologists. Indeed, there seemed little reason to consider it, given that women had such a small presence in the institutions of criminal justice. As rates of female arrests and incarceration have grown, however, the subject of disparate treatment of female offenders is being examined more closely.

According to Joanne Belknap of the University of Colorado at Boulder, criminologists consider three hypotheses when discussing sex discrimination in criminal justice:

- The *equal treatment hypothesis,* which holds that there is no discrimination and that men and women are treated equally.

- The *chivalry* or *paternalism hypothesis,* which holds that females are treated more leniently than males.

- The *evil woman hypothesis,* which holds that women are treated more harshly than men for similar offenses.[74]

In a strictly legal sense, the equal treatment hypothesis seems to dominate. Since the 1970s, when all remaining state prostitution laws that specifically applied to women were extended to apply to males as well, American law has been **gender-neutral.** That is, criminal and sentencing laws do not differentiate between men and women offenders. The day-to-day operations of criminal justice, however, are conducted on principles of discretion rather than statute, and, as we know, discretion allows room for personal tendencies to seep into the system.

GENDER-NEUTRAL
Criminal sanctions and sentencing provisions that do not take into consideration whether the suspect or convict is male or female. American law is considered gender-neutral.

The Police and Female Offenders

Many researchers have noted a tendency among police officers to use the "evil woman" model when dealing with juvenile offenders. These attitudes are significant, as police play an important role in determining whether a case of juvenile misconduct will lead to contact with the juvenile justice system. Juvenile delinquency researchers Jean E. Rhodes and Karla Fischer have found that girls are more likely than boys to be detained for noncriminal statute offenses, such as running away or engaging in underage sex.[75] Police are tougher on "wayward" girls because their behavior does not conform to sexual stereotypes, and the officer may feel that the juvenile justice system can "salvage" a girl who is heading in the wrong direction. In contrast, such activity by boys is seen as normal adolescent behavior and more often ignored.[76]

Despite the widespread belief that attractive women who exhibit a "friendly" attitude are given lenient treatment from male law enforcement officers, there is little statistical evidence that police treat adult women differently than men.[77] One area in which disparate treatment is evident is prostitution. Though, by law, both the provider and the consumer of illicit sexual relations have committed crimes, the female provider is much more likely to be arrested than the male consumer. Women are approximately 63 time more likely to be arrested for prostitution and commercialized vice than are men.[78] This could be the result of operational strategy rather than individual police discretion, however.

Female Offenders in the Courts

Women who are convicted of crimes are less likely to go to prison than men, and those who are incarcerated are given shorter sentences (see Figure 18.8). One study attributes these differences to the elements of female criminality: in property crimes, women are usually accessories, and in violent crimes, women are usually reacting to physical abuse. In both cases, the mitigating circumstances would lead to lesser punishment.[79] Wider evidence suggests, however, that the chivalry effect plays a large part in the decisions of prosecutors, judges, and juries.

Data compiled by the Federal Sentencing Commission show that prosecutors are more likely to offer women beneficial plea bargains.[80] Several self-report studies have shown that judges may treat female defendants more "gently" than male ones, and that judges will be influenced by mitigating factors such as a woman's marital status and family background that they would ignore with men.[81] Juries' leniency toward women can be most clearly seen in death penalty cases. Though women account for 13 percent of all murder arrests, they represent only 1.5 percent of the prisoners on death row. According to Karen Jo Koonan, an Oakland jury consultant, jurors do not want to believe that a woman, in her role as nurturer, could also be a cold-blooded killer.[82]

Figure 18.8 Sentence Lengths by Sex

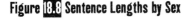

SOURCE: Bureau of Justice Statistics, *State Court Sentencing of Convicted Felons, 1994* (Washington, D.C.: U.S. Department of Justice, 1998), 20.

Is Chivalry Dead?

There are signs, however, that the public's desire for equal treatment is changing some of these attitudes. On January 16, 1996, the day she was scheduled to be executed for the double murder of her baby daughter and husband, Guinevere Garcia was pardoned by Illinois Governor Jim Edgar. The move was unpopular with Edgar's constituency, who were generally of the opinion that Garcia would have been put to death for the same crimes if she had been a man. Two years later, in 1998, after a twenty-five-year stretch when only one woman was executed in the United States, three were put to death, though in Texas support for the death penalty dropped from 86 percent to 68 percent following the execution of Karla Faye Tucker.[83]

Judicial Leniency. Similarly, sentencing reforms designed to limit judicial discretion have had far-reaching implications that can be seen in the increased incarceration of women. In fact, some observers are now supporting the practice of judicial leniency for women and claim that gender-neutral sentencing laws exact a heavy price on society. By separating increasing numbers of nonviolent female offenders from their children, the sentencing guidelines are placing the cost of caring for these children on the taxpayer.[84] Furthermore, by increasing the chances that the children will have emotional problems themselves due to lack of an active parent, such laws increase the probability that these children will become delinquent. Instead of sending nonviolent offenders who are pregnant or have children to jail or prison, the argument goes, the correctional system should place them in community-based programs where they can continue to care for their offspring.

Race and the Chivalry Effect. It must be noted that to whatever degree the chivalry effect has existed, it has primarily benefited white women as opposed to minority women.[85] According to prison historian Nicole Rafter, the criminal justice system has traditionally tried to reform white female offenders, while viewing the courts and correctional facilities as means to punish and incarcerate African American female prisoners.[86] To a certain extent, this theory is supported by data. The prison incarceration rate for black women today is greater than it was for white males in 1980,[87] a remarkable statistic given the difference in population percentages between the two groups.

CHALLENGES FOR THE NEW PRISON CULTURE

It is estimated that nearly 80 percent of female inmates are mothers, with an average of two dependent children each. In an attempt to reduce the negative effects of separation for both mothers and children, a number of correctional facilities have set up programs for them. The Maryland Correctional Institute for Women, for example, has formed a Girl Scout troop made up of daughters of inmates. Two Saturdays a month, the scouts make a trip to the prison to visit their mothers.[88] Such efforts reflect one of the challenges of the changing composition of American prisons and jails. As the make-up of inmate populations has shifted, prison culture has changed in response. In this section, we will examine the realities of the prison culture with regard to minorities and women.

Issues of Race and Ethnicity in Men's Prisons

Over the past three decades, African Americans and Hispanics have become the majority in many penal institutions. As a result of such changes in prison

SECURITY THREAT GROUPS (STGs)
The official term for prison gangs, or groups of inmates who bond together for protection and to run illegal activities within the correctional facility.

"The Bloods started because Latin Kings and Netas were trying to oppress black people."

—Sherman "Sherm da Worm" Adams, *describing the formation of the New York chapter of the United Blood Nation gang (the Bloods) in the state's penal system (1998)*

populations, issues of race and ethnicity have become increasingly important to prison administrators and researchers.

The "Balkanization" of Prisons. As early as the 1950s, researchers were noticing the different group structures in inmate life. At that time, for example, prisoners at California's Soledad prison informally segregated themselves according to geography as well as race: Tejanos (Mexicans raised in Texas), Chicanos, blacks from California, blacks from the South and Southwest, and the majority whites all formed separate social worlds.[89]

Leo Carroll, professor of sociology at the University of Rhode Island, has written extensively on how today's prisons are "balkanized," with race determining nearly every aspect of an inmate's life, including friends, job assignments, and cell location.[90] In further studies, Carroll has shown that cliques of African American inmates generally adhere to a set of values and roles brought with them from outside society. As racial tensions are prevalent in that outside society, it should not be surprising that blacks, or any other minority group, have seized upon race to help form their prison identity. Carroll defined the typical relationship between imprisoned African Americans as one of "brotherhood." One inmate Carroll interviewed said:

> As long as a man's a brother, you ain't gonna let nothing happen to him. If he's got a beef, then it's your beef. If you got a beef, then it's his.[91]

Prison Gangs. Racial and ethnic identification is often the primary focus of prison gangs, or cliques of inmates that are linked to illegal and violent activities within prisons. Prostitution, extortion, drug selling, gambling, loan sharking—such activities are invariably operated by prison gangs. In many instances, administrators believe, gangs have "taken over" a number of prison systems in the country. In Illinois, for example, officials estimate that 54 percent of the inmates in state prisons are gang members.

Gang Violence. From their beginnings, gangs have relied on violence to meet their economic and social goals. In 1967, a group of young Chicanos incarcerated in California's San Quentin began to force drugs on other prisoners. After a time, fellow inmates began to resent the intrusions of the "Mexican Mafia," as the group came to be known. Finally, the Mafia was attacked, and, in a series of knife fights, several dozen prisoners were wounded and one killed. The Mafia survived, and the battle inspired its opponents to form their own group, La Nuestra Familia. In a pattern that has repeated itself numerous times in numerous prison organizations, the conflict between the two groups continued outside the California prison system, as members carried their gang identities beyond prison walls.[92]

Though the stereotypical gang is comprised of African Americans or Hispanics, in truth the array of different racial and ethnic prison groups is extensive. One of the most violent and extensive prison gangs is, for example, the Aryan Brotherhood, whose members are dedicated to principles of white supremacy. Regardless of make-up, however, gangs share the same purpose:

> Their members have done in prison what many people do elsewhere when they feel personally powerless, threatened, and vulnerable: They align themselves with others, organize to fight back, and enhance their own status and control through their connection to a more powerful group.[93]

Administrative Response. Gangs have come to dominate prison culture in a number of states, including California, Texas, and New York. Prison officials have reacted inconsistently to this phenomenon, and many states are only now organizing programs to combat **security threat groups (STGs)**. In

Massachusetts, for example, the Department of Corrections recently announced that inmates identified as members of three Hispanic gangs—La Familia, the Latin Kings, and NETA—would be segregated in "restrictive housing" at the Massachusetts Correctional Institution in Cedar Junction.[94] To justify separating gang members from other inmates, corrections officials point to data that show that gang-affiliated inmates are more violent and more likely to have been the subject of disciplinary efforts within the prison. Because supposed gang members do not enjoy due process during the determination of whether they are in fact part of an STG, however, many prisoner's rights advocates criticize such measures as unjust and racist.[95]

Inside the Women's Prison

Eleven times as many research projects are conducted in men's prisons as in women's prisons.[96] This disparity can partly be attributed to the small number of female inmates compared to male inmates, but it is also doubtless the result of the traditional lack of interest in women in the corrections system. Nonetheless, the research that has been done provides insight into the social world of a women's prison. (See *Careers in Criminal Justice* on page 655.)

Adaptive Roles of Female Inmates. While studying the District of Columbia's Women's Reformatory in Occoquan, Virginia, researcher Esther Hefferman found that women conform to three general roles in adapting to the prison environment:

1. *In the life.* An inmate "in the life" is a repeat offender whose antisocial values assure that she will be spending a great deal of time in penal institutions. For these women, the prison community is their only community, and they feel comfortable within the confines of life behind bars.

2. *Squares.* A "square," in contrast, accepts and conforms to society's norms and values. For the most part, these are not habitual criminals but women who may have committed a crime in a moment of rage. While in prison, the "square" tries to maintain her outside values and may be labeled (not without a hint of scorn) as a "good Christian woman."

3. *Cool.* A "cool" inmate is one who accepts a prison stay as part of a life of crime and aims to do her time without a great deal of discomfort while procuring an early release.[97]

Hefferman found that these personality traits were brought with the inmates from the outside and did not tend to change over the period of incarceration—giving further credibility to the importation model of prisonization discussed in Chapter 14.

The Pseudo-Family. As with males, a system of prisonization is evident in women's prisons. The adaptation process in the female institution, however, relies on tightly knit cliques of prisoners that mimic the traditional family structure. The more experienced convicts adopt the role of the "father" or "mother" and act as parent-figures for younger, inexperienced "sons" or "daughters." Inmates choose their role depending on appearance, personality, and background. As in "real" families, prison families restrict sexual contact between members, relying on each other primarily for emotional support.[98]

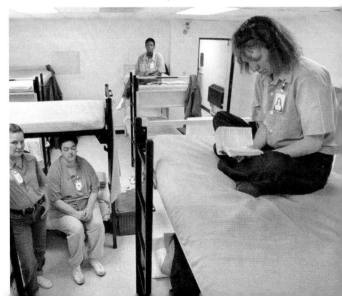

Inmates relax at the Iowa Correctional Institution for Women in Mitchellville, Iowa. Researchers have found that women in prison react differently to each other than do male inmates. What are some of the distinctive features of the culture in a women's correctional facility?

Homosexuality often manifests itself in a women's prison through formation of another traditional family model: the monogamous couple. One member of the couple chooses the role of the husband, and the other becomes the wife.[99] In general, sex between inmates plays a different role in women's prisons than in men's prisons. In the latter, rape is considered an act of aggression and power rather than sex, and "true" homosexuals are relegated to the lowest rungs of the social hierarchy. By contrast, women who engage in sexual activity in prison are not automatically labeled homosexual, and lesbians are not hampered in their social-climbing efforts.[100]

Researchers have also found that female inmates share a great deal more than their male counterparts. In a men's prison, self-sufficiency and autonomy are valued, whereas in women's prisons members of cliques and families allocate cosmetics, foods, clothes, and other goods.[101] (One observer points out that this greater tendency to share may be attributed to the fact that women are allowed more personal belongings in prison than men are.[102])

DIVERSITY IN CRIMINAL JUSTICE EMPLOYMENT

To this point, this chapter has concentrated on offenders in the criminal justice system. We now turn our attention to diversity among criminal justice employees. Despite legislation designed to encourage new hiring practices, their racial and gender make-up underrepresents both the diversity of the American population at large and the diversity of the people served by the criminal justice system. In this section, we will discuss efforts to improve the situation with regard to police officers, correctional officers, and judges.

Diversity in the Police Workforce

For many years, the typical American police officer was primarily white and male. As recently as 1968, the National Advisory Commission on Civil Disorder found that African Americans represented only 5 percent of all sworn officers in the United States.[103] Only in the past twenty-five years has this inconsistency been addressed, and only in the past decade have many police departments been actively trying to recruit women, African Americans, Hispanics, Asian Americans, and other minorities into the workforce.

To be sure, these steps were not taken entirely without external pressure. The 1964 Civil Rights Act and its 1972 amendments guaranteed minorities and woman equal access to jobs in law enforcement, and the Equal Employment Opportunity Act of 1972 set the stage for affirmative action in hiring and promotion. Court decisions also played a role in the transformation of the American police force. As a result of Supreme Court decisions in *Griggs v. Duke Power Company* (1971) and *Albermarle Paper Co. v. Moody* (1975),[104] police departments could be found in violation of federal law if their hiring and promotion policies were tainted by racial discrimination. In 1987, the Supreme Court upheld the constitutionality of an Alabama judge's order that the state's Department of Public Safety promote one qualified African American officer for every white officer who received a promotion. This order was based on the fact that no blacks had been hired as state troopers in nearly forty years in Alabama.[105]

Not all diversity efforts in law enforcement agencies have been ordered by legislators and the courts. Many departments, particularly those in urban areas, have realized that a culturally diverse police force can offer a number of benefits, including improved community relations and higher levels of service. The results of these changing attitudes, while not to the satisfaction of many observers, can be seen in the latest available figures on women and minorities in law enforcement agencies, which are summarized in Figure 18.9.

Figure 18.9 Minorities and Women as Law Enforcement Agents

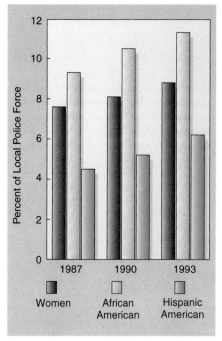

SOURCE: Brian Reaves, Local Police Departments, 1993 (Washington, D.C.: National Institute of Justice, 1996).

Minority Officers. The integration of African Americans and other minorities into the nation's police forces has been a slow process. Chicago hired its first black police officer in 1872, but African Americans still made up only 2 percent of the city's force in 1930. That same year, blacks made up 4 percent of police officers in Philadelphia, 2 percent in Pittsburgh, and less than 1 percent in such major cities as New York and Cleveland.[106]

Careers in Criminal Justice

MEDA CHESNEY-LIND, CRIMINOLOGIST

I have always felt that you should only study or do something if you have a passion for it. Otherwise, you will disappoint not only yourself but everyone else around you. From my earliest days as a student, I had a passion for learning, discovery, and human behavior, and I was deeply concerned about social justice and women's issues. Through the help of teachers and mentors, I have found a career that enables me to mix my interests in the local community, crime and victimization while teaching and creating new knowledge in the area of criminology. Although I received my B.A. and Ph.D. in sociology, I knew fairly quickly that the field of criminology was my intellectual home. I am now a Professor of Women's Studies at the University of Hawaii at Manoa, where I specialize in the study of the treatment of girls and women in the criminal justice system.

About fifteen years ago, when I was reading files compiled on youth referred to Honolulu's family court during the first half of this century, I ran across what I considered to be a bizarre pattern. Over half of the girls had been referred to court for "immorality," and another third were charged with being "Wayward." In reading the files, I discovered that this meant that the young women were suspected of being sexually active. Evidence of this "exposure" was vigorously pursued in all cases—and this was not subtle. Virtually all of the girls' files contained reports of gynecological examinations.

Later analysis of the data revealed the harsh sanctions imposed on girls found guilty of these offenses. Contrary to the widespread assumption about the chivalrous treatment of female offenders, the then skimpy literature on women's crime showed that a large number of girls were being incarcerated for noncriminal offenses.

Reflecting on this pattern, it occurred to me that girls were being treated in this fashion as the field of criminology was developing. So while criminologists, mostly male, were paying a lot of attention to the male delinquent, large numbers of girls were being processed, punished, and incarcerated. Indeed, one of the classic excuses for neglecting female offenders—their relatively small numbers—did not hold during these years. I found, for example, that girls made up half of those committed to Hawaii training schools well into the 1950s.

One reason for the neglect of girls may have been the inability of researchers to identify with their problems or situations. By contrast, I was not able to distance myself from their lives. At that time, the women's movement was a major part of my life. For the first time, I was seeing the connections between my life and the lives of other women.

As a young scholar working on my masters thesis, it was apparent that the delinquency theories I studied at the university could not account for the administration of these medical examinations, the use of examinations to categorize girls as "immoral," wayward or incorrigible offenders, and the harsh treatment of these girls. The extensive focus of criminological theory on disadvantaged males in public settings meant that the victimization of girls and the relationship between girls' problems and women's crime had been systematically ignored.

Through my own research, as well as the work of other feminist scholars, I have come to understand that we need to revise and expand criminological theory in order to include the experiences of girls and women. This has been a driving force in my career as a criminologist, and I am working to make sure that women and girls are not ignored in the theories that shape both the study and everyday practice of the criminal justice system.

These numbers changed with the implementation of affirmative action, but it would be a mistake to see minority representation on police forces solely in the traditional light of this policy. In general, affirmative action programs strive to increase opportunities for African Americans as a remedy for past injustices. In police departments, the programs have also sought to improve the overall effectiveness of the force.

For example, after a series of racially motivated riots in 1967, Detroit decided to increase its ratio of black police officers—which had been 5 percent in a city that was more than 50 percent African American. In a court case challenging the constitutionality of the use of quotas, the city argued that it needed a representative police force to fulfill its duties to the citizens of Detroit. The court agreed, noting that the presence of a "mostly white police force in minority communities can be a 'dangerous irritant' which can trig-

Tom Sanchez raises his hand as he is sworn in as the new chief of the Denver Police Department in 1998. Sanchez is the first Hispanic police chief in that city's history. The Hispanic community of Denver reacted favorably to the appointment. "Anytime we in the Hispanic community have someone put in a position like this, I believe it's a positive, in terms of leadership and being a role model," said Pete Salas, president of Denver's Hispanic League. What specific benefits do you believe come from having a member of a minority group assume a position of power in the criminal justice system, be it a police chief, judge, or prison warden?

ger" a destructive response.[107] In 1986, Supreme Court Justice John Paul Stevens concurred, stating that police administrators "might reasonably conclude that an integrated police force could develop a better relationship with the community and thereby do a more effective job of maintaining law and order than a force composed of white officers."[108]

The Limits of Progress. To a certain extent, the increase in minority representation in local police forces that we saw in Figure 18.9 has also occurred in leadership positions. In the past three decades, African Americans have been appointed as police commissioners or chiefs in some of the nation's police departments. The list includes William Hart (Detroit), Benjamin Ward (New York City), and Willie Williams (Los Angeles). Smaller cities are also becoming more open to minority leadership of their police forces, with African Americans taking control of police departments in Tacoma (Washington), Evansville (Indiana), and Portsmouth (Virginia) in 1998. Other minorities are seeing progress as well: in 1996 Fred Lau became the first Asian American appointed police chief in the history of the San Francisco Police Department.

Despite these hirings, the problems that have historically faced minority police officers have not been solved. First, the extensive programs to recruit minority officers have not been as successful as many observers had hoped. This has been attributed to a lack of aggressiveness on the part of police recruiters and the continuing negative view of law enforcement in minority communities, which discourages African Americans and Hispanics from applying for the jobs.[109] There are also other indications that discrimination still exists in the law enforcement community:

- In 1998, the New York City Police Department released a study acknowledging that minority officers are more likely to face punishment for breaking department rules than are white officers. African American and Hispanic officers, who account for 11.9 percent and 14 percent of the department's force, respectively, accounted for 19.2 percent and 17.8 percent of all disciplinary cases.[110]

- In 1996, the Bureau of Alcohol, Tobacco, and Firearms paid $5.9 million in damages and legal fees to a group of African American agents who had filed a lawsuit claiming they were discriminated against in promotions and pay.[111]

Many African American police officers also find that they must accept a racially charged work atmosphere as "part of the job." An African American sergeant in the Los Angeles Police Department recalled, "I had one fellow officer who was white, tell me that if he calls blacks niggers it shouldn't offend me because I'm blue, not black."[112]

Female Officers. Since the formation of the earliest police departments in the nineteenth century, policing has been seen as "man's work"—only men were considered to have the physical strength necessary to deal with the dangers of the street.[113] Statistically, the advance of women into police work has been even slower than that of minorities. The first female to serve in a police department was Lola Baldwin of Portland, Oregon, who was hired in 1905 to protect women and children from drunks during the Lewis and Clark Exposition. The first full-time female police officer was Alice Stebbin Wells, who joined the Los Angeles Police Department in 1910. By 1946, only 141 out of 417 American cities had any policewomen at all, and it was not until 1968 that a city—Indianapolis—had two female patrol officers on the force.[114]

Though the legal barriers to employment have for the most part fallen, policewomen must still contend with a number of on-the-job issues. In 1997,

The International Association of Women Police (at **www.iawp.org/**) **and the National Center for Women and Policing** (at **www.feminist.org/police/ ncwp.html**) **both offer Web sites with information and advice for women police officers.**

three female police officers in Visalia (California) filed a lawsuit that enumerated many of these issues. The lawsuit alleged that

- Female officers were not given their own rest rooms, changing rooms, and showers.
- Supervisors and other male officers made inappropriate, derogatory, and degrading comments of a sexual nature.
- Female officers were inappropriately touched.
- Female officers were not provided with backup support in the field.
- Female officers were passed over for promotion and advancement.[115]

That same year, a Minneapolis judge fined the city's police department $1.5 million for sexual harassment and gender discrimination. During the trial, one female officer testified that a male peer carried a pair of women's panties, which he used to wipe the sweat off his face.[116] (See Figure 18.10 for the results of a wide-ranging 1998 survey on women in policing.)

Policewoman are also under "constant pressures to demonstrate their competence and effectiveness vis-à-vis their male counterparts," says criminologist Susan Martin.[117] One female police officer describes this experience:

> I go to a call. They send another male officer and then another male officer. The attitude is—get a *guy*. I'm there with the one male officer and when the other guy shows up, the first male officer says to the second, this is right in front of me—"I'm glad you came."[118]

A number of studies have shown, however, that policewomen can be as effective as men in most situations, and sometimes more so. Citizens appear to prefer female police officers to males for service calls—especially those that involve domestic violence.[119] In general, policewomen are less aggressive and more likely to reduce the potential for a violent situation by relying on verbal skills rather than their authority as law enforcement agents.[120] Following its study of police brutality, which showed that none of the 120 officers with the highest-recorded levels of use of force were women, the Christopher Commission suggested that hiring more female police officers was one of the keys to reducing that particular problem.[121]

Female Corrections Officers

Traditionally, female corrections officers have been employed only in women's penal institutions. Since 1972, however, when Congress amended Title VII of the 1964 Civil Rights Act to prohibit employment discrimination on the basis of sex in government agencies,[122] the number of women working as custodial staff in all federal correctional facilities has grown to almost 12 percent. Questions of privacy and perceptions of female weakness still conspire, however, to make the correctional work environment a difficult one for women.

Figure 18.10 Female Police Officers: Still Facing Bias and Harassment

In 1998, the International Association of Chiefs of Police surveyed 800 police departments to provide a thorough analysis of women in policing. The results gave a valuable overview of the position of women in law enforcement.

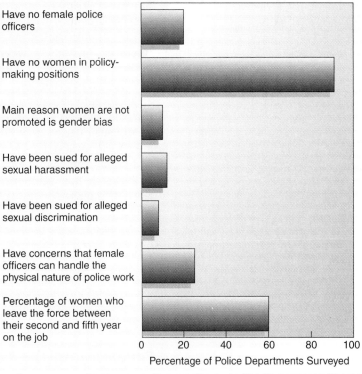

Percentage of Police Departments Surveyed

SOURCE: INTERNATIONAL ASSOCIATION OF CHIEFS OF POLICE, AD HOC COMMITTEE ON WOMEN IN POLICING, THE FUTURE OF WOMEN IN POLICING: MANDATES FOR ACTION (ALEXANDRIA, VA: INTERNATIONAL ASSOCIATION OF CHIEFS OF POLICE).

The entrance of female custodial employees into the prison environment has been the basis for a number of inmate Section 1983 lawsuits. One typical suit in this area, for example, alleged that prison officials violated male inmates' privacy rights by allowing female guards to view them in states of partial or total nudity when showering, dressing, or using the toilet.[123] Another lawsuit challenged a female guard's ability to strip-search male inmates.[124] In deciding these cases, many courts have relied on the precedent set by the Supreme Court in *Bell v. Wolfish* (1979),[125] which established that a prisoner's constitutional rights must be balanced against prison security. Therefore, inmates enjoy diminished privacy expectations. The need for correctional officers of both sexes to do their duties outweighs any discomfort that an inmate may experience while being searched by a member of the opposite sex.

The Supreme Court has heard only one case that dealt specifically with employment issues of female correctional guards. In *Dothard v. Rawlinson* (1977),[126] the justices held that although the state of Alabama could not discriminate against women in its general hiring practices, it did have the right to preclude women from "contact positions"—those requiring close proximity to male inmates. The Court's reasoning that inmates would attack a female guard simply because of her gender permeates the "real world" of prisons and jails. One study found that female correctional officers in men's prisons actually exhibited more aggressive behavioral tendencies than their male counterparts, probably as a defense mechanism against the belief that they were "too soft" for the job.[127] As in other areas of the criminal justice system, sexism and sexual harassment continue to plague the corrections workplace.[128]

Minority Corrections Officers

Traditionally, the ranks of corrections officers have been drawn from the rural areas in which prisons are located, meaning that most of the officers were white. Today, 23 percent of correctional officers employed by the Federal Bureau of Prisons are African American and 12 percent are Hispanic. Many observers believe that, ultimately, the percentage of minority correctional officers should match the percentage of minority inmates. The theory is that the racial tensions between officers and inmates could be alleviated if more of the officers were of the same race and ethnicity as the prisoners. At least with regard to juvenile correctional facilities, a judge has upheld this theory as an acceptable reason for hiring African American officers based solely on the color of their skin. In *Wittmer v. Peters* (1996),[129] the Seventh Circuit Court of Appeals ruled that an Illinois boot camp where 68 percent of the offenders are African American was justified in using race as the main factor in hiring additional staff members.

Research has been inconclusive in establishing whether similar backgrounds improve relations between officers and inmates in adult facilities. A survey of 179 correctional officers carried out by University of Arizona professor Nancy C. Jurik found that hiring minority officers had little effect on negative staff views of inmates.[130] Another study done at the Texas Department of Corrections discovered that the race of correctional officers did not lessen punitive and aggressive attitudes toward inmates.[131] One explanation for this may be that prison administrators only hire correctional officers—no matter what their race—who are generally unsympathetic toward inmates.[132]

Diversity on the Bench

The process by which judges are "hired" is not, as we saw in Chapter 8, comparable to the employment of police or custodial officers. The issue of gender and race is inherent in the unwritten "golden rule" of judicial selection: who becomes a judge is often a reflection of who selects judges. A criticism of the Missouri Plan (see page 284), for example, is that the members of the selection committees, who are mostly white, upper-class attorneys, nominate mostly white, upper-class attorneys.[133] In South Carolina, the state legislature chooses judicial candidates; not surprisingly, a disproportionate number of South Carolina state judges are ex-legislators. Only 6 percent of Georgia's state judges are African American, compared to 27 percent of the state's population—a disproportionality mirrored throughout the United States.

Diversity in State Courts. The average state court judge is a white, educated, male ex-attorney. It was not until 1979 that every state had a woman on the bench, and today only about 10 percent of state judges are female. Given that the primary background of judges is in the law, as more women become lawyers the number of female state judges is expected to increase. A number of studies have tried to determine whether female judges rule differently than their male counterparts, but have reached no conclusive results.[134]

The underrepresentation of minority judges on state courts also continues to present a challenge. Although the number of minorities employed by state judicial system is close to 20 percent (higher than the general population) most of those jobs are clerical and menial. Traditionally, efforts to diversify state judges have met with resistance from those who insist that judges must be impartial, so by definition it makes no difference whether a judge is African American, Asian American, Hispanic American, or white. Sherrilyn A. Ifill of the University of Maryland School of Law rejects this argument, pointing out that judicial elections are often justified for their role in "connecting" judges to the communities they serve.[135] According to Ifill, the lack of diversity on many state trial courts has a number of consequences:

1. Disproportionate sentencing of African American youths versus white youths who have committed similar crimes.
2. Disproportionate denial of bail to African American offenders.
3. Unfair imposition of the death penalty on African American defendants accused of killing white victims.
4. Preference given to the testimony of white witnesses over comparable black witnesses.

Ifill suggests that the Voting Rights Act of 1965, which shifted district boundaries to increase representation of minorities in legislatures, should be applied to state judgeships as well. The Supreme Court has also held this opinion, ruling in 1991 that the act, as amended in 1982, applies to judicial elections as well.[136] The effect of this decision can be seen in the states that hold judicial elections, such as Arkansas, where ten new judicial seats were recently created in predominantly African American communities.

Diversity in Federal Courts. Determining the causes of diversification in federal courts is a relatively simple task because the selection process relies primarily on the political will of the sitting president. For example, nearly two out of every three federal judges appointed by President Bill Clinton were women or minorities. By comparison, only 27.6 percent of those appointed by his predecessor, George Bush, were women or minorities.

Of the 108 justices who have served on the Supreme Court, only two have been women and two have been members of a minority group. Sandra Day O'Connor became the first woman appointed to the Supreme Court (by President Ronald Reagan) in 1981, and Clinton appointed the second, Ruth Bader Ginsburg, in 1993. Both continue to sit on the Court. Thurgood Marshall (1970–1991) and Clarence Thomas (1991–present), both African American, have been the only two minorities represented.

Stanley Mills has served as a circuit court judge in Florida since 1989. What are some of the challenges that members of minority groups face when being named to the bench in state courts?

Criminal Justice in Action
Hate Crimes and the Law

The American legal system continues to expand and evolve to match the needs of a changing social and political landscape. As minorities and women gain greater access to the pathways of power in the United States, their concerns are more likely to be met by society's institutions, such as the criminal justice system. In this chapter, we have noted some of the ways in which diversity has affected the way we make and implement criminal laws in this country. Here we look a relatively new set of statutes designed to protect those Americans who have not always enjoyed sanctuary in the law.

A BRUTAL CRIME

On October 8, 1998, the body of twenty-one-year-old University of Wyoming freshman Matthew Shepard was found tied to a deer fence off Snowy Mountain View Road, one mile east of Laramie. Shepard's head and face had been brutally beaten, his arms were scorched with burn marks, and he had been left unconscious and bleeding on the fence for nearly eighteen hours. Five days later, he died in a local hospital while on life support. In investigating the crime, local police found that the two men who had beaten Shepard had been at least partly motivated by the fact that their victim was homosexual. According to friends of suspects Russel Henderson and Aaron McKinney, Shepard had embarrassed the two men by making passes at them at a local bar. Following the incident, Henderson and McKinney pretended to be gay themselves to lure Shepard into a pickup truck, whereupon they beat him, drove him out of town, stole his money, and tied him to the fence.

Shephard was one of the approximately 10,000 Americans victimized by hate crimes each year because of race, ethnicity, sexual orientation, religion, or disability (see Figure 18.11). Wyoming is one of only nine states that does not have a **hate crime law**—a fact raised numerous times in the wake of Shepard's death by those who felt the lack of such a law created a climate in which verbal and physical attacks against homosexuals were subtly tolerated. Hate crime laws provide for greater sanctions against those who commit crimes motivated by animosity against a person or group because of race, ethnicity, religion, gender, sexual orientation, disability, or age. Shepard's murder also provided a platform for President Clinton to urge Congress to pass the Federal Hate Crimes Prevention Act, something it had failed to do earlier in the year. Opponents, however, continue to debate the necessity of such laws and question their validity given the First Amendment protection of freedom of speech.

HATE CRIME LAW
A statute that provides for greater sanctions against those who commit crimes motivated by animosity against an individual or a group based on race, ethnicity, religion, gender, sexual orientation, disability, or age.

PENALTY ENHANCEMENT STATUTES

In fact, some hate crime legislation already exists at the federal level. As noted earlier in the chapter, violence motivated by gender can be prosecuted under the Violence Against Women Act of 1994.[137] The Hate Crime Statistics Act of 1990 ordered the Federal Bureau of Investigation to gather data on hate crimes from local law enforcement agencies.[138]

Figure 18.11 Offenses Motivated by Bias

In 1997, the Federal Bureau of Investigation reported 9,861 bias-motivated offenses. This chart shows the percentage distribution of the motivating factors.

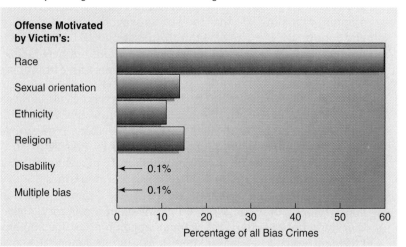

Offense Motivated by Victim's:

- Race
- Sexual orientation
- Ethnicity
- Religion
- Disability ← 0.1%
- Multiple bias ← 0.1%

Percentage of all Bias Crimes (0, 10, 20, 30, 40, 50, 60)

SOURCE: ADAPTED FROM FEDERAL BUREAU OF INVESTIGATION, CRIME IN THE UNITED STATES, 1997 (WASHINGTON, D.C.: U.S. DEPARTMENT OF JUSTICE, 1998), CHART 2.18 AT PAGE 61.

Judy and Dennis Shepard speak at a news conference in Casper, Wyoming, following the death of their son, Matthew.

The full weight of prosecuting hate crimes, however, has fallen for the most part on those states that have passed relevant laws. In general, these laws are based on a model created by the Anti-Defamation League (ADL) in 1981. The ADL model was centered around the concept of "penalty enhancement": just as someone who robs a convenience store using a gun will face a greater penalty than if he or she had been unarmed, so will someone who commits a crime because of prejudice against her or his victim or victims.[139] In 1997, for example, Gunner Lindbergh, the leader of a white supremacist gang, was convicted of first degree murder in Santa Ana, California, for killing a young Vietnamese American named Thien Minh Ly. Because a jury decided that the homicide has been motivated by the victim's ethnicity, Lindbergh was eligible for, and received, the death penalty.[140]

The specifics of hate crime legislation vary from jurisdiction to jurisdiction. Not all states follow the penalty enhancement model, preferring instead to create new categories of crimes committed "because of" or "by reason of" the victim's characteristics. Some states do not specify which groups are protected by the legislation, while others list some aspects, such as race, but not others, such as mental or physical disability. Furthermore, some states establish training in dealing with hate crimes for law enforcement personnel. A number of police departments have created specialized bias units to prevent and collect data on hate crimes.

INFOTRAC®
COLLEGE EDITION

Humm, Andy. **Social insecurity. need to give equal rights**

SUPREME COURT RULINGS

The legal basis for hate crime legislation was established by two cases heard by the Supreme Court in the early 1990s. In *R.A.V. v. St. Paul* (1992),[141] the Court reviewed a case involving a group of white teenagers who burned a cross on the lawn of an African American family in St. Paul, Minnesota. One of the youths, who had been arrested and convicted under the city's Bias-Motivated Crime Ordinance, claimed that the law violated his right to free speech. The Minnesota Supreme Court upheld the conviction, ruling that the law was constitutional because it applied only to "fighting words," or speech that is likely to evoke a violent response. The Supreme Court, however, reversed the state court's decision, holding that the statute was too broad and therefore could be used to outlaw forms of expression that are protected under the First Amendment, as well as "fighting words."

The following year, however, the Supreme Court upheld Wisconsin's Penalty Enhancement Statute in *State of Wisconsin v. Todd Mitchell* (1993).[142] The case involved Todd Mitchell, a nineteen-year-old African American who incited his friends to attack a white teenager after viewing the film *Mississippi Burning.* The victim was left in a coma for two days, and Mitchell was convicted of felony aggravated battery and sentenced to two years in prison, plus an additional two years under the state's hate crime law. The Court upheld the statute, reasoning that the results of hate crime, such as community fear, justify harsher punishments. Furthermore, it ruled that speech could be used as evidence of motive, and because motive is an integral part of sentencing, hate speech could be used to augment sentences.

PROTECTING SPEECH, NOT ACTIONS

In sum, the Supreme Court had ruled that whereas the city of St. Paul was punishing the white teenager for his beliefs, which is unconstitutional, Wisconsin was punishing Todd Mitchell for acting on his beliefs, which is not. In other words, the First Amendment protects the right to be a racist and to make racist statements, but not to take part in racist attacks.[143] To assure that constitutional requirements are met, most state hate crime laws require prosecutors to clearly establish the link between a wrongdoer's selection of a particular victim and the victim's race, religion, gender, or other characteristic.

Supporters of hate crime legislation believe that such laws are important because the intended victim is usually not an individual, but an entire group of citizens.[144] By passing laws protecting a minority group, society allows that group to feel less isolated and safer and makes a strong statement about what type of behavior is considered unacceptable. (The lack of such laws, many residents believe, was severely felt in Matthew Shepard's Wyoming.) Furthermore, as with any law that increases penalties for specific criminal acts, supporters of hate crime legislation believe these statutes deter such actions.

QUESTIONING HATE LAWS

Many of those who question the validity of hate crime legislation do so on First Amendment grounds. Punish Todd Mitchell for his acts, they say, but not for his beliefs, which he has a constitutional right to hold. Some of these opponents also question laws that seem to indicate that some victims are worthy of more protection than others. They find it disturbing that Mitchell would have received a lesser sentence if he and his friends had beaten an African American youth instead of a white youth.[145]

In addition, James B. Jacobs, a professor of law at New York University, points out that it is difficult enough to establish the *mens rea* (intent) of someone who has committed a criminal act without trying to establish his or her motivation.[146] Jacobs envisions court cases bogged down by prosecutors trying to establish the defendant's levels of prejudice and bias, a difficult task considering the deep psychological and sociological roots of such feelings. Law enforcement officials are also wary of the demands of hate crime legislation. "I'm very fearful of the concept of thought police," said a commander in the Kenosha (Wisconsin) police department. "It makes me nervous."[147]

Key Terms

discrimination 645

disparity 645

frustration-aggression theory 643

gender-neutral 649

hate crime law 660

liberal feminist theory 644

masculinity hypothesis 643

security threat groups (STGs) 652

social reality of crime 642

Chapter Summary

1. **Indicate the two reasons why it is important to study diversity in the criminal justice system.** First, by observing patterns of criminality and victimization, members of the criminal justice system can adjust crime-fighting strategies accordingly. Secondly, if certain minority groups or women are found to be treated in a discriminatory manner, then the system must adjust its methods to correct these inconsistencies.

2. **Outline the basic racial, ethnic, and gender trends in crime.** Although two-thirds of the persons arrested and a majority of prisoners are white, minorities are arrested in disproportionate numbers to their populations, and relative to their populations, there are more than seven times as many minorities in prison than whites. Women, in contrast, are involved in about 20 percent of all arrests and constitute a small percentage of the prison population. The rate of incarcerated women is growing at almost twice the rate of men, however.

3. **Briefly describe the social reality of crime theory.** This theory hypothesizes that the criminal justice system is a tool of society's most powerful classes, such that criminal law reflects a set of "rules" through which those who hold power can control and subdue those who do not. It follows that conflicts between the "haves" and "have-nots" will be decided in favor of the "haves." Violations of the law are therefore inherently political acts, not criminal ones. Given that African Americans have been "have-nots" for several hundred years, they suffer at the hands of the "haves." The same theory applies to women.

4. **Trace the progression of theories about the causes of female criminality from the late 1800s until today.** Early criminologists upheld the masculinity hypothesis, concluding that female criminals were abnormal women, and biologically more like men. Then the socialization theory argued that boys were given the freedom to develop physical skills and male rituals that prepared them for delinquency, whereas girls were expected to be ladylike and were subject to more restrictions. Next the liberal feminist theory of female criminality became popular in the mid-1970s; it argued that crime should be viewed in terms of the power relationship between men and women. Finally, postfeminist theories argue that the new female criminal is a single mother with children who commits property crimes out of need or abuses drugs as an avenue of escape from a difficult situation.

5. **Contrast the disparity view with the discrimination view of disproportionate crime statistics for minorities.** The disparity view argues that inconsistencies in arrests and incarceration rates for minorities result from legitimate factors in the decision-making processes of judges, prosecutors, police officers, and other criminal justice system authority figures. In contrast, the discrimination view argues that all such disparities are based on illegitimate influences, such as a suspect's race.

6. **Explain why crack sentencing laws have been viewed as racist.** The Omnibus Crime Prevention Act of 1986 established a ratio of 100:1 for the punishment of selling or using crack cocaine as compared to powder cocaine. Even though about half of crack users are white, they make up only 4 percent of all convictions on crack-related charges. Eighty-five percent of federal crack convictions involve African Americans.

7. **Outline the reasons why female offenders are less likely to go to prison than male offenders or, if sent to prison, why they receive shorter sentences.** First, in property crimes women are usually accessories, and in violent crimes women are usually reacting to physical abuse. The chivalry effect may also be at work in the decisions of prosecutors, judges, and juries. Prosecutors are more likely to offer women beneficial plea bargains. Judges seem to be influenced by mitigating factors, such as marital status and family background, which they often ignore when sentencing men.

8. **Define balkanization as it relates to prisons.** Balkanization refers to informal segregation within a population. Today's prisons are balkanized almost exclusively on the basis of race and ethnicity. In some cases balkanization continues within racial units based on the geographical homes of the prisoners. Prison gangs almost exclusively follow racial and ethnic lines.

9. **Explain why the presence of female custodial employees in jails and prisons has instigated inmate Section 1983 lawsuits.** Most of these lawsuits involve male prisoners arguing that female prison guards violate male inmates' privacy rights. The Supreme Court has indicated, though,

that it is constitutional for inmates to enjoy diminished privacy expectations.

10. **List some of the purported consequences of the lack of diversity in state trial courts.** (a) Disproportionate sentencing for minorities versus majorities committing similar crimes, particularly with respect to juveniles; (b) disproportionate denial of bail to minority offenders; (c) unfair imposition of the death penalty on African Americans accused of killing whites; and (d) preference given to the testimony of white witnesses over comparable black witnesses.

Questions for Critical Analysis

1. What is the main problem in using the FBI's Uniform Crime Reports to obtain data about the relationship between crime and race or ethnicity?

2. Some criminologists have suggested that the way to reduce crime is by helping inner-city residents move to the suburbs. What is the reasoning behind this suggestion?

3. How might the culture of the inner city lead to increased male criminality there?

4. What might cause police officers to concentrate on arresting more minorities in inner cities compared to whites in suburbia?

5. What additional cost has been imposed on society due to the application of mandatory minimum sentences to female criminals?

6. How does the adaptation process in a women's prison differ from that in a men's prison?

7. Have Congress and the judicial system been the only factors in causing police departments to become more racially diverse? Explain your answer.

8. Under what circumstances might a female police officer be more effective than a male officer?

9. How does the concept of penalty enhancement relate to hate crime laws?

10. Provide the arguments for and against hate crime laws.

Selected Print and Electronic Resources

SUGGESTED READINGS

Daly, Kathleen, *Gender, Crime, and Punishment*, New Haven: Yale University Press, 1996. The author examines women's and men's offenses, including homicide, robbery, larceny, and aggravated assault, that are routinely processed in felony courts. She discovers sentencing disparity according to gender. Her results are presented both numerically and narratively.

Jacobs, James B., and Kimberly Potter, *Hate Crimes: Criminal Law and Identity Politics*, New York: Oxford University Press, 1998. This book presents the controversial view that the definitions of hate crimes are often too vague to be meaningful. The authors argue

that the development of hate crime legislation is wrongheaded. Indeed, they argue that virtually every crime is motivated by hate of one kind or another. Specifically, they state that all individuals who are victims deserve equal protection under the law.

Kappeler, Victor E., et al., *Forces of Deviance: Understanding the Dark Side of Policing*, Prospect Heights, IL: Waveland Press, 1998. These authors look at the discretionary authority and power granted to the police. They argue that such a situation creates opportunities for deviance, which may result in gender discrimination as well as discrimination according to race.

Kennedy, Randall, *Race, Crime, and the Law*, New York: Pantheon, 1997. This is a provocative book. Kennedy looks at views both from the right and from the left, conservative and liberal, with respect to the issue of crime and race. He points out when and how racial issues become obstacles to the fair workings of our criminal justice system. He argues that liberals and conservatives have more common ground on race and law than it seems at first blush.

Russell, Katheryn K., *The Color of Crime*, New York: New York University Press, 1998. The author illustrates through examples the lasting damage that occurs when racial stereotypes are manipulated and exploited. She examines numerous racial hoaxes that have been used to protect various individuals from being accused of crimes.

MEDIA RESOURCES

In the Heat of the Night (1967) It's a dark night in the deep South—Sparta, Mississippi, to be exact. After a patrol officer stumbles across a dead body, the local police arrest the most obvious suspect in town: Virgil Tibbs (Sidney Poitier), a well-dressed stranger who is implicated solely because he is African American. Tibbs, as it turns out, is a Philadelphia homicide detective, and after local sheriff Bill Gillespie (Rod Steiger) decides that Tibbs is not a suspect, he convinces the northerner to stay and help solve the case. At the time of its release, *In the Heat of the Night* was remarkable for both its frank treatment of racism and its casting of an African American in a starring role.

Critically analyze this film:

1. *In the Heat of the Night* was released more than thirty years ago. Are the issues that the film addresses still relevant? Explain your answer.

2. How does Tibbs react to Sheriff Gillespie's overt racism? How does he overcome it? What do you think is the "message" of the relationship between the two men, if there is one?

3. How does this film implicitly support the argument that minority police officers lessen instances of discrimination in law enforcement?

4. Does this film rely too heavily on racial and geographical stereotypes, by today's standards? For example, are Americans justified in thinking that such attitudes toward African Americans still exist in the South?

Logging On

Court TV has developed a mini-unit on justice and the law that concerns hate crimes. Though the lessons in this unit are designed for adolescents, they do offer an overview of how to make people aware of the hate crime problem in the United States. Go to:

http://staging.courttv.com/choices/curriculum/hatecrime/

If you want to read a private view of "whiteness" in police departments, you can go to a Web site at the University of California at Berkeley:

http://garnet.berkeley.edu/~annaleen/whiteness_police.html

You can find out more about women and prisons by going to the following web site:

www.prisonactivist.org/women/

Using the internet for Criminal Justice Analysis

INFOTRAC® COLLEGE EDITION

1. Go to your InfoTrac College Edition at www.infotrac-college.com/wadsworth/. After you log on, type in the words: RACE AND THE PROBLEM OF CRIME IN "TIME" AND "NEWSWEEK" COVER STORIES

The author of this article argues, after intensive study, that the media have led to the popular stereotyping of "young black males" as criminals. Both *Time* and *Newsweek* are accused of portraying crime as mainly a problem of urban blacks. Read the article and answer the following questions:

a. When does the author date the first news reports on violence that led to the association between crime and urban African Americans?

b. What is the author's thesis of how and when crime began to be racialized?

c. How does the author contend whites in middle-class communities would react if the same police tactics were used there that are used in urban underclass ghettos?

d. Go to the conclusion and summarize the author's findings.

2. You can discover statistics on victims according to race/ethnicity. Go to the Sourcebook of Criminal Justice Statistics, which can be found at: **www.albany.edu/sourcebook**

Once you are there, click on *searching by key words*. Then on the next page, click on "search" in one of the boxes at the bottom of the page. On the next page, click on "*Search the Index*." Then go down and click on *victimization*. Next click on the file under assault labeled *Race/ethnicity of victim*. Once there, answer the following questions:

a. For the latest year, is there a difference between the rates at which black and white, households are victims of violent crimes?

b. In Table 3.3 can you find a category of crime for which blacks constitute a higher percentage of victims than whites?

c. For which categories of violent crimes were Hispanics more victimized than non-Hispanics?

d. Do you see a major difference in victimization rates for violent crimes between Hispanics and non-Hispanics?

Notes

1. Dennis B. Roddy, "Young Black Males Taught Lesson in Caution," *Pittsburgh Post-Gazette* (November 5, 1995), A1.
2. Mark Clements, "Findings from Parade's National Survey on Law and Order," *Chicago Sun-Times* (April 18, 1993), 4.
3. Randall Kennedy, *Race, Crime, and the Law* (New York: Pantheon, 1997), 14.
4. Katheryn K. Russell, *The Color of Crime* (New York: New York University Press, 1998), 123.
5. *The Prosecution of Felony Arrests* (Washington, D.C.: Office of Justice Programs, U.S. Department of Justice, 1987).
6. *The Violence against Women Act of 1991: The Civil Rights Remedy: A National Call for Protection against Violent Gender-Based Discrimination,* U.S. Senate Report No. 197, 102nd Congress, 1st Session, 37.
7. Margaret Farnworth, Raymond H. C. Teske, Jr., and Gina Thurman, "Ethnic, Racial, and Minority Disparity in Felony Court Processing," in *Race and Criminal Justice,* ed. Michael J. Lynch and E. Britt Patterson (New York: Harrow & Heston, 1991), 55–7.
8. Russell, 111–29.
9. Robert Tillman, "The Size of the 'Criminal Population': The Prevalence and Incidence of Adult Arrests," *Criminology* (Fall 1987), 335–47.
10. Marvin D. Free, Jr., *African Americans and the Criminal Justice System* (New York: Garland Publishing, 1996), 7–8.
11. Kenneth F. Schoen and Julie Peterson, "How Powerful Is Prison as a Crime Fighting Tool?" *Perspectives* (Summer 1996), 36.
12. The Report of the National Criminal Justice Association, *The Real War on Crime* (New York: HarperPerennial, 1996), 106–7.
13. Bureau of Justice Statistics, *Survey of State Prison Inmates 1991* (Washington, D.C.: U.S. Department of Justice, 1993), 6.
14. Bureau of Justice Statistics, *Prison and Jail Inmates at Midyear 1997* (Washington, D.C.: U.S. Department of Justice, 1997), 4.
15. Tracy L. Snell, *Women in Prison: Survey of State Prison Inmates, 1991* (Washington, D.C.: U.S. Department of Justice, 1994), 3.
16. Bureau of Justice Statistics, *Sourcebook of Criminal Justice Statistics, 1996* (Washington, D.C.: U.S. Department of Justice, 1997), 340.
17. Angela Browne and Kirk R. Williams, "Exploring the Effect of Resource Availability and the Likelihood of Female-Perpetrated Homicides," *Law and Society Review* 23 (1989), 75–94.
18. 42 U.S.C. Section 13981(b) (1994).
19. Stephanie Stapleton, "Surgeon General Nominee Has Smooth Sailing So Far," *American Medical News* (October 27, 1997), 6.
20. John H. DiIulio, *Rethinking the Criminal Justice System* (Washington, D.C.: Bureau of Justice Statistics, 1994).
21. U.S. Department of Justice, *Criminal Victimization in the United States, 1991* (Washington, D.C.: U.S. Government Printing Office, 1992).
22. Darnell F. Hawkins, "The Nations Within: Race, Class, Religion and American Lethal Violence," *University of Colorado Law Review* 69 (Fall 1998), 905.
23. Russell, 126.
24. *Ibid.,* 114.
25. Jody D. Armour, "Race Ipsa Loquitur," *Stanford Law Review* 46 (1994), 781–7.

26. Charles M. Sennott, "Case Confirms Some Fears of Racism in S.C. Town," *Boston Globe* (November 6, 1994), 22.

27. James Q. Wilson, "Fear of Black Crime Is Justified," in *Crime and Criminals: Opposing Viewpoints,* ed. Paul A. Winters (San Diego, CA: Greenhaven Press, 1995), 253.

28. Randy L. Lagrange and Kenneth F. Ferraro, "Assessing Age and Gender Differences in Perceived Risk and Fear of Crime," *Criminology* 27 (1989), 697–718.

29. *Ibid.*

30. Joanne Belknap, *The Invisible Woman: Gender, Crime, and Gender* (Belmont, CA: Wadsworth Publishing Co., 1996), 124.

31. Tracy L. Snell, *Women in Prison: Survey of State Prison Inmates, 1991* (Washington, D.C.: U.S. Department of Justice, 1994), Table 8 at page 5.

32. Dorothy S. McCellan, David Farabee, and Ben M. Crouch, "Early Victimization, Drug Use, and Criminality," *Criminal Justice and Behavior* 24 (December 1997), 456–8.

33. Richard Quinney, *The Social Reality of Crime* (Boston: Little, Brown, 1970).

34. Jeffrey H. Birnbaum, "Fannie Mae: Spinning Idealism into Gold," *Fortune* (August 3, 1998), 101.

35. Dan R. Dalton and Catherine Daily, "Women in the Boardroom Are Still on the Outside," *Chicago Tribune* (March 14, 1999), 7.

36. Nicole Hahn Rafter, *Partial Justice: Women, Prisons, and Social Control* (New Brunswick: Transaction Publishers, 1990).

37. Jerome Miller and Barry Holman, *Hobbling a Generation: African American Males in the Disctrict of Columbia's Criminal Justice System* (Washington, D.C.: National Center on Institutions and Alternatives, March 1992).

38. Dave Huizinga and Delbert Elliot, "Juvenile Offenders: Prevalence, Offender Incidence, and Arrest Rates by Race," *Crime and Delinquency* 33 (1987), 206–23.

39. Willie Dantzler, Jr., *Why Black Males Are Conditioned to Fail* (East St. Louis, IL: Essai Seay Publications, 1991).

40. Coramae R. Mann, *Unequal Justice: A Question of Color* (Bloomington, IN: Indiana University Press, 1993).

41. James P. Comer, "Black Violence and Public Policy," in *American Violence and Public Policy,* ed. Lynn Curtis (New Haven, CT: Yale University Press, 1985), 81.

42. Carol Smart, *Woman, Crime, and Criminology: A Feminist Critique* (London: Routledge & Kegan Paul, 1976), 33.

43. Dale Hoffman-Bustamante, "The Nature of Female Criminality," *Issues in Criminology* 8 (1973), 117–23.

44. Rita James Simon, *Women and Crime* (Lexington, MA: Lexington Books, 1975).

45. Freda Adler, *Sisters in Crime: The Rise of the New Female Criminal* (New York: McGraw-Hill, 1975).

46. Jane Roberts Chapman, *Economic Realities and Female Crime* (Lexington, MA: Lexington, Books, 1980).

47. Stefanie Fleischer Seldin, "A Strategy for Advocacy on Behalf of Women Offenders," *Columbia Journal of Gender and Law* 1 (1995), 1.

48. Kathleen Daly, "Women's Pathways to Felony Court: Feminist Theory of Lawbreaking and Problems of Representation," *Review of Law and Women's Studies* 2 (1992), 11–52.

49. William N. Brownsberger, *Profile of Anti-Drug Law Enforcement in Urban Poverty Areas of Massachusetts* (Cambridge, MA; Harvard University Press, November 1997).

50. Larry Michael Fehr, "Racial and Ethnic Disparities in Prosecution and Sentencing: Empirical Research of the Washington State Minority and Justice Commission," *Gonzaga Law Review* 32 (1996–1997), 577.

51. Ian Ayres and Joel Wadfogel, "A Market Test for Race Discrimination in Bail Setting," *Stanford Law Review* 46 (May 1994), 987.

52. Bureau of Justice Statistics, *Police Use of Force: Collection of National Data* (Washington, D.C.: U.S. Department of Justice, November 1997).

53. Sean Hecker, "Race and Pretextual Traffic Stops: An Expanded Role for Civilian Review," *Columbia Human Rights Law Review* 28 (Spring 1997), 551.

54. Memorandum in Support of Plaintiffs' Motion for Enforcement of Settlement Agreement and for Further Relief, *Wilkins v. Maryland State Police,* Civil Action No. CCB-93-468, 1. (This study is available at http://www.aclu.org/court/mspset.html.)

55. William J. Chambliss, "Policing the Ghetto Underclass: The Politics of Law and Law Enforcement," *Social Problems* 41 (May 1994), 177–94.

56. *Ibid.,* 179.

57. Randall L. Kennedy, "*McCleskey v. Kemp,* Race, Capital Punishment, and the Supreme Court," *Harvard Law Review* 101 (1988), 1436–8.

58. Douglas A. Smith, "Minorities and the Police: Attitudinal and Behavioral Questions," *Race and Criminal Justice,* ed. Michael J. Lynch and E. Britt Patterson (New York: Harrow & Heston, 1991), 28–30.

59. Sarah Lee Browning, "Race and Getting Hassled by the Police: A Research Note," *Police Studies* 17 (1994), 3.

60. Willard Gaylin, *Partial Justice: A Study of Bias in Sentencing* (New York: Knopf, 1974), 162, 165.

61. See *United States Sentencing Common Guidelines Manual* Section 2D1.1(c) (1994).

62. William Spade, Jr., "Beyond the 100:1 Ratio: Towards a Rational Cocaine Sentencing Policy," *Arizona Law Review* 38 (Winter 1996), 1233.

63. U.S. Sentencing Commission, *Cocaine and Federal Sentencing Policy* (Washington, D.C.: The Commission, 1995), 156.

64. 517 U.S. 456 (1996).

65. Tracey L. McCain, "The Interplay of Editorial and Prosecutorial Discretion in the Perpetuation of Racism in the Criminal Justice System," *Columbia Journal of Law and Social Problems* 25 (1992), 601.

66. Scott Shepherd, "More Blacks Agreeing with Death Penalty, Data Show," *Fresno Bee* (April 18, 1998) A6.

67. Janice Joseph, "Young, Black, and Sentenced to Die: Black Males and the Death Penalty," *Challenge: A Journal of Research on African American Men* 7 (December 1996), 68.

68. 481 U.S. 279 (1987).

69. David C. Baldus, George Woodworth, and Charles A. Pulaski, *Equal Justice and the Death Penalty: A Legal and Empirical Analysis* (Boston: Northeastern University Press, 1990), 140–97, 306.

70. Alfred Blumstein, "Research on Sentencing," *Justice System Journal* 7 (1982), 307–30.

71. Ayres and Wadfogel, 988.

72. Brownsberger.

73. Free, 102.

74. Belknap, 69–70.

75. Jean E. Rhodes and Karla Fischer, "Spanning the Gender Gap: Gender Differences in Delinquency among Inner-City Adolescents," *Adolescence* 28 (1993), 879–83.

76. Anne Bowen Poulin, "Female Delinquents: Defining Their Place in the Justice System," *Wisconsin Law Review* (1996), 541.

77. Belknap, 78–9.

78. Federal Bureau of Investigation, *Crime in the United States, 1997* (Washington, D.C.: U.S. Department of Justice, 1998) Table 42 at page 239.

79. Clarice Feinman, *Women in the Criminal Justice System*, 3d ed. (Westport, CT: Praeger), 35.

80. Ilene H. Nagel and Barry L. Johnson, "The Role of Gender in a Structured Sentencing System: Equal Treatment, Policy Choices, and the Sentencing of Female Offenders under the United States Sentencing Guidelines," *Journal of Criminal Law and Criminology* 85 (1994), 181–90.

81. Darrell Steffensmeir, John Kramer and Cathy Streifel, "Gender and Imprisonment Decisions," *Criminology* 31 (1993), 411; and David P. Farrington and Allison M. Morris, "Sex, Sentencing, and Reconvictions," *British Journal of Criminology* 23 (1983), 229.

82. Quoted in Raymond Smith, "Death Penalty Rare for Women," *Press-Enterprise* (Riverside, California) (July 30, 1998), A12.

83. John Moritz, "Support for Death Penalty Declines among Texans," *Forth Worth Star-Telegram* (March 15, 1998), 1.

84. Myrna S. Raeder, "Gender and Sentencing: Single Moms, Battered Women, and Other Sex-Based Anomalies in the Gender-Free World of the Federal Sentencing Guidelines," *Pepperdine Law Review* 20 (1993), 948.

85. Clarice Feinman, *Women in the Criminal Justice System*, 33–37.

86. Rafter, 155.

87. Elliot Currie, *Crime and Punishment in America* (New York: Metropolitan Books, 1998), 14.

88. Marilyn C. Moses, *Keeping Incarcerated Mothers and Their Daughters Together: Girl Scouts behind Bars* (Washington, D.C.: National Institute of Justice, October 1995).

89. John Irwin, *Prisons in Turmoil* (Boston: Little, Brown, 1980), 47

90. Leo Carroll, "Race, Ethnicity and the Social Order of the Prison," in *The Pains of Imprisonment*, ed. R. Johnson and H. Toch (Beverly Hills, CA: Sage, 1982).

91. Quoted in Leo Carroll, *Hacks, Blacks, and Cons: Race Relations in a Maximum-Security Prison* (Lexington, MA: Lexington Books, 1988), 78.

92. Irwin, 48.

93. Craig Haney, "Psychology and the Limits to Prison Pain," *Psychology, Public Policy, and Law* 3 (December 1997), 499.

94. Phillip Kassel, "The Gang Crackdown in 'Massachusetts' Prisons: Arbitrary and Harsh Treatment Can Only Make Matters Worse," *New England Journal on Criminal and Civil Confinement* 24 (Winter 1998), 37.

95. C. Roland Huff and Matthew Meyer, "Managing Prison Gangs and Other Security Threat Groups," *Corrections Management Quarterly* (Fall 1997), 11.

96. Leanne Fiftal Alarid, "Female Inmate Subcultures," in *Correction Contexts: Contemporary and Classical Readings*, ed. James W. Marquart and Jonathan R. Sorenson (Los Angeles: Roxbury Publishing Co., 1997), 137.

97. Esther Hefferman, *Making It in Prison: The Square, the Cool, and the Life* (New York: Wiley, 1972), 41–2.

98. *Ibid.*, 91.

99. *Ibid.*, 88

100. Alarid, 136–7.

101. James G. Fox, *Organizational and Racial Conflict in Maximum Security Prisons* (Lexington, MA: Lexington Books, 1982).

102. Lee H. Bowker, "Gender Differences in Prisoner Subcultures," in *Women and Crime in America*, ed. Lee H. Bowker (New York: Macmillan, 1981), 409–19.

103. National Advisory Committee on Civil Disorder, *Report* (Washington, D.C.: U.S. Government Printing Officer, 1968), Chapter 11.

104. *Griggs v. Duke Power Company*, 401 U.S. 424 (1971); and *Albermarle Paper Co. v. Moody*, 422 U.S. 405 (1975).

105. *United States v. Paradise*, 480 U.S. 149 (1987).

106. Samuel Walker, *Popular Justice* (New York: Oxford University Press, 1980), 243.

107. *Detroit Police Officers' Association v. Young*, 608 F.2d 671, 695 (6th Cir. 1979).

108. *Wygant v. Jackson Board of Education*, 476 U.S. 314 (1986).

109. George F. Cole, *The American System of Criminal Justice*, 5th ed. (Pacific Grove, CA: Brooks/Cole 1989), 291.

110. Kit R. Roane, "Police Admit Minority Officers Are Punished More Often," *New York Times* (March 14, 1998), B3.

111. "The High Cost of Discrimination," *Law Enforcement News* (December 31, 1996), 19.

112. Lena Williams, "Police Officers Tell of Strains of Living as a 'Black in Blue,'" *Annual Additions: Criminal Justice—90/91*, ed. John J. Sullivan (Guilford, CT: Dushkin Publishing, 1990), 112.

113. D. C. Hale and C. L. Bennett, "Realities of Women in Policing: An Organizational Cultural Perspective," in *Women, Law, and Social Control*, (Boston: Allyn & Bacon, 1995), 41–54.

114. Lawrence M. Friedman, *Crime and Punishment in American History* (New York: Basic Books, 1993), 364–5.

115. Lewis Griswold, "Female Officers Sue City of Visalia," *Fresno Bee* (April 15, 1997), A1.

116. Jim Adams, "Judge Finds Pattern of Gender Bias in Police Department," *Minneapolis-St. Paul Star Tribune* (November 6, 1997), 1A.

117. Susan Martin, "Women Police and Stress," *Police Chief* 50 (1983), 107–9.

118. Susan Fletcher, *Breaking & Entering: Women Cops Talk about Life in the Ultimate Men's Club* (New York: HarperCollins, 1995), 196.

119. Lewis J. Sherman, "An Evaluation of Policewomen in Patrol in a Suburban Patrol Department," *Journal of Police Science and Administration* 3 (1975), 434–8.

120. Patricia W. Lunnenbourg, *Women Police Officers: Current Career Profiles* (Springfield, IL: Charles C. Thomas, 1989).

121. *Report by the Women's Advisory Council to the Los Angeles Police Commission*, September 1993.

122. Civil Rights Act of 1964, 42 Sections 2000e–2000e15 (1964) (amended in 1972.)

123. *Grummett v. Rushen*, 779 F.2d 491–3 (9th Cir. 1985).

124. *Smith v. Fairman*, 678 F.2d 52 (7th Cir. 1982), cert. denied, 461 U.S. 907 (1983).

125. 441 U.S. 520 (1979).

126. 433 U.S. 334 (1977).

127. Denise L. Jenne and Robert C. Kersting, "Aggression and Women Correctional Officers in Male Prisons," *The Prison Journal* (December 1996), 442–60.

128. Mark. R. Pogrebin and Eric D. Poole, "The Sexualized Work Environment: A Look at Women Jail Officers," *The Prison Journal* (March 1997), 41–57.

129. 87 F.3d 916, 917 (7th Cir. 1996).

130. Nancy C. Jurik, "Individual and Organizational Determinants of Correctional Officer Attitudes toward Inmates," *Criminology* 23 (1985), 523–39.

131. B. M. Crouch and G. P. Alpert, "Sex and Occupational Socialization among Prison Guards: A Longitudinal Study," *Criminal Justice and Behavior* 9 (1982), 159–176.

132. J. B. Jacobs and L. J. Kraft, "Integrating the Keepers: A Comparison of Black and White Prison Guards in Illinois," *Social Problems* 25 (1978), 304–18.

133. Richard Watson and Robert G. Downing, *The Politics of the Bench and Bar: Judicial Selection under the Missouri Nonpartisan Court Plan* (New York: John Wiley & Sons, 1969).

134. Sue Davis, Susan Haire, and Donald Songer, "Voting Behavior and Gender on the U.S. Court of Appeals," *Judicature* 77 (1993), 129–33.

135. Sherrilyn A. Ifill, "Judging the Judges: Racial Diversity, Impartiality, and Representation on State Trial Courts," *Boston College Law Review* 39 (December 1997), 95.

136. *Chisom v. Roemer*, 501 U.S. 380 (1991).

137. Pub. L. No. 103-322, 108 Stat. 1796.

138. Pub. L. No. 101-275, Section 2(a)-(b), 104 Stat. 140, 141 (1990), codified in part at 28 U.S.C. Section 534 note (1994).

139. Steven M. Freeman, "Hate Crime Laws: Punishment Which Fits the Crime," *Annual Survey of American Law* no. 4 (1992/93), 581–5.

140. Greg Hernandez, "O.C. Jury Votes Death for Hate Crime," *Los Angeles Times* (October 10, 1997), A1.

141. 505 U.S. 377 (1992).

142. 508 U.S. 476 (1993).

143. Nadine Strossen, "Yes: Discriminatory Crimes," *ABA Journal* (May 1993), 44.

144. Julie Brienza, "Hate Crimes Against Gays Hurt Body and Soul," *Trial* (January 1998), 95.

145. Nat Hentoff, "Letting Loose the Hate Crimes Police," *The Village Voice* (July 13, 1993).

146. James B. Jacobs, "Should Hate Be a Crime?" *The Public Interest* (Fall 1993), 3–14.

147. Quoted in Hentoff.

Glossary

A

ABANDONMENT DOCTRINE The legal principle that, in cases involving searches and seizures, when a person abandons an item, he or she no longer enjoys the protection of constitutional privacy laws with regard to that item.

ACQUITTAL A declaration following a trial that the individual accused of the crime is innocent in the eyes of the law and thus absolved from the charges.

ACTUS REUS (pronounced *ak-tus ray-uhs*). A guilty (prohibited) act. The commission of a prohibited act is one of the two essential elements required for criminal liability, the other element being the intent to commit a crime.

ADJUDICATORY HEARING The process through which a juvenile court determines whether there is sufficient evidence to support the initial petition.

ADVERSARY SYSTEM A legal system in which the prosecution and defense are opponents, or adversaries, and present their cases in the light most favorable to themselves. The court arrives at a just solution based on the evidence presented by the contestants and determines who wins and who loses.

AGE OF ONSET The age at which a juvenile first exhibits delinquent behavior. The earlier the age of onset, according to some observers, the greater the chance a person will become a career offender.

AGGRAVATING CIRCUMSTANCES Any circumstances accompanying the commission of a crime that may justify a harsher sentence.

AGING OUT A term used to explain the fact that criminal activity declines with age.

ALLEN CHARGE An instruction by a judge to a deadlocked jury with only a few dissenters that asks the jurors in the minority to reconsider the majority opinion.

ANOMIE A condition in which the individual suffers from the breakdown or absence of social norms. According to this theory, this condition occurs when a person is disconnected from these norms or rejects them as inconsistent with his or her personal goals.

APPEAL The process of seeking a higher court's review of a lower court's decision for the purpose of correcting or changing the lower court's judgment or decision.

APPELLATE COURTS Courts that review decisions made by lower courts, such as trial courts. Also known as courts of appeals.

ARRAIGNMENT A court proceeding in which the suspect is formally charged with the criminal offense stated in the indictment. The suspect enters a plea (guilty, not guilty, *nolo contendere*) in response.

ARREST To take into custody a person suspected of criminal activity. Police may use only reasonable levels of force in making an arrest.

ARREST WARRANT A written order, based on probable cause and issued by a judge or magistrate, commanding that the person named on the warrant be arrested by the police.

ASSET FORFEITURE LAW A statute that allows law enforcement agents to seize any equipment used in manufacturing, storing or transporting illicit drugs and any profits or property gained from the sale of the drugs, as well as the drugs themselves.

ATTORNEY GENERAL The chief law officer of a state; also, the chief law officer of the nation.

ATTORNEY-CLIENT PRIVILEGE A rule of evidence requiring that communications between a client and his or her attorney be kept confidential, unless the client consents to disclosure.

AUTHENTICATION Establishing the genuineness of an item that is to be introduced as evidence in a trial.

AUTHORITY The power designated to an agent of the law over a person who has broken the law.

AUTOMATIC TRANSFER The process by which a juvenile is transferred to adult court as a matter of state law. In some states, for example, a juvenile who is suspected of murder is automatically transferred to adult court.

B

BAIL The amount or conditions set by the court to ensure that an individual accused of a crime will appear for further criminal proceedings. If the accused person provides bail, whether in cash or by means of a bail bond, then she or he is released from jail.

BAIL BONDSPERSON An businessperson who agrees, for a fee, to pay the bail amount if the accused fails to appear in court as ordered.

BEHAVIOR THERAPY Treatment programs that attempt to change an inmate's behavior patterns to eliminate or lessen criminal tendencies.

BENCH TRIAL A trial conducted without a jury, in which a judge makes the determination of the defendant's guilt or innocence.

BEYOND A REASONABLE DOUBT The standard used to determine the guilt or innocence of a person charged with a crime. To be guilty of a crime, a suspect must be proved guilty "beyond and to the exclusion of a reasonable doubt."

BILL OF RIGHTS The first ten amendments to the U.S. Constitution.

BLUE CURTAIN A metaphorical term used to refer to the value placed on secrecy and the general mistrust of the outside world shared by many police officers.

BOOKING The process of entering a suspect's name, offense, and arrival time into the police log following her or his arrest.

BOOT CAMP A correctional facility based on militaristic principles of discipline and physical conditioning; reserved primarily for juvenile and first-time offenders serving terms of less than six months, with the ultimate goal of deterring further criminal behavior.

BOYKIN FORM A form that must be completed by a defendant who pleads guilty; the defendant states that she or he has done so voluntarily and with full comprehension of the consequences.

BROKEN WINDOWS THEORY Wilson and Kelling's theory that a neighborhood in disrepair signals that criminal activity is tolerated in the area. Thus, by cracking down on quality-of-life crimes, police can reclaim the neighborhood and encourage law-abiding citizens to live and work there.

BUREAUCRACY A hierarchically structured administrative organization that carries out specific functions.

BURNOUT A mental state that occurs when a person suffers from exhaustion and is incapable of maintaining acceptable standards of performance as the result of overwork and stress.

C

CAPITAL PUNISHMENT The use of the death penalty to punish wrongdoers for certain crimes.

CASE ATTRITION The process through which prosecutors, by deciding whether or not to prosecute each person arrested, effect an overall reduction in the number of persons prosecuted. As a result, the number of persons convicted and sentenced is much smaller than the number of persons arrested.

CASE LAW The rules of law announced in court decisions. Case law includes the aggregate of reported cases that interpret judicial precedents, statutes, regulations, and constitutional provisions.

CHALLENGE FOR CAUSE A *voir dire* challenge for which an attorney states the reason why a prospective juror should not be included on the jury.

CHARGE The judge's instructions to the jury following the attorneys' closing arguments; the charge sets forth the rules of law that the jury must apply in reaching its decision, or verdict.

CHILD ABUSE Mistreatment of children by causing physical, emotional, or sexual damage without any plausible explanation, such as an accident.

CHILD NEGLECT A form of child abuse in which the child is denied certain necessities such as shelter, food, care, and love. Neglect is justification for a government agency to assume responsibility for a child in place of the parents or legal guardian.

CHOICE THEORY A school of criminology that holds that wrongdoers act as if they weigh the possible benefits of criminal or delinquent activity against the costs of being apprehended. When the benefits are greater than the costs, the offender will make a rational choice to commit a crime or delinquent act.

CHRONIC OFFENDER A delinquent or criminal who commits multiple offenses, and is considered part of a small group of wrongdoers who are responsible for a majority of the antisocial activity in any given community.

CIRCUMSTANTIAL EVIDENCE Indirect evidence that is offered to establish, by inference, the likelihood of a fact that is in question.

CITIZEN OVERSIGHT The process by which citizens review complaints brought against individual police officers or police departments. The citizens often do not have the power to discipline misconduct, but can recommend that action be taken by police administrators.

CIVIL LAW The branch of law dealing with the definition and enforcement of all private or public rights, as opposed to criminal matters.

CLASSICAL CRIMINOLOGY A school of criminology based on the belief that individuals have free will to engage in any behavior, including criminal behavior. To deter criminal behavior, society must hold wrongdoers responsible for their actions by punishing them.

CLASSIFICATION The process that determines the security and treatment needs of an inmate upon her or his initial contact with the correctional system.

CLOSING ARGUMENTS Arguments made by each side's attorney after the cases for the plaintiff and defendant have been presented.

COHORT A group of persons statistically gathered for study because they share a certain characteristic, such as age, income, or criminal background.

COLD HIT A term used to describe a match between a sample in a DNA database and the DNA of a suspect who was unknown to police when evidence from the crime scene was submitted to the laboratory for testing.

COMMON LAW The body of law developed from custom or judicial decisions in English and U.S. courts and not attributable to a legislature.

COMMUNITY POLICING A policing philosophy that emphasizes community support for and cooperation with the police in preventing crime. Community policing stresses a police role that is less centralized and more proactive than reform era policing strategies.

CONCURRING OPINIONS Separate opinions prepared by judges who support the decision of the majority of the court but who want to make or clarify a particular point or to voice disapproval of the grounds on which the decision was made.

CONFIDENTIAL INFORMANT (CI) A human source for police who provides information concerning illegal activity in which he or she is involved.

CONFLICT MODEL A criminal justice model in which the content of criminal law is determined by the groups that hold economic, political, and social power in a community.

CONGREGATE SYSTEM A nineteenth-century penitentiary system developed in New York in which inmates were kept in separate cells during the night but worked together in the daytime under a code of enforced silence.

CONSENSUS MODEL A criminal justice model in which the majority of citizens in a society share the same values and beliefs. Criminal acts are those acts that conflict with these values and beliefs and are deemed harmful to society.

CONSENT SEARCHES Searches by police that are made after the subject of the search has agreed to the action. In these situations, consent, if given of free will, validates a warrantless search.

CONSOLIDATION A corrections model in which the inmates who pose the highest security risk are housed in a single facility to separate them from the general prison population.

CONSTITUTIONAL LAW Law based on the U.S. Constitution and the constitutions of the various states.

CONTAMINATED When evidence of a crime is rendered useless because of exposure to a foreign agent or improper removal from a crime scene.

CONTINUUM-OF-SANCTIONS A corrections strategy in which offenders are not assigned a single punishment, but rather are initially sentenced based on their criminal act and then moved toward harsher or more lenient forms of sanction depending on their behavior within the corrections system.

CONTRACT LABOR SYSTEM The system in which a correctional facility would sell inmate labor to a private employer, who would provide the inmates with the raw materials to produce goods for sale.

CONTROL THEORIES A series of theories that assume that all individuals have the potential for criminal behavior, but are restrained by the damage that such actions would do to their relationships with family, friends, and members of the community. Criminality occurs when these bonds are broken or nonexistent.

CORONER The medical examiner of a county, usually elected by popular vote.

CORPUS DELICTI The body of circumstances that must exist for a criminal act to have occurred.

COURTROOM WORK GROUP The social organization consisting of the judge, prosecutor, defense attorney, and other court workers. The relationships among these persons have a far-reaching impact on the day-to-day operations of any court.

CRIME CONTROL MODEL A criminal justice model that places primary emphasis on the right of society to be protected from crime and violent criminals. Crime control values emphasize speed and efficiency in the criminal justice process; the benefits of lower crime rates outweigh any possible costs to individual rights.

CRIME SCENE The physical area that contains or is believed to contain evidence of a crime.

CRIMINAL MODEL OF ADDICTION An approach to drug abuse that holds that drug offenders harm society by their actions to the same extent as other criminals and should face the same punitive sanctions.

CRIMINOLOGY The scientific study of crime and the causes of criminal behavior.

CROSS-EXAMINATION The questioning of an opposing witness during the trial.

CULTURAL DEVIANCE THEORY A branch of social structure theory based on the assumption that members of certain subcultures reject the values of the dominant culture through deviant behavior patterns.

CUSTODIAL INTERROGATION The questioning of a suspect after that person has been taken in custody. In this situation, the suspect *must* be read his or her *Miranda* rights before interrogation can begin.

CUSTODY The forceful detention of a person, or the perception that a person is not free to leave the immediate vicinity.

D

DARK FIGURE OF CRIME A term used to describe the actual amount of crime that takes place. The "figure" is "dark," or impossible to detect, because a great number of crimes are never reported to the police.

DAY REPORTING CENTER A community-based corrections center to which offenders report on a daily basis for purposes of treatment, education, and incapacitation.

DEADLY FORCE Force applied by a police officer that is likely or intended to cause death.

DECRIMINALIZATION A policy that combines the elimination of criminal penalties on drug use with restrictions to discourage use such as high taxes and limitations on advertising of drugs.

DEFENSE ATTORNEY The lawyer representing the defendant.

DELEGATION OF AUTHORITY The principles of command on which most police departments are based; personnel take orders from and are responsible to those in positions of power directly above them.

"DELIBERATE INDIFFERENCE" A standard that must be met by inmates trying to prove that their Eighth Amendment rights were violated by a correctional facility. It occurs when prison officials are aware of harmful conditions of confinement but fail to take steps to remedy those conditions.

DEPARTURE A stipulation in many federal and state sentencing guidelines that allows a judge to adjust his or her sentencing decision based on the special circumstances of particular cases.

DEPRIVATION MODEL A theory that inmate aggression is the result of the frustration inmates feel at being deprived of freedom, consumer goods, sex, and other staples of life outside the institution.

DETECTIVE The primary police investigator of crimes.

DETENTION The temporary custody of a juvenile in a state facility after a petition has been filed and before the adjudicatory process begins.

DETENTION HEARING A hearing to determine whether a juvenile should be detained, or remain detained, while waiting for the adjudicatory process to begin.

DETERRENCE The strategy of preventing crime through the threat of punishment. Assumes that potential criminals will weigh the costs of punishments versus the benefits of the criminal act; therefore, punishments should be severe.

DIFFERENTIAL RESPONSE A strategy for answering calls for service in which response time is adapted to the seriousness of the call.

DIRECT EVIDENCE Evidence that establishes the existence of a fact that is in question without relying on inference.

DIRECT EXAMINATION The examination of a witness by the attorney who calls the witness to the stand to testify.

DIRECT SUPERVISION APPROACH A process of prison and jail administration in which correctional officers are in continuous physical contact with inmates during the day.

DIRECTED PATROL Patrol strategies that are designed to respond to a specific criminal activity at a specific time.

DISCOVERY Formal investigation prior to trial. During discovery, the defense uses various methods to obtain information from the prosecution to prepare for trial.

DISCRETION The ability of individuals in the criminal justice system to make operational decisions based on personal judgment instead of formal rules or official information.

DISCRETIONARY RELEASE The release of an inmate into a community supervision program at the discretion of the parole board within limits set by state or federal law.

DISCRIMINATION Inconsistencies in the treatment of an individual that can be attributed to extralegal variables such as the defendant's race, ethnicity, gender, sexual orientation, or economic standing.

DISPARITY Inconsistencies between the treatment of minorities and nonminorities that result from legitimate factors in the decision-making process of the criminal justice system.

DISPERSION A corrections model in which high-risk inmates are spread throughout the general prison population, in the hopes that they will be absorbed without causing misconduct problems.

DISPOSITION HEARING Similar to the sentencing hearing for adults, a hearing in which the juvenile judge or officer decides the appropriate punishment for a youth found to be delinquent or a status offender.

DISSENTING OPINIONS Separate opinions in which judges disagree with the conclusion reached by the majority of the court and expand on their own views about the case.

DIVERSION In the context of corrections, a strategy to divert those offenders who qualify away from prison and jail and toward community-based and intermediate sanctions.

DOCKET The list of cases entered on a court's calendar and thus scheduled to be heard by the court.

DOMESTIC VIOLENCE An act of physical aggression against a spouse or intimate partner.

DOUBLE JEOPARDY To twice place at risk (jeopardize) a person's life or liberty. The Fifth Amendment to the U.S. Constitution prohibits a second prosecution for the same criminal offense.

DOUBLE-CELLING The practice of placing two inmates in a cell that is designed for one; usually occurs in facilities with prison populations that exceed the institution's capacity.

DRUG Any substance that modifies behavior; in particular, an illegal substance with those properties.

DRUG ABUSE The use of drugs that results in physical or psychological problems for the user, as well as disruption of personal relationships and employment.

DRUG COURTS Courts whose jurisdiction is limited to drug offenses. Offenders are offered treatment as an alternative to incarceration.

DUAL COURT SYSTEM The separate but interrelated court system of the United States, made up of the courts on the national level and the courts on the state level.

DUE PROCESS CLAUSE The provisions of the Fifth and Fourteenth Amendments to the Constitution that guarantee that no person shall be deprived of life, liberty, or property without due process of law. Similar clauses are found in most state constitutions.

DUE PROCESS MODEL A criminal justice model that places primacy on the right of the individual to be protected from the power of the government. Due process values hold that the state must prove a person's guilt within the confines of a process designed to safeguard personal liberties as enumerated in the Bill of Rights.

DURESS Unlawful pressure brought to bear upon a person, causing the person to perform an act that he or she would not otherwise perform.

DURHAM RULE A test of criminal responsibility adopted in a 1954 case: "an accused is not criminally responsible if his unlawful act was the product of mental disease or mental defect."

DUTY The moral sense of a police officer that she or he should apply authority in a certain manner.

E

ELECTRONIC MONITORING A technique of probation supervision in which the offender's whereabouts, though not his or her actions, are kept under surveillance by an electronic device; often used in conjunction with home confinement.

ENTRAPMENT A defense in which the defendant claims that he or she was induced by a public official—usually an undercover agent or police officer—to commit a crime that he or she would otherwise not have committed.

ETHICS The rules or standards of behavior governing a profession; aimed at ensuring the fairness and rightness of actions.

EVIDENCE Anything that is used to prove the existence or nonexistence of a fact.

EXCLUSIONARY RULE A rule under which any evidence that is obtained in violation of the accused's rights under the Fourth, Fifth, and Sixth Amendments, as well as any evidence derived from illegally obtained evidence, will not be admissible in criminal court.

EXIGENT CIRCUMSTANCES Situations that require extralegal or exceptional actions by the police. In these circumstances, police officers are justified in not following procedural rules, such as those pertaining to search and arrest warrants.

EXONERATE The removal of a charge of wrongdoing against a police officer by determining that the act in question was justified under the circumstances.

EXPERT WITNESS A witness with professional training or substantial experience qualifying her or him to testify on a certain subject.

F

FEDERAL BUREAU OF INVESTIGATION (FBI) The branch of the Department of Justice responsible for investigating violations of federal law. The bureau also collects national crime statistics and provides training and other forms of aid to local law enforcement agencies.

FEDERALISM A form of government in which a written constitution provides for a division of powers between a central government and several regional governments. In the United States, the division of powers between the federal government and the fifty states is established by the Constitution.

FELONY A serious crime punishable by death or by imprisonment in a federal or state corrections facility for more than a year.

FIELD TRAINING The segment of a police recruit's training in which he or she is removed from the classroom and placed on the beat, under the supervision of a senior officer.

FOLLOW-UP INVESTIGATION The steps taken by investigative personnel once it has been determined, based on the results of the preliminary investigation, that the crime is solvable.

FORENSICS The application of scientific methods to finding and utilizing criminal evidence.

LOW-VISIBILITY DECISION MAKING A term used to describe the discretionary power police have in determining what to do with misbehaving juveniles. For the most part, this power goes unchallenged and unnoticed by citizens.

M

M'NAUGHTEN RULE A common law test of criminal responsibility derived from *M'Naughten's case* in 1843 that relies on the defendant's inability to distinguish right from wrong.

MAGISTRATE A public civil officer or official with limited judicial authority within a particular geographical area, such as the authority to issue an arrest warrant.

MALA IN SE A descriptive term for acts that are inherently wrong, regardless of whether they are prohibited by law.

MALA PROHIBITA A descriptive term for acts that are made illegal by criminal statute and are not necessarily wrong of themselves.

MANDATORY ARREST A statutory requirement that law enforcement agents shall arrest a person suspected of committing a specific illegal act.

MANDATORY RELEASE Release from prison that occurs when an offender has served the length of his or her sentence, with time taken off for good behavior.

MANDATORY SENTENCING GUIDELINES Statutorily determined punishments that must be applied to those who are convicted of specific crimes.

MASCULINITY HYPOTHESIS The theory that women who commit crimes are biologically and psychologically similar to men.

MASTER JURY LIST The list of citizens in a court's district from which a jury can be selected; often compiled from voter registration lists, driver's license lists, and other sources.

MAXIMUM-SECURITY PRISON A correctional institution designed and organized to control and discipline dangerous felons, as well as prevent escape with intense supervision, cement walls, and electronic, barbed wire fences.

MEDICAL MODEL A model of corrections in which the psychological and biological roots of an inmate's criminal behavior are identified and treated.

MEDICAL MODEL OF ADDICTION An approach to drug addiction that treats drug abuse as a mental illness and focuses on treating and rehabilitating offenders rather than punishing them.

MEDIUM-SECURITY PRISON A correctional institution that houses less dangerous inmates, and therefore uses less restrictive measures to avoid violence and escapes.

MENS REA (pronounced *mehns ray*-uh). Mental state, or intent. A wrongful mental state is as necessary as a wrongful act to establish criminal liability.

MINIMUM-SECURITY PRISON A correctional institution designed to allow inmates, most of whom pose low security risks, a great deal of freedom of movement and contact with the outside world.

MIRANDA RIGHTS The constitutional rights of accused persons taken into custody by law enforcement officials. Following the United States Supreme Court's decision *Miranda v. Arizona,* on taking an accused person into custody, the arresting officer must inform the person of certain constitutional rights, such as the right to remain silent and the right to counsel.

MISDEMEANOR Any crime that is not a felony; punishable by a fine or by confinement for up to a year.

MISSOURI PLAN A method of selecting judges that combines appointment and election. Under the plan, the state governor or another government official selects judges from a group of nominees chosen by a nonpartisan committee. After a year on the bench, the judges face a popular election to determine whether the public wishes to keep them in office.

MITIGATING CIRCUMSTANCES Any circumstances accompanying the commission of a crime that may justify a lighter sentence.

MOONLIGHTING The practice of a police officer holding a second job in the private security field.

MOTION FOR A DIRECTED VERDICT A motion requesting that the court grant judgment in favor of the defense on the ground that the prosecution has not produced sufficient evidence to support the state's claim.

N

NECESSITY A defense against criminal liability in which the defendant asserts that circumstances required her or him to commit an illegal act.

NEGLIGENCE The failure to use the care that a reasonable person would use under the given circumstances.

NEW GENERATION JAIL A type of jail that is distinguished architecturally from its predecessors by a design that encourages interaction between inmates and jailers and that offers greater opportunities for treatment.

NOLO CONTENDERE Latin for "I will not contest it." A criminal defendant's plea, in which he or she chooses not to challenge, or contest, the charges brought by the government. Although the defendant may still be sentenced or fined, the plea neither admits nor denies guilt.

NONPARTISAN ELECTIONS Elections in which candidates are presented on the ballot without any party affiliation.

O

OPENING STATEMENTS The attorneys' statements to the jury at the beginning of the trial. Each side briefly outlines the evidence that will be offered during the trial and the legal theory that will be pursued.

OPIATES Drugs containing opium or its derivatives; have the effects of dulling sensations including pain and anxiety, producing a feeling of euphoria, and causing general inaction.

OPINION A statement by the court expressing the reasons for its decision in a case.

ORAL ARGUMENTS The verbal arguments presented in person by attorneys to an appellate court. Each attorney presents reasons why the court should rule in his or her client's favor.

ORGANIZED CRIME A conspiratorial relationship between any number of persons engaged in the market for illegal goods or services, such as illicit drugs or firearms.

P

PARDON An act of executive clemency that overturns a conviction and erases mention of the crime from the person's criminal record.

PARENS PATRIAE A doctrine that holds that the state has a responsibility to look after the well-being of children and to assume the role of parent if necessary.

PAROLE The conditional release of an inmate before his or her sentence has expired. The remainder of the sentence is served in the community under the supervision of correctional officers, and the offender can be returned to incarceration if he or she breaks the conditions of parole, as determined by a parole board.

PAROLE BOARD A body of appointed civilians that decides whether a convict should be granted conditional release before the end of his or her sentence.

PAROLE CONTRACT An agreement between the state and the offender that establishes the conditions under which the latter will be allowed to serve the remainder of her or his prison term in the community.

PAROLE GRANT HEARING A hearing in which the entire parole board or a subcommittee reviews information, meets the offender, and hears testimony from relevant witnesses to determine whether to grant parole.

PAROLE GUIDELINES Employed to remove discretion from the parole process, these guidelines attempt to measure the risks of an offender recidivating, and then use these measurements to determine whether early release will be granted and under what conditions.

PAROLE REVOCATION When a parolee breaks the conditions of parole, the process of withdrawing parole and returning the person to prison.

PART II OFFENSES All crimes recorded by the FBI that do not fall into the catergory of Part I offenses. Include both misdemeanors and felonies.

PARTISAN ELECTIONS Elections in which candidates are affiliated with and receive support from political parties; the candidates are listed in conjunction with their party on the ballot.

PATRONAGE SYSTEM A form of corruption in which the political party in power hires and promotes police officers, receiving job-related "favors" in return.

PENITENTIARY An early form of correctional facility that emphasized separating inmates from society and from each other so that they would have an environment in which to reflect on their wrongdoing and ponder their reformation.

PEREMPTORY CHALLENGES *Voir dire* challenges to exclude potential jurors from serving on the jury without any supporting reason or cause.

PETITION The document filed with a juvenile court alleging that the juvenile is a delinquent or a status offender, and asking the court to either hear the case itself or transfer it to an adult court.

PLAIN VIEW DOCTRINE The legal principle that objects in plain view of a law enforcement agent who has the right to be in a position to have that view may be seized without a warrant and introduced as evidence.

PLEA BARGAINING The process by which the accused and the prosecutor work out a mutually satisfactory conclusion to the case, subject to court approval. Usually, plea bargaining involves the defendant's pleading guilty to a lesser offense in return for a lighter sentence.

PODULAR DESIGN The architectural style of the new generation jail. Each "pod" consists of between twelve and twenty-four one-person cells and a communal "day room" to allow for social interaction.

POLICE CORRUPTION The abuse of authority by a law enforcement officer for personal gain.

POLICE CYNICISM The suspicion that citizens are weak, corrupt, and dangerous. This outlook is the result of a police officer being constantly exposed to civilians at their worst and can negatively affect the officer's performance.

POLICE SUBCULTURE The values and perceptions that are shared by members of a police department and, to a certain extent, by all law enforcement agents. These values and perceptions are shaped by the unique and isolated existence of the police officer.

POSITIVISM A school of social science that sees criminal and delinquent behavior as the result of biological, psychological, and social forces. Because wrongdoers are driven to deviancy by external factors, they should not be punished but treated to lessen the influence of those factors.

PRECEDENT A court decision that furnishes an example of authority for deciding subsequent cases involving identical or similar facts.

PREDISPOSITION REPORT A report prepared during the disposition process that provides the judge with relevant background material to aid in the disposition decision.

PRELIMINARY HEARING An initial hearing in which a magistrate decides if there is probable cause to believe that the defendant committed the crime with which he or she is charged.

PRELIMINARY INVESTIGATION The procedure, usually conducted by a patrol officer, that must be followed immediately upon initial arrival at a crime scene. Includes securing the crime scene, interviewing witnesses and suspects, and searching the scene for evidence.

PRESENTENCE INVESTIGATIVE REPORT An investigative report on an offender's background that assists a judge in determining the proper sentence.

PRESUMPTIVE PAROLE DATE The date, provided to a convict at the time of sentencing, at which he or she will be eligible for parole.

PRETRIAL DETAINEES Individuals who cannot post bail after arrest and are therefore forced to spend the time prior to their trial incarcerated in jail.

PRETRIAL DIVERSION PROGRAM An alternative to trial offered by a judge or prosecutor, in which the offender agrees to participate in a specified counseling or treatment program in return for withdrawal of the charges.

PREVENTIVE DETENTION The retention of an accused person in custody due to fears that she or he will commit a crime if released before a trial.

PRINCIPLE OF LEAST ELIGIBILITY The belief that, as part of their punishment, prisoners should not have access to any goods or services that are not available to citizens who have not broken the law.

PRISONIZATION The socialization process through which a new inmate learns the accepted norms and values of the prison population.

PRIVATE PRISONS Correctional facilities operated by private corporations instead of the government, and therefore reliant on profit for survival.

PRIVATE SECURITY The practice of private corporations or individuals offering services traditionally performed by police officers.

PROBABLE CAUSE Reasonable grounds to believe the existence of facts warranting certain actions, such as the search or arrest of a person.

PROBATION A criminal sanction in which a convict is allowed to remain in the community rather than be imprisoned as long as she or he follows certain conditions set by the court.

PROBLEM-SOLVING POLICING A policing philosophy that requires police to identify potential criminal activity and develop strategies to prevent or respond to that activity.

PROCEDURAL CRIMINAL LAW Rules that define the manner in which the rights and duties of individuals may be enforced.

PROFESSIONAL MODEL A style of policing advocated by August Vollmer and O. W. Wilson that emphasizes centralized police organizations, increased use of technology, and a limitation of police discretion through regulations and guidelines.

PROHIBITION A period in American history, lasting from the passage of the Eighteenth Amendment in 1919 until its repeal in 1933, during which the production and consumption of alcohol were prohibited by federal law.

PROPERTY CRIME Crimes committed against property, including larceny/theft, burglary, and arson.

PROSECUTORIAL WAIVER A procedure in which juvenile court judges have the discretion to transfer a juvenile case to adult court, when certain predetermined conditions as to the seriousness of the offense and the age of the offender are met.

PSYCHOACTIVE DRUGS Chemicals that affect the brain, causing changes in emotions, perceptions, and behavior.

PSYCHOTHERAPY The treatment of psychological disorders in order to determine the causes of and rehabilitate criminal behavior.

PUBLIC DEFENDERS Court-appointed attorneys who are paid by the state to represent defendants who are unable to hire private counsel.

PUBLIC ORDER CRIME Behavior that has been labeled criminal because it is contrary to shared social values, customs, and norms.

PUBLIC PROSECUTORS Individuals, acting as trial lawyers, who initiate and conduct cases in the government's name and on behalf of the people.

Q

QUALIFIED IMMUNITY A defense against civil litigation used by police officers in which they try to prove that their discretionary actions fell within the boundaries of reasonable behavior.

R

REAL EVIDENCE Evidence that is brought into court and seen by the jury, as opposed to evidence that is described for a jury.

"REAL OFFENSE" The actual offense committed, as opposed to the charge levied by a prosecutor as the result of a plea bargain. Judges who make sentencing decisions based on the real offense are often seen as undermining the plea bargain process.

REALITY THERAPY A form of social therapy that encourages inmates to take responsibility for their actions and for the consequences of those actions.

REASONABLE FORCE The degree of force that is appropriate to protect the police officer or other citizens and is not excessive.

REBUTTAL Evidence given to counteract or disprove evidence presented by the opposing party.

REHABILITATION The philosophy that society is best served when wrongdoers are not simply punished, but provided the resources needed to eliminate criminality from their behavioral pattern.

REINTEGRATION A goal of corrections that focuses on preparing the offender for a return to the community unmarred by further criminal behavior.

RELATIVE DEPRIVATION The theory that inmate aggression is caused when freedoms and services that the inmate has come to accept as normal are decreased or eliminated.

RELEASE ON RECOGNIZANCE (ROR) A judge's order that releases an accused from jail with the understanding that he or she will return for further proceedings of his or her own will; used instead of setting a monetary bond.

RELEVANT EVIDENCE Evidence tending to make a fact in question more or less probable than it would be without the evidence. Only relevant evidence is admissible in court.

RESIDENTIAL TREATMENT PROGRAMS Government-run facilities for juveniles whose offenses are not deemed serious enough to warrant incarceration in a training school.

RESPONSE TIME A measurement of police efficiency based on the rapidity with which calls for service are answered.

RETRIBUTION The philosophy that those who commit criminal acts should be punished based on the severity of the crime, and no other factors need be considered.

RULE OF FOUR A rule of the United States Supreme Court that the Court will not issue a writ of *certiorari* unless at least four justices approve of the decision to hear the case.

S

SCHOOLYARD STATUTES Laws that intensify the penalties for drug offenses if they occur on or near school property.

SEARCH The process by which police examine a person or property to find evidence that will used to prove guilt in a criminal trial.

SEARCH WARRANT A written order, based on probable cause and issued by a judge or magistrate, commanding that police officers or criminal investigators search a specific person, place, or property to obtain evidence.

SEARCHES AND SEIZURES The legal term, as found in the Fourth Amendment of the U.S. Constitution, that generally refers to the searching for and the confiscating of evidence by law enforcement agents.

SEARCHES INCIDENTAL TO ARREST Searches of persons who have just been arrested for weapons and evidence. The fruit of such searches is admissible if any items found are within the immediate vicinity or control of the suspect.

SECTION 1983 VIOLATIONS Violations of a citizen's constitutional rights by a police officer or other government agent.

SEDATIVES Drugs that slow the signals sent from the brain to other parts of the body, thereby inducing sleep or reducing anxiety.

SEIZURE The forcible taking of a person or property in response to a violation of the law.

SELF-DEFENSE The legally recognized privilege to protect one's self or property by injury by another. The privilege of self-defense protects only acts that are reasonably necessary to protect one's self or property.

SELF-REPORT SURVEYS A method of gathering crime data that relies on participants to reveal and detail their own criminal or delinquent behavior.

SENTENCING DISCRIMINATION A situation in which the length of a sentence appears to be influenced by a defendant's race, gender, economic status, or other factor not directly related to the crime he or she committed.

SENTENCING DISPARITY A situation in which those convicted of similar crimes do not receive similar sentences.

SEPARATE CONFINEMENT A nineteenth-century penitentiary system developed in Pennsylvania in which inmates were kept separate from each other at all times, with daily activities taking place in individual cells.

SHERIFF The primary law enforcement officer in a county, usually elected to the post by a popular vote.

SHIRE-REEVE The chief law enforcement officer in an early English shire, or county. The forerunner of the modern sheriff.

SHOCK INCARCERATION A short period of incarceration that is designed to deter further criminal activity by "shocking" the offender with the hardships of imprisonment.

SOCIAL CONFLICT THEORIES A school of criminology that views criminal behavior as the result of class conflict. Certain behavior is labeled illegal not because it is inherently criminal, but because the ruling class has an economic or social interest in restricting such behavior in order to protect the *status quo*.

SOCIAL DISORGANIZATION THEORY The theory that deviant behavior is more likely in communities where social institutions such as the family, schools, and criminal justice system fail to exert control over the population.

SOCIAL PROCESS THEORIES A school of criminology that considers criminal behavior to be the predictable result of a person's interaction with his or her environ-ment. According to these theories, everybody has the potential for wrongdoing. Those who act upon this potential are conditioned to do so by family or peer groups, or institutions such as the media.

SOCIAL REALITY OF CRIME The theory that criminal laws are designed by those in power (the rich) to help them keep power at the expense of those who do not have power (the poor). This would explain, for example, why the punishment for white-collar crime, mostly committed by members of the upper and middle classes, is less severe than the punishment for property and violent crimes, mostly committed by members of the lower class.

SOCIALIZATION The process through which a police officer is taught the values and expected behavior of the police subculture.

SOLVABILITY FACTORS Those factors that affect the probability that a case will be solved.

SPECIALTY COURTS Lower courts that have jurisdiction over one specific area of criminal activity, such as illegal drugs or domestic violence.

SPLIT SENTENCE PROBATION A sentence that consists of incarceration in a prison or jail, followed by a probationary period in the community.

STARE DECISIS (pronounced *ster*-ay dih-*si*-*ses*). A common law doctrine under which judges are obligated to follow the precedents established under prior decisions.

STATE USE SYSTEM A system of using inmate labor under which the goods produced by such labor can only be sold to other government industries or organizations and cannot compete on the free market.

STATUS OFFENDER A juvenile who has been found to have engaged in behavior deemed unacceptable for those under a certain, statutorily determined age.

STIMULANTS Drugs such as cocaine or amphetamine that stimulate the central nervous system, thereby quickening motor functions of the body.

STOP A brief detention of a person by law enforcement agents for questioning. The agents must have a reasonable suspicion of the person before making a stop.

STRAIN THEORY The assumption that crime is the result of frustration felt by individuals who cannot reach their financial and personal goals through legitimate means.

STRESSORS The aspects of police work and life that lead to feelings of stress.

STRICT LIABILITY Certain crimes, such as traffic violations, in which the defendant is guilty regardless of her or his state of mind at the time of the act.

SUBCULTURE A group exhibiting certain values and behavior patterns that distinguish it from the dominant culture.

SUBSTANTIAL CAPACITY TEST From the Model Penal Code, a test that states that a person is not responsible for criminal behavior if when committing the act "as a result of mental disease or defect he lacks substantial capacity either to appreciate the wrongfulness of his conduct or to conform his conduct to the requirements of law."

SUBSTANTIVE CRIMINAL LAW Law that defines the rights and duties of individuals with respect to each other.

SUPERMAX PRISON A correctional facility reserved for those inmates who have extensive records of misconduct in maximum-security prisons; characterized by extremely strict control and supervision over the inmates, including extensive use of solitary confinement.

SUPPLY-SIDE ENFORCEMENT The law enforcement strategy of combating the use of illegal drugs by concentrating on the suppliers of the drugs rather than the buyers. Thus, agents will focus on a single drug dealer rather than on his or her many clients.

SUSPENDED SENTENCE A judicially imposed condition in which an offender is sentenced after being convicted of a crime, but is not required to begin the sentence immediately. The judge may revoke the suspended sentence and remit the offender to prison or jail if he or she does not follow certain conditions.

T

TECHNICAL VIOLATION An action taken by a probationer that, although not criminal, breaks the terms of probation as designated by the court; can result in the revocation of probation and a return to prison or jail.

TEN PERCENT CASH BAIL An alternative to traditional bail in which defendants may gain pretrial release by posting 10 percent of their bond amount to the court instead of seeking a bail bondsperson.

TERRORISM The use or threat of violence to achieve political objectives.

TESTIMONY Verbal evidence given by witnesses under oath.

THEORY OF DIFFERENTIAL ASSOCIATION Sutherland's theory that criminality is the result of the values an individual is exposed to by family, friends, and other members of the community. When these values favor deviant behavior over conventional norms, criminal activity is more likely.

TIME SERVED The period of time a person denied bail has spent in jail prior to his or her trial. If the suspect is found guilty and sentenced to a jail or prison term, the judge will often lessen the duration of the sentence based on the amount of time served as a pretrial detainee.

TITHING SYSTEM In Anglo-Saxon England, a system of law enforcement in which groups of ten families, known as tithings, were collectively responsible for law and order within their group.

TOKEN ECONOMY A form of behavior therapy that offers inmates incentives (in the form of tokens that can be used to purchase desired goods or services) to abide by the rules of the institution.

TOTAL INSTITUTION An institution, such as a prison, that provides all of the necessities for existence to those who live within its boundaries.

TRAINING SCHOOLS Correctional institutions for juveniles found to be delinquent or status offenders.

TRIAL COURTS Courts in which most cases usually begin and in which questions of fact are examined.

U

UNIFORM CRIME REPORT (UCR) An annual report compiled by the FBI to give an indication of criminal activity in the United States. The FBI collects data from local, state, and federal law enforcement agencies in preparing this report.

UTILITARIANISM An approach to ethical reasoning in which the "correct" decision is the one that results in the greatest amount of good for the greatest number of people affected by that decision.

V

VENIRE The group of citizens from which the jury is selected.

VERDICT A formal decision made by the jury.

VICTIM SURVEYS A method of gathering crime data that directly surveys participants to determine their experiences as victims of crime.

VIOLENT CRIME Crimes committed against persons, including murder, rape, assault and battery, and robbery.

VOIR DIRE The preliminary questions that the trial attorneys ask prospective jurors to determine whether they are biased or have any connection with the defendant or a witness.

W

WARDEN The prison official who is ultimately responsible for the organization and performance of a correctional facility.

WAREHOUSE PRISONS A perception of modern prisons as institutions that subject inmates to an idle and regimented existence while providing few opportunities for rehabilitation.

WARRANTLESS ARREST An arrest made without first seeking a warrant for the action; permitted under certain circumstances, such as when the arresting officer has witnessed the crime or has a reasonable belief that the suspect has committed a felony.

WATCH SYSTEM A community law enforcement system in medieval England in which citizens were regularly required to spend a night guarding against disturbances of the peace and property crimes.

"WEDDING CAKE" MODEL A wedding cake–shaped model that explains why different cases receive different treatment in the criminal justice system. The cases at the "top" of the cake receive the most attention and have the greatest effect on public perception of criminal justice, while those cases at the "bottom" are disposed of quickly and virtually ignored by the media.

WHITE-COLLAR CRIME Nonviolent crimes committed by corporations and individuals to gain a personal or business advantage.

WIDEN THE NET The criticism that intermediate sanctions designed to divert offenders from prison actually increase the number of citizens who are under the control and surveillance of the American corrections system.

WORK RELEASE PROGRAM Temporary release of convicts from prison for purposes of employment. The offenders may spend their days on the job, but must return to the correctional facility at night and during the weekend.

WRIT OF CERTIORARI A request from a higher court asking a lower court for the record of a case. In essence, the request signals the higher court's willingness to review the case.

WRONGFUL DEATH A type of civil lawsuit brought by the beneficiaries of a person who has died because of the alleged action or inaction of a police officer.

Y

YOUTH GANGS Self-formed groups of youths with several identifiable characteristics, including a gang name and other recognizable symbols, a geographic territory, a leadership structure, a meeting pattern, and participation in illegal activities.

Case Index

Name Index

A

Abramsoan, Jeffrey, 357
Abramson, Leslie, 322
Abu-Jamal, Mumia, 647
Adams, John, 361
Adams, Sherman "Sherm da Worm," 652
Adler, Freda, 644
Agunabo, Mecca, 646
Alford, Henry, 324, 325
Ali, Mohammed Haroon, 421
Allen, George, 548
Anderson, Robin, 29
Arafat, Rami, 87
Arafat, Rania, 87
Aristotle, 76
Arpaio, Joe, 475
Auden, W. H., 7
Augustus, John, 421, 422
Aung San Suu Kyi, 438
Avila, Jeffrey, 407

B

Baer, Harold, Jr., 199
Bailey, Eno, 90
Bailey, William C., 248
Baily, Penny, 137
Baitinger, William E., 255
Baldwin, James, 122
Baldwin, Lola, 656
Ballock, Scott T., 429
Barak, Gregg, 29
Barber, Jeremy W., 346
Barr, Bob, 305
Barrow, Clyde, 122
Bataille, Georges, 56
Batson, James Kirkland, 348
Bazelon, David, 93–94
Bean, Roy, 276
Beccaria, Cesare, 54, 406
Beck, Allen J., 524
Becker, Charles, 119
Becker, Ronald F., 253–254
Becker-Darling, Judy, 353
Bedau, Hugo, 402, 403
Belknap, Joanne, 640, 649
Bell, Sam, 470
Bellair, Paul E., 59
Bennett, William, 611
Bentham, Jeremy, 54, 377, 378
Bercal, Thomas, 136
Berk, Richard, 140

Berns, Walter, 403
Berra, Bill, 28
Bertsch, Dale, 295
Bessette, Joseph, 403
Beto, George, 467–468
Bevilacqua, Joseph, 286
Bierce, Ambrose, 362
Biletnikoff, Tracey, 421
Bittner, Egon, 134, 161
Black, Hugo, 294, 362, 367
Blackstone, Sir William, 76
Blake, Brandi, 83
Blucker, Michael, 505
Blumberg, Abraham S., 309
Blumstein, Alfred, 458–459, 462, 588, 649
Bobbit, Lorena, 366
Bonn, Robert L., 432
Boswell, James, 182
Bourgeois, Phillipe, 615
Bouza, Anthony, 161
Bowker, Lee, 638
Bowker, Lee H., 495
Bradley, Keith, Jr., 224
Braga, Anthony A., 589
Brandl, Steven G., 167
Brando, Marlon, 9
Bratton, William, 185, 251
Brecher, Edward, 604
Brennan, William, 364, 398, 399
Breyer, Charles, 5
Bright, Stephen, 294, 395
Brockway, Zebulon, 456–457, 462, 533
Broderick, Vincent, 394
Brougham, Lord, 328
Brown, Nicole, 84, 362
Browne, Angela, 637
Browning, Kelly, 570
Brucker, Joseph, 356
Brummall, Marcus L., 186
Buenoano, Judias, 4
Bullush, Sheila, 272
Bundy, Ted, 4
Burge, Tim, 358
Burger, Warren, 324–325, 546
Burgess, Ernest, 59
Burgos, Anthony, 588
Burns, Robert, 514
Burrell, Garland E., Jr., 270
Burris, Damien "Pookie," 15
Bush, George, 622, 659
Bush, George W., 4
Butler, Paul, 361

Byrd, James, Jr., 342
Byrne, William, 354

C

Cabranes, José A., 384
Cage, Nicholas, 540
Campbell, Aaron, 200–201
Campbell, Charles Rodman, 404
Campbell, Luther, 349
Camus, Albert, 462
Canetti, Elias, 23
Capano, Thomas, 351
Capone, Al, 133, 605
Carboni, William, 138
Cardozo, Benjamin, 351
Caroline (queen of Great Britain), 328
Carrey, Jim, 328
Carroll, Leo, 652
Carter, Rubin "Hurricane," 402
Casper, Jonathan D., 307–308
Cassell, Paul, 226, 401–402
Castille, Ton, 305
Caulfield, Regina, 304
Causey, Damon, 295
Chambliss, William, 646
Chapman, Jane Roberts, 644
Chapman, Kelly, 508
Chenoweth, James H., 234
Chermack, Steven M., 259
Chesney-Lind, Meda, 585, 655
Chester, Donna, 430
Chestnut, Jacob J., 93
Christiansen, Karl, 57
Cicero, 77
Clark, Marcia, 367
Clark, Ramsey, 249
Clark, Tom, 196
Clear, Todd R., 531, 544
Clemmer, Donald, 492
Clinton, Bill, 11, 27, 66, 104, 133, 176, 214, 598, 606, 616, 620, 659, 660
Cochran, John K., 46
Coffee, John C., 389
Cole, David, 105
Cole, George F., 531
Coleridge, Lord, 99
Collins, Robert, 286
Comer, James P., 643
Condon, Charles, 19
Connor, M. S., 247
Contreraz, Nicholaus, 578
Cooksey, Kazi, 85

Cooper, Karla, 533
Coppola, Francis Ford, 9
Cordner, Gary W., 161, 166
Corrigan, Christina, 88
Cosmides, Leda, 56
Costanzo, Mark, 396
Cox, Michael, 257
Crandell, Sherry, 186
Cressey, Donald, 492–493
Crocker, Daniel Leroy, 389
Crofton, Sir Walter, 533
Cruz, Rolando, 320, 402
Cunanan, Andrew, 29, 58
Cundiff, Ellsworth, 387
Cunningham, William, 134
Cuny, Duane, 153
Cuomo, Mario, 273

D

Dahmer, Jeffrey, 4, 95, 430
Dally, Sherri, 349
Daly, Kathleen, 644
D'Amato, Alphonse, 319
Dantzler, Willie, Jr., 643
Darley, John M., 378–379
Darwin, Charles, 615
Davis, Gray, 377
Davis, Kenneth Culp, 317
Davis, Len, 295
Davis, Richard Allen, 547
Dean, Jerry Lynn, 4
del Carmen, Rolando V., 203–204
Del Toro, Joey, 272, 273
Dempsey, John S., 172
Denny, Reginald, 357
Dershowitz, Alan M., 200, 219, 295
DeSantis, John, 259
Diallo, Amadou, 649
Diamond, John L., 83
DiAngelo, Rio, 156
Dick, Philip K., 608
Dickerson, Charles T., 220
DiIulio, John, Jr., 50, 470, 586–587, 639
Dillenkoffer, Karl, 153
Dillinger, John, 121–122
Dimmick, Carolyn, 285
Donaldson, Stephen, 498
Dorschner, John, 250
Dotts, Jodi, 401
Douglas, William O., 398
Drega, Carl, 23
Droulette, Louis, 119
Drummond, Edward, 93
Dudley, Kevin, 432
Dugan, Brian, 402
Duke, Jim, 43
Duncan, Birt, 640

Durk, David, 251
Durkheim, Emile, 53, 60
Dye, Delores, 338

E

Eappen, Matthew, 4
Eastwood, Clint, 253
Eck, John E., 167, 173
Edgar, Jim, 651
Edwards, Daniel, Jr., 152
Egelhoff, James Allen, 96
Ehrenreich, Barbara, 604
Ehrlich, Isaac, 379, 401
Einhorn, Ira, 273
Einstein, Albert, 366
Eisenstein, James, 309
Ellis, Lee, 56
Ellsworth, Oliver, 278
Ellsworth, Phoebe, 96
Ely, John Hart, 200
Esmerado, John G., 304
Esola, Frank, 119
Estes, Ken, 5
Evans, Kris, 545
Everett, Quincy, 138
Ewing, Charles, 315

F

Fagan, Jeffrey, 574
Farrell, John, 186
Faulder, Joseph, 272
Fay, Michael, 378
Fay, Thomas, 285–286
Feeley, Malcolm, 309
Feld, Barry C., 575
Felipe, Luis, 384
Felker, Ellis Wayne, 365
Felson, Marcus, 40
Ferrara, Vic, Jr., 152
Fesquez, Tracy, 389
Fielding, Henry, 115–116
Fields, Ejuanda, 570
Figlio, Robert, 53
Finley, LeTisia, 51
Fischer, Karla, 650
Flanagan, Timothy J., 422
Flatlow, Alisa, 105
Flavin, Jeanne, 140
Fleissner, James P., 22
Flood, John, 419
Foglia, Michael, 356
Fontaneau, John, 178
Foote, Caleb, 312
Fortas, Abe, 563, 565
Foucault, Michael, 498
Frank, James, 167
Frank, Jerome, 338

Frank, Leo, 329
Frankel, Marvin E., 382, 634
Frankfurter, Felix, 199
Frawley, Michael, 349
Free, Marvin D., Jr., 636
Freitag, Angela, 392
Freud, Sigmund, 57
Friedman, Lawrence M., 18, 83
Friedman, Milton, 618
Frost, Robert, 347
Fujisaki, Hiroshi, 366
Fyfe, James J., 139–140, 234

G

Gabbard, Harold Don, 475
Gacy, John Wayne, 53
Gaddis, William, 76
Gaethe-Leonard, Teresa, 97
Gambino, Carlo, 9
Garcia, Guinevere, 651
Garner, Edward, 246
Garner, Wayne, 513
Gault, Gerald, 565
Gay, William G., 160–161
Gaylin, Willard, 646–647
Gebelein, Richard S., 281
Gelacak, Michael S., 394
Gelernter, David, 66, 302
Gemelli, Salvatore, 471
Genovese, Vito, 9
Gere, Richard, 308
Gertz, Alejandro, 135
Gibson, John M., 93
Gigante, Vincent "Chin," 308
Gilbert, Sir William, 376
Gilmore, Gary Mark, 4, 396, 398–399
Ginsburg, Ruth Bader, 659
Giuliani, Rudolph, 245
Glasser, William, 528
Glatzke, Mary, 175
Glueck, Sheldon, 422
Goetz, Bernhard, 98, 640
Goffman, Erving, 490, 501–502
Golden, Andrew, 562
Goldkamp, John, 312
Goldman, Ron, 84, 362
Goldstein, Herman, 180–181
Goldstein, Joseph, 569
Goldstein, Paul, 609
Gonzalez, Samuel, 272
Goodson, Joe, 172
Gottfredson, Don M., 539
Gottfredson, Michael, 177, 583
Gottfredson, Stephen D., 539
Gotti, John, 9
Gotti, John A. "Junior," 8
Graham, Dethorne, 247
Grasso, Thomas, 273

Subject Index